MW00527161

PARALLEL CLASSIC COMMENTARY *on the* PSALMS

CHARLES
Spurgeon

JOHN
Calvin

MATTHEW
Henry

God's Word to you is our highest calling.

Parallel Classic Commentary on the Psalms
AMG Publishers
6815 Shallowford Road
Chattanooga, Tennessee 37421

Typography: BookDesign™, London, UK

ISBN-13: 978-0-89957-455-4
ISBN-10: 0-89957-455-6

Printed in Canada
17 16 15 –M– 9 8 7 6 5 4

Contents

Introduction

The Parallel Commentary on the Psalms consists of edited versions of pbably the three greatest classic commentaries ever written on the book of Psalms: C.H. Spurgeon's even-volume commentary, entitled, *The Treasury of David*; John Calvin's five-volume commentary ntitled, *Commentary on the Psalms*; and Matthew's Henry commentary on the Psalms from his C mentary on the Whole Bible, which was first published in 1710, and has never been out of print si e.
These three commentaries on the Psalms are laid out side by side each double page, next to the relevant King James Version passage of the Psalms.

Contributors

Charles H. Spurgeon, 1834-1892

C.H. Spurgeon's greatest writing, running to over 3,000 pages consists of an exposition of every verse of every psalm. They took the great Baptist preacher twenr one years to research, and write. They were published between 1869 and 1883 in weekly in allments in the London Metropolitan Tabernacle's periodical, "The Sword and the Trowel." By 895, 120,000 copies of the seven-volume work had been sold. *The Treasury of David* is rightly regar d as Spurgeon's magnum opus. Spurgeon's wife said that if Spurgeon had never written any other ork, *The Treasury of David* would have been Spurgeon's "permanent literary memorial."

James Stalker, a Scottish scholar-preacher and yo nger contemporary of Spurgeon once wrote of The Treasury of David, "For many years it has been y wont, week after week to read over Spurgeon's commentary on the Psalms along with the best an most learned commentaries in existence. That is the best test, and the severest test. Mr. Spurgeon s nds the test well. Not only do you everywhere feel the presence of a vigorous and vigilant mind, an a heart in thorough sympathy with the spirit of the Psalms; but I have often been perfectly astonish d to observe how, without any parade of learning, he shows himself to be thoroughly acquainted wi h the results of the most advanced scholarship; and the truth is that there is scarcely a point in the Psalms of real importance—scarcely a point on which scholarship can give us anything of real imp rtance—as to which there are not sufficient hints to the intelligent reader of Mr. Spurgeon's work."

More recently, J. I. Packer has writter that, "Spurgeon on the Psalms has indeed classic status."

John Calvin, 1509-1564

C. H. Spurgeon commended Calvin'scommentaries on the Psalms in the following way: "Calvin is a tree whose 'leaf also shall not withe '; whatsoever he has written lives on, and is never out of date, because he expounded the word wi hout bias or partiality."

The version of Calvin's commentary on the Psalms used in The Parallel Commentary on the Psalms has been taken from Rev. James Anderson's translation from the original Latin, which he collated with Calvin's French ersion, and then published in 1849.

Calvin used his own tra slation of the Psalms and this accounts for the occasional differences between some of the words and phrases he uses and those used in the KJV of the Psalms.

Matthew Henry, 1662-1714

Spurgeon also rated Matthew Henry's Bible commentary very highly: "He is most pious and pithy, sound and sensible, suggestive and sober, terse and trustworthy." Spurgeon recommended that, "every minister ought to read Matthew Henry entirely and carefully through once at least."

The Psalms

The following three quotations underline the importance of using and understanding the Psalms today. Calvin wholeheartedly supported the practice of singing the Psalms in Christian worship. In his Preface to the Geneva Psalter (1543), he argued, "For what St. Augustine said is true, that one can sing nothing worthy of God save what one has received from Him. Wherefore though we look far and wide we will find no better songs nor songs more suitable to that purpose than the Psalms of David, which the Holy Spirit made and imparted to him. Thus, singing them we may be sure that our words come from God just as if He were to sing in us for His own exaltation."

"Every emotion of the renewed heart Godwards finds adequate expression in the Book of Psalms." John "Rabbi" Duncan, Scottish theologian, and contemporary of Spurgeon.

"Read the psalms and you will find that they glory in the endless power of God." D. Martyn Lloyd-Jones.

C. H. Spurgeon's Introduction to the Psalms

Preface

My Preface shall at least possess the virtue of brevity, as I find it difficult to impart to it any other.

The delightful study of the Psalms has yielded me boundless profit and ever-growing pleasure; common gratitude constrains me to communicate to others a portion of the benefit, with the prayer that it may induce them to search further for themselves. That I have nothing better of my own to offer upon this peerless book is to me a matter of deepest regret; that I have anything whatever to present is subject for devout gratitude to the Lord of grace. I have done my best, but, conscious of many defects, I heartily wish I could have done far better.

The exposition here given is my own. I consulted a few authors before penning it, to aid me in interpretation and arouse my thoughts; but, still I can claim originality for my comments, at least so I honestly think. Whether they are better or worse for that, I know not; at least I know I have sought heavenly guidance while writing them, and therefore I look for a blessing on the printing of them.

Should this first volume meet with the approbation of the judicious, I shall hope by God's grace to continue the work as rapidly as I can consistently with the research demanded and my incessant pastoral duties. Another volume will follow in all probability in twelve months' time, if life be spared and strength be given.

C. H. Spurgeon, Clapham, December, 1869

John Calvin's Introduction to the Psalms

The Author's Preface

To the godly and ingenuous readers, greeting.

Writing in French and Latin

If the reading of these my Commentaries confer as much benefit on the Church of God as I myself have reaped advantage from the composition of them, I shall have no reason to regret that I have undertaken this work. Having expounded here, in our small school, the Book of Psalms, about three years ago, I thought that I had by this means sufficiently discharged my duty, and had resolved not to publish to the world what I had familiarly taught those of my own household. And, in fact, before I had undertaken to expound this book in my lectures, at the request of my brethren, I said what was true, that I had kept away from this subject, because that most faithful teacher of the Church of God, Martin Bucer, had labored in this field with such singular learning, diligence, fidelity, and success, that at least there was not so great need that I should put my hand to the work. And had the Commentaries of Wolphangus Musculus at that time been published, I would not have omitted to do them justice, by mentioning them in the same way, since he too, in the judgment of good men, has earned no small praise by his diligence and industry in this walk. I had not yet come to the end of the book, when, lo! I am urged by renewed solicitations not to suffer my lectures, which certain persons had carefully, faithfully, and not without great labor, taken down, to be lost to the world. My purpose still remained unaltered; only I promised what for a long time I had been thinking of, to write something on the subject in the French language, that my countrymen might not be without the means of being enabled to understand so useful a book when perusing it. Whilst I am thinking of making this attempt, suddenly, and contrary to my first design, it occurred to me, by what impulse I know not, to compose in Latin, only as it were in the way of trial, an exposition of one Psalm. When I found that my success corresponded to my desire far beyond what I had ventured to anticipate, I was encouraged, and accordingly began to make the same attempt in a few other Psalms. On perceiving this, my intimate friends, as if in this way they held me bound, urged me with the greater confidence not to desist from my course. One reason which made me comply with their solicitations, and which also had from the commencement induced me to make this first attempt, was an apprehension that at some future period notes that had been taken down from my lectures, might be published to the world contrary to my wishes or at least without my knowledge. I can truly say, that I was drawn to execute this work rather from such an apprehension, than led to it from my own free will. At the same time, as I continued to prosecute the work, I began to perceive more distinctly that this was by no means a superfluous undertaking, and I have also felt from my own individual experience, that to readers who are not so exercised, I would furnish important assistance in understanding The Psalms.

"An Anatomy of all the Parts of the Soul"

The resplendid riches which are contained it this treasury it is no easy matter to express in words; so much so, that I well know that whatever I shall be able to say will be far from approaching the excellence of the subject. But as it is better to give to my readers some taste, however small, of the wonderful advantages they will derive from the study of this book, than to be entirely silent on the point, I may be permitted briefly to advert to a matter, the greatness of which does not admit of being fully unfolded. I have been accustomed to call this book, I think not inappropriately, "An Anatomy of all the Parts of the Soul;" for there is not an emotion of which any one can be conscious that is not here represented as in a mirror. Or rather, the Holy Spirit has here drawn to the life all the griefs, sorrows, fears, doubts, hopes, cares, perplexities, in short, all the distracting emotions with which the minds of men are wont to be agitated. The other parts of Scripture contain the commandments which God enjoined his servants to announce to us. But here the prophets themselves, seeing they are exhibited to us as speaking to God, and laying open all their inmost thoughts and affections, call, or rather draw, each of us to the examination of himself in particulars in order that none of the many infirmities to which we are subject, and of the many vices with which we abound, may remain concealed. It is certainly a rare and singular advantage, when all lurking places are discovered, and the heart is brought into the light, purged from that most baneful infection, hypocrisy.

In short, as calling upon God is one of the principal means of securing our safety, and as a better and more unerring rule for guiding us in this exercise cannot be found elsewhere than in The Psalms, it follows, that in proportion to the proficiency which a man shall have attained in understanding them, will be his knowledge of the most important part of celestial doctrine.

Prayer and the Psalms

Genuine and earnest prayer proceeds first from a sense of our need, and next, from faith in the promises of God. It is by perusing these inspired compositions, that men will be most effectually awakened to a sense of their maladies, and, at the same time, instructed in seeking remedies for their cure. In a word, whatever may serve to encourage us when we are about to pray to God, is taught us in this book. And not only are the promises of God presented to us in it, but oftentimes there is exhibited to us one standing, as it were, amidst the invitations of God on the one hand, and the impediments of the flesh on the other, girding and preparing himself for prayer: thus teaching us, if at any time we are agitated with a variety of doubts, to resist and fight against them, until the soul, freed and disentangled from all these impediments, rise up to God; and not only so, but even when in the midst of doubts, fears, and apprehensions, let us put forth our efforts in prayer, until we experience some consolation which may calm and bring contentment to our minds. Although distrust may shut the gate against our prayers, yet we must not allow ourselves to give way, whenever our hearts waver or are agitated with inquietude, but must persevere until faith finally come forth victorious from these conflicts. In many places we may perceive the exercise of the servants of God in prayer so fluctuating, that they are almost overwhelmed by the alternate hope of success and apprehension of failure, and gain the prize only by strenuous exertions. We see on the one hand, the flesh manifesting its infirmity; and on the other, faith putting forth its power; and if it is not so valiant and courageous as might be desired, it is at least prepared to fight until by degrees it acquire perfect strength. But as those things which serve to teach us the true method of praying aright will be found scattered through the whole of this Commentary, I will not now stop to treat of topics which it will be necessary afterwards to repeat, nor detain my readers from proceeding to the work itself. Only it appeared to me to be requisite to show in passing, that this book makes known to us this privilege, which is desirable above all others—that not only is there opened up to us familiar access to God, but also that we have permission and freedom granted us to lay open before him our infirmities which we would be ashamed to confess before men. Besides there is also here prescribed to us an infallible rule for directing us with respect to the right manner of offering to God the sacrifice of praise, which he declares to be most precious in his sight, and of the sweetest odor.

Bearing the cross

There is no other book in which there is to be found more express and magnificent commendations, both of the unparalleled liberality of God towards his Church, and of all his works; there is no other book in which there is recorded so many deliverances nor one in which the evidences and experiences of the fatherly providence and solicitude which God exercises towards us are celebrated with such splendor of diction, and yet with the strictest adherence to truth, in short, there is no other book in which we are more perfectly taught the right manner of praising God, or in which we are more powerfully stirred up to the performance of this religious exercise. Moreover although The Psalms are replete with all the precepts which serve to frame our life to every part of holiness, piety, and righteousness, yet they will principally teach and train us to bear the cross; and the bearing of the cross is a genuine proof of our obedience, since by doing this, we renounce the guidance of our own affections and submit ourselves entirely to God, leaving him to govern us, and to dispose of our life according to his will, so that the afflictions which are the bitterest and most severe to our nature, become sweet to us, because they proceed from him. In one word, not only will we here find general commendations of the goodness of God, which may teach men to repose themselves in him alone, and to seek all their happiness solely in him; and which are intended to teach true believers with their whole hearts confidently to look to him for help in all their necessities; but we will also find that the free remission of sins, which alone reconciles God towards us and procures for us settled peace with him, is so set forth and magnified, as that here there is nothing wanting which relates to the knowledge of eternal salvation.

The purpose of the writers of the Psalms and Calvin's life

Now, if my readers derive any fruit and advantage from the labor which I have bestowed in writing these commentaries, I would have them to understand that the small measure of experience which I have had by the conflicts with which the Lord has exercised me, has in no ordinary degree assisted me, not only in applying to present use whatever instruction could be gathered from these divine compositions, but also in more easily comprehending the design of each of the writers. And as David holds the principal place among them, it has greatly aided me in understanding more fully the complaints made by him of the internal afflictions which the Church had to sustain through those who gave themselves out to be her members, that I had suffered the same or similar things from the domestic enemies of the Church. For although I follow David at a great distance, and come far short of equaling him; or rather, although in aspiring slowly and with great difficulty to attain to the many virtues in which he excelled, I still feel myself tarnished with the contrary vices; yet if I have any things in common with him, I have no hesitation in comparing myself with him. In reading the instances of his faith, patience, fervor, zeal, and integrity, it has, as it ought, drawn from me unnumbered groans and sighs, that I am so far from approaching them; but it has, notwithstanding, been of very great advantage to me to behold in him as in a mirror, both the commencement of my calling, and the continued course of my function; so that I know the more assuredly, that whatever that most illustrious king and prophet suffered, was exhibited to me by God as an example for imitation. My conditions no doubt, is much inferior to his, and it is unnecessary for me to stay to show this. But as he was taken from the sheepfold, and elevated to the rank of supreme authority; so God having taken me from my originally obscure and humble condition, has reckoned me worthy of being invested with the honorable office of a preacher and minister of the gospel. When I was as yet a very little boy, my father had destined me for the study of theology. But afterwards when he considered that the legal profession commonly raised those who followed it to wealth this prospect induced him suddenly to change his purpose. Thus it came to pass, that I was withdrawn from the study of philosophy, and was put to the study of law. To this pursuit I endeavored faithfully to apply myself in obedience to the will of my father; but God, by the secret guidance of his providence, at length gave a different direction to my course. And first, since I was too obstinately devoted to the superstitions of Popery to be easily extricated from so profound an abyss of mire, God by a sudden conversion subdued and brought my mind to a teachable frame, which was more hardened in such matters than might have been expected from one at my early period of life Having thus received some taste and knowledge of true godliness I was immediately inflamed with so intense a desire to make progress therein, that although I did not altogether leave off other studies, I yet pursued them with less ardor. I was quite surprised to find that before a year had elapsed, all who had any desire after purer doctrine were continually coming to me to learn, although I myself was as yet but a mere novice and tyro. Being of a disposition somewhat unpolished and bashful, which led me always to love the shade and retirement, I then began to seek some secluded corner where I might be withdrawn from the public view; but so far from being able to accomplish the object of my be desire, all my retreats were like public schools.

In short, whilst my one great object was to live in seclusion without being known, God so led me about through different turnings and changes, that he never permitted me to rest in any place, until, in spite of my natural disposition, he brought me forth to public notice. Leaving my native country, France, I in fact retired into Germany, expressly for the purpose of being able there to enjoy in some obscure corner the repose which I had always desired, and which had been so long denied me. But lo! whilst I lay hidden at Basle, and known only to a few people, many faithful and holy persons were burnt alive in France; and the report of these burnings having reached foreign nations, they excited the strongest disapprobation among a great part of the Germans, whose indignation was kindled against the authors of such tyranny. In order to allay this indignation, certain wicked and lying pamphlets were circulated, stating that none were treated with such cruelty but Anabaptists and seditious persons, who by their perverse ravings and false opinions, were overthrowing not only religion but also all civil order. Observing that the object which these instruments of the court aimed at by their disguises, was not only that the disgrace of shedding so much innocent blood might remain buried under the false charges and calumnies which they brought against the holy martyrs after their death, but also, that afterwards they might be able to proceed to the utmost extremity in murdering the poor saints without exciting compassion towards them in the breasts of any, it appeared to me, that unless I opposed them to the utmost of my ability, my silence could not be vindicated from the charge of cowardice and treachery.

Institute of Christian Religion

This was the consideration which induced me to publish my Institute of the Christian Religion. My objects were, first, to prove that these reports were false and calumnious, and thus to vindicate my brethren, whose death was precious in the sight of the Lord; and next, that as the same cruelties might very soon after be exercised against many unhappy individuals, foreign nations might be touched with at least some compassion towards them and solicitude about them. When it was then published, it was not that copious and labored work which it now is, but only a small treatise containing a summary of the principal truths of the Christian religion, and it was published with no other design than that men might know what was the faith held by those whom I saw basely and wickedly defamed by those flagitious and perfidious flatterers. That my object was not to acquire fame, appeared from this, that immediately after I left Basle, and particularly from the fact that nobody there knew that I was the author.

Geneva

Wherever else I have gone, I have taken care to conceal that I was the author of that performance; and I had resolved to continue in the same privacy and obscurity, until at length William Farel detained me at Geneva, not so much by counsel and exhortation, as by a dreadful imprecation, which I felt to be as if God had from heaven laid his mighty hand upon me to arrest me. As the most direct road to Strasburg, to which I then intended to retire, was as shut up by the wars, I had resolved to pass quickly by Geneva, without staying longer than a single night in that city. A little before this, Popery had been driven from it by the exertions of the excellent person whom I have named, and Peter Viret; but matters were not yet brought to a settled state, and the city was divided into unholy and dangerous factions. Then an individual who now basely apostatized and returned to the Papists, discovered me and made me known to others.

Upon this, Farel, who burned with an extraordinary zeal to advance the gospel, immediately strained every nerve to detain me. And after having learned that my heart was set upon devoting myself to private studies for which I wished to keep myself free from other pursuits, and finding that he gained nothing by entreaties, he proceeded to utter an imprecation that God would curse my retirement, and the tranquility of the studies which I sought, if I should withdraw and refuse to give assistance, when the necessity seas so urgent. By this imprecation I was so stricken with terror, that I desisted from the journey which I had undertaken; but sensible of my natural bashfulness and timidity, I would not bring myself under obligation to discharge any particular office. After that, four months had scarcely elapsed, when, on the one hand, the Anabaptists began to assail us, and, on the other, a certain wicked apostate, who being secretly supported by the influence of some of the magistrates of the city, was thus enabled to give us a great deal of trouble. At the same time, a succession of dissensions fell out in the city which strangely afflicted us. Being, as I acknowledge, naturally of a timid, softer and pusillanimous disposition, I was compelled to encounter these violent tempests as part of my early training; and although I did not sink under themes yet I was not sustained by such greatness of mind, as not to rejoice more than it became me, when, in consequence of certain commotions, I was banished from Geneva. By this means set at liberty and loosed from the tie of my vocational I resolved to live in a private station, free from the burden and cares of any public charge, when that most excellent servant of Christ, Martin Bucer, employing a similar kind of remonstrance and protestation as that to which Farel had recourse before, drew me back to a new station. Alarmed by the example of Jonas which he set before me, I still continued in the work of teaching. And although I always continued like myself, studiously avoiding celebrity; yet I was carried, I know not how, as it were by force to the Imperial assemblies, where, willing or unwilling, I was under the necessity of appearing before the eyes of many. Afterwards, when the Lord having compassion on this city, had allayed the hurtful agitations and broils which prevailed in it, and by his wonderful power had defeated both the wicked counsels and the sanguinary attempts of the disturbers of the Republic, necessity was imposed upon me of returning to my former charge, contrary to my desire and inclination. The welfare of this church, it is true, lay so near my heart, that for its sake I would not have hesitated to lay down my life; but my timidity nevertheless suggested to me many reasons for excusing myself from again willingly taking upon my shoulders so heavy a burden. At length, however, a solemn and conscientious regard to my duty, prevailed with me to consent to return to the flock from which I had been torn; but with what grief, tears, great anxiety and distress I did this, the Lord is my best witness, and many godly persons who would have wished to see me delivered from this painful state, had it not been that that which I feared, and which made me give my consent, prevented them and shut their mouths. Were I to narrate the various conflicts by which the Lord has exercised me since that time, and by what trials he has proved me, it would make a long history.

"David showed me the way"

But that I may not become tedious to my readers by a waste of words, I shall content myself with repeating briefly what I have touched upon a little before, that in considering the whole course of the life of David, it seemed to me that by his own footsteps he showed me the way, and from this I have experienced no small consolation. As that holy king was harassed by the Philistines and other foreign enemies with continual wars, while he was much more grievously afflicted by the malice and wickedness of some perfidious men amongst his own people, so I can say as to myself, that I have been assailed on all sides, and have scarcely been able to enjoy repose for a single moment, but have always had to sustain some conflict either from enemies without or within the Church. Satan has made many attempts to overthrow the fabric of this Church; and once it came to this, that I, altogether feeble and timorous as I am, was compelled to break and put a stop to his deadly assaults by putting my life in danger, and opposing my person to his blows. Afterwards, for the space of five years, when some wicked libertines were furnished with undue influence, and also some of the common people, corrupted by the allurements and perverse discourse of such persons, desired to obtain the liberty of doing whatever they pleased, without controls I was under the necessity of fighting without ceasing to defend and maintain the discipline of the Church. To these irreligious characters. and despisers of the heavenly doctrine, it was a matter of entire indifference, although the Church should sink into ruin, provided they obtained what they sought,—the power of acting just as they pleased. Many, too, harassed by poverty and hunger, and others impelled by insatiable ambition or avarice and a desire of dishonest gain, were become so frantic, that they chose rather, by throwing all things into confusion, to involve themselves and us in one common ruin, than to remain quiet by living peaceably and honestly. During the whole of this lengthened period, I think that there is scarcely any of the weapons which are forged in the workshop of Satan, which has not been employed by them in order to obtain their object. And at length matters had come to such a state, that an end could be put to their machinations in no other way than cutting them off by an ignominious death; which was indeed a painful and pitiable spectacle to me. They no doubt deserved the severest punishment, but I always rather desired that they might live in prosperity, and continue safe and untouched; which would have been the case had they not been altogether incorrigible, and obstinately refused to listen to wholesome admonition. The trial of these five years was grievous and hard to bear; but I experienced not less excruciating pain from the malignity of those who ceased not to assail myself and my ministry with their envenomed calumnies. A great proportion of them, it is true, are so blinded by a passion for slander and detraction, that to their great disgracers they betray at once their impudence, while others, however crafty and cunning, cannot so cover or disguise themselves as to escape being shamefully convicted and disgraced; yet when a man has been a hundred times found innocent of a charge brought against him, and when the charge is again repeated without any cause or occasion, it is an indignity hard to bear.

God's secret providence

Because I affirm and maintain that the world is managed and governed by the secret providence of God, a multitude of presumptuous men rise lip against me, and allege that I represent God as the author of sin. This is so foolish a calumny, that it would of itself quickly come to nothing, did it not meet with persons who have tickled ears, and who take pleasure in feeding upon such discourse. But there are many whose minds are so filled with envy and spleen, or ingratitude, or malignity, that there is no falsehood, however preposterous, yea, even monstrous, which they do not receive, if it is spoken to them. Others endeavor to overthrow God's eternal purpose of predestination, by which he distinguishes between the reprobate and the elect; others take upon them to defend free will; and forthwith many throw themselves into their ranks, not so much through ignorance as by a perversity of zeal which I know not how to characterize. If they were open and avowed enemies who brought these troubles upon me, the thing might in some way be borne. But that those who shroud themselves under the name of brethren, and not only eat Christ's sacred bread, but also administer it to others, that those, in short, who loudly boast of being preachers of the gospel, should wage such nefarious war against me, how detestable is it? In this matter I may very justly complain with David,

> "Yea, mine own familiar friend, in whom I trusted, who did eat of my bread,
> hath lifted up his heel against me,"
> (Psalm 41:9.)
>
> "For it was not an enemy that reproached me;
> but it was thou, a man mine equal, my guide, and mine acquaintance.
> We took sweet counsel together, and walked unto the house of God in company,"
> (Psalm 55:12, 13, 14.)

Others circulated ridiculous reports concerning my treasures; others, of the extravagant authority and enormous influence which they say I possess; others speak of my delicacies and magnificence. But when a man is content with scanty food and common clothing and does not require from the humblest more frugality than he shows and practices himself, shall it be said that such an one is too sumptuous, and lives in too high a style? As to the power and influence of which they envy me, I wish I could discharge this burden upon them; for they estimate my power by the multitude of affairs, and the vast weight of labors with which I am overwhelmed. And if there are some whom I cannot persuade whilst I am alive that I am not rich, my death at length will prove it. I confess, indeed, that I am not poor; for

I desire nothing more than what I have. All these are invented stories, and there is no color whatever for any one of them; but many nevertheless are very easily persuaded of their truth, and applaud them; and the reason is, because the greatest part judge that the only means of cloaking their enormities is to throw all things into disorder, and to confound black and white; and they think that the best and shortest way by which they can obtain full liberty to live with impunity just as they please, is to destroy the authority of Christ's servants. In addition to these, there are "the hypocritical mockers in feasts," of whom David complains, (Psalm 35:16;) and I mean by these not only lick-dish characters who seek a meal to fill their belly, but all those who by false reports seek to obtain the favor of the great. Having been long accustomed to swallow such wrongs as these, I have become almost hardened; yet when the insolence of such characters increased I cannot but sometimes feel my heart wounded with bitter pangs. Nor was it enough that I should be so inhumanly treated by my neighbors. In addition to this, in a distant country towards the frozen ocean, there was raised I know not how, by the frenzy of a few, a storm which afterwards stirred up against me a vast number of persons, who are too much at leisure, and have nothing to do but by their bickering to hinder those who are laboring for the edification of the Church. I am still speaking of the internal enemies of the Church-of those who, boasting mightily of the gospel of Christ, nevertheless rush against me with greater impetuosity than against the open adversaries of the Church, because I do not embrace their gross and fictitious notion concerning a carnal way of eating Christ in the sacrament; and of whom I may protest, after the example of David, "I am for peace; but when I speak, they are for war," (Psalm 120:7.) Moreover, the cruel ingratitude of all of them is manifest in this, that they scruple not to assail both in flank and rear a man who strenuously exerts himself to maintain a cause which they have in common with him and whom therefore they ought to aid and succor. Certainly, if such persons were possessed of even a small portion of humanity, the fury of the Papists which is directed against me with such unbridled violence, would appease the most implacable animosity which they may bear towards me. But since the condition of David was such, that though he had deserved well of his own people, he was nevertheless bitterly hated by many without a cause, as he complains in Psalm 69:4, "I restored that which I took not away," it afforded me no small consolation when I was groundlessly assailed by the hatred of those who ought to have assisted and solaced me, to conform myself to the example of so great and so excellent a person. This knowledge and experience have been of much service in enabling me to understand The Psalms, so that in my meditations upon them, I did not wander, as it were, in an unknown region. My readers, too, if I mistake not, will observe, that in unfolding the internal affections both of David and of others I discourse upon them as matters of which I have familiar experience.

A treasure for all the people of God

Moreover, since I have labored faithfully to open up this treasure for the use of all the people of God, although what I have done has not been equal to my wishes, yet the attempt which I have made deserves to be received with some measure of favor. Still I only ask that each may judge of my labors with justice and candor, according to the advantage and fruit which he shall derive from them. Certainly, as I have said before, in reading these Commentaries, it will be clearly seen that I have not sought to please, unless in so far as I might at the same time be profitable to others. And, therefore, I have not only observed throughout a simple style of teaching, but in order to be removed the farther from all ostentation, I have also generally abstained from refuting the opinions of others, although this presented a more favorable opportunity for plausible display, and of acquiring the applause of those who shall favor my book with a perusal. I have never touched upon opposite opinions, unless where there was reason to fear, that by being silent respecting them, I might leave my readers in doubt and perplexity. At the same time, I am sensible that it would have been much more agreeable to the taste of many, had I heaped together a great mass of materials which has great show, and acquires fame for the writer; but I have felt nothing to be of more importance than to have a regard to the edification of the Church. May God, who has implanted this desire in my heart, grant by his grace that the success may correspond thereto!

John Calvin, Geneva, July 22, 1557.

Matthew Henry's Introduction to the Psalms

An exposition, with practical observations, of the book of Psalms

We have now before us one of the choicest and most excellent parts of all the Old Testament; nay, so much is there in it of Christ and his gospel, as well as of God and his law, that it had been called the abstract, or summary, of both Testaments. The History of Israel, which we were long upon, let us to camps and council-boards, and there entertained and instructed us in the knowledge of God. The book of Job brought us into the schools, and treated us with profitable disputations concerning God and his providence. But this book brings us into the sanctuary, draws us off from converse with men, with the politicians, philosophers, or disputers of this world, and directs us into communion with God, by solacing and reposing our souls in him, lifting up and letting out our hearts towards him. Thus may we be in the mount with God; and we understand not our interests if we say not, It is good to be here. Let us consider,

I. The title of this book.
It is called, 1. The Psalms; under that title it is referred to, Luke xxiv. 44. The Hebrew calls it Tehillim, which properly signifies Psalms of praise, because many of them are such; but Psalms is a more general word, meaning all metrical compositions fitted to be sung, which may as well be historical, doctrinal, or supplicatory, as laudatory. Though singing be properly the voice of joy, yet the intention of songs is of a much greater latitude, to assist the memory, and both to express and to excite all the other affections as well as this of joy. The priests had a mournful muse as well as joyful ones; and the divine institution of singing psalms is thus largely intended; for we are directed not only to praise God, but to teach and admonish ourselves and one another in psalms, and hymns, and spiritual songs, Col. iii. 16.

2. It is called the Book of Psalms; so it is quoted by St. Peter, Acts i. 20. It is a collection of psalms, of all the psalms that were divinely inspired, which, though composed at several times and upon several occasions, are here put together without any reference to or dependence upon one another; thus they were preserved from being scattered and lost, and were in so much greater readiness for the service of the church. See what a good master we serve, and what pleasantness there is in wisdom's ways, when we are not only commanded to sing at our work, and have cause enough given us to do so, but have words also put in our mouths and songs prepared to our hands.

II. The author of this book.
It is, no doubt, derived originally from the blessed Spirit. They are spiritual songs, words which the Holy Ghost taught. The penman of most of them was David the son of Jesse, who is therefore called the sweet psalmist of Israel, 2 Sam. xxiii.

Some that have not his name in their titles yet are expressly ascribed to him elsewhere, as Ps. ii. (Acts iv. 25) and Ps. xcvi. and cv. (1 Chron. xvi.) One psalm is expressly said to be the prayer of Moses (Ps. xc.); and that some of the psalms were penned by Asaph is intimated, 2 Chron. xxix. 30, where they are said to praise the Lord in the words of David and Asaph, who is there called a seer or prophet. Some of the psalms seem to have been penned long after, as Ps. cxxxvii., at the time of the captivity in Babylon; but the far greater part of them were certainly penned by David himself, whose genius lay towards poetry and music, and who was raised up, qualified, and animated, for the establishing of the ordinance of singing psalms in the church of God, as Moses and Aaron were, in their day, for the settling of the ordinances of sacrifice; theirs is superseded, but his remains, and will to the end of time, when it shall be swallowed up in the songs of eternity. Herein David was a type of Christ, who descended from him, not from Moses, because he came to take away sacrifice (the family of Moses was soon lost and extinct), but to establish and perpetuate joy and praise; for of the family of David in Christ there shall be no end.

III. The scope of it.
It is manifestly intended, 1. To assist the exercises of natural religion, and to kindle in the souls of men those devout affections which we owe to God as our Creator, owner, ruler, and benefactor. The book of Job helps to prove our first principles of the divine perfections and providence; but this helps to improve

them in prayers and praises, and professions of desire towards him, dependence on him, and an entire devotedness and resignation to him. Other parts of scripture show that God is infinitely above man, and his sovereign Lord; but this shows us that he may, notwithstanding, be conversed with by us sinful worms of the earth; and there are ways in which, if it be not our own fault, we may keep up communion with him in all the various conditions of human life.

2. To advance the excellencies of revealed religion, and in the most pleasing powerful manner to recommend it to the world. There is indeed little or nothing of the ceremonial law in all the book of Psalms. Though sacrifice and offering were yet to continue many ages, yet they are here represented as things which God did not desire (Ps. xl. 6, li. 16), as things comparatively little, and which in time were to vanish away. But the word and law of God, those parts of it which are moral and of perpetual obligation are here all along magnified and made honorable, nowhere more. And Christ, the crown and center of revealed religion, the foundation, corner, and top-stone, of that blessed building, is here clearly spoken of in type and prophecy, his sufferings and the glory that should follow, and the kingdom that he should set up in the world, in which God's covenant with David, concerning his kingdom, was to have its accomplishment. What a high value does this book put upon the word of God, his statutes and judgments, his covenant and the great and precious promises of it; and how does it recommend them to us as our guide and stay, and our heritage for ever!

IV. The use of it.

All scripture, being given by inspiration of God, is profitable to convey divine light into our understandings; but this book is of singular use with that to convey divine life and power, and a holy warmth, into our affections. There is no one book of scripture that is more helpful to the devotions of the saints than this, and it has been so in all ages of the church, ever since it was written and the several parts of it were delivered to the chief musician for the service of the church

1. It is of use to be sung. Further than David's psalms we may go, but we need not, for hymns and spiritual songs. What the rules of the Hebrew meter were even the learned are not certain. But these psalms ought to be rendered according to the meter of every language, at least so as that they may be sung for the edification of the church. And methinks it is a great comfort to us, when we are singing David's psalms, that we are offering the very same praises to God that were offered to him in the days of David and the other godly kings of Judah. So rich, so well made, are these divine poems, that they can never be exhausted, can never be worn thread-bare.

2. It is of use to be read and opened by the ministers of Christ, as containing great and excellent truths, and rules concerning good and evil. Our Lord Jesus expounded the psalms to his disciples, the gospel psalms, and opened their understandings (for he had the key of David) to understand them, Luke xxiv. 44. 3. It is of use to be read and meditated upon by all good people. It is a full fountain, out of which we may all be drawing water with joy.

(1.) The Psalmist's experiences are of great use for our direction, caution, and encouragement. In telling us, as he often does, what passed between God and his soul, he lets us know what we may expect from God, and what he will expect, and require, and graciously accept, from us. David was a man after God's own heart, and therefore those who find themselves in some measure according to his heart have reason to hope that they are renewed by the grace of God, after the image of God, and many have much comfort in the testimony of their consciences for them that they can heartily say Amen to David's prayers and praises.

(2.) Even the Psalmist's expressions too are of great use; and by them the Spirit helps our praying infirmities, because we know not what to pray for as we ought. In all our approaches to God, as well as in our first returns to God, we are directed to take with us words (Hos. xiv. 2), these words, words which the Holy Ghost teaches. If we make David's psalms familiar to us, as we ought to do, whatever errand we have at the throne of grace, by way of confession, petition, or thanksgiving, we may thence be assisted in the delivery of it; whatever devout affection is working in us, holy desire or hope, sorrow or joy, we may there find apt words wherewith to clothe it, sound speech which cannot be condemned. It will be good to collect the most proper and lively expressions of devotion which we find here, and to methodize them, and reduce them to the several heads of prayer, that they may be the more ready to us. Or we may take sometimes one choice psalm and sometimes another, and pray it over, that is, enlarge upon each verse in our own thoughts, and offer up our meditations to God as they arise from the expressions we find there.

The learned Dr. Hammond, in his preface to his paraphrase on the Psalms (sect. 29), says, "That going over a few psalms with these interpunctions of mental devotion, suggested, animated, and maintained, by the native life and vigor which is in the psalms, is much to be preferred before the saying over the whole Psalter, since nothing is more fit to be averted in religious offices than their degenerating into heartless dispirited recitations." If, as St. Austin advises, we form our spirit by the affection of the psalm, we may then be sure of acceptance with God in using the language of it. Nor is it only our devotion, and the affections of our mind, that the book of Psalms assists, teaching us how to offer praise so as to glorify God, but, it is also a directory to the actions of our lives, and teaches us how to order our conversation aright, so as that, in the end, we may see the salvation of God, Ps. i. 23. The Psalms were thus serviceable to the Old-Testament church, but to us Christians they may be of more use than they could be to those who lived before the coming of Christ; for, as Moses' sacrifices, so David's songs, are expounded and made more intelligible by the gospel of Christ, which lets us within the veil; so that if to David's prayers and praises we add St. Paul's prayers in his epistles, and the new songs in the Revelation, we shall be thoroughly furnished for this good work; for the scripture, perfected, makes the man of God perfect.

As to the division of this book, we need not be solicitous; there is no connection (or very seldom) between one psalm and another, nor any reason discernible for the placing of them in the order wherein we here find them; but it seems to be ancient, for that which is now the second psalm was so in the apostles' time, Acts xiii. 33. The vulgar Latin joins the 9th and 10th together; all popish authors quote by that, so that, thenceforward, throughout the book, their number is one short of ours; our xi. is their x., our cxix. is their cxviii. But they divide the 147th into two, and so make up the number of 150.

Some have endeavored to reduce the psalms to proper heads, according to the matter of them, but there is often such a variety of matter in one and the same psalm that this cannot be done with any certainty. But the seven penitential Psalms have been in a particular manner singled out by the devotions of many. They are reckoned to be Ps. vi., xxxii., xxxviii., li., cii., cxxx., cxliii. The Psalms were divided into five books, each concluding with Amen, Amen, or Hallelujah; the first ending with Ps. xli., the second with Ps. lxxii., the third with Ps. lxxxix., the fourth with Ps. cvi., the fifth with Ps. cl. Others divide them into three fifties; others into sixty parts, two for every day of the month, one for the morning, the other for the evening. Let good Christians divide them for themselves, so as may best increase their acquaintance with them, that they may have them at hand upon all occasions and may sing them in the spirit and with the understanding.

Matthew Henry, *Commentary on the Whole Bible,* 1710

Book One: Psalms 1-41

Psalm 1

1 Blessed is the man that walketh not in the counsel of the ungodly, nor standeth in the way of sinners, nor sitteth in the seat of the scornful.
2 But his delight is in the law of the LORD; and in his law doth he meditate day and night.
3 And he shall be like a tree planted by the rivers of water, that bringeth forth his fruit in his season; his leaf also shall not wither; and whatsoever he doeth shall prosper.
4 The ungodly are not so: but are like the chaff which the wind driveth away.
5 Therefore the ungodly shall not stand in the judgment, nor sinners in the congregation of the righteous.
6 For the LORD knoweth the way of the righteous: but the way of the ungodly shall perish.

Book One: Psalms 1-41

Psalm 1

TITLE. This Psalm may be regarded as THE PREFACE PSALM, having in it a notification of the contents of the entire Book. It is the psalmists's desire to teach us the way to blessedness, and to warn us of the sure destruction of sinners. This, then, is the matter of the first Psalm, which may be looked upon, in some respects, as the text upon which the whole of the Psalms make up a divine sermon.

DIVISION. This Psalm consists of two parts: in the first (from verse 1 to the end of the 3rd) David sets out wherein the felicity and blessedness of a godly man consisteth, what his exercises are, and what blessings he shall receive from the Lord. In the second part (from verse 4 to the end) he contrasts the state and character of the ungodly, reveals the future, and describes, in telling language, his ultimate doom.

EXPOSITION
Verse 1. "BLESSED"—see how this Book of Psalms opens with a benediction, even as did the famous Sermon of our Lord upon the Mount! The word translated "blessed" is a very expressive one. We might read it, "Oh, the blessednesses!" and we may well regard it as a joyful acclamation of the gracious man's felicity. May the like benediction rest on us!
Verse 2. And now mark his positive character. "His delight is in the law of the Lord." He is not under the law as a curse and condemnation, but he is in it, and he delights to be in it as his rule of life; he delights, moreover, to meditate in it, to read it by day, and think upon it by night. He takes a text and carries it with him all day long; and in the night-watches, when sleep forsakes his eyelids, he museth upon the Word of God.
Verse 3. "And he shall be like a tree planted"—not a wild tree, but "a tree planted," chosen, considered as property, cultivated and secured from the last terrible uprooting, for "every plant which my heavenly Father hath not planted, shall be rooted up:" Matthew 15:13.
Verse 4. We have now come to the second head of the Psalm. In this verse the contrast of the ill estate of the wicked is employed to heighten the coloring of that fair and pleasant picture which precedes it.
Verse 5. They shall stand there to be judged, but not to be acquitted. Fear shall lay hold upon them there; they shall not stand their ground; they shall flee away; they shall not stand in their own defence; for they shall blush and be covered with eternal contempt.
Verse 6. Or, as the Hebrew hath it yet more fully, "The Lord is knowing the way of the righteous." He is constantly looking on their way, and though it may be often in mist and darkness, yet the Lord knoweth it. "But the way of the ungodly shall perish." Not only shall they perish themselves, but their way shall perish too. The righteous man ploughs the furrows of earth, and sows a harvest here, which shall never be fully reaped till he enters the enjoyments of eternity; but as for the wicked, he ploughs the sea, and though there may seem to be a shining trail behind his keel, yet the waves shall pass over it, and the place that knew him shall know him no more for ever. The very "way" of the ungodly shall perish. If it exist in remembrance, it shall be in the remembrance of the bad; for the Lord will cause the name of the wicked to rot, to become a stench in the nostrils of the good, and to be only known to the wicked themselves by its putridity. May the Lord cleanse our hearts and our ways, that we may escape the doom of the ungodly, and enjoy the blessedness of the righteous!

JOHN CALVIN

Book One: Psalms 1-41

Psalm 1

He who collected the Psalms into one volume, whether Ezra or some other person, appears to have placed this Psalm at the beginning, by way of preface, in which he inculcates upon all the godly the duty of meditating upon the law of God. The sum and substance of the whole is, that they are blessed who apply their hearts to the pursuit of heavenly wisdom; whereas the profane despisers of God, although for a time they may reckon themselves happy, shall at length have a most miserable end.

1. Blessed is the man. The meaning of the Psalmist is that it shall be always well with God's devout servants, whose constant endeavor it is to make progress in the study of his law. The sum of the whole is that the servants of God must endeavor utterly to abhor the life of ungodly men.
2. In the second verse, the Psalmist does not simply pronounce those happy who fear God, as in other places, but designates godliness by the study of the law, teaching us that God is only rightly served when that law is obeyed. It is not left to every man to frame a system of religion according to his own judgment, but the standard of godliness is to be taken from the Word of God.
3. The Psalmist here illustrates, and, at the same time, confirms by a metaphor the statement made in the preceding verse; for he shows in what respect those who fear God are to be accounted happy. There is in the words an implied contrast between the vigor of a tree planted in a situation well watered, and the decayed appearance of one which, although it may flourish beautifully for a time, yet soon withers on account of the barrenness of the soil in which it is placed.
4. The meaning is that although the ungodly now live prosperously, yet by and by they shall be like chaff; for when the Lord has brought them low, he shall drive them hither and thither with the blast of his wrath. Besides, by this form of speech, the Holy Spirit teaches us to contemplate with the eye of faith, what might otherwise seem incredible; for although the ungodly man rise high, and appear to great advantage, like a stately tree, we may rest assured that he will be even as chaff or refuse, whenever God chooses to cast him down from his high estate, with the breath of his mouth.
5. In the fifth verse, the prophet teaches that a happy life depends on a good conscience, and that, therefore, it is not wonderful, if the ungodly suddenly fall from the happiness of which they fancied themselves in possession.
6. According to all outward appearance, the servants of God may derive no advantage from their uprightness; but as it is the peculiar office of God to defend them and take care of their safety, they must be happy under his protection. And from this we may also conclude that, as he is the certain avenger of wickedness, although, for a time, he may seem to take no notice of the ungodly, yet at length he will visit them with destruction.

MATTHEW HENRY

Book One: Psalms 1-41

Psalm 1

1-3 The happy man.
The psalmist begins with the character and condition of a godly man, that those may first take the comfort of that to whom it belongs.
A godly man, that he may avoid the evil, utterly renounces the companionship of evil-doers, and will not be led by them (v. 1): He walks not in the council of the ungodly, &c. This part of his character is put first, because those that will keep the commandments of their God must say to evil-doers, Depart from us (Ps. cxix. 115), and departing from evil is that in which wisdom begins.

A godly man, that he may do that which is good and cleave to it, submits to the guidance of the word of God and makes that familiar to him, v. 2. This is that which keeps him out of the way of the ungodly. By the words of thy lips I have kept me from the path of the deceiver, Ps. xvii. 4.

His blessedness is here illustrated by a similitude (v. 3): He shall be like a tree, fruitful and flourishing.

4-6 Description and doom of the ungodly.
Here is,
I. The description of the ungodly given, v. 4.
In general, they are the reverse of the righteous, both in character and condition: They are not so. The LXX. emphatically repeats this: Not so the ungodly; they are not so; they are led by the counsel of the wicked, in the way of sinners, to the seat of the scornful; they have no delight in the law of God, nor ever think of it; they bring forth no fruit but grapes of Sodom; they cumber the ground.
II. The doom of the ungodly read, v. 5.
They will be cast, upon their trial, as traitors convicted: They shall not stand in the judgment, that is, they shall be found guilty, shall hang down the head with shame and confusion, and all their pleas and excuses will be overruled as frivolous. There is a judgment to come, in which every man's present character and work, though ever so artfully concealed and disguised, shall be truly and perfectly discovered, and appear in their own colors, and accordingly every man's future state will be, by an irreversible sentence, determined for eternity.
III. The reason rendered of this different state of the godly and wicked, v. 6.
God must have all the glory of the prosperity and happiness of the righteous.

In singing these verses, and praying over them, let us possess ourselves with a holy dread of the wicked man's portion, and with a holy care to approve ourselves to God in every thing, entreating his favor with our whole hearts.

Psalm 2

1-6
1 Why do the heathen rage, and the people imagine a vain thing?
2 The kings of the earth set themselves, and the rulers take counsel together, against the LORD, and against his anointed, saying,
3 Let us break their bands asunder, and cast away their cords from us.
4 He that sitteth in the heavens shall laugh: the LORD shall have them in derision.
5 Then shall he speak unto them in his wrath, and vex them in his sore displeasure.
6 Yet have I set my king upon my holy hill of Zion.

Psalm 2

TITLE. We shall not greatly err in our summary of this sublime Psalm if we call it THE PSALM OF MESSIAH THE PRINCE; for it sets forth, as in a wondrous vision, the tumult of the people against the Lord's anointed, the determinate purpose of God to exalt his own Son, and the ultimate reign of that Son over all his enemies.

DIVISION. This Psalm will be best understood if it be viewed as a four-fold picture. (In verses 1, 2, 3) the Nations are raging; (4 to 6) the Lord in heaven derides them; (7 to 9) the Son proclaims the decree; and (from 10 to end) advice is given to the kings to yield obedience to the Lord's anointed. This division is not only suggested by the sense, but is warranted by the poetic form of the Psalm, which naturally falls into four stanzas of three verses each.

EXPOSITION
1-6
1. We have, in these first three verses, a description of the hatred of human nature against the Christ of God. The Psalm begins abruptly with an angry interrogation; and well it may: it is surely but little to be wondered at, that the sight of creatures in arms against their God should amaze the psalmist's mind. We see the heathen raging, roaring like the sea, tossed to and fro with restless waves, as the ocean in a storm; and then we mark the people in their hearts imagining a vain thing against God.
4. Let us now turn our eyes from the wicked counsel-chamber and raging tumult of man, to the secret place of the majesty of the Most High. What doth God say? What will the King do unto the men who reject his only-begotten Son, the Heir of all things?
5. After he has laughed he shall speak; he needs not smite; the breath of his lips is enough. At the moment when their power is at its height, and their fury most violent, then shall his Word go forth against them. And what is it that he says?—it is a very galling sentence—"Yet," says he, "despite your malice, despite your tumultuous gatherings, despite the wisdom of your counsels, despite the craft of your lawgivers, 'yet have I set my king upon my holy hill of Zion'."

7-10
7. This Psalm wears something of a dramatic form, for now another person is introduced as speaking. We have looked into the council-chamber of the wicked, and to the throne of God, and now we behold the Anointed declaring his rights of sovereignty, and warning the traitors of their doom.
8. "Ask of me." It was a custom among great kings, to give to favored ones whatever they might ask. (See Esther 5:6; Matthew 14:7.)
So Jesus hath but to ask and have. Here he declares that his very enemies are his inheritance. To their face he declares this decree, and "Lo! here," cries the Anointed One, as he holds aloft in that once pierced hand the scepter of his power, "He hath given me this, not only the right to be a king, but the power to conquer." Yes! Jehovah hath given to his Anointed a rod of iron with which he shall break rebellious nations in pieces, and, despite their imperial strength, they shall be but as potters' vessels, easily dashed into shivers, when the rod of iron is in the hand of the omnipotent Son of God. Those who will not bend must break. Potters' vessels are not to be restored if dashed in pieces, and the ruin of sinners will be hopeless if Jesus shall smite them.

10-12
10. The scene again changes, and counsel is given to those who have taken counsel to rebel. They are exhorted to obey, and give the kiss of homage and affection to him whom they have hated.

JOHN CALVIN

Psalm 2

David boasts that his kingdom, though assailed by a vast multitude of powerful enemies, would, notwithstanding, be perpetual, because it was upheld by the hand and power of God. He adds, that in spite of his enemies, it would be extended even to the uttermost ends of the earth. And, therefore, he exhorts kings and other rulers to lay aside their pride, and receive, with submissive minds, the yoke laid upon them by God; as it would be vain for them to attempt to shake it off. All this was typical and contains a prophecy concerning the future kingdom of Christ.

1-3
We know how many conspired against David, and endeavored to prevent his coming to the throne, and from their hostile attempts, had he judged according to the eye of sense and reason, he might have been so full of apprehension, as forthwith to have given up all hope of ever becoming king. And, doubtless, he had often to struggle sorrowfully with very grievous temptations. But, as he had the testimony of an approving conscience, that he had attempted nothing rashly nor acted as ambition and depraved desire impel many to seek changes in the government of kingdoms; as he was, on the contrary, thoroughly persuaded that he had been made king by divine appointment, when he coveted no such thing, nor even thought of it; he encouraged himself by strong confidence in God against the whole world, just as in these words, he nobly pours contempt both on kings and their armies.

4-6
After David has told us of the tumult and commotions, the counsels and pride, the preparation and resources the strength and efforts of his enemies, in opposition to all these he places the power of God alone, which he concludes would be brought to bear against them, from their attempting to frustrate his decree. And, as a little before, by terming them kings of the earth, he expressed their feeble and perishable condition; so now, by the lofty title of He that dwelleth in heaven, he extols the power of God, as if he had said, that power remains intact and unimpaired, whatever men may attempt against it. Let them exalt themselves as they may, they shall never be able to reach to heaven; yea, while they think to confound heaven and earth together, they resemble so many grasshoppers, and the Lord, meanwhile, undisturbed beholds from on high their infatuated evolutions. And David ascribes laughter to God on two accounts; first, to teach us that he does not stand in need of great armies to repress the rebellion of wicked men, as if this were an arduous and difficult matter, but, on the contrary, could do this as often as he pleases with the most perfect ease. In the second place, he would have us to understand that when God permits the reign of his Son to be troubled, he does not cease from interfering because he is employed elsewhere; but he purposely delays the inflictions of his wrath to the proper time.

MATTHEW HENRY

Psalm 2

1-6 The enemies of Messiah.
Observe here the mighty opposition that would be given to the Messiah and his kingdom, to his holy religion and all the interests of it, v. 1-3. One would have expected that so great a blessing to this world would be universally welcomed and embraced, and that every sheaf would immediately bow to that of the Messiah and all the crowns and scepters on earth would be laid at his feet; but it proves quite contrary. Never were the notions of any sect of philosophers, though ever so absurd, nor the powers of any prince or state, though ever so tyrannical, opposed with so much violence as the doctrine and government of Christ—a sign that it was from heaven, for the opposition was plainly from hell originally.

We are here told what it is they are exasperated at and what they aim at in this opposition (v. 3): Let us break their bands asunder. They will not be under any government; they are children of Belial, that cannot endure the yoke, at least the yoke of the Lord and his anointed.

Those that engage in this mighty struggle are the people of the earth, and the kings of the earth, who, being of the earth, are earthy; but he whom they contest with is one that sits in the heavens, v. 4. He is in the heaven, a place of such a vast prospect that he can oversee them all and all their projects; and such is his power that he can overcome them all and all their attempts. He sits there, as one easy and at rest, out of the reach of all their impotent menaces and attempts.

Sometimes God is said to awake, and arise, for the vanquishing of his enemies; here he is said to sit still and vanquish them; for the utmost operations of God's omnipotence create no difficulty at all, nor the least disturbance to his eternal rest. They are justly punished, v. 5.

They are certainly defeated, and all their counsels turned headlong (v. 6): Yet have I set my king upon my holy hill of Zion. David was advanced to the throne, and became master of the strong-hold of Zion.

7-9 The triumphs of Messiah.
We have heard what the kings of the earth have to say against Christ's kingdom, and have heard it gainsaid by him that sits in heaven; let us now hear what the Messiah himself has to say for his kingdom, to make good his claims, and it is what all the powers on earth cannot gainsay.
I. The kingdom of the Messiah is founded upon a decree, an eternal decree, of God the Father. It was not a sudden resolve. The transactions between the Father and the Son concerning man's redemption, represented by the covenant of royalty made with David and his seed, Ps. lxxxix. 3. This our Lord Jesus often referred to as that which, all along in his

Psalm 2

7-12
7 I will declare the decree: the LORD hath said unto me, Thou art my Son; this day have I begotten thee.
8 Ask of me, and I shall give thee the heathen for thine inheritance, and the uttermost parts of the earth for thy possession.
9 Thou shalt break them with a rod of iron; thou shalt dash them in pieces like a potter's vessel.
10 Be wise now therefore, O ye kings: be instructed, ye judges of the earth.
11 Serve the LORD with fear, and rejoice with trembling.
12 Kiss the Son, lest he be angry, and ye perish from the way, when his wrath is kindled but a little. Blessed are all they that put their trust in him.

"Be wise."—It is always wise to be willing to be instructed, especially when such instruction tends to the salvation of the soul. "Be wise now, therefore;" delay no longer, but let good reason weigh with you. Your warfare cannot succeed, therefore desist and yield cheerfully to him who will make you bow if you refuse his yoke. O how wise, how infinitely wise is obedience to Jesus, and how dreadful is the folly of those who continue to be his enemies!

"Serve the Lord with fear;" let reverence and humility be mingled with your service. He is a great God, and ye are but puny creatures; bend ye, therefore, in lowly worship, and let a filial fear mingle with all your obedience to the great Father of the Ages.

"Rejoice with trembling,"—There must ever be a holy fear mixed with the Christian's joy. This is a sacred compound, yielding a sweet smell, and we must see to it that we burn no other upon the altar. Fear, without joy, is torment; and joy, without holy fear, would be presumption. Mark the solemn argument for reconciliation and obedience. It is an awful thing to perish in the midst of sin, in the very way of rebellion; and yet how easily could his wrath destroy us suddenly. It needs not that his anger should be heated seven times hotter; let the fuel kindle but a little, and we are consumed. O sinner! Take heed of the terrors of the Lord; for "our God is a consuming fire."

Note the benediction with which the Psalm closes: "Blessed are all they that put their trust in him." Have we a share in this blessedness? Do we trust in him? Our faith may be slender as a spider's thread; but if it be real, we are in our measure blessed. The more we trust, the more fully shall we know this blessedness. We may therefore close the Psalm with the prayer of the apostles: "Lord, increase our faith."

The first Psalm was a contrast between the righteous man and the sinner; the second Psalm is a contrast between the tumultuous disobedience of the ungodly world and the sure exaltation of the righteous Son of God.

In the first Psalm, we saw the wicked driven away like chaff; in the second Psalm we see them broken in pieces like a potter's vessel.

In the first Psalm, we beheld the righteous like a tree planted by the rivers of water; and here, we contemplate Christ the Covenant Head of the righteous, made better than a tree planted by the rivers of water, for he is made king of all the islands, and all the heathen bow before him and kiss the dust; while he himself gives a blessing to all those who put their trust in him.

The two Psalms are worthy of the very deepest attention; they are, in fact, the preface to the entire Book of Psalms, and were by some of the ancients, joined into one.

They are, however, two Psalms; for Paul speaks of this as the second Psalm. (Acts 13:33.) The first shows us the character and lot of the righteous; and the next teaches us that the Psalms are Messianic, and speak of Christ the Messiah—the Prince who shall reign from the river even unto the ends of the earth. That they have both a far-reaching prophetic outlook we are well assured, but we do not feel competent to open up that matter, and must leave it to abler hands.

7-8
7. I will declare, etc. David, to take away all pretense of ignorance from his enemies, assumes the office of a preacher in order to publish the decree of God; or at least he protests that he did not come to the throne without a sure and clear proof of his calling; as if he had said, I did not, without consideration, publicly go forward to usurp the kingdom, but I brought with me the command of God.
8. Ask of me. Christ, it is true, besought his Father (John 17:5) to "glorify him with the glory which he had with him before the world was;" yet the more obvious meaning is, that the Father will deny nothing to his Son which relates to the extension of his kingdom to the uttermost ends of the earth. But, in this wonderful matter, Christ is introduced as presenting himself before the Father with prayers, in order to illustrate the free liberality of God in conferring upon men the honor of constituting his own Son governor over the whole world.
9. This is expressly stated to teach us that Christ is furnished with power by which to reign even over those who are averse to his authority, and refuse to obey him. The language of David implies that all will not voluntarily receive his yoke, but that many will be stiff-necked and rebellious, whom notwithstanding he shall subdue by force, and compel to submit to him. It is true, the beauty and glory of the kingdom of which David speaks are more illustriously displayed when a willing people run to Christ.

10-11
David having, as a preacher of the judgments of God, set forth the vengeance which God would take upon his enemies proceeds now, in the character of a prophet and teacher, to exhort the unbelieving to repentance, that they may not, when it is too late, be compelled to acknowledge, from dire experience, that the divine threatenings are neither idle nor ineffectual. And he addresses by name kings and rulers, who are not very easily brought to a submissive state of mind, and who are, besides, prevented from learning what is right by the foolish conceit of their own wisdom with which they are puffed up. And if David spare not even kings themselves, who seem unrestrained by laws, and exempted from ordinary rules, much more does his exhortation apply to the common class of men, in order that all, from the highest to the lowest, may humble themselves before God.
12. David expresses yet more distinctly what kind of fear and service God requires. Since it is the will of God to reign by the hand of his Son, and since he has engraved on his person the marks and insignia of his own glory, the proper proof of our obedience and piety towards him is reverently to embrace his Son, whom he has appointed king over us, according to the declaration, "He that honoureth not the Son, honoureth not the Father who hath sent him," (John 5:23).

The term kiss refers to the solemn token or sign of honor which subjects were wont to yield to their sovereigns. The sum is, that God is defrauded of his honor if he is not served in Christ.

undertaking, he governed himself by; This is the will of him that sent me, John vi. 40. This commandment have I received of my Father, John x. 18; xiv. 31.
II. There is a declaration of that decree as far as is necessary for the satisfaction of all those who are called and commanded to yield themselves subjects to this king, and to leave those inexcusable who will not have him to reign over them. The decree was secret; it was what the Father said to the Son, when he possessed him in the beginning of his way, before his works of old; but it is declared by a faithful witness, who had lain in the bosom of the Father from eternity, and came into the world as the prophet of the church, to declare him, John i. 18.

The fountain of all being is, without doubt, the fountain of all power; and it is by, from, and under him, that the Messiah claims. He has his right to rule from what Jehovah said to him, by whose word all things were made and are governed. Christ here makes a two-fold title to his kingdom:
1. A title by inheritance (v. 7): Thou art my Son, this day have I begotten thee. This scripture the apostle quotes (Heb. i. 5) to prove that Christ has a more excellent name than the angels, but that he obtained it by inheritance, v. 4. He is the Son of God, not by adoption, but his begotten Son, the only begotten of the Father, John i. 14.
2. A title by agreement, v. 8, 9. The agreement is, in short, this: the Son must undertake the office of an intercessor, and, upon that condition, he shall have the honor and power of a universal monarch; see Isa. liii. 12.

10-12 Warning to the enemies of Messiah.
We have here the practical application of this gospel doctrine concerning the kingdom of the Messiah, by way of exhortation to the kings and judges of the earth. They hear that it is in vain to oppose Christ's government; let them therefore be so wise for themselves as to submit to it. He that has power to destroy them shows that he has no pleasure in their destruction, for he puts them into a way to make themselves happy, v. 10.

We are exhorted, to reverence God and to stand in awe of him, v. 11. This is the great duty of natural religion. God is great, and infinitely above us, just and holy, and provoked against us, and therefore we ought to fear him and tremble before him; yet he is our Lord and Master, and we are bound to serve him, our friend and benefactor, and we have reason to rejoice in him.

We are also exhorted to welcome Jesus Christ and to submit to him, v. 12. This is the great duty of the Christian religion; it is that which is required of all, even kings and judges, and it is our wisdom and interest to do it.

In singing this, and praying it over, we should have our hearts filled with a holy awe of God, but at the same time borne up with a cheerful confidence in Christ.

Psalm 3

Title
A Psalm of David, when he fled from Absalom his son.

1 Lord, how are they increased that trouble me! many are they that rise up against me.
2 Many there be which say of my soul, There is no help for him in God. Selah.
3 But thou, O LORD, art a shield for me; my glory, and the lifter up of mine head.
4 I cried unto the LORD with my voice, and he heard me out of his holy hill. Selah.
5 I laid me down and slept; I awaked; for the LORD sustained me.
6 I will not be afraid of ten thousands of people, that have set themselves against me round about.
7 Arise, O LORD; save me, O my God: for thou hast smitten all mine enemies upon the cheek bone; thou hast broken the teeth of the ungodly.
8 Salvation belongeth unto the LORD: thy blessing is upon thy people. Selah.

Psalm 3

TITLE. "A Psalm of David, when he fled from Absalom his Son." You will remember the sad story of David's flight from his own palace, when in the dead of the night, he forded the brook Kedron, and went with a few faithful followers to hide himself for awhile from the fury of his rebellious son. Remember that David in this was a type of the Lord Jesus Christ. He, too, fled; he, too, passed over the brook Kedron when his own people were in rebellion against him, and with a feeble band of followers he went to the garden of Gethsemane. He, too, drank of the brook by the way, and therefore doth he lift up the head. By very many expositors this is entitled THE MORNING HYMN. May we ever wake with holy confidence in our hearts, and a song upon our lips!

DIVISION. This Psalm may be divided into four parts of two verses each. Indeed, many of the Psalms cannot be well understood unless we attentively regard the parts into which they should be divided. They are not continuous descriptions of one scene, but a set of pictures of many kindred subjects. As in our modern sermons, we divide our discourse into different heads, so is it in these Psalms. There is always unity, but it is the unity of a bundle of arrows, and not of a single solitary shaft. Let us now look at the Psalm before us. In the first two verses you have David making a complaint to God concerning his enemies; he then declares his confidence in the Lord (3, 4), sings of his safety in sleep (5, 6), and strengthens himself for future conflict (7, 8).

EXPOSITION
Verse 1. The poor broken-hearted father complains of the multitude of his enemies: and if you turn to 2 Samuel 15:12, you will find it written that "the conspiracy was strong; for the people increased continually with Absalom," while the troops of David constantly diminished! "Lord how are they increased that trouble me!" Here is a note of exclamation to express the wonder of woe which amazed and perplexed the fugitive father.
Verse 3. Here David avows his confidence in God. "Thou, O Lord, art a shield for me." The word in the original signifies more than a shield; it means a buckler round about, a protection which shall surround a man entirely, a shield above, beneath, around, without and within. Oh! what a shield is God for his people!
Verse 4. "I cried unto the Lord with my voice." Why doth he say, "with my voice?" Surely, silent prayers are heard. Yes, but good men often find that, even in secret, they pray better aloud than they do when they utter no vocal sound.
Verse 5. David's faith enabled him to lie down; anxiety would certainly have kept him on tiptoe, watching for an enemy. Yea, he was able to sleep, to sleep in the midst of trouble, surrounded by foes. "So he giveth his beloved sleep."
Verse 6. Buckling on his harness for the day's battle, our hero sings, "I will not be afraid of ten thousands of people, that have set themselves against me round about."
Verse 7. His only hope is in his God, but that is so strong a confidence, that he feels the Lord hath but to arise and he is saved. It is enough for the Lord to stand up, and all is well.
Verse 8. This verse contains the sum and substance of Calvinistic doctrine. Search Scripture through, and you must, if you read it with a candid mind, be persuaded that the doctrine of salvation by grace alone is the great doctrine of the word of God: "Salvation belongeth unto the Lord."

JOHN CALVIN

Psalm 3

David, although driven from his kingdom, and pressed down with utter despair of relief from every earthly quarter, ceases not to call upon God, and supports himself from his promise against the greatest terrors, against the mockery and cruel assaults of his enemies; and, finally, against death itself, which then forced itself upon his consideration. In the end of the psalm, he congratulates himself and the whole Church on the happy issue of all.

1-2
Sacred history teaches that David was not only dethroned, but forsaken by almost all men; so that he had well nigh as many enemies as he had subjects. It is true there accompanied him in his flight a few faithful friends; but he escaped in safety, not so much by their aid and protection as by the hiding-places of the wilderness. It is therefore not wonderful though he was affrighted by the great numbers who were opposed to him, for nothing could have taken place more unlooked for, on his part, than so sudden a rebellion.

3-4
Having mourned over their own sins, and humbly betaken themselves to the mercy of God, they ought to keep their eyes fixed on the obvious and immediate cause of their afflictions, that they may entertain no doubt of the help of God when undeservedly subjected to evil treatment.
4. With my voice have I cried unto the Lord. He here informs us that he had never been so broken by adversity, or cast down by impious scornings, as to be prevented from addressing his prayers to God.

5-6
He had doubtless been tossed amidst the merciless waves of anxiety, but it is certain their violence had been allayed by means of faith, so that however much he was disquieted, he reposed in God. Thus the godly never fail in ultimately proving victorious over all their fears, whereas the ungodly, who do not rely upon God, are overwhelmed with despair, even when they meet with the smallest perils.

7-8
7. Arise, O Lord. As in the former verses David boasted of his quiet state, it would now appear he desires of the Lord to be preserved in safety during the whole of his life; as if he had said, Lord, since thou hast overthrown my enemies, grant that this thy goodness may follow me, and be continued even to the end of my course. But because it is no uncommon thing for David, in the Psalms, to mingle together various affections, it seems more probable, that, after having made mention of his confidence in God, he returns again to make the same prayers as at the beginning.
8. Salvation belongeth unto the Lord. By these words, David not only claims the office of saving for God alone, tacitly opposing his power to all human succor; but also declares, that although a thousand deaths hang over his people, yet this cannot render God unable to save them.

MATTHEW HENRY

Psalm 3

1-3 Distress and confidence.
The first three verses apply to God. Whither else should we go but to him when any thing grieves us or frightens us? David was now at a distance from his own closet, and from the courts of God's house, where he used to pray; and yet he could find away open heaven-ward. Wherever we are we may have access to God, and may draw nigh to him whithersoever we are driven. David, in his flight, attends his God,
I. With a representation of his distress, v. 1, 2.
He looks round, and as it were takes a view of his enemies' camp, or receives information of their designs against him, which he brings to God, not to his own council-board.
II. A profession of his dependence upon God, v. 3.
An active believer, the more he is beaten off from God, either by the rebukes of Providence or the reproaches of enemies, the faster hold he will take of him and the closer will he cleave to him; so David here, when his enemies said, There is no help for him in God, cries out with so much the more assurance, "But thou, O Lord! art a shield for me; let them say what they will, I am sure thou wilt never desert me, and I am resolved I will never distrust thee." See what God is to his people, what he will be, what they have found him, what David found in him.

4-8 Confidence in God.
David, having stirred up himself by the irritations of his enemies to take hold on God as his God, and so gained comfort in looking upward when, if he looked round about him, nothing appeared but what was discouraging, here looks back with pleasing reflections upon the benefit he had derived from trusting in God and looks forward with pleasing expectations of a very bright and happy issue to which the dark dispensation he was now under would shortly be brought.
I. See with what comfort he looks back upon the communion he had had with God, and the communications of his favor to him, either in some former trouble he had been in, and through God's goodness got through, or in this hitherto. David had been exercised with many difficulties, often oppressed and brought very low; but still he had found God all-sufficient.
II. See with what confidence he looks forward to the dangers he had yet in prospect. Having put himself under God's protection and often found the benefit of it, his fears were all stilled and silenced, v. 6, and his prayers were quickened and encouraged, v. 7. He believed God was his Savior, and yet prays; nay, he therefore prays, Arise, O Lord! save me, O my God! Promises of salvation do not supersede, but engage, our petitions for it. He will for this be enquired of.

Psalm 4

Title
To the chief Musician on Neginoth, a Psalm of David.

1 Hear me when I call, O God of my righteousness: thou hast enlarged me when I was in distress; have mercy upon me, and hear my prayer.
2 O ye sons of men, how long will ye turn my glory into shame? how long will ye love vanity, and seek after leasing? Selah.
3 But know that the LORD hath set apart him that is godly for himself: the LORD will hear when I call unto him.
4 Stand in awe, and sin not: commune with your own heart upon your bed, and be still. Selah.
5 Offer the sacrifices of righteousness, and put your trust in the LORD.
6 There be many that say, Who will shew us any good? LORD, lift thou up the light of thy countenance upon us.
7 Thou hast put gladness in my heart, more than in the time that their corn and their wine increased.
8 I will both lay me down in peace, and sleep: for thou, LORD, only makest me dwell in safety.

Psalm 4

TITLE. This Psalm is apparently intended to accompany the third, and make a pair with it. If the last may be entitled THE MORNING PSALM, this from its matter is equally deserving of the title of THE EVENING HYMN. May the choice words of the 8th verse be our sweet song of rest as we retire to our repose!

The Inspired title runs thus: "To the chief Musician on Neginoth, a Psalm of David." The chief musician was the master or director of the sacred music of the sanctuary. Concerning this person carefully read 1 Chronicles 6:31, 32; 15:16-22; 25:1, 7. In these passages will be found much that is interesting to the lover of sacred song, and very much that will throw a light upon the mode of praising God in the temple. Some of the titles of the Psalms are, we doubt not, derived from the names of certain renowned singers, who composed the music to which they were set.
On Neginoth, that is, on stringed instruments, or hand instruments, which were played on with the hand alone, as harps and cymbals. The joy of the Jewish church was so great that they needed music to set forth the delightful feelings of their souls.

DIVISION. In the first verse David pleads with God for help. In the second he expostulates with his enemies, and continues to address them to the end of verse 5. Then from verse 6 to the close he delightfully contrasts his own satisfaction and safety with the disquietude of the ungodly in their best estate. The Psalm was most probably written upon the same occasion as the preceding, and is another choice flower from the garden of affliction. Happy is it for us that David was tried, or probably we should never have heard these sweet sonnets of faith.

EXPOSITION
Verse 1. This is another instance of David's common habit of pleading past mercies as a ground for present favor.
Verse 2. In this second division of the Psalm, we are led from the closet of prayer into the field of conflict. Remark the undaunted courage of the man of God. He allows that his enemies are great men but still he believes them to be foolish men, and so chides them, as though they were but children.
Verse 3. "But know." Fools will not learn, and therefore they must again and again be told the same thing, especially when it is such a bitter truth which is to be taught them, viz.: the fact that the godly are the chosen of God, and are, by distinguishing grace, set apart and separated from among men. Election is a doctrine which unrenewed men cannot endure.
Verse 4. "Tremble and sin not." How many reverse this counsel and sin but tremble not.
Verse 5. Provided that the rebels had obeyed the voice of the last verse, they would now be crying, "What shall we do to be saved?"
Verse 6. We have now entered upon the third division of the Psalm, in which the faith of the afflicted one finds utterance in sweet expressions of contentment and peace.
Verse 7. "It is better," said one, "to feel God's favor one hour in our repenting souls, that to sit whole ages under the warmest sunshine that this world affordeth."
Verse 8. Sweet Evening Hymn! I shall not sit up to watch through fear, but I will lie down; and then I will not lie awake listening to every rustling sound, but I will lie down in peace and sleep, for I have nought to fear. He that hath the wings of God above him needs no other curtain. Better than bolts or bars is the protection of the Lord.

JOHN CALVIN

Psalm 4

1. In these words there is shown the faith of David, who, although brought to the uttermost distress, and indeed almost consumed by a long series of calamities, did not sink under his sorrow; nor was he so broken in heart as to be prevented from betaking himself to God his deliverer. By his praying, he testified, that when utterly deprived of all earthly succor, there yet remained for him hope in God.

2-3
2. O ye sons of men. The happy result of the prayer of David was, that resuming courage, he was able not only to repel the fury of his enemies, but also to challenge them on his part, and fearlessly to despise all their machinations. That our confidence, therefore, may remain unshaken, we ought not, when assailed by the wicked, to enter into conflict without being furnished like David with the same armor. The sum is, that since God was determined to defend David by his own power, it was in vain for all the men in the world to endeavor to destroy him.
3. Know that Jehovah hath set apart, etc This is a confirmation of the preceding verse, for it shows that the cause of David's boldness consisted in this, that he depended upon God, the founder of his kingdom. And surely we may then safely triumph over our enemies when we are assured of having the call of God to the office which we hold, or the work in which we are engaged.

4-5
4. Tremble then. Now he exhorts his enemies to repentance, if peradventure, their madness was not wholly incorrigible. In the first place, he bids them tremble, or be troubled; a word by which he rebukes their stupidity in running headlong in their wicked course, without any fear of God, or any sense of danger.
5. Sacrifice ye. Let us learn from this passage, that, in contending with the corrupters of true religion, who may have the name of God continually in their mouth, and vaunt themselves on account of their observance of his outward worship, we may safely rebuke their boasting, because they do not offer the right sacrifices.

6-8
6. David uses the expression, The light of God's countenance, to denote his serene and pleasant countenance—the manifestations of his favor and love; just as, on the other hand, the face of God seems to us dark and clouded when he shows the tokens of his anger.
7. Thou hast given more joy to my heart. The sum is, that he had more satisfaction in seeing the reconciled countenance of God beaming upon him, than if he had possessed garners full of corn, and cellars full of wine.
8. He concludes, by stating, that as he is protected by the power of God, he enjoys as much security and quiet as if he had been defended by all the garrisons on earth. Now, we know, that to be free from all fear, and from the torment and vexation of care, is a blessing to be desired above all other things.

MATTHEW HENRY

Psalm 4

1-5 Expostulation with sinners.
I. David addresses himself to God, v. 1. Whether the sons of men, to whom he is about to speak, will hear, or whether they will forbear, he hopes and prays that God will give him a generous audience, and an answer of peace: "Hear me when I call, and accept my adorations, grant my petitions, and judge upon my appeals; have mercy upon me, and hear me." All the notice God is pleased to take of our prayers, and all the returns he is pleased to make to them, must be ascribed, not to our merit, but purely to his mercy. "Hear me for thy mercy-sake" is our best plea.
II. He addresses himself to the children of men, for the conviction and conversion of those that are yet strangers to God, and that will not have the Messiah, the Son of David, to reign over them. He endeavors to convince them of the folly of their impiety (v. 2). 2. He shows them the peculiar favor which God has for good people, the special protection they are under, and the singular privileges to which they are entitled, v. 3.

He warns them against sin, and exhorts them both to frighten and to reason themselves out of it (v. 4): "Stand in awe and sin not" (be angry and sin not, so the LXX., and some think the apostle takes that exhortation from him, Eph. iv. 26); "commune with your own hearts; be converted, and, in order thereunto, consider and fear."

He counsels them to make conscience of their duty (v. 5): Offer to God the sacrifice of righteousness. We must not only cease to do evil, but learn to do well.

6-8 The good man's desire.
We have here,
I. The foolish wish of worldly people: There be many that say, Who will show us any good? Who will make us to see good? What good they meant is intimated, v. 7. It was the increase of their corn and wine; all they desired was plenty of the wealth of this world, that they might enjoy abundance of the delights of sense.
II. The wise choice which godly people make. David, and the pious few that adhered to him, dissented from that wish, and joined in this prayer, Lord, lift thou up the light of thy countenance upon us.
1. He disagrees from the vote of the many. God had set him apart for himself by distinguishing favors, and therefore he sets himself apart by a distinguishing character. "They are for any good, for worldly good, but so am not I; I will not say as they say; any good will not serve my turn; the wealth of the world will never make a portion for my soul, and therefore I cannot take up with it."
2. He and his friends agree in their choice of God's favor as their felicity; it is this which in their account is better than life and all the comforts of life.

Psalm 5

Title
To the chief Musician upon Neginoth, a Psalm of David.

1-6
1 Give ear to my words, O LORD, consider my meditation.
2 Hearken unto the voice of my cry, my King, and my God: for unto thee will I pray.
3 My voice shalt thou hear in the morning, O LORD; in the morning will I direct my prayer unto thee, and will look up.
4 For thou art not a God that hath pleasure in wickedness: neither shall evil dwell with thee.
5 The foolish shall not stand in thy sight: thou hatest all workers of iniquity.
6 Thou shalt destroy them that speak leasing: the LORD will abhor the bloody and deceitful man.

Psalm 5

TITLE. "To the Chief Musician upon Nehiloth, a Psalm of David." The Hebrew word Nehiloth is taken from another word, signifying "to perforate;" "to bore through," whence it comes to mean a pipe or a flute; so that this song was probably intended to be sung with an accompaniment of wind instruments, such as the horn, the trumpet, flute, or cornet. However, it is proper to remark that we are not sure of the interpretation of these ancient titles, for the Septuagint translates it, "For him who shall obtain inheritance," and Aben Ezra thinks it denotes some old and well known melody to which this Psalm was to be played. The best scholars confess that great darkness hangs over the precise interpretation of the title; nor is this much to be regretted, for it furnishes an internal evidence of the great antiquity of the Book. Throughout the first, second, third, and forth Psalms, you will have noticed that the subject is a contrast between the position, the character, and the prospects of the righteous and of the wicked. In this Psalm you will note the same. The Psalmist carries out a contrast between himself made righteous by God's grace, and the wicked who opposed him. To the devout mind there is here presented a precious view of the Lord Jesus, of whom it is said that in the days of his flesh, he offered up prayers and supplications with strong crying and tears.

DIVISION. The Psalm should be divided into two parts, from the first to the seventh verse, and then from the eighth to the twelfth. In the first part of the Psalm David most vehemently beseeches the Lord to hearken to his prayer, and in the second part he retraces the same ground.

EXPOSITION
Verse 1. There are two sorts of prayers—those expressed in words, and the unuttered longings which abide as silent meditations. Words are not the essence but the garments of prayer. Moses at the Red Sea cried to God, though he said nothing. Yet the use of language may prevent distraction of mind, may assist the powers of the soul, and may excite devotion. David, we observe, uses both modes of prayer, and craves for the one a hearing, and for the other a consideration. What an expressive word! "Consider my meditation." If I have asked that which is right, give it to me; if I have omitted to ask that which I most needed, fill up the vacancy in my prayer.
Verse 2. "The voice of my cry." In another Psalm we find the expression, "The voice of my weeping." Weeping has a voice—a melting, plaintive tone, an ear-piercing shrillness, which reaches the very heart of God; and crying hath a voice—a soul-moving eloquence; coming from our heart it reaches God's heart. Ah! my brothers and sisters, sometimes we cannot put our prayers into words: they are nothing but a cry: but the Lord can comprehend the meaning, for he hears a voice in our cry. To a loving father his children's cries are music, and they have a magic influence which his heart cannot resist.
Verse 3. Observe, this is not so much a prayer as a resolution, "'My voice shalt thou hear;' I will not be dumb, I will not be silent, I will not withhold my speech, I will cry to thee for the fire that dwells within compels me to pray." We can sooner die than live without prayer. None of God's children are possessed with a dumb devil.
Verse 4. And now the Psalmist having thus expressed his resolution to pray, you hear him putting up his prayer. He is pleading against his cruel and wicked enemies. He uses a most mighty argument. He begs of God to put them away from him, because they were displeasing to God himself. "For thou art not a God that hath pleasure in wickedness: neither shall evil dwell with thee." "When I pray against my tempters," says David, "I pray against the very things which thou thyself abhorrest." Thou hatest evil: Lord, I beseech thee, deliver me from it!

Psalm 5

1-2
I presume not positively to determine whether David, in this psalm, bewails the wrongs which he suffered from his enemies at some particular time, or whether he complains generally of the various persecutions with which, for a long time, he was harassed under Saul. Some of the Jewish commentators apply the psalm even to Absalom; because, by the bloody and deceitful man, they think Doeg and Ahithophel are pointed out. To me, however, it appears more probable, that when David, after the death of Saul, had got peaceable possession of the kingdoms he committed to writing the prayers which he had meditated in his afflictions and dangers.
3. The expression, To direct unto God, I take to signify the same thing as directly to approach to God. Many, as if the language were elliptical, supply the words, my prayer. But in my judgment, David rather intends to declare that he was not turned hither and thither, nor drawn different ways by the temptations to which he was exposed, but that to betake himself to God was the settled order of his life.
4. Here David makes the malice and wickedness of his enemies an argument to enforce his prayer for the divine favor towards him. The language is indeed abrupt, as the saints in prayer will often stammer; but this stammering is more acceptable to God than all the figures of rhetoric, be they ever so fine and glittering. Besides, the great object which David has in view, is to show, that since the cruelty and treachery of his enemies had reached their utmost height, it was impossible but that God would soon arrest them in their course. His reasoning is grounded upon the nature of God. Since righteousness and upright dealing are pleasing to him, David, from this, concludes that he will take vengeance on all the unjust and wicked.

One use, then, which may be made of this doctrine is this,—when we see the wicked indulging themselves in their lusts, and when, in consequence, doubts steal into our minds as to whether God takes any care of us, we should learn to satisfy ourselves with the consideration that God, who hates and abhors all iniquity, will not permit them to pass unpunished, and although he bear with them for a time, he will at length ascend into the judgment-seat, and show himself an avenger, as he is the protector and defender of his people.
7. The scope of the passage leads us to understand David as promising to give thanks to God. He had before spoken of his enemies as hated of God; and now, being persuaded that God will keep him in safety, he calls himself to the exercise of gratitude. I will come into thy temples says he, in the multitude of thy mercy; as if he had said, I may now seem to be in a condition almost desperate, but by the favor of God, I shall be kept in perfect safety. This passage, therefore, teaches us, that when we are afflicted by the most distressing temptations, we ought to set the grace of God before our eyes, in order thereby to be supported with the hope of the divine interposition amidst the greatest dangers.

Psalm 5

1-6 Prayer for guidance and protection.
In these verses David had an eye to God,
I. As a prayer-hearing God; such he has always been ever since men began to call upon the name of the Lord, and yet is still as ready to hear prayer as ever. Observe how David here styles him: O Lord (v. 1, 3), Jehovah, a self-existent, self-sufficient, Being, whom we are bound to adore, and, "my King and my God (v. 2), whom I have avouched for my God, to whom I have sworn allegiance, and under whose protection I have put myself as my King." We believe that the God we pray to is a King, and a God.
II. As a sin-hating God, v. 4-6.
David takes notice of this,
1. As a warning to himself, and all other praying people, to remember that, as the God with whom we have to do is gracious and merciful, so he is pure and holy; though he is ready to hear prayer, yet, if we regard iniquity in our heart, he will not hear our prayers, Ps. lxvi. 18.
2. As an encouragement to his prayers against his enemies; they were wicked men, and therefore enemies to God, and such as he had not pleasure in. In singing these verses, and praying them over, we must engage and stir up ourselves to the duty of prayer, and encourage ourselves in it, because we shall not seek the Lord in vain; and must express our detestation of sin, and our awful expectation of that day of Christ's appearing which will be the day of the perdition of ungodly men.

7-12 Delight in public worship; happiness of the righteous.

In these verses David gives three characters: of himself, of his enemies, and of all the people of God, and subjoins a prayer to each of them.
I. He gives an account of himself and prays for himself, v. 7, 8.

First, he is steadfastly resolved to keep closely to God and to his worship. Sinners go away from God, and so make themselves odious to his holiness and obnoxious to his justice: "But, as for me, that shall not keep me from thee." God's holiness and justice are so far from being a terror to the upright in heart, to drive them from God, that they are rather by them invited to cleave to him.

Second, he earnestly prays that God, by his grace, would guide and preserve him always in the way of his duty (v. 8): Lead me in thy righteousness, because of my enemies: Heb. "Because of those who observe me, who watch for my halting and seek occasion against me." See here,
(1.) The good use which David made of the malice of his enemies against him. The more curious they were in spying faults in him, that they might have whereof to accuse him, the more cautious he was to avoid sin and all appearances of it, and the more solicitous to

Psalm 5

7-12
7 But as for me, I will come into thy house in the multitude of thy mercy: and in thy fear will I worship toward thy holy temple.
8 Lead me, O LORD, in thy righteousness because of mine enemies; make thy way straight before my face.
9 For there is no faithfulness in their mouth; their inward part is very wickedness; their throat is an open sepulcher; they flatter with their tongue.
10 Destroy thou them, O God; let them fall by their own counsels; cast them out in the multitude of their transgressions; for they have rebelled against thee.
11 But let all those that put their trust in thee rejoice: let them ever shout for joy, because thou defendest them: let them also that love thy name be joyful in thee.
12 For thou, LORD, wilt bless the righteous; with favor wilt thou compass him as with a shield.

Verse 5. "The foolish shall not stand in thy sight." Sinners are fools written large. A little sin is a great folly, and the greatest of all folly is great sin. Such sinful fools as these must be banished from the court of heaven. Earthly kings were wont to have fools in their trains, but the only wise God will have no fools in his palace above.
Verse 6. Observe, that evil speakers must be punished as well as evil workers, for "thou shalt destroy them that speak leasing." All liars shall have their portion in the lake which burneth with fire and brimstone. A man may lie without danger of the law of man, but he will not escape the law of God. Liars have short wings, their flight shall soon be over, and they shall fall into the fiery floods of destruction.
Verse 7. With this verse the first part of the Psalm ends. The Psalmist has bent his knee in prayer; he has described before God, as an argument for his deliverance, the character and the fate of the wicked; and now he contrasts this with the condition of the righteous. "But as for me, I will come into thy house." I will not stand at a distance, I will come into thy sanctuary, just as a child comes into his father's house. But I will not come there by my own merits; no, I have a multitude of sins, and therefore I will come in the multitude of thy mercy. I will approach thee with confidence because of thy immeasurable grace. God's judgments are all numbered, but his mercies are innumerable; he gives his wrath by weight, but without weight his mercy.
Verse 8. Now we come to the second part, in which the Psalmist repeats his arguments, and goes over the same ground again.

"Lead me, O Lord," as a little child is led by its father, as a blind man is guided by his friend. It is safe and pleasant walking when God leads the way. "In thy righteousness," not in my righteousness, for that is imperfect, but in thine, for thou art righteousness itself. "Make thy way," not my way, "straight before my face."
Verse 9. This description of depraved man has been copied by the Apostle Paul, and, together with some other quotations, he has placed it in the second chapter of Romans, as being an accurate description of the whole human race, not of David's enemies only, but of all men by nature. Note that remarkable figure, "Their throat is an open sepulcher," a sepulcher full of loathsomeness, of miasma, of pestilence and death.
Verse 10. "Against thee:" not against me. If they were my enemies I would forgive them, but I cannot forgive thine. We are to forgive our enemies, but God's enemies it is not in our power to forgive. These expressions have often been noticed by men of over refinement as being harsh, and grating on the ear. "Oh!" say they, "they are vindictive and revengeful." Let us remember that they might be translated as prophecies, not as wishes; but we do not care to avail ourselves of this method of escape.
Verse 11. Joy is the privilege of the believer. When sinners are destroyed our rejoicing shall be full. They laugh first and weep ever after; we weep now, but shall rejoice eternally. When they howl we shall shout, and as they must groan for ever, so shall we ever shout for joy. This holy bliss of ours has a firm foundation, for, O Lord, we are joyful in thee.
Verse 12. As for the defense which the believer needs in this land of battles, it is here promised to him in the fullest measure. There were vast shields used by the ancients as extensive as a man's whole person, which would surround him entirely. So says David, "With favor wilt thou compass him as with a shield." According to Ainsworth there is here also the idea of being crowned, so that we wear a royal helmet, which is at once our glory and defense. O Lord, ever give to us this gracious coronation!

8-10
8. The righteousness of God in this passage, as in many others, is to be understood of his faithfulness and mercy which he shows in defending and preserving his people. Consequently, in thy righteousness means the same thing as for or according to thy righteousness. David, desiring to have God as the guide of his path, encourages himself in the hope of obtaining his request, because God is righteous; as if he had said, Lord, as thou art righteous, defend me with thine aid, that I may escape from the wicked plots of my enemies. Of the same import is the last clause of the verse, where he prays that the way of God may be made straight before his face, in other words, that he might be delivered by the power of God from the distresses with which he was so completely surrounded, that, according to the judgment of the flesh, he never expected to find a way of escape.
9. For there is no faithfulness in their mouth. He still repeats the same complaints which he made before, in order thereby to render his enemies the more odious in the sight of God, and to call forth in his own behalf the mercy of God, who has promised to succor those who are unjustly oppressed. And this is to be particularly attended to, that the more our enemies manifest their cruelty against us, or the more wickedly they vex us, we ought, with so much the greater confidence, to send up our groanings to heaven, because God will not suffer their rage to proceed to the uttermost, but will bring forth their malice and wicked devices to the light.
10. If we are afraid of the snares and deceits of men, and if we find those who desire to do us mischief to be clear-headed and sharp-witted persons, let us remember, that it is the continual office of God to strike with stupidity and madness those who are wise to commit iniquity. In short, David wishes God to lay his hand upon his enemies, and to put a stop to their wicked deliberations.

11-12
11. This passage teaches us, that true joy proceeds from no other source than from the protection of God. We may be exposed to a thousand deaths, but this one consideration ought abundantly to suffice us, that we are covered and defended by the hand of God. And this will be the case, if the vain shadows of this world do not so beguile us as to excite us to take shelter under them. We ought also particularly to notice the statement, that those who trust in the Lord love his name. The remembrance of God must be sweet to us, and fill our hearts with joy, or rather ravish us with love to him, after he has caused us to taste of his goodness.
12. For thou, Jehovah, wilt bless the righteous. The Psalmist here confirms the concluding sentence of the preceding verse, namely, that all the servants of God in common will take support to their faith from what he had experienced, for he would have us from one example to form our judgment of the immutability and perpetuity of God's grace towards all the godly. Again, by this he teaches us that there is no true and right joy but that which is derived from the sense of God's fatherly love.

be always found in the good way of God and duty. Thus, by wisdom and grace, good may come out of evil.
(2.) The right course which David took for the baffling of those who sought occasion against him. He committed himself to a divine guidance, begged of God both by his providence and by his grace to direct him in the right way, and keep him from turning aside out of it, at any time, in any instance whatsoever, that the most critical and captious of his enemies, like Daniel's, might find no occasion against him. The way of our duty is here called God's way, and his righteousness, because he prescribes to us by his just and holy laws, which if we sincerely set before us as our rule, we may in faith beg of God to direct us in all particular cases. How this prayer of David's was answered to him see 1 Sam. xviii. 14, 15.
II. He gives an account of his enemies, and prays against them, v. 9, 10. If his account of them is true, as no doubt it is, they have a very bad character; and, if they had not been bad men indeed, they could not have been enemies to a man after God's own heart. He had spoken (v. 6) of God's hating the bloody and deceitful man. "Now, Lord," says he, "that is the character of my enemies: they are deceitful; there is no trusting them, for there is no faithfulness in their mouth." They thought it was no sin to tell a deliberate lie if it might but blemish David, and render him odious. "Lord, lead me," says he (v. 8), "for such as these are the men I have to do with, against whose slanders innocency itself is no security. Do they speak fair? Do they talk of peace and friendship? They flatter with their tongues; it is designed to cover their malice, and to gain their point the more securely. Whatever they pretend of religion or friendship, two sacred things, they are true to neither: Their inward part is wickedness itself; it is very wickedness. They are likewise bloody; for their throat is an open sepulcher, cruel as the grave, gaping to devour and to swallow up, insatiable as the grave.
III. He gives an account of the people of God, and prays for them, concluding with an assurance of their bliss, which he doubted not of his own interest in. Observe,
1. The description he gives of God's people. They are the righteous (v. 12); for they put their trust in God, are well assured of his power and all-sufficiency, venture their all upon his promise, and are confident of his protection in the way of their duty; and they love his name, are well pleased with all that by which God has made himself known, and take delight in their acquaintance with him. This is true and pure religion, to live a life of complacency in God and dependence on him.
2. His prayer for them: "Let them rejoice; let them have cause to rejoice and hearts to rejoice; fill them with joy, with great joy and unspeakable; let them shout for joy, with constant joy and perpetual."

Psalm 6

Title
To the chief Musician on Niginoth upon Sheminith, a Psalm of David.

1-5
1 O LORD, rebuke me not in thine anger, neither chasten me in thy hot displeasure.
2 Have mercy upon me, O LORD; for I am weak: O LORD, heal me; for my bones are vexed.
3 My soul is also sore vexed: but thou, O LORD, how long?
4 Return, O LORD, deliver my soul: oh save me for thy mercies' sake.
5 For in death there is no remembrance of thee: in the grave who shall give thee thanks?

Psalm 6

TITLE. This Psalm is commonly known as the first of the PENITENTIAL PSALMS, (The other six are 32, 38, 51, 102, 130, 143) and certainly its language well becomes the lip of a penitent, for it expresses at once the sorrow, (verses 3, 6, 7), the humiliation (verses 2 and 4), and the hatred of sin (verse 8), which are the unfailing marks of the contrite spirit when it turns to God. O Holy Spirit, beget in us the true repentance which needeth not to be repented of. The title of this Psalm is "To the chief Musician on Neginoth upon Sheminith (1 Chronicle 15:21), A Psalm of David," that is, to the chief musician with stringed instruments, upon the eighth, probably the octave. Some think it refers to the bass or tenor key, which would certainly be well adapted to this mournful ode. But we are not able to understand these old musical terms, and even the term "Selah," still remains untranslated. This, however, should be no difficulty in our way. We probably lose but very little by our ignorance, and it may serve to confirm our faith. It is a proof of the high antiquity of these Psalms that they contain words, the meaning of which is lost even to the best scholars of the Hebrew language. Surely these are but incidental (accidental I might almost say, if I did not believe them to be designed by God), proofs of their being, what they profess to be, the ancient writings of King David of olden times.

DIVISION. You will observe that the Psalm is readily divided into two parts. First, there is the Psalmist's plea in his great distress, reaching from the first to the end of the seventh verse. Then you have, from the eighth to the end, quite a different theme. The Psalmist has changed his note. He leaves the minor key, and betakes himself to sublimer strains. He tunes his note to the high key of confidence, and declares that God hath heard his prayer, and hath delivered him out of all his troubles.

EXPOSITION
Verse 1. Having read through the first division, in order to see it as a whole, we will now look at it verse by verse. "O Lord, rebuke me not in thine anger." The Psalmist is very conscious that he deserves to be rebuked, and he feels, moreover, that the rebuke in some form or other must come upon him, if not for condemnation, yet for conviction and sanctification. "Corn is cleaned with wind, and the soul with chastenings." It were folly to pray against the golden hand which enriches us by its blows. He does not ask that the rebuke may be totally withheld, for he might thus lose a blessing in disguise; but, "Lord, rebuke me not in thine anger." If thou remindest me of my sin, it is good; but, oh, remind me not of it as one incensed against me, lest thy servant's heart should sink in despair. Thus saith Jeremiah, "O Lord, correct me, but with judgment; not in thine anger, lest thou bring me to nothing."
Verse 2. "Have mercy upon me, O Lord; for I am weak." Though I deserve destruction, yet let thy mercy pity my frailty. This is the right way to plead with God if we would prevail. Urge not your goodness or your greatness, but plead your sin and your littleness. Cry, "I am weak," therefore, O Lord, give me strength and crush me not. Send not forth the fury of thy tempest against so weak a vessel. Temper the wind to the shorn lamb. Be tender and pitiful to a poor withering flower, and break it not from its stem. Surely this is the plea that a sick man would urge to move the pity of his fellow if he were striving with him, "Deal gently with me, 'for I am weak.'" A sense of sin had so spoiled the Psalmist's pride, so taken away his vaunted strength, that he found himself weak to obey the law, weak through the sorrow that was in him, too weak, perhaps, to lay hold on the promise.
Verse 3. "O Lord, heal me; for my bones are vexed." Here he prays for healing, not merely the mitigation of the ills he endured, but their entire removal, and the curing of the wounds which had arisen therefrom. His

Psalm 6

David, being afflicted by the hand of God, acknowledges that he had provoked the Divine wrath by his sins, and, therefore, in order to obtain relief, he prays for forgiveness. At the same time, he regrets, that by being taken out of the world, he would be deprived of an opportunity of praising God. Then, having obtained confidence, he celebrates the grace of God, and directs his discourse to his enemies, who triumphed over his calamities.

Title
The name of Song shows that David composed this psalm, in which he describes the passionate workings of his grief in the time of his troubles after he had obtained deliverance from the evils which he deplores. What the kind of chastisement was of which he speaks is uncertain.

1. The calamity which David now experienced had, perhaps, been inflicted by men, but he wisely considers that he has to deal with God. Those persons are very unsuitably exercised under their afflictions who do not immediately take a near and a steady view of their sins, in order thereby to produce the conviction that they have deserved the wrath of God. And yet we see how thoughtless and insensible almost all men are on this subject; for while they cry out that they are afflicted and miserable, scarcely one among a hundred looks to the hand which strikes. From whatever quarter, therefore, our afflictions come, let us learn to turn our thoughts instantly to God, and to acknowledge him as the Judge who summons us as guilty before his tribunal, since we, of our own accord, do not anticipate his judgment.
2. Have mercy upon me. As he earnestly calls upon God to be merciful to him, it is from this the more clearly manifest, that by the terms anger and indignation he did not mean cruelty or undue severity, but only such judgment as God executes upon the reprobate, whom he does not spare in mercy as he does his own children. If he had complained of being unjustly and too severely punished, he would now have only added something to this effect: Restrain thyself, that in punishing me thou mayest not exceed the measure of my offense.
3. And thou, O Jehovah, how long? This elliptical form of expression serves to express more strongly the vehemence of grief, which not only holds the minds of men bound up, but likewise their tongues, breaking and cutting short their speech in the middle of the sentence. God, in his compassion towards us, permits us to pray to him to make haste to succor us; but when we have freely complained of his long delay, that our prayers or sorrow, on this account, may not pass beyond bounds we must submit our case entirely to his will, and not wish him to make greater haste than shall seem good to him.
4. Return, O Lord. In the preceding verses the Psalmist bewailed the absence of God, and now he earnestly requests the tokens of his presence, for our happiness consists in this, that we are the objects of the Divine regard, but we think he

Psalm 6

1-7 David's complaints.
These verses speak the language of a heart truly humbled under humbling providences, of a broken and contrite spirit under great afflictions, sent on purpose to awaken conscience and mortify corruption. Those heap up wrath who cry not when God binds them; but those are getting ready for mercy who, under God's rebukes, sow in tears, as David does here. Let us observe here,
I. The representation he makes to God of his grievances. He pours out his complaint before him.
1. He complains of bodily pain and sickness (v. 2): My bones are vexed. His bones and his flesh, like Job's, were touched. Though David was a king, yet he was sick and pained; his imperial crown could not keep his head from aching. Great men are men, and subject to the common calamities of human life.
2. He complains of inward trouble: My soul is also sorely vexed; and that is much more grievous than the vexation of the bones. The spirit of a man will sustain his infirmity, if that be in good plight; but, if that be wounded, the grievance is intolerable. David's sickness brought his sin to his remembrance, and he looked upon it as a token of God's displeasure against him; that was the vexation of his soul; that made him cry, I am weak, heal me.
II. The impression which his troubles made upon him. They lay very heavily; he groaned till he was weary, wept till he made his bed to swim, and watered his couch (v. 6), wept till he had almost wept his eyes out (v. 7): My eye is consumed because of grief. David had more courage and consideration than to mourn thus for any outward affliction; but, when sin sat heavily upon his conscience and he was made to possess his iniquities, when his soul was wounded with the sense of God's wrath and his withdrawings from him, then he thus grieves and mourns in secret, and even his soul refuses to be comforted.
III. The petitions which he offers up to God in this sorrowful and distressed state. That which he dreads as the greatest evil is the anger of God. This was the wormwood and the gall in the affliction and the misery; it was the infusion of this that made it indeed a bitter cup; and therefore he prays (v. 1), O Lord! rebuke me not in thy anger, though I have deserved it, neither chasten me in thy hot displeasure. He does not pray, "Lord, rebuke me not; Lord, chasten me not;" for, as many as God loves he rebukes and chastens, as a father the son in whom he delights.
IV. The pleas with which he enforces his petitions, not to move God (he knows our cause and the true merits of it better than we can state them), but to move himself. He pleads God's mercy; and thence we take some of our best encouragements in prayer: Save me, for thy mercies' sake. He pleads God's glory (v. 5): "For in death there is no remembrance of thee. Lord, if thou deliver me and comfort me, I will

Psalm 6

6-10

6 I am weary with my groaning; all the night make I my bed to swim; I water my couch with my tears.
7 Mine eye is consumed because of grief; it waxeth old because of all mine enemies.
8 Depart from me, all ye workers of iniquity; for the LORD hath heard the voice of my weeping.
9 The LORD hath heard my supplication; the LORD will receive my prayer.
10 Let all mine enemies be ashamed and sore vexed: let them return and be ashamed suddenly.

bones were "shaken," as the Hebrew has it. His terror had become so great that his very bones shook; not only did his flesh quiver, but the bones, the solid pillars of the house of manhood, were made to tremble. "My bones are shaken." Ah, when the soul has a sense of sin, it is enough to make the bones shake; it is enough to make a man's hair stand up on end to see the flames of hell beneath him, an angry God above him, and danger and doubt surrounding him. Well might he say, "My bones are shaken." Lest, however, we should imagine that it was merely bodily sickness—although bodily sickness might be the outward sign—the Psalmist goes on to say, "My soul is also sore vexed." Soul-trouble is the very soul of trouble.

Verse 4. "Return, O Lord; deliver my soul." As God's absence was the main cause of his misery, so his return would be enough to deliver him from his trouble. "Oh save me for thy mercies' sake." He knows where to look, and what arm to lay hold upon. He does not lay hold on God's left hand of justice, but on his right hand of mercy. He knew his iniquity too well to think of merit, or appeal to anything but the grace of God.

Verse 5. And now David was in great fear of death—death temporal, and perhaps death eternal. Read the passage as you will, the following verse is full of power. "For in death there is no remembrance of thee; in the grave who shall give thee thanks?" Churchyards are silent places; the vaults of the sepulcher echo not with songs. Damp earth covers dumb mouths. "O Lord!" saith he, "if thou wilt spare me I will praise thee. If I die, then must my mortal praise at least be suspended; and if I perish in hell, then thou wilt never have any thanksgiving from me. Songs of gratitude cannot rise from the flaming pit of hell. True, thou wilt doubtless be glorified, even in my eternal condemnation, but then O Lord, I cannot glorify thee voluntarily; and among the sons of men, there will be one heart the less to bless thee."

Verse 6. The Psalmist gives a fearful description of his long agony: "I am weary with my groaning." He has groaned till his throat was hoarse; he had cried for mercy till prayer became a labor. God's people may groan, but they may not grumble. Yea, they must groan, being burdened, or they will never shout in the day of deliverance.

Verse 7. "I water my couch with my tears. Mine eye is consumed because of grief; it waxeth old because of all my enemies." As an old man's eye grows dim with years, so, says David, my eye is grown red and feeble through weeping. Conviction sometimes has such an effect upon the body, that even the outward organs are made to suffer.

Verse 8. David has found peace, and rising from his knees he begins to sweep his house of the wicked. "Depart from me, all ye workers of iniquity." The best remedy for us against an evil man is a long space between us both. "Get ye gone; I can have no fellowship with you." Repentance is a practical thing. A pardoned sinner will hate the sins which cost the Savior his blood. Grace and sin are quarrelsome neighbors, and one or the other must go to the wall.

Verse 9. "The Lord hath heard my supplication." The Holy Spirit had wrought into the Psalmist's mind the confidence that his prayer was heard. This is frequently the privilege of the saints. Praying the prayer of faith, they are often infallibly assured that they have prevailed with God.

Verse 10. "Let all mine enemies be ashamed and sore vexed." This is rather a prophecy than an imprecation, it may be read in the future, "All my enemies shall be ashamed and sore vexed." They shall return and be ashamed instantaneously,—in a moment;—their doom shall come upon them suddenly.

is alienated front us, if he does not give us some substantial evidence of his care for us. That David was at this time in the utmost peril, we gather from these words, in which he prays both for the deliverance of his soul, as it were, from the jaws of death, and for his restoration to a state of safety. Yet no mention is made of any bodily disease, and, therefore, I give no judgment with respect to the kind of his affliction.
5. For in death there is no remembrance of thee. After God has bestowed all things freely upon us, he requires nothing in return but a grateful remembrance of his benefits. To this gratitude reference is made when David says, that there will be no remembrance of God in death, nor any celebration of his praise in the grave His meaning is, that if, by the grace of God, he shall be delivered from death, he will be grateful for it, and keep it in remembrance. And he laments, that if he should be removed out of the world, he would be deprived of the power and opportunity of manifesting his gratitude, since in that case he would no longer mingle in the society of men, there to commend or celebrate the name of God.

6-7
These forms of expression are hyperbolical, but it must not be imagined that David, after the manner of poets, exaggerates his sorrow; but he declares truly and simply how severe and bitter it had been. It should always be kept in mind, that his affliction did not proceed so much from his having been severely wounded with bodily distress; but regarding God as greatly displeased with him, he saw, as it were, hell open to receive him; and the mental distress which this produces exceeds all other sorrows. Indeed, the more sincerely a man is devoted to God, he is just so much the more severely disquieted by the sense of his wrath; and hence it is that holy persons, who were otherwise endued with uncommon fortitude, have showed in this respect the greatest softness and want of resolution. And nothing prevents us at this day from experiencing in ourselves what David describes concerning himself but the stupidity of our flesh. Those who have experienced, even in a moderate degree, what it is to contend with the fear of eternal death, will be satisfied that there is nothing extravagant in these words.

8-10
After David has disburdened his griefs and troubles into the bosom of God, he now, as it were, assumes a new character. And, without doubt, he had been afflicted with long-continued despondency of spirit before he could recover himself, and attain to such a degree of assurance as he here displays. Directing his discourse against his adversaries, he represents it as not the least part of his temptations that ungodly men triumphed over him, and derided him as lost, and in a hopeless condition; for we know with what insolence their pride and cruelty magnify themselves against the children of God, when they see them oppressed under the cross. And to this Satan moves them, in order to drive the faithful to despair, when they see their hope made the subject of mockery.

not only give thee thanks for my deliverance, and stir up others to join with me in these thanksgivings, but I will spend the new life thou shalt entrust me with in thy service and to thy glory, and all the remainder of my days I will preserve a grateful remembrance of thy favors to me, and be quickened thereby in all instances of service to thee; but, if I die, I shall be cut short of that opportunity of honoring thee and doing good to others, for in the grave who will give the thanks?"
8-10 Confidence in God
What a sudden change is here for the better! He that was groaning, and weeping, and giving up all for gone (v. 6, 7), here looks and speaks very pleasantly. Having made his requests known to God, and lodged his case with him, he is very confident the issue will be good and his sorrow is turned into joy.
I. He distinguishes himself from the wicked and ungodly, and fortifies himself against their insults (v. 8): Depart from me, all you workers of iniquity.
II. He assures himself that God was, and would be, propitious to him, notwithstanding the present intimations of wrath which he was under. He is confident of a gracious answer to this prayer which he is now making. While he is yet speaking, he is aware that God hears (as Isa. lxv. 24, Dan. ix. 20), and therefore speaks of it as a thing done, and repeats it with an air of triumph, "The Lord hath heard" (v. 8), and again (v. 9), "The Lord hath heard." By the workings of God's grace upon his heart he knew his prayer was graciously accepted, and therefore did not doubt but it would in due time be effectually answered. His tears had a voice, a loud voice, in the ears of the God of mercy: The Lord has heard the voice of my weeping. Silent tears are not speechless ones.
III. He either prays for the conversion or predicts the destruction of his enemies and persecutors, v. 10.
1. It may very well be taken as a prayer for their conversion: "Let them all be ashamed of the opposition they have given me and the censures they have passed upon me. Let them be (as all true penitents are) vexed at themselves for their own folly; let them return to a better temper and disposition of mind, and let them be ashamed of what they have done against me and take shame to themselves."
2. If they be not converted, it is a prediction of their confusion and ruin. They shall be ashamed and sorely vexed (so it maybe read), and that justly. They rejoiced that David was vexed (v. 2, 3), and therefore, as usually happens, the evil returns upon themselves; they also shall be sorely vexed. Those that will not give glory to God shall have their faces filled with everlasting shame.

In singing this, and praying over it, we must give glory to God, as a God ready to hear prayer, must own his goodness to us in hearing our prayers, and must encourage ourselves to wait upon him and to trust in him in the greatest straits and difficulties.

Psalm 7

Title
Shiggaion of David, which he sang unto the Lord, concerning the words of Cush the Benjamite.

1-6
1 O LORD my God, in thee do I put my trust: save me from all them that persecute me, and deliver me:
2 Lest he tear my soul like a lion, rending it in pieces, while there is none to deliver.
3 O LORD my God, If I have done this; if there be iniquity in my hands;
4 If I have rewarded evil unto him that was at peace with me; (yea, I have delivered him that without cause is mine enemy:)
5 Let the enemy persecute my soul, and take it; yea, let him tread down my life upon the earth, and lay mine honor in the dust. Selah.
6 Arise, O LORD, in thine anger, lift up thyself because of the rage of mine enemies: and awake for me to the judgment that thou hast commanded.

Psalm 7

TITLE. "Shiggaion of David, which he sang unto the Lord, concerning the word of Cush the Benjamite." "Shiggaion of David." As far as we can gather from the observations of learned men, and from a comparison of this Psalm with the only other Shiggaion in the Word of God, (Habakkuk 3:1), this title seems to mean "variable songs," with which also the idea of solace and pleasure is associated. Truly our life-psalm is composed of variable verses; one stanza rolls along with the sublime meter of triumph, but another limps with the broken rhythm of complaint. There is much bass in the saint's music here below. Our experience is as variable as the weather in England. From the title we learn the occasion of the composition of this song. It appears probable that Cush the Benjamite had accused David to Saul of treasonable conspiracy against his royal authority. This the king would be ready enough to credit, both from his jealousy of David, and from the relation which most probably existed between himself, the son of Kish, and this Cush, or Kish, the Benjamite. He who is near the throne can do more injury to a subject than an ordinary slanderer.
This may be called the SONG OF THE SLANDERED SAINT. Even this sorest of evils may furnish occasion for a Psalm. What a blessing it would be if we could turn even the most disastrous event into a theme for song, and so turn the tables upon our great enemy. Let us learn a lesson from Luther, who once said, "David made Psalms; we also will make Psalms, and sing them as well as we can to the honor of our Lord, and to spite and mock the devil."

DIVISION. In the first and second verses the danger is stated, and prayer offered. Then the Psalmist most solemnly avows his innocence. (3, 4, 5). The Lord is pleaded with to arise to judgment (6, 7). The Lord, sitting upon his throne, hears the renewed appeal of the Slandered Supplicant (8, 9). The Lord clears his servant, and threatens the wicked (10, 11, 12, 13). The slanderer is seen in vision bringing a curse upon his own head, (14, 15, 16), while David retires from trial singing a hymn of praise to his righteous God. We have here a noble sermon upon that text: "No weapon that is formed against thee shall prosper, and every tongue that riseth against thee in judgment thou shalt condemn."

EXPOSITION
Verse 1. David appears before God to plead with him against the Accuser, who had charged him with treason and treachery. The case is here opened with an avowal of confidence in God. Whatever may be the emergency of our condition we shall never find it amiss to retain our reliance upon our God. "O Lord my God," mine by a special covenant, sealed by Jesus' blood, and ratified in my own soul by a sense of union to thee; "in thee," and in thee only, "do I put my trust," even now in my sore distress. I shake, but my rock moves not. It is never right to distrust God, and never vain to trust him.
Verse 2. "Lest he tear my soul." Here is the plea of fear co-working with the plea of faith. There was one among David's foes mightier that the rest, who had both dignity, strength, and ferocity, and was, therefore, "like a lion." From this foe he urgently seeks deliverance. We must be ready for this trial, for it will surely come upon us. If God was slandered in Eden, we shall surely be maligned in this land of sinners. Gird up your loins, ye children of the resurrection, for this fiery trial awaits you all.
Verses 3-5. The second part of this wandering hymn contains a protestation of innocence, and an invocation of wrath upon his own head, if he were not clear from the evil imputed to him. So far from hiding treasonable intentions in his hands, or ungratefully requiting the peaceful deeds of a friend, he had even suffered his enemy to escape when he had him completely in his power. Twice had he spared Saul's life; once in the cave of Adullam, and

Psalm 7

1-2
At the commencement of the psalm, David speaks of having many enemies, and in the second verse he specifies some one in the singular number. And certainly, since the minds of all men were inflamed against him, he had very good reason for praying to be delivered from all his persecutors. But as the wicked cruelty of the king, like a firebrand, had kindled against him, though an innocent person, the hatred of the whole people, he had good reason also for turning his pen particularly against him. Thus, in the first verse, he describes the true character of his own circumstances—he was a persecuted man; and, in the second verse, the fountain or cause of the calamity he was enduring. There is great emphasis in these words which he uses in the beginning of the Psalms O Jehovah my Godly in thee do I trust.

3-5
3. O Jehovah my God Here David, to induce God to show him favor, protests that he is molested unjustly, and without being guilty of any crime. To give his protestation the greater weight, he uses an imprecation. If he has done any wrong, he declares his readiness to bear the blame; yea, he offers to endure the severest punishment, if he is not altogether innocent of the crime of which all men thought him almost convicted. And by entreating God to succor him upon no other condition than this, that his integrity should upon trial be found to be untarnished, he teaches us, by his example, that as often as we have recourse to God, we must make it our first care to be well assured in our own consciences with respect to the righteousness of our cause; for we do him great wrong if we wish to engage him as the advocate and defender of a bad cause.
5. Let mine enemy pursue It is a striking proof of the great confidence which David had in his own integrity, when he is willing to endure any kind of punishment, however dreadful, provided he should be found guilty of any crime. If we could bring a good conscience like this before God, his hand would be more quickly stretched forth to afford us immediate assistance.

6-8
6. Arise, O Jehovah David here sets the anger of God in opposition to the rage of his enemies; and when we are in similar circumstances we should act in the same manner. When the ungodly are inflamed against us, and cast forth their rage and fury to destroy us, we ought humbly to beseech God to be inflamed also on his side; in other words, to show in truth that he has, no less zeal and power to preserve us, than they have inclination to destroy us. The word, Arise, is taken in a figurative sense, for to ascend into a judgment-seat, or rather to prepare one's self to make resistance; and it is here applied to God, because, while he delays to succor us, we are very apt to think him asleep. Accordingly, David also, a little after, beseeches him to awake; for it seemed on the part

Psalm 7

David prays against his enemies; prayer for sinners and saints.

1-9
In these verses,
I. He puts himself under God's protection and flies to him for succor and shelter (v. 1): "Lord, save me, and deliver me from the power and malice of all those that persecute me, that they may not have their will against me." He pleads,
1. His relation to God. "Thou art my God, and therefore whither else should I go but to thee? Thou art my God, and therefore my shield (Gen. xv. 1), my God, and therefore I am one of thy servants, who may expect to be protected."
2. His confidence in God: "Lord, save me, for I depend upon thee: In thee do I put my trust, and not in any arm of flesh." Men of honor will not fail those that repose a trust in them, especially if they themselves have encouraged them to do so, which is our case.
3. The rage and malice of his enemies, and the imminent danger he was in of being swallowed up by them: "Lord, save me, or I am gone; he will tear my soul like a lion tearing his prey," with so much pride, and pleasure, and power, so easily, so cruelly. St. Paul compares Nero to a lion (2 Tim. iv. 17), as David here compares Saul.
4. The failure of all other helpers: "Lord, be thou pleased to deliver me, for otherwise there is none to deliver," v. 2. It is the glory of God to help the helpless.
II. He makes a solemn protestation of his innocency as to those things whereof he was accused, and by a dreadful imprecation appeals to God, the searcher of hearts, concerning it, v. 3-5. Observe, in general,
1. When we are falsely accused by men it is a great comfort if our own consciences acquit us, and not only they cannot prove their calumnies (Acts xxiv. 13), but our hearts can disprove them, to our own satisfaction.
2. God is the patron of wronged innocency. David had no court on earth to appeal to. His prince, who should have righted him, was his sworn enemy. But he had the court of heaven to fly to, and a righteous Judge there, whom he could call his God.
III. Having this testimony of his conscience concerning his innocency, he humbly prays to God to appear for him against his persecutors, and backs every petition with a proper plea, as one that knew how to order his cause before God.
1. He prays that God would manifest his wrath against his enemies, and pleads their wrath against him: "Lord, they are unjustly angry at me, be thou justly angry with them and let them know that thou art so, v. 6. In thy anger lift up thyself to the seat of judgment, and make thy power and justice conspicuous, because of the rage, the furies, the outrages (the word is plural) of my enemies." Those need not fear

Psalm 7

7-12

7 So shall the congregation of the people compass thee about: for their sakes therefore return thou on high.
8 The LORD shall judge the people: judge me, O LORD, according to my righteousness, and according to mine integrity that is in me.
9 Oh let the wickedness of the wicked come to an end; but establish the just: for the righteous God trieth the hearts and reins.
10 My defense is of God, which saveth the upright in heart.
11 God judgeth the righteous, and God is angry with the wicked every day.
12 If he turn not, he will whet his sword; he hath bent his bow, and made it ready.

again when he found him sleeping in the midst of his slumbering camp: he could, therefore, with a clear conscience, make his appeal to heaven. He needs not fear the curse whose soul is clear of guilt.

Selah. David enhances the solemnity of this appeal to the dread tribunal of God by the use of the usual pause.

Verse 6. We now listen to a fresh prayer, based upon the avowal which he has just made. We cannot pray too often, and when our heart is true, we shall turn to God in prayer as naturally as the needle to its pole.

Verse 7. "So shall the congregation of the people compass thee about." Thy saints shall crowd to thy tribunal with their complaints, or shall surround it with their solemn homage: "for their sakes therefore return thou on high." As when a judge travels at the assizes, all men take their cases to his court that they may be heard, so will the righteous gather to their Lord. Here he fortifies himself in prayer by pleading that if the Lord will mount the throne of judgment, multitudes of the saints would be blessed as well as himself. If I be too base to be remembered, yet, "for their sakes," for the love thou bearest to thy chosen people, come forth from thy secret pavilion, and sit in the gate dispensing justice among the people. When my suit includes the desires of all the righteous it shall surely speed, for, "shall not God avenge his own elect?"

Verse 8. If I am not mistaken, David has now seen in the eye of his mind the Lord ascending to his judgment-seat, and beholding him seated there in royal state, he draws near to him to urge his suit anew. In the last two verses he besought Jehovah to arise, and now that he is arisen, he prepares to mingle with "the congregation of the people" who compass the Lord about. The royal heralds proclaim the opening of the court with the solemn words, "The Lord shall judge the people." Our petitioner rises at once, and cries with earnestness and humility, "Judge me, O Lord, according to my righteousness, and according to mine integrity that is in me." His hand is on an honest heart, and his cry is to a righteous Judge.

Verse 9. He sees a smile of complacency upon the face of the King, and in the name of all the assembled congregation he cries aloud, "Oh let the wickedness of the wicked come to an end; but establish the just." Is not this the universal longing of the whole company of the elect? When shall we be delivered from the filthy conversation of these men of Sodom? When shall we escape from the filthiness of Mesech and the blackness of the tents of Kedar?

What a solemn and weighty truth is contained in the last sentence of the ninth verse! How deep is the divine knowledge!—"He trieth." How strict, how accurate, how intimate his search!—"he trieth the hearts," the secret thoughts, "and reins," the inward affections. "All things are naked and opened to the eyes of him with whom we have to do."

Verse 10. The judge has heard the cause, has cleared the guiltless, and uttered his voice against the persecutors. Let us draw near, and learn the results of the great assize. Yonder is the slandered one with his harp in hand, hymning the justice of his Lord, and rejoicing aloud in his own deliverance. "My defense is of God, which saveth the upright in heart." Oh, how good to have a true and upright heart. Crooked sinners, with all their craftiness, are foiled by the upright in heart. God defends the right. Filth will not long abide on the pure white garments of the saints, but shall be brushed off by divine providence, to the vexation of the men by whose base hands it was thrown upon the godly. When God shall try our cause, our sun has risen, and the sun of the wicked is set for ever. Truth, like oil, is ever above, no power of our enemies can drown it; we shall refute their slanders in the day when the trumpet wakes the dead, and we shall shine in honor when lying lips are put to silence. O believer, fear not all that thy foes can do or say against thee, for the tree which God plants no winds can hurt.

Verse 11. "God judgeth the righteous," he hath not given thee up to be condemned by the lips of persecutors. Thine enemies cannot sit on God's of God something like the forgetfulness of sleep to give no assistance to an individual who was so much afflicted and oppressed on all hands.

7. And a congregation of peoples Some limit this sentence exclusively to the people of Israel, as if David promised that, as soon as he should ascend the throne, he would endeavor to reunite together, in the pure worship of God, the people who before had been as it were in a state of dispersion. Under the reign of Saul, religion had been neglected, or such an unrestrained license in wickedness had prevailed, that few paid any regard to God.

8. Jehovah shall judge the nations This sentence is closely connected with the preceding verse. David had prayed God to show himself as judge to the nations; and now he takes it for a certain and admitted truth, that it is the peculiar office of God to judge the nations: for the word put in the future tense, and rendered shall judge, denotes here a continued act; and this is the signification of the future tense in general sentences. Besides, he does not here speak of one nation only, but comprehends all nations. As he acknowledges God to be the judge of the whole world, he concludes a little after from this, that he will maintain his cause and right. And as often as we seem to be forsaken and oppressed, we should recall this truth to our remembrance, that as God is the governor of the world, it is as utterly impossible for him to abdicate his office as to deny himself. From this source there will flow a continual stream of comfort, although a long succession of calamities may press upon us: for from this truth we may assuredly conclude, that he will take care to defend our innocence.

9-11

9. Let the malice of the wicked come to an endow I beseech thee. David prays that God would restrain the malice of his enemies, and bring it to an end; from which it follows, that his affliction had been of long duration.

10. My shield It is not wonderful that David often mingles meditations with his prayers, thereby to inspire himself with true confidence. We may go to God in prayer with great alacrity; but our fervor, if it does not gather new strength, either immediately fails or begins to languish. David, therefore, in order to continue in prayer with the same ardor of devotion and affection with which he commenced, brings to his recollection some of the most common truths of religion, and by this means fosters and invigorates his faith. He declares, that as God saves the upright in heart, he is perfectly safe under his protection. Whence it follows, that he had the testimony of an approving conscience. And, as he does not simply say the righteous, but the upright in heart, he appears to have an eye to that inward searching of the heart and reins mentioned in the preceding verse.

11. God judgeth the righteous etc. As Saul and his accomplices had, by their calumnious reports, so far succeeded in their wicked design as to have produced a general prejudice against David, so that he was condemned by almost the whole people, the holy man supports himself

men's wrath against them who have God's wrath for them. Who knows the power of his anger?

2. He prays that God would plead his cause.

(1.) He prays, Awake for me to judgment (that is, let my cause have a hearing), to the judgment which thou hast commanded; this speaks, The divine power; as he blesses effectually, and is therefore said to command the blessing, so he judges effectually, and is therefore said to command the judgment, which is such as none can countermand; for it certainly carries execution along with it. The divine purpose and promise: "It is the judgment which thou hast determined to pass upon all the enemies of thy people. Thou hast commanded the princes and judges of the earth to give redress to the injured and vindicate the oppressed; Lord, awaken thyself to that judgment."

(2.) He prays (v. 7), "Return thou on high, maintain thy own authority, resume thy royal throne of which they have despised the sovereignty, and the judgment-seat of which they have despised the sentence. Return on high, that is, visibly and in the sight of all, that it may be universally acknowledged that heaven itself owns and pleads David's cause."

(3.) He prays again (v. 8), "Judge me, judge for me, give sentence on my side." He pleads that his cause was now brought into the proper court: The Lord shall judge the people, v. 8. He is the Judge of all the earth, and therefore no doubt he will do right and all will be obliged to acquiesce in his judgment.

3. He prays, in general, for the conversion of sinners and the establishment of saints (v. 9): "O let the wickedness, not only of my wicked enemies, but of all the wicked, come to an end! but establish the just."

10-17 The persecutor's doom.

David having lodged his appeal with God by prayer and a solemn profession of his integrity, in the former part of the psalm, in this latter part does, as it were, take out judgment upon the appeal, by faith in the word of God, and the assurance it gives of the happiness and safety of the righteous and the certain destruction of wicked people that continue impenitent.

I. David is confident that he shall find God his powerful protector and Savior, and the patron of his oppressed innocency (v. 10): "My defense is of God. Not only, God is my defender, and I shall find him so; but I look for defense and safety in no other; my hope for shelter in a time of danger is placed in God alone; if I have defense, it must be of God." My shield is upon God (so some read it); there is that in God which gives an assurance of protection to all that are his. His name is a strong tower, Prov. xviii. 10.

II. He is no less confident of the destruction of all his persecutors, even as many of them as would not repent, to give glory to God. He reads their doom here, for their good, if possible, that they might cease from their enmity, or, however, for his own comfort,

Psalm 7

13-17

13 He hath also prepared for him the instruments of death; he ordaineth his arrows against the persecutors.
14 Behold, he travaileth with iniquity, and hath conceived mischief, and brought forth falsehood.
15 He made a pit, and digged it, and is fallen into the ditch which he made.
16 His mischief shall return upon his own head, and his violent dealing shall come down upon his own pate.
17 I will praise the LORD according to his righteousness: and will sing praise to the name of the LORD most high.

throne, nor blot thy name out of his book. Let them alone, then, for God will find time for his revenge.

"God is angry with the wicked every day." He not only detests sin, but is angry with those who continue to indulge in it. We have no insensible and stolid God to deal with; he can be angry, nay, he is angry to-day and every day with you, ye ungodly and impenitent sinners. The best day that ever dawns on a sinner brings a curse with it. Sinners may have many feast days, but no safe days.

Verse 12. "If he turn not, he will whet his sword." What blows are those which will be dealt by that long uplifted arm! God's sword has been sharpening upon the revolving stone of our daily wickedness, and if we will not repent, it will speedily cut us in pieces. Turn or burn is the sinner's only alternative. "He hath bent his bow and made it ready."

Verse 13. Even now the thirsty arrow longs to wet itself with the blood of the persecutor. The bow is bent, the aim is taken, the arrow is fitted to the string, and what, O sinner, if the arrow should be let fly at thee even now! Remember, God's arrows never miss the mark, and are, every one of them, "instruments of death." Judgment may tarry, but it will not come too late. The Greek proverb saith, "The mill of God grinds late, but grinds to powder."

Verse 14. In three graphic pictures we see the slanderer's history. A woman in travail furnishes the first metaphor. "He travaileth with iniquity." He is full of it, pained until he can carry it out, he longs to work his will, he is full of pangs until his evil intent is executed. "He hath conceived mischief." This is the original of his base design. The devil has had doings with him, and the virus of evil is in him. And now behold the progeny of this unhallowed conception.

Verse 15. "He made a pit, and digged it." He was cunning in his plans, and industrious in his labors. He stooped to the dirty work of digging. He did not fear to soil his own hands, he was willing to work in a ditch if others might fall therein. What mean things men will do to wreak revenge on the godly. They hunt for good men, as if they were brute beasts; nay, they will not give them the fair chase afforded to the hare or the fox, but must secretly entrap them, because they can neither run them down nor shoot them down. Our enemies will not meet us to the face, for they fear us as much as they pretend to despise us.

Verse 16. The rod which he lifted on high, has smitten his own back. He shot an arrow upward, and it has "returned upon his own head." He hurled a stone at another and it has "come down upon his own pate." Curses are like young chickens, they always come home to roost. Ashes always fly back in the face of him that throws them. "As he loved cursing, so let it come unto him." (Psalm 109:17.)

Verse 17. We conclude with the joyful contrast. In this all these Psalms are agreed; they all exhibit the blessedness of the righteous, and make its colors the more glowing by contrast with the miseries of the wicked. The bright jewel sparkles in a black foil. Praise is the occupation of the godly, their eternal work, and their present pleasure. Singing is the fitting embodiment for praise, and therefore do the saints make melody before the Lord Most High. The slandered one is now a singer.

from this one consideration, that whatever may be the confusion of things in the world, God, notwithstanding, can easily discern between the righteous and the wicked. He, therefore, appeals from the false judgments of men to Him who can never be deceived. It may, however, be asked, How does the Psalmist represent God as judging every day, when we see him delaying punishment frequently for a long time? The sacred writings certainly most justly celebrate his long-suffering; but, although he exercises patience long, and does not immediately execute his judgments, yet, as no time passes, yea, not even a day, in which he does not furnish the clearest evidence that he discerns between the righteous and the wicked, notwithstanding the confusion of things in the world, it is certain that he never ceases to execute the office of a judge.

12-14
12. David, I have no doubt, by relating the dreadful attempts of his enemies against him, intended thereby to illustrate more highly the grace of God; for when these malicious men, strengthened by powerful military forces, and abundantly provided with armor, furiously rushed upon him in the full expectation of destroying him, who would not have said that it was all over with him? Moreover, there is implied in the words a kind of irony, when he pretends to be afraid of their putting him to death. They mean the same thing as if he had said, "If my enemy do not alter his purpose, or turn his fury and his strength in another direction, who can preserve me from perishing by his hands? He has an abundant supply of arms, and he is endeavoring, by all methods, to accomplish my death." But Saul is the person of whom he particularly speaks, and therefore he says, he hath made fit his arrows for the persecutors This implies that Saul had many agents in readiness who would willingly put forth their utmost efforts in seeking to destroy David. The design of the prophet, therefore, was to magnify the greatness of the grace of God, by showing the greatness of the danger from which he had been delivered by him.
14. Behold, he shall travail David has hitherto shown how great and formidable the danger was which was near him. In this verse, laughing to scorn the presumptuous and foolish attempts of Saul, and his magnificent preparations, he declares that they had failed to achieve their goal.

15-16
Here David says not only that their wicked devices were without success, but that, by the wonderful providence of God, the result was the very opposite of what had been contemplated. He sets this forth, metaphorically, by employing the figure of a pit and a ditch; and then he expresses the same thing in simple terms without figure, declaring, that the mischief intended for others returned upon the head of him who had devised it.
17. I will praise Jehovah according to his righteousness; and I will sing to the name of Jehovah, Most High. As the design of God in the deliverances which he vouchsafes to his servants is, that they may render to him in return the sacrifices of praise, David here promises that he will gratefully acknowledge the deliverance which he had received, and at the same time affirms that his preservation from death was the undoubted and manifest work of God.

that he might not be afraid of them nor aggrieved at their prosperity and success for a time.
They are children of death, as all the children of wrath are, sons of perdition, marked out for ruin.
1. God will destroy them. The destruction they are reserved for is destruction from the Almighty, which ought to be a terror to every one of us, for it comes from the wrath of God, v. 13, 14.

It is here intimated, That the destruction of sinners may be prevented by their conversion, for it is threatened with that proviso: If he turn not from his evil way, if he do not let fall his enmity against the people of God, then let him expect it will be his ruin; but, if he turn, it is implied that his sin shall be pardoned and all shall be well. Thus even the threatenings of wrath are introduced with a gracious implication of mercy, enough to justify God for ever in the destruction of those that perish; they might have turned and lived, but they chose rather to go on and die and their blood is therefore upon their own heads. That, if it be not thus prevented by the conversion of the sinner, it will be prepared for him by the justice of God. In general (v. 13), He has prepared for him the instruments of death, of all that death which is the wages of sin. If God will slay, he will not want instruments of death for any creature; even the least and weakest may be made so when he pleases.

First, Here is variety of instruments, all which breathe threatenings and slaughter. Here is a sword, which wounds and kills at hand, a bow and arrows, which wound and kill at a distance those who think to get out of the reach of God's vindictive justice. If the sinner flees from the iron weapon, yet the bow of steel shall strike him through, Job xx. 24.

Secondly, These instruments of death are all said to be made ready. God has them not to seek, but always at hand. Judgments are prepared for scorners. Tophet is prepared of old.
2. They will destroy themselves, v. 14-16. The sinner is here described as taking a great deal of pains to ruin himself, more pains to damn his soul than, if directed aright, would save it. His conduct is described, By the pains of a laboring woman that brings forth a false conception, v. 14. The sinner's head with its politics conceives mischief, contrives it with a great deal of art, lays the plot deep, and keeps it close; the sinner's heart with its passions travails with iniquity, and is in pain to be delivered of the malicious projects it is hatching against the people of God. But what does it come to when it comes to the birth? It is falsehood; it is a cheat upon himself; it is a lie in his right hand. He cannot compass what he intended, nor, if he gain his point, will he gain the satisfaction he promised himself. He brings forth wind (Isa. xxvi. 18), stubble (Isa. xxxiii. 11), death (James i. 15), that is, falsehood. By the pains of a laboring man that works hard to dig a pit, and then falls into it and perishes in it.

Psalm 8

Title
To the Chief Musician upon Gittith, a Psalm of David.

1-4
1 O LORD, our Lord, how excellent is thy name in all the earth! who hast set thy glory above the heavens.
2 Out of the mouth of babes and sucklings hast thou ordained strength because of thine enemies, that thou mightest still the enemy and the avenger.
3 When I consider thy heavens, the work of thy fingers, the moon and the stars, which thou hast ordained;
4 What is man, that thou art mindful of him? and the son of man, that thou visitest him?

Psalm 8

TITLE. "To the Chief Musician upon Gittith, a Psalm of David." The term Gittith is applied to two other Psalms, (81 and 84) both of which, being of a joyous character, it may be concluded, that where we find that word in the title, we may look for a hymn of delight.
We may style this Psalm the Song of the Astronomer: let us go abroad and sing it beneath the starry heavens at eventide, for it is very probable that in such a position, it first occurred to the poet's mind.

DIVISION. The first and last verses are a sweet song of admiration, in which the excellence of the name of God is extolled. The intermediate verses are made up of holy wonder at the Lord's greatness in creation, and at his condescension towards man. Poole, in his annotations, has well said, "It is a great question among interpreters, whether this Psalm speaks of man in general, and of the honor which God puts upon him in his creation; or only of the man Christ Jesus. Possibly both may be reconciled and put together, and the controversy if rightly stated, may be ended, for the scope and business of this Psalm seems plainly to be this: to display and celebrate the great love and kindness of God to mankind, not only in his creation, but especially in his redemption by Jesus Christ, whom, as he was man, he advanced to the honor and dominion here mentioned, that he might carry on his great and glorious work. So Christ is the principal subject of this Psalm, and it is interpreted of him, both by our Lord himself (Matthew 21:16), and by his holy apostle (1 Corinthians 15:27; Hebrews 2:6,7).

EXPOSITION
Verse 1. Unable to express the glory of God, the Psalmist utters a note of exclamation. O Jehovah our Lord! We need not wonder at this, for no heart can measure, no tongue can utter, the half of the greatness of Jehovah. The whole creation is full of his glory and radiant with the excellency of his power; his goodness and his wisdom are manifested on every hand. The countless myriads of terrestrial beings, from man the head, to the creeping worm at the foot, are all supported and nourished by the Divine bounty. The solid fabric of the universe leans upon his eternal arm. Universally is he present, and everywhere is his name excellent. God worketh ever and everywhere. There is no place where God is not. The miracles of his power await us on all sides. Traverse the silent valleys where the rocks enclose you on either side, rising like the battlements of heaven till you can see but a strip of the blue sky far overhead; you may be the only traveler who has passed through that glen; the bird may start up affrighted, and the moss may tremble beneath the first tread of human foot; but God is there in a thousand wonders, upholding yon rocky barriers, filling the flowercups with their perfume, and refreshing the lonely pines with the breath of his mouth. Everywhere, and in every place, God dwells and is manifestly at work. Nor on earth alone is Jehovah extolled, for his brightness shines forth in the firmament above the earth. His glory exceeds the glory of the starry heavens; above the region of the stars he hath set fast his everlasting throne, and there he dwells in light ineffable.
Note the fact that even the heavens cannot contain his glory, it is set above the heavens, since it is and ever must be too great for the creature to express.
Verse 2. Nor only in the heavens above is the Lord seen, but the earth beneath is telling forth his majesty. In the sky, the massive orbs, rolling in their stupendous grandeur, are witnesses of his power in great things, while here below, the lisping utterances of babes are the manifestations of his strength in little ones. How often will children tell us of a God whom we have forgotten! How doth their simple prattle refute those learned fools who deny the being of God! Many men have been made to hold their tongues, while

Psalm 8

David, reflecting upon God's fatherly beneficence towards mankind, is not content with simply giving thanks for it, but is enraptured by the contemplation of it.

1. There is presented to us in the whole order of nature, the most abundant matter for showing forth the glory of God, but, as we are unquestionably more powerfully affected with what we ourselves experience, David here, with great propriety, expressly celebrates the special favor which God manifests towards mankind; for this, of all the subjects which come under our contemplation, is the brightest mirror in which we can behold his glory.
2. He now enters upon the proof of the subject which he had undertaken to discourse upon, declaring, that the providence of God, in order to make itself known to mankind, does not wait till men arrive at the age of maturity, but even from the very dawn of infancy shines forth so brightly as is sufficient to confute all the ungodly, who, through their profane contempt of God, would wish to extinguish his very name.

3-4
3. When the Psalmist calls the heavens God's heavens, and the works of his fingers, he has a reference to the same subject, and intends to illustrate it. How is it that God comes forth from so noble and glorious a part of his works, and stoops down to us, poor worms of the earth, if it is not to magnify and to give a more illustrious manifestation of his goodness? From this, also, we learn, that those are chargeable with a very presumptuous abuse of the goodness of God, who take occasion from it to be proud of the excellence which they possess, as if they had either obtained it by their own skill, or as if they possessed it on account of their own merit; whereas their origin should rather remind them that it has been gratuitously conferred upon those who are otherwise vile and contemptible creatures, and utterly unworthy of receiving any good from God. Whatever estimable quality, therefore, we see in ourselves, let it stir us up to celebrate the free and undeserved goodness of God in bestowing it upon us.

5-6
5. If any person object that David first put the question, What is man? because God has so abundantly poured forth his favor upon a creature, so miserable, contemptible, and worthless; but that there is no cause for such admiration of God's favor for Christ, who is not an ordinary man, but the only begotten Son of God. The answer is easy, and it is this: What was bestowed upon Christ's human nature was a free gift; nay, more, the fact that a mortal man, and the son of Adam, is the only Son of God, and the Lord of glory, and the head of angels, affords a bright illustration of the mercy of God. At the same time, it is to be observed, that whatever gifts he has received ought to be considered as proceeding from the free grace of God, so much the more for this reason,

Psalm 8

1-2 Glory of God in his works.
Two things David here admires:
I. How plainly God displays his glory himself, v. 1. He addresses himself to God with all humility and reverence, as the Lord and his people's Lord: O Lord our Lord! If we believe that God is the Lord, we must avouch and acknowledge him to be ours. He is ours, for he made us, protects us, and takes special care of us. He must be ours, for we are bound to obey him and submit to him; we must own the relation, not only when we come to pray to God, as a plea with him to show us mercy, but when we come to praise him, as an argument with ourselves to give him glory: and we shall never think we can do that with affection enough if we consider how brightly God's glory shines even in this lower world.
II. How powerfully he proclaims it by the weakest of his creatures (v. 2): Out of the mouth of babes and sucklings hast thou ordained strength, or perfected praise, the praise of thy strength, Matt. xxi. 16. This intimates the glory of God in the kingdom of nature. The care God takes of little children (when they first come into the world the most helpless of all animals), the special protection they are under, and the provision nature has made for them, ought to be acknowledged by every one of us, to the glory of God, as a great instance of his power and goodness, and the more sensibly because we have all had the benefit of it, for to this we owe it that we died not from the womb, that the knees then prevented us, and the breasts, that we should suck. "This is such an instance of thy goodness, as may for ever put to silence the enemies of thy glory, who say, There is no God."

3-9 Condescension of God.
David here goes on to magnify the honor of God by recounting the honors he has put upon man, especially the man Christ Jesus. The condescensions of the divine grace call for our praises as much as the elevations of the divine glory. How God has condescended in favor to man the psalmist here observes with wonder and thankfulness, and recommends it to our thoughts. See here,
I. What it is that leads him to admire the condescending favor of God to man; it is his consideration of the luster and influence of the heavenly bodies, which are within the view of sense (v. 3): I consider thy heavens, and there, particularly, the moon and the stars. But why does he not take notice of the sun, which much excels them all? Probably because it was in a night-walk, but moon-light, that he entertained and instructed himself with this meditation, when the sun was not within view, but only the moon and the stars, which, though they are not altogether so serviceable to man as the sun is, yet are no less demonstrations of the wisdom, power, and goodness of the Creator.

Psalm 8

5-9

5 For thou hast made him a little lower than the angels, and hast crowned him with glory and honor.
6 Thou madest him to have dominion over the works of thy hands; thou hast put all things under his feet:
7 All sheep and oxen, yea, and the beasts of the field;
8 The fowl of the air, and the fish of the sea, and whatsoever passeth through the paths of the seas.
9 O LORD our Lord, how excellent is thy name in all the earth!

sucklings have borne witness to the glory of the God of heaven. It is singular how clearly the history of the church expounds this verse. Did not the children cry "Hosannah!" in the temple, when proud Pharisees were silent and contemptuous? and did not the Savior quote these very words as a justification of their infantile cries? He who delights in the songs of angels is pleased to honor himself in the eyes of his enemies by the praises of little children. What a contrast between the glory above the heavens, and the mouths of babes and sucklings! yet by both the name of God is made excellent.

Verses 3, 4. At the close of that excellent little manual entitled "The Solar System," written by Dr. Dick, we find an eloquent passage which beautifully expounds the text: A survey of the solar system has a tendency to moderate the pride of man and to promote humility. Pride is one of the distinguishing characteristics of puny man, and has been one of the chief causes of all the contentions, wars, devastations, systems of slavery, and ambitious projects which have desolated and demoralized our sinful world. Yet there is no disposition more incongruous to the character and circumstances of man. Perhaps there are no rational beings throughout the universe among whom pride would appear more unseemly or incompatible than in man, considering the situation in which he is placed. He is exposed to numerous degradations and calamities, to the rage of storms and tempests, the devastations of earthquakes and volcanoes, the fury of whirlwinds, and the tempestuous billows of the ocean, to the ravages of the sword, famine, pestilence, and numerous diseases; and at length he must sink into the grave, and his body must become the companion of worms! The most dignified and haughty of the sons of men are liable to these and similar degradations as well as the meanest of the human family. Yet, in such circumstances, man—that puny worm of the dust, whose knowledge is so limited, and whose follies are so numerous and glaring—has the effrontery to strut in all the haughtiness of pride, and to glory in his shame.

Verses 5-8. These verses may set forth man's position among the creatures before he fell; but as they are, by the apostle Paul, appropriated to man as represented by the Lord Jesus, it is best to give most weight to that meaning. In order of dignity, man stood next to the angels, and a little lower than they; in the Lord Jesus this was accomplished, for he was made a little lower than the angels by the suffering of death. Man in Eden had the full command of all creatures, and they came before him to receive their names as an act of homage to him as the vice-regent of God to them. Jesus in his glory, is now Lord, not only of all living, but of all created things, and, with the exception of him who put all things under him, Jesus is Lord of all, and his elect, in him, are raised to a dominion wider than that of the first Adam, as shall be more clearly seen at his coming. Thou madest him a little lower than the angels—a little lower in nature, since they are immortal, and but a little, because time is short; and when that is over, saints are no longer lower than the angels. Under our feet we must keep the world, and we must shun that base spirit which is content to let worldly cares and pleasures sway the empire of the immortal soul.

Verse 9. Here, like a good composer, the poet returns to his key-note, falling back, as it were, into his first state of wondering adoration. What he started with as a proposition in the first verse, he closes with as a well proven conclusion, with a sort of quod erat demonstrandum. O for grace to walk worthy of that excellent name which has been named upon us, and which we are pledged to magnify!

that they are intended principally to be conferred upon us. His excellence and heavenly dignity, therefore, are extended to us also, seeing it is for our sake he is enriched with them. What the apostle therefore says in that passage concerning the abasement of Christ for a short time, is not intended by him as an explanation of this text; but for the purpose of enriching and illustrating the subject on which he is discoursing, he introduces and accommodates to it what had been spoken in a different sense. The same apostle did not hesitate, in Romans 10:6, in the same manner to enrich and to employ, in a sense different from their original one, the words of Moses in Deuteronomy 30:12: "Who shall go up for us to heaven and bring it to us, that we may hear it and do it?" etc. The apostle, therefore, in quoting this psalm, had not so much an eye to what David meant; but making an allusion to these words, Thou hast made him a little lower; and again, Thou hast crowned him with honor, he applies this diminution to the death of Christ, and the glory and honor to his resurrection.

6. Thou hast set him over. David now comes to the second point, which I have just now spoken of, namely, that from the dominion over all things which God has conferred upon men, it is evident how great is the love which he has borne towards them, and how much account he has made of them.

7-9

7. We are not to understand David as meaning that it is a proof that man is invested with dominion over all the works of God, because he clothes himself with the wool and the skins of beasts, because he lives upon their flesh, and because he employs their labor for his own advantage; for this would be inconclusive reasoning. He only brings forward this as an example, and as a mirror in which we may behold and contemplate the dominion over the works of his hands, with which God has honored man. The sum is this: God, in creating man, gave a demonstration of his infinite grace and more than fatherly love towards him, which ought justly to strike us with amazement; and although, by the fall of man, that happy condition has been almost entirely ruined, yet there is still in him some remains of the liberality which God then displayed towards him, which should suffice to fill us with admiration. In this mournful and wretched overthrow, it is true, the legitimate order which God originally established no longer shines forth, but the faithful whom God gathers to himself, under Christ their head, enjoy so much of the fragments of the good things which they lost in Adam, as may furnish them with abundant matter of wonder at the singularly gracious manner in which God deals with them. David here confines his attention to God's temporal benefits, but it is our duty to rise higher, and to contemplate the invaluable treasures of the kingdom of heaven which he has unfolded in Christ, and all the gifts which belong to the spiritual life, that by reflecting upon these our hearts may be inflamed with love to God, that we may be stirred up to the practice of godliness, and that we may not suffer ourselves to become slothful and remiss in celebrating his praises.

II. How he expresses this admiration (v. 4): "Lord, what is man (enosh, sinful, weak, miserable man, a creature so forgetful of thee and his duty to thee) that thou art thus mindful of him, that thou takest cognizance of him and of his actions and affairs, that in the making of the world thou hadst a respect to him! What is the son of man, that thou visitest him, that thou not only feedest him and clothest him, protectest him and providest for him, in common with other creatures, but visited him as one friend visits another, art pleased to converse with him and concern thyself for him! What is man—(so mean a creature), that he should be thus honored—(so sinful a creature), that he should be thus countenanced and favored!"
Now this refers,

1. To mankind in general. Though man is a worm, and the son of man is a worm (Job xxv. 6), yet God puts a respect upon him, and shows him abundance of kindness; man is, above all the creatures in this lower world, the favorite and darling of Providence. For,

(1.) He is of a very honorable rank of beings. We may be sure he takes precedence of all the inhabitants of this lower world, for he is made but a little lower than the angels (v. 5), lower indeed, because by his body he is allied to the earth and to the beasts that perish, and yet by his soul, which is spiritual and immortal, he is so near akin to the holy angels that he may be truly said to be but a little lower than they, and is, in order, next to them.

(2.) He is invested with a sovereign dominion over the inferior creatures, under God, and is constituted their lord. He that made them, and knows them, and whose own they are, has made man to have dominion over them, v. 6.

He specifies some of the inferior animals (v. 7, 8), not only sheep and oxen, which man takes care of and provides for, but the beasts of the field, as well as those of the flood, yea, and those creatures which are most at a distance from man, as the fowl of the air, yea, and the fish of the sea, which live in another element and pass unseen through the paths of the seas. Man has arts to take these; though many of them are much stronger and many of them much swifter than he, yet, one way or other, he is too hard for them, Jam. iii. 7. Every kind of beasts, and birds, and things in the sea, is tamed, and has been tamed. He has likewise liberty to use them as he has occasion. Rise, Peter, kill and eat, Acts x. 13. Every time we partake of fish or of fowl we realize this dominion which man has over the works of God's hands; and this is a reason for our subjection to God, our chief Lord, and to his dominion over us.

In singing this and praying it over, though we must not forget to acknowledge, with suitable affections, God's common favors to mankind, particularly in the serviceableness of the inferior creatures to us, yet we must especially set ourselves to give glory to our Lord Jesus, by confessing that he is Lord, submitting to him as our Lord.

Psalm 9

Title
To the Chief Musician upon Muth-labben, a Psalm of David.

1-6
1 I will praise thee, O LORD, with my whole heart; I will shew forth all thy marvelous works.
2 I will be glad and rejoice in thee: I will sing praise to thy name, O thou most High.
3 When mine enemies are turned back, they shall fall and perish at thy presence.
4 For thou hast maintained my right and my cause; thou satest in the throne judging right.
5 Thou hast rebuked the heathen, thou hast destroyed the wicked, thou hast put out their name for ever and ever.
6 O thou enemy, destructions are come to a perpetual end: and thou hast destroyed cities; their memorial is perished with them.

Psalm 9

TITLE. To the Chief Musician upon Muth-labben, a Psalm of David. From a considerable company of learned witnesses we gather that the title signifies a Psalm concerning the death of the Son. The Chaldee has, "concerning the death of the Champion who went out between the camps," referring to Goliath of Gath, or some other Philistine, on account of whose death many suppose this Psalm to have been written in after years by David. Believing that out of a thousand guesses this is at least as consistent with the sense of the Psalm as any other, we prefer it; and the more especially so because it enables us to refer it mystically to the victory of the Son of God over the champion of evil, even to enemy of souls (verse 6).
DIVISION. The strain so continually changes, that it is difficult to give an outline of it methodically arranged: we give the best we can make. From verses 1 to 6 is a song of jubilant thanksgiving; from 7 to 12, there is a continued declaration of faith as to the future. Prayer closes the first great division of the Psalm in verses 13 and 14. The second portion of this triumphal ode, although much shorter, is parallel in all its parts to the first portion, and is a sort of rehearsal of it. Observe the song for past judgments, verses 15, 16; the declaration of trust in future justice, 17, 18; and the closing prayer, 19, 20. Let us celebrate the conquests of the Redeemer as we read this Psalm, and it cannot but be a delightful task if the Holy Ghost be with us.

EXPOSITION
Verse 1. With a holy resolution the songster begins his hymn; I will praise thee, O Lord. It sometimes needs all our determination to face the foe, and bless the Lord in the teeth of his enemies; vowing that whoever else may be silent we will bless his name; here, however, the overthrow of the foe is viewed as complete, and the song flows with sacred fullness of delight. It is our duty to praise the Lord; let us perform it as a privilege. Observe that David's praise is all given to the Lord. Praise is to be offered to God alone; we may be grateful to the intermediate agent, but our thanks must have long wings and mount aloft to heaven. With my whole heart. Half heart is no heart.
Verse 2. Gladness and joy are the appropriate spirit in which to praise the goodness of the Lord. Birds extol the Creator in notes of overflowing joy, the cattle low forth his praise with tumult of happiness, and the fish leap up in his worship with excess of delight. Moloch may be worshipped with shrieks of pain, and Juggernaut may be honored by dying groans and inhuman yells, but he whose name is Love is best pleased with the holy mirth, and sanctified gladness of his people.
Verse 3. God's presence is evermore sufficient to work the defeat of our most furious foes, and their ruin is so complete when the Lord takes them in hand, that even flight cannot save them, they fall to rise no more when he pursues them. We must be careful, like David, to give all the glory to him whose presence gives the victory. If we have here the exultings of our conquering Captain, let us make the triumphs of the Redeemer the triumphs of the redeemed, and rejoice with him at the total discomfiture of all his foes.
Verse 4. One of our nobility has for his motto, "I will maintain it;" but the Christian has a better and more humble one, "Thou hast maintained it." "God and my right," are united by my faith: while God lives my right shall never be taken from me. If we seek to maintain the cause and honor of our Lord we may suffer reproach and misrepresentation, but it is a rich comfort to remember that he who sits on the throne knows our hearts, and will not leave us to the ignorant and ungenerous judgment of erring man.
Verse 5. God rebukes before he destroys, but when he once comes to blows with the wicked he ceases not until he has dashed them in pieces so

JOHN CALVIN

Psalm 9

David, after having recounted the former victories which he had gained, and exalted in lofty strains the grace and power of God in their happy issue, now again, when he sees new enemies and dangers rising up, implores the protection of the same God by whom he had before been delivered, and beseeches him to overthrow the pride of his enemies.

1-3

1. I will praise the Lord. David begins the psalm in this way, to induce God to succor him in the calamities with which he was now afflicted. As God continues his favor towards his own people without intermission, all the good he has hitherto done to us should serve to inspire us with confidence and hope, that he will be gracious and merciful to us in the time to come.

2. I will rejoice and exult in thee. Observe how the faithful praise God sincerely and without hypocrisy, when they do not rest on themselves for happiness, and are not intoxicated with foolish and carnal presumption, but rejoice in God alone; which is nothing else than to seek the matter of their joy from the favor of God, and from no other source, since in it perfect happiness consists.

3. While my enemies are turned back. In these words he assigns the reason why he undertakes to sing the praises of God, namely, because he acknowledges that his frequent victories had been achieved, not by his own power, nor by the power of his soldiers, but by the free favor of God.

4-5

4. The Psalmist proceeds a step farther in the 4th verse, declaring that God stretched forth his hand to give him succor, because he was unrighteously afflicted by his enemies. And surely if we desire to be favored with the assistance of God, we ought to see to it that we fight under his standard. David, therefore, calls him a judge of righteousness, or, which is the same thing, a righteous judge; as if he had said, God has acted towards me according to his ordinary manner and constant principle of acting, for it is his usual way to undertake the defense of good causes.

When he says, Thou hast blotted out their name for ever, it may be understood as meaning, that they were destroyed without any hope of ever being able to rise again, and devoted to everlasting shame.

6-8

6. O thou enemy, desolations are come to an end for ever. This contrast between the power of the enemies of God and his people, and the work of God in breaking up their proceedings, very well illustrates the wonderful character of the succor which he granted to his people. The ungodly had set to themselves no limit in the work of doing mischief, save in the utter destruction of all things, and at the commencement complete destruction seemed to be at hand; but when things were in this state of confusion, God seasonably made his appearance for the help of his people.

MATTHEW HENRY

Psalm 9

1-10 Devout acknowledgments.

I. David excites and engages himself to praise God for his mercies and the great things he had of late done for him and his government, v. 1, 2. Note,

1. God expects suitable returns of praise from those for whom he has done marvelous works.

2. If we would praise God acceptably, we must praise him in sincerity, with our hearts, and not only with our lips, and be lively and fervent in the duty, with our whole heart.

3. When we give thanks for some one particular mercy we should take occasion thence to remember former mercies and so to show forth all his marvelous works.

II. He acknowledges the almighty power of God as that which the strongest and stoutest of his enemies were no way able to contest with or stand before, v. 3. But,

1. They are forced to turn back. Their policy and their courage fail them, so that they cannot, they dare not, push forward in their enterprises, but retire with precipitation.

2. When once they turn back, they fall and perish; even their retreat will be their ruin, and they will save themselves no more by flying than by fighting.

III. He gives to God the glory of his righteousness, in his appearing on his behalf (v. 4): "Thou hast maintained my right and my cause, that is, my righteous cause; when that came on, thou satest in the throne, judging right."

IV. He records, with joy, the triumphs of the God of heaven over all the powers of hell and attends those triumphs with his praises, v. 5. By three steps the power and justice of God had proceeded against the heathen, and wicked people, who were enemies to the king God had lately set up upon his holy hill of Zion.

He had checked them: "Thou hast rebuked the heathen, hast given them real proofs of thy displeasure against them." This he did before he destroyed them, that they might take warning by the rebukes of Providence and so prevent their own destruction.

V. He exults over the enemy whom God thus appears against (v. 6): Thou hast destroyed cities. Either, "Thou, O enemy! hast destroyed our cities, at least in intention and imagination," or "Thou, O God! hast destroyed their cities by the desolation brought upon their country." It may be taken either way; for the psalmist will have the enemy to know that their destruction is just and that God was but reckoning with them for all the mischief which they had done and designed against his people.

VI. He comforts himself and others in God, and pleases himself with the thoughts of him.

1. With the thoughts of his eternity. On this earth we see nothing durable, even strong cities are buried in

Psalm 9

7-12

7 But the LORD shall endure for ever: he hath prepared his throne for judgment.
8 And he shall judge the world in righteousness, he shall minister judgment to the people in uprightness.
9 The LORD also will be a refuge for the oppressed, a refuge in times of trouble.
10 And they that know thy name will put their trust in thee: for thou, LORD, hast not forsaken them that seek thee.
11 Sing praises to the LORD, which dwelleth in Zion: declare among the people his doings.
12 When he maketh inquisition for blood, he remembereth them: he forgetteth not the cry of the humble.

small that their very name is forgotten, and like a noisome snuff their remembrance is put out for ever and ever.

Verse 6. Here the Psalmist exults over the fallen foe. He bends as it were, over his prostrate form, and insults his once vaunted strength. He plucks the boaster's song out of his mouth, and sings it for him in derision. After this fashion doth our Glorious Redeemer ask of death, "Where is thy sting?" and of the grave, "Where is thy victory?" The spoiler is spoiled, and he who made captive is led into captivity himself.

Verse 7. The enduring existence and unchanging dominion of our Jehovah, are the firm foundations of our joy. The enemy and his destructions shall come to a perpetual end, but God and his throne shall endure for ever. The eternity of divine sovereignty yields unfailing consolation. By the throne being prepared for judgment, are we not to understand the swiftness of divine justice. In heaven's court suitors are not worn out with long delays.

Verse 8. Whatever earthly courts may do, heaven's throne ministers judgment in uprightness. Partiality and respect of persons are things unknown in the dealings of the Holy One of Israel. How the prospect of appearing before the impartial tribunal of the Great King should act as a check to us when tempted to sin, and as a comfort when we are slandered or oppressed.

Verse 9. He who gives no quarter to the wicked in the day of judgment, is the defense and refuge of his saints in the day of trouble. There are many forms of oppression; both from man and from Satan oppression comes to us; and for all its forms, a refuge is provided in the Lord Jehovah. There were cities of refuge under the law, God is our refuge-city under the gospel.

Verse 10. Ignorance is worst when it amounts to ignorance of God, and knowledge is best when it exercises itself upon the name of God. This most excellent knowledge leads to the most excellent grace of faith. O, to learn more of the attributes and character of God. Unbelief, that hooting night bird, cannot live in the light of divine knowledge, it flies before the sun of God's great and gracious name.

Verse 11. Being full of gratitude himself, our inspired author is eager to excite others to join the strain, and praise God in the same manner as he himself vowed to do in the first and second verses. The heavenly spirit of praise is gloriously contagious, and he that hath it is never content unless he can excite all who surround him to unite in his sweet employ. Singing and preaching, as means of glorifying God, are here joined together, and it is remarkable that, connected with all revivals of gospel ministry, there has been a sudden outburst of the spirit of song. Luther's Psalms and Hymns were in all men's mouths, and in the modern revival under Wesley and Whitefield, the strains of Charles Wesley, Cennick, Berridge, Toplady, Hart, Newton, and many others, were the outgrowth of restored piety. The singing of the birds of praise fitly accompanies the return of the gracious spring of divine visitation through the proclamation of the truth. Sing on brethren, and preach on, and these shall both be a token that the Lord still dwelleth in Zion. It will be well for us when coming up to Zion, to remember that the Lord dwells among his saints, and is to be had in peculiar reverence of all those that are about him.

Verse 12. When an inquest is held concerning the blood of the oppressed, the martyred saints will have the first remembrance; he will avenge his own elect. Those saints who are living shall also be heard; they shall be exonerated from blame, and kept from destruction, even when the Lord's most terrible work is going on; the man with the inkhorn by his side shall mark them all for safety, before the slaughtermen are permitted to smite the Lord's enemies. The humble cry of the poorest saints shall neither be drowned by the voice of the thundering justice nor by the shrieks of the condemned.

Verse 13. Memories of the past and confidences concerning the future conducted the man of God to the mercy seat to plead for the needs of the

8. And he shall judge the world in righteousness. As David has just now testified, that the power of God is not inactive, so that he dwells in heaven only indulging himself in pleasures; but that it is a constantly operating power which he exercises in preserving his authority, and governing the world in righteousness and equity; so in this verse he adds the use of this doctrine, which is this, that the power of God is not shut up in heaven, but manifests itself in succoring men.

9-12

9. And Jehovah will be a refuge for the poor. David here furnishes a remedy for the temptation which greatly afflicts the weak, when they see themselves, and those who are like them, abandoned to the will of the ungodly, while God keeps silence. He reminds us that God delays his aid, and to outward appearance forsakes his faithful ones, in order at length to succor them at a more convenient season, according to the greatness of their necessity and affliction.

10. In the tenth verse, the Psalmist teaches us, that when the Lord delivers the righteous, the fruit which results from it is, that they themselves, and all the rest of the righteous, acquire increasing confidence in his grace; for, unless we are fully persuaded that God exercises a care about men and human affairs, we must necessarily be troubled with constant disquietude.

11. Sing unto Jehovah. David, not contented with giving thanks individually, and on his own account, exhorts the faithful to unite with him, praising God, and to do this not only because it is their duty to stir up one another to this religious exercise, but because the deliverances of which he treats were worthy of being publicly and solemnly celebrated; and this is expressed more clearly in the second clause, where he commands them to be published among the nations.

12. There is here a repetition of what the Psalmist had said a little before, that we ought to consider God's power, as it is manifested in the mercy which he exercises towards his servants, who are unrighteously persecuted by wicked men. From the numerous works of God, he selects one which he commends as especially worthy of being remembered, namely, his work in delivering the poor from death.

13-14

13. Have mercy upon me, O Jehovah. I think that this is the second part of the psalm. The Psalmist, in the first place, strengthens his faith from his past experience, inasmuch as he had often been delivered from the greatest dangers. And, in the second place, he assures himself of deliverance, even in the very jaws of death; because God is accustomed not only to succor his servants, and to deliver them from their calamities by ordinary means, but also to bring them from the grave, even after all hope of life is cut off; for the gates of death is a metaphorical expression, denoting the utmost perils which threaten destruction, or rather, which lay the grave open before us.

14. That I may recount. David's meaning simply is, that he will celebrate the praises of God in all assemblies, and,

rubbish and forgotten; but the Lord shall endure for ever, v. 7. There is no change of his being; his felicity, power, and perfection, are out of the reach of all the combined forces of hell and earth; they may put an end to our liberties, our privileges, our lives, but our God is still the same, and sits even upon the floods, unshaken, undisturbed, Ps. xxix. 10; xciii. 2.

2. With the thoughts of his justice and righteousness in all the administrations of his government. He does all every day, he will do all at the last day, according to the eternal unalterable rules of equity (v. 8): He shall judge the world, all persons and all controversies, shall minister judgment to the people (shall determine their lot both in this and in the future state) in righteousness and in uprightness, so that there shall not be the least color of exception against it.

3. With the thoughts of that peculiar favor which God bears to his own people and the special protection which he takes them under. The Lord, who endures for ever, is their everlasting strength and protection; he that judges the world will be sure to judge for them, when at any time they are injured or distressed (v. 9): He will be a refuge for the oppressed, a high place, a strong place, for the oppressed, in times of trouble. It is the lot of God's people to be oppressed in this world and to have troublous times appointed to them.

4. With the thoughts of that sweet satisfaction and repose of mind which those have that make God their refuge (v. 10): "Those that know thy name will put their trust in thee, as I have done" (for the grace of God is the same in all the saints), "and then they will find, as I have found, that thou dost not forsake those that seek thee;" for the favor of God is the same towards all the saints.

11-20 A call to praise God; certain ruin of the wicked. In these verses,

I. David, having praised God himself, calls upon and invites others to praise him likewise, v. 11. Those who believe God is greatly to be praised not only desire to do that work better themselves, but desire that others also may join with them in it and would gladly be instrumental to bring them to it: Sing praises to the Lord who dwelleth in Zion. As the special residence of his glory is in heaven, so the special residence of his grace is in his church, of which Zion was a type.

Take notice of the justice of God in avenging the blood of his people Israel on the Philistines and their other wicked neighbors, who had, in making war upon them, used them barbarously and given them no quarter, v. 12. When God comes to make inquisition for blood by his judgments on earth, before he comes to do it by the judgment of the great day, he remembers them, remembers every drop of the innocent blood which they have shed, and will return it sevenfold upon the head of the blood-thirsty; he will give them blood to drink, for they are worthy.

Psalm 9

13-20
13 Have mercy upon me, O LORD; consider my trouble which I suffer of them that hate me, thou that liftest me up from the gates of death:
14 That I may shew forth all thy praise in the gates of the daughter of Zion: I will rejoice in thy salvation.
15 The heathen are sunk down in the pit that they made: in the net which they hid is their own foot taken.
16 The LORD is known by the judgment which he executeth: the wicked is snared in the work of his own hands. Higgaion. Selah.
17 The wicked shall be turned into hell, and all the nations that forget God.
18 For the needy shall not alway be forgotten: the expectation of the poor shall not perish for ever.
19 Arise, O LORD; let not man prevail: let the heathen be judged in thy sight.
20 Put them in fear, O LORD: that the nations may know themselves to be but men. Selah.

present. Between praising and praying he divided all his time. How could he have spent it more profitably? His first prayer is one suitable for all persons and occasions, it breathes a humble spirit, indicates self-knowledge, appeals to the proper attributes, and to the fitting person.

Verse 14. We must not overlook David's object in desiring mercy, it is God's glory: "that I may show forth all thy praise." Saints are not so selfish as to look only to self; they desire mercy's diamond that they may let others see it flash and sparkle, and may admire Him who gives such priceless gems to his beloved.

Here ends the first part of this instructive Psalm, and in pausing awhile we feel bound to confess that our exposition has only flitted over its surface and has not digged into the depths. The verses are singularly full of teaching, and if the Holy Spirit shall bless the reader, he may go over this Psalm, as the writer has done scores of times, and see on each occasion fresh beauties.

Verse 15. In considering this terrible picture of the Lord's overwhelming judgments of his enemies, we are called upon to ponder and meditate upon it with deep seriousness by the two untranslated words, Higgaion, Selah. Meditate, pause. Consider, and tune your instrument. Bethink yourselves and solemnly adjust your hearts to the solemnity which is so well becoming the subject. Let us in a humble spirit approach these verses, and notice, first, that the character of God requires the punishment of sin.

Verse 16. Jehovah is known by the judgment which he executeth; his holiness and abhorrence of sin is thus displayed. A ruler who winked at evil would soon be known by all his subjects to be evil himself, and he, on the other hand, who is severely just in judgment reveals his own nature thereby.

Verse 17. The justice which has punished the wicked, and preserved the righteous, remains the same, and therefore in days to come, retribution will surely be meted out. How solemn is the seventeenth verse, especially in its warning to forgetters of God.

Verse 18. Mercy is as ready to her work as ever justice can be. Needy souls fear that they are forgotten; well, if it be so, let them rejoice that they shall not alway be so. Satan tells poor tremblers that their hope shall perish, but they have here the divine assurance that their expectation shall not perish for ever.

Verse 19. Prayers are the believer's weapons of war. When the battle is too hard for us, we call in our great ally, who, as it were, lies in ambush until faith gives the signal by crying out, "Arise, O Lord." Although our cause be all but lost, it shall be soon won again, if the Almighty doth but bestir himself.

Verse 20. One would think that men would not grow so vain as to deny themselves to be but men, but it appears to be a lesson which only a divine schoolmaster can teach to some proud spirits. Crowns leave their wearers but men, degrees of eminent learning make their owners not more than men, velour and conquest cannot elevate beyond the dead level of "but men;" and all the wealth of Croesus, the wisdom of Solon, the power of Alexander, the eloquence of Demosthenes, if added together, would leave the possessor but a man. May we ever remember this lest like those in the text, we should be put in fear.

wherever there is the greatest concourse of people, (for at that time it was the custom to hold assemblies at the gates of cities;) but, at the same time, there seems to be an allusion to the gates of death, of which he has just spoken, as if he had said, After I am delivered from the grave, I will do my endeavor to bear testimony, in the most public manner, to the goodness of God, manifested in my deliverance.

15-16
15. The heathen are sunk. David being now raised up to holy confidence, triumphs over his enemies. In the first place, he says metaphorically, that they were taken in their own craftiness and snares. He next expresses the same thing without figure, that they were snared in their own wickedness. And he affirms that this happened not by chance, but was the work of God, and a striking proof of his judgment.
16. The word Higgaion, which properly signifies meditation, is inserted here because David intended to fix the minds of the godly in meditation upon the judgments of God. The word Selah was intended to answer the same purpose, and as I have said before, regulated the singing in such a manner as to make the music correspond to the words and the sentiment.

17-18
17. The faithful, also, it is true, descend into the grave, but not with such fearful violence as plunges them into it without hope of coming out again. So far is this from being the case, that even when shut up in the grave, they dwell already in heaven by hope.
18. For the poor shall not always be forgotten. The assertion that God will not forsake the poor and afflicted for ever, is a confirmation of the preceding sentence. By it he intimates, that they may indeed seem to be forsaken for a time. Let us, therefore, remember that God has promised his assistance to us, not in the way of preventing our afflictions, but of at length succoring us after we have been long subdued under the cross. David speaks expressly of hope or expectation, thereby to encourage us to prayer.

19-20
19. Arise, O Jehovah. When David beseeches God to arise, the expression does not strictly apply to God, but it refers to external appearance and to our senses; for we do not perceive God to be the deliverer of his people except when he appears before our eyes, as it were sitting upon the judgment-seat.
20. With respect to the chosen of God, it becomes them to be humbled under a sense of their own weakness, and willingly to divest themselves of all vain confidence and presumption. And this will be the case if they remember that they are but men. Augustine has well and wisely said, that the whole humility of man consists in the knowledge of himself. Moreover, since pride is natural to all, God requires to strike terror into all men, that, his own people may learn to be humble, and that the wicked, may be put back with shame and confusion.

II. David, having praised God for former mercies and deliverances, earnestly prays that God would still appear for him; for he sees not all things put under him.
1. He prays that God would be compassionate to him (v. 13): "Have mercy upon me, who, having misery only, and no merit, to speak for me, must depend upon mercy for relief."
2. He pleads his sincere purpose to praise God when his victories should be completed (v. 14): "Lord, save me, not that I may have the comfort and credit of the deliverance, but that thou mayest have the glory, that I may show forth all thy praise, and that publicly, in the gates of the daughter of Zion;" there God was said to dwell (v. 11) and there David would attend him, with joy in God's salvation, typical of the great salvation which was to be wrought out by the Son of David.
III. David by faith foresees and foretells the certain ruin of all wicked people, both in this world and in that to come.
1. In this world, v. 15, 16. God executes judgment upon them when the measure of their iniquities is full, and does it so as to put shame upon them and make their fall inglorious; for they sink into the pit which they themselves digged (Ps. vii. 15), they are taken in the net which they themselves laid for the ensnaring of God's people, and they are snared in the work of their own hands. In all the struggles David had with the Philistines they were the aggressors, 2 Sam. v. 17, 22.
2. In the other world (v. 17): The wicked shall be turned into hell, as captives into the prison-house, even all the nations that forget God.
IV. David encourages the people of God to wait for his salvation, though it should be long deferred, v. 18. The needy may think themselves forgotten for a while, and their expectation of help from God may seem to have perished and to have been for ever frustrated. But he that believes does not make haste; the vision is for an appointed time, and at the end it shall speak.
V. He concludes with prayer that God would humble the pride, break the power, and blast the projects, of all the wicked enemies of his church: "Arise, O Lord! (v. 19), stir up thy self, exert thy power, take thy seat, and deal with all these proud and daring enemies of thy name, and cause, and people."
1. "Lord, restrain them, and set bounds to their malice: Let not man prevail; consult thy own honor, and let not weak and mortal men prevail against the kingdom and interest of the almighty and immortal God. Shall mortal man be too hard for God, too strong for his Maker?"
2. "Lord, frighten them: Put them in fear, O Lord! (v. 20), strike a terror upon them, make them afraid with thy judgments." God knows how to make the strongest and stoutest of men to tremble and to flee when none pursues, and thereby he makes them know and own that they are but men; they are but weak men, unable to stand before the holy God.

Psalm 10

1-6

1 Why standest thou afar off, O LORD? why hidest thou thyself in times of trouble?
2 The wicked in his pride doth persecute the poor: let them be taken in the devices that they have imagined.
3 For the wicked boasteth of his heart's desire, and blesseth the covetous, whom the LORD abhorreth.
4 The wicked, through the pride of his countenance, will not seek after God: God is not in all his thoughts.
5 His ways are always grievous; thy judgments are far above out of his sight: as for all his enemies, he puffeth at them.
6 He hath said in his heart, I shall not be moved: for I shall never be in adversity.

Psalm 10

Since this Psalm has no title of its own, it is supposed by some to be a fragment of Psalm 9. We prefer, however, since it is complete in itself, to consider it as a separate composition. We have had instances already of Psalms which seem meant to form a pair (Psalm 1 and 2, Psalm 3 and 4) and this, with the ninth, is another specimen of the double Psalm.

The prevailing theme seems to be the oppression and persecution of the wicked, we will, therefore, for our own guidance, entitle it, THE CRY OF THE OPPRESSED.

DIVISION. The first verse, in an exclamation of surprise, explains the intent of the Psalm, viz., to invoke the interposition of God for the deliverance of his poor and persecuted people. From verse 2 to 11, the character of the oppressor is described in powerful language. In verse 12, the cry of the first verse bursts forth again, but with a clearer utterance. In the next place (verses 13-15), God's eye is clearly beheld as regarding all the cruel deeds of the wicked; and as a consequence of divine omniscience, the ultimate judgment of the oppressed is joyously anticipated (verses 16-18). To the Church of God during times of persecution, and to individual saints who are smarting under the hand of the proud sinner, this Psalm furnishes suitable language both for prayer and praise.

EXPOSITION

Verse 1. To the tearful eye of the sufferer the Lord seemed to stand still, as if he calmly looked on, and did not sympathize with his afflicted one. Nay, more, the Lord appeared to be afar off, no longer "a very present help in trouble," but an inaccessible mountain, into which no man would be able to climb. The presence of God is the joy of his people, but any suspicion of his absence is distracting beyond measure. Let us, then, ever remember that the Lord is nigh us.

Verse 2. The second verse contains the formal indictment against the wicked: "The wicked in his pride doth persecute the poor." The accusation divides itself into two distinct charges—pride and tyranny; the one the root and cause of the other. The second sentence is the humble petition of the oppressed: "Let them be taken in the devices that they have imagined." The prayer is reasonable, just, and natural.

Verse 3. The indictment being read, and the petition presented, the evidence is now heard upon the first count. The evidence is very full and conclusive upon the matter of pride, and no jury could hesitate to give a verdict against the prisoner at the bar. Let us, however, hear the witnesses one by one. The first testifies that he is a boaster. "For the wicked boasteth of his heart's desire." He is a very silly boaster, for he glories in a mere desire.

Verse 4. The proud boastings and lewd blessings of the wicked have been received in evidence against him, and now his own face confirms the accusation, and his empty closet cries aloud against him. "The wicked, through the pride of his countenance, will not seek after God." Proud hearts breed proud looks and stiff knees. It is an admirable arrangement that the heart is often written on the countenance, just as the motion of the wheels of a clock find their record on its face. A brazen face and a broken heart never go together.

Verse 5. "His ways are always grievous." To himself they are hard. Men go a rough road when they go to hell. God has hedged-up the way of sin: O what folly to leap these hedges and fall among the thorns! To others, also, his ways cause much sorrow and vexation; but what cares he? He sits like the idol god upon his monstrous car, utterly regardless of the crowds who are crushed as he rolls along. "Thy judgments are far above out of his sight:" he looks high, but not high enough. As God is forgotten, so are his judgments. He is not able to comprehend the things of God; a swine may

Psalm 10

1-2
1. Lord, why standest thou afar off? We here see how the prophet, seeking a remedy for his calamities, which were apparently past hope, directly addresses himself to God at the very commencement. And the rule which we should observe, when we are in trouble and sorrow, is this: We should seek comfort and solace in the providence of God; for amidst our agitations, vexations, and cares, we ought to be fully persuaded that it is his peculiar office to give relief to the wretched and afflicted.
2. The ungodly in his pride, etc Before uttering his prayer against the ungodly, the Psalmist briefly sets forth their wickedness in cruelly vexing the afflicted, for no other reason but because they disdain and despise them, through the pride with which they are inflated.

3-4
3. What is this desire of soul? In my opinion, desire of soul here denotes rather lust, and the intemperate gratification of passion and appetite; and thus the meaning is, that they indulge themselves with delight in their depraved desires, and, despising the judgment of God, fearlessly absolve themselves from all guilt, maintain their innocence. David, indeed, says a little after, that the ungodly abuse their prosperity, by flattering themselves; but here, in my judgment, he expresses something more weighty, namely, that they acquire praise from their presumptuousness, and glory in their wickedness; and this foolish confidence, or bold assurance, is the cause of their throwing off all restraint and breaking forth into every kind of excess.
4. David simply means, that the ungodly, without examination, permit themselves to do any thing, or do not distinguish between what is lawful and unlawful, because their own lust is their law, yea, rather, as if superior to all laws, they fancy that it is lawful for them to do whatever they please.

5-6
5. As the ungodly enjoy a continued course of prosperity, they dream that God is bound or plighted to them, and hence they put his judgments far from them; and if any man oppose them, they are confident they can immediately put him down, or dash him to pieces with a puff or breath. Now, we understand the simple meaning of the prophet to be, that the ungodly mock God, taking encouragement from his forbearance. Hence it is, that they put far from them the judgments of God.
6. The Psalmist confirms these statements in the next verse, where he tells us that the persons of whom he speaks are fully persuaded in their hearts that they are beyond all danger of change. He saith in his heart, I shall not be moved from generation to generation The ungodly often pour forth proud language to this effect.

Psalm 10

1-11 The character of the wicked; the character of persecutors.
David, in these verses, discovers,
I. A very great affection to God and his favor; for, in the time of trouble, that which he complains of most feelingly is God's withdrawing his gracious presence (v. 1): "Why standest thou afar off, as one unconcerned in the indignities done to thy name and the injuries done to the people?"
II. A very great indignation against sin, the sins that made the times perilous, 2 Tim. iii. 1. he beholds the transgressors and is grieved, is amazed, and brings to his heavenly Father their evil report, not in a way of vain-glory, boasting before God that he was not as these publicans (Luke xviii. 11), much less venting any personal resentments, piques, or passions, of his own; but as one that laid to he art that which is offensive to God and all good men, and earnestly desired a reformation of manners. passionate and satirical invectives against bad men do more hurt than good; if we will speak of their badness, let it be to God in prayer, for he alone can make them better. This long representation of the wickedness of the wicked is here summed up in the first words of it (v. 2), The wicked in his pride doth persecute the poor, where two things are laid to their charge, pride and persecution, the former the cause of the latter.
1. They are proud, very proud, and extremely conceited of themselves; justly therefore did he wonder that God did not speedily appear against them, for he hates pride, and resists the proud. He proudly casts off the thoughts of God, and all dependence upon him and devotion to him (v. 4): The wicked, through the pride of his countenance, that pride of his heart which appears in his very countenance (Prov. vi. 17), will not seek after God, nor entertain the thoughts of him. God is not in all his thoughts, not in any of them. He proudly makes light of God's commandments and judgments (v. 5): His wings are always grievous; he is very daring and resolute in his sinful courses; he will have his way, though ever so tiresome to himself and vexatious to others; he travails with pain in his wicked courses, and yet his pride makes him willful and obstinate in them.

He proudly sets trouble at defiance and is confident of the continuance of his own prosperity (v. 6): He hath said in his heart, and pleased himself with the thought, I shall not be moved, my goods are laid up for many years, and I shall never be in adversity; like Babylon, that said, I shall be a lady for ever, Isa. xlvii. 7; Rev. xviii. 7. Those are nearest ruin who thus set it furthest from them.
2. They are persecutors, cruel persecutors. For the gratifying of their pride and covetousness, and in opposition to God and religion, they are very oppressive to all within their reach. Observe,

Psalm 10

7-12

7 His mouth is full of cursing and deceit and fraud: under his tongue is mischief and vanity.
8 He sitteth in the lurking places of the villages: in the secret places doth he murder the innocent: his eyes are privily set against the poor.
9 He lieth in wait secretly as a lion in his den: he lieth in wait to catch the poor: he doth catch the poor, when he draweth him into his net.
10 He croucheth, and humbleth himself, that the poor may fall by his strong ones.
11 He hath said in his heart, God hath forgotten: he hideth his face; he will never see it.
12 Arise, O LORD; O God, lift up thine hand: forget not the humble.

sooner look through a telescope at the stars than this man study the Word of God to understand the righteousness of the Lord.

Verse 6. The testimony of the sixth verse concludes the evidence against the prisoner upon the first charge of pride, and certainly it is conclusive in the highest degree. The present witness has been prying into the secret chambers of the heart, and has come to tell us what he has heard. "He hath said in his heart, I shall not be moved: for I shall never be in adversity." O impertinence runs to seed! The man thinks himself immutable, and omnipotent too, for he, he is never to be in adversity. He counts himself a privileged man. He sits alone, and shall see no sorrow. His nest is in the stars, and he dreams not of a hand that shall pluck him thence. But let us remember that this man's house is built upon the sand, upon a foundation no more substantial than the rolling waves of the sea.

Verse 7. Let us now hear the witnesses in court. Let the wretch speak for himself, for out of his own mouth he will be condemned. "His mouth is full of cursing and deceit and fraud." There is not only a little evil there, but his mouth is full of it. A three-headed serpent hath stowed away its coils and venom within the den of its black mouth. There is cursing which he spits against both God and men, deceit with which he entraps the unwary, and fraud by which, even in his common dealings, he robs his neighbors. Beware of such a man: have no sort of dealing with him: none but the silliest of geese would go to the fox's sermon, and none but the most foolish will put themselves into the society of knaves. But we must proceed. Let us look under this man's tongue as well as in his mouth; "under his tongue is mischief and vanity." Deep in his throat are the unborn words which shall come forth as mischief and iniquity.

Verse 8. Despite the bragging of this base wretch, it seems that he is as cowardly as he is cruel. "He sitteth in the lurking places of the villages: in the secret places doth he murder the innocent: his eyes are privily set against the poor." He acts the part of the highwayman, who springs upon the unsuspecting traveler in some desolate part of the road.

Verse 9. The picture becomes darker, for here is the cunning of the lion, and of the huntsman, as well as the stealthiness of the robber. Surely there are some men who come up to the very letter of this description. With watching, perversion, slander, whispering, and false swearing, they ruin the character of the righteous, and murder the innocent; or, with legal quibbles, mortgages, bonds, writs, and the like, they catch the poor, and draw them into a net. Chrysostom was peculiarly severe upon this last phase of cruelty, but assuredly not more so than was richly merited. Take care, brethren, for there are other traps besides these. Hungry lions are crouching in every den, and fowlers spread their nets in every field.

Verse 11. As upon the former count, so upon this one; a witness is forthcoming, who has been listening at the keyhole of the heart. Speak up, friend, and let us hear your story. "He hath said in his heart, God hath forgotten: he hideth his face; he will never see it." This cruel man comforts himself with the idea that God is blind, or, at least, forgetful: a fond and foolish fancy, indeed. Men doubt Omniscience when they persecute the saints. If we had a sense of God's presence with us, it would be impossible for us to ill-treat his children. In fact, there can scarcely be a greater preservation from sin than the constant thought of "Thou, God, seest me." Thus has the trial proceeded. The case has been fully stated; and now it is but little wonder that the oppressed petitioner lifts up the cry for judgment, which we find in the following verse.

Verse 12. With what bold language will faith address its God! and yet what unbelief is mingled with our strongest confidence. Fearlessly the Lord is stirred up to arise and lift up his hand, yet timidly he is begged not to forget the humble; as if Jehovah could ever be forgetful of his saints. This verse is the incessant cry of the Church, and she will never refrain therefrom until her Lord shall come in his glory to avenge her of all her adversaries.

7-10

7. His mouth is full of cursing. The scope of these four verses is this: If God intends to succor his servants, it is now a proper time for doing so, inasmuch as the lawlessness of the ungodly has burst forth to the utmost possible excess. In the first place, he complains that their tongues are full of perjuries and deceits, and that they carry or hide mischief and wrongs, it being impossible to have any dealings with them in any matter without loss and damage.

8. David describes what ungodly men are accustomed to do. And, in the first place, he compares them to highwaymen, who lie in wait at the narrow parts of roads, and choose for themselves hiding-places from which they may fall upon travelers when off their guard. He says also, that their eyes are bent or leering, by a similitude borrowed from the practice of dart-shooters, who take their aim with leering, or half shut eyes, in order to hit the mark the surer.

9. In the next verse, he sets forth their cruelty in a light still more aggravated, by another comparison, saying, that they thirst for their prey like lions in their dens Now, it is a step higher in wickedness to equal in cruelty wild beasts than to make havoc after the manner of robbers.

10. He again repeats all this in the tenth verse, giving a beautiful and graphic description of the very gesture of such wicked men, just as if he set before our eyes a picture of them. The obvious meaning of the Psalmist is, that the ungodly are to be dreaded on all sides, because they dissemble their cruelty, till they find those caught in their toils whom they wish to devour.

11-13

11. He hath said in his heart. The Psalmist again points out the source from which the presumption of the ungodly proceeds. Because God seems to take no notice of their wicked practices, they flatter themselves with the hope of escaping unpunished. As, however, they do not openly utter with their mouth the detestable blasphemy, that God hath forgotten their conduct, and hath shut his eyes that he may never see it, but hide their thoughts in the deep recesses of their own hearts, as Isaiah declares, (Isaiah 29:15) the Psalmist uses the same form of expression which he used before, and which he repeats a little after the third time, namely, that the ungodly say to themselves, in their hearts, that God takes no concern whatever in the affairs of men.

12. Arise, O Jehovah. It is a disease under which men in general labor, to imagine, according to the judgment of the flesh, that when God does not execute his judgments, he is sitting idle, or lying at ease. There is, however, a great difference with respect to this between the faithful and the wicked. The latter cherish the false opinion which is dictated by the weakness of the flesh, and in order to soothe and flatter themselves in their vices, they indulge in slumbering, and render their conscience stupid, until at length, through their wicked obstinacy, they harden themselves into a gross contempt of God. But the former soon shake from their minds that false imagination, and chastise themselves,

concerning these persecutors that they are very bitter and malicious (v. 7): His mouth is full of cursing. Those he cannot do a real mischief to, yet he will spit his venom at, and breathe out the slaughter which he cannot execute. Thus have God's faithful worshippers been anathematized and cursed, with bell, book, and candle.

They are very cunning and crafty in carrying on their designs. They have ways and means to concert what they intend, that they may the more effectually accomplish it. Like Esau, that cunning hunter, he sits in the lurking places, in the secret places, and his eyes are privily set to do mischief (v. 8), not because he is ashamed of what he does (if he blushed, there were some hopes he would repent), not because he is afraid of the wrath of God, for he imagines God will never call him to an account (v. 11), but because he is afraid lest the discovery of his designs should be the breaking of them. Perhaps it refers particularly to robbers and highwaymen, who lie in wait for honest travelers, to make a prey of them and what they have. They are base and hypocritical (v. 10): He crouches and humbles himself, as beasts of prey do, that they may get their prey within their reach.

12-18 Prayer against persecutors.

David here, upon the foregoing representation of the inhumanity and impiety of the oppressors, grounds an address to God, wherein observe,

I. What he prays for.

1. That God would himself appear (v. 12): "Arise, O Lord! O God! lift up thy hand, manifest thy presence and providence in the affairs of this lower world. Arise, O Lord! to the confusion of those who say that thou hidest thy face. Manifest thy power, exert it for the maintaining of thy own cause, lift up thy hand to give a fatal blow to these oppressors; let thy everlasting arm be made bare."

2. That he would appear for his people: "Forget not the humble, the afflicted, that are poor, that are made poorer, and are poor in spirit. Their oppressors, in their presumption, say that thou hast forgotten them; and they, in their despair, are ready to say the same. Lord, make it to appear that they are both mistaken."

3. That he would appear against their persecutors, v. 15.

(1.) That he would disable them from doing any mischief: Break thou the arm of the wicked, take away his power, that the hypocrite reign not, lest the people be ensnared, Job xxxiv. 30. We read of oppressors whose dominion was taken away, but their lives were prolonged (Dan. vii. 12), that they might have time to repent.

(2.) That he would deal with them for the mischief they had done: "Seek out his wickedness; let that be all brought to light which he thought should for ever lie undiscovered; let that be all brought to account which he thought should for ever go unpunished; bring it out till thou find none, that is, till none of his evil deeds

Psalm 10

13-18
13 Wherefore doth the wicked contemn God? he hath said in his heart, Thou wilt not require it.
14 Thou hast seen it; for thou beholdest mischief and spite, to requite it with thy hand: the poor committeth himself unto thee; thou art the helper of the fatherless.
15 Break thou the arm of the wicked and the evil man: seek out his wickedness till thou find none.
16 The LORD is King for ever and ever: the heathen are perished out of his land.
17 LORD, thou hast heard the desire of the humble: thou wilt prepare their heart, thou wilt cause thine ear to hear:
18 To judge the fatherless and the oppressed, that the man of the earth may no more oppress.

Verse 13. In these verses the description of the wicked is condensed, and the evil of his character traced to its source, viz., atheistical ideas with regard to the government of the world. We may at once perceive that this is intended to be another urgent plea with the Lord to show his power, and reveal his justice. When the wicked call God's righteousness in question, we may well beg him to teach them terrible things in righteousness. In verse 13, the hope of the infidel and his heart-wishes are laid bare. He despises the Lord, because he will not believe that sin will meet with punishment.

Verse 14. This vile suggestion receives its answer in verse 14. "Thou hast seen it; for thou beholdest mischief and spite, to requite it with thy hand." God is all-eye to see, and all-hand to punish his enemies. From Divine oversight there is no hiding, and from Divine justice there is no fleeing. Wanton mischief shall meet with woeful misery, and those who harbor spite shall inherit sorrow. Verily there is a God which judgeth in the earth. Nor is this the only instance of the presence of God in the world; for while he chastises the oppressor, he befriends the oppressed. "The poor committeth himself unto thee." They give themselves up entirely into the Lord's hands. Resigning their judgment to his enlightenment, and their wills to his supremacy, they rest assured that he will order all things for the best. Nor does he deceive their hope. He preserves them in times of need, and causes them to rejoice in his goodness. "Thou art the helper of the fatherless." God is the parent of all orphans. When the earthly father sleeps beneath the sod, a heavenly Father smiles from above. By some means or other, orphan children are fed, and well they may when they have such a Father.

Verse 15. In this verse we hear again the burden of the psalmist's prayer: "Break thou the arm of the wicked and the evil man." Let the sinner lose his power to sin; stop the tyrant, arrest the oppressor, weaken the loins of the mighty, and dash in pieces the terrible. They deny thy justice: let them feel it to the full. Indeed, they shall feel it; for God shall hunt the sinner for ever: so long as there is a grain of sin in him it shall be sought out and punished. It is not a little worthy of note, that very few great persecutors have ever died in their beds: the curse has manifestly pursued them, and their fearful sufferings have made them own that divine justice at which they could at one time launch defiance. God permits tyrants to arise as thorn-hedges to protect his church from the intrusion of hypocrites, and that he may teach his backsliding children by them, as Gideon did the men of Succoth with the briers of the wilderness; but he soon cuts up these Herods, like the thorns, and casts them into the fire. To the men who had neither justice nor mercy for the saints, there shall be rendered justice to the full, but not a grain of mercy.

Verses 16, 17, 18. The Psalm ends with a song of thanksgiving to the great and everlasting King, because he has granted the desire of his humble and oppressed people, has defended the fatherless, and punished the heathen who trampled upon his poor and afflicted children. Let us learn that we are sure to speed well, if we carry our complaint to the King of kings. Rights will be vindicated, and wrongs redressed, at his throne. His government neglects not the interests of the needy, nor does it tolerate oppression in the mighty. Great God, we leave ourselves in thine hand; to thee we commit thy church afresh.

returning of their own accord to a due consideration of what is the truth on this subject.
13. Why doth the wicked despise God? It is, indeed, superfluous to bring arguments before God, for the purpose of persuading him to grant us what we ask; but still he permits us to make use of them, and to speak to him in prayer, as familiarly as a son speaks to an earthly father. It should always be observed, that the use of praying is, that God may be the witness of all our affections; not that they would otherwise be hidden from him, but when we pour out our hearts before him, our cares are hereby greatly lightened, and our confidence of obtaining our requests increases. Thus David, in the present passage, by setting before himself how unreasonable and intolerable it would be for the wicked to be allowed to despise God according to their pleasure, thinking he will never bring them to an account, was led to cherish the hope of deliverance from his calamities.

14-15
14. Thou hast seen it; for thou, etc Here David, suddenly kindled with a holy zeal, enters into conflict, and, armed with the shield of faith, courageously repels these execrable opinions; but as he could derive no advantage by making his appeal to men, he has recourse to God, and addresses him. As the ungodly imagine themselves to be far beyond his reach; so, on the contrary, the faithful ought carefully to keep themselves aloof from those wild opinions, which are afloat in the world, and with minds lifted upward, to speak to God as if present with them.
15. Break thou the arm. This form of expression just means breaking the power of the wicked. And it is not simply a prayer; it may also be regarded as a prophecy.

16-18
16. Jehovah is King for ever and ever. David now, as if he had obtained the desires of his heart, rises up to holy rejoicing and thanksgiving. When he calls God King for ever and ever, it is a token of his confidence and joy. By the title of King, he vindicates God's claim to the government of the world, and when he describes him as King for ever and ever, this shows how absurd it is to think to shut him up within the narrow limits of time.
17. O Jehovah, thou hast heard the desire of the needy. In these words the prophet confirms that when hypocrites prevail in the Church, or exceed the faithful in number, we ought, unceasingly, to beseech God to root them out; for such a confused and shameful state of things ought surely to be matter of deep grief to all the true servants of God.
18. That the man who is of earth may no more terrify them. David again commends the power of God in destroying the ungodly; and he does it for this purpose,—that in the midst of their tumultuous assaults we may have this principle deeply fixed in our minds, that God, whenever he pleases, can bring all their attempts to nothing.

The design of the Psalmist is indirectly to condemn their infatuated presumption, in that, forgetful of their condition, they breathe out cruel and terrible threatenings, as if it were beyond the power of even God himself to repress the violence of their rage.

remain unreckoned for, none of his evil designs undefeated, and none of his partisans undestroyed."
II. What he pleads for the encouraging of his own faith in these petitions.
1. He pleads the great affronts which these proud oppressors put upon God himself: "Lord, it is thy own cause that we beg thou wouldst appear in; the enemies have made it so, and therefore it is not for thy glory to let them go unpunished" (v. 13): Wherefore do the wicked contemn God? He does so; for he says, "Thou wilt not require it; thou wilt never call us to an account for what we do," than which they could not put a greater indignity upon the righteous God.
2. He pleads the notice God took of the impiety and iniquity of these oppressors (v. 14): "Do the persecutors encourage themselves with a groundless fancy that thou wilt never see it? Let the persecuted encourage themselves with a well-grounded faith, not only that thou hast seen it, but that thou doest behold it, even all the mischief that is done by the hands, and all the spite and malice that lurk in the hearts, of these oppressors; it is all known to thee, and observed by thee; nay, not only thou hast seen it and dost behold it, but thou wilt requite it, wilt recompense it into their bosoms, by thy just and avenging hand."
3. He pleads the dependence which the oppressed had upon him: "The poor commits himself unto thee, each of them does so, I among the rest. They rely on thee as their patron and protector, they refer themselves to thee as their Judge, in whose determination they acquiesce and at whose disposal they are willing to be. They leave themselves with thee" (so some read it), "not prescribing, but subscribing, to thy wisdom and will. They thus give thee honor as much as their oppressors dishonor thee. They are thy willing subjects, and put themselves under thy protection; therefore protect them."
4. He pleads the relation in which God is pleased to stand to us, as a great God. He is King for ever and ever, v. 16.
5. He pleads the experience which God's church and people had had of God's readiness to appear for them. He had dispersed and extirpated their enemies (v. 16): "The heathen have perished out of his land, and this is an encouragement to us to hope that God will, in like manner, break the arm of the oppressive Israelites, who were, in some respects, worse than heathens."
6. He pleads their expectations from God pursuant to their experience of him: "Thou hast heard, therefore thou will cause thy ear to hear," as, Ps. vi. 9. Observe what he will do in answer to prayer, v. 18. He will plead the cause of the persecuted, will judge the fatherless and oppressed, will judge for them, clear up their innocency, restore their comforts, and recompense them for all the loss and damage they have sustained. He will put an end to the fury of the persecutors. Hitherto they shall come, but no further; here shall the proud waves of their malice be stayed.

Psalm 11

Title
To the chief Musician, a Psalm of David.

1 In the LORD put I my trust: how say ye to my soul, Flee as a bird to your mountain?
2 For, lo, the wicked bend their bow, they make ready their arrow upon the string, that they may privily shoot at the upright in heart.
3 If the foundations be destroyed, what can the righteous do?
4 The LORD is in his holy temple, the LORD's throne is in heaven: his eyes behold, his eyelids try, the children of men.
5 The LORD trieth the righteous: but the wicked and him that loveth violence his soul hateth.
6 Upon the wicked he shall rain snares, fire and brimstone, and an horrible tempest: this shall be the portion of their cup.
7 For the righteous LORD loveth righteousness; his countenance doth behold the upright.

Psalm 11

SUBJECT. To assist us to remember this short, but sweet Psalm, we will give it the name of "THE SONG OF THE STEADFAST."
DIVISION. From 1 to 3, David describes the temptation with which he was assailed, and from 4 to 7, the arguments by which his courage was sustained.

EXPOSITION
Verse 1. These verses contain an account of a temptation to distrust God, with which David was, upon some unmentioned occasion, greatly exercised. It may be, that in the days when he was in Saul's court, he was advised to flee at a time when this flight would have been charged against him as a breach of duty to the king, or a proof of personal cowardice.
Verse 2. How forcibly the case is put! The bow is bent, the arrow is fitted to the string: "Flee, flee, thou defenseless bird, thy safety lies in flight; begone, for thine enemies will send their shafts into thy heart; haste, haste, for soon wilt thou be destroyed!"
Verse 3. It was equally correct that the very foundations of law and justice were destroyed under Saul's unrighteous government: but what were all these things to the man whose trust was in God alone? He could brave the dangers, could escape the enemies, and defy the injustice which surrounded him.
Verse 4. David here declares the great source of his unflinching courage. He borrows his light from heaven—from the great central orb of deity. The God of the believer is never far from him; he is not merely the God of the mountain fastnesses, but of the dangerous valleys and battle plains.
Verse 5. "The Lord trieth the righteous:" he doth not hate them, but only tries them. They are precious to him, and therefore he refines them with afflictions. None of the Lord's children may hope to escape from trial, nor, indeed, in our right minds, would any of us desire to do so, for trial is the channel of many blessings.
Verse 6. "But the wicked and him that loveth violence his soul hateth:" why, then, shall I flee from these wicked men? If God hateth them, I will not fear them. Haman was very great in the palace until he lost favor, but when the king abhorred him, how bold were the meanest attendants to suggest the gallows for the man at whom they had often trembled! Look at the black mark upon the faces of our persecutors, and we shall not run away from them. If God is in the quarrel as well as ourselves, it would be foolish to question the result, or avoid the conflict.
Verse 7. The delightful contrast of the last verse is well worthy of our observation, and it affords another overwhelming reason why we should be steadfast, unmoveable, not carried away with fear, or led to adopt carnal expedients in order to avoid trial. "For the righteous Lord loveth righteousness." It is not only his office to defend it, but his nature to love it. He would deny himself if he did not defend the just. It is essential to the very being of God that he should be just; fear not, then, the end of all your trials, but "be just, and fear not." God approves, and, if men oppose, what matters it? "His countenance doth behold the upright." We need never be out of countenance, for God countenances us. He observes, he approves, he delights in the upright. He sees his own image in them, an image of his own fashioning, and therefore with complacency he regards them. Shall we dare to put forth our hand unto iniquity in order to escape affliction? Let us not hearken to the voice of the charmer, but seek an increase of faith, that we may wrestle with principalities and powers, and follow the Lord, fully going without the camp, bearing his reproach.

JOHN CALVIN

Psalm 11

1-3
1. In Jehovah do I put my trust. The psalm should be divided into two parts. Before celebrating the righteousness of God, which he displays in the preservation of the godly, the Psalmist shows how he had encountered even death itself, and yet, through faith and an upright conscience, had obtained the victory. As all men advised him to leave his country, and retire into some place of exile, where he might be concealed, inasmuch as there remained for him no hope of life, unless he should relinquish the kingdom, which had been promised to him; in the beginning of the psalm, he opposes to this perverse advice the shield of his trust in God.
2. David here continues his account of the trying circumstances in which he was placed. His design is not only to place before our view the dangers with which he was surrounded, but to show us that he was exposed even to death itself. He therefore says, that wherever he might hide himself, it was impossible for him to escape from the hands of his enemies. Now, the description of so miserable a condition illustrates the more strikingly the grace of God in the deliverance which he afterwards granted him.
3. David complains, that, in the eyes of the world, he was utterly overthrown, inasmuch as all that he possessed was completely destroyed. In the last clause, he again repeats, that to be persecuted so cruelly was what he did not deserve: What hath the righteous one done? And he asserts his own innocence, partly to comfort himself in his calamities from the testimony of a good conscience, and partly to encourage himself in the hope of obtaining deliverance.

4-5
4. Jehovah is in the palace of his holiness. In what follows, the Psalmist glories in the assurance of the favor of God. Being destitute of human aid, he betakes himself to the providence of God. It is a signal proof of faith to take and to borrow, so to speak, light from heaven to guide us to the hope of salvation, when we are surrounded in this world with darkness on every side.

6-7
6. He will rain upon the ungodly. David now lays it down as a certain truth, that although God, for a time, may be still and delay his judgments, yet the hour of vengeance will assuredly come. Thus we see how by degrees he rises up to the hope of a happy issue to his present affliction, and he uses his efforts to attain this, that the social and moral disorder, which he saw prevailing around him, might not weaken his faith.

The portion of their cup. By this expression he testifies that the judgments of God will certainly take effect, although ungodly men may delude themselves by deceitful flattery.
7. For the righteous Jehovah loveth righteousness. The Psalmist concludes that God will be the defender of the good and the upright.

MATTHEW HENRY

Psalm 11

1-3 Confidence in God.
Here is,
I. David's fixed resolution to make God his confidence: In the Lord put I my trust, v. 1. Those that truly fear God and serve him are welcome to put their trust in him, and shall not be made ashamed of their doing so. And it is the character of the saints, who have taken God for their God, that they make him their hope.
II. His resentment of a temptation to the contrary: "How say you to my soul, which has thus returned to God as its rest and reposes in him, Flee as a bird to your mountain, to be safe there out of the reach of the fowler?"

They would have him flee because he could not be safe where he was, v. 2. "Observe," say they, "how the wicked bend their bow; Saul and his instruments aim at thy life, and the uprightness of thy heart will not be thy security."

He resists the temptation with a gracious abhorrence, v. 3. He looks upon this suggestion as striking at the foundations which every Israelite builds upon: "If you destroy the foundations, if you take good people off from their hope in God, if you can persuade them that their religion is a cheat and a jest and can banter them out of that, you ruin them, and break their hearts indeed, and make them of all men the most miserable."

4-7
Consider,
I. That there is a God in heaven: The Lord is in his holy temple above, where, though he is out of our sight, we are not out of his. Let not the enemies of the saints insult over them, as if they were at a loss and at their wits' end: no, they have a God, and they know where to find him and how to direct their prayer unto him, as their Father in heaven.
II. That, if he afflict good people, it is for their trial and therefore for their good, v. 5. The Lord tries all the children of men that he may do them good in their latter end, Deut. viii. 16.
III. That, however persecutors and oppressors may prosper and prevail awhile, they now lie under, and will for ever perish under, the wrath of God. He is a righteous Judge, and therefore he will punish them, v. 6.
IV. That, though honest good people may be run down and trampled upon, yet God owns them, and favor them, and smile upon them, and that is the reason why God will severely reckon with persecutors and oppressors, because those whom they oppress and persecute are dear to him; so that whosoever toucheth them toucheth the apple of his eye, v. 7. We must herein be followers of God, must love righteousness as he does, that we may keep ourselves always in his love.

Psalm 12

Title
To the Chief Musician upon Sheminith, a Psalm of David.

1 Help, LORD; for the godly man ceaseth; for the faithful fail from among the children of men.
2 They speak vanity every one with his neighbor: with flattering lips and with a double heart do they speak.
3 The LORD shall cut off all flattering lips, and the tongue that speaketh proud things:
4 Who have said, With our tongue will we prevail; our lips are our own: who is lord over us?
5 For the oppression of the poor, for the sighing of the needy, now will I arise, saith the LORD; I will set him in safety from him that puffeth at him.
6 The words of the LORD are pure words: as silver tried in a furnace of earth, purified seven times.
7 Thou shalt keep them, O LORD, thou shalt preserve them from this generation for ever.
8 The wicked walk on every side, when the vilest men are exalted.

Psalm 12

TITLE. This Psalm is headed "To the Chief Musician upon Sheminith, a Psalm of David," which title is identical with that of the sixth Psalm, except that Neginoth is here omitted. The subject will be the better before the mind's eye if we entitle this Psalm: "GOOD THOUGHTS IN BAD TIMES." It is supposed to have been written while Saul was persecuting David, and those who favored his cause.
DIVISION. In the first and second verses David spreads his plaint before the Lord concerning the treachery of his age; verses 3 and 4 denounce judgments upon proud traitors; in verse 5, Jehovah himself thunders out his wrath against oppressors; hearing this, the Chief Musician sings sweetly of the faithfulness of God and his care of his people, in verses 6 and 7; but closes on the old key of lament in verse 8, as he observes the abounding wickedness of his times. Those holy souls who dwell in Mesech, and sojourn in the tents of Kedar, may read and sing these sacred stanzas with hearts in full accord with their mingled melody of lowly mourning and lofty confidence.

EXPOSITION
Verse 1. "Help, Lord." A short but sweet, suggestive, seasonable, and serviceable prayer; a kind of angel's sword, to be turned every way, and to be used on all occasions. Ainsworth says the word rendered "help," is largely used for all manner of saving, helping, delivering, preserving, etc.
Verse 2. "They speak vanity every one with his neighbor." They utter that which is vain to hear, because of its frivolous, foolish, want of worth; vain to believe, because it was false and lying; vain to trust to, since it was deceitful and flattering; vain to regard, for it lifted up the hearer, filling him with proud conceit of himself. Flattery is the sign of the tavern where duplicity is the host. The Chinese consider a man of two hearts to be a very base man, and we shall be safe in reckoning all flatteries to be such.
Verses 3, 4. Total destruction shall overwhelm the lovers of flattery and pride, but meanwhile how they hector and fume! Well did the apostle call them "raging waves of the sea, foaming out their own shame." Free-thinkers are generally very free-talkers, and they are never more at ease than when railing at God's dominion, and arrogating to themselves unbounded license.
Verse 5. In due season the Lord will hear his elect ones, who cry day and night unto him, and though he bear long with their oppressors, yet will he avenge them speedily.
Verse 6. What a contrast between the vain words of man, and the pure words of Jehovah. Man's words are yea and nay, but the Lord's promises are yea and amen. For truth, certainty, holiness, faithfulness, the words of the Lord are pure as well-refined silver. In the original there is an allusion to the most severely purifying process known to the ancients, through which silver was passed when the greatest possible purity was desired; the dross was all consumed, and only the bright and precious metal remained; so clear and free from all alloy of error or unfaithfulness is the book of the words of the Lord.
Verse 7. To fall into the hands of an evil generation, so as to be baited by their cruelty, or polluted by their influence, is an evil to be dreaded beyond measure; but it is an evil foreseen and provided for in the text.
Verse 8. Here we return to the fount of bitterness, which first made the psalmist run to the wells of salvation, namely, the prevalence of wickedness. When those in power are vile, their underlings will be no better. As a warm sun brings out noxious flies, so does a sinner in honor foster vice everywhere.

JOHN CALVIN

Psalm 12

1-2
1. I understand these words as meaning that there is no longer any beneficence or truth remaining among men. He has expressed in these words in what true righteousness consists. As there are two kinds of unrighteousness, violence and deceit; so men live righteously when, in their intercourse with each other, they conscientiously abstain from doing any wrong or injury to one another, and cultivate peace and mutual friendship; when they are neither lions nor foxes. When, however, we see the world in such a state of disorder as is here described, and are afflicted thereby, we ought to be careful not to howl with the wolves, nor to suffer ourselves to be carried away with the dissipation and overflowing flood of iniquity which we see prevailing around us, but should rather imitate the example of David.
2. Every man speaketh deceit. David in this verse sets forth that part of unrighteousness which is contrary to truth. He says that there is no sincerity or uprightness in their speech, because the great object upon which they are bent is to deceive. He next describes the manner in which they deceive, namely, that every man endeavors to ensnare his neighbor by flattery. He also points out the fountain and first cause of this, They speak with a double heart. This doubleness of heart, as I may term it, makes men double and variable in their speech, in order thereby to disguise themselves in different ways, or to make themselves appear to others different from what they really are.

3-4
3. To his complaint in the preceding verse he now subjoins an imprecation, that God would cut off deceitful tongues.
4. Who have said, we will be strengthened by our tongues. Those must be possessed of great authority who think that, in the very falsehood to which they are addicted, they have enough of strength to accomplish their purposes, and to protect themselves.

5-6
5. Because of the spoiling of the needy. David now sets before himself as matter of consolation, the truth that God will not suffer the wicked thus to make havoc without end and measure. The more effectually to establish himself and others in the belief of this truth, he introduces God himself as speaking.
6. The words of Jehovah. The Psalmist now declares, that God is sure, faithful, and steadfast in his promises.

7-8
7. David, animated with holy confidence, boasts of the certain safety of all the godly, of whom God, who neither can deceive nor lie, avows himself to be the guardian.
8. The ungodly walk about on every side. They possess the whole land; as if the Psalmist had said, Wherever I turn my eyes, I see troops of them on every side. In the next clause he complains that mankind are shamefully and basely oppressed by their tyranny.

MATTHEW HENRY

Psalm 12

1-7 Complaints of the times.
I. Let us see here what it is that makes the times bad, and when they may be said to be so. Ask the children of this world what it is in their account that makes the times bad, and they will tell you, Scarcity of money, decay of trade, and the desolations of war, make the times bad. But the scripture lays the badness of the times upon causes of another nature. 2 Tim. iii. 1, Perilous times shall come, for iniquity shall abound; and that is the thing David here complains of.
1. When there is a general decay of piety and honesty among men the times are then truly bad (v. 1): When the godly man ceases and the faithful fail.
2. When dissimulation and flattery have corrupted and debauched all conversation, then the times are very bad (v. 2), when men are generally so profligate that they make no conscience of a lie.
3. When proud sinners have arrived at such a pitch of impiety as to say, "With our tongue will we prevail against the cause of virtue; our lips are our own and we may say what we will; who is lord over us, either to restrain us or to call us to an account?" v. 4.
4. When the poor and needy are oppressed, and abused, and puffed at, then the times are very bad. This is implied (v. 5) where God himself takes notice of the oppression of the poor.
5. When wickedness abounds, and goes barefaced, under the protection and countenance of those in authority, then the times are very bad, v. 8.
II. Let us now see what good thoughts we are here furnished with for such bad times; and what times we may yet be reserved for we cannot tell. When times are thus bad it is comfortable to think,
1. That we have a God to go to, from whom we may ask and expect the redress of all our grievances. This he begins with (v. 1): "Help, Lord, for the godly man ceaseth. All other helps and helpers fail; even the godly and faithful, who should lend a helping hand to support the dying cause of religion, are gone, and therefore whither shall we seek but to thee?"
2. That God will certainly reckon with false and proud men, and will punish and restrain their insolence. He will pluck out the tongue that speaks proud things against God and religion, v. 3.
3. That God will, in due time, work deliverance for his oppressed people, and shelter them from the malicious designs of their persecutors (v. 5).
4. That, though men are false, God is faithful; though they are not to be trusted, God is. They speak vanity and flattery, but the words of the Lord are pure words (v. 6).
5. That God will secure his chosen remnant to himself, how bad soever the times are (v. 7). In times of general apostasy the Lord knows those that are his, and they shall be enabled to keep their integrity.

Psalm 13

Title
To the chief Musician, a Psalm of David.

1 How long wilt thou forget me, O LORD? for ever? how long wilt thou hide thy face from me?
2 How long shall I take counsel in my soul, having sorrow in my heart daily? how long shall mine enemy be exalted over me?
3 Consider and hear me, O LORD my God: lighten mine eyes, lest I sleep the sleep of death;
4 Lest mine enemy say, I have prevailed against him; and those that trouble me rejoice when I am moved.
5 But I have trusted in thy mercy; my heart shall rejoice in thy salvation.
6 I will sing unto the LORD, because he hath dealt bountifully with me.

Psalm 13

OCCASION. The Psalm cannot be referred to any especial event or period in David's history. All attempts to find it a birthplace are but guesses. It was, doubtless, more than once the language of that much tried man of God, and is intended to express the feelings of the people of God in those ever-returning trials which beset them. We have been wont to call this the "How Long Psalm." We had almost said the Howling Psalm, from the incessant repetition of the cry "how long?"
DIVISION. This Psalm is very readily to be divided into three parts: the question of anxiety, 1, 2; the cry of prayer, 3, 4; the song of faith, 5, 6.

EXPOSITION
Verse 1. "How long?" This question is repeated no less than four times. It betokens very intense desire for deliverance, and great anguish of heart. And what if there be some impatience mingled therewith; is not this the more true a portrait of our own experience? It is not easy to prevent desire from degenerating into impatience. O for grace that, while we wait on God, we may be kept from indulging a murmuring spirit!
Verse 2. "How long shall I take counsel, in my soul, having sorrow in my heart daily?" There is in the original the idea of "laying up" counsels in his heart, as if his devices had become innumerable but unavailing. Herein we have often been like David, for we have considered and reconsidered day after day, but have not discovered the happy device by which to escape from our trouble. Such store is a sad sore. Ruminating upon trouble is bitter work.
Verse 3. But now prayer lifteth up her voice, like the watchman who proclaims the daybreak. Now will the tide turn, and the weeper shall dry his eyes. The mercy-seat is the life of hope and the death of despair. The gloomy thought of God's having forsaken him is still upon the psalmist's soul, and he therefore cries, "Consider and hear me." He remembers at once the root of his woe, and cries aloud that it may be removed. The final absence of God is Tophet's fire, and his temporary absence brings his people into the very suburbs of hell. God is here entreated to see and hear, that so he may be doubly moved to pity. What should we do if we had no God to turn to in the hour of wretchedness?
Verse 4. Another plea is urged in the fourth verse, and it is one which the tried believer may handle well when on his knees. We make use of our arch-enemy for once, and compel him, like Samson, to grind in our mill while we use his cruel arrogance as an argument in prayer. It is not the Lord's will that the great enemy of our souls should overcome his children. This would dishonor God, and cause the evil one to boast.
Verse 5. What a change is here! Lo, the rain is over and gone, and the time of the singing of birds is come. The mercy-seat has so refreshed the poor weeper, that he clears his throat for a song. If we have mourned with him, let us now dance with him. David's heart was more often out of tune than his harp, He begins many of his psalms sighing, and ends them singing; and others he begins in joy and ends in sorrow; "so that one would think," says Peter Moulin, "that those Psalms had been composed by two men of a contrary humor." It is worthy to be observed that the joy is all the greater because of the previous sorrow. "Sorrows remembered sweeten present joy."
Verse 6. The Psalm closes with a sentence which is a refutation of the charge of forgetfulness which David had uttered in the first verse, "He hath dealt bountifully with me." So shall it be with us if we wait awhile. The complaint which in our haste we utter shall be joyfully retracted, and we shall witness that the Lord hath dealt bountifully with us.

Psalm 13

The subject of this psalm is almost the same as that of the preceding. David, being afflicted, not only with the deepest distress, but also feeling himself, as it were, overwhelmed by a long succession of calamities and multiplied afflictions, implores the aid and succor of God, the only remedy which remained for him; and, in the close, taking courage, he entertains the assured hope of life from the promise of God, even amidst the terrors of death.

1-2

1. How long, O Jehovah. To acknowledge in the midst of our afflictions that God has really a care about us, is not the usual way with men, or what the feelings of nature would prompt; but by faith we apprehend his invisible providence. Thus, it seemed to David, so far as could be judged from beholding the actual state of his affairs, that he was forsaken of God. At the same time, however, the eyes of his mind, guided by the light of faith, penetrated even to the grace of God, although it was hidden in darkness.

3-4

3. Look upon me, answer me. As when God does not promptly afford assistance to his servants, it seems to the eye of sense that he does not behold their necessities, David, for this reason, asks God, in the first place, to look upon him, and, in the second place, to succor him. Neither of these things, it is true, is prior or posterior in respect of God; but it has been already stated in a preceding psalm, and we will have occasion afterwards frequently to repeat the statement, that the Holy Spirit purposely accommodates to our understanding the models of prayer recorded in Scripture. To enlighten the eyes signifies the same thing in the Hebrew language as to give the breath of life.

4. Lest my enemy. David again repeats what he had a little before said concerning the pride of his enemies, namely, how it would be a thing ill becoming the character of God were he to abandon his servant to the mockery of the ungodly. David's enemies lay, as it were, in ambush watching the hour of his ruin, that they might deride him when they saw him fall. And as it is the peculiar office of God to repress the audacity and insolence of the wicked, as often as they glory in their wickedness, David beseeches God to deprive them of the opportunity of indulging in such boasting.

5. The Psalmist does not as yet feel how much he has profited by praying; but depending upon the hope of deliverance, which the faithful promise of God enabled him to entertain, he makes use of this hope as a shield to repel those temptations with the terror of which he might be greatly distressed. He declares it to be his resolution to continue firm in his reliance upon the grace of God, and in the hope of salvation. With the very same confidence ought all the godly to be furnished and sustained, that they may duly persevere in prayer. Whence, also, we gather that it is by faith we apprehend the grace of God, which is hidden from and unknown to the understanding of the flesh.

Psalm 13

David's complaints and prayers turned into praises.

I. His troubles extort complaints (v. 1, 2); and the afflicted have liberty to pour out their complaint before the Lord, Ps. cii. title. It is some ease to a troubled spirit to give vent to its griefs, especially to give vent to them at the throne of grace, where we are sure to find one who is afflicted in the afflictions of his people and is troubled with the feeling of their infirmities; thither we have boldness of access by faith, and there we have parresia—freedom of speech.

II. His complaints stir up his prayers, v. 3, 4. We should never allow ourselves to make any complaints but what are fit to be offered up to God and what drive us to our knees. Observe here,

1. What his petitions are: Consider my case, hear my complaints, and enlighten my eyes, that is,

(1.) "Strengthen my faith;" for faith is the eye of the soul, with which it sees above, and sees through, the things of sense. "Lord, enable me to look beyond my present troubles and to foresee a happy issue of them."

(2.) "Guide my way; enable me to look about me, that I may avoid the snares which are laid for me."

2. What his pleas are. He mentions his relation to God and interest in him (O Lord my God!) and insists upon the greatness of the peril, which called for speedy relief and succor.

III. His prayers are soon turned into praises (v. 5, 6): But my heart shall rejoice and I will sing to the Lord. What a surprising change is here in a few lines! In the beginning of the psalm we have him drooping, trembling, and ready to sink into melancholy and despair; but, in the close of it, rejoicing in God, and elevated and enlarged in his praises. See the power of faith, the power of prayer, and how good it is to draw near to God. If we bring our cares and griefs to the throne of grace, and leave them there, we may go away like Hannah, and our countenance will be no more sad, 1 Sam. i. 18. And here observe the method of his comfort.

1. God's mercy is the support of his faith. "My case is bad enough, and I am ready to think it deplorable, till I consider the infinite goodness of God; but, finding I have that to trust to, I am comforted, though I have no merit of my own. In former distresses I have trusted in the mercy of God, and I never found that it failed me; his mercy has in due time relieved me and my confidence in it has in the mean time supported me.

2. His joy in God's salvation would fill his mouth with songs of praise (v. 6): "I will sing unto the Lord, sing in remembrance of what he has done formerly; though I should never recover the peace I have had, I will die blessing God that ever I had it. He has dealt bountifully with me formerly, and he shall have the glory of that, however he is pleased to deal with me now. I will sing in hope of what he will do for me at last, being confident that all will end well."

Psalm 14

Title
To the chief Musician, a Psalm of David.

1 The fool hath said in his heart, There is no God. They are corrupt, they have done abominable works, there is none that doeth good.
2 The LORD looked down from heaven upon the children of men, to see if there were any that did understand, and seek God.
3 They are all gone aside, they are all together become filthy: there is none that doeth good, no, not one.
4 Have all the workers of iniquity no knowledge? who eat up my people as they eat bread, and call not upon the LORD.
5 There were they in great fear: for God is in the generation of the righteous.
6 Ye have shamed the counsel of the poor, because the LORD is his refuge.
7 Oh that the salvation of Israel were come out of Zion! when the LORD bringeth back the captivity of his people, Jacob shall rejoice, and Israel shall be glad.

Psalm 14

TITLE. This admirable ode is simply headed, "To the Chief Musician, by David." The dedication to the Chief Musician stands at the head of fifty-three of the Psalms, and clearly indicates that such psalms were intended, not merely for the private use of believers, but to be sung in the great assemblies by the appointed choir at whose head was the overseer, or superintendent, called in our version, "the Chief Musician," and by Ainsworth, "the Master of the Music."

As no distinguishing title is given to this Psalm, we would suggest as an assistance to the memory, the heading—CONCERNING PRACTICAL ATHEISM.

DIVISION. The world's foolish creed (verse 1); its practical influence in corrupting morals, 1, 2, 3. The persecuting tendencies of sinners, 4; their alarms, 5; their ridicule of the godly, 6; and a prayer for the manifestation of the Lord to his people's joy.

EXPOSITION

Verse 1. "The fool." The Atheist is the fool pre-eminently, and a fool universally. He would not deny God if he were not a fool by nature, and having denied God it is no marvel that he becomes a fool in practice. Sin is always folly, and as it is the height of sin to attack the very existence of the Most High, so it is also the greatest imaginable folly. To say there is no God is to stifle consciousness, which is madness.

Verse 2. "The Lord looked down from heaven upon the children of men." As from a watchtower, or other elevated place of observation, the Lord is represented as gazing intently upon men. He will not punish blindly, nor like a tyrant command an indiscriminate massacre because a rumor of rebellion has come up to his ears. What condescending interest and impartial justice are here imaged!

Verse 3. "They are all gone aside." Without exception, all men have apostatized from the Lord their Maker, from his laws, and from all the eternal principles of right. Like stubborn heifers they have sturdily refused to receive the yoke, like errant sheep they have found a gap and left the right field.

Verse 4. Hatred of God and corruptness of life are the motive forces which produce persecution. Men who having no saving knowledge of divine things, enslave themselves to become workers of iniquity, have no heart to cry to the Lord for deliverance, but seek to amuse themselves with devouring the poor and despised people of God.

Verse 5. Oppressors have it not all their own way, they have their fits of trembling and their appointed seasons of overthrow. There—where they denied God and hectored against his people; there—where they thought of peace and safety, they were made to quail.

Verse 6. Notwithstanding their real cowardice, the wicked put on the lion's skin and lord it over the Lord's poor ones. Though fools themselves, they mock at the truly wise as if the folly were on their side; but this is what might be expected, for how should brutish minds appreciate excellence, and how can those who have owl's eyes admire the sun? The special point and butt of their jest seems to be the confidence of the godly in their Lord.

Verse 7. Natural enough is this closing prayer, for what would so effectually convince atheists, overthrow persecutors, stay sin, and secure the godly, as the manifest appearance of Israel's great Salvation? The coming of Messiah was the desire of the godly in all ages, and though he has already come with a sin-offering to purge away iniquity, we look for him to come a second time, to come without a sin-offering unto salvation.

JOHN CALVIN

Psalm 14

1. The fool hath said. As the Hebrew word, nabal, signifies not only a fool, but also a perverse, vile, and contemptible person, it would not have been unsuitable to have translated it so in this place; yet I am content to follow the more generally received interpretation, which is, that all profane persons, who have cast off all fear of God and abandoned themselves to iniquity, are convicted of madness. David does not bring against his enemies the charge of common foolishness, but rather inveighs against the folly of those whom the world accounts eminent for their wisdom. We commonly see that those who, in the estimation both of themselves and of others, highly excel in sagacity and wisdom, employ their cunning in laying snares, and exercise the ingenuity of their minds in despising and mocking God.

2-3
2. Jehovah looked down from heaven. God himself is here introduced as speaking on the subject of human depravity, and this renders the discourse of David more emphatic than if he had pronounced the sentence in his own person. When God is exhibited to us as sitting on his throne to take cognizance of the conduct of men, unless we are stupefied in an extraordinary degree, his majesty must strike us with terror.

To see if there were any that did understand As the whole economy of a good and righteous life depends upon our being governed and directed by the light of understanding, David has justly taught us in the beginning of the psalm, that folly is the root of all wickedness.
4. This question is added to give a more amplified illustration of the preceding doctrine. The prophet had said that God observed from heaven the doings of men, and had found all of them gone out of the way; and now he introduces him exclaiming with astonishment, What madness is this, that they who ought to cherish my people, and assiduously perform to them every kind office, are oppressing and falling upon them like wild beasts, without any feeling of humanity?

5-6
5. There did they tremble with fear. The prophet now encourages himself and all the faithful with the best of all consolations, namely, that God will not forsake his people even to the end, but will at length show himself to be their defender.
6. Ye deride the counsel of the poor. He inveighs against those giants who mock at the faithful for their simplicity, in calmly expecting, in their distresses, that God will show himself to be their deliverer.
7. David, after having laid down the doctrine of consolation, again returns to prayers and groanings. By this he teaches us, that although God may leave us for a long time to languish, yet we ought not to weary, or lose courage, but should always glory in him; and, again, that while our troubles continue, the most effectual solace we can have is often to return to the exercise of prayer.

MATTHEW HENRY

Psalm 14

1-3 Human depravity.
If we apply our hearts as Solomon did (Eccl. vii. 25) to search out the wickedness of folly, even of foolishness and madness, these verses will assist us in the search and will show us that sin is exceedingly sinful. Sin is the disease of mankind, and it appears here to be malignant and epidemic.
1. See how malignant it is (v. 1) in two things:
(1.) The contempt it puts upon the honor of God: for there is something of practical atheism at the bottom of all sin. The fool hath said in his heart, There is no God. We are sometimes tempted to think, "Surely there never was so much atheism and profaneness as there is in our days;" but we see the former days were no better; even in David's time there were those who had arrived at such a height of impiety as to deny the very being of a God and the first and self-evident principles of religion.
(2.) The disgrace and debasement it puts upon the nature of man. Sinners are corrupt, quite degenerated from what man was in his innocent estate: They have become filthy (v. 3), putrid. All their faculties are so disordered that they have become odious to their Maker and utterly incapable of answering the ends of their creation. They are corrupt indeed; for, They do no good, but are the unprofitable burdens of the earth; they do God no service, bring him no honor, nor do themselves any real kindness. They do a great deal of hurt. They have done abominable works, for such all sinful works are.
2. See how epidemic this disease is; it has infected the whole race of mankind. To prove this, God himself is here brought in for a witness, and he is an eye-witness, v. 2, 3.

4-7
In these verses the psalmist endeavors,
I. To convince sinners of the evil and danger of the way they are in, how secure soever they are in that way. Three things he shows them, which, it may be, they are not very willing to see their wickedness, their folly, and their danger, while they are apt to believe themselves very wise, and good, and safe.
II. He endeavors to comfort the people of God,
1. With what they have. They have God's presence (v. 5): He is in the generation of the righteous. They have his protection (v. 6): The Lord is their refuge. This is as much their security as it is the terror of their enemies, who may jeer them for their confidence in God, but cannot jeer them out of it. In the judgment-day it will add to the terror and confusion of sinners to see God own the generation of the righteous, which they have hated and bantered.
2. With what they hope for; and that is the salvation of Israel, v. 7. When David was driven out by Absalom he comforted himself with an assurance that God would in due time turn again his captivity.

Psalm 15

Title
A Psalm of David.

1 Lord, who shall abide in thy tabernacle? who shall dwell in thy holy hill?
2 He that walketh uprightly, and worketh righteousness, and speaketh the truth in his heart.
3 He that backbiteth not with his tongue, nor doeth evil to his neighbor, nor taketh up a reproach against his neighbor.
4 In whose eyes a vile person is contemned; but he honoreth them that fear the LORD. He that sweareth to his own hurt, and changeth not.
5 He that putteth not out his money to usury, nor taketh reward against the innocent. He that doeth these things shall never be moved.

Psalm 15

SUBJECT, &c. This Psalm of David bears no dedicatory title at all indicative of the occasion upon which it was written, but it is exceedingly probable that, together with the twenty-fourth Psalm, to which it bears a striking resemblance, its composition was in some way connected with the removal of the ark to the holy hill of Zion.
DIVISION. The first verse asks the question; the rest of the verses answer it. We will call the Psalm THE QUESTION AND ANSWER.

EXPOSITION
Verse 1. THE QUESTION. Jehovah. Thou high and holy One, who shall be permitted to have fellowship with thee? The heavens are not pure in thy sight, and thou chargest thine angels with folly, who then of mortal mould shall dwell with thee, thou dread consuming fire? A sense of the glory of the Lord and of the holiness which becomes his house, his service, and his attendants, excites the humble mind to ask the solemn question before us. Where angels bow with veiled faces, how shall man be able to worship at all? The unthinking many imagine it to be a very easy matter to approach the Most High, and when professedly engaged in his worship they have no questionings of heart as to their fitness for it; but truly humbled souls often shrink under a sense of utter unworthiness, and would not dare to approach the throne of the God of holiness if it were not for him, our Lord, our Advocate, who can abide in the heavenly temple, because his righteousness endureth for ever.
Verse 2. THE ANSWER. The Lord in answer to the question informs us by his Holy Spirit of the character of the man who alone can dwell in his holy hill. In perfection this holiness is found only in the Man of Sorrows, but in a measure it is wrought in all his people by the Holy Ghost. Faith and the graces of the Spirit are not mentioned, because this is a description of outward character, and where fruits are found the root may not be seen, but it is surely there.
Verse 3. After the positive comes the negative. "He that backbiteth not with his tongue." There is a sinful way of backbiting with the heart when we think too hardly of a neighbor, but it is the tongue which does the mischief. Some men's tongues bite more than their teeth. The tongue is not steel, but it cuts, and it's wounds are very hard to heal; its worst wounds are not with its edge to our face, but with its back when our head is turned.
Verse 4. "In whose eyes a vile person is contemned; but he honoureth them that fear the Lord." We must be as honest in paying respect as in paying our bills. Honor to whom honor is due. To all good men we owe a debt of honor, and we have no right to hand over what is their due to vile persons who happen to be in high places. When base men are in office, it is our duty to respect the office; but we cannot so violate our consciences as to do otherwise than contemn the men; and on the other hand, when true saints are in poverty and distress, we must sympathize with their afflictions and honor the men none the less.
Verse 5. "He that putteth not out his money to usury." Usury was and is hateful both to God and man. That a lender should share with the borrower in gains made by his money is most fitting; but that the man of property should eat up the poor wretch who unfortunately obtained a loan of him is abominable. Those who grind poor tradesmen, and such like, by charging them interest at intolerable rates, will find that their gold, and their silver are cankered. The man who shall ascend into the hill of the Lord must shake off this sin as Paul shook the viper into the fire. "Nor taketh reward against the innocent." Bribery is a sin both in the giver and the receiver.

Psalm 15

This psalm teaches us upon what condition God made choice of the Jews to be his people, and placed his sanctuary in the midst of them. This condition was, that they should show themselves to be a peculiar and holy people, by leading a just and upright life.

1-2

1. O Jehovah, who shall dwell in thy tabernacle? As nothing is more common in the world than falsely to assume the name of God, or to pretend to be his people, and as a great part of men allow themselves to do this without any apprehension of the danger it involves, David, without stopping to speak to men, addresses himself to God, which he considers the better course; and he intimates, that if men assume the title of the people of God, without being so in deed and in truth, they gain nothing by their self-delusion, for God continues always like himself, and as he is faithful himself, so will he have us to keep faith with him in return.

The sum is, that hypocrites, who occupy a place in the temple of God, in vain pretend to be his people, for he acknowledges none as such but those who follow after justice and uprightness during the whole course of their life. David saw the temple crowded with a great multitude of men who all made a profession of the same religion, and presented themselves before God as to the outward ceremony; and, therefore, assuming the person of one wondering at the spectacle, he directs his discourse to God, who, in such a confusion and medley of characters, could easily distinguish his own people from strangers.

2. He that walketh in integrity. Here we should mark, that in the words there is an implied contrast between the vain boasting of those who are only the people of God in name, or who make only a bare profession of being so, which consists in outward observances, and this indubitable and genuine evidence of true godliness which David commends.

3. David, after having briefly set forth the virtues with which all who desire to have a place in the Church ought to be endued, now enumerates certain vices from which they ought to be free.

4. The man who sees the wicked honored, and by the applause of the world rendered more obstinate in their wickedness, and who willingly gives his consent or approbation to this, does he not, by so doing, exalt vice to authority, and invest it with sovereign power?

5. In this verse David enjoins the godly neither to oppress their neighbors by usury, nor to suffer themselves to be corrupted with bribes to favor unrighteous causes.

He who doeth these things. This conclusion warns us again, that all who thrust themselves into the sanctuary of God are not permanent citizens of "the holy Jerusalem which is above;" but that hypocrites, and all who falsely assume the title of saints, shall at length be "cast out" with Ishmael whom they resemble.

Psalm 15

The citizen of Zion.

Here is,

I. A very serious and weighty question concerning the characters of a citizen of Zion (v. 1): "Lord, who shall abide in thy tabernacle? Let me know who shall go to heaven." Not, who by name (in this way the Lord only knows those that are his), but who by description: "What kind of people are those whom thou wilt own and crown with distinguishing and everlasting favors?" This supposes that it is a great privilege to be a citizen of Zion, an unspeakable honor and advantage.

II. A very plain and particular answer to this question. Those that desire to know their duty, with a resolution to do it, will find the scripture a very faithful director and conscience a faithful monitor. Let us see then the particular characters of a citizen of Zion.

1. He is one that is sincere and entire in his religion: He walketh uprightly, according to the condition of the covenant (Gen. xvii. 1), "Walk before me, and be thou perfect" (it is the same word that is here used) "and then thou shalt find me a God all-sufficient."

2. He is one that contrives to do all the good he can to his neighbors, but is very careful to do hurt to no man, and is, in a particular manner, tender of his neighbor's reputation, v. 3. He does no evil at all to his neighbor willingly or designedly, nothing to offend or grieve his spirit, nothing to prejudice the health or ease of his body, nothing to injure him in his estate or secular interests, in his family or relations; but walks by that golden rule of equity, To do as he would be done by.

3. He is one that values men by their virtue and piety, and not by the figure they make in the world, v. 5.

4. He is one that always prefers a good conscience before any secular interest or advantage whatsoever; for, if he has promised upon oath to do any thing, though afterwards it appear much to his damage and prejudice in his worldly estate, yet he adheres to it and changes not, v. 4.

5. He is one that will not increase his estate by any unjust practices, v. 5.

(1.) Not by extortion: He putteth not out his money to usury, that he may live at ease upon the labors of others.

(2.) Not by bribery: He will not take a reward against the innocent; if he be any way employed in the administration of public justice, he will not, for any gain, or hope of it, to himself, do any thing to the prejudice of a righteous cause.

III. The psalm concludes with a ratification of this character of the citizen of Zion. He is like Zion-hill itself, which cannot be moved, Ps. cxxv. 1. Every true living member of the church is built upon a rock, which the gates of hell cannot prevail against.

KING JAMES VERSION

Psalm 16

Title
Michtam of David.

1-5
1 Preserve me, O God: for in thee do I put my trust.
2 O my soul, thou hast said unto the LORD, Thou art my Lord: my goodness extendeth not to thee;
3 But to the saints that are in the earth, and to the excellent, in whom is all my delight.
4 Their sorrows shall be multiplied that hasten after another god: their drink offerings of blood will I not offer, nor take up their names into my lips.
5 The LORD is the portion of mine inheritance and of my cup: thou maintainest my lot.

CHARLES H. SPURGEON

Psalm 16

TITLE. MICHTAM OF DAVID. This is usually understood to mean THE GOLDEN PSALM, and such a title is most appropriate, for the matter is as the most fine gold. Ainsworth calls it "David's jewel, or notable song." Dr. Alexander thinks that the word is most probably a simple derivative of a word signifying to hide, and signifies a secret or mystery, and indicates the depth of doctrinal and spiritual import in these sacred compositions. If this be the true interpretation the psalm can be entitled: THE PSALM OF THE PRECIOUS SECRET.
SUBJECT. We are not left to human interpreters for the key to this golden mystery, for, speaking by the Holy Ghost, Peter tells us, "David speaketh concerning HIM." (Acts 2:25.)
DIVISION. The whole is so compact that it is difficult to draw sharp lines of division. It may suffice to note our Lord's prayer of faith, verse 1, avowal of faith in Jehovah alone, 2, 3, 4, 5, the contentment of his faith in the present, 6, 7, and the joyous confidence of his faith for the future (8, 11).

EXPOSITION
Verse 1. "Preserve me," keep, or save me, or as Horsley thinks, "guard me," even as bodyguards surround their monarch, or as shepherds protect their flocks. Tempted in all points like as we are, the manhood of Jesus needed to be preserved from the power of evil; and though in itself pure, the Lord Jesus did not confide in that purity of nature, but as an example to his followers, looked to the Lord, his God, for preservation. One of the great names of God is "the Preserver of men," (Job 7:20,) and this gracious office the Father exercised towards our Mediator and Representative.
Verse 2. "O my soul, thou hast said unto the Lord, Thou art my Lord." In his inmost heart the Lord Jesus bowed himself to do service to his Heavenly Father, and before the throne of Jehovah his soul vowed allegiance to the Lord for our sakes. We are like him when our soul, truly and constantly in the presence of the heart-searching God, declares her full consent to the rule and government of the Infinite Jehovah, saying, "Thou art my Lord." To avow this with the lip is little, but for the soul to say it, especially in times of trial, is a gracious evidence of spiritual health. This sentence may also be viewed as the utterance of appropriating faith, laying hold upon the Lord by personal covenant and enjoyment; in this sense may it be our daily song in the house of our pilgrimage.
Verse 3. "But to the saints that are in the earth." These sanctified ones, although still upon the earth, partake of the results of Jesus' mediatorial work, and by his goodness are made what they are. The peculiar people, zealous for good works, and hallowed to sacred service, are arrayed in the Savior's righteousness and washed in his blood, and so receive of the goodness treasured up in him; these are the persons who are profited by the work of the man Christ Jesus; but that work added nothing to the nature, virtue, or happiness of God, who is blessed for evermore.
Verse 4. The same loving heart which opens towards the chosen people is fast closed against those who continue in their rebellion against God. Jesus hates all wickedness, and especially the high crime of idolatry. The text while it shows our Lord's abhorrence of sin, shows also the sinner's greediness after it. Professed believers are often slow towards the true Lord, but sinners "hasten after another god." They run like madmen where we creep like snails. Let their zeal rebuke our tardiness. Yet theirs is a case in which the more they haste the worse they speed, for their sorrows are multiplied by their diligence in multiplying their sins.
Verse 5. "The Lord is the portion of mine inheritance and of my cup." With what confidence and bounding joy does Jesus turn to Jehovah, whom his soul possessed and delighted in! Content beyond measure with his portion in the Lord his God, he had not a single desire with which to hunt after other

Psalm 16

In the beginning David commends himself to the protection of God. He then meditates upon the benefits which he received from God, and thereby stirs himself up to thanksgiving. By his service, it is true, he could in no respect be profitable to God, but he, notwithstanding, surrenders and devotes himself entirely to him, protesting that he will have nothing to do with superstitions. He also states the reason of this to be, that full and substantial happiness consists in resting in God alone, who never suffers his own people to want any good thing.

1. This is a prayer in which David commits himself to the protection of God. He does not, however, here implore the aid of God, in some particular emergency, as he often does in other psalms, but he beseeches him to show himself his protector during the whole course of his life, and indeed our safety both in life and in death depends entirely upon our being under the protection of God. What follows concerning trust, signifies much the same thing as if the Holy Spirit assured us by the mouth of David, that God is ready to succor all of us, provided we rely upon him with a sure and steadfast faith; and that he takes under his protection none but those who commit themselves to him with their whole heart. At the same time, we must be reminded that David, supported by this trust, continued firm and unmoved amidst all the storms of adversity with which he was buffeted.

2-3
2. Thou shalt say unto Jehovah. David begins by stating that he can bestow nothing upon God, not only because God stands in no need of any thing, but also because mortal man cannot merit the favor of God by any service which he can perform to him. At the same time, however, he takes courage, and, as God accepts our devotion, and the service which we yield to him, David protests that he will be one of his servants.
3. Unto the saints who are on the earth. Almost all are agreed in understanding this place, as if David, after the sentence which we have just now been considering, had added, The only way of serving God aright is to endeavor to do good to his holy servants. And the truth is, that God, as our good deeds cannot extend to him, substitutes the saints in his place, towards whom we are to exercise our charity. When men, therefore, mutually exert themselves in doing good to one another, this is to yield to God right and acceptable service. We ought, doubtless, to extend our charity even to those who are unworthy of it, as our heavenly Father "maketh his sun to rise on the evil and on the good," (Matthew 5:45;) but David justly prefers the saints to others, and places them in a higher rank.
4. The Psalmist now describes the true way of maintaining brotherly concord with the saints, by declaring that he will have nothing to do with unbelievers and the superstitious. We cannot be united into the one body of the Church under God, if we do not break off all the bonds of impiety, separate

Psalm 16

1-7 Believing confidence; consecration to God.
This psalm is entitled Michtam, which some translate a golden psalm, a very precious one, more to be valued by us than gold, yea, than much fine gold, because it speaks so plainly of Christ and his resurrection, who is the true treasure hidden in the field of the Old Testament.
I. David here flies to God's protection with a cheerful believing confidence in it (v. 1): "Preserve me, O God! from the deaths, and especially from the sins, to which I am continually exposed; for in thee, and in thee only, do I put my trust." Those that by faith commit themselves to the divine care, and submit themselves to the divine guidance, have reason to hope for the benefit of both. This is applicable to Christ, who prayed, Father, save me from this hour, and trusted in God that he would deliver him.
II. He recognizes his solemn dedication of himself to God as his God (v. 2): "O my soul! thou hast said unto the Lord, Thou art my Lord, and therefore thou mayest venture to trust him." It is the duty and interest of every one of us to acknowledge the Lord for our Lord, to subject ourselves to him, and then to stay ourselves upon him. Adonai signifies My stayer, the strength of my heart
III. He devotes himself to the honor of God in the service of the saints (v. 2, 3): My goodness extends not to thee, but to the saints. Observe,
1. Those that have taken the lord for their Lord must, like him, be good and do good; we do not expect happiness without goodness.
2. Whatever good there is in us, or is done by us, we must humbly acknowledge that it extends not to God; so that we cannot pretend to merit any thing by it.
IV. He disclaims the worship of all false gods and all communion with their worshippers, v. 4. Here he reads the doom of idolaters, who hasten after another God, being mad upon their idols, and pursuing them as eagerly as if they were afraid they would escape from them: Their sorrows shall be multiplied, both by the judgments they bring upon themselves from the true God whom they forsake and by the disappointment they will meet with in the false gods they embrace.
V. He repeats the solemn choice he had made of God for his portion and happiness (v. 5), takes to himself the comfort of the choice (v. 6), and gives God the glory of it, v. 7. This is very much the language of a devout and pious soul in its gracious exercises.
1. Choosing the Lord for its portion and happiness. "Most men take the world for their chief good, and place their felicity in the enjoyments of it; but this I say, The Lord is the portion of my inheritance and of my cup, the portion I make choice of, and will gladly take up with, how poor soever my condition is in this world. Let me have the love and favor of God, and be accepted of him; let me have the comfort of

Psalm 16

6-11

6 The lines are fallen unto me in pleasant places; yea, I have a goodly heritage.

7 I will bless the LORD, who hath given me counsel: my reins also instruct me in the night seasons.

8 I have set the LORD always before me: because he is at my right hand, I shall not be moved.

9 Therefore my heart is glad, and my glory rejoiceth: my flesh also shall rest in hope.

10 For thou wilt not leave my soul in hell; neither wilt thou suffer thine Holy One to see corruption.

11 Thou wilt shew me the path of life: in thy presence is fullness of joy; at thy right hand there are pleasures for evermore.

gods; his cup was full, and his heart was full too; even in his sorest sorrows he still laid hold with both his hands upon his Father, crying, "My God, my God;" he had not so much as a thought of falling down to worship the prince of this world, although tempted with an "all these will I give thee."

Verse 6. Jesus found the way of obedience to lead into "pleasant places." Notwithstanding all the sorrows which marred his countenance, he exclaimed, "Lo, I come; in the volume of the book it is written of me, I delight to do thy will, O my God: yea, thy law is within my heart." It may seem strange, but while no other man was ever so thoroughly acquainted with grief, it is our belief that no other man ever experienced so much joy and delight in service, for no other served so faithfully and with such great results in view as his recompense of reward. The joy which was set before him must have sent some of its beams of splendor a-down the rugged places where he endured the cross, despising the shame, and must have made them in some respects pleasant places to the generous heart of the Redeemer.

Verse 7. "I will bless the Lord, who hath given me counsel." Praise as well as prayer was presented to the Father by our Lord Jesus, and we are not truly his followers unless our resolve be, "I will bless the Lord." Jesus is called Wonderful, Counselor, but as man he spake not of himself, but as his Father had taught him. Read in confirmation of this, John 7:16; 8:28; and 12:49, 50; and the prophecy concerning him in Isaiah 11:2, 3. It was our Redeemer's wont to repair to his Father for direction, and having received it, he blessed him for giving him counsel.

Verse 8. The fear of death at one time cast its dark shadow over the soul of the Redeemer, and we read that, "he was heard in that he feared." There appeared unto him an angel, strengthening him; perhaps the heavenly messenger reassured him of his glorious resurrection as his people's surety, and of the eternal joy into which he should admit the flock redeemed by blood. Then hope shone full upon our Lord's soul, and, as recorded in these verses, he surveyed the future with holy confidence because he had a continued eye to Jehovah, and enjoyed his perpetual presence.

Verse 9. He clearly foresaw that he must die, for he speaks of his flesh resting, and of his soul in the abode of separate spirits; death was full before his face, or he would not have mentioned corruption; but such was his devout reliance upon his God, that he sang over the tomb, and rejoiced in vision of the sepulcher.

Verse 10. Our Lord Jesus was not disappointed in his hope. He declared his Father's faithfulness in the words, "thou wilt not leave my soul in hell," and that faithfulness was proven on the resurrection morning. Among the departed and disembodied Jesus was not left; he had believed in the resurrection, and he received it on the third day, when his body rose in glorious life, according as he had said in joyous confidence, "neither wilt thou suffer thine Holy One to see corruption."

Verse 11. "Thou wilt shew me the path of life." To Jesus first this way was shown, for he is the first begotten from the dead, the first-born of every creature. He himself opened up the way through his own flesh, and then trod it as the forerunner of his own redeemed. The thought of being made the path of life to his people, gladdened the soul of Jesus. "In thy presence is fullness of joy." Christ being raised from the dead ascended into glory, to dwell in constant nearness to God, where joy is at its full for ever: the foresight of this urged him onward in his glorious but grievous toil.

ourselves from idolaters, and keep ourselves pure and at a distance from all the pollutions which corrupt and vitiate the holy service of God.

5-6
5. The Lord is the portion of mine inheritance. Here the Psalmist explains why he separates himself from idolaters, and resolves to continue in the church of God, why he shuns, with abhorrence, all participation in their errors, and cleaves to the pure worship of God; namely, because he rests in the only true God as his portion.
6. The lines have fallen to me. The Psalmist confirms more fully what he had already said in the preceding verse with respect to his resting, with a composed and tranquil mind, in God alone; or rather, he so glories in God as nobly to despise all that the world imagines to be excellent and desirable without him. By magnifying God in such honorable and exalted strains, he gives us to understand that he does not desire any thing more as his portion and felicity.
7. Last of all, David confesses that it was entirely owing to the pure grace of God that he had come to possess so great a good, and that he had been made a partaker of it by faith. It would be of no advantage to us for God to offer himself freely and graciously to us, if we did not receive him by faith, seeing he invites to himself both the reprobate and the elect in common; but the former, by their ingratitude, defraud themselves of this inestimable blessing.

8-9
8. I have set Jehovah, etc. The Psalmist again shows the firmness and stability of his faith. To set God before us is nothing else than to keep all our senses bound and captive, that they may not run out and go astray after any other object.
9. Therefore my heart is glad. In this verse the Psalmist commends the inestimable fruit of faith, of which Scripture every where makes mention, in that, by placing us under the protection of God, it makes us not only to live in the enjoyment of mental tranquility, but, what is more, to live joyful and cheerful.
10. The Psalmist goes on to explain still more fully the preceding doctrine, by declaring that as he is not afraid of death, there is nothing wanting which is requisite to the completion of his joy.
11. David next adds, that when God is reconciled to us, we have all things which are necessary to perfect happiness. The phrase, the countenance of God, may be understood either of our being beheld by him, or of our beholding him; but I consider both these ideas as included, for his fatherly favor, which he displays in looking upon us with a serene countenance, precedes this joy, and is the first cause of it, and yet this does not cheer us until, on our part, we behold it shining upon us. David testifies that true and solid joy in which the minds of men may rest will never be found any where else but in God; and that, therefore, none but the faithful, who are contented with his grace alone, can be truly and perfectly happy.

communion with God, and satisfaction in the communications of his graces and comforts; let me have an interest in his promises, and a title by promise to everlasting life and happiness in the future state; and I have enough, I need no more, I desire no more, to complete my felicity."
2. Rejoicing in this portion, and taking a complacency in it (v. 6): The lines have fallen to me in pleasant places. Those have reason to say so that have God for their portion; they have a worthy portion, a goodly heritage. What can they have better? What can they desire more? Return unto thy rest, O my soul! and look no further.
3. Giving thanks to God for it, and for grace to make this wise and happy choice (v. 7): "I will bless the Lord who has given me counsel, this counsel, to take him for my portion and happiness." So ignorant and foolish are we that, if we be left to ourselves, our hearts will follow our eyes, and we shall choose our own delusions, and forsake our own mercies for lying vanities; and therefore, if we have indeed taken God for our portion and preferred spiritual and eternal blessings before those that are sensible and temporal, we must thankfully acknowledge the power and goodness of divine grace directing and enabling us to make that choice.

8-11 Prophecy relating to the Messiah; sufferings and consequent glory of Christ.
All these verses are quoted by St. Peter in his first sermon, after the pouring out of the Spirit on the day of Pentecost (Acts ii. 25-28); and he tells us expressly that David in them speaks concerning Christ and particularly of his resurrection. Something we may allow here of the workings of David's own pious and devout affections towards God, depending upon his grace to perfect every thing that concerned him, and looking for the blessed hope, and happy state on the other side death, in the enjoyment of God; but in these holy elevations towards God and heaven he was carried by the spirit of prophecy quite beyond the consideration of himself and his own case, to foretell the glory of the Messiah, in such expressions as were peculiar to that, and could not be understood of himself. The New Testament furnishes us with a key to let us into the mystery of these lines.

These verses must certainly be applied to Christ; of him speaks the prophet this, as did many of the Old-Testament prophets, who testified beforehand the sufferings of Christ and the glory that should follow (1 Pet. i. 11), and that is the subject of this prophecy here. It is foretold that Christ should suffer, and rise from the dead, 1 Cor. xv. 3, 4.

That he should suffer and die. This is implied here when he says (v. 8), I shall not be moved; he supposed that he should be struck at, and have a dreadful shock given him, as he had in his agony, when his soul was exceedingly sorrowful, and he prayed that the cup might pass from him.

Psalm 17

Title
A prayer of David.
1-7

1 Hear the right, O LORD, attend unto my cry, give ear unto my prayer, that goeth not out of feigned lips.
2 Let my sentence come forth from thy presence; let thine eyes behold the things that are equal.
3 Thou hast proved mine heart; thou hast visited me in the night; thou hast tried me, and shalt find nothing; I am purposed that my mouth shall not transgress.
4 Concerning the works of men, by the word of thy lips I have kept me from the paths of the destroyer.
5 Hold up my goings in thy paths, that my footsteps slip not.
6 I have called upon thee, for thou wilt hear me, O God: incline thine ear unto me, and hear my speech.
7 Shew thy marvelous loving kindness, O thou that savest by thy right hand them which put their trust in thee from those that rise up against them.

Psalm 17

TITLE and SUBJECT. A prayer of David. David would not have been a man after God's own heart, if he had not been a man of prayer. He was a master in the sacred art of supplication. He flies to prayer in all times of need, as a pilot speeds to the harbor in the stress of tempest. So frequent were David's prayers that they could not be all dated and entitled; and hence this simply bears the author's name, and nothing more. The smell of the furnace is upon the present psalm, but there is evidence in the last verse that he who wrote it came unharmed out of the flame. We have in the present plaintive song, AN APPEAL TO HEAVEN from the persecutions of earth. A spiritual eye may see Jesus here.
DIVISIONS. There are no very clear lines of demarcation between the parts; but we prefer the division adopted by that precious old commentator, David Dickson. In verses 1-4, David craves justice in the controversy between him and his oppressors. In verses 5 and 6, he requests of the Lord grace to act rightly while under the trial. From verse 7-12, he seeks protection from his foes, whom he graphically describes; and in verses 13 and 14, pleads that they may be disappointed; closing the whole in the most comfortable confidence that all would certainly be well with himself at the last.

EXPOSITION
Verse 1. "Hear the right, O Lord." He that has the worst cause makes the most noise; hence the oppressed soul is apprehensive that its voice may be drowned, and therefore pleads in this one verse for a hearing no less than three times. The troubled heart craves for the ear of the great Judge, persuaded that with him to hear is to redress. If our God could not or would not hear us, our state would be deplorable indeed; and yet some professors set such small store by the mercy-seat, that God does not hear them for the simple reason that they neglect to plead. As well have no house if we persist like gypsies in living in the lanes and commons; as well have no mercy-seat as be always defending our own cause and never going to God. There is more fear that we will not hear the Lord than that the Lord will not hear us.
Verse 2. "Let my sentence come forth from thy presence." The psalmist has now grown bold by the strengthening influence of prayer, and he now entreats the Judge of all the earth to give sentence upon his case. He has been libeled, basely and maliciously libeled; and having brought his action before the highest court, he, like an innocent man, has no desire to escape the enquiry, but even invites and sues for judgment.
Verse 3, "Thou hast proved mine heart." Like Peter, David uses the argument, "Thou knowest all things, thou knowest that I love thee." It is a most assuring thing to be able to appeal at once to the Lord, and call upon our Judge to be a witness for our defense. "Beloved, if our heart condemn us not, then have we confidence toward God." "Thou hast visited me in the night." As if he had said, "Lord, thou hast entered my house at all hours; and thou hast seen me when no one else was nigh; thou hast come upon me unawares and marked my unrestrained actions, and thou knowest whether or no I am guilty of the crimes laid at my door."
Verse 4. "Concerning the works of men." While we are in the midst of men we shall have their works thrust under our notice, and we shall be compelled to keep a corner of our diary headed "concerning the works of men." To be quite clear from the dead works of carnal humanity is the devout desire of souls who are quickened by the Holy Spirit.
Verse 5. Under trial it is not easy to behave ourselves aright; a candle is not easily kept alight when many envious mouths are puffing at it. In evil times prayer is peculiarly needful, and wise men resort to it at once. Plato said to one of his disciples, "When men speak ill of thee, live so that no one will

JOHN CALVIN

Psalm 17

This psalm contains a mournful complaint against the cruel pride of David's enemies. He protests that he did not deserve to be persecuted with such inhumanity, inasmuch as he had given them no cause for exercising their cruelty against him. At the same time, he beseeches God, as his protector, to put forth his power for his deliverance. The inscription of the psalm does not refer to any particular time, but it is probable that David here complains of Saul and his associates.

1-2
1. Hear my righteousness, O Jehovah. The Psalmist begins the psalm by setting forth the goodness of his cause. He does this because God has promised that he will not suffer the innocent to be oppressed, but will always, at length, succor them.
2. From the presence of thy countenance. Literally it is, from before thy face, or, before thy face. By these words David intimates that if God does not rise up as the vindicator of his cause, he will be overwhelmed with calumnies though innocent, and will be looked upon as a guilty and condemned person. The cognizance which God will take of his cause is tacitly set in opposition to the dark inventions of falsehood which were spread against him.

3-4
3. Thou hast proved my heart. What David intended to express is certainly very evident. As he was unjustly and falsely charged with crime, and could obtain neither justice nor humanity at the hands of men, he appeals to God, requesting he would become judge in the matter. But not to do this rashly, he subjects himself to an impartial examination, seeing God, whose prerogative it is to search the secret recesses of the heart, cannot be deceived by the external appearance.
4. If we would have a good rule for governing ourselves, when our enemies, by their mischievous actions, provoke us to treat them in a similar manner, let us learn, after the example of David, to meditate upon the word of God, and to keep our eyes fixed upon it. By this means our minds will be preserved from ever being blinded, and we shall always avoid the paths of wickedness, seeing God will not only keep our affections under restraint by his commandments, but will also train them to patience by his promises.

5-6
5. Uphold my steps. If we take God's paths for the precepts of his law, the sense will be evident, namely, that although David had spoken according to truth, in boasting of having, in the midst of the most grievous temptations which assailed him, constantly practiced righteousness with a pure heart, yet, conscious of his own weakness, he commits himself to God to be governed by him, and prays for grace to enable him to persevere.
6. I have called upon thee, etc. This verb being put in the past tense denotes a continued act; and, therefore, it includes the

MATTHEW HENRY

Psalm 17

1-7 Sincere and importunate prayer.
This psalm is a prayer. Our believing dependence upon God is a good plea to enforce our desires towards him. Let us now see,
I. What his appeal is; and here observe,
1. What the court is to the cognizance and determination of which he makes his appeal; it is the court of heaven. "Lord, do thou hear the right, for Saul is so passionate, so prejudiced, that he will not hear it. Lord, let my sentence come forth from thy presence, v. 2. Men sentence me to be pursued and cut off as an evil-doer. Lord, I appeal from them to thee." This he did in a public remonstrance before Saul's face (1 Sam. xxiv. 12, The Lord judge between me and thee), and he repeats it here in his private devotions.
2. What the evidence is by which he hopes to make good his appeal; it is the trial God had made of him (v. 3): Thou hast proved my heart. God's sentence is therefore right, because he always proceeds upon his knowledge, which is more certain and infallible than that which men attain to by the closest views and the strictest investigations.
II. What his petition is; it is, in short, this, That he might experience the good work of God in him, as an evidence of and qualification for the good will of God towards him: this is grace and peace from God the Father.

8-15 Prayer for protecting mercy; character of David's enemies.
We may observe, in these verses,
I. What David prays for. Being compassed about with enemies that sought his life, he prays to God to preserve him safely through all their attempts against him, to the crown to which he was anointed. This prayer is both a prediction of the preservation of Christ through all the hardships and difficulties of his humiliation, to the glories and joys of his exalted state, and a pattern to Christians to commit the keeping of their souls to God, trusting him to preserve them to his heavenly kingdom. He prays,
1. That he himself might be protected (v. 8): "Keep me safe, hide me close, where I may not be found, where I may not be come at. Deliver my soul, not only my mortal life from death, but my immortal spirit from sin." Those who put themselves under God's protection may in faith implore the benefit of it.
2. That all the designs of his enemies to bring him either into sin or into trouble might be defeated (v. 13): "Arise, O Lord! appear for me, disappoint him, and cast him down in his own eyes by the disappointment." While Saul persecuted David, how often did he miss his prey, when he thought he had him sure! And how were Christ's enemies disappointed by his resurrection, who thought they had gained their point when they had put him to death!

Psalm 17

8-15
8 Keep me as the apple of the eye, hide me under the shadow of thy wings,
9 From the wicked that oppress me, from my deadly enemies, who compass me about.
10 They are enclosed in their own fat: with their mouth they speak proudly.
11 They have now compassed us in our steps: they have set their eyes bowing down to the earth;
12 Like as a lion that is greedy of his prey, and as it were a young lion lurking in secret places.
13 Arise, O LORD, disappoint him, cast him down: deliver my soul from the wicked, which is thy sword:
14 From men which are thy hand, O LORD, from men of the world, which have their portion in this life, and whose belly thou fillest with thy hid treasure: they are full of children, and leave the rest of their substance to their babes.
15 As for me, I will behold thy face in righteousness: I shall be satisfied, when I awake, with thy likeness.

believe them;" good enough advice, but he did not tell us how to carry it out. We have a precept here incorporated in an example; if we would be preserved, we must cry to the Preserver, and enlist divine support upon our side.

Verse 6. "I have called upon thee, for thou wilt hear me, O God." Thou hast always heard me, O my Lord, and therefore I have the utmost confidence in again approaching thine altar. Experience is a blessed teacher. He who has tried the faithfulness of God in hours of need, has great boldness in laying his case before the throne.

Verse 7. "Shew thy marvelous lovingkindness." Marvelous in its antiquity, its distinguishing character, its faithfulness, its immutability, and above all, marvelous in the wonders which it works. That marvelous grace which has redeemed us with the precious blood of God's only begotten, is here invoked to come to the rescue.

Verse 8. "Keep me as the apple of the eye." No part of the body more precious, more tender, and more carefully guarded than the eye; and of the eye, no portion more peculiarly to be protected than the central apple, the pupil, or as the Hebrew calls it, "the daughter of the eye." The all-wise Creator has placed the eye in a well-protected position; it stands surrounded by projecting bones like Jerusalem encircled by mountains.

Verse 9. "From the wicked that oppress me, from my deadly enemies, who compass me about." The foes from whom David sought to be rescued were wicked men. It is hopeful for us when our enemies are God's enemies. They were deadly enemies, whom nothing but his death would satisfy.

Verse 10. "They are inclosed in their own fat." Luxury and gluttony beget vainglorious fatness of heart, which shuts up its gates against all compassionate emotions and reasonable judgments. The old proverb says that full bellies make empty skulls, and it is yet more true that they frequently make empty hearts. The rankest weeds grow out of the fattest soil.

Verse 11. "They have now compassed us in our steps." The fury of the ungodly is aimed not at one believer alone, but at all the band; they have compassed us. All the race of the Jews were but a morsel for Haman's hungry revenge, and all because of one Mordecai. The prince of darkness hates all the saints for their Master's sake. The Lord Jesus is one of the us, and herein is our hope.

Verse 12. Lions are not more greedy, nor their ways more cunning than are Satan and his helpers when engaged against the children of God. The blood of souls the adversary thirsts after, and all his strength and craft are exerted to the utmost to satisfy his detestable appetite.

Verse 13. "Arise, O Lord." The more furious the attack, the more fervent the Psalmist's prayer. His eye rests singly upon the Almighty, and he feels that God has but to rise from the seat of his patience, and the work will be performed at once.

Verse 14. Having styled the ungodly a sword in his Father's hand, he now likens them to that hand itself, to set forth his conviction that God could as easily remove their violence as a man moves his own hand.

Verse 15. "As for me." "I neither envy nor covet these men's happiness, but partly have and partly hope for a far better." To behold God's face and to be changed by that vision into his image, so as to partake in his righteousness, this is my noble ambition; and in the prospect of this I cheerfully waive all my present enjoyments. My satisfaction is to come; I do not look for it as yet. I shall sleep awhile, but I shall wake at the sound of the trumpet; wake to everlasting joy, because I arise in thy likeness, O my God and King!

present time. David, in my judgment, here encourages and animates himself to call upon God, from the confident hope of being heard, as if he had said, Since I call upon thee, surely, O God, thou wilt not despise my prayers. Immediately after he beseeches God to bestow upon him the blessings of which he told us he entertained an assured hope.

7-9

7. David, in my judgment, perceiving that he could only be delivered from the perilous circumstances in which he was placed by singular and extraordinary means, betakes himself to the wonderful or miraculous power of God. Those who think he desires God to withhold his grace from his persecutors do too great violence to the scope of the passage. By this circumstance there is expressed the extreme danger to which David was exposed.

9. From the face of the ungodly. The Psalmist, by again accusing his enemies, intends to set forth his own innocence, as an argument for his obtaining the favor of God. At the same time, he complains of their cruelty, that God may be the more inclined to aid him.

10-12

10. They have enclosed themselves in their own fat. By the word fat, I think, is denoted the pride with which they were filled and swollen, as it were, with fatness. It is a very appropriate and expressive metaphor to represent them as having their hearts choked up with pride, in the manner in which corpulent persons are affected from the fat within them.

11. They have now compassed me round about in our steps. The Psalmist confirms what he has said before concerning the furious passion for doing mischief with which his enemies were inflamed. He says they were so cruelly bent on accomplishing his destruction, that in whatever way he directed or altered his course, they ceased not to follow close upon him.

13-14

13. Arise, O Jehovah. The more furiously David was persecuted by his enemies, he beseeches God the more earnestly to afford him immediate aid; for he uses the word face to denote the swift impetuosity of his adversary, to repress which there was need of the greatest haste. By these words, the Holy Spirit teaches us, that when death shows itself to be just at hand, God is provided with remedies perfectly prepared, by which he can effect our deliverance in a moment. The Psalmist not only attributes to God the office of delivering his people; he at the same time arms him with power to crush and break in pieces the wicked.

15. Having with anguish of heart declared before God the troubles which afflicted and tormented him, that he might not be overwhelmed with the load of temptations which pressed upon him, he now takes, as it were, the wings of faith and rises up to a region of undisturbed tranquility, where he may behold all things arranged and directed in due order.

II. What he pleads for the encouraging of his own faith in these petitions, and his hope of speeding. He pleads,

1. The malice and wickedness of his enemies: "They are such as are not fit to be countenanced, such as, if I be not delivered from them by the special care of God himself, will be my ruin. Lord, see what wicked men those are that oppress me, and waste me, and run me down."

(1.) "They are very spiteful and malicious; they are my deadly enemies, that thirst after my blood, my heart's blood-enemies against the soul," so the word is.

(2.) "They are very secure and sensual, insolent and haughty (v. 10): They are enclosed in their own fat, wrap themselves, hug themselves, in their own honor, and power, and plenty, and then make light of God, and set his judgments at defiance, Ps. lxxiii. 7; Job xv. 27.

(3.) "They are restless and unwearied in their attempts against me: They compass me about, v. 9. They have now in a manner gained their point; they have surrounded us, they have compassed us in our steps, they track us wherever we go, follow us as close as the hound does the hare, and take all advantages against us, being both too many and too quick for us.

(4.) "The ringleader of them (that was Saul) is in a special manner bloody and barbarous, politic and projecting (v. 12), like a lion that lives by prey and is therefore greedy of it." It is as much the meat and drink of a wicked man to do mischief as it is of a good man to do good. He is like a young lion lurking in secret places, disguising his cruel designs.

2. The power God had over them, to control and restrain them. He pleads, "Lord, they are thy sword; and will any father suffer his sword to be drawn against his own children?"

3. Their outward prosperity (v. 14): "Lord, appear against them, for, "They are entirely devoted to the world, and care not for thee and thy favor. They are men of the world, actuated by the spirit of the world, walking according to the course of this world, in love with the wealth and pleasure of this world, eager in the pursuits of it (making them their business) and at ease in the enjoyments of it—making them their bliss."

4. He pleads his own dependence upon God as his portion and happiness. "They have their portion in this life, but as for me (v. 15) I am none of them, I have but little of the world. Nec habeo, nec careo, nec curo—I neither have, nor need, nor care for it. It is the vision and fruition of God that I place my happiness in; that is it I hope for, and comfort myself with the hopes of, and thereby distinguish myself from those who have their portion in this life." Beholding God's face with satisfaction may be considered as our duty and comfort in this world. We must in righteousness by faith behold God's face and set him always before us, must entertain ourselves from day to day with the contemplation of the beauty of the Lord. We must be satisfied with his likeness set before us in his word.

Psalm 18

Title

To the Chief Musician a Psalm of David, the servant of the Lord, who spake unto the Lord the words of this song in the day that the Lord delivered him from the hand of all his enemies, and from the hand of Saul: and he said,

1-8

1 I will love thee, O LORD, my strength.
2 The LORD is my rock, and my fortress, and my deliverer; my God, my strength, in whom I will trust; my buckler, and the horn of my salvation, and my high tower.
3 I will call upon the LORD, who is worthy to be praised: so shall I be saved from mine enemies.
4 The sorrows of death compassed me, and the floods of ungodly men made me afraid.
5 The sorrows of hell compassed me about: the snares of death prevented me.
6 In my distress I called upon the LORD, and cried unto my God: he heard my voice out of his temple, and my cry came before him, even into his ears.
7 Then the earth shook and trembled; the foundations also of the hills moved and were shaken, because he was wroth.
8 There went up a smoke out of his nostrils, and fire out of his mouth devoured: coals were kindled by it.

Psalm 18

TITLE. "To the Chief Musician a Psalm of David, the servant of the Lord, who spake unto the Lord the words of this song in the day that the Lord delivered him from the hand of all his enemies, and from the hand of Saul." We have another form of this Psalm, with significant variations (2 Samuel 22), and this suggests the idea that it was sung by David at different times when he reviewed his own remarkable history, and observed the gracious hand of God in it all. This Psalm is the song of a grateful heart overwhelmed with a retrospect of the manifold and marvelous mercies of God. We will call it THE GRATEFUL RETROSPECT.

The title deserves attention. David, although at this time a king, calls himself, "the servant of Jehovah," but makes no mention of his royalty; hence we gather that he counted it a higher honor to be the Lord's servant than to be Judah's king. Right wisely did he judge. Being possessed of poetic genius, he served the Lord by composing this Psalm for the use of the Lord's house; and it is no mean work to conduct or to improve that delightful part of divine worship, the singing of the Lord's praises. Would that more musical and poetical ability were consecrated, and that our chief musicians were fit to be trusted with devout and spiritual psalmody. It should be observed that the words of this song were not composed with the view of gratifying the taste of men, but were spoken unto Jehovah. It were well if we had a more single eye to the honor of the Lord in our singing, and in all other hallowed exercises. That praise is little worth which is not directed solely and heartily to the Lord. David might well be thus direct in his gratitude, for he owed all to his God, and in the day of his deliverance he had none to thank but the Lord, whose right hand had preserved him. We too should feel that to God and God alone we owe the greatest debt of honor and thanksgiving.

If it be remembered that the second and the forty-ninth verses are both quoted in the New Testament (Hebrews 2:13; Romans 15:9) as the words of the Lord Jesus, it will be clear that a greater than David is here. Reader, you will not need our aid in this respect; if you know Jesus you will readily find him in his sorrows, deliverance, and triumphs all through this wonderful psalm.

DIVISION. The first three verses are the proem or preface in which the resolve to bless God is declared. Delivering mercy is most poetically extolled from verse 4 to verse 19; and then the happy songster from verse 20 to 28, protests that God had acted righteously in thus favoring him. Filled with grateful joy he again pictures his deliverance, and anticipates future victories from verse 29-45; and in closing speaks with evident prophetic foresight of the glorious triumphs of the Messiah, David's seed and the Lord's anointed.

EXPOSITION

Verse 1. "I will love thee, O Lord." With strong, hearty affection will I cling to thee; as a child to its parent, or a spouse to her husband. The word is intensely forcible, the love is of the deepest kind. "I will love heartily, with my inmost bowels." Here is a fixed resolution to abide in the nearest and most intimate union with the Most High. Our triune God deserves the warmest love of all our hearts. Father, Son and Spirit have each a claim upon our love.

Verse 2. "The Lord is my rock and my fortress." Dwelling among the crags and mountain fastnesses of Judea David had escaped the malice of Saul, and here he compares his God to such a place of concealment and security. Believers are often hidden in their God from the strife of tongues and the fury of the storm of trouble.

Verse 3. In this verse the happy poet resolves to invoke the Lord in joyful song, believing that in all future conflicts his God would deal as well with

JOHN CALVIN

Psalm 18

1-2

1. It is to be observed, that love to God is here laid down as constituting the principal part of true godliness; for there is no better way of serving God than to love him. No doubt, the service which we owe him is better expressed by the word reverence, that thus his majesty may prominently stand forth to our view in its infinite greatness. But as he requires nothing so expressly as to possess all the affections of our heart, and to have them going out towards him, so there is no sacrifice which he values more than when we are bound fast to him by the chain of a free and spontaneous love; and, on the other hand, there is nothing in which his glory shines forth more conspicuously than in his free and sovereign goodness.

3-6

3. I will call upon the praised Jehovah. Calling upon God frequently comprehends the whole of his service; but as the effect or fruit of prayer is particularly mentioned in what follows, this phrase in the passage before us, I have no doubt, signifies to have recourse to God for protection, and to ask by prayer deliverance from him. David having said in the second verse, that he trusted in God, now subjoins this as an evidence of his trust; for every one who confides in God will earnestly beseech his aid in the time of need.

4. The cords of death had compassed me about. David now begins to recount the undoubted and illustrious proofs by which he had experienced that the hand of God is sufficiently strong and powerful to repel all the dangers and calamities with which he may be assailed. And we need not wonder that those things which might have been described more simply, and in an unadorned style, are clothed in poetical forms of expression, and set forth with all the elegancies and ornaments of language.

6. In my distress, etc. It was a very evident proof of uncommon faith in David, when, being almost plunged into the gulf of death, he lifted up his heart to heaven by prayer. Let us therefore learn, that such an example is set before our eyes, that no calamities, however great and oppressive, may hinder us from praying, or create an aversion to it. It was prayer which brought to David the fruits or wonderful effects of which he speaks a little after, and from this it appears still more clearly that his deliverance was effected by the power of God.

7-11

7. Then the earth shook. David, convinced that the aid of God, which he had experienced, was of such a character, that it was impossible for him to extol it sufficiently and as it deserved, sets forth an image of it in the sky and the earth, as if he had said, It has been as visible as the changes which give different appearances to the sky and the earth. If natural things always flowed in an even and uniform course, the power of God would not be so perceptible. But when he changes the face of the sky by sudden rain, or by loud thunder, or by dreadful tempests, those who before were, as it were, asleep and

MATTHEW HENRY

Psalm 18

1-19 David's triumphs in God; devout confidence.
In these verses,

I. He triumphs in God and his relation to him. The first words of the psalm, I will love thee, O Lord! my strength, are here prefixed as the scope and contents of the whole. Love to God is the first and great commandment of the law, because it is the principle of all our acceptable praise and obedience; and this use we should make of all the mercies God bestows upon us, our hearts should thereby be enlarged in love to him. This he requires and will accept; and we are very ungrateful if we grudge him so poor a return. An interest in the person loved is the lover's delight; this string therefore he touches, and on this he harps with much pleasure (v. 2): "The Lord Jehovah is my God; and then he is my rock, my fortress, all that I need and can desire in my present distress." For there is that in God which is suited to all the exigencies and occasions of his people that trust in him. "He is my rock, and strength, and fortress;" that is,

1. "I have found him so in the greatest dangers and difficulties."

2. "I have chosen him to be so, disclaiming all others, and depending upon him alone to protect me." Those that truly love God may thus triumph in him as theirs, and may with confidence call upon him, v. 3. This further use we should make of our deliverances, we must not only love God the better, but love prayer the better, call upon him as long as we live, especially in time of trouble, with an assurance that so we shall be saved; for thus it is written, Whosoever shall call upon the name of the Lord shall be saved: "And it shall come to pass, that whosoever shall call on the name of the Lord shall be saved", Acts ii. 21.

II. He sets himself to magnify the deliverances God had wrought for him, that he might be the more affected in his returns of praise. It is good for us to observe all the circumstances of a mercy, which magnify the power of God and his goodness to us in it.

1. The more imminent and threatening the danger was out of which we were delivered the greater is the mercy of the deliverance. David now remembered how the forces of his enemies poured in upon him, which he calls the floods of Belial, shoals of the children of Belial, likely to overpower him with numbers. They surrounded him, compassed him about; they surprised him, and by that means were very near seizing him; their snares prevented him, and, when without were fightings, within were fears and sorrows, v. 4, 5. His spirit was overwhelmed, and he looked upon himself as a lost man; see Ps. cxvi. 3, "The sorrows of death compassed me, and the pains of hell gat hold upon me: I found trouble and sorrow."

2. The more earnest we have been with God for deliverance, and the more direct answer it is to our prayers, the more we are obliged to be thankful.

Psalm 18

9-16
9 He bowed the heavens also, and came down: and darkness was under his feet.
10 And he rode upon a cherub, and did fly: yea, he did fly upon the wings of the wind.
11 He made darkness his secret place; his pavilion round about him were dark waters and thick clouds of the skies.
12 At the brightness that was before him his thick clouds passed, hail stones and coals of fire.
13 The LORD also thundered in the heavens, and the Highest gave his voice; hail stones and coals of fire.
14 Yea, he sent out his arrows, and scattered them; and he shot out lightnings, and discomfited them.
15 Then the channels of waters were seen, and the foundations of the world were discovered at thy rebuke, O LORD, at the blast of the breath of thy nostrils.
16 He sent from above, he took me, he drew me out of many waters.

him as in the past. It is well to pray to God as to one who deserves to be praised, for then we plead in a happy and confident manner. If I feel that I can and do bless the Lord for all his past goodness, I am bold to ask great things of him.
Verses 4-19. In most poetical language the Psalmist now describes his experience of Jehovah's delivering power.
Verse 4. "The sorrows of death compassed me." Death like a cruel conqueror seemed to twist round about him the cords of pain. He was environed and hemmed in with threatening deaths of the most appalling sort.
Verse 5. "The sorrows of hell compassed me about." From all sides the hell-hounds barked furiously. A cordon of devils hemmed in the hunted man of God; every way of escape was closed up. Satan knows how to blockade our coasts with the iron warships of sorrow, but, blessed be God, the port of all prayer is still open, and grace can run the blockade bearing messages from earth to heaven, and blessings in return from heaven to earth.
Verse 6. "In my distress I called upon the Lord, and cried unto my God." Prayer is that postern gate which is left open even when the city is straitly besieged by the enemy; it is that way upward from the pit of despair to which the spiritual miner flies at once when the floods from beneath break forth upon him.
Verse 7. There was no great space between the cry and its answer. The Lord is not slack concerning his promise, but is swift to rescue his afflicted.
Verse 8. "There went up a smoke out of his nostrils." A violent oriental method of expressing fierce wrath. Since the breath from the nostrils is heated by strong emotion, the figure portrays the Almighty Deliverer as pouring forth smoke in the heat of his wrath and the impetuousness of his zeal.
Verse 9. Amid the terror of the storm Jehovah the Avenger descended, bending beneath his foot the arch of heaven. "He bowed the heavens also, and came down." He came in haste, and spurned everything which impeded his rapidity.
Verse 10. There is inimitable grandeur in this verse. Without speculating upon the mysterious and much-disputed subject of the cherubim, it may be enough to remark that angels are doubtless our guards and ministering friends, and all their powers are enlisted to rescue the afflicted.
Verse 11. The storm thickened, and the clouds pouring forth torrents of rain combined to form the secret chamber of the invisible but wonder-working God. "Pavilioned in impervious shade" faith saw him, but no other eye could gaze through the "thick clouds of the skies." Blessed is the darkness which encurtains my God; if I may not see him, it is sweet to know that he is working in secret for my eternal good.
Verse 12. Suddenly the terrible artillery of heaven was discharged; the brightness of lightning lit up the clouds as with a glory proceeding from him who was concealed within the cloudy pavilion; and volleys of hailstones and coals of fire were hurled forth upon the enemy.
Verse 13. Over all this splendor of tempest pealed the dread thunder. "The Lord also thundered in the heavens, and the Highest gave his voice." Fit accompaniment for the flames of vengeance. How will men bear to hear it at the last when addressed to them in proclamation of their doom, for even now their hearts are in their mouths if they do but hear it muttering from afar? In all this terror David found a theme for song, and thus every believer finds even in the terrors of God a subject for holy praise.
Verse 14. The lightnings were darted forth as forked arrows upon the hosts of the foe, and speedily "scattered them." Boastful sinners prove to be great cowards when Jehovah enters the lists with them. They despise his words, and are very tongue-valiant, but when it comes to blows they fly apace.
Verse 15. So tremendous was the shock of God's assault in arms that the order of nature was changed, and the bottoms of rivers and seas were laid bare.

JOHN CALVIN

insensible, must necessarily be awakened, and be tremblingly conscious of the existence of a presiding God.

8. The Psalmist means, that God, without great labor or effort, as soon as he shall have sent forth a breath or blast from his nostrils, and opened his mouth, will kindle such a fire that its smoke will darken the whole world, and its intense heat devour it.

10. He rode also upon a cherub. The Psalmist having exhibited to us a sign of the wrath of God in the clouds, and in the darkening of the air, representing him as if he breathed out smoke, from his nostrils, and descended with a threatening countenance, to afflict men by the dreadful weight of his power; and having also represented lightnings and thunderbolts as flaming fire proceeding from his mouths—he now introduces him as riding upon the winds and tempests, to take a survey of the whole world with rapid speed, or rather with the swiftness of flying.

12-19

12. At the brightness, etc. The Psalmist again returns to the lightnings which, by dividing and as it were cleaving the clouds, lay open the heaven; and, therefore, he says, that the clouds of God passed away at the brightness which was before him These sudden changes affect us with a much more lively sense of the power and agency of God than natural phenomena which move on in one uniform course.

13. Jehovah thundered. David here repeats the same thing in different words, declaring that God thundered from heaven; and he calls the thunder the yoke of God, that we may not suppose it is produced merely by chance or by natural causes, independent of the appointment and will of God.

We should remember that David, under these figures, describes to us the dreadful power of God, the better to exalt and magnify the divine grace, which was manifested in his deliverance. He declares a little after, that this was his intention; for, when speaking of his enemies, he says, (verse 14,) that they were scattered, or put to flight, by the arrows of God; as if he had said, They have been overthrown, not by the hands or swords of men, but by God, who openly launched his thunderbolts against them. Not that he means to affirm that this happened literally, but he speaks in this metaphorical language, because those who were uninstructed and slow to acknowledge the power of God, could not otherwise be brought to perceive that God was the author of his deliverance.

15. And the sources of the waters were seen. In this verse, David doubtless alludes to the miracle which was wrought when the chosen tribes passed through the Red Sea. As all the special benefits which God in old time conferred upon any of the children of Abraham as individuals, were so many testimonies by which he recalled to their remembrance the covenant which he had once entered into with the whole people, to assure them that he would always continue his grace towards them, and that one deliverance might be to them a token or pledge of their perpetual safety, and of the protection of God, David fitly conjoins with that ancient deliverance of the Church the assistance which God had sent from heaven to

MATTHEW HENRY

David's deliverances were so, v. 6. David was found a praying man, and God was found a prayer-hearing God. If we pray as he did, we shall speed as he did. Though distress drive us to prayer, God will not therefore be deaf to us; nay, being a God of pity, he will be the more ready to succor us.

3. The more wonderful God's appearances are in any deliverance the greater it is: such were the deliverances wrought for David, in which God's manifestation of his presence and glorious attributes is most magnificently described, v. 7, &c. Little appeared of man, but much of God, in these deliverances.

(1.) He appeared a God of almighty power; for he made the earth shake and tremble, and moved even the foundations of the hills (v. 7), as of old at Mount Sinai. When the men of the earth were struck with fear, then the earth might be said to tremble; when the great men of the earth were put into confusion, then the hills moved.

(2.) He showed his anger and displeasure against the enemies and persecutors of his people: He was wroth, v. 7. His wrath smoked, it burned, it was fire, it was devouring fire (v. 8), and coals were kindled by it. Those that by their own sins make themselves as coals (that is, fuel) to this fire will be consumed by it. He that ordains his arrows against the persecutors sends them forth when he pleases, and they are sure to hit the mark and do execution; for those arrows are lightnings, v. 14.

(3.) He showed his readiness to plead his people's cause and work deliverance for them; for he rode upon a cherub and did fly, for the maintaining of right and the relieving of his distressed servants, v. 10. No opposition, no obstruction, can be given to him who rides upon the wings of the wind, who rides on the heavens, for the help of his people, and, in his excellency, on the skies.

(4.) He showed his condescension, in taking cognizance of David's case: He bowed the heavens and came down (v. 9), did not send an angel, but came himself, as one afflicted in the afflictions of his people.

(5.) He wrapped himself in darkness, and yet commanded light to shine out of darkness for his people: "Verily thou art a God that hidest thyself, O God of Israel, the Savior", Isa. xlv. 15. He is a God that hideth himself; for he made darkness his pavilion, v. 11. his glory is invisible, his counsels are unsearchable, and his proceedings unaccountable, and so, as to us, clouds and darkness are round about him; we know not the way that he takes, even when he is coming towards us in ways of mercy; but, when his designs are secret, they are kind; for, though he hide himself, he is the God of Israel, the Savior. And, at his brightness, the thick clouds pass (v. 12), comfort returns, the face of affairs is changed, and that which was gloomy and threatening becomes serene and pleasant.

Psalm 18

17-24
17 He delivered me from my strong enemy, and from them which hated me: for they were too strong for me.
18 They prevented me in the day of my calamity: but the LORD was my stay.
19 He brought me forth also into a large place; he delivered me, because he delighted in me.
20 The LORD rewarded me according to my righteousness; according to the cleanness of my hands hath he recompensed me.
21 For I have kept the ways of the LORD, and have not wickedly departed from my God.
22 For all his judgments were before me, and I did not put away his statutes from me.
23 I was also upright before him, and I kept myself from mine iniquity.
24 Therefore hath the LORD recompensed me according to my righteousness, according to the cleanness of my hands in his eyesight.

Verse 16. Now comes the rescue. The Author is divine, "He sent;" the work is heavenly, "from above;" the deliverance is marvelous, "He drew me out of many waters." Here David was like another Moses, drawn from the water; and thus are all believers like their Lord, whose baptism in many waters of agony and in his own blood has redeemed us from the wrath to come.

Verse 17. When we have been rescued, we must take care to ascribe all the glory to God by confessing our own weakness, and remembering the power of the conquered enemy. God's power derives honor from all the incidents of the conflict.

Verse 18. It was an ill day, a day of calamity, of which evil foes took cruel advantage, while they used crafty means utterly to ruin him, yet David could say, "but the Lord is my stay." What a blessed but which cuts the Gordian knot, and slays the hundred-headed hydra! There is no fear of deliverance when our stay is in Jehovah.

Verse 19. "He brought me forth also into a large place." After pining awhile in the prison-house Joseph reached the palace, and from the cave of Adullam David mounted to the throne. Sweet is pleasure after pain.

Verse 20. David's early troubles arose from the wicked malice of envious Saul, who no doubt prosecuted his persecutions under cover of charges brought against the character of "the man after God's own heart." These charges David declares to have been utterly false, and asserts that he possessed a grace-given righteousness which the Lord had graciously rewarded in defiance of all his calumniators.

Verse 21. Here the assertion of purity is repeated, both in a positive and a negative form. There is "I have" and "I have not," both of which must be blended in a truly sanctified life; constraining and restraining grace must each take its share.

Verse 22. "For all his judgments were before me." The word, the character, and the actions of God should be evermore before our eyes; we should learn, consider, and reverence them. Men forget what they do not wish to remember, but the excellent attributes of the Most High are objects of the believer's affectionate and delighted admiration. We should keep the image of God so constantly before us that we become in our measure conformed unto it. This inner love to the right must be the main spring of Christian integrity in our public walk.

Verse 23. "I was also upright before him." Sincerity is here claimed; sincerity, such as would be accounted genuine before the bar of God. Whatever evil men might think of him, David felt that he had the good opinion of his God. Moreover, freedom from his one great besetting sin he ventures also to plead, "I kept myself from mine iniquity." It is a very gracious sign when the most violent parts of our nature have been well guarded. If the weakest link in the chain is not broken, the stronger links will be safe enough.

Verse 24. God first gives us holiness, and then rewards us for it. We are his workmanship; vessels made unto honor; and when made, the honor is not withheld from the vessel; though, in fact, it all belongs to the Potter upon whose wheel the vessel was fashioned. The prize is awarded to the flower at the show, but the gardener reared it; the child wins the prize from the schoolmaster, but the real honor of his schooling lies with the master, although instead of receiving he gives the reward.

Verse 25. The dealings of the Lord in his own case, cause the grateful singer to remember the usual rule of God's moral government; he is just in his dealings with the sons of men, and metes out to each man according to his measure. "With the merciful thou wilt shew thyself merciful; with an upright man thou wilt shew thyself upright." Every man shall have his meat weighed in his own scales, his corn meted in his own bushel, and his land measured with his own rod. No rule can be more fair, to ungodly men more terrible, or to the generous man more honorable. How would men throw

him in particular. As the grace which he declares God had shown towards him was not to be separated from that first deliverance, since it was, so to speak, a part and an appendage of it, he beholds, as it were at a glance, or in an instant, both the ancient miracle of the drying up of the Red Sea, and the assistance which God granted to himself.
16. He sent down from above. Here there is briefly shown the drift of the sublime and magnificent narrative which has now passed under our review, namely, to teach us that David at length emerged from the profound abyss of his troubles, neither by his own skill, nor by the aid of men, but that he was drawn out of them by the hand of God. When God defends and preserves us wonderfully and by extraordinary means, he is said in Scripture language to send down succor from above; and this sending is set in opposition to human and earthly aids, on which we usually place a mistaken and an undue confidence.
18. They had prevented me in the day of my calamity. The Psalmist here confirms in different words the preceding sentence, namely, that he had been sustained by the aid of God, when there was no way of escaping by the power of man. He tells us how he had been besieged on all sides, and that not by an ordinary siege, inasmuch as his enemies, in persecuting him, always molested him most in the time of his calamity. From this circumstance it is the more evident that he had obtained enlargement by no other means than by the hand of God.

Ambitious and turbulent men, who are carried headlong by their unruly lusts, inconsiderately to attempt any thing, and who, by their rashness, involve themselves in dangers, may often accomplish their undertakings by vigorous and resolute efforts, but at length a reverse takes place, and they are stopped short in their career of success, for they are unworthy of being sustained and prospered by God, since, without having any warrant or foundation for what they do in his call, they would raise their insane structures even to heaven, and disturb all around them.

20-24
20. Jehovah rewarded me. David might seem at first sight to contradict himself; for, while a little before he declared that all the blessings which he possessed were to be traced to the good pleasure of God, he now boasts that God rendered to him a just recompense. But if we remember for what purpose he connects these commendations of his own integrity with the good pleasure of God, it will be easy to reconcile these apparently conflicting statements. He has before declared that God was the sole author and originator of the hope of coming to the kingdom which he entertained, and that he had not been elevated to it by the suffrages of men, nor had he rushed forward to it through the mere impulse of his own mind, but accepted it because such was the will of God. Now he adds, in the second place, that he had yielded faithful obedience to God, and had never turned aside from his will.
21. For I have kept the ways of Jehovah. He had spoken in the preceding verse of the cleanness of his hands, but finding that men judged of him perversely, and were very active in

4. The greater the difficulties are that lie in the way of deliverance the more glorious the deliverance is. For the rescuing of David, the waters were to be divided till the very channels were seen; the earth was to be cloven till the very foundations of it were discovered, v. 15. There were waters deep and many, waters out of which he was to be drawn (v. 16), as Moses, who had his name from being drawn out of the water literally, as David was figuratively. His enemies were strong, and they hated him; had he been left to himself, they would have been too strong for him, v. 17. And they were too quick for him; for they prevented him in the day of his calamity, v. 18. But, in the midst of his troubles, the Lord was his stay, so that he did not sink. Note, God will not only deliver his people out of their troubles in due time, but he will sustain them and bear them up under their troubles in the mean time.
5. That which especially magnified the deliverance was that his comfort was the fruit of it and God's favor was the root and fountain of it.
(1.) It was an introduction to his preferment, v. 19. "He brought me forth also out of my straits into a large place, where I had room, not only to turn, but to thrive in."
(2.) It was a token of God's favor to him, and that made it doubly sweet: "He delivered me because he delighted in me, not for my merit, but for his own grace and good-will." Compare this with 2 Sam. xv. 26, If he thus say, I have no delight in thee, here I am. We owe our salvation, that great deliverance, to the delight God had in the Son of David, in whom he has declared himself to be well pleased.

20-28 Devout thanksgivings; devout confidence
Here,
I. David reflects with comfort upon his own integrity, and rejoices in the testimony of his conscience that he had had his conversation in godly sincerity and not with fleshly wisdom: "For our rejoicing is this, the testimony of our conscience, that in simplicity and godly sincerity, not with fleshly wisdom, but by the grace of God, we have had our conversation in the world, and more abundantly to you-ward", 2 Cor. i. 12. His deliverances were an evidence of this, and this was the great comfort of his deliverances. His enemies had misrepresented him, and perhaps, when his troubles continued long, he began to suspect himself; but, when God visibly took his part, he had both the credit and the comfort of his righteousness.
1. His deliverances cleared his innocency before men, and acquitted him from those crimes which he was falsely accused of. This he calls rewarding him according to his righteousness (v. 20, 24), that is, determining the controversy between him and his enemies, according to the justice of his cause and the cleanness of his hands, from that sedition, treason, and rebellion, with which he was charged. He had

Psalm 18

25-32
25 With the merciful thou wilt shew thyself merciful; with an upright man thou wilt shew thyself upright;
26 With the pure thou wilt shew thyself pure; and with the froward thou wilt shew thyself froward.
27 For thou wilt save the afflicted people; but wilt bring down high looks.
28 For thou wilt light my candle: the LORD my God will enlighten my darkness.
29 For by thee I have run through a troop; and by my God have I leaped over a wall.
30 As for God, his way is perfect: the word of the LORD is tried: he is a buckler to all those that trust in him.
31 For who is God save the LORD? or who is a rock save our God?
32 It is God that girdeth me with strength, and maketh my way perfect.

away their light weights, and break their short yards, if they could but believe that they themselves are sure to be in the end the losers by their knavish tricks! Note that even the merciful need mercy; no amount of generosity to the poor, or forgiveness to enemies, can set us beyond the need of mercy. Lord, have mercy upon me, a sinner.
Verse 26. "With the pure thou wilt shew thyself pure; and with the froward thou wilt shew thyself froward." The sinner's frowardness is sinful and rebellious, and the only sense in which the term can be applied to the Most Holy God is that of judicial opposition and sternness, in which the Judge of all the earth will act at cross-purposes with the offender, and let him see that all things are not to be made subservient to wicked whims and willful fancies.
Verse 27. "For thou wilt save the afflicted people." This is a comforting assurance for the poor in spirit whose spiritual griefs admit of no sufficient solace from any other than a divine hand. They cannot save themselves nor can others do it, but God will save them. "But will bring down high looks." Those who look down on others with scorn shall be looked down upon with contempt ere long. The Lord abhors a proud look. What a reason for repentance and humiliation! How much better to be humble than to provoke God to humble us in his wrath! A considerable number of clauses occur in this passage in the future tense; how forcibly are we thus brought to remember that our present joy or sorrow is not to have so much weight with us as the great and eternal future!
Verse 28. "For thou wilt light my candle." Even the children of the day sometimes need candle-light. In the darkest hour light will arise; a candle shall be lit, it will be comfort such as we may fittingly use without dishonesty—it will be our own candle; yet God himself will find the holy fire with which the candle shall burn; our evidences are our own, but their comfortable light is from above. Candles which are lit by God the devil cannot blow out. All candles are not shining, and so there are some graces which yield no present comfort; but it is well to have candles which may by and by be lit, and it is well to possess graces which may yet afford us cheering evidences.
Verses 29-45. Some repetitions are not vain repetitions. Second thoughts upon God's mercy should be and often are the best. Like wines on the lees our gratitude grows stronger and sweeter as we meditate upon divine goodness. The verses which we have now to consider are the ripe fruit of a thankful spirit; they are apples of gold as to matter, and they are placed in baskets of silver as to their language. They describe the believer's victorious career and his enemies' confusion.
Verse 29. "For by thee have I run through a troop; and by my God have I leaped over a wall." Whether we meet the foe in the open field or leap upon them while they lurk behind the battlements of a city, we shall by God's grace defeat them in either case; if they hem us in with living legions, or environ us with stone walls, we shall with equal certainty obtain our liberty.
Verse 30. "As for God, his way is perfect." Far past all fault and error are God's dealings with his people; all his actions are resplendent with justice, truth, tenderness, mercy, and holiness. Every way of God is complete in itself, and all his ways put together are matchless in harmony and goodness. Is it not very consolatory to believe that he who has begun to bless us will perfect his work, for all his ways are "perfect." Nor must the divine "word" be without its song of praise. "The word of the Lord is tried," like silver refined in the furnace. The doctrines are glorious, the precepts are pure, the promises are faithful, and the whole revelation is superlatively full of grace and truth. David had tried it, thousands have tried it, we have tried it, and it has never failed. It was meet that when way and word had been extolled, the Lord himself should be magnified; hence it is added, "He is a buckler to all those that trust in him." No armor of proof or shield of brass so well secures the warrior as the covenant God of Israel protects his

spreading evil reports concerning him, he affirms that he had kept the ways of the Lord, which is equivalent to his appealing the matter to the judgment-seat of God.

22. For all his judgments were before me. He now shows how he came to possess that unbending rectitude of character, by which he was enabled to act uprightly amidst so many and so grievous temptations, namely, because he always applied his mind to the study of the law of God. As Satan is daily making new assaults upon us, it is necessary for us to have recourse to arms, and it is meditation upon the Divine Law which furnishes us with armor to resist. Whoever, therefore, would desire to persevere in uprightness and integrity of life, let them learn to exercise themselves daily in the study of the word of God; for, whenever a man despises or neglects instruction, he easily falls into carelessness and stupidity, and all fear of God vanishes from his mind.

23. I was also upright with him. All the verbs in this verse are put by David in the future tense, I will be upright, etc. because he does not boast of one act only, or of a good work performed by fits and starts, but of steady perseverance in an upright course. What I have said before, namely, that David takes God for his judge, as he saw that he was wrongfully and unrighteously condemned by men, appears still more clearly from what he here says, "I have been upright with him." The Scriptures, indeed, sometimes speak in similar terms of the saints, to distinguish them from hypocrites, who content themselves with wearing the outward mask of religious observances; but it is to disprove the false reports which were spread against him that David thus confidently appeals to God with respect to them.

25-27

25. With the merciful, etc. David here prosecutes the same subject. In considering the grace of God by which he had been delivered, he brings it forward as a proof of his integrity, and thus triumphs over the unfounded and disgraceful calumnies of his enemies. Hypocrites, I confess, are also accustomed to act in the same way; for prosperity and the success of their affairs so elates them that they are not ashamed proudly to vaunt themselves not only against men, but even against God. As such persons, however, openly mock God, when, by his long-suffering, he allures them to repentance, their wicked and unhappy presumption has no resemblance to the boasting by which we here see David encouraging himself.

27. For thou wilt save the afflicted people. This verse contains the correction of a mistake into which we are very ready to fall. As experience shows that the merciful are often severely afflicted, and the sincere involved in troubles of a very distressing description, to prevent any from regarding the statement as false that God deals mercifully with the merciful, David admonishes us that we must wait for the end; for although God does not immediately run to succor the good, yet, after having exercised their patience for a time, he lifts them up from the dust on which they lay prostrate, and brings effectual relief to them, even when they were in despair. Whence it follows, that we ought only to judge by the issue

often appealed to God concerning his innocency; and now God had given judgment upon the appeal (as he always will) according to equity.

2. They confirmed the testimony of his own conscience for him, which he here reviews with a great deal of pleasure, v. 21-23: "For I have kept the ways of the Lord, and have not wickedly departed from my God. For all his judgments were before me, and I did not put away his statutes from me. I was also upright before him, and I kept myself from mine iniquity." His own heart knows, and is ready to attest it, that he had kept his eye upon the rule of God's commands (v. 22): "All his judgments were before me; and I had a respect to them all, despised none as little, disliked none as hard, but made it my care and business to conform to them all. His statutes I did not put away from me, out of my sight, out of my mind, but kept my eye always upon them, and did not as those who, because they would quit the ways of the Lord, desire not the knowledge of those ways."

II. He takes occasion thence to lay down the rules of God's government and judgment, that we may know not only what God expects from us, but what we may expect from him, v. 25, 26.

III. Hence he speaks comfort to the humble ("Thou wilt save the afflicted people, that are wronged and bear it patiently"), terror to the proud ("Thou wilt bring down high looks, that aim high, and look with scorn and disdain upon the poor and pious"), and encouragement to himself, "Thou wilt light my candle, that is, thou wilt revive and comfort my sorrowful spirit, and not leave me melancholy; thou wilt recover me out of my troubles and restore me to peace and prosperity; thou wilt make my honor bright, which is now eclipsed; thou wilt guide my way, and make it plain before me, that I may avoid the snares laid for me; thou wilt light my candle to work by, and give me an opportunity of serving thee and the interests of thy kingdom among men."

29-50 Grateful remembrance of past deliverances; confidence in the divine goodness.

In these verses,

I. David looks back, with thankfulness, upon the great things which God had done for him. He had not only wrought deliverance for him, but had given him victory and success, and made him triumph over those who thought to triumph over him. When we set ourselves to praise God for one mercy we must be led by that to observe the many more with which we have been compassed about, and followed, all our days. Many things had contributed to David's advancement, and he owns the hand of God in them all, to teach us to do likewise, in reviewing the several steps by which we have risen to our prosperity.

1. God had given him all his skill and understanding in military affairs, which he was not bred up to nor designed for, his genius leading him more to music,

Psalm 18

33-40

33 He maketh my feet like hinds' feet, and setteth me upon my high places.
34 He teacheth my hands to war, so that a bow of steel is broken by mine arms.
35 Thou hast also given me the shield of thy salvation: and thy right hand hath holden me up, and thy gentleness hath made me great.
36 Thou hast enlarged my steps under me, that my feet did not slip.
37 I have pursued mine enemies, and overtaken them: neither did I turn again till they were consumed.
38 I have wounded them that they were not able to rise: they are fallen under my feet.
39 For thou hast girded me with strength unto the battle: thou hast subdued under me those that rose up against me.
40 Thou hast also given me the necks of mine enemies; that I might destroy them that hate me.

warring people. He himself is the buckler of trustful ones; what a thought is this! What peace may every trusting soul enjoy!

Verse 31. Having mentioned his God, the psalmist's heart burns, and his words sparkle; he challenges heaven and earth to find another being worthy of adoration or trust in comparison with Jehovah. His God, as Matthew Henry says, is a None-such. The idols of the heathen he scorns to mention, snuffing them all out as mere nothings when Deity is spoken of. "Who is God save the Lord?"

Verse 32. Surveying all the armor in which he fought and conquered, the joyful victor praises the Lord for every part of the panoply. The girdle of his loins earns the first stanza: "It is God that girdeth me with strength, and maketh my way perfect." Girt about the loins with power from heaven, the warrior was filled with vigor, far above all created might; and, whereas, without this wondrous belt he would have been feeble and effeminate, with relaxed energies and scattered forces, he felt himself, when braced with the girdle of truth, to be compact in purpose, courageous in daring, and concentrated in power; so that his course was a complete success, so undisturbed by disastrous defeat as to be called "perfect."

Verse 33. The conqueror's feet had been shod by a divine hand, and the next note must, therefore, refer to them. "He maketh my feet like hinds' feet, and setteth me upon my high places." Pursuing his foes the warrior had been swift of foot as a young roe, but, instead of taking pleasure in the legs of a man, he ascribes the boon of swiftness to the Lord alone. When our thoughts are nimble, and our spirits rapid, like the chariots of Amminadib, let us not forget that our best Beloved's hand has given us the choice favor.

Verse 34. "He teacheth my hands to war." Martial prowess and skill in the use of weapons are gratefully acknowledged to be the result of divine teaching; no sacrifice is offered at the shrine of self in praise of natural dexterity, or acquired skillfulness; but, regarding all warlike prowess as a gift of heavenly favor, thankfulness is presented to the Giver. The Holy Spirit is the great Drillmaster of heavenly soldiers. "So that a bow of steel is broken by mine arms." A bow of brass is probably meant, and these bows could scarcely be bent by the arms alone, the archer had to gain the assistance of his foot; it was, therefore, a great feat of strength to bend the bow, so far as even to snap it in halves.

Verse 35. "Thou hast also given me the shield of thy salvation." Above all we must take the shield of faith, for nothing else can quench Satan's fiery darts; this shield is of celestial workmanship, and is in all cases a direct gift from God himself; it is the channel, the sign, the guarantee, and the earnest of perfect salvation. "Thy right hand hath holden me up." Secret support is administered to us by the preserving grace of God, and at the same time Providence kindly yields us manifest aid.

Verse 36. "Thou hast enlarged my steps." A smooth pathway leading to spacious possessions and camping-grounds had been opened up for him. Instead of threading the narrow mountain paths, and hiding in the cracks and corners of caverns, he was able to traverse the plains and dwell under his own vine and fig tree. It is no small mercy to be brought into full Christian liberty and enlargement, but it is a greater favor still to be enabled to walk worthily in such liberty, not being permitted to slip with our feet. To stand upon the rocks of affliction is the result of gracious upholding, but that aid is quite as much needed in the luxurious plains of prosperity.

Verse 37. The preservation of the saints bodes ill for their adversaries. The Amelekites thought themselves clear away with their booty, but when David's God guided him in the pursuit, they were soon overtaken and cut in pieces. When God is with us sins and sorrows flee, and all forms of evil are "consumed" before the power of grace. What a noble picture this and the following verses present to us of the victories of our glorious Lord Jesus!

how God shows himself merciful towards the merciful and pure towards the pure. If he did not keep his people in suspense and waiting long for deliverance from affliction, it could not be said that it is his prerogative to save the afflicted. And it is no small consolation, in the midst of our adversities, to know that God purposely delays to communicate his assistance, which otherwise is quite prepared, that we may experience his goodness in saving us after we have been afflicted and brought low.

28-32

28. For thou shalt light my lamp. It was by the grace of God that David, who had been plunged in darkness, returned to the light. David does not simply give thanks to God for having lighted up a lamp before him, but also for having converted his darkness into light. He, therefore, acknowledges that he had been reduced to such extremity of distress, that he was like a man whose condition was forlorn and hopeless; for he compares the confused and perplexed state of his affairs to darkness. This, indeed, by the transference of material things to things spiritual, may be applied to the spiritual illumination of the understanding; but, at the same time, we must attend to the subject of which David treats, that we may not depart from the true and proper meaning. Now, as he acknowledges that he had been restored to prosperity by the favor of God, which was to him, as it were, a life-giving light, let us, after his example, regard it as certain that we will never have the comfort of seeing our adversities brought to an end, unless God disperse the darkness which envelops us, and restore to us the light of joy.

30. The way of God is perfect. The phrase, The way of God, is not here taken for his revealed will, but for his method of dealing towards his people. The meaning, therefore, is, that God never disappoints or deceives his servants, nor forsakes them in the time of need, (as may be the case with men who do not aid their dependants, except in so far as it contributes to their own particular advantage,) but faithfully defends and maintains those whom he has once taken under his protection. But we will never have any nearness to God, unless he first come near to us by his word; and, for this reason, David, after having asserted that God aids his people in good earnest, adds, at the same time, that his word is purified.

31. For who is God besides Jehovah? David here, deriding the foolish inventions of men, who, according to their own fancy, make for themselves tutelary gods, confirms that he never undertook any thing but by the authority and command of God. If he had passed beyond the limits of his calling, he could not with such confidence have said that God was on his side. Besides, although in these words he opposes to the true God all the false gods invented by men, his purpose, at the same time, is to overthrow all the vain hopes in which the world is wrapped up, and by which it is carried about, and prevented from resting in God. The question which David here treats of is not the bare title and name of God, but he declares that whatever assistance we need we should seek it from God, and from no other quarter, because he alone is endued with power:

and poetry, and a contemplative life: He teaches my hands to war, v. 34.

2. God had given him bodily strength to go through the business and fatigue of war: God girded him with strength (v. 32, 39), to such a degree that he could break even a bow of steel, v. 34. What service God designs men for he will be sure to fit them for.

3. God had likewise given him great swiftness, not to flee from the enemies but to fly upon them (v. 33): He makes my feet like hinds' feet, v. 36. "Thou hast enlarged my steps under me; but" (whereas those that take large steps are apt to tread awry) "my feet did not slip." He was so swift that he pursued his enemies and overtook them, v. 37.

4. God had made him very bold and daring in his enterprises, and given him spirit proportionable to his strength. If a troop stood in his way, he made nothing of running through them; if a wall, he made nothing of leaping over it (v. 29); if ramparts and bulwarks, he soon mounted them, and by divine assistance set his feet upon the high places of the enemy, v. 33.

5. God had protected him, and kept him safe, in the midst of the greatest perils. Many a time he put his life in his hand, and yet it was wonderfully preserved: "Thou hast given me the shield of thy salvation (v. 35), and that has compassed me on every side. By that I have been delivered from the strivings of the people who aimed at my destruction (v. 43), particularly from the violent man" (v. 48), that is, Saul, who more than once threw a javelin at him.

6. God had prospered him in his designs; he it was that made his way perfect (v. 32) and it was his right hand that held him up, v. 35.

7. God had given him victory over his enemies, the Philistines, Moabites, Ammonites, and all that fought against Israel: those especially he means, yet not excluding the house of Saul, which opposed his coming to the crown, and the partisans of Absalom and Sheba, who would have deposed him. He enlarges much upon the goodness of God to him in defeating his enemies, attributing his victories, not to his own sword or bow, nor to the velour of his mighty men, but to the favor of God: I pursued them (v. 37), I wounded them (v. 38); for thou hast girded me with strength (v. 39), else I could not have done it. All the praise is ascribed to God: Thou hast subdued them under me, v. 39. Thou hast given me their necks (v. 40), not only to trample upon them (as Josh. x. 24, "And it came to pass, when they brought out those kings unto Joshua, that Joshua called for all the men of Israel, and said unto the captains of the men of war which went with him, Come near, put your feet upon the necks of these kings. And they came near, and put their feet upon the necks of them."), but to cut them off. Even those who hated David whom God loved, and were enemies to the Israel of God, in their distress cried unto the Lord: but in vain; he answered them not. How could they expect he should when it was he whom they fought against? And, when he

Psalm 18

41-45

41 They cried, but there was none to save them: even unto the LORD, but he answered them not.
42 Then did I beat them small as the dust before the wind: I did cast them out as the dirt in the streets.
43 Thou hast delivered me from the strivings of the people; and thou hast made me the head of the heathen: a people whom I have not known shall serve me.
44 As soon as they hear of me, they shall obey me: the strangers shall submit themselves unto me.
45 The strangers shall fade away, and be afraid out of their close places.

Verse 38. The destruction of our spiritual enemies is complete. We may exult over sin, death, and hell, as disarmed and disabled for us by our conquering Lord; may he graciously give them a like defeat within us.
Verses 39 and 40. It is impossible to be too frequent in the duty of ascribing all our victories to the God of our salvation. It is true that we have to wrestle with our spiritual antagonists, but the triumph is far more the Lord's than ours. We must not boast like the ambitious votaries of vainglory, but we may exult as the willing and believing instruments in the Lord's hand of accomplishing his great designs.
Verse 41. "They cried, but there was none to save them; even unto the Lord, but he answered them not." Prayer is so notable a weapon that even the wicked will take to it to in their fits of desperation. Bad men have appealed to God against God's own servants, but all in vain; the kingdom of heaven is not divided, and God never succors his foes at the expense of his friends. There are prayers to God which are no better than blasphemy, which bring no comfortable reply, but rather provoke the Lord to greater wrath.
Verse 42. The defeat of the nations who fought with King David was so utter and complete that they were like powders pounded in a mortar; their power was broken into fragments and they became as weak as dust before the wind, and as mean as the mire of the roads. Thus powerless and base are the enemies of God now become through the victory of the Son of David upon the cross. Arise, O my soul, and meet thine enemies, for they have sustained a deadly blow, and will fall before thy bold advance.
Verse 43. "Thou hast delivered me from the strivings of the people." Internal strife is very hard to deal with. A civil war is war in its most miserable form; it is a subject for warmest gratitude when concord rules within. Our poet praises Jehovah for the union and peace which smiled in his dominions, and if we have peace in the three kingdoms of our spirit, soul, and body, we are in duty bound to give Jehovah a song. Unity in a church should assuredly excite like gratitude. "Thou hast made me the head of the heathen; a people whom I have not known shall serve me." The neighboring nations yielded to the sway of Judah's prince. Oh, when shall all lands adore King Jesus, and serve him with holy joy? Surely there is far more of Jesus than of David here. Missionaries may derive rich encouragement from the positive declaration that heathen lands shall own the Headship of the Crucified.
Verse 44. "As soon as they hear of me, they shall obey me." Thus readily did the once struggling captain become a far-renowned victor, and thus easy shall be our triumphs. We prefer, however, to speak of Jesus. In many cases the gospel is speedily received by hearts apparently unprepared for it. Those who have never heard the gospel before, have been charmed by its first message, and yielded obedience to it; while others, alas! who are accustomed to its joyful sound, are rather hardened than softened by its teachings. The grace of God sometimes runs like fire among the stubble, and a nation is born in a day. "Love at first sight" is no uncommon thing when Jesus is the wooer. He can write Caesar's message without boasting, Veni, vidi, vici; his gospel is in some cases no sooner heard than believed. What inducements to spread abroad the doctrine of the cross!
Verse 45. "The strangers shall fade away." Like sear leaves or blasted trees our foes and Christ's foes shall find no sap and stamina remaining in them. Those who are strangers to Jesus are strangers to all lasting happiness; those must soon fade who refuse to be watered from the river of life. "And be afraid out of their close places." Out of their mountain fastnesses the heathen crept in fear to own allegiance to Israel's king, and even so, from the castles of self-confidence and the dens of carnal security, poor sinners come bending before the Savior, Christ the Lord. Our sins which have entrenched themselves in our flesh and blood as in impregnable forts, shall yet be driven forth by the sanctifying energy of the Holy Spirit, and we shall serve the Lord in singleness of heart.

Who is strong except our God? We should, however, attend to the design of David, which I have first adverted to, namely, that, by confidently representing God as opposed to all his enemies, and as the leader, under whose standard he had valiantly fought against them, he means to affirm that he had attempted nothing according to his own fancy, or with an evil and condemning conscience.

32. It is God who hath girded. This is a metaphor taken either from the belt or girdle of a warrior, or from the reins, in which the Scripture sometimes places a man's vigor or strength. It is, therefore, as if he had said, I, who would otherwise have been feeble and effeminate, have been made strong and courageous by the power of God.

33-36

33. David, having taken many strongholds which, on account of their steep and difficult access, were believed to be impregnable, extols the grace of God in this particular. When he says that God had given him feet like hinds' feet, he means that he had given him unusual swiftness, and such as does not naturally belong to men. The sense, therefore, is, that he had been aided by God in an extraordinary manner, so that like a roe he climbed with amazing speed over inaccessible rocks. He calls the strongholds, which, as conqueror, he had obtained by right of war, his high places; for he could justly boast that he took possession of nothing which belonged to another man, inasmuch as he knew that he had been called to occupy these fortresses by God.

37-40

37. The point on which David insists so much is, that of showing from the effect or issue, that all his victories were to be traced to the favor of God; and from this it follows that his cause was good and just. God, no doubt, sometimes grants successes even to the ungodly and wicked; but he at length shows by the issue, that he was all the while opposed to them and their enemy. It is his servants alone who experience such tokens of his favor as he shewed towards David, and he intends by these to testify that they are approved and accepted by him. We are apt to think that David here speaks too much after the manner of a soldier, in declaring that he will not cease from the work of slaughter until he has destroyed all his enemies; or rather that he has forgotten the gentleness and meekness which ought to shine in all true believers, and in which they should resemble their heavenly Father; but as he attempted nothing without the command of God, and as his affections were governed and regulated by the Holy Spirit, we may be assured that these are not the words of a man who was cruel, and who took pleasure in shedding blood, but of a man who faithfully executed the judgment which God had committed to him. And, indeed, we know that he was so distinguished for gentleness of disposition as to abhor the shedding of even a single drop of blood, except in so far as duty and the necessity of his office required. We must, therefore, take into consideration David's vocation, and also his pure zeal, which was free from all perturbation of the flesh.

disowned them (as he will all those that act against his people), no other succors could stand them in stead: There was none to save them, v. 41. Those whom God has abandoned are easily vanquished: Then did I beat them small as the dust, v. 42. But those whose cause is just he avenges (v. 47), and those whom he favors will certainly be lifted up above those that rise up against them, v. 48.

8. God had raised him to the throne, and not only delivered him and kept him alive, but dignified him and made him great (v. 35): Thy gentleness has increased me—thy discipline and instruction; so some. The good lessons David learned in his affliction prepared him for the dignity and power that were intended him; and the lessening of him helped very much to increase his greatness. God made him not only a great conqueror, but a great ruler: Thou hast made me the head of the heathen (v. 43); all the neighboring nations were tributaries to him.

II. David looks up with humble and reverent adorations of the divine glory and perfection. When God had, by his providence, magnified him, he endeavors, with his praises, to magnify God, to bless him and exalt him, v. 46. He gives honor to him,

1. As a living God: The Lord liveth, v. 46. We had our lives at first from, and we owe the continuance of them to, that God who has life in himself and is therefore fitly called the living God. The gods of the heathen were dead gods. The best friends we have among men are dying friends. But God lives, lives for ever, and will not fail those that trust in him, but, because he lives, they shall live also; for he is their life.

2. As a finishing God: As for God, he is not only perfect himself, but his way is perfect, v. 30. He is known by his name Jehovah: "And I appeared unto Abraham, unto Isaac, and unto Jacob, by the name of God Almighty, but by my name JEHOVAH was I not known to them" (Exod. vi. 3), a God performing and perfecting what he begins in providence as well as creation, Gen. ii. 1. If it was God that made David's way perfect (v. 32), much more is his own way so. There is no flaw in God's works, nor any fault to be found with what he does: "I know that, whatsoever God doeth, it shall be for ever: nothing can be put to it, nor any thing taken from it: and God doeth it, that men should fear before him," Eccl. iii. 14. And what he undertakes he will go through with, whatever difficulties lie in the way; what God begins to build he is able to finish.

3. As a faithful God: The word of the Lord is tried. "I have tried it" (says David), "and it has not failed me." All the saints, in all ages, have tried it, and it never failed any that trusted in it. It is tried as silver is tried, refined from all such mixture and alloy as lessen the value of men's words. David, in God's providences concerning him, takes notice of the performance of his promises to him, which, as it puts sweetness into the providence, so it puts honor upon the promise.

Psalm 18

46-50
46 The LORD liveth; and blessed be my rock; and let the God of my salvation be exalted.
47 It is God that avengeth me, and subdueth the people under me.
48 He delivereth me from mine enemies: yea, thou liftest me up above those that rise up against me: thou hast delivered me from the violent man.
49 Therefore will I give thanks unto thee, O LORD, among the heathen, and sing praises unto thy name.
50 Great deliverance giveth he to his king; and sheweth mercy to his anointed, to David, and to his seed for evermore.

Thus with remembrance of conquests in the past, and with glad anticipations of victories yet to come, the sweet singer closes the description, and returns to exercise of more direct adoration of his gracious God.

Verse 46. "The Lord liveth." Possessing underived, essential, independent and eternal life. We serve no inanimate, imaginary, or dying God. He only hath immortality. Like loyal subjects let us cry, Live on, O God. Long live the King of kings. By thine immortality do we dedicate ourselves afresh to thee. As the Lord our God liveth so would we live to him. "And blessed be my rock." He is the ground of our hope, and let him be the subject of our praise. Our hearts bless the Lord, with holy love extolling him.

Verse 47. "It is God that avengeth me, and subdueth the people under me." To rejoice in personal revenge is unhallowed and evil, but David viewed himself as the instrument of vengeance upon the enemies of God and his people, and had he not rejoiced in the success accorded to him he would have been worthy of censure.

Verse 48. From all enemies, and especially from one who was pre-eminent in violence, the Lord's anointed was preserved, and at the last over the head of Saul and all other adversaries he reigned in honor. The like end awaits every saint, because Jesus who stooped to be lightly esteemed among men is now made to sit far above all principalities and powers.

Verse 49. Paul cites this verse (Romans 15:9): "And that the Gentiles might glorify God for his mercy; as it is written, For this cause I will confess to thee among the Gentiles, and sing unto thy name." This is clear evidence that David's Lord is here, but David is here too, and is to be viewed as an example of a holy soul making its boast in God even in the presence of ungodly men. Who are the despisers of God that we should stop our mouths for them? We will sing to our God whether they like it or no, and force upon them the knowledge of his goodness. Too much politeness to traitors may be treason to our King.

Verse 50. This is the winding up verse into which the writer throws a fullness of expression, indicating the most rapturous delight of gratitude. "Great deliverance." The word "deliverance" is plural, to show the variety and completeness of the salvation; the adjective "great" is well placed if we consider from what, to what, and how we are saved. All this mercy is given to us in our King, the Lord's Anointed, and those are blessed indeed who as his seed may expect mercy to be built up for evermore

The Psalm concludes in the same loving spirit which shone upon its commencement; happy are they who can sing on from love to love, even as the pilgrims marched from strength to strength.

41-45

41. They shall cry, etc. The change of the tense in the verb from the past to the future does not break the continuity of the narration; and, therefore, the words should be explained thus: Although they cried to God, yet their prayers were rejected by him. He pursues the same subject which it was his object to illustrate before, namely, that it was at length manifest from the issue that his enemies falsely boasted of having the support and countenance of God, who showed that he had turned away from them. It is true, that when their affairs continued to go on prosperously, they sometimes received such applause and commendation, that it was commonly believed that God was favorable to them, while, at the same time he seemed to be opposed to David, who although he cried night and day to him, found it of no avail. But after God had sufficiently tried the patience of his servant, he cast them down, and disappointed them of their vain hope; yea, rather he would not deign to hear their prayers. We now perceive the design of David in these words. As the ungodly had long wickedly abused the name of God, by pretending that he favored their unjust proceedings, the Psalmist derides their vain boasting, in which they were completely disappointed.

43. Thou shalt deliver me from the contentions of the people. David states, in a few words, that he had experienced the assistance of God in all variety of ways. He was in great danger from the tumults which sometimes arose among his own subjects, if God had not wonderfully allayed them, and subdued the fierceness of the people.

44. At the simple fame of my name they shall obey me. This is of the same import with the last clause of the preceding verse. Although David, by his victories, had acquired such reputation and renown, that many laid down their arms and came voluntarily to surrender themselves to him; yet, as they also had been subdued through the dread of the power of his arms, which they saw their neighbors had experienced to their smart, it cannot be said, properly speaking, that at the simple fame of the name of David they submitted themselves to him. This applies more truly to the person of Christ, who, by means of his word, subdues the world to himself.

46. Whenever God withdraws the working of his power from before our eyes, the sense and cognizance of the truth, "God liveth," also evanishes from our minds. He is, therefore, said to live, inasmuch as he shows, by evident proofs of his power, that it is he who preserves and upholds the world. And as David had known, by experience, this life of God, he celebrates it with praises and thanksgiving.

47. The God who giveth me vengeance. The Psalmist again attributes to God the victories which he had obtained. As he could never have expected to obtain them unless he had been confident that he would receive the aid of God, so now he acknowledges God to be the sole author of them.

49. Therefore will I praise thee, O Jehovah! In this verse he teaches us that the blessings God had conferred upon him, of which he had spoken, are worthy of being celebrated with extraordinary and unusual praises, that the fame of them might reach even the heathen.

4. As the protector and defender of his people. David had found him so to him: "He is the God of my salvation (v. 46), by whose power and grace I am and hope to be saved; but not of mine only: he is a buckler to all those that trust in him (v. 30); he shelters and protects them all, is both able and ready to do so."

5. As a non—such in all this, v. 31. There is a God, and who is God save Jehovah? That God is a rock, for the support and shelter of his faithful worshippers; and who is a rock save our God? Thus he not only gives glory to God, but encourages his own faith in him.

III. David looks forward, with a believing hope that God would still do him good. He promises himself,

1. That his enemies should be completely subdued, and that those of them that yet remained should be made his footstool,—that his government should be extensive, so that even a people whom he had not known should serve him (v. 43),—that his conquests, and, consequently, his requests, should be easy (As soon as they hear of me they shall obey me, v. 44),—and that his enemies should be convinced that it was to no purpose to oppose him; even those that had retired to their fastnesses should not trust to them, but be afraid out of their close places, having seen so much of David's wisdom, courage, and success. Thus the Son of David, though he sees not yet all things put under him, yet knows he shall reign till all opposing rule, principality, and power shall be quite put down.

2. That his seed should be forever continued in the Messiah, who, he foresaw, should come from his loins, v. 50. He shows mercy to his anointed, his Messiah, to David himself, the anointed of the God of Jacob in the type, and to his seed for evermore. He saith not unto seeds, as of many, but to his seed, as of one, that is Christ: "Now to Abraham and his seed were the promises made. He saith not, And to seeds, as of many; but as of one, And to thy seed, which is Christ. And this I say, that the covenant, that was confirmed before of God in Christ, the law, which was four hundred and thirty years after, cannot disannul, that it should make the promise of none effect. For if the inheritance be of the law, it is no more of promise: but God gave it to Abraham by promise. Wherefore then serveth the law? It was added because of transgressions, till the seed should come to whom the promise was made; and it was ordained by angels in the hand of a mediator." Gal. iii. 16-19. It is he only that shall reign for ever, and of the increase of whose government and peace there shall be no end. Christ is called David: "Afterward shall the children of Israel return, and seek the LORD their God, and David their king; and shall fear the LORD and his goodness in the latter days." Hos. iii. 5. God has called him his king: "Yet have I set my king upon my holy hill of Zion." Ps. ii. 6. Great deliverance God does give, and will give to him, and to his church and people, here called his seed, for evermore.

Psalm 19

Title
To the chief Musician, a Psalm of David.

1-7
1 The heavens declare the glory of God; and the firmament sheweth his handywork.
2 Day unto day uttereth speech, and night unto night sheweth knowledge.
3 There is no speech nor language, where their voice is not heard.
4 Their line is gone out through all the earth, and their words to the end of the world. In them hath he set a tabernacle for the sun,
5 Which is as a bridegroom coming out of his chamber, and rejoiceth as a strong man to run a race.
6 His going forth is from the end of the heaven, and his circuit unto the ends of it: and there is nothing hid from the heat thereof.
7 The law of the LORD is perfect, converting the soul: the testimony of the LORD is sure, making wise the simple.

Psalm 19

SUBJECT. It would be idle to enquire into the particular period when this delightful poem was composed, for their is nothing in its title or subject to assist us in the enquiry. The heading, "To the Chief Musician, a Psalm of David," informs us that David wrote it, and that it was committed to the Master of the service of song in the sanctuary for the use of the assembled worshippers. In his earliest days the psalmist, while keeping his father's flock, had devoted himself to the study of God's two great books—nature and Scripture; and he had so thoroughly entered into the spirit of these two only volumes in his library that he was able with a devout criticism to compare and contrast them, magnifying the excellency of the Author as seen in both. How foolish and wicked are those who instead of accepting the two sacred tomes, and delighting to behold the same divine hand in each, spend all their wits in endeavoring to find discrepancies and contradictions. We may rest assured that the true "Vestiges of Creation" will never contradict Genesis, nor will a correct "Cosmos" be found at variance with the narrative of Moses. He is wisest who reads both the world-book, and the Word-book as two volumes of the same work, and feels concerning them, "My Father wrote them both."
DIVISION. This song very distinctly divides itself into three parts, very well described by the translators in the ordinary heading of our version. The creatures show God's glory, 1-6. The word showeth his grace, 7-11. David prayeth for grace, 12-14. Thus praise and prayer are mingled, and he who here sings the work of God in the world without, pleads for a work of grace in himself within.

EXPOSITION
Verse 1. "The heavens declare the glory of God." The book of nature has three leaves, heaven, earth, and sea, of which heaven is the first and the most glorious, and by its aid we are able to see the beauties of the other two. Any book without its first page would be sadly imperfect, and especially the great Natural Bible, since its first pages, the sun, moon, and stars, supply light to the rest of the volume, and are thus the keys, without which the writing which follows would be dark and undiscerned.
Verse 2. "Day unto day uttereth speech, and night unto night sheweth knowledge." As if one day took up the story where the other left it, and each night passed over the wondrous tale to the next. The original has in it the thought of pouring out or welling over, with speech; as though days and nights were but as a fountain flowing evermore with Jehovah's praise.
Verse 3. "There is no speech nor language, where their voice is not heard." Every man may hear the voices of the stars. Many are the languages of terrestrials, to celestials there is but one, and that one may be understood by every willing mind. The lowest heathen are without excuse, if they do not discover the invisible things of God in the works which he has made. Sun, moon, and stars are God's traveling preachers; they are apostles upon their journey confirming those who regard the Lord, and judges on circuit condemning those who worship idols.
Verse 4. "Their line is gone out through all the earth, and their words to the end of the world." Although the heavenly bodies move in solemn silence, yet in reason's ear they utter precious teachings. They give forth no literal words, but yet their instruction is clear enough to be so described.
Verse 5. "Which is as a bridegroom coming out of his chamber." A bridegroom comes forth sumptuously appareled, his face beaming with a joy which he imparts to all around; such, but with a mighty emphasis, is the rising Sun. "And rejoiceth as a strong man to run a race." As a champion girt for running cheerfully addresses himself to the race, so does the sun speed onward with matchless regularity and unwearying swiftness in his appointed orbit. It is but mere play to him; there are no signs of effort,

JOHN CALVIN

Psalm 19

1-6
1. The heavens declare the glory of God. There is certainly nothing so obscure or contemptible, even in the smallest corners of the earth, in which some marks of the power and wisdom of God may not be seen; but as a more distinct image of him is engraven on the heavens, David has particularly selected them for contemplation, that their splendor might lead us to contemplate all parts of the world. When a man, from beholding and contemplating the heavens, has been brought to acknowledge God, he will learn also to reflect upon and to admire his wisdom and power as displayed on the face of the earth, not only in general, but even in the minutest plants.
2. Day unto day uttereth speech. Philosophers, who have more penetration into those matters than others, understand how the stars are arranged in such beautiful order, that notwithstanding their immense number there is no confusion; but to the ignorant and unlettered, the continual succession of days is a more undoubted proof of the providence of God. David, therefore, having spoken of the heavens, does not here descend from them to other parts of the world; but, from an effect more sensible and nearer our apprehension, he confirms what he has just now said, namely, that the glory of God not only shines, but also resounds in the heavens.
3. There is no language nor speech [where] their voice is not heard. The import of his language is, Different nations differ from each other as to language; but the heavens have a common language to teach all men without distinction, nor is there any thing but their own carelessness to hinder even those who are most strange to each other, and who live in the most distant parts of the world, from profiting, as it were, at the mouth of the same teacher.
4. Their writing has gone forth, etc. Here the inspired writer declares how the heavens preach to all nations indiscriminately, namely, because men, in all countries and in all parts of the earth, may understand that the heavens are set before their eyes as witnesses to bear testimony to the glory of God.

7-9
7. The law of the Lord. Here the second part of the psalm commences. After having shown that the creatures, although they do not speak, nevertheless serve as instructors to all mankind, and teach all men so clearly that there is a God, as to render them inexcusable, the Psalmist now turns towards the Jews, to whom God had communicated a fuller knowledge of himself by means of his word.
While the heavens bear witness concerning God, their testimony does not lead men so far as that thereby they learn truly to fear him, and acquire a well-grounded knowledge of him; it serves only to render them inexcusable.
8. The statutes of Jehovah are right. The Psalmist at first view may seem to utter a mere common-place sentiment when he calls the statutes of the Lord right. If we, however, more attentively consider the contrast which he no doubt makes

MATTHEW HENRY

Psalm 19

1-6 God's glory seen in the creation.
Observe here,
I. What that is which the creatures notify to us. They are in many ways useful and serviceable to us, but in nothing so much as in this, that they declare the glory of God, by showing his handy-works, v. 1. They plainly speak themselves to be God's handy-works; for they could not exist from eternity; all succession and motion must have had a beginning; they could not make themselves, that is a contradiction; they could not be produced by a casual hit of atoms, that is an absurdity, fit rather to be bantered than reasoned with: therefore they must have a Creator, who can be no other than an eternal mind, infinitely wise, powerful, and good.
II. What are some of those things which notify this?
1. The heavens and the firmament—the vast expanse of air and ether, and the spheres of the planets and fixed stars. Man has this advantage above the beasts, in the structure of his body, that whereas they are made to look downwards, as their spirits must go, he is made erect, to look upwards, because upwards his spirit must shortly go and his thoughts should now rise.
2. The constant and regular succession of day and night (v. 2): Day unto day, and night unto night, speak the glory of that God who first divided between the light and the darkness, and has, from the beginning to this day, preserved that established order without variation, according to God's covenant with Noah (Gen. viii. 22), that, while the earth remains, day and night shall not cease, to which covenant of providence the covenant of grace is compared for its stability, Jer. xxxiii. 20; xxxi. 35.
III. To whom this declaration is made of the glory of God. It is made to all parts of the world (v. 3, 4): There is no speech nor language (no nation, for the nations were divided after their tongues, Gen. x. 31, 32) where their voice is not heard. Their line has gone through all the earth (the equinoctial line, suppose) and with it their words to the end of the world, proclaiming the eternal power of God of nature, v. 4.

7-14 The excellency of the scriptures.
Observe here,
I. The psalmist gives an account of the excellent properties and uses of the word of God, in six sentences (v. 7-9), in each of which the name Jehovah is repeated, and no vain repetition, for the law has its authority and all its excellency from the law-maker. Here are six several titles of the word of God, to take in the whole of divine revelation, precepts and promises, and especially the gospel. Here are several good properties of it, which proves its divine original, which recommend it to our affection, and which extol it above all other laws whatsoever. Here are several good effects of the law

Psalm 19

8-14

8 The statutes of the LORD are right, rejoicing the heart: the commandment of the LORD is pure, enlightening the eyes.
9 The fear of the LORD is clean, enduring for ever: the judgments of the LORD are true and righteous altogether.
10 More to be desired are they than gold, yea, than much fine gold: sweeter also than honey and the honeycomb.
11 Moreover by them is thy servant warned: and in keeping of them there is great reward.
12 Who can understand his errors? cleanse thou me from secret faults.
13 Keep back thy servant also from presumptuous sins; let them not have dominion over me: then shall I be upright, and I shall be innocent from the great transgression.
14 Let the words of my mouth, and the meditation of my heart, be acceptable in thy sight, O LORD, my strength, and my redeemer.

flagging, or exhaustion. No other creature yields such joy to the earth as her bridegroom the sun; and none, whether they be horse or eagle, can for an instant compare in swiftness with that heavenly champion.

Verse 6. "His going forth is from the end of the heaven, and his circuit unto the ends of it." He bears his light to the boundaries of the solar heavens, traversing the zodiac with steady motion, denying his light to none who dwell within his range. "And there is nothing hid from the heat thereof." Above, beneath, around, the heat of the sun exercises an influence. The bowels of the earth are stored with the ancient produce of the solar rays, and even yet earth's inmost caverns feel their power. Where light is shut out, yet heat and other more subtle influences find their way.

Verse 7. "The law of the Lord is perfect;" by which he means not merely the law of Moses but the doctrine of God, the whole run and rule of sacred Writ. The doctrine revealed by God he declares to be perfect, and yet David had but a very small part of the Scriptures, and if a fragment, and that the darkest and most historical portion, be perfect, what must the entire volume be? How more than perfect is the book which contains the clearest possible display of divine love, and gives us an open vision of redeeming grace.

Verse 8. "The statutes of the Lord are right." His precepts and decrees are founded in righteousness, and are such as are right or fitted to the right reason of man. As a physician gives the right medicine, and a counselor the right advice, so does the Book of God. "Rejoicing the heart." Mark the progress; he who was converted was next made wise and is now made happy; that truth which makes the heart right then gives joy to the right heart. Free-grace brings heart-joy.

Verse 9. "The fear of the Lord is clean." The doctrine of truth is here described by its spiritual effect, viz., inward piety, or the fear of the Lord; this is clean in itself, and cleanses out the love of sin, sanctifying the heart in which it reigns.

Verse 10. "More to be desired are they than fine gold, yea, than much fine gold." Bible truth is enriching to the soul in the highest degree; the metaphor is one which gathers force as it is brought out; gold—fine gold—much fine gold; it is good, better, best, and therefore it is not only to be desired with a miser's avidity, but with more than that. As spiritual treasure is more noble than mere material wealth, so should it be desired and sought after with greater eagerness.

Verse 11. "Moreover by them is thy servant warned." We are warned by the Word both of our duty, our danger, and our remedy. On the sea of life there would be many more wrecks, if it were not for the divine storm-signals, which give to the watchful a timely warning.

Verse 12. "Who can understand his errors?" A question which is its own answer. It rather requires a note of exclamation than of interrogation. By the law is the knowledge of sin, and in the presence of divine truth, the psalmist marvels at the number and heinousness of his sins.

Verse 13. "Keep back thy servant also from presumptuous sins; let them not have dominion over me." This earnest and humble prayer teaches us that saints may fall into the worst of sins unless restrained by grace, and that therefore they must watch and pray lest they enter into temptation.

Verse 14. "Let the words of my mouth, and the meditation of my heart, be acceptable in thy sight, O Lord, my strength, and my Redeemer." A sweet prayer, and so spiritual that it is almost as commonly used in Christian worship as the apostolic benediction.

between the rectitude of the law and the crooked ways in which men entangle themselves when they follow their own understandings, we will be convinced that this commendation implies more than may at first sight appear. We know how much every man is wedded to himself, and how difficult it is to eradicate from our minds the vain confidence of our own wisdom. It is therefore of great importance to be well convinced of this truth, that a man's life cannot be ordered aright unless it is framed according to the law of God, and that without this he can only wander in labyrinths and crooked bypaths.

9. The fear of Jehovah is clean. By the fear of God we are here to understand the way in which God is to be served; and therefore it is taken in an active sense for the doctrine which prescribes to us the manner in which we ought to fear God.

10-11

10. More to be desired are they than gold. The Psalmist now exalts the law of God both on account of its price and sweetness. This commendation depends on the commendations given in the preceding verses; for the many and great advantages which he has just now enumerated, ought justly to make us account heavenly truth the highest and most excellent treasure, and to despise, when compared with it, all the gold and silver of the world.

11. Moreover, by them is thy servant made circumspect. These words may be extended generally to all the people of God; but they are properly to be understood of David himself, and by them he testifies that he knew well, from his own experience, all that he had stated in the preceding verses respecting the law. No man will ever speak truly and in good earnest of heavenly truth, but he who has it deeply fixed in his own heart.

12-14

12. Who can understand his errors? This exclamation shows us what use we should make of the promises of the law, which have a condition annexed to them. It is this: As soon as they come forth, every man should examine his own life, and compare not only his actions, but also his thoughts, with that perfect rule of righteousness which is laid down in the law.

13. Keep back thy servant also from presumptuous sins. By presumptuous sins he means known and evident transgressions,] accompanied with proud contempt and obstinacy. By the word keep back, he intimates, that such is the natural propensity of the flesh to sin, that even the saints themselves would immediately break forth or rush headlong into it, did not God, by his own guardianship and protection, keep them back.

14. Let the words of my mouth, and the meditation of my heart. David asks still more expressly to be fortified by the grace of God, and thus enabled to live an upright and holy life. The substance of the verse is this: I beseech thee, O God, not only to keep me from breaking forth into the external acts of transgression, but also to frame my tongue and my heart to the obedience of thy law.

upon the minds of men, which show what it is designed for, what use we are to make of it, and how wonderful the efficacy of divine grace is, going along with it, and working by it.

II. He expresses the great value he had for the word of God, and the great advantage he had, and hoped to have, from it, v. 10, 11.

1. See how highly he prized the commandments of God. It is the character of all good people that they prefer their religion and the word of God.

2. See what use he made of the precepts of God's word: By them is thy servant warned. The word of God is a word of warning to the children of men; it warns us of the duty we are to do, the dangers we are to avoid, and the deluge we are to prepare for, Ezek. iii. 17; xxxiii. 7. It warns the wicked not to go on in his wicked way, and warns the righteous not to turn from his good way. All that are indeed God's servants take this warning.

3. See what advantage he promised himself by his obedience to God's precepts: In keeping them there is great reward. Those who make conscience of their duty will not only be no losers by it, but unspeakable gainers. There is a reward, not only after keeping, but in keeping, God's commandments, a present great reward of obedience. Religion is health and honor; it is peace and pleasure; it will make our comforts sweet and our crosses easy, life truly valuable and death itself truly desirable.

III. He draws some good inferences from this pious meditation upon the excellency of the word of God. Such thoughts as these should excite in us devout affections, and they are to good purpose.

1. He takes occasion hence to make a penitent reflection upon his sins; for by the law is the knowledge of sin. "Is the commandment thus holy, just, and good? Then who can understand his errors? I cannot, whoever can."

2. He takes occasion hence to pray against sin. All the discoveries of sin made to us by the law should drive us to the throne of grace, there to pray, as David does here, For grace to help in time of need. Having prayed that his sins of infirmity might be pardoned, he prays that presumptuous sins might be prevented, v. 13. All that truly repent of their sins, and have them pardoned, are in care not to relapse into sin, nor to return again to folly, as appears by their prayers, which concur with David's here.

3. He takes occasion humbly to beg the divine acceptance of those his thoughts, v. 14. Observe the connection of this with what goes before. He prays to God to keep him from sin, and then begs he would accept his performances; for, if we favor our sins, we cannot expect God should favor us or our services, Ps. lxvi. 18. Observe What his services were—the words of his mouth and the meditations of his heart, his holy affections offered up to God.

Psalm 20

Title
To the chief Musician, a Psalm of David.

1-4
1 The LORD hear thee in the day of trouble; the name of the God of Jacob defend thee;
2 Send thee help from the sanctuary, and strengthen thee out of Zion;
3 Remember all thy offerings, and accept thy burnt sacrifice; Selah.
4 Grant thee according to thine own heart, and fulfill all thy counsel.

Psalm 20

SUBJECT. We have before us a National Anthem, fitted to be sung at the outbreak of war, when the monarch was girding on his sword for the fight. If David had not been vexed with wars, we might never have been favored with such psalms as this. There is a needs be for the trials of one saint, that he may yield consolation to others. A happy people here plead for a beloved sovereign, and with loving hearts cry to Jehovah, "God save the King." We gather that this song was intended to be sung in public, not only from the matter of the song, but also from its dedication "To the Chief Musician." We know its author to have been Israel's sweet singer, from the short title, "A Psalm of David." The particular occasion which suggested it, it would be mere folly to conjecture, for Israel was almost always at war in David's day. His sword may have been hacked, but it was never rusted. Kimchi reads the title, concerning David, or, for David, and it is clear that the king is the subject as well as the composer of the song. It needs but a moment's reflection to perceive that this hymn of prayer is prophetical of our Lord Jesus, and is the cry of the ancient church on behalf of her Lord, as she sees him in vision enduring a great fight of afflictions on her behalf. The militant people of God, with the great Captain of salvation at their head, may still in earnest plead that the pleasure of the Lord may prosper in his hand. We shall endeavor to keep to this view of the subject in our brief exposition, but we cannot entirely restrict out remarks to it.
DIVISION. The first four verses are a prayer for the success of the king. Verses 5, 6, and 7 express unwavering confidence in God and his Anointed; verse 8 declares the defeat of the foe, and verse 9 is a concluding appeal to Jehovah.

EXPOSITION
Verse 1. "The Lord hear thee in the day of trouble." All loyal subjects pray for their king, and most certainly citizens of Zion have good cause to pray for the Prince of Peace. In times of conflict loving subjects redouble their pleas, and surely in the sorrows of our Lord his church could not but be in earnest. All the Savior's days were days of trouble, and he also made them days of prayer; the church joins her intercession with her Lord's, and pleads that he may be heard in his cries and tears. The agony in the garden was especially a gloomy hour, but he was heard in that he feared. He knew that his Father heard him always, yet in that troublous hour no reply came until thrice he had fallen on his face in the garden; then sufficient strength was given in answer to prayer, and he rose a victor from the conflict.
Verse 2. "Send thee help from the sanctuary." Out of heaven's sanctuary came the angel to strengthen our Lord, and from the precious remembrance of God's doings in his sanctuary our Lord refreshed himself when on the tree. There is no help like that which is of God's sending, and no deliverance like that which comes out of his sanctuary. The sanctuary to us is the person of our blessed Lord, who was typified by the temple, and is the true sanctuary which God has pitched, and not man: let us fly to the cross for shelter in all times of need and help will be sent to us.
Verse 3. "Remember all thy offerings, and accept thy burnt sacrifice. Selah." Before war kings offered sacrifice, upon the acceptance of which the depended for success; our blessed Lord presented himself as a victim, and was a sweet savor unto the Most High, and then he met and routed the embattled legions of hell. Still does his burnt sacrifice perfume the courts of heaven, and through him the offerings of his people are received as his sacrifices and oblations. We ought in our spiritual conflicts to have an eye to the sacrifice of Jesus, and never venture to war until first the Lord has given us a token for good at the altar of the cross, where faith beholds her bleeding Lord.

Psalm 20

This psalm contains a common prayer of the Church in behalf of the King of Israel, that God would succor him in danger; and in behalf of his kingdom, that God would maintain it in safety, and cause it to prosper: for in the person of David the safety and well-being of the whole community centered. To this there is added a promise, that God will preside over that kingdom of which he was the founder, and so effectually watch over it as to secure its continual preservation.

1-2

1. May Jehovah hear thee, etc. The Holy Spirit, by introducing the people as praying that God would answer the prayers of the king, is to be viewed as at the same time admonishing kings that it is their duty to implore the protection of God in all their affairs. When he says, In the day of trouble, he shows that they will not be exempted from troubles, and he does this that they may not become discouraged, if at any time they should happen to be in circumstances of danger. In short, the faithful, that the body may not be separated from the head, further the king's prayers by their common and united supplications.

The name of God is here put for God himself and not without good reason; for the essence of God being incomprehensible to us, it behoves us to trust in him, in so far as his grace and power are made known to us. From his name, therefore, proceeds confidence in calling upon him.

2. May he send thee help. That is to say, may he succor thee out of mount Sion, where he commanded the ark of the covenant to be placed, and chose for himself a dwelling-place. The weakness of the flesh will not suffer men to soar up to heaven, and, therefore, God comes down to meet them, and by the external means of grace shows that he is near them.

3-5

3. May he remember. I understand the word remember as meaning to have regard to, as it is to be understood in many other places; just as to forget often signifies to neglect, or not to deign to regard, nor even to behold, the object to which it is applied. It is, in short, a prayer that God would actually show that the king's sacrifices were acceptable to him.

5. That we may rejoice in thy salvation. The expression, In thy salvation, may be referred to God as well as to the king; for the salvation which God bestows is often called the salvation of God; but the context requires that it should be rather understood of the king. The people lived "under the shadow of the king," to use the words of Jeremiah, (Lamentations 4:20;) and, therefore, the faithful now testify, that as long as he is safe and in prosperity, they will all be joyful and happy.

6-9

6. Now I know. Here there follows grateful rejoicing, in which the faithful declare that they have experienced the goodness of God in the preservation of the king. To this there is at the

Psalm 20

1-5 Petitions against sin.

Observe here,

I. What it is that they are taught to ask of God for the king.

1. That God would answer his prayers: The Lord hear thee in the day of trouble (v. 1), and the Lord fulfill all thy petitions, v. 5. Note,

(1.) Even the greatest of men may be much in trouble. It was often a day of trouble with David himself, of disappointment and distress, of treading down and of perplexity. Neither the crown on his head nor the grace in his heart would exempt him from the trouble.

(2.) Even the greatest of men must be much in prayer. David, though a man of business, a man of war, was constant to his devotions; though he had prophets, and priests, and many good people among his subjects, to pray for him, he did not think that excused him from praying for himself. Let none expect benefit by the prayers of the church, or of their ministers or friends for them, who are capable of praying for themselves, and yet neglect it. The prayers of others for us must be desired, not to supersede, but to second, our own for ourselves. Happy the people that have praying princes, to whose prayers they may thus say, Amen.

2. That God would protect his person, and preserve his life, in the perils of war: "The name of the God of Jacob defend thee, and set thee out of the reach of thy enemies."

(1.) "Let God by his providence keep thee safe, even the God who preserved Jacob in the days of his trouble." David had mighty men for his guards, but he commits himself, and his people commit him, to the care of the almighty God.

(2.) "Let God by his grace keep thee easy from the fear of evil, Prov. xviii. 10, The name of the Lord is a strong tower, into which the righteous run by faith, and are safe; let David be enabled to shelter himself in that strong tower, as he has done many a time."

3. That God would testify his gracious acceptance of the sacrifices he offered with his prayers, according to the law of that time, before he went out on a dangerous expedition: The Lord remember all thy offerings and accept thy burnt-sacrifices (v. 3), or turn them to ashes; that is, "The Lord give thee the victory and success which thou didst by prayer with sacrifices ask of him, and thereby give as full proof of his acceptance of the sacrifice as ever he did by kindling it with fire from heaven." By this we may now know that God accepts our spiritual sacrifices, if by his Spirit he kindles in our souls a holy fire of pious and divine affection and with that makes our hearts burn within us.

5. That God would crown all his enterprises and noble designs for the public welfare with the desired success (v. 4): The Lord grant thee according to thy own heart. This they might in faith pray for, because

Psalm 20

5-9

5 We will rejoice in thy salvation, and in the name of our God we will set up our banners: the LORD fulfill all thy petitions.
6 Now know I that the LORD saveth his anointed; he will hear him from his holy heaven with the saving strength of his right hand.
7 Some trust in chariots, and some in horses: but we will remember the name of the LORD our God.
8 They are brought down and fallen: but we are risen, and stand upright.
9 Save, LORD: let the king hear us when we call.

Verse 4. "Grant thee according to thine own heart, and fulfill all thy counsel." Christ's desire and counsel were both set upon the salvation of his people; the church of old desired for him good speed in his design, and the church in these latter days, with all her heart desires the complete fulfillment of his purpose. In Christ Jesus sanctified souls may appropriate this verse as a promise; they shall have their desire, and their plans to glorify their Master shall succeed. We may have our own will, when our will is God's will. This was always the case with our Lord, and yet he said, "not as I will, but as thou wilt." What need for submission in our case; if it was necessary to him, how much more for us?

Verse 5. "We will rejoice in thy salvation." In Jesus there is salvation; it is his own, and hence it is called thy salvation; but it is ours to receive and ours to rejoice in. We should fixedly resolve that come what may, we will rejoice in the saving arm of the Lord Jesus. The people in this psalm, before their king went to battle, felt sure of victory, and therefore began to rejoice beforehand; how much more ought we to do this who have seen the victory completely won! Unbelief begins weeping for the funeral before the man is dead; why should not faith commence piping before the dance of victory begins? Buds are beautiful, and promises not yet fulfilled are worthy to be admired.

Verse 6. "Now know I that the Lord saveth his anointed." We live and learn, and what we learn we are not ashamed to acknowledge. He who thinks he knows everything will miss the joy of finding out new truth; he will never be able to cry, "now know I," for he is so wise in his own conceit that he knows all that can be revealed and more. Souls conscious of ignorance shall be taught of the Lord, and rejoice as they learn. Earnest prayer frequently leads to assured confidence.

Verse 7. Contrasts frequently bring out the truth vividly, and here the church sets forth the creature confidences of carnal men in contrast with her reliance upon the Prince Immanuel and the invisible Jehovah. "Some trust in chariots, and some in horses." Chariots and horses make an imposing show, and with their rattling, and dust, and fine caparisons, make so great a figure that vain man is much taken with them; yet the discerning eye of faith sees more in an invisible God than in all these.

"We will remember the name of the Lord our God." "Our God" in covenant, who has chosen us and whom we have chosen; this God is our God. The name of our God is JEHOVAH, and this should never be forgotten; the self-existent, independent, immutable, ever-present, all-filling I AM. Let us adore that matchless name, and never dishonor it by distrust or creature confidence.

Verse 8. How different the end of those whose trusts are different! The enemies of God are uppermost at first, but they ere long are brought down by force, or else fall of their own accord. Their foundation is rotten, and therefore when the time comes it gives way under them; their chariots are burned in the fire, and their horses die of pestilence, and where is their boasted strength? As for those who rest on Jehovah, they are often cast down at the first onset, but an Almighty arm uplifts them, and they joyfully stand upright. The victory of Jesus is the inheritance of his people.

Verse 9. The Psalm is here recapitulated. That Jesus might himself be delivered, and might then, as our King, hear us, is the two-fold desire of the Psalm. The first request is granted, and the second is sure to all the seed; and therefore we may close the Psalm with the hearty shout, "God save the King." "God save King Jesus, and may he soon come to reign."

same time added a doctrine of faith, namely, that God showed by the effect that he put forth his power in maintaining the kingdom of David, because it was founded upon his calling. The meaning is, It appears from certain experience, that God is the guardian of the kingdom which he himself set up, and of which he is the founder. For David is called Messiah, or anointed, that the faithful might be persuaded that he was a lawful and sacred king, whom God had testified, by outward anointing, to be chosen by himself. Thus, then, the faithful ascribe to the grace of God the deliverance which had been wrought for David from the greatest dangers, and at the same time, particularly mention the cause of this to be, that God had determined to protect and defend him who, by his commandment, had been anointed king over his people. They confirm still more clearly their hope, with respect to the future, in the following clause: God will hear him out of heaven I do not translate the verb which is here used into the past tense, but retain the future: for I have no doubt, that from the experience which God had already given them of his goodness, they concluded that it would be hereafter exercised in the continual preservation of the kingdom.

7. Some trust in chariots. I do not restrict this to the enemies of Israel, as is done by other interpreters. I am rather inclined to think that there is here a comparison between the people of God and all the rest of the world. We see how natural it is to almost all men to be the more courageous and confident the more they possess of riches, power and military forces. The people of God, therefore, here protest that they do not place their hope, as is the usual way with men, in their military forces and warlike apparatus, but only in the aid of God. As the Holy Spirit here sets the assistance of God in opposition to human strength, it ought to be particularly noticed, that whenever our minds come to be occupied by carnal confidence, they fall at the same time into a forgetfulness of God. It is impossible for him, who promises himself victory by confiding in his own strength, to have his eyes turned towards God. The inspired writer, therefore, uses the word remember, to show, that when the saints betake themselves to God, they must cast off every thing which would hinder them from placing an exclusive trust in him.

8. They are bowed down. It is probable that there is here pointed out, as it were with the finger, the enemies of Israel, whom God had overthrown, when they regarded no event as less likely to happen. There is contained in the words a tacit contrast between the cruel pride with which they had been lifted up for a time when they audaciously rushed forward to make havoc of all things on the one hand, and the oppression of the people of God on the other.

9. Save, O Jehovah! etc. Some read in one sentence, O Jehovah! save the king; perhaps because they think it wrong to attribute to an earthly king what is proper to God only,—to be called upon, and to hear prayer. But if we turn our eyes towards Christ, as it becomes us to do, we will no longer wonder that what properly belongs to him is attributed in a certain sense to David and his successors, in so far as they were types of Christ.

they knew David was a man after God's own heart, and would design nothing but what was pleasing to him. Those who make it their business to glorify God may expect that God will, in one way or other, gratify them: and those who walk in his counsel may promise themselves that he will fulfill theirs. Thou shalt devise a thing and it shall be established unto thee.

II. What confidence they had of an answer of peace to these petitions for themselves and their good king (v. 5): "We will rejoice in thy salvation. We that are subjects will rejoice in the preservation and prosperity of our prince;" or, rather, "In thy salvation, O God! in thy power and promise to save, will we rejoice; that is it which we depend upon now, and which, in the issue, we shall have occasion greatly to rejoice in." Those that have their eye still upon the salvation of the Lord shall have their hearts filled with the joy of that salvation: In the name of our God will we set up our banners.

6-9 The subject's prayer for the sovereign.

Here is, I. Holy David himself triumphing in the interest he had in the prayers of good people (v. 6): "Now know I (I that pen the psalm know it) that the Lord saveth his anointed, because he hath stirred up the hearts of the seed of Jacob to pray for him." Note, It bodes well to any prince and people, and may justly be taken as a happy presage, when God pours upon them a spirit of prayer.

II. His people triumphing in God and their relation to him, and his revelation of himself to them, by which they distinguish themselves from those that live without God in the world.

1. See the difference between worldly people and godly people, in their confidences, v. 7. The children of this world trust in second causes, and think all is well if those do but smile upon them; they trust in chariots and in horses, and the more of them they can bring into the field the more sure they are of success in their wars; probably David has here an eye to the Syrians, whose forces consisted much of chariots and horsemen, as we find in the history of David's victories over them, 2 Sam. viii. 4; x. 18.

2. See the difference in the issue of their confidences and by that we are to judge of the wisdom of the choice; things are as they prove; see who will be ashamed of their confidence and who not, v. 8. "Those that trusted in their chariots and horses are brought down and fallen, and their chariots and horses were so far from saving them that they helped to sink them, and made them the easier and the richer prey to the conqueror, 2 Sam. viii. 4.

III. They conclude their prayer for the king with a Hosanna, "Save, now, we beseech thee, O Lord!" v. 9. As we read this verse, it may be taken as a prayer that God would not only bless the king, "Save, Lord, give him success," but that he would make him a blessing to them, "Let the king hear us when we call to him for justice and mercy." Those that would have good of their magistrates must thus pray for them.

Psalm 21

Title
To the chief Musician, a Psalm of David.

1-6
1 The king shall joy in thy strength, O LORD; and in thy salvation how greatly shall he rejoice!
2 Thou hast given him his heart's desire, and hast not withholden the request of his lips. Selah.
3 For thou preventest him with the blessings of goodness: thou settest a crown of pure gold on his head.
4 He asked life of thee, and thou gavest it him, even length of days for ever and ever.
5 His glory is great in thy salvation: honor and majesty hast thou laid upon him.
6 For thou hast made him most blessed for ever: thou hast made him exceeding glad with thy countenance.

Psalm 21

SUBJECT. The title gives us but little information; it is simply, To the chief Musician, a Psalm of David. Probably written by David, sung by David, relating to David, and intended by David to refer in its fullest reach of meaning to David's Lord. It is evidently the fit companion of Psalm Twenty, and is in its proper position next to it. Psalm Twenty anticipates what this regards as realized. If we pray to-day for a benefit and receive it, we must, ere the sun goes down, praise God for that mercy, or we deserve to be denied the next time. It has been called David's triumphant song, and we may remember it as The Royal Triumphal Ode. "The king" is most prominent throughout, and we shall read it to true profit if our meditation of him shall be sweet while perusing it. We must crown him with the glory of our salvation; singing of his love, and praising his power, The next psalm will take us to the foot of the cross, this introduces us to the steps of the throne.
DIVISION. The division of the translators will answer every purpose. A thanksgiving for victory, verses 1 to 6. Confidence of further success, verses 7 to 13.

EXPOSITION
Verse 1. "The king shall joy in thy strength, O Lord." Jesus is a Royal Personage. The question, "Art thou a King then?" received a full answer from the Savior's lips: "Thou sayest that I am a King. To this end was I born, and for this purpose came I into the world, that I might bear witness unto the truth." He is not merely a King, but the King; King over minds and hearts, reigning with a dominion of love, before which all other rule is but mere brute force. He was proclaimed King even on the cross, for there, indeed, to the eye of faith, he reigned as on a throne, blessing with more than imperial munificence the needy sons of earth.
Verse 2. "Thou hast given him his heart's desire." That desire he ardently pursued when he was on earth, both by his prayer, his actions, and his suffering; he manifested that his heart longed to redeem his people, and now in heaven he has his desire granted him, for he sees his beloved coming to be with him where he is.
Verse 3. "For thou preventest him with the blessings of goodness." The word prevent formerly signified to precede or go before, and assuredly Jehovah preceded his Son with blessings. Before he died saints were saved by the anticipated merit of his death, before he came believers saw his day and were glad, and he himself had his delights with the sons of men.
Verse 4. "He asked life of thee, and thou gavest it him, even length of days for ever and ever." The first words may suit King David, but the length of days for ever and ever can only refer to the King Messiah.
Verse 5. "His glory is great in thy salvation." Immanuel bears the palm; he once bore the cross. The Father has glorified the Son, so that there is no glory like unto that which surroundeth him.
Verse 6. "For thou hast made him most blessed for ever." He is most blessed in himself, for he is God over all, blessed for ever; but this relates to him as our Mediator, in which capacity blessedness is given to him as a reward.
Verse 7. "For the king trusteth in the Lord." Our Lord, like a true King and leader, was a master in the use of the weapons, and could handle well the shield of faith, for he has set us a brilliant example of unwavering confidence in God. He felt himself safe in his Father's care until his hour was come, he knew that he was always heard in heaven; he committed his cause to him that judgeth right, and in his last moments he committed his spirit into the same hands. The joy expressed in the former verses was the joy of faith, and the victory achieved was due to the same precious grace. A holy confidence in Jehovah is the true mother of victories. This psalm of

Psalm 21

1-3

1. The king will rejoice in thy strength, O Jehovah! David could have given thanks to God in private for the victories and other signal favors which he had received from him; but it was his intention to testify not only that it was God who elevated him to the throne, but also that whatever blessings God had conferred upon him redounded to the public good, and the advantage of all the faithful. In the beginning of the psalm the believing Israelites express their firm persuasion that God, who had created David to be king, had undertaken to defend and maintain him.

2. In the second verse there is pointed out the cause of this joy. The cause was this: that God had heard the prayers of the king, and had liberally granted him whatever he desired. It was important to be known, and that the faithful should have it deeply impressed on their minds, that all David's successes were so many benefits conferred upon him by God, and at the same time testimonies of his lawful calling.

3. For thou wilt prevent him. When it is said, Thou wilt prevent him, the meaning is, that such will be the liberality and promptitude of God, in spontaneously bestowing blessings, that he will not only grant what is asked from him, but, anticipating the requests of the king, will load him with every kind of good things far beyond what he had ever expected. By blessings we are to understand abundance or plenteousness.

4-6

4. He asked life from thee. This verse confirms that this psalm is not to be limited to the person of any one man. David's life, it is true, was prolonged to an advanced period, so that, when he departed from this world, he was an old man, and full of days; but the course of his life was too short to be compared to this length of days, which is said to consist of many ages.

5. His glory is great. By these words the people intimate that their king, through the protection which God afforded him, and the deliverances which he wrought for him, would become more renowned than if he had reigned in peace with the applause of all men, or had been defended by human wealth and human strength, or, finally, had continued invincible by his own power and policy; for thereby it appeared the more clearly that he had only attained to the royal dignity by the favor, conduct, and commandment of God.

6. For thou hast set him to be blessings for ever. We must carefully mark what is said immediately after concerning joy: Thou hast gladdened him with joy before thy countenance. The people not only mean that God did good to the king, seeing he looked upon him with a benignant and fatherly eye, but they also point out the proper cause of this joy, telling us that it proceeded from the knowledge which the king had of his being the object of the Divine favor.

Psalm 21

1-6 The subject's thanksgiving.

David here speaks for himself in the first place, professing that his joy was in God's strength and in his salvation, and not in the strength or success of his armies. He also directs his subjects herein to rejoice with him, and to give God all the glory of the victories he had obtained; and all with an eye to Christ, of whose triumphs over the powers of darkness David's victories were but shadows.

1. They here congratulate the king on his joys and concur with him in them (v. 1): "The king rejoices, he uses to rejoice in thy strength, and so do we; what pleases the king pleases us," 2 Sam. iii. 36. Happy the people the character of whose king it is that he makes God's strength his confidence and God's salvation his joy, that is pleased with all the advancements of God's kingdom and trusts God to bear him out in all he does for the service of it. Our Lord Jesus, in his great undertaking, relied upon help from heaven, and pleased himself with the prospect of that great salvation which he was thereby to work out.

2. They gave God all the praise of those things which were the matter of their king's rejoicing.

(1.) That God had heard his prayers (v. 2): Thou hast given him his heart's desire (and there is no prayer accepted but what is the heart's desire), the very thing they begged of God for him, Ps. xx. 4.

(2.) That God had surprised him with favors, and much outdone his expectations (v. 3): Thou preventest him with the blessings of goodness. All our blessings are blessings of goodness, and are owing, not at all to any merit of ours, but purely and only to God's goodness.

(3.) That God had assured him of the perpetuity of his kingdom, and therein had done more for him than he was able either to ask or think (v. 4): "When he went forth upon a perilous expedition he asked his life of thee, which he then put into his hand, and thou not only gavest him that, but withal gavest him length of days for ever and ever, didst not only prolong his life far beyond his expectation, but didst assure him of a blessed immortality in a future state and of the continuance of his kingdom in the Messiah that should come of his loins."

(4.) That God had advanced him to the highest honor and dignity (v. 5): "His glory is great, far transcending that of all the neighboring princes, in the salvation thou hast wrought for him and by him." The glory which every good man is ambitious of is to see the salvation of the Lord.

(5.) That God had given him the satisfaction of being the channel of all bliss to mankind (v. 6): "Thou hast set him to be blessings for ever" (so the margin reads it), "thou hast made him to be a universal blessing to the world, in whom the families of the earth are, and shall be blessed; and so thou hast made him exceedingly

Psalm 21

7-13

7 For the king trusteth in the LORD, and through the mercy of the most High he shall not be moved.
8 Thine hand shall find out all thine enemies: thy right hand shall find out those that hate thee.
9 Thou shalt make them as a fiery oven in the time of thine anger: the LORD shall swallow them up in his wrath, and the fire shall devour them.
10 Their fruit shalt thou destroy from the earth, and their seed from among the children of men.
11 For they intended evil against thee: they imagined a mischievous device, which they are not able to perform.
12 Therefore shalt thou make them turn their back, when thou shalt make ready thine arrows upon thy strings against the face of them.
13 Be thou exalted, LORD, in thine own strength: so will we sing and praise thy power.

triumph was composed long before our Lord's conflict began, but faith overleaps the boundaries of time.

Verse 8. "Thine hand shall find out all thine enemies: thy right hand shall find out those that hate thee." The destruction of the wicked is a fitting subject for joy to the friends of righteousness; hence here, and in most scriptural songs, it is noted with calm thanksgiving. "Thou hast put down the mighty from their seats," is a note of the same song which sings, "and hast exalted them of low degree." We pity the lost for they are men, but we cannot pity them as enemies of Christ. None can escape from the wrath of the victorious King, nor is it desirable that they should. Without looking for his flying foes he will find them with his hand, for his presence is about and around them. In vain shall any hope for escape, he will find out all, and be able to punish all, and that too with the ease and rapidity which belong to the warrior's right hand.

Verse 9. "Thou shalt make them as a fiery oven in the time of thine anger." They themselves shall be an oven to themselves, and so their own tormentors. Those who burned with anger against thee shall be burned by thine anger. The fire of sin will be followed by the fire of wrath. Even as the smoke of Sodom and Gomorrah went up to heaven, so shall the enemies of the Lord Jesus be utterly and terribly consumed.

Verse 10. "Their fruit shalt thou destroy from the earth." Their life's work shall be a failure, and the result of their toil shall be disappointment. That in which they prided themselves shall be forgotten; their very names shall be wiped out as abominable, "and their seed from among the children of men." Their posterity following in their footsteps shall meet with a similar overthrow, till at last the race shall come to an end. Doubtless the blessing of God is often handed down by the righteous to their sons, as almost a heirloom in the family, while the dying sinner bequeaths a curse to his descendants. If men will hate the Son of God, they must not wonder if their own sons meet with no favor.

Verse 11. "For they intended evil against thee." God takes notice of intentions. He who would but could not is as guilty as he who did. Christ's church and cause are not only attacked by those who do not understand it, but there are many who have the light and yet hate it. Intentional evil has a virus in it which is not found in sins of ignorance; now as ungodly men with malice aforethought attack the gospel of Christ, their crime is great, and their punishment will be proportionate.

Verse 12. "Therefore shalt thou make them turn their back, when thou shalt make ready thine arrows upon thy strings against the face of them." For a time the foes of God may make bold advances, and threaten to overthrow everything, but a few ticks of the clock will alter the face of their affairs. At first they advance impudently enough, but Jehovah meets them to their teeth, and a taste of the sharp judgment of God speedily makes them flee in dismay. The original has in it the thought of the wicked being set as a butt for God to shoot at, a target for his wrath to aim at.

Verse 13. "Be thou exalted, Lord, in thine own strength." A sweet concluding verse. Our hearts shall join in it. It is always right to praise the Lord when we call to remembrance his goodness to his Son, and the overthrow of his foes. The exaltation of the name of God should be the business of every Christian; but since such poor things as we fail to honor him as he deserves, we may invoke his own power to aid us. Be high, O God, but do thou maintain thy loftiness by thine own almightiness, for no other power can worthily do it.

7-10
7. For the king trusteth. Here again the pious Israelites glory that their king shall be established, because he relies upon God; and they express at the same time how he relies upon him, namely, by hope or trust. The cause or the ground of this hope or trust is at the same time expressed, and it is this, that God mercifully cherishes his own people, whom he has once graciously received into his favor.
8. Thy hand shall find. Hitherto the internal happiness of the kingdom has been described. Now there follows, as it was necessary there should, the celebration of its invincible strength against its enemies. What is said in this verse is of the same import as if the king had been pronounced victorious over all his enemies.
9. Thou shalt put them as it were into a furnace of fire. The Psalmist here describes a dreadful kind of vengeance, from which we gather, that he does not speak of every kind of enemies in general, but of the malicious and frantic despisers of God, who, after the manner of the giants of old, rise up against his only begotten Son. The very severity of the punishment shows the greatness of the wickedness.
The expression, In the time of thy wrath, admonishes us that we ought patiently to bear the cross as long as it shall please the Lord to exercise and humble us under it. If, therefore, he does not immediately put forth his power to destroy the ungodly, let us learn to extend our hope to the time which our heavenly Father has appointed in his eternal purpose for the execution of his judgment, and when our King, armed with his terrible power, will come forth to execute vengeance.
10. Thou shalt destroy their fruit from the earth. David amplifies the greatness of God's wrath, from the circumstance that it shall extend even to the children of the wicked. It is a doctrine common enough in Scripture, that God not only inflicts punishment upon the first originators of wickedness, but makes it even to overflow into the bosom of their children.

11-13
11. For they have spread out. In this verse David shows that the ungodly had deserved the awful ruin which he predicted would befall them, since they had not only molested mortal man, but had also rushed forth in the fury of their pride to make war against God himself.
12. For thou wilt set them as a butt. The great object which the Psalmist has in view is doubtless to teach us to exercise patience, until God, at the fit time, bring the ungodly to their end.
13. Raise thyself, O Jehovah! The psalm is at length concluded with a prayer, which again confirms that the kingdom which is spoken of is so connected with the glory of God, that his power is reflected from it. This was no doubt true with respect to the kingdom of David; for God in old time displayed his power in exalting him to the throne. But what is here stated was only fully accomplished in Christ, who was appointed by the heavenly Father to be King over us, and who is at the same time God manifest in the flesh.

glad with the countenance thou hast given to his undertaking and to him in the prosecution of it."

7-13 The subject's hope.
The psalmist, having taught his people to look back with joy and praise on what God had done for him and them, here teaches them to look forward with faith, and hope, and prayer, upon what God would further do for them: The king rejoices in God (v. 1), and therefore we will be thankful; the king trusteth in God (v. 7), therefore will we be encouraged.
I. They are confident of the stability of David's kingdom. Through the mercy of the Most High, and not through his own merit or strength, he shall not be moved.
II. They are confident of the destruction of all the impenitent implacable enemies of David's kingdom. The success with which God had blessed David's arms hitherto was an earnest of the rest which God would give him from all his enemies round about, and a type of the total overthrow of all Christ's enemies who would not have him to reign over them. Observe,
1. The description of his enemies. They are such as hate him, v. 8. They hated David because God had set him apart for himself, hated Christ because they hated the light; but both were hated without any just cause, and in both God was hated, John xv. 23, 25.
2. The designs of his enemies (v. 11): They intended evil against thee, and imagined a mischievous device; they pretended to fight against David only, but their enmity was against God himself.
3. The disappointment of them: "They devise what they are not able to perform," v. 11. Their malice is impotent, and they imagine a vain thing, Ps. ii. 1.
4. The discovery of them (v. 8): "Thy hand shall find them out. Though ever so artfully disguised by the pretences and professions of friendship, though mingled with the faithful subjects of this kingdom and hardly to be distinguished from them, though flying from justice and absconding in their close places, yet thy hand shall find them out wherever they are."
5. The destruction of them; it will be an utter destruction (Luke xix. 27); they shall be swallowed up and devoured, v. 9. Hell, the portion of all Christ's enemies, is the complete misery both of body and soul. Their fruit and their seed shall be destroyed, v. 10. The enemies of God's kingdom, in every age, shall fall under the same doom, and the whole generation of them will at last be rooted out, and all opposing rule, principality, and power, shall be put down. The arrows of God's wrath shall confound them and put them to flight, being leveled at the face of them, v. 12. That will be the lot of daring enemies that face God. The fire of God's wrath will consume them (v. 9).
III. In this confidence they beg of God that he would still appear for his anointed (v. 13), that he would act for him in his own strength, by the immediate operations of his power as Lord of hosts. Hereby he would exalt himself and glorify his own name.

Psalm 22

Title
To the chief Musician upon Aijeleth Shahar. A Psalm of David.

1-8
1 My God, my God, why hast thou forsaken me? why art thou so far from helping me, and from the words of my roaring?
2 O my God, I cry in the day time, but thou hearest not; and in the night season, and am not silent.
3 But thou art holy, O thou that inhabitest the praises of Israel.
4 Our fathers trusted in thee: they trusted, and thou didst deliver them.
5 They cried unto thee, and were delivered: they trusted in thee, and were not confounded.
6 But I am a worm, and no man; a reproach of men, and despised of the people.
7 All they that see me laugh me to scorn: they shoot out the lip, they shake the head, saying,
8 He trusted on the LORD that he would deliver him: let him deliver him, seeing he delighted in him.

Psalm 22

TITLE. "To the chief Musician upon Aijeleth Shahar. A Psalm of David." This ode of singular excellence was committed to the most excellent of the temple songsters; the chief among ten thousand is worthy to be extolled by the chief Musician; no meaner singer must have charge of such a strain; we must see to it that we call up our best abilities when Jesus is the theme of praise. The words Aijeleth Shahar are enigmatical, and their meaning is uncertain; some refer them to a musical instrument used upon mournful occasions, but the majority adhere to the translation of our margin, "Concerning the kind of the morning." This last interpretation is the subject of much enquiry and conjecture. Our Lord Jesus is so often compared to a hind, and his cruel huntings are so pathetically described in this most affecting psalm, that we cannot but believe that the title indicates the Lord Jesus under a well-known poetical metaphor; at any rate, Jesus is the Hind of the morning concerning whom David here sings.
SUBJECT. This is beyond all others THE PSALM OF THE CROSS. It may have been actually repeated word by word by our Lord when hanging on the tree; it would be too bold to say that it was so, but even a casual reader may see that it might have been. It begins with, "My God, my God, why hast thou forsaken me?" and ends, according to some, in the original with "It is finished." For plaintive expressions uprising from unutterable depths of woe we may say of this psalm, "there is none like it." It is the photograph of our Lord's saddest hours, the record of his dying words, the lachrymatory of his last tears, the memorial of his expiring joys. David and his afflictions may be here in a very modified sense, but, as the star is concealed by the light of the sun, he who sees Jesus will probably neither see nor care to see David. Before us we have a description both of the darkness and of the glory of the cross, the sufferings of Christ and the glory which shall follow. Oh for grace to draw near and see this great sight! We should read reverently, putting off our shoes from off our feet, as Moses did at the burning bush, for if there be holy ground anywhere in Scripture it is in this psalm.
DIVISION. From the commencement to the twenty-first verse is a most pitiful cry for help, and from verse 21 to 31 is a most precious foretaste of deliverance. The first division may be subdivided at the tenth verse, from verse 1 to 10 being an appeal based upon covenant relationship; and from verse 10 to 21 being an equally earnest plea derived from the imminence of his peril.
EXPOSITION
Verse 1. "My God, my God, why hast thou forsaken me?" This was the startling cry of Golgotha: Eloi, Eloi, lama sabacthani. The Jews mocked, but the angels adored when Jesus cried this exceeding bitter cry. Nailed to the tree we behold our great Redeemer in extremities, and what see we? Having ears to hear let us hear, and having eyes to see let us see! Let us gaze with holy wonder, and mark the flashes of light amid the awful darkness of that midday-midnight. Our Lord keeps his hold upon his God with both hands and cries twice, "My God, my God!" The spirit of adoption was strong within the suffering Son of Man, and he felt no doubt about his interest in his God.
Verse 2. "O my God, I cry in the daytime, but thou hearest not." For our prayers to appear to be unheard is no new trial, Jesus felt it before us, and it is observable that he still held fast his believing hold on God, and cried still, "My God."
Verse 3. "But thou art holy, O thou that inhabitest the praises of Israel." However ill things may look, there is no ill in thee, O God! We are very apt to think and speak hardly of God when we are under his afflicting hand, but not so the obedient Son. He knows too well his Father's goodness to let outward circumstances libel his character. There in no unrighteousness with the God of Jacob, he deserves no censure; let him do what he will, he

JOHN CALVIN

Psalm 22

1-2

1. My God! The first verse contains two remarkable sentences, which, although apparently contrary to each other, are yet ever entering into the minds of the godly together. When the Psalmist speaks of being forsaken and cast off by God, it seems to be the complaint of a man in despair; for can a man have a single spark of faith remaining in him, when he believes that there is no longer any succor for him in God? And yet, in calling God twice his own God, and depositing his groanings into his bosom, he makes a very distinct confession of his faith. With this inward conflict the godly must necessarily be exercised whenever God withdraws from them the tokens of his favor, so that, in whatever direction they turn their eyes, they see nothing but the darkness of night.

As our Savior Jesus Christ, when hanging on the cross, and when ready to yield up his soul into the hands of God his Father, made use of these very words, (Matthew 27:46,) we must consider how these two things can agree, that Christ was the only begotten Son of God, and that yet he was so penetrated with grief, seized with so great mental trouble, as to cry out that God his Father had forsaken him. As he became our representative, and took upon him our sins, it was certainly necessary that he should appear before the judgment-seat of God as a sinner. From this proceeded the terror and dread which constrained him to pray for deliverance from death; not that it was so grievous to him merely to depart from this life; but because there was before his eyes the curse of God, to which all who are sinners are exposed.

2. O my God! I cry in the day-time. In this verse the Psalmist expresses the long continuance of his affliction, which increased his disquietude and weariness. It was a temptation even still more grievous, that his crying seemed only to be lost labor; for, as our only means of relief under our calamities is in calling upon God, if we derive no advantage from our prayers, what other remedy remains for us?

3-8

3. Yet thou art holy. The subject here treated is not what God is in heaven, but what he has shown himself to be towards men. He, therefore, not only meant to ask how it was that God, who had always dealt mercifully with his people, should now, forgetting as it were his own nature, thus leave a miserable man without any succor or solace; but he also takes a shield with which to defend himself against the fiery darts of Satan. He calls God holy, because he continues always like himself.

4. Our fathers trusted in thee. Here the Psalmist assigns the reason why God sitteth amidst the praises of the tribes of Israel. The reason is, because his hand had been always stretched forth to preserve his faithful people.

In short, to show that this confidence was neither cold nor dead, David tells us, at the same time, that they cried unto God. He who pretends that he trusts in God, and yet is so listless and indifferent under his calamities that he does not implore his aid, lies shamefully. By prayer, then, true faith is

MATTHEW HENRY

Psalm 22

1-10 Sorrowful complaints.

In these verses we have,

I. A sad complaint of God's withdrawings, v. 1, 2.

1. This may be applied to David, or any other child of God, in the want of the tokens of his favor, pressed with the burden of his displeasure, roaring under it, as one overwhelmed with grief and terror, crying earnestly for relief, and, in this case, apprehending himself forsaken of God, unhelped, unheard, yet calling him, again and again, "My God," and continuing to cry day and night to him and earnestly desiring his gracious returns.

2. But is must be applied to Christ: for, in the first words of this complaint, he poured out his soul before God when he was upon the cross (Matt. xxvii. 46); probably he proceeded to the following words, and, some think, repeated the whole psalm, if not aloud (because they caviled at the first words), yet to himself.

II. Encouragement taken, in reference hereunto, v. 3-5. Though God did not hear him, did not help him, yet,

1. He will think well of God: "But thou art holy, not unjust, untrue, nor unkind, in any of thy dispensations. Though thou dost not immediately come in to the relief of thy afflicted people, yet thou lovest them, art true to thy covenant with them, and dost not countenance the iniquity of their persecutors, Hab. i. 13. And, as thou art infinitely pure and upright thyself, so thou delightest in the services of thy upright people: Thou inhabitest the praises of Israel; thou art pleased to manifest thy glory, and grace, and special presence with thy people, in the sanctuary, where they attend thee with their praises. There thou art always ready to receive their homage, and of the tabernacle of meeting thou hast said, This is my rest for ever."

2. He will take comfort from the experiences which the saints in former ages had of the benefit of faith and prayer (v. 4, 5): "Our fathers trusted in thee, cried unto thee, and thou didst deliver them; therefore thou wilt, in due time, deliver me, for never any that hoped in thee were made ashamed of their hope, never any that sought thee sought thee in vain. And thou art still the same in thyself and the same to thy people that ever thou wast. They were our fathers, and thy people are beloved for the fathers' sake," Rom. xi. 28.

III. The complaint renewed of another grievance, and that is the contempt and reproach of men. This complaint is by no means so bitter as that before of God's withdrawings; but, as that touches a gracious soul, so this a generous soul, in a very tender part, v. 6-8. Our fathers were honored, the patriarchs in their day, first or last, appeared great in the eye of the world, Abraham, Moses, David; but Christ is a worm, and no man. It was great condescension that he became man, a step downwards, which is, and will be, the wonder of angels; yet, as if it were too much,

Psalm 22

9-16

9 But thou art he that took me out of the womb: thou didst make me hope when I was upon my mother's breasts.
10 I was cast upon thee from the womb: thou art my God from my mother's belly.
11 Be not far from me; for trouble is near; for there is none to help.
12 Many bulls have compassed me: strong bulls of Bashan have beset me round.
13 They gaped upon me with their mouths, as a ravening and a roaring lion.
14 I am poured out like water, and all my bones are out of joint: my heart is like wax; it is melted in the midst of my bowels.
15 My strength is dried up like a potsherd; and my tongue cleaveth to my jaws; and thou hast brought me into the dust of death.
16 For dogs have compassed me: the assembly of the wicked have enclosed me: they pierced my hands and my feet.

is to be praised, and to reign enthroned amid the songs of his chosen people.

Verse 4. "Our fathers trusted in thee: they trusted, and thou didst deliver them." This is the rule of life with all the chosen family. Three times over is it mentioned, they trusted, and trusted, and trusted, and never left off trusting, for it was their very life; and they fared well too, for thou didst deliver them.

Verse 5. "They cried unto thee, and were delivered: they trusted in thee, and were not confounded." As if he had said, "How is it that I am now left without succor in my overwhelming griefs, while all others have been helped? We may remind the Lord of his former lovingkindnesses to his people, and beseech him to be still the same. This is true wrestling; let us learn the art.

Verse 6. "But I am a worm, and no man." This verse is a miracle in language. How could the Lord of glory be brought to such abasement as to be not only lower than the angels, but even lower than men. What a contrast between "I AM" and "I am a worm"! yet such a double nature was found in the person of our Lord Jesus when bleeding upon the tree. He felt himself to be comparable to a helpless, powerless, down-trodden worm, passive while crushed, and unnoticed and despised by those who trod upon him.

Verse 7. "All they that see me laugh me to scorn." Read the evangelistic narrative of the ridicule endured by the Crucified One, and then consider, in the light of this expression, how it grieved him. The iron entered into his soul.

Verse 8. "Saying, He trusted on the Lord that he would deliver him: let him deliver him, seeing he delighted in him." Here the taunt is cruelly aimed at the sufferer's faith in God, which is the tenderest point in a good man's soul, the very apple of his eye.

Verse 9. "But thou art he that took me out of the womb." Kindly providence attends with the surgery of tenderness at every human birth; but the Son of Man, who was marvelously begotten of the Holy Ghost, was in an especial manner watched over by the Lord when brought forth by Mary.

Verse 10. "I was cast upon thee from the womb." Into the Almighty arms he was first received, as into those of a loving parent. This is a sweet thought. God begins his care over us from the earliest hour. We are dandled upon the knee of mercy, and cherished in the lap of goodness; our cradle is canopied by divine love, and our first totterings are guided by his care. "Thou art my God from my mother's belly." The psalm begins with "My God, my God," and here, not only is the claim repeated, but its early date is urged. Oh noble perseverance of faith, thus to continue pleading with holy ingenuity of argument! Our birth was our weakest and most perilous period of existence; if we were then secured by Omnipotent tenderness, surely we have no cause to suspect that divine goodness will fail us now. He who was our God when we left our mother, will be with us till we return to mother earth, and will keep us from perishing in the belly of hell.

Verses 11-21. The crucified Son of David continues to pour out his complaint and prayer. We need much grace that while reading we may have fellowship with his sufferings. May the blessed Spirit conduct us into a most clear and affecting sight of our Redeemer's woes.

Verse 11. "Be not far from me." This is the petition for which he has been using such varied and powerful pleas. His great woe was that God had forsaken him, his great prayer is that he would be near him. A lively sense of the divine presence is a mighty stay to the heart in times of distress. "For trouble is near; for there is none to help." There are two "fors," as though faith gave a double knock at mercy's gate; that is a powerful prayer which is full of holy reasons and thoughtful arguments.

Verse 12. "Many bulls have compassed me: strong bulls of Bashan have beset me round." The mighty ones in the crowd are here marked by the tearful eye of their victim. The priests, elders, scribes, Pharisees, rulers, and captains bellowed round the cross like wild cattle, fed in the fat and

JOHN CALVIN

known, as the goodness of a tree is known by its fruit. It ought also to be observed, that God regards no other prayers as right but those which proceed from faith, and are accompanied with it. It is therefore not without good reason that David has put the word cried in the middle between these words, They trusted in thee, they trusted, in the fourth verse, and these words, They trusted in thee, in the fifth verse.

6. But I am a worm, and not a man. David does not murmur against God as if God had dealt hardly with him; but in bewailing his condition, he says, in order the more effectually to induce God to show him mercy, that he is not accounted so much as a man. This, it is true, seems at first sight to have a tendency to discourage the mind, or rather to destroy faith; but it will appear more clearly from the sequel, that so far from this being the case, David declares how miserable his condition is, that by this means he may encourage himself in the hope of obtaining relief.

7. All those who see me mock at me. This is an explanation of the preceding sentence. He had said that he was an object of scorn to the lowest of men, and, as it were, to the refuse of the people. He now informs us of the ignominy with which he had been treated,—that not content with opprobrious language, they also showed their insolence by their very gesture, both by shooting out their lips, and by shaking their heads.

9-11

9. Surely thou. David again here raises a new fortress, in order to withstand and repel the machinations of Satan. He briefly enumerates the benefits which God had bestowed upon him, by which he had long since learned that he was his father. Yea, he declares that even before he was born God had shown towards him such evidence of his fatherly love, that although now overwhelmed with the darkness of death, he might upon good ground venture to hope for life from him. And it is the Holy Spirit who teaches the faithful the wisdom to collect together, when they are brought into circumstances of fear and trouble, the evidences of the goodness of God, in order thereby to sustain and strengthen their faith.

11. Depart not far from me. Here he employs another argument to induce God to show him mercy, alleging that he is sorely pressed and hemmed in by the greatest distress. He doubtless set before his eyes the office which the Scriptures every where attribute to God of succoring the miserable, and of being the more ready to help us the more we are afflicted.

12-16

12. Strong bulls have encompassed me. The Psalmist now complains of the cruelty and barbarous rage of his enemies; and he compares them first to bulls, secondly to lions, and thirdly to dogs. When the anger of bulls is kindled, we know how fierce and terrible they are. The lion, also, is a cruel beast, and dreadful to mankind. And the eager and fierce boldness with which dogs, when once they are irritated, rush upon a man to do him injury, is well known. In short, David's enemies were so blood-thirsty and cruel, that they more resembled wild beasts than men.

MATTHEW HENRY

too great, to be a man, he becomes a worm, and no man. See what abuses were put upon him.

1. He was reproached as a bad man, as a blasphemer, a sabbath-breaker, a wine-bibber, a false prophet, an enemy to Cæsar, a confederate with the prince of the devils.

2. He was despised of the people as a mean contemptible man, not worth taking notice of, his country in no repute, his relations poor mechanics, his followers none of the rulers, or the Pharisees, but the mob.

3. He was ridiculed as a foolish man, and one that not only deceived others, but himself too. Those that saw him hanging on the cross laughed him to scorn. So far were they from pitying him, or concerning themselves for him, that they added to his afflictions, with all the gestures and expressions of insolence upbraiding him with his fall. They make mouths at him, make merry over him, and make a jest of his sufferings: They shoot out the lip, they shake their head, saying, This was he that said he trusted God would deliver him; now let him deliver him. David was sometimes taunted for his confidence in God; but in the sufferings of Christ this was literally and exactly fulfilled. Those very gestures were used by those that reviled him (Matt. xxvii. 39); they wagged their heads, nay, and so far did their malice make them forget themselves that they used the very words (v. 43), He trusted in God; let him deliver him. Our Lord Jesus, having undertaken to satisfy for the dishonor we had done to God by our sins, did it by submitting to the lowest possible instance of ignominy and disgrace.

IV. Encouragement taken as to this also (v. 9, 10): Men despise me, but thou art he that took me out of the womb. David and other good men have often, for direction to us, encouraged themselves with this, that God was not only the God of their fathers, as before (v. 4), but the God of their infancy, who began by times to take care of them, as soon as they had a being, and therefore, they hope, will never cast them off. He that did so well for us in that helpless useless state will not leave us when he has reared us and nursed us up into some capacity of serving him.

11-21 The sufferings of the Messiah; the Messiah supported in His sufferings.

In these verses we have Christ suffering and Christ praying, by which we are directed to look for crosses and to look up to God under them.

I. Here is Christ suffering. David indeed was often in trouble, and beset with enemies; but many of the particulars here specified are such as were never true of David, and therefore must be appropriated to Christ in the depth of his humiliation.

1. He is here deserted by his friends: Trouble and distress are near, and there is none to help, none to uphold, v. 11. He trod the wine-press alone; for all his disciples forsook him and fled. It is God's honor to help when all other helps and succors fail.

Psalm 22

17-24

17 I may tell all my bones: they look and stare upon me.
18 They part my garments among them, and cast lots upon my vesture.
19 But be not thou far from me, O LORD: O my strength, haste thee to help me.
20 Deliver my soul from the sword; my darling from the power of the dog.
21 Save me from the lion's mouth: for thou hast heard me from the horns of the unicorns.
22 I will declare thy name unto my brethren: in the midst of the congregation will I praise thee.
23 Ye that fear the LORD, praise him; all ye the seed of Jacob, glorify him; and fear him, all ye the seed of Israel.
24 For he hath not despised nor abhorred the affliction of the afflicted; neither hath he hid his face from him; but when he cried unto him, he heard.

solitary pastures of Bashan, full of strength and fury; they stamped and foamed around the innocent One, and longed to gore him to death with their cruelties.

Verse 13. "They gaped upon me with their mouths, as a ravening and a roaring lion." Like hungry cannibals they opened their blasphemous mouths as if they were about to swallow the man whom they abhorred. They could not vomit forth their anger fast enough through the ordinary aperture of their mouths, and therefore set the doors of their lips wide open like those who gape.

Verse 14. Turning from his enemies, our Lord describes his own personal condition in language which should bring the tears into every loving eye. "I am poured out like water." He was utterly spent, like water poured upon the earth; his heart failed him, and had no more firmness in it than running water, and his whole being was made a sacrifice, like a libation poured out before the Lord.

Verse 15. "My strength is dried up like a potsherd." Most complete debility is here portrayed; Jesus likens himself to a broken piece of earthenware, or an earthen pot, baked in the fire till the last particle of moisture is driven out of the clay. No doubt a high degree of feverish burning afflicted the body of our Lord. All his strength was dried up in the tremendous flames of avenging justice, even as the paschal lamb was roasted in the fire.

Verse 16. We are to understand every item of this sad description as being urged by the Lord Jesus as a plea for divine help; and this will give us a high idea of his perseverance in prayer. "For dogs have compassed me." Here he marks the more ignoble crowd, who, while less strong than their brutal leaders, were not less ferocious, for there they were howling and barking like unclean and hungry dogs.

Verse 17. So emaciated was Jesus by his fastings and sufferings that he says, "I may tell all my bones." He could count and recount them. The posture of the body on the cross, Bishop Horne thinks, would so distend the flesh and skin as to make the bones visible, so that they might be numbered.

Verse 18. "They part my garments among them, and cast lots upon my vesture." The garments of the executed were the perquisites of the executioners in most cases, but it was not often that they cast lots at the division of the spoil; this incident shows how clearly David in vision saw the day of Christ, and how surely the Man of Nazareth is he of whom the prophets spake: "these things, therefore, the soldiers did." He who gave his blood to cleanse us gave his garments to clothe us. As Ness says, "this precious Lamb of God gave up his golden fleece for us."

Verse 19. "But be thou not far from me, O Lord." Invincible faith returns to the charge, and uses the same means, viz., importunate prayer. He repeats the petition so piteously offered before. He wants nothing but his God, even in his lowest state. He does not ask for the most comfortable or nearest presence of God, he will be content if he is not far from him; humble requests speed at the throne.

Verse 20. "Deliver my soul from the sword." By the sword is probably meant entire destruction, which as a man he dreaded; or perhaps he sought deliverance from the enemies around him, who were like a sharp and deadly sword to him. The Lord had said, "Awake, O sword," and now from the terror of that sword the Shepherd would fain be delivered as soon as justice should see fit.

Verse 21. "Save me from the lion's mouth: for thou hast heard me from the horns of the unicorns." Having experienced deliverance in the past from great enemies, who were strong as the unicorns, the Redeemer utters his last cry for rescue from death, which is fierce and mighty as the lion. This prayer was heard, and the gloom of the cross departed.

Verses 22-31. The transition is very marked; from a horrible tempest all is changed into calm. The darkness of Calvary at length passed away from

JOHN CALVIN

14. I am poured out like water. Hitherto he has informed us that being surrounded by wild beasts, he was not far from death, as if he had been at the point of being devoured every moment. He now bewails, in addition to this, his inward distress; from which we learn that he was not stupid or insensible in dangers.
15. My strength is dried up. He means the vigor which is imparted to us by the radical moisture, as physicians call it. What he adds in the next clause, My tongue cleaveth to my jaws, is of the same import. We know that excessive grief not only consumes the vital spirits, but also dries up almost all the moisture which is in our bodies. He next declares, that in consequence of this, he was adjudged or devoted to the grave: Thou hast brought me to the dust of death. By this he intimates, that all hope of life was taken from him; and in this sense Paul also says, (2 Corinthians 1:9,) that "he had received the sentence of death in himself." But David here speaks of himself in hyperbolical language, and he does this in order to lead us beyond himself to Christ.

17-21
17. David complains that his body was so lean and wasted, that the bones appeared protruding from all parts of it; for he adds immediately after, that his enemies took pleasure in seeing him in so pitiable a condition. The cruelty of his enemies was so insatiable, that beholding a wretched man wasted with grief, and as it were pining away, they took pleasure in feeding their eyes with so sad a spectacle.
18. What follows in the next verse concerning his garments is metaphorical. It is as if he had said, that all his goods were become a prey to his enemies, even as conquerors are accustomed to plunder the vanquished, or to divide the spoil among themselves, by casting lots to determine the share which belongs to each.
19. Be not thou, then, far from me, O Jehovah! We must keep in mind all that David has hitherto related concerning himself. As his miseries had reached the utmost height, and as he saw not even a single ray of hope to encourage him to expect deliverance, it is a wonderful instance of the power of faith, that he not only endured his afflictions patiently, but that from the abyss of despair he arose to call upon God.
21. When it is said in the end of the 21st verse, Answer me, or, Hear me from the horns of the unicorns, this Hebrew manner of speaking may seem strange and obscure to our ears, but the sense is not at all ambiguous. The cause is only put instead of the effect; for our deliverance is the consequence or effect of God's hearing us.

22-24
22. I will declare thy name. David, in promising that when he is delivered he will not be ungrateful, confirms that he had never been so cast down by temptation as not to take courage to resist it. How could he be putting himself in readiness, as he is doing here, to offer to God the sacrifice of thanksgiving, if he had not beforehand entertained the assured hope of deliverance?

MATTHEW HENRY

2. He is here insulted and surrounded by his enemies, such as were of a higher rank, who for their strength and fury, are compared to bulls, strong bulls of Bashan (v. 12), fat and fed to the full, haughty and sour; such were the chief priests and elders that persecuted Christ; and others of a lower rank, who are compared to dogs (v. 16), filthy and greedy, and unwearied in running him down. There was an assembly of the wicked plotting against him (v. 16); for the chief priests sat in council, to consult of ways and means to take Christ. These enemies were numerous and unanimous: "Many, and those of different and clashing interests among themselves, as Herod and Pilate, have agreed to compass me. They have carried their plot far, and seem to have gained their point, for they have beset me round, v. 12. They have enclosed me, v. 16. They are formidable and threatening (v. 13): They gaped upon me with their mouths, to show me that they would swallow me up; and this with as much strength and fierceness as a roaring ravening lion leaps upon his prey."
3. He is here crucified. The very manner of his death is described, though never in use among the Jews: They pierced my hands and my feet (v. 16), which were nailed to the accursed tree, and the whole body left so to hang, the effect of which must needs be the most exquisite pain and torture. There is no one passage in all the Old Testament which the Jews have so industriously corrupted as this, because it is such an eminent prediction of the death of Christ and was so exactly fulfilled.
4. He is here dying (v. 14, 15), dying in pain and anguish, because he was to satisfy for sin, which brought in pain, and for which we must otherwise have lain in everlasting anguish.
5. He was stripped. The shame of nakedness was the immediate consequence of sin; and therefore our Lord Jesus was stripped of his clothes, when he was crucified, that he might clothe us with the robe of his righteousness, and that the shame of our nakedness might not appear. Now here we are told,
(1.) How his body looked when it was thus stripped: I may tell all my bones, v. 17. His blessed body was lean and emaciated with labor, grief, and fasting, during the whole course of his ministry, which made him look as if he was nearly 50 years old when he was yet but 33, as we find, John viii. 57.
(2.) What they did with his clothes, which they took from him (v. 18): They parted my garments among them, to every soldier a part, and upon my vesture, the seamless coat, do they cast lots. This very circumstance was exactly fulfilled, John xix. 23, 24. And though it was no great instance of Christ's suffering, yet it is a great instance of the fulfilling of the scripture in him. Thus it was written, and therefore thus it behoved Christ to suffer. Let this therefore confirm our faith in him as the true Messiah, and inflame our love to him as the best of friends, who loved us and suffered all this for us.

Psalm 22

25-31
25 My praise shall be of thee in the great congregation: I will pay my vows before them that fear him.
26 The meek shall eat and be satisfied: they shall praise the LORD that seek him: your heart shall live for ever.
27 All the ends of the world shall remember and turn unto the LORD: and all the kindreds of the nations shall worship before thee.
28 For the kingdom is the LORD's: and he is the governor among the nations.
29 All they that be fat upon earth shall eat and worship: all they that go down to the dust shall bow before him: and none can keep alive his own soul.
30 A seed shall serve him; it shall be accounted to the Lord for a generation.
31 They shall come, and shall declare his righteousness unto a people that shall be born, that he hath done this.

the face of nature, and from the soul of the Redeemer, and beholding the light of his triumph and its future results the Savior smiled.

Verse 22. "I will declare thy name unto my brethren." The delights of Jesus are always with his church, and hence his thoughts, after much distraction, return at the first moment of relief to their usual channel; he forms fresh designs for the benefit of his beloved ones. He is not ashamed to call them brethren, "Saying, I will declare thy name unto my brethren, in the midst of the church will I sing praise unto thee."

Verse 23. "Ye that fear the Lord praise him." The reader must imagine the Savior as addressing the congregation of the saints. He exhorts the faithful to unite with him in thanksgiving. The description of "fearing the Lord" is very frequent and very instructive; it is the beginning of wisdom, and is an essential sign of grace.

Verse 24. "For he hath not despised nor abhorred the affliction of the afflicted." Here is good matter and motive for praise. The experience of our covenant Head and Representative should encourage all of us to bless the God of grace.

Verse 25. "My praise shall be of thee in the great congregation." The one subject of our Master's song is the Lord alone. The Lord and the Lord only is the theme which the believer handleth when he gives himself to imitate Jesus in praise.

Verse 26. "The meek shall eat and be satisfied." Mark how the dying Lover of our souls solaces himself with the result of his death. The spiritually poor find a feast in Jesus, they feed upon him to the satisfaction of their hearts.

Verse 27. In reading this verse one is struck with the Messiah's missionary spirit. It is evidently his grand consolation that Jehovah will be known throughout all places of his dominion. "All the ends of the world shall remember and turn unto the Lord." Out from the inner circle of the present church the blessing is to spread in growing power until the remotest parts of the earth shall be ashamed of their idols.

Verse 28. "For the kingdom is the Lord's." As an obedient Son the dying Redeemer rejoiced to know that his Father's interests would prosper through his pains. "The Lord reigneth" was his song as it is ours.

Verse 29. "All they that be fat upon earth," the rich and great are not shut out. Grace now finds the most of its jewels among the poor, but in the latter days the mighty of the earth "shall eat," shall taste of redeeming grace and dying love.

Verse 30. "A seed shall serve him." Posterity shall perpetuate the worship of the Most High. The kingdom of truth on earth shall never fail. As one generation is called to its rest, another will arise in its stead.

Verse 31. "They shall come." Sovereign grace shall bring out from among men the bloodbought ones. Nothing shall thwart the divine purpose. The chosen shall come to life, to faith, to pardon, to heaven. In this the dying Savior finds a sacred satisfaction. Toiling servant of God, be glad at the thought that the eternal purpose of God shall suffer neither let nor hindrance.

JOHN CALVIN

23. Ye who fear Jehovah. Here, again, the Psalmist expresses more distinctly the fruit of public and solemn thanksgiving, declaring, that by engaging in this exercise, every man in his own place invites and stirs up the church by his example to praise God.
24. For he hath not despised. To rejoice in one another's good, and to give thanks in common for each other's welfare, is a branch of that communion which ought to exist among the people of God, as Paul also teaches, "That for the gift bestowed upon us by the means of many persons, thanks may be given by many on our behalf" (2 Corinthians 1:11.)

25-29
25. My praise shall proceed from thee. The Hebrew manner of expression here requires this sense that David will take the matter of his song of praise from God. Accordingly, I supply the verb shall proceed, or shall flow,—My praise shall proceed or flow from thee; and he made this statement in order to testify that he owed his deliverance entirely to God.
26. The poor shall eat. The Psalmist has a reference to the custom which was at that time prevalent among the Jews, of feasting on their sacrifices, as is very well known. He here promises this feast, in order to exercise and prove his charity.
27. All the ends of the earth shall remember. This passage, beyond all doubt, shows that David stops not at his own person, but that under himself, as a type, he describes the promised Messiah. For even then, it ought to have been a well-known point, that he had been created king by God, that the people might be united together and enjoy a happy life under one head; and this was at length completely fulfilled in Christ.
29. All the fat ones of the earth shall eat and worship. Lest it should be thought inconsistent that now the fat ones of the earth are admitted as guests to this banquet, which David seemed immediately before to have appointed only for the poor, let us remember that the first place was given to the poor, because to them principally comfort was set forth in the example of David.

30-31
30. Their seed shall serve him. The more to exalt the greatness of the benefit, he declares that it will be of such a character that posterity will never forget it. And he shows how it will come to be perpetuated, namely, because the conversion of the world, of which he has spoken, will not be for a short time only but will continue from age to age.
31. They shall come, and shall declare. The Psalmist here confirms that since the fathers will transmit the knowledge of this benefit to their children the name of God will be always renowned. So it is by the preaching of the grace of God alone that the Church is kept from perishing. At the same time, let it be observed, that care and diligence in propagating divine truth are here enjoined upon us, that it may continue after we are removed from this world. The Holy Spirit prescribes it as a duty incumbent on all the faithful to be diligent in instructing their children.

MATTHEW HENRY

II. Here is Christ praying, and with that supporting himself under the burden of his sufferings. Christ, in his agony, prayed earnestly, prayed that the cup might pass from him. When the prince of this world with his terrors set upon him, gaped upon him as a roaring lion, he fell upon the ground and prayed. And of that David's praying here was a type. He calls God his strength, v. 19. He prays,
1. That God would be with him, and not set himself at a distance from him: Be not thou far from me (v. 11), and again, v. 19. "Whoever stands aloof from my sore, Lord, do not thou." The nearness of trouble should quicken us to draw near to God and then we may hope that he will draw near to us.
2. That he would help him and make haste to help him, help him to bear up under his troubles, that he might not fail nor be discouraged, that he might neither shrink from his undertaking nor sink under it. And the Father heard him in that he feared (Heb. v. 7) and enabled him to go through with his work.
3. That he would deliver him and save him, v. 20, 21.

22-31 The Messiah's triumphs; extension and perpetuity of the Church.
Five things are here spoken of, the view of which were the satisfaction and triumph of Christ in his sufferings:
I. That he should have a church in the world, and that those that were given him from eternity should, in the fullness of time, be gathered in to him. This is implied here; that he should see his seed, Isa. liii. 10.
II. That God should be greatly honored and glorified in him by that church. His Father's glory was that which he had in his eye throughout his whole undertaking (John xvii. 4), particularly in his sufferings, which he entered upon with this solemn request, Father, glorify thy name, John xii. 27, 28.
III. That all humble gracious souls should have a full satisfaction and happiness in him, v. 26. It comforted the Lord Jesus in his sufferings that in and through him all true believers should have everlasting consolation.
IV. That the church of Christ, and with it the kingdom of God among men, should extend itself to all the corners of the earth and should take in all sorts of people.
V. That the church of Christ, and with it the kingdom of God among men, should continue to the end, through all the ages of time. Mankind is kept up in a succession of generations; so that there is always a generation passing away and a generation coming up. Now, as Christ shall have honor from that which is passing away and leaving the world so he shall have honor from that which is rising up, and setting out, in the world, v. 30.

Psalm 23

Title
A Psalm of David.

1 The LORD is my shepherd; I shall not want.
2 He maketh me to lie down in green pastures: he leadeth me beside the still waters.
3 He restoreth my soul: he leadeth me in the paths of righteousness for his name's sake.
4 Yea, though I walk through the valley of the shadow of death, I will fear no evil: for thou art with me; thy rod and thy staff they comfort me.
5 Thou preparest a table before me in the presence of mine enemies: thou anointest my head with oil; my cup runneth over.
6 Surely goodness and mercy shall follow me all the days of my life: and I will dwell in the house of the LORD for ever.

Psalm 23

There is no inspired title to this psalm, and none is needed, for it records no special event, and needs no other key than that which every Christian may find in his own bosom. It is David's Heavenly Pastoral; a surpassing ode, which none of the daughters of music can excel. The clarion of war here gives place to the pipe of peace, and he who so lately bewailed the woes of the Shepherd tunefully rehearses the joys of the flock. Sitting under a spreading tree, with his flock around him, like Bunyan's shepherd-boy in the Valley of Humiliation, we picture David singing this unrivalled pastoral with a heart as full of gladness as it could hold; or, if the psalm be the product of his after-years, we are sure that his soul returned in contemplation to the lonely water-brooks which rippled among the pastures of the wilderness, where in early days she had been wont to dwell. This is the pearl of psalms whose soft and pure radiance delights every eye; a pearl of which Helicon need not be ashamed, though Jordan claims it. Of this delightful song it may be affirmed that its piety and its poetry are equal, its sweetness and its spirituality are unsurpassed.

EXPOSITION
Verse 1. "The Lord is my shepherd." What condescension is this, that the infinite Lord assumes towards his people the office and character of a Shepherd! It should be the subject of grateful admiration that the great God allows himself to be compared to anything which will set forth his great love and care for his own people. David had himself been a keeper of sheep, and understood both the needs of the sheep and the many cares of a shepherd. He compares himself to a creature weak, defenseless, and foolish, and he takes God to be his Provider, Preserver, Director, and, indeed, his everything.
Verse 2. "He maketh me to lie down in green pastures: he leadeth me beside the still waters." The Christian life has two elements in it, the contemplative and the active, and both of these are richly provided for.
Verse 3. "He restoreth my soul." When the soul grows sorrowful he revives it; when it is sinful he sanctifies it; when it is weak he strengthens it. "He" does it. His ministers could not do it if he did not. His Word would not avail by itself. "He restoreth my soul." Are any of us low in grace? Do we feel that our spirituality is at its lowest ebb? He who turns the ebb into the flood can soon restore our soul. Pray to him, then, for the blessing—"Restore thou me, thou Shepherd of my soul!"
Verse 4. "Yea, though I walk through the valley of the shadow of death, I will fear no evil: for thou art with me; thy rod and thy staff they comfort me." This unspeakably delightful verse has been sung on many a dying bed, and has helped to make the dark valley bright times out of mind. Every word in it has a wealth of meaning. "Yea, though I walk," as if the believer did not quicken his pace when he came to die, but still calmly walked with God.
Verse 5. "Thou preparest a table before me in the presence of mine enemies." The good man has his enemies. He would not be like his Lord if he had not. If we were without enemies we might fear that we were not the friends of God, for the friendship of the world is enmity to God. Yet see the quietude of the godly man in spite of, and in the sight of, his enemies.
Verse 6. "Surely goodness and mercy shall follow me all the days of my life." This is a fact as indisputable as it is encouraging, and therefore a heavenly verily, or "surely" is set as a seal upon it. This sentence may be read, "only goodness and mercy," for there shall be unmingled mercy in our history. These twin guardian angels will always be with me at my back and my beck.

Psalm 23

1-4

1. Jehovah is my shepherd. Although God, by his benefits, gently allures us to himself, as it were by a taste of his fatherly sweetness, yet there is nothing into which we more easily fall than into a forgetfulness of him, when we are in the enjoyment of peace and comfort. Yea, prosperity not only so intoxicates many, as to carry them beyond all bounds in their mirth, but it also engenders insolence, which makes them proudly rise up and break forth against God. Accordingly, there is scarcely a hundredth part of those who enjoy in abundance the good things of God, who keep themselves in his fear, and live in the exercise of humility and temperance, which would be so becoming.

2. He maketh me to lie down in pastures of grass. In this verse, and in the verses following, he explains the last clause of the first verse, I shall not want. He relates how abundantly God had provided for all his necessities, and he does this without departing from the comparison which he employed at the commencement. The amount of what is stated is, that the heavenly Shepherd had omitted nothing which might contribute to make him live happily under his care.

3. He restoreth my soul As it is the duty of a good shepherd to cherish his sheep, and when they are diseased or weak to nurse and support them, David declares that this was the manner in which he was treated by God. The restoring of the soul, as we have translated it, or the conversion of the soul, as it is, literally rendered, is of the same import as to make anew, or to recover.

4. Though I should walk. True believers, although they dwell safely under the protection of God, are, notwithstanding, exposed to many dangers, or rather they are liable to all the afflictions which befall mankind in common, that they may the better feel how much they need the protection of God. David, therefore, here expressly declares, that if any adversity should befall him, he would lean upon the providence of God. Thus he does not promise himself continual pleasures; but he fortifies himself by the help of God courageously to endure the various calamities with which he might be visited.

5-6

5. Thou wilt prepare. These words, which are put in the future tense, here denote a continued act. David, therefore, now repeats, without a figure, what he has hitherto declared, concerning the beneficence of God, under the similitude of a shepherd. He tells us that by his liberality he is supplied with all that is necessary for the maintenance of this life.

6. Surely goodness and mercy. Having recounted the blessings which God had bestowed upon him, he now expresses his undoubted persuasion of the continuance of them to the end of his life. He does not say, My cup shall be always full, or, My head shall be always perfumed with oil; but in general he entertains the hope that as the goodness of God never fails, he will be favorable towards him even to the end.

Psalm 23

The divine Shepherd.

I. From God's being his shepherd he infers that he shall not want anything that is good for him, v. 1. See here,

1. The great care that God takes of believers. He is their shepherd, and they may call him so.

2. The great confidence which believers have in God: "If the Lord is my shepherd, my feeder, I may conclude I shall not want any thing that is really necessary and good for me."

II. From his performing the office of a good shepherd to him he infers that he needs not fear any evil in the greatest dangers and difficulties he could be in, v. 2-4. He experiences the benefit of God's presence with him and care of him now, and therefore expects the benefit of them when he most needs it. See here,

1. The comforts of a living saint. God is his shepherd and his God—a God all-sufficient to all intents and purposes. David found him so, and so have we. See the happiness of the saints as the sheep of God's pasture.

2. See here the courage of a dying saint (v. 4): "Having had such experience of God's goodness to me all my days, in six troubles and in seven, I will never distrust him, no, not in the last extremity."

III. From the good gifts of God's bounty to him now he infers the constancy and perpetuity of his mercy, v. 5, 6. Here we may observe,

1. How highly he magnifies God's gracious vouchsafements to him (v. 5): "Thou preparest a table before me; thou hast provided for me all things pertaining both to life and godliness, all things requisite both for body and soul, for time and eternity:" such a bountiful benefactor is God to all his people; and it becomes them abundantly to utter his great goodness.

2. How confidently he counts upon the continuance of God's favors, v. 6. He had said (v. 1), I shall not want; but now he speaks more positively, more comprehensively: Surely goodness and mercy shall follow me all the days of my life. His hope rises, and his faith is strengthened, by being exercised. Observe,

(1.) What he promises himself—goodness and mercy.

(2.) The manner of the conveyance of it: It shall follow me, as the water out of the rock followed the camp of Israel through the wilderness; it shall follow into all places and all conditions, shall be always ready.

(3.) The continuance of it: It shall follow me all my life long, even to the last; for whom God loves he loves to the end.

(4.) The constancy of it: All the days of my life, as duly as the day comes; it shall be new every morning (Lam. iii. 22, 23) like the manna that was given to the Israelites daily.

Psalm 24

Title
A Psalm of David.

1-5
1 The earth is the LORD's, and the fullness thereof; the world, and they that dwell therein.
2 For he hath founded it upon the seas, and established it upon the floods.
3 Who shall ascend into the hill of the LORD? or who shall stand in his holy place?
4 He that hath clean hands, and a pure heart; who hath not lifted up his soul unto vanity, nor sworn deceitfully.
5 He shall receive the blessing from the LORD, and righteousness from the God of his salvation.

Psalm 24

TITLE. A Psalm of David. From the title we learn nothing but the authorship: but this is interesting and leads us to observe the wondrous operations of the Spirit upon the mind of Israel's sweet singer, enabling him to touch the mournful string in Psalm twenty-two, to pour forth gentle notes of peace in Psalm twenty-three, and here to utter majestic and triumphant strains. We can do or sing all things when the Lord strengtheneth us.

This sacred hymn was probably written to be sung when the ark of the covenant was taken up from the house of Obed-edom, to remain within curtains upon the hill of Zion. The words are not unsuitable for the sacred dance of joy in which David led the way upon that joyful occasion. The eye of the psalmist looked, however, beyond the typical upgoing of the ark to the sublime ascension of the King of glory. We will call it The Song of the Ascension.

Division. The Psalm makes a pair with the fifteenth Psalm. It consists of three parts. The first glorifies the true God, and sings of his universal dominion; the second describes the true Israel, who are able to commune with him; and the third pictures the ascent of the true Redeemer, who has opened heaven's gates for the entrance of his elect.

EXPOSITION

Verse 1. How very different is this from the ignorant Jewish notion of God which prevailed in our Savior's day? The Jews said, "The holy land is God's, and the seed of Abraham are his only people;" but their great Monarch had long before instructed them—"The earth is the Lord's, and the fullness thereof." The whole round world is claimed for Jehovah, "and they that dwell therein" are declared to be his subjects.

The term "world" indicates the habitable regions, wherein Jehovah is especially to be acknowledged as Sovereign. He who rules the fish of the sea and the fowl of the air should not be disobeyed by man, his noblest creature. Jehovah is the Universal King, all nations are beneath his sway.

Verse 2. In the second verse we have the reason why the world belongs to God, namely, because he has created it, which is a title beyond all dispute. "For he hath founded it upon the seas." It is God who lifts up the earth from out of the sea, so that the dry land, which otherwise might in a moment be submerged, as in the days of Noah, is kept from the floods. The hungry jaws of ocean would devour the dry land if a constant fiat of Omnipotence did not protect it. "He hath established it upon the floods." The world is Jehovah's, because from generation to generation he preserves and upholds it, having settled its foundations. Providence and Creation are the two legal seals upon the title-deeds of the great Owner of all things. He who built the house and bears up its foundations has surely a first claim upon it. Let it be noted, however, upon what insecure foundations all terrestrial things are founded. Founded on the seas! Established on the floods! Blessed be God the Christian has another world to look forward to, and rests his hopes upon a more stable foundation than this poor world affords.

Verses 3-6. Here we have the true Israel described. The men who shall stand as courtiers in the palace of the living God are not distinguished by race, but by character; they are not Jews only, nor Gentiles only, nor any one branch of mankind peculiarly, but a people purified and made meet to dwell in the holy hill of the Lord.

Verse 3. "Who shall ascend into the hill of the Lord?" It is uphill work for the creature to reach the Creator. Where is the mighty climber who can scale the towering heights? Nor is it height alone; it is glory too. Whose eye shall see the King in his beauty and dwell in his palace? In heaven he reigns most gloriously, who shall be permitted to enter into his royal presence? God has made all, but he will not save all; there is a chosen company who shall have the singular honor of dwelling with him in his high abode.

Psalm 24

As God stands related to all mankind as their Creator and Governor, David, from this consideration, magnifies the special favor which God manifested towards the children of Abraham, in choosing them to be his peculiar people, in preference to the rest of mankind, and in erecting his sanctuary as his house that he might dwell among them. He shows, at the same time, that although the sanctuary was open to all the Jews, God was not near to all of them, but only to those who feared and served him in sincerity, and who had cleansed themselves from the pollutions of the world, in order to devote themselves to holiness and righteousness. Moreover, as the grace of God was more clearly manifested after the temple was built, he celebrates that grace in a strain of splendid poetry, to encourage true believers with the more alacrity to persevere in the exercise of serving and honoring him.

1-4
1. The earth is Jehovah's. We will find in many other places the children of Abraham compared with all the rest of mankind, that the free goodness of God, in selecting them from all other nations, and in embracing them with his favor, may shine forth the more conspicuously. The object of the beginning of the psalm is to show that the Jews had nothing of themselves which could entitle them to approach nearer or more familiarly to God than the Gentiles. As God by his providence preserves the world, the power of his government is alike extended to all, so that he ought to be worshipped by all, even as he also shows to all men, without exception, the fatherly care he has about them. But since he preferred the Jews to all other nations, it was indispensably necessary that there should be some sacred bond of connection between him and them, which might distinguish them from the heathen nations. By this argument David invites and exhorts them to holiness.
2. For he hath founded it upon the seas. The Psalmist here confirms the truth, that men are rightfully under the authority and power of God, so that in all places and countries they ought to acknowledge him as King.
3. Who shall ascend unto. It being very well known that it was of pure grace that God erected his sanctuary, and chose for himself a dwelling-place among the Jews, David makes only a tacit reference to this subject. He insists principally on the other point contained in the verse, that of distinguishing true Israelites from the false.
4. He who is clean of hands, and pure of heart. Under the purity of the hands and of the heart, and the reverence of God's name, he comprehends all religion, and denotes a well ordered life. True purity, no doubt, has its seat in the heart, but it manifests its fruits in the works of the hands. The Psalmist, therefore, very properly joins to a pure heart the purity of the whole life; for that man acts a ridiculous part who boasts of having a sound heart, if he does not show by his fruits that the root is good.

Psalm 24

1-2 God's absolute propriety.
Here is,
I. God's absolute propriety in this part of the creation where our lot is cast, v. 1. We are not to think that the heavens, even the heavens only, are the Lord's, and the numerous and bright inhabitants of the upper world, and that this earth, being so small and inconsiderable a part of the creation, and at such a distance from the royal palace above, is neglected, and that he claims no interest in it. No, even the earth is his, and this lower world; and, though he has prepared the throne of his glory in the heavens, yet his kingdom rules over all, and even the worms of this earth are not below his cognizance, nor from under his dominion.
II. The ground of this propriety. The earth is his by an indisputable title, for he hath founded it upon the seas and established it upon the floods, v. 2. It is his; for,
1. He made it, formed it, founded it, and fitted it for the use of man. The matter is his, for he made it out of nothing; the form is his, for he made it according to the eternal counsels and ideas of his own mind. He made it himself, he made it for himself; so that he is sole, entire, and absolute owner, and none can let us a title to any part, but by, from, and under him; see Ps. lxxxix. 11, 12.
2. He made it so as no one else could. It is the creature of omnipotence, for it is founded upon the seas, upon the floods, a weak and unstable foundation (one would think) to build the earth upon, and yet, if almighty power please, it shall serve to bear the weight of this earth. The waters which at first covered the earth, and rendered it unfit to be a habitation for man, were ordered under it, that the dry land might appear, and so they are as a foundation to it; see Ps. civ. 8, 9. 3.

3-6 The character of true Israelites.
From this world, and the fullness thereof, the psalmist's meditations rise, of a sudden to the great things of another world, the foundation of which is not on the seas, nor on the floods. The things of this world God has given to the children of men and we are much indebted to his providence for them; but they will not make a portion for us. And therefore,
I. Here is an enquiry after better things, v. 3. This earth is God's footstool; but, if we had ever so much of it, we must be here but a while, must shortly go hence, and Who then shall ascend into the hill of the Lord? Who shall go to heaven hereafter, and, as an earnest of that, shall have communion with God in holy ordinances now? A soul that knows and considers its own nature, origin, and immortality, when it has viewed the earth and the fullness thereof, will sit down unsatisfied; there is not found among all the creatures a help meet for man, and therefore it will think of ascending towards God, towards heaven,

Psalm 24

6-10

6 This is the generation of them that seek him, that seek thy face, O Jacob. Selah.

7 Lift up your heads, O ye gates; and be ye lift up, ye everlasting doors; and the King of glory shall come in.

8 Who is this King of glory? The LORD strong and mighty, the LORD mighty in battle.

9 Lift up your heads, O ye gates; even lift them up, ye everlasting doors; and the King of glory shall come in.

10 Who is this King of glory? The LORD of hosts, he is the King of glory. Selah.

Verse 4. "He that hath clean hands." Outward, practical holiness is a very precious mark of grace. To wash in water with Pilate is nothing, but to wash in innocency is all-important. It is to be feared that many professors have perverted the doctrine of justification by faith in such a way as to treat good works with contempt; if so, they will receive everlasting contempt at the last great day.

Verse 5. It must not be supposed that the persons who are thus described by their inward and outward holiness are saved by the merits of their works; but their works are the evidences by which they are known. The present verse shows that in the saints grace reigns and grace alone. Such men wear the holy livery of the Great King because he has of his own free love clothed them therewith. The true saint wears the wedding garment, but he owns that the Lord of the feast provided it for him, without money and without price.

Verse 6. "This is the generation of them that seek him, that seek thy face, O Jacob." These are the regeneration, these are in the line of grace; these are the legitimate seed. Yet they are only seekers; hence learn that true seekers are very dear in God's esteem, and are entered upon his register. Even seeking has a sanctifying influence; what a consecrating power must lie in finding and enjoying the Lord's face and favor!

Verse 7. These last verses reveal to us the great representative man, who answered to the full character laid down, and therefore by his own right ascended the holy hill of Zion. Our Lord Jesus Christ could ascend into the hill of the Lord because his hands were clean and his heart was pure, and if we by faith in him are conformed to his image we shall enter too. We have here a picture of our Lord's glorious ascent. We see him rising from amidst the little group upon Olivet, and as the cloud receives him, angels reverently escort him to the gates of heaven.

Verse 8. The watchers at the gate hearing the song look over the battlements and ask, "Who is this King of glory?" A question full of meaning and worthy of the meditations of eternity. Who is he in person, nature, character, office and work? What is his pedigree? What his rank and what his race? The answer given in a mighty wave of music is, "The Lord strong and mighty, the Lord mighty in battle." We know the might of Jesus by the battles which he has fought, the victories which he has won over sin, and death, and hell, and we clap our hands as we see him leading captivity captive in the majesty of his strength. Oh for a heart to sing his praises! Mighty hero, be thou crowned for ever King of kings and Lord of lords.

Verse 9. "Lift up your heads, O ye gates; even lift them up, ye everlasting doors; and the King of glory shall come in." The words are repeated with a pleasing variation. There are times of deep earnest feeling when repetitions are not vain but full of force. Doors were often taken from their hinges when Easterns would show welcome to a guest, and some doors were drawn up and down like a portcullis, and may possibly have protruded from the top; thus literally lifting up their heads. The picture is highly poetical, and shows how wide heaven's gate is set by the ascension of our Lord. Blessed be God, the gates have never been shut since. The opened gates of heaven invite the weakest believer to enter.

Verse 10. The closing note is inexpressibly grand. Jehovah of hosts, Lord of men and angels, Lord of the universe, Lord of the worlds, is the King of glory. All true glory is concentrated upon the true God, for all other glory is but a passing pageant, the painted pomp of an hour. The ascended Savior is here declared to be the Head and Crown of the universe, the King of Glory.

JOHN CALVIN

5-6
5. He shall receive blessing. The more effectually to move the minds of the Israelites, David declares that nothing is more desirable than to be numbered among the flock of God, and to be members of the church. We must here consider that there is an implied contrast between true Israelites and those of them who were degenerate.
6. This is the generation. It is, no doubt, truly said in many other places, as in Psalm 27, that those sought the face of God who, to testify their godliness, exercised themselves in the ceremonies before the ark of the covenant; that is to say, if they were brought thither by a pure and holy affection. But as hypocrites seek God externally in a certain way, as well as true saints, while yet they shun him by their false pretences. David here declares that God is not sought in truth unless there go before a zealous cultivation of holiness and righteousness.

7-10
7. Lift up your heads, O ye gates! The magnificent and splendid structure of the temple, in which there was more outward majesty than in the tabernacle, not being yet erected, David here speaks of the future building of it. By doing this, he encourages the pious Israelites to employ themselves more willingly, and with greater confidence, in the ceremonial observances of the law. It was no ordinary token of the goodness of God that he condescended to dwell in the midst of them by a visible symbol of his presence, and was willing that his heavenly dwelling-place should be seen upon earth. This doctrine ought to be of use to us at this day; for it is an instance of the inestimable grace of God, that so far as the infirmity of our flesh will permit, we are lifted up even to God by the exercises of religion.
8. Who is this King of glory? etc The praises by which the power of God is here magnified are intended to tell the Jews that he did not sit idle in his temple, but took up his abode in it, in order to show himself ready to succor his people.
It is to be observed, that there is great weight both in the interrogation, and in the repetition of the same sentence. The prophet assumes the person of one who wonders thereby to express with greater effect that God comes armed with invincible power to maintain and save his people, and to keep the faithful in safety under his shadow.

The amount of what is stated is, that whenever the people should call upon God in the temple, it would manifestly appear, from the effect which would follow, that the ark of the covenant was not a vain and an illusory symbol of the presence of God, because he would always stretch forth his omnipotent arm for the defense and protection of his people. The repetition teaches us that true believers cannot be too constant and diligent in meditation on this subject. The Son of God, clothed with our flesh, has now shown himself to be King of glory and Lord of hosts, and he is not entered into his temple only by shadows and figures, but really and in very deed, that he may dwell in the midst of us.

MATTHEW HENRY

will ask, "What shall I do to rise to that high place, that hill, where the Lord dwells and manifests himself, that I may be acquainted with him, and to abide in that happy holy place where he meets his people and makes them holy and happy? What shall I do that I may be of those whom God owns for his peculiar people and who are his in another manner than the earth is his and its fullness?" This question is much the same with that, Ps. xv. 1. The hill of Zion on which the temple was built typified the church, both visible and invisible. When the people attended the ark to its holy place David puts them in mind that these were but patterns of heavenly things, and therefore that by them they should be led to consider the heavenly things themselves.
II. An answer to this enquiry, in which we have,

1. The properties of God's peculiar people, who shall have communion with him in grace and glory.
(2.) They are a praying people (v. 6): This is the generation of those that seek him. In every age there is a remnant of such as these, men of this character, who are accounted to the Lord for a generation, Ps. xxii. 30.

2. The privileges of God's peculiar people, v. 5. They shall be made truly and for ever happy. They shall be blessed: they shall receive the blessing from the Lord, all the fruits and gifts of God's favor, according to his promise; and those whom God blesses are blessed indeed, for it is his prerogative to command the blessing.

7-10 The King of glory.
What is spoken once is spoken a second time in these verses; such repetitions are usual in songs, and have much beauty in them. Here is,
1. Entrance once and again demanded for the King of glory; the doors and gates are to be thrown open, thrown wide open, to give him admission, for behold he stands at the door and knocks, ready to come in.
2. Enquiry once and again made concerning this mighty prince, in whose name entrance is demanded: Who is this King of glory? As, when any knock at our door, it is common to ask, Who is there?
3. Satisfaction once and again given concerning the royal person that makes the demand: It is the Lord, strong and mighty, the Lord, mighty in battle, the Lord of hosts, v. 8, 10. Now,
I. This splendid entry here described it is probable refers to the solemn bringing in of the ark into the tent David pitched for it or the temple Solomon built for it; for, when David prepared materials for the building of it, it was proper for him to prepare a psalm for the dedication of it.
II. Doubtless it points at Christ, of whom the ark, with the mercy-seat, was a type. We may apply it to the ascension of Christ into heaven and the welcome given to him there. When he had finished his work on earth he ascended in the clouds of heaven, Dan. vii. 13, 14.

Psalm 25

Title
A Psalm of David.

1-8
1 Unto thee, O LORD, do I lift up my soul.
2 O my God, I trust in thee: let me not be ashamed, let not mine enemies triumph over me.
3 Yea, let none that wait on thee be ashamed: let them be ashamed which transgress without cause.
4 Shew me thy ways, O LORD; teach me thy paths.
5 Lead me in thy truth, and teach me: for thou art the God of my salvation; on thee do I wait all the day.
6 Remember, O LORD, thy tender mercies and thy lovingkindnesses; for they have been ever of old.
7 Remember not the sins of my youth, nor my transgressions: according to thy mercy remember thou me for thy goodness' sake, O LORD.
8 Good and upright is the LORD: therefore will he teach sinners in the way.

Psalm 25

TITLE. A Psalm of David. David is pictured in this Psalm as in a faithful miniature. His holy trust, his many conflicts, his great transgression, his bitter repentance, and his deep distresses are all here; so that we see the very heart of "the man after God's own heart." It is evidently a composition of David's later days, for he mentions the sins of his youth, and from its painful references to the craft and cruelty of his many foes, it will not be too speculative a theory to refer it to the period when Absalom was heading the great rebellion against him. This has been styled the second of the seven Penitential Psalms. It is the mark of a true saint that his sorrows remind him of his sins, and his sorrow for sin drives him to his God.

SUBJECT AND DIVISION. The twenty-two verses of this Psalm begin in the original with the letters of the Hebrew alphabet in their proper order. It is the first instance we have of an inspired acrostic or alphabetical song. This method may have been adopted by the writer to assist the memory; and the Holy Spirit may have employed it to show us that the graces of style and the arts of poetry may lawfully be used in his service. Why should not all the wit and ingenuity of man be sanctified to noblest ends by being laid upon the altar of God? From the singularity of the structure of the Psalm, it is not easy to discover any marked divisions; there are great changes of thought, but there is no variation of subject; the moods of the writer's mind are twofold-prayer and meditation; and as these appear in turns, we should thus divide the verses. Prayer from Ps 25:1-7; meditation, Ps 25:8-10; prayer, Ps 25:11; meditation, Ps 25:12-15; prayer, Ps 25:16-22.

EXPOSITION

Verse 1. Unto thee, O Lord. See how the holy soul flies to its God like a dove to its cote. When the storm winds are out, the Lord's vessels put about and make for their well remembered harbor of refuge. What a mercy that the Lord will condescend to hear our cries in time of trouble, although we may have almost forgotten him in our hours of fancied prosperity. Unto thee, O Jehovah, do I lift up my soul. It is but a mockery to uplift the hands and the eyes unless we also bring our souls into our devotions. True prayer may be described as the soul rising from earth to have fellowship with heaven; it is taking a journey upon Jacob's ladder, leaving our cares and fears at the foot, and meeting with a covenant God at the top.

Verse 2. O my God. This title is more dear than the name Jehovah, which is used in the first sentence. Already the sweet singer has drawn nearer to his heavenly helper, for he makes bold to grasp him with the hand of assured possession, calling him, my God.

Verse 3. Yea, let none that wait on thee be ashamed. Suffering enlarges the heart by creating the power to sympathize. If we pray eagerly for ourselves, we shall not long be able to forget our fellow sufferers. None pity the poor like those who have been or are still poor, none have such tenderness for the sick as those who have been long in ill health themselves. We ought to be grateful for occasional griefs if they preserve us from chronic hardheartedness; for of all afflictions, an unkind heart is the worst, it is a plague to its possessor, and a torment to those around him.

Verse 4. Shew me thy ways, O Lord. Unsanctified natures clamor for their own way, but gracious spirits cry, "Not my will, but thine be done." We cannot at all times discern the path of duty, and at such times it is our wisdom to apply to the Lord himself. Frequently the dealings of God with us are mysterious, and then also we may appeal to him as his own interpreter, and in due time he will make all things plain. Moral, providential and mental forms of guidance are all precious gifts of a gracious God to a teachable people.

Verse 5. Lead me in thy truth, and teach me. The same request as in the last verse. The little child having begun to walk, asks to be still led onward

JOHN CALVIN

Psalm 25

1-3
1. Unto thee, O Jehovah! etc The Psalmist declares at the very outset, that he is not driven hither and thither, after the manner of the ungodly, but that he directs all his desires and prayers to God alone. Nothing is more inconsistent with true and sincere prayer to God, than to waver and gaze about as the heathen do, for some help from the world; and at the same time to forsake God, or not to betake ourselves directly to his guardianship and protection.
2. O my God! I have put my trust in thee. By this verse we learn that David had to do with men; but as he was persuaded that his enemies were, as it were, the scourges of God, he with good reason asks that God would restrain them by his power, lest they should become more insolent, and continue, to exceed all bounds.
3. Yea, none of those, etc. If these words should be explained in the form of a desire, as if David had said, Let none who wait on thee be put to shame, then, in this verse, he continues his prayer, and extends to all the faithful in common what he had spoken of himself alone. But I am rather inclined to understand the words in a different sense, and to view them as meaning that David shows the fruit of divine grace which should proceed from his deliverance.

Psalm 25:4-7
4. O Jehovah! make me to know thy ways. By the ways of the Lord, David sometimes means the happy and prosperous issue of affairs, but more frequently he uses this expression to denote the rule of a holy and righteous life. As the term truth occurs in the immediately following verse, the prayer which he offers up in this place is, in my opinion, to this effect: Lord, keep thy servant in the firm persuasion of thy promises, and do not suffer him to turn aside to the right hand or to the left.
6. Remember, O Jehovah; From this it appears that David was grievously afflicted and tried, so much so that he had lost all sense of God's mercy: for he calls upon God to remember for him his favor, in such a manner as if he had altogether forgotten it. This, therefore, is the complaint of a man suffering extreme anguish, and overwhelmed with grief. We may learn from this, that although God, for a time, may withdraw from us every token of his goodness, and, apparently regardless of the miseries which afflict us, should, as if we were strangers to him, and not his own people, forsake us, we must fight courageously, until, set free from this temptation, we cordially present the prayer which is here recorded, beseeching God, that, returning to his former manner of dealing, he would again begin to manifest his goodness towards us, and to deal with us in a more gracious manner.
7. Remember not the sins of my youth. As our sins are like a wall between us and God, which prevents him from hearing our prayers, or stretching forth his hand to help us, David now removes this obstruction. It is indeed true, in general,

MATTHEW HENRY

Psalm 25

1-7 Earnest supplications.
I. David professes his desire towards God: Unto thee, O Lord! do I lift up my soul, v. 1. In the foregoing psalm (v. 4) it was made the character of a good man that he has not lifted up his soul to vanity; and a call was given to the everlasting gates to lift up their heads for the King of glory to come in, v. 1. To this character, to this call, David here answers, "Lord, I lift up my soul, not to vanity, but to thee."
II. He professes his dependence upon God and begs for the benefit and comfort of that dependence (v. 2): O my God! I trust in thee. His conscience witnessed for him that he had no confidence in himself nor in any creature, and that he had no diffidence of God or of his power or promise.
III. He begs direction from God in the way of his duty, v. 4, 5. Once and again he here prays to God to teach him. He was a knowing man himself, but the most intelligent, the most observant, both need and desire to be taught of God; from him we must be ever learning.
IV. He appeals to God's infinite mercy, and casts himself upon that, not pretending to any merit of his own (v. 6): "Remember, O Lord! thy tender mercies, and, for the sake of those mercies, lead me, and teach me; for they have been ever of old."
V. He is in a special manner earnest for the pardon of his sins (v. 7): "O remember not the sins of my youth. Lord, remember thy mercies (v. 6), which speak for me, and not my sins, which speak against me." Here is an implicit confession of sin; he specifies particularly the sins of his youth.

8-14 Divine goodness and mercy.
God's promises are here mixed with David's prayers. Many petitions there were in the former part of the psalm, and many we shall find in the latter; and here, in the middle of the psalm, he meditates upon the promises, and by a lively faith sucks and is satisfied from these breasts of consolation; for the promises of God are not only the best foundation of prayer, telling us what to pray for and encouraging our faith and hope in prayer, but they are a present answer to prayer. Let the prayer be made according to the promise, and then the promise may be read as a return to the prayer; and we are to believe the prayer is heard because the promise will be performed. But, in the midst of the promises, we find one petition which seems to come in somewhat abruptly, and should have followed upon v. 7. It is that (v. 11), Pardon my iniquity. But prayers for the pardon of sin are never impertinent; we mingle sin with all our actions, and therefore should mingle such prayers with all our devotions. He enforces this petition with a double plea. The former is very natural: "For thy name's sake pardon my iniquity, because thou hast proclaimed thy name gracious and merciful,

Psalm 25

9-16
9 The meek will he guide in judgment: and the meek will he teach his way.
10 All the paths of the LORD are mercy and truth unto such as keep his covenant and his testimonies.
11 For thy name's sake, O LORD, pardon mine iniquity; for it is great.
12 What man is he that feareth the LORD? him shall he teach in the way that he shall choose.
13 His soul shall dwell at ease; and his seed shall inherit the earth.
14 The secret of the LORD is with them that fear him; and he will shew them his covenant.
15 Mine eyes are ever toward the LORD; for he shall pluck my feet out of the net.
16 Turn thee unto me, and have mercy upon me; for I am desolate and afflicted.

by its parent's helping hand, and to be further instructed in the alphabet of truth. Experimental teaching is the burden of this prayer. Lead me according to thy truth, and prove thyself faithful; lead me into truth that I may know its preciousness, lead me by the way of truth that I may manifest its spirit.
Verse 6. Remember, O Lord, thy tender mercies and thy lovingkindnesses. We are usually tempted in seasons of affliction to fear that our God has forgotten us, or forgotten his usual kindness towards us; hence the soul doth as it were put the Lord in remembrance, and beseech him to recollect those deeds of love which once he wrought towards it. There is a holy boldness which ventures thus to deal with the Most High, let us cultivate it; but there is also an unholy unbelief which suggests our fears, let us strive against it with all our might.
Verse 7. Remember not the sins of my youth. Sin is the stumbling block. This is the thing to be removed. Lord, pass an act of oblivion for all my sins, and especially for the hot blooded wanton follies of my younger years. Those offences which we remember with repentance God forgets, but if we forget them, justice will bring them forth to punishment. The world winks at the sins of younger men, and yet they are none so little after all; the bones of our youthful feastings at Satan's table will stick painfully in our throats when we are old men. He who presumes upon his youth is poisoning his old age.
Verses 8-10. These three verses are a meditation upon the attributes and acts of the Lord. He who toils in the harvest field of prayer should occasionally pause awhile and refresh himself with a meal of meditation.
Verse 8. Good and upright is the Lord: therefore will he teach sinners in the way. Here the goodness and rectitude of the divine character are beheld in friendly union; he who would see them thus united in bonds of perfect amity must stand at the foot of the cross and view them blended in the sacrifice of the Lord Jesus. It is no less true than wonderful that through the atonement the justice of God pleads as strongly as his grace for the salvation of the sinners whom Jesus died to save.
Verse 9. The meek will he guide in judgment. Meek spirits are in high favor with the Father of the meek and lowly Jesus, for he sees in them the image of his only begotten Son. They know their need of guidance, and are willing to submit their own understandings to the divine will, and therefore the Lord condescends to be their guide. Humble spirits are in this verse endowed with a rich inheritance; let them be of good cheer.
Verse 10. This is a rule without exception. God is good to those that be good. Mercy and faithfulness shall abound towards those who through mercy are made faithful. Whatever outward appearances may threaten we should settle it steadfastly in our minds that while grace enables us to obey the Lord's will we need not fear that Providence will cause us any real loss.
Verse 11. This sentence of prayer would seem out of place were it not that prayer is always in its place, whether in season or out of season. Meditation having refreshed the Psalmist, he falls to his weighty work again, and wrestles with God for the remission of his sin. For thy name's sake, O Lord. Here is a blessed, never failing plea. Not for our sakes or our merit's sake, but to glorify thy mercy, and to show forth the glory of thy divine attributes.
Verse 12. What man is he that feareth the Lord? Let the question provoke self examination. Gospel privileges are not for every pretender. Art thou of the seed royal or no? Him shall he teach in the way that he shall choose. Those whose hearts are right shall not err for want of heavenly direction.
Verse 13. He who fears God has nothing else to fear. His soul shall dwell at ease. He shall lodge in the chamber of content. One may sleep as soundly in the little bed in the corner as in the Great Bed of Ware; it is not abundance but content that gives true ease. Even here, having learned by grace both to abound and be empty, the believer dwells at ease; but how profound will be the ease of his soul for ever!

that men pray in a wrong way, and in vain, unless they begin by seeking the forgiveness of their sins. There is no hope of obtaining any favor from God unless he is reconciled to us.

8-11
8. Good and upright is Jehovah. Pausing for a little as it were in the prosecution of his prayer, he exercises his thoughts in meditation upon the goodness of God, that he may return with renewed ardor to prayer. The faithful feel that their hearts soon languish in prayer, unless they are constantly stirring themselves up to it by new incitements; so rare and difficult a thing is it to persevere steadfastly and unweariedly in this duty.
9. He will guide the poor in judgment. The Psalmist here specifies the second manifestation of his grace which God makes towards those who, being subdued by his power, and brought under his yoke, bear it willingly, and submit themselves to his government. But never will this docility be found in any man, until the heart, which is naturally elated and filled with pride, has been humbled and subdued.
10. All the ways of Jehovah. The amount of what is said is, that God acts in such a manner towards his people, as that, in all respects, they may find from experience that he is merciful and faithful. David is not here speaking of the character in which God acts towards mankind in general, but what his own children find him to be.
11. I connect this verse with the preceding one in this way: The prophet, having reflected upon this, that God is kind and faithful to those who serve him, now examines his own heart, and acknowledges that he cannot be accounted of their number, unless God grant unto him the forgiveness of his sins; and, therefore, he betakes himself to prayer for pardon: as in Psalm 19:13, after having spoken of the reward which is laid up for the faithful who keep the law, he instantly exclaims, "Who can understand his errors?" Accordingly, although David is not ignorant that God promises liberally to bestow upon those who keep his covenant every thing which pertains to a life of happiness, yet, at the same time, considering how far he is as yet from the perfect righteousness of the law, he does not rest his confidence upon it, but seeks a remedy for the manifold offenses of which he feels himself to be guilty.

12-15
12. Who is the man. By again recalling to his mind the character in which God manifests himself towards his servants, he derives new strength and courage.
13. His soul shall dwell in good. If the supreme felicity of man consists in undertaking or attempting nothing except by the warrant of God, it follows that it is also a high and incomparable benefit to have him for our conductor and guide through life, that we may never go astray. But, in addition to this, an earthly blessing is here promised, in which the fruit of the preceding grace is distinctly shown.
14. The counsel of Jehovah. The Psalmist here confirms what he had just said in a preceding verse, namely, that God will faithfully discharge the office of a teacher and master to all

pardoning iniquity, for thy glory-sake, for thy promise-sake, for thy own sake," Isa. xliii. 25. But the latter is very surprising: "Pardon my iniquity, for it is great, and the greater it is the more will divine mercy be magnified in the forgiveness of it." It is the glory of a great God to forgive great sins, to forgive iniquity, transgression, and sin, Exod. xxxiv. 7. "It is great, and therefore I an undone, for ever undone, if infinite mercy do not interpose for the pardon of it. It is great; I see it to be so." The more we see of the heinousness of our sins the better qualified we are to find mercy with God. When we confess sin we must aggravate it.

15-22 Precious promises; petitions.
David, encouraged by the promises he had been meditating upon, here renews his addresses to God, and concludes the psalm, as he began, with professions of dependence upon God and desire towards him.
I. He lays open before God the calamitous condition he was in. His feet were in the net, held fast and entangled, so that he could not extricate himself out of his difficulties, v. 15. He was desolate and afflicted, v. 16. It is common for those that are afflicted to be desolate; their friends desert them then, and they are themselves disposed to sit alone and keep silence, Lam. iii. 28. David calls himself desolate and solitary because he depended not upon his servants and soldiers, but relied as entirely upon God as if he had no prospect at all of help and succor from any creature. Being in distress, in many distresses, the troubles of his heart were enlarged (v. 17), he grew more and more melancholy and troubled in mind. Sense of sin afflicted him more than any thing else: this it was that broke and wounded his spirit, and made his outward troubles lie heavily upon him. He was in affliction and pain, v. 18. His enemies that persecuted him were many and malicious (they hated him), and very barbarous; it was with a cruel hatred that they hated him, v. 19. Such were Christ's enemies and the persecutors of his church.
II. He expresses the dependence he had upon God in these distresses (v. 15): My eyes are ever towards the Lord. Idolaters were for gods that they could see with their bodily eyes, and they had their eyes ever towards their idols, Isa. xvii. 7, 8. But it is an eye of faith that we must have towards God, who is a Spirit, Zech. ix. 1.
Those that have their eye ever towards God shall not have their feet long in the net. He repeats his profession of dependence upon God (v. 20)—Let me not be ashamed, for I put my trust in thee; and of expectation from him—I wait on thee, v. 21. It is good thus to hope and quietly wait for the salvation of the Lord.
III. He prays earnestly to God for relief and succor,
1. For himself.
(1.) See how he begs,

Psalm 25

17-22

17 The troubles of my heart are enlarged: O bring thou me out of my distresses.
18 Look upon mine affliction and my pain; and forgive all my sins.
19 Consider mine enemies; for they are many; and they hate me with cruel hatred.
20 O keep my soul, and deliver me: let me not be ashamed; for I put my trust in thee.
21 Let integrity and uprightness preserve me; for I wait on thee.
22 Redeem Israel, O God, out of all his troubles.

Verse 14. The secret of the Lord is with them that fear him. Some read it "the friendship:" it signifies familiar intercourse, confidential intimacy, and select fellowship. This is a great secret. Carnal minds cannot guess what is intended by it, and even believers cannot explain it in words, for it must be felt to be known.

Verse 15. Mine eyes are ever toward the Lord. The writer claims to be fixed in his trust, and constant in his expectation; he looks in confidence, and waits in hope. We may add to this look of faith and hope the obedient look of service, the humble look of reverence, the admiring look of wonder, the studious look of meditation, and the tender look of affection. Happy are those whose eyes are never removed from their God.

Verse 16. His own eyes were fixed upon God, but he feared that the Lord had averted his face from him in anger. Oftentimes unbelief suggests that God has turned his back upon us. If we know that we turn to God we need not fear that he will turn from us, but may boldly cry, Turn thee unto me.

Verse 17. The troubles of my heart are enlarged. When trouble penetrates the heart it is trouble indeed. In the case before us, the heart was swollen with grief like a lake surcharged with water by enormous floods; this is used as an argument for deliverance, and it is a potent one.

Verse 18. Look upon mine affliction and my pain. Note the many trials of the saints; here we have no less than six words all descriptive of woe. "Desolate, and afflicted, troubles enlarged, distresses, affliction, and pain." But note yet more the submissive and believing spirit of a true saint; all he asks for is, "Lord, look upon my evil plight;" he does not dictate, or even express a complaint; a look from God will content him, and that being granted he asks no more.

Verse 19. Consider mine enemies. Watch them, weigh them, check them, defeat them. For they are many. They need the eyes of Argus to watch them, and the arms of Hercules to match them, but the Lord is more than sufficient to defeat them. The devils of hell and the evils of earth are all vanquished when the Lord makes bare his arm.

Verse 20. O keep my soul out of evil, and deliver me when I fall into it. This is another version of the prayer, "Lead us not into temptation, but deliver us from evil." Let me not be ashamed. This is the one fear which like a ghost haunted the psalmist's mind. He trembled lest his faith should become the subject of ridicule through the extremity of his affliction. Noble hearts can brook anything but shame.

Verse 21. Let integrity and uprightness preserve me. What better practical safeguards can a man require? If we do not prosper with these as our guides, it is better for us to suffer adversity. Even the ungodly world admits that "honesty is the best policy."

Verse 22. Redeem Israel, O God, out of all his troubles. This is a very comprehensive prayer, including all the faithful and all their trials. Sorrow had taught the psalmist sympathy, and given him communion with the tried people of God; he therefore remembers them in his prayers. Jesus is the Redeemer from trouble as well as sin, he is a complete Redeemer, and from every evil he will rescue every saint. Redemption by blood is finished: O God, send us redemption by power. Amen and Amen.

JOHN CALVIN

the godly; and, after his usual manner, he repeats the same sentiment twice in the same verse for the covenant of God is nothing else than his secret or counsel.

15. Mine eyes are continually towards Jehovah. David here speaks of his own faith, and of its perseverance, not in the way of boasting, but to encourage himself in the hope of obtaining his requests, so that he might give himself the more readily and cheerfully to prayer.

16-22

16. Have respect unto me. As the flesh is ever ready to suggest to our minds that God has forgotten us, when he ceases to manifest his power in aiding us, David here follows the order which nature dictates, in asking God to have respect unto him, as if he had altogether neglected him before. Now, it appears to me that the words might be explained thus: Have respect unto me, in order to pity me. He accounts it at once the cause and the source of his salvation to be regarded of God; and then he adds the effect of it: for as soon as God, of his own good pleasure, shall vouchsafe to regard us, his hand also will be ready to help us.

17. The troubles of my heart are enlarged. In this verse he acknowledges not only that he had to contend outwardly with his enemies and the troubles which they occasioned him, but that he was also afflicted inwardly with sorrow and anguish of heart.

18. Look upon mine affliction. By repeating these complaints so frequently, he plainly shows that the calamities with which he was assailed were not some slight and trivial evils. And this ought to be carefully marked by us, so that when trials and afflictions shall have been measured out to us after the same manner, we may be enabled to lift up our souls to God in prayer; for the Holy Spirit has set before our view this representation, that our minds may not fail us under the multitude or weight of afflictions.

19. Behold mine enemies. In this verse David complains of the number and cruelty of his enemies, because the more the people of God are oppressed, the more is he inclined to aid them; and in proportion to the magnitude of the danger by which they are surrounded, he assists them the more powerfully.

21. Let integrity and uprightness preserve me. Whosoever waits upon God with a meek and quiet spirit, will rather suffer any thing which men can inflict, than allow himself to contend unrighteously with his enemies.

22. Do thou, O God! redeem Israel. By this conclusion David shows of what character the enemies were of whom he complained. From this it would appear that they were domestic enemies, who, like some disease raging within the bowels, were now the cause of trouble and vexation to the people of God. By the word redeem, which he here employs, we may infer that the Church was at that time oppressed with hard bondage; and, therefore, I have no doubt that in this psalm he alludes to Saul and others who reigned with him in a tyrannical manner. At the same time, he shows that he has respect not merely to his own benefit, but that he comprehends in his prayer the state of the whole realm.

MATTHEW HENRY

[1.] For the remission of sin (v. 18): Forgive all my sins. Those were his heaviest burdens, and which brought upon him all other burdens. He had begged (v. 7) for the pardon of the sins of his youth, and (v. 11) for the pardon of some one particular iniquity that was remarkably great, which some think, was his sin in the matter of Uriah. But here he prays, Lord, forgive all, take away all iniquity. It is observable that, as to his affliction, he asks for no more than God's regard to it: "Look upon my affliction and my pain, and do with it as thou pleasest." But, as to his sin, he asks for no less than a full pardon: Forgive all my sins. Yet he prays,

[2.] For the redress of his grievances. His mind was troubled for God's withdrawings from him and under the sense he had of his displeasure against him for his sins; and therefore he prays (v. 16), Turn thou unto me. And, if God turn to us, no matter who turns from us. His condition was troubled, and, in reference to that, he prays, "O bring thou me out of my distresses. I see no way of deliverance open; but thou canst either find one or make one."

(2.) Four things he mentions by way of plea to enforce these petitions, and refers himself and them to God's consideration:

[1.] He pleads God's mercy: Have mercy upon me. Men of the greatest merits would be undone if they had not to do with a God of infinite mercies.

[2.] He pleads his own misery, the distress he was in, his affliction and pain, especially the troubles of his heart, all which made him the proper object of divine mercy.

[3.] He pleads the iniquity of his enemies: "Lord, consider them, how cruel they are, and deliver me out of their hands."

[4.] He pleads his own integrity, v. 12. He did not expect to be safe any longer than he continued in his integrity and uprightness, and that, while he did continue in it, he did not doubt of being safe.

Sincerity will be our best security in the worst of times.Integrity and uprightness will be a man's preservation more than the wealth and honor of the world can be. These will preserve us to the heavenly kingdom. We should therefore pray to God to preserve us in our integrity and then be assured that that will preserve us.

2. For the church of God (v. 22): Redeem Israel, O God! out of all his troubles. David was now in trouble himself, but he thinks it not strange, since trouble is the lot of all God's Israel.

Good men have little comfort in their own safety while the church is in distress and danger. This prayer is a prophecy that God would, at length, give David rest, and therewith give Israel rest from all their enemies round about. It is a prophecy of the sending of the Messiah in due time to redeem Israel from his iniquities (Ps. cxxx. 8) and so to redeem them from their troubles. It refers also to the happiness of the future state. In heaven, and in heaven only, will God's Israel be perfectly redeemed from all troubles.

Psalm 26

Title
A Psalm of David.

1-6
1 Judge me, O LORD; for I have walked in mine integrity: I have trusted also in the LORD; therefore I shall not slide.
2 Examine me, O LORD, and prove me; try my reins and my heart.
3 For thy loving kindness is before mine eyes: and I have walked in thy truth.
4 I have not sat with vain persons, neither will I go in with dissemblers.
5 I have hated the congregation of evil doers; and will not sit with the wicked.
6 I will wash mine hands in innocency: so will I compass thine altar, O LORD:

Psalm 26

TITLE. A Psalm of David. The sweet singer of Israel appears before us in this Psalm as one enduring reproach; in this he was the type of the great Son of David, and is an encouraging example to us to carry the burden of slander to the throne of grace. It is an ingenious surmise that this appeal to heaven was written by David at the time of the assassination of Ishbosheth, by Baanah and Rechab, to protest his innocence of all participation in that treacherous murder; the tenor of the Psalm certainly agrees with the supposed occasion, but it is not possible with such a slender clue to go beyond conjecture.
DIVISION. Unity of subject is so distinctly maintained, that there are no sharp divisions. David Dickson has given an admirable summary in these words—"He appeals to God", the supreme Judge, in the testimony of a good conscience, bearing him witness; first, of his endeavor to walk uprightly as a believer, Ps 26:1-3; secondly, of his keeping himself from the contagion of the evil counsel, sinful causes, and examples of the wicked, Ps 26:4-5; thirdly, of his purpose still to behave himself holily and righteously, out of love to be partaker of the public privileges of the Lord's people in the congregation, Ps 26:6-8 Whereupon he prayeth to be free of the judgment coming upon the wicked, Ps 26:9-10 according as he had purposed to eschew their sins, Ps 26:11 and he closes the prayer with comfort and assurance of being heard, Ps 26:12.

EXPOSITION
Verse 1. Judge me, O Jehovah. A solemn appeal to the just tribunal of the heart searching God, warranted by the circumstances of the writer, so far as regarded the particular offences with which he was wrongly charged. Worried and worn out by the injustice of men, the innocent spirit flies from its false accusers to the throne of Eternal Right. He had need have a clear case who dares to carry his suit into the King's Bench of heaven.
Verse 2. There are three modes of trial here challenged, which are said in the original to refer to trial by touch, trial by smell, and trial by fire. The psalmist was so clear from the charge laid against him, that he submitted himself unconditionally to any form of examination which the Lord might see fit to employ. Examine me, O Lord. Look me through and through; make a minute survey; put me to the question, cross examine my evidence.
Verse 3. For thy lovingkindness is before mine eyes. An object of memory and a ground of hope. A sense of mercy received sets a fair prospect before the faithful mind in its gloomiest condition, for it yields visions of mercies yet to come, visions not visionary but real. Dwell, dear reader, upon that celestial word lovingkindness. It has a heavenly savor.
Verses 4-5. So far from being himself an open offender against the laws of God, the psalmist had not even associated with the lovers of evil. He had kept aloof from the men of Belial. A man is known by his company, and if we have kept ourselves apart from the wicked, it will always be evidence in our favor should our character be impugned. He who was never in the parish is not likely to have stolen the corn. He who never went to sea is clearly not the man who scuttled the ship.
Verse 4. I have not sat with vain persons. True citizens have no dealings with traitors. David had no seat in the parliament of triflers. They were not his boon companions at feasts, nor his advisers in council, nor his associates in conversation. We must needs see, and speak, and trade, with men of the world, but we must on no account take our rest and solace in their empty society. Not only the profane, but the vain are to be shunned by us. All those who live for this life only are vain, chaffy, frothy men, quite unworthy of a Christian's friendship.
Verse 5. I have hated the congregation of evil doers. A severe sentence, but not too severe. A man who does not hate evil terribly, does not love good

Psalm 26

1-4

1. Judge me, O Jehovah! I have just said, that David betakes himself to the judgment of God, because he found neither equity nor humanity among men. The Hebrew word which is rendered to judge, signifies to undertake the cognizance of a cause. The meaning here, therefore, is as if David called upon God to be the defender of his right. When God leaves us for a time to the injuries and petulance of our enemies, he seems to neglect our cause; but when he restrains them from assailing us at their pleasure he clearly demonstrates that the defense of our cause is the object of his care.

2. Prove me, O Jehovah! The more that David observed himself basely and undeservedly pursued with calumnies, the more powerfully was he excited by the vehemence of his grief fearlessly to assert his rectitude. Nor does he merely clear himself of outward sins; he glories also in the uprightness of his heart, and the purity of its affections, tacitly comparing himself, at the same time, with his enemies.

3. For thy goodness is before mine eyes. It is a remarkable difference between the children of God and worldly men, that the former, in the hope of a favorable issue at the Lord's hand, rely upon his word, and are not driven by restlessness to mischievous practices; while the latter, although they maintain a good cause, yet because they are ignorant of the providence of God, are hurried hither and thither; follow unlawful counsels; betake themselves to craftiness; and, in short, have no other object than to overcome evil with evil. Whence, accordingly, their miserable and sorrowful, and often their tragic ends, but because, despising the favor of God, they give themselves up to cunning and deceit?

4. I have not sat with vain men. He again declares the very great dissimilarity which existed between him and his adversaries. For the contrast is always to be observed, that wicked men, by all the harm and mischief they wrought against him, could never drive him from the path of rectitude. This verse might likewise be joined with the former, as if completing the sentence, in this way, That David, by confiding in the favor of God, had withdrawn himself from deceivers. The words, sitting and walking, denote sharing in counsel and fellowship in working, according to what is said in the first psalm.

5-7

5. I hate the assembly. The Psalmist protests again how greatly he abhorred the ungodly. Formerly he denied that he had any fellowship with them; now he still more explicitly declares that he fled from their company with loathing, for that is the meaning of the phrase, I hate. It is indeed true, that the wicked are everywhere hated; but how few withdraw themselves from them, that they may not imitate their vices!

6. I will wash my hands in purity. Referring, in these words, to the ordinary use of the sacrifices, he makes a distinction between himself and those who professed to offer the same divine worship, and thrust themselves forward in the services

Psalm 26

1-5 Devout appeals.

I. David appeals to God's righteous sentence (v. 1): "Judge me, O God! be thou Judge between me and my accusers, between the persecutor and the poor prisoner; bring me off with honor, and put those to shame that falsely accuse me." Saul, who was himself supreme judge in Israel, was his adversary, so that in a controversy with him he could appeal to no other than to God himself. As to his offences against God, he prays, Lord, enter not into judgment with me (Ps. cxliii. 2), remember not my transgressions (Ps. xxv. 7), in which he appeals to God's mercy; but, as to his offences against Saul, he appeals to God's justice and begs of him to judge for him, as Ps. xliii. 1.

II. He submits to his unerring search (v. 2): Examine me, O Lord! and prove me, as gold is proved, whether it be standard. God knows every man's true character, for he knows the thoughts and intents of the heart, as sees through every disguise. David prays, Lord, examine me, which intimates that he was well pleased that God did know him and truly desirous that he would discover him to himself and discover him to all the world.

III. He solemnly protests his sincerity (v. 1): "I have walked in my integrity; my conversation had agreed with my profession, and one part of it has been of a piece with another." It is vain to boast of our integrity unless we can make it out that by the grace of God we have walked in our integrity, and that our conversation in the world has been in simplicity and godly sincerity.

1. He had a constant regard to God and to his grace, v. 3. He aimed at God's good favor as his end and chief good: Thy loving-kindness is before my eyes. This will be a good evidence of our sincerity, if what we do in religion we do from a principle of love to God, and good thoughts of him as the best of beings and the best of friends and benefactors, and from a grateful sense of God's goodness to us in particular, which we have had the experience of all our days.

2. He had no fellowship with the unfruitful works of darkness, nor with the workers of those works, v. 4, 5.

6-12 Delight in divine ordinances.

In these verses,

I. David mentions, as further evidence of his integrity,

1. The sincere affection he had to the ordinances of God, the constant care he took about them, and the pleasure he took in them. Hypocrites and dissemblers may indeed be found attending on God's ordinances, as the proud Pharisee went up to the temple to pray with the penitent publican; but it is a good sign of sincerity if we attend upon them as David here tells us he did, v. 6-8.

2. He was very diligent and serious in his attendance upon them: I will compass thy altar, alluding to the

Psalm 26

7-12

7 That I may publish with the voice of thanksgiving, and tell of all thy wondrous works.
8 LORD, I have loved the habitation of thy house, and the place where thine honor dwelleth.
9 Gather not my soul with sinners, nor my life with bloody men:
10 In whose hands is mischief, and their right hand is full of bribes.
11 But as for me, I will walk in mine integrity: redeem me, and be merciful unto me.
12 My foot standeth in an even place: in the congregations will I bless the LORD.

heartily. Men, as men, we must always love, for they are our neighbors, and therefore to be loved as ourselves; but evil doers, as such, are traitors to the Great King, and no loyal subject can love traitors. What God hates we must hate. The congregation or assembly of evil doers, signifies violent men in alliance and conclave for the overthrow of the innocent; such synagogues of Satan are to be held in abhorrence.

Verse 6. I will wash mine hands in innocency. He would publicly avow himself to be altogether clear of the accusations laid against him, and if any fault in other matters could be truthfully alleged against him, he would for the future abstain from it.

Verse 7. That I may publish with the voice of thanksgiving. David was so far instructed that he does not mention the typical offering, but discerns the spiritual offering which was intended thereby, not the groans of bullocks, but songs of gratitude the spiritual worshipper presents.

Verse 8. Lord, I have loved the habitation of thy house. Into the abodes of sin he would not enter, but the house of God he had long loved, and loved it still. We were sad children if we did not love our Father's dwelling place. Though we own no sacred buildings, yet the church of the living God is the house of God, and true Christians delight in her ordinances, services, and assemblies.

Verse 9. Gather not my soul with sinners. Lord, when, like fruit, I must be gathered, put me not in the same basket with the best of sinners, much less with the worst of them. The company of sinners is so distasteful to us here, that we cannot endure the thought of being bound up in the same bundle with them to all eternity. Our comfort is, that the Great Husbandman discerns the tares from the wheat, and will find a separate place for distinct characters. In the former verses we see that the psalmist kept himself clear of profane persons, and this is to be understood as a reason why he should not be thrust into their company at the last.

Verse 10. In whose hands is mischief. They have both hands full of it, plotting it and carrying it out. And their right hand, with which they are most dexterous, is full of bribes; like thieves who would steal with impunity, they carry a sop for the dogs of justice. He who gives bribes is every way as guilty as the man who takes them, and in the matter of our parliamentary elections the rich villain who give the bribe is by far the worse.

Verse 11. Here is the lover of godliness entering his personal protest against unrighteous gain. He is a Nonconformist, and is ready to stand alone in his Nonconformity. Like a live fish, he swims against the stream. Trusting in God, the psalmist resolves that the plain way of righteousness shall be his choice, and those who will, may prefer the tortuous paths of violence and deceit. Yet, he is by no means a boaster, or a self righteous vaunter of his own strength, for he cries for redemption and pleads for mercy.

Verse 12. The song began in the minor, but it has now reached the major key. Saints often sing themselves into happiness. The even place upon which our foot stands is the sure, covenant faithfulness, eternal promise and immutable oath of the Lord of Hosts; there is no fear of falling from this solid basis, or of its being removed from under us. Established in Christ Jesus, by being vitally united to him, we have nothing left to occupy our thoughts but the praises of our God. Let us not forsake the assembling of ourselves together, and when assembled, let us not be slow to contribute our portion of thanksgiving.

of the sanctuary, as if they alone had the sole right to perform them. As David, therefore, and these hypocrites were one in this respect, that they entered the sanctuary, and surrounded the sacred altar together, he proceeds to show that he was a true worshipper, declaring, that he not only diligently attended to the external rites, but came to worship God with unfeigned devotion.

7. That I may make men to hear, etc In these words, he shows that he referred the sacrifices to their proper use and design, which hypocrites were far from doing. They neither know, nor do they consider, for what purpose God appointed the services of worship, but think it sufficient to thrust themselves into the divine presence with the pomp and form of their dissimulation.

8-11

8. O Jehovah! I have loved, etc In this verse he confirms what he had said before, that he came not into the sanctuary in a careless manner, but with serious devotion. Irreligious men, although they often resort to the sacred assemblies, frequent them merely as lurking places, where they may escape the eye of God. On the contrary, the truly pious and pure in heart resort to them as they are sincerely bent on seeking God, they willingly and affectionately employ the helps which he there affords them; and the advantage which they derive from them creates love to them in their hearts, and longings after them.

9. Gather not my soul with wicked men. Having now affirmed his innocence, he has recourse again to prayer, and calls upon God to defend him.

10. When he says, Their right hands are full of bribes, we may infer from this, that it was not the common people whom he pointed out for observation, but the nobility themselves, who were most guilty of practicing this corruption. Although the common sort of men may be hired for reward, and suborned as agents in wickedness, yet we know that bribes are offered chiefly to judges, and other great men who are in power.

11. But I will walk in mine integrity. In this repetition there is to be remarked a circumstance which more clearly illustrates David's righteousness; namely, that, in the midst of so many temptations, he steadily held on his way. He saw many become suddenly rich by gifts, as we still see those who sit at the helm of affairs accumulating to themselves, in a very brief space, a great abundance of wealth, building sumptuous palaces, and extending their lands far and wide. He, therefore, beseeches God to redeem him, because, being oppressed with wrongs, and tempted in various ways, he relied only on God, trusting that he would deliver him. From this we may conclude, that he was at this time reduced to great straits.

12. David celebrates the grace of God towards him, and, at the same time, vows his gratitude. He tells us that he was preserved in safety. And as he knew that it was the hand of God alone which enabled him to stand, he therefore addresses himself to the exercise of praise and thanksgiving.

custom of the priests, who, while the sacrifice was in offering, walked round the altar, and probably the offerers likewise did so at some distance, denoting a diligent regard to what was done and a dutiful attendance in the service.

3. In all his attendance on God's ordinances he aimed at the glory of God and was much in the thankful praise and adoration of him. He had an eye to the place of worship as the place where God's honor dwelt (v. 8), and therefore made it his business there to honor God and to give him the glory due to his name, to publish with the voice of thanksgiving all God's wondrous works. God's gracious works, which call for thanksgiving, are all wondrous works, which call for our admiration.

4. He did this with delight and from a principle of true affection to God and his institutions. Touching this he appeals to God: "Lord, thou knowest how dearly I have loved the habitation of thy house (v. 8), the tabernacle where thou art pleased to manifest thy residence among thy people and receive their homage, the place where thy honor dwells."

II. David, having given proofs of his integrity, earnestly prays, with a humble confidence towards God (such as those have whose hearts condemn them not), that he might not fall under the doom of the wicked (v. 9, 10). Gather not my soul with sinners, Here,

1. David describes these sinners, whom he looked upon to be in a miserable condition, so miserable that he could not wish the worst enemy he had in the world to be in a worse. "They are bloody men, that thirst after blood and lie under a great deal of the guilt of blood. "

2. He dreaded having his lot with them. He never loved them, nor associated with them, in this world, and therefore could in faith pray that he might not have his lot with them in the other world.

III. David, with a holy humble confidence, commits himself to the grace of God, v. 11, 12.

1. He promises that by the grace of God he would persevere in his duty: "As for me, whatever others do, I will walk in my integrity." Note, When the testimony of our consciences for us that we have walked in our integrity is comfortable to us this should confirm our resolutions to continue therein.

2. He prays for the divine grace both to enable him to do so and to give him the comfort of it: "Redeem me out of the hands of my enemies, and be merciful to me, living and dying." Be we ever so confident of our integrity, yet still we must rely upon God's mercy and the great redemption Christ has wrought out, and pray for the benefit of them.

3. He pleases himself with his steadiness: "My foot stands in an even place, where I shall not stumble and whence I shall not fall." This he speaks as one that found his resolutions fixed for God and godliness.

4. He promises himself that he should yet have occasion to praise the Lord, that he should be furnished with matter for praise.

Psalm 27

Title
A Psalm of David.

1-7
1 The LORD is my light and my salvation; whom shall I fear? the LORD is the strength of my life; of whom shall I be afraid?
2 When the wicked, even mine enemies and my foes, came upon me to eat up my flesh, they stumbled and fell.
3 Though an host should encamp against me, my heart shall not fear: though war should rise against me, in this will I be confident.
4 One thing have I desired of the LORD, that will I seek after; that I may dwell in the house of the LORD all the days of my life, to behold the beauty of the LORD, and to enquire in his temple.
5 For in the time of trouble he shall hide me in his pavilion: in the secret of his tabernacle shall he hide me; he shall set me up upon a rock.
6 And now shall mine head be lifted up above mine enemies round about me: therefore will I offer in his tabernacle sacrifices of joy; I will sing, yea, I will sing praises unto the LORD.
7 Hear, O LORD, when I cry with my voice: have mercy also upon me, and answer me.

Psalm 27

TITLE AND SUBJECT. Nothing whatever can be drawn from the title as to the time when this Psalm was written, for the heading, "A Psalm of David," is common to so many of the Psalms; but if one may judge from the matter of the song, the writer was pursued by enemies, Ps 27:2-3, was shut out from the house of the Lord, Ps 27:4, was just parting from father and mother, Ps 27:10, and was subject to slander, Ps 27:12; do not all these meet in the time when Doeg, the Edomite, spake against him to Saul? It is a song of cheerful hope, well fitted for those in trial who have learned to lean upon the Almighty arm. The Psalm may with profit be read in a threefold way, as the language of David, of the Church, and of the Lord Jesus. The plenitude of Scripture will thus appear the more wonderful.
DIVISION. The poet first sounds forth his sure confidence in his God, Ps 27:1-3, and his love of communion with him, Ps 27:4-6. He then betakes himself to prayer, Ps 27:7-12, and concludes with an acknowledgment of the sustaining power of faith in his own case, and an exhortation to others to follow his example.

EXPOSITION
Verse 1. The Lord is my light and my salvation. Here is personal interest, "my light," "my salvation;" the soul is assured of it, and therefore, declaring it boldly. "My light;"—into the soul at the new birth divine light is poured as the precursor of salvation; where there is not enough light to see our own darkness and to long for the Lord Jesus, there is no evidence of salvation. Salvation finds us in the dark, but it does not leave us there; it gives light to those who sit in the valley of the shadow of death. After conversion our God is our joy, comfort, guide, teacher, and in every sense our light; he is light within, light around, light reflected from us, and light to be revealed to us.
Verse 2. This verse records a past deliverance, and is an instance of the way in which experience should be employed to reassure our faith in times of trial. Each word is instructive. When the wicked. It is a hopeful sign for us when the wicked hate us; if our foes were godly men it would be a sore sorrow, but as for the wicked their hatred is better than their love.
Verse 3. Though an host should encamp against me, my heart shall not fear. Before the actual conflict, while as yet the battle is untried, the warrior's heart, being held in suspense, is very liable to become fluttered. The encamping host often inspires greater dread than the same host in actual affray.
Verse 4. One thing. Divided aims tend to distraction, weakness, disappointment. The man of one book is eminent, the man of one pursuit is successful. Let all our affections be bound up in one affection, and that affection set upon heavenly things. Have I desired what we cannot at once attain, it is well to desire. God judges us very much by the desire of our hearts. He who rides a lame horse is not blamed by his master for want of speed, if he makes all the haste he can, and would make more if he could; God takes the will for the deed with his children.
Verse 5. This verse gives an excellent reason for the psalmist's desire after communion with God, namely, that he was thus secured in the hour of peril. For in the time of trouble, that needy time, that time when others forsake me, he shall hide me in his pavilion: he shall give me the best of shelter in the worst of danger. The royal pavilion was erected in the center of the army, and around it all the mighty men kept guard at all hours; thus in that divine sovereignty which almighty power is sworn to maintain, the believer peacefully is hidden, hidden not by himself furtively, but by the king, who hospitably entertains him. In the secret of his tabernacle shall he hide me. Sacrifice aids sovereignty in screening the elect from harm.
Verse 6. And now shall mine head be lifted up above mine enemies round about me. He is quite sure of it. Godly men of old prayed in faith, nothing

JOHN CALVIN

Psalm 27

1-3

1. Jehovah is my light. This commencement may be understood as meaning that David, having already experienced God's mercy, publishes a testimony of his gratitude. But I rather incline to another meaning, namely, that, perceiving the conflict he had to wage with the sharpest temptations, he fortifies himself beforehand, and as it were brings together matter for confidence: for it is necessary that the saints earnestly wrestle with themselves to repel or subdue the doubts which the flesh is so prone to cherish, that they may cheerfully and speedily betake themselves to prayer.

2. When the wicked, etc. I connect this verse with the following one. In the former, David recalls to mind the triumphs which, by God's help, he had already obtained; and from this he concludes, that by what hosts soever he may be environed, or whatever mischief his enemies may devise against him, he would fearlessly stand up against them.

3. Though armies should encamp. He infers from his former experience that whatever adversity may befall him, he ought to hope well, and to have no misgivings about the divine protection, which had been so effectually vouchsafed to him in his former need. He had asserted this, indeed, in the first verse, but now, upon farther proof of it, he repeats it. Under the terms, camps and armies, he includes whatever is most formidable in the world: as if he had said, Although all men should conspire for my destruction, I will disregard their violence, because the power of God, which I know is on my side, is far above theirs.

4-6

4. One thing have I desired. Although David was banished from his country, despoiled of his wife, bereft of his kinsfolk; and, in fine, dispossessed of his substance, yet he was not so desirous for the recovery of these, as he was grieved and afflicted for his banishment from God's sanctuary, and the loss of his sacred privileges. Under the word one, there is an implied antithesis, in which David, disregarding all other interests, displays his intense affection for the service of God; so that it was bitterer to him to be an exile from the sanctuary, than to be denied access to his own house.

5. For he shall hide me in his tent. Here the Psalmist promises himself that his prayer would not be in vain. Although he is deprived of the visible sanctuary for a time, he doubts not that, wherever he may be, he shall experience the protecting power of God. And he alludes to the temple, because it was a symbol to the faithful of the divine presence; as if he had said, that in making the request which he mentioned he by no means lost his labor; for every one who shall seek God sincerely, and with a pure heart, shall be safely concealed under the wings of his protection. The figure of the temple, he therefore affirms, was not an unmeaning one, for there God, so to speak, spread forth his wings to gather true believers under his protection.

6. And I will offer sacrifices of triumph in his tabernacle. By making a solemn vow of thanksgiving, after he shall have been

MATTHEW HENRY

Psalm 27

1-6 Devout confidence; encouragement in prayers.
We may observe here,

I. With what a lively faith David triumphs in God, glories in his holy name, and in the interest he had in him.

1. The Lord is my light. David's subjects called him the light of Israel, 2 Sam. xxi. 17. And he was indeed a burning and a shining light: but he owns that he shone, as the moon does, with a borrowed light; what light God darted upon him reflected upon them: The Lord is my light. God is a light to his people, to show them the way when they are in doubt, to comfort and rejoice their hearts when they are in sorrow. It is in his light that they now walk on in their way, and in his light they hope to see light for ever.

2. "He is my salvation, in whom I am safe and by whom I shall be saved."

3. "He is the strength of my life, not only the protector of my exposed life, who keeps me from being slain, but the strength of my frail weak life, who keeps me from fainting, sinking, and dying away." God, who is a believer's light, is the strength of his life, not only by whom, but in whom, he lives and moves. In God therefore let us strengthen ourselves.

II. With what an undaunted courage he triumphs over his enemies; no fortitude like that of faith. If God be for him, who can be against him? Whom shall I fear? Of whom shall I be afraid? If God be his light, he fears no shades; if God be his salvation, he fears no colors. He triumphs over his enemies that were already routed, v. 2.

III. With what a gracious earnestness he prays for a constant communion with God in holy ordinances, v. 4. It greatly encouraged his confidence in God that he was conscious to himself of an entire affection to God and to his ordinances, and that he was in his element when in the way of his duty and in the way of increasing his acquaintance with him.

7-14 Confidence in divine goodness.
David in these verses expresses,

I. His desire towards God, in many petitions. If he cannot now go up to the house of the Lord, yet, wherever he is, he can find a way to the throne of grace by prayer.

1. He humbly bespeaks, because he firmly believes he shall have, a gracious audience: "Hear, O Lord, when I cry, not only with my heart, but, as one in earnest, with my voice too." He bespeaks also an answer of peace, which he expects, not from his own merit, but God's goodness: Have mercy upon me, and answer me, v. 7. If we pray and believe, God will graciously hear and answer.

2. He takes hold of the kind invitation God had given him to this duty, v. 8. It is presumption for us to come into the presence of the King of kings uncalled, nor can we draw near with any assurance unless he hold

Psalm 27

7-14

8 When thou saidst, Seek ye my face; my heart said unto thee, Thy face, LORD, will I seek.

9 Hide not thy face far from me; put not thy servant away in anger: thou hast been my help; leave me not, neither forsake me, O God of my salvation.

10 When my father and my mother forsake me, then the LORD will take me up.

11 Teach me thy way, O LORD, and lead me in a plain path, because of mine enemies.

12 Deliver me not over unto the will of mine enemies: for false witnesses are risen up against me, and such as breathe out cruelty.

13 I had fainted, unless I had believed to see the goodness of the LORD in the land of the living.

14 Wait on the LORD: be of good courage, and he shall strengthen thine heart: wait, I say, on the LORD.

wavering, and spoke of their answer to their prayers as a certainty. David was by faith so sure of a glorious victory over all those who beset him, that he arranged in his own heart what he would do when his foes lay all prostrate before him; that arrangement was such as gratitude suggested.

Verse 7. Hear, O Lord, when I cry with my voice. The pendulum of spirituality swings from prayer to praise. The voice which in the last verse was tuned to music is here turned to crying. As a good soldier, David knew how to handle his weapons, and found himself much at home with the weapon of "all prayer."

Verse 8. In this verse we are taught that if we would have the Lord hear our voice, we must be careful to respond to his voice. The true heart should echo the will of God as the rocks among the Alps repeat in sweetest music the notes of the peasant's horn. Observe, that the command was in the plural, to all the saints, Seek ye; but the man of God turned it into the singular by a personal application, Thy face, Lord, will I seek. The voice of the Lord is very effectual where all other voices fail. When thou saidst, then my heart, my inmost nature was moved to an obedient reply.

Verse 9. Hide not thy face far from me. The word "far" is not in the original, and is a very superfluous addition of the translators, since even the least hiding of the Lord's face is a great affliction to a believer.

Verse 10. When my father and my mother forsake me. These dear relations will be the last to desert me, but if the milk of human kindness should dry up even from their breasts, there is a Father who never forgets.

Verse 11. Teach me thy way, O Lord. He does not pray to be indulged with his own way, but to be informed as to the path in which the righteous Jehovah would have him walk. This prayer evinces an humble sense of personal ignorance, great teachableness of spirit, and cheerful obedience of heart. Lead me in a plain path. Help is here sought as well as direction; we not only need a map of the way, but a guide to assist us in the journey.

Verse 12. Deliver me not over unto the will of mine enemies; or I should be like a victim cast to the lions, to be rent in pieces and utterly devoured. God be thanked that our foes cannot have their way with us, or Smithfield would soon be on a blaze again.

Verse 13. Faintness of heart is a common infirmity; even he who slew Goliath was subject to its attacks. Faith puts its bottle of cordial to the lip of the soul, and so prevents fainting. Hope is heaven's balm for present sorrow. In this land of the dying, it is our blessedness to be looking and longing for our fair portion in the land of the living, whence the goodness of God has banished the wickedness of man, and where holy spirits charm with their society those persecuted saints who were vilified and despised among men.

Verse 14. Wait on the Lord. Wait at his door with prayer; wait at his foot with humility; wait at his table with service; wait at his window with expectancy. Suitors often win nothing but the cold shoulder from earthly patrons after long and obsequious waiting; he speeds best whose patron is in the skies. Be of good courage. A soldier's motto. Be it mine. Courage we shall need, and for the exercise of it we have as much reason as necessity, if we are soldiers of King Jesus. And he shall strengthen thine heart. He can lay the plaister right upon the weak place. Let the heart be strengthened, and the whole machine of humanity is filled with power; a strong heart makes a strong arm. What strength is this which God himself gives to the heart?

delivered from dangers, he confirms himself again in the hope of deliverance.

7-9

7. Hear, O Jehovah! my voice. The Psalmist returns again to prayer, and in doing so, he declares with what armor he was furnished to break through his temptations. By the word cry, he expresses his vehemence that he may thereby move God the sooner to help him.

8. The term, face, is commonly explained to mean help or succor; as if it had been said, Seek me. But I am persuaded that the allusion here is also to the sanctuary, and that David refers to the mode of manifestation in which God was wont to render himself in some degree visible.

9. Hide not thy face from me. The Psalmist elegantly continues the same form of speech, but with a different meaning. The face of God is now employed to describe the sensible effects of his grace and favor: as if it had been said, Lord, make me truly to experience that thou hast been near to me, and let me clearly behold thy power in saving me.

10-12

10. When my father and my mother shall forsake me. As it appears from the sacred history, that Jesse, so far as his opportunity admitted, performed his duty to his son David, some are of opinion that the nobles and councilors are here mentioned allegorically; but this is not suitable. Nor is it with any reason that they urge this scruple. David does not complain that he was unnaturally betrayed by his father or mother; but by this comparison he magnifies the grace of God, declaring, that he would ever find him ready to help him, although he might be forsaken of all men.

11. Teach me thy way, O Jehovah! He sets the right path in opposition to the difficulties and impediments which are in places which are rough, and of difficult access, to overcome which he was unequal, unless God undertook the office of a guide to lead him.

12. Give me not up to the desire of mine oppressors. If the ungodly should at any time rise against us, not only with menaces and cruel violence, but to give the semblance of justice to their enmity, should slander us with lies, let us remember the example of David, who was assaulted in both ways; nay, let us recall to mind that Christ the Son of God suffered no less injury from lying tongues than from violence.

13-14

13. Unless I had believed to see the goodness of Jehovah. We ought all to hope that, although God may not openly work deliverance for us, or show us his favor in a visible manner, he will, nevertheless, be always merciful to us, even in the present life.

14. Wait thou on Jehovah. He again repeats what he had said about waiting on God: Wait thou alone on Jehovah.

forth to us the golden scepter. David therefore going to pray fastens, in his thoughts, upon the call God had given him to the throne of his grace, and reverently touches, as it were, the top of the golden scepter which was thereby held out to him.

3. He is very particular in his requests.

(1.) For the favor of God, that he might not be shut out from that (v. 9): "Thy face, Lord, will I seek, in obedience to thy command; therefore hide not thy face from me; let me never want the reviving sense of the favor; love me, and let me know that thou lovest me; put not thy servant away in anger."

(2.) For the continuance of his presence with him: "Thou hast been my help formerly, and thou are the God of my salvation; and therefore whither shall I go but to thee? O leave me not, neither forsake me; withdraw not the operations of thy power from me, for then I am helpless; withdraw not the tokens of thy good-will to me, for then I am comfortless."

(3.) For the benefit of divine guidance (v. 11): "Teach me thy way, O Lord! give me to understand the meaning of thy providences towards me and make them plain to me; and give me to know my duty in every doubtful case, that I may not mistake it, but may walk rightly, and that I may not do it with hesitation, but may walk surely."

(4.) For the benefit of a divine protection (v. 12): "Deliver me not over to the will of my enemies. Lord, let them not gain their point, for it aims at my life, and no less, and in such a way as that I have no fence against them, but thy power over their consciences; for false witnesses have risen up against me, that aim further than to take away my reputation or estate, for they breathe out cruelty; it is the blood, the precious blood, they thirst after."

II. He expresses his dependence upon God,

1. That he would help and succor him when all other helps and succors failed him (v. 10): "When my father and my mother forsake me, the nearest and dearest friends I have in the world, from whom I may expect most relief and with most reason, when they die, or are at a distance from me, or are disabled to help me in time of need, or are unkind to me or unmindful of me, and will not help me, when I am as helpless as ever poor orphan was that was left fatherless and motherless, then I know the Lord will take me up, as a poor wandering sheep is taken up, and saved from perishing."

2. That in due time he should see the displays of his goodness, v. 13. He believed he should see the goodness of the Lord in the land of the living; and, if he had not done so, he would have fainted under his afflictions.

3. That in the mean time he should be strengthened to bear up under his burdens (v. 14); whether he says it to himself, or to his friends, it comes all to one; this is that which encourages him: He shall strengthen thy heart, shall sustain thy spirit, and then the spirit shall sustain the infirmity.

Psalm 28

Title
A Psalm of David.

1-4
1 Unto thee will I cry, O LORD my rock; be not silent to me: lest, if thou be silent to me, I become like them that go down into the pit.
2 Hear the voice of my supplications, when I cry unto thee, when I lift up my hands toward thy holy oracle.
3 Draw me not away with the wicked, and with the workers of iniquity, which speak peace to their neighbors, but mischief is in their hearts.
4 Give them according to their deeds, and according to the wickedness of their endeavors: give them after the work of their hands; render to them their desert.

Psalm 28

TITLE AND SUBJECT. Again, the title "A Psalm of David," is too general to give us any clue to the occasion on which it was written. Its position, as following the twenty-seventh, seems to have been designed, for it is a most suitable pendant and sequel to it. It is another of those "songs in the night" of which the pen of David was so prolific. The thorn at the breast of the nightingale was said by the old naturalists to make it sing: David's griefs made him eloquent in holy psalmody. The main pleading of this Psalm is that the suppliant may not be confounded with the workers of iniquity for whom he expresses the utmost abhorrence; it may suit any slandered saint, who being misunderstood by men, and treated by them as an unworthy character, is anxious to stand aright before the bar of God. The Lord Jesus may be seen here pleading as the representative of his people.
DIVISION. The first and second verses earnestly entreat audience of the Lord in a time of dire emergency. From Ps 28:2-5, the portion of the wicked is described and deprecated. In Ps 28:6-8, praise is given for the Lord's mercy in hearing prayer, and the Psalm concludes with a general petition for the whole host of militant believers.

EXPOSITION
Verse 1. Unto thee will I cry, O Lord, my rock. A cry is the natural expression of sorrow, and is a suitable utterance when all other modes of appeal fail us; but the cry must be alone directed to the Lord, for to cry to man is to waste our entreaties upon the air. When we consider the readiness of the Lord to hear, and his ability to aid, we shall see good reason for directing all our appeals at once to the God of our salvation, and shall use language of firm resolve like that in the text, "I will cry." The immutable Jehovah is our rock, the immovable foundation of all our hopes and our refuge in time of trouble: we are fixed in our determination to flee to him as our stronghold in every hour of danger.
Verse 2. This is much to the same effect as the first verse, only that it refers to future as well as present pleadings. Hear me! Hear me! Hear the voice of my supplications! This is the burden of both verses. We cannot be put off with a refusal when we are in the spirit of prayer; we labor, use importunity, and agonize in supplications until a hearing is granted us. The word "supplications," in the plural, shows the number, continuance, and variety of a good man's prayers, while the expression "hear the voice," seems to hint that there is an inner meaning, or heart voice, about which spiritual men are far more concerned than for their outward and audible utterances. A silent prayer may have a louder voice than the cries of those priests who sought to awaken Baal with their shouts.
Verse 3. Draw me not away with the wicked. They shall be dragged off to hell like felons of old drawn on a hurdle to Tyburn, like logs drawn to the fire, like fagots to the oven. David fears lest he should be bound up in their bundle, drawn to their doom; and the fear is an appropriate one for every godly man. The best of the wicked are dangerous company in time, and would make terrible companions for eternity; we must avoid them in their pleasures, if we would not be confounded with them in their miseries. And with the workers of iniquity. These are overtly sinful, and their judgment will be sure; Lord, do not make us to drink of their cup. Activity is found with the wicked even if it be lacking to the righteous. Oh! to be "workers" for the Lord. Which speak peace to their neighbors, but mischief is in their hearts. They have learned the manners of the place to which they are going: the doom of liars is their portion for ever, and lying is their conversation on the road. Soft words, oily with pretended love, are the deceitful meshes of the infernal net in which Satan catches the precious life; many of his children are learned in his abominable craft, and fish with their father's nets, almost as cunningly as he himself could do it.

JOHN CALVIN

Psalm 28

After being delivered by God's help from great dangers, David, in this psalm, according to his custom, first records the vows that he had made in the midst of his difficulties, and then his thanksgivings and praises to God, to induce others to follow his example. It is probable that he speaks of his persecutions by Saul.

1-2
1. Unto thee, O Jehovah! will I cry. The Psalmist begins by declaring that he would betake himself to the help of God alone, which shows both his faith and his sincerity. Although men labor every where under a multitude of troubles, yet scarcely one in a hundred ever has recourse to God. Almost all having their consciences burdened with guilt, and having never experienced the power of divine grace which might lead them to betake themselves to it, either proudly gnaw the bit or fill the air with unavailing complaints, or, giving way to desperation, faint under their afflictions. By calling God his strength, David more fully shows that he confided in God's assistance, not only when he was in the shade and in peace, but also when he was exposed to the severest temptations.
2. Hear the voice of my prayers when I cry to thee. This repetition is a sign of a heart in anguish. David's ardor and vehemence in prayer are also intimated by the noun signifying voice, and the verb signifying to cry. He means that he was so stricken with anxiety and fear, that he prayed not coldly, but with burning, vehement desire, like those who, under the pressure of grief, vehemently cry out. In the second clause of the verse, by synecdoche, the thing signified is indicated by the sign. It has been a common practice in all ages for men to lift up their hands in prayer. Nature has extorted this gesture even from heathen idolaters, to show by a visible sign that their minds were directed to God alone.

3-5
3. Draw me not away with wicked men. The meaning is, that in circumstances so dissimilar, God should not mingle the righteous with the wicked in the same indiscriminate destruction. Undoubtedly, too, in speaking of his enemies, he indirectly asserts his own integrity. But he did not pray in this manner, because he thought that God was indiscriminately and unreasonably angry with men; he reasons rather from the nature of God, that he ought to cherish good hope, because it was God's prerogative to distinguish between the righteous and the wicked, and to give every one his due reward.
4. Give them according to their works. Having thus requested God to have a regard to his innocence, the Psalmist thunders forth a curse against his enemies. And the accumulation of words shows that he had groaned long and grievously under the burden before he broke forth to desire such vengeance. He intimates that the wicked of whom he speaks had transgressed not once, nor for a short time, nor in one way, but that they had proceeded so far in their constant evil doings, that their audacity was no longer to be endured. We know how

MATTHEW HENRY

Psalm 28

1-5 Prayer for deliverance.
In these verses David is very earnest in prayer.
I. He prays that God would graciously hear and answer him, now that, in his distress, he called upon him, v. 1, 2. Observe his faith in prayer: O Lord, my rock, denoting his belief of God's power (he is a rock) and his dependence upon that power—"He is my rock, on whom I build my hope." Observe his fervency in prayer: "To thee will I cry, as one in earnest, being ready to sink, unless thou come in with seasonable succor." And observe how solicitous he is to obtain an answer: "Be not silent to me, as one angry at my prayers, Ps. lxxx. 4. Lord, speak to me, answer me with good words and comfortable words (Zech. i. 13); though the thing I pray for has not been given me, yet let God speak to me joy and gladness, and make me to hear them. Lord, speak for me, in answer to my prayers, plead my cause, command deliverances for me, and thus hear and answer the voice of my supplications."
II. He deprecates the doom of wicked people, as before (Ps. xxvi. 9, "Gather not my soul with sinners): Lord, I attend thy holy oracle, draw me not away from that with the wicked, and with the workers of iniquity," v. 3.
III. He imprecates the just judgments of God upon the workers of iniquity (v. 4): Give them according to their deeds. This is not the language of passion or revenge, nor is it inconsistent with the duty of praying for our enemies.
IV. He foretells their destruction for their contempt of God and his hand (v. 5): "Because they regard not the works of the Lord and the operations of his hands, by which he manifests himself and speaks to the children of men, he will destroy them in this world and in the other, and not build them up." Note, A stupid regardlessness of the works of God is the cause of their ruin. Why do men question the being or attributes of God, but because they do not duly regard his handiworks, which declare his glory, and in which the invisible things of him are clearly seen? Why do men forget God, and live without him, nay, affront God, and live in rebellion against him, but because they consider not the instances of that wrath of his which is revealed from heaven against all ungodliness and unrighteousness of men? Why do the enemies of God's people hate and persecute them, and devise mischief against them, but because they regard not the works God has wrought for his church, by which he has made it appear how dear it is to him? See Isa. v. 12.

In singing this we must arm ourselves against all temptations to join with the workers of iniquity, and animate ourselves against all the troubles we may be threatened with by the workers of iniquity.

Psalm 28

5-9

5 Because they regard not the works of the LORD, nor the operation of his hands, he shall destroy them, and not build them up.
6 Blessed be the LORD, because he hath heard the voice of my supplications.
7 The LORD is my strength and my shield; my heart trusted in him, and I am helped: therefore my heart greatly rejoiceth; and with my song will I praise him.
8 The LORD is their strength, and he is the saving strength of his anointed.
9 Save thy people, and bless thine inheritance: feed them also, and lift them up for ever.

Verse 4. When we view the wicked simply as such, and not as our fellow men, our indignation against sin leads us entirely to coincide with the acts of divine justice which punish evil, and to wish that justice might use her power to restrain by her terrors the cruel and unjust; but still the desires of the present verse, as our version renders it, are not readily made consistent with the spirit of the Christian dispensation, which seeks rather the reformation than the punishment of sinners.

Verse 5. Because they regard not the works of the Lord, nor the operation of his hands. God works in creation—nature teems with proofs of his wisdom and goodness, yet purblind atheists refuse to see him: he works in providence, ruling and overruling, and his hand is very manifest in human history, yet the infidel will not discern him: he works in grace—remarkable conversions are still met with on all hands, yet the ungodly refuse to see the operations of the Lord. Where angels wonder, carnal men despise. God condescends to teach, and man refuses to learn. He shall destroy them: he will make them "behold, and wonder, and perish." If they would not see the hand of judgment upon others, they shall feel it upon themselves. Both soul and body shall be overwhelmed with utter destruction for ever and ever. And not build them up. God's cure is positive and negative; his sword has two edges, and cuts right and left. Their heritage of evil shall prevent the ungodly receiving any good; the ephah shall be too full of wrath to contain a grain of hope.

Verse 6. Blessed be the Lord. Saints are full of benedictions; they are a blessed people, and a blessing people; but they give their best blessings, the fat of their sacrifices, to their glorious Lord. Our Psalm was prayer up to this point, and now it turns to praise. They who pray well, will soon praise well: prayer and praise are the two lips of the soul; two bells to ring out sweet and acceptable music in the ears of God; two angels to climb Jacob's ladder: two altars smoking with incense; two of Solomon's lilies dropping sweet smelling myrrh; they are two young roes that are twins, feeding upon the mountain of myrrh and the hill of frankincense.

Verse 7. Here is David's declaration and confession of faith, coupled with a testimony from his experience. The Lord is my strength. The Lord employs his power on our behalf, and moreover, infuses strength into us in our weakness. The psalmist, by an act of appropriating faith, takes the omnipotence of Jehovah to be his own. Dependence upon the invisible God gives great independence of spirit, inspiring us with confidence more than human.

Verse 8. The Lord is their strength. The heavenly experience of one believer is a pattern of the life of all. To all the militant church, without exception, Jehovah is the same as he was to his servant David, "the least of them shall be as David." They need the same aid and they shall have it, for they are loved with the same love, written in the same book of life, and one with the same anointed Head. And he is the saving strength of his anointed.

Verse 9. This is a prayer for the church militant, written in short words, but full of weighty meaning. We must pray for the whole church, and not for ourselves alone. Save thy people. Deliver them from their enemies, preserve them from their sins. There is a plea hidden in the expression, "thy people:" for it may be safely concluded that God's interest in the church, as his own portion, will lead him to guard it from destruction. Bless thine inheritance. Grant positive blessings, peace, plenty, prosperity, happiness; make all thy dearly purchased and precious heritage to be comforted by thy Spirit.

troublesome and grievous a temptation it is to see the ungodly proceeding without measure or end, as if God connived at their wickedness. David, therefore, wearied as it were with continual forbearing, and fainting under the burden, implores God, at length, to restrain the wantonness of his enemies, who of late ceased not to heap wickedness upon wickedness. Thus we perceive that there is nothing superfluous in this verse, when to works he adds the wickedness of their doings, and the work of their hands, and thrice petitions that they may receive the reward which they have deserved.
5. Because they regard not the doings of Jehovah. In this verse he lays open the root of impiety, declaring that the ungodly are so bold to do mischief, because, while they are thus indulging their hatred, and perpetrating every species of wickedness, they think that they have nothing to do with God. And when conscience stings them, they soothe themselves with false hopes, and at last stubbornly harden themselves into insensibility.

6-8
6. Blessed be Jehovah, who hath heard. This is the second part of the psalm in which the prophet begins to give thanks to God. By this thanksgiving he teaches us that his prayers were not in vain. Thus he confirms by his own example, that God is ready to bring help to his people whenever they seek him in truth and sincerity. He declares the same truth more fully in the next verse, calling God his strength and his shield; for he was persuaded that God had heard him from this, that he had been wonderfully preserved. He adds, that he had been helped in respect of his confidence and hope; for it often comes to pass, that those who call upon God, notwithstanding come short of his grace through their own unbelief. Thirdly, he says that he will add to his joy a testimony of his gratitude. Wicked men and hypocrites flee to God when they are overwhelmed with difficulties, but as soon as they escape from them, forgetting their deliverer, they rejoice with frantic mirth. In short, David trusted not in vain, since he truly found by experience that God possesses ever present power to preserve his servants; and that this was matter of true and solid joy to him, that he found God ever favorable to him.
8. Jehovah is their strength. By way of explanation, he repeats what he had said before, that God had been his strength; namely, because he had blessed his armies. David had indeed employed the hand and labor of men, but to God alone he ascribes the victory.
9. In this verse he shows that it was not so much his own welfare as the welfare of the whole Church which was the object of his concern, and that he neither lived nor reigned for himself, but for the common good of the people. He well knew that he was appointed king for no other end. In this he declares himself to be a type of the Son of God, of whom, when Zechariah (Zechariah 9:9) predicts that he would come "having salvation," there is no doubt that he promises nothing to him apart from his members, but that the effects of this salvation would diffuse themselves throughout his whole body.

6-9 Devout thanksgiving and praise.
In these verses,
I. David gives God thanks for the audience of his prayers as affectionately as a few verses before he had begged it: Blessed be the Lord, v. 6. How soon are the saints' sorrows turned into songs and their prayers into praises! It was in faith that David prayed (v. 2), Hear the voice of my supplications; and by the same faith he gives thanks (v. 6) that God has heard the voice of his supplications.
II. He encourages himself to hope in God for the perfecting of every thing that concerned him. Having given to God the glory of his grace (v. 6), he is humbly bold to take the comfort of it, v. 7. This is the method of attaining peace: let us begin with praise that is attainable. Let us first bless God and then bless ourselves.
III. He pleases himself with the interest which all good people, through Christ, have in God (v. 8): "The Lord is their strength; not mine only, but the strength of every believer." Note, The saints rejoice in their friends' comforts as well as their own; for, as we have not the less benefit from the light of the sun, so neither from the light of Gods' countenance, for others' sharing therein; for we are sure there is enough for all and enough for each. This is our communion with all saints, that God is their strength and ours, Christ their Lord and ours, 1 Cor. i. 2. He is their strength, the strength of all Israel, because he is the saving strength of his anointed, that is,
1. Of David in the type. God, in strengthening him that was their king and fought their battles, strengthened the whole kingdom. He calls himself God's anointed because it was the unction he had received that exposed him to the envy of his enemies, and therefore entitled him to the divine protection.
2. Of Christ, his anointed, his Messiah, in the anti-type. God was his saving strength, qualified him for his undertaking and carried him through it; see Ps. lxxxix. 21; Isa. xlix. 5; l. 7, 9. And so he becomes their strength, the strength of all the saints; he strengthened him that is the church's head, and from him diffuses strength to all the members, has commanded his strength, and so strengthens what he has wrought for us; Ps. lxviii. 28; lxxx. 17, 18.
IV. He concludes with a short but comprehensive prayer for the church of God, v. 9. He prays for Israel, not as his people ("save my people, and bless my inheritance"), though they were so, but, "thine." God's interest in them lay nearer his heart than his own. We are thy people is a good plea, Isa. lxiv. 9; lxiii. 19. I am thine, save me. God's people are his inheritance, dear to him, and precious in his eyes; what little glory he has from this world he has from them. The Lord's portion is his people. That which he begs of God for them is,
1. That he would save them from their enemies and the dangers they were exposed to.
2. That he would bless them with all good, flowing from his favor, in performance of his promise, and amounting to a happiness for them.

Psalm 29

Title
A Psalm of David.

1-5
1 Give unto the LORD, O ye mighty, give unto the LORD glory and strength.
2 Give unto the LORD the glory due unto his name; worship the LORD in the beauty of holiness.
3 The voice of the LORD is upon the waters: the God of glory thundereth: the LORD is upon many waters.
4 The voice of the LORD is powerful; the voice of the LORD is full of majesty.
5 The voice of the LORD breaketh the cedars; yea, the LORD breaketh the cedars of Lebanon.

Psalm 29

TITLE. A Psalm of David. The title affords us no information beyond the fact that David is the author of this sublime song.
SUBJECT. It seems to be the general opinion of modern annotators, that this Psalm is meant to express the glory of God as heard in the pealing thunder, and seen in the equinoctial tornado. Just as the eighth Psalm is to be read by moonlight, when the stars are bright, as the nineteenth needs the rays of the rising sun to bring out its beauty, so this can be best rehearsed beneath the black wing of tempest, by the glare of the lightning, or amid that dubious dusk which heralds the war of elements. The verses march to the tune of thunderbolts. God is everywhere conspicuous, and all the earth is hushed by the majesty of his presence. The word of God in the law and gospel is here also depicted in its majesty of power. True ministers are sons of thunder, and the voice of God in Christ Jesus is full of majesty. Thus we have God's works and God's word joined together: let no man put them asunder by a false idea that theology and science can by any possibility oppose each other. We may, perhaps, by a prophetic glance, behold in this Psalm the dread tempests of the latter days, and the security of the elect people.
DIVISION. The first two verses are a call to adoration. From Ps 29:3-10 the path of the tempest is traced, the attributes of God's word are rehearsed, and God magnified in all the terrible grandeur of his power; and the last verse sweetly closes the scene with the assurance that the omnipotent Jehovah will give both strength and peace to his people. Let heaven and earth pass away, the Lord will surely bless his people.

EXPOSITION
Verse 1. Give, i.e., ascribe. Neither men nor angels can confer anything upon Jehovah, but they should recognize his glory and might, and ascribe it to him in their songs and in their hearts. Unto the Lord, and unto him alone, must honor be given. Natural causes, as men call them, are God in action, and we must not ascribe power to them, but to the infinite Invisible who is the true source of all. O ye mighty. Ye great ones of earth and of heaven, kings and angels, join in rendering worship to the blessed and only Potentate; ye lords among men need thus to be reminded, for ye often fail where humbler men are ardent; but fail no longer, bow your heads at once, and loyally do homage to the King of kings.
Verse 2. Give unto the Lord the glory due unto his name. A third time the admonition is given, for men are backward in glorifying God, and especially great men, who are often too much swollen with their own glory to spare time to give God his rightful praise, although nothing more is asked of them than is most just and right. Surely men should not need so much pressing to give what is due, especially when the payment is so pleasant. Unbelief and distrust, complaining and murmuring, rob God of his honor; in this respect, even the saints fail to give due glory to their King. Worship the Lord, bow before him with devout homage and sacred awe, and let your worship be such as he appoints.
Verse 3. The voice of the Lord is upon the waters. The thunder is not only poetically but instructively called "the voice of God," since it peals from on high; it surpasses all other sounds, it inspires awe, it is entirely independent of man, and has been used on some occasions as the grand accompaniment of God's speech to Adam's sons. There is a peculiar terror in a tempest at sea, when deep calleth unto deep, and the raging sea echoes to the angry sky. No sight more alarming than the flash of lightning around the mast of the ship; and no sound more calculated to inspire reverent awe than the roar of the storm. The children of heaven have often enjoyed the tumult with humble joy peculiar to the saints, and even those who know not God have been forced into unwilling reverence while the storm has lasted.

Psalm 29

David, that he may humble all men before God, from the highest to the lowest, celebrates his terrible power in the various wonders of nature, which he affirms are not less fitted to arouse us to give glory to God, than if he were to assert his empire and majesty with his own voice. After he has struck fear into the proud, who are reluctant to yield, and addressed an exhortation to them accompanied by a gentle reproof, he sweetly invites the faithful voluntarily to fear the Lord.

1-4

1. Give unto Jehovah, ye sons of the mighty. It was no doubt David's design to lead all men to worship and reverence God; but as it is more difficult to reduce great men, who excel in rank, to order, he expressly addresses himself to them.

By the brightness of God's sanctuary is to be understood, not heaven as some think, but the tabernacle of the covenant, adorned with the symbols of the divine glory, as is evident from the context.

3. The voice of Jehovah is upon the waters. David now rehearses the wonders of nature and well indeed does he celebrate the power of God as well as his goodness, in his works. As there is nothing in the ordinary course of nature, throughout the whole frame of heaven and earth, which does not invite us to the contemplation of God, he might have brought forward, as in Psalm 19:1, the sun and the stars, and the whole host of heaven, and the earth with its riches; but he selects only those works of God which prove not only that the world was at first created by him, and is governed by his power.

5-8

5. The voice of Jehovah breaketh the cedars. We see how the prophet, in order to subdue the stubbornness of men, shows, by every word, that God is terrible. He also seems to rebuke, in passing, the madness of the proud, and of those who swell with vain presumption, because they hearken not to the voice of God in his thunders, rending the air with his lightnings, shaking the lofty mountains, prostrating and overthrowing the loftiest trees. What a monstrous thing is it, that while all the irrational portion of the creation tremble before God, men alone, who are endued with sense and reason, are not moved! Moreover, though they possess genius and learning, they employ enchantments to shut their ears against God's voice, however powerful, lest it should reach their hearts.

9-11

9. The voice of Jehovah maketh the hinds to bring forth. A tacit comparison is here made. It is worse than irrational, it is monstrous, that men are not moved at God's voice, when it has such power and influence on wild beasts. It is base ingratitude, indeed, in men not to perceive his providence and government in the whole course of nature; but it is a detestable insensibility that at least his unusual and extraordinary works, which compel even wild beasts to obey

Psalm 29

1-11 The glory of the Lord.

In this psalm we have,

I. A demand of the homage of the great men of the earth to be paid to the great God. Every clap of thunder David interpreted as a call to himself and other princes to give glory to the great God. Observe who they are that are called to this duty: "O you mighty (v. 1), you sons of the mighty, who have power, and on whom that power is devolved by succession and inheritance, who have royal blood running in your veins!" It is much for the honor of the great God that the men of this world should pay their homage to him; and they are bound to do it, not only because, high as they are, he is infinitely above them, and therefore they must bow to him, but because they have their power from him, and are to use it for him, and this tribute of acknowledgment they owe to him for it.

II. Good reason given for this demand. We shall see ourselves bound to give glory to God if we consider,

1. His sufficiency in himself, intimated in his name Jehovah—I am that I am, which is repeated here no fewer than eighteen times in this short psalm, twice in every verse but three, and once in two of those three; I do not recollect that there is the like in all the book of psalms. Let the mighty ones of the earth know him by this name and give him the glory due to it.

2. His sovereignty over all things. Let those that rule over men know there is a God that rules over them, that rules over all. The psalmist here sets forth God's dominion,

(1.) In the kingdom of nature. In the wonderful effects of natural causes, and the operations of the powers of nature, we ought to take notice of God's glory and strength, which we are called upon to ascribe to him; in the thunder, and lightning, and rain, we may see,

[1.] His glory. To speak it the voice of the God of glory, it is here said to be upon the water, upon many waters (v. 3); it reaches over the vast ocean, the waters under the firmament; it rattles among the thick clouds, the waters above the firmament. Every one that hears the thunder (his ear being made to tingle with it) will own that the voice of the Lord is full of majesty (Ps. xxix. 4), enough to make the highest humble (for none can thunder with a voice like him) and the proudest tremble—for, if his voice be so terrible, what is his arm? Every time we hear it thunder, let our hearts be thereby filled with great, and high, and honorable thoughts of God, in the holy adorings and admirings of whom the power of godliness does so much consist. O Lord our God! thou art very great.

[2.] His power (v. 4): The voice of the Lord is powerful, as appears by the effects of it; for it works wonders. Those that write natural histories relate the prodigious effects of thunder and lightning, even out of the ordinary course of natural causes, which must be resolved into the omnipotence of the God of nature.

Psalm 29

6-11
6 He maketh them also to skip like a calf; Lebanon and Sirion like a young unicorn.
7 The voice of the LORD divideth the flames of fire.
8 The voice of the LORD shaketh the wilderness; the LORD shaketh the wilderness of Kadesh.
9 The voice of the LORD maketh the hinds to calve, and discovereth the forests: and in his temple doth every one speak of his glory.
10 The LORD sitteth upon the flood; yea, the LORD sitteth King for ever.
11 The LORD will give strength unto his people; the LORD will bless his people with peace.

Verse 4. The voice of the Lord is powerful. An irresistible power attends the lightning of which the thunder is the report. In an instant, when the Lord wills it, the force of electricity produces amazing results. A writer upon this subject, speaks of these results as including a light of the intensity of the sun in his strength, a heat capable of fusing the most compact metals, a force in a moment paralyzing the muscles of the most powerful animals; a power suspending the all pervading gravity of the earth, and an energy capable of decomposing and recomposing the closest affinities of the most intimate combinations.

Verse 5. The voice of the Lord breaketh the cedars. Noble trees fall prostrate beneath the mysterious bolt, or stand in desolation as mementoes of its power. Lebanon itself is not secure, high as it stands, and ancient as are its venerable woods: Yea, the Lord breaketh the cedars of Lebanon. The greatest and most venerable of trees or men, may not reckon upon immunity when the Lord is abroad in his wrath. The gospel of Jesus has a like dominion over the most inaccessible of mortals; and when the Lord sends the word, it breaks hearts far stouter than the cedars.

Verse 6. He maketh them also to skip like a calf; Lebanon and Sirion like a young unicorn. Not only the trees, but the mountains themselves move as though they frisked and leaped like young bulls or antelopes.

Verse 7. The voice of the Lord divideth the flames of fire. As when sparks fly from the anvil by blows of a ponderous hammer, so the lightning attends the thundering strokes of Jehovah.

Verse 8. As the storm traveled, it burst over the desert. The voice of the Lord shaketh the wilderness; the Lord shaketh the wilderness of Kadesh. God courts not the applause of men—his grandest deeds are wrought where man's inquisitive glance is all unknown. Where no sound of man was heard, the voice of God was terribly distinct. The vast and silent plains trembled with affright. Silence did homage to the Almighty voice.

Verse 9. The voice of the Lord maketh the hinds to calve, those timid creatures, in deadly fear of the tempest, drop their burdens in an untimely manner. Perhaps a better reading is, "the oaks to tremble," especially as this agrees with the next sentence, and discovereth the forests. The dense shades of the forest are lit up with the lurid glare of the lightning, and even the darkest recesses are for a moment laid bare.

Verse 10. The Lord sitteth upon the flood. Flood follows tempest, but Jehovah is ready for the emergency. No deluge can undermine the foundation of his throne. He is calm and unmoved, however much the deep may roar and be troubled: his government rules the most unstable and boisterous of created things.

Verse 11. Power was displayed in the hurricane whose course this Psalm so grandly pictures; and now, in the cool calm after the storm, that power is promised to be the strength of the chosen. He who wings the unerring bolt, will give to his redeemed the wings of eagles; he who shakes the earth with his voice, will terrify the enemies of his saints, and give his children peace. Why are we weak when we have divine strength to flee to? Why are we troubled when the Lord's own peace is ours? Jesus the mighty God is our peace—what a blessing is this today! What a blessing it will be to us in that day of the Lord which will be in darkness and not light to the ungodly! Dear reader, is not this a noble Psalm to be sung in stormy weather? Can you sing amid the thunder? Will you be able to sing when the last thunders are let loose, and Jesus judges quick and dead? If you are a believer, the last verse is your heritage, and surely that will set you singing.

JOHN CALVIN

him, will not teach them wisdom. Some interpreters think that hinds are mentioned, rather than other beasts, on account of their difficulty in bringing forth their young; which I disapprove not. The voice of the Lord is also said to discover or make bare the forests, either because there is no covering which can prevent it from penetrating into the most secret recesses and caverns; or, because lightnings, rains, and stormy winds, beat off the leaves and make the trees bare. Either sense is appropriate.

In his temple. God's voice fills the whole world, and spreads itself to its farthest limits; but the prophet declares that his glory is celebrated only in his church, because God not only speaks intelligibly and distinctly there, but also there gently allures the faithful to himself. His terrible voice, which thunders in various ways in the air, strikes upon the ears, and causes the hearts of men to beat in such a manner, as to make them shrink from rather than approach him not to mention that a considerable portion turn a deaf ear to its sound in storms, rains, thunder, and lightnings. As men, therefore, profit not so much in this common school as to submit themselves to God, David wisely says especially that the faithful sing the praises of God in his temple, because, being familiarly instructed there by his fatherly voice, they devote and consecrate themselves wholly to his service. No man proclaims the glory of God aright but he who worships him willingly. This may be understood likewise as a complaint, in which David reproves the whole world of being silent in so far as the glory of God is concerned, and laments that although his voice resounds through all regions, yet his praises are no where sung but in his temple alone. He appears, however, after the example of all the godly, to exhort the whole of mankind to praise God's name, and designedly to erect a temple as a receptacle for his glory, for the purpose of teaching us, that in order truly to know God, and praise him as is his due, we need another voice than that which is heard in thunders, showers, and storms in the air, in the mountains, and in the forests; for if he teach us not in plain words, and also kindly allure us to himself, by giving us a taste of his fatherly love, we will continue dumb.

10. Jehovah sitteth upon the flood. David mentions this among other proofs of God's power, that even when the elements appear to be mingled and confounded together by the utmost fury of the weather, God controls and moderates these commotions from his throne in heaven. He accordingly adds, for the sake of explanation, God sits King for ever.

11. Jehovah will give strength to his people. He returns to his former doctrine, namely, that although God exhibits his visible power to the view of the whole world indiscriminately, yet he exerts it in a peculiar manner in behalf of his elect people. Moreover, he here describes him in a very different manner from what he did formerly; that is to say, not as one who overwhelms with fear and dread those to whom he speaks, but as one who upholds, cherishes, and strengthens them.

MATTHEW HENRY

First, Trees have been rent and split by thunderbolts, v. 5, 6. The voice of the Lord, in the thunder, often broke the cedars, even those of Lebanon, the strongest, the stateliest. Earthquakes also shook the ground itself on which the trees grew, and made Lebanon and Sirion to dance; the wilderness of Kadesh also was in like manner shaken (v. 8), the trees by winds, the ground by earthquakes, and both by thunders, of which I incline rather to understand it.
Secondly. Fires have been kindled by lightnings and houses and churches thereby consumed; hence we read of hot thunderbolts (Ps. lxxviii. 48); accordingly the voice of the Lord, in the thunder, is here said to divide the flames of fire (v. 7), that is, to scatter them upon the earth, as God sees fit to direct them and do execution by them.
Thirdly, The terror of thunder makes the hinds to calve sooner, and some think more easily, than otherwise they would. The hind is a timorous creature, and much affected with the noise of thunder; and no marvel, when sometimes proud and stout men have been made to tremble at it.

(2.) In the kingdom of providence, v. 10. God is to be praised as the governor of the world of mankind. He sits upon the flood; he sits King for ever. He not only sits at rest in the enjoyment of himself, but he sits as King in the throne which he has prepared in the heavens (Ps. ciii. 19), where he takes cognizance of, and gives orders about, all the affairs of the children of men, and does all according to his will, according to the counsel of his will.

(3.) In the kingdom of grace. Here his glory shines most brightly,

[1.] In the adorations he receives from the subjects of that kingdom (v. 9). In his temple, where people attend his discoveries of himself and his mind and attend him with their praises, every one speaks of his glory. In the world every man sees it, or at least may behold it afar off (Job xxxvi. 25); but it is only in the temple, in the church, that it is spoken of to his honor. All his works do praise him (that is, they minister matter for praise), but his saints only do bless him, and speak of his glory of his works, Ps. cxlv. 10.

[2.] In the favors he bestows upon the subjects of that kingdom, v. 11. First, He will qualify them for his service: He will give strength to his people, to fortify them against every evil work and to furnish them for every good work; out of weakness they shall be made strong; nay, he will perfect strength in weakness. Secondly, He will encourage them in his service: He will bless his people with peace. Peace is a blessing of inestimable value, which God designs for all his people. The work of righteousness is peace (great peace have those that love thy law); but much more the crown of righteousness: the end of righteousness is peace; it is endless peace.

Psalm 30

Title
A Psalm and Song at the dedication of the house of David.

1-6
1 I will extol thee, O LORD; for thou hast lifted me up, and hast not made my foes to rejoice over me.
2 O LORD my God, I cried unto thee, and thou hast healed me.
3 O LORD, thou hast brought up my soul from the grave: thou hast kept me alive, that I should not go down to the pit.
4 Sing unto the LORD, O ye saints of his, and give thanks at the remembrance of his holiness.
5 For his anger endureth but a moment; in his favor is life: weeping may endure for a night, but joy cometh in the morning.
6 And in my prosperity I said, I shall never be moved.

Psalm 30

TITLE. A Psalm and Song at the Dedication of the House of David; or rather, A Psalm; a Song of Dedication for the House. By David. A song of faith since the house of Jehovah, here intended, David never lived to see. A Psalm of praise, since a sore judgment had been stayed, and a great sin forgiven. From our English version it would appear that this Psalm was intended to be sung at the building of that house of cedar which David erected for himself, when he no longer had to hide himself in the Cave of Adullam, but had become a great king. If this had been the meaning, it would have been well to observe that it is right for the believer when removing, to dedicate his new abode to God.
Throughout this Psalm there are indications that David had been greatly afflicted, both personally and relatively, after having, in his presumption, fancied himself secure. When God's children prosper one way, they are generally tried another, for few of us can bear unmingled prosperity. Even the joys of hope need to be mixed with the pains of experience, and the more surely so when comfort breeds carnal security and self confidence. Nevertheless, pardon soon followed repentance, and God's mercy was glorified. The Psalm is a song, and not a complaint. Let it be read in the light of the last days of David, when he had numbered the people, and God had chastened him, and then in mercy had bidden the angel sheathe his sword. On the floor of Ornan, the poet received the inspiration which glows in this delightful ode. It is the Psalm of the numbering of the people, and of the dedication temple which commemorated the staying of the plague. DIVISION. In Ps 30:1-3, David extols the Lord for delivering him. Ps 30:4-5 he invites the saints to unite with him in celebrating divine compassion. In Ps 30:6-7 he confesses the fault for which he was chastened, Ps 30:8-10 repeats the supplication which he offered, and concludes with commemorating his deliverance and vowing eternal praise.

EXPOSITION
Verse 1. I will extol thee. I will have high and honorable conceptions of thee, and give them utterance in my best music. Others may forget thee, murmur at thee, despise thee, blaspheme thee, but "I will extol thee," for I have been favored above all others. I will extol thy name, thy character, thine attributes, thy mercy to me, thy great forbearance to my people; but, especially will I speak well of thyself; "I will extol thee," O Jehovah; this shall be my cheerful and constant employ.
Verse 2. O Lord my God, I cried unto thee, and thou hast healed me. David sent up prayers for himself and for his people when visited with the pestilence. He went at once to head quarters, and not roundabout to fallible means. God is the best physician, even for our bodily infirmities. We do very wickedly and foolishly when we forget God.
Verse 3. O Lord, thou hast brought up my soul from the grave. Mark, it is not "I hope so;" but it is, "Thou hast; thou hast; thou hast"—three times over. David is quite sure, beyond a doubt, that God has done great things for him, whereof he is exceeding glad. He had descended to the brink of the sepulcher, and yet was restored to tell of the forbearance of God; nor was this all, he owned that nothing but grace had kept him from the lowest hell, and this made him doubly thankful.
Verse 4. Sing unto the Lord, O ye saints of his. "Join my song; assist me to express my gratitude." He felt that he could not praise God enough himself, and therefore he would enlist the hearts of others. Sing unto the Lord, O ye saints of his. David would not fill his choir with reprobates, but with sanctified persons, who could sing from their hearts. He calls to you, ye people of God, because ye are saints: and if sinners are wickedly silent, let your holiness constrain you to sing. You are his saints—chosen, blood

JOHN CALVIN

Psalm 30

1-3
1. I will extol thee, O Jehovah! As David had been brought, as it were, from the grave to the life-giving air, he promises to extol the name of God. It is God who lifts us up with his own hand when we have been plunged into a profound gulf; and therefore it is our duty, on our part, to sing his praises with our tongues. By the foes who, he says, obtained no matter of rejoicing over him, we may understand both domestic and foreign enemies.
2. In the second verse, he concludes that he was preserved by the favor of God, alleging in proof of this, that when he was at the very point of death he directed his supplications to God alone, and that he immediately felt that he had not done so in vain. When God hears our prayers, it is a proof which enables us to conclude with certainty that he is the author of our salvation, and of the deliverance which we obtain.
3. For the sake of amplification, accordingly, he immediately adds, Thou hast brought up my soul from the grave He reckoned that he could not sufficiently express in words the magnitude of the favor which God had conferred upon him, unless he compared the darkness of that period to a grave and pit, into which he had been forced to throw himself hastily, to protect his life by hiding, until the flame of insurrection was quenched.

4-5
4. Sing unto Jehovah. The better to testify his gratitude, David calls upon all the saints to join with him in singing the praises of God; and under one class he describes the whole body. As he had been preserved beyond all expectation, and by this instance had been instructed concerning God's continual and infinite goodness towards all the godly, he breaks forth into this exhortation, in which he includes the general deliverance of the whole church as well as his own.
5. For his anger is only for a moment. It is beyond all controversy that life is opposed here to for a moment, and consequently signifies long continuance, or the constant progress of time from day to day. David thus intimates that if God at any time chastise his people, he not only mitigates the rigor of their punishment, but is immediately appeased, and moderates his anger; whereas he prolongs his kindness and favor for a long time.

6-10
6. And in my tranquility I had said. This is the confession in which David acknowledges that he had been justly and deservedly punished for his foolish and rash security, in forgetting his mortal and mutable condition as a man, and in setting his heart too much on prosperity. By the term tranquility, he means the quiet and flourishing state of his kingdom.
7. O Jehovah! of thy good pleasure. This verse describes the difference which exists between the confidence which is founded upon the word of God and the carnal security which

MATTHEW HENRY

Psalm 30

1-5 Thanksgiving and praise.
I. David does himself give God thanks for the great deliverances he had wrought for him (v. 1): "I will extol thee, O Lord! I will exalt thy name, will praise thee as one high and lifted up, I will do what I can to advance the interest of thy kingdom among men. I will extol thee, for thou hast lifted me up, not only up out of the pit in which I was sinking, but up to the throne of Israel." He raiseth up the poor out of the dust. In consideration of the great things God has done to exalt us, both by his providence and by his grace, we are bound, in gratitude, to do all we can to extol his name, though the most we can do is but little. Three things magnify David's deliverance:
1. That it was the defeat of his enemies. They were not suffered to triumph over him, as they would have done (though it is a barbarous thing) if he had died of this sickness or perished in this distress: see Ps. xli. 11.
2. That it was an answer to his prayers (v. 2): I cried unto thee. All the expressions of the sense we have of our troubles should be directed to God, and every cry be a cry to him; and giving way, in this manner, to our grief, will ease a burdened spirit. "I cried to thee, and thou hast not only heard me, but healed me, healed the distempered body, healed the disturbed and disquieted mind, healed the disordered distracted affairs of the kingdom." This is what God glories in, I am the Lord that healeth thee (Exod. xv. 26), and we must give him the glory of it.
3. That it was the saving of his life; for he was brought to the last extremity, dropping into the grave, and ready to go down into the pit, and yet rescued and kept alive, v. 3. The more imminent our dangers have been, the more eminent our deliverances have been, the more comfortable are they to ourselves and the more illustrious proofs of the power and goodness of God. A life from the dead ought to be spent in extolling the God of our life.
II. He calls upon others to join with him in praise, not only for the particular favors God has bestowed upon him, but for the general tokens of his good-will to all his saints (v. 4): Sing unto the Lord, O you saints of his! All that are truly saints he owns for his.

6-12 Prayer and praise.
We have, in these verses, an account of three several states that David was in successively, and of the workings of his heart towards God in each of those states—what he said and did, and how his heart stood affected; in the first of these we may see what we are too apt to be, and in the other two what we should be.
I. He had long enjoyed prosperity, and then he grew secure and over-confident of the continuance of it (v. 6, 7): "In my prosperity, when I was in health of body and God had given me rest from all my enemies,

Psalm 30

7-12

7 LORD, by thy favor thou hast made my mountain to stand strong: thou didst hide thy face, and I was troubled.

8 I cried to thee, O LORD; and unto the LORD I made supplication.

9 What profit is there in my blood, when I go down to the pit? Shall the dust praise thee? shall it declare thy truth?

10 Hear, O LORD, and have mercy upon me: LORD, be thou my helper.

11 Thou hast turned for me my mourning into dancing: thou hast put off my sackcloth, and girded me with gladness;

12 To the end that my glory may sing praise to thee, and not be silent. O LORD my God, I will give thanks unto thee for ever.

bought, called, and set apart for God; sanctified on purpose that you should offer the daily sacrifice of praise. Abound ye in this heavenly duty.

Verse 5. For his anger endureth but a moment. David here alludes to those dispensations of God's providence which are the chastisement ordered in his paternal government towards his erring children, such as the plague which fell upon Jerusalem for David's sins; these are but short judgments, and they are removed as soon as real penitence sues for pardon and presents the great and acceptable sacrifice. What a mercy is this, for if the Lord's wrath smoked for a long season, flesh would utterly fail before him.

Verse 6. In my prosperity. When all his foes were quiet, and his rebellious son dead and buried, then was the time of peril. Many a vessel founders in a calm. No temptation is so bad as tranquility. I said, I shall never be moved. Ah! David, you said more than was wise to say, or even to think, for God has founded the world upon the floods, to show us what a poor, mutable, moveable, inconstant world it is. Unhappy he who builds upon it! He builds himself a dungeon for his hopes. Instead of conceiving that we shall never be moved, we ought to remember that we shall very soon be removed altogether.

Verse 7. Lord, by thy favor thou hast made my mountain to stand strong. He ascribed his prosperity to the Lord's favor—so far good, it is well to own the hand of the Lord in all our stability and wealth. But observe that the good in a good man is not unmingled good, for this was alloyed with carnal security. His state he compares to a mountain, a molehill would have been nearer—we never think too little of ourselves.

Verse 8. I cried to thee, O Lord. Prayer is the unfailing resource of God's people. If they are driven to their wit's end, they may still go to the mercy seat. When an earthquake makes our mountain tremble, the throne of grace still stands firm, and we may come to it. Let us never forget to pray, and let us never doubt the success of prayer. The hand which wounds can heal: let us turn to him who smites us, and he will be entreated of us.

Verse 9. In this verse we learn the form and method of David's prayer. It was an argument with God, an urging of reasons, a pleading of his cause. It was not a statement of doctrinal opinions, nor a narration of experience, much less a sly hit at other people under pretence of praying to God, although all these things and worse have been substituted for holy supplication at certain prayer meetings.

Verse 10. Hear, O Lord, and have mercy upon me. A short and comprehensive petition, available at all seasons, let us use it full often. It is the publican's prayer; be it ours. If God hears prayer, it is a great act of mercy; our petitions do not merit a reply. Lord, be thou my helper. Another compact, expressive, ever fitting prayer.

Verse 11. Observe the contrast, God takes away the mourning of his people; and what does he give them instead of it? Quiet and peace? Aye, and a great deal more than that. Thou hast turned for me my mourning into dancing. He makes their hearts to dance at the sound of his name.

Verse 12. To the end—namely, with this view and intent—that my glory—that is, my tongue or my soul—may sing praise to thee, and not be silent. It would be a shameful crime, if, after receiving God's mercies, we should forget to praise him. God would not have our tongues lie idle while so many themes for gratitude are spread on every hand. He would have no dumb children in the house. They are all to sing in heaven, and therefore they should all sing on earth.

springs from presumption. True believers, when they rely upon God, are not on that account neglectful of prayer. On the contrary, looking carefully at the multitude of dangers by which they are beset, and the manifold instances of human frailty which pass before their eyes, they take warning from them, and pour out their hearts before God. The prophet now failed in duty as to this matter; because, by anchoring himself on his present wealth and tranquility, or spreading his sails to the prosperous winds, he depended not on the free favor of God in such a manner as to be ready at any time to resign into his hands the blessings which he had bestowed upon him.

8. O Jehovah! I cried unto thee. Now follows the fruit of David's chastisement. He had been previously sleeping profoundly, and fostering his indolence by forgetfulness; but being now awakened all on a sudden with fear and terror, he begins to cry to God. As the iron which has contracted rust cannot be put to any use until it be heated again in the fire, and beaten with the hammer, so in like manner, when carnal security has once got the mastery, no one can give himself cheerfully to prayer, until he has been softened by the cross, and thoroughly subdued.

9. What profit is there in my blood? Some explain the verse after this manner: What will it avail me to have lived, unless thou prolongest my life till I shall have finished the course of my vocation? But this exposition seems too strained, especially as the term blood here signifies death, not life: as if David had said, What profit wilt thou derive from my death? This interpretation is farther confirmed by the following clause, where he complains that his lifeless body will then be useless for celebrating the praises of God.

10. Hear, O Jehovah! In this clause the Psalmist softens and corrects his former complaint; for it would have been absurd to expostulate with God like one who despaired of safety, and to leave off in this fretful temper.

11-12

11. Thou hast turned my mourning into dancing. David concludes the psalm as he had begun it, with thanksgiving. He affirms that it was by the help and blessing of God that he had escaped safe; and he then adds, that the final object of his escape was, that he might employ the rest of his life in celebrating the praises of God. Moreover, he shows us that he was not insensible or obdurate under his afflictions, but mourned in heaviness and sorrow; and he also shows that his very mourning had been the means of leading him to pray to God to deprecate his wrath.

12. That my glory may sing praise to thee. In this verse he more fully expresses his acknowledgement of the purpose for which God had preserved him from death, and that he would be careful to render him a proper return of gratitude. That every man may celebrate thy glory; as if the prophet had said, This is a blessing worthy of being celebrated by the public praises of all men.

I said I shall never be moved; I never thought either of having my body distempered or my government disturbed, not had any apprehensions of danger upon any account."

II. On a sudden he fell into trouble, and then he prayed to God, and pleaded earnestly for relief and succor.

1. His mountain was shaken and he with it; it proved, when he grew secure, that he was least safe: "Thou didst hide thy face and I was troubled, in mind, body, or estate." In every change of his condition he still kept his eye upon God, and, as he ascribed his prosperity to God's favor, so in his adversity he observed the hiding of God's face, to be the cause of it. If God hide his face, a good man is certainly troubled, though no other calamity befall him; when the sun sets night certainly follows, and the moon and all the stars cannot make day.

2. When his mountain was shaken he lifted up his eyes above the hills. Prayer is a salve for every sore; he made use of it accordingly. Is any afflicted? Is any troubled? Let him pray. Though God hid his face from him, yet he prayed. If God, in wisdom and justice, turn from us, yet it will be in us the greatest folly and injustice imaginable if we turn from him. No; let us learn to pray in the dark (v. 8): I cried to thee, O Lord! It seems God's withdrawings made his prayers the more vehement. We are here told, for it seems he kept account of it,

(1.) What he pleaded, v. 9.

[1.] That God would be no gainer by his death: What profit is there in my blood? implying that he would willingly die if he could thereby do any real service to God or his country (Phil. ii. 17), but he saw not what good could be done by his dying in the bed of sickness, as might be if he had died in the bed of honor. "Lord," says he, "wilt thou sell one of thy own people for nought and not increase thy wealth by the price?" Ps. xliv. 12. Nay

[2.] That, in his honor, God would seem to be a loser by his death: Shall the dust praise thee? The sanctified spirit, which returns to God, shall praise him, shall be still praising him; but the dust, which returns to the earth, shall not praise him, nor declare his truth.

(2.) What he prayed for, v. 10. He prayed for mercy to pardon (Have mercy upon me), and for grace to help in time of need—Lord, be thou my helper. On these two errands we also may come boldly to the throne of grace, Heb. iv. 16.

III. In due time God delivered him out of his troubles and restored him to his former prosperity. His prayers were answered and his mourning was turned into dancing, v. 11. God's anger now endured but for a moment, and David's weeping but for a night. The sackcloth with which, in a humble compliance with the divine Providence, he had clad himself, was loosed.

He tells us, v. 12. that his complaints were turned into praises and that these praises were likely to be forever.

Psalm 31

Title
To the chief Musician, a Psalm of David.

1-8
1 In thee, O LORD, do I put my trust; let me never be ashamed: deliver me in thy righteousness.
2 Bow down thine ear to me; deliver me speedily: be thou my strong rock, for an house of defense to save me.
3 For thou art my rock and my fortress; therefore for thy name's sake lead me, and guide me.
4 Pull me out of the net that they have laid privily for me: for thou art my strength.
5 Into thine hand I commit my spirit: thou hast redeemed me, O LORD God of truth.
6 I have hated them that regard lying vanities: but I trust in the LORD.
7 I will be glad and rejoice in thy mercy: for thou hast considered my trouble; thou hast known my soul in adversities;
8 And hast not shut me up into the hand of the enemy: thou hast set my feet in a large room.

Psalm 31

TITLE. To the Chief Musician—a Psalm of David. The dedication to the chief musician proves that this song of mingled measures and alternate strains of grief and woe was intended for public singing, and thus a deathblow is given to the notion that nothing but praise should be sung. Perhaps the Psalms, thus marked, might have been set aside as too mournful for temple worship, if special care had not been taken by the Holy Spirit to indicate them as being designed for the public edification of the Lord's people. May there not also be in Psalms thus designated a peculiar distinct reference to the Lord Jesus? He certainly manifests himself very clearly in the twenty-second, which bears this title; and in the one before us we plainly hear his dying voice in the fifth verse. Jesus is chief everywhere, and in all the holy songs of his saints he is the chief musician.
SUBJECT. The psalmist in dire affliction appeals to his God for help with much confidence and holy importunity, and ere long finds his mind so strengthened that he magnifies the Lord for his great goodness. Some have thought that the occasion in his troubled life which led to this Psalm, was the treachery of the men of Keilah, and we have felt much inclined to this conjecture; but after reflection it seems to us that its very mournful tone, and its allusion to his iniquity demand a later date, and it may be more satisfactory to illustrate it by the period when Absalom had rebelled, and his courtiers were fled from him, while lying lips spread a thousand malicious rumors against him. It is perhaps quite as well that we have no settled season mentioned, or we might have been so busy in applying it to David's case as to forget its suitability to our own.
DIVISION. There are no great lines of demarcation; throughout the strain undulates, falling into valleys of mourning, and rising with hills of confidence. However, we may for convenience arrange it thus: David testifying his confidence in God pleads for help, Ps 31:1-6; expresses gratitude for mercies received, Ps 31:7-8; particularly describes his case, Ps 31:9-13; vehemently pleads for deliverance, Ps 31:14-18; confidently and thankfully expects a blessing, Ps 31:19-22; and closes by showing the bearing of his case upon all the people of God.

EXPOSITION
Verse 1. In thee, O Lord, do I put my trust. Nowhere else do I fly for shelter, let the tempest howl as it may. The psalmist has one refuge, and that the best one. He casts out the great sheet anchor of his faith in the time of storm. Let other things be doubtful, yet the fact that he relies on Jehovah, David lays down most positively; and he begins with it, lest by stress of trial he should afterwards forget it. This avowal of faith is the fulcrum by means of which he labors to uplift and remove his trouble; he dwells upon it as a comfort to himself and a plea with God.
Verse 2. Bow down thine ear to me. Condescend to my low estate; listen to me attentively as one who would hear every word. Heaven with its transcendent glories of harmony might well engross the divine ear, but yet the Lord has an hourly regard to the weakest moanings of his poorest people. Deliver me speedily. We must not set times or seasons, yet in submission we may ask for swift as well as sure mercy.
Verse 3. For thou art my rock and my fortress. Here the tried soul avows yet again its full confidence in God. Faith's repetitions are not vain. The avowal of our reliance upon God in times of adversity is a principle method of glorifying him.
Verse 4. Pull me out of the net that they have laid privily for me. The enemies of David were cunning as well as mighty; if they could not conquer him by power, they would capture him by craft. Our own spiritual foes are of the same order—they are of the serpent's brood, and seek to ensnare us by their guile.

JOHN CALVIN

Psalm 31

1-4

1. In thee, O Jehovah! have I put my trust. Some are of opinion that this psalm was composed by David, after he had most unexpectedly escaped out of the wilderness of Maon; to which I do not object, although it is only a doubtful conjecture. Certainly he celebrates one or more of the greatest of his dangers. In the commencement he tells us what kind of prayer he offered in his agony and distress; and its language breathes affection of the most ardent nature. He takes it for a ground of hope that he trusted in the Lord, or continued to trust in him; for the verb in the past tense seems to denote a continued act.

2. Incline thine ear unto me. These words express with how much ardor David's soul was stimulated to pray. He affects no splendid or ornate language, as rhetoricians are wont to do; but only describes in suitable figures the vehemence of his desire. In praying that he may be delivered speedily there is shown the greatness of his danger, as if he had said, All will soon be over with my life, unless God make haste to help me.

3. For thou art my rock. David, by interjecting this reflection, encourages himself not only to earnestness in prayer, but also in the confident hope of obtaining his requests. We know that it is usual with him to mingle such things in his prayers as may serve to remove his doubts, and to confirm his assurance. Having, therefore, expressed his need, he assures himself, in order to encourage and animate himself, that his prayer shall certainly have a happy answer.

4. In the next verse, under the metaphor of a net, he appears to designate the snares and artifices with which his enemies encompassed him. We know that conspiracies were frequently formed against his life, which would have left him no room for escape; and as his enemies were deeply skilled in policy, and hating him with an inconceivable hatred, were eagerly bent on his destruction, it was impossible for him to be saved from them by any human power.

5-8

5. Into thy hand I commit my spirit. David again declares his faith to God, and affirms that he had such high thoughts of his providence, as to cast all his cares upon it. Whoever commits himself into God's hand and to his guardianship, not only constitutes him the arbiter of life and death to him, but also calmly depends on him for protection amidst all his dangers.

6. I hate all that give heed to lying vanities. In order the better to express that his faith was firmly fixed on God, he affirms that he was free from the vile affections which usually turn away our minds from God, and under which unbelievers for the most part labor. For we know that by contrasting things which are opposite, a subject is better illustrated.

7. I will be glad and rejoice in thy goodness. Here is inserted a thanksgiving, although many are rather of opinion that David's prayer is suspended, and that he makes a vow, when he shall be delivered from present danger. But as no condition is annexed, I am rather inclined to think that stopping all at

MATTHEW HENRY

Psalm 31

1-8 Prayer for deliverance; profession of confidence in God.

David prays,

1. That God would deliver him (v. 1), that his life might be preserved from the malice of his enemies, and that an end might be put to their persecutions of him, that God, not only in his mercy, but in righteousness, would deliver him, as a righteous Judge betwixt him and his unrighteous persecutors, that he would bow down his ear to his petitions, to his appeals, and deliver him, v. 2. It is condescension in God to take cognizance of the case of the greatest and best of men; he humbles himself to do it.

2. That if he did not immediately deliver him out of his troubles, yet he would protect and shelter him in his troubles; "Be thou my strong rock, immovable, impregnable, as a fastness framed by nature, and my house of defense, a fortress framed by art, and all to save me."

3. That his case having much in it of difficulty, both in respect of duty and in respect of prudence, he might be under the divine guidance: "Lord, lead me and guide me (v. 3), so order my steps, so order my spirit, that I may never do any thing unlawful and unjustifiable—against my conscience, nor unwise and indiscreet—against my interest." Those that resolve to follow God's direction may in faith pray for it.

4. That his enemies being very crafty, as well as very spiteful, God would frustrate and baffle their designs against him (v. 4): "Pull me out of the net that they have laid privily for me, and keep me from the sin, the trouble, the death, they aim to entrap me in."

II. In this prayer he gives glory to God by a repeated profession of his confidence in him and dependence on him. This encouraged his prayers and qualified him for the mercies he prayed for (v. 1): "In thee, O Lord! do I put my trust, and not in myself, or any sufficiency of my own, or in any creature; let me never be ashamed, let me not be disappointed of any of that good which thou hast promised me and which therefore I have promised myself in thee."

1. He had chosen God for his protector, and God had, by his promise, undertaken to be so (v. 3): "Thou art my rock and my fortress, by thy covenant with me and my believing consent to that covenant; therefore be my strong rock," v. 2. Those that have in sincerity avouched the Lord for theirs may expect the benefit of his being so; for God's relations to us carry with them both name and thing. Thou art my strength, v. 4. If God be our strength, we may hope that he will both put his strength in us and put forth his strength for us.

2. He gave up his soul in a special manner to him (v. 5): Into thy hands I commit my spirit. If David here looks upon himself as a dying man, by these words he resigns his departing soul to God who gave it, and to whom, at death, the spirit returns. "Men can but kill

Psalm 31

9-16

9 Have mercy upon me, O LORD, for I am in trouble: mine eye is consumed with grief, yea, my soul and my belly.
10 For my life is spent with grief, and my years with sighing: my strength faileth because of mine iniquity, and my bones are consumed.
11 I was a reproach among all mine enemies, but especially among my neighbors, and a fear to mine acquaintance: they that did see me without fled from me.
12 I am forgotten as a dead man out of mind: I am like a broken vessel.
13 For I have heard the slander of many: fear was on every side: while they took counsel together against me, they devised to take away my life.
14 But I trusted in thee, O LORD: I said, Thou art my God.
15 My times are in thy hand: deliver me from the hand of mine enemies, and from them that persecute me.
16 Make thy face to shine upon thy servant: save me for thy mercies' sake.

Verse 5. Into thine hand I commit my spirit. These living words of David were our Lord's dying words, and have been frequently used by holy men in their hour of departure. Be assured that they are good, choice, wise, and solemn words; we may use them now and in the last tremendous hour.
Verse 6. I have hated them that regard lying vanities. Those who will not lean upon the true arm of strength, are sure to make to themselves vain confidences. Man must have a god, and if he will not adore the only living and true God, he makes a fool of himself, and pays superstitious regard to a lie, and waits with anxious hope upon a base delusion.
Verse 7. I will be glad and rejoice in thy mercy. For mercy past he is grateful, and for mercy future, which he believingly anticipates, he is joyful. In our most importunate intercessions, we must find breathing time to bless the Lord: praise is never a hindrance to prayer, but rather a lively refreshment therein. It is delightful at intervals to hear the notes of the high sounding cymbals when the dolorous sackbut rules the hour.
Verse 8. And hast not shut me up into the hand of the enemy. To be shut up in one's hand is to be delivered over absolutely to his power; now, the believer is not in the hand of death or the devil, much less is he in the power of man. The enemy may get a temporary advantage over us, but we are like men in prison with the door open; God will not let us be shut up, he always provides a way of escape.
Verse 9. Have mercy upon me, O Lord, for I am in trouble. Now, the man of God comes to a particular and minute description of his sorrowful case. He unbosoms his heart, lays bare his wounds, and expresses his inward desolation. This first sentence pithily comprehends all that follows, it is the text for his lamenting discourse. Misery moves mercy—no more reasoning is needed. "Have mercy" is the prayer; the argument is as prevalent as it is plain and personal, "I am in trouble."
Verse 10. For my life is spent with grief, and my years with sighing. It had become his daily occupation to mourn; he spent all his days in the dungeon of distress. The sap and essence of his existence was being consumed, as a candle is wasted while it burns. His adversities were shortening his days, and digging for him an early grave.
Verse 11. I was a reproach among all mine enemies. They were pleased to have something to throw at me; my mournful estate was music to them, because they maliciously interpreted it to be a judgment from heaven upon me. Reproach is little thought of by those who are not called to endure it, but he who passes under its lash knows how deep it wounds.
Verse 12. I am forgotten as a dead man out of mind. All David's youthful prowess was now gone from remembrance; he had been the savior of his country, but his services were buried in oblivion. Men soon forget the deepest obligations; popularity is evanescent to the last degree: he who is in every one's mouth today may be forgotten by all tomorrow.
Verse 13. For I have heard the slander of many. One slanderous viper is death to all comfort—what must be the venom of a whole brood? What the ear does not hear the heart does not rue.
Verses 14-18. In this section of the Psalm he renews his prayers, urging the same pleas as at first: earnest wrestlers attempt over and over again the same means of gaining their point.
Verse 14. But I trusted in thee, O Lord. Notwithstanding all afflicting circumstances, David's faith maintained its hold, and was not turned aside from its object. What a blessed saving clause is this! So long as our faith, which is our shield, is safe, the battle may go hard, but its ultimate result is no matter of question; if that could be torn from us, we should be as surely slain as were Saul and Jonathan upon the high places of the field.
Verse 15. My times are in thy hand. The sovereign arbiter of destiny holds in his own power all the issues of our life; we are not waifs and strays upon the ocean of fate, but are steered by infinite wisdom towards our desired

once in the middle of his prayer, he promises himself a deliverance, for which he will have abundant matter for giving thanks.

8. This is also farther intimated by the following sentence, Thou hast set my feet in a large place, which denotes a sudden and unexpected change.

9-13

9. Have mercy upon me, O Jehovah! To move God to succor him, he magnifies the greatness of his misery and grief by the number of his complaints; not that God needs arguments to persuade him, but because he allows the faithful to deal familiarly with him, that they may disburden themselves of their cares. The greater the number of afflictions with which they are oppressed, the more do they encourage themselves, while bewailing them before God, in the hope of obtaining his assistance.

10. And although it is true that David was accustomed to ascribe the afflictions which he at any time suffered to his own fault, yet, as he is only recounting his miseries here, without mentioning the cause of them, it is probable that, according to his usual manner, he expresses the same thing twice by different words.

11. David was everywhere hated, and his enemies had induced almost the whole realm to take part with them against him, he had an evil name even among his friends and neighbors; just as popular opinion, like a violent tempest, usually carries all before it.

12. I am forgotten as one dead. The Psalmist still pursues the same idea, and complains that he was as completely blotted out of all men's remembrance as if he had been dead. The memory of some men after their death flourishes for a time among survivors, but it more frequently vanishes; for there is no longer any intercourse between the quick and the dead, nor can the living be of any farther service to the dead. David illustrates this idea by the metaphor of a broken vessel, which denotes utter contempt and meanness.

13. He adds, in fine, that he was railed upon by the multitude, and agitated with terrors. When great men, who are often as powerful in judgment as in authority, slander and defame us as wicked persons, this adds to the indignity with which we are treated, because, whatever they say in condemnation of us has the effect of prejudicing the common people against us.

14-18

14. Yet have I trusted in thee, O Jehovah! David, setting the steadfastness of his faith in opposition to the assaults of the temptations of which he has made mention, denies that he had ever fainted, but rather maintains, on the contrary, that he stood firm in his hope of deliverance from God.

15. My times are in thy hand. That he might the more cheerfully commit the preservation of his person to God, he assures us, that, trusting to his divine guardianship, he did not trouble himself about those casual and unforeseen events which men commonly dread. The import of his language is, Lord, it is thy prerogative, and thou alone hast the power, to dispose of both my life and my death.

the body, but I trust in God to redeem my soul from the power of the grave," Ps. xlix. 15. He is willing to die if God will have it so; but let my soul fall into the hands of the Lord, for his mercies are great.

III. He disclaimed all confederacy with those that made an arm of flesh their confidence (v. 6): I have hated those that regard lying vanities—idolaters (to some), who expect aid from false gods, which are vanity and a lie—astrologers, and those that give heed to them, so others. David abhorred the use of enchantments and divinations; he consulted not, nor even took notice of, the flight of birds or entrails of beasts, good omens or bad omens; they are lying vanities, and he not only did not regard them himself, but hated the wickedness of those that did. He trusted in God only, and not in any creature.

IV. He comforted himself with his hope in God, and made himself, not only easy, but cheerful, with it, v. 7. Having relied on God's mercy, he will be glad and rejoice in it; and those know not how to value their hope in God who cannot find joy enough in that hope to counterbalance their grievances and silence their griefs.

V. He encouraged himself in this hope with the experiences he had had of late, and formerly, of God's goodness to him, which he mentions to the glory of God; he that has delivered doth and will.

9-18 sorrowful complaints; humble and believing prayer.

In the foregoing verses David had appealed to God's righteousness, and pleaded his relation to him and dependence on him; here he appeals to his mercy, and pleads the greatness of his own misery, which made his case the proper object of that mercy. Observe,

I. The complaint he makes of his trouble and distress (v. 9): "Have mercy upon me, O Lord! for I am in trouble, and need thy mercy." The remembrance he makes of his condition is not much unlike some even of Job's complaints.

1. His troubles had fixed a very deep impression upon his mind and made him a man of sorrows. So great was his grief that his very soul was consumed with it, and his life spent with it, and he was continually sighing, v. 9, 10. Herein he was a type of Christ,—who was intimately acquainted with grief and often in tears.

2. His body was afflicted with the sorrows of his mind (v. 10): My strength fails, my bones are consumed, and all because of my iniquity.

3. His friends were unkind and became shy of him. He was a fear to his acquaintance, when they saw him they fled from him, v. 11. They durst not harbor him nor give him any assistance, durst not show him any countenance, nor so much as be seen in his company, for fear of being brought into trouble by it, now that Saul had proclaimed him a traitor and outlawed him.

4. His enemies were unjust in their censures of him. They would not have persecuted him as they did if

Psalm 31

17-24

17 Let me not be ashamed, O LORD; for I have called upon thee: let the wicked be ashamed, and let them be silent in the grave.
18 Let the lying lips be put to silence; which speak grievous things proudly and contemptuously against the righteous.
19 Oh how great is thy goodness, which thou hast laid up for them that fear thee; which thou hast wrought for them that trust in thee before the sons of men!
20 Thou shalt hide them in the secret of thy presence from the pride of man: thou shalt keep them secretly in a pavilion from the strife of tongues.
21 Blessed be the LORD: for he hath shewed me his marvelous kindness in a strong city.
22 For I said in my haste, I am cut off from before thine eyes: nevertheless thou heardest the voice of my supplications when I cried unto thee.
23 O love the LORD, all ye his saints: for the LORD preserveth the faithful, and plentifully rewardeth the proud doer.
24 Be of good courage, and he shall strengthen your heart, all ye that hope in the LORD.

haven. Providence is a soft pillow for anxious heads, an anodyne for care, a grave for despair.

Verse 16. Make thy face to shine upon thy servant. Give me the sunshine of heaven in my soul, and I will defy the tempests of earth. Permit me to enjoy a sense of thy favor, O Lord, and a consciousness that thou art pleased with my manner of life, and all men may frown and slander as they will.

Verse 17. Let me not be ashamed, O Lord; for I have called upon thee. Put not my prayers to the blush! Do not fill profane mouths with jeers at my confidence in my God.

Verse 18. Let the lying lips be put to silence. A right good and Christian prayer; who but a bad man would give liars more license than need be? May God silence them either by leading them to repentance, by putting them to thorough shame, or by placing them in positions where what they may say will stand for nothing.

Verses 19-22. Being full of faith, the psalmist gives glory to God for the mercy which he is assured will be his position.

Verse 19. Oh how great is thy goodness. Is it not singular to find such a joyful sentence in connection with so much sorrow? Truly the life of faith is a miracle.

Verse 20. Thou shalt hide them in the secret of thy presence from the pride of man. Pride is a barbed weapon: the proud man's contumely is iron which entereth into the soul; but those who trust in God, are safely housed in the Holy of holies, the innermost court, into which no man may dare intrude; here in the secret dwelling place of God the mind of the saint rests in peace, which the foot of pride cannot disturb.

Verse 21. Blessed be the Lord. When the Lord blesses us we cannot do less than bless him in return. For he hath shewed me his marvelous kindness in a strong city.

Verse 22. Confession of faults is always proper; and when we reflect upon the goodness of God, we ought to be reminded of our own errors and offences. For I said in my haste. We generally speak amiss when we are in a hurry. Hasty words are but for a moment on the tongue, but they often lie for years on the conscience.

Verse 23. O love the Lord, all ye his saints. A most affecting exhortation, showing clearly the deep love of the writer to his God: there is the more beauty in the expression, because it reveals love toward a smiting God, love which many waters could not quench. To bless him who gives is easy, but to cling to him who takes away is a work of grace.

Verse 24. Be of good courage. Keep up your spirit, let no craven thoughts blanch your cheek. Fear weakens, courage strengthens. Victory waits upon the banners of the brave. And he shall strengthen your heart. Power from on high shall be given in the most effectual manner by administering force to the fountain of vitality. So far from leaving us, the Lord will draw very near to us in our adversity, and put his own power into us. All ye that hope in the Lord. Every one of you, lift up your heads and sing for joy of heart. God is faithful, and does not fail even his little children who do but hope, wherefore then should we be afraid?

16. Make thy face to shine upon thy servant. This form of speech is taken from the common apprehension of men, who think that God regards them not, unless he really show his care of them by its effects. According to the judgment of sense, afflictions hide his countenance, just as clouds obscure the brightness of the sun.
17. O Jehovah! let me not be ashamed. In these words, the Psalmist continues his prayer, and to strengthen his hopes, he contrasts himself with his enemies; for it would have been more than absurd to permit those who by their wickedness so openly provoked the wrath of God to escape with impunity, and that one who relied upon God should be disappointed and made a laughing-stock.
18. In the very next verse, therefore, he adds, Let lying lips be put to silence, which, in my opinion, includes both their craftiness, and the false pretences and calumnies by which they endeavor to accomplish their designs, and also the vain boasting in which they indulge themselves. For he tells us that they speak with harshness and severity against the righteous, in pride and scorn; because it was their froward conceit, which almost always begets contempt, that made David's enemies so bold in lying.

19-21
19. O how great is thy goodness which thou hast hidden for them that fear thee! In this verse the Psalmist exclaims that God is incomprehensibly good and beneficent towards his servants. Goodness here means those divine blessings which are the effects of it.
20. Thou shalt hide them in the secret of thy countenance. In this verse the Psalmist specially commends the grace of God, because it preserves and protects the faithful against all harm.
21. Blessed be Jehovah! These general truths the Psalmist here proceeds to apply to his own circumstances, and he declares that the goodness of God in preserving his life was wondrously displayed.

22-24
22. And I said in my fear. David here confesses that for his distrust he deserved to be deserted by God and left to perish. It is true that to confess this before men he felt to be a shameful thing; but that he may the more fully illustrate the grace of God to him, he hesitates not to publish the shame of his fault.
23. O love Jehovah, all ye his meek ones! In my opinion, the Psalmist does not here exhort the saints to fear and reverence God, as many think, but encourages them to confide in him; or, in other words, to devote themselves wholly to him, to put all their hope in him, and to rely entirely upon him, without seeking to any other.
24. Be of good courage. This exhortation is to be understood in the same way as the preceding; for the steadfastness which the Psalmist here enjoins is founded on the love of God of which he had spoken, when renouncing all the enticements of the world, we embrace with our whole hearts the defense and protection which he promises.

they had not first represented him as a bad man; he was a reproach among all his enemies, but especially among his neighbors, v. 11.
5. His life was aimed at and he went in continual peril of it. Fear was on every side, and he knew that, whatever counsel his enemies took against him, the design was not to take away his liberty, but to take away his life (v. 13), a life so valuable, so useful, to the good services of which all Israel owed so much, and which was never forfeited.
II. His confidence in God in the midst of these troubles. Every thing looked black and dismal round about him, and threatened to drive him to despair: "But I trusted in thee, O Lord! (v. 14) and was thereby kept from sinking." His enemies robbed him of his reputation among men, but they could not rob him of his comfort in God, because they could not drive him from his confidence in God.
III. His petitions to God, in this faith and confidence.
1. He prays that God would deliver him out of the hand of his enemies (v. 15), and save him (v. 16), and this for his mercies' sake, and not for any merit of his own.
2. That God would give him the comfort of his favor in the mean time (v. 16): "Make thy face to shine upon thy servant; let me have the comfortable tokens and evidences of thy favor to me, and that shall put gladness in my heart in the midst of all my griefs."
3. That his prayers to God might be answered and his hopes in God accomplished (v. 17): "Let me not be ashamed of my hopes and prayers, for I have called upon thee, who never saidst to thy people, Seek in vain, and hope in vain."

19-24 Triumphant praise.
We have three things in these verses:
I. The believing acknowledgment which David makes of God's goodness to his people in general, v. 19, 20.
II. The thankful returns which David makes for God's goodness to him in particular, v. 21, 22. Having admired God's goodness to all the saints, he here owns how good he had found him.
III. The exhortation and encouragement which he hereupon gives to all the saints, v. 23, 24.
1. He would have them set their love on God (v. 23): O love the Lord! all you his saints. Those that have their own hearts full of love to God cannot but desire that others also may be in love with him; for in his favor there is no need to fear a rival.
2. He would have them set their hope in God (v. 24): "Be of good courage; have a good heart on it; whatever difficulties or dangers you may meet with, the God you trust in shall by that trust strengthen your heart." Those that hope in God have reason to be of good courage, and let their hearts be strong, for, as nothing truly evil can befall them, so nothing truly good for them shall be wanting to them.

Psalm 32

Title
A Psalm of David, Maschil.

1-5
1 Blessed is he whose transgression is forgiven, whose sin is covered.
2 Blessed is the man unto whom the LORD imputeth not iniquity, and in whose spirit there is no guile.
3 When I kept silence, my bones waxed old through my roaring all the day long.
4 For day and night thy hand was heavy upon me: my moisture is turned into the drought of summer. Selah.
5 I acknowledge my sin unto thee, and mine iniquity have I not hid. I said, I will confess my transgressions unto the LORD; and thou forgavest the iniquity of my sin. Selah.

Psalm 32

TITLE. A Psalm of David, Maschil. That David wrote this gloriously evangelic Psalm is proved not only by this heading, but by the words of the apostle Paul, in Ro 4:6-8. "Even as David also describeth the blessedness of the man unto whom God imputeth righteousness without works," &c. Probably his deep repentance over his great sin was followed by such blissful peace, that he was led to pour out his spirit in the soft music of this choice song. In the order of history it seems to follow the fifty-first. Maschil is a new title to us, and indicates that this is an instructive or didactic Psalm. The experience of one believer affords rich instruction to others, it reveals the footsteps of the flock, and so comforts and directs the weak. Perhaps it was important in this case to prefix the word, that doubting saints might not imagine the Psalm to be the peculiar utterance of a singular individual, but might appropriate it to themselves as a lesson from the Spirit of God. David promised in the fifty-first Psalm to teach transgressors the Lord's ways, and here he does it most effectually. Grotius thinks that this Psalm was meant to be sung on the annual day of the Jewish expiation, when a general confession of their sins was made.
DIVISION. In our reading we have found it convenient to note the benediction of the pardoned, Ps 32:1-2; David's personal confession, Ps 32:3-5; and the application of the case to others, Ps 32:6-7. The voice of God is heard by the forgiven one in Ps 32:8-9; and the Psalm then concludes with a portion for each of the two great classes of men, Ps 32:10-11.

EXPOSITION
Verse 1. Blessed. Like the sermon on the mount on the mount, this Psalm begins with beatitudes. This is the second Psalm of benediction. The first Psalm describes the result of holy blessedness, the thirty-second details the cause of it. The first pictures the tree in full growth, this depicts it in its first planting and watering. He who in the first Psalm is a reader of God's book, is here a suppliant at God's throne accepted and heard. Blessed is he whose transgression is forgiven. He is now blessed and ever shall be. Be he ever so poor, or sick, or sorrowful, he is blessed in very deed. Pardoning mercy is of all things in the world most to be prized, for it is the only and sure way to happiness. To hear from God's own Spirit the words, "absolvo te" is joy unspeakable.
Verse 2. Blessed is the man unto whom the Lord imputeth not iniquity. The word blessed is in the plural, oh, the blessednesses! the double joys, the bundles of happiness, the mountains of delight! Note the three words so often used to denote our disobedience: transgression, sin, and iniquity, are the three headed dog at the gates of hell, but our glorious Lord has silenced his barkings for ever against his own believing ones. The trinity of sin is overcome by the Trinity of heaven.
Verses 3-5. David now gives us his own experience: no instructor is so efficient as one who testifies to what he has personally known and felt. He writes well who like the spider spins his matter out of his own bowels.
Verse 3. When I kept silence. When through neglect I failed to confess, or through despair dared not do so, my bones, those solid pillars of my frame, the stronger portions of my bodily constitution, waxed old, began to decay with weakness, for my grief was so intense as to sap my health and destroy my vital energy. What a killing thing is sin! It is a pestilent disease! A fire in the bones! While we smother our sin it rages within, and like a gathering wound swells horribly and torments terribly.
Verse 4. For day and night thy hand was heavy upon me. God's finger can crush us—what must his hand be, and that pressing heavily and continuously! Under terrors of conscience, men have little rest by night, for the grim thoughts of the day dog them to their chambers and haunt their

JOHN CALVIN

Psalm 32

David having largely and painfully experienced what a miserable thing it is to feel God's hand heavy on account of sin, exclaims that the highest and best part of a happy life consists in this, that God forgives a man's guilt, and receives him graciously into his favor. After giving thanks for pardon obtained, he invites others to fellowship with him in his happiness, showing, by his own example, the means by which this may be obtained.

1-2

1. Blessed are they whose iniquity is forgiven. This exclamation springs from the fervent affection of the Psalmist's heart as well as from serious consideration. Since almost the whole world turning away their thoughts from God's judgment, bring upon themselves a fatal forgetfulness, and intoxicate themselves with deceitful pleasures; David, as if he had been stricken with the fear of God's wrath, that he might betake himself to Divine mercy, awakens others also to the same exercise, by declaring distinctly and loudly that those only are blessed to whom God is reconciled, so as to acknowledge those for his children whom he might justly treat as his enemies.

2. In whose spirit there is no guile. In this clause the Psalmist distinguishes believers both from hypocrites and from senseless despisers of God, neither of whom care for this happiness, nor can they attain to the enjoyment of it. The wicked are, indeed, conscious to themselves of their guilt, but still they delight in their wickedness; harden themselves in their impudence, and laugh at threatenings; or, at least, they indulge themselves in deceitful flatteries, that they may not be constrained to come into the presence of God.

3-4

3. When I kept silence, my bones wasted away. Here David confirms, by his own experience, the doctrine which he had laid down; namely, that when humbled under the hand of God, he felt that nothing was so miserable as to be deprived of his favor: by which he intimates, that this truth cannot be rightly understood until God has tried us with a feeling of his anger. Nor does he speak of a mere ordinary trial, but declares that he was entirely subdued with the extremest rigor.

4. For day and night thy hand was heavy upon me. In this verse he explains more fully whence such heavy grief arose; namely, because he felt the hand of God to be sore against him. The greatest of all afflictions is to be so heavily pressed with the hand of God, that the sinner feels he has to do with a Judge whose indignation and severity involve in them many deaths, besides eternal death.

5-7

5. I have acknowledged my sin unto thee. The prophet now describes the issue of his misery, in order to show to all the ready way of obtaining the happiness of which he makes mention. When his feeling of divine wrath sorely vexed and

MATTHEW HENRY

Psalm 32

1-6 Who are blessed.

In particular, we are here instructed,

I. Concerning the nature of the pardon of sin. This is that which we all need and are undone without; we are therefore concerned to be very solicitous and inquisitive about it.

1. It is the forgiving of transgression. Sin is the transgression of the law. Upon our repentance, the transgression is forgiven; that is, the obligation to punishment which we lay under, by virtue of the sentence of the law, is vacated and cancelled; it is lifted off (so some read it), that by the pardon of it we may be eased of a burden, a heavy burden, like a load on the back, that makes us stoop, or a load on the stomach, that makes us sick, or a load on the spirits, that makes us sink. The remission of sins gives rest and relief to those that were weary and heavily laden, Matt. xi. 28.

2. It is the covering of sin, as nakedness is covered, that it may not appear to our shame, Rev. iii. 18. One of the first symptoms of guilt in our first parents was blushing at their own nakedness. Sin makes us loathsome in the sight of God and utterly unfit for communion with him.

3. It is the not imputing of iniquity, not laying it to the sinner's charge, not proceeding against him for it according to the strictness of the law, not dealing with him as he deserves. The righteousness of Christ being imputed to us, and we being made the righteousness of God in him, our iniquity is not imputed, God having laid upon him the iniquity of us all and made him sin for us.

II. Concerning the character of those whose sins are pardoned: in whose spirit there is no guile. He does not say, "There is no guilt" (for who is there that lives and sins not?), but no guile; the pardoned sinner is one that does not dissemble with God in his professions of repentance and faith, nor in his prayers for peace or pardon, but in all these is sincere and means as he says—that does not repent with a purpose to sin again, and then sin with a purpose to repent again, as a learned interpreter glosses upon it.

III. Concerning the happiness of a justified state: Blessednesses are to the man whose iniquity is forgiven, all manner of blessings, sufficient to make him completely blessed. That is taken away which incurred the curse and obstructed the blessing; and then God will pour out blessings till there be no room to receive them. The forgiveness of sin is that article of the covenant which is the reason and ground of all the rest.

IV. Concerning the uncomfortable condition of an unhumbled sinner, that sees his guilt, but is not yet brought to make a penitent confession of it. This David describes very pathetically, from his own sad experience (v. 3, 4): While I kept silence my bones

Psalm 32

6-11

6 For this shall every one that is godly pray unto thee in a time when thou mayest be found: surely in the floods of great waters they shall not come nigh unto him.
7 Thou art my hiding place; thou shalt preserve me from trouble; thou shalt compass me about with songs of deliverance. Selah.
8 I will instruct thee and teach thee in the way which thou shalt go: I will guide thee with mine eye.
9 Be ye not as the horse, or as the mule, which have no understanding: whose mouth must be held in with bit and bridle, lest they come near unto thee.
10 Many sorrows shall be to the wicked: but he that trusteth in the LORD, mercy shall compass him about.
11 Be glad in the LORD, and rejoice, ye righteous: and shout for joy, all ye that are upright in heart.

dreams, or else they lie awake in a cold sweat of dread. God's hand is very helpful when it uplifts, but it is awful when it presses down: better a world on the shoulder, like Atlas, than God's hand on the heart, like David. My moisture is turned into the drought of summer.

Verse 5. I acknowledged my sin unto thee. After long lingering, the broken heart bethought itself of what it ought to have done at the first, and laid bare its bosom before the Lord. The lancet must be let into the gathering ulcer before relief can be afforded. The least thing we can do, if we would be pardoned, is to acknowledge our fault; if we are too proud for this we double deserve punishment.

Verse 6. For this shall every one that is godly pray unto thee in a time when thou mayest be found. If the psalmist means that on account of God's mercy others would become hopeful, his witness is true. Remarkable answers to prayer very much quicken the prayerfulness of other godly persons. Where one man finds a golden nugget others feel inclined to dig. The benefit of our experience to others should reconcile us to it. No doubt the case of David has led thousands to seek the Lord with hopeful courage who, without such an instance to cheer them, might have died in despair.

Verse 7. Thou art my hiding place. Terse, short sentences make up this verse, but they contain a world of meaning. Personal claims upon our God are the joy of spiritual life. To lay our hand upon the Lord with the clasp of a personal "my" is delight at its full. Observe that the same man who in the fourth verse was oppressed by the presence of God, here finds a shelter in him. See what honest confession and full forgiveness will do! The gospel of substitution makes him to be our refuge who otherwise would have been our judge.

Verse 8. I will instruct thee and teach thee in the way which thou shalt go. Here the Lord is the speaker, and gives the psalmist an answer to his prayer. Our Savior is our instructor. The Lord himself deigns to teach his children to walk in the way of integrity, his holy word and the monitions of the Holy Spirit are the directors of the believer's daily conversation.

Verse 9. Be ye not as the horse, or as the mule, which have no understanding. Understanding separates man from a brute—let us not act as if we were devoid of it. Men should take counsel and advice, and be ready to run where wisdom points them the way. Alas! we need to be cautioned against stupidity of heart, for we are very apt to fall into it.

Verse 10. Many sorrows shall be to the wicked. Like refractory horses and mules, they have many cuts and bruises. Here and hereafter the portion of the wicked is undesirable. Their joys are evanescent, their sorrows are multiplying and ripening. He who sows sin will reap sorrow in heavy sheaves.

Verse 11. Be glad. Happiness is not only our privilege, but our duty. Truly we serve a generous God, since he makes it a part of our obedience to be joyful. How sinful are our rebellious murmurings! How natural does it seem that a man blest with forgiveness should be glad! We read of one who died at the foot of the scaffold of overjoy at the receipt of his monarch's pardon; and shall we receive the free pardon of the King of kings, and yet pine in inexcusable sorrow? "In the Lord." Here is the directory by which gladness is preserved from levity. We are not to be glad in sin, or to find comfort in corn, and wine, and oil, but in our God is to be the garden of our soul's delight. That there is a God and such a God, and that he is ours, ours for ever, our Father and our reconciled Lord, is matter enough for a never ending psalm of rapturous joy. And rejoice, ye righteous, redouble your rejoicing, peal upon peal.

tormented him, his only relief was unfeignedly to condemn himself before God, and humbly to flee to him to crave his forgiveness. He does not say, however, that his sins merely came to his remembrance, for so also did the sins of Cain and Judas, although to no profit; because, when the consciences of the wicked are troubled with their sins, they cease not to torment themselves, and to fret against God: yea, although he forces them unwillingly to his bar, they still eagerly desire to hide themselves.

6. Therefore shall every one that is meek pray unto thee. Here the Psalmist expressly states that whatever he has hitherto set forth in his own person belongs in common to all the children of God. And this is to be carefully observed, because, from our native unbelief, the greater part of us are slow and reluctant to appropriate the grace of God.

7. Whatever adversity may befall him, he is persuaded that God will be his deliverer. By the word compass, he means manifold and various kinds of deliverance; as if he had said, that he should be under obligation to God in innumerable ways, and that he should, on every side, have most abundant matter for praising him. We may observe in the meantime, how he offers his service of gratitude to God, according to his usual method, putting songs of deliverance instead of help.

8-11

8. I will instruct thee, and teach thee. That his exhortation may have the greater force, the divine speaker directs his discourse to every man individually; for the doctrine which is spoken penetrates the mind more readily, when every man applies it particularly to himself. When the way of salvation is here shown to the children of God, the greatest care must be taken that no man depart from it in the slightest degree.

9. Be not like the horse or mule. David now briefly explains the amount of the counsel which he formerly said he would give. He exhorts all to learn with quietness, to lay aside stubbornness, and to put on the spirit of meekness. There is much wisdom, too, in the advice which he gives to the godly to correct their hardihood; for if we were as attentive to God's corrections as we ought, every one would eagerly hasten to seek his favor.

10. Many sorrows shall be to the wicked. Without a figure he here declares what will be the condition of the rebellious and stiff-necked. He mentioned before that God wanted not bridles and bits with which to restrain their frowardness; and now he adds, that there would be no end or measure of their miseries until they were utterly consumed.

11. Be glad in Jehovah. After teaching how ready and accessible true happiness is to all the godly, David, with much reason, exhorts them to gladness. He commands them to rejoice in the Lord, as if he had said, There is nothing to prevent them from assuring themselves of God's favor, seeing he so liberally and so kindly offers to be reconciled to them. In the meantime, we may observe that this is the incomparable fruit of faith which Paul likewise commends, namely, when the consciences of the godly being quiet and cheerful, enjoy peace and spiritual joy.

waxed old. Those may be said to keep silence who stifle their convictions.

V. Concerning the true and only way to peace of conscience. We are here taught to confess our sins, that they may be forgiven, to declare them, that we may be justified. This course David took: I acknowledged my sin unto thee, and no longer hid my iniquity, v. 5.

VI. Concerning God's readiness to pardon sin to those who truly repent of it: "I said, I will confess (I sincerely resolved upon it, hesitated no longer, but came to a point, that I would make a free and ingenuous confession of my sins) and immediately thou forgavest the iniquity of my sin, and gavest me the comfort of the pardon in my own conscience; immediately I found rest to my soul."

VII. Concerning the good use that we are to make of the experience David had had of God's readiness to forgive his sins (v. 6): For this shall every one that is godly pray unto thee.

7-11 Devout confidence.

David is here improving the experience he had had of the comfort of pardoning mercy.

I. He speaks to God, and professes his confidence in him and expectation from him, v. 7. Having tasted the sweetness of divine grace to a penitent sinner, he cannot doubt of the continuance of that grace to a praying saint, and that in that grace he should find both safety and joy.

1. Safety: "Thou art my hiding-place; when by faith I have recourse to thee I see all the reason in the world to be easy, and to think myself out of the reach of any real evil. Thou shalt preserve me from trouble, from the sting of it, and from the strokes of it as far as is good for me. Thou shalt preserve me from such trouble as I was in while I kept silence," v. 3. When God has pardoned our sins, if he leaves us to ourselves, we shall soon run as far in debt again as ever and plunge ourselves again into the same gulf; and therefore, when we have received the comfort of our remission, we must fly to the grace of God to be preserved from returning to folly again.

2. Joy: "Thou shalt not only deliver me, but compass me about with songs of deliverance; which way soever I look I shall see occasion to rejoice and to praise God; and my friends also shall compass me about in the great congregation, to join with me in songs of praise: they shall join their songs of deliverance with mine. As every one that is godly shall pray with me, so they shall give thanks with me."

II. He turns his speech to the children of men. Here is a word of caution to sinners, and a good reason is given for it. The caution is, not to be unruly and ungovernable: Be you not as the horse and the mule, which have no understanding, v. 9. The reason for this caution is because the way of sin which we would persuade you to forsake will certainly end in sorrow (v. 10).

Psalm 33

1-8

1 Rejoice in the LORD, O ye righteous: for praise is comely for the upright.
2 Praise the LORD with harp: sing unto him with the psaltery and an instrument of ten strings.
3 Sing unto him a new song; play skillfully with a loud noise.
4 For the word of the LORD is right; and all his works are done in truth.
5 He loveth righteousness and judgment: the earth is full of the goodness of the LORD.
6 By the word of the LORD were the heavens made; and all the host of them by the breath of his mouth.
7 He gathereth the waters of the sea together as an heap: he layeth up the depth in storehouses.
8 Let all the earth fear the LORD: let all the inhabitants of the world stand in awe of him.

Psalm 33

TITLE. This song of praise bears no title or indication of authorship; to teach us, says Dickson, "to look upon Holy Scripture as altogether inspired of God, and not put price upon it for the writers thereof."
SUBJECT AND DIVISION. The praise of Jehovah is the subject of this sacred song. The righteous are exhorted to praise him, Ps 33:1-3; because of the excellency of his character, Ps 33:4-5; and his majesty in creation, Ps 33:6-7. Men are bidden to fear before Jehovah because his purposes are accomplished in providence, Ps 33:8-11. His people are proclaimed blessed, Ps 33:12. The omniscience and omnipotence of God, and his care for his people are celebrated, in opposition to the weakness of an arm of flesh, Ps 33:13-19; and the Psalm concludes with a fervent expression of confidence, Ps 33:20-21, and an earnest prayer, Ps 33:22.

EXPOSITION
Verse 1. Rejoice in the Lord. Joy is the soul of praise. To delight ourselves in God is most truly to extol him, even if we let no notes of song proceed from our lips. That God is, and that he is such a God, and our God, ours for ever and ever, should wake within us an unceasing and overflowing joy. To rejoice in temporal comforts is dangerous, to rejoice in self is foolish, to rejoice in sin is fatal, but to rejoice in God is heavenly.
Verse 2. Praise the Lord with harp. Men need all the help they can get to stir them up to praise. This is the lesson to be gathered from the use of musical instruments under the old dispensation. Israel was at school, and used childish things to help her to learn; but in these days, when Jesus gives us spiritual manhood, we can make melody without strings and pipes.
Verse 3. Sing unto him a new song. All songs of praise should be unto him. Singing for singing's sake is nothing worth; we must carry our tribute to the King, and not cast it to the winds.
Verse 4. For the word of the Lord is right. His ordinances both natural, moral, and spiritual, are right, and especially his incarnate Word, who is the Lord our righteousness. Whatever God has ordained must be good, and just, and excellent. There are no anomalies in God's universe, except what sin has made; his word of command made all things good.
Verse 5. He loveth righteousness and judgment. The theory and practice of right he intensely loves. He doth not only approve the true and the just, but his inmost soul delights therein. The character of God is a sea, every drop of which should become a wellhead of praise for his people. The righteousness of Jesus is peculiarly dear to the Father, and for its sake he takes pleasure in those to whom it is imputed. Sin, on the other hand, is infinitely abhorrent to the Lord, and woe unto those who die in it; if he sees no righteousness in them, he will deal righteously with them, and judgment stern and final will be the result.
Verse 6. By the word of the Lord were the heavens made. The angelic heavens, the sidereal heavens, and the firmament or terrestrial heavens, were all made to start into existence by a word; what if we say by the Word, "For without him was not anything made that is made." It is interesting to note the mention of the Spirit in the next clause, and all the host of them by the breath of his mouth; the breath is the same as is elsewhere rendered Spirit. Thus the three persons of the Godhead unite in creating all things.
Verse 7. He gathereth the waters of the sea together as an heap. The waters were once scattered like corn strewn upon a threshing floor: they are now collected in one spot as an heap. Who else could have gathered them into one channel but their great Lord, at whose bidding the waters fled away? The miracle of the Red Sea is repeated in nature day by day, for the sea which now invades the shore under the impulse of sun and moon, would soon devour the land if bounds were not maintained by the divine decree.

Psalm 33

1-4

1. Rejoice in Jehovah, ye righteous. Here the inspired writer addresses believers or the righteous by name, because they alone are capable of proclaiming the glory of God. Unbelievers, who have never tasted his goodness, cannot praise him from the heart, and God has no pleasure in his name being pronounced by their unholy tongues.

2. Praise Jehovah upon the harp. It is evident that the Psalmist here expresses the vehement and ardent affection which the faithful ought to have in praising God, when he enjoins musical instruments to be employed for this purpose. He would have nothing omitted by believers which tends to animate the minds and feelings of men in singing God's praises. The name of God, no doubt, can, properly speaking, be celebrated only by the articulate voice; but it is not without reason that David adds to this those aids by which believers were wont to stimulate themselves the more to this exercise; especially considering that he was speaking to God's ancient people.

3. Sing unto him a new song. As the Psalmist afterwards treats of the mighty works of God, and particularly concerning the preservation of the Church, it is not wonderful that he exhorts the righteous to sing a new, that is, a rare and choice song.

4. For the word of Jehovah is right. The amount of what is stated is, that whatever God appoints and commands is right; and whatever he brings to pass in actual operation is faithful and true. Meanwhile, it ought to be observed, that the term word is not to be understood of doctrine, but of the method by which God governs the world.

5-9

5. He loveth righteousness and judgment. This is a confirmation of the preceding verse, and intimates to us that God of his own nature loves righteousness and equity. It therefore follows, that froward affections cannot hurry him, after the manner of men, to evil devices. At first sight, indeed, this appears but a common commendation of God, and of small importance, because all confess that he observes the most perfect rule of righteousness in all his works.

6. By the word of Jehovah. That he may stir us up to think more closely of God's works, he brings before us the creation of the world itself; for until God be acknowledged as the Creator and Framer of the world, who will believe that he attends to the affairs of men, and that the state of the world is controlled by his wisdom and power? But the creation of the world leads us by direct consequence to the providence of God.

7. He gathered together the waters of the sea as into a heap. Here the Psalmist does not speak of all that might have been said of every part of the world, but under one department he comprehends all the rest. He celebrates, however, a signal and remarkable miracle which we see in looking on the surface of the earth; namely, that God gathers together the element of water, fluid and unstable as it is, into a solid heap, and holds it so at his pleasure.

Psalm 33

1-11 An exhortation to praise God.

Four things the psalmist expresses in these verses:

I. The great desire he had that God might be praised. He did not think he did it so well himself, but that he wished others also might be employed in this work; the more the better, in this concert: it is the more like heaven.

1. Holy joy is the heart and soul of praise, and that is here pressed upon all good people (v. 1): Rejoice in the Lord, you righteous; so the foregoing psalm concluded and so this begins; for all our religious exercises should both begin and end with a holy complacency and triumph in God as the best of being and best of friends.

2. Thankful praise is the breath and language of holy joy; and that also is here required of us (v. 2): "Praise the Lord; speak well of him, and give him the glory due to his name."

3. Religious songs are the proper expressions of thankful praise; those are here required (v. 3): "Sing unto him a new song, the best you have, not that which by frequent use is worn, thread-bare, but that which, being new, is most likely to move the affections, a new song for new mercies and upon every new occasion, for those compassions which are new every morning."

II. The high thoughts he had of God, and of his infinite perfections, v. 4, 5. God makes himself known to us, in his word, here put for all divine revelation, all that which God at sundry times and in divers manners spoke to the children of men, and that is all right, there is nothing amiss in it; his commands exactly agree with the rules of equity and the eternal reasons of good and evil.

III. The conviction he was under of the almighty power of God, evidenced in the creation of the world. We "believe in God," and therefore we praise him as "the Father Almighty, maker of heaven and earth," so we are here taught to praise him. Observe,

1. How God made the world, and brought all things into being. He spoke, and he commanded (v. 9), and that was enough; there needed no more.

2. What he made. He made all things, but notice is here taken,

(1.) Of the heavens, and the host of them, v. 6. The visible heavens, and the sun, moon, and stars, their hosts.

(2.) Of the waters, and the treasures of them, v. 7.

3. What use is to be made of this (v. 8): Let all the earth fear the Lord, and stand in awe of him; that is, let all the children of men worship him and give glory to him, Ps. xc. 5, 6. The everlasting gospel gives this as the reason why we must worship God, because he made the heaven, and the earth, and the sea, Rev. xiv. 6, 7.

IV. The satisfaction he had of God's sovereignty and dominion, v. 10, 11. He over-rules all the counsels of

Psalm 33

9-16
9 For he spake, and it was done; he commanded, and it stood fast.
10 The LORD bringeth the counsel of the heathen to nought: he maketh the devices of the people of none effect.
11 The counsel of the LORD standeth for ever, the thoughts of his heart to all generations.
12 Blessed is the nation whose God is the LORD; and the people whom he hath chosen for his own inheritance.
13 The LORD looketh from heaven; he beholdeth all the sons of men.
14 From the place of his habitation he looketh upon all the inhabitants of the earth.
15 He fashioneth their hearts alike; he considereth all their works.
16 There is no king saved by the multitude of an host: a mighty man is not delivered by much strength.

Verse 8. Let all the earth fear the Lord. Not only Jews, but Gentiles. The psalmist was not a man blinded by national prejudice, he did not desire to restrict the worship of Jehovah to the seed of Abraham. He looks for homage even to far off nations. If they are not well enough instructed to be able to praise, at least let them fear.
Verse 9. For he spake, and it was done. Creation was the fruit of a word. Jehovah said, "Light be," and light was. The Lord's acts are sublime in their ease and instantaneousness. "What a word is this?" This was the wondering enquiry of old, and it may be ours to this day. He commanded, and it stood fast. Out of nothing creation stood forth, and was confirmed in existence.
Verse 10. The Lord bringeth the counsel of the heathen to nought. While his own will is done, he takes care to anticipate the willfulness of his enemies. Before they come to action he vanquishes them in the council chamber; and when, well armed with craft, they march to the assault, he frustrates their knaveries, and makes their promising plots to end in nothing. Not only the folly of the heathen, but their wisdom too, shall yield to the power of the cross of Jesus: what a comfort is this to those who have to labor where sophistry, and philosophy, falsely so called, are set in opposition to the truth as it is in Jesus.
Verse 11. The counsel of the Lord standeth for ever. He changes not his purpose, his decree is not frustrated, his designs are accomplished. God has a predestination according to the counsel of his will, and none of the devices of his foes can thwart his decree for a moment. Men's purposes are blown to and from like the thread of the gossamer or the down of the thistle, but the eternal purposes are firmer than the earth. The thoughts of his heart to all generations. Men come and go, sons follow their sires to the grave, but the undisturbed mind of God moves on in unbroken serenity, producing ordained results with unerring certainty. No man can expect his will or plan to be carried out from age to age; the wisdom of one period is the folly of another, but the Lord's wisdom is always wise, and his designs run on from century to century. His power to fulfill his purposes is by no means diminished by the lapse of years. He who was absolute over Pharaoh in Egypt is not one whit the less today the King of kings and Lord of lords; still do his chariot wheels roll onward in imperial grandeur, none being for a moment able to resist his eternal will.
Verse 12. Blessed is the nation whose God is the Lord. Israel was happy in the worship of the only true God. It was the blessedness of the chosen nation to have received a revelation from Jehovah. While others groveled before their idols, the chosen people were elevated by a spiritual religion which introduced them to the invisible God, and led them to trust in him. All who confide in the Lord are blessed in the largest and deepest sense, and none can reverse the blessing. And the people whom he hath chosen for his own inheritance. Election is at the bottom of it all. The divine choice rules the day; none take Jehovah to be their God till he takes them to be his people. What an ennobling choice this is! We are selected to no mean estate, and for no ignoble purpose: we are made the peculiar domain and delight of the Lord our God. Being so blessed, let us rejoice in our portion, and show the world by our lives that we serve a glorious Master.
Verse 13. The Lord looketh from heaven. The Lord is represented as dwelling above and looking down below; seeing all things, but peculiarly observing and caring for those who trust in him. It is one of our choicest privileges to be always under our Father's eye, to be never out of sight of our best Friend. He beholdeth all the sons of men. All Adam's sons are as well watched as was Adam himself, their lone progenitor in the garden. Ranging from the frozen pole to the scorching equator, dwelling in hills and valleys, in huts and palaces, alike doth the divine eye regard all the members of the family of man.

8. Let all the earth fear Jehovah. The Psalmist concludes that there is just reason why the whole world should reverently submit itself to the government of God, who gave it being, and who also preserves it. To fear Jehovah, and to stand in awe of him, just means to do honor to, and to reverence his mighty power.
9. The prophet alludes to both these things, affirming that the world appeared as soon as God spake, and that it is upheld in being by his commandment; for it would not have been enough for the world to have been created in a moment, if it had not been supported in existence by the power of God. He did not employ a great array of means in creating the world, but to prove the inconceivable power of his word, he ordered that so soon as he should as it were pronounce the word, the thing should be done.

10-12
10. Jehovah scattereth the counsel of the nations. After briefly touching upon the creation of the world, the Psalmist returns to his former subject, namely, to show that the events which daily come to pass are undoubted proofs of the providence of God. And lest any man should be surprised, that he should exhibit God as an adversary to men, scattering their counsels rather than establishing and bringing them to a happy issue, he selects an instance which had the greatest power to comfort the saints.
11. The counsel of Jehovah. The prophet extols the infinite power of God in such a manner as that he may build up our faith in its greatness; for he does not here commend a counsel of God which is hidden in heaven, and which he would have us to honor and revere at a distance. But as the Lord everywhere in Scripture testifies that he loveth righteousness and truth; that he cares for the righteous and good; and that he is ever inclined to succor his servants when they are wrongfully oppressed;—the prophet means, that all this shall remain sure and steadfast. Thus he declares for what end God bringeth to nought the counsels of the nations, namely, because without discrimination they run headlong into the violation of all order.
12. Blessed are the people whose God is Jehovah. This verse excellently agrees with the preceding, because it would profit us little to observe what is said of the stability of God's counsel if that counsel referred not to us. The prophet, therefore, in proclaiming that they are blessed whom God receives into his protection, reminds us that the counsel which he had just mentioned is not a secret which remains always hidden in God, but is displayed in the existence of the Church, and may there be beheld.

13-17
13. Jehovah looked down from heaven. The Psalmist still proceeds with the same doctrine, namely, that human affairs are not tossed hither and thither fortuitously, but that God secretly guides and directs all that we see taking place. Now he here commends God's inspection of all things, that we on our part may learn to behold, and to contemplate with the eye of faith, his invisible providence. There are, no doubt, evident proofs of it continually before our eyes; but the great majority

men, and makes them, contrary to their intention, serviceable to his counsels. Come and see with an eye of faith God in the throne, as he frustrates the devices of his enemies and fulfills his own decrees: The counsel of the Lord standeth for ever. It is immutable in itself, for he is in one mind, and who can turn him?

12-22 God's sovereign power.
We are here taught to give to God the glory,
I. Of his common providence towards all the children of men. Though he has endued man with understanding and freedom of will, yet he reserves to himself the government of him, and even of those very faculties by which he is qualified to govern himself.
1. The children of men are all under his eye, even their hearts are so; and all the motions and operations of their souls, which none know but they themselves, he knows better than they themselves, v. 13, 14.
2. Their hearts, as well as their times, are all in his hand: He fashions their hearts. He made them at first, formed the spirit of each man within him, then when he brought him into being. Hence he is called the Father of spirits: and this is a good argument to prove that he perfectly knows them. The artist that made the clock, can account for the motions of every wheel. David uses this argument with application to himself, Ps. cxxxix. 1, 14. He still moulds the hearts of men, turns them as the rivers of water, which way soever he pleases, to serve his own purposes, darkens or enlightens men's understandings, stiffens or bows their wills, according as he is pleased to make use of them.
3. They, and all they do, are obnoxious to his judgment; for he considers all their works, not only knows them, but weighs them, that he may render to every man according to his works, in the day, in the world, of retribution, in the judgment, and to eternity.
4. All the powers of the creature have a dependence upon him, and are of no account, of no avail at all, without him, v. 16, 17. It is much for the honor of God that not only no force can prevail in opposition to him, but that no force can act but in dependence on him and by a power derived from him.
II. We are to give God the glory of his special grace. In the midst of his acknowledgments of God's providence he pronounces those blessed that have Jehovah for their God, who governs the world, and has wherewithal to help them in every time of need, while those were miserable who had this and the other Baal for their god, which was so far from being able to hear and help them that it was itself senseless and helpless (v. 12): Blessed is the nation whose God is the Lord, even Israel, who had the knowledge of the true God and were taken into covenant with him, and all others who own God for theirs and are owned by him; for they also, whatever nation they are of, are of the spiritual seed of Abraham.

Psalm 33

17-22
17 An horse is a vain thing for safety: neither shall he deliver any by his great strength.
18 Behold, the eye of the LORD is upon them that fear him, upon them that hope in his mercy;
19 To deliver their soul from death, and to keep them alive in famine.
20 Our soul waiteth for the LORD: he is our help and our shield.
21 For our heart shall rejoice in him, because we have trusted in his holy name.
22 Let thy mercy, O LORD, be upon us, according as we hope in thee.

Verse 14. From the place of his habitation he looketh upon all the inhabitants of the earth. Here the sentiment is repeated: it is worth repeating, and it needs repeating, for man is most prone to forget it. As great men sit at their windows and watch the crowd below, so doth the Lord; he gazes intently upon his responsible creatures, and forgets nothing of what he sees.
Verse 15. He fashioneth their hearts alike. By which is meant that all hearts are equally fashioned by the Lord, kings' hearts as well as the hearts of beggars. The text does not mean that all hearts are created originally alike by God, such a statement would scarcely be true, since there is the utmost variety in the constitutions and dispositions of men. All men equally owe the possession of life to the Creator, and have therefore no reason to boast themselves.
Verse 16. There is no king saved by the multitude of an host. Mortal power is a fiction, and those who trust in it are dupes. Serried ranks of armed men have failed to maintain an empire, or even to save their monarch's life when a decree from the court of heaven has gone forth for the empire's overthrow. The all seeing God preserves the poorest of his people when they are alone and friendless, but ten thousand armed men cannot ensure safety to him whom God leaves to destruction.
Verse 17. An horse is a vain thing for safety. Military strength among the Orientals lay much in horses and scythed chariots, but the psalmist calls them a lie, a deceitful confidence. Surely the knight upon his gallant steed may be safe, either by velour or by flight? Not so, his horse shall bear him into danger or crush him with its fall. Neither shall he deliver any by his great strength. Thus the strongest defenses are less than nothing when most needed.
Verse 18. Behold. For this is a greater wonder than hosts and horses, a surer confidence than chariots or shields. The eye of the Lord is upon them that fear him. That eye of peculiar care is their glory and defense. None can take them at unawares, for the celestial watcher foresees the designs of their enemies, and provides against them.
Verse 19. To deliver their soul from death. The Lord's hand goes with his eye; he sovereignly preserves those whom he graciously observes. Rescues and restorations hedge about the lives of the saints; death cannot touch them till the King signs his warrant and gives him leave, and even then his touch is not so much mortal as immortal; he doth not so much kill us as kill our mortality.
Verse 20. Our soul waits for the Lord. Here the godly avow their reliance upon him whom the Psalm extols. To wait is a great lesson. To be quiet in expectation, patient in hope, single in confidence, is one of the bright attainments of a Christian.
Verse 21. For our hearts shall rejoice in him. The duty commended and commanded in the first verse is here presented to the Lord. We, who trust, cannot but be of a glad heart, our inmost nature must triumph in our faithful God. Because we have trusted in his holy name. The root of faith in due time bears the flower of rejoicing. Doubts breed sorrow, confidence creates joy.
Verse 22. Here is a large and comprehensive prayer to close with. It is an appeal for mercy, which even joyful believers need; and it is sought for in a proportion which the Lord has sanctioned. "According to your faith be it unto you," is the Master's word, and he will not fall short of the scale which he has himself selected. Yet, Master, do more than this when hope is faint, and bless us far above what we ask or even think.

JOHN CALVIN

of men, notwithstanding, see nothing of them, and, in their blindness, imagine that all things are under the conduct of a blind fortune.
15. He who fashioned their hearts altogether. It appears that this is added for the express purpose of assuredly persuading believers, that, however the wicked might craftily, deceitfully, and by secret stratagems, attempt to withdraw themselves from God's sight, and hide themselves in caverns, yet his eyes would penetrate into their dark hiding-places.
16. It therefore follows, A king is not saved for the multitude of his host, etc. By this the inspired writer means to teach us, that the safety of men's lives depends not upon their own strength, but upon the favor of God. He names particularly kings and giants rather than others; because, as they are not of the common class of men, but of a higher condition, they appear to themselves to be beyond the reach of all danger from darts, and if any adversity befall them, they promise themselves an easy deliverance from it.
17. A horse is a deceitful thing for safety. In this verse, the Psalmist, by the figure synecdoche under the name of horse, is to be understood as meaning any kind of help. The sense is, that in general those who conceive that their life is well protected by earthly means, are commonly disappointed at the very crisis of danger, and are miserably beguiled to their utter undoing, so that God therein clearly shows them their folly.

18-19
18. Behold, the eye of Jehovah is upon them that fear him. Having shown that what men account their best defenses often profit them nothing, or rather are utterly worthless, when men depend upon them; the Psalmist now shows, on the other hand, that believers, although they are neither men of great power nor of great wealth, are nevertheless sufficiently protected by God's favor alone, and shall be safe for ever.
19. Again, when it is affirmed, that God, in times of famine and dearth, has remedies in readiness to preserve the lives of the godly, we are taught that the faithful only pay due honor to his providence when they allow not their hearts to despond in the extremest indigence; but, on the contrary, raise their hopes even from the grave.

20-22
20. Our soul waiteth upon Jehovah. What the Psalmist has hitherto spoken concerning God's providence, and particularly concerning that faithful guardianship by which he protects his people, he has spoken not so much from himself as from the mouth of the Holy Spirit.
21. Surely our heart shall rejoice in him. Experience undoubtedly proves, that when men are overwhelmed with sorrow, and pine away with care, grief, and anxiety, it is that they may receive the recompense of their folly; seeing that there is nothing to which they are led with more difficulty, than to set their hopes on God alone.
22. Let thy mercy be on us, O Jehovah! The psalm concludes with a prayer that God would make them feel from the effect that they have not relied on the divine goodness in vain.

MATTHEW HENRY

1. It is their wisdom that they take the Lord for their God, that they direct their homage and adoration there where it is due and where the payment of it will not be in vain.
2. It is their happiness that they are the people whom God has chosen for his own inheritance, whom he is pleased with, and honored in, and whom he protects and takes care of, whom he cultivates and improves as a man does his inheritance, Deut. xxxii. 9. Now let us observe here, to the honor of divine grace,
(1.) The regard which God has to his people, v. 18, 19. God beholds all the sons of men with an eye of observation, but his eye of favor and complacency is upon those that fear him. He looks upon them with delight, as the father on his children, as the bridegroom on his spouse, Isa. lxii. 5. Those that have the Lord for their God shall find him their help and their shield, v. 20. In their difficulties he will assist them; they shall be helped over them, helped through them. In their dangers he will secure them; they shall be helped over them, helped through them. In their dangers he will secure them, so that they shall not receive any real damage.
(2.) The regard which God's people have to him and which we ought to have in consideration of this.
[1.] We must wait for God. We must attend the motions of his providence, and accommodate ourselves to them, and patiently accommodate ourselves to them, and patiently expect the issue of them. Our souls must wait for him, v. 20. We must not only in word and tongue profess a believing regard to God, but it must be inward and sincere, a secret and silent attendance on him.
[2.] We must rely on God, hope in his mercy, in the goodness of his nature, though we have not an express promise to depend upon. Those that fear God and his wrath must hope in God and his mercy; for there is no flying from God, but by flying to him. These pious dispositions will not only consist together, but befriend each other, a holy fear of God and yet at the same time a hope in his mercy. This is trusting in his holy name (v. 21), in all that whereby he has made known himself to us, for our encouragement to serve him.
[3.] We must rejoice in God, v. 21. Those do not truly rest in God, or do not know the unspeakable advantage they have by so doing, who do not rejoice in him at all times; because those that hope in God hope for an eternal fullness of joy in his presence.
[4.] We must seek to him for that mercy which we hope in, v. 22. Our expectations from God are not to supersede, but to quicken and encourage, our applications to him; he will be sought unto for that which he has promised, and therefore the psalm concludes with a short but comprehensive prayer

Psalm 34

Title
Psalm of David, when he changed his behavior before Abimelech; who drove him away, and he departed.

1-8
1 I will bless the LORD at all times: his praise shall continually be in my mouth.
2 My soul shall make her boast in the LORD: the humble shall hear thereof, and be glad.
3 O magnify the LORD with me, and let us exalt his name together.
4 I sought the LORD, and he heard me, and delivered me from all my fears.
5 They looked unto him, and were lightened: and their faces were not ashamed.
6 This poor man cried, and the LORD heard him, and saved him out of all his troubles.
7 The angel of the LORD encampeth round about them that fear him, and delivereth them.
8 O taste and see that the LORD is good: blessed is the man that trusteth in him.

Psalm 34

TITLE. Psalm of David, when he changed his behavior before Abimelech; who drove him away, and he departed. Of this transaction, which reflects no credit upon David's memory, we have a brief account in 1Sa 21:1-15. Although the gratitude of the psalmist prompted him thankfully to record the goodness of the Lord in vouchsafing an undeserved deliverance, yet he weaves none of the incidents of the escape into the narrative, but dwells only on the grand fact of his being heard in the hour of peril. We may learn from his example not to parade our sins before others, as certain vainglorious professors are wont to do who seem as proud of their sins as old Greenwich pensioners of their battles and their wounds. David played the fool with singular dexterity, but he was not so real a fool as to sing of his own exploits of folly. In the original, the title does not teach us that the psalmist composed this poem at the time of his escape from Achish, the king or Abimelech of Gath, but that it is intended to commemorate that event, and was suggested by it. It is well to mark our mercies with well carved memorials. God deserves our best handiwork. David in view of the special peril from which he was rescued, was at great pains with this Psalm, and wrote it with considerable regularity, in almost exact accordance with the letters of the Hebrew alphabet. This is the second alphabetical Psalm, the twenty-fifth being the first.

DIVISION. The Psalm is split into two great divisions at the close of Ps 34:10, when the Psalmist having expressed his praise to God turns in direct address to men. The first ten verses are A HYMN, and the last twelve A SERMON. For further assistance to the reader we may subdivide thus: In Ps 34:1-3, David vows to bless the Lord, and invites the praise of others; from Ps 34:4-7 he relates his experience, and in Ps 34:8-10 exhorts the godly to constancy of faith. In Ps 34:1-14, he gives direct exhortation, and follows it up by didactic teaching from Ps 34:15-22 to the close.

EXPOSITION

Verse 1. I will bless the Lord at all times. He is resolved and fixed, I will; he is personally and for himself determined, let others so as they may; he is intelligent in head and inflamed in heart—he knows to whom the praise is due, and what is due, and for what and when. To Jehovah, and not to second causes our gratitude is to be rendered. The Lord hath by right a monopoly in his creatures praise. Even when a mercy may remind us of our sin with regard to it, as in this case David's deliverance from the Philistine monarch was sure to do, we are not to rob God of his need of honor because our conscience justly awards a censure to our share in the transaction.

Verse 2. My soul shall make her boast in the Lord. Boasting is a very natural propensity, and if it were used as in this case, the more it were indulged the better. The exultation of this verse is no mere tongue bragging, "the soul" is in it, the boasting is meant and felt before it is expressed. What scope there is for holy boasting in Jehovah! His person, attributes, covenant, promises, works, and a thousand things besides, are all incomparable, unparalleled, matchless; we may cry them up as we please, but we shall never be convicted of vain and empty speech in so doing.

Verse 3. O magnify the Lord with me. Is this request addressed to the humble? If so it is most fitting. Who can make God great but those who feel themselves to be little? He bids them help him to make the Lord's fame greater among the sons of men. Jehovah is infinite, and therefore cannot really be made greater, but his name grows in manifested glory as he is made known to his creatures, and thus he is said to be magnified.

Verse 4. I sought the Lord, and he heard me. It must have been in a very confused manner that David prayed, and there must have been much of self sufficiency in his prayer, or he would not have resorted to methods of

JOHN CALVIN

Psalm 34

1-6
1. I will bless Jehovah at all times. David here extols the greatness of God, promising to keep in remembrance during his whole life the goodness which he had bestowed upon him. God assists his people daily, that they may continually employ themselves in praising him; yet it is certain that the blessing which is said to be worthy of everlasting remembrance is distinguished by this mark from other benefits which are ordinary and common.
2. My soul shall make her boast in Jehovah. The term soul in this place signifies not the vital spirit, but the seat of the affections; as if David had said, I shall always have ground of boasting with my whole heart in God alone, so that I shall never suffer myself to fall into forgetfulness of so great a deliverance. In the second clause he specifies this as the fruit of his thanksgiving, that the afflicted and miserable shall derive from it ground of hope.
3. Magnify Jehovah with me. The Psalmist shows still another fruit which would be the result of his giving thanks to God, namely, that he shall induce others by his example to the same exercise of devotion; nay more, he calls upon all the godly to unite with him in this exercise, inviting and exhorting them heartily and with one consent to extol the Lord.
4. I sought Jehovah, and he answered me. The Psalmist here explains more plainly and more fully what he had said concerning joy. He tells us that his prayers had been heard. This he applies to all the godly, that, encouraged by a testimony so precious, they might stir themselves up to prayer.
5. They shall look to him, and shall flow to him. I have already intimated, that this verse and the following should be read in connection with the preceding verse. In relating his own experience David has furnished an example to others, that they should freely and without fear approach God in order to present their prayers before him. Now, he says that they shall come, and this too with a happy issue.
6. This poor man cried, and Jehovah heard him. David here introduces all the godly speaking of himself, the more emphatically to express how much weight there is in his example to encourage them. This poor man, say they, cried; therefore God invites all the poor to cry to him.

7-10
7. The angel of Jehovah encampeth round about them that fear him. David here discourses in general of God's fatherly favor towards all the godly; and as the life of man is exposed to innumerable dangers, he at the same time teaches us that God is able to deliver them. The faithful especially, who are as sheep in the midst of wolves, beset as it were with death in every form, are constantly harassed with the dread of some approaching danger.
8. Taste and see that Jehovah is good. In this verse the Psalmist indirectly reproves men for their dullness in not perceiving the goodness of God, which ought to be to them

MATTHEW HENRY

Psalm 34

1-10 Praise and thanksgiving.
I. David engages and excites himself to praise God. Though it was his fault that he changed his behavior, yet it was God's mercy that he escaped, and the mercy was so much the greater in that God did not deal with him according to the desert of his dissimulation, and we must in every thing give thanks. He resolves,
1. That he will praise God constantly: I will bless the Lord at all times, upon all occasions. He resolves to keep up stated times for this duty, to lay hold of all opportunities for it, and to renew his praises upon every fresh occurrence that furnished him with matter. If we hope to spend our eternity in praising God, it is fit that we should spend as much as may be of our time in this work.
2. That he will praise him openly: His praise shall continually be in my mouth. Thus he would show how forward he was to own his obligations to the mercy of God and how desirous to make others also sensible of theirs.
3. That he will praise him heartily: "My soul shall make her boast in the Lord, in my relation to him, my interest in him, and expectations from him." It is not vainglory to glory in the Lord.
II. He calls upon others to join with him herein. He expects they will (v. 2): "The humble shall hear thereof, both of my deliverance and of my thankfulness, and be glad that a good man has so much favor shown him and a good God so much honor done him." Those have most comfort in God's mercies, both to others and to themselves, that are humble, and have the least confidence in their own merit and sufficiency. It pleased David to think that God's favors to him would rejoice the heart of every Israelite. Three things he would have us all to concur with him in:
1. In great and high thoughts of God, which we should express in magnifying him and exalting his name, v. 3. We cannot make God greater or higher than he is; but if we adore him as infinitely great, and higher than the highest, he is pleased to reckon this magnifying and exalting him. This we must do together. God's praises sound best in concert, for so we praise him as the angels do in heaven. Those that share in God's favor, as all the saints do, should concur in his praises; and we should be as desirous of the assistance of our friends in returning thanks for mercies as in praying for them.
2. He would have us to join with him in kind and good thoughts of God (v. 8): O taste and see that the Lord is good! The goodness of God includes both the beauty and amiableness of his being and the bounty and beneficence of his providence and grace.
3. He would have us join with him in a resolution to seek God and serve him, and continue in his fear (v. 9): O fear the Lord! you his saints. When we taste and see that he is good we must not forget that he is great

Psalm 34

9-16

9 O fear the LORD, ye his saints: for there is no want to them that fear him.

10 The young lions do lack, and suffer hunger: but they that seek the LORD shall not want any good thing.

11 Come, ye children, hearken unto me: I will teach you the fear of the LORD.

12 What man is he that desireth life, and loveth many days, that he may see good?

13 Keep thy tongue from evil, and thy lips from speaking guile.

14 Depart from evil, and do good; seek peace, and pursue it.

15 The eyes of the LORD are upon the righteous, and his ears are open unto their cry.

16 The face of the LORD is against them that do evil, to cut off the remembrance of them from the earth.

such dubious morality as pretending to be mad and behaving as a lunatic; yet his poor limping prayer had an acceptance and brought him succor: the more reason for then celebrating the abounding mercy of the Lord. We may seek God even when we have sinned.

Verse 5. They looked unto him, and were lightened. The psalmist avows that his case was not at all peculiar, it was matched in the lives of all the faithful; they too, each one of them on looking to their Lord were brightened up, their faces began to shine, their spirits were uplifted. What a means of blessing one look at the Lord may be!

Verse 6. This poor man cried. Here he returns to his own case. He was poor indeed, and so utterly friendless that his life was in great jeopardy; but he cried in his heart to the protector of his people and found relief. His prayer was a cry, for brevity and bitterness, for earnestness and simplicity, for artlessness and grief; it was a poor man's cry, but it was none the less powerful with heaven, for the Lord heard him, and to be heard of God is to be delivered; and so it is added that the Lord saved him out of all his troubles.

Verse 7. The angel of the Lord. The covenant angel, the Lord Jesus, at the head of all the bands of heaven, surrounds with his army the dwellings of the saints. Like hosts entrenched so are the ministering spirits encamped around the Lord's chosen, to serve and succor, to defend and console them.

Verse 8. O taste and see. Make a trial, an inward, experimental trial of the goodness of God. You cannot see except by tasting for yourself; but if you taste you shall see, for this, like Jonathan's honey, enlightens the eyes. That the Lord is good. You can only know this really and personally by experience. There is the banquet with its oxen and fatlings; its fat things full of marrow, and wine on the lees well refined; but their sweetness will be all unknown to you except you make the blessings of grace your own, by a living, inward, vital participation in them.

Verse 9. O fear the Lord, ye his saints. Pay to him humble childlike reverence, walk in his laws, have respect to his will, tremble to offend him, hasten to serve him. Fear not the wrath of men, neither be tempted to sin through the virulence of their threats; fear God and fear nothing else. For there is no want to them that fear him. Jehovah will not allow his faithful servants to starve. He may not give luxuries, but the promise binds him to supply necessaries, and he will not run back from his word.

Verse 10. The young lions do lack, and suffer hunger. They are fierce, cunning, strong, in all the vigor of youth, and yet they sometimes howl in their ravenous hunger, and even so crafty, designing, and oppressing men, with all their sagacity and unscrupulousness, often come to want; yet simple minded believers, who dare not act as the greedy lions of earth, are fed with food convenient for them. To trust God is better policy than the craftiest politicians can teach or practice.

Verse 11. Come, ye children. Though a warrior and a king, the psalmist was not ashamed to teach children. Teachers of youth belong to the true peerage; their work is honorable, and their reward shall be glorious.

Verse 12. Life spent in happiness is the desire of all, and he who can give the young a receipt for leading a happy life deserves to be popular among them. Mere existence is not life; the art of living, truly, really, and joyfully living, it is not given to all men to know.

Verse 13. Keep thy tongue from evil. Guard with careful diligence that dangerous member, the tongue, lest it utter evil, for that evil will recoil upon thee, and mar the enjoyment of thy life. Men cannot spit forth poison without feeling some of the venom burning their own flesh. And thy lips from speaking guile. Deceit must be very earnestly avoided by the man who desires happiness.

Verse 14. Depart from evil. Go away from it. Not merely take your hands off, but yourself off. Live not near the pest house. Avoid the lion's lair, leave the

JOHN CALVIN

more than matter of simple knowledge. By the word taste he at once shows that they are without taste; and at the same time he assigns the reason of this to be, that they devour the gifts of God without relishing them, or through a vitiated loathing ungratefully conceal them.

9. Fear Jehovah, ye his saints. Here the people of God are exhorted to the pursuit of holiness and righteousness, that they may open up a channel for divine blessings. We know that men are accustomed to provide for their wants, by resorting to fraud, plunder, and even to wrongful violence.

10. The Psalmist illustrates this doctrine by a very apposite comparison, namely, that God provides every thing necessary for his people, and relieves their wants, whilst the lions, which surpass in ferocity all the wild beasts of the earth, prowl about in a famishing condition for their prey. David simply asserts, that those who guard against all unrighteousness should profit more by so doing than by rapine and plunder; because the Lord feeds his people, while even the lions and other beasts of prey often suffer hunger.

11-14

11. Come, children, hearken unto me. The Psalmist continues, with increased earnestness, to exhort the faithful, that they may know that nothing can be more profitable for them than to conduct themselves justly and harmlessly towards all men. As the greater part of men imagine that the best and the shortest way to attain a life of happiness and ease consists in striving to surpass other men in violence, fraud, injustice, and other means of mischief, it is necessary frequently to repeat this doctrine.

12. Who is the man who desireth life? The prophet does not inquire if there be any man so disposed, as if all men voluntarily brought upon themselves the miseries which befall them; for we know that all men without exception desire to live in the enjoyment of happiness.

13. Keep thy tongue from evil The precept which David here delivers relates to a virtue which is very rare, namely, that we should be truthful and free from deceit in our discourse. We should not speak deceitfully with our neighbors, so as that our words may prove the means of ensnaring them.

14. Turn away from evil, and do good. Here the Psalmist commands the children of God to abstain from all evil, and to devote themselves to the work of doing good to their neighbors. This verse is generally quoted as if David here treated of the two parts of repentance. The first step in the work of repentance is, that the sinner forsake the vices to which he is addicted, and renounce his former manner of life; and the second, that he frame his behavior according to righteousness.

15. The eyes of Jehovah are upon the righteous. The best support of our patience is a firm persuasion that God regards us, and that according as every man perseveres in a course of uprightness and equity, so shall he be preserved in peace and safety under his protection. In order, therefore, that the faithful may not think that they are exposed to the caprice of the world, while they are endeavoring to keep themselves

MATTHEW HENRY

and greatly to be feared; nay, even his goodness is the proper object of a filial reverence and awe. They shall fear the Lord and his goodness, Hos. iii. 5. Fear the Lord; that is, worship him, and make conscience of your duty to him in every thing, not fear him and shun him, but fear him and seek him (v. 10) as a people seek unto their God; address yourselves to him and portion yourselves in him.

11-22 An exhortation to fear God; the privileges of the righteous.

David, in this latter part of the psalm, undertakes to teach children. Though a man of war, and anointed to be king, he did not think it below him; though now he had his head so full of cares and his hands of business, yet he could find heart and time to give good counsel to young people, from his own experience. It does not appear that he had now any children of his own, at least any that were grown up to a capacity of being taught; but, by divine inspiration, he instructs the children of his people. Those that were in years would not be taught by him, though he had offered them his service (Ps. xxxii. 8); but he had hopes that the tender branches will be more easily bent and that children and young people will be more tractable, and therefore he calls together a congregation of them (v. 11).

I. He supposes that we all aim to be happy (v. 12): What man is he that desireth life? that is, as it follows, not only to see many days, but to see good comfortable days.

II. He prescribes the true and only way to happiness both in this world and that to come, v. 13, 14. Would we pass comfortably through this world, and out of the world, our constant care must be to keep a good conscience; and, in order to that,

1. We must learn to bridle our tongues, and be careful what we say, that we never speak amiss, to God's dishonor or our neighbors prejudice: Keep thy tongue from evil speaking, lying, and slandering.

2. We must be upright and sincere in every thing we say, and not double-tongued. Our words must be the indications of our minds; our lips must be kept from speaking guile either to God or man.

3. We must leave all our sins, and resolve we will have no more to do with them. We must depart from evil, from evil works and evil workers; from the sins others commit and which we have formerly allowed ourselves in.

4. It is not enough not to do hurt in the world, but we must study to be useful, and live to some purpose. We must not only depart from evil, but we must do good.

5. Since nothing is more contrary to that love which never fails (which is the summary both of law and gospel, both of grace and glory) than strife and contention, which bring confusion and every evil work, we must seek peace and pursue it.

III. He enforces these directions by setting before us the happiness of the godly in the love and favor of God and the miserable state of the wicked under his

Psalm 34

17-22

17 The righteous cry, and the LORD heareth, and delivereth them out of all their troubles.
18 The LORD is nigh unto them that are of a broken heart; and saveth such as be of a contrite spirit.
19 Many are the afflictions of the righteous: but the LORD delivereth him out of them all.
20 He keepeth all his bones: not one of them is broken.
21 Evil shall slay the wicked: and they that hate the righteous shall be desolate.
22 The LORD redeemeth the soul of his servants: and none of them that trust in him shall be desolate.

viper's nest. Set a distance between yourself and temptation. And do good. Be practical, active, energetic, persevering in good.

Verse 15. The eyes of the Lord are upon the righteous. He observes them with approval and tender consideration; they are so dear to him that he cannot take his eyes off them; he watches each one of them as carefully and intently as if there were only that one creature in the universe.

Verse 16. The face of the Lord is against them that do evil. God is not indifferent to the deeds of sinners, but he sets his face against them, as we say, being determined that they shall have no countenance and support, but shall be thwarted and defeated. He is determinately resolved that the ungodly shall not prosper; he sets himself with all his might to overthrow them.

Verse 17. The righteous cry. Like Israel in Egypt, they cry out under the heavy yoke of oppression, both of sin, temptation, care, and grief. And the Lord heareth; he is like the night watchman, who no sooner hears the alarm bell than he flies to relieve those who need him.

Verse 18. The Lord is nigh unto them that are of a broken heart. Near in friendship to accept and console. Broken hearts think God far away, when he is really most near them; their eyes are holden so that they see not their best friend. Indeed, he is with them, and in them, but they know it not. They run hither and thither, seeking peace in their own works, or in experiences, or in proposals and resolutions, whereas the Lord is nigh them, and the simple act of faith will reveal him.

Verse 19. Many are the afflictions of the righteous. Thus are they made like Jesus their covenant Head. Scripture does not flatter us like the story books with the idea that goodness will secure us from trouble; on the contrary, we are again and again warned to expect tribulation while we are in this body.

Verse 20. He keepeth all his bones: not one of them is broken. David had come off with kicks and cuffs, but no broken bones. No substantial injury occurs to the saints. Eternity will heal all their wounds. Their real self is safe; they may have flesh wounds, but no part of the essential fabric of their being shall be broken. This verse may refer to frequent providential protections vouchsafed to the saints; but as good men have had broken limbs as well as others, it cannot absolutely be applied to bodily preservations; but must, it seems to me, be spiritually applied to great injuries of soul, which are for ever prevented by divine love.

Verse 21. Evil shall slay the wicked. Their adversaries shall be killing; they are not medicine, but poison. Ungodly men only need rope enough and they will hang themselves; their own iniquities shall be their punishment. Hell itself is but evil fully developed, torturing those in whom it dwells. Oh! happy they who have fled to Jesus to find refuge from their former sins, such, and such only will escape.

Verse 22. The Lord redeemeth the soul of his servants—with price and with power, with blood and with water. All providential helps are a part of the redemption by power, hence the Lord is said still to redeem. All thus ransomed belong to him who bought them—this is the law of justice and the verdict of gratitude. Faith is the mark of the ransomed, and wherever it is seen, though in the least and meanest of the saints, it ensures eternal salvation. Believer, thou shalt never be deserted, forsaken, given up to ruin. God, even thy God, is thy guardian and friend, and bliss is thine.

innocent, and that they may not, under the influence of this fear, go astray from the right path, David exhorts them to reflect upon the providence of God, and to rest assured that they are safe under his wings.

16. On the other hand, he declares, that although God sometimes appears to wink at the misdeeds of men, and seems to overlook them, because he does not inflict immediate punishment upon them, yet nothing escapes his inspection. Whilst the wicked, says he, by reason of their impunity harden themselves in sin, God is watching, that he may cut off their remembrance from the earth, (1 Peter 5:10.)

17. They cried, and Jehovah heard them. The Psalmist's meaning is, that they are heard as often as they cry. This is a doctrine applicable to all times; and David does not merely relate what God has done once or twice, but what he is accustomed to do. It is also a confirmation of the preceding sentence, where he had said that the ears of the Lord are open to the cry of the righteous; for he now demonstrates by the effect, that God is not deaf when we lay our complaints and groanings before him.

18-22

18. Jehovah is nigh to those who are broken of heart. David here exemplifies and extends still more the preceding doctrine, that God is the deliverer of his people, even when they are brought very low, and when they are, as it were, half-dead. It is a very severe trial, when the grace of God is delayed, and all experience of it so far withdrawn, as that our spirits begin to fail; nay more, to say that God is nigh to the faithful, even when their hearts faint and fall them, and they are ready to die, is altogether incredible to human sense and reason.

19. Many are the afflictions of the righteous. The Psalmist here anticipates the thought which often arises in the mind, "How can it be that God has a care about the righteous, who are continually harassed with so many calamities and trials? for what purpose does the protection of God serve, unless those who are peaceably inclined enjoy peace and repose? and what is more unreasonable, than that those who cause trouble to no one should themselves be tormented and afflicted in all variety of ways?"

20. What he adds concerning their bones, seems not a little to illustrate the truth of this doctrine, and to teach us that those who are protected by God shall be free from all danger. He therefore declares, that God will take care that not one of their bones shall be broken; in which sense Christ also says, that "the very hairs of our head are all numbered," (Luke 12:7.)

21. But malice shall slay the wicked. As David taught before, that there was no defense better than a just and blameless life, so now he declares, that all the wicked enterprises of the wicked, even though no one should in any thing oppose them, shall turn to their own destruction. Let this, therefore, be to us as a wall of brass and sure defense; that however numerous the enemies which beset us may be, we should not be afraid, because they are already devoted to destruction. The same thing David confirms in the last verse, in which he says, that Jehovah redeems the soul of his servants.

displeasure. Here are life and death, good and evil, the blessing and the curse, plainly stated before us, that we may choose life and live. See Isa. iii. 10, 11.

1. Woe to the wicked, it shall be ill with them, however they may bless themselves in their own way.

(1.) God is against them, and then they cannot but be miserable. Sad is the case of that man who by his sin has made his Maker his enemy, his destroyer. The face of the Lord is against those that do evil, v. 16. Sometimes God is said to turn his face from them (Jer. xviii. 17), because they have forsaken him; here he is said to set his face against them, because they have fought against him; and most certainly God is able to out-face the most proud and daring sinners and can frown them into hell.

(2.) Ruin is before them; this will follow of course if God be against them, for he is able both to kill and to cast into hell.

2. Yet say to the righteous, It shall be well with them. All good people are under God's special favor and protection. We are here assured of this under a great variety of instances and expressions.

(1.) God takes special notice of good people, and takes notice who have their eyes ever to him and who make conscience of their duty to him: The eyes of the Lord are upon the righteous (v. 15), to direct and guide them, to protect and keep them.

(2.) They are sure of an answer of peace to their prayers. All God's people are a praying people, and they cry in prayer, which denotes great importunity; but is it to any purpose? Yes, God takes notice of what we say (v. 17): They cry, and the Lord hears them, and hears them so as to make it appear he has a regard to them. His ears are open to their prayers, to receive them all, and to receive them readily and with delight.

(3.) They are taken under the special protection of the divine government (v. 20): He keepeth all his bones; not only his soul, but his body; not only his body in general, but every bone in it: Not one of them is broken. He that has a broken heart shall not have a broken bone; for David himself had found that, when he had a contrite heart, the broken bones were made to rejoice, Ps. li. 8, 17.

(4.) They are, and shall be, delivered out of their troubles.

[1.] It is supposed that they have their share of crosses in this world, perhaps a greater share than others. In the world they must have tribulation, that they may be conformed both to the will of God and to the example of Christ (v. 19); Many are the afflictions of the righteous, witness David and his afflictions, Ps. cxxxii.

1. There are those that hate them (v. 21) and they are continually aiming to do them a mischief; their God loves them, and therefore corrects them.

[2.] God has engaged for their deliverance and salvation: He delivers them out of all their troubles (v. 17, 19); he saves them (v. 18), so that, though they may fall into trouble, it shall not be their ruin. This promise of their deliverance is explained, v. 22.

Psalm 35

Title
A Psalm of David

1-7
1 Plead my cause, O LORD, with them that strive with me: fight against them that fight against me.
2 Take hold of shield and buckler, and stand up for mine help.
3 Draw out also the spear, and stop the way against them that persecute me: say unto my soul, I am thy salvation.
4 Let them be confounded and put to shame that seek after my soul: let them be turned back and brought to confusion that devise my hurt.
5 Let them be as chaff before the wind: and let the angel of the LORD chase them.
6 Let their way be dark and slippery: and let the angel of the LORD persecute them.
7 For without cause have they hid for me their net in a pit, which without cause they have digged for my soul.

Psalm 35

TITLE. A Psalm of David. Here is all we know concerning this Psalm, but internal evidence seems to fix the date of its composition in those troublous times when Saul hunted David over hill and dale, and when those who fawned upon the cruel king, slandered the innocent object of his wrath, or it may be referred to the unquiet days of frequent insurrections in David's old age. The whole Psalm is the appeal to heaven of a bold heart and a clear conscience, irritated beyond measure by oppression and malice. Beyond a doubt David's Lord may be seen here by the spiritual eye.
DIVISION. The most natural mode of dividing this Psalm is to note its triple character. Its complaint, prayer, and promise of praise are repeated with remarkable parallelism three times, even as our Lord in the Garden prayed three times, using the same words. The first portion occupies from Ps 35:1-10, the second from Ps 35:11-18, and the last from Ps 35:19-28; each section ending with a note of grateful song.

EXPOSITION
Verse 1. Plead my cause, O Lord, with them that strive with me. Plead against those who plead against me; strive with my strivers; contend with my contenders. If they urge their suit in the law court, Lord, meet them there, and beat them at their own weapons. Every saint of God shall have this privilege: the accuser of the brethren shall be met by the Advocate of the saints.
Verse 2. Take hold of shield and buckler, and stand up for mine help. In vivid metaphor the Lord is pictured as coming forth armed for battle, and interposing himself between his servant and his enemies. The greater and lesser protections of providence may be here intended by the two defensive weapons, and by the Lord's standing up is meant his active and zealous preservation of his servant in the perilous hour.
Verse 3. Draw out also the spear, and stop the way against them that persecute me. Before the enemy comes to close quarters the Lord can push them off as with a long spear. To stave off trouble is no mean act of lovingkindness. As when some valiant warrior with his lance blocks up a defile, and keeps back a host until his weaker brethren have made good their escape, so does the Lord often hold the believer's foes at bay until the good man had taken breath, or clean fled from his foes.
Verse 4. Let them be confounded and put to shame that seek after my soul. There is nothing malicious here, the slandered man simply craves for justice, and the petition is natural and justifiable. Guided by God's good spirit the psalmist foretells the everlasting confusion of all the haters of the righteous. Shameful disappointment shall be the portion of the enemies of the gospel, nor would the most tender hearted Christian have it otherwise: viewing sinners as men, we love them and seek their good, but regarding them as enemies of God, we cannot think of them with anything but detestation, and a loyal desire for the confusion of their devices.
Verse 6. Let their way be dark and slippery. What terrors are gathered Here! No light, no foothold, and a fierce avenger at their heels! What a doom is appointed for the enemies of God! They may rage and rave today, but how altered will be their plight ere long! And let the angel of the Lord persecute them. He will follow them hot foot, as we say, never turning aside, but like a trusty pursuivant serving the writ of vengeance upon them, and arresting them in the name of unflinching justice. Woe, woe, woe, unto those who touch the people of God; their destruction is both swift and sure.
Verse 7. In this verse the psalmist brings forward the gravamen of his charge against the servants of the devil. For without cause—without my having injured, assailed, or provoked them; out of their own spontaneous malice have they hid for me their net in a pit, even as men hunt for their game with cunning and deception. Innocent persons have often been

Psalm 35

1-3
1. Plead my cause, O Jehovah! As the enemies of David not only avowedly sought to take away his life, but also troubled him by calumny and misrepresentation, he pleads for the redress of both these grievances. In the first place, by appealing to God for his aid in defense of his cause, he intimates, that he has to do with wicked and maligning men. In the second place, by urging him to take up arms, he shows that he was grievously oppressed. It was a very dishonorable thing, that this holy man, alike eminent for his beneficence and inoffensiveness towards all men, and who by his courtesy and meekness had merited, both in public and private, the esteem and favor of all, was not permitted to escape the reproach and calumny of wicked men; but it is important for us to know this, and it sets before us a very profitable example.
2. Take the shield. These words certainly cannot be applied, in the strict and proper sense, to God, who has no need of the spear or buckler: for by the breath of his mouth alone, or merely with his nod, he is able to overthrow all his enemies. But although such figures at first sight appear rude, yet the Holy Ghost employs them in accommodation to the weakness of our understanding, for the purpose of impressing more effectually upon our minds the conviction that God is present to aid us.
3. Say to my soul. Some expound these words thus: Declare to me by secret inspiration; and others, Make me to feel indeed that my salvation is in thy hand. In my opinion, David desires to have it thoroughly fixed in his mind, and to be fully persuaded that God is the author of his salvation. This he was unable, from the present aspect of things, to ascertain and determine; for such is the insensibility and dullness of our natures, that God often delivers us whilst we sleep and are ignorant of it.

4-7
4. Let those who seek my soul be confounded. David now calls upon God to take vengeance upon his enemies; and he asks not only that he would disappoint and destroy their designs, but also that he would recompense them according to their deserts.
5. The same thing he expresses more clearly in the following verse, praying that the angel of the Lord would drive them through dark and slippery places, so that reason and understanding might fail them, and that they might not know whither to go, nor what to become, nor have even time given them to draw their breath.
7. For they have hid for me without a cause. He here declares that he did not take the name of God in vain, nor call upon him for protection without just cause, for he openly asserts his innocence, and complains that he was thus severely afflicted without having committed any crime, or given any occasion to his enemies. It becomes us carefully to mark this, so that no one may rush unadvisedly into God's presence, nor call upon him for vengeance, without the assurance and

Psalm 35

1-10 Prayer for divine protection.
In these verses we have,
I. David's representation of his case to God, setting forth the restless rage and malice of his persecutors. He was God's servant, expressly appointed by him to be what he was, followed his guidance, and aimed at his glory in the way of duty, had lived (as St. Paul speaks) in all good conscience before God unto this day; and yet there were those that strove with him, that did their utmost to oppose his advancement, and made all the interest they could against him; they fought against him (v. 1), not only undermined him closely and secretly, but openly avowed their opposition to him and set themselves to do him all the mischief they could. They persecuted him with an unwearied enmity, sought after his soul (v. 4), that is, his life, no less would satisfy their bloody minds; they aimed to disquiet his spirit and put that into disorder. Nor was it a sudden passion against him that they harbored, but inveterate malice: They devised his hurt, laid their heads together, and set their wits on work, not only to do him a mischief, but to find out ways and means to ruin him. They treated him, who was the greatest blessing of his country, as if he had been the curse and plague of it; they hunted him as a dangerous beast of prey; they digged a pit for him and laid a net in it, that they might have him at their mercy, v. 7. They took a great deal of pains in persecuting him, for they digged a pit (Ps. vii. 15); and very close and crafty they were in carrying on their designs; the old serpent taught them subtlety: they hid their net from David and his friends; but in vain, for they could not hide it from God. And, lastly, he found himself an unequal match for them. His enemy, especially Saul, was too strong for him (v. 10), for he had the army at his command.
II. His appeal to God concerning his integrity and the justice of his cause. If a fellow-subject had wronged him, he might have appealed to his prince, as St. Paul did to Cæsar; but, when his prince wronged him, he appealed to his God, who is prince and Judge of the kings of the earth: Plead my cause, O Lord! v. 1.
III. His prayer to God to manifest himself both for him and to him, in this trial.
1. For him. He prays that God would fight against his enemies, so as to disable them to hurt him, and defeat their designs against him (v. 1), that he would take hold of shield and buckler, for the Lord is a man of war (Exod. xv. 3), and that he would stand up for his help (v. 2), for he had few that would stand up for him, and, if he had ever so many, they would stand him in no stead without God. He prays that God would stop their way (v. 3), that they might not overtake him when he fled from them. This prayer we may put up against our persecutors, that God would restrain them and stop their way.

Psalm 35

8-14

8 Let destruction come upon him at unawares; and let his net that he hath hid catch himself: into that very destruction let him fall.
9 And my soul shall be joyful in the LORD: it shall rejoice in his salvation.
10 All my bones shall say, LORD, who is like unto thee, which deliverest the poor from him that is too strong for him, yea, the poor and the needy from him that spoileth him?
11 False witnesses did rise up; they laid to my charge things that I knew not.
12 They rewarded me evil for good to the spoiling of my soul.
13 But as for me, when they were sick, my clothing was sackcloth: I humbled my soul with fasting; and my prayer returned into mine own bosom.
14 I behaved myself as though he had been my friend or brother: I bowed down heavily, as one that mourneth for his mother.

ruined by traps set for them, into which they have fallen as guilelessly as beasts which stumble into concealed pits, and are taken as in a net. It is no little thing to be able to feel that the enmity which assails us is undeserved—not caused by any willful offence on our part.

Verse 8. Let destruction come upon him at unawares. This tremendous imprecation is frequently fulfilled. God's judgments are often sudden and signal. Death enters the persecutor's house without pausing to knock at the door. The thunderbolt of judgment leaps from its hiding place, and in one crash the wicked are broken for ever. And let his net that he hath hid catch himself: into that very destruction let him fall. There is a lex talionis with God which often works most wonderfully.

Verse 9. And my soul shall be joyful in the Lord. Thus rescued, David ascribes all the honor to the Judge of the right; to his own valorous arm he offers no sacrifice of boasting. He turns away from his adversaries to his God, and finds a deep unbroken joy in Jehovah, and in that joy his spirit revels. It shall rejoice in his salvation. We do not triumph in the destruction of others, but in the salvation given to us of God. Prayer heard should always suggest praise. It were well if we were more demonstrative in our holy rejoicing. We rob God by suppressing grateful emotions.

Verse 10. As the tongue were not enough to bless God with, David makes every limb vocal—All my bones shall say, Lord, who is like unto thee? His whole anatomy he would make resonant with gratitude. Those bones which were to have been broken by my enemies shall now praise God; every one of them shall bring its tribute, ascribing unrivalled excellence to Jehovah the Savior of his people. Even if worn to skin and bone, yet my very skeleton shall magnify the Lord, which deliverest the poor from him that is too strong for him, yea, the poor and the needy from him that spoileth him. God is the champion, the true knight errant of all oppressed ones.

Verse 11. False witnesses did rise up. This is the old device of the ungodly, and we must not wonder if it be used against us as against our Master. To please Saul, there were always men to be found mean enough to impeach David. They laid to my charge things that I knew not. He had not even a though of sedition; he was loyal even to excess; yet they accused him of conspiring against the Lord's anointed. He was not only innocent, but ignorant of the fault alleged. It is well when our hands are so clean that no trace of dirt is upon them.

Verse 12. They rewarded me evil for good. This is devilish; but men have learned the lesson well of the old Destroyer, and practice it most perfectly. To the spoiling of my soul. They robbed him of comfort, and even would have taken his life had it not been for special rescues from the hand of God. The wicked would strip the righteous naked to their very soul: they know no pity. There are only such limits to human malice as God himself may see fit to place.

Verse 13. But as for me, when they were sick, my clothing was sackcloth. David had been a man of sympathy; he had mourned when Saul was in ill health, putting on the weeds of sorrow for him as though he were a near and dear friend. His heart went into mourning for his sick master. Humbled my soul with fasting. He prayed for his enemy, and made the sick man's case his own, pleading and confessing as if his own personal sin had brought on the evil. This showed a noble spirit in David, and greatly aggravated the baseness of those who now so cruelly persecuted him. And my prayer returned into mine own bosom. Prayer is never lost: if it bless not those for whom intercession is made, it shall bless the intercessors. Clouds do not always descend in showers upon the same spot from which the vapors ascended, but they come down somewhere; and even so do supplications in some place or other yield their showers of mercy. If our dove find no rest for the sole of her foot among our enemies, it shall fly into our bosoms and bring an olive branch of peace in its mouth. How sharp is the contrast all through this Psalm between the righteous testimony of a good conscience. When he says that he was assailed by stratagem, fraud, and wicked practices, there is implied in this a tacit commendation of his own integrity.

8-10

8. Let confusion of which he is not aware come upon him. David again prays that God would cause to return upon the head of his enemies the mischief which they had directed against a just and an inoffensive man.

9. And my soul is joyful in Jehovah. David here declares that he will not forget the favor which God had bestowed upon him. My soul, says he, shall rejoice, not in a deliverance of the author of which it is ignorant, but in the salvation of God.

10. O Jehovah! who is like thee? Here he explains more fully the nature of his joy in the salvation of God of which he had spoken, showing that it consisted in his ascribing entirely to God the deliverance which he had obtained. Men, in general, praise God in such a manner that he scarcely obtains the tenth part of his due. But David, distinguishing him from all others, distinctly declares that the whole glory of his deliverance is due to him alone.

11-15

11. Violent witnesses rise up. The Hebrew is, they shall rise up; but in using the future tense, the Psalmist intimates that he is speaking of what he had suffered for a long time. And he complains that he was so oppressed with calumny that he had no opportunity of defending himself; than which nothing more grievous and painful can ever happen to those of an ingenuous mind, and who are conscious of no blame.

12. They render me evil for good. David again shows that the malice of his enemies was of a very aggravated character, because they not only oppressed him wrongfully, seeing he was innocent, and had given them no occasion of offense, but also because even those who had received much enjoyment and many favors from him, recompensed him in a very strange and ungrateful manner. Such disgraceful conduct wounds the feelings of good men very severely, and seems quite intolerable.

15. David was shamefully treated by the lowest dregs of the people. The words, I knew not, may be referred to the cause as well as to the persons. I, however, explain it as referring to the persons in this sense: So far from having any cause to complain that I have offended them, or done them any harm, I did not even know them. At the same time, these words may be understood as implying a complaint on the part of David, that the people were enraged against him without any cause, since he is conscious of no crime, and can conceive of no ground for such fierce hatred towards him.

16-18

16. David simply relates the combination of his enemies. And the meaning of the expression is to this effect, That among men of a crafty disposition, who had been addicted to deceit, and were consequently lost to all sense of shame, the only and the constant subject of their deliberations was, how

2. To him: "Say unto my soul, I am thy salvation; let me have inward comfort under all these outward troubles, to support my soul which they strike at. Let God be my salvation, not only my Savior out of my present troubles, but my everlasting bliss. Let me have that salvation not only which he is the author of, but which consists in his favor; and let me know my interest in it; let me have the comfortable assurance of it in my own breast." If God, by his Spirit, witness to our spirits that he is our salvation, we have enough, we need desire no more to make us happy; and this is a powerful support when men persecute us. If God be our friend, no matter who is our enemy.

IV. His prospect of the destruction of his enemies, which he prays for, not in malice or revenge. We find how patiently he bore Shimei's curses (so let him curse, for the Lord has bidden him); and we cannot suppose that he who was so meek in his conversation would give vent to any intemperate heat or passion in his devotion. David here prays,

1. Against his many enemies (v. 4-6): Let them be confounded, &c. Or, as Dr. Hammond reads it, They shall be confounded, they shall be turned back. This may be taken as a prayer for their repentance, for all penitents are put to shame for their sins and turned back from them. Or, if they were not brought to repentance, David prays that they might be defeated and disappointed in their designs against him and so put to shame. Though they should in some degree prevail, yet he foresees that it would be to their own ruin at last: They shall be as chaff before the wind, so unable will wicked men be to stand before the judgments of God and so certainly will they be driven away by them, Ps. i. 4. Their way shall be dark and slippery, darkness and slipperiness (so the margin reads it); the way of sinners is so, for they walk in darkness and in continual danger of falling into sin, into hell; and it will prove so at last, for their foot shall slide in due time, Deut. xxxii. 35.

2. Against his one mighty enemy (v. 8): Let destruction come upon him. It is probable that he means Saul, who laid snares for him and aimed at his destruction. David vowed that his hand should not be upon him; he would not be judge in his own cause. But, at the same time, he foretold that the Lord would smite him (1 Sam. xxvi. 10), and here that the net he had hidden should catch himself, and into that very destruction he should fall. This was remarkably fulfilled in the ruin of Saul; for he had laid a plot to make David fall by the hand of the Philistines (1 Sam. xviii. 25), that was the net which he hid for him under pretence of doing him honor, and in that very net was he himself taken, for he fell by the hand of the Philistines when his day came to fall.

V. His prospect of his own deliverance, which, having committed his cause to God, he did not doubt of, v. 9, 10.

1. He hoped that he should have the comfort of it: "My soul shall be joyful, not in my own ease and safety,

Psalm 35

15-21

15 But in mine adversity they rejoiced, and gathered themselves together: yea, the abjects gathered themselves together against me, and I knew it not; they did tear me, and ceased not:
16 With hypocritical mockers in feasts, they gnashed upon me with their teeth.
17 Lord, how long wilt thou look on? rescue my soul from their destructions, my darling from the lions.
18 I will give thee thanks in the great congregation: I will praise thee among much people.
19 Let not them that are mine enemies wrongfully rejoice over me: neither let them wink with the eye that hate me without a cause.
20 For they speak not peace: but they devise deceitful matters against them that are quiet in the land.
21 Yea, they opened their mouth wide against me, and said, Aha, aha, our eye hath seen it.

and his enemies! We must be earnest to keep the line of demarcation broad and clear.

Verse 14. I behaved myself as though he has been my friend or brother: I waited upon him assiduously, comforted him affectionately, and sympathized with him deeply. This may refer to those days when David played on the harp, and chased away the evil spirit from Saul. I bowed down heavily, as one that mourneth for his mother. He bowed his head as mourners do. The strongest natural grief was such as he felt when they were in trouble. The mother usually wins the deepest love, and her loss is most keenly felt: such was David's grief. How few professors in these days have such bowels of compassion; and yet under the gospel there should be far more tender love than under the law. Had we more hearty love to manhood, and care for its innumerable ills, we might be far more useful; certainly we should be infinitely more Christ like. "He prayeth best that lovest best."

Verse 15. But in mine adversity they rejoiced. In my halting they were delighted. My lameness was sport to them. Danger was near, and they sang songs over my expected defeat. How glad are the wicked to see a good man limp! "Now," say they, "he will meet with his downfall." And gathered themselves together, like kites and vultures around a dying sheep. They found a common joy in my ruin, and a recreation in my sorrow, and therefore met together to keep the feast. They laid their heads together to devise, and their tongues to deceive. Yea, the abjects gathered themselves together against me. Those who deserved horsewhipping, fellows the soles of whose feet were needing the bastinado, came together to plot, and held hole and corner meetings. Like curs around a sick lion, the mean wretches taunted and insulted one whose name had been their terror. The very cripples hobbled out to join the malicious crew. How unanimous are the powers of evil; how heartily do men serve the devil; and none decline his service because they are not endowed with great abilities! I knew it not. It was all done behind my back. What a fluster the world may be in, and the cause of it all may not even know that he has given offence. They did tear me, and ceased not. It is such dainty work to tear to pieces a good man's character, that when slanderers have their hand in they are loath to leave off.

Verse 16. With hypocritical mockers in feasts, they gnashed upon me with their teeth. Like professional buffoons who grin around the banquet to make sport, so they made a business of jeering at the good man; not, however, out of mirth, but from violent, insatiable hatred. Like cake scoffers, or men who will jeer for a bit of bread, these hireling miscreants persecuted David in order to get a bellyful for themselves from Saul's table: having moreover an inward grudge against the son of Jesse because he was a better man than themselves. Very forcibly might our Lord have used the words of these verses! Let us not forget to see the Despised and Rejected of men here painted to the life. Calvary and the ribald crew around the cross seem brought before our eyes.

Verse 17. Lord, how long wilt thou look on? Why be a mere spectator? Why so neglectful of thy servant? Art thou indifferent? Carest thou not that we perish? We may thus reason with the Lord. He permits us this familiarity. There is a time for our salvation, but to our impatience it often seems to be very slow in coming; yet wisdom has ordained the hour, and nothing shall delay it. Rescue my soul from their destructions. From their many devices; their multiplied assaults, be pleased to set me free. ["My darling,"] my lovely, only, precious soul, do thou rescue ["from the lions."] His enemies were fierce, cunning, and strong as young lions; God only could deliver him from their jaws, to God he therefore addresses himself.

Verse 20. "For they speak not peace." They love it not; how can they speak it? They are such troublers themselves that they cannot judge others to be peaceable. Out of the mouth comes what is in the heart. Riotous men

they might destroy this afflicted man. David again reverts to the leaders of the people, and to those in power, as the source whence all the mischief took its rise; for this description could not apply to a great part of the common people, who acted rather by thoughtless impulse.
17. O Lord! how long wilt thou look on? The meaning of the word which I have translated how long, is ambiguous in the Hebrew. In Latin it signifies, How long wilt thou see it, and suffer it without uttering a word? But the other interpretation is equally appropriate, namely, After having seemed to take no notice of the matter for a long time, when wilt thou at length begin to see it? The meaning, however, is substantially the same, for David complains of God's long forbearance, declaring that while the wicked are running to every excess, God connives at them, and delays too much to take vengeance.
18. I will magnify thee in the great congregation. In this verse David again engages to give thanks to God for all his goodness, since the faithful can render him no other recompense than the sacrifice of praise, as we shall see in Psalm 116:17. Thus even whilst he was surrounded by the impetuous billows of fear and danger, he sets himself to the exercise of giving thanks, as if he had already obtained his desire; and by this he intended to encourage and confirm himself in the assurance of obtaining his requests.

19-23
19. Let not those who are my enemies wrongfully rejoice over me. Because David's enemies already exulted in the hope of seeing his overthrow and destruction, he prays that God would not suffer them to realize a desire so wicked. In order to render God favorable to his cause, he again protests that they hated him without any fault or occasion on his part, and that it was their own malice which urged them to such cruelty against him; for in order to secure the help of God, it is necessary to come before him with the testimony of a good conscience.
20. In the following verse, that he may cherish still greater confidence in God, David again declares, that he has to do with enemies of an irreconcilable character, and who are fully bent upon cruelty. Of this we ought to be firmly persuaded, that the more grievously we are oppressed, so much the more certainly ought we to expect deliverance.
22. O Jehovah! thou hast also seen it. There is in these words an implied contrast between the view which God is here represented as taking, and the sight at which, as we are told in the preceding verse, the ungodly rejoiced. The import of David's language is, You have rejoiced exceedingly at the sight of my miseries; but God also sees and takes notice of the cruelty and malice of those who feel a pleasure and gratification in seeing others afflicted and in trouble. David, however, in thus speaking, stays not to reason with his enemies, but rather addresses himself directly to God, and sets his providence as a rampart of defense in opposition to all the assaults of those who sought to shake his confidence, and who caused him much trouble.

but in the Lord and in his favor, in his promise and in his salvation according to the promise." Joy in God and in his salvation is the only true, solid, satisfying joy. Those whose souls are sorrowful in the Lord, who sow in tears and sorrow after a godly sort, need not question but that in due time their souls shall be joyful in the Lord; for gladness is sown for them, and they shall at last enter into the joy of their Lord.
2. He promised that then God should have the glory of it (v. 10): All my bones shall say, Lord, who is like unto thee?
(1.) He will praise God with the whole man, with all that is within him, and with all the strength and vigor of his soul, intimated by his bones, which are within the body and are the strength of it.
(2.) He will praise him as one of peerless and unparalleled perfection. We cannot express how great and good God is, and therefore must praise him by acknowledging him to be a non-such.

11-16 Prayer for deliverance; sorrowful complaints.
Two very wicked things David here lays to the charge of his enemies, to make good his appeal to God against them—perjury and ingratitude.
I. Perjury, v. 11. When Saul would have David attainted of treason, in order to his being outlawed, perhaps he did it with the formalities of a legal prosecution, produced witnesses who swore some treasonable words or overt acts against him, and he being not present to clear himself (or, if he was, it was all the same), Saul adjudged him a traitor. This he complains of here as the highest piece of injustice imaginable: False witnesses did rise up, who would swear anything; they laid to my charge things that I knew not, nor ever thought of.
II. Ingratitude. Call a man ungrateful and you can call him no worse. This was the character of David's enemies (v. 12): They rewarded me evil for good. A great deal of good service he had done to his king, witness his harp, witness Goliath's sword, witness the foreskins of the Philistines; and yet his king vowed his death, and his country was made too hot for him. This is to the spoiling of his soul; this base unkind usage robs him of his comfort, and cuts him to the heart, more than anything else.
1. How tenderly, and with what a cordial affection, he had behaved towards them in their afflictions (v. 13, 14): They were sick. Note, Even the palaces and courts of princes are not exempt from the jurisdiction of death and the visitation of sickness.
2. How basely and insolently and with what a brutish enmity, and worse than brutish, they had behaved towards him (v. 15, 16); In my adversity they rejoiced. When he fell under the frowns of Saul, was banished the court, and persecuted as a criminal, they were pleased, were glad at his calamities, and got together in their drunken clubs to make themselves and one another merry with the disgrace of this great favorite. Well, might he call them abjects, for nothing could be

Psalm 35

22-28

22 This thou hast seen, O LORD: keep not silence: O Lord, be not far from me.

23 Stir up thyself, and awake to my judgment, even unto my cause, my God and my Lord.

24 Judge me, O LORD my God, according to thy righteousness; and let them not rejoice over me.

25 Let them not say in their hearts, Ah, so would we have it: let them not say, We have swallowed him up.

26 Let them be ashamed and brought to confusion together that rejoice at mine hurt: let them be clothed with shame and dishonor that magnify themselves against me.

27 Let them shout for joy, and be glad, that favor my righteous cause: yea, let them say continually, Let the LORD be magnified, which hath pleasure in the prosperity of his servant.

28 And my tongue shall speak of thy righteousness and of thy praise all the day long.

charge others with sedition. "They devise deceitful matters against them that are quiet in the land." David would fain have been an orderly citizen, but they labored to make him a rebel. He could do nothing aright, all his dealings were misrepresented.

Verse 21. "Yea, they opened their mouth wide against me." As if they would swallow him. Uttering great lies which needed wide mouths. They set no bounds to their infamous charges, but poured out wholesale abuse, trusting that if all did not stick, some of it would. "And said, Aha, aha, our eye hath seen it." Glad to find out a fault or a misfortune, or to swear they had seen evil where there was none. Malice has but one eye; it is blind to all virtue in its enemy.

Verse 22. "This thou hast seen, O Lord." Here is comfort. Our heavenly Father knows all our sorrow. Omniscience is the saint's candle which never goes out. A father will not long endure to see his child abused. Shall not God avenge his own elect? "Keep not silence." Rebuke thine enemies and mine, O Lord. A word will do it. Clear my character, comfort my heart. "O Lord, be not far from me." Walk the furnace with me. Stand in the pillory at my side. The sweet presence of God is the divine cordial of the persecuted; his painful absence would be their seepest misery.

Verse 23. "Stir up thyself." Be upon thy mettle. Prove that thou art no indifferent witness to all this infamy. "Awake to my judgement." Take the scepter and summon the great assize; vindicate justice, avenge oppression. Do not tarry as men do who sleep. "Even unto my cause, my God and my Lord." He claims a nearness to his God, he holds him with both hands; he leaves his case with the righteous Judge.

Verse 24. The appeal is here repeated; the plaintiff feels that the joy of his accusers will be short-lived as soon as impartial justice rules. The oppressors' wrong, the proud man's contumely, the fool's grimace—all, all will cease when the righteous Lord sits down upon the judgment seat.

Verse 25. "Let them not say in their hearts, Ah, so would we have it: let them not say, We have swallowed him up." Disappoint them of their prey when their mouths are ready to swallow it. Saints are too dear a morsel for the powers of evil; God will not give his sheep over to the wolfish jaws of persecutors. Just when they are tuning their pipes to celebrate their victory, they shall be made to laugh on the other side of their mouths.

Verse 26. Here is the eternal result of all the laborious and crafty devices of the Lord's enemies. God will make little of them, though they "magnified themselves;" he will shame them for shaming his people, bring them to confusion for making confusion, pull off their fine apparel and give them a beggarly suit of dishonor, and turn all their rejoicing into weeping and wailing, and gnashing of teeth. Truly, the saints can afford to wait.

Verse 27. "Let them shout for joy, and be glad, that favor my righteous cause." Even those who could not render him active aid, but in their hearts favored him, David would have the Lord reward most abundantly. Men of tender heart set great store by the good wishes and prayers of the Lord's people. Jesus also prizes those whose hearts are with his cause.

Verse 28. Unceasing praise is here vowed to the just and gracious God. From morning till evening the grateful tongue would talk and sing, and glorify the Lord. O for such a resolve carried out by us all!

24-28
24. Judge me, O Jehovah my God! David here confirms the prayer of the preceding verse that God would be his defender, and would maintain his righteous cause. Having been for a time subjected to suffering as one who had been forsaken and forgotten, he sets before himself the righteousness of God, which forbids that he should altogether abandon the upright and the just. It is, therefore, not simply a prayer, but a solemn appeal to God, that as he is righteous, he would manifest his righteousness in defending his servant in a good cause. And certainly, when we seem to be forsaken and deprived of all help, there is no remedy which we can employ, more effectual to overcome temptation than this consideration, that the righteousness of God, on which our deliverance depends, can never fail. Accordingly, the Apostle Paul, in exhorting the faithful to patience, says in 2 Thessalonians 1:6, "It is a righteous thing with God to recompense tribulation to them that trouble you."
26. Let those who rejoice at thy hurt be ashamed and confounded together. This imprecation has already been expounded; and it is only necessary to remark, that there is peculiar force in the expression, together, or at once. It shows that it was not only one or two, but a great multitude, who waged war against him, and that he yielded not to the influence of fear, but believed that as soon as God should lift up his hand, he could at one stroke easily overthrow them all. When it is said that they seek after and rejoice in David's hurt, this shows that they were filled with cruel hatred against him. And when it is said, that they magnify themselves against him, this is a token of pride.
27. Let those who favor my righteous cause rejoice and be glad. David here extols the deliverance which he asks of God, and exults in the results which should flow from it; namely, that it would be an occasion of general rejoicing and good hope to all the godly, while at the same time it would stir them up to celebrate the praises of God. He attributes to all the faithful the credit of desiring, that as an innocent man his righteous cause should be maintained. David, it is true, was the object of almost universal hatred among the simple and unsuspecting, who were imposed upon by false and unjust reports made concerning him; but it is certain that there were among the people some who formed a just and impartial estimate of things, and who were sorely grieved that a holy man, and one too whose benevolence was well known, should have been so unjustly and so wrongfully oppressed. And surely the common feelings of humanity require, that when we see men unjustly oppressed and afflicted, if we are not able to help them, we should at least pity them. When David uses the language, Jehovah be magnified, his design seems to be tacitly to set this in opposition to the pride of the wicked, of which he made mention above.
28. Finally, the Psalmist again declares, in the conclusion of the psalm, his resolution to celebrate in appropriate praises the righteousness of God, by which he had been preserved and delivered.

more vile and sordid than to triumph in the fall of a man of such unstained honor and consummate virtue.

17-28 Sorrowful complaints; David's appeal and prayer to God.
In these verses, as before,
I. David describes the great injustice, malice, and insolence, of his persecutors, pleading this with God as a reason why he should protect him from them and appear against them.
1. They were very proud and scornful (v. 21): They opened their mouth wide against me; they shouted and huzzaed when they saw his fall; they bawled after him when he was forced to quit the court, "Aha! aha! this is the day we longed to see."
2. They were very barbarous and base, for they trampled upon him when he was down, rejoiced at his hurt, and magnified themselves against him, v. 26. Thus, when the Son of David was run upon by the rulers, the people cried, Crucify him, crucify him.
3. They set themselves against all the sober good people that adhered to David (v. 20): They devised deceitful matters, to trepan and ruin those that were quiet in the land.
II. He appeals to God against them, the God to whom vengeance belongs, appeals to his knowledge (v. 22): This thou hast seen. They had falsely accused him, but God, who knows all things, knew that he did not falsely accuse them, nor make them worse than really they were. They had carried on their plots against him with a great degree of secrecy (v. 15).
III. He prays earnestly to God to appear graciously for him and his friends, against his and their enemies, that by his providence the struggle might issue to the honor and comfort of David and to the conviction and confusion of his persecutors. He prays that God would act for him, and not stand by as a spectator (v. 17): "Lord, how long wilt thou look on? How long wilt thou connive at the wickedness of the wicked? Rescue my soul from the destructions they are plotting against it; rescue my darling, my only one, from the lions. My soul is my only one, and therefore the greater is the shame if I neglect it and the greater the loss if I lose it: it is my only one, and therefore ought to be my darling, ought to be carefully protected and provided for. It is my soul that is in danger; Lord, rescue it. It does, in a peculiar manner, belong to the Father of spirits, therefore claim thy own; it is thine, save it. Lord, keep not silence, as if thou didst consent to what is done against me! Lord, be not far from me (v. 22), as if I were a stranger that thou wert not concerned for; let not me beheld afar off, as the proud are."
IV. The mercy he hoped to win by prayer he promises to wear with praise: "I will give thee thanks, as the author of my deliverance (v. 18), and my tongue shall speak of thy righteousness, the justice of thy judgments and the equity of all thy dispensations."

Psalm 36

Title
To the Chief Musician. A Psalm of David the servant of the Lord.

1-6
1 The transgression of the wicked saith within my heart, that there is no fear of God before his eyes.
2 For he flattereth himself in his own eyes, until his iniquity be found to be hateful.
3 The words of his mouth are iniquity and deceit: he hath left off to be wise, and to do good.
4 He deviseth mischief upon his bed; he setteth himself in a way that is not good; he abhorreth not evil.
5 Thy mercy, O LORD, is in the heavens; and thy faithfulness reacheth unto the clouds.
6 Thy righteousness is like the great mountains; thy judgments are a great deep: O LORD, thou preservest man and beast.

Psalm 36

TITLE. To the Chief Musician, He who had the leadership of the Temple service was charged with the use of this song in public worship. What is everybody's business is never done. It was well to have one person specially to attend to the service of song in the house of the Lord. Of David the servant of the Lord. This would seem to indicate that the Psalm peculiarly befits one who esteems it an honor to be called Jehovah's servant. It is THE SONG OF HAPPY SERVICE; such a one as all may join in who bear the easy yoke of Jesus. The wicked are contrasted with the righteous, and the great Lord of devout men is heartily extolled; thus obedience to so good a Master is indirectly insisted on, and rebellion against him is plainly condemned.
DIVISION. From Ps 36:1-4 David describes the rebellious: in Ps 36:5-9 he extols the various attributes of the Lord; in Ps 36:10-11 he addresses the Lord in prayer, and in the last verse his faith sees in vision the overthrow of all the workers of iniquity.

EXPOSITION
Verse 1. The transgression of the wicked. His daring and wanton sin; his breaking the bounds of law and justice. Saith within my heart, that there is no fear of God before his eyes. Men's sins have a voice to godly ears. They are the outer index of an inner evil. It is clear that men who dare to sin constantly and presumptuously cannot respect the great Judge of all. Despite the professions of unrighteous men, when we see their unhallowed actions our heart is driven to the conclusion that they have no religion whatever. Unholiness is clear evidence of ungodliness.
Verse 2. For. Here is the argument to prove the proposition laid down in the former verse. David here runs over the process of reasoning by which he had become convinced that wicked men have no proper idea of God or respect for him. God fearing men see their sins and bewail them, where the reverse is the case we may be sure there is no fear of God.
Verse 3. The words of his mouth are iniquity and deceit. This pair of hell dogs generally hunt together, and what one does not catch the other will; if iniquity cannot win by oppression, deceit will gain by chicanery. When the heart is so corrupt as to flatter itself, the tongue follows suit. The open sepulcher of the throat reveals the foulness of the inner nature. God fearing men make a conscience of their words, and if they sin through infirmity they do not invent excuses, or go about to boast of their wickedness: but because wicked men think little of evil and artful speeches, we may be clear that God rules not in their souls.
Verse 4. He deviseth mischief upon his bed. His place of rest becomes the place for plotting. His bed is a hot bed for poisonous weeds. God fearing men meditate upon God and his service; but when men turn all their thoughts and inventive faculties towards evil, their godlessness is proved to a demonstration. He hath the devil for his bed fellow who lies abed and schemes how to sin. God is far from him. He setteth himself in a way that is not good. When he gets up he resolutely and persistently pursues the mischief which he planned.
Verses 5-9. From the baseness of the wicked the psalmist turns his contemplation to the glory of God. Contrasts are impressive.
Verse 5. Thy mercy, O Lord, is in the heavens. Like the ethereal blue, it encompasses the whole earth, smiling upon universal nature, acting as a canopy for all the creatures of earth, surmounting the loftiest peaks of human provocations, and rising high above the mists of mortal transgression. Clear sky is evermore above, and mercy calmly smiles above the din and smoke of this poor world. Darkness and clouds are but of earth's lower atmospheres: the heavens are evermore serene, and bright with innumerable stars. Divine mercy abides in its vastness of expanse, and matchless patience, all unaltered by the rebellions of man.

JOHN CALVIN

Psalm 36

1-4
1. Ungodliness saith to the wicked in the midst of my heart. It is to be observed, that the prophet speaks not of outward faults, but penetrates even to the very source; as if he had said, Although the wicked cloak their malice with wily dissimulation, yet I know it so well that I seem to hear it speaking. It is indeed true, that as the ungodly and profane rush headlong into every kind of wickedness, as if they were never to be called to render up an account of it, the judgment which David here expresses may be formed even from their life; but his language is much more emphatic when he says, that the servants of God openly perceive the depravity of such persons hidden within the heart.
2. For he flattereth himself in his own eyes. Here the Psalmist shows by their fruits or the marks of their character, that there is no fear of God among the wicked, seeing they take such pleasure in committing deeds of wickedness, that, although hateful in the sight of all other men, they still cherish the natural obstinacy of their hearts, and willfully harden themselves in their evil course.
3. The words of his mouth are iniquity and deceit. The two clauses of this verse may be understood as referring to the same thing, namely, that the wicked indulging in deceit and vanity, will not receive or admit the light of understanding. This, I apprehend, is the meaning of David. He reproves the wicked not merely for circumventing others by their wiles and stratagems, but especially because they are altogether destitute of uprightness and sincerity.
4. He meditates iniquity upon his bed. Here the sacred writer shows that the wickedness of the ungodly man is of a secret and very determined character.

5-9
5. O Jehovah! thy mercy is unto the heavens. After having spoken of the very great depravity of men, the prophet, afraid lest he should become infected by it, or be carried away by the example of the wicked, as by a flood, quits the subject, and recovers himself by reflecting on a different theme. It usually happens, that in condemning the wicked, the contagion of their malice insinuates itself into our minds when we are not conscious of it; and there is scarcely one in a hundred who, after having complained of the malice of others, keeps himself in true godliness, pure and unpolluted. The meaning therefore is, Although we may see among men a sad and frightful confusion, which, like a great gulf, would swallow up the minds of the godly, David, nevertheless, maintains that the world is full of the goodness and righteousness of God, and that he governs heaven and earth on the strictest principles of equity.
6. Thy righteousness is as the mountains of God. In this verse there is a commendation of God's righteousness, which the sacred writer compares to the high mountains, because his glory shines forth more clearly there. In the last place, it is said, that his judgments are like a great and bottomless abyss.

MATTHEW HENRY

Psalm 36

1-4 The character of the wicked.
I. Here is the root of bitterness, from which all the wickedness of the wicked comes. It takes rise,
1. From their contempt of God and the want of a due regard to him (v. 1): "The transgression of the wicked (as it is described afterwards, v. 3, 4) saith within my heart (makes me to conclude within myself) that there is no fear of God before his eyes; for, if there were, he would not talk and act so extravagantly as he does; he would not, he durst not, break the laws of God, and violate his covenants with him, if he had any awe of his majesty or dread of his wrath." Fitly therefore is it brought into the form of indictments by our law that the criminal, not having the fear of God before his eyes, did so and so.
2. From their conceit of themselves and a cheat they willfully put upon their own souls (v. 2): He flattereth himself in his own eyes; that is, while he goes on in sin, he thinks he does wisely and well for himself, and either does not see or will not own the evil and danger of his wicked practices; he calls evil good and good evil; his licentiousness he pretends to be but his just liberty, his fraud passes for his prudence and policy, and his persecuting the people of God, he suggests to himself, is a piece of necessary justice. If his own conscience threaten him for what he does, he says, God will not require it; I shall have peace though I go on.
II. Here are the cursed branches which spring from this root of bitterness. The sinner defies God, and even deifies himself, and then what can be expected but that he should go all to naught? These two were the first inlets of sin. Men do not fear God, and therefore they flatter themselves, and then,
1. They make no conscience of what they say, true of false, right or wrong (v. 3): The words of his mouth are iniquity and deceit, contrived to do wrong, and yet to cover it with specious and plausible pretences. It is no marvel if those that deceive themselves contrive how to deceive all mankind; for to whom will those be true who are false to their own souls?
2. What little good there has been in them is gone; the sparks of virtue are extinguished, their convictions baffled, their good beginnings come to nothing: They have left off to be wise and to do good. They seemed to be under the direction of wisdom and the government of religion, but they have broken these bonds asunder; they have shaken off their religion, and therewith their wisdom. Note, Those that leave off to do good leave off to be wise.
3. Having left off to do good, they contrive to do hurt and to be vexatious to those about them that are good and do good (v. 4): He devises mischief upon his bed.

5-12 The amazing goodness of God; favor of God towards His people; David's prayers, intercessions and triumphs.

Psalm 36

7-12

7 How excellent is thy loving kindness, O God! therefore the children of men put their trust under the shadow of thy wings.

8 They shall be abundantly satisfied with the fatness of thy house; and thou shalt make them drink of the river of thy pleasures.

9 For with thee is the fountain of life: in thy light shall we see light.

10 O continue thy loving kindness unto them that know thee; and thy righteousness to the upright in heart.

11 Let not the foot of pride come against me, and let not the hand of the wicked remove me.

12 There are the workers of iniquity fallen: they are cast down, and shall not be able to rise.

Verse 6. Thy righteousness is like the great mountains. Firm and unmoved, lofty and sublime. As winds and hurricanes shake not an Alp, so the righteousness of God is never in any degree affected by circumstances; he is always just. Who can bribe the Judge of all the earth, or who can, by threatening, compel him to pervert judgment? Not even to save his elect would the Lord suffer his righteousness to be set aside. No awe inspired by mountain scenery can equal that which fills the soul when it beholds the Son of God slain as a victim to vindicate the justice of the Inflexible Lawgiver.

Verse 7. How excellent is thy lovingkindness, O God. Here we enter into the Holy of Holies. Benevolence, and mercy, and justice, are everywhere, but the excellence of that mercy only those have known whose faith has lifted the veil and passed into the brighter presence of the Lord; these behold the excellency of the Lord's mercy.

Verse 8. They shall be abundantly satisfied with the fatness of thy house. Those who learn to put their trust in God shall be received into his house, and shall share in the provision laid up therein. The dwelling place of the Lord is not confined to any place, and hence reside where we may, we may regard our dwelling, if we be believers, as one room in the Lord's great house; and we shall, both in providence and grace, find a soul contenting store supplied to us as the result of living by faith in nearness to the Lord.

Verse 9. For with thee is the fountain of life. This verse is made of simple words, but like the first chapter of John's Gospel, it is very deep. From the Lord, as from an independent self sufficient spring, all creature life proceeds, by him is sustained, through him alone can it be perfected. Life is in the creature, but the fountain of it is only in the Creator.

Verse 10. O continue thy lovingkindness unto them that know thee. We ask no more than a continuance of the past mercy. Lord, extend this grace of thine to all the days of all who have been taught to know thy faithful love, thy tenderness, thine immutability and omnipotence. As they have been taught of the Lord to know the Lord, so go on to instruct them and perfect them. This prayer is the heart of the believer asking precisely that which the heart of his God is prepared to grant. It is well when the petition is but the reflection of the promise.

Verse 11. Let not the foot of pride come against me. The general prayer is here turned into a particular and personal one for himself. Pride is the devil's sin. Good men may well be afraid of proud men, for the serpent's seed will never cease to bite the heel of the godly. Fain would proud scoffers spurn the saints or trample them under foot: against their malice prayer lifts up her voice. No foot shall come upon us, no hand shall prevail against us, while Jehovah is on our side.

Verse 12. There are the workers of iniquity fallen. Faith sees them scattered on the plain. There! before our very eyes sin, death, and hell, lie prostrate. Behold the vanquished foes! They are cast down. Providence and grace have dashed them from their vantage ground. Jesus has already thrown all the foes of his people upon their faces, and in due time all sinners shall find it so. And shall not be able to rise. The defeat of the ungodly and of the powers of evil is final, total, irretrievable. Glory be to God, however high the powers of darkness may carry it at this present, the time hastens on when God shall defend the right, and give to evil such a fall as shall for ever crush the hopes of hell; while those who trust in the Lord shall eternally praise him and rejoice in his holy name.

JOHN CALVIN

By these words he teaches us, that to whatever side we turn our eyes, and whether we look upward or downward, all things are disposed and ordered by the just judgment of God.
7. The metaphorical expression of wings, as applied to God, is common enough in Scripture. By it God teaches us that we are preserved in safety under his protecting care, even as the hen cherishes her chickens under her wings; and thus he invites us kindly and affectionately to return to him.
8. They shall be abundantly satisfied with the fatness of that house. I have no doubt that by the fatness of God's house the prophet means the abundance of good things which is not designed for all men indiscriminately, but is laid up in store for the children of God who commit themselves wholly to his protection.
9. For with thee is the fountain of life. The Psalmist here confirms the doctrine of the preceding verse, the knowledge of which is so profitable that no words can adequately express it.

10-12
10. Prolong thy mercy to them that know thee. David now sets himself to pray. And, he asks in general, that God would continue his mercy to all the godly, and then he pleads particularly in his own behalf, imploring the help of God against his enemies.
With the mercy of God he connects his righteousness, combining them as cause and effect. We have already said in another place, that the righteousness of God is manifested in his undertaking the defense of his own people, vindicating their innocence, avenging their wrongs, restraining their enemies, and in proving himself faithful in the preservation of their welfare and happiness against all who assail them. Now, since all this is done for them freely by God, David, with good reason, makes mention particularly of his goodness, and places it first in order, that we may learn to depend entirely upon his favor. We ought also to observe the epithets by which he describes true believers; first, he says, that they know God; and, secondly, that they are upright in heart. We learn from this that true godliness springs from the knowledge of God, and again, that the light of faith must necessarily dispose us to uprightness of heart.
11. Let not the foot of pride come upon me. The Psalmist here applies to his own circumstances the prayer which he had offered. But by including in his prayer in the preceding verse all the children of God, he designed to show that he asked nothing for himself apart from others, but only desired that as one of the godly and upright, who have their eyes directed to God, he might enjoy his favor.
12. There the workers of iniquity are fallen. Here he derives confidence from his prayer, not doubting that he has already obtained his request. And thus we see how the certainty of faith directs the saints to prayer. Besides, still farther to confirm his confidence and hope in God, he shows, as it were, by pointing to it with the finger, the certain destruction of the wicked, even though it lay as yet concealed in the future.

MATTHEW HENRY

David, having looked round with grief upon the wickedness of the wicked, here looks up with comfort upon the goodness of God, a subject as delightful as the former was distasteful and very proper to be set in the balance against it. Observe,
I. His meditations upon the grace of God. He sees the world polluted, himself endangered, and God dishonored, by the transgressions of the wicked; but, of a sudden, he turns his eye, and heart, and speech, to God "However it be, yet thou art good." He here acknowledges the peculiar favor of God to the saints. Observe,
(1.) Their character, v. 7. They are such as are allured by the excellency of God's loving-kindness to put their trust under the shadow of his wings.
(2.) Their privilege. Happy, thrice happy, the people whose God is the Lord, for in him they have, or may have, or shall have, a complete happiness.
II. We have here David's prayers, intercessions, and holy triumphs, grounded upon these meditations.
1. He intercedes for all saints, begging that they may always experience the benefit and comfort of God's favor and grace, v. 10.
(1.) The persons he prays for are those that know God, that are acquainted with him, acknowledge him, and avouch him for theirs—the upright in heart, that are sincere in their profession of religion, and faithful both to God and man. Those that are not upright with God do not know him as they should.
(2.) The blessing he begs for them is God's loving-kindness (that is, the tokens of his favor towards them) and his righteousness (that is, the workings of his grace in them); or his loving-kindness and righteousness are his goodness according to promise; they are mercy and truth.
(3.) The manner in which he desires this blessing may be conveyed: O continue it, draw it out, as the mother draws out her breasts to the child, and then the child draws out the milk from the breasts. Let it be drawn out to a length equal to the line of eternity itself. The happiness of the saints in heaven will be in perfection, and yet in continual progression (as some thing); for the fountain there will be always full and the streams always flowing. In these is continuance, Isa. lxiv. 5.
2. He prays for himself, that he might be preserved in his integrity and comfort (v. 11): "Let not the foot of pride come against me, to trip up my heels, or trample upon me; and let not the hand of the wicked, which is stretched out against me, prevail to remove me, either from my purity and integrity, by any temptation, or from my peace and comfort, by any trouble." Let not those who fight against God triumph over those who desire to cleave to him.

Psalm 37

Title
A Psalm of David.

1-8
1 Fret not thyself because of evildoers, neither be thou envious against the workers of iniquity.
2 For they shall soon be cut down like the grass, and wither as the green herb.
3 Trust in the LORD, and do good; so shalt thou dwell in the land, and verily thou shalt be fed.
4 Delight thyself also in the LORD: and he shall give thee the desires of thine heart.
5 Commit thy way unto the LORD; trust also in him; and he shall bring it to pass.
6 And he shall bring forth thy righteousness as the light, and thy judgment as the noonday.
7 Rest in the LORD, and wait patiently for him: fret not thyself because of him who prospereth in his way, because of the man who bringeth wicked devices to pass.
8 Cease from anger, and forsake wrath: fret not thyself in any wise to do evil.

Psalm 37

TITLE. Of David. There is but this word to denote the authorship; whether it was a song or a meditation we are not told. It was written by David in his old age Ps 37:25, and is the more valuable as the record of so varied an experience.
SUBJECT. The great riddle of the prosperity of the wicked and the affliction of the righteous, which has perplexed so many, is here dealt with in the light of the future; and fretfulness and repining are most impressively forbidden. It is a Psalm in which the Lord hushes most sweetly the too common repinings of his people, and calms their minds as to his present dealings with his own chosen flock, and the wolves by whom they are surrounded. It contains eight great precepts, is twice illustrated by autobiographical statements, and abounds in remarkable contrasts.
DIVISION. The Psalm can scarcely be divided into considerable sections. It resembles a chapter of the book of Proverbs, most of the verses being complete in themselves. It is an alphabetical Psalm: in somewhat broken order, the first letters of the verses follow the Hebrew alphabet. This may have been not only a poetical invention, but a help to memory. The reader is requested to read the Psalm through without comment before he turns to our exposition.

EXPOSITION
Verse 1. The Psalm opens with the first precept. It is alas! too common for believers in their hours of adversity to think themselves harshly dealt with when they see persons utterly destitute of religion and honesty, rejoicing in abundant prosperity. Much needed is the command, Fret not thyself because of evildoers. To fret is to worry, to have the heartburn, to fume, to become vexed.
Verse 2. For they shall soon be cut down like the grass. The scythe of death is sharpening. Green grows the grass, but quick comes the scythe. The destruction of the ungodly will be speedy, sudden, sure, overwhelming, irretrievable. The grass cannot resist or escape the mower. And wither as the green herb. The beauty of the herb dries up at once in the heat of the sun, and so all the glory of the wicked shall disappear at the hour of death. Death kills the ungodly man like grass, and wrath withers him like hay; he dies, and his name rots.
Verse 3. Trust in the Lord. Here is the second precept, and one appropriate to the occasion. Faith cures fretting. Sight is cross-eyed, and views things only as they seem, hence her envy: faith has clearer optics to behold things as they really are, hence her peace. And do good. True faith is actively obedient. Doing good is a fine remedy for fretting. There is a joy in holy activity which drives away the rust of discontent. So shalt thou dwell in the land. In "the land" which floweth with milk and honey; the Canaan of the covenant.
Verse 4. There is an ascent in this third precept. He who was first bidden not to fret, was then commanded actively to trust, and now is told with holy desire to delight in God. Delight thyself also in the Lord. Make Jehovah the joy and rejoicing of thy spirit. Bad men delight in carnal objects; do not envy them if they are allowed to take their fill in such vain idols; look thou to thy better delight, and fill thyself to the full with thy more sublime portion. In a certain sense imitate the wicked; they delight in their portion—take care to delight in yours, and so far from envying you will pity them.
Verse 5. Commit thy way unto the Lord. Roll the whole burden of life upon the Lord. Leave with Jehovah not thy present fretfulness merely, but all thy cares; in fact, submit the whole tenor of thy way to him. Cast away anxiety, resign thy will, submit thy judgment, leave all with the God of all. What a medicine is this for expelling envy! What a high attainment does this fourth precept indicate! How blessed must he be who lives every day in obedience

JOHN CALVIN

Psalm 37

1-6
1. Fret not thyself because of the wicked. David lays down this as a general principle, that the prosperity of the wicked, in which they greatly rejoice, should on no account vex or disquiet the children of God, because it will soon fade away. On the other hand, although the people of God are afflicted for a time, yet the issue of their afflictions shall be such, that they have every reason to be contented with their lot. Now all this depends upon the providence of God; for unless we are persuaded that the world is governed by him in righteousness and truth, our minds will soon stagger, and at length entirely fail us.
2. David tells us that the judgment of God, like a scythe in the hand of man, shall cut down the wicked, so that they shall suddenly perish.
3. Put thy trust in Jehovah, and do good. The inspired writer now goes on, in the second place, to say, that every thing in the end shall be well with the righteous, because they are under the protection of God. But as there is nothing better or more desirable than to enjoy the fostering and protecting care of God, he exhorts them to put their trust in him, and at the same time to follow after goodness and truth.
4. And delight thyself in Jehovah. This delight is set in opposition to the vain and deceitful allurements of the world, which so intoxicate the ungodly, that despising the blessing of God, they dream of no other happiness than what presents itself for the time before their eyes.
5. Roll thy ways upon Jehovah. Here David illustrates and confirms the doctrine contained in the preceding verse. In order that God may accomplish our desires, it behoves us to cast all our cares upon him in the exercise of hope and patience. Accordingly, we are taught from this passage how to preserve our minds in tranquility amidst anxieties, dangers, and floods of trouble.
6. And he will bring forth thy righteousness as the light. This David says, in order to anticipate the misgivings which often trouble us when we seem to lose our labor in faithfully serving God, and in dealing uprightly with our neighbors; nay, when our integrity is either exposed to the calumnies of the wicked, or is the occasion of injury to us from men; for then it is thought to be of no account in the sight of God.

7-11
7. Be silent to Jehovah. The Psalmist continues the illustration of the same doctrine, namely, that we should patiently and meekly bear those things that usually disquiet our minds; for amid innumerable sources of disquietude and conflict there is need of no small patience. By the similitude of silence, which often occurs in the sacred writings, he declares most aptly the nature of faith; for as our affections rise in rebellion against the will of God, so faith, restoring us to a state of humble and peaceful submission, appeases all the tumults of our hearts.
8. David next repeats what he had said in the first verse, Fret not because of the man who prospereth in his way, or who

MATTHEW HENRY

Psalm 37

1-6 Exhortations and promises.
I. We are here cautioned against discontent at the prosperity and success of evil-doers (v. 1, 2): Fret not thyself, neither be thou envious. We may suppose that David speaks this to himself first, and preaches it to his own heart (in his communing with that upon his bed), for the suppressing of those corrupt passions which he found working there, and then leaves it in writing for instruction to others that might be in similar temptation. That is preached best, and with most probability of success, to others, which is first preached to ourselves. Now,
1. When we look abroad we see the world full of evil-doers and workers of iniquity, that flourish and prosper, that have what they will and do what they will, that live in ease and pomp themselves and have power in their hands to do mischief to those about them. So it was in David's time; and therefore, if it is so still, let us not marvel at the matter, as though it were some new or strange thing.
2. When we look within we find ourselves tempted to fret at this, and to be envious against these scandals and burdens, these blemishes and common nuisances, of this earth. We are apt to fret at God, as if he were unkind to the world and unkind to his church in permitting such men to live, and prosper, and prevail, as they do. Yet that is not all; for,
3. When we look forward with an eye of faith we shall see no reason to envy wicked people their prosperity, for their ruin is at the door and they are ripening apace for it, v. 2. They flourish, but as the grass, and as the green herb, which nobody envies nor frets at. The flourishing of a godly man is like that of a fruitful tree (Ps. i. 3), but that of the wicked man is like grass and herbs, which are very short-lived.
II. We are here counseled to live a life on confidence and complacency in God, and that will keep us from fretting at the prosperity of evil-doers; if we do well for our own souls, we shall see little reason to envy those that do so ill for theirs. Here are three excellent precepts, which we are to be ruled by, and, to enforce them, three precious promises, which we may rely upon.
1. We must make God our hope in the way of duty and then we shall have a comfortable subsistence in this world, v. 3. It is required that we trust in the Lord and do good, that we confide in God and conform to him.
2. We must make God our heart's delight and then we shall have our heart's desire, v. 4. We must not only depend upon God, but solace ourselves in him.
3. We must make God our guide, and submit in every thing to his guidance and disposal; and then all our affairs, even those that seem most intricate and perplexed, shall be made to issue well and to our satisfaction, v. 5, 6.

Psalm 37

9-16

9 For evildoers shall be cut off: but those that wait upon the LORD, they shall inherit the earth.
10 For yet a little while, and the wicked shall not be: yea, thou shalt diligently consider his place, and it shall not be.
11 But the meek shall inherit the earth; and shall delight themselves in the abundance of peace.
12 The wicked plotteth against the just, and gnasheth upon him with his teeth.
13 The LORD shall laugh at him: for he seeth that his day is coming.
14 The wicked have drawn out the sword, and have bent their bow, to cast down the poor and needy, and to slay such as be of upright conversation.
15 Their sword shall enter into their own heart, and their bows shall be broken.
16 A little that a righteous man hath is better than the riches of many wicked.

to it! Trust also in him; and he shall bring it to pass. Our destiny shall be joyfully accomplished if we confidently entrust all to our Lord.
Verse 6. And he shall bring forth thy righteousness as the light. In the matter of personal reputation we may especially be content to be quiet, and leave our vindication with the Judge of all the earth. The more we fret in this case the worse for us.
Verse 7. Rest in the Lord. This fifth is a most divine precept, and requires much grace to carry it out. To hush the spirit, to be silent before the Lord, to wait in holy patience the time for clearing up the difficulties of Providence—that is what every gracious heart should aim at.
Verse 8. Cease from anger and forsake wrath. Especially anger against the arrangements of Providence, and jealousies of the temporary pleasures of those who are so soon to be banished from all comfort. Anger anywhere is madness, here it is aggravate insanity. Yet since anger will try to keep us company, we must resolvedly forsake it. Fret not thyself in any wise to do evil. By no reasonings and under no circumstances be led into such a course. Fretfulness lies upon the verge of great sin.
Verse 9. For evil doers shall be cut off. Their death shall be a penal judgment; not a gentle removal to a better state, but an execution in which the axe of justice will be used. But those that wait upon the Lord—those who in patient faith expect their portion in another life—they shall inherit the earth. Even in this life they have the most of real enjoyment, and in the ages to come theirs shall be the glory and the triumph. Passion, according to Bunyan's parable, has his good things first, and they are soon over; Patience has his good things last, and they last for ever.
Verse 10. For yet a little while, and the wicked shall not be. When bad men reach to greatness, the judgments of God frequently sweep them away; their riches melt, their power decays, their happiness turns to wretchedness; they themselves cease any longer to be numbered with the living. The shortness of life makes us see that the glitter of the wicked great is not true gold.
Verse 11. But the meek shall inherit the earth. Above all others they shall enjoy life. Even if they suffer, their consolations shall overtop their tribulations. By inheriting the land is meant obtaining covenant privileges and the salvation of God. Such as are truly humble shall take their lot with the rest of the heirs of grace, to whom all good things come by a sacred birthright.
Verses 12-15. Here is the portrait of a proud oppressor armed to the teeth.
Verse 12. The wicked plotteth against the just. Why can he not let the good man alone? Because there is enmity between the serpent's seed and the seed of the woman. Why not attack him fairly? Why plot and scheme? Because it is according to the serpent's nature to be very subtle. Plain sailing does not suit those who are on board of "The Apollyon." And gnashed upon him with his teeth. The wicked show by their gestures what they would do if they could; if they cannot gnaw they will gnash; if they may not bite they will at least bark. This is precisely what the graceless world did with "that just One," the Prince of Peace. Yet he took no vengeance upon them, but like a silent lamb received injuries in patience.
Verse 13. The Lord shall laugh at him. The godly man needs not trouble himself, but leave well deserved vengeance to be dealt out by the Lord, who will utterly deride the malice of the good man's enemies. Let the proud scorner gnash his teeth and foam at the mouth; he has one to deal with who will look down upon him and his ravings with serene contempt.
Verse 14. The wicked have drawn out the sword. They hold their weapon out of its sheath, and watch for a time to use it. And have bent their bow. One weapon is not enough, they carry another ready for action. They carry so strong a bow that they have trodden upon it to bend it—they will lose nothing for want of force or readiness. To cast down the poor and needy. These are their game, the objects of their accursed malice.

brings his ways to a happy issue; nor against the man who behaveth himself wickedly, or who accomplishes his devices.

9. For the wicked shall be cut off. It is not without cause that he repeatedly inculcates the same thing, namely, that the happiness and prosperity which the ungodly enjoy is only a mask or phantom; for the first sight of it so dazzles our senses, that we are unable to form a proper estimate of what will be its issue, in the light of which alone we ought to judge of the value of all that has preceded.

10. Yet a little while, and the wicked shall not be. This is a confirmation of the preceding verse. It is hope alone which of itself produces meekness; for, by restraining the impetuosity of the flesh, and allaying its vehemence, it trains to equanimity and patience those who submit themselves to God. From this passage it would seem, that Christ has taken that which is written in Matthew 5:5.

11. The word peace is generally employed in the Hebrew to denote the prosperous and happy issue of things; yet another sense will agree better with this place, namely, that while the ungodly shall be agitated with inward trouble, and God shall encompass them on every side with terror, the faithful shall rejoice in the abundance of peace. It is not meant that they are exempted from trouble, but they are sustained by the tranquility of their minds; so that accounting all the trials which they endure to be only temporary, they now rejoice in hope of the promised rest.

12-15

12. The wicked plotteth against the righteous. David here anticipates an objection which might have been taken to the preceding verse. Where, it might be said, can tranquility and joy be found when the wicked are mad with rage, and plot every kind of mischief against the children of God? And how shall they cherish good hope for the future who see themselves surrounded with innumerable sources of death? David therefore replies, That although the life of the godly should be assailed by many dangers, yet they are secure in the aid and protection of God; and that however much the wicked should plot against them, they shall be continually preserved.

13. And lest the flesh should still murmur and complain, demanding why God should only laugh at the wicked, and not rather take vengeance upon them, the reason is added, that he sees the day of their destruction at hand: For he seeth that his day is coming. Whence is it that the injuries we sustain from the wickedness of man so trouble us, if it be not that, when not obtaining a speedy redress, we begin to despair of ever seeing a better state of things? But he who sees the executioner standing behind the aggressor with drawn sword no longer desires revenge, but rather exults in the prospect of speedy retribution.

14. The wicked draw their sword, and bend their bow. David now goes on to say, that the ungodly, being armed with sword and bow, threaten with death the children of God; and this he does in order to meet the temptation which would otherwise overwhelm them. The promises of God do not have place in a time of quietness and peace, but in the midst of severe and terrible conflicts. And, therefore, David now teaches us that

7-20 Exhortations and promises.

In these verses we have,

I. The foregoing precepts inculcated; for we are so apt to disquiet ourselves with needless fruitless discontents and distrusts that it is necessary there should be precept upon precept, and line upon line, to suppress them and arm us against them.

1. Let us compose ourselves by believing in God: "Rest in the Lord, and wait patiently for him (v. 7), that is, be well reconciled to all he does and acquiesce in it, for that is best that is, because it is what God has appointed; and be well satisfied that he will still make all to work for good to us, though we know not how or which way."

2. Let us not discompose ourselves at what we see in this world: "Fret not thyself because of him who prospers in his wicked way, who, though he is a bad man, yet thrives and grows rich and great in the world; no, nor because of him who does mischief with his power and wealth, and brings wicked devices to pass against those that are virtuous and good, who seems to have gained his point and to have run them down. If thy heart begins to rise at it, stroke down thy folly, and cease from anger (v. 8), check the first stirrings of discontent and envy, and do not harbor any hard thoughts of God and his providence upon this account."

II. The foregoing reasons, taken from the approaching ruin of the wicked notwithstanding their prosperity, and the real happiness of the righteous notwithstanding their troubles, are here much enlarged upon and the same things repeated in a pleasing variety of expression. We were cautioned (v. 7) not to envy the wicked either worldly prosperity or the success of their plots against the righteous, and the reasons here given respect these two temptations severally:

1. Good people have no reason to envy the worldly prosperity of wicked people, nor to grieve or be uneasy at it, because the prosperity of the wicked will soon be at an end (v. 9).

2. Good people have no reason to fret at the occasional success of the designs of the wicked against the just. Though they do bring some of their wicked devices to pass, which makes us fear they will gain their point and bring them all to pass, yet let us cease from anger, and not fret ourselves so as to think of giving up the cause. For their plots will be their shame, v. 12, 13. It is true the wicked plotteth against the just; there is a rooted enmity in the seed of the wicked one against the righteous seed; their aim is, if they can, to destroy their righteousness, or, if that fail, then to destroy them. With this end in view they have acted with a great deal both of cursed policy and contrivance (they plot, they practice, against the just), and of cursed zeal and fury—they gnash upon them with their teeth, so desirous are they, if they could get it into their power, to eat them up, and so full of rage and indignation are they

Psalm 37

17-24

17 For the arms of the wicked shall be broken: but the LORD upholdeth the righteous.
18 The LORD knoweth the days of the upright: and their inheritance shall be for ever.
19 They shall not be ashamed in the evil time: and in the days of famine they shall be satisfied.
20 But the wicked shall perish, and the enemies of the LORD shall be as the fat of lambs: they shall consume; into smoke shall they consume away.
21 The wicked borroweth, and payeth not again: but the righteous sheweth mercy, and giveth.
22 For such as be blessed of him shall inherit the earth; and they that be cursed of him shall be cut off.
23 The steps of a good man are ordered by the LORD: and he delighteth in his way.
24 Though he fall, he shall not be utterly cast down: for the LORD upholdeth him with his hand.

Verse 15. Their sword shall enter into their own heart. Like Haman they shall be hanged upon the gallows built by themselves for Mordecai. Hundreds of times has this been the case. Saul, who sought to slay David, fell on his own sword; and the bow, his favorite weapon, the use of which he taught the children of Israel, was not able to deliver him on Gilboa. And their bows shall be broken. Their inventions of evil shall be rendered useless.

Verse 16. A little that a righteous man hath is better than the riches of many wicked. This is a fine proverb. The little of one good man is contrasted with the riches of many wicked, and so the expression is rendered the more forcible. There is more happiness in the godly dinner of herbs than in the stalled ox of profane rioters.

Verse 17. For the arms of the wicked shall be broken. Their power to do mischief shall be effectually taken away, for the arms which they lifted up against God shall be crushed even to the bone. God often makes implacable men incapable men. What is a more contemptible sight than toothless malice, armless malevolence! But the Lord upholdeth the righteous. Their cause and course shall be safe, for they are in good keeping. The sword of two edges smites the wicked and defends the just.

Verse 18. The Lord knoweth the days of the upright. His foreknowledge made him laugh at the proud, but in the case of the upright he sees a brighter future, and treats them as heirs of salvation. Ever is this our comfort, that all events are known to our God, and that nothing in our future can take him at unawares. No arrow can pierce us by accident, no danger smite us by stealth; neither in time nor eternity can any unforeseen ill occur to us. Futurity shall be but a continual development of the good things which the Lord has laid up in store for us.

Verse 19. They shall not be ashamed in the evil time. Calamities will come, but deliverances will come also. As the righteous never reckoned upon immunity from trouble, they will not be disappointed when they are called to take their share of it, but the rather they will cast themselves anew upon their God, and prove again his faithfulness and love. God is not a friend in the sunshine only, he is a friend indeed and a friend in need.

Verse 20. But the wicked shall perish. Whatever phantom light may mock their present, their future is black with dark, substantial night. Judgment has been given against them, they are but reserved for execution. Let them flaunt their scarlet and fine linen, and fare sumptuously every day; the sword of Damocles is above their heads, and if their wits were a little more awake, their mirth would turn to misery.

Verse 21. The wicked borroweth, and payeth not again. Partly because he will not, but mainly because he cannot. Want follows upon waste, and debt remains undischarged. Often are the wicked thus impoverished in this life. Their wanton extravagance brings them down to the usurer's door and to the bankrupt's suit. But the righteous sheweth mercy, and giveth, Mercy has given to him, and therefore he gives in mercy. He is generous and prosperous. He is not a borrower, but a giver.

Verse 22. For such as be blessed of him shall inherit the earth. God's benediction is true wealth after all. True happiness, such as the covenant secures to all the chosen of heaven, lies wrapped up in the divine favor. And they that be cursed of him shall be cut off. His frown is death; nay, more, It is hell.

Verse 23. The steps of a good man are ordered by the Lord. All his course of life is graciously ordained, and in lovingkindness all is fixed, settled, and maintained. No reckless fate, no fickle chance rules us; our every step is the subject of divine decree. He delighteth in his way. As parents are pleased with the tottering footsteps of their babes. All that concerns a saint is interesting to his heavenly Father.

Verse 24. Though he fall. Disasters and reverses may lay him low; he may, like Job, be stripped of everything; like Joseph, be put in prison; like Jonah, the righteous are not deprived of that peace of which he had spoken a little before, although the wicked should threaten them with instant death.

15. David is not speaking of the laughter of God, but is denouncing vengeance against the ungodly, just as we have already seen in the second psalm, at the fourth verse, that although God, by conniving at the wicked, has often suffered them for a time to run to every excess in mirth and rioting, yet he at length speaks to them in his anger to overthrow them.

16-19

16. Better is the little of the righteous, etc. David is here speaking, not so much of external grandeur and wealth, as of the secret blessing of God which truly enriches the righteous; for although they live from hand to mouth, yet are they fed from heaven as it were with manna; while the ungodly are always hungry, or else waste away in the very midst of their abundance.

17. To this also belongs the reason which is added in the next verse, namely, that there is nothing stable in the world except it be sustained by the power of God; but we are plainly told that the righteous only are upheld by him, and that the power of the ungodly shall be broken. Here again we see, that in order to form a right and proper estimate of true felicity, we must look forward to the future, or contemplate by the eye of faith the secret grace of God, and his hidden judgments.

18. Jehovah knoweth the days of the upright. It is not without good reason that David so frequently inculcates this doctrine, that the righteous are blessed because God provides for their necessities.

19. They shall not be ashamed in the season of adversity. This verse also shows us, that the faithful have no right to expect such exemption as the flesh would desire from affliction and trial, but they are assured of deliverance in the end; which, though it be indeed obtained, yet it is of such a nature as can be realized only by faith. We must regard these two things as inseparably connected, namely, that as the faithful are mingled among the wicked in this world, so hunger and adversity are common to both. The only difference betwixt them is, that God stretches forth his hand towards his own people in the time of their need, while he abandons the ungodly, and takes no care of them.

20-22

20. For the wicked shall perish. We learn from this what another prophet likewise teaches, that the ungodly are fattened for the day of slaughter; so that the more sumptuously they shall have lived, the more suddenly shall their destruction come upon them. To be consumed into smoke is of the same import as to vanish away quickly; as if it had been said, There is no stability or substance in them.

21. The wicked borroweth, and payeth not again. Those are mistaken who suppose that the wicked are here blamed for their treachery in carrying off the goods of others by fraud and deception; and that, on the other hand, the children of God are commended for their kindness in being always ready to

because it is not in their power; but by all this they do but make themselves ridiculous. Those that are not suddenly cut off shall yet be so disabled for doing any further mischief that the interests of the church shall be effectually secured: Their bows shall be broken (v. 15); the instruments of their cruelty shall fail them and they shall lose those whom they had made tools of to serve their bloody purposes with; nay, their arms shall be broken, so that they shall not be able to go on with their enterprises, v. 17. But the Lord upholds the righteous, so that they neither sink under the weight of their afflictions nor are crushed by the violence of their enemies. He upholds them both in their integrity and in their prosperity; and those that are so upheld by the rock of ages have no reason to envy the wicked the support of their broken reeds.

21-33 Exhortations and promises.

These verses are much to the same purport with the foregoing verses of this psalm, for it is a subject worthy to be dwelt upon. Observe here,

I. What is required of us as the way to our happiness, which we may learn both from the characters here laid down and from the directions here given. If we would be blessed of God,

1. We must make conscience of giving every body his own; for the wicked borrows and pays not again, v. 21. It is the first thing which the Lord our God requires of us, that we do justly, and render to all their due.

2. We must be ready to all acts of charity and beneficence; for, as it is an instance of God's goodness to the righteous that he puts it into the power of his hand to be kind and to do good, so it is an instance of the goodness of the righteous man that he has a heart proportionable to his estate: He shows mercy, and gives, v. 21.

3. We must leave our sins, and engage in the practice of serious godliness (v. 27): Depart from evil and do good. Cease to do evil and abhor it; learn to do well and cleave to it; this is true religion.

4. We must abound in good discourse, and with our tongues must glorify God and edify others. It is part of the character of a righteous man (v. 30) that his mouth speaketh wisdom; not only he speaks wisely, but he speaks wisdom, like Solomon himself, for the instruction of those about him.

5. We must have our wills brought into an entire subjection to the will and word of God (v. 31): The law of God, of his God, is in his heart; and in vain do we pretend that God is our God if we do not receive his law into our hearts and resign ourselves to the government of it. It is but a jest and a mockery to speak wisdom, and to talk of judgment (v. 30), unless we have the law in our hearts, and we think as we speak.

II. What is assured to us, as instances of our happiness and comfort, upon these conditions.

Psalm 37

25-32
25 I have been young, and now am old; yet have I not seen the righteous forsaken, nor his seed begging bread.
26 He is ever merciful, and lendeth; and his seed is blessed.
27 Depart from evil, and do good; and dwell for evermore.
28 For the LORD loveth judgment, and forsaketh not his saints; they are preserved for ever: but the seed of the wicked shall be cut off.
29 The righteous shall inherit the land, and dwell therein for ever.
30 The mouth of the righteous speaketh wisdom, and his tongue talketh of judgment.
31 The law of his God is in his heart; none of his steps shall slide.
32 The wicked watcheth the righteous, and seeketh to slay him.

be cast into the deep. He shall not be utterly cast down. He shall not be altogether prostrate. He shall be brought on his knees, but not on his face; or, if laid prone for a moment, he shall be up again ere long. No saint shall fall finally or fatally.

Verse 25. This was David's observation, I have been young, and now am old; yet have I not seen the righteous forsaken, nor his seed begging bread. It is not my observation just as it stands, for I have relieved the children of undoubtedly good men, who have appealed to me as common mendicants. But this does not cast a doubt upon the observation of David. He lived under a dispensation more outward, and more of this world than the present rule of personal faith.

Verse 26. He is ever merciful, and lendeth. The righteous are constantly under generous impulses; they do not prosper through parsimony, but through bounty. Like the bounteous giver of all good, of whom they are the beloved sons, they delight in doing good.

Verses 27-29. Here we have the seventh precept, which takes a negative and positive form, and is the quintessence of the entire Psalm

Verse 27. Depart from evil, and do good. We must not envy the doers of evil, but depart altogether from their spirit and example. As Lot left Sodom without casting a look behind, so must we leave sin. No truce or parley is to be held with sin, we must turn away from it without hesitation, and set ourselves practically to work in the opposite direction. He who neglects to do good will soon fall into evil. And dwell for evermore. Obtain an abiding and quiet inheritance. Short lived are the gains and pleasures of evil, but eternal are the rewards of grace.

Verse 28. For the Lord loveth judgment. The awarding of honor to whom honor is due is God's delight, especially when the upright man has been traduced by his fellow men. It must be a divine pleasure to right wrongs, and to defeat the machinations of the unjust. The great Arbiter of human destinies is sure to deal out righteous measure both to rich and poor, to good and evil, for such judgment is his delight.

Verse 29. The righteous shall inherit the land. As heirs with Jesus Christ, the Canaan above, which is the antitype of "the land," shall be theirs with all covenant blessing. And dwell therein for ever. Tenures differ, but none can match the holding which believers have of heaven. Paradise is theirs for ever by inheritance, and they shall live for ever to enjoy it. Who would not be a saint on such terms? Who would fret concerning the fleeting treasures of the godless?

Verse 30. The mouth of the righteous speaketh wisdom. Where the whole Psalm is dedicated to a description of the different fates of the just and the wicked, it was meet to give a test by which they could be known. A man's tongue is no ill index of his character. The mouth betrays the heart. Good men, as a rule, speak that which is to edifying, sound speech, religious conversation, consistent with the divine illumination which they have received. Righteousness is wisdom in action, hence all good men are practically wise men, and well may the speech be wise. His tongue talketh of judgment. He advocates justice, gives an honest verdict on things and men, and he foretells that God's judgments will come upon the wicked, as in the former days. His talk is neither foolish nor ribald, neither vapid nor profane. Our conversation is of far more consequence than some men imagine.

Verse 31. The law of his God is in his heart; none of his steps shall slide. The best thing in the best place, producing the best results. Well might the man's talk be so admirable when his heart was so well stored. To love holiness, to have the motives and desires sanctified, to be in one's inmost nature obedient to the Lord—this is the surest method of making the whole run of our life efficient for its great ends, and even for securing the details of it, our steps from any serious mistake. To keep the even tenor of one's way, in such times as these, is given only to those whose hearts are sound relieve the wants of their poorer brethren. The prophet rather extols, on the one hand, the blessing of God towards the godly; and declares, on the other, that the ungodly never have enough. The meaning therefore is, that God deals bountifully with his own people, that they may be able to aid others; but that the ungodly are always in want, so that their poverty leads them to have recourse to fraud and rapine.

22. The meaning is simply this, that whatever we need for the preservation and maintenance of life, and for the exercise of humanity towards others, comes to us neither from the heavens nor from the earth, but only from the favor and blessing of God; and that if he once withdraw his grace, the abundance of the whole world would not satisfy us.

23-26

23. The footsteps of a man are directed by Jehovah. Some join together these two things, first, that the footsteps of the godly are ordered by the grace of God, since men do not in their own strength follow what is just and right, but only in so far as the Spirit of God directs them; and hence the second follows, namely, that God favors and approves what is his own.

24. Though he fall, he shall not be utterly cast down. This verse has generally been interpreted proverbially, and as meaning, that though the righteous may fall into sin, his fall is not deadly; but this is not at all in accordance with the design of the prophet, who is discoursing of the happiness of the godly. The meaning is, that when God visits his servants with severe afflictions, he at the same time mitigates them that they may not faint under them.

25. I have been young, I am also become old. The meaning of these words is not in the least doubtful, namely, that David, even when he was become an old man, had not seen any of the righteous, or any of their children, begging their bread. But here there arises a question of some difficulty with respect to the fact stated; for it is certain that many righteous men have been reduced to beggary. And what David here declares as the result of his own experience pertains to all ages.

26. He is daily merciful. The Psalmist here repeats what he had already said, that the grace of God is a fountain of all blessings which can never be exhausted; and, therefore, while it is displayed towards the faithful, they not only have enough for the supply of their own wants, but are able also liberally to assist others.

27-29

27. Depart from evil, and do good. In this verse David argues, that, in order to realize the blessedness of which he has spoken, we must abstain from all evil, perform the duties of humanity, and exert ourselves in doing good to our neighbors.

28. For Jehovah loveth judgement. This, it ought to be observed, is a confirmation of the doctrine contained in the preceding sentence; and it is here made to rest upon a higher principle, namely, that God takes pleasure in righteousness and truth.

29. The righteous shall inherit the earth. The repetition of the same doctrine here is not superfluous, since it is so very difficult to impress it deeply upon our minds.

1. That we shall have the blessing of God, and that blessing shall be the spring, and sweetness, and security of all our temporal comforts and enjoyments (v. 22): Such as are blessed of God, as all the righteous are, with a Father's blessing, by virtue of that shall inherit the earth, or the land (for so the same word is translated, v. 29), the land of Canaan, that glory of all lands.

2. That God will direct and dispose of our actions and affairs so as may be most for his glory (v. 23): The steps of a good man are ordered by the Lord. By his grace and Holy Spirit he directs the thoughts, affections, and designs of good men. He has all hearts in his hand, but theirs by their own consent. By his providence he overrules the events that concern them, so as to make their way plain before them, both what they should do and what they may expect.

3. That God will keep us from being ruined by our falls either into sin or into trouble (v. 24): Though he fall, he shall not be utterly cast down.

4. That we shall not want the necessary supports of this life (v. 25): "I have been young and now am old, and, among all the changes I have seen in men's outward condition and the observations I have made upon them, I never saw the righteous forsaken of God and man, as I have sometimes seen wicked people abandoned both by heaven and earth; nor do I ever remember to have seen the seed of the righteous reduced to such an extremity as to beg their bread."

5. That God will not desert us, but graciously protect us in our difficulties and straits (v. 28): The Lord loves judgment; he delights in doing justice himself and he delights in those that do justice; and therefore he forsakes not his saints in affliction when others make themselves strange to them and become shy of them, but he takes care that they be preserved for ever, that is, that the saint in every age be taken under his protection, that the succession be preserved to the end of time, and that particular saints be preserved from all the temptations and through all the trials of this present time, to that happiness which shall be for ever. He will preserve them to his heavenly kingdom; that is a preservation for ever, 2 Tim. iv. 18; Ps. xii. 7.

6. That we shall have a comfortable settlement in this world, and in a better when we leave this. That we shall dwell for evermore (v. 27), and not be cut off as the seed of the wicked, v. 28. Those shall not be tossed that make God their rest and are at home in him. But on this earth there is no dwelling for ever, no continuing city; it is in heaven only, that city which has foundations, that the righteous shall dwell for ever; that will be their everlasting habitation.

7. That we shall not become a prey to our adversaries, who seek our ruin, v. 32, 33. There is an adversary that takes all opportunities to do us a mischief, a wicked one that watches the righteous (as a roaring lion watches his prey) and seeks to slay him.

Psalm 37

33-40

33 The LORD will not leave him in his hand, nor condemn him when he is judged.
34 Wait on the LORD, and keep his way, and he shall exalt thee to inherit the land: when the wicked are cut off, thou shalt see it.
35 I have seen the wicked in great power, and spreading himself like a green bay tree.
36 Yet he passed away, and, lo, he was not: yea, I sought him, but he could not be found.
37 Mark the perfect man, and behold the upright: for the end of that man is peace.
38 But the transgressors shall be destroyed together: the end of the wicked shall be cut off.
39 But the salvation of the righteous is of the LORD: he is their strength in the time of trouble.
40 And the LORD shall help them, and deliver them: he shall deliver them from the wicked, and save them, because they trust in him.

towards God, who can, as in the text, call God their God. Policy slips and trips, it twists and tacks, and after all is worsted in the long run, but sincerity plods on its plain pathway and reaches the goal.

Verse 32. The wicked watcheth the righteous, and seeketh to slay him. If it were not for the laws of the land, we should soon see a massacre of the righteous. Jesus was watched by his enemies, who were thirsting for his blood: his disciples must not look for favor where their Master found hatred and death.

Verse 33. The Lord will not leave him in his hand. God often appears to deliver his servants, and when he does not do so in this life as to their bodies, he gives their souls such joy and peace that they triumphantly rise beyond their tormentors' power. We may be in the enemy's hand for awhile, as Job was, but we cannot be left there.

Verse 34. Wait on the Lord. We have here the eighth precept, and it is a lofty eminence to attain to. Tarry the Lord's leisure. Wait in obedience as a servant, in hope as an heir, in expectation as a believer. This little word "wait" is easy to say, but hard to carry out, yet faith must do it.

Verse 35. A second time David turns to his diary, and this time in poetic imagery tells us of what he had observed. It were well if we too took notes of divine providences.

Verse 36. Yet he passed away. Tree and man both gone, the son of man as surely as the child of the forest. What clean sweeps death makes! And, lo, he was not. To the surprise of all men the great man was gone, his estates sold, his business bankrupt, his house alienated, his name forgotten, and all in a few months.

Verse 37. Mark the perfect man, and behold the upright. After having watched with surprise the downfall of the wicked, give your attention to the sincerely godly man, and observe the blessed contrast. Good men are men of mark, and are worth our study. Upright men are marvels of grace, and worth beholding.

Verse 38. But the transgressors shall be destroyed together. A common ruin awaits those who are joined in common rebellion.

Verse 39. But the salvation of the righteous is of the Lord. Sound doctrine this. The very marrow of the gospel of free grace. By salvation is meant deliverance of every kind; not only the salvation which finally lands us in glory, but all the minor rescues of the way; these are all to be ascribed unto the Lord, and to him alone.

Verse 40. And the Lord shall help them. In all future time Jehovah will stand up for his chosen. Our Great Ally will bring up his forces in the heat of the battle. He shall deliver them from the wicked. As he rescued Daniel from the lions, so will he preserve his beloved from their enemies; they need not therefore fret, nor be discouraged. And save them, because they trust in him. Faith shall ensure the safety of the elect.

JOHN CALVIN

30-33

30, 31. The mouth of the righteous will speak wisdom. As it is customary with hypocrites confidently to draw to their own advantage whatever the Spirit of God declares concerning the just and upright, David here gives a definition of the righteousness which God requires on the part of his children, and divides it into three principal parts—that their speech should be in sincerity and truth; that the law of God should reign in their heart; and that they should order their conversation aright.

32, 33. The wicked watcheth the righteous, etc. David here illustrates more plainly the nature of the possession of the earth, of which he had spoken, namely, that God preserves his own people, though they are beset with enemies round about.

34-36

34. Wait upon Jehovah, and keep his way. David again returns to the style of exhortation, in order that the faithful, trusting to God's promises and sustained by them, may not suffer themselves to be drawn hither and thither by any temptations through devious and sinful ways, but may persevere steadfastly in the service of God.

35,.36. I have seen the wicked terrible, etc. David here confirms from his own experience what I have just said, namely, that although the wicked are intoxicated with their prosperity, and held in admiration by all on account of it, yet their happiness is transitory and evanescent, and, therefore, nothing else than a mere illusion. In the 35th verse he tells us, that it is no strange thing for the ungodly, puffed up with their prosperity, to spread themselves far and wide, and to give occasion of terror to the innocent.

37-40

37, 38. Observe the perfect man. David exhorts the faithful diligently to consider every instance they may meet with of the grace of God, as well as of his judgment; but he teaches, at the same time, that it is in vain for any to sit in judgment upon the first aspect of things.

But if a man extend his view, as if it were from a watch-tower, to a great distance, he will find that it has been said with truth, that the end of the reprobate and the end of the righteous respectively are at length very different. This clause, with respect to the end of these two classes of men, seems to be added by way of caution, that we may learn to suspend our judgment, if God should not immediately accomplish what he has spoken.

39, 40. The salvation of the righteous is from Jehovah. The sum of the whole is, that whatever may happen, the righteous shall be saved, because they are in the hand of God, and can never be forgotten by him. This ought to be particularly noticed, that those who are greatly afflicted may be sustained by the assurance that the salvation which they expect from God is infallibly certain, because God is eternal, and governs the world by his power.

MATTHEW HENRY

34-40 Exhortations and promises.

The psalmist's conclusion of this sermon (for that is the nature of this poem) is of the same purport with the whole, and inculcates the same things.

I. The duty here pressed upon us is still the same (v. 34): Wait on the Lord and keep his way. Duty is ours, and we must mind it and make conscience of it, keep God's way and never turn out of it nor loiter in it, keep close, keep going; but events are God's and we must refer ourselves to him for the disposal of them; we must wait on the Lord, attend the motions of his providence, carefully observe them, and conscientiously accommodate ourselves to them.

II. The reasons to enforce this duty are much the same too, taken from the certain destruction of the wicked and the certain salvation of the righteous. Observe,

1. The misery of the wicked at last, however they may prosper awhile: The end of the wicked shall be cut off (v. 38); and that cannot be well that will undoubtedly end so ill. The wicked, in their end, will be cut off from all good and all hopes of it; a final period will be put to all their joys, and they will be for ever separated from the fountain of life to all evil.

2. The blessedness of the righteous, at last. Let us see what will be the end of God's poor despised people.

(1.) Preferment. There have been times the iniquity of which has been such that men's piety has hindered their preferment in this world, and put them quite out of the way of raising estates; but those that keep God's way may be assured that in due time he will exalt them, to inherit the land (v. 34); he will advance them to a place in the heavenly mansions, to dignity, and honor, and true wealth, in the New Jerusalem, to inherit that good land, that land of promise, of which Canaan was a type; he will exalt them above all contempt and danger.

(2.) Peace, v. 37. Let all people mark the perfect man, and behold the upright; take notice of him to admire him and imitate him, keep your eye upon him to observe what comes of him, and you will find that the end of that man is peace. However, if all his days continue dark and cloudy, perhaps his dying day may prove comfortable to him and his sun may set in brightness; or, if it should set under a cloud, yet his future state will be peace, everlasting peace. Those that walk in their uprightness while they live shall enter into peace when they die, Isa. live. 2.

(3.) Salvation, v. 39, 40. The salvation of the righteous (which may be applied to the great salvation of which the prophets enquired and searched diligently, 1 Pet. i. 10) is of the Lord; it will be the Lord's doing. The eternal salvation, that salvation of God which those shall see that order their conversation aright (Ps. l. 23), is likewise of the Lord. And he that intends Christ and heaven for them will be a God all-sufficient to them: He is their strength in time of trouble, to support them under it and carry them through it.

Psalm 38

Title
A Psalm of David, to bring to remembrance.

1-8
1 O Lord, rebuke me not in thy wrath: neither chasten me in thy hot displeasure.
2 For thine arrows stick fast in me, and thy hand presseth me sore.
3 There is no soundness in my flesh because of thine anger; neither is there any rest in my bones because of my sin.
4 For mine iniquities are gone over mine head: as an heavy burden they are too heavy for me.
5 My wounds stink and are corrupt because of my foolishness.
6 I am troubled; I am bowed down greatly; I go mourning all the day long.
7 For my loins are filled with a loathsome disease: and there is no soundness in my flesh.
8 I am feeble and sore broken: I have roared by reason of the disquietness of my heart.

Psalm 38

TITLE. A Psalm of David, to bring remembrance. David felt as if he had been forgotten of his God, and, therefore, he recounted his sorrows and cried mightily for help under them. The same title is given to Psalm 70, where in like manner the psalmist pours out his complaint before the Lord. It would be foolish to make a guess as to the point in David's history when this was written; it may be a commemoration of his own sickness and endurance of cruelty; it may, on the other hand, have been composed by him for the use of sick and slandered saints, without special reference to himself.
DIVISION. The Psalm opens with a prayer, Ps 38:1; continues in a long complaint, Ps 38:2-8; pauses to dart an eye to heaven, Ps 38:9; proceeds with a second tale of sorrow, Ps 38:10-14; interjects another word of hopeful address to God, Ps 38:15; a third time pours out a flood of griefs, Ps 38:16-20; and then closes as it opened, with renewed petitioning, Ps 38:21-22.

EXPOSITION
Verse 1. O Lord, rebuke me not in thy wrath. Rebuked I must be, for I am an erring child and thou a careful Father, but throw not too much anger into the tones of thy voice; deal gently although I have sinned grievously. The anger of others I can bear, but not thine. As thy love is most sweet to my heart, so thy displeasure is most cutting to my conscience.
Verse 2. For thine arrows stick fast in me. By this he means both bodily and spiritual griefs, but we may suppose, especially the latter, for these are most piercing and stick the fastest. God's law applied by the Spirit to the conviction of the soul of sin, wounds deeply and rankles long; it is an arrow not lightly to be brushed out by careless mirthfulness, or to be extracted by the flattering hand of self righteousness. The Lord knows how to shoot so that his bolts not only strike but stick.
Verse 3. There is no soundness in my flesh because of thine anger. Mental depression tells upon the bodily frame; it is enough to create and foster every disease, and is in itself the most painful of all diseases. Soul sickness tells upon the entire frame; it weakens the body, and then bodily weakness reacts upon the mind. One drop of divine anger sets the whole of our blood boiling with misery. Neither is there any rest in my bones because of my sin. Deeper still the malady penetrates, till the bones, the more solid parts of the system, are affected.
Verse 4. For mine iniquities are gone over mine head. Like waves of the deep sea; like black mire in which a man utterly sinks. Above my hopes, my strength, my life itself, my sin rises in its terror. Unawakened sinners think their sins to be mere shallows, but when conscience is aroused they find out the depth of iniquity. As an heavy burden they are too heavy for me. It is well when sin is an intolerable load, and when the remembrance of our sins burdens us beyond endurance. This verse is the genuine cry of one who feels himself undone by his transgressions and as yet sees not the great sacrifice.
Verse 5. My wounds stink and are corrupt because of my foolishness. Apply this to the body, and it pictures a sad condition of disease; but read it of the soul, and it is to the life. Conscience lays on stripe after stripe till the swelling becomes a wound and suppurates, and the corruption within grows offensive.
Verse 6. I am troubled. I am wearied with distress, writhing with pain, in sore travail on account of sin revealed within me. I am bowed down greatly. I am brought very low, grievously weakened and frightfully depressed. Nothing so pulls a man down from all loftiness as a sense of sin and of divine wrath concerning it. I go mourning all the day long. The mourner's soul sorrow knew no intermission, even when he went about such business as he was

Psalm 38

1-5

1. O Jehovah! rebuke me not in thy wrath. David does not expressly ask that his afflictions should be removed, but only that God would moderate the severity of his chastisements. Hence we may infer, that David did not give loose reins to the desires of the flesh, but offered up his earnest prayer in a duly chastened spirit of devotion. All men would naturally desire that permission should be granted them to sin with impunity. But David lays a restraint upon his desires, and does not wish the favor and indulgence of God to be extended beyond measure, but is content with a mitigation of his affliction.
2. For thy arrows go down in me. He shows that he was constrained by dire necessity to ask an alleviation of his misery; for he was crushed under the weight of the burden which he sustained. This rule is always to be observed in our prayers—to keep God's promises present to our view.
3. There is no soundness in my flesh because of thy anger. Others translate, There is no beauty; but this does not seem to be so suitable. In the clause which follows, David ascribes to God the praise of righteousness, without which, the acknowledgement which he formerly made would be of little avail; nay, instead of this, such an acknowledgement sometimes rather exasperates the minds of men, so that they provoke the wrath of God still more, by charging him with cruelty, and pouring forth horrible blasphemies against him.
4. For my iniquities have passed over my head. Here he complains that he is overwhelmed by his sins as by a heavy burden, so that he utterly faints under their weight; and yet he again confirms the doctrine which we have already stated, that he deservedly suffered the wrath of God, which had been inflicted on him in a manner so severe and dreadful.
5. My wounds have become putrid. In this verse, he pleads the long continuance of his disease as an argument for obtaining some alleviation. The object which David has in view, in complaining of the long continuance of his misery is that when he had endured the punishment which he had merited, he might at length obtain deliverance.

6-10

6. I am bent. This description clearly shows that this holy man was oppressed with extreme grief, so much so, that it is marvelous how, under such a vast accumulation of miseries, his faith was sufficiently strong to bear up his mind. When he says bowed down, he seems tacitly to contrast his humility and dejection with the pride and stubbornness of many, who refuse to be humbled by the many chastisements with which God afflicts them, but rather harden themselves, daring to resist and oppose him.
7. In my opinion, the sense simply is, that his reins, or flanks, or thighs, were filled with an inflammatory disease, or at least were covered over with putrid sores; for these parts of the body are most subject to inflammation, and most liable to contract putrid humors. Some expound it allegorically, as

Psalm 38

1-11 Sorrowful Complaints.

I. He deprecates the wrath of God and his displeasure in his affliction (v. 1): O Lord! rebuke me not in thy wrath. With this same petition he began another prayer for the visitation of the sick, Ps. vi. 1. This was most upon his heart, and should be most upon ours when we are in affliction, that, however God rebukes and chastens us, it may not be in wrath and displeasure, for that will be wormwood and gall in the affliction and misery. Those that would escape the wrath of God must pray against that more than any outward affliction, and be content to bear any outward affliction while it comes from, and consists with, the love of God.

II. He bitterly laments the impressions of God's displeasure upon his soul (v. 2): Thy arrows stick fast in me. Let Job's complaint (Job vii. 4) expound this of David. By the arrows of the Almighty he means the terrors of God, which did set themselves in array against him. He was under a very melancholy frightful apprehension of the wrath of God against him for his sins, and thought he could look for nothing but judgment and fiery indignation to devour him. God's arrows, as they are sure to hit the mark, so they are sure to stick where they hit, to stick fast, till he is pleased to draw them out and to bind up with his comforts the wound he has made with his terrors. This will be the everlasting misery of the damned—the arrows of God's wrath will stick fast in them and the wound will be incurable. "Thy hand, thy heavy hand, presses me sore, and I am ready to sink under it; it not only lies hard upon me, but it lies long; and who knows the power of God's anger, the weight of his hand?"

III. He acknowledges his sin to be the procuring provoking cause of all his troubles, and groans more under the load of guilt than any other load, v. 3. He complains that his flesh had no soundness, his bones had no rest, so great an agitation he was in. "It is because of thy anger; that kindles the fire which burns so fiercely;" but, in the next words, he justifies God herein, and takes all the blame upon himself: "It is because of my sin. I have deserved it, and so have brought it upon myself. My own iniquities do correct me." If our trouble be the fruit of God's anger, we may thank ourselves; it is our sin that is the cause of it. It is sin therefore that this good man complains most of,
1. As a burden, a heavy burden (v. 4): "My iniquities have gone over my head, as proud waters over a man that is sinking and drowning, or as a heavy burden upon my head, pressing me down more than I am able to bear or to bear up under."
2. As wounds, dangerous wounds (v. 5): "My wounds stink and are corrupt (as wounds in the body rankle, and fester, and grow foul, for want of being dressed and looked after), and it is through my own foolishness." Sins are wounds (Gen. iv. 23), painful

Psalm 38

9-16

9 Lord, all my desire is before thee; and my groaning is not hid from thee.
10 My heart panteth, my strength faileth me: as for the light of mine eyes, it also is gone from me.
11 My lovers and my friends stand aloof from my sore; and my kinsmen stand afar off.
12 They also that seek after my life lay snares for me: and they that seek my hurt speak mischievous things, and imagine deceits all the day long.
13 But I, as a deaf man, heard not; and I was as a dumb man that openeth not his mouth.
14 Thus I was as a man that heareth not, and in whose mouth are no reproofs.
15 For in thee, O LORD, do I hope: thou wilt hear, O Lord my God.
16 For I said, Hear me, lest otherwise they should rejoice over me: when my foot slippeth, they magnify themselves against me.

able to attend, he went forth like a mourner who goes to the tomb, and his words and manners were like the lamentations of those who follow the corpse. The whole verse may be the more clearly understood if we picture the Oriental mourner, covered with sackcloth and ashes, bowed as in a heap, sitting amid squalor and dirt, performing contortions and writhings expressive of his grief; such is the awakened sinner, not in outward guise, but in very deed.

Verse 7. For my loins are filled with a loathsome disease—a hot, dry, parching disorder, probably accompanied by loathsome ulcers. Spiritually, the fire burns within when the evil of the heart is laid bare. Note the emphatic words, the evil is loathsome, it is in the loins, its seat is deep and vital—the man is filled with it.

Verse 9. Lord, all my desire is before thee. If unuttered, yet perceived. Blessed be God, he reads the longings of our hearts; nothing can be hidden from him; what we cannot tell to him he perfectly understands. The psalmist is conscious that he has not exaggerated, and therefore appeals to heaven for a confirmation of his words. The good Physician understands the symptoms of our disease and sees the hidden evil which they reveal, hence our case is safe in his hands.

Verse 10. My heart panteth. Here begins another tale of woe. He was so dreadfully pained by the unkindness of friends, that his heart was in a state of perpetual palpitation. Sharp and quick were the beatings of his heart; he was like a hunted roe, filled with distressing alarms, and ready to fly out of itself with fear. The soul seeks sympathy in sorrow, and if it finds none, its sorrowful heart throbs are incessant.

Verse 11. My lovers and my friends stand aloof from my sore. Whatever affection they might pretend to, they kept out of his company, lest as a sinking vessel often draws down boats with it, they might be made to suffer through his calamities. It is very hard when those who should be the first to come to the rescue, are the first to desert us. In times of deep soul trouble, even the most affectionate friends cannot enter into the sufferer's case; let them be as anxious as they may, the sores of a tender conscience they cannot bind up.

Verse 12. They also that seek after my life lay snares for me. Alas! for us when in addition to inward griefs, we are beset by outward temptations. David's foes endeavored basely to ensnare him. If fair means would not overthrow him, foul should be tried. This snaring business is a vile one, the devil's own poachers alone condescend to it; but prayer to God will deliver us, for the craft of the entire college of tempters can be met and overcome by those who are led of the Spirit.

Verse 13. But I, as a deaf man, heard not. Well and bravely was this done. A sacred indifference to the slanders of malevolence is true courage and wise policy. It is well to be as if we could not hear or see. Perhaps the psalmist means that this deafness on his part was unavoidable because he had no power to answer the taunts of the cruel, but felt much of the truth of their ungenerous accusations. And I was as a dumb man that openeth not his mouth. David was bravely silent, and herein was eminently typical of our Lord Jesus, whose marvelous silence before Pilate was far more eloquent than words. To abstain from self defense is often most difficult, and frequently most wise.

Verse 14. Thus I was as a man that heareth not, and in whose mouth are no reproofs. He repeats the fact of his silence that we may note it, admire it, and imitate it. We have an advocate, and need not therefore plead our own cause. The Lord will rebuke our foes, for vengeance belongs to him; we may therefore wait patiently and find it our strength to sit still.

Verse 15. David committed himself to him that judgeth righteously, and so in patience was able to possess his soul. Hope in God's intervention, and belief in the power of prayer, are two most blessed stays to the soul in time of adversity.

meaning, that David seemed loathsome in his own eyes, when he thought of his reproach; but this appears too forced. When he adds that he was weakened and sore broken, he still farther confirms what he had said in the preceding verses: for by these various terms he wished to express the intolerable vehemence of his grief. Now, as a man, who is distinguished by courage, does not cry out and complain, and as we know that David did not shrink in bearing his afflictions, we may gather from this, that his sufferings were severe and painful in the extreme, inasmuch as he not only wept bitterly, but was also forced to cry out and complain.

8. The noun which I have rendered roaring, may be derived from another verb than that which David has here used; but the meaning is obvious, namely, that the incontrollable emotions of his heart forced him to cry out.

9. O Lord! thou knowest all my desire. He adds this, not so much in respect of God, as to strengthen himself in the hope of obtaining some alleviation of his trouble, and thus to animate himself to persevering prayer.

10. My heart hath turned round. The verb which David here uses signifies to travel or wander hither and thither; but here it is taken for the agitation or disquietude which distress of heart engenders when we know not what to do. According as men are disquieted in mind, so do they turn themselves on all sides, and so their heart may be said to turn round, or to run to and fro.

11-14

11. My friends and my companions stand away from my sore. Here David enumerates other circumstances to show the aggravated character of his misery, that he might excite the compassion of God. One of these is, that he finds no help or solace among men.

12. They also that sought for my life have laid snares for me, etc.. Here another circumstance is added, that the enemies of David laid snares for him, and talked about his destruction, and framed deceits among themselves. The purport of what is stated is, that while his friends cowardly sit still and will do nothing to aid him, his enemies vigorously bestir themselves, and seek by every means to destroy him.

13. But I, as a deaf man, hear not, etc. The inspired writer here compares himself to a dumb and deaf man, for two reasons. In the first place, he intimates that he was so overwhelmed with the false and wicked judgments of his enemies, that he was not even permitted to open his mouth in his own defense. In the second place, he alleges before God his own patience, as a plea to induce God the more readily to have pity upon him; for such meekness and gentleness, not only with good reason, secures favor to the afflicted and the innocent, but it is also a sign of true piety. Those who depend upon the world if they cannot avenge the injuries that are done them, plainly show by their loud complaints the burning rage and fury of their hearts. In order, therefore, that a man may quietly and patiently endure the insolence, violence, calumny, and deceit of his enemies, it is necessary that he trust in God.

mortal wounds. Our wounds by sin are often in a bad condition, no care taken of them, no application made to them, and it is owing to the sinner's foolishness in not confessing sin, Ps. xxxii. 3, 4. A slight sore, neglected, may prove of fatal consequence, and so may a slight sin slighted and left unrepented of.

IV. He bemoans himself because of his afflictions, and gives ease to his grief by giving vent to it and pouring out his complaint before the Lord.

1. He was troubled in mind, his conscience was pained, and he had no rest in his own spirit; and a wounded spirit who can bear? He was troubled, or distorted, bowed down greatly, and went mourning all the day long, v. 6. He was always pensive and melancholy, which made him a burden and terror to himself. His spirit was feeble and sorely broken, and his heart disquieted, v. 8. Herein David, in his sufferings, was a type of Christ, who, being in his agony, cried out, My soul is exceedingly sorrowful. This is a sorer affliction than any other in this world; whatever God is pleased to lay upon us, we have no reason to complain as long as he preserves to us the use of our reason and the peace of our consciences.

2. He was sick and weak in body; his loins were filled with a loathsome disease, some swelling, or ulcer, or inflammation (some think a plague-sore, such as Hezekiah's boil), and there was no soundness in his flesh, but, like Job, he was all over distempered. He was feeble and sorely broken, v. 8. His heart panted, and was in a continual palpitation, v. 10. His strength and limbs failed him. As for the light of his eyes, that had gone from him, either with much weeping or by a defluxion of rheum upon them, or perhaps through the lowness of his spirits and the frequent returns of fainting.

3. His friends were unkind to him (v. 11): My lovers (such as had been merry with him in the day of his mirth) now stand aloof from my sore; they would not sympathize with him in his griefs, nor so much as come within hearing of his complaints, but, like the priest and Levite (Luke x. 31), passed on the other side.

V. In the midst of his complaints, he comforts himself with the cognizance God graciously took both of his griefs and of his prayers (v. 9): "Lord, all my desire is before thee. Thou knowest what I want and what I would have: My groaning is not hidden from thee. Thou knowest the burdens I groan under and the blessings I groan after."

12-22 Sorrowful Complaints.

In these verses,

I. David complains of the power and malice of his enemies, who, it should seem, not only took occasion from the weakness of his body and the trouble of his mind to insult over him, but took advantage thence to do him a mischief. He has a great deal to say against them, which he humbly offers as a reason why God should appear for him, as Ps. xxv. 19, Consider my enemies.

Psalm 38

17-22

17 For I am ready to halt, and my sorrow is continually before me.
18 For I will declare mine iniquity; I will be sorry for my sin.
19 But mine enemies are lively, and they are strong: and they that hate me wrongfully are multiplied.
20 They also that render evil for good are mine adversaries; because I follow the thing that good is.
21 Forsake me not, O LORD: O my God, be not far from me.
22 Make haste to help me, O Lord my salvation.

Verse 16. For I said, hear me, lest otherwise they should rejoice over me. The good man was not insensible, he dreaded the sharp stings of taunting malice; he feared lest either by his conduct or his condition, he should give occasion to the wicked to triumph. This fear his earnest desires used as an argument in prayer as well as an incentive to prayer.

Verse 17. For I am ready to halt. Like one who limps, or a person with tottering footsteps, in danger of falling. How well this befits us all. "Let him that thinketh he standeth, take heed lest he fall." How small a thing will lame a Christian, how insignificant a stumbling block may cause him to fall! This passage refers to a weakness caused by pain and sorrow; the sufferer was ready to give up in despair; he was so depressed in spirit that he stumbled at a straw. Some of us painfully know what it is to be like dry tinder for the sparks of sorrow; ready to halt, ready to mourn, and sigh and cry upon any occasion, and for any cause.

Verse 18. For I will declare mine iniquity. The slander of his enemies he repudiates, but the accusations of his conscience he admits. Open confession is good for the soul. When sorrow leads to hearty and penitent acknowledgment of sin it is blessed sorrow, a thing to thank God for most devoutly. I will be sorry for my sin. My confession will be salted with briny tears.

Verse 19. But mine enemies are lively, and they are strong. However weak and dying the righteous man may be, the evils which oppose him are sure to be lively enough. Neither the world, the flesh, nor the devil, are ever afflicted with debility or inertness; this trinity if evils labor with mighty unremitting energy to overthrow us. If the devil were sick, or our lusts feeble, or Madame Bubble infirm, we might slacken prayer; but with such lively and vigorous enemies we must not cease to cry mightily unto our God. And they that hate me wrongfully are multiplied. Here is another misery, that as we are no match for our enemies in strength, so also they outnumber us as a hundred to one. Wrong as the cause of evil is, it is a popular one.

Verse 20. They also that render evil for good are mine adversaries. Such would a wise man wish his enemies to be. Why should we seek to be beloved of such graceless souls? It is a fine plea against our enemies when we can without injustice declare them to be like the devil, whose nature it is to render evil for good. Because I follow the thing that good is. If men hate us for this reason we may rejoice to bear it: their wrath is the unconscious homage which vice renders to virtue.

Verse 21. Forsake me not, O Lord. Now is the time I need thee most. When sickness, slander, and sin, all beset a saint, he requires the especial aid of heaven, and he shall have it too. He is afraid of nothing while God is with him, and God is with him evermore.

Verse 22. Make haste to help me. Delay would prove destruction. The poor pleader was far gone and ready to expire, only speedy help would serve his turn. See how sorrow quickens the importunity of prayer! Here is one of the sweet results of affliction, it gives new life to our pleading, and drives us with eagerness to our God. O Lord my salvation. Not my Savior only, but my salvation. He who has the Lord on his side has salvation in present possession. Faith foresees the blessed issue of all her pleas, and in this verse begins to ascribe to God the glory of the expected mercy. We shall not be left of the Lord. His grace will succor us most opportunely, and in heaven we shall see that we had not one trial too many, or one pang too severe.

JOHN CALVIN

15-20

15. For on thee, O Jehovah! do I wait. David here shows the source of his patience. It consisted in this, that, trusting in the grace of God, he overcame all the temptations of the world. And certainly, the mind of man will never be framed to gentleness, nor will he be able to subdue his passions, until he has learned never to give up hope.

16. For I said, lest they rejoice over me. Here he also confirms his faith and his earnestness in prayer from this consideration, that if he should be forsaken of God, his enemies would triumph. This indignity, on their part, is of no small weight in inducing God to help us; for the wicked, in thus magnifying themselves against us, and indulging in derision, not only make war with our flesh, but also directly assail our faith and endeavor to destroy whatever there is of religion and the fear of God in our hearts. What is the object of all their mockery, but to persuade us that what God has promised is vain and worthless? The Psalmist immediately adds, that it is not without cause that he is struck with the fear that his enemies would rejoice over him, since he had already had experience of their proud boastings.

17. Surely I am ready to halt. I think that David here employs a metaphorical mode of expression, and that his meaning is, that if God did not soon come to his aid, there was no hope of his ever being restored to his former condition; and that he was so greatly afflicted, that he would walk as if he had been maimed or lame all the days of his life.

18, 19. Surely I declare my iniquity. By comparison, he amplifies what he had just said concerning the pride and the reproachful conduct of his enemies; for he says, that whilst he is lying in a filthy and wretched condition, like a wicked man, and one abandoned by God, they fly about in mirth and gladness, nay, they carry their heads high, because they are rich and powerful. But first, it is proper to notice in what sense it is that he declares his sin.

20. David declares that they requited him evil for the good which he had done them. More than this, however, is implied in the language of David. It implies that he not only abstained from all hurtful dealing towards his enemies, but that he had done them all the good which was in his power; and on this account the rage of the wicked is the less excusable, which not only moves them to do harm to others without cause, but which likewise cannot be appeased by any marks of kindness exercised towards them.

21-22

In these concluding verses, David briefly states the chief point which he desired, and the sum of his whole prayer; namely, that whereas he was forsaken of men, and grievously afflicted in every way, God would receive him and raise him up again. He uses three forms of expression; first, that God would not forsake him, or cease to take care of him; secondly, that he would not be far from him; and, thirdly, that he would make haste to help him. David was, indeed, persuaded that God is always near to his servants, and that he delays not a single moment longer than is necessary.

MATTHEW HENRY

1. "They are very spiteful and cruel: They seek my hurt; nay, they seek after my life," v. 12. That life which was so precious in the sight of the Lord and all good men was aimed at, as if it had been forfeited, or a public nuisance. Such is the enmity of the serpent's seed against the seed of the woman; it would wound the head, though it can but reach the heel. It is the blood of the saints that is thirsted after.

2. "They are very subtle and politic. They lay snares, they imagine deceits, and herein they are restless and unwearied: they do it all the day long. They speak mischievous things one to another; every one has something or other to propose that may be a mischief to me." Mischief, covered and carried on by deceit, may well be called a snare.

3. "They are not only unjust, but very ungrateful: They hate me wrongfully, v. 19. I never did them any ill turn, nor so much as bore them any ill-will, nor ever gave them any provocation; nay, they render evil for good, v. 20. Many a kindness I have done them, for which I might have expected a return of kindness; but for my love they are my adversaries," Ps. cix. 4.

4. "They are many and mighty: They are lively; they are strong; they are multiplied, v. 19. Lord, how are those increased that trouble me?" Ps. iii. 1.

II. He reflects, with comfort, upon his own peaceable and pious behavior under all the injuries and indignities that were done him. It is then only that our enemies do us a real mischief when they provoke us to sin (Neh. vi. 13), when they prevail to put us out of the possession of our own souls, and drive us from God and our duty. If by divine grace we are enabled to prevent this mischief, we quench their fiery darts, and are saved from harm. If still we hold fast our integrity and our peace, who can hurt us? This David did here. He kept his temper, and was not ruffled nor discomposed by any of the slights that were put upon him or the mischievous things that were said or done against him (v. 13, 14): "I, as a deaf man, heard not; I took no notice of the affronts put upon me, much less did I meditate revenge, or study to return the injury."

III. He here bewails his own follies and infirmities. He was very sensible of the present workings of corruption in him, and that he was now ready to repine at the providence of God and to be put into a passion by the injuries men did him: I am ready to halt, v. 17. This will best be explained by a reflection like this which the psalmist made upon himself in a similar case (Ps. lxxiii. 2): My feet were almost gone, when I saw the prosperity of the wicked. So here: I was ready to halt, ready to say, I have cleansed my hands in vain. His sorrow was continual: All the day long have I been plagued, (Ps. lxxiii. 13, 14), and it was continually before him; he could not forbear poring upon it, and that made him almost ready to halt between religion and irreligion.

Psalm 39

Title
To the Chief Musician, even to Jeduthun. A Psalm of David.

1-6
1 I said, I will take heed to my ways, that I sin not with my tongue: I will keep my mouth with a bridle, while the wicked is before me.
2 I was dumb with silence, I held my peace, even from good; and my sorrow was stirred.
3 My heart was hot within me, while I was musing the fire burned: then spake I with my tongue,
4 LORD, make me to know mine end, and the measure of my days, what it is: that I may know how frail I am.
5 Behold, thou hast made my days as an handbreadth; and mine age is as nothing before thee: verily every man at his best state is altogether vanity. Selah.
6 Surely every man walketh in a vain shew: surely they are disquieted in vain: he heapeth up riches, and knoweth not who shall gather them.

Psalm 39

TITLE. To the Chief Musician, even to Jeduthun. Jeduthun's name, which signifies praising or celebrating, was a most appropriate one for a leader in sacred psalmody. He was one of those ordained by the King's order "for song in the house of the Lord with cymbals, psalteries, and harps" 1Ch 15:6, and his children after him appear to have remained in the same hallowed service, even so late as the days of Nehemiah. To have a name and a place in Zion is no small honor, and to hold this place by a long entail of grace is an unspeakable blessing. O that our household may never lack a man to stand before the Lord God of Israel to do him service. David left this somewhat sorrowful ode in Jeduthun's hands because he thought him most fit to set it to music, or because he would distribute the sacred honor of song among all the musicians who in their turn presided in the choir. A Psalm of David. Such as his chequered life would be sure to produce; fit effusions for a man so tempted, so strong in his passions, and yet so firm in faith.

DIVISION. The psalmist, bowed down with sickness and sorrow, is burdened with unbelieving thoughts, which he resolves to stifle, lest any evil should come from their expression, Ps 39:1-2. But silence creates an insupportable grief, which at last demands utterance, and obtains it in the prayer of Ps 39:3-6, which is almost a complaint and a sigh for death, or at best a very desponding picture of human life. From Ps 39:7-13 the tone is more submissive, and the recognition of the divine hand more distinct; the cloud has evidently passed, and the mourner's heart is relieved.

EXPOSITION

Verse 1. I said. I steadily resolved and registered a determination. In his great perplexity his greatest fear was lest he should sin; and, therefore, he cast about for the most likely method for avoiding it, and he determined to be silent. It is right excellent when a man can strengthen himself in a good course by the remembrance of a well and wisely formed resolve. "What I have written I have written, "or what I have spoken I will perform, may prove a good strengthener to a man in a fixed course of right. I will take heed to my ways. To avoid sin one had need be very circumspect, and keep one's actions as with a guard or garrison. Unguarded ways are generally unholy ones. Heedless is another word for graceless.

Verse 2. I was dumb with silence. He was as strictly speechless as if he had been tongueless—not a word escaped him. He was as silent as the dumb. I held my peace, even from good. Neither bad nor good escaped his lips. Perhaps he feared that if he began to talk at all, he would be sure to speak amiss, and, therefore, he totally abstained. It was an easy, safe, and effectual way of avoiding sin, if it did not involve a neglect of the duty which he owed to God to speak well of his name.

Verse 3. My heart was hot within me. The friction of inward thoughts produced an intense mental heat. The door of his heart was shut, and with the fire of sorrow burning within, the chamber of his soul soon grew unbearable with heat. Silence is an awful thing for a sufferer, it is the surest method to produce madness. Mourner, tell your sorrow; do it first and most fully to God, but even to pour it out before some wise and godly friend is far from being wasted breath.

Verse 4. Lord. It is well that the vent of his soul was toward God and not towards man. Oh! if my swelling heart must speak, Lord let it speak with thee; even if there be too much of natural heat in what I say, thou wilt be more patient with me than man, and upon thy purity it can cast no stain; whereas if I speak to my fellows, they may harshly rebuke me or else learn evil from my petulance. Make me to know mine end. Did he mean the same as Elias in his agony, "Let me die, I am no better than my father"? Perhaps so. At any rate, he rashly and petulantly desired to know the end of his

JOHN CALVIN

Psalm 39

1-3

1. I said, I will take heed to my ways. David explains and illustrates the greatness of his grief by this circumstance, that, contrary to his inclination and resolution, he broke forth into the severest complaints. The meaning substantially is, that although he had subdued his heart to patience, and resolved to keep silence, yet the violence of his grief was such that it forced him to break his resolution, and extorted from him, if we might so speak, expressions which indicate that he had given way to an undue degree of sorrow.

2. I was dumb in silence. He now declares that this resolution of which he has spoken had not been a mere passing and momentary thought, but that he had shown by his conduct that it was indeed a resolution deeply fixed in his heart. He says, then, that he held his peace for a time, just as if he had been deaf, which was a singular manifestation of his patience.

3. My heart became hot within me. He now illustrates the greatness of his grief by the introduction of a simile, telling us that his sorrow, being internally suppressed, became so much the more inflamed, until the ardent passion of his soul continued to increase in strength. From this we may learn the very profitable lesson, that the more strenuously any one sets himself to obey God, and employs all his endeavors to attain the exercise of patience, the more vigorously is he assailed by temptation: for Satan, whilst he is not so troublesome to the indifferent and careless, and seldom looks near them, displays all his forces in hostile array against that individual.

4-6

4. O Jehovah! cause me to know my end. It appears from this, that David was transported by an improper and sinful excess of passion, seeing he finds fault with God. This will appear still more clearly from the following verses. It is true, indeed, that in what follows he introduces pious and becoming prayers, but here he complains, that, being a mortal man, whose life is frail and transitory, he is not treated more mildly by God.

5. The expression, wholly or altogether vanity, implies that among the whole human race there is nothing but vanity. He declares this of men, even whilst they are standing; that is to say, when, being in the prime and vigor of life, they wish to be held in estimation, and seem to themselves to be men possessed of considerable influence and power. It was the pangs of sorrow which forced David to give utterance to these complaints; but it is to be observed, that it is chiefly when men are sore oppressed by adversity that they are made to feel their nothingness in the sight of God.

6. Surely man walketh in a shadow. He still prosecutes the same subject. By the word shadow, he means, that there is nothing substantial in man, but that he is only, as we say, a vain show, and has I know not how much of display and ostentation. David spoke under the influence of a distempered and troubled state of mind; but there is included in his language this very profitable lesson, that there is no

MATTHEW HENRY

Psalm 39

1-6 Devout reflections; brevity and vanity of life.

I. David remembered the covenants he had made with God to walk circumspectly, and to be very cautious both of what he did and what he said. When at any time we are tempted to sin, and are in danger of falling into it, we must call to mind the solemn vows we have made against sin, against the particular sin we are upon the brink of. God can, and will, remind us of them (Jer. ii. 20, Thou saidst, I will not transgress), and therefore we ought to remind ourselves of them. So David did here.

1. He remembers that he had resolved, in general, to be very cautious and circumspect in his walking (v. 1): I said, I will take heed to my ways; and it was well said, and what he would never unsay and therefore must never gainsay.

2. He remembers that he had in particular covenanted against tongue-sins—that he would not sin with his tongue, that he would not speak amiss, either to offend God or offend the generation of the righteous, Ps. lxxiii. 15.

II. Pursuant to these covenants he made a shift with much ado to bridle his tongue (v. 2): I was dumb with silence; I held my peace even from good. His silence was commendable; and the greater the provocation was the more praiseworthy was his silence. Watchfulness and resolution, in the strength of God's grace, will do more towards the bridling of the tongue than we can imagine, though it be an unruly evil.

III. The less he spoke the more he thought and the more warmly. Binding the distempered part did but draw the humor to it: My sorrow was stirred, my heart was hot within me, v. 3. He could bridle his tongue, but he could not keep his passion under; though he suppressed the smoke, that was as a fire in his bones, and, while he was musing upon his afflictions and upon the prosperity of the wicked, the fire burned.

IV. When he did speak, at last, it was to the purpose: At the last I spoke with my tongue. Some make what he said to be the breach of his good purpose, and conclude that, in what he said, he sinned with his tongue; and so they make what follows to be a passionate wish that he might die, like Elijah (1 Kings xix. 4) and Job vi. 8, 9.

7-13 Confidence in God; David pleading with God. The psalmist, having meditated on the shortness and uncertainty of life, and the vanity and vexation of spirit that attend all the comforts of life, here, in these verses, turns his eyes and heart heaven-ward. When there is no solid satisfaction to be had in the creature it is to be found in God, and in communion with him; and to him we should be driven by our disappointments in the world. David here expresses,

I. His dependence on God, v. 7. Seeing all is vanity, and man himself is so, he despairs of a happiness in the things of the world, and disclaims all expectations from it: "Now, Lord, what wait I for? Even nothing from

Psalm 39

7-13
7 And now, Lord, what wait I for? my hope is in thee.
8 Deliver me from all my transgressions: make me not the reproach of the foolish.
9 I was dumb, I opened not my mouth; because thou didst it.
10 Remove thy stroke away from me: I am consumed by the blow of thine hand.
11 When thou with rebukes dost correct man for iniquity, thou makest his beauty to consume away like a moth: surely every man is vanity. Selah.
12 Hear my prayer, O LORD, and give ear unto my cry; hold not thy peace at my tears: for I am a stranger with thee, and a sojourner, as all my fathers were.
13 O spare me, that I may recover strength, before I go hence, and be no more.

wretched life, that he might begin to reckon the days till death should put a finish to his woe. Impatience would pry between the folded leaves. As if there were no other comfort to be had, unbelief would fain hide itself in the grave and sleep itself into oblivion. David was neither the first nor the last who have spoken unadvisedly in prayer.
Verse 5. Behold, thou hast made my days as an handbreadth. Upon consideration, the psalmist finds little room to bewail the length of life, but rather to bemoan its shortness. What changeful creatures we are! One moment we cry to be rid of existence, and the next instant beg to have it prolonged! A handbreadth is one of the shortest natural measures, being the breadth of four fingers; such is the brevity of life, by divine appointment; God hath made it so, fixing the period in wisdom.
Verse 6. Surely every man walketh in a vain shew. Life is but a passing pageant. This alone is sure, that nothing is sure. All around us shadows mock us; we walk among them, and too many live for them as if the mocking images were substantial; acting their borrowed parts with zeal fit only to be spent on realities, and lost upon the phantoms of this passing scene.
Verse 7. And now, Lord, what wait I for? What is there in these phantoms to enchant me? Why should I linger where the prospect is so uninviting, and the present so trying? It were worse than vanity to linger in the abodes of sorrow to gain a heritage of emptiness. The psalmist, therefore, turns to his God, in disgust of all things else; he has thought on the world and all things in it, and is relieved by knowing that such vain things are all passing away; he has cut all cords which bound him to earth, and is ready to sound "Boot and saddle, up and away."
Verse 8. Deliver me from all my transgressions. How fair a sign it is when the psalmist no longer harps upon his sorrows, but begs freedom from his sins! What is sorrow when compared with sin! Let but the poison of sin be gone from the cup, and we need not fear its gall, for the bitter will act medicinally. None can deliver a man from his transgression but the blessed One who is called Jesus.
Verse 9. I was dumb, I opened not my mouth; because thou didst it. This had been far clearer if it had been rendered, "I am silenced, I will not open my mouth." Here we have a nobler silence, purged of all sullenness, and sweetened with submission.
Verse 10. Remove thy stroke away from me. Silence from all repining did not prevent the voice of prayer, which must never cease. In all probability the Lord would grant the psalmist's petition, for he usually removes affliction when we are resigned to it; if we kiss the rod, our Father always burns it.
Verse 11. When thou with rebukes dost correct man for iniquity. God does not trifle with his rod; he uses it because of sin, and with a view to whip us from it; hence he means his strokes to be felt, and felt they are. Thou makest his beauty to consume away like a moth. As the moth frets the substance of the fabric, mars all its beauty, and leaves it worn out and worthless, so do the chastisements of God discover to us our folly, weakness, and nothingness, and make us feel ourselves to be as worn out vestures, worthless and useless.
Verse 12. Hear my prayer, O Lord. Drown not my pleadings with the sound of thy strokes. Thou hast heard the clamor of my sins, Lord; hear the laments of my prayers. And give ear unto my cry. Here is an advance in intensity: a cry is more vehement, pathetic, and impassioned, than a prayer. The main thing was to have the Lord's ear and heart.

remedy better fitted for enabling us to rise above all unnecessary cares, than the recollection that the brief period of our life is only, as it were, a hand-breadth.

7-9

7. And now, O Lord! what do I wait for? David, having acknowledged that his heart had been too much under the influence of ardent and impetuous emotion, from which he had experienced great disquietude, now returns to a calm and settled state of mind; and from this what I have before stated is rendered still more obvious, namely, that this psalm consists partly of appropriate prayers and partly of inconsiderate complaints.

8. Deliver me from all my sins. In this verse the Psalmist still continues his godly and holy prayer. He is now no longer carried away by the violence of his grief to murmur against God, but, humbly acknowledging himself guilty before God, he has recourse to his mercy. In asking to be delivered from his transgressions, he ascribes the praise of righteousness to God, while he charges upon himself the blame of all the misery which he endures; and he blames himself, not only on account of one sin, but acknowledges that he is justly chargeable with manifold transgressions.

9. I was dumb. Here David blames himself, because he had not preserved that silence which, as we have already seen, the violence of his grief forced him to break. When he says then that he was dumb, he does not mean this as a commendation of the uniform and persevering restraint which he had exercised over himself. It is rather a correction of his error, as if reproving his own impatience.

10. Take away thy stroke from me. David here confirms the prayer which he had already presented, namely, that having obtained pardon from God, he might, at the same time, be gently dealt with by him.

11. This sentence, that every man is vanity, is again very properly repeated; for until we are overcome by the power of God, and as it were humbled in the dust, we never search into our own hearts, that the knowledge of our own vanity may divest us of all presumption.

12-13

12. Hear my prayer, O Jehovah! David gradually increases his vehemence in prayer. He speaks first of prayer; in the second place, of crying; and in the third place, of tears. This gradation is not a mere figure of rhetoric, which serves only to adorn the style, or to express the same thing in different language.

13. Let me alone, that I may recover strength. This concluding verse of the psalm relates to the disquietude and sinful emotions which he had experienced according to the flesh; for he seems in the way of complaining of God, to ask that at least time might be granted him to die. We might, indeed, regard the prayer as allowable, by understanding it in this sense: Lord, as it will not be possible for me to endure thy stroke any longer, but I must, indeed, miserably perish, if thou continuest to afflict me severely, at least grant me relief for a little season, that in calmness and peace I may commit my soul into thy hands.

the things of sense and time; I have nothing to wish for, nothing to hope for, from this earth." Note, The consideration of the vanity and frailty of human life should deaden our desires to the things of this world and lower our expectations from it. "If the world be such a thing as this, God deliver me from having, or seeking, my portion in it." We cannot reckon upon constant health and prosperity, nor upon comfort in any relation; for it is all as uncertain as our continuance here. "Though I have sometimes foolishly promised myself this and the other from the world, I am now of another mind."

II. His submission to God, and his cheerful acquiescence in his holy will, v. 9. If our hope be in God for a happiness in the other world, we may well afford to reconcile ourselves to all the dispensations of his providence concerning us in this world: "I was dumb; I opened not my mouth in a way of complaint and murmuring." He now again recovered that serenity and sedateness of mind which were disturbed, v. 2. Whatever comforts he is deprived of, whatever crosses he is burdened with, he will be easy. "Because thou didst it; it did not come to pass by chance, but according to thy appointment."

III. His desire towards God, and the prayers he puts up to him. Is any afflicted? let him pray, as David here,

1. For the pardoning of his sin and the preventing of his shame, v. 8. Before he prays (v. 10), Remove thy stroke from me, he prays (v. 8), "Deliver me from all my offences, from the guilt I have contracted, the punishment I have deserved, and the power of corruption by which I have been enslaved." When God forgives our sins he delivers us from them, he delivers us from them all.

2. For the removal of his affliction, that he might speedily be eased of his present burdens (v. 10): Remove thy stroke away from me. Note, When we are under the correcting hand of God our eye must be to God himself, and not to any other, for relief. He only that inflicts the stroke can remove it; and we may then in faith, and with satisfaction, pray that our afflictions may be removed, when our sins are pardoned (Isa. xxxviii. 17).

3. He pleads the great extremity he was reduced to by his affliction, which made him the proper object of God's compassion: I am consumed by the blow of thy hand. His sickness prevailed to such a degree that his spirits failed, his strength was wasted, and his body emaciated. "The blow, or conflict, of thy hand has brought me even to the gates of death."

4. He prays for a reprieve yet a little longer (v. 13): "O spare me, ease me, raise me up from this illness that I may recover strength both in body and mind, that I may get into a more calm and composed frame of spirit, and may be better prepared for another world, before I go hence by death, and shall be no more in this world." I take this as a pious prayer that God would continue him here till by his grace he had made him fit to go hence.

Psalm 40

Title
To the chief Musician, a Psalm of David.

1-5
1 I waited patiently for the LORD; and he inclined unto me, and heard my cry.
2 He brought me up also out of an horrible pit, out of the miry clay, and set my feet upon a rock, and established my goings.
3 And he hath put a new song in my mouth, even praise unto our God: many shall see it, and fear, and shall trust in the LORD.
4 Blessed is that man that maketh the LORD his trust, and respecteth not the proud, nor such as turn aside to lies.
5 Many, O LORD my God, are thy wonderful works which thou hast done, and thy thoughts which are to us-ward: they cannot be reckoned up in order unto thee: if I would declare and speak of them, they are more than can be numbered.

Psalm 40

TITLE. To the Chief Musician. Well might so exceedingly precious a Psalm be specially committed to the most skilled of the sacred musicians. The noblest music should be made tributary to a subject so incomparable. The dedication shows that the song was intended for public worship, and was not a merely personal hymn, as its being in the first person singular might lead us to suppose. A Psalm of David. This is conclusive as to the authorship: lifted by the Holy Spirit into the region of prophecy, David was honored to write concerning a far greater than himself.
SUBJECT. Jesus is evidently here, and although it might not be a violent wresting of language to see both David and his Lord, both Christ and the church, the double comment might involve itself in obscurity, and therefore we shall let the sun shine even though this should conceal the stars. Even if the New Testament were not so express upon it, we should have concluded that David spoke of our Lord in Ps 40:6-9, but the apostle in Heb 10:5-9, puts all conjecture out of court, and confines the meaning to him who came into the world to do the Father's will.
DIVISION. From Ps 40:1-3, is a personal thanksgiving, followed by a general declaration of Jehovah's goodness to his saints, Ps 40:4-5. In Ps 40:6-10, we have an avowal of dedication to the Lord's will; Ps 40:11-17, contains a prayer for deliverance from pressing trouble, and for the overthrow of enemies.

EXPOSITION
Verse 1. I waited patiently for the Lord. Patient waiting upon God was a special characteristic of our Lord Jesus. Impatience never lingered in his heart, much less escaped his lips. All through his agony in the garden, his trial of cruel mockings before Herod and Pilate, and his passion on the tree, he waited in omnipotence of patience. No glance of wrath, no word of murmuring, no deed of vengeance came from God's patient Lamb; he waited and waited on; was patient, and patient to perfection, far excelling all others who have according to their measure glorified God in the fires. Job on the dunghill does not equal Jesus on the cross. The Christ of God wears the imperial crown among the patient. Did the Only Begotten wait, and shall we be petulant and rebellious? And he inclined unto me, and heard my cry. Neither Jesus the head, nor any one of the members of his body, shall ever wait upon the Lord in vain.
Verse 2. He brought me up also out of an horrible pit. When our Lord bore in his own person the terrible curse which was due to sin, he was so cast down as to be like a prisoner in a deep, dark, fearful dungeon, amid whose horrible glooms the captive heard a noise as of rushing torrents, while overhead resounded the tramp of furious foes. Our Lord in his anguish was like a captive in the oubliettes, forgotten of all mankind, immured amid horror, darkness, and desolation. Yet the Lord Jehovah made him to ascend from all his abasement; he retraced his steps from that deep hell of anguish into which he had been cast as our substitute.
Verse 3. And he hath put a new song in my mouth, even praise unto our God. At the Passover, before his passion, our Lord sang one of the grand old Psalms of praise; but what is the music of his heart now, in the midst of his redeemed! What a song is that in which his glad heart for ever leads the chorus of the elect!
Verse 4. Blessed. This is an exclamation similar to that of the first Psalm, "Oh, the happiness of the man." God's blessings are emphatic, "I wot that he whom thou blessest is blessed," indeed and in very truth. Is that man that maketh the Lord his trust. Faith obtaineth promises. A simple single eyed confidence in God is the sure mark of blessedness.
Verse 5. Many, O Lord my God, are thy wonderful works which thou hast done. Creation, providence, and redemption, teem with wonders as the sea

Psalm 40

David, being delivered from some great danger, and it may be, not from one only, but from many, extols very highly the grace of God, and by means of this, his soul is filled with admiration of the providence of God, which extends itself to the whole human race. Then he protests that he will give himself wholly to the service of God, and defines briefly in what manner God is to be served and honored. Afterwards, he again returns to the exercise of thanksgiving, and celebrates the praises of the Eternal by rehearsing many of his glorious and powerful deeds. Lastly, when he has complained of his enemies, he concludes the psalm with a new prayer.

1-3

1. In waiting I waited. The beginning of this psalm is an expression of thanksgiving, in which David relates that he had been delivered, not only from danger, but also from present death. Some are of opinion, but without good reason, that it ought to be understood of sickness. It is rather to be supposed that David here comprehends a multitude of dangers from which he had escaped.

2. And he drew me out of the roaring pit. Here an allusion to the deep gulfs, where the waters gush with a tumultuous force. By this similitude he shows that he was placed in as imminent peril of death as if he had been cast into a deep pit, roaring with the impetuous rage of waters. To the same purpose also is the similitude of the miry clay, by which he intimates that he had been so nearly overwhelmed by the weight of his calamities, that it was no easy matter to extricate him from them. Next, there follows a sudden and incredible change, by which he makes manifest to all the greatness of the grace which had been bestowed upon him. He declares that his feet were set upon a rock, whereas formerly he had been overwhelmed with water; and that his steps were established or upheld, whereas before they were not only unsteady and slippery, but were also stuck fast in the mire.

3. And he hath put into my mouth a new song. In the first clause of the verse he concludes the description of what God had done for him. By God's putting a new song into his mouth he denotes the consummation of his deliverance. In whatever way God is pleased to succor us, he asks nothing else from us in return but that we should be thankful for and remember it. As often, therefore, as he bestows benefits upon us, so often does he open our mouths to praise his name. Since God, by acting liberally towards us, encourages us to sing his praises, David with good reason reckons, that having been so wonderfully delivered, the matter of a new song had been furnished to him.

4-5

4. Blessed is the man who hath set Jehovah for his confidence. David here relates what ground for good hope his deliverance would give to all the faithful; inasmuch as, setting aside all the allurements of the world, they would thereby be encouraged to commit themselves with

Psalm 40

1-5 The benefit of confidence in God.

In these verses we have,

I. The great distress and trouble that the psalmist had been in. He had been plunged into a horrible pit and into miry clay (v. 2), out of which he could not work himself, and in which he found himself sinking yet further. He says nothing here either of the sickness of his body or the insults of his enemies, and therefore we have reason to think it was some inward disquiet and perplexity of spirit that was now his greatest grievance. Despondency of spirit under the sense of Gods withdrawings, and prevailing doubts and fears about the eternal state, are indeed a horrible pit and miry clay, and have been so to many a dear child of God.

II. His humble attendance upon God and his believing expectations from him in those depths: I waited patiently for the Lord, v. 1. Waiting, I waited. He expected relief from no other than from God; the same hand that tears must heal, that smites must bind up (Hos. vi. 1), or it will never be done. From God he expected relief, and he was big with expectation, not doubting but it would come in due time. There is power enough in God to help the weakest, and grace enough in God to help the unworthiest, of all his people that trust in him. But he waited patiently, which intimates that the relief did not come quickly; yet he doubted not but it would come, and resolved to continue believing, and hoping, and praying, till it did come. Those whose expectation is from God may wait with assurance, but must wait with patience. Now this is very applicable to Christ. His agony, both in the garden and on the cross, was the same continued, and it was a horrible pit and miry clay. Then was his soul troubled and exceedingly sorrowful; but then he prayed, Father, glorify thy name; Father, save me; then he kept hold of his relation to his Father, "My God, my God," and thus waited patiently for him.

III. His comfortable experience of God's goodness to him in his distress, which he records for the honor of God and his own and others' encouragement.

God silenced his fears, and stilled the tumult of his spirits, and gave him a settled peace of conscience (v. 2): "He brought me up out of that horrible pit of despondency and despair, scattered the clouds, and shone brightly upon my soul, with the assurances of his favor; and not only so, but set my feet upon a rock and established my goings." Those that have been under the prevalency of a religious melancholy, and by the grace of God have been relieved, may apply this very feelingly to themselves; they are brought up out of a horrible pit.

IV. The good improvement that should be made of this instance of God's goodness to David.

1. David's experience would be an encouragement to many to hope in God, and, for that end, he leaves it here upon record: Many shall see, and fear, and trust

Psalm 40

6-11
6 Sacrifice and offering thou didst not desire; mine ears hast thou opened: burnt offering and sin offering hast thou not required.
7 Then said I, Lo, I come: in the volume of the book it is written of me,
8 I delight to do thy will, O my God: yea, thy law is within my heart.
9 I have preached righteousness in the great congregation: lo, I have not refrained my lips, O LORD, thou knowest.
10 I have not hid thy righteousness within my heart; I have declared thy faithfulness and thy salvation: I have not concealed thy loving kindness and thy truth from the great congregation.
11 Withhold not thou thy tender mercies from me, O LORD: let thy loving kindness and thy truth continually preserve me.

with life. Our special attention is called by this passage to the marvels which cluster around the cross and flash from it. The accomplished redemption achieves many ends, and compasses a variety of designs; the outgoings of the atonement are not to be reckoned up, the influences of the cross reach further than the beams of the sun. Wonders of grace beyond all enumeration take their rise from the cross; adoption, pardon, justification, and a long chain of godlike miracles of love proceed from it. Note that our Lord here speaks of the Lord as "my God." The man Christ Jesus claimed for himself and us a covenant relationship with Jehovah. Let our interest in our God be ever to us our peculiar treasure.

Verse 6. Here we enter upon one of the most wonderful passages in the whole of the Old Testament, a passage in which the incarnate Son of God is seen not through a glass darkly, but as it were face to face. Sacrifice and offering thou didst not desire. In themselves considered, and for their own sakes, the Lord saw nothing satisfactory in the various offerings of the ceremonial law. Neither the victim pouring forth its blood, nor the fine flour rising in smoke from the altar, could yield content to Jehovah's mind; he cared not for the flesh of bulls or of goats, neither had he pleasure in corn and wine, and oil. Typically these offerings had their worth, but when Jesus, the Antitype, came into the world, they ceased to be of value, as candles are of no estimation when the sun has arisen.

Verse 7. Then said I. That is to say, when it was clearly seen that man's misery could not be remedied by sacrifices and offerings. It being certain that the mere images of atonement, and the bare symbols of propitiation were of no avail, the Lord Jesus, in propria persona, intervened. O blessed "then said I." Lord, ever give us to hear and feed on such living words as these, so peculiarly and personally thine own. Lo, I come. Behold, O heavens, and thou earth, and ye places under the earth! Here is something worthy of your most intense gaze.

Verse 8. I delight to do thy will, O my God. Our blessed Lord alone could completely do the will of God. The law is too broad for such poor creatures as we are to hope to fulfill it to the uttermost: but Jesus not only did the Father's will, but found a delight therein; from old eternity he had desired the work set before him; in his human life he was straitened till he reached the baptism of agony in which he magnified the law, and even in Gethsemane itself he chose the Father's will, and set aside his own.

Verse 9. I have preached righteousness in the great congregation. The purest morality and the highest holiness were preached by Jesus. Righteousness divine was his theme. Our Lord's whole life was a sermon, eloquent beyond compare, and it is heard each day by myriads. Moreover, he never shunned in his ministry to declare the whole counsel of God; God's great plan of righteousness he plainly set forth. He taught openly in the temple, and was not ashamed to be a faithful and a true witness. He was the great evangelist; the master of itinerant preachers; the head of the clan of open air missionaries. O servants of the Lord, hide not your lights, but reveal to others what your God has revealed to you; and especially by your lives testify for holiness, be champions for the right, both in word and deed.

Verse 10. I have not hid thy righteousness within my heart. On the contrary, "Never man spake like this man." God's divine plan of making men righteous was well known to him, and he plainly taught it. What was in our great Master's heart he poured forth in holy eloquence from his lips. The doctrine of righteousness by faith he spake with great simplicity of speech. Law and gospel equally found in him a clear expositor. I have declared thy faithfulness and thy salvation. Jehovah's fidelity to his promises and his grace in saving believers were declared by the Lord Jesus on many occasions, and are blessedly blended in the gospel which he came to preach. God, faithful to his own character, law and threatenings, and yet saving sinners, is a peculiar revelation of the gospel.

confidence to the protection of God; persuaded not only that they are happy who trust in him alone, but that all other expectations at variance with this are deceitful and cursed. This assurance is not natural to us, but is derived partly from the word of God, and partly from his works; although the contemplation alone of the works of God would not kindle this light within us, unless God, illuminating us by his word, should show us his benevolence.
5. Many are thy wonderful works which thou hast done, O Jehovah! Interpreters are not entirely agreed as to these words; but it is generally admitted that David here contemplates with admiration the providence of God in the government of mankind. He exclaims that the wonders of God's works are great or many; meaning by this, that God in his inscrutable wisdom so governs human affairs, that his works, which come to be little thought of by men, from their constant familiarity with them, far surpass the comprehension of the human understanding. Thus we find, that from one particular species he ascends to the whole class; as if he had said, God has proved not only by this particular act the paternal care which he exercises towards men, but that, in general, his wonderful providence shines forth in the several parts of creation. Then he adds, that the counsels of God concerning us are so high and so hidden, that it is impossible to reckon them up in order distinctly and agreeably to their nature.
6-8
6. In sacrifice and oblation thou hast not taken pleasure. Here David offers not only the sacrifice of praise, or, as the prophet Hosea calls it, (Hosea 14:2,) "the calves of the lips," but, in token of his gratitude, offers and consecrates himself entirely to God; as if he had said, I am now wholly devoted to God, because, having been delivered by his wonderful power, I am doubly indebted to him for my life.
7. Then said I, Lo! I come. Here true obedience is very properly distinguished from a constrained and slavish subjection. Whatever service, therefore, men may offer to God, it is vain and offensive in his sight, unless at the same time they offer themselves; and, moreover, this offering of one's self is of no value unless it be done willingly.
In the roll of the book. The voice of God resounds throughout the whole world, so that all who do not obey it are rendered inexcusable; but it penetrates into the hearts of the godly alone, for whose salvation it is ordained. As a general, therefore, enrolls the names of his soldiers, that he may know their exact number, and as a schoolmaster writes the names of his scholars in a scroll, so has God written the names of his children in the book of life, that he may retain them under the yoke of his own discipline.

9-11
9. I have proclaimed thy righteousness in the great assembly. Here David again brings forward his own thankfulness, and for no other reason but to induce God to continue his goodness towards him. God, whenever he manifests his liberality towards us, encourages us to render thanks to him;

in the Lord. They shall fear the Lord and his justice, which brought David, and the Son of David, into that horrible pit, and shall say, If this be done to the green tree, what shall be done to the dry? They shall fear the Lord and his goodness, in filling the mouth of David, and the Son of David, with new songs of joy and praise. There is a holy reverent fear of God, which is not only consistent with, but the foundation of, our hope in him.
2. The joyful sense he had of this mercy led him to observe, with thankfulness, the many other favors he had received from God, v. 5. When God puts new songs into our mouth we must not forget our former songs, but repeat them: "Many, O Lord my God! are thy wonderful works which thou hast done, both for me and others; this is but one of many." Many are the benefits with which we are daily loaded both by the providence and by the grace of God.

6-10 Insufficiency of the legal sacrifices; the efficacy of Christ's sacrifice.
The psalmist, being struck with amazement at the wonderful works that God had done for his people, is strangely carried out here to foretell that work of wonder which excels all the rest and is the foundation and fountain of all, that of our redemption by our Lord Jesus Christ. God's thoughts, which were to us-ward concerning that work, were the most curious, the most copious, the most gracious, and therefore to be most admired. This paragraph is quoted by the apostle (Heb. x. 5, &c.) and applied to Christ and his undertaking for us. As in the institutions, so in the devotions, of the Old Testament saints were aware of; and, when the apostle would show us the Redeemer's voluntary undertaking of his work, he does not fetch his account out of the book of God's secret counsels, which belong not to us, but from the things revealed. Observe,
I. The utter insufficiency of the legal sacrifices to atone for sin in order to our peace with God and our happiness in him: Sacrifice and offering thou didst not desire; thou wouldst not have the Redeemer to offer them. Something he must have to offer, but not these (Heb. viii. 3); therefore he must not be of the house of Aaron, Heb. vii. 14. Or, In the days of the Messiah burnt-offering and sin-offering will be no longer required, but all those ceremonial institutions will be abolished.
II. The designation of our Lord Jesus to the work and office of Mediator: My ears hast thou opened. God the Father disposed him to the undertaking (Isa. l. 5, 6) and then obliged him to go through with it. My ear hast thou digged. It is supposed to allude to the law and custom of binding servants to serve for ever by boring their ear to the doorpost; see Exod. xxi. 6. Our Lord Jesus was so in love with his undertaking that he would not go out free from it, and therefore engaged to persevere for ever in it; and for this reason he is able to save us to the uttermost, because he

Psalm 40

12-17

12 For innumerable evils have compassed me about: mine iniquities have taken hold upon me, so that I am not able to look up; they are more than the hairs of mine head: therefore my heart faileth me.
13 Be pleased, O LORD, to deliver me: O LORD, make haste to help me.
14 Let them be ashamed and confounded together that seek after my soul to destroy it; let them be driven backward and put to shame that wish me evil.
15 Let them be desolate for a reward of their shame that say unto me, Aha, aha.
16 Let all those that seek thee rejoice and be glad in thee: let such as love thy salvation say continually, The LORD be magnified.
17 But I am poor and needy; yet the Lord thinketh upon me: thou art my help and my deliverer; make no tarrying, O my God.

Verse 11. Withhold not thou thy tender mercies from me, O Lord. Alas! these were to be for awhile withheld from our Lord while on the accursed tree, but meanwhile in his great agony he seeks for gentle dealing; and the coming of the angel to strengthen him was a clear answer to his prayer.

Verse 12. For innumerable evils have compassed me about. On every side he was beset with evils; countless woes environed the great Substitute for our sins. Our sins were innumerable, and so were his griefs. There was no escape for us from our iniquities, and there was no escape for him from the woes which we deserved. From every quarter evils accumulated about the blessed One, although in his heart evil found no place.

Verse 13. Be pleased, O Lord, to deliver me: O Lord, make haste to help me. How touching! How humble! How plaintive! The words thrill us as we think that after this sort our Lord and Master prayed. His petition is not so much that the cup should pass away undrained, but that he should be sustained while drinking it, and set free from its power at the first fitting moment. He seeks deliverance and help; and he entreats that the help may not be slow in coming; this is after the manner of our pleadings. Is it not? Note, reader, how our Lord was heard in that he feared, for there was after Gethsemane a calm endurance which made the fight as glorious as the victory.

Verse 14. Let them be ashamed and confounded together that seek after my soul to destroy it. Whether we read this as a prayer or a prophecy it matters not, for the powers of sin, and death, and hell, may well be ashamed as they see the result of their malice for ever turned against themselves.

Verse 15. Let them be desolate, or amazed; even as Jesus was desolate in his agony, so let his enemies be in their despair when he defeats them. The desolation caused in the hearts of evil spirits and evil men by envy, malice, chagrin, disappointment, and despair, shall be a fit recompense for their cruelty to the Lord when he was in their hands.

Verse 16. Let all those that seek thee, rejoice and be glad in thee. We have done with Ebal and turn to Gerizim. Here our Lord pronounces benedictions on his people. Note who the blessed objects of his petition are: not all men, but some men, "I pray for them, I pray not for the world." He pleads for seekers: the lowest in the kingdom, the babes of the family; those who have true desires, longing prayers, and consistent endeavors after God. Let seeking souls pluck up heart when they hear of this. What riches of grace, that in his bitterest hour Jesus should remember the lambs of the flock!

Verse 17. But I am poor and needy. The man of sorrows closes with another appeal, based upon his affliction and poverty. Yet the Lord thinketh upon me. Sweet was this solace to the holy heart of the great sufferer. The Lord's thoughts of us are a cheering subject of meditation, for they are ever kind and never cease. Thou art my help and my deliverer. His unmoved confidence stayed itself alone on God. O that all believers would imitate more fully their great Apostle and High Priest in his firm reliance upon God, even when afflictions abounded and the light was veiled. Make no tarrying, O my God. The peril was imminent, the need urgent, the suppliant could not endure delay, nor was he made to wait, for the angel came to strengthen, and the brave heart of Jesus rose up to meet the foe. Lord Jesus, grant that in all our adversities we may possess like precious faith, and be found like thee, more than conquerors.

JOHN CALVIN

and he continues to act in a similar manner towards us when he sees that we are thankful and mindful of what he has done for us.
10. I have not hidden thy righteousness within my heart. Salvation is the effect of righteousness, for God continues to manifest his free favor to his people, daily affording them aid and assistance, until he has completely saved them.
11. O thou Jehovah! withhold not thy tender mercies from me. We now see more clearly, what I have just adverted to, that David speaks of his own thankfulness, that he might secure a continuance of God's favor towards him; and that he opened his mouth in the praises of God, that he might continue to acquire new favors, against which our perverse and ungrateful silence very often closes the gate.

12-15
12. For innumerable evils have compassed me on all sides. We must understand this fainting or failing of the heart as referring to the sense of the flesh; for his perseverance in prayer is a certain proof that his faith was never altogether extinguished. But since he was, in so far as man was concerned, destitute of counsel, and was altogether without strength, it is not without cause that he says that his heart failed him.
13. Be thou pleased, O Jehovah! to deliver me. We must maintain it as a fixed principle, that the more unjustly our enemies afflict us, and the more cruelly they wrong us, God is so much the more disposed to give us help. And it is no slight consolation that the mercy of God strives against their wickedness, so that the more fiercely our enemies pursue us to effect our hurt, the more ready is he to bring us help.
14, 15. When the Psalmist prays that his enemies may be destroyed for a reward of their shame, the meaning is this: As their sole desire has been to overwhelm me with shame, in order that, while thus dismayed and confounded, they might make me the object of their derision; so let a similar confusion fall upon their own heads.

16-17
16. Let all those that seek thee be glad and rejoice in thee. David here uses another argument—one which he often adduces elsewhere—in order to obtain deliverance; not that it is necessary to allege reasons to persuade God, but because it is profitable to confirm our faith by such supports. As, then, it is the will of God that he should be known in his gracious character, not only of one or two, but generality of all men, whenever he vouchsafes deliverance to any of his children, it is a common benefit which all the faithful ought to apply to themselves when they see in the person of one man in what manner God, who is never inconsistent with himself, will act towards all his people.
17. But I am poor and needy. In this concluding clause he mingles prayer with thanksgiving, although it may be that he records a request which he had made when he was placed in extreme danger.

MATTHEW HENRY

has engaged to serve his Father to the uttermost, who upholds him in it, Isa. xlii. 1.
III. His own voluntary consent to this undertaking: "Then said I, Lo, I come; then, when sacrifice and offering would not do, rather than the work should be undone; I said, Lo, I come, to enter the lists with the powers of darkness, and to advance the interests of God's glory and kingdom."
IV. The pleasure he took in his undertaking. Having freely offered himself to it, he did not fail, nor was discouraged, but proceeded with all possible satisfaction to himself (v. 8, 9): I delight to do thy will, O my God! It was to Christ his meat and drink to go on with the work appointed to him (John iv. 34); and the reason here given is, Thy law is within my heart; it is written there, it rules there.
VI. The publication of the gospel to the children of men, even in the great congregation, v. 9, 10. The same that as a priest wrought out redemption for us, as a prophet, by his own preaching first, then by his apostles, and still by his word and Spirit, makes it known to us.

11-17 Encouragement in prayer.
The psalmist, having meditated upon the work of redemption, and spoken of it in the person of the Messiah, now comes to make improvement of the doctrine of his mediation between us and God, and therefore speaks in his own person. Christ having done his Father's will, and finished his work, and given orders for the preaching of the gospel to every creature, we are encouraged to come boldly to the throne of grace, for mercy and grace.
I. This may encourage us to pray for the mercy of God, and to put ourselves under the protection of that mercy, v. 11. "Lord, thou hast not spared thy Son, nor withheld him; withhold not thou thy tender mercies then, which thou hast laid up for us in him; for wilt thou not with him also freely give us all things? Rom. viii. 32. Let thy lovingkindness and thy truth continually preserve me." The best saints are in continual danger, and see themselves undone if they be not continually preserved by the grace of God; and the everlasting lovingkindness and truth of God are what we have to depend upon for our preservation to the heavenly kingdom, Ps. lxi. 7.
II. This may encourage us in reference to the guilt of sin, that Jesus Christ has done that towards our discharge from it which sacrifice and offering could not do. Note the frightful sight he had of sin, v. 12.
III. This may encourage us to hope for victory over our spiritual enemies that seek after our souls to destroy them (v. 14), the roaring lion that goes about continually seeking to devour.
IV. This may encourage all that seek God, and love his salvation, to rejoice in him and to praise him, v. 16.
V. This may encourage the saints, in distress and affliction, to trust in God and comfort themselves in him, v. 17.

Psalm 41

Title
To the chief Musician, a Psalm of David.

1-7
1 Blessed is he that considereth the poor: the LORD will deliver him in time of trouble.
2 The LORD will preserve him, and keep him alive; and he shall be blessed upon the earth: and thou wilt not deliver him unto the will of his enemies.
3 The LORD will strengthen him upon the bed of languishing: thou wilt make all his bed in his sickness.
4 I said, LORD, be merciful unto me: heal my soul; for I have sinned against thee.
5 Mine enemies speak evil of me, When shall he die, and his name perish?
6 And if he come to see me, he speaketh vanity: his heart gathereth iniquity to itself; when he goeth abroad, he telleth it.
7 All that hate me whisper together against me: against me do they devise my hurt.

Psalm 41

TITLE. To the Chief Musician. A Psalm of David. This title has frequently occurred before, and serves to remind us of the value of the Psalm, seeing that it was committed to no mean songster; and also to inform us as to the author who has made his own experience the basis of a prophetic song, in which a far greater than David is set forth. How wide a range of experience David had! What power it gave him to edify future ages! And how full a type of our Lord did he become! What was bitterness to him has proved to be a fountain of unfailing sweetness to many generations of the faithful.
Jesus Christ betrayed by Judas Iscariot is evidently the great theme of this Psalm, but we think not exclusively. He is the antitype of David, and all his people are in their measure like him; hence words suitable to the Great Representative are most applicable to those who are in him. Such as receive a vile return for long kindness to others, may read this song with much comfort, for they will see that it is alas! too common for the best of men, to be rewarded for their holy charity with cruelty and scorn; and when they have been humbled by falling into sin, advantage has been taken of their low estate, their good deeds have been forgotten and the vilest spite has been vented upon them.
DIVISION. The psalmist in Ps 41:1-3, describes the mercies which are promised to such as consider the poor, and this he uses as a preface to his own personal plea for succor: from Ps 41:4-9 he states his own case, proceeds to prayer in Ps 41:10, and closes with thanksgiving, Ps 41:11-13.

EXPOSITION
Verse 1. Blessed is he that considereth the poor. This is the third Psalm opening with a benediction, and there is a growth in it beyond the first two. To search the word of God comes first, pardoned sin is second, and now the forgiven sinner brings forth fruit unto God available for the good of others.
Verse 2. The Lord will preserve him, and keep him alive. His noblest life shall be immortal, and even his mortal life shall be sacredly guarded by the power of Jehovah. Jesus lived on till his hour came, nor could the devices of crafty Herod take away his life till the destined hour had struck; and even then no man took his life from him, but he laid it down of himself, to take it again.
Verse 3. The Lord will strengthen him upon the bed of languishing. The everlasting arms shall stay up his soul as friendly hands and downy pillows stay up the body of the sick. How tender and sympathizing is this image; how near it brings our God to our infirmities and sicknesses! Whoever heard this of the old heathen Jove, or of the gods of India or China? This is language peculiar to the God of Israel; he it is who deigns to become nurse and attendant upon good men.
Verses 4-9. Here we have a controversy between the pleader and his God. He has been a tender friend to the poor, and yet in the hour of his need the promised assistance was not forthcoming. In our Lord's case there was a dark and dreary night in which such arguments were well befitting himself and his condition.
Verse 4. I said—said it in earnest prayer—Lord, be merciful unto me. Prove now thy gracious dealings with my soul in adversity, since thou didst aforetime give me grace to act liberally in my prosperity. No appeal is made to justice; the petitioner but hints at the promised reward, but goes straightforward to lay his plea at the feet of mercy. How low was our Redeemer brought when such petitions could come from his reverend mouth, when his lips like lilies dropped such sweet smelling but bitter myrrh!
Verse 5. Mine enemies speak evil of me. It was their nature to do and speak evil; it was not possible that the child of God could escape them. The viper fastened on Paul's hand: the better the man the more likely, and the more

JOHN CALVIN

Psalm 41

1-3
1. Blessed is he that judgeth wisely of the poor. Interpreters are generally of opinion that the exercise of kindness and compassion manifested in taking care of the miserable, and helping them, is here commended. Those, however, who maintain that the Psalmist here commends the considerate candor of those who judge wisely and charitably of men in adversity, form a better judgment of his meaning.
2. Jehovah will keep him, and preserve him in life. Here David follows out the same sentiment expressed in the preceding verse, when he says that the Lord will keep the afflicted, whose destruction cruel and unjust men represent as inevitable. It is likewise necessary always to bear in mind the contrast which is stated between the day of evil and the blessing of deliverance. In this verse the expressions denoting restoration to life, and blessedness on the earth, are of similar import.

4-6
4. I have said, O Jehovah! have mercy upon me. By this verse he shows that in his adversity he did not seek to soothe his mind by flattery, as the greater part of men do, who endeavor to assuage their sorrows by some vain consolation. And, certainly, the man who is guided by the Spirit of God will, when warned of God by the afflictions with which he is visited, frankly acknowledge his sins, and quietly submit to the admonitions of his brethren, nay, he will even anticipate them by a voluntary confession.
5. My enemies have spoken evil of me. To speak is here used in the sense of to imprecate. In thus describing the unbecoming conduct of his enemies, he seeks, as has been elsewhere said, to induce God to have mercy upon him: because the more that God sees his own people cruelly treated, he is so much the more disposed mercifully to succor them.
6. And if he come to see me, he speaketh lies. What is contained in this verse relates to his false and treacherous friends. Those who were his professed enemies made no secret of their enmity against him, but openly persecuted him; and that he has already shown in the preceding verse.

7-9
7. All they that hate me whisper together against me. Here he seems generally to include both classes of his enemies; those who sought to oppress him in an open manner, and in the character of avowed enemies; and those who, under the pretense of friendship, attempted to do the same thing by deceit and stratagem.
8. An evil deed of Belial cleaved fast to him. From this verse it appears that they had thus conspired together for his destruction, on the ground that they regarded him as a wicked man, and a person worthy of a thousand deaths. The insolence and arrogance which they manifested towards him proceeded from the false and wicked judgment which they had formed concerning him, and of which he made mention in the beginning of the psalm.

MATTHEW HENRY

Psalm 41

1-4 Promises to those who consider the poor.
In these verses we have,
I. God's promises of succor and comfort to those that consider the poor; and, we may suppose that David makes mention of these with application either,

1. To his friends, who were kind to him, and very considerate of his case, now that he was in affliction: Blessed is he that considers poor David. Here and there he met with one that sympathized with him, and was concerned for him. The provocations which his enemies gave him did but endear his friends so much the more to him. Or,

2. To himself. He had the testimony of his conscience for him that he had considered the poor, that when he was in honor and power at court he had taken cognizance of the wants and miseries of the poor and had provided for their relief, and therefore was sure God would, according to his promise, strengthen and comfort him in his sickness.
II. David's prayer, directed and encouraged by these promises (v. 4): I said, Heal my soul. It is good for us to keep some account of our prayers, that we may not unsay, in our practices, any thing that we said in our prayers.

5-13 David complains of his enemies; David's comfort in God.
David often complains of the insolent conduct of his enemies towards him when he was sick, which, as it was very barbarous in them, so it could not but be very grievous to him. They had not indeed arrived at that modern pitch of wickedness of poisoning his meat and drink, or giving him something to make him sick; but, when he was sick, they insulted over him (v. 5): My enemies speak evil of me, designing thereby to grieve his spirit, to ruin his reputation, and so to sink his interest. Let us enquire,
I. What was the conduct of his enemies towards him.
1. They longed for his death: When shall he die, and his name perish with him? He had but an uncomfortable life, and yet they grudged him that.
2. They picked up every thing they could to reproach him with (v. 6): "If he come to see me" (as it has always been reckoned a piece of neighborly kindness to visit the sick) "he speaks vanity; that is, he pretends friendship, and that his errand is to mourn with me and to comfort me; he tells me he is very sorry to see me so much indisposed, and wishes me my health; but it is all flattery and falsehood."
3. They promised themselves that he would never recover from this sickness, nor ever wipe off the odium with which they had loaded him. They whispered together against him (v. 7), speaking that secretly in one another's ears which they could not for shame speak out, and which, if they did, they knew would be confuted. Whisperers and backbiters are put together among the worst of sinners, Rom. i. 29, 30.

Psalm 41

8-13

8 An evil disease, say they, cleaveth fast unto him: and now that he lieth he shall rise up no more.

9 Yea, mine own familiar friend, in whom I trusted, which did eat of my bread, hath lifted up his heel against me.

10 But thou, O LORD, be merciful unto me, and raise me up, that I may requite them.

11 By this I know that thou favorest me, because mine enemy doth not triumph over me.

12 And as for me, thou upholdest me in mine integrity, and settest me before thy face for ever.

13 Blessed be the LORD God of Israel from everlasting, and to everlasting. Amen, and Amen.

venomous the slander. Evil tongues are busy tongues, and never deal in truth. Jesus was traduced to the utmost, although no offence was in him.

Verse 6. And if he come to see me, he speaketh vanity. His visits of sympathy are visitations of mockery. When the fox calls on the sick lamb his words are soft, but he licks his lips in hope of the carcass. It is wretched work to have spies haunting one's bedchamber, calling in pretence of kindness, but with malice in their hearts.

Verse 7. All that hate me whisper together against me. The spy meets his comrades in conclave and sets them all a whispering. Why could they not speak out? Were they afraid of the sick warrior? Or were their designs so treacherous that they must needs be hatched in secrecy? Mark the unanimity of the wicked—all. How heartily the dogs unite to hunt the stag! Would God we were half as united in holy labor as persecutors in their malicious projects, and were half as wise as they are crafty, for their whispering was craft as well as cowardice, the conspiracy must not be known till all is ready.

Verse 8. An evil disease, say they, cleaveth fast unto him. They whisper that some curse has fallen upon him, and is riveted to him. They insinuate that a foul secret stains his character, the ghost whereof haunts his house, and never can be laid. An air of mystery is cast around this doubly dark saying, as if to show how indistinct are the mutterings of malice. Even thus was our Lord accounted "smitten of God and afflicted."

Verse 9. Yea. Here is the climax of the sufferer's woe, and he places before it the emphatic affirmation, as if he thought that such villainy would scarcely be believed. Mine own familiar friend. "The man of my peace," so runs the original, with whom I had no differences, with whom I was in league, who had aforetime ministered to my peace and comfort. This was Ahithophel to David, and Iscariot with our Lord. Judas was an apostle, admitted to the privacy of the Great Teacher, hearing his secret thoughts, and, as it were, allowed to read his very heart. "Et tu Brute?" said the expiring Caesar. The kiss of the traitor wounded our Lord's heart as much as the nail wounded his hand.

Verse 10. But thou, O Lord, be merciful unto me. How the hunted and affrighted soul turns to her God! How she seems to take breath with a "but, thou!" How she clings to the hope of mercy from God when every chance of pity from man is gone!

Verse 11. We are all cheered by tokens for good, and the psalmist felt it to be an auspicious omen, that after all his deep depression he was not utterly given over to his foe.

Verse 12. And as for me, despite them all and in the sight of them all, thou upholdest me in mine integrity; thy power enables me to rise above the reach of slander by living in purity and righteousness. Our innocence and consistency are the result of the divine upholding.

Verse 13. The Psalm ends with a doxology. Blessed be the Lord, i.e., let him be glorified. The blessing at the beginning from the mouth of God is returned from the mouth of his servant. We cannot add to the Lord's blessedness, but we can pour out our grateful wishes, and these he accepts, as we receive little presents of flowers from children who love us. Jehovah is the personal name of our God. God of Israel is his covenant title, and shows his special relation to his elect people. From everlasting and to everlasting. The strongest way of expressing endless duration. This last verse may serve for the prayer of the universal church in all ages, but none can sing it so sweetly as those who have experienced as David did the faithfulness of God in times of extremity.

JOHN CALVIN

9. Even the man of my peace. As the very height of all his miseries, David here declares that he had found the same treachery in some one, or, indeed, in many of his greatest friends. For the change of number is very frequent in the Hebrew language, so that he may speak of several individuals as if they were only one person. Thus the meaning would be: Not only the common people, or strangers of whom I had no knowledge or acquaintance, but my greatest friends, nay, even those with whom I was most intimate, and those of my own household, whom I admitted to eat and drink with me at my table, vaunt themselves reproachfully against me. Among the Hebrews, the expression, men of peace, denotes their kinsfolk and connections; but it was a much closer alliance, and one which ought to have secured a stricter observance of the laws of friendship, to eat the bread of David in company with himself: for it is as if he had employed the appellation, My companion.

10-13

10. Do thou, O Jehovah I have mercy upon me. From a consideration of the wrongful cruelty of his enemies, he again takes encouragement to pray. And there is included in what he says a tacit contrast between God and men; as if he had said, Since there is to be found no aid or help in the world, but as, on the contrary, a strange degree of cruelty, or secret malice, every where prevails, be thou, at least, O Lord! pleased to succor me by thy mercy.

11. By this I know that I have been acceptable to thee. David was not destitute of faith, but for the confirmation of it he took advantage of the helps which God had afterwards added to his word. In speaking thus, he seems to refer not only to the favor and good-will which God bears to all the faithful in common, but to the special favor which God had conferred upon him in choosing him to be king; as if he had said, Now, Lord, I am more and more confirmed in the belief that thou hast vouchsafed to adopt me to be the first-born among the kings of the earth. Thus he extends to the whole state of the realm the help of God, by means of which he had been delivered from some particular calamity.

12. And as for me, thou wilt uphold me in my integrity. God will never cease to manifest his favor, until he has preserved his servants in safety, even to the end. As to the form of expression, that God establishes them before his face, this is said of those whom he defends and preserves in such a manner, that he shows by evident tokens the paternal care which he exercises over them; as, on the other hand, when he seems to have forgotten his own people, he is said to hide his face from them.

13. Blessed be Jehovah, the God of Israel, for ever and ever. Here the Psalmist confirms and repeats the expression of thanksgiving contained in a preceding verse. By calling God expressly the God of Israel, he testifies that he cherished in his heart a deep and thorough impression of the covenant which God had made with the Fathers; because it was the source from which his deliverance proceeded.

MATTHEW HENRY

4. There was one particularly, in whom he had reposed a great deal of confidence, that took part with his enemies and was as abusive to him as any of them (v. 9): My own familiar friend; probably he means Ahithophel, who had been his bosom-friend and prime-minister of state, in whom he trusted as one inviolably firm to him, whose advice he relied much upon in dealing with his enemies, and who did eat of his bread, that is, with whom he had been very intimate and whom he had taken to sit at the table with him, nay, whom he had maintained and given a livelihood to, and so obliged, both in gratitude and interest, to adhere to him. Those that had their maintenance from the king's palace did not think it meet for them to see the king's dishonor (Ezra iv. 14), much less to do him dishonor. Yet this base and treacherous confidant of David's forgot all the eaten bread, and lifted up his heel against him that had lifted up his head; not only deserted him, but insulted him, kicked at him, endeavored to supplant him.

II. How did David bear this insolent ill-natured conduct of his enemies towards him?

1. He prayed to God that they might be disappointed. He said nothing to them, but turned himself to God: O Lord! be thou merciful to me, for they are unmerciful, v. 10. He had prayed in reference to the insults of his enemies, Lord, be merciful to me, for this is a prayer which will suit every case. God's mercy has in it a redress for every grievance, "They endeavor to run me down, but, Lord, do thou raise me up from this bed of languishing, from which they think I shall never arise. Raise me up that I may requite them, that I may render them good for evil" (so some), for that was David's practice, Ps. vii. 4; xxxv. 13. A good man will even wish for an opportunity of making it to appear that he bears no malice to those that have been injurious to him, but, on the contrary, that he is ready to do them any good office.

2. He assured himself that they would be disappointed (v. 11): "By this I know that thou favourest me and my interest, because my enemy doth not triumph over me." They hoped for his death, but he found himself, through mercy, recovering, and this would add to the comfort of his recovery.

3. The psalm concludes with a solemn doxology, or adoration of God as the Lord God of Israel, v. 13. It is not certain whether this verse pertains to this particular psalm (if so, it teaches us this, That a believing hope of our preservation through grace to glory is enough to fill our hearts with joy and our mouths with everlasting praise, even in our greatest straits) or whether it was added as the conclusion of the first book of Psalms, which is reckoned to end here (the like being subjoined to lxxii., lxxxix, cvi.), and then it teaches us to make God the Omega who is the Alpha, to make him the end who is the beginning of every good work.

**Book Two:
Psalms 42-72**

Psalm 42

Title
To the chief Musician, Maschil, for the sons of Korah.

1-5
1 As the hart panteth after the water brooks, so panteth my soul after thee, O God.
2 My soul thirsteth for God, for the living God: when shall I come and appear before God?
3 My tears have been my meat day and night, while they continually say unto me, Where is thy God?
4 When I remember these things, I pour out my soul in me: for I had gone with the multitude, I went with them to the house of God, with the voice of joy and praise, with a multitude that kept holyday.
5 Why art thou cast down, O my soul? and why art thou disquieted in me? hope thou in God: for I shall yet praise him for the help of his countenance.

Book Two: Psalms 42-72

Psalm 42

TITLE. To the chief Musician, Maschil, for the sons of Korah. Dedicated to the Master of Music, this Psalm is worthy of his office; he who can sing best can have nothing better to sing. It is called, Maschil, or an instructive ode; and full as it is of deep experimental expressions, it is eminently calculated to instruct those pilgrims whose road to heaven is of the same trying kind as David's was. It is always edifying to listen to the experience of a thoroughly gracious and much afflicted saint.
SUBJECT. It is the cry of a man far removed from the outward ordinances and worship of God, sighing for the long loved house of his God; and at the same time it is the voice of a spiritual believer, under depressions, longing for the renewal of the divine presence, struggling with doubts and fears, but yet holding his ground by faith in the living God. Most of the Lord's family have sailed on the sea which is here so graphically described. It is probable that David's flight from Absalom may have been the occasion for composing this Maschil.
DIVISION. The structure of the song directs us to consider it in two parts which end with the same refrain; Ps 42:1-5 and then Ps 42:6-11.
EXPOSITION
Verse 1. As the hart panteth after the water brooks, so panteth my soul after the, O God. As after a long drought the poor fainting hind longs for the streams, or rather as the hunted hart instinctively seeks after the river to lave its smoking flanks and to escape the dogs, even so my weary, persecuted soul pants after the Lord my God. Debarred from public worship, David was heartsick. Ease he did not seek, honor he did not covet, but the enjoyment of communion with God was an urgent need of his soul; he viewed it not merely as the sweetest of all luxuries, but as an absolute necessity, like water to a stag. Like the parched traveler in the wilderness, whose skin bottle is empty, and who finds the wells dry, he must drink or die—he must have his God or faint.
Verse 2. My soul. All my nature, my inmost self. Thirsteth. Which is more than hungering; hunger you can palliate, but thirst is awful, insatiable, clamorous, deadly. O to have the most intense craving after the highest good! this is no questionable mark of grace. For God. Not merely for the temple and the ordinances, but for fellowship with God himself. None but spiritual men can sympathies with this thirst. For the living God. Because he lives, and gives to men the living water; therefore we, with greater eagerness, desire him. A dead God is a mere mockery; we loathe such a monstrous deity; but the ever living God, the perennial fountain of life and light and love, is our soul's desire.
Verse 3. My tears have been my meat day and night. Salt meats, but healthful to the soul. When a man comes to tears, constant tears, plenteous tears, tears that fill his cup and trencher, he is in earnest indeed. As the big tears stand in the stag's eyes in her distress, so did the salt drops glitter in the eyes of David. His appetite was gone, his tears not only seasoned his meat, but became his only meat, he had no mind for other diet. Perhaps it was well for him that the heart could open the safety valves; there is a dry grief far more terrible than showery sorrows.
Verse 4. When I remember these things, I pour out my soul in me. When he harped upon his woes his heart melted into water and was poured out upon itself. God hidden, and foes raging, a pair of evils enough to bring down the stoutest heart! Yet why let reflections so gloomy engross us, since the result is of no value: merely to turn the soul on itself, to empty it from itself into itself is useless, how much better to pour out the heart before the Lord! The prisoner's tread wheel might sooner land him in the skies than mere inward questioning raise us nearer to consolation.

JOHN CALVIN

Book Two: Psalms 42-72

Psalm 42

In the first place, David shows that when he was forced to flee by reason of the cruelty of Saul, and was living in a state of exile, what most of all grieved him was, that he was deprived of the opportunity of access to the sanctuary; for he preferred the service of God to every earthly advantage. In the second place, he shows that being tempted with despair, he had in this respect a very difficult contest to sustain. In order to strengthen his hope, he also introduces prayer and meditation on the grace of God. Last of all, he again makes mention of the inward conflict which he had with the sorrow which he experienced.

1-3
1, 2. As the hart crieth for the fountains of water, etc. The meaning of these two verses simply is, that David preferred to all the enjoyments, riches, pleasures, and honors of this world, the opportunity of access to the sanctuary, that in this way he might cherish and strengthen his faith and piety by the exercises prescribed in the Law.
When he says that he cried for the living God, we are not to understand it merely in the sense of a burning love and desire towards God: but we ought to remember in what manner it is that, God allures us to himself, and by what means he raises our minds upwards. He does not enjoin us to ascend forthwith into heaven, but, consulting our weakness, he descends to us.
3. My tears have been my bread. Here the Psalmist mentions another sharp piercing shaft with which the wicked and malevolent grievously wounded his heart. There can be no doubt that Satan made use of such means as these to fan the flame that consumed him with grief. "What," we may suppose that adversary to say, "wouldst thou have? Seest thou not that God hath cast thee off? For certainly he desires to be worshipped in the tabernacle, to which you have now no opportunity of access, and from which you are as it were banished." These were violent assaults, and enough to have overturned the faith of this holy man, unless, supported by the power of the Spirit in a more than ordinary degree, he had made a strong and vigorous resistance. It is evident that his feelings had been really and strongly affected.

4-6
4. When I remember these things. This verse is somewhat obscure, on account of the variation of the tenses in the Hebrew. And yet I have no doubt that the true and natural sense is, that David, when he called to remembrance his former condition, experienced so much the greater sadness by comparing it with his present condition. The remembrance, I say, of the past had no small influence in aggravating his misery, from the thought that he, who had formerly acted the part of a leader and standard-bearer in conducting others to the holy assemblies, should now be debarred from access to the temple.

MATTHEW HENRY

Book Two: Psalms 42-72

Psalm 42

1-5 Desiring communion with God; mourning for the loss of public ordinances.
Here is,
I. Holy love thirsting, love upon the wing, soaring upwards in holy desires towards the Lord and towards the remembrance of his name (v. 1, 2): "My soul panteth, thirsteth, for God, for nothing more than God, but still for more and more of him." Now observe,
1. When it was that David thus expressed his vehement desire towards God. It was,
(1.) When he was debarred from his outward opportunities of waiting on God, when he was banished to the land of Jordan, a great way off from the courts of God's house.
(2.) When he was deprived, in a great measure, of the inward comfort he used to have in God. He now went mourning, but he went on panting.
2. What is the object of his desire and what it is he thus thirsts after. He pants after God, he thirsts for God, not the ordinances themselves, but the God of the ordinances. A gracious soul can take little satisfaction in God's courts if it do not meet with God himself there: "O that I knew where I might find him! that I might have more of the tokens of his favor, the graces and comforts of his Spirit, and the earnests of his glory."
II. Holy love mourning for God's present withdrawings and the want of the benefit of solemn ordinances (v. 3): "My tears have been my meat day and night during this forced absence from God's house." His circumstances were sorrowful, and he accommodated himself to them, received the impressions and returned the signs of sorrow. Even the royal prophet was a weeping prophet when he wanted the comforts of God's house.
Two things aggravated his grief:
1. The reproaches with which his enemies teased him: They continually say unto me, Where is thy God? This was because he was absent from the ark, the token of God's presence. Judging of the God of Israel by the gods of the heathen, they concluded he had lost his God.
2. The remembrance of his former liberties and enjoyments, v. 4. Son, remember thy good things, is a great aggravation of evil things, so much do our powers of reflection and anticipation add to the grievance of this present time. David remembered the days of old, and then his soul was poured out in him; he melted away, and the thought almost broke his heart. He poured out his soul within him in sorrow, and then poured out his soul before God in prayer.
III. Holy love hoping (v. 5): Why art thou cast down, O my soul? His sorrow was upon a very good account, and yet it must not exceed its due limits, nor prevail to

Psalm 42

6-11

6 O my God, my soul is cast down within me: therefore will I remember thee from the land of Jordan, and of the Hermonites, from the hill Mizar.
7 Deep calleth unto deep at the noise of thy waterspouts: all thy waves and thy billows are gone over me.
8 Yet the LORD will command his loving kindness in the day time, and in the night his song shall be with me, and my prayer unto the God of my life.
9 I will say unto God my rock, Why hast thou forgotten me? why go I mourning because of the oppression of the enemy?
10 As with a sword in my bones, mine enemies reproach me; while they say daily unto me, Where is thy God?
11 Why art thou cast down, O my soul? and why art thou disquieted within me? hope thou in God: for I shall yet praise him, who is the health of my countenance, and my God.

Verse 5. Why art thou cast down, O my soul? As though he were two men, the psalmist talks to himself. His faith reasons with his fears, his hope argues with his sorrows. These present troubles, are they to last forever? The rejoicings of my foes, are they more than empty talk? My absence from the solemn feasts, is that a perpetual exile? Why this deep depression, this faithless fainting, this chicken hearted melancholy? As Trapp says, "David chides David out of the dumps;" and herein he is an example for all desponding ones. To search out the cause of our sorrow is often the best surgery for grief. Self ignorance is not bliss; in this case it is misery.
Verse 6. O my God, my soul is cast down within me. Here the song begins again upon the bass. So sweet an ending deserves that for the sake of a second hopeful close the Psalm should even begin again. Perhaps the psalmist's dejection continued, the spasm of despondency returned; well, then, he will down with his harp again, and try again its power upon himself, as in his younger days, he saw its influence upon Saul when the evil spirit came upon him. With God the song begins a second time more nearly than at first. The singer was also a little more tranquil. Outward expression of desire was gone; there was no visible panting; the sorrow was not all restrained within doors.
Verse 7. Deep calleth unto deep at the noise of thy waterspouts. Thy severe dealings with me seem to excite all creation to attack me; heaven, and earth, and hell, call to each other, stirring each other up in dreadful conspiracy against my peace. As in a waterspout, the deeps above and below clasp hands, so it seemed to David that heaven and earth united to create a tempest around him. His woes were incessant and overwhelming.
Verse 8. Yet the Lord will command his lovingkindness in the daytime. Come what may there shall be "a certain secret something" to sweeten all. Lovingkindness is a noble life belt in a rough sea. The day may darken into a strange and untimely midnight, but the love of God ordained of old to be the portion of the elect, shall be by sovereign decree meted out to them.
Verse 9. I will say unto God my rock, Why hast thou forgotten me? Faith is allowed to enquire of her God the causes of his displeasure, and she is even permitted to expostulate with him and put him in mind of his promises, and ask why apparently they are not fulfilled.
Verse 10. As with a sword in my bones, mine enemies reproach me. Cruel mockeries cut deeper than the flesh, they reach the soul as though a rapier were introduced between the ribs to prick the heart. If reproaches kill not, yet they are killing, the pain caused is excruciating. The tongue cuts to the bone, and its wounds are hard to cure. While they say daily unto me, Where is thy God? This is the most unkind cut of all, reflecting as it does both upon the Lord's faithfulness and his servant's character.
Verse 11. Why art thou cast down, O my soul? and why art thou disquieted within me? In the rehearsal of his sorrow, he finds after all no sufficient ground for being disquieted. Looked in the face, his fears were not so overwhelming as they seemed when shrouded in obscurity. Hope thou in God. Let the anchor still keep its hold. God is faithful, God is love, therefore there is room and reason for hope. Who is the health of my countenance, and my God. This is the same hopeful expression as that contained in verse five, but the addition of and my God shows that the writer was growing in confidence, and was able defiantly to reply to the question, "Where is thy God?" Here, even here, he is, ready to deliver me. I am not ashamed to own him amid your sneers and taunts, for he will rescue me out of your hands.

JOHN CALVIN

5. O my soul! why art thou cast down? From this it appears that David contended strongly against his sorrow, lest he should yield to temptation: but what we ought chiefly to observe is, that he had experienced a strong and bitter contest before he obtained the victory over it; or we might rather say, that he was not delivered from it after one alarming assault, but was often called upon to enter into new scenes of conflict.
6. O my God! my soul is cast down within me. The import of the whole verse will is this, I am now living in a state of exile, banished from the temple, and seem to be an alien from the household of God; but this will not prevent me from regarding him, and having recourse to him. I am now deprived of the accustomed sacrifices, of which I stand much in need, but he has not taken from me his word.

7-8
7. Depth calleth unto depth. These words express the grievousness, as well as the number and long continuance, of the miseries which he suffered; as if he had said, I am oppressed not only with one kind of misery, but various kinds of distress return one after another, so that there seems to be neither end nor measure to them.
8. Jehovah will command his loving-kindness by day. The argument of David is to this effect: Why should I not expect that God will be merciful to me, so that in the day-time his loving-kindness may be manifested towards me, and by night upon my bed a song of joy be with me? He, no doubt, places this ground of comfort in opposition to the sorrow which he might well apprehend from the dreadful tokens of the divine displeasure, which he has enumerated in the preceding verse.

9-11
9. I will say to God my rock. The meaning here is: Since I expect that God will be favorable to me, inasmuch as by day he manifests his favor towards me, and continues to do this, so that even by night I have occasion to praise him, I will bewail the more frankly my miseries before him, saying, O Lord! my rock, why hast thou forgotten me? In making such a complaint, the faithful are not to be understood as meaning that God has utterly rejected them: for if they did not believe that they were under his care and protection, it were in vain for them to call upon him. But they speak in this manner according to the sense of the flesh.
10. It is as a slaughter in my bones. David here affirms that the grief which he experienced from the reproaches of his enemies, wounded him in no degree less than if they had pierced through his bones.
11. O my soul! why art thou cast down? This repetition shows us that David had not so completely overcome his temptations in one encounter, or by one extraordinary effort, as to render it unnecessary for him to enter anew into the same conflict. By this example, therefore, we are admonished, that although Satan, by his assaults, often subjects us to a renewal of the same trouble, we ought not to lose our courage, or allow ourselves to be cast down.

MATTHEW HENRY

depress his spirits; he therefore communes with his own heart, for his relief. "Come, my soul, I have something to say to thee in thy heaviness." Let us consider,
1. The cause of it. "Thou art cast down, as one stooping and sinking under a burden, Prov. xii. 25. Thou art disquieted, in confusion and disorder; now why are thou so?" Our disquietudes would in many cases vanish before a strict scrutiny into the grounds and reasons of them.
2. The cure of it: Hope thou in God, for I shall yet praise him. A believing confidence in God is a sovereign antidote against prevailing despondency and disquietude of spirit.

6-11 Complaints and consolations.
Complaints and comforts here, as before, take their turn, like day and night in the course of nature.
I. He complains of the dejections of his spirit, but comforts himself with the thoughts of God, v. 6.
1. In his troubles. His soul was dejected, and he goes to God and tells him so: O my God! my soul is cast down within me.
2. In his devotions. His soul was elevated, and, finding the disease very painful, he had recourse to that as a sovereign remedy. "My soul is plunged; therefore, to prevent its sinking, I will remember thee, meditate upon thee, and call upon thee, and try what that will do to keep up my spirit."
II. He complains of the tokens of God's displeasure against him, but comforts himself with the hopes of the return of his favor in due time.
1. He saw his troubles coming from God's wrath, and that discouraged him (v. 7): "Deep calls unto deep, one affliction comes upon the neck of another, as if it were called to hasten after it; and thy water-spouts give the signal and sound the alarm of war."
2. He expected his deliverance to come from God's favor (v. 8): Yet the Lord will command his lovingkindness. Things are bad, but they shall not always be so. Though affairs are now in an evil plight, they may not always be so.
III. He complains of the insolence of his enemies, and yet comforts himself in God as his friend, v. 9-11.
1. His complaint is that his enemies oppressed him, and this made a great impression upon him.
2. His comfort is that God is his rock (v. 9)—a rock to build upon, a rock to take shelter in. He repeats what he had before said (v. 5), and concludes with it (v. 11): Why art thou cast down, O my soul? His griefs and fears were clamorous and troublesome; they were not silenced though they were again and again answered. But, at length, his faith forced the enemies to quit the field. And he gains this victory,
(1.) By repeating what he had before said.
(2.) By adding one word to it. He adds, and my God, "related to me, in covenant with me; all that he is, all that he has, is mine, according to the true intent and meaning of the promise."

Psalm 43

1 Judge me, O God, and plead my cause against an ungodly nation: O deliver me from the deceitful and unjust man.
2 For thou art the God of my strength: why dost thou cast me off? why go I mourning because of the oppression of the enemy?
3 O send out thy light and thy truth: let them lead me; let them bring me unto thy holy hill, and to thy tabernacles.
4 Then will I go unto the altar of God, unto God my exceeding joy: yea, upon the harp will I praise thee, O God my God.
5 Why art thou cast down, O my soul? and why art thou disquieted within me? hope in God: for I shall yet praise him, who is the health of my countenance, and my God.

Psalm 43

TITLE. On account of the similarity of the structure of this Psalm to that of Psalm forty-two, it has been supposed to be a fragment wrongly separated from the preceding song; but it is always dangerous to allow these theories of error in Holy Scripture, and in this instance it would be very difficult to show just cause for such an admission.

As an appendix it needed no title. David complains of his enemies, and asks the privilege of communion with God as his surest deliverance from them.

DIVISION. The psalmist cried to God in prayer, Ps 43:1-3. Promises praise in the anticipation of an answer, Ps 43:4, and chides himself for his despondency, Ps 43:5.

EXPOSITION

Verse 1. Judge me, O God. Others are unable to understand my motives, and unwilling to give me a just verdict. My heart is clear as to intent and therefore I bring my case before thee, content that thou wilt impartially weigh my character, and right my wrongs. If thou wilt judge, thy acceptance of my conduct will be enough for me; I can laugh at human misrepresentation if my conscience knows that thou art on my side; thou art the only one I care for; and besides, thy verdict will not sleep, but thou wilt see practical justice done to thy slandered servant.

Verse 2. For. Here is argument, which is the very sinew of prayer. If we reasoned more with the Lord we should have more victories in supplication. Thou art the God of my strength. All my strength belongs to thee—I will not, therefore, use it on my own behalf against my personal foes. All my strength comes from thee, I therefore seek help from thee, who art able to bestow it.

Verse 3. O send out thy light and thy truth. The joy of thy presence and the faithfulness of thy heart; let both of these be manifest to me. Reveal my true character by thy light, and reward me according to thy truthful promise. As the sun darts forth his beams, so does the Lord send forth his favor and his faithfulness towards all his people; and as all nature rejoices in the sunshine, even so the saints triumph in the manifestation of the love and fidelity of their God, which, like the golden sunbeam, lights up even the darkest surroundings with delightful splendor.

Verse 4. Then will I go unto the altar of God. If David might but be favored with such a deliverance as would permit his return, it would not be his own house or heritage which would be his first resort, but to the altar of God his willing feet should conduct him. His whole heart would go as sacrifice to the altar, he himself counting it his greatest happiness to be permitted to lie as a burnt offering wholly dedicated to the Lord. With what exultation should believers draw near unto Christ, who is the antitype of the altar! clearer light should give greater intensity of desire. Unto God my exceeding joy. It was not the altar as such that the psalmist cared for, he was no believer in the heathenism of ritualism: his soul desired spiritual fellowship, fellowship with God himself in very deed. What are all the rites of worship unless the Lord be in them; what, indeed, but empty shells and dry husks?

Verse 5. Why art thou cast down, O my soul? If God be thine, why this dejection? If he uplifts thee, why art thou so near the ground? The dew of love is falling, O withering heart, revive. And why art thou disquieted within me? What cause is there to break the repose of thy heart? Wherefore indulge unreasonable sorrows, which benefit no one, fret thyself, and dishonor thy God? Why overburden thyself with forebodings? Hope in God, or wait for God. There is need of patience, but there is ground for hope.

Psalm 43

This psalm is very similar to the preceding one. David, who probably was the author of it, being chased and driven out of his country by the unjust violence and tyranny of his enemies, calls upon God for vengeance, and encourages himself to hope for restoration.

1-5

1. Judge me, O God! David, in the first place, complains of the extreme cruelty of his enemies; but in the verses which immediately follow, he shows that there was nothing which he felt to be more grievous, than to be deprived of the opportunity of access to the sanctuary. We have an evidence of his enjoying the testimony of a good conscience in this, that he commends the defense of his cause to God.

2. For thou art the God of my strength. This verse differs very little from the ninth verse of the preceding psalm, and the difference consists more in words than in matter. Setting as a shield against temptation the fact, that he had experienced the power of God to be present with him, he complains that his life is spent in mourning, because he sees himself as it were abandoned to the will of his enemies.

3. The term light is to be understood as denoting favor; for as adversities not only obscure the face of God, but also overcast the heavens, as it were, with clouds and fogs, so also, when we enjoy the divine blessing which makes rich, it is like the cheerful light of a serene day shining around us; or rather the light of life, dispelling all that thick obscurity which overwhelmed us in sorrow. By this word the Psalmist intimates two things; first, that all our miseries arise from no other source than this, that God withdraws from us the tokens of his paternal love; and, secondly, that as soon as he is pleased to manifest towards us his serene and gracious countenance, deliverance and salvation also arise to us. He adds truth, because he expected this light only from the promises of God.

4. And I will go to the altar of God. Here he promises to God a solemn sacrifice, in commemoration of the deliverance which he should obtain from him; for he speaks not only of the daily or ordinary service, but in making mention of the altar on which it was customary to offer the peace-offerings, he expresses the token of gratitude and thanksgiving of which I have spoken. For this reason, also, he calls God the God of his joy, because, being delivered from sorrow, and restored to a state of joy, he resolves to acknowledge openly so great a benefit. And he calls him the joy of his rejoicing, that he may the more illustriously set forth the grace of his deliverance. The second word in the genitive is added by way of an epithet, and by it he signifies that his heart had been filled with joy of no common kind, when God restored him, contrary to the expectation of all.

Psalm 43

1-5 Appeals and petitions.

David here makes application to God, by faith and prayer, as his judge, his strength, his guide, his joy, his hope, with suitable affections and expressions.

I. As his Judge, his righteous Judge, who he knew would judge him, and who (being conscious of his own integrity) he knew would judge for him (v. 1): Judge me, O God! and plead my cause. There were those that impeached him; against them he is defendant, and from their courts, where he stood unjustly convicted and condemned, he appeals to the court of heaven, the supreme judicature, praying to have their judgment given against him reversed and his innocency cleared. There were those that had injured him; against them he is plaintiff, and exhibits his complaint to him who is the avenger of wrong, praying for justice for himself and upon them.

II. As his strength, his all-sufficient strength; so he eyes God (v. 2): "Thou art the God of my strength, my God, my strength, from whom all my strength is derived, in whom I strengthen myself, who hast often strengthened me, and without whom I am weak as water and utterly unable either to do or suffer any thing for thee." David now went mourning, destitute of spiritual joys, yet he found God to be the God of his strength. If we cannot comfort ourselves in God, we may stay ourselves upon him, and may have spiritual supports when we want spiritual delights.

III. As his guide, his faithful guide (v. 3): Lead me, bring me to thy holy hill. He prays that God by his providence would bring him back from his banishment, and open a way for him again to the free enjoyment of the privileges of God's sanctuary. His heart is upon the holy hill and the tabernacles, not upon his family-comforts, his court-preferments, or his diversions; he could bear the want of these, but he is impatient to see God's tabernacles again; nothing so amiable in his eyes as those; thither he would gladly be brought back.

IV. As his joy, his exceeding joy. If God guide him to his tabernacles, if he restore him to his former liberties, he knows very well what he has to do: Then will I go unto the altar of God, v. 4. He will get as near as he can unto God, his exceeding joy.

V. As his hope, his never-failing hope, v. 5. Here, as before, David quarrels with himself for his dejections and despondencies, and owns he did ill to yield to them, and that he had no reason to do so: Why art thou cast down, O my soul? He then quiets himself in the believing expectation he had of giving glory to God (Hope in God, for I shall yet praise him) and of enjoying glory with God: He is the health of my countenance and my God. That is what we cannot too much insist upon, for it is what we must live and die by.

Psalm 44

Title
To the Chief Musician for the sons of Korah, Maschil.

1-6
1 We have heard with our ears, O God, our fathers have told us, what work thou didst in their days, in the times of old.
2 How thou didst drive out the heathen with thy hand, and plantedst them; how thou didst afflict the people, and cast them out.
3 For they got not the land in possession by their own sword, neither did their own arm save them: but thy right hand, and thine arm, and the light of thy countenance, because thou hadst a favor unto them.
4 Thou art my King, O God: command deliverances for Jacob.
5 Through thee will we push down our enemies: through thy name will we tread them under that rise up against us.
6 For I will not trust in my bow, neither shall my sword save me.

Psalm 44

TITLE. To the Chief Musician for the sons of Korah, Maschil. The title is similar to the forty-second, and although this is no proof that it is by the same author it makes it highly probable. No other writer should be sought for to father any of the Psalms when David will suffice, and therefore we are loathe to ascribe this sacred song to any but the great psalmist, yet as we hardly know any period of his life which it would fairly describe, we feel compelled to look elsewhere. Some Israelitish patriot fallen on evil times, sings in mingled faith and sorrow, his country's ancient glory and her present griefs, her traditions of former favor and her experience of pressing ills. By Christians it can best be understood if put into the mouth of the church when persecution is peculiarly severe. The last verses remind us of Milton's famous lines on the massacre of the Protestants among the mountains of Piedmont. The song before us is fitted for the voices of the saved by grace, the sons of Korah, and is to them and to all others full of teaching, hence the title Maschil.
DIVISION. From Ps 44:1-3, the Lord's mighty works for Israel are rehearsed, and in remembrance of them faith in the Lord is expressed Ps 44:4-8. Then the notes of complaint are heard Ps 44:9-16, the fidelity of the people to their God is aroused, Ps 44:17-22, and the Lord is entreated to interpose, Ps 44:23-26.

EXPOSITION
Verse 1. We have heard with our ears, O God. Thy mighty acts have been the subjects of common conversation; not alone in books have we read thy famous deeds, but in the ordinary talk of the people we have heard of them. Among the godly Israelites the biography of their nation was preserved by oral tradition, with great diligence and accuracy. This mode of preserving and transmitting history has its disadvantages, but it certainly produces a more vivid impression on the mind than any other; to hear with the ears affects us more sensitively than to read with the eyes; we ought to note this, and seize every possible opportunity of telling abroad the gospel of our Lord Jesus viva voce, since this is the most telling mode of communication.
Verse 2. How thou didst drive out the heathen with thy hand. The destruction of the Canaanites from the promised land is the work here brought to remembrance. A people numerous, warlike, gigantic and courageous, firmly established and strongly fortified, were driven out by a far feebler nation, because the Lord was against them in the fight. It is clear from Scripture that God sent a plague (so that the land ate up the inhabitants thereof), and also a visitation of hornets against the Canaanites, and by other means dispirited them, so that the easy victories of Joshua were but the results of God's having worked beforehand against the idolatrous nation.
Verse 3. For they got not the land in possession by their own sword. Behold how the Lord alone was exalted in bringing his people to the land which floweth with milk and honey! He, in his distinguishing grace, had put a difference between Canaan and Israel, and therefore, by his own effectual power, he wrought for his chosen and against their adversaries.
Verse 4. Thou art my King, O God. Knowing right well thy power and grace my heart is glad to own thee for her sovereign prince. Who among the mighty are so illustrious as thou art? To whom, then, should I yield my homage or turn for aid? God of my fathers in the olden time, thou art my soul's monarch and liege Lord. Command deliverances for Jacob. To whom should a people look but to their king? he it is who, by virtue of his office, fights their battles for them. In the case of our King, how easy it is for him to scatter all our foes! O Lord, the King of kings, with what ease canst thou rescue thy people; a word of thine can do it, give but the command and thy persecuted people shall be free.

JOHN CALVIN

Psalm 44

1-3
1. O God! we have heard with our ears. The people of God here recount the goodness which he had formerly manifested towards their fathers, that, by showing the great dissimilarity of their own condition, they may induce God to alleviate their miseries. They begin by declaring that they speak not of things unknown or doubtful, but that they related events, the truth of which was authenticated by unexceptionable witnesses.
2. Thou hast expelled the heathen with thy hand. This is an illustration of the preceding verse: for the inspired writer had not yet expressly referred to that work of God, the fame of which had been preserved by their fathers.
3. For they got not possession of the land by their own sword. Here the sacred writer confirms by contrast what he has just said; for if they obtained not possession of the land by their own power and skill, it follows that they were planted in it by the hand of another.

4-8
4. Thou, even thou, art my King, O God! In this verse the faithful express that the goodness of God was not only apparent in the deliverance of his people, but also flowed upon them in continued succession from age to age; and therefore it is said, Thou, even thou, art my King.
5. Through thee we have pushed, or smitten, with the horn our adversaries. The prophet here declares in what respect God had manifested himself to be the King of this people. He did so by investing them with such strength and power, that all their enemies stood in fear of them. The similitude, taken from bulls, which he here uses, tends to show, that they had been endued with more than human strength, by which they were enabled to assail, overturn, and trample under foot, every thing which opposed them.
7. They again declare that they were saved by the power of God, and that he also had chased away and put to shame their enemies.
8. In God we will boast all the day. This is the conclusion of the first part of the psalm. To express the meaning in a few words, they acknowledge, that in all ages the goodness of God had been so great towards the children of Abraham, that it furnished them with continual matter of thanksgiving. As if the thing were still present to their view, they acknowledge that, without ceasing, they ought to give praise to God, because they had flourished and triumphed, not merely for one age, or a short period of time, but because they had continued to do so successively from age to age, for whatever prosperity had befallen them, they ascribe it to the grace of God.

9-14
9. Nevertheless thou hast abhorred us. Here follows a complaint, in which they bewail their present miseries and extreme calamity. There is here described such a change as

MATTHEW HENRY

Psalm 44

1-7 Grateful acknowledgment of past mercies; consecration to God.
Observe,
I. Their commemoration of the great things God had formerly done for them.

1. In general (v. 1): Our fathers have told us what work thou didst in their days. Observe,
(1.) The many operations of providence are here spoken of as one work—"They have told us the work which thou didst;" for there is a wonderful harmony and uniformity in all that God does, and the many wheels make but one wheel (Ezek. x. 13), many works make but one work.
(2.) It is a debt which every age owes to posterity to keep an account of God's works of wonder, and to transmit the knowledge of them to the next generation.
(3.) We must not only make mention of the work God has done in our own days, but must also acquaint ourselves and our children with what he did in the times of old, long before our own days; and of this we have in the scripture a sure word of history, as sure as the word of prophecy.
(4.) Children must diligently attend to what their parents tell them of the wonderful works of God, and keep it in remembrance, as that which will be of great use to them.
(5.) Former experiences of God's power and goodness are strong supports to faith and powerful pleas in prayer under present calamities. See how Gideon insists upon it (Judg. vi. 13): Where are all his miracles which our fathers told us of?

2. In particular, their fathers had told them,
(1.) How wonderfully God planted Israel in Canaan at first, v. 2, 3. He drove out the natives, to make room for Israel, afflicted them, and cast them out, gave them as dust to Israel's sword and as driven stubble to their bow. The many complete victories which Israel obtained over the Canaanites, under the command of Joshua, were not to be attributed to themselves, nor could they challenge the glory of them.
(2.) How frequently he had given them success against their enemies that attempted to disturb them in the possession of that good land (v. 7): Thou hast, many a time, saved us from our enemies, and hast put to flight, and so put to shame, those that hated us, witness the successes of the judges against the nations that oppressed Israel. Many a time have the persecutors of the Christian church, and those that hate it, been put to shame by the power of truth, Acts vi. 10.
II. The good use they make of this record, and had formerly made of it, in consideration of the great things God had done for their fathers of old.

1. They had taken God for their sovereign Lord, had sworn allegiance to him, and put themselves

Psalm 44

7-12
7 But thou hast saved us from our enemies, and hast put them to shame that hated us.
8 In God we boast all the day long, and praise thy name for ever. Selah.
9 But thou hast cast off, and put us to shame; and goest not forth with our armies.
10 Thou makest us to turn back from the enemy: and they which hate us spoil for themselves.
11 Thou hast given us like sheep appointed for meat; and hast scattered us among the heathen.
12 Thou sellest thy people for nought, and dost not increase thy wealth by their price.

Verse 5. Through thee will we push down our enemies. The fight was very close, bows were of no avail, and swords failed to be of service, it came to daggers drawing, and hand to hand wrestling, pushing and tugging. Jacob's God was renewing in the seed of Jacob their father's wrestling. And how fared it with faith then? Could she stand foot to foot with her foe and hold her own? Yea, verily, she came forth victorious from the encounter, for she is great at a close push, and overthrows all her adversaries, the Lord being her helper.

Verse 6. For I will not trust in my bow, neither shall my sword save me. Thy people Israel, under thy guidance, shouldered out the heathen, and gained their land, not by skill of weapons or prowess of arms, but by thy power alone; therefore will we renounce for ever all reliance upon outward confidences, of which other men make such boast, and we will cast ourselves upon the omnipotence of our God. Bows having been newly introduced by king Saul, were regarded as very formidable weapons in the early history of Israel, but they are here laid aside together with the all conquering sword, in order that there may be room for faith in the living God.

Verse 7. But thou hast saved us from our enemies. In ages past all our rescues have been due to thee, O God. Never hast thou failed us. Out of every danger thou has brought us. And hast put them to shame that hated us. With the back of thy saving hand thou hast given them a cuff which has made them hide their faces; thou hast defeated them in such a manner as to make them ashamed of themselves to be overthrown by such puny adversaries as they thought the Israelites to be.

Verse 8. In God we boast all the day long. We have abundant reason for doing so while we recount his mighty acts. What blessed boasting is this! it is the only sort of boasting that is bearable. All other manna bred worms and stank except that which was laid up before the Lord, and all other boasting is loathsome save this glorying in the Lord, which is laudable and pleasing. And praise thy name for ever. Praise should be perpetual.

Verse 9. But thou hast cast off, and put us to shame. Here the patriot bard begins to contrast the past glories of the nation's history with its present sadness and distress; which he does not ascribe to the death of some human champion, or to the accidents of war, but solely and alone to the withdrawal of Israel's God. It seemed to the mourner that Jehovah had grown weary of his people and put them away in abhorrence, as men lay aside leprous garments, loathing the sight of them. To show his displeasure he had made his people to be ridiculed by the heathen, whose easy victories over their largest armies covered Israel with disgrace.

Verse 10. Thou makest us to turn back from the enemy. The humiliating consciousness that the Lord has left them soon makes men cowards. Flight closes the fight of those who have not the Lord in the van. And they which hate us spoil for themselves. After defeat and retreat, comes spoliation.

Verse 11. Thou hast given us like sheep appointed for meat. As sheep are slaughtered for food, so were the people slain in flocks, with ease, and frequency. Not with dignity of sacrifice, but with the cruelty of the shambles, were they put to death. God appeared to give them up like sheep allotted to the butcher, to abandon them as the hireling abandons the flock to wolves. The complaint is bitterly eloquent. And hast scattered us among the heathen. Many were carried into captivity, far off from the public worship of the temple of God, to pine as exiles among idolaters. All this is ascribed to the Lord, as being allowed by him, and even appointed by his decree. It is well to trace the hand of God in our sorrows, for it is surely there.

Verse 12. Thou sellest thy people for nought. As men sell merchandise to any one who cares to have it, so the Lord seemed to hand over his people to any nation who might choose to make war upon them. Meanwhile no good result was perceptible from all the miseries of Israel; so far as the psalmist could discover, the Lord's name received no honor from the showed not only that God had ceased to exercise towards them his accustomed favor, but also, that he was openly adverse and hostile to his people.

10. Thou hast made us to turn back from the enemy. Here the people of God still further complain, that he had made them to flee before their enemies, and had given them up as a prey to be devoured by them. As the saints firmly believe that men are strong and valiant only in so far as God upholds them by his secret power, they also conclude, that when men flee, and are seized with trembling, it is God who strikes them with terror, so that the poor wretched creatures are deprived of reason, and both their skill and courage fail them.

11. To the same purpose is that other comparison, in which they say that they were given as sheep for food. By this the prophet intimates, that being already vanquished previous to the battle, they fell down, as it were, upon the earth before their enemies, ready to be devoured by them, and not fit for any thing else than to gratify their insatiable cruelty.

12. Thou hast sold thy people, and not become rich. In saying that they were sold without any gain, it is meant that they were exposed to sale as slaves that are contemptible, and of no value. In the second clause, too, And hast not increased the price of them, there seems to be an allusion to the custom of exposing things to auction, and selling them to the highest bidder. We know that those slaves who were sold were not delivered to the buyers till the price of them had been increased by bidding. Thus the faithful mean, that they were cast out as being altogether worthless, so that their condition had been worse than that of any bond-slave.

13. Thou hast made us a reproach to our neighbors. Here the Psalmist speaks of their neighbors, who were all actuated either by some secret ill-will, or avowed enmity to the people of God. And certainly it often happens, that neighborhood, which ought to be the means of preserving mutual friendship, engenders all discord and strife. But there was a special reason in respect of the Jews; for they had taken possession of the country in spite of all men, and their religion being hateful to others, so to speak, served as a trumpet to stir up war, and inflamed their neighbors with rage against them.

14. They add that they were a proverb, a byword, or jest, even among the nations that were far off.

15-21

15. My reproach is daily before me. The reason is added why they were so overwhelmed with shame, that they dared not to lift up their eyes and their face, namely, because they had no respite, but were incessantly subjected to the insolence and reproach of their enemies. Had they been allowed to hide themselves in some corner, they might have endured, as well as they were able, their calamities in secret; but when their enemies openly derided them with the greatest insolence, it served to redouble the wound inflicted upon them. They, therefore, complain that their calamities had accumulated to such an extent, that they were forced unceasingly to hear blasphemies and bitter reproaches.

under his protection (v. 4): Thou art my King, O God! He speaks in the name of the church, as (Ps. lxxiv. 12), Thou art my King of old. God, as a king, has made laws for his church, provided for the peace and good order of it, judged for it, pleaded its cause, fought its battles, and protected it; it is his kingdom in the world, and ought to be subject to him, and to pay him tribute.

2. They had always applied to him by prayer for deliverance when at any time they were in distress: Command deliverances for Jacob.

3. They had trusted and triumphed in him. As they owned it was not their own sword and bow that had saved them (v. 3), so neither did they trust to their own sword or bow to save them for the future (v. 6): "I will not trust in my bow, nor in any of my military preparations, as if those would stand me in stead without God. No; through thee will we push down our enemies (v. 5); we will attempt it in thy strength."

4. They had made him their joy and praise (v. 8): "In God we have boasted; in him we do and will boast, every day, and all the day long." When their enemies boasted of their strength and successes, as Sennacherib and Rabshakeh hectored Hezekiah, they owned they had nothing to boast of, in answer thereunto, but their relation to God and their interest in him; and, if he were for them, they could set all the world at defiance.

9-16 Afflicted condition of Israel.

The people of God here complain to him of the low and afflicted condition that they were now in, under the prevailing power of their enemies and oppressors. Let us see what the complaint is.

I. That they wanted the usual tokens of God's favor to them and presence with them (v. 9): "Thou hast cast off; thou seemest to have cast us off and our cause, and to have cast off thy wonted care of us and concern for us, and so hast put us to shame, for we boasted of the constancy and perpetuity of thy favor. Our armies go forth as usual, but they are put to flight; we gain no ground, but lose what we have gained, for thou goest not forth with them, for, if thou didst, which way soever they turned they would prosper; but it is quite contrary."

II. That they were put to the worst before their enemies in the field of battle (v. 10): Thou makest us to turn back from the enemy, as Joshua complained when they met with a repulse at Ai (Josh. vii. 8): "We are dispirited, and have lost the ancient velour of Israelites; we flee, we fall, before those that used to flee and fall before us; and then those that hate us have the plunder of our camp and of our country; they spoil for themselves, and reckon all their own that they can lay their hands on. Attempts to shake off the Babylonish yoke have been ineffectual, and we have rather lost ground by them."

III. That they were doomed to the sword and to captivity (v. 11): "Thou hast given us like sheep appointed for meat. They make no more scruple of killing an Israelite

Psalm 44

13-18

13 Thou makest us a reproach to our neighbors, a scorn and a derision to them that are round about us.

14 Thou makest us a byword among the heathen, a shaking of the head among the people.

15 My confusion is continually before me, and the shame of my face hath covered me,

16 For the voice of him that reproacheth and blasphemeth; by reason of the enemy and avenger.

17 All this is come upon us; yet have we not forgotten thee, neither have we dealt falsely in thy covenant.

18 Our heart is not turned back, neither have our steps declined from thy way;

sorrows of his people; they were given away to their foes as if they were so little valued as not to be worth the ordinary price of slaves, and the Lord did not care to gain by them so long as they did but suffer. The woe expressed in this line is as vinegar mingled with gall: the expression is worthy of the weeping prophet.

Verse 13. Thou makest us a reproach to our neighbors. Scorn is always an intensely bitter ingredient in the cup of the oppressed. The taunts and jeers of the victors pain the vanquished almost as much as their swords and spears. It was a mystery indeed that God should suffer his royal nation, his peculiar people, to be taunted by all who dwelt near them.

Verse 14. Thou makest us a byword among the heathen, a shaking of the head among the people. The lamentation is here repeated. They had sunk so low that none did them reverence, but universally and publicly they were treated as infamous and despicable. Those who reviled others dragged in Israel's name by the way as a garnish to their insults, and if perchance they saw one of the seed of Jacob in the street they used lewd gestures to annoy him. Those whose heads were emptiest wagged them at the separated people.

Verse 15. My confusion is continually before me. The poet makes himself the representative of his nation, and declares his own constant distress of soul. He is a man of ill blood who is unconcerned for the sorrows of the church of which he is a member, or the nation of which he is a citizen; the better the heart the greater its sympathy.

Verse 16. For the voice of him that reproacheth and blasphemeth. It seems that from mocking the people of God, the adversaries advanced to reviling God himself, they proceeded from persecution to the sin which is next of kin, namely blasphemy.

Verse 17. All this is come upon us; yet have we not forgotten thee. Here the psalmist urges that Israel had not turned away from her allegiance to Jehovah. When in the midst of many griefs we can still cling to God in loving obedience, it must be well with us. True fidelity can endure rough usage. Those who follow God for what they get, will leave him when persecution is stirred up, but not so the sincere believer; he will not forget his God, even though the worst come to the worst. Neither have we dealt falsely in thy covenant. No idol was set up, the ordained worship was not relinquished, God was still nationally acknowledged, and therefore the psalmist is more earnest that the Lord should interpose. This and the succeeding verses are suitable for the lips of martyrs, indeed the entire psalm might be called the martyr's complaint.

Verse 18. Our heart is not turned back, neither have our steps declined from thy way. Heart and life were agreed, and both were true to the Lord's way. Neither within nor without had the godly sufferers offended; they were not absolutely perfect, but they were sincerely free from all willful transgression. It was a healthy sign for the nation that her prophet poet could testify to her uprightness before God, both in heart and act; far oftener the case would have worn quite another color, for the tribes were all too apt to set up other gods and forsake the rock of their salvation.

Verse 19. Though thou hast sore broken us in the place of dragons. Though utterly crushed and rendered desolate and driven as it were to associate with creatures such as jackals, owls, serpents, which haunt deserted ruins, yet Israel remained faithful. To be true to a smiting God, even when the blows lay our joys in ruinous heaps, is to be such as the Lord delighteth in. Better to be broken by God than from God. Better to be in the place of dragons than of deceivers. And covered us with the shadow of death. The language is very strong. The nation is described as completely enveloped in the dense darkness of despair and death, covered up as though confined in hopelessness. Yet the claim is made that they still remained mindful of their God, and a glorious plea it is. Better death than false of faith. Those who are true to God shall never find him false to them.

16. They describe their enemies by the epithet avengers, a term which, among the Hebrews, denotes barbarity and cruelty, accompanied with pride.
17. All this has come upon us, etc. As they have already attributed to God all the afflictions which they endured, if they should now say that they were undeservedly afflicted, it would be the same thing as to accuse God of injustice; and thus what is here spoken would no longer be a holy prayer, but rather an impious blasphemy. It is, however, to be observed, that the faithful, although in their adversities they do not perceive any obvious reason for being so dealt with, yet they rest assured of this, and regard it as a fixed principle, that God has some good reasons for treating them so severely.
18. The complaint which is here made amounts rather to this, That the faithful are like poor wretched creatures wandering in desert places, seeing God had withdrawn his hand from them. The expression, The paths of God, does not always refer to doctrine, but sometimes to prosperous and desirable events.
19. Although thou hast broken us in the place of dragons. The faithful repeat more largely what we have already seen, namely, that although plunged into the greatest depth of miseries, yet they continued steadfast in their resolution, and in the right way. If we consider the distressing circumstances in which they were placed, it will not appear to us a hyperbolical mode of speech, when they say that they were broken even within the depths of the sea; for by the place of dragons I understand not the deserts and solitary places, but the deepest gulfs of the sea.
20. We have not stretched out our hands to a strange god. By these words they intimate, that, contented with God alone, they did not suffer their hopes to be divided on different objects, nor gazed around them in search of other means of assistance. Hence we learn, that those whose hearts are thus divided and distracted by various expectations are forgetful of the true God, to whom we fail to yield the honor which is due to him, if we do not repose with confidence in him alone. And certainly, in the true and rightful service of God, faith and supplication which proceeds from it hold the first place: for we are guilty of depriving him of the chief part of his glory, when we seek apart from him in the least degree our own welfare. Let us then bear in mind, that it is a true test of our piety, when, being plunged into the lowest depths of disasters, we lift up our eyes, our hopes, and our prayers, to God alone.
21. Shall not God search this out? We have here a solemn and emphatic protestation, in which the people of God dare to appeal to him as the judge of their integrity and uprightness. From this it appears, that they did not plead their cause openly before men, but communed with themselves as if they had been before the judgment-seat of God; and moreover, as a token of still greater confidence, they add, that nothing is hidden from God. Why is it that hypocrites often call God to witness, if it is not because they imagine that, by concealing their wickedness under some specious disguise, they have escaped the judgment of God? and thus they would represent the character of God to be different from what it is, as if by their deceptions they could dazzle his eyes. Whenever,

than of killing a sheep; nay, like the butcher, they make a trade of it, they take a pleasure in it as a hungry man in his meat; and we are led with as much ease, and as little resistance, as a lamb to the slaughter; many are slain, and the rest scattered among the heathen, continually insulted by their malice or in danger of being infected by their iniquities." They looked upon themselves as bought and sold, and charged it upon God, Thou sellest thy people, when they should have charged it upon their own sin. For your iniquities have you sold yourselves, Isa. 1. 1.
IV. That they were loaded with contempt, and all possible ignominy was put upon them. In this also they acknowledge God: "Thou makest us a reproach; thou bringest those calamities upon us which occasion the reproach, and thou permittest their virulent tongues to smite us." They complain,
1. That they were ridiculed and bantered, and were looked upon as the most contemptible people under the sun; their troubles were turned to their reproach, and upon the account of them they were derided.
2. That their neighbors, those about them, from whom they could not withdraw, were most abusive to them, v. 13.
3. That the heathen, the people that were strangers to the commonwealth of Israel and aliens to the covenants of promise, made them a by-word, and shook the head at them, as triumphing in their fall, v. 14.
4. That the reproach was constant and incessant (v. 15): My confusion is continually before me. The church in general, the psalmist in particular, were continually teased and vexed with the insults of the enemy. Concerning those that are going down every one cries, "Down with them."
5. That it was very grievous, and in a manner overwhelmed him: The shame of my face has covered me. He blushed for sin, or rather for the dishonor done to God, and then it was a holy blushing.
6. That it reflected upon God himself; the reproach which the enemy and the avenger cast upon them was downright blasphemy against God, v. 16, and 2 Kings xix. 3. There was therefore strong reason to believe that God would appear for them. As there is no trouble more grievous to a generous and ingenuous mind than reproach and calumny, so there is none more grievous to a holy gracious soul than blasphemy and dishonor done to God.

17-26 Israel's appeal to God.
The people of God, being greatly afflicted and oppressed, here apply to him; whither else should they go?
I. By way of appeal, concerning their integrity, which he only is an infallible judge of, and which he will certainly be the rewarder of. Two things they call God to witness to:
1. That, though they suffered these hard things, yet they kept close to God and to their duty (v. 17): "All this

Psalm 44

19-26
19 Though thou hast sore broken us in the place of dragons, and covered us with the shadow of death.
20 If we have forgotten the name of our God, or stretched out our hands to a strange god;
21 Shall not God search this out? for he knoweth the secrets of the heart.
22 Yea, for thy sake are we killed all the day long; we are counted as sheep for the slaughter.
23 Awake, why sleepest thou, O Lord? arise, cast us not off for ever.
24 Wherefore hidest thou thy face, and forgettest our affliction and our oppression?
25 For our soul is bowed down to the dust: our belly cleaveth unto the earth.
26 Arise for our help, and redeem us for thy mercies' sake.

Verse 20. An appeal is now made to the omniscience of God; he is himself called in to bear witness that Israel had not set up another God. If we have forgotten the name of our God. This would be the first step in apostasy; men first forget the true, and then adore the false. Or stretched out our hands to a strange god. Stretching out the hands was the symbol of adoration or of entreaty in prayer; this they had not offered to any of the idols of the heathens.

Verse 21. Shall not God search this out? Could such idolatry be concealed from him? Would he not with holy indignation have detected unfaithfulness to itself, even had it been hidden in the heart and unrevealed in the life? For he knoweth the secrets of the heart. He is acquainted with the inner workings of the mind, and therefore this could not have escaped him. Not the heart only which is secret, but the secrets of the heart, which are secrets of the most secret thing, are as open to God as a book to a reader. The reasoning is that the Lord himself knew the people to be sincerely his followers, and therefore was not visiting them for sin; hence, then, affliction evidently came from quite another cause.

Verse 22. Yea, i.e., assuredly, certainly, for thy sake, not for our offences, but for obeying thee; the trials of these suppliants came upon them because they were loyal to their God. Are we killed all the day long. Persecution never ceased to hound them to the death, they had no respite and found no door of escape; and all in God's behalf, because they would not forsake their covenant God and King. We are counted as sheep for the slaughter; as if we were only meant to be killed, and made on purpose to be victims; as if it were as easy and as innocent a thing to slay us as to slaughter sheep.

Verse 23. Awake, why sleepest thou, O Lord. God sleepeth not, but the psalmist puts it so, as if on no other theory he could explain the divine inaction. He would fain see the great Judge ending oppression and giving peace to the holy, therefore does he cry "Awake;" he cannot understand why the reign of tyranny and the oppression of virtue are permitted, and therefore he enquires "Why sleepest thou?"

Verse 24. Wherefore hidest thou thy face, and forgettest our affliction and our oppression? Not petulantly, but piteously and inquiringly, we may question the Lord when his dealings are mysterious. We are permitted to order our case with arguments, and plead the right before the face of the august Majesty. Why, Lord, dost thou become oblivious of thy children's woes? This question is far more easily asked than answered; it is hard in the midst of persecution to see the reason why we are left to suffer so severely.

Verse 25. For our soul is bowed down to the dust. Our heart is low as low can be, as low as the dust beneath the soles of men's feet. When the heart sinks, the man is down indeed. Heart sorrow is the very heart of sorrow.

Verse 26. Arise for our help. A short, but sweet and comprehensive prayer, much to the point, clear, simple, urgent, as all prayers should be. And redeem us for thy mercies' sake. Here is the final plea. The favor is redemption, the plea is mercy; and this, too, in the case of faithful sufferers who had not forgotten their God. Mercy is always a safe plea, and never will any man find a better.

therefore, we come before God, let us at the same time remember, that there is nothing to be gained by any vain pretense in his presence, inasmuch as he knows the heart.

22-26

22. Surely for thy sake we are killed all the day. Here the faithful urge another reason why God should show mercy to them, namely, that they are subjected to sufferings not on account of crimes committed by themselves, but simply because the ungodly, from hatred to the name of God, are opposed to them.

23. Arise, O Lord! why sleepest thou? Here the saints desire that God, having pity upon them, would at length send them help and deliverance. Although God allows the saints to plead with him in this babbling manner, when in their prayers they desire him to rise up or awake; yet it is necessary that they should be fully persuaded that he keeps watch for their safety and defense. We must guard against the notion of Epicurus, who framed to himself a god who, having his abode in heaven, delighted only in idleness and pleasure. But as the insensibility of our nature is so great, that we do not at once comprehend the care which God has of us, the godly here request that he would be pleased to give some evidence that he was neither forgetful of them nor slow to help them. We must, indeed, firmly believe that God ceases not to regard us, although he appears not to do so; yet as such an assurance is of faith, and not of the flesh, that is to say, is not natural to us, the faithful familiarly give utterance before God to this contrary sentiment, which they conceive from the state of things as it is presented to their view; and in doing so, they discharge from their breasts those morbid affections which belong to the corruption of our nature, in consequence of which faith then shines forth in its pure and native character.

25. For our soul is humbled to the dust. The people of God again deplore the greatness of their calamities, and in order that God may be the more disposed to help them, they declare to him that they are afflicted in no ordinary manner. By the metaphors which they here employ, they mean not only that they are cast down, but also that they are crushed and laid upon the earth, so that they are not able to rise again. Some take the word soul for the body, so that there would be in this verse a repetition of the same sentiment; but I would rather take it for the part in which the life of man consists; as if they had said, We are cast down to the earth, and lie prostrate upon our belly, without any hope of getting up again.

26. After this complaint they subjoin a prayer, that God would arise for their help. By the word redeem they mean not ordinary kind of help, for there was no other means of securing their preservation but by redeeming them. And yet there can be no doubt, that they were diligently employed in meditating upon the great redemption from which all the deliverances which God is daily effecting in our behalf, when he defends us from dangers by various means, flow as streams from their source. They are contented to ascribe their salvation to the unmerited goodness of God as the alone cause of it.

has come upon us, and it is as bad perhaps as bad can be, yet have we not forgotten thee, neither cast off the thoughts of thee nor deserted the worship of thee; for, though we cannot deny but that we have dealt foolishly, yet we have not dealt falsely in thy covenant, so as to cast thee off and take to other gods. Though thou hast seemed to forsake us and withdraw from us, yet we have not therefore forsaken thee." The trouble they had been long in was very great: " We have been wrapped up in obscurity, and buried alive; and thou hast thus broken us, thou hast thus covered us (v. 19), yet we have not harbored any hard thoughts of thee, nor meditated a retreat from thy service. Though thou hast slain us, we have continued to trust in thee: Our heart has not turned back; we have not secretly withdrawn our affections from thee, neither have our steps, either in our religious worship or in our conversation, declined from thy way (v. 18), the way which thou hast appointed us to walk in." For the proof of their integrity they take God's omniscience to witness, which is as much the comfort of the upright in heart as it is the terror of hypocrites (v. 20, 21): "If we have forgotten the name of our God, under pretence that he had forgotten us, or in our distress have stretched out our hands to a strange god, as more likely to help us, shall not God search this out? "

2. That they suffered these hard things because they kept close to God and to their duty (v. 22): "It is for thy sake that we are killed all the day long, because we stand related to thee, are called by thy name, call upon thy name, and will not worship other gods."

II. By way of petition, with reference to their present distress, that God would, in his own due time, work deliverance for them. Their request is very importunate: Awake, arise, v. 23. Arise for our help; redeem us (v. 26); come speedily and powerfully to our relief, Ps. lxxx. 2. Stir up thy strength, and come and save us. They had complained (v. 12) that God had sold them; here they pray (v. 26) that God would redeem them; for there is no appealing from God, but by appealing to him. If he sell us, it is not any one else that can redeem us; the same hand that tears must heal, that smites must bind up, Hos. vi. 1. They had complained (v. 9), Thou hast cast us off; but here they pray (v. 23), "Cast us not off forever; let us not be finally forsaken of God." The expostulations are very moving: Why sleepest thou? v. 23. He that keeps Israel neither slumbers nor sleeps; but, when he does not immediately appear for the deliverance of his people, they are tempted to think he sleeps. The pleas are very proper, not their own merit and righteousness, though they had the testimony of their consciences concerning their integrity, but they plead the poor sinner's pleas.

1. Their own misery, which made them the proper objects of the divine compassion (v. 25).

2. God's mercy: (Exod. xxxiv. 6), and those sure mercies of David are conveyed by the covenant to all his spiritual seed.

Psalm 45

Title
To the Chief Musician upon Shoshannim. For the sons of Korah. Maschil. A Song of loves.

1-5
1 My heart is inditing a good matter: I speak of the things which I have made touching the king: my tongue is the pen of a ready writer.
2 Thou art fairer than the children of men: grace is poured into thy lips: therefore God hath blessed thee for ever.
3 Gird thy sword upon thy thigh, O most mighty, with thy glory and thy majesty.
4 And in thy majesty ride prosperously because of truth and meekness and righteousness; and thy right hand shall teach thee terrible things.
5 Thine arrows are sharp in the heart of the king's enemies; whereby the people fall under thee.

Psalm 45

TITLE. The many titles of this Psalm mark its royalty, its deep and solemn import, and the delight the writer had in it. To the Chief Musician upon Shoshannim. The most probable translation of this word is upon the lilies, and it is either a poetical title given to this noblest of songs after the Oriental manner, or it may relate to the tune to which it was set, or to the instrument which was meant to accompany it. We incline to the first theory, and if it be the true one, it is easy to see the fitness of borrowing a name for so beautiful, so pure, so choice, so matchless a poem from the golden lilies, whose bright array outshone the glory of Solomon. For the sons of Korah. Special singers are appointed for so divine a hymn. King Jesus deserves to be praised not with random, ranting ravings, but with the sweetest and most skilful music of the best trained choristers. The purest hearts in the spiritual temple are the most harmonious songsters in the ears of God; acceptable song is not a matter so much of tuneful voices as of sanctified affections, but in no case should we sing of Jesus with unprepared hearts. Maschil, an instructive ode, not an idle lay, or a romancing ballad, but a Psalm of holy teaching, didactic and doctrinal. This proves that it is to be spiritually understood. Blessed are the people who know the meaning of its joyful sound. A Song of loves. Not a carnal sentimental love song, but a celestial canticle of everlasting love fit for the tongues and ears of angels.
SUBJECT. Some here see Solomon and Pharaoh's daughter only—they are short sighted; others see both Solomon and Christ—they are cross eyed; well focused spiritual eyes see here Jesus only, or if Solomon be present at all, it must be like those hazy shadows of by passers which cross the face of the camera, and therefore are dimly traceable upon a photographic landscape. "The King," the God whose throne is for ever and ever, is no mere mortal and his everlasting dominion is not bounded by Lebanon and Egypt's river. This is no wedding song of earthly nuptials, but an Epithalamium for the Heavenly Bridegroom and his elect spouse.
DIVISION. Ps 45:1 is an announcement of intention, a preface to the song; Ps 45:3 adores the matchless beauty of Messiah; and from Ps 45:3-9, he is addressed in admiring ascriptions of praise. Ps 45:10-12 are spoken to the bride. The church is further spoken of in Ps 45:13-15, and the Psalm closes with another address to the King, foretelling his eternal fame, Ps 45:16-17.

EXPOSITION
Verse 1. My heart. There is no writing like that dictated by the heart. Heartless hymns are insults to heaven. Is inditing a good matter. A good heart will only be content with good thoughts. Where the fountain is good good streams will flow forth. The learned tell us that the word may be read overflows, or as others, boils or bubbles up, denoting the warmth of the writer's love, the fullness of his heart, and the consequent richness and glow of his utterance, as though it were the ebullition of his inmost soul, when most full of affection.
Verse 2. Thou. As though the King himself had suddenly appeared before him, the psalmist lost in admiration of his person, turns from his preface to address his Lord. A loving heart has the power to realize its object. The eyes of a true heart see more than the eyes of the head. Moreover, Jesus reveals himself when we are pouring forth our affections towards him. It is usually the case that when we are ready Christ appears. If our heart is warm it is an index that the sun is shining, and when we enjoy his heat we shall soon behold his light. Thou art fairer than the children of men. In person, but especially in mind and character, the King of saints is peerless in beauty. The Hebrew word is doubled, "Beautiful, beautiful art thou." Jesus is so emphatically lovely that words must be doubled, strained, yea, exhausted before he can be described.

JOHN CALVIN

Psalm 45

In this psalm, the grace and beauty of Solomon, his virtues in ruling the kingdom, and also his power and riches, are illustrated and described in terms of high commendation. More especially, as he had taken to wife a stranger out of Egypt, the blessing of God is promised to him in this relationship, provided the newly espoused bride, bidding adieu to her own nation, and renouncing all attachment to it, devote herself wholly to her husband. At the same time, there can be no doubt, that under this figure the majesty, wealth, and extent of Christ's kingdom are described and illustrated by appropriate terms, to teach the faithful that there is no felicity greater or more desirable than to live under the reign of this king, and to be subject to his government.

1-5

1. My heart is boiling over with a good matter. This preface shows sufficiently that the subject of the psalm is no common one; for whoever the author of it may have been, he here intimates, at the very outset, that he will treat of great and glorious things. The Holy Spirit is not accustomed to inspire the servants of God to utter great swelling words, and to pour forth empty sounds into the air; and, therefore, we may naturally conclude, that the subject here treated of is not merely a transitory and earthly kingdom, but sortie-thing more excellent. Were not this the case, what end would it serve to announce, as the prophet does in such a magnificent style, that his heart was boiling over, from his ardent desire to be employed in rehearsing the praises of the king? It is as if the inspired writer had said, My heart is ready to breathe forth something excellent and worthy of being remembered. He afterwards expresses the harmony between the tongue and the heart, when he compares his tongue to the pen of a swift and ready writer.

2. Thou art fairer than the sons of men. The Psalmist commences his subject with the commendation of the beauty of the king, and then he proceeds also to praise his eloquence. Personal excellence is ascribed to the king, not that the beauty of the countenance, which of itself is not reckoned among the number of the virtues, ought to be very highly valued; but because a noble disposition of mind often shines forth in the very countenance of a man.

3. Gird thy sword upon thy thigh. Here Solomon is praised as well for his warlike valor, which strikes terror into]his enemies, as for his virtues which give him authority among his subjects, and secure him their reverence. On the one hand, no king will be able to preserve and defend his subjects, unless he is formidable to his enemies; and, on the other hand, it will be to little purpose to make war boldly upon foreign realms, if the internal state of his own kingdom is not established and regulated in uprightness and justice.

5. Thy arrows are sharp, etc. Here the Psalmist again refers to warlike power, when he says that the arrows of the king shall be sharp, so that they shall pierce the hearts of his enemies; by which he intimates that he has weapons in his hand with

MATTHEW HENRY

Psalm 45

1-5 Nuptial song; glories of the Messiah.

Some make Shoshannim, in the title, to signify an instrument of six strings; others take it in its primitive signification for lilies or roses, which probably were strewed, with other flowers, at nuptial solemnities; and then it is easily applicable to Christ who calls himself the rose of Sharon and the lily of the valleys, Cant. ii. 1. It is a song of loves, concerning the holy love that is between Christ and his church. It is a song of the well-beloved, the virgins, the companions of the bride (v. 14), prepared to be sung by them. The virgin-company that attend the Lamb on Mount Zion are said to sing a new song, Rev. xiv. 3, 4.

I. The preface (v. 1) speaks,

1. The dignity of the subject. It is a good matter, and it is a pity that such a moving art as poetry should ever be employed about a bad matter. It is touching the King, King Jesus, and his kingdom and government. Note, Those that speak of Christ speak of a good matter, no subject so noble, so copious, so fruitful, so profitable, and so well-becoming us; it is a shame that this good matter is not more the matter of our discourse.

2. The excellency of the management. This song was a confession with the mouth of faith in the heart concerning Christ and his church.

II. In these verses the Lord Jesus is represented,

1. As most beautiful and amiable in himself. It is a marriage-song; and therefore the transcendent excellencies of Christ are represented by the beauty of the royal bridegroom (v. 2): Thou art fairer than the children of men, than any of them. He proposed (v. 1) to speak of the King, but immediately directs his speech to him. Those that have an admiration and affection for Christ love to go to him and tell him so.

2. As the great favorite of heaven. He is fairer than the children of men, for God has done more for him than for any of the children of men, and all his kindness to the children of men is for his sake, and passes through his hands, through his mouth.

3. As victorious over all his enemies. The royal bridegroom is a man of war, and his nuptials do not excuse him from the field of battle (as was allowed by the law, Deut. xxiv. 5); nay, they bring him to the field of battle, for he is to rescue his spouse by dint of sword out of her captivity, to conquer her, and to conquer for her, and then to marry her.

6-9 Majesty and glory of Christ.

We have here the royal bridegroom filling his throne with judgment and keeping his court with splendor.

I. He here fills his throne with judgment. It is God the Father that says to the Son here, Thy throne, O God! is forever and ever, as appears Heb. i. 8, 9, where this is quoted to prove that he is God and has a more excellent name than the angels. The Mediator is God, else he neither would have been able to do the

Psalm 45

6-11

6 Thy throne, O God, is for ever and ever: the scepter of thy kingdom is a right scepter.
7 Thou lovest righteousness, and hatest wickedness: therefore God, thy God, hath anointed thee with the oil of gladness above thy fellows.
8 All thy garments smell of myrrh, and aloes, and cassia, out of the ivory palaces, whereby they have made thee glad.
9 Kings' daughters were among thy honorable women: upon thy right hand did stand the queen in gold of Ophir.
10 Hearken, O daughter, and consider, and incline thine ear; forget also thine own people, and thy father's house;
11 So shall the king greatly desire thy beauty: for he is thy Lord; and worship thou him.

Verse 3. Gird thy sword upon thy thigh. Loving spirits jealous of the Redeemer's glory long to see him putting forth his power to vindicate his own most holy cause. Why should the sword of the Spirit lie still, like a weapon hung up in an armory; it is sharp and strong, both for cutting and piercing: O that the divine power of Jesus were put forth to use against error. The words before us represent our great King as urged to arm himself for battle, by placing his sword where it is ready for use. Christ is the true champion of the church, others are but underlings who must borrow strength from him; the single arm of Immanuel is the sole hope of the faithful. Our prayer should be that of this verse.

Verse 4. And in thy majesty ride prosperously. The hero monarch armed and appareled is now entreated to ascend his triumphal car. Would to God that our Immanuel would come forth in the chariot of love to conquer our spiritual foes and seize by power the souls whom he has bought with blood. Because of truth and meekness and righteousness. These words may be rendered, ride forth upon truth and meekness and righteousness.—Three noble chargers to draw the war chariot of the gospel. In the sense of our translation it is a most potent argument to urge with our Lord that the cause of the true, the humble, and the good, calls for his advocacy.

Verse 5. Thine arrows. Our King is master of all weapons: he can strike those who are near and those afar off with equal force. Are sharp. Nothing that Jesus does is ill done, he uses no blunted shafts, no pointless darts. In the heart of the King's enemies. Our Captain aims at men's hearts rather than their heads, and he hits them too; point blank are his shots, and they enter deep into the vital part of man's nature. Whether for love or vengeance, Christ never misses aim, and when his arrows stick, they cause a smart not soon forgotten, a wound which only he can heal. Jesus' arrows of conviction are sharp in the quiver of his word, and sharp when on the bow of his ministers, but they are most known to be so when they find a way into careless hearts.

Verse 6. Thy throne, O God, is for ever and ever. To whom can this be spoken but our Lord? The psalmist cannot restrain his adoration. His enlightened eye sees in the royal Husband of the church, God, God to be adored, God reigning, God reigning everlastingly. Blessed sight! Blind are the eyes that cannot see God in Christ Jesus! We never appreciate the tender condescension of our King in becoming one flesh with his church, and placing her at his right hand, until we have fully rejoiced in his essential glory and deity.

Verse 7. Thou lovest righteousness, and hatest wickedness. Christ Jesus is not neutral in the great contest between right and wrong: as warmly as he loves the one he abhors the other. What qualifications for a sovereign! what grounds of confidence for a people! The whole of our Lord's life on earth proved the truth of these words; his death to put away sin and bring in the reign of righteousness, sealed the fact beyond all question; his providence by which he rules from his mediatorial throne, when rightly understood, reveals the same; and his final assize will proclaim it before all worlds.

Verse 8. All thy garments smell of myrrh, and aloes, and cassia. The divine anointing causes fragrance to distil from the robes of the Mighty Hero. He is delightful to every sense, to the eyes most fair, to the ear most gracious, to the spiritual nostril most sweet. The excellences of Jesus are all most precious, comparable to the rarest spices; they are most varied, and to be likened not to myrrh alone, but to all the perfumes blended in due proportion. The Father always finds a pleasure in him, in him he is well pleased; and all regenerated spirits rejoice in him, for he is made of God unto us, "wisdom, righteousness, sanctification, and redemption."

Verse 9. King's daughters were among thy honorable women. Our Lord's courts lack not for courtiers, and those the fairest and noblest. Virgin souls are maids of honor to the court, the true lilies of heaven. The lowly and pure in heart are esteemed by the Lord Jesus as his most familiar friends, their

JOHN CALVIN

which to strike, even at a distance, all his enemies, whoever they may be, who resist his authority. In the same sense also he says that the people shall fall under him; as if it had been said, Whoever shall engage in the attempt to shake the stability of his kingdom shah miserably perish, for the king has in his hand a sufficiency of power to break the stubbornness of all such persons.

6-7

6. Thy throne, O God! is for ever and ever. In this verse the Psalmist commends other princely virtues in Solomon, namely, the eternal duration of his throne, and then the justice and rectitude of his mode of government. The simple and natural sense is, that Solomon reigns not tyrannically, as the most of kings do, but by just and equal laws, and that, therefore, his throne shall be established for ever. Although he is called God, because God has imprinted some mark of his glory in the person of kings, yet this title cannot well be applied to a mortal man; for we nowhere read in Scripture that man or angel has been distinguished by this title without some qualification.

7. This verse sets before us a fuller statement of the righteousness for which this monarch is distinguished; for we are told that he is no less strict in, the punishment of iniquity than in maintaining justice. We know how many and great evils are engendered by impunity and license in doing evil, when kings are negligent and slack in punishing crimes. Hence the old proverb, That it is better to live under a prince who gives no allowance, than under one who imposes no restraint.

8-12

8. All thy garments smell of myrrh. It is sufficient that we understand the prophet as meaning that the garments of the king are perfumed with precious and sweet-smelling odors. He describes Solomon coming forth from his ivory palace amidst shoutings of universal applause and joy.

9. The daughter of the king of Egypt, whom Solomon had married, was his principal wife, and the first in rank but it appears that the others, whom sacred history describes as occupying an inferior rank, were provided for in a liberal and honorable manner. These the prophet calls the daughters of kings, because some of them were descended of the royal blood. In what sense, then, it might be asked, does the prophet account it among the praises of Solomon that he had many wives,—a thing which God condemns in all private persons, but expressly in kings? (Deuteronomy 17:17.) Doubtless it may easily be inferred that in commending, according to a common practice, the wealth and glory of the king, as the prophet here does, he did not mean to approve of the abuse of them. It was not his design to set forth the example of a man in opposition to the law of God.

10. Hearken, O daughter! and consider. I have no doubt, that what is here said is spoken of the Egyptian woman, whom the prophet has described as standing at the right hand of the king. It was not, indeed, lawful for Solomon to marry a strange woman; but this of itself is to be accounted among the

MATTHEW HENRY

Mediator's work nor fit to wear the Mediator's crown. Concerning his government observe,

1. The eternity of it; it is for ever and ever. It shall continue on earth throughout all the ages of time, in despite of all the opposition of the gates of hell; and in the blessed fruits and consequences of it shall last as long as the days of heaven, and run parallel with the line of eternity itself.

2. The equity of it: The scepter of thy kingdom, the administration of thy government, is right, exactly according to the eternal counsel and will of God, which is the eternal rule and reason of good and evil. Whatever Christ does he does none of his subjects any wrong, but gives redress to those that do suffer wrong: He loves righteousness, and hates wickedness, v. 7. He himself loves to do righteousness, and hates to do wickedness; and he loves those that do righteousness, and hates those that do wickedness.

3. The establishment and elevation of it: Therefore God, even thy God (Christ, as Mediator, called God his God, John xx. 17, as commissioned by him, and the head of those that are taken into covenant with him), has anointed thee with the oil of gladness.

II. He keeps his court with splendor and magnificence.

1. His robes of state, wherein he appears, are taken notice of, not for their pomp, which might strike an awe upon the spectator, but their pleasantness and the gratefulness of the odors with which they were perfumed (v. 8): They smell of myrrh, aloes, and cassia (the oil of gladness with which he and his garments were anointed): these were some of the ingredients of the holy anointing oil which God appointed.

2. His royal palaces are said to be ivory ones, such as were then reckoned most magnificent. We read of an ivory house that Ahab made, 1 Kings xxii. 39. The mansions of light above are the ivory palaces, whence all the joys both of Christ and believers come, and where they will be for ever in perfection; for by them he is made glad, and all that are his with him; for they shall enter into the joy of their Lord.

3. The beauties of his court shine very brightly. In public appearances at court, when the pomp of it is shown, nothing is supposed to contribute so much to it as the splendor of the ladies, which is alluded to here, v. 9.

10-17 The Glory of the Church.

This latter part of the psalm is addressed to the royal bride, standing on the right hand of the royal bridegroom. God, who said to the Son, Thy throne is for ever and ever, says this to the church, which, upon the account of her espousals to the Son, he here calls his daughter.

I. He tells her of the duties expected from her, which ought to be considered by all those that come into relation to the Lord Jesus: "Hearken, therefore, and consider this, and incline thy ear, that is, submit to

Psalm 45

12-17

12 And the daughter of Tyre shall be there with a gift; even the rich among the people shall intreat thy favor.

13 The king's daughter is all glorious within: her clothing is of wrought gold.

14 She shall be brought unto the king in raiment of needlework: the virgins her companions that follow her shall be brought unto thee.

15 With gladness and rejoicing shall they be brought: they shall enter into the king's palace.

16 Instead of thy fathers shall be thy children, whom thou mayest make princes in all the earth.

17 I will make thy name to be remembered in all generations: therefore shall the people praise thee for ever and ever.

place in his palace is not among the menials but near the throne. The day will come when those who are "king's daughters" literally will count it their greatest honor to serve the church, and, meanwhile every believing sister is spiritually a King's daughter, a member of the royal family of heaven.

Verse 10. Hearken, O daughter, and consider. Ever is this the great duty of the church. Faith cometh by hearing, and confirmation by consideration. No precept can be more worthy of the attention of those who are honored to be espoused to Christ that that which follows. And incline thine ear. Lean forward so that no syllable may be unheard. The whole faculties of the mind should be bent upon receiving holy teaching. Forget also thine own people, and thy father's house. To renounce the world is not easy, but it must be done by all who are affianced to the Great King, for a divided heart he cannot endure; it would be misery to the beloved one as well as dishonor to her Lord.

Verse 11. So shall the king greatly desire thy beauty. Wholehearted love is the duty and bliss of the marriage state in every case, but especially so in this lofty mystic marriage. The church must forsake all others and cleave to Jesus only, or she will not please him nor enjoy the full manifestation of his love. What less can he ask, what less may she dare propose than to be wholly his? Jesus sees a beauty in his church, a beauty which he delights in most when it is not marred by worldliness.

Verse 12. And the daughter of Tyre shall be there with a gift. When the church abounds in holiness, she shall know no lack of homage from the surrounding people. Her glory shall then impress and attract the heathen around, till they also unite in doing honor to her Lord. The power of missions abroad lies at home: a holy church will be a powerful church.

Verse 13. The king's daughter is all glorious within. Within her secret chambers her glory is great. Though unseen of men her Lord sees her, and commends her.

Verse 14. She shall be brought unto the king in raiment of needlework. The day comes when the celestial marriage shall be openly celebrated, and these words describe the nuptial procession wherein the queen is brought to her royal Husband attended by her handmaidens. In the latter-day glory, and in the consummation of all things, the glory of the bride, the Lamb's wife, shall be seen by all the universe with admiration.

Verse 15. With gladness and rejoicing shall they be brought. Joy becomes a marriage feast. What joy will that be which will be seen at the feasts of paradise when all the redeemed shall be brought home! Gladness in the saints themselves, and rejoicing from the angels shall make the halls of the New Jerusalem ring again with shoutings.

Verse 16. Instead of thy fathers shall be thy children. The ancient saints who stood as fathers in the service of the Great King have all passed away; but a spiritual seed is found to fill their places. The veterans depart, but volunteers fill up the vacant places. The line of grace never becomes extinct. As long as time shall last, the true apostolical succession will be maintained.

Verse 17. I will make thy name to be remembered in all generations. Jehovah by the prophet's mouth promises to the Prince of Peace eternal fame as well as a continuous progeny. His name is his fame, his character, his person; these are dear to his people now—they never can forget them.

gifts of God, that a king so powerful as the king of Egypt was, sought his alliance. At the same time, as by the appointment of the Law, it was required that the Jews, previous to entering into the marriage relation, should endeavor to instruct their wives in the pure worship of God, and emancipate them from superstition; in the present instance, in which the wife spoken of was descended from a heathen nation, and who, by her present marriage, was included in the body of the Church, the prophet, in order to withdraw her from her evil training, exhorts her to forget her own country and her father's house, and to assume a new character and other manners.

12. And the daughter of Tyre with a gift. This also is a part of the recompense which the prophet promises to the queen in order to mitigate or rather to extinguish entirely, the longing desire she might still feel after her former condition. He says: that the Tyrians will come humbly to pay her reverence, bringing presents with them. Tyre, we know, was formerly a city of great renown, and, therefore, he accounts it a very high honor that men will come from a city so distinguished and opulent to greet her and to testify their submission to her.

13-17

13. The daughter of the King is all glorious within. This verse may be understood in a twofold sense; either as meaning that the queen, not only when she appears in public before all the people, but also when sitting in private in her own chamber, is always sumptuously appareled; or, that the splendor and gorgeous appearance of her attire is not merely a thing of display, designed to dazzle the eyes of the simple, but consists of expensive and really substantial material. The prophet accordingly enhances the happy and lofty condition of the queen by the circumstance, that she has not only sumptuous apparel in which she may appear on particular occasions, but also for her ordinary and daily attire.

16. Instead of thy fathers shall be thy children. This also serves to show the glory and transcendent excellence of this kingdom, namely, that the children will not be inferior in dignity to their fathers, and that the nobility of the race will not be diminished after the death of Solomon; for the children which shall be born to him will equal those who had preceded them in the most excellent virtues. Then it is added, that they shall be princes in all the earth, because the empire shall enjoy such an extent of dominion on every side, that it might easily be divided into many kingdoms.

17. I will make thy name to be remembered, etc. This also is equally inapplicable to Solomon, who, by his shameful and impious rebellion, stained the memory of his name with disgrace. In polluting by superstitious abominations the land which was consecrated to God, did he not bring upon himself indelible ignominy and shame? For this deed alone his name deserves to be buried in everlasting oblivion. Nor was his son Rehoboam in any degree more deserving of praise; for through his own foolish presumption he lost the better part of his kingdom. To find, therefore, the true accomplishment of what is here said, we must come to Christ, the memory of whose name continues to prosper and prevail.

those conditions of thy espousals, and bring thy will to comply with them." This is the method of profiting by the word of God. He that has ears, let him hear, let him hearken diligently; he that hearkens, let him consider and weigh it duly; he that considers, let him incline and yield to the force of what is laid before him.

II. He tells her of the honors designed for her.

1. Great court should be made to her, and rich presents brought her (v. 12): "The daughter of Tyre," a rich and splendid city, "the daughter of the King of Tyre shall be there with a gift; every royal family round about shall send a branch, as a representative of the whole, to seek thy favor and to make an interest in thee; even the rich among the people, whose wealth might be thought to exempt them from dependence at court, even they shall entreat thy favor, for his sake to whom thou art espoused, that by thee they may make him their friend."

2. She shall be very splendid, and highly esteemed in the eyes of all,

(1.) For her personal qualifications, the endowments of her mind, which every one shall admire (v. 13): The king's daughter is all glorious within.

3. Her nuptials shall be celebrated with a great deal of honor and joy (v. 14, 15): She shall be brought to the king, as the Lord God brought the woman to the man (Gen. ii. 22), which was a type of this mystical marriage between Christ and his church. None are brought to Christ but whom the Father brings, and he has undertaken to do it; none besides are so brought to the king (v. 14) as to enter into the king's palace, v. 15.

4. The progeny of this marriage shall be illustrious (v. 16): Instead of thy fathers shall be thy children. Instead of the Old-Testament church a Gentile-church, that shall be grafted into the same olive and partake of its root and fatness (Rom. xi. 17); more and more eminent shall be the children of the desolate than the children of the married wife, Isa. liv. 1.

5. The praise of this marriage shall be perpetual in the praises of the royal bridegroom (v. 18): I will make thy name to be remembered. His Father has given him a name above every name, and here promises to make it perpetual, by keeping up a succession of ministers and Christians in every age, that shall bear up his name, which shall thus endure for ever (Ps. lxxii. 17), by being remembered in all the generations of time; for the entail of Christianity shall not be cut off. "Therefore, because they shall remember thee in all generations, they shall praise thee for ever and ever." Those that help to support the honor of Christ on earth shall in heaven see his glory, and share in it, and be for ever praising him. In the believing hope of our everlasting happiness in the other world let us always keep up the remembrance of Christ, as our only way thither, in our generation; and, in assurance of the perpetuating of the kingdom of the Redeemer in the world, let us transmit the remembrance of him to succeeding generations, that his name may endure for ever and be as the days of heaven.

Psalm 46

Title
To the chief Musician, for the Sons of Korah. A Song upon Alamoth.

1-5
1 God is our refuge and strength, a very present help in trouble.
2 Therefore will not we fear, though the earth be removed, and though the mountains be carried into the midst of the sea;
3 Though the waters thereof roar and be troubled, though the mountains shake with the swelling thereof. Selah.
4 There is a river, the streams whereof shall make glad the city of God, the holy place of the tabernacles of the most High.
5 God is in the midst of her; she shall not be moved: God shall help her, and that right early.

Psalm 46

TITLE. To the Chief Musician. He who could sing other Psalms so well was fitly entrusted with this noble ode. Trifles may be left to commoner songsters, but the most skilful musician in Israel must be charged with the due performance of this song, with the most harmonious voices and choicest music. For the Sons of Korah. One alone cannot fulfill the praise, there must be picked choristers under him, whose joyful privilege it shall be to celebrate the service of song in the house of the Lord. As to why the sons of Korah were selected, see our remarks at the head of Psalm 42. It may be well to add that they were a division of the Levites who took their turn in serving at the temple. All the works of holy service ought not to be monopolized by one order of talent, each company of believers should in due course enjoy the privilege. None ought to be without a share in the service of God.
A Song upon Alamoth. Which may denote that the music was to be pitched high for the treble or soprano voices of the Hebrew virgins. They went forth in their dances to sing the praises of David when he smote the Philistine, it was meet that they should make merry and be glad when the victories of Jehovah became their theme. We need to praise God upon virgin hearts, with souls chaste towards his fear, with lively and exalted expressions, and happy strains. Or the word Alamoth may refer to shrill sounding instruments, as in 1Ch 15:20, where we read that Zechariah, and Eliab, and Benaiah were to praise the Lord "with psalteries on Alamoth." We are not always, in a slovenly manner, to fall into one key, but with intelligence are to modulate our praises and make them fittingly expressive of the occasion and the joy it creates in our souls. These old musical terms cannot be interpreted with certainty, but they are still useful because they show that care and skill should be used in our sacred music.
SUBJECT. Happen what may, the Lord's people are happy and secure, this is the doctrine of the Psalm, and it might, to help our memories, be called THE SONG OF HOLY CONFIDENCE, were it not that from the great reformer's love to this soul-stirring hymn it will probably be best remembered as LUTHER'S PSALM.
DIVISION. It is divided by inspired authority into three parts, each of which ends with Selah.

EXPOSITION
Verse 1. God is our refuge and strength. Not our armies, or our fortresses. Israel's boast is in Jehovah, the only living and true God. Others vaunt their impregnable castles, placed on inaccessible rocks, and secured with gates of iron, but God is a far better refuge from distress than all these: and when the time comes to carry the war into the enemy's territories, the Lord stands his people in better stead than all the velour of legions or the boasted strength of chariot and horse. Soldiers of the cross, remember this, and count yourselves safe, and make yourselves strong in God.
Verse 2. Therefore. How fond the psalmist is of therefores! his poetry is no poetic rapture without reason, it is as logical as a mathematical demonstration. The next words are a necessary inference from these. Will not we fear. With God on our side, how irrational would fear be! Where he is all power is, and all love, why therefore should we quail? Though the earth be removed, though the basis of all visible things should be so convulsed as to be entirely changed.
Verse 3. Though the waters thereof roar and be troubled. When all things are excited to fury, and reveal their utmost power to disturb, faith smiles serenely. She is not afraid of noise, nor even of real force, she knows that the Lord stilleth the raging of the sea, and holdeth the waves in the hollow of his hand. Though the mountains shake with the swelling thereof. Alps and Andes may tremble, but faith rests on a firmer basis, and is not to be moved

JOHN CALVIN

Psalm 46

This psalm seems to be an expression of thanksgiving rather for some particular deliverance, than for the constant aid by which God has always protected and preserved his Church. It may be inferred from it that the city of Jerusalem. when stricken with great terror, and placed in extreme danger, was preserved, contrary to all expectation, by the unlooked for and miraculous power of God. The prophet, therefore, whoever composed the psalm, commending a deliverance so singularly vouchsafed by God, exhorts the faithful to commit themselves confidently to his protection, and not to doubt that, relying fearlessly upon him as their guardian and the protector of their welfare, they shall be continually preserved in safety from all the assaults of their enemies, because it is his peculiar office to quell all commotions.

1-2
1. God is our refuge and strength. Here the Psalmist begins with a general expression or sentiment, before he comes to speak of the more particular deliverance. He begins by premising that God is sufficiently able to protect his own people, and that he gives them sufficient ground to expect it.
2. When, however, the sacred poet says, We will not fear, he is not to be understood as meaning that the minds of the godly are exempt from all solicitude or fear, as if they were destitute of feeling, for there is a great difference between insensibility and the confidence of faith. He only shows that whatever may happen they are never overwhelmed with terror, but rather gather strength and courage sufficient to allay all fear. Though the earth be moved, and the mountains fall into the midst of the sea, are hyperbolical modes of expression, but they nevertheless denote a revolution, and turning upside down of the whole world.

Psalm 46:3-5
3, 4. Though the waters thereof roar, etc. This verse ought to be read in connection with the verse which follows, because it is necessary to complete the sense, as if it had been said: Though the waters of the sea roar and swell, and by their fierce impetuosity shake the very mountains—even in the midst of these dreadful tumults, the holy city of God will continue to enjoy comfort and peace, satisfied with her small streams. The prophet intended simply to say, that the small streams of a river would afford to the holy city abundant cause of rejoicing, though the whole world should be moved and destroyed.
5. God is in the midst of her; she shall not be moved. The Psalmist now shows that the great security of the Church consists in this, that God dwells in the midst of her; for the verb which we translate, shall be moved, is of the feminine gender, nor can it be referred to God, as if it were designed to teach that God is immovable. The sentence must be explained in this way, The holy city shall not be moved or shaken, because God dwells there, and is always ready to help her. The expression, the dawn of the morning denotes daily,

MATTHEW HENRY

Psalm 46

1-5 God the protection of His people.
The psalmist here teaches us by his own example.
I. To triumph in God, and his relation to us and presence with us, especially when we have had some fresh experiences of his appearing in our behalf (v. 1): God is our refuge and strength; we have found him so, he has engaged to be so, and he ever will be so. Are we pursued? God is our refuge to whom we may flee, and in whom we may be safe and think ourselves so; secure upon good grounds, Prov. xviii. 10. Are we oppressed by troubles? Have we work to do and enemies to grapple with? God is our strength, to bear us up under our burdens, to fit us for all our services and sufferings; he will by his grace put strength into us, and on him we may stay ourselves.
II. To triumph over the greatest dangers: God is our strength and our help, a God all-sufficient to us; therefore will not we fear. Those that with a holy reverence fear God need not with any amazement to be afraid of the power of hell or earth. If God be for us, who can be against us; to do us any harm? It is our duty, it is our privilege, to be thus fearless; it is an evidence of a clear conscience, of an honest heart, and of a lively faith in God and his providence and promise: "We will not fear, though the earth be removed, though all our creature-confidences fail us and sink us; nay, though that which should support us threaten to swallow us up, as the earth did Korah," for whose sons this psalm was penned, and, some think, by them; yet while we keep close to God, and have him for us, we will not fear, for we have no cause to fear.
Observe here,
1. How threatening the danger is. We will suppose the earth to be removed, and thrown into the sea, even the mountains, the strongest and firmest parts of the earth, to lie buried in the unfathomed ocean; we will suppose the sea to roar and rage, and make a dreadful noise, and its foaming billows to insult the shore with so much violence as even to shake the mountains, v. 3.
2. How well-grounded the defiance of this danger is, considering how well guarded the church is, and that interest which we are concerned for. Here is,
(1.) Joy to the church, even in the most melancholy and sorrowful times (v. 4): There is a river the streams whereof shall make it glad, even then when the waters of the sea roar and threaten it. It alludes to the waters of Siloam, which went softly by Jerusalem (Isa. viii. 6, 7): though of no great depth or breadth, yet the waters of it were made serviceable to the defense of Jerusalem in Hezekiah's time, Isa. xxii. 10, 11. But this must be understood spiritually; the covenant of grace is the river, the promises of which are the streams.
(2.) Establishment to the church. Though heaven and earth are shaken, yet God is in the midst of her, she

Psalm 46

6-11

6 The heathen raged, the kingdoms were moved: he uttered his voice, the earth melted.
7 The LORD of hosts is with us; the God of Jacob is our refuge. Selah.
8 Come, behold the works of the LORD, what desolations he hath made in the earth.
9 He maketh wars to cease unto the end of the earth; he breaketh the bow, and cutteth the spear in sunder; he burneth the chariot in the fire.
10 Be still, and know that I am God: I will be exalted among the heathen, I will be exalted in the earth.
11 The LORD of hosts is with us; the God of Jacob is our refuge. Selah.

by swelling seas. Evil may ferment, wrath may boil, and pride may foam, but the brave heart of holy confidence trembles not.

Verse 4. There is a river. Divine grace like a smoothly flowing, fertilizing, full, and never failing river, yields refreshment and consolation to believers. This is the river of the water of life, of which the church above as well as the church below partakes evermore. It is no boisterous ocean, but a placid stream, it is not stayed in its course by earthquakes or crumbling mountains, it follows its serene course without disturbance.

Verse 5. God is in the midst of her. His help is therefore sure and near. Is she besieged, then he is himself besieged within her, and we may be certain that he will break forth upon his adversaries. How near is the Lord to the distresses of his saints, since he sojourns in their midst! Let us take heed that we do not grieve him; let us have such respect to him as Moses had when he felt the sand of Horeb's desert to be holy, and put off his shoes from off his feet when the Lord spake from the burning bush.

Verse 6. The heathen raged. The nations were in a furious uproar, they gathered against the city of the Lord like wolves ravenous for their prey; they foamed, and roared, and swelled like a tempestuous sea. The kingdoms were moved. A general confusion seized upon society; the fierce invaders convulsed their own dominions by draining the population to urge on the war, and they desolated other territories by their devastating march to Jerusalem.

Verse 7. The Lord of hosts is with us. This is the reason for all Zion's security, and for the overthrow of her foes. The Lord rules the angels, the stars, the elements, and all the hosts of heaven; and the heaven of heavens are under his sway.

Verse 8. Come, behold the works of the Lord. The joyful citizens of Jerusalem are invited to go forth and view the remains of their enemies, that they may mark the prowess of Jehovah and the spoil which his right hand hath won for his people. It were well if we also carefully noted the providential dealings of our covenant God, and were quick to perceive his hand in the battles of his church.

Verse 9. He maketh wars to cease unto the end of the earth. His voice quiets the tumult of war, and calls for the silence of peace. However remote and barbarous the tribe, he awes the people into rest. He crushes the great powers till they cannot provoke strife again; he gives his people repose.

Verse 10. Be still, and know that I am God. Hold off your hands, ye enemies! Sit down and wait in patience, ye believers! Acknowledge that Jehovah is God, ye who feel the terrors of his wrath! Adore him, and him only, ye who partake in the protection of his grace. Since none can worthily proclaim his nature, let "expressive silence muse his praise." The boasts of the ungodly and the timorous forebodings of the saints should certainly be hushed by a sight of what the Lord has done in past ages.

Verse 11. The Lord of hosts is with us; the God of Jacob is our refuge. It was meet to sing this twice over. It is a truth of which no believer wearies, it is a fact too often forgotten, it is a precious privilege which cannot be too often considered. SELAH. Here as before, lift up the heart. SELAH bids the music rest.

Pause in silence soft and blest;
SELAH bids uplift the strain,
Harps and voices tune again;
SELAH ends the vocal praise,
Still your hearts to God upraise.

as soon as the sun rises upon the earth. The sum of the whole is, If we desire to be protected by the hand of God, we must be concerned above all things that he may dwell amongst us; for all hope of safety depends upon his presence alone. And he dwells amongst us for no other purpose than to preserve us uninjured.

6-11

6. The peoples raged. Since the Church of God is never without enemies, and these very powerful, and such as consequently fight against her with cruel and unbridled fury, the prophet now confirms from experience the doctrine which he had advanced concerning the impregnable character of the divine protection. He then deduces from it this general ground of consolation, That it belongs continually to God to restrain and quell all commotions, and that his arm is strong enough to break all the efforts of the enemy.

7. Jehovah of armies is with us. In this verse we are taught how we shall be able to apply to our own use the things which the Scriptures everywhere record concerning the infinite power of God. We shall be able to do this when we believe ourselves to be of the number of those whom God has embraced with his fatherly love, and whom he will cherish.

8. Come ye, consider the works of Jehovah. The Psalmist seems still to continue in this verse the history of a deliverance by which God had given abundant evidence that he is the most efficient and faithful protector of his Church, that the godly might derive from it both courage and strength to enable them to overcome whatever temptations might afterwards arise. The manifestations which God has given of his favor towards us in preserving us, ought to be kept continually before our eyes as a means of establishing in our hearts a persuasion of the stability of his promises. By this exhortation we have tacitly rebuked the indifference and stupidity of those who do not make so great account of the power of God as they ought to do; or rather, the whole world is charged with ingratitude, because there is scarcely one in a hundred who acknowledges that he has abundant help and security in God, so that they are all blinded to the works of God, or rather willfully shut their eyes at that which would, nevertheless, prove the best means of strengthening their faith.

10. Be still, and know that I am God. The Psalmist seems now to turn his discourse to the enemies of the people of God, who indulge their lust of mischief and revenge upon them: for in doing injury to the saints they do not consider that they are making war against God. Imagining that they have only to do with men, they presumptuously assail them, and therefore the prophet here represses their insolence; and that his address may have the more weight, he introduces God himself as speaking to them. In the first place, he bids them be still, that they may know that he is God; for we see that when men are carried away without consideration, they go beyond all bounds and measure.

shall not be moved, v. 5. God has assured his church of his special presence with her and concern for her; his honor is embarked in her, he has set up his tabernacle in her and has undertaken the protection of it, and therefore she shall not be moved.

(3.) Deliverance to the church, though her dangers be very great: God shall help her; and who then can hurt her? He shall help her under her troubles, that she shall not sink; nay, that the more she is afflicted the more she shall multiply. God shall help her out of her troubles, and that right early—when the morning appears; that is, very speedily, for he is a present help (v. 1), and very seasonably, when things are brought to the last extremity and when the relief will be most welcome.

6-11 Confidence in God.

These verses give glory to God both as King of nations and as King of saints.

I. As King of nations, ruling the world by his power and providence, and overruling all the affairs of the children of men to his own glory; he does according to his will among the inhabitants of the earth, and none may say, What doest thou?

1. He checks the rage and breaks the power of the nations that oppose him and his interests in the world (v. 6): The heathen raged at David's coming to the throne, and at the setting up of the kingdom of the Son of David; compare Ps. ii. 1, 2.

2. When he pleases to draw his sword, and give it commission, he can make great havoc among the nations and lay all waste (v. 8): Come, behold the works of the Lord; they are to be observed (Ps. lxvi. 5), and to be sought out, Ps. cxi. 2. All the operations of Providence must be considered as the works of the Lord, and his attributes and purposes must be taken notice of in them.

3. When he pleases to sheathe his sword, he puts an end to the wars of the nations and crowns them with peace, v. 9. War and peace depend on his word and will, as much as storms and calms at sea do, Ps. cvii. 25, 29.

II. As King of saints, and as such we must own that great and marvelous are his works, Rev. xv. 3. He does and will do great things,

1. For his own glory (v. 10): Be still, and know that I am God.

(1.) Let his enemies be still, and threaten no more.

(2.) Let his own people be still; let them be calm and sedate, and tremble no more.

2. For his people's safety and protection. He triumphs in the former: I will be exalted; they triumph in this, v. 7 and again v. 11.

(1.) They have the presence of a God of power, of all power.

(2.) They are under the protection of a God in covenant, who not only is able to help them, but is engaged in honor and faithfulness to help them.

Psalm 47

Title
To the chief Musician. A Psalm for the Sons of Korah.

1-4
1 O clap your hands, all ye people; shout unto God with the voice of triumph.
2 For the LORD most high is terrible; he is a great King over all the earth.
3 He shall subdue the people under us, and the nations under our feet.
4 He shall choose our inheritance for us, the excellency of Jacob whom he loved. Selah.

Psalm 47

TITLE. To the Chief Musician. Many songs were dedicated to this leader of the chorus, but he was not overloaded thereby. God's service is such delight that it cannot weary us; and that choicest part of it, the singing of his praises, is so pleasurable that we cannot have too much of it. Doubtless, the chief musician, as he was commissioned with so many sacred songs, felt that the more the merrier. A Psalm for the Sons of Korah. We cannot agree with those who think that the sons of Korah were the authors of these Psalms; they have all the indications of David's authorship that one could expect to see. Our ear has grown accustomed to the ring of David's compositions, and we are morally certain that we hear it in this Psalm. Every expert would detect here the autography of the Son of Jesse, or we are greatly mistaken. The Sons of Korah sang these Psalms, but we believe they did not write them. Fit singers were they whose origin reminded them of sin, whose existence was a proof of sovereign grace, and whose name has a close connection with the name of Calvary.
SUBJECT. Whether the immediate subject of this Psalm be the carrying up of the ark from the house of Obededom to Mount Zion, or the celebration of some memorable victory, it would be hard to decide. As even the doctors differ, who should dogmatise? But it is very clear that both the present sovereignty of Jehovah, and the final victories of our Lord, are here fitly hymned, while his ascension, as the prophecy of them, is sweetly gloried in.
DIVISION. In so short a Psalm, there is no need of any other division than that indicated by the musical pause at the end of Ps 47:4.

EXPOSITION
Verse 1. O clap your hands. The most natural and most enthusiastic tokens of exultation are to be used in view of the victories of the Lord, and his universal reign. Our joy in God may be demonstrative, and yet he will not censure it. All ye people. The joy is to extend to all nations; Israel may lead the van, but all the Gentiles are to follow in the march of triumph, for they have an equal share in that kingdom where there is neither Greek nor Jew, but Christ is all and in all.
Verse 2. For the Lord, or JEHOVAH, the self existent and only God; Most high, most great in power, lofty in dominion, eminent in wisdom, elevated in glory. Is terrible, none can resist his power or stand before his vengeance; yet as these terrors are wielded on the behalf of his subjects, they are fit reasons for rejoicing. Omnipotence, which is terrible to crush, is almighty to protect.
Verse 3. He, with whom is infinite power, shall subdue the people under us. The battle is not ours but the Lord's. He will take his own time, but he will certainly achieve victory for his church. Truth and righteousness shall through grace climb to the ascendant. We wage no doubtful warfare. Hearts the most rebellious, and wills the most stubborn, shall submit to all conquering grace. All the Lord's people, whether Jews or Gentiles, may clap their hands at this, for God's victory will be theirs; but surely apostles, prophets, ministers, and those who suffer and labor the most, may take the largest share in the joy.
Verse 4. While as yet we see not all things put under him, we are glad to put ourselves and our fortunes at his disposal. He shall choose our inheritance for us. We feel his reign to be so gracious that we even now ask to be in the fullest degree the subjects of it. We submit our will, our choice, our desire, wholly to him. Our heritage here and hereafter we leave to him, let him do with us as seemeth him good. The excellency of Jacob whom he loved. He gave his ancient people their portion, he will give us ours, and we ask nothing better; this is the most spiritual and real manner of clapping our hands because of his sovereignty, namely, to leave all our affairs in his

JOHN CALVIN

Psalm 47

Some think that this psalm was composed at the time when the temple was dedicated, and the ark of the covenant placed in the sanctuary. But as this is a conjecture which has little to support it, it is better, if I am not mistaken, instead of detaining ourselves with this, to consider the subject-matter of the psalm, and the use to which it ought especially to be applied. It was no doubt appointed for the stated holy assemblies, as may be easily gathered from the whole tenor of the poem; and perhaps it was composed by David, and delivered by him to the Levites, to be sung by them before the temple was built, and when the ark as yet abode in the tabernacle. But whoever was its author, he exhorts not only the Israelites, but also all nations, to worship the only true God. It chiefly magnifies the favor which, according to the state of things at that time, God had graciously vouchsafed to the offspring of Abraham; and salvation to the whole world was to proceed from this source. It however contains, at the same time, a prophecy of the future kingdom of Christ. It teaches that the glory which then shone under the figure of the material sanctuary will diffuse its splendor far and wide; when God himself will cause the beams of his grace to shine into distant lands, that kings and nations may be united into fellowship with the children of Abraham.

1-4

1. Clap your hands, all ye peoples. As the Psalmist requires the nations, in token of their joy and of their thanksgiving; to God, to clap their hands, or rather exhorts them to a more than ordinary joy, the vehemence of which breaks forth and manifests itself by external expressions, it is certain that he is here speaking of the deliverance which God had wrought for them.

3. He hath set in order the people under us. The prophet when he declares that the Gentiles Will be subdued, so that they will not refuse to obey the chosen people, is describing that kingdom of which he had previously spoken. We are not to suppose that he here treats of that secret providence by which God governs the whole world, but of the special power which he exercises by means of his word; and, therefore, in order that he may be properly called a King, his own people must necessarily acknowledge him as such.

4. He hath chosen our inheritance for us. The inspired poet here celebrates more distinctly the special grace which God, in his goodness, had bestowed upon the chosen and holy seed of Abraham. As he passed by all the rest of the word, and adopted to himself a people who were few in number and contemptible; so it was proper that such a signal pledge of his fatherly love should be distinguished from his common beneficence, which is extended to all mankind without distinction. The word chosen is therefore peculiarly emphatic, implying that God had not dealt with the children of Abraham as he had been accustomed indiscriminately to deal with other nations; but that he had bestowed upon them, as it were by hereditary right, a peculiar dignity by which they excelled all others.

MATTHEW HENRY

Psalm 47

1-4 Exhortation to praise God.

The psalmist, having his own heart filled with great and good thoughts of God, endeavors to engage all about him in the blessed work of praise, as one convinced that God is worthy of all blessing and praise, and as one grieved at his own and others' backwardness to and barrenness in this work. Observe, in these verses,

I. Who are called upon to praise God: "All you people, all you people of Israel;" those were his own subjects, and under his charge, and therefore he will engage them to praise God, for on them he has an influence. Whatever others do, he and his house, he and his people, shall praise the Lord. Or, "All you people and nations of the earth;" and so it may be taken as a prophecy of the conversion of the Gentiles and the bringing of them into the church; see Rom. xv. 11.

II. What they are called upon to do: "O clap your hands, in token of your own joy and satisfaction in what God has done for you, of your approbation, nay, your admiration, of what God has done in general, and of your indignation against all the enemies of God's glory, Job xxvii. 23. Clap your hands, as men transported with pleasure, that cannot contain themselves; shout unto God, not to make him hear (his ear is not heavy), but to make all about you hear, and take notice how much you are affected and filled with the works of God.

III. What is suggested to us as matter for our praise.

1. That the God with whom we have to do is a God of awful majesty (v. 2): The Lord most high is terrible. He is infinitely above the noblest creatures, higher than the highest; there are those perfections in him that are to be reverenced by all, and particularly that power, holiness, and justice, that are to be dreaded by all those that contend with him.

2. That he is a God of sovereign and universal dominion. He is a King that reigns alone, and with an absolute power, a King over all the earth; all the creatures, being made by him, are subject to him, and therefore he is a great King, the King of kings.

3. That he takes a particular care of his people and their concerns, has done so and ever will;

(1.) In giving them victory and success (v. 3), subduing the people and nations under them, both those that stood in their way (Ps. xliv. 2) and those that made attempts upon them.

(2.) In giving them rest and settlement (v. 4): He shall choose our inheritance for us. He had chosen the land of Canaan to be an inheritance for Israel; it was the land which the Lord their God spied out for them; see Deut. xxxii. 8.

5-9 Exhortation to praise God.

We are here most earnestly pressed to praise God, and to sing his praises; so backward are we to this duty that we have need to be urged to it by precept

Psalm 47

5-9

5 God is gone up with a shout, the LORD with the sound of a trumpet.
6 Sing praises to God, sing praises: sing praises unto our King, sing praises.
7 For God is the King of all the earth: sing ye praises with understanding.
8 God reigneth over the heathen: God sitteth upon the throne of his holiness.
9 The princes of the people are gathered together, even the people of the God of Abraham: for the shields of the earth belong unto God: he is greatly exalted.

hands, for then our hands are empty of all care for self, and free to be used in his honor. He was the boast and glory of Israel, he is and shall be ours. He loved his people and became their greatest glory; he loves us, and he shall be our exceeding joy.

Verse 5. God is gone up with a shout. Faith hears the people already shouting. The command of the first verse is here regarded as a fact. The fight is over, the conqueror ascends to his triumphant chariot, and rides up to the gates of the city which is made resplendent with the joy of his return. The words are fully applicable to the ascension of the Redeemer.

Verse 6. Sing praises. What jubilation is here, when five times over the whole earth is called upon to sing to God! He is worthy, he is Creator, he is goodness itself. Sing praises, keep on with the glad work. Never let the music pause. He never ceases to be good, let us never cease to be grateful. Strange that we should need so much urging to attend to so heavenly an exercise.

Verse 7. For God is the King of all the earth. The Jews of our Savior's time resented this truth, but had their hearts been right they would have rejoiced in it. They would have kept their God to themselves, and not even have allowed the Gentile dogs to eat the crumbs from under his table. Alas! how selfishness turns honey into wormwood. Jehovah is not the God of the Jews only, all the nations of the earth are, through the Messiah, yet to own him Lord.

Verse 8. Now at this moment, over the most debased idolaters, God holds a secret rule; here is work for faith. How we ought to long for the day when this truth shall be changed in its aspect, and the rule now unrecognized shall be delighted in! The great truth that God reigneth in providence is the guarantee that in a gracious gospel sense his promises shall be fulfilled, and his kingdom shall come.

Verse 9. The princes of the people are gathered together. The prophetic eye of the psalmist sees the willing subjects of the great King assembled to celebrate his glory. Not only the poor and the men of low estate are there, but nobles bow their willing necks to his sway. "All kings shall bow down before him." No people shall be unrepresented; their great men shall be good men, their royal ones regenerate ones. How august will be the parliament where the Lord Jesus shall open the court, and princes shall rise up to do him honor! Even the people of the God of Abraham. That same God, who was known only to here and there a patriarch like the father of the faithful, shall be adored by a seed as many as the stars of heaven. The covenant promise shall be fulfilled, "In thee and in thy seed shall all the nations of the earth be blessed." Shiloh shall come, and "to him shall the gathering of the people be." Babel's dispersion shall be obliterated by the gathering arm of the Great Shepherd King.

For the shields of the earth belong unto God. The insignia of pomp, the emblems of rank, the weapons of war, all must pay loyal homage to the King of all. Right honorables must honor Jesus, and majesties must own him to be far more majestic. Those who are earth's protectors, the shields of the commonwealth, derive their might from him, and are his. All principalities and powers must be subject unto Jehovah and his Christ, for He is greatly exalted. In nature, in power, in character, in glory, there is none to compare with him. Oh, glorious vision of a coming era! Make haste, ye wheels of time! Meanwhile, ye saints, "Be ye steadfast, unmovable, always abounding in the work of the Lord, forasmuch as ye know that your labor is not in vain in the Lord."

5-9

5. God is gone up with triumph. There is here an allusion to the ancient ceremony which was observed under the Law. As the sound of trumpets was wont to be used in solemnizing the holy assemblies, the prophet says that God goes up, when the trumpets encourage and stir up the people to magnify and extol his power. When this ceremony was performed in old time, it was just as if a king, making his entrance among his subjects, presented himself to them in magnificent attire and great splendor, by which he gained their admiration and reverence.

7. For God is King of all the earth. The Psalmist, having called God in the close of the preceding verse King of the chosen people, now calls him King of all the earth; and thus, while he claims to the Jews the right and honor of primogeniture, he at the same time joins to them the Gentiles as associates and partakers with them of the same blessing. By these words he intimates that the kingdom of God would be much more magnificent and glorious at the coming of the Messiah, than it was under the shadowy dispensation of the Law, inasmuch as it would be extended to the utmost boundaries of the earth. To show the greater earnestness in his exhortation, he repeats the words, Sing praises to God, five times.

8. He hath obtained the kingdom over the heathen. The prophet repeatedly informs us that God reigns over the Gentiles; and from this it is easy to gather that he here treats of a new and a previously unheard of manner of reigning. There is an implied contrast between the time of the Law, when God confined his empire, or kingdom, within the boundaries of Judea, and the coming of Christ, when he extended it far and wide, so as to occupy the whole world from one end to the other. The majesty of God sent forth some sparks of its brightness among the heathen nations, when David made them tributary; but the prophet could not, on that account, have properly said that God reigned among them, since they both contemned his worship and the true religion, and also wished to see the Church completely extinguished.

9. The princes of the peoples are gathered together. The Psalmist enriches and amplifies by various expressions the preceding sentence. He again declares that the way in which God obtained dominion over the Gentiles was, that those who before were aliens united in the adoption of the same faith with the Jews; and thus different nations, from a state of miserable dispersion, were gathered together into one body. When the doctrine of the Gospel was manifested and shone forth, it did not remove the Jews from the covenant which God had long before made with them. On the contrary, it has rather joined us to them. As then the calling of the Gentiles was nothing else than the means by which they were grafted and incorporated into the family of Abraham, the prophet justly states, that strangers or aliens from every direction were gathered together to the chosen people, that by such an increase the kingdom of God might be extended through all quarters of the globe.

upon precept, and line upon line; so we are here (v. 6): Sing praises to God, and again, Sing praises, Sing praises to our King, and again, Sing praises. This intimates that it is a very necessary and excellent duty, that it is a duty we ought to be frequent and abundant in; we may sing praises again and again in the same words, and it is no vain repetition if it be done with new affections. Should not a people praise their God? Dan. v. 4. Should not subjects praise their king? God is our God, our King, and therefore we must praise him; we must sing his praises, as those that are pleased with them and that are not ashamed of them.

Three things are mentioned in these verses as just matter for our praises, and each of them will admit of a double sense:

I. We must praise God going up (v. 5): God has gone up with a shout, which may refer,

1. To the carrying up of the ark to the hill of Zion, which was done with great solemnity, David himself dancing before it, the priests, it is likely, blowing the trumpets, and the people following with their loud huzzas.

2. To the ascension of our Lord Jesus into heaven, when he had finished his work on earth, Acts i. 9.

II. We must praise God reigning, v. 7, 8. God is not only our King, and therefore we owe our homage to him, but he is King of all the earth (v. 7), over all the kings of the earth, and therefore in every place the incense of praise is to be offered up to him. Now this may be understood,

1. Of the kingdom of providence. God, as Creator, and the God of nature, reigns over the heathen, disposes of them and all their affairs, as he pleases, though they know him not, nor have any regard to him: He sits upon the throne of his holiness, which he has prepared in the heavens, and there he rules over all, even over the heathen, serving his own purposes by them and upon them.

2. Of the kingdom of the Messiah. Jesus Christ, who is God, and whose throne is for ever and ever reigns over the heathen; not only he is entrusted with the administration of the providential kingdom, but he shall set up the kingdom of his grace in the Gentile world, and rule in the hearts of multitudes that were bred up in heathenism, Eph. ii. 12, 13.

III. We must praise God as attended and honored by the princes of the people, v. 9. This may be understood,

1. Of the congress or convention of the states of Israel, the heads and rulers of the several tribes, at the solemn feasts, or to despatch the public business of the nation.

2. It may be applied to the calling of the Gentiles into the church of Christ, and taken as a prophecy that in the days of the Messiah the kings of the earth and their people should join themselves to the church, and bring their glory and power into the New Jerusalem.

Psalm 48

Title
A Song and Psalm for the sons of Korah.

1-7
1 Great is the LORD, and greatly to be praised in the city of our God, in the mountain of his holiness.
2 Beautiful for situation, the joy of the whole earth, is mount Zion, on the sides of the north, the city of the great King.
3 God is known in her palaces for a refuge.
4 For, lo, the kings were assembled, they passed by together.
5 They saw it, and so they marveled; they were troubled, and hasted away.
6 Fear took hold upon them there, and pain, as of a woman in travail.
7 Thou breakest the ships of Tarshish with an east wind.

Psalm 48

TITLE. A Song and Psalm for the Sons of Korah. A song for joyfulness and a Psalm for reverence. Alas! every song is not a Psalm, for poets are not all heaven born, and every Psalm is not a song, for in coming before God we have to utter mournful confessions as well as exulting praises. The Sons of Korah were happy in having so large a selection of song; the worship where such a variety of music was used could not become monotonous, but must have given widest scope for all the sacred passions of gracious souls.
SUBJECT AND DIVISION. It would be idle dogmatically to attribute this song to any one event of Jewish history. Its author and date are unknown. It records the withdrawal of certain confederate kings from Jerusalem, their courage failing them before striking a blow. The mention of the ships of Tarshish may allow us to conjecture that the Psalm was written in connection with the overthrow of Ammon, Moab, and Edom in the reign of Jehoshaphat; and if the reader will turn to 2 Chronicles 20, and note especially 2Ch 20:19,25,36, he will probably accept the suggestion. Ps 48:1-3, are in honor of the Lord and the city dedicated to his worship. From Ps 48:4-8 the song records the confusion of Zion's foes, ascribing all the praise to God; Ps 48:9-11 extolling Zion, and avowing Jehovah to be her God for evermore.

EXPOSITION
Verse 1. Great is the Lord. How great Jehovah is essentially none can conceive; but we can all see that he is great in the deliverance of his people, great in their esteem who are delivered, and great in the hearts of those enemies whom he scatters by their own fears. Instead of the mad cry of Ephesus, "Great is Diana," we bear the reasonable, demonstrable, self evident testimony, "Great is Jehovah." There is none great in the church but the Lord. Jesus is "the great Shepherd," he is "a Savior, and a great one," our great God and Savior, our great High Priest; his Father has divided him a portion with the great, and his name shall be great unto the ends of the earth.
Verse 2. Beautiful for situation. Jerusalem was so naturally, she was styled the Queen of the East; the church is so spiritually, being placed near God's heart, within the mountain of his power, upon the hills of his faithfulness, in the center of providential operations. The elevation of the church is her beauty.
Verse 3. God is known in her palaces for a refuge. We worship no unknown God. We know him as our refuge in distress, we delight in him as such, and run to him in every time of need. We know nothing else as our refuge. Though we are made kings, and our houses are palaces, yet we have no confidence in ourselves, but trust in the Lord Protector, whose well known power is our bulwark.
Verse 4. The kings were assembled, they passed by together. They came and they went. No sooner together than scattered. They came one way and fled twenty ways. Boastful the gathering hosts with their royal leaders, despairing the fugitive bands with their astonished captains. They came like foam on the angry sea, like foam they melted away.
Verse 5. They saw it, and so they marveled. They came, they saw, but they did not conquer. There was no veni, vidi, vici for them. No sooner did they perceive that the Lord was in the Holy City, than they took to their heels. Before the Lord came to blows with them, they were faint hearted, and beat a retreat. They were troubled and hasted away. The troublers were troubled. Their haste in coming was nothing to their hurry in going. Panic seized them, horses were not fleet enough; they would have borrowed the wings of the wind. They fled ignominiously, like children in a fright. Glory be to God, it shall be even thus with the foes of his church; when the Lord cometh to our help, our enemies shall be as nothing. Could they foresee their ignominious defeat, they would not advance to the attack.

JOHN CALVIN

Psalm 48

1-3

1. Great is Jehovah, and greatly to be praised. The prophet, before proceeding to make mention of that special example of the favor of God towards them, to which I have adverted, teaches in general that the city of Jerusalem was happy and prosperous, because God had been graciously pleased to take upon him the charge of defending and preserving it. In this way he separates and distinguishes the Church of God from all the rest of the world; and when God selects from amongst the whole human race a small number whom he embraces with his fatherly love, this is an invaluable blessing which he bestows upon them.

2. Beautiful for situation, the joy of the whole earth, is mount Zion. For the confirmation of the statement made in the preceding sentence, the prophet celebrates the excellencies for which mount Zion was at that time renowned; and in them was to be seen the glory of God, of which I have just now spoken. The beauty of its situation, which he mentions in the first place, was indeed natural; but by it he gives us to understand, that from the very commencement the agreeable appearance of the city had engraven upon it marks of the favor of God, so that the sight of it alone showed that God had in a special manner adorned and enriched that place, with the view of its being, at some future period, consecrated to sacred purposes.

3. God in her palaces is known for a defense. Here the sacred poet again brings forward, for the purpose of setting forth the dignity of the city of Jerusalem, the protection which God afforded it.

4-7

4. For, behold! the kings assembled. Here that special deliverance of which I have spoken is touched upon. The prophet relates how, when the kings were assembled together to destroy Jerusalem, their efforts passed away without producing any effect, even as clouds in the atmosphere vanish away; yea, he tells us, that by a simple look at the city, they were defeated and undone, and that not after an ordinary manner, but like a woman who, when the hour of child-birth has come upon her, finds herself suddenly afflicted with pain and sorrow.

5, 6. When the Psalmist says that upon beholding the city they marveled—were frightened—fled precipitately—and were seized with sorrow, like the pangs of a woman in travail—he heaps together as many and varied expressions as possible, in order to set forth the greatness of the miracle which God had wrought in the overthrow of such a vast and formidable host. The language should be resolved thus: As soon as they saw the city they marveled. It is related of Caesar in ancient times, that when speaking of the ease with which he subdued Egypt, he made use of the laconic saying, "I came, I saw, I conquered;" but the prophet here states, on the contrary, that the ungodly were struck with amazement at the mere sight of the city, as if God had dazzled their eyes with the splendor of his glory.

MATTHEW HENRY

Psalm 48

1-7 The beauty and strength of Zion.

The psalmist is designing to praise Jerusalem and to set forth the grandeur of that city; but he begins with the praises of God and his greatness (v. 1), and ends with the praises of God and his goodness, v. 14. For, whatever is the subject of our praises, God must be both the Alpha and Omega of them. And, particularly, whatever is said to the honor of the church must redound to the honor of the church's God.

What is here said to the honor of Jerusalem is,

I. That the King of heaven owns it: it is the city of our God (v. 1), which he chose out of all the cities of Israel to put his name there. Of Zion he said kinder things than ever he said of any other place upon earth. This is my rest for ever; here will I dwell, for I have desired it, Ps. cxxxii. 13, 14. It is the city of the great King (v. 2), the King of all the earth, who is pleased to declare himself in a special manner present there.

1. It is enlightened with the knowledge of God. In Judah God is known, and his name is great, but especially in Jerusalem, the head-quarters of the priests, whose lips were to keep this knowledge. In Jerusalem God is great (v. 1) who in other places was made little of, was made nothing of. There God is known (v. 3) and where he is known he will be great; none contemn God but those that are ignorant of him.

2. It is devoted to the honor of God. It is therefore called the mountain of his holiness, for holiness to the Lord is written upon it and all the furniture of it, Zech. xiv. 20, 21.

3. It is the place appointed for the solemn service and worship of God; there he is greatly praised, and greatly to be praised, v. 1.

4. It is taken under his special protection (v. 3): He is known for a refuge; that is, he has approved himself such a one, and as such a one he is there applied to by his worshippers.

5. Upon all these accounts, Jerusalem, and especially Mount Zion, on which the temple was built, were universally beloved and admired—beautiful for situation, and the joy of the whole earth, v. 2. The situation must needs be every way agreeable, when Infinite Wisdom chose it for the place of the sanctuary; and that which made it beautiful was that it was the mountain of holiness, for there is a beauty in holiness.

II. That the kings of the earth were afraid of it. That God was known in their palaces for a refuge they had had a late instance, and a very remarkable one. Whatever it was,

1. They had had but too much occasion to fear their enemies; for the kings were assembled, v. 4. The neighboring princes were confederate against Jerusalem; their heads and horns, their policies and powers, were combined for its ruin; they were assembled with all their forces; they passed, advanced, and marched on together, not doubting but

Psalm 48

8-14
8 As we have heard, so have we seen in the city of the LORD of hosts, in the city of our God: God will establish it for ever. Selah.
9 We have thought of thy loving kindness, O God, in the midst of thy temple.
10 According to thy name, O God, so is thy praise unto the ends of the earth: thy right hand is full of righteousness.
11 Let mount Zion rejoice, let the daughters of Judah be glad, because of thy judgments.
12 Walk about Zion, and go round about her: tell the towers thereof.
13 Mark ye well her bulwarks, consider her palaces; that ye may tell it to the generation following.
14 For this God is our God for ever and ever: he will be our guide even unto death.

Verse 6. Fear took hold upon them there. They were in Giant Despair's grip. Where they hoped to triumph, there they quivered with dismay. They did not take the city, but fear took hold on them. And pain, as of a woman in travail. They were as much overcome as a woman whose fright causes premature delivery; or, as full of pain as a poor mother in her pangs—a strong expression, commonly employed by Orientals to set forth the extremity of anguish. When the Lord arises for the help of his church, the proudest of his foes shall be as trembling women, and their dismay shall be but the beginning of eternal defeat.
Verse 7. Thou breakest the ships of Tarshish with an east wind. As easily as vessels are driven to shipwreck, dost thou overturn the most powerful adversaries; or it may mean the strength of some nations lies in their ships, whose wooden walls are soon broken; but our strength is in our God, and therefore, it fails not; or there may be another meaning, though thou art our defense, yet thou takest vengeance on our inventions, and while thou dost preserve us, yet our ships, our comforts, our earthly ambitions, are taken from us that we may look alone to thee.
Verse 8. As we have heard, so have we seen in the city of the Lord of hosts, in the city of our God. Our father's stories are reproduced before our very eyes. We heard the promise, and we have seen the fulfillment. The records of Zion, wonderful as they are, are proved to be truthful, because present facts are in perfect harmony therewith.
Verse 9. We have thought. Holy men are thoughtful men; they do not suffer God's wonders to pass before their eyes and melt into forgetfulness, but they meditate deeply upon them. Of thy lovingkindness, O God. What a delightful subject! Devout minds never tire of so divine a theme. It is well to think of past lovingkindness in times of trial, and equally profitable to remember it in seasons of prosperity. Grateful memories sweeten sorrows and sober joys. In the midst of thy temple. Fit place for so devout a meditation. Where God is most seen he is best loved.
Verse 10. According to thy name, O God, so is thy praise unto the ends of the earth. Great fame is due to his great name. The glory of Jehovah's exploits overleaps the boundaries of earth; angels behold with wonder, and from every star delighted intelligences proclaim his fame beyond the ends of the earth.
Verse 11. Let mount Zion rejoice. As the first of the cities of Judah, and the main object of the enemies' attack, let her lead the song. Let the daughters of Judah be glad, let the smaller towns join the chorus, for they join in the common victory.
Verse 12. Walk about Zion; often beat her bounds, even as Israel marched around Jericho. With leisurely and careful inspection survey her. And go round about her. Encircle her again and again with loving perambulations. We cannot too frequently or too deeply consider the origin, privileges, history, security, and glory of the church.
Verse 13. Mark ye well her bulwarks. Consider most attentively how strong are her ramparts, how safely her inhabitants are entrenched behind successive lines of defense.
Verse 14. For this God is our God for ever and ever. A good reason for preserving a record of all that he has wrought. Israel will not change her God so as to wish to forget, nor will the Lord change so as to make the past mere history. He will be the covenant God of his people world without end. There is no other God, we wish for no other, we would have no other even if there were.

JOHN CALVIN

7. By the east wind thou breakest in pieces the ships of Tarshish. The enemies of the Church were overthrown and plunged into destruction, just as God by suddenly raising storms sinks the ships of Cilicia to the bottom of the sea. The Psalmist celebrates the power which God is accustomed to display in great and violent storms; and his language implies that it is not to be wondered at if God, who breaks by the violence of the winds the strongest ships, had also overthrown his enemies, who were inflated with the presumptuous confidence which they reposed in their own strength. By the sea of Tarshish the Hebrews mean the Mediterranean Sea.

8-10
8. The concluding clause of the verse distinguishes Jerusalem from all the other cities of the world, which are subject to vicissitudes, and flourish only for a time.
9. O God! we have waited for thy mercy. This verse teaches us that the faithful were preserved by the power of God; for, when all things were in a state of the greatest confusion, they continued tranquil and patient until God at length, having pity upon them, brought them help.
10. As is thy name, O God! so is thy praise. The meaning of the inspired poet is, That the names of false gods prevailed, and were renowned among men, although they had done nothing to furnish matter of true praise; but that it was altogether different with respect to the God of Israel: for wherever the report of him was carried, all would understand that he was the deliverer of his people.

11-14
11. Mount Zion shall rejoice. The Psalmist now concludes his exhortation to rejoicing, telling us that Jerusalem and the other cities of Judea shall have cause to commend the righteousness of God, because they had found from undoubted experience that he was the protector of their welfare.
12, 13. Encompass Zion, etc. Here the prophet again commends the situation and beauty of Jerusalem, intimating that the city was strongly fortified and impregnable; and he does this, because in these external things the blessing of God in some respect shone forth. We must always bear in mind what he stated in a preceding verse, that "God in her palaces is known for a fortress." In making mention here of her towers and walls, he sets them before us as a mirror in which the character of God may be seen.
14. For this God is our God for ever and ever. From these words it appears still more clearly, that when the prophet spake of the palaces of Jerusalem, it was not that the godly should keep their eyes fixed upon them, but that by the aid of these outward things they should elevate their minds to the contemplation of the glory of God. God would have them to behold, as it were, the marks of his grace engraven wherever they turned themselves, or rather, to recognize him as present in these marks. From this we conclude, that whatever dignity shines forth in the Church, we are not to consider it otherwise than as the means of presenting God to our view, that we may magnify and praise him in his gifts.

MATTHEW HENRY

they should soon make themselves masters of that city which should have been the joy, but was the envy of the whole earth.
2. God made their enemies to fear them. The very sight of Jerusalem struck them into a consternation and gave check to their fury, as the sight of the tents of Jacob frightened Balaam from his purpose to curse Israel (Num. xxiv. 2): They saw it and marveled, and hasted away, v. 5. Not Veni, vidi, vici—I came, I saw, I conquered; but, on the contrary, Veni vidi victus sum—I came, I saw, I was defeated. Not that there was any thing to be seen in Jerusalem that was so very formidable; but the sight of it brought to mind what they had heard concerning the special presence of God in that city. Though they were kings, though they were many in confederacy, yet they knew themselves an unequal match for Omnipotence, and therefore fear came upon them, and pain, v. 6.

8-14 God's care of His Church.
We have here the good use and improvement which the people of God are taught to make of his late glorious and gracious appearances for them against their enemies, that they might work for their good.
I. Let our faith in the word of God be hereby confirmed. If we compare what God has done with what he has spoken, we shall find that, as we have heard, so have we seen (v. 8), and what we have seen obliges us to believe what we have heard.
II. Let our hope of the stability and perpetuity of the church be hereby encouraged. "From what we have seen, compared with what we have heard, in the city of our God, we may conclude that God will establish it for ever."
III. Let our minds be hereby filled with good thoughts of God. "From what we have heard, and seen, and hope for, we may take occasion to think much of God's loving-kindness, whenever we meet in the midst of his temple," v. 9.
IV. Let us give to God the glory of the great things which he has done for us, and mention them to his honor (v. 10): "According to thy name, O God! so is thy praise, not only in Jerusalem, but to the ends of the earth."
V. Let all the members of the church in particular take to themselves the comfort of what God does for his church in general (v. 11): "Let Mount Zion rejoice: let the women in their songs and dances, as usual on occasion of public joys, celebrate with thankfulness the great salvation which God has wrought for us."
VI. Let us diligently observe the instances and evidences of the church's beauty, strength, and safety, and faithfully transmit our observations to those that shall come after us (v. 12, 13).
VII. Let us triumph in God, and in the assurances we have of his everlasting lovingkindness, v. 14. Tell this to the generation following

Psalm 49

Title
To the chief Musician, a Psalm for the sons of Korah.

1-7
1 Hear this, all ye people; give ear, all ye inhabitants of the world:
2 Both low and high, rich and poor, together.
3 My mouth shall speak of wisdom; and the meditation of my heart shall be of understanding.
4 I will incline mine ear to a parable: I will open my dark saying upon the harp.
5 Wherefore should I fear in the days of evil, when the iniquity of my heels shall compass me about?
6 They that trust in their wealth, and boast themselves in the multitude of their riches;
7 None of them can by any means redeem his brother, nor give to God a ransom for him:

Psalm 49

TITLE. To the Chief Musician, a Psalm for the sons of Korah. This is precisely the same as on former occasions, and no remark is needed.
DIVISION. The poet musician sings, to the accompaniment of his harp, the despicable character of those who trust in their wealth, and so he consoles the oppressed believer. The first four verses are a preface; from Ps 49:5-12 all fear of great oppressors is removed by the remembrance of their end and their folly; Ps 49:13 contains an expression of wonder at the perpetuity of folly; Ps 49:14-15 contrast the ungodly and the righteous in their future; and from Ps 49:16-20 the lesson from the whole is given in an admonitory form. Note the chorus in Ps 49:2,20, and also the two Selahs.

EXPOSITION
Verses 1-4. In these four verses the poet prophet calls universal humanity to listen to his didactic hymn.
Verse 1. Hear this, all ye people. All men are concerned in the subject, it is of them, and therefore to them that the psalmist would speak. It is not a topic which men delight to consider, and therefore he who would instruct them must press them to give ear. Where, as in this case, the theme claims to be wisdom and understanding, attention is very properly demanded; and when the style combines the sententiousness of the proverb with the sweetness of poesy, interest is readily excited.
Verse 2. Both low and high, rich and poor, together. Sons of great men, and children of mean men, men of large estate, and ye who pine in poverty, ye are all bidden to hear the inspired minstrel as he touches his harp to a mournful but instructive lay. The low will be encouraged, the high will be warned, the rich will be sobered, the poor consoled, there will be a useful lesson for each if they are willing to learn it.
Verse 3. My mouth shall speak of wisdom. Inspired and therefore lifted beyond himself, the prophet is not praising his own attainments, but extolling the divine Spirit which spoke in him. He knew that the Spirit of truth and wisdom spoke through him. He who is not sure that his matter is good has no right to ask a hearing. And the meditation of my heart shall be of understanding. The same Spirit who made the ancient seers eloquent, also made them thoughtful.
Verse 4. I will incline mine ear to a parable. He who would have others hear, begins by hearing himself. As the minstrel leans his ear to his harp, so must the preacher give his whole soul to his ministry. The truth came to the psalmist as a parable, and he endeavored to unriddle it for popular use; he would not leave the truth in obscurity, but he listened to its voice till he so well understood it as to be able to interpret and translate it into the common language of the multitude.
Verse 5. Wherefore should I fear in the days of evil, when the iniquity of my heels shall compass me about? The man of God looks calmly forward to dark times when those evils which have dogged his heels shall gain a temporary advantage over him. Iniquitous men, here called in the abstract iniquity, lie in wait for the righteous, as serpents that aim at the heels of travelers: the iniquity of our heels is that evil which aims to trip us up or impede us.
Verse 6. What if the good man's foes be among the great ones of the earth! yet he need not fear them. They that trust in their wealth. Poor fools, to be content with such a rotten confidence. When we set our rock in contrast with theirs, it would be folly to be afraid of them. Even though they are loud in their brags, we can afford to smile. What if they glory and boast themselves in the multitude of their riches? yet while we glory in our God we are not dismayed by their proud threatenings. Great strength, position, and estate, make wicked men very lofty in their own esteem, and tyrannical towards others; but the heir of heaven is not overawed by their dignity, nor cowed by

JOHN CALVIN

Psalm 49

1-4

1. Hear this, all ye people. Whoever may have been the penman of this psalm, it discusses one of the most important principles in divine philosophy, and there is a propriety in the elevated terms designed to awaken and secure attention, with which the Psalmist announces his purpose to discourse of things of a deep and momentous nature. As God's providence of the world is not presently apparent, we must exercise patience, and rise superior to the suggestions of carnal sense in anticipating the favorable issue. That it is our duty to maintain a resolute struggle with our afflictions, however severe these may be, and that it were foolish to place happiness in the enjoyment of such fleeting possessions as the riches, honors, or pleasures of this world, may be precepts which even the heathen philosophers have enforced, but they have uniformly failed in setting before us the true source of consolation.

3. My mouth shall speak of wisdom. The prophet was warranted in applying these commendatory terms to the doctrine which he was about to communicate. It is, no doubt, by plain appeals to observation that we find him reproving human folly; but the general principle upon which his instruction proceeds is one by no means obvious to the common sense of mankind, not to say that his design in using such terms is less to assert the dignity of his subject than simply to awaken attention.

4. I will incline my ear to a parable. The Psalmist, when he adds that he will open his dark saying, shows that nothing was farther from his intention than to wrap the subject of his discourse in perplexing and intricate obscurity. The truths of revelation are so high as to exceed our comprehension; but, at the same time, the Holy Spirit has accommodated them so far to our capacity, as to render all Scripture profitable for instruction.

5-9

5. Wherefore should I fear in the days of evil? The Psalmist now enters upon the point on which he proposed to discourse, That the people of God must not yield to despondency even in the most distressing circumstances, when their enemies may seem to have enclosed them on every side, but must rest assured that God, although he connives for a time, is awake to their condition, and only watches the best opportunity of executing his judgments.

6. They trust in their wealth. We are now furnished with the reason why the suffering children of God should dismiss their apprehensions, and keep themselves from despondency, even when reduced to extremity by the violence and treachery of their enemies. Any boasted power which they possess is fleeting and evanescent. The Psalmist would convince us that the fear of man is unwarrantable; that it argues ignorance of what man is even at his best; and that it were as reasonable to startle at a shadow or a specter.

7. None can give a price to God for the ransom of another, where he adverts to the truth that men's lives are absolutely

MATTHEW HENRY

Psalm 49

1-5 A call to attention.

I. The psalmist demands the attention of others to that which he was about to say (v. 1, 2): Hear this, all you people; hear it and heed it, hear it and consider it; what is spoken once, hear twice. He gives a good reason why his discourse should be regarded (v. 3): My mouth shall speak of wisdom; what he had to say,

1. Was true and good. It is wisdom and understanding; it will make those wise and intelligent that receive it and submit to it. It is not doubtful but certain, not trivial but weighty, not a matter of nice speculation but of admirable use to guide us in the right way to our great end.

2. It was what he had himself well digested. What his mouth spoke was the meditation of his heart (as Ps. xix. 14; xlv. 1); it was what God put into his mind, what he had himself seriously considered, and was fully apprized of the meaning of and convinced of the truth of.

II. He engages his own attention (v. 4): I will incline my ear to a parable. It is called a parable, not because it is figurative and obscure, but because it is a wise discourse and very instructive. It is the same word that is used concerning Solomon's proverbs. The psalmist will himself incline his ear to it.

III. He promises to make the matter as plain and as affecting as he could: I will open my dark saying upon the harp. What he learned for himself he would not conceal or confine to himself, but would communicate, for the benefit of others.

IV. He begins with the application of it to himself, and that is the right method in which to treat of divine things. We must first preach to ourselves before we undertake to admonish or instruct others. Before he comes to set down the folly of carnal security (v. 6), he here lays down, from his own experience, the benefit and comfort of a holy gracious security, which those enjoy who trust in God, and not in their worldly wealth: Wherefore should I fear? he means, Wherefore should I fear their fear (Isa. viii. 12), the fears of worldly people.

6-14 The vanity of worldly riches; the end of the wicked.

In these verses we have,

I. A description of the spirit and way of worldly people, whose portion is in this life, Ps. xvii. 14. It is taken for granted that they have wealth, and a multitude of riches (v. 6), houses and lands of inheritance, which they call their own, v. 11. God often gives abundance of the good things of this world to bad men who live in contempt of him and rebellion against him, by which it appears that they are not the best things in themselves (for then God would give most of them to his best friends), and that they are not the best things for us, for then those would not have so much of them who, being marked for ruin, are to be ripened for it by their prosperity, Prov. i. 32.

Psalm 49

8-14

8 (For the redemption of their soul is precious, and it ceaseth for ever:)

9 That he should still live for ever, and not see corruption.

10 For he seeth that wise men die, likewise the fool and the brutish person perish, and leave their wealth to others.

11 Their inward thought is, that their houses shall continue for ever, and their dwelling places to all generations; they call their lands after their own names.

12 Nevertheless man being in honor abideth not: he is like the beasts that perish.

13 This their way is their folly: yet their posterity approve their sayings. Selah.

14 Like sheep they are laid in the grave; death shall feed on them; and the upright shall have dominion over them in the morning; and their beauty shall consume in the grave from their dwelling.

their haughtiness. He sees the small value of riches, and the helplessness of their owners in the hour of death, and therefore he is not so mean as to be afraid of an ephemera, a moth, a bubble.

Verse 7. None of them can by any means redeem his brother. With all their riches, the whole of them put together could not rescue a comrade from the chill grasp of death. They boast of what they will do with us, let them see to themselves. Let them weigh their gold in the scales of death, and see how much they can buy therewith from the worm and the grave. The poor are their equals in this respect; let them love their friend ever so dearly, they cannot give to God a ransom for him.

Verse 8. For the redemption of their soul is precious, and it ceaseth for ever. Too great is the price, the purchase is hopeless. For ever must the attempt to redeem a soul with money remain a failure. Death comes and wealth cannot bribe him; hell follows and no golden key can unlock its dungeon.

Verse 9. No price could secure for any man that he should still live for ever, and not see corruption. Mad are men now after gold, what would they be if it could buy the elixir of immortality? Gold is lavished out of the bag to cheat the worm of the poor body by embalming it, or enshrining it in a coffin of lead, but it is a miserable business, a very burlesque and comedy. As for the soul, it is too subtle a thing to be detained when it hears the divine command to soar through tracks unknown. Never, therefore, will we fear those base nibblers at our heels, whose boasted treasure proves to be so powerless to save.

Verse 10. For he seeth that wise men die. Every one sees this. The proud persecuting rich man cannot help seeing it. He cannot shut his eyes to the fact that wiser men than he are dying, and that he also, with all his craft, must die. Likewise the fool and the brutish person perish. Folly has no immunity from death. Off goes the jester's cap, as well as the student's gown. Jollity cannot laugh off the dying hour; death who visits the university, does not spare the tavern. Thoughtlessness and brutishness meet their end as surely as much care and wasting study. In fact, while the truly wise, so far as this world is concerned, die, the fool has a worse lot, for he perishes, is blotted out of remembrance, bewailed by none, remembered no more. And leave their wealth to others. Not a farthing can they carry with them. Whether heirs male of their own body, lawfully begotten, inherit their estates, or they remain unclaimed, it matters not, their hoardings are no longer theirs; friends may quarrel over their property, or strangers divide it as spoil, they cannot interfere. Ye boasters, hold ye your own, before ye dream of despoiling the sons of the living God. Keep shoes to your own feet in death's dark pilgrimage, ere ye seek to bite our heels.

Verse 11. Their inward thought is, their houses shall continue for ever, and their dwelling places to all generations. He is very foolish who is more a fool in his inmost thought than he dare to be in his speech. Such rotten fruit, rotten at the core, are worldlings. Down deep in their hearts, though they dare not say so, they fancy that earthly goods are real and enduring. Foolish dreamers! The frequent dilapidation of their castles and manor houses should teach them better, but still they cherish the delusion. They cannot tell the mirage from the true streams of water; they fancy rainbows to be stable, and clouds to be the everlasting hills. They call their lands after their own names. Common enough is this practice. His grounds are made to bear the groundling's name, he might as well write it on the water. Men have even called countries by their own names, but what are they the better for the idle compliment, even if men perpetuate their nomenclature?

Verse 12. Nevertheless man being in honor abideth not. He is but a lodger for the hour, and does not stay a night: even when he dwells in marble halls his notice to quit is written out. Eminence is evermore in imminence of peril.

Verse 13. Their vain confidences are not casual aberrations from the path of wisdom, but their way, their usual and regular course; their whole life is regulated by such principles. Their life path is essential folly. They are fools at the disposal of God, and that they never can be extended by any human arrangement one moment beyond the period which God has fixed.

8. He enforces the same lesson in the verse which follows, where he states that the redemption of their soul is precious, an expression not to be understood as implying merely that it is an event of rare occurrence, but that it never can take place, as 1 Samuel 3:1, where the word of the Lord is said to have been precious under the priesthood of Eli, when it is evidently meant that it had ceased altogether. The Psalmist would assert that no man can hope to purchase an immortality either for himself or others in this world.

9. That he should still live for ever, more fully express the truth, that it is not merely impossible to redeem the life of men when they are dead, but impossible while they are yet living, to extend the term of their existence. A definite limit has been assigned to every man's life. This he cannot pass over, and the Psalmist would impress the fact upon us as one which stamps folly upon the conduct of the wicked, who will cherish their unfounded confidence even at the moment when they are upon the brink of the grave.

10-12

10. For he shall see that wise men die. I consider the ninth and tenth verses to be connected, and that it is the intention of the Psalmist to censure the folly of those who dream of spending an eternity in this world, and set themselves seriously to establish a permanent settlement in it, though they cannot but see their fellow-creatures cut down daily before their eyes by the stroke of death. It is a common proverb, that experience teaches fools, and they may be looked upon as something worse who will not lay to heart their mortality, when surrounded by so many convincing illustrations of it. This seems obviously to be the connection.

11. Their desire should be to have their names written in the book of life, and to be blessed before God and his holy angels; but their ambition is of another kind—to be renowned and extolled upon earth. By the expression, calling out, it is insinuated that the fame of ungodly men is but an empty sound.

12. And man shall not abide in honor. Having exposed the vain and delusory nature of the fancies entertained by the ungodly, he next shows that however fondly they may cherish them, they must experience the same fate with the beasts of the field. It is true that there is a great difference, so far as the soul is concerned, between man and the brute creation; but the Psalmist speaks of things as they appear in this world, and in this respect he was warranted to say of the ungodly that they die as the beasts.

13-15

13. This their way is foolishness. The Psalmist means that the event proves them to be wholly destitute of wisdom, in placing their happiness upon earthly objects, and brands them, notwithstanding all the pretensions they make to foresight and shrewdness, with ridicule and contempt. And

II. A demonstration of their folly herein. In general (v. 13), This their way is their folly. Note, The way of worldliness is a very foolish way: those that lay up their treasure on earth, and set their affections on things below, act contrary both to right reason and to their true interest.

1. That with all their wealth they cannot save the life of the dearest friend they have in the world, nor purchase a reprieve for him when he is under the arrest of death (v. 7-9): None of them can by any means redeem his brother, his brother worldling, who would give counter-security out of his own estate, if he would but be bail for him: and gladly he would, in hopes that he might do the same kindness for him another time. But their words will not be taken one for another, nor will one man's estate be the ransom of another man's life. God does not value it; it is of no account with him; and the true value of things is as they stand in his books. His justice will not accept it by way of commutation or equivalent. The Lord of our brother's life is the Lord of our estate, and may take both if he please, without either difficulty to himself or wrong to us; and therefore one cannot be ransom for another.

2. That with all their wealth they cannot secure themselves from the stroke of death. The worldling sees, and it vexes him to see it, that wise men die, likewise the fool and the brutish person perish, v. 10. Therefore he cannot but expect that it will, at length, come to his own turn; he cannot find any encouragement to hope that he himself shall continue for ever, and therefore foolishly comforts himself with this, that, though he shall not, his house shall.

3. That, as their wealth will stand them in no stead in a dying hour, so neither will their honor (v. 12): Man, being in honor, abides not. We will suppose a man advanced to the highest pinnacle of preferment, as great and happy as the world can make him, man in splendor; yet then he abides not.

4. That their condition on the other side of death will be very miserable. The world they dote upon will not only not save them from death, but will sink them so much the lower into hell (v. 14): Like sheep they are laid in the grave. Their prosperity did but feed them like sheep for the slaughter (Hos. iv. 16), and then death comes.

15-20 Privilege of the godly.

Good reason is here given to good people,

I. Why they should not be afraid of death.

1. There is no cause for that fear if they have such a comfortable prospect as David here has of a happy state on the other side death, v. 15. He had shown (v. 14) how miserable the dead are that die in their sins, where he shows how blessed the dead are that die in the Lord. The distinction of men's outward condition, how great a difference soever it makes in life, makes none at death; rich and poor meet in the grave. But the distinction of men's spiritual state, though, in this

Psalm 49

15-20

15 But God will redeem my soul from the power of the grave: for he shall receive me. Selah.
16 Be not thou afraid when one is made rich, when the glory of his house is increased;
17 For when he dieth he shall carry nothing away: his glory shall not descend after him.
18 Though while he lived he blessed his soul: and men will praise thee, when thou doest well to thyself.
19 He shall go to the generation of his fathers; they shall never see light.
20 Man that is in honor, and understandeth not, is like the beasts that perish.

ingrain. From first to last brutishness is their characteristic, groveling stupidity the leading trait of their conduct. Yet their posterity approve their sayings. Those who follow them in descent follow them in folly, quote their worldly maxims, and accept their mad career as the most prudent mode of life.

Verse 14. Like sheep they are laid in the grave. As dumb driven cattle, they are hurried to their doom, and are penned in within the gates of destruction. As sheep that go whither they are driven, and follow their leader without thought, so these men who have chosen to make this world their all, are urged on by their passions, till they find themselves at their journey's end, that end the depths of Hades.

Verse 15. But God will redeem my soul from the power of the grave. Forth from that temporary resting place we shall come in due time, quickened by divine energy. Like our risen Head we cannot be holden by the bands of the grave; redemption has emancipated us from the slavery of death. No redemption could man find in riches, but God has found it in the blood of his dear Son.

Verse 16. In these last verses the psalmist becomes a preacher, and gives admonitory lessons which he has himself gathered from experience. Be not thou afraid when one is made rich. Let it not give thee any concern to see the godless prosper. Raise no questions as to divine justice; suffer no foreboding to cloud thy mind.

Verse 17. For when he dieth he shall carry nothing away. He has but a leasehold of his acres, and death ends his tenure. Through the river of death man must pass naked. Not a rag of all his raiment, not a coin of all his treasure, not a joy of all his honor, can the dying worldling carry with him. Why then fret ourselves about so fleeting a prosperity? His glory shall not descend after him. As he goes down, down, down for ever, none of his honors or possessions will follow him.

Verse 18. Though while he lived he blessed his soul. He pronounced himself happy. He had his good things in this life. His chief end and aim were to bless himself. He was charmed with the adulation of flatterers. Men will praise thee, when thou doest well to thyself. The generality of men worship success, however it may be gained.

Verse 19. He shall go to the generation of his fathers. Where the former generations lie, the present shall also slumber. The sires beckon to their sons to come to the same land of forgetfulness. Mortal fathers beget not immortal children. As our ancestors have departed, so also must we.

Verse 20. The song ends with the refrain, Man that is in honor, and understandeth not, is like the beasts that perish. From the loftiest elevation of worldly honor to the uttermost depths of death is but a step. Saddest of all is the reflection, that though men are like beasts in all the degradation of perishing, yet not in the rest which animal perishing secures, for, alas! it is written, "These shall go away into everlasting punishment." So ends the minstrel's lay. Comforting as the theme is to the righteous, it is full of warning to the worldly. Hear ye it, O ye rich and poor. Give ear to it, ye nations of the earth.

JOHN CALVIN

this he states, to show in a more aggravated light the madness of their posterity, who will not be instructed by the fate of their predecessors.
14. Like sheep they are laid in the grave; death shall feed them. The figure is striking. They go down into the grave as sheep are gathered into the fold by the shepherd. The entire world might not seem vast enough for men of a haughty spirit.
15. But God will redeem my soul. The prophet does not deny his liability to death; but he looks to God as He who would defend and redeem him from it. We have here a convincing proof of that faith in which the saints under the Law lived and died. It is evident that their views were directed to another and a higher life, to which the present was only preparatory.

16-20
16. Be not thou afraid. The Psalmist repeats, in the form of an exhortation, the same sentiment which he had formerly expressed, that the children of God have no reason to dread the wealth and power of their enemies, or to envy their evanescent prosperity; and as the best preservative against despondency, he would have them to direct their eyes habitually to the end of life. The effect of such a contemplation will be at once to check any impatience we might be apt to feel under our short-lived miseries, and to raise our minds in holy contempt above the boasted but delusory grandeur of the wicked.
17. So much is implied in the words, He shall not carry away all these things when he dieth. Be their lives ever so illustrious in the eyes of their fellow-creatures, this glory is necessarily bounded by the present world. The same truth is further asserted in the succeeding clause of the verse, His glory shall not descend after him.
18. For he will bless his soul in his lifetime. There can be little doubt that the reference is to the children of the world. It is said that they bless their own soul so long as they live on earth, by which is meant, that they indulge and pamper themselves with earthly pleasures.
19. He shall come to the age of his fathers. He proceeds to show how false are the flatteries by which the wicked deceive themselves, and are deceived by others. Be they ever so intoxicated with the praises of the world, or with their own vain imaginations, yet they cannot live beyond the age of their fathers; and, granting their life to be extended to the longest term, it can never stretch into eternity.
20. Man is in honor, and will not understand. Here the prophet qualifies his former statements by a single word, importing that those whom he reprehends have reduced themselves to the level of the beasts that perish, by senselessly devouring the blessings which God has bestowed, and thus divesting themselves of that honor which God had put upon them. It is against the abuse of this world that the prophet has been directing his censures. They are aimed at those who devote themselves in an infatuated manner to the passing glory of this world, instead of contemplating heavenly things.

MATTHEW HENRY

life, it makes a small difference, where all things come alike to all, yet, at and after death, it makes a very great one.
2. That he will receive them to himself. He redeems their souls, that he may receive them. Ps. xxxi. 5, Into thy hands I commit my spirit, for thou has redeemed it. He will receive them into his favor, will admit them into his kingdom, into the mansions that he prepared for them (John xiv. 2, 3), those everlasting habitations, Luke xvi. 9.
II. Why they should not be afraid of the prosperity and power of wicked people in this world, which, as it is their pride and joy, has often been the envy, and grief, and terror of the righteous, which yet, all things considered, there is no reason for.
1. He supposes the temptation very strong to envy the prosperity of sinners, and to be afraid that they will carry all before them with a high hand, that with their wealth and interest they will run down religion and religious people, and that they will be found the truly happy people; for he supposes,
(1.) That they are made rich, and so are enabled to give law to all about them and have every thing at command.
(2.) That the glory of their house, from very small beginnings, is increased greatly, which naturally makes men haughty, insolent, and imperious, Ps. v. 16. Thus they seem to be the favorites of heaven, and therefore formidable.
(3.) That they are very easy and secure in themselves and in their own minds (v. 18): In his life-time he blessed his soul; that is, he thought himself a very happy man, such a one as he would be, and a very good man, such a one as he should be, because he prospered in the world.
2. He suggests that which is sufficient to take off the strength of the temptation, by directing us to look forward to the end of prosperous sinners (Ps. lxxiii. 17): "Think what they will be in the other world, and you will see no cause to envy them what they are and have in this world."
(1.) In the other world they will be never the better for all the wealth and prosperity they are now so fond of. It is a miserable portion, which will not last so long as they must (v. 17): When he dies it is taken for granted that he goes into another world himself, but he shall carry nothing away with him of all that which he has been so long heaping up.
(2.) In the other world they will be infinitely the worse for all their abuses of the wealth and prosperity they enjoyed in this world (v. 19): The soul shall go to the generation of his worldly wicked fathers, whose sayings he approved and whose steps he trod in, his fathers who would not hearken to the word of God, Zech. i. 4. He shall go to be there where they are that shall never see light.

Psalm 50

Title
A Psalm of Asaph.

1-8
1 The mighty God, even the LORD, hath spoken, and called the earth from the rising of the sun unto the going down thereof.
2 Out of Zion, the perfection of beauty, God hath shined.
3 Our God shall come, and shall not keep silence: a fire shall devour before him, and it shall be very tempestuous round about him.
4 He shall call to the heavens from above, and to the earth, that he may judge his people.
5 Gather my saints together unto me; those that have made a covenant with me by sacrifice.
6 And the heavens shall declare his righteousness: for God is judge himself. Selah.
7 Hear, O my people, and I will speak; O Israel, and I will testify against thee: I am God, even thy God.
8 I will not reprove thee for thy sacrifices or thy burnt offerings, to have been continually before me.

Psalm 50

TITLE. A Psalm of Asaph. This is the first of the Psalms of Asaph, but whether the production of that eminent musician, or merely dedicated to him, we cannot tell. The titles of twelve Psalms bear his name, but it could not in all of them be meant to ascribe their authorship to him, for several of these Psalms are of too late a date to have been composed by the same writer as the others. There was an Asaph in David's time, who was one of David's chief musicians, and his family appear to have continued long after in their hereditary office of temple musicians. An Asaph is mentioned as a recorder or secretary in the days of Hezekiah 2Ki 18:18, and another was keeper of the royal forests under Artaxerxes. That Asaph did most certainly write some of the Psalms is clear from 2Ch 29:30, where it is recorded that the Levites were commanded to "sing praises unto the Lord with the words of David, and of Asaph the seer," but that other Asaphic Psalms were not of his composition, but were only committed to his care as a musician, is equally certain from 1Ch 16:7, where David is said to have delivered a Psalm into the hand of Asaph and his brethren. It matters little to us whether he wrote or sang, for poet and musician are near akin, and if one composes words and another sets them to music, they rejoice together before the Lord.
DIVISION. The Lord is represented as summoning the whole earth to hear his declaration, Ps 50:1-6; he then declares the nature of the worship which he accepts, Ps 50:7-15, accuses the ungodly of breaches of the precepts of the second table, Ps 50:16-21, and closes the court with a word of threatening, Ps 50:22, and a direction of grace, Ps 50:23.

EXPOSITION
Verse 1. The mighty God, even the Lord. El, Elohim, Jehovah, three glorious names for the God of Israel. To render the address the more impressive, these august titles are mentioned, just as in royal decrees the names and dignities of monarchs are placed in the forefront. Here the true God is described as Almighty, as the only and perfect object of adoration and as the self existent One.
Verse 2. Out of Zion, the perfection of beauty, God hath shined. The Lord is represented not only as speaking to the earth, but as coming forth to reveal the glory of his presence to an assembled universe. God of old dwelt in Zion among his chosen people, but here the beams of his splendor are described as shining forth upon all nations. The sun was spoken of in the first verse, but here is a far brighter sun. The majesty of God is most conspicuous among his own elect, but is not confined to them; the church is not a dark lantern, but a candlestick. God shines not only in Zion, but out of her.
Verse 3. Our God shall come. The psalmist speaks of himself and his brethren as standing in immediate anticipation of the appearing of the Lord upon the scene. "He comes," they say, "our covenant God is coming;" they can hear his voice from afar, and perceive the splendor of his attending train.
Verse 4. He shall call to the heavens from above, and to the earth. Angels and men, the upper and the lower worlds, are called to witness the solemn scene. The whole creation shall stand in court to testify to the solemnity and the truth of the divine pleading.
Verse 5. Gather my saints together unto me. Go, ye swift winged messengers, and separate the precious from the vile. Gather out the wheat of the heavenly garner. Let the long scattered, but elect people, known by my separating grace to be my sanctified ones, be now assembled in one place. All are not saints who seem to be so—a severance must be made; therefore let all who profess to be saints be gathered before my throne of judgment, and let them hear the word which will search and try the whole, that the false may be convicted and the true revealed.

JOHN CALVIN

Psalm 50

1-5
1. The God of gods, even Jehovah, hath spoken. God is here represented as citing all the nations of the earth to his tribunal, not with the view of prescribing the rule of piety to an assembled world, or collecting a church for his service, but with the design of alarming the hypocrite, and terrifying him out of his self-complacency. It would serve as a spur to conviction, thus to be made aware that the whole world was summoned as a witness to their dissimulation, and that they would be stripped of that pretended piety of which they were disposed to boast.
2. When God speaks out of Zion he necessarily sanctions the authority of the Law; and the Prophets, when at any time they make use of this form of speech, declare themselves to be interpreters of the Law. That holy mountain was not chosen of man's caprice, and therefore stands identified with the Law. The prophet thus cuts off any pretext which the Jews might allege to evade his doctrine.
3. Our God shall come, and shall not keep silence. He repeats that God would come, in order to confirm his doctrine, and more effectually arouse them. He would come, and should not always keep silence, lest they should be encouraged to presume upon his forbearance.
4. He shall call to the heavens from above. It is plain from this verse for what purpose God, as he had already announced, would call upon the earth. This was to witness the settlement of his controversy with his own people the Jews, against whom judgment was to be pronounced, not in the ordinary manner as by his prophets, but with great solemnity before the whole world.
5. The prophet here declares that sacrifices were of no value whatever except as seals of God's covenant, an interpretative handwriting of submission to it, or in general as means employed for ratifying it. There is an allusion to the custom then universally prevalent of interposing sacrifices, that covenants might be made more solemn, and be more religiously observed. In like manner, the design with which sacrifices were instituted by God was to bind his people more closely to himself, and to ratify and confirm his covenant.

6-13
6. And the heavens shall declare his righteousness. The Jews were vain enough to imagine that their idle and fantastic service was the perfection of righteousness; but they are here warned by the prophet, that God, who had seemed to connive at their folly, was about to reveal his own righteousness from heaven, and expose their miserable devices.
7. Hear, O my people! and I will speak. Hitherto the prophet has spoken as the herald of God, throwing out several expressions designed to alarm the minds of those whom he addressed. But from this to the end of the psalm God himself is introduced as the speaker; and to show the importance of the subject, he uses additional terms to awaken attention, calling them his own people, that he might challenge the

MATTHEW HENRY

Psalm 50

1-6 The Majesty of Messiah.
Here is,
I. The court called, in the name of the King of kings (v. 2): The mighty God, even the Lord, hath spoken—El, Elohim, Jehovah, the God of infinite power justice and mercy, Father, Son, and Holy Ghost. God is the Judge, the Son of God came for judgement into the world, and the Holy Ghost is the Spirit of judgment. All the earth is called to attend, not only because the controversy God had with his people Israel for their hypocrisy and ingratitude might safely be referred to any man of reason but because all the children of men are concerned to know the right way of worshipping God, in spirit and in truth.
II. The judgment set, and the Judge taking his seat. As, when God gave the law to Israel in the wilderness, it is said, He came from Sinai, and rose up from Seir, and shone forth from Mount Paran, and came with ten thousands of his saints, and then from his right hand went a fiery law (Deut. xxxiii. 2), so, with allusion to that, when God comes to reprove them for their hypocrisy, and to send forth his gospel to supersede the legal institutions, it is said here,
1. That he shall shine out of Zion, as then from the top of Sinai, v. 2.
2. That he shall come, and not keep silence, shall no longer seem to wink at the sins of men, as he had done (v. 21), but shall show his displeasure at them.
3. That his appearance should be very majestic and terrible: A fire shall devour before him. The fire of his judgments shall make way for the rebukes of his word.
4. That as on Mount Sinai he came with ten thousands of his saints, so he shall now call to the heavens from above, to take notice of this solemn process (v. 4).
III. The issue of this solemn trial foretold (v. 6): The heavens shall declare his righteousness, those heavens that were called to be witnesses to the trial (v. 4); the people in heaven shall say, Hallelujah. True and righteous are his judgments, Rev. xix. 1, 2. The righteousness of God in all the rebukes of his word and providence, in the establishment of his gospel (which brings in an everlasting righteousness, and in which the righteousness of God is revealed), and especially in the judgment of the great day, is what the heavens will declare; that is,
1. It will be universally known, and proclaimed to all the world. As the heavens declare the glory, the wisdom and power, of God the Creator (Ps. xix. 1), so they shall no less openly declare the glory, the justice and righteousness, of God the Judge; and so loudly do they proclaim both that there is no speech nor language where their voice is not heard, as it follows there, v. 3.
2. It will be incontestably owned and proved; who can deny what the heavens declare? Even sinners' own

Psalm 50

9-16
9 I will take no bullock out of thy house, nor he goats out of thy folds.
10 For every beast of the forest is mine, and the cattle upon a thousand hills.
11 I know all the fowls of the mountains: and the wild beasts of the field are mine.
12 If I were hungry, I would not tell thee: for the world is mine, and the fullness thereof.
13 Will I eat the flesh of bulls, or drink the blood of goats?
14 Offer unto God thanksgiving; and pay thy vows unto the most High:
15 And call upon me in the day of trouble: I will deliver thee, and thou shalt glorify me.
16 But unto the wicked God saith, What hast thou to do to declare my statutes, or that thou shouldest take my covenant in thy mouth?

Verse 6. And the heavens shall declare his righteousness. Celestial intelligences and the spirits of just men made perfect, shall magnify the infallible judgment of the divine tribunal. Now they doubtless wonder at the hypocrisy of men; then they shall equally marvel at the exactness of the severance between the true and the false.
Verses 7-15. The address which follows is directed to the professed people of God. It is clearly, in the first place, meant for Israel; but is equally applicable to the visible church of God in every age. It declares the futility of external worship when spiritual faith is absent, and the mere outward ceremonial is rested in.
Verse 7. Hear, O my people, and I will speak. Because Jehovah speaks and they are avowedly his own people, they are bound to give earnest heed. "Let me speak," saith the great I AM. The heavens and earth are but listeners, the Lord is about both to testify and to judge. O Israel, and I will testify against thee. Their covenant name is mentioned to give point to the address; it was a double evil that the chosen nation should become so carnal, so unspiritual, so false, so heartless to their God.
Verse 8. I will not reprove thee for thy sacrifices or thy burnt offerings, to have been ever before me. Though they had not failed in maintaining his outward worship, or even if they had, he was not about to call them to account for this: a more weighty matter was now under consideration. They thought the daily sacrifices and the abounding burnt offerings to be everything: he counted them nothing if the inner sacrifice of heart devotion had been neglected.
Verse 9. I will take no bullock out of thy house. Foolishly they dreamed that bullocks with horns and hoofs could please the Lord, when indeed he sought for hearts and souls. Impiously they fancied that Jehovah needed these supplies, and that if they fed his altar with their fat beasts, he would be content.
Verse 10. For every beast of the forest is mine. How could they imagine that the Most High God, possessor of heaven and earth, had need of beasts, when all the countless hordes that find shelter in a thousand forests and wildernesses belong to him? And the cattle upon a thousand hills. Not alone the wild beasts, but also the tamer creatures are all his own. Even if God cared for these things, he could supply himself.
Verse 11. I know all the fowls of the mountain. All the winged creatures are under my inspection and near my hand; what then can be the value of your pairs of turtledoves, and your two young pigeons? The great Lord not only feeds all his creatures, but is well acquainted with each one; how wondrous is this knowledge! And the wild beasts of the fields are mine. The whole population moving over the plain belongs to me; why then should I seek you rams?
Verse 12. If I were hungry, I would not tell thee. Strange conception, a hungry God! Yet if such an absurd ideal could be truth, and if the Lord hungered for meat, he would not ask it of men. He could provide for himself out of his own possessions; he would not turn suppliant to his own creatures. Even under the grossest ideal of God, faith in outward ceremonies is ridiculous. Do men fancy that the Lord needs banners, and music, and incense, and fine linen?
Verse 13. Will I eat the flesh of bulls, or drink the blood of goats? Are you so infatuated as to think this? Is the great I AM subject to corporeal wants, and are they to be thus grossly satisfied? Heathens thought thus of their idols, but dare ye think thus of the God who made the heavens and the earth? Can ye have fallen so low as to think thus of me, O Israel? What vivid reasoning is here! How the fire flashes dart into the idiot faces of trusters in outward forms!
Verse 14. Offer unto God thanksgiving. No longer look at your sacrifices as in themselves gifts pleasing to me, but present them as the tributes of your gratitude; it is then that I will accept them, but not while your poor souls have no love and no thankfulness to offer me.

higher authority to his words, and intimating, that the following address is not of a mere ordinary description, but an expostulation with them for the infraction of his covenant.
8. I will not reprove thee for thy sacrifices, etc. God now proceeds to state the charge which he adduced against them. He declares, that he attached no value whatsoever to sacrifices in themselves considered.
9. I will take no calf out thy house. Two reasons are given in this and the succeeding verses to prove that he cannot set any value upon sacrifices. The first is, that supposing him to depend upon these, he needs not to be indebted for them to man, having all the fullness of the earth at his command; and the second, that he requires neither food nor drink as we do for the support of our infirm natures. There may be nothing new in the truths here laid down by the Psalmist; but, considering the strong propensity we have by nature to form our estimate of God from ourselves, and to degenerate into a carnal worship, they convey a lesson by no means unnecessary, and which contains profound wisdom, that man can never benefit God by any of his services, as we have seen in Psalm 16:2, "My goodness extendeth not unto thee."

14-15
14. These verses cast light upon the preceding context. Had it been stated in unqualified terms that sacrifices were of no value, we might have been perplexed to know why in that case they were instituted by God; but the difficulty disappears when we perceive that they are spoken of only in comparison with the true worship of God. From this we infer, that when properly observed, they were far from incurring divine condemnation. There is in all men by nature a strong and ineffaceable conviction that they ought to worship God. Indisposed to worship him in a pure and spiritual manner, it becomes necessary that they should invent some specious appearance as a substitute; and however clearly they may be persuaded of the vanity of such conduct, they persist in it to the last, because they shrink from a total renunciation of the service of God.
15. In the fifteenth verse we have first an injunction to prayer, then a promise of its being answered, and afterwards a call to thanksgiving. We are enjoined to pray in the day of trouble, but not with the understanding that we are to pray only then, for prayer is a duty incumbent upon us every day, and every moment of our lives. Be our situation ever so comfortable and exempt from disquietude, we must never cease to engage in the exercise of supplication, remembering that, if God should withdraw his favor for a moment, we would be undone.

16-20
16. But unto the wicked, etc. He now proceeds to direct his censures more openly against those whose whole religion lies in an observance of ceremonies, with which they attempt to blind the eyes of God. An exposure is made of the vanity of seeking to shelter impurity of heart and life under a veil of outward services, a lesson which ought to have been received by all with true consent, but which was peculiarly ungrateful to Jewish ears.

consciences will subscribe to it, and hell as well as heaven will be forced to acknowledge the righteousness of God.

7-15 The inefficacy of legal sacrifices.
God is here dealing with those that placed all their religion in the observances of the ceremonial law, and thought those sufficient.
I. He lays down the original contract between him and Israel, in which they had avouched him to be their God, and he them to be his people, and so both parties were agreed (v. 7): Hear, O my people! and I will speak. Note, It is justly expected that whatever others do, when he speaks, his people should give ear; who will, if they do not?
II. He puts a slight upon the legal sacrifices, v. 8, &c. Now,
1. This may be considered as looking back to the use of these under the law. God had a controversy with the Jews; but what was the ground of the controversy? Not their neglect of the ceremonial institutions; no, they had not been wanting in the observance of them, their burnt-offerings had been continually before God, they took a pride in them, and hoped by their offerings to procure a dispensation for their lusts, as the adulterous woman, Prov. vii. 14. Their constant sacrifices, they thought, would both expiate and excuse their neglect of the weightier matters of the law; but God here shows them the contrary,
(1.) That he did not need their sacrifices. What occasion had he for their bullocks and goats who has the command of all the beasts of the forest, and the cattle upon a thousand hills (v. 9, 10), has an incontestable propriety in them and dominion over them, has them all always under his eye and within his reach, and can make what use he pleases of them; they all wait on him, and are all at his disposal? Ps. civ. 27-29. Can we add any thing to his store whose all the wild fowl and wild beasts are, the world itself and the fullness thereof? v. 11, 12. God's infinite self-sufficiency proves our utter insufficiency to add any thing to him.
(2.) That he could not be benefited by their sacrifices. Their goodness, of this kind, could not possibly extend to him, nor, if they were in this matter righteous, was he the better (v. 13): Will I eat the flesh of bulls? It is as absurd to think that their sacrifices could, of themselves, and by virtue of any innate excellency in them, add any pleasure of praise to God, as it would be to imagine that an infinite Spirit could be supported by meat and drink, as our bodies are.
2. This may be considered as looking forward to the abolishing of these by the gospel of Christ. Thus Dr. Hammond understands it. When God shall set up the kingdom of the Messiah he shall abolish the old way of worship by sacrifice and offerings; he will no more have those to be continually before him (v. 8); he will

Psalm 50

17-23
17 Seeing thou hatest instruction, and casteth my words behind thee.
18 When thou sawest a thief, then thou consentedst with him, and hast been partaker with adulterers.
19 Thou givest thy mouth to evil, and thy tongue frameth deceit.
20 Thou sittest and speakest against thy brother; thou slanderest thine own mother's son.
21 These things hast thou done, and I kept silence; thou thoughtest that I was altogether such an one as thyself: but I will reprove thee, and set them in order before thine eyes.
22 Now consider this, ye that forget God, lest I tear you in pieces, and there be none to deliver.
23 Whoso offereth praise glorifieth me: and to him that ordereth his conversation aright will I shew the salvation of God.

Verse 15. And call upon me in the day of trouble. Oh blessed verse! Is this then true sacrifice? Is it an offering to ask an alms of heaven? It is even so. The King himself so regards it. For herein is faith manifested, herein is love proved, for in the hour of peril we fly to those we love. It seems a small think to pray to God when we are distressed, yet is it a more acceptable worship than the mere heartless presentation of bullocks and he goats. This is a voice from the throne, and how full of mercy it is!

Verses 16-21. Here the Lord turns to the manifestly wicked among his people; and such there were even in the highest places of his sanctuary. If moral formalists had been rebuked, how much more these immoral pretenders to fellowship with heaven? If the lack of heart spoiled the worship of the more decent and virtuous, how much more would violations of the law, committed with a high hand, corrupt the sacrifices of the wicked?

Verse 16. But unto the wicked God saith. To the breakers of the second table he now addresses himself; he had previously spoken to the neglectors of the first.

Verse 17. Seeing thou hatest instruction. Profane professors are often too wise to learn, too besotted with conceit to be taught of God. What a monstrosity that men should declare those statutes which with their hearts they do not know, and which in their lives they openly disavow! Woe unto the men who hate the instruction which they take upon themselves to give.

Verse 18. When thou sawest a thief, then thou consentedst with him. Moral honesty cannot be absent where true grace is present. Those who excuse others in trickery are guilty themselves; those who use others to do unjust actions for them are doubly so. If a man be ever so religious, if his own actions do not rebuke dishonesty, he is an accomplice with thieves.

Verse 19. Thou givest thy mouth to evil. Sins against the ninth commandment are here mentioned. The man who surrenders himself to the habit of slander is a vile hypocrite if he associates himself with the people of God.

Verse 20. Thou sittest and speakest against thy brother. He sits down to it, makes it his meat, studies it, resolves upon it, becomes a master of defamation, occupies the chair of calumny.

Verse 21. These things hast thou done, and I kept silence. No swift judgment overthrew the sinner—longsuffering reigned; no thunder was heard in threatening, and no bolt of fire was hurled in execution.

Verse 22. Now or oh! it is a word of entreaty, for the Lord is loath even to let the most ungodly run on to destruction. Consider this; take these truths to heart, ye who trust in ceremonies and ye who live in vice, for both of you sin in that ye forget God. Think how unaccepted you are, and turn to the Lord.

Verse 23. Whoso offereth praise glorifieth me. Praise is the best sacrifice; true, hearty, gracious thanksgiving from a renewed mind. Not the lowing of bullocks bound to the altar, but the songs of redeemed men are the music which the ear of Jehovah delights in. Holy living is a choice evidence of salvation. He who submits his whole way to divine guidance, and is careful to honor God in his life, brings an offering which the Lord accepts through his dear Son. He needs salvation, for the best ordering of the life cannot save us, but that salvation he shall have. Not to ceremonies, not to unpurified lips, is the blessing promised, but to grateful hearts and holy lives.

17. Also thou hatest correction. Here hypocrites are challenged with treacherous duplicity in denying, by their life and their works, that godliness which they have professed with the lip. Their contempt of God he proves from their want of reverential deference to his Word; subjection to the Word of God, and cordial submission to his precepts and instructions, being the surest test of religious principle. One way in which hypocrisy usually displays itself is, by the ingenious excuses it invents for evading the duty of obedience. The Psalmist points to this as the mainspring of their ungodliness, that they had cast the Word of God behind their back, while he insinuates that the principle from which all true worship flows is the obedience of faith. He adverts also to the cause of their perversity, which lies in the unwillingness of their corrupt heart to suffer the yoke of God.
18. The Psalmist next proceeds to specify some of those works of ungodliness, informing us that hypocrites, who were addicted to theft and adultery, mixed up and polluted the holy name of God with their wickedness.
19. The charge here brought against hypocrites, that they put forth their mouth to evil, may include not merely slander, but all the different kinds of speaking which injure their neighbors, for it immediately follows, my tongue frameth deceit. It is well known in what a variety of ways the lying and deceitful tongue may inflict injury and pain.

21-23
21. These things hast thou done. Hypocrites, until they feel the hand of God against them, are ever ready to surrender themselves to a state of security, and nothing is more difficult than to awaken their apprehensions. By this alarming language the Psalmist aims at convincing them of the certainty of destruction should they longer presume upon the forbearance of God, and thus provoke his anger the more, by imagining that he can favor the practice of sin.
22. Now consider this, ye that forget God. Here we have more of that severe expostulation which is absolutely necessary in dealing with hardened hypocrites, who otherwise will only deride all instruction. While, however, the Psalmist threatens and intends to alarm them, he would, at the same time, hold out to them the hope of pardon, upon their hastening to avail themselves of it.
23. Whoso offereth praise will glorify me. This is the third time that the Psalmist has inculcated the truth, that the most acceptable sacrifice in God's sight is praise, by which we express to him the gratitude of our hearts for his blessings. The repetition is not a needless one, and that on two accounts. In the first place, there is nothing with which we are more frequently chargeable than forgetfulness of the benefits of the Lord. And, secondly, we do not assign that importance to the duty of praise which it deserves. We are apt to neglect it as something trivial; whereas it constitutes the chief exercise of godliness, in which God would have us to be engaged during the whole of our life. In the words before us, the sacrifice of praise is asserted to form the true and proper worship of God.

no more require of his worshippers to bring him their bullocks and their goats, to be burnt upon his altar, v. 9.
III. He directs to the best sacrifices of prayer and praise as those which, under the law, were preferred before all burnt-offerings and sacrifices, and on which then the greatest stress was laid, and which now, under the gospel, come in the room of those carnal ordinances which were imposed until the times of reformation. He shows us here (v. 14, 15) what is good, and what the Lord our God requires of us, and will accept, when sacrifices are slighted and superseded.

16-23 The character of the wicked.
God, by the psalmist, having instructed his people in the right way of worshipping him and keeping up their communion with him, here directs his speech to the wicked, to hypocrites, whether they were such as professed the Jewish or the Christian religion: hypocrisy is wickedness for which God will judge. Observe here,
I. The charge drawn up against them.
1. They are charged with invading and usurping the honors and privileges of religion (v. 16): What has thou to do, O wicked man! to declare my statutes?
2. They are charged with transgressing and violating the laws and precepts of religion.
(1.) They are charged with a daring contempt of the word of God (v. 17): Thou hatest instruction.
(2.) A close confederacy with the worst of sinners (v. 18): "When thou sawest a thief, instead of reproving him and witnessing against him, as those should do that declare God's statutes, thou consentedst with him, didst approve of his practices, and desire to be a partner with him and to share in the profits of his cursed trade; and thou hast been partaker with adulterers, hast done as they did, and encouraged them to go on in their wicked courses, hast done these things and hast had pleasure in those that do them," Rom. i. 32.
(3.) A constant persisting in the worst of tongue-sins (v. 19): "Thou givest thy mouth to evil, not only allowest thyself in, but addictest thyself wholly to, all manner of evil-speaking."
II. The proof of this charge (v. 21): "These things thou hast done; the fact is too plain to be denied, the fault too bad to be excused; these things God knows, and thy own heart knows, thou hast done."
III. The fair warning given of the dreadful doom of hypocrites (v. 22): "Now consider this, you that forget God, consider that God knows and keeps account of all your sins."
V. Full instructions given to us all how to prevent this fearful doom. Let us hear the conclusion of the whole matter; we have it, v. 23, which directs us what to do that we may attain our chief end.

Psalm 51

Title
To the chief Musician. A Psalm of David. When Nathan the prophet came unto him, after he had gone in to Bathsheba.

1-6
1 Have mercy upon me, O God, according to thy loving kindness: according unto the multitude of thy tender mercies blot out my transgressions.
2 Wash me throughly from mine iniquity, and cleanse me from my sin.
3 For I acknowledge my transgressions: and my sin is ever before me.
4 Against thee, thee only, have I sinned, and done this evil in thy sight: that thou mightest be justified when thou speakest, and be clear when thou judgest.
5 Behold, I was shapen in iniquity; and in sin did my mother conceive me.
6 Behold, thou desirest truth in the inward parts: and in the hidden part thou shalt make me to know wisdom.

Psalm 51

TITLE. To the Chief Musician. Therefore not written for private meditation only, but for the public service of song. Suitable for the loneliness of individual penitence, this matchless Psalm is equally well adapted for an assembly of the poor in spirit. A Psalm of David. It is a marvel, but nevertheless a fact, that writers have been found to deny David's authorship of this Psalm, but their objections are frivolous, the Psalm is David like all over. It would be far easier to imitate Milton, Shakespeare, or Tennyson, than David. His style is altogether sui generis, and it is as easily distinguished as the touch of Rafaelle or the coloring of Rubens. "When Nathan the prophet came unto him, after he had gone in to Bathsheba." When the divine message had aroused his dormant conscience and made him see the greatness of his guilt, he wrote this Psalm. He had forgotten his psalmody while he was indulging his flesh, but he returned to his harp when his spiritual nature was awakened, and he poured out his song to the accompaniment of sighs and tears. The great sin of David is not to be excused, but it is well to remember that his case has an exceptional collection of specialities in it. He was a man of very strong passions, a soldier, and an Oriental monarch having despotic power; no other king of his time would have felt any compunction for having acted as he did, and hence there were not around him those restraints of custom and association which, when broken through, render the offence the more monstrous. He never hints at any form of extenuation, nor do we mention these facts in order to apologize for his sin, which was detestable to the last degree; but for the warning of others, that they reflect that the licentiousness in themselves at this day might have even a graver guilt in it than in the erring King of Israel. When we remember his sin, let us dwell most upon his penitence, and upon the long series of chastisements which rendered the after part of his life such a mournful history.
DIVISION. It will be simplest to note in the first twelve verses the penitent's confessions and plea for pardon, and then in the last seven his anticipatory gratitude, and the way in which he resolves to display it.

EXPOSITION
Verse 1. Have mercy upon me, O God. He appeals at once to the mercy of God, even before he mentions his sin. The sight of mercy is good for eyes that are sore with penitential weeping. Pardon of sin must ever be an act of pure mercy, and therefore to that attribute the awakened sinner flies. According to thy lovingkindness. Act, O Lord, like thyself; give mercy like thy mercy. Show mercy such as is congruous with thy grace.
Verse 2. Wash me throughly. It is not enough to blot out the sin; his person is defiled, and he fain would be purified. He would have God himself cleanse him, for none but he could do it effectually. The washing must be thorough, it must be repeated, therefore he cries, "Multiply to wash me." The dye is in itself immovable, and I, the sinner, have lain long in it, till the crimson is ingrained; but, Lord, wash, and wash, and wash again, till the last stain is gone, and not a trace of my defilement is left.
Verse 3. For I acknowledge my transgressions. Here he sees the plurality and immense number of his sins, and makes open declaration of them. He seems to say, I make a full confession of them. Not that this is my plea in seeking forgiveness, but it is a clear evidence that I need mercy, and am utterly unable to look to any other quarter for help. My pleading guilty has barred me from any appeal against the sentence of justice: O Lord, I must cast myself on thy mercy, refuse me not, I pray thee.
Verse 4. Against thee, thee only have I sinned. The virus of sin lies in its opposition to God: the psalmist's sense of sin towards others rather tended to increase the force of this feeling of sin against God. All his wrong doing centered, culminated, and came to a climax, at the foot of the divine throne.

JOHN CALVIN

Psalm 51

1-2

1. Have mercy upon me. David begins by praying for pardon; and his sin having been of an aggravated description, he prays with unwonted earnestness. He does not satisfy himself with one petition. Having mentioned the loving-kindness of the Lord, he adds the multitude of his compassions, to intimate that mercy of an ordinary kind would not suffice for so great a sinner. Had he prayed God to be favorable, simply according to his clemency or goodness, even that would have amounted to a confession that his case was a bad one; but when he speaks of his sin as remissible, only through the countless multitude of the compassions of God, he represents it as peculiarly atrocious.

2. Multiply to wash me. David felt the stain of his sin to be deep, and to require multiplied washings. It is not as if God could experience any difficulty in cleansing the worst sinner, but the more aggravated a man's sin is, the more earnest naturally are his desires to be delivered from the terrors of conscience.

3-6

3. For If know my sins. He now discovers his reason for imploring pardon with so much vehemency, and this was the painful disquietude which his sins caused him, and which could only be relieved by his obtaining reconciliation with God. This proves that his prayer did not proceed from dissimulation, as many will be found commending the grace of God in high terms, although, in reality, they care little about it, having never felt the bitterness of being exposed to his displeasure.

4. Against thee, thee only, have I sinned. Though all the world should pardon him, he felt that God was the Judge with whom he had to do, that conscience hailed him to his bar, and that the voice of man could administer no relief to him, however much he might be disposed to forgive, or to excuse, or to flatter.

5. Behold, I was born in iniquity, etc. He now proceeds further than the mere acknowledgement of one or of many sins, confessing that he brought nothing but sin with him into the world, and that his nature was entirely depraved. He is thus led by the consideration of one offense of peculiar atrocity to the conclusion that he was born in iniquity, and was absolutely destitute of all spiritual good. Indeed, every sin should convince us of the general truth of the corruption of our nature.

6. Behold, thou hast desired truth, etc. This verse confirms that David was far from seeking to invent an apology for his sin, when he traced it back to the period of his conception, and rather intended by this to acknowledge that from his very infancy he was an heir of eternal death. He thus represents his whole life to have been obnoxious to condemnation.

7-9

7. Thou shalt purge me with hyssop. He still follows out the same strain of supplication; and the repetition of his requests

MATTHEW HENRY

Psalm 51

1-6 Penitential petitions.

In these words we have,

I. David's humble petition, v. 1, 2. His prayer is much the same with that which our Savior puts into the mouth of his penitent publican in the parable: God be merciful to me a sinner! Luke xviii. 13. Observe,

1. What his plea is for this mercy: "have mercy upon me, O God! not according to the dignity of my birth, as descended from the prince of the tribe of Judah, not according to my public services as Israel's champion, or my public honors as Israel's king;" his plea is not, Lord, remember David and all his afflictions, how he vowed to build a place for the ark (Ps. cxxxii. 1, 2); a true penitent will make no mention of any such thing; but "Have mercy upon me for mercy's sake. I have nothing to plead with thee but,"

(1.) "The freeness of thy mercy, according to thy lovingkindness, thy clemency, the goodness of thy nature, which inclines thee to pity the miserable."

(2.) "The fullness of thy mercy. There are in thee not only lovingkindness and tender mercies, but abundance of them, a multitude of tender mercies for the forgiveness of many sinners, of many sins, to multiply pardons as we multiply transgressions."

2. What is the particular mercy that he begs—the pardon of sin. Blot out my transgressions, as a debt is blotted or crossed out of the book, when either the debtor has paid it or the creditor has remitted it. "Wipe out my transgressions, that they may not appear to demand judgment against me, nor stare me in the face to my confusion and terror." The blood of Christ, sprinkled upon the conscience, to purify and pacify that, blots out the transgression, and, having reconciled us to God, reconciles up to ourselves, v. 2.

II. David's penitential confessions, v. 3-5.

1. He was very free to own his guilt before God: I acknowledge my transgressions; this he had formerly found the only way of easing his conscience, Ps. xxxii. 4, 5. Nathan said, Thou art the man. I am, says David; I have sinned.

2. He had such a deep sense of it that the was continually thinking of it with sorrow and shame. His contrition for his sin was not a slight sudden passion, but an abiding grief: "My sin is ever before me, to humble me and mortify me, and make me continually blush and tremble. It is ever against me" (so some); "I see it before me as an enemy, accusing and threatening me." David was, upon all occasions, put in mind of his sin, and was willing to be so, for his further abasement. He never walked on the roof of his house without a penitent reflection on his unhappy walk there when thence he saw Bathsheba; he never lay down to sleep without a sorrowful thought of the bed of his uncleanness, never sat down to meat, never sent his servant on an errand, or took his pen in hand, but it put him in mind of his making Uriah

Psalm 51

7-12

7 Purge me with hyssop, and I shall be clean: wash me, and I shall be whiter than snow.

8 Make me to hear joy and gladness; that the bones which thou hast broken may rejoice.

9 Hide thy face from my sins, and blot out all mine iniquities.

10 Create in me a clean heart, O God; and renew a right spirit within me.

11 Cast me not away from thy presence; and take not thy holy spirit from me.

12 Restore unto me the joy of thy salvation; and uphold me with thy free spirit.

Verse 5. Behold, I was shapen in iniquity. He is thunderstruck at the discovery of his inbred sin, and proceeds to set it forth. This was not intended to justify himself, but it rather meant to complete the confession. It is as if he said, not only have I sinned this once, but I am in my very nature a sinner. The fountain of my life is polluted as well as its streams. My birth tendencies are out of the square of equity; I naturally lean to forbidden things.

Verse 6. Behold. Here is the great matter for consideration. God desires not merely outward virtue, but inward purity, and the penitent's sense of sin is greatly deepened as with astonishment he discovers this truth, and how far he is from satisfying the divine demand. The second "Behold" is fitly set over against the first; how great the gulf which yawns between them! Thou desirest truth in the inward parts. Reality, sincerity, true holiness, heart fidelity, these are the demands of God. He cares not for the pretence of purity, he looks to the mind, heart, and soul.

Verse 7. Purge me with hyssop. Sprinkle the atoning blood upon me with the appointed means. Give me the reality which legal ceremonies symbolize. Nothing but blood can take away my blood stains, nothing but the strongest purification can avail to cleanse me. Let the sin offering purge my sin. Let him who was appointed to atone, execute his sacred office on me; for none can need it more than I.

Verse 8. Make me to hear joy and gladness. He prays about his sorrow late in the Psalm; he began at once with his sin; he asks to hear pardon, and then to hear joy. He seeks comfort at the right time and from the right source. His ear has become heavy with sinning, and so he prays, "Make me to hear." No voice could revive his dead joys but that which quickeneth the dead. Pardon from God would give him double joy—"joy and gladness." No stinted bliss awaits the forgiven one; he shall not only have a double blooming joy, but he shall hear it; it shall sing with exultation.

Verse 9. Hide thy face from my sins. Do not look at them; be at pains not to see them. They thrust themselves in the way; but, Lord, refuse to behold them, lest if thou consider them, thine anger burn, and I die. Blot out all mine iniquities. He repeats the prayer of the first verse with the enlargement of it by the word "all." All repetitions are not "vain repetitions." Souls in agony have no space to find variety of language: pain has to content itself with monotones.

Verse 10. Create. What! has sin so destroyed us, that the Creator must be called in again? What ruin then doth evil work among mankind! Create in me. I, in my outward fabric, still exist; but I am empty, desert, void. Come, then, and let thy power be seen in a new creation within my old fallen self. Thou didst make a man in the world at first; Lord, make a new man in me!

Verse 11. Cast me not away from thy presence. Throw me not away as worthless; banish me not, like Cain, from thy face and favor. Permit me to sit among those who share thy love, though I only be suffered to keep the door. I deserve to be forever denied admission to thy courts; but, O good Lord, permit me still the privilege which is dear as life itself to me.

Verse 12. Restore unto me the joy of thy salvation. Salvation he had known, and had known it as the Lord's own; he had also felt the joy which arises from being saved in the Lord, but he had lost it for a while, and therefore he longed for its restoration. None but God can give back this joy; he can do it; we may ask it; he will do it for his own glory and our benefit. This joy comes not first, but follows pardon and purity: in such order it is safe, in any other it is vain presumption or idiotic delirium.

Verse 13. Then will I teach transgressors thy ways. It was his fixed resolve to be a teacher of others; and assuredly none instruct others so well as those who have been experimentally taught of God themselves. Reclaimed poachers make the best gamekeepers.

Verse 14. Deliver me from bloodguiltiness. He had been the means of the death of Uriah, the Hittite, a faithful and attached follower, and he now for pardon proves how earnestly he desired it. He speaks of hyssop, in allusion to the ceremonies of the law; and though he was far from putting his trust in the mere outward symbol of purification, he knew that, like every other legal rite, it was instituted for an important end. The sacrifices were seals of the grace of God. In them, therefore, he was anxious to find assurance of his reconciliation; and it is highly proper that, when our faith is disposed at any time to waver, we should confirm it by improving such means of divine support.

8, 9. In the two verses which follow, the Psalmist prays that God would be pacified towards him. He prays, in general, for testimonies of the divine favor. When he speaks of his bones as having been broken, he alludes to the extreme grief and overwhelming distress to which he had been reduced. The joy of the Lord would reanimate his soul; and this joy he describes as to be obtained by hearing; for it is the word of God alone which can first and effectually cheer the heart of any sinner.

10-12

10. Create in me a clean heart, O God! In the previous part of the psalm David has been praying for pardon. He now requests that the grace of the Spirit, which he had forfeited, or deserved to have forfeited, might be restored to him. The two requests are quite distinct, though sometimes confounded together, even by men of learning. He passes from the subject of the gratuitous remission of sin to that of sanctification. And to this he was naturally led with earnest anxiety, by the consciousness of his having merited the loss of all the gifts of the Spirit, and of his having actually, in a great measure, lost them.

11. As he had already been endued with the Spirit, he prays in the latter part of the verse that God would renew a right spirit within him. But by the term create, which he had previously employed, he acknowledges that we are indebted entirely to the grace of God, both for our first regeneration, and, in the event of our falling, for subsequent restoration. He does not merely assert that his heart and spirit were weak, requiring divine assistance, but that they must remain destitute of all purity and rectitude till these be communicated from above.

12. Restore unto me the joy of thy salvation. He cannot dismiss his grief of mind until he have obtained peace with God. This he declares once and again, for David had no sympathy with those who can indulge themselves in ease when they are lying under the divine displeasure. In the latter clause of the verse, he prays as in the verses preceding, that the Holy Spirit might not be taken away from him.

13. I will teach transgressors thy ways. Here he speaks of the gratitude which he would feel should God answer his prayer, and engages to show it by exerting himself in effecting the conversion of others by his example.

14. Deliver me from bloods. His recurring so often to petitions for pardon, proves how far David was from flattering himself with unfounded hopes, and what a severe struggle he sustained with inward terrors. According to some, he prays in this verse to be delivered from the guilt of the blood of Uriah, and, in general, of the whole army. But the term bloods in

drunk, the treacherous message he sent by him, and the fatal warrant he wrote and signed for his execution.

(1.) He confesses his actual transgressions (v. 4): Against thee, thee only, have I sinned. David was a very great man, and yet, having done amiss, submits to the discipline of a penitent, and thinks not his royal dignity will excuse him from it.

(2.) He confesses his original corruption (v. 5): Behold, I was shapen in iniquity. He does not call upon God to behold it, but upon himself. "Come, my soul, look unto the rock out of which I was hewn, and thou wilt find I was shapen in iniquity. Had I duly considered this before, I find I should not have made so bold with the temptation, nor have ventured among the sparks with such tinder in my heart; and so the sin might have been prevented."

III. David's acknowledgment of the grace of God (v. 6), both his good-will towards us ("thou desirest truth in the inward parts, thou wouldst have us all honest and sincere, and true to our profession") and his good work in us—"In the hidden part thou hast made," or shalt make, "me to know wisdom." Truth and wisdom will go very far towards making a man a good man. A clear head and a sound heart (prudence and sincerity) bespeak the man of God perfect.

7-13 Penitential petitions.

I. See here what David prays for. Many excellent petitions he here puts up, to which if we do but add, "for Christ's sake," they are as evangelical as any other.

1. He prays that God would cleanse him from his sins and the defilement he had contracted by them (v. 7): "Purge me with hyssop; that is, pardon my sins, and let me know that they are pardoned, that I may be restored to those privileges which by sin I have forfeited and lost." The expression here alludes to a ceremonial distinction, that of cleansing the leper, or those that were unclean by the touch of a body by sprinkling water, or blood, or both upon them with a bunch of hyssop, by which they were, at length, discharged from the restraints they were laid under by their pollution.

2. He prays that, his sins being pardoned, he might have the comfort of that pardon. He asks not to be comforted till first he is cleansed; but if sin, the bitter root of sorrow, be taken away, he can pray in faith, "Make me to hear joy and gladness (v. 8), that is, let me have a well-grounded peace, of thy creating, thy speaking, so that the bones which thou hast broken by convictions and threatenings may rejoice, may not only be set again, and eased from the pain, but may be sensibly comforted, and, as the prophet speaks, may flourish as a herb."

3. He prays for a complete and effectual pardon. This is that which he is most earnest for as the foundation of his comfort (v. 9): "Hide thy face from my sins, that is, be not provoked by them to deal with me as

Psalm 51

13-19

13 Then will I teach transgressors thy ways; and sinners shall be converted unto thee.
14 Deliver me from blood guiltiness, O God, thou God of my salvation: and my tongue shall sing aloud of thy righteousness.
15 O Lord, open thou my lips; and my mouth shall shew forth thy praise.
16 For thou desirest not sacrifice; else would I give it: thou delightest not in burnt offering.
17 The sacrifices of God are a broken spirit: a broken and a contrite heart, O God, thou wilt not despise.
18 Do good in thy good pleasure unto Zion: build thou the walls of Jerusalem.
19 Then shalt thou be pleased with the sacrifices of righteousness, with burnt offering and whole burnt offering: then shall they offer bullocks upon thine altar.

confesses that fact. Besides, his sin of adultery was a capital offence, and he puts himself down as one worthy to die the death. Honest penitents do not fetch a compass and confess their sins in an elegant periphrasis, but they come to the point, call a spade a spade, and make a clean breast of all. What other course is rational in dealing with the Omniscient? O God, thou God of my salvation. He had not ventured to come so near before. It had been, O God, up till now, but here he cries, Thou God of my salvation. Faith grows by the exercise of prayer.

Verse 15. O Lord, open thou my lips. He is so afraid of himself that he commits his whole being to the divine care, and fears to speak till the Lord unstops his shame silenced mouth. How marvelously the Lord can open our lips, and what divine things can we poor simpletons pour forth under his inspiration! This prayer of a penitent is a golden petition for a preacher, Lord, I offer it for myself and my brethren.

Verse 16. For thou desirest not sacrifice. This was the subject of the last Psalm. The psalmist was so illuminated as to see far beyond the symbolic ritual; his eye of faith gazed with delight upon the actual atonement. Else would I give it. He would have been glad enough to present tens of thousands of victims if these would have met the case.

Verse 17. The sacrifices of God are a broken spirit. All sacrifices are presented to thee in one, by the man whose broken heart presents the Savior's merit to thee. When the heart mourns for sin, thou art better pleased than when the bullock bleeds beneath the axe. "A broken heart" is an expression implying deep sorrow, embittering the very life; it carries in it the idea of all but killing anguish in that region which is so vital as to be the very source of life.

Verse 18. Do good in thy good pleasure unto Zion. Let blessings according to thy wont be poured upon thy holy hill and chosen city. Zion was David's favorite spot, whereon he had hoped to erect a temple. The ruling passion is so strong on him, that when he has discharged his conscience he must have a word for Zion. He felt he had hindered the project of honoring the Lord there as he desired, but he prayed God still to let the place of his ark be glorious, and to establish his worship and his worshipping people.

Verse 19. In those days of joyful prosperity thy saints shall present in great abundance the richest and holiest thank offerings to thee, and thou shalt be pleased to accept them. A saved soul expects to see its prayers answered in a revived church, and then is assured that God will be greatly glorified. Though we bring no more sacrifices for sin, yet as priests unto God our solemn praises and votive gifts are thank offerings acceptable to God by Jesus Christ. We bring not the Lord our least things—our doves and pigeons; but we present him with our best possessions—our bullocks. We are glad that in this present time we are able to fulfill in person the declaration of this verse: we also, forecasting the future, wait for days of the divine presence, when the church of God, with unspeakable joy, shall offer gifts upon the altar of God, which will far eclipse anything beheld in these less enthusiastic days. Hasten it, O Lord.

Hebrew may denote any capital crime, and, in my opinion, he is here to be considered as alluding to the sentence of death, to which he felt himself to be obnoxious, and from which he requests deliverance. By the righteousness of God, which he engages to celebrate, we are to understand his goodness; for this attribute, as usually ascribed to God in the Scriptures, does not so much denote the strictness with which he exacts vengeance, as his faithfulness in fulfilling the promises and extending help to all who seek him in the hour of need.

15. He prays that his lips may be opened; in other words, that God would afford him matter of praise. David seems to intimate that his mouth must be shut until God called him to the exercise of thanksgiving by extending pardon. In another place we find him declaring that a new song had been put in his mouth, (Psalm 40:3,) and it seems to be in this sense that he here desires his lips to be opened.

16-19

16. For thou wilt not accept a sacrifice. By this language he expresses his confidence of obtaining pardon, although he brought nothing to God in the shape of compensation, but relied entirely upon the riches of Divine mercy. He confesses that he comes to God both poor and needy; but is persuaded that this will not prevent the success of his suit, because God attaches no importance to sacrifices.

17. The sacrifices of God are a broken spirit. He had shown that sacrifices have no such efficacy in procuring the Divine favor as the Jews imagined; and now he declares that he needed to bring nothing whatever to God but a contrite and humbled heart. Nothing more is necessary, on the part of the sinner, than to prostrate himself in supplication for Divine mercy.

18. Do good to Zion in thy good pleasure: build thou the walls of Jerusalem. From prayer in his own behalf he now proceeds to offer up supplications for the collective Church of God, a duty which he may have felt to be the more incumbent upon him from the circumstance of his having done what he could by his fall to ruin it, Raised to the throne, and originally anointed to be king for the very purpose of fostering the Church of God, he had by his disgraceful conduct nearly accomplished its destruction.

19. Then shalt thou accept sacrifices of righteousness. In these words there is an apparent, but only an apparent, inconsistency with others which he had used in the preceding context. He had declared sacrifices to be of no value when considered in themselves, but now he acknowledges them to be acceptable to God when viewed as expressions or symbols of faith, penitence, and thanksgiving. He calls them distinctly sacrifices of righteousness, right, warrantable, and such as are offered in strict accordance with the commandment of God. The expression is the same employed in Psalm 4:5, where David uses it with a tacit condemnation of those who gloried in the mere outward form of ceremonies. We find him again exciting himself and others by his example to the exercise of gratitude, and to the expression of it openly in the solemn assembly.

I deserve; they are ever before me, let them be cast behind thy back. Blot out all my iniquities out of the book of thy account; blot them out, as a cloud is blotted out and dispelled by the beams of the sun," Isa. xliv. 22.

4. He prays for sanctifying grace; and this every true penitent is as earnest for as for pardon and peace, v. 10. He does not pray, "Lord, preserve me my reputation," as Saul, I have sinned, yet honor me before this people. No; his great concern is to get his corrupt nature changed.

5. He prays for the continuance of God's good-will towards him and the progress of his good work in him, v. 11.

6. He prays for the restoration of divine comforts and the perpetual communications of divine grace, v. 12.

II. See what David here promises, v. 13. Observe,

1. What good work he promises to do: I will teach transgressors thy ways. David had been himself a transgressor, and therefore could speak experimentally to transgressors.

2. What good effect he promises himself from his doing this: "Sinners shall be converted unto thee, and shall neither persist in their wanderings from thee, nor despair of finding mercy in their returns to thee."

14-17 Penitential petitions.

I. David prays against the guilt of sin, and prays for the grace of God, enforcing both petitions from a plea taken from the glory of God, which he promises with thankfulness to show forth.

1. He prays against the guilt of sin, that he might be delivered from that, and promises that then he would praise God, v. 14.

2. He prays for the grace of God and promises to improve that grace to his glory (v. 15): "O Lord! open thou my lips, not only that I may teach and instruct sinners."

II. David offers the sacrifice of a penitent contrite heart, as that which he knew God would be pleased with. He knew well that the sacrificing of beasts was in itself of no account with God (v. 16): Thou desirest not sacrifice (else would I give it with all my heart to obtain pardon and peace); thou delightest not in burnt-offering.

III. David intercedes for Zion and Jerusalem, with an eye to the honor of God. See what a concern he had,

1. For the good of the church of God (v. 18): Do good in thy good pleasure unto Zion; that is, "To all the particular worshippers in Zion, to all that love and fear thy name; keep them from falling into such wounding wasting sins as these of mine; defend and succor all that fear thy name."

2. For the honor of the churches of God, v. 19. If God would show himself reconciled to him and his people, as he had prayed, then they should go on with the public services of his house.

Psalm 52

Title
To the chief Musician. Maschil. A Psalm of David. When Doeg the Edomite came and told Saul, and said unto him, David is come to the house of Ahimelech.

1-4
1 Why boastest thou thyself in mischief, O mighty man? the goodness of God endureth continually.
2 The tongue deviseth mischiefs; like a sharp razor, working deceitfully.
3 Thou lovest evil more than good; and lying rather than to speak righteousness. Selah.
4 Thou lovest all devouring words, O thou deceitful tongue.

Psalm 52

TITLE. To the Chief Musician. Even short Psalms, if they record but one instance of the goodness of the Lord, and rebuke but briefly the pride of man, are worthy of our best minstrelsy. When we see that each Psalm is dedicated to "the chief musician," it should make us value our psalmody, and forbid us to praise the Lord carelessly. Maschil. An Instructive. Even the malice of a Doeg may furnish instruction to a David. A Psalm of David. He was the prime object of Doeg's doggish hatred, and therefore the most fitting person to draw from the incident the lesson concealed within it. When Doeg the Edomite came and told Saul, and saith unto him, David is come to the house of Ahimelech. By this deceitful tale bearing, he procured the death of all the priests at Nob: though it had been a crime to have succored David as a rebel, they were not in their intent and knowledge guilty of the fault. David felt much the villainy of this arch enemy, and here he denounces him in vigorous terms; it may be also that he has Saul in his eye.
DIVISION. We shall follow the sacred pauses marked by the Selahs of the poet.

EXPOSITION
Verse 1. Why boasteth thyself in mischief, O mighty man? Doeg had small matter for boasting in having procured the slaughter of a band of defenseless priests. A mighty man indeed to kill men who never touched a sword! He ought to have been ashamed of his cowardice. He had no room for exultation! Honorable titles are but irony where the wearer is mean and cruel. If David alluded to Saul, he meant by these words pityingly to say, "How can one by nature fitted for nobler deeds, descend to so low a level as to find a theme for boasting in a slaughter so heartless and mischievous?" The goodness of God endureth continually. A beautiful contrast. The tyrant's fury cannot dry up the perennial stream of divine mercy. If priests be slain their Master lives. If Doeg for awhile triumphs the Lord will outlive him, and right the wrongs which he has done. This ought to modify the proud exultations of the wicked, for after all, while the Lord liveth, iniquity has little cause to exalt itself.
Verse 2. Thy tongue deviseth mischiefs. Thou speakest with an ulterior design. The information given was for Saul's assistance apparently, but in very deed in his heart the Edomite hated the priests of the God of Jacob. It is a mark of deep depravity, when the evil spoken is craftily intended to promote a yet greater evil. Like a sharp razor, working deceitfully. David represents the false tongue as being effectual for mischief, like a razor which, unawares to the person operated on, is making him bald; so softly and deftly do Oriental barbers perform their work. Or he may mean that as with a razor a man's throat may be cut very speedily, under the pretence of shaving him, even thus keenly, basely, but effectually Doeg destroyed the band of the priests. Whetted by malice, and guided by craft, he did his cruel work with accursed thoroughness.
Verse 3. Thou lovest evil more than good. He loved not good at all. If both had been equally profitable and pleasant, he would have preferred evil. And lying rather than to speak righteousness. He was more at home at lying than at truth. He spake not the truth except by accident, but he delighted heartily in falsehood. SELAH. Let us pause and look at the proud blustering liar. Doeg is gone, but other dogs bark at the Lord's people. Saul's cattle master is buried, but the devil still has his drovers, who fain would hurry the saints like sheep to the slaughter.
Verse 4. Thou lovest. Thou hast a taste, a gusto for evil language. All devouring words. There are words that, like boa constrictors, swallow men whole, or like lions, rend men to pieces; these words evil minds are fond of. Their oratory is evermore furious and bloody. That which will most readily provoke the lowest passions they are sure to employ, and they think such

Psalm 52

This psalm was composed by David at the time when the death of Abimelech and the other priests had spread universal tenor among the people, indisposing them for lending any countenance to his cause, and when Doeg was triumphing in the successful issue of his information. Supported, even in these circumstances, by the elevating influence of faith, he inveighs against the cruel treachery of that unprincipled informer, and encourages himself by the reflection, that God, who is judge in heaven, will vindicate the interests of such as fear him, and punish the pride of the ungodly.

1-4

1. Why boastest thou of thy wickedness? The success which crowned the treachery of Doeg must have tended considerably to stagger David's faith; and he seems to have adopted the strain of holy defiance with which the psalm commences, in order to arm himself more effectually against this temptation. He begins by charging Doeg with an aggravation of his guilt, in boasting of the power which he had acquired by an act of consummate villainy. This power may have been sufficiently considerable to attract the notice which is here taken of it; for although he is only said to have been "master of the king's herdsmen," the designation does not imply that he was personally occupied in herding cattle, but may have been an honorary title; as in modern courts we speak of "The Master of the Horse." he is reminded that there was no reason why he should applaud himself in his greatness, so long as he abused it to purposes of wickedness; nor why he should be vain of any new honor which the king might have conferred upon him in consideration of his late crime, as integrity is the only sure pathway to power and preferment. Any triumph which may be obtained by violence, treachery, or other unjustifiable means, is short-lived.

2-4. Thy tongue reckons up mischiefs. David is not to be considered as here venting a flood of reproaches against his adversary, as many who have been unjustly injured are in the habit of doing, merely to gratify a feeling of revenge. He brings these charges against him in the sight of God, with a view to encourage himself in the hopefulness of his own cause: for it is plain that the farther our enemies proceed in the practice of iniquity, they proportionally provoke the anger of the Lord, and are nearer to that destruction which must issue in our deliverance. His object, therefore, is not to blacken the character of Doeg in the estimation of the world, but rather to set before his own eyes the divine punishment which the flagrant offenses he specifies were certain to draw down upon his head. Amongst these he singles out, as more especially worthy of reprobation, the hidden treachery with which he had been chargeable in accomplishing the destruction of the priesthood.

5-7

5. God shall likewise destroy thee for ever. From these words it is made still more evident that his object in dwelling upon

Psalm 52

1-5 The wickedness of Doeg.

The title is a brief account of the story which the psalm refers to. David now, at length, saw it necessary to quit the court, and shift for his own safety, for fear of Saul, who had once and again attempted to murder him. Being unprovided wit harms and victuals, he, by a wile, got Ahimelech the priest to furnish him with both. Doeg an Edomite happened to be there, and he went and informed Saul against Ahimelech, representing him as confederate with a traitor, upon which accusation Saul grounded a very bloody warrant, to kill all the priests; and Doeg, the prosecutor, was the executioner, 1 Sam. xxii. 9, &c.

In these verses,

I. David argues the case fairly with this proud and mighty man, v. 1. Doeg probably was mighty in respect of bodily strength; but, if he was, he gained no reputation to it by his easy victory over the unarmed priests of the Lord; it is no honor for those that wear a sword to hector those that wear an ephod. However, he was, by his office, a mighty man, for he was set over the servants of Saul, chamberlain of the household. This was he that boasted himself, not only in the power he had to do mischief, but in the mischief he did. Now note:

1. The sinfulness of his sin: "God is continually doing good, and those that therein are like him have reason to glory in their being so; but thou art continually doing mischief, and therein art utterly unlike him, and contrary to him, and yet gloriest in being so."

2. The folly of it: "Thou thinkest, with the mischief which thou boastest of (so artfully contrived and so successfully carried on), to run down and ruin the people of God; but thou wilt find thyself mistaken: the goodness of God endures continually for their preservation, and then they need not fear what man can do unto them." The enemies in vain boast in their mischief while we have God's mercy to boast in.

II. He draws up a high charge against him in the court of heaven, as he had drawn up a high charge against Ahimelech in Saul's court, v. 2-4. He accuses him of the wickedness of his tongue (that unruly evil, full of deadly poison) and the wickedness of his heart, which that was an evidence of. Four things he charges him with:

1. Malice. His tongue does mischief, not only pricking like a needle, but cutting like a sharp razor. Scornful bantering words would not content him; he loved devouring words, words that would ruin the priests of the Lord, whom he hated.

2. Falsehood. It was a deceitful tongue that he did this mischief with (v. 4); he loved lying (v. 3), and this sharp razor did work deceitfully (v. 2), that is, before he had this occasion given him to discover his malice against the priests, he had acted very plausibly towards them; though he was an Edomite, he attended the altars, and brought his offerings, and

Psalm 52

5-9

5 God shall likewise destroy thee for ever, he shall take thee away, and pluck thee out of thy dwelling place, and root thee out of the land of the living. Selah.
6 The righteous also shall see, and fear, and shall laugh at him:
7 Lo, this is the man that made not God his strength; but trusted in the abundance of his riches, and strengthened himself in his wickedness.
8 But I am like a green olive tree in the house of God: I trust in the mercy of God for ever and ever.
9 I will praise thee for ever, because thou hast done it: and I will wait on thy name; for it is good before thy saints.

pandering to the madness of the wicked to be eloquence of a high order. O thou deceitful tongue. Men can manage to say a great many furious things, and yet cover all over with the pretext of justice. They claim that they are jealous for the right, but the truth is they are determined to put down truth and holiness, and craftily go about it under this transparent pretence.

Verse 5. God shall likewise destroy thee for ever. Fain would the persecutor destroy the church, and therefore God shall destroy him, pull down his house, pluck up his roots, and make an end of him. He shall take thee away. God shall extinguish his coal and sweep him away like the ashes of the hearth; he would have quenched the truth, and God shall quench him. And pluck thee out of thy dwelling place, like a plant torn from the place where it grew, or a captive dragged from his home. Ahimelech and his brother priests were cut off from their abode, and so should those be who compassed and contrived their murder. And root thee out of the land of the living. The persecutor shall be eradicated, stubbed up by the root, cut up root and branch. He sought the death of others and death shall fall upon him. He troubled the land of the living, and he shall be banished to that land where the wicked cease from troubling. Those who will not "let live" have no right to "live." God will turn the tables on malicious men, and mete to them a portion with their own measure. "SELAH." Pause again, and behold the divine justice proving itself more than a match for human sin.

Verse 6. The righteous—the object of the tyrant's hatred—shall outlive his enmity, and also shall see, before his own face, the end of the ungodly oppressor. God permits Mordecai to see Haman hanging on the gallows. David had brought to him the tokens of Saul's death on Gilboa. And fear. Holy awe shall sober the mind of the good man; he shall reverently adore the God of providence. And shall laugh at him. If not with righteous joy, yet with solemn contempt. Schemes so far reaching all baffled, plans so deep, so politic, all thwarted. Mephistopheles outwitted, the old serpent taken in his own subtlety. This is a good theme for that deep seated laughter which is more akin to solemnity than merriment.

Verse 7. Lo. Look ye here, and read the epitaph of a mighty man, who lorded it proudly during his little hour, and set his heel upon the necks of the Lord's chosen. This is the man that made not God his strength. Behold the man! The great vainglorious man. He found a fortress, but not in God; he gloried in his might, but not in the Almighty.

Verse 8. But I, hunted and persecuted though I am, am like a green olive tree. I am not plucked up or destroyed, but am like a flourishing olive, which out of the rock draws oil, and amid the drought still lives and grows. In the house of God. He was one of the divine family, and could not be expelled from it; his place was near his God, and there was he safe, despite all the machinations of his foes. He was bearing fruit, and would continue to do so when all his enemies were withered like branches lopped from the tree.

Verse 9. I will praise thee for ever. Like thy mercy shall my thankfulness be. While others boast in their riches I will boast in my God; and when their glorying is silenced for ever in the tomb, my song shall continue to proclaim the lovingkindness of Jehovah. Because thou hast done it. Thou hast vindicated the righteous, and punished the wicked. God's memorable acts of providence, both to saints and sinners, deserve, and must have our gratitude. David views his prayer as already answered, the promise of God as already fulfilled, and therefore at once lifts up the sacred Psalm. And I will wait on thy name. God shall still be the psalmist's hope; he will not in future look elsewhere.

the aggravated guilt of Doeg, was to prove the certainty of his approaching doom, and this rather for his own conviction and comfort, than with a view to alarming the conscience of the offender. Accordingly, he declares his persuasion that God would not allow his treachery to pass unpunished, though he might for a time connive at the perpetration of it. The ungodly are disposed, so long as their prosperity continues, to indulge in undisturbed security; and the saint of God, when he sees the power of which they are possessed, and witnesses their proud contempt of the divine judgments, is too apt to be overwhelmed with unbelieving apprehensions.

6. The righteous also shall see, and fear. He here adduces, as another reason why the ruin of Doeg might be expected, that an important end would be obtained by it, in so far as it would promote religion in the hearts of the Lord's people, and afford them a refreshing display of the Divine justice. Should it take place, it would be witnessed by the ungodly as well as by the righteous; but there are two reasons why the Psalmist represents it as being seen especially by the latter.

7. Lo! this is the man that made not God his strength. Some think that these words are given as what should afterwards be proverbially applied to Doeg; but they would not appear to have been intended in that restricted signification. They merely express the improvement which the people of God would make of the judgment. It would teach them, on the one hand, to be patient under the insolence of the ungodly, which is so speedily humbled; and, on the other, to beware of indulging a similarly infatuated spirit themselves.

8-9

8. But I am like a green olive-tree. We have seen that David was enabled, by the exercise of faith, to look down upon the worldly grandeur of Doeg with a holy contempt; and now we find him rising superior to all that was presently afflictive in his own condition. Though, to appearance, he more resembled the withered trunk of a tree which rots upon the ground, he compares himself, in the confidence of coming prosperity, to a green olive. I need not say that the destruction of Doeg could only communicate comfort to his mind, in the way of convincing him that God was the avenging judge of human cruelty, and leading him to infer that, as he had punished his wrongs, so he would advance him to renewed measures of prosperity.

9. I will praise thee, etc. He concludes the psalm with thanksgiving, and shows that he is sincere in this, by the special acknowledgement which he makes of the fact that this had been the work of God. Such is the corruption of the human heart, that out of a hundred who profess gratitude to God with their lips, scarcely one man seriously reflects upon the benefits which he has received as coming from his hand. David declares, therefore, that it was entirely owing to the divine protection that he had escaped from the treachery of Doeg, and from all his subsequent dangers, and promises to retain a grateful sense of it throughout the whole of his life.

paid his respects to the priests, as decently as any Israelite; and thus he gained an opportunity of doing them so much the greater mischief.

3. Subtlety in sin: "Thy tongue devises mischiefs; that is, it speaks the mischief which thy heart devises." The more there is of craft and contrivance in any wickedness the more there is of the devil in it.

4. Affection to sin: "Thou lovest evil more than good; that is, thou lovest evil, and hast no love at all to that which is good; thou takest delight in lying, and makest no conscience of doing right. Thou wouldst rather please Saul by telling a lie than please God by speaking truth."

III. He reads his doom and denounces the judgments of God against him for his wickedness (v. 5): "Thou hast destroyed the priests of the Lord and cut them off, and therefore God shall likewise destroy thee for ever." Sons of perdition actively shall be sons of perdition passively, as Judas and the man of sin.

6-9 The ruin of Doeg predicted.

David was at this time in great distress; the mischief Doeg had done him was but the beginning of his sorrows; and yet here we have him triumphing, and that is more than rejoicing, in tribulation. Blessed Paul, in the midst of his troubles, is in the midst of his triumphs, 2 Cor. ii. 14. David here triumphs,

I. In the fall of Doeg. Yet, lest this should look like personal revenge, he does not speak of it as his own act, but the language of other righteous persons. They shall observe God's judgments on Doeg, and speak of them,

1. To the glory of God: They shall see and fear (v. 6); that is, they shall reverence the justice of God, as a God of almighty power, before whom the we ought every one of us to humble ourselves.

2. To the shame of Doeg. They shall laugh at him, not with a ludicrous, but a rational serious laughter, as he that sits in heaven shall laugh at him, Ps. ii. 4. He shall appear ridiculous, and worthy to be laughed at. We are told how they shall triumph in God's just judgments on him (v. 7): Lo, this is the man that made not God his strength.

II. In his own stability, v. 8, 9. "This mighty man is plucked up by the roots; but I am like a green olive-tree, planted and rooted, fixed and flourishing; he is turned out of God's dwelling-place, but I am established in it, not detained, as Doeg, by any thing but the abundant satisfaction I meet with there."

We must live a life of thankfulness and holy joy in God (v. 9): "I will praise thee for ever, because thou hast done it, has avenged the blood of thy priests upon their bloody enemy, and given him blood to drink, and hast performed thy promise to me," which he was as sure would be done in due time as if it were done already.

Psalm 53

Title
To the chief Musician. Upon Mahalath. Maschil. A Psalm of David.

1 The fool hath said in his heart, There is no God. Corrupt are they, and have done abominable iniquity: there is none that doeth good.
2 God looked down from heaven upon the children of men, to see if there were any that did understand, that did seek God.
3 Every one of them is gone back: they are altogether become filthy; there is none that doeth good, no, not one.
4 Have the workers of iniquity no knowledge? who eat up my people as they eat bread: they have not called upon God.
5 There were they in great fear, where no fear was: for God hath scattered the bones of him that encampeth against thee: thou hast put them to shame, because God hath despised them.
6 Oh that the salvation of Israel were come out of Zion! When God bringeth back the captivity of his people, Jacob shall rejoice, and Israel shall be glad.

Psalm 53

It is not a copy of the fourteenth Psalm, emended and revised by a foreign hand; it is another edition by the same author, emphasized in certain parts, and rewritten for another purpose.

All repetitions are not vain repetitions. We are slow to learn, and need line upon line. David after a long life, found men no better than they were in his youth. Holy Writ never repeats itself needlessly, there is good cause for the second copy of this Psalm; let us read it with more profound attention than before. If our age has advanced from fourteen to fifty-three, we shall find the doctrine of this Psalm more evident than in our youth.

Psalm 53

This psalm being almost identical with the fourteenth, it has not been considered necessary to subjoin any distinct commentary.

Psalm 53

See Psalm 14.

Psalm 54

Title
To the chief Musician on Neginoth. Maschil. A Psalm of David, when the Ziphims came and said to Saul, Doth not David hide himself with us?

1 Save me, O God, by thy name, and judge me by thy strength.
2 Hear my prayer, O God; give ear to the words of my mouth.
3 For strangers are risen up against me, and oppressors seek after my soul: they have not set God before them. Selah.
4 Behold, God is mine helper: the Lord is with them that uphold my soul.
5 He shall reward evil unto mine enemies: cut them off in thy truth.
6 I will freely sacrifice unto thee: I will praise thy name, O LORD; for it is good.
7 For he hath delivered me out of all trouble: and mine eye hath seen his desire upon mine enemies.

Psalm 54

TITLE. To the Chief Musician on Neginoth. The music was to be that of stringed instruments. Variety is to be studied in our tunes, and in all other matters relating to sacred song. Monotony is often the death of congregational praise. Providence is varied, and so should our recording songs be. Maschil. We are to learn and to teach by what we sing. Edification must not be divorced from psalmody. A Psalm of David. David's productions were as plentiful as they are profitable. His varied life was for our benefit, for from it we derive these hymns, which at this hour are as fresh and as precious as when he wrote them. When the Ziphims came and said to Saul, Doth not David hide himself with us? To curry favor with Saul they were guilty of gross inhospitality. What cared they what innocent blood was shed so that they earned the graceless monarch's smile! David came quietly among them, hoping for a little rest in his many flights, but they deserted him in his solitary abode, and betrayed him. He turns to God in prayer, and so strong was his faith that he soon sang himself into delightful serenity.
DIVISION. From Ps 54:1-3, where the Selah makes a pause for us, the psalmist pleads with God, and then in the rest of the song, laying aside all doubt, he chants a hymn of joyful triumph. The vigor of faith is the death of anxiety, and the birth of security.

EXPOSITION
Verse 1. Save me, O God. Thou art my Savior; all around me are my foes and their eager helpers. No shelter is permitted me. Every land rejects me and denies me rest.
Verse 2. Hear my prayer, O God. This has ever been the defense of saints.
Verse 3. For strangers are risen up against me. Those who had no cause for ill will had gone against him; persons to whom he could have given no offence, for they were strangers to him.
Verse 4. Behold, God is mine helper. He saw enemies everywhere, and now to his joy as he looks upon the band of his defenders he sees one whose aid is better than all the help of men.
Verse 5. He shall reward evil unto mine enemies. They worked for evil, and they shall have their wages. It cannot be that malice should go unavenged.
Verse 6. I will freely sacrifice unto thee. Spontaneously will I bring my freewill offerings.
Verse 7. For he hath delivered me out of all trouble. Up to that time deliverance had come, and for that danger also he felt that rescue was near. David lived a life of dangers, yet he was always safe.

Psalm 54

1-3

1. Save me, O God! As David was at this time placed beyond the reach of human assistance, he must be understood as praying to be saved by the name and the power of God. Though all help must ultimately come from God, there are ordinary methods by which he generally extends it. When these fail, and every earthly stay is removed, he must then take the work into his own hands. It was in such a situation that David here fled to the saints' last asylum, and sought to be saved by a miracle of divine power.

2. Hear my prayer, O God! The language is expressive of his earnestness. He was led to this fervor of supplication by the extremity of his present circumstances, which is alluded to in the following verse, where he complains of being surrounded by men fierce, barbarous, and unrestrained by a sense of religion.

3. He adds, that they sought after his soul, to denote that nothing would content their insatiable cruelty but his life. And the better to express the unbridled nature of their fury, he tells us that they had no respect to God.

Psalm 54:4-7

4. Behold! God is my helper. Such language as this may show us that David did not direct his prayers at random into the air, but offered them in the exercise of a lively faith.

5. He shall reward evil unto mine enemies. With the view of confirming his hopes, David adverts particularly to the truth of God; for nothing can support us in the hour of temptation, when the Divine deliverance may be long delayed, but a firm persuasion that God is true, and that he cannot deceive us by his divine promises.

6. I will freely sacrifice unto thee. According to his usual custom, he engages, provided deliverance should be granted, to feel a grateful sense of it; and there can be no doubt that he here promises also to return thanks to God, in a formal manner, when he should enjoy an opportunity of doing so. Though God principally looks to the inward sentiment of the heart, that would not excuse the neglect of such rites as the Law had prescribed.

7. We are now to suppose him relieved from his anxieties, and subjoining a fresh expression of his gratitude: nor is it improbable that, he refers to mercies which he had experienced at other periods of his history, and which were recalled to his memory by the one more immediately brought under our notice in the preceding verses; so that he is to be understood as declaring, in a more general sense, that the name of God was good, and that he had been delivered out of all trouble.

Psalm 54

1-3 Complaints.

We may observe here,

1. The great distress that David was now in, which the title gives an account of. The Ziphim came of their own accord, and informed Saul where David was, with a promise to deliver him into his hand.

2. His prayer to God for succor and deliverance, v. 1, 2. He appeals to God's strength, by which he was able to help him, and to his name, by which he was engaged to help him, and begs he would save him from his enemies and judge him, that is, plead his cause and judge for him. This would be the effectual answer of his prayers (v. 2), which even in his flight, when he had not opportunity for solemn address to God, he was ever and anon lifting up to heaven: Hear my prayer, which comes from my heart, and give ear to the words of my mouth.

3. His plea, which is taken from the character of his enemies, v. 3. They are strangers; such were the Ziphites, unworthy the name of Israelites. "They have used me more basely and barbarously than the Philistines themselves would have done."

4-7 Consolations.

We have here the lively actings of David's faith in his prayer, by which he was assured that the issue would be comfortable, though the attempt upon him was formidable.

I. He was sure that he had God on his side, that God took his part (v. 4); he speaks it with an air of triumph and exultation, Behold, God is my helper. If we be for him, he is for us; and, if he be for us, we shall have such help in him that we need not fear any power engaged against us.

II. God taking part with him, he doubted not but his enemies should both flee and fall before him (v. 5): "He shall reward evil unto my enemies that observe me, seeking an opportunity to do me a mischief. The evil they designed against me the righteous God will return upon their own heads."

III. He promises to give thanks to God for all the experiences he had had of his goodness to him (v. 6): I will sacrifice unto thee. Though sacrifices were expensive, yet, when God required that his worshippers should in that way praise him, David would not only offer them, but offer them freely and without grudging.

IV. He speaks of his deliverance as a thing done (v. 7): I will praise thy name, and say, "He has delivered me; this shall be my song then." He has delivered me from all trouble; and a deliverance to his heart's content, 1 Sam. xxiii. 27, 28.

Psalm 55

Title
To the chief Musician on Neginoth. Maschil. A Psalm of David.

1-8

1 Give ear to my prayer, O God; and hide not thyself from my supplication.
2 Attend unto me, and hear me: I mourn in my complaint, and make a noise;
3 Because of the voice of the enemy, because of the oppression of the wicked: for they cast iniquity upon me, and in wrath they hate me.
4 My heart is sore pained within me: and the terrors of death are fallen upon me.
5 Fearfulness and trembling are come upon me, and horror hath overwhelmed me.
6 And I said, Oh that I had wings like a dove! for then would I fly away, and be at rest.
7 Lo, then would I wander far off, and remain in the wilderness. Selah.
8 I would hasten my escape from the windy storm and tempest.

Psalm 55

TITLE. To the Chief Musician on Neginoth. Another song to be accompanied by stringed instruments. The strain is at one time mournful, and at another softly sweet. It needed the chief musician's best care to see that the music was expressive of the sentiment. Maschil. It is not a mere personal hymn, there is teaching in it for us all, and where our Lord shines through David, his personal type, there is a great deep of meaning. Of David. The man of many conditions, much tried, and much favored, persecuted but delivered and exalted, was from experience enabled to write such precious verses in which he sets forth not only the sorrows of common pilgrims, but of the Lord of the way himself.

SUBJECT. It would be idle to fix a time, and find an occasion for this Psalm with any dogmatism. It reads like a song of the time of Absalom and Ahithophel. It was after David had enjoyed peaceful worship (Ps 55:14), when he was or had just been a dweller in a city (Ps 55:9-11), and when he remembered his former roamings in the wilderness. Altogether it seems to us to relate to that mournful era when the King was betrayed by his trusted counselor. The spiritual eye ever and anon sees the Son of David and Judas, and the chief priests appearing and disappearing upon the glowing canvas of the Psalm.

DIVISION. From Ps 55:1-8, the suppliant spreads his case in general before his God; in Ps 55:9-11, he portrays his enemies; in Ps 55:12-14, he mentions one special traitor, and cries for vengeance, or foretells it in Ps 55:15. From Ps 55:16-19 he consoles himself by prayer and faith; in Ps 55:20-21 he again mentions the deceitful covenant breaker, and closes with a cheering exhortation to the saints (Ps 55:22), and a denunciation of destruction upon the wicked and deceitful (Ps 55:22).

EXPOSITION

Verse 1. Give ear to my prayer, O God. The fact is so commonly before us, otherwise we should be surprised to observe how universally and constantly the saints resort to prayer in seasons of distress. From the Great Elder Brother down to the very least of the divine family, all of them delight in prayer. They run as naturally to the mercy seat in time of trouble as the little chickens to the hen in the hour of danger. But note well that it is never the bare act of prayer which satisfies the godly, they crave an audience with heaven, and an answer from the throne, and nothing less will content them.

Verse 2. Attend unto me, and hear me. This is the third time he prays the same prayer. He is in earnest, in deep and bitter earnest. If his God do not hear, he feels that all is over with him. He begs for his God to be a listener and an answerer.

Verse 3. Because of the voice of the enemy. The enemy was vocal and voluble enough, and found a voice where his godly victim had nothing better than a "noise." Slander is seldom short of expression, it prates and prattles evermore.

Verse 4. My heart is sore pained within me. His spirit writhed in agony, like a poor worm; he was mentally as much in pain as a woman in travail physically. His inmost soul was touched; and a wounded spirit who can bear? If this were written when David was attacked by his own favorite son, and ignominiously driven from his capital, he had reason enough for using these expressions. And the terrors of death are fallen upon me. Mortal fears seized him, he felt like one suddenly surrounded with the glooms of the shadow of death, upon whom the eternal night suddenly descends.

Verse 5. Fearfulness and trembling are come upon me. Like house breakers these robbers were entering his soul. Like one who feels a fainting fit coming over him, so the oppressed suppliant was falling into a state of terror. His fear was so great as to make him tremble. He did not know what would happen next, or how soon the worst should come. The sly,

JOHN CALVIN

Psalm 55

1-3
1-2. Give ear to my prayer, O God! From the language with which the psalm opens, we may conclude that David at this time was laboring under heavy distress. It could be no ordinary amount of it which produced such an overwhelming effect upon a saint of his distinguished courage.
3. The affliction of the wicked is here to be understood in the active sense of persecution. And in applying the term wicked to his enemies, he does not so much level an accusation against them as implicitly assert his own innocence. Our greatest comfort under persecution is conscious rectitude, the reflection that we have not deserved it; for there springs from this the hope that we will experience the help of the Lord, who is the shield and defense of the distressed.

4-8
4. My heart trembles within me. Here we have additional evidence of the extremity of David's sufferings. He that uses these words was no soft or effeminate person, but one who had given indubitable proofs of constancy. Nor is it merely of the atrocious injuries inflicted upon him by his enemies that he complains. He exclaims that he is overwhelmed with terrors, and thus acknowledges that his heart was not insensible to his afflictions.
6. And I said, Who will give me wings like a dove? These words mean more than merely that he could find no mode of escape. They are meant to express the deplorableness of his situation, which made exile a blessing to be coveted, and this not the common exile of mankind, but such as that of the dove when it flies far off to some deserted hiding-place. They imply that he could only escape by a miracle. They intimate that even the privilege of retreat by common banishment was denied him, so that it fared worse with him than with the poor bird of heaven, which can at least fly from its pursuer. It seems most probable that David meant by this comparison, that he longed to escape from his cruel enemies, as the timid and defenseless dove flies from the hawk. Great, indeed, must have been the straits to which he was reduced, when he could so far forget the promise made to him of the kingdom as, in the agitation of his spirits, to contemplate a disgraceful flight, and speak of being content to hide himself far from his native country, and the haunts of human society, in some solitude of the wilderness.

9-11
9. Destroy, O Lord; and divide their tongue. Having now composed, as it were, his mind, he resumes the exercise of prayer. Had he indulged longer in the strain of complaint, he might have given his sanction to the folly of those who do themselves more harm than good by the excessive use of this barren species of comfort. There will occasionally escape from the lips of a saint, when he prays, some complaining exclamations which cannot be altogether justified, but he soon recalls himself to the exercise of believing supplication.

MATTHEW HENRY

Psalm 55

1-8 Supplications of David in distress.
In these verses we have,
I. David praying. Prayer is a salve for every sore and a relief to the spirit under every burden: Give ear to my prayer, O God! v. 1, 2. He does not set down the petitions he offered up to God in his distress, but begs that God would hear the prayers which, at every period, his heart lifted up to God, and grant an answer of peace to them: Attend to me, hear me. Saul would not hear his petitions; his other enemies regarded not his pleas; but, "Lord, be thou pleased to hearken to me. Hide not thyself from my supplication, either as one unconcerned and not regarding it, nor seeming to take any notice of it, or as one displeased, angry at me, and therefore at my prayer."
II. David weeping; for in this he was a type of Christ that he was a man of sorrows and often in tears (v. 2): "I mourn in my complaint" (or in my meditation, my melancholy musings), "and I make a noise; I cannot forbear such sighs and groans, and other expressions of grief, as discover it to those about me." Great griefs are sometimes noisy and clamorous, and thus are, in some measure, lessened, while those increase that are stifled, and have no vent given them. But what was the matter? v. 3. It is because of the voice of the enemy, the menaces and insults of Absalom's party, that swelled, and hectored, and stirred up the people to cry out against David, and shout him out of his palace and capital city, as afterwards the chief priests stirred up the mob to cry out against the Son of David, Away with him—Crucify him.
III. David trembling, and in great consternation. We may well suppose him to be so upon the breaking out of Absalom's conspiracy and the general defection of the people, even those that he had little reason to suspect.
1. See what fear seized him. David was a man of great boldness, and in some very eminent instances had signalized his courage, and yet, when the danger was surprising and imminent, his heart failed him. Let not the stout man therefore glory in his courage any more than the strong man in his strength. Now David's heart is sorely pained within him; the terrors of death have fallen upon him, v. 4. Fearfulness of mind and trembling of body came upon him, and horror covered and overwhelmed him, v. 5. When without are fightings no marvel that within are fears; and, if it was upon the occasion of Absalom's rebellion, we may suppose that the remembrance of his sin in the matter of Uriah, which God was now reckoning with him for, added as much more to the fright.
2. See how desirous he was, in this fright, to retire into a desert, any where to be far enough from hearing the voice of the enemy and seeing their oppressions. He said (v. 6), said it to God in prayer, said it to himself in meditation, said it to his friends in

Psalm 55

9-16
9 Destroy, O Lord, and divide their tongues: for I have seen violence and strife in the city.
10 Day and night they go about it upon the walls thereof: mischief also and sorrow are in the midst of it.
11 Wickedness is in the midst thereof: deceit and guile depart not from her streets.
12 For it was not an enemy that reproached me; then I could have borne it: neither was it he that hated me that did magnify himself against me; then I would have hid myself from him:
13 But it was thou, a man mine equal, my guide, and mine acquaintance.
14 We took sweet counsel together, and walked unto the house of God in company.
15 Let death seize upon them, and let them go down quick into hell: for wickedness is in their dwellings, and among them.
16 As for me, I will call upon God; and the LORD shall save me.

mysterious whisperings of slander often cause a noble mind more fear than open antagonism; we can be brave against an open foe, but cowardly, plotting conspiracies bewilder and distract us. And horror hath overwhelmed me. He was as one enveloped in a darkness that might be felt.
Verse 6. And I said, Oh that I had wings like a dove! for then would I fly away, and be at rest. If he could not resist as an eagle, he would escape as a dove. Swiftly, and unobserved, on strong, untiring pinions would he h away from the abodes of slander and wickedness. His love of peace made him sigh for an escape from the scene of strife.
Verse 7. Lo, then would I wander far off. Yet when David was far off, he sighed to be once more near Jerusalem; thus, in our ill estate we ever think the past to be better than the present. We shall be called to fly far enough away, and perchance we shall be loath to go; we need not indulge vain notions of premature escape from earth.
Verse 8. I would hasten my escape. He tried to pause but could not, like a horse which when pulled up slips on a little because of the speed at which he was going. David declares that he would not waste a moment, or stay to bid adieu to his friends, but up and away at once, for fear he should be too late, and because he could bear the clamor of his foes no longer.
Verse 9. Destroy, O Lord. Put mine enemies to the rout. Let them be devoured by the sword, since they have unsheathed it against me. How could we expect the exiled monarch to offer any other prayer than this against the rebellious bands of Absalom, and the crafty devices of Ahithophel? Divide their tongues. Make another Babel in their debates and councils of war. Set them at cross purposes. Divide the pack that the hunted one may escape.
Verse 10. Day and night they go about it upon the walls thereof. The city, the holy city had become a den of wickedness; conspirators met in the dark, and talked in little knots in the streets even in broad daylight. Meanwhile the country was being roused to revolt, and the traitors without threatened to environ the city, and act in concert with the rebels within.
Verse 11. Wickedness is in the midst thereof. The very heart of the city was base. In her places of authority crime went hand in hand with calamity. All the wilder and more wicked elements were uppermost; the canaille were commanders; the scum floated uppermost; justice was at a discount; the population was demoralized; prosperity had vanished and order with it.
Verse 12. The reader will do well to observe how accurately the psalmist described his own Psalm when he said, "I mourn in my complaint," or rather "give loose to my thoughts," for he proceeds from one point of his sorrow to another, wandering on like one in a maze, making few pauses, and giving no distinct intimations that he is changing the subject. Now from the turbulent city his mind turns to the false hearted councilor.
Verse 13. But it was thou. He sees him. The poetic fury is upon him, he sees the traitor as though he stood before him in flesh and blood. He singles him out, he points his finger at him, he challenges him to his face. But thou. Et tu, Brute. And thou, Ahithophel, art thou here? Judas, betrayest thou the Son of Man? A man mine equal. Treated by me as one of my own rank, never looked upon as an inferior, but as a trusted friend. My guide, a counselor so sage that I trusted thine advice and found it prudent to do so.
Verse 14. We took sweet counsel together. It was not merely the counsel which men take together in public or upon common themes, their fellowship had been tender and confidential. The traitor had been treated lovingly, and trusted much. Solace, mutual and cheering, had grown out of their intimate communings. There were secrets between them of no common kind.
Verse 15. Not thus would Jesus pray, but the rough soldier David so poured out the anguish of his spirit, under treachery and malice seldom equaled and altogether unprovoked. The soldier, as such, desires the overthrow of his foes, for this very end he fights; and viewed as a matter of law and

In the expression, divide their tongue, there seems an allusion to the judgment which fell upon the builders of Babel, (Genesis 31:7.) He means in general to pray that God would break their criminal confederacies, and distract their impious counsels, but evidently with an indirect reference to that memorable proof which God gave of his power to thwart the designs of the wicked by confounding their communication. It is thus that to this day he weakens the enemies of the Church, and splits them into factions, through the force of mutual animosities, rivalries, and disagreements in opinion. For his own encouragement in prayer, the Psalmist proceeds to insist upon the wickedness and malignity of his adversaries, this being a truth never to be lost sight of, that just in proportion as men grow rampant in sin, may it be anticipated that the divine judgments are about to descend upon them. From the unbridled license prevailing amongst them, he comforts himself with the reflection that the deliverance of God cannot be far distant; for he visits the proud, but gives more grace to the humble. Before proceeding to pray for divine judgments against them, he would intimate that he had full knowledge of their evil and injurious character. Interpreters have spent an unnecessary degree of labor in determining whether the city here spoken of was that of Jerusalem or of Keilah, for David by this term would appear merely to denote the open and public prevalence of crime in the country. The city stands opposed to places more hidden and obscure, and he insinuates that strife was practiced with unblushing publicity.

12-15
12. Of a truth, it was not an enemy that cast reproach upon me. He informs us of one circumstance which added bitterness to the injuries under which he suffered, that they came from the hands not only of his professed enemies, but of such as pretended to be his friends.
The sum of David's complaint in this passage is, that he was assailed by treachery of that secret description which rendered self-defense impossible. With regard to the individual whom he had particularly in view, when he preferred this accusation, I do not imagine that it was Ahitophel, for the psalm itself would not appear to have been written upon the persecution of Absalom. Whether it may have been some notorious traitor in the city of Keilah, it is impossible to determine. Not the least probable conjecture is, that it may have been some great man at court, whose intimacy with David was generally known. Possibly he may have had more than one in his eye, courtiers who had sacrificed former friendship to a desire of rising in the royal favor, and lent their influence to destroy him. These, with some more eminent person at their head, may be the parties aimed at.
15. Let death seize upon them. He now denounces the whole faction, not the nation generally, but those who had taken a prominent part in the persecution of him. In imprecating this curse he was not influenced by any bad feeling towards them, and must be understood as speaking not in his own cause but in that of God, and under the immediate guidance of his Spirit.

complaint, O that I had wings like a dove! Much as he had been sometimes in love with Jerusalem, now that it had become a rebellious city he longed to get clear of it, and, like the prophet, wished he had in the wilderness a lodging place of way-faring men, that he might leave his people and go from them.

9-15 Prophetic imprecations.
David here complains of his enemies, whose wicked plots had brought him, though not to his faith's end, yet to his wits' end, and prays against them by the spirit of prophecy. Observe here,
I. The character he gives of the enemies he feared. They were of the worst sort of men, and his description of them agrees very well with Absalom and his accomplices.
1. He complains of the city of Jerusalem, which strangely fell in with Absalom and fell off from David, so that he had none there but his own guards and servants that he could repose any confidence in: David, with his own eyes, did himself see nothing but violence and strife in the city (v. 9). If he walked the rounds upon the walls of the city, he saw that violence and strife went about it day and night, and mounted its guards, v. 10. Deceit and guile, and all manner of treacherous dealing, departed not from her streets, v. 11.
2. He complains of one of the ringleaders of the conspiracy, that had been very industrious to foment jealousies, to misrepresent him and his government, and to incense the city against him. All this must needs be very grievous to an ingenuous mind, and yet this was not all; this traitor had seemed a saint, else he had never been David's bosom-friend (v. 14): "We took counsel together, spent many an hour together, with a great deal of pleasure, in religious discourse."
II. His prayers against them, which we are both to stand in awe of and to comfort ourselves in, as prophecies, but not to copy into our prayers against any particular enemies of our own. He prays,
1. That God would disperse them, as he did the Babel-builders (v. 9): "Destroy, O Lord! and divide their tongues; that is, blast their counsels, by making them to disagree among themselves, and clash with one another. Send an evil spirit among them, that they may not understand one another, but be envious and jealous one of another."
2. That God would destroy them, as he did Dathan and Abiram. This was then a new thing which God executed, Num. xvi. 30. But David prays that it might now be repeated, or something equivalent (v. 15): "Let death seize upon them by divine warrant, and let them go down quickly into hell; let them be dead, and buried, and so utterly destroyed, in a moment; for wickedness is wherever they are; it is in the midst of them."

Psalm 55

17-23

17 Evening, and morning, and at noon, will I pray, and cry aloud: and he shall hear my voice.

18 He hath delivered my soul in peace from the battle that was against me: for there were many with me.

19 God shall hear, and afflict them, even he that abideth of old. Selah. Because they have no changes, therefore they fear not God.

20 He hath put forth his hands against such as be at peace with him: he hath broken his covenant.

21 The words of his mouth were smoother than butter, but war was in his heart: his words were softer than oil, yet were they drawn swords.

22 Cast thy burden upon the LORD, and he shall sustain thee: he shall never suffer the righteous to be moved.

23 But thou, O God, shalt bring them down into the pit of destruction: bloody and deceitful men shall not live out half their days; but I will trust in thee.

justice, David was right in his wish; he was waging a just, defensive war against men utterly regardless of truth and justice. Read the words as a warrior's imprecation. Let death seize upon them. Traitors such as these deserve to die, there is no living with them, earth is polluted by their tread; if spies are shot, much more these sneaking villains.

Verse 16. As for me, I will call upon God. The psalmist would not endeavor to meet the plots of his adversaries by counterplots, or imitate their incessant violence, but in direct opposition to their godless behavior would continually resort to his God. Thus Jesus did, and it has been the wisdom of all believers to do the same.

Verse 17. Evening and morning, and at noon, will I pray. Often but none too often. Seasons of great need call for frequent seasons of devotion. The three periods chosen are most fitting; to begin, continue, and end the day with God is supreme wisdom. Where time has naturally set up a boundary, there let us set up an altar stone. The psalmist means that he will always pray; he will run a line of prayer right along the day, and track the sun with his petitions.

Verse 18. He hath delivered my soul in peace from the battle that was against me. The deliverance has come. Joab has routed the rebels. The Lord has justified the cause of his anointed. Faith sees as well as foresees; to her foresight is sight. He is not only safe but serene, delivered in peace—peace in his inmost soul. For there were many with me; many contending against me.

Verse 19. God shall hear, and afflict them. They make a noise as well as I, and God will hear them. The voice of slander, malice, and pride, is not alone heard by those whom it grieves, it reaches to heaven, it penetrates the divine ear, it demands vengeance, and shall have it. God hears and delivers his people, he hears and destroys the wicked.

Verse 20. The psalmist cannot forget the traitor's conduct, and returns again to consider it. He hath put forth his hands against such as be at peace with him. He smites those to whom he had given the hand of friendship, he breaks the bonds of alliance, he is perfidious to those who dwell at ease because of his friendly profession.

Verse 22. Thy burden, or what thy God lays upon thee, lay thou it upon the Lord. His wisdom casts it on thee, it is thy wisdom to cast it on him. He cast thy lot for thee, cast thy lot on him. He gives thee thy portion of suffering, accept it with cheerful resignation, and then take it back to him by thine assured confidence.

Verse 23. For the ungodly a sure, terrible, and fatal overthrow is appointed. Climb as they may, the pit yawns for them, God himself will cause them to descend into it, and destruction there shall be their portion. Bloody and deceitful men, with double iniquity of cruelty and craft upon them, shall not live out half their days; they shall be cut off in their quarrels, or being disappointed in their artifices, vexation shall end them. They were in heart murderers of others, and they became in reality self murderers. Doubt not that virtue lengthens life, and that vice tends to shorten it. But I will trust in thee. A very wise, practical conclusion. We can have no better ground of confidence. The Lord is all, and more than all that faith can need as the foundation of peaceful dependence. Lord, increase our faith evermore.

JOHN CALVIN

16-19

16. I will call upon God. He does not content himself with saying that he will pray, for many do this in a perfunctory manner, and soon become wearied with the exercise; but he resolves to display both assiduity and vehemency. From the particular mention he makes of evening, morning, and noon, we are left to infer that these must have been the stated hours of prayer amongst the godly at that period. Sacrifices were offered daily in the temple morning and evening, and by this they were taught to engage privately in prayer within their own houses. At noon also it was the practice to offer additional sacrifices. As we are naturally indisposed for the duty of prayer, there is a danger that we may become remiss, and gradually omit it altogether, unless we restrict ourselves to a certain rule. In appointing particular fixed hours to be observed for his worship, there can be no doubt that God had respect to the infirmity of our nature, and the same principle should be applied to the secret as to the public services of devotion, as appears from the passage now before us, and from the example of Daniel, (Daniel 9:3.) Sacrifices are no longer to be observed in the Church, but as there remains the same indisposition on our part to the duty, and an equal need of incitements to overcome it, we should still prescribe certain hours to ourselves to be observed in prayer.

18. He hath redeemed my soul into peace. We may suppose that either he was so confident of being delivered that he speaks as if he actually were so already, or that he inserts what was the substance of his meditations at different times; it being sufficiently common, when mention is made of prayers, to subjoin a statement of the event which followed from them.

19. God shall hear, and afflict them. Having said that God would hear him, he adds that he would answer him, in the way of avenging his cause, in the punishment of his enemies. The epithet, or descriptive title, which he applies to God, is one calculated to comfort the pious mind in times of trouble and confusion.

20-23

20. He hath sent his hands against those that were at peace with him. It is well known how many fair promises and flatteries Saul addressed to David with a view to entrap him, and we may conjecture that the same arts were practiced by his courtiers. It is one special trial of the Lord's people, that they are exposed to such attempts on the part of crafty men to seduce them into destruction. Here the Holy Spirit puts a mark of reprobation upon all subtlety of this kind, and particularly upon treacherous flatteries, exhorting us to cultivate simplicity of intention.

22. Cast thy giving upon Jehovah. There is no other method of relieving our anxious souls, but by reposing ourselves upon the providence of the Lord.

23. Thou, O God! shalt cast them into the pit of corruption. He returns to speak of his enemies, designing to show the very different end which awaits them, from that which may be expected by the righteous.

MATTHEW HENRY

16-23 Confidence in God.

In these verses,

I. David perseveres in his resolution to call upon God, being well assured that he should not seek him in vain (v. 16): "As for me, let them take what course they please to secure themselves, let violence and strife be their guards, prayer shall be mine; this I have found comfort in, and therefore this will I abide by: I will call upon God, and commit myself to him, and the Lord shall save me."

II. He assures himself that God would in due time give an answer of peace to his prayers.

1. That he himself should be delivered and his fears prevented; those fears with which he was much disordered (v. 4, 5) by the exercise of faith were now silenced, and he begins to rejoice in hope (v. 18): God has delivered my soul in peace, that is, he will deliver it; David is as sure of the deliverance as if it were already wrought.

2. That his enemies should be reckoned with, and brought down. They had frightened him with their menaces (v. 3), but here he says enough to frighten them and make them tremble with more reason, and no remedy; for they could not ease themselves of their fears as David could, by faith in God.

(1.) David here gives their character as the reason why he expected God would bring them down.

[1.] They are impious and profane, and stand in no awe of God, of his authority or wrath (v. 19).

[2.] They are treacherous and false, and will not be held by the most sacred and solemn engagements (v. 20).

[3.] They are base and hypocritical, pretending friendship while they design mischief (v. 21).

(2.) David here foretells their ruin.

[1.] God shall afflict them, and bring them into straits and frights, and recompense tribulation to those that have troubled his people, and this in answer to the prayers of his people.

[2.] God shall bring them down, not only to the dust, but to the pit of destruction (v. 23), to the bottomless pit, which is called destruction, Job xxvi. 6. He afflicted them (v. 19) to see if that would humble and reform them; but, they not being wrought upon by that, he shall at last bring them to ruin.

III. He encourages himself and all good people to commit themselves to God, with confidence in him. He himself resolves to do so (v. 23): "I will trust in thee, in thy providence, and power, and mercy, and not in my own prudence, strength, or merit; when bloody and deceitful men are cut off in the midst of their days I shall still live by faith in thee." And this he will have others to do (v. 22): "Cast thy burden upon the Lord," whoever thou art that art burdened, and whatever the burden is. If we do so, it is promised,

1. That he will sustain us, both support and supply us.

2. That he will never suffer the righteous to be moved, to be so shaken by any troubles as to quit either their duty to God or their comfort in him.

Psalm 56

Title
To the chief Musician. Upon Jonathelemrechokim. Michtam of David. When the Philistines took him in Gath.

1-6
1 Be merciful unto me, O God: for man would swallow me up; he fighting daily oppresseth me.
2 Mine enemies would daily swallow me up: for they be many that fight against me, O thou most High.
3 What time I am afraid, I will trust in thee.
4 In God I will praise his word, in God I have put my trust; I will not fear what flesh can do unto me.
5 Every day they wrest my words: all their thoughts are against me for evil.
6 They gather themselves together, they hide themselves, they mark my steps, when they wait for my soul.

Psalm 56

TITLE. To the Chief Musician. That mighty minstrel by degrees acquired a noble repertoire of hallowed songs, and set them all to music. Upon Jonathelemrechokim—this was probably the title of the tune, as we should say Old Hundred, or Sicilian Mariners. Perhaps the title may however belong to the Psalm, and if so it is instructive, for it has been translated "the silent dove in distant places." We have here the songs of God's servant, who rejoices once more to return from banishment, and to leave those dangerous places where he was compelled to hold his peace even from good. There is such deep spiritual knowledge in this Psalm that we might say of it, "Blessed art thou David Barjonas, for flesh and blood hath not revealed this unto thee." When David plays the Jonah he is not like the prophet of that name; in David the love of the dove predominates, but in Jonah its moaning and complaining are most notable. Michtam of David. This is the second golden Psalm, we had the first in Psalm 16, to which this Psalm has a great likeness, especially in its close, for it ends in the joyful presence. A golden mystery, the gracious secret of the life of faith is in both these Psalms most sweetly unveiled, and a pillar is set up because of God's truth. When the Philistines took him in Gath. He was like a dove in strangers' hands, and on his escape he records his gratitude.
DIVISION. In Ps 56:1-2, he pours out his complaint; in Ps 56:3-4 he declares his confidence in God; in Ps 56:5-6 he returns to his complaining, but pleads in earnest hope in Ps 56:7-9, and sings a grateful song from Ps 56:10 to the close.

EXPOSITION
Verse 1. Be merciful unto me, O God. In my deep distress my soul turns to thee, my God. Man has no mercy on me, therefore double thy mercy to me. If thy justice has let loose my enemies, let thy mercy shorten their chain. It is sweet to see how the tender dove like spirit of the psalmist flies to the most tender attribute for succor in the hour of peril. For man would swallow me up. He is but thy creature, a mere man, yet like a monster he is eager for blood, he pants, he gapes for me; he would not merely wound me, or feed on my substance, but he would fain swallow me altogether, and so make an end of me. The open mouths of sinners when they rage against us should open our mouths in prayer. We may plead the cruelty of men as a reason for the divine interposition—a father is soon aroused when his children are shamefully entreated. He fighting daily oppresseth me. He gives me no interval—he fights daily. He is successful in his unrighteous war—he oppresses me, he crushes me, he presses me sore.
Verse 2. Mine enemies would daily swallow me up. Their appetite for blood never fails them. With them there is no truce or armistice. They are many, but one mind animates them. Nothing I can do can make them relent. Unless they can quite devour me they will never be content. The ogres of nursery tales exist in reality in the enemies of the church, who would crush the bones of the godly, and make a mouthful of them if they could. For they be many that fight against me. Sinners are gregarious creatures.
Verse 3. What time I am afraid. David was no braggart, he does not claim never to be afraid, and he was no brutish Stoic free from fear because of the lack of tenderness. David's intelligence deprived him of the stupid heedlessness of ignorance, he saw the imminence of his peril, and was afraid. We are men, and therefore liable to overthrow; we are feeble, and therefore unable to prevent it; we are sinful men, and therefore deserving it, and for all these reasons we are afraid.
Verse 4. In God I will praise his word. Faith brings forth praise. He who can trust will soon sing. God's promise, when fulfilled, is a noble subject for praise, and even before fulfillment it should be the theme of song. It is in or through God that we are able to praise. We praise as well as pray in the

Psalm 56

1-4

1. Be merciful unto me, O God! for man swallows me up. It would be difficult to determine whether he speaks here of foreign or domestic enemies. When brought to King Achish he was as a sheep between two bands of wolves, an object of deadly hatred to the Philistines on the one hand, and exposed to equal persecutions from his own fellow-countrymen.

3. In the day that I was afraid, etc. He acknowledges his weakness, in so far as he was sensible of fear, but denies having yielded to it. Dangers might distress him, but could not induce him to surrender his hope. He makes no pretensions to that lofty heroism which contemns danger, and yet while he allows that he felt fear, he declares his fixed resolution to persist in a confident expectation of the divine favor. The true proof of faith consists in this, that when we feel the solicitations of natural fear, we can resist them, and prevent them from obtaining an undue ascendancy.

4. In God I will praise his word. Here he grows more courageous in the exercise of hope, as generally happens with the people of God. They find it difficult at first to reach this exercise. It is only after a severe struggle that they rise to it, but the effort being once made, they emerge from their fears into the fullness of confidence, and are prepared to grapple with the most formidable enemies. To praise, is here synonymous with glorying or boasting. He was now in possession of a triumphant confidence, and rejoiced in the certainty of hope.

5-8

5. Every day my words vex me. David confesses his own lack of wisdom and foresight, shown in the abortive issue of every plan which he devised. It aggravated the evil, that his enemies were employing their united counsels to plot his ruin. He adds, that they gathered themselves together; and this made his case the more calamitous, matched as he was, a single individual, against this numerous host. In mentioning that they hide themselves, he adverts to the subtle devices which they framed for surprising him into destruction. He tells us that they pressed upon him in every direction, and as it were trod upon his heels, so that he had no respite. And he points at their implacable hatred as the cause of their eager pursuit of him; for nothing, he informs us, would satisfy them but his death.

7. After their mischief they think to escape. The beginning of this verse is read by some interrogatively, Shall they escape in their iniquity? But there is no necessity for having recourse to this distant meaning. It is much better to understand the words in the sense which they naturally suggest when first read, That the wicked think to escape in their iniquity, but that God will cast them down. He alludes to the fact that the ungodly, when allowed to proceed without interruption in their evil courses, indulge the idea that they have a license to perpetrate the worst wickedness with impunity. In these our own times, we see many such profane characters, who display an unmeasured audacity under the assurance that God's hand

Psalm 56

1-7 Prayer for help under oppression; confidence in God.

I. David complains to God of the malice and wickedness of his enemies, to show what reason he had to fear them, and what cause, what need, there was that God should appear against them (v. 1): Be merciful unto me, O God! That petition includes all the good we come to the throne of grace for; if we obtain mercy there, we obtain all we can desire, and need no more to make us happy.

He complains,

1. That his enemies were very numerous (v. 2): "They are many that fight against me, and think to overpower me with numbers; take notice of this, O thou Most High! and make it to appear that wherein they deal proudly thou art above them."

2. That they were very barbarous: they would swallow him up, v. 1 and again v. 2. They sought to devour him; no less would serve; they came upon him with the utmost fury, like beasts of prey, to eat up his flesh, Ps. xxvii. 2. Man would swallow him up, those of his own kind, from whom he might have expected humanity. The ravenous beasts prey not upon those of their own species; yet a bad man would devour a good man if he could. "They are men, weak and frail; make them to know that they are so," Ps. ix. 20.

3. That they were very unanimous (v. 6): They gather themselves together; though they were many, and of different interests among themselves, yet they united and combined against David, as Herod and Pilate against the Son of David.

4. That they were very powerful, quite too hard for him if God did not help him: "They fight against me (v. 2); they oppress me, v. 1. I am almost overcome and borne down by them, and reduced to the last extremity."

5. That they were very subtle and crafty (v. 6): "They hide themselves; they industriously cover their designs, that they may the more effectually prosecute and pursue them. They hide themselves as a lion in his den, that they may mark my steps;" that is, "they observe every thing I say and do with a critical eye, that they may have something to accuse me of."

6. That they were very spiteful and malicious. They put invidious constructions upon every thing he said, though ever so honestly meant and prudently expressed (v. 5): "They wrest my words, put them upon the rack, to extort that out of them which was never in them."

7. That they were very restless and unwearied. They continually waited for his soul; it was the life, the precious life, they hunted for; it was his death they longed for, v. 6. They fought daily against him (v. 1), and would daily swallow him up (v. 2), and every day they wrested his words, v. 5. Their malice would not admit the least cessation of arms, or the acts of hostility, but they were continually pushing at him.

Psalm 56

7-13

7 Shall they escape by iniquity? in thine anger cast down the people, O God.
8 Thou tellest my wanderings: put thou my tears into thy bottle: are they not in thy book?
9 When I cry unto thee, then shall mine enemies turn back: this I know; for God is for me.
10 In God will I praise his word: in the LORD will I praise his word.
11 In God have I put my trust: I will not be afraid what man can do unto me.
12 Thy vows are upon me, O God: I will render praises unto thee.
13 For thou hast delivered my soul from death: wilt not thou deliver my feet from falling, that I may walk before God in the light of the living?

Spirit. Or we may read it—in extolling the Lord one of the main points for thanksgiving is his revealed will in the Scriptures, and the fidelity with which he keeps his word of promise.

Verse 5. Every day they wrest my words. This is a common mode of warfare among the ungodly. They put our language on the rack, they extort meanings from it which it cannot be made fairly to contain. Thus our Savior's prophecy concerning the temple of his body, and countless accusations against his servants, were founded on willful perversions. They who do this every day become great adepts in the art. A wolf can always find in a lamb's discourse a reason for eating him.

Verse 6. They gather themselves together. Firebrands burn the fiercer for being pushed together. They are afraid to meet the good man till their numbers place terrible odds against him. Come out, ye cowards, man to man, and fight the old hero! No, ye wait till ye are assembled like thieves in bands, and even then ye waylay the man.

Verse 7. Shall they escape by iniquity? Will such wickedness as this stand them in good stead? Can it be that this conduct shall enable them to avoid the sentence of earthly punishment? They slander the good man to screen themselves—will this avail them? They have cunningly managed hitherto, but will there not be an end to their games? In thine anger cast down the people, O God. Trip them up in their tricks.

Verse 8. Thou tellest my wanderings. Every step which the fugitive had taken when pursued by his enemies, was not only observed but thought worthy of counting and recording. We perhaps are so confused after a long course of trouble, that we hardly know where we have or where we have not been; but the omniscient and considerate Father of our spirits remembers all in detail; for he has counted them over as men count their gold, for even the trial of our faith is precious in his sight.

Verse 9. When I cry unto thee, then shall mine enemies turn back. So soon as I pray they shall fly. So surely as I cry they shall be put to the rout. The machinery of prayer is not always visible, but it is most efficient. God inclines us to pray, we cry in anguish of heart, he hears, he acts, the enemy is turned back.

Verse 10. In God will I praise his word. Now comes the thanksgiving. He is a wretch who, having obtained help, forgets to return a grateful acknowledgment. The least we can do is to praise him from whom we receive such distinguished favors.

Verse 11. In God have I put my trust. This and the former verse are evidently the chorus of the Psalm. We cannot be too careful of our faith, or see too sedulously that it is grounded on the Lord alone. I will not be afraid what man can do unto me. Faith has banished fear.

Verse 12. Thy vows are upon me, O God. Vows made in his trouble he does not lightly forget, nor should we. We voluntarily made them, let us cheerfully keep them.

Verse 13. For thou hast delivered my soul from death. His enemies were defeated in their attempts upon his life, and therefore he vowed to devote his life to God. Wilt not thou deliver my feet from falling? One mercy is a plea for another, for indeed it may happen that the second is the necessary complement of the first. Thus in this short Psalm, we have climbed from the ravenous jaws of the enemy into the light of Jehovah's presence, a path which only faith can tread.

can never reach them. They not only look to go unpunished, but found their hopes of success upon their evil deeds, and encourage themselves to farther wickedness, by cherishing the opinion that they will contrive a way of escape from every adversity. David has no sooner stated this vain confident persuasion of the wicked, than he refutes it by an appeal to the judgment of God, declaring his conviction that, however proudly they might exalt themselves, the hour of vengeance would come when God would cast down the peoples.
8. Thou hast taken account of my wanderings. The words run in the form of an abrupt prayer. Having begun by requesting God to consider his tears, suddenly, as if he had obtained what he asked, he declares that they were written in God's book. It is possible, indeed, to understand the interrogation as a prayer; but he would seem rather to insinuate by this form of expression, that he stood in no need of multiplying words, and that God had already anticipated his desire.

9-11
9. When I cry, then shall mine enemies turn back. Here he boasts of victory with even more confidence than formerly, specifying, as it were, the very moment of time when his enemies were to be turned back. He had no sensible evidence of their approaching destruction but from the firm reliance which he exercised upon the promise, he was able to anticipate the coming period, and resolved to wait for it with patience. Though God might make no haste to interpose, and might not scatter his enemies at the very instant when he prayed, he was confident that his prayers would not be disappointed: and his ground for believing this was just a conviction of the truth, that God never frustrates the prayers of his own children.
10. In God will I praise his word. How desirable is it that the Lord's people generally would accustom themselves to think in the same manner, and find, in the word of God, matter of never-failing praise amidst their worst trials!
11. In God have I hoped, etc. We shall find men universally agreed in the opinion that God is an all-sufficient protector; but observation proves how ready we are to distrust him under the slightest temptation.

12-13
12. Thy vows are upon me, O God! I hinted, from the outset, that it is probable this psalm was written by David after he had escaped the dangers which he describes; and this may account for the thanksgiving here appended to it.
13. For thou hast delivered my soul from death. Contemplating the greatness of his danger, he considers his escape as nothing less than miraculous. It is our duty, when rescued from any peril, to retain in our recollection the circumstances of it, and all which rendered it peculiarly formidable. To walk in the light of the living means nothing else than to enjoy the vital light of the sun. The words, before God, which are interjected in the verse, point to the difference between the righteous, who make God the great aim of their life, and the wicked, who wander from the right path and turn their back upon God.

II. He encourages himself in God, and in his promises, power, and providence, v. 3, 4. In the midst of his complaints, and before he has said what he has to say of his enemies, he triumphs in the divine protection.
1. He resolves to make God his confidence, then when dangers were most threatening and all other confidences failed: "What time I am afraid, in the day of my fear, when I am most terrified from without and most timorous within, then I will trust in thee, and thereby my fears shall be silenced."
2. He resolves to make God's promises the matter of his praises, and so we have reason to make them (v. 4): "In God I will praise, not only his work which he has done, but his word which he has spoken; I will give him thanks for a promise, though not yet performed. In God (in his strength and by his assistance) I will both glory in his word and give him the glory of it."
3. Thus supported, he will bid defiance to all adverse powers: "When in God I have put my trust, I am safe, I am easy, and I will not fear what flesh can do unto me; it is but flesh, and cannot do much; nay, it can do nothing but by divine permission."
III. He foresees and foretells the fall of those that fought against him, and of all others that think to establish themselves in and by any wicked practices (v. 7): Shall they escape by iniquity? They hope to escape God's judgments, as they escape men's, by violence and fraud, and the arts of injustice and treachery; but shall they escape? No, they shall not.

8-13 Comfort under affliction; confidence in God.
Several things David here comforts himself with in the day of his distress and fear.
I. That God took particular notice of all his grievances and all his griefs, v. 8.
II. That his prayers would be powerful for the defeat and discomfiture of his enemies, as well as for his own support and encouragement (v. 9): "When I cry unto thee, then shall my enemies turn back; I need no other weapons than prayers and tears; this I know, for God is for me, to plead my cause, to protect and deliver me; and, if God be for me, who can be against me so as to prevail?"
III. That his faith in God would set him above the fear of man, v. 10, 11. Here he repeats, with a strong pathos, what he had said (v. 4), "In God will I praise his word; that is, I will firmly depend upon the promise for the sake of him that made it, who is true and faithful, and has wisdom, power, and goodness enough to make it good."
IV. That he was in bonds to God (v. 12).
V. That he should still have more and more occasion to praise him: I will render praises unto thee. Two things he will praise God for:
1. For what he had done for him (v. 13).
2. For what he would do for him: "Thou hast begun a good work, and therefore thou wilt carry it on and perfect it."

Psalm 57

Title

To the chief Musician. Altaschith. Michtam of David. When he fled from Saul in the cave.

1-5

1 Be merciful unto me, O God, be merciful unto me: for my soul trusteth in thee: yea, in the shadow of thy wings will I make my refuge, until these calamities be overpast.

2 I will cry unto God most high; unto God that performeth all things for me.

3 He shall send from heaven, and save me from the reproach of him that would swallow me up. Selah. God shall send forth his mercy and his truth.

4 My soul is among lions: and I lie even among them that are set on fire, even the sons of men, whose teeth are spears and arrows, and their tongue a sharp sword.

5 Be thou exalted, O God, above the heavens; let thy glory be above all the earth.

Psalm 57

TITLE. To the Chief Musician. So glad a song as this becomes ere it closes, should be in the keeping of the most skilled of all the temple minstrels. Altaschith, i.e., DESTROY NOT. This petition is a very sententious prayer, as full as it is brief, and well worthy to be the motto for a sacred song. David had said, "destroy not," in reference to Saul, when he had him in his power, and now he takes pleasure in employing the same words in supplication to God. We may infer from the spirit of the Lord's prayer, that the Lord will spare us as we spare our foes. There are four of these "Destroy not" Psalms, namely, the 57th, 58th, 59th, and 75th. In all of them there is a distinct declaration of the destruction of the wicked and the preservation of the righteous, and they all have probably a reference to the overthrow of the Jews, on account of their persecution of the great Son of David: they will endure heavy chastisement, but concerning them it is written in the divine decree, "Destroy them not." Michtam of David. For quality this Psalm is called golden, or a secret, and it well deserves the name. We may read the words and yet not know the secret joy of David, which he has locked up in his golden casket. When he fled from Saul in the cave. This is a song from the bowels of the earth, and, like Jonah's prayer from the bottom of the sea, it has a taste of the place. The poet is in the shadow of the cave at first, but he comes to the cavern's mouth at last, and sings in the sweet fresh air, with his eye on the heavens, watching joyously the clouds floating therein.
DIVISION. We have here prayer, Ps 57:1-6, and praise, Ps 57:7-11. The hunted one takes a long breath of prayer, and when he is fully inspired, he breathes out his soul in jubilant song.

EXPOSITION

Verse 1. Be merciful unto me, O God, be merciful unto me. Urgent need suggests the repetition of the cry, for thus intense urgency of desire is expressed. If "he gives twice who gives quickly," so he who would receive quickly must ask twice. For mercy the psalmist pleads at first, and he feels he cannot improve upon his plea, and therefore returns to it. God is the God of mercy, and the Father of mercies, it is most fit therefore that in distress he should seek mercy from him in whom it dwells.

Verse 2. I will cry. He is quite safe, but yet he prays, for faith is never dumb. We pray because we believe. We exercise by faith the spirit of adoption whereby we cry. He says not I do cry, or I have cried, but I will cry, and indeed, this resolution may stand with all of us until we pass through the gates of pearl; for while we are here below we shall still have need to cry. Unto God most high.—Prayers are for God only; the greatness and sublimity of his person and character suggest and encourage prayer; however high our enemies, our heavenly Friend is higher, for he is Most high, and he can readily send from the height of his power the succor which we need.

Verse 3. He shall send from heaven. If there be no fit instruments on earth, heaven shall yield up its legions of angels for the succor of the saints. We may in times of great straits expect mercies of a remarkable kind; like the Israelites in the wilderness, we shall have our bread hot from heaven, new every morning; and for the overthrow of our enemies God shall open his celestial batteries, and put them to utter confusion. Wherever the battle is more fierce than ordinary, there shall come succors from headquarters, for the Commander in chief sees all.

Verse 4. My soul is among lions. He was a very Daniel. Howled at, hunted, wounded, but not slain. His place was in itself one of extreme peril, and yet faith made him feel himself secure, so that he could lie down. The cave may have reminded him of a lion's den, and Saul and his band shouting and yelling in their disappointment at missing him, were the lions; yet beneath the divine shelter he finds himself safe. And I lie even among them that are

JOHN CALVIN

Psalm 57

This psalm consists of two parts. In the first, David gives expression to the anxiety which he felt, imploring Divine assistance against Saul and his other enemies. In the second, he proceeds upon the confident expectation of deliverance, and stirs up his soul to the exercise of praise.

1-3

1. Be merciful unto me, O God! The repetition of the prayer proves that the grief, the anxiety, and the apprehension, with which David was filled at this time, must have been of no common description. It is noticeable, that his plea for mercy is, his having hoped in God. His soul trusted in him; and this is a form of expression the force of which is not to be overlooked: for it implies that the trust which he exercised proceeded from his very innermost affections,—that it was of no volatile character, but deeply and strongly rooted. He declares the same truth in figurative terms, when he adds his persuasion that God would cover him with the shadow of his wings.

2. In addressing God, he applies to him an honorable title, commending him as the God who performed whatsoever he had promised, or (as we may understand the expression) who carries forward to perfection the work which he has begun.

3. He shall send from heaven, and save me. David interlaces his prayers with holy meditations for the comfort of his own soul, in which he contemplates his hopes as already realized in the event. In the words before us, he glories in the divine help with as much assurance as if he had already seen the hand of God interposed in his behalf.

4-6

4. My soul is among lions. He again insists upon the cruelty of his enemies as a plea to prevail with God for his speedier interposition. He compares them to lions, speaks of them as inflamed with fury or implacable hatred, and likens their teeth to spears and arrows. In what he says of their tongue, he alludes to the virulent calumnies which are vended by the wicked, and which inflict a deeper wound than any sword upon the innocent party who suffers from them. David, as is well known, encountered no heavier trial than the false and calumnious charges which were leveled against him by his enemies. When we hear of the cruel persecution of different kinds which this saint was called upon to endure, we should account it no hardship to be involved in the same conflict, but be satisfied so long as we may bring our complaints to the Lord, who can bridle the false tongue, and put an arrest upon the hand of violence.

5. To him we find David appealing in the words that follow, Exalt thyself, O God! above the heavens: let thy glory be above all the earth. To perceive the appropriateness of this prayer, it is necessary that we reflect upon the height of audacity and pride to which the wicked proceed, when unrestrained by the providence of God, and upon the formidable nature of that conspiracy which was directed

MATTHEW HENRY

Psalm 57

1-6 Prayer in affliction.

The title of this psalm has one word new in it, Al-taschith—Destroy not. Some make it to be only some known tune to which this psalm was set; others apply it to the occasion and matter of the psalm. Destroy not; that is, David would not let Saul be destroyed, when now in the cave there was a fair opportunity of killing him, and his servants would fain have done so. No, says David, destroy him not, 1 Sam. xxiv. 4, 6. Or, rather, God would not let David be destroyed by Saul; he suffered him to persecute David, but still under this limitation, Destroy him hot; as he permitted Satan to afflict Job, Only save his life. David must not be destroyed, for a blessing is in him (Isa. lxv. 8), even Christ, the best of blessings. When David was in the cave, in imminent peril, he here tells us what were the workings of his heart towards God; and happy are those that have such good thoughts as these in their minds when they are in danger!

I. He supports himself with faith and hope in God, and prayer to him, v. 1, 2. Seeing himself surrounded with enemies, he looks up to God with that suitable prayer: Be merciful to me, O Lord! which he again repeats, and it is no vain repetition: Be merciful unto me. It was the publican's prayer, Luke xviii. 13.

1. That all his dependence is upon God: My soul trusteth in thee, v. 1. He did not only profess to trust in God, but his soul did indeed rely on God only, with a sincere devotion and self-dedication, and an entire complacency and satisfaction. He goes to God, and, at the footstool of the throne of his grace, humbly professes his confidence in him: In the shadow of thy wings will I make my refuge, as the chickens take shelter under the wings of the hen when the birds of prey are ready to strike at them, until these calamities be over-past.

2. That all his desire is towards God (v. 2): "I will cry unto God most high, for succor and relief; to him that is most high will I lift up my soul, and pray earnestly, even unto God that performs all things for me."

3. That all his expectation is from God (v. 3): He shall send from heaven, and save me. Those that make God their only refuge, and fly to him by faith and prayer, may be sure of salvation, in his way and time.

II. He represents the power and malice of his enemies (v. 4): My soul is among lions. So fierce and furious was Saul, and those about him, against David, that he might have been as safe in a den of lions as among such men, who were continually roaring against him and ready to make a prey of him. They are set on fire, and breathe nothing but flame; they set on fire the course of nature, inflaming one another against David, and they were themselves set on fire of hell, Jam. iii. 6. He describes their malicious projects against him (v. 6) and shows the issue of them: "They have prepared a net for my steps, in which to take me, that I might not

Psalm 57

6-11

6 They have prepared a net for my steps; my soul is bowed down: they have digged a pit before me, into the midst whereof they are fallen themselves. Selah.
7 My heart is fixed, O God, my heart is fixed: I will sing and give praise.
8 Awake up, my glory; awake, psaltery and harp: I myself will awake early.
9 I will praise thee, O Lord, among the people: I will sing unto thee among the nations.
10 For thy mercy is great unto the heavens, and thy truth unto the clouds.
11 Be thou exalted, O God, above the heavens: let thy glory be above all the earth.

set on fire. Perhaps Saul and his band kindled a fire in the cavern while they halted in it, and David was thus reminded of the fiercer fire of their hate which burned within their hearts.

Verse 5. Be thou exalted, O God, above the heavens. This is the chorus of the Psalm. Before he has quite concluded his prayer the good man interjects a verse of praise; and glorious praise too, seeing it comes from the lion's den and from amid the coals of fire. Higher than the heavens is the Most High, and so high ought our praises to rise. Above even the power of cherubim and seraphim to express it, the glory of God is revealed and is to be acknowledged by us. Let thy glory be above all the earth. As above, so below, let thy praises, O thou great Jehovah, be universally proclaimed. As the air surrounds all nature, so let thy praises gird the earth with a zone of song.

Verse 6. They have prepared a net for my steps. The enemies of the godly spare no pains, but go about their wicked work with the coolest deliberation. As for each sort of fish, or bird, or beast, a fitting net is needed, so do the ungodly suit their net to their victim's circumstances and character with a careful craftiness of malice. Whatever David might do, and whichever way he might turn, his enemies were ready to entrap him in some way or other. My soul is bowed down. He was held down like a bird in a trap; his enemies took care to leave him no chance of comfort.

Verse 7. My heart is fixed. One would have thought he would have said, "My heart is fluttered; "but no, he is calm, firm, happy, resolute, established. When the central axle is secure, the whole wheel is right. If our great bower anchor holds, the ship cannot drive. O God, my heart is fixed. I am resolved to trust thee, to serve thee, and to praise thee. Twice does he declare this to the glory of God who thus comforts the souls of his servants. Reader, it is surely well with thee, if thy once roving heart is now firmly fixed upon God and the proclamation of his glory.

Verse 8. Awake up, my glory. Let the noblest powers of my nature bestir themselves: the intellect which conceives thought, the tongue which expresses it, and the inspired imagination which beautifies it—let all be on the alert now that the hour for praise has come. Awake, psaltery and harp. Let all the music with which I am familiar be well attuned for the hallowed service of praise.

Verse 9. I will praise thee, O Lord, among the people. Gentiles shall hear my praise. Here is an instance of the way in which the truly devout evangelic spirit overleaps the boundaries which bigotry sets up. The ordinary Jew would never wish the Gentile dogs to hear Jehovah's name, except to tremble at it; but this grace taught psalmist has a missionary spirit, and would spread the praise and fame of his God. I will sing unto thee among the nations. However far off they may be, I would make them hear of thee through my glad psalmody.

Verse 10. For thy mercy is great unto the heavens. Right up from man's lowliness to heaven's loftiness mercy reaches. Imagination fails to guess the height of heaven, and even thus the riches of mercy exceed our highest thoughts. The psalmist, as he sits at the cave's mouth and looks up to the firmament, rejoices that God's goodness is more vast and more sublime than even the vaulted skies.

Verse 11. Be thou exalted, O God, above the heavens. A grand chorus. Take it up, ye angels and ye spirits made perfect, and join in it, ye sons of men below, as ye say, Let thy glory be above all the earth. The prophet in the previous verse spoke of mercy "unto the heavens," but here his song flies "above the heavens;" praise rises higher, and knows no bounds.

against David by Saul, and the nation in general, all which demanded a signal manifestation of divine power on his behalf. Nor is it a small comfort to consider that God, in appearing for the help of his people, at the same time advances his own glory.

6. The Psalmist reverts to the language of complaint. He had spoken of the cruel persecution to which he was subjected, and now bewails the treachery and deceit which were practiced against him. His soul he describes as being bowed down, in allusion to the crouching of the body when one is under the influence of fear, or to birds when terrified by the fowler and his nets, which dare not move a feather, but lie flat upon the ground.

7-11

7. My heart is prepared, O God! The ready heart is here contrasted by David to the mere lip-service of the hypocrite, on the one hand, and to dead or sluggish service, on the other. He addressed himself to this voluntary sacrifice with a sincere fervor of spirit, casting aside sloth, and whatever might prove a hindrance in the duty.

8. Awake up, my tongue. David here expresses, in poetical terms, the ardor with which his soul was inspired. He calls upon tongue, psaltery, and harp, to prepare for the celebration of the name of God.

9. I will praise thee, O Lord! among the peoples. As the nations and peoples are here said to be auditors of the praise which he offered, we must infer that David, in the sufferings spoken of throughout the psalm, represented Christ. This it is important to observe, as it proves that our own state and character are set before us in this psalm as in a glass. That the words have reference to Christ's kingdom, we have the authority of Paul for concluding, (Romans 15:9,) and, indeed, might sufficiently infer in the exercise of an enlightened judgment upon the passage. To proclaim the praises of God to such as are deaf, would be an absurdity much greater than singing them to the rocks and stones; it is therefore evident that the Gentiles are supposed to be brought to the knowledge of God when this declaration of his name is addressed to them.

10. He touches briefly upon what he designed as the sum of his song of praise, when he adds, that the whole world is full of the goodness and truth of God. It is of his mere goodness that God is induced to promise so readily and so liberally. On the other hand, his faithfulness is commended to our notice, to convince us that he is as constant in fulfilling his promises as he is ready and willing to make them.

12. The Psalmist concludes with a prayer that God would arise, and not suffer his glory to be obscured, or the audacity of the wicked to become intolerable by conniving longer at their impiety. The words, however, may be understood in another sense, as a prayer that God would hasten the calling of the Gentiles, of which he had already spoken in the language of prediction, and illustrate his power by executing not only an occasional judgment in Judea for the deliverance of distressed innocence, but his mighty judgments over the whole world for the subjection of the nations.

again escape out of their hands; they have digged a pit before me, that I might, ere I was aware, run headlong into it."

III. He prays to God to glorify himself and his own great name (v. 5): "Whatever becomes of me and my interest, be thou exalted, O God! above the heavens, be thou praised by the holy angels, those glorious inhabitants of the upper world; and let thy glory be above or over all the earth; let all the inhabitants of this earth be brought to know and praise thee." Thus God's glory should lie nearer our hearts, and we should be more concerned for it, than for any particular interests of our own.

7-11 Prayer turned to praise.

How strangely is the tune altered here! David's prayers and complaints, by the lively actings of faith, are here, all of a sudden, turned into praises and thanksgivings; his sackcloth is loosed, he is girded with gladness, and his hallelujahs are as fervent as his hosannas. This should make us in love with prayer, that, sooner or later, it will be swallowed up in praise. Observe,

I. How he prepares himself for the duty of praise (v. 7): My heart is fixed, O God! my heart is fixed. My heart is erect, or lifted up (so some), which was bowed down, v. 6.

II. How he excites himself to the duty of praise (v. 8): Awake up my glory, that is, my tongue (our tongue is our glory, and never more so than when it is employed in praising God), or my soul, that must be first awakened; dull and sleepy devotions will never be acceptable to God. We must stir up ourselves, and all that is within us, to praise God; with a holy fire must that sacrifice be kindled, and ascend in a holy flame.

III. How he pleases himself, and (as I may say) even prides himself, in the work of praise; so far is he from being ashamed to own his obligations to God, and dependence upon him, that he resolves to praise him among the people and to sing unto him among the nations, v. 9.

IV. How he furnishes himself with matter for praise, v. 10. That which was the matter of his hope and comfort (God shall send forth his mercy and his truth, v. 3) is here the matter of his thanksgiving: Thy mercy is great unto the heavens, great beyond conception and expression; and thy truth unto the clouds, great beyond discovery, for what eye can reach that which is wrapped up in the clouds? God's mercy and truth reach to the heavens, for they will bring all such to heaven as lay up their treasure in them and build their hopes upon them.

V. How he leaves it at last to God to glorify his own name (v. 11): Be thou exalted, O God! The same words which he had used (v. 5) to sum up his prayers in here he uses again (and no vain repetition) to sum up his praises in: "Lord, I desire to exalt thy name, and that all the creatures may exalt it; but what can the best of us do towards it? Lord, take the work into thy own hands; do it thyself: Be thou exalted, O God!"

Psalm 58

Title
To the chief Musician. Altaschith. Michtam of David.

1-5
1 Do ye indeed speak righteousness, O congregation? do ye judge uprightly, O ye sons of men?
2 Yea, in heart ye work wickedness; ye weigh the violence of your hands in the earth.
3 The wicked are estranged from the womb: they go astray as soon as they be born, speaking lies.
4 Their poison is like the poison of a serpent: they are like the deaf adder that stoppeth her ear;
5 Which will not hearken to the voice of charmers, charming never so wisely.

Psalm 58

TITLE. To the Chief Musician. Although David had his own case in his mind's eye, yet he wrote not as a private person, but as an inspired prophet, and therefore his song is presented, for public and perpetual use, to the appointed guardian of the Temple psalmody. Altaschith. The wicked are here judged and condemned, but over the godly the sacred "Destroy not" is solemnly pronounced. Michtam of David. This is the fourth of the Psalms of the Golden Secret, and the second of the "Destroy nots." These names if they serve for nothing else may be useful to aid the memory. Men give names to their horses, jewels, and other valuables, and these names are meant not so much to describe as to distinguish them, and in some cases to set forth the owner's high esteem of his treasure; after the same fashion the Oriental poet gave a title to the song he loved, and so aided his memory, and expressed his estimation of the strain. We are not always to look for a meaning in these superscriptions, but to treat them as we would the titles of poems, or the names of tunes.
DIVISION. The ungodly enemy is accused, Ps 58:1-5; judgment is sought from the judge, Ps 58:6-8; and seen in prophetic vision as already executed, Ps 58:9-11.

EXPOSITION
Verse 1. Do ye indeed speak righteousness, O congregation? The enemies of David were a numerous and united band, and because they so unanimously condemned the persecuted one, they were apt to take it for granted that their verdict was a right one. "What everybody says must be true," is a lying proverb based upon the presumption which comes of large combinations. Have we not all agreed to hound the man to the death, and who dare hint that so many great ones can be mistaken? Yet the persecuted one lays the axe at the root by requiring his judges to answer the question whether or not they were acting according to justice. It were well if men would sometimes pause, and candidly consider this.
Verse 2. Yea, in heart ye work wickedness. Down deep in your very souls ye hold a rehearsal of the injustice ye intend to practice, and when your opportunity arrives, ye wreak vengeance with a gusto; your hearts are in your wicked work, and your hands are therefore ready enough. Those very men who sat as judges, and pretended to so much indignation at the faults imputed to their victim, were in their hearts perpetrating all manner of evil. Ye weigh the violence of your hands in the earth. They were deliberate sinners, cold, calculating villains. As righteous judges ponder the law, balance the evidence, and weigh the case, so the malicious dispense injustice with malice aforethought in cold blood.
Verse 3. The wicked are estranged from the womb. It is small wonder that some men persecute the righteous seed of the woman, since all of them are of the serpent's brood, and enmity is set between them. No sooner born than alienated from God—what a condition to be found in! Do we so early leave the right track? Do we at the same moment begin to be men and commence to be sinners? They go astray as soon as they be born, speaking lies. Every observer may see how very soon infants act lies. Before they can speak they practice little deceptive arts.
Verse 4. Their poison is like the poison of a serpent. Is man also a poisonous reptile? Yes, and his venom is even as that of a serpent. The viper has but death for the body in his fangs; but unregenerate man carries poison under his tongue, destructive to the nobler nature. They are like the deaf adder that stoppeth her ear.
Verse 5. Which will not hearken to the voice of charmers, charming never so wisely. Ungodly men are not to be won to right by arguments the most logical, or appeals the most pathetic. Try all your arts, ye preachers of the word! Lay yourselves out to meet the prejudices and tastes of sinners, and

JOHN CALVIN

Psalm 58

The following psalm consists of two parts. In the commencement, David vindicates his personal integrity from the calumnies cast upon him by his enemies. Having expressed his sense of the grievous injuries which they had inflicted, their cruelty and their treachery, he concludes by an appeal to the judgment of God, and by praying that they might be visited with deserved destruction.

1-5
1. Do ye indeed speak righteousness? In putting this question to his enemies, by way of challenge, David displays the boldness of conscious rectitude. It argues that the justice of our cause is demonstratively evident when we venture to appeal to the opposite party himself; for were there any ground to question its justice, it would show an absurd degree of confidence to challenge the testimony of an adversary. David comes forward with the openness of one who was supported by a sense of his integrity, and repels, by a declaration forced from their own lips, the base charges with which they blackened his character in the estimation of such as were simple enough to believe them.
2. Yea, rather, in heart ye plot wickedness. In the former verse he complained of the gross shamelessness manifested in their conduct. Now he charges them both with entertaining wickedness in their thoughts, and practicing it with their hands.
3. They are estranged, being wicked from the womb. He adduces, in aggravation of their character, the circumstance, that they were not sinners of recent date, but persons born to commit sin. We see some men, otherwise not so depraved in disposition, who are drawn into evil courses through levity of mind, or bad example, or the solicitation of appetite, or other occasions of a similar kind; but David accuses his enemies of being leavened with wickedness from the womb, alleging that their treachery and cruelty were born with them.
4. Their poison is like the poison of a serpent: they are like the deaf adder. He prosecutes his description; and, though he might have insisted on the fierceness which characterized their opposition, he charges them more particularly, here as elsewhere, with the malicious virulence of their disposition. Some read, their fury; but this does not suit the figure, by which they are here compared to serpents. No objection can be drawn to the translation we have adopted from the etymology of the word, which is derived from heat. It is well known, that while some poisons kill by cold, others consume the vital parts by a burning heat. David then asserts of his enemies, in this passage, that they were as full of deadly malice as serpents are full of poison.
5. The more emphatically to express their consummate subtlety, he compares them to deaf serpents, which shut their ears against the voice of the charmer—not the common kind of serpents, but such as are famed for their cunning, and are upon their guard against every artifice of that description.

MATTHEW HENRY

Psalm 58

1-5 A reproof to wicked judges.
We have reason to think that this psalm refers to the malice of Saul and his janizaries against David, because it bears the same inscription (Al-taschith, and Michtam of David) with that which goes before and that which follows, both which appear, by the title, to have been penned with reference to that persecution through which God preserved him (Al-taschith—Destroy not), and therefore the psalms he then penned were precious to him, Michtams—David's jewels, as Dr. Hammond translates it.

In these verses David, not as a king, for he had not yet come to the throne, but as a prophet, in God's name arraigns and convicts his judges, with more authority and justice than they showed in prosecuting him. Two things he charges them with:
I. The corruption of their government. They were a congregation, a bench of justices, nay, perhaps, a congress or convention of the states, from whom one might have expected fair dealing, for they were men learned in the laws, had been brought up in the study of these statutes and judgments, which were so righteous that those of other nations were not to be compared with them. So it was in Saul's time.
1. The judges would not do right, would not protect or vindicate oppressed innocency (v. 1): "Do you indeed speak righteousness, or judge uprightly? No; you are far from it; your own consciences cannot but tell you that you do not discharge the trust reposed in you as magistrates, by which you are bound to be a terror to evil-doers and a praise to those that do well."
2. They did a great deal of wrong; they used their power for the support of injury and oppression (v. 2): In heart you work wickedness (all the wickedness of the life is wrought in the heart). It intimates that they wrought with a great deal of plot and management, not by surprise, but with premeditation and design, and with a strong inclination to it and resolution in it.
II. The corruption of their nature. This was the root of bitterness from which that gall and wormwood sprang (v. 3): The wicked, who in heart work wickedness, are estranged from the womb, estranged from God and all good, alienated from the divine life, and its principles, powers, and pleasures, Eph. iv. 18. Three instances are here given of the corruption of nature: falsehood, malice, and intractableness. They are malicious, and nothing will work upon them, no reason, no kindness, to mollify them, and bring them to a better temper. They are like the deaf adder that stops her ear, v. 4, 5. The psalmist, having compared these wicked men, whom he here complains of, to serpents, for their poisonous malice, takes occasion thence, upon another account, to compare them to the deaf adder or viper.

Psalm 58

6-11

6 Break their teeth, O God, in their mouth: break out the great teeth of the young lions, O LORD.
7 Let them melt away as waters which run continually: when he bendeth his bow to shoot his arrows, let them be as cut in pieces.
8 As a snail which melteth, let every one of them pass away: like the untimely birth of a woman, that they may not see the sun.
9 Before your pots can feel the thorns, he shall take them away as with a whirlwind, both living, and in his wrath.
10 The righteous shall rejoice when he seeth the vengeance: he shall wash his feet in the blood of the wicked.
11 So that a man shall say, Verily there is a reward for the righteous: verily he is a God that judgeth in the earth.

ye shall yet have to cry, "Who hath believed our report?" It is not in your music, but in the sinner's ear that the cause of failure lies, and it is only the power of God that can remove it.

Verse 6. Break their teeth, O God, in their mouth. If they have no capacity for good, at least deprive them of their ability for evil. Treat them as the snake charmers do their serpents, extract their fangs, break their teeth. The Lord can do this, and he will. He will not suffer the malice of the wicked to triumph, he will deal them such a blow as shall disable them from mischief.

Verse 7. Let them melt away as waters which run continually. Like mountain torrents dried up by the summer heats let them disappear; or like running streams whose waters are swiftly gone, so let them pass away; or like water spilt which none can find again, so let them vanish out of existence. Begone, ye foul streams, the sooner ye are forgotten the better for the universe. When he bendeth his bow to shoot his arrows, let them be as cut in pieces. When the Lord goes forth to war, let his judgments so tell upon these persecutors that they may be utterly cut in pieces as a mark shattered by many shafts.

Verse 8. As a snail which melteth, let every one of them pass away. As the snail makes its own way by its slime, and so dissolves as it goes, or as its shell is often found empty, as though the inhabitant had melted away, so shall the malicious eat out their own strength while they proceed upon their malevolent designs, and shall themselves disappear. To destroy himself by envy and chagrin is the portion of the ill disposed. Like the untimely birth of a woman, that they may not see the sun. Solemn is this curse, but how surely does it fall on many graceless wretches!

Verse 9. Before your pots can feel the thorns. So sudden is the overthrow of the wicked, so great a failure is their life, that they never see joy. Their pot is put upon the hook to prepare a feast of joy, and the fuel is placed beneath, but before the thorns are lit, before any heat can be brought to bear upon the pot, yea, even as soon as the fuel has touched the cooking vessel, a storm comes and sweeps all away; the pot is overturned, the fuel is scattered far and wide. Perhaps the figure may suppose the thorns, which are the fuel, to be kindled, and then the flame is so rapid that before any heat can be produced the fire is out, the meat remains raw, the man is disappointed, his work is altogether a failure.

Verse 10. The righteous shall rejoice when he seeth the vengeance. He will have no hand in meting out, neither will he rejoice in the spirit of revenge, but his righteous soul shall acquiesce in the judgments of God, and he shall rejoice to see justice triumphant. There is nothing in Scripture of that sympathy with God's enemies which modern traitors are so fond of parading as the finest species of benevolence.

Verse 11. So that a man shall say. Every man however ignorant shall be compelled to say, Verily, in very deed, assuredly, there is a reward for the righteous. If nothing else be true this is. The godly are not after all forsaken and given over to their enemies; the wicked are not to have the best of it, truth and goodness are recompensed in the long run. Verily he is a God that judgeth in the earth. All men shall be forced by the sight of the final judgment to see that there is a God, and that he is the righteous ruler of the universe. Two things will come out clearly after all—there is a God and there is a reward for the righteous. Time will remove doubts, solve difficulties, and reveal secrets; meanwhile faith's foreseeing eye discerns the truth even now, and is glad thereat.

JOHN CALVIN

6-9
6. Break their teeth, O God! in their mouth. From this part of the psalm he assumes the language of imprecation, and solicits the vengeance of God, whose peculiar prerogative it is to repel oppression and vindicate injured innocence.
7. In the next verse, and in the several succeeding verses, he prosecutes the same purpose, employing a variety of apt similitudes. He prays that God would make them flow away like waters, that is, swiftly. The expression indicates the greatness of his faith. His enemies were before his eyes in all the array of their numbers and resources; he saw that their power was deeply rooted and firmly established; the whole nation was against him, and seemed to rise up before him like a hopeless and formidable barrier of rocky mountains. To pray that this solid and prodigious opposition should melt down and disappear, evidenced no small degree of courage, and the event could only appear credible to one who had learnt to exalt the power of God above all intervening obstacles.
8. Let him vanish like a snail, which melts away. The two comparisons in this verse are introduced with the same design as the first, expressing his desire that his enemies might pass away quietly, and prove as things in their own nature the most evanescent. He likens them to snails, and it might appear ridiculous in David to use such contemptible figures when speaking of men who were formidable for their strength and influence, did we not reflect that he considered God as able in a moment, without the slightest effort, to crush and annihilate the mightiest opposition.
9. Before your pots can feel the fire of your thorns. David refers to the swiftness of that judgment which God would execute upon his enemies, and prays that he would carry them away as by a whirlwind, either before they arrived at the full growth of their strength, like the thorn sprung to the vigorous plant, or before they came to maturity and readiness, like flesh which has been boiled in the pot.

10-11
10. The righteous shall rejoice when he seeth the vengeance. It might appear at first sight that the feeling here attributed to the righteous is far from being consistent with the mercy which ought to characterize them; but we must remember that the affection which David means to impute to them is one of a pure and well-regulated kind; and in this case there is nothing absurd in supposing that believers, under the influence and guidance of the Holy Spirit, should rejoice in witnessing the execution of divine judgments.
11. There is subjoined the reason why the righteous cannot fail to reap the reward of their piety, because God is the judge of the world; it being impossible, on the supposition of the world being ruled by the providence of God, that he should not, sooner or later, distinguish between the good and the evil. He is said more particularly to judge in the earth, because men have sometimes profanely alleged that the government of God is confined to heaven, and the affairs of this world abandoned to blind chance.

MATTHEW HENRY

6-11 Prophetic imprecations.
In these verses we have,
I. David's prayers against his enemies, and all the enemies of God's church and people; for it is as such that he looks upon them, so that he was actuated by a public spirit in praying against them, and not by any private revenge.
1. He prays that they might be disabled to do any further mischief (v. 6): Break their teeth, O God! Not so much that they might not feed themselves as that they might not be able to make prey of others, Ps. iii. 7.
2. That they might be disappointed in the plots they had already laid, and might not gain their point: "When he bends his bow, and takes aim to shoot his arrows at the upright in heart, let them be as cut in pieces, v. 7. Let them fall at his feet, and never come near the mark."
3. That they and their interest might waste and come to nothing, that they might melt away as waters that run continually. He prays (v. 8) that they might melt as a snail, which wastes by its own motion, in every stretch it makes leaving some of its moisture behind, which, by degrees, must needs consume it, though it makes a path to shine after it. He that like a snail in her house is plenus sui—full of himself.
II. His prediction of their ruin (v. 9): "Before your pots can feel the heat of a fire of thorns made under them (which they will presently do, for it is a quick fire and violent while it lasts), so speedily, with such a hasty and violent flame, God shall hurry them away, as terribly and as irresistibly as with a whirlwind, as it were alive, as it were in fury."
1. The proverbial expressions are somewhat difficult, but the sense is plain, that the judgments of God often surprise wicked people in the midst of their jollity, and hurry them away of a sudden.
2. There are two things which the psalmist promises himself as the good effects of sinners' destruction:
(1.) That saints would be encouraged and comforted by it (v. 10): The righteous shall rejoice when he sees the vengeance. The pomp and power, the prosperity and success, of the wicked, are a discouragement to the righteous; they sadden their hearts, and weaken their hands, and are sometimes a strong temptation to them to question their foundations, Ps. lxxiii. 2, 13.
(2.) That sinners would be convinced and converted by it, v. 11. The vengeance God sometimes takes on the wicked in this world will bring men to say, Verily, there is a reward for the righteous. Any man may draw this inference from such providences, and many a man shall, who before denied even these plain truths or doubted of them. Some shall have this confession extorted from them, others shall have their minds so changed that they shall willingly own it, and thank God who has given them to see it and see it with satisfaction, that God is, and, that he is the bountiful rewarder of his saints and servants.

Psalm 59

Title
To the chief Musician. Altaschith. Michtam of David. When Saul sent, and they watched the house to kill him.

1-5
1 Deliver me from mine enemies, O my God: defend me from them that rise up against me.
2 Deliver me from the workers of iniquity, and save me from bloody men.
3 For, lo, they lie in wait for my soul: the mighty are gathered against me; not for my transgression, nor for my sin, O LORD.
4 They run and prepare themselves without my fault: awake to help me, and behold.
5 Thou therefore, O LORD God of hosts, the God of Israel, awake to visit all the heathen: be not merciful to any wicked transgressors. Selah.

Psalm 59

TITLE. To the Chief Musician. Strange that the painful events in David's life should end in enriching the repertoire of the national minstrelsy. Out of a sour, ungenerous soil spring up the honey bearing flowers of psalmody. Had he never been cruelly hunted by Saul, Israel and the church of God in after ages would have missed this song. The music of the sanctuary is in no small degree indebted to the trials of the saints. Affliction is the tuner of the harps of sanctified songsters. Altaschith. Another "destroy not" Psalm. Whom God preserves Satan cannot destroy. The Lord can even preserve the lives of his prophets by the very ravens that would naturally pick out their eyes. David always found a friend to help him when his case was peculiarly dangerous, and that friend was in his enemy's household; in this instance it was Michal, Saul's daughter, as on former occasions it had been Jonathan, Saul's son. Michtam of David. This is the Fifth of the Golden Secrets of David: God's chosen people have many such. When Saul sent, and they watched the house to kill him. Great efforts were made to carry the Psalms away to other authors and seasons than those assigned in the headings, it being the fashion just now to prove one's learning by disagreeing with all who have gone before. Perhaps in a few years the old titles will be as much reverenced as they are now rejected. There are spasms in these matters, and in many other things among the would be "intellectuals" of the schools. We are not anxious to show our readiness at conjecture, and therefore are content with reading this Psalm in the light of the circumstances here mentioned; it does not seem unsuitable to any verse, and in some the words are very appropriate to the specified occasion.
DIVISION. In Ps 59:1-2 he prays, in Ps 59:3-4 he complains of his woes, and again in Ps 59:5 he prays. Here he inserts a Selah, and ends one portion of his song. In Ps 59:6-7 he renews his complaint, in Ps 59:8-10 declares his confidence in God, and in Ps 59:11-13 lifts up his heart in prayer; closing another part of his Psalm with Selah. Then he prays again in Ps 59:14-15, and afterwards betakes himself to singing.

EXPOSITION
Verse 1. Deliver me from mine enemies, O my God. They were all round the house with the warrant of authority, and a force equal to the carrying of it out. He was to be taken dead or alive, well or ill, and carried to the slaughter. No prowess could avail him to break the cordon of armed men, neither could any eloquence stay the hand of his bloody persecutor. He was taken like a bird in a net, and no friend was near to set him free.
Verse 2. Deliver me from the workers of iniquity. Saul was treating him very unjustly, and besides that was pursuing a tyrannical and unrighteous course towards others, therefore David the more vehemently appeals against him. Evil men were in the ascendant at court, and were the ready tools of the tyrant, against these also he prays. Bad men in a bad cause may be pleaded against without question. When a habitation is beset by thieves, the good man of the house rings the alarm bell; and in these verses we may hear it ring out loudly, "deliver me," "defend me," "deliver me," "save me." Saul had more cause to fear than David had, for the invincible weapon of prayer was being used against him, and heaven was being aroused to give him battle.
Verse 3. For, lo, they lie in wait for my soul. They were in ambuscade for the good man's life. He knew their design and cried to God to be rescued from it. Like wild beasts they crouched, and waited to make the fatal spring; but their victim used effectual means to baffle them, for he laid the matter before the Lord. While the enemy lies waiting in the posture of a beast, we wait before God in the posture of prayer, for God waits to be gracious to us and terrible towards our foes.

JOHN CALVIN

Psalm 59

The title, which immediately follows, informs us upon what occasion this psalm was written, which bears a considerable resemblance to the preceding. He begins by insisting upon the injustice of that cruel hostility which his enemies showed to him, and which he had done nothing to deserve. His complaint is followed up by prayer to God for help; and afterwards, as his hopes revive in the exercise of devout meditation, he proceeds to prophesy their calamitous destruction. At the close, he engages to preserve a grateful remembrance of his deliverance, and to praise the goodness of God.

1-5

1. Deliver me from mine enemies, O my God! He insists upon the strength and violence of his enemies, with the view of exciting his mind to greater fervor in the duty of prayer. These he describes as rising up against him, in which expression he alludes not simply to the audacity or fierceness of their assaults, but to the eminent superiority of power which they possessed; and yet he asks that he may be lifted up on high, as it were, above the reach of this over-swelling inundation. His language teaches us that we should believe in the ability of God to deliver us even upon occasions of emergency, when our enemies have an overwhelming advantage.

2. In the verse which follows, while he expresses the extremity to which he was reduced, he adverts at the same time to the injustice and cruelty of his persecutors.

3. Immediately afterwards, he connects the two grounds of his complaint together: on the one hand, his complete helplessness under the danger, and, on the other, the undeserved nature of the assaults from which he suffered.

4. Awake to hasten for my help, and behold. In using this language, he glances at the eagerness with which his enemies, as he had already said, were pressing upon him, and states his desire that God would show the same haste in extending help as they did in seeking his destruction. With the view of conciliating the divine favor, he once more calls upon God to be the witness and judge of his cause, adding, and behold. The expression is one which savors at once of faith and of the infirmity of the flesh. In speaking of God, as if his eyes had been hitherto shut to the wrongs which he had suffered, and needed now for the first time to be opened for the discovery of them, he expresses himself according to the weakness of our human apprehension. On the other hand, in calling upon God to behold his cause, he shows his faith by virtually acknowledging that nothing was hid from his providential cognizance. Though David may use language of this description, suited to the infirmity of sense, we must not suppose him to have doubted before this time that his afflictions, his innocence, and his wrongs, were known to God. Now, however, he lays the whole before God for examination and decision.

5. He prosecutes the same prayer with still greater vehemency in the verse which succeeds. He addresses God under new titles, calling him Jehovah, God of Hosts, and the God of Israel, the first of which appellations denotes the immensity of

MATTHEW HENRY

Psalm 59

1-7 Prayer for deliverance.

The title of this psalm acquaints us particularly with the occasion on which it was penned; it was when Saul sent a party of his guards to beset David's house in the night, that they might seize him and kill him; we have the story 1 Sam. xix. 11. It was when his hostilities against David were newly begun, and he had but just before narrowly escaped Saul's javelin. These first eruptions of Saul's malice could not but put David into disorder and be both grievous and terrifying, and yet he kept up his communion with God, and such a composure of mind as that he was never out of frame for prayer and praises. In these verses,

I. David prays to be delivered out of the hands of his enemies, and that their cruel designs against him might be defeated (v. 1, 2): "Deliver me from my enemies, O my God! thou art God, and cast deliver me, my God, under whose protection I have put myself; and thou hast promised me to be a God all-sufficient, and therefore, in honor and faithfulness, thou wilt deliver me. Set me on high out of the reach of the power and malice of those that rise up against me, and above the fear of it. Let me be safe, and see myself so, safe and easy, safe and satisfied. O deliver me! and save me." He cries out as one ready to perish, and that had his eye to God only for salvation and deliverance. He prays (v. 4), "Awake to help me, take cognizance of my case, behold that with an eye of pity, and exert thy power for my relief."

II. He pleads for deliverance. Our God gives us leave not only to pray, but to plead with him, to order our cause before him and to fill our mouth with arguments, not to move him, but to move ourselves. David does so here.

1. He pleads the bad character of his enemies.

2. He pleads their malice against him, and the imminent danger he was in from them, v. 3. "Their spite is great; they aim at my soul, my life, my better part. They are subtle and very politic: They lie in wait, taking an opportunity to do me a mischief. They are all mighty, men of honor and estates, and interest in court and country. They are in a confederacy; they are united by league, and actually gathered together against me, combined both in consultation and action. They are very ingenious in their contrivances, and very industrious in the prosecution of them (v. 4): They run and prepare themselves, with the utmost speed and fury, to do me a mischief." He takes particular notice of the brutish conduct of the messengers that Saul sent to take him (v. 6): "They return at evening from the posts assigned them in the day, to apply themselves to their works of darkness (their night-work, which may well be their day-shame), and then they make a noise like a hound in pursuit of the hare."

3. He pleads his own innocency, not as to God (he was never backward to own himself guilty before

Psalm 59

6-11

6 They return at evening: they make a noise like a dog, and go round about the city.

7 Behold, they belch out with their mouth: swords are in their lips: for who, say they, doth hear?

8 But thou, O LORD, shalt laugh at them; thou shalt have all the heathen in derision.

9 Because of his strength will I wait upon thee: for God is my defense.

10 The God of my mercy shall prevent me: God shall let me see my desire upon mine enemies.

11 Slay them not, lest my people forget: scatter them by thy power; and bring them down, O Lord our shield.

Verse 4. They run and prepare themselves without my fault. They are all alive and active, they are swift to shed blood. They prepare and use their best tactics; they besiege me in my house, and lay their ambuscades as for some notable enemy. They come up fully armed to the attack, and assail me with all the vigor and skill of a host about to storm a castle; and all for no cause, but out of gratuitous malice. So quick are they to obey their cruel master, that they never stay to consider whether their errand is a good one or not; they run at once, and buckle on their harness as they run. To be thus gratuitously attacked is a great grief.

Verse 5. Thou, thyself, work for me personally, for the case needs thine interposition. Therefore, because I am unjustly assailed, and cannot help myself. O Lord, ever living, God of Hosts, able to rescue me; the God of Israel, pledged by covenant to redeem thine oppressed servant; awake to visit all the heathen, arouse thy holy mind, bestow thy sacred energies, punish the heathen among thine Israel, the false hearted who say they are Jews and are not, but do lie. And when thou art about the business, let all the nations of thine enemies, and all the heathenish people at home and abroad know that thou art judging and punishing. It is the mark of a thoughtful prayer that the titles which are in it applied to God are appropriate.

Verse 6. They return at evening. Like wild beasts that roam at night, they come forth to do mischief. If foiled in the light, they seek the more congenial darkness in which to accomplish their designs. They mean to break into the house in the dead of might. They make a noise like a dog, and go round about the city. Howling with hunger for their prey, they sneak round and round the walls, prowling with stealthy footstep, and barking in unamiable concert. David compares his foes to Eastern dogs, unowned, loathsome, degraded, lean, and hungry, and he represents them as howling with disappointment, because they cannot find the food they seek.

Verse 7. Behold they belch out with their mouth. The noisy creatures are so remarkable in their way, that attention is called to them with a behold. Ecce homines, might we not say, Ecce canes! Their malicious speech gushes from them as from a bubbling fountain. The wicked are voluble in slander; their vocabulary of abuse is copious, and as detestable as it is abundant. What torrents of wrathful imprecation will they pour on the godly! They need no prompters, their feelings force for themselves their own vent, and fashion their own expressions. Swords are in their lips. They speak daggers.

Verse 8. But thou, O Lord, shalt laugh at them. He speaks to God, as to one who is close at hand. He points to the liars in wait and speaks to God about them. They are laughing at me, and longing for my destruction, but thou hast the laugh of them seeing thou hast determined to send them away without their victim, and made fools of by Michal. The greatest, cleverest, and most malicious of the enemies of the church are only objects of ridicule to the Lord; their attempts are utterly futile, they need give no concern to our faith.

Verse 9. Because of his strength will I wait upon thee. Is my persecutor strong? Then, my God, for this very reason I will turn myself to thee, and leave my matters in thy hand. It is a wise thing to find in the greatness of our difficulties a reason for casting ourselves on the Lord. For God is my defense, my high place, my fortress, the place of my resort in the time of my danger. If the foe be too strong for me to cope with him, I will retreat into my castle, where he cannot reach me.

Verse 10. The God of my mercy shall prevent me. God who is the giver and fountain of all the undeserved goodness I have received, will go before me and lead my way as I march onward. He will meet me in my time of need. Not alone shall I have to confront my foes, but he whose goodness I have long tried and proved will gently clear my way, and be my faithful protector.

Verse 11. Slay them not, lest my people forget. It argues great faith on David's part, that even while his house was surrounded by his enemies he

JOHN CALVIN

his power, and the second the special care which he exerts over the Church, and over all his people.

6-9
6. They will return at evening. He compares his enemies to famished and furious dogs which hunger impels to course with endless circuits in every direction, and under this figure accuses their insatiable fierceness, shown in the ceaseless activity to which they were instigated by the desire of mischief. He says that they return in the evening, to intimate, not that they rested at other times, but were indefatigable in pursuing their evil courses. If they came no speed through the day, yet the night would find them at their work. The barking of dogs aptly expressed as a figure the formidable nature of their assaults.
7. In the verse which follows, he describes their fierceness. The expression, prating, or belching out with their mouth, denotes that they proclaimed their infamous counsels openly, and without affecting concealment.
8. But thou, O Jehovah! shalt laugh at them. In the face of all this opposition, David only rises to greater confidence. When he says that God would laugh at his enemies, he employs a figure which is well fitted to enhance the power of God, suggesting that, when the wicked have perfected their schemes to the uttermost, God can, without any effort, and, as it were, in sport, dissipate them all. No sooner does God connive at their proceedings, than their pride and insolence take occasion to manifest themselves: for they forget that even when he seems to have suspended operation, he needs but nod, and his judgments shall be executed. David, accordingly, in contempt of his adversaries, tells them that God was under no necessity to make extensive preparations, but, at the moment when he saw fit to make retribution, would, by a mere play of his power, annihilate them all. He in this manner conveys a severe rebuke to that blind infatuation which led them to boast so intemperately of their own powers, and to imagine that God was slumbering in the heavens. In the close of the verse, mention is made of all nations, to intimate that though they might equal the whole world in numbers, they would prove a mere mockery with all their influence and resources. Or the words may be read—Even As thou hast all the nations in derision. One thing is obvious, that David ridicules the vain boasting of his enemies, who thought no undertaking too great to be accomplished by their numbers.
9. I will intrust his strength to thee. It is evident that David is here enabled, from the eminence of faith, to despise the violent opposition of his enemy, convinced that he could do nothing without the divine permission.

10-12
10. The God of my mercy will prevent me. The scope of the words is that God will interpose at the very moment when it is required, however much he may retard or defer his assistance.
11. Slay them not, lest my people forget. David very properly suggests this to his own mind, as a consideration which should produce patience. We are apt to think, when God has not annihilated our enemies at once, that they have escaped out of

MATTHEW HENRY

him), but as to his persecutors; what they charged him with was utterly false, nor had he ever said or done any thing to deserve such treatment from them (v. 3): "Not for my transgression, nor for my sin, O Lord! thou knowest, who knowest all things." And again (v. 4), without my fault.

4. He pleads that his enemies were profane and atheistic, and bolstered themselves up in their enmity to David, with the contempt of God: For who, say they, doth hear? v. 7.

III. He refers himself and his cause to the just judgment of God, v. 5. "The Lord, the Judge, be Judge between me and my persecutors." In this appeal to God he has an eye to him as the Lord of hosts, that has power to execute judgment, having all creatures, even hosts of angels, at his command; he views him also as the God of Israel, to whom he was. Mark that.
1. If David had been conscious to himself that he was a wicked transgressor, he would not have expected to find mercy; but, as to his enemies, he would say he was no transgressor at all (v. 3, 4): "Not for my transgression, and therefore thou wilt appear for me."
2. He knew his enemies were wicked transgressors, willful, malicious, and hardened in their transgressions both against God and man, and therefore he sues for justice against them, judgment without mercy.

8-17 Confidence in God.
David here encourages himself, in reference to the threatening power of his enemies, with a pious resolution to wait upon God and a believing expectation that he should yet praise him.
I. He resolves to wait upon God (v. 9): "Because of his strength" (either the strength of his enemies, the fear of which drove him to God, or because of God's strength, the hope of which drew him to God) "Will I wait upon thee, with a believing dependence upon thee and confidence in thee." It is our wisdom and duty, in times of danger and difficulty, to wait upon God; for he is our defense, our high place, in whom we shall be safe. He hopes,
1. That God will be to him a God of mercy (v. 10): "The God of my mercy shall prevent me with the blessings of his goodness and the gifts of his mercy, prevent my fears, prevent my prayers, and be better to me than my own expectations."
2. That he will be to his persecutors a God of vengeance. His expectation of this he expresses partly by way of prediction and partly by way of petition, which come all to one; for his prayer that it might be so amounts to a prophecy that it shall be so. Here are several things which he foretells concerning his enemies, or observers, that sought occasions against him and opportunity to do him a mischief, in all which he should see his desire, not a passionate or revengeful desire, but a believing desire upon them, v. 10.
(1.) He foresees that God would expose them to scorn, as they had indeed made themselves

Psalm 59

12-17

12 For the sin of their mouth and the words of their lips let them even be taken in their pride: and for cursing and lying which they speak.
13 Consume them in wrath, consume them, that they may not be: and let them know that God ruleth in Jacob unto the ends of the earth. Selah.
14 And at evening let them return; and let them make a noise like a dog, and go round about the city.
15 Let them wander up and down for meat, and grudge if they be not satisfied.
16 But I will sing of thy power; yea, I will sing aloud of thy mercy in the morning: for thou hast been my defense and refuge in the day of my trouble.
17 Unto thee, O my strength, will I sing: for God is my defense, and the God of my mercy.

is yet so fully sure of their overthrow, and so completely realizes it in his own mind, that he puts in a detailed petition that they may not be too soon or too fully exterminated. God's victory over the craft and cruelty of the wicked is so easy and so glorious that it seems a pity to end the conflict too soon. To sweep away the plotters all at once were to end the great drama of retribution too abruptly. Nay, let the righteous be buffeted a little longer, and let the boasting oppressor puff and brag through his little hour, it will help to keep Israel in mind of the Lord's justice, and make the brave party who side with God's champion accustomed to divine interpositions.

Verse 12. For the sin of their mouth and the words of their lips let them even be taken in their pride. Such dreadful language of atheism and insolence deserves a fit return. As they hope to take their victims, so let them be taken themselves, entangled in their own net, arrested in the midst of their boastful security. Sins of the lips are real sins, and punishable sins.

Verse 13. Consume them in wrath. As if he had changed his mind and would have them brought to a speedy end, or if spared would have them exist as ruins, he cries, consume them, and he redoubles his cry, consume them; nay, he gives a triple note, that they may not be. Revilers of God whose mouths pour forth such filth as David was on this occasion obliged to hear, are not to be tolerated by a holy soul; indignation must flame forth, and cry to God against them.

Verse 14. Here verse six is repeated, as if the songster defied his foes and reveled in the thought of their futile search, their malice, their disappointment, their rage, their defeated vigilance, their wasted energy. He laughs to think that all the city would know how they were deceived, and all Israel would ring with the story of the image and the goats' hair in the bed. Nothing was more a subject of Oriental merriment than a case in which the crafty are deceived, and nothing more makes a man the object of derision than to be outwitted by a woman, as in this instance Saul and his base minions were by Michal. The warrior poet hears in fancy the howl of rage in the council of his foes when they found their victim clean escaped from their hands.

Verse 15. Let them wander up and down for meat. Like dogs that have missed the expected carcass, let them go up and down dissatisfied, snapping at one another, and too disappointed to be quiet and take the matter easily. And grudge if they be not satisfied. Let them act like those who cannot believe that they have lost their prey: like a herd of Oriental dogs, unhoused, unkennelled, let them prowl about seeking a prey which they shall never find.

Verse 16. But I will sing of thy power. The wicked howl, but I sing and will sing. Their power is weakness, but thine is omnipotence; I see them vanquished and thy power victorious, and for ever and ever will I sing of thee.

Verse 17. Unto thee, O my strength, will I sing. What transport is here! What a monopolizing of all his emotions for the one object of praising God! Strength has been overcome by strength; not by the hero's own prowess, but by the might of God alone. See how the singer girds himself with the almightiness of God, and calls it all his own by faith. Sweet is the music of experience, but it is all for God; there is not even a stray note for man, for self, or for human helpers. For God is my defense, and the God of my mercy. With full assurance he claims possession of the Infinite as his protection and security.

his hands altogether; and we look upon it as properly no punishment, that they should be gradually and slowly destroyed. Such being the extravagant desire which almost all, without exception, have, to see their enemies at once exterminated, David checks himself, and dwells upon the judgment of God to be seen in the lesser calamities which overtake the wicked. It is true, that were not our eyes blinded, we would behold a more evident display of divine retribution in cases where the destruction of the ungodly is sudden; but these are so apt to fade away from our remembrance, that he had good reason to express his desire that the spectacle might be one constantly renewed, and thus our knowledge of the judgments of God be more deeply graven upon our hearts.

12. The sin of their mouth, the words of their lips. It is as if David had said that no lengthened proof was necessary to convict them of sin, which plainly showed itself in the mischievous tendency of their discourse. Wickedness, he tells us, proceeded from their mouth., They vomited out their pride and cruelty.

13-17

13. Consume, consume them in wrath, that they may not be. David may seem to contradict himself in praying for the utter destruction of his enemies, when immediately before he had expressed his desire that they might not be exterminated at once.

14. And at evening they shall return. It is of no consequence whether we read the words in the future tense or in the subjunctive, understanding it to be a continuance of the preceding prayer. But it seems more probable that David, after having brought his requests to a close, anticipates the happy issue which he desired. And he makes an apt allusion to what he had already said of their insatiable hunger. The words which he had formerly used he repeats, but with a different application, ironically declaring that they would be ravenous in another sense, and that matters would issue otherwise than they had looked for. Above he had complained that they made a noise like dogs, adverting to the eagerness and fierceness with which they were bent upon mischief; now he derides their malicious efforts, and says, that after wearying themselves with their endless pursuit all day, they would go disappointed of their purpose.

16. But I will sing of thy power. By this he does not mean merely that he would have occasion to sing at some future period, but prepares himself presently for the exercise of thanksgiving; and he proceeds to acknowledge that his deliverance would be at once an illustrious effect of Divine power, and conferred of mere grace.

17. My strength is with thee, I will sing psalms. He expresses still more explicitly the truth, that he owed his safety entirely to God. Formerly he had said that the strength of his enemy was with God, and now he asserts the same thing of his own. David, weak as he was in himself, maintains that he had strength sufficient in the Lord; and accordingly adds, that he had good reason to engage in praise, as James the inspired apostle exhorts those who are merry to sing psalms, (James 5:13.)

ridiculous, v. 8. "They think God does not hear them, does not heed them; but thou, O Lord! shalt laugh at them for their folly, to think that he who planted the ear shall not hear, and thou shalt have not them only, but all such other heathenish people that live without God in the world, in derision."

(2.) That God would make them standing monuments of his justice (v. 11): Slay them not; let them not be killed outright, lest my people forget. If the execution be soon done, the impressions of it will not be deep, and therefore will not be durable, but will quickly wear off. Swift destructions startle men for the present, but they are soon forgotten, for which reason he prays that this might be gradual: "Scatter them by thy power, and let them carry about with them, in their wanderings, such tokens of God's displeasure as may spread the notice of their punishment to all parts of the country."

II. He expects to praise God, that God's providence would find him matter for praise and that God's grace would work in him a heart for praise, v. 16, 17. Observe,

1. What he would praise God for.

(1.) He would praise his power and his mercy; both should be the subject-matter of his song. Power, without mercy, is to be dreaded; mercy, without power, is not what a man can expect much benefit from; but God's power by which he is able to help us, and his mercy by which he is inclined to help us, will justly be the everlasting praise of all the saints.

(2.) He would praise him because he had, many a time, and all along, found him his defense and his refuge in the day of trouble. God brings his people into trouble, that they may experience his power and mercy in protecting and sheltering them, and may have occasion to praise him.

(3.) He would praise him because he had still a dependence upon him and a confidence in him, as his strength to support him and carry him on in his duty.

2. How he would praise God.

(1.) He would sing. As that is a natural expression of joy, so it is an instituted ordinance for the exerting and exciting of holy joy and thankfulness.

(2.) He would sing aloud, as one much affected with the glory of God, that was not ashamed to own it, and that desired to affect others with it. He will sing of God's power, but he will sing aloud of his mercy; the consideration of that raises his affections more than any thing else.

(3.) He would sing aloud in the morning, when his spirits were most fresh and lively. God's compassions are new every morning, and therefore it is fit to begin the day with his praises.

(4.) He would sing unto God (v. 17), to his honor and glory, and with him in his eye. As we must direct our prayers to God, so to him we must direct our praises, and must look up, making melody to the Lord.

Psalm 60

Title
To the chief Musician upon Shushaneduth. Michtam of David. To teach, when he strove with Aramnaharaim and with Aramzobah, when Joab returned, and smote of Edom in the valley of salt twelve thousand.

1-6
1 O God, thou hast cast us off, thou hast scattered us, thou hast been displeased; O turn thyself to us again.
2 Thou hast made the earth to tremble; thou hast broken it: heal the breaches thereof; for it shaketh.
3 Thou hast shewed thy people hard things: thou hast made us to drink the wine of astonishment.
4 Thou hast given a banner to them that fear thee, that it may be displayed because of the truth. Selah.
5 That thy beloved may be delivered; save with thy right hand, and hear me.
6 God hath spoken in his holiness; I will rejoice, I will divide Shechem, and mete out the valley of Succoth.

Psalm 60

TITLE. Here is a lengthy title, but it helps us much to expound the Psalm. To the Chief Musician upon Shushaneduth, or the Lily of Testimony. The forty-fifth was on the lilies, and represented the kingly warrior in his beauty going forth to war; here we see him dividing the spoil and bearing testimony to the glory of God.
Michtam of David, to teach. David obeyed the precept to teach the children of Israel; he recorded the Lord's mighty acts that they might be rehearsed in the ears of generations to come. Golden secrets are to be told on the house tops; these things were not done in a corner and ought not to be buried in silence. We ought gladly to learn what inspiration so beautifully teaches. When he strove with Aramnaharaim and with Aramzobah. The combined Aramean tribes sought to overcome Israel, but were signally defeated. When Joab returned. He had been engaged in another region, and the enemies of Israel took advantage of his absence, but on his return with Abishai the fortunes of war were changed. And smote of Edom in the valley of salt twelve thousand. More than this appear to have fallen according to 1Ch 18:12, but this commemorates one memorable part of the conflict. Terrible must have been the battle, but decisive indeed were the results, and the power of the enemy was utterly broken. Well did the Lord deserve a song from his servant.
DIVISION. Properly the song may be said to consist of three parts: the complaining verses, Ps 60:1-3; the happy, Ps 60:4-8; the prayerful, Ps 60:9-12. We have divided it as the sense appeared to change.

EXPOSITION
Verse 1. Before the days of Saul, Israel had been brought very low; during his government it had suffered from internal strife, and his reign was closed by an overwhelming disaster at Gibeon. David found himself the possessor of a tottering throne, troubled with the double evil of factions at home, and invasion from abroad. He traced at once the evil to its true source, and began at the fountainhead.
Verse 2. Thou hast made the earth to tremble. Things were as unsettled as though the solid earth had been made to quake; nothing was stable; the priests had been murdered by Saul, the worst men had been put in office, the military power had been broken by the Philistines, and the civil authority had grown despicable through insurrections and intestine contests.
Verse 3. Thou hast showed thy people hard things. Hardships had been heaped upon them, and the psalmist traces these rigorous providences to their fountainhead. Nothing had happened by chance, but all had come by divine design and with a purpose.
Verse 4. Here the strain takes a turn. The Lord has called back to himself his servants, and commissioned them for his service, presenting them with a standard to be used in his wars. Thou hast given a banner to them that fear thee. Their afflictions had led them to exhibit holy fear, and then being fitted for the Lord's favor, he gave them an ensign, which would be both a rallying point for their hosts, a proof that he had sent them to fight, and a guarantee of victory. The bravest men are usually intrusted with the banner, and it is certain that those who fear God must have less fear of man than any others.
Verse 5. That thy beloved may be delivered. David was the Lord's beloved, his name signifies "dear, or beloved," and there was in Israel a remnant according to the election of grace, who were the beloved of the Lord; for their sakes the Lord wrought great marvels, and he had an eye to them in all his mighty acts. God's beloved are the inner seed, for whose sake he preserves the entire nation, which acts as a husk to the vital part. This is the main design of providence, That thy beloved may be delivered; if it were not for their sakes he would neither give a banner nor send victory to it.

JOHN CALVIN

Psalm 60

1-3

1. O God! thou hast cast us off. With the view of exciting both himself and others to a more serious consideration of the goodness of God, which they presently experienced, he begins the psalm with prayer; and a comparison is instituted, designed to show that the government of Saul had been under the divine reprobation. He complains of the sad confusions into which the nation had been thrown, and prays that God would return to it in mercy, and re-establish its affairs.

2. He next describes the confusions which reigned by a metaphor, representing the country as opened, or cleft asunder; not that there had been a literal earthquake, but that the kingdom, in its rent and shattered condition, presented that calamitous aspect which generally follows upon an earthquake. The affairs of Saul ceased to prosper from the time that he forsook God; and when he perished at last, he left the nation in a state little short of ruin.

3. Thou hast showed thy people hard things. He says, first, that the nation had been dealt with severely, and then adds a figure which may additionally represent the grievousness of its calamities, speaking of it as drunk with the wine of stupor or astonishment. It is evident that the Psalmist alludes to some kind of poisoned drink, which deprives a person of his senses, insinuating that the Jews were stupefied by their calamities. He would place, in short, before their eyes the curse of God, which had pressed upon the government of Saul, and induce them to abandon their obstinate attempts to maintain the interests of a throne which lay under the divine reprobation.

4-8

4. Thou hast given a banner to them that fear thee. David uses the language of congratulation, and, by pointing to the change which had taken place, calls attention to the evident appearances of the divine favor. He returns thanks to God, in the name of all the people, for having raised a standard which might at once cheer their hearts, and unite their divided numbers.

5. He next proceeds to address God again in prayer. In the previous verse he calls them fearers of the Lord, and now his beloved; implying that, when God rewards such as fear and worship him, it is always with a respect to his own free love. And prayer is subjoined: for however great may be the favors which God has bestowed upon us, modesty and humility will teach us always to pray that he would perfect what his goodness has begun.

6. God hath spoken in his holiness; I will rejoice. Hitherto he has adverted to the proofs which had come under their own observation, and from which they might easily see that God had manifested his favor in a manner new, and for many years unprecedented. He had raised the nation from a state of deep distress to prosperity, and had changed the aspect of affairs so far, that one victory was following another in rapid

MATTHEW HENRY

Psalm 60

1-5 David's complaints and petitions.

In these verses, which begin the psalm, we have,

I. A melancholy memorial of the many disgraces and disappointments which God had, for some years past, put the people under. During the reign of Saul, especially in the latter end of it, and during David's struggle with the house of Saul, while he reigned over Judah only, the affairs of the kingdom were much perplexed, and the neighboring nations were vexatious to them.

1. He complains of hard things which they had seen (that is, which they had suffered), while the Philistines and other ill-disposed neighbors took all advantages against them, v. 3.

2. He owns God's displeasure to be the cause of all the hardships they had undergone: "Thou hast been displeased by us, displeased against us (v. 1), and in thy displeasure hast cast us off and scattered us, hast put us out of thy protection, else our enemies could not have prevailed thus against us. They would never have picked us up and made a prey of us if thou hadst not broken the staff of bands (Zech. xi. 14) by which we were united, and so scattered us."

3. He laments the ill effects and consequences of the miscarriages of the late years. The whole nation was in a convulsion: Thou hast made the earth (or the land) to tremble, v. 2. The generality of the people had dreadful apprehensions of the issue of these things. The good people themselves were in a consternation: "Thou hast made us to drink the wine of astonishment (v. 3); we were like men intoxicated, and at our wits' end, not knowing how to reconcile these dispensations with God's promises and his relation to his people; we are amazed, can do nothing, nor know we what to do." Now this is mentioned here to teach, that is, for the instruction of the people.

II. A thankful notice of the encouragement God had given them to hope that, though things had been long bad, they would now begin to mend (v. 4): "Thou hast given a banner to those that fear thee (for, as bad as the times are, there is a remnant among us that desire to fear thy name, for whom thou hast a tender concern), that it may be displayed by thee, because of the truth of thy promise which thou wilt perform, and to be displayed by them, in defense of truth and equity," Ps. xlv. 4.

III. A humble petition for seasonable mercy.

1. That God would be reconciled to them, though he had been displeased with them. In his displeasure their calamities began, and therefore in his favor their prosperity must begin: O turn thyself to us again! (v. 1) smile upon us, and take part with us; be at peace with us, and in that peace we shall have peace.

2. That they might be reconciled to one another, though they had been broken and wretchedly divided among themselves: "Heal the breaches of our land

Psalm 60

7-12

7 Gilead is mine, and Manasseh is mine; Ephraim also is the strength of mine head; Judah is my lawgiver;
8 Moab is my washpot; over Edom will I cast out my shoe: Philistia, triumph thou because of me.
9 Who will bring me into the strong city? who will lead me into Edom?
10 Wilt not thou, O God, which hadst cast us off? and thou, O God, which didst not go out with our armies?
11 Give us help from trouble: for vain is the help of man.
12 Through God we shall do valiantly: for he it is that shall tread down our enemies.

Verse 6. God hath spoken in his holiness. Faith is never happier than when it can fall back upon the promise of God. She sets this over against all discouraging circumstances; let outward providences say what they will, the voice of a faithful God drowns every sound of tear. God had promised Israel victory, and David the kingdom; the holiness of God secured the fulfillment of his own covenant, and therefore the king spake confidently.

Verse 7. Gilead is mine, and Manasseh is mine. He claims the whole land on account of the promise. Two other great divisions of the country he mentions, evidently delighting to survey the goodly land which the Lord had given him. All things are ours, whether things present or things to come; no mean portion belongs to the believer, and let him not think meanly of it.

Verse 8. Having looked at home with satisfaction, the hero king now looks abroad with exultation. Moab, so injurious to me in former years, is my washpot. The basin into which the water falls when it is poured from an ewer upon my feet. A mere pot to hold the dirty water after my feet have been washed in it. Once she defiled Israel, according to the counsel of Balaam, the son of Beor; but she shall no longer be able to perpetrate such baseness; she shall be a washpot for those whom she sought to pollute. The wicked as we see in them the evil, the fruit, and the punishment of sin, shall help on the purification of the saints. This is contrary to their will, and to the nature of things, but faith finds honey in the lion, and a washpot in filthy Moab. David treats his foes as but insignificant and inconsiderable; a whole nation he counts but as a footbath for his kingdom.

Verse 9. As yet the interior fortresses of Edom had not been subdued. Their invading bands had been slain in the valley of salt, and David intended to push his conquests even to Petra the city of the rock, deemed to be impregnable.

Verse 10. Wilt not thou, O God, which hadst cast us off? Yes, the chastising God is our only hope. He loves us still. For a small moment doth he forsake, but with great mercy does he gather his people. Strong to smite, he is also strong to save. He who proved to us our need of him by showing us what poor creatures we are without him, will now reveal the glory of his help by conducting great enterprises to a noble issue.

Verse 11. Give us help from trouble. Help us to overcome the disasters of civil strife and foreign invasion; save us from further incursions from without and division within. Do thou, O Lord, work this deliverance, for vain is the help of man. We have painfully learned the utter impotence of armies, kings, and nations without thine help.

Verse 12. Through God we shall do valiantly. From God all power proceeds, and all we do well is done by divine operation; but still we, as soldiers of the great king, are to fight, and to fight valiantly too. Divine working is not an argument for human inaction, but rather is it the best excitement for courageous effort. Helped in the past, we shall also be helped in the future, and being assured of this we resolve to play the man. For he it is that shall tread down our enemies. From him shall the might proceed, to him shall the honor be given. Like straw on the threshing floor beneath the feet of the oxen shall we tread upon our abject foes, but it shall rather be his foot which presses them down than ours. In the case of Christians there is much encouragement for a resolve similar to that of the first clause. We shall do valiantly, we will not be ashamed of our colors, afraid of our foes, or fearful of our cause. The Lord is with us, omnipotence sustains us, and we will not hesitate, we dare not be cowards. O that our King, the true David, were come to claim the earth, for the kingdom is the Lord's, and he is the governor among the nations.

succession. But now he calls their attention to a point of still greater importance, the divine promise—the fact that God had previously declared all this with his own mouth. However numerous and striking may be the practical demonstrations we receive of the favor of God, we can never recognize them, except in connection with his previously revealed promise.

7. So with Gilead and Manasseh. As Ephraim was the most populous of all the tribes, he appropriately terms it the strength of his head, that is, of his dominions. To procure the greater credit to the oracle, by showing that it derived a sanction from antiquity, he adds, that Judah would be his lawgiver, or chief; which was equivalent to saying, that the posterity of Abraham could never prosper unless, in agreeableness to the prediction of the patriarch Jacob, they were brought under the government of Judah, or of one who was sprung from that tribe. He evidently alludes to what is narrated by Moses, (Genesis 49:10,) "The scepter shall not depart from Judah, nor a lawgiver from between his feet, until Shiloh come." No government could stand which was not resident in the tribe of Judah, this being the decree and the good pleasure of God.

8. Moab is my wash-pot. In proceeding to speak of foreigners, he observes a wide distinction between them and his own countrymen. The posterity of Abraham he would govern as brethren, and not as slaves; but it was allowable for him to exercise greater severities upon the profane and the uncircumcised, in order to their being brought under forcible subjection.

9-12

9. Who will bring me into the fortified city? Anticipating an objection which might be alleged, he proceeds to state that he looked to God for the accomplishment of what remained to be done in the capture of the fortified places of his enemies, and the consolidation of his victories.

10. With a view to prove his legitimate call to the government, he amplifies a second time the marks of the divine favor which it had received, by contrasting it with that which preceded. "The God," he says, "who had formerly cast us off, and abandoned us to unsuccessful warfare, will now lay open before me the gates of hostile cities, and enable me to break through all their fortifications."

11. Give us help from trouble: for vain is the help of man. Again he reverts to the exercise of prayer, or rather is led to it naturally by the very confidence of hope, which we have seen that he entertained. He expresses his conviction, that should God extend his help, it would be sufficient of itself, although no assistance should be received from any other quarter.

12. And to confirm this position, he declares in the last verse of the psalm, that as, on the one hand, we can do nothing without him, so, on the other, we can do all things by his help. Even in our controversy with creatures like ourselves, we are not at liberty to share the honor of success with God. Those who arrogate the least fraction of strength to themselves apart from God, only ruin themselves through their own pride.

(v. 2), not only the breaches made upon us by our enemies, but the breaches made among ourselves by our unhappy divisions."

3. That thus they might be preserved out of the hands of their enemies (v. 5): "That thy beloved may be delivered, and not made a prey of, save with thy right hand, with thy own power and by such instruments as thou art pleased to make the men of thy right hand, and hear me."

6-12 Rejoicing in hope.

David is here rejoicing in hope and praying in hope; such are the triumphs of the saints, not so much upon the account of what they have in possession as of what they have in prospect (v. 6).

I. David here rejoices; and it is in prospect of two things:

1. The perfecting of this revolution in his own kingdom. God having spoken in his holiness that David shall be king, he doubts not but the kingdom is all his own, as sure as if it were already in his hand: I will divide Shechem (a pleasant city in Mount Ephraim) and mete out the valley of Succoth, as my own. Gilead is mine, and Manasseh is mine, and both are entirely reduced, v. 7.

2. The conquering of the neighboring nations, which had been vexatious to Israel, were still dangerous, and opposed the throne of David, v. 8. Moab shall be enslaved, and put to the meanest drudgery. The Moabites became David's servants, 2 Sam. viii. 2.

II. He prays in hope. His prayer is, Give us help from trouble, v. 11. The hope with which they support themselves in this prayer has two things in it:

1. A diffidence of themselves and all their creature-confidences: Vain is the help of man. Then only we are qualified to receive help from God when we are brought to own the insufficiency of all creatures to do that for us which we expect him to do.

2. A confidence in God, and in his power and promise (v. 12): "Through God we shall do valiantly, and so we shall do victoriously; for he it is, and he only, that shall tread down our enemies, and shall have the praise of doing it." Note,

(1.) Our confidence in God must be so far from superseding that it must encourage and quicken our endeavors in the way of our duty. Though it is God that performs all things for us, yet there is something to be done by us.

(2.) Hope in God is the best principle of true courage.

(3.) It is only through God, and by the influence of his grace, that we do valiantly; it is he that puts strength into us, and inspires us, who of ourselves are weak and timorous, with courage and resolution.

(4.) Though we do ever so valiantly, the success must be attributed entirely to him. All our victories, as well as our velour, are from him, and therefore at his feet all our crown must be cast.

Psalm 61

Title
To the chief Musician upon Neginah, a Psalm of David.

1 Hear my cry, O God; attend unto my prayer.
2 From the end of the earth will I cry unto thee, when my heart is overwhelmed: lead me to the rock that is higher than I.
3 For thou hast been a shelter for me, and a strong tower from the enemy.
4 I will abide in thy tabernacle for ever: I will trust in the covert of thy wings. Selah.
5 For thou, O God, hast heard my vows: thou hast given me the heritage of those that fear thy name.
6 Thou wilt prolong the king's life: and his years as many generations.
7 He shall abide before God for ever: O prepare mercy and truth, which may preserve him.
8 So will I sing praise unto thy name for ever, that I may daily perform my vows.

Psalm 61

TITLE. To the Chief Musician upon Neginah, a Psalm of David. The original indicates that both the hymn and the musical instrument were David's. He wrote the verses and himself sang them to the stringed instrument whose sound he loved so well. We have left the Psalms entitled Michtam, but we shall still find much precious meaning though the golden name be wanting. We have met with the title of this Psalm before, in Psalms 4, 6, 54, and 55, but with this difference, that in the present case the word is in the singular number: the Psalm itself is very personal, and well adapted for the private devotion of a single individual.

SUBJECT AND DIVISION. This Psalm is a pearl. It is little, but precious. To many a mourner it has furnished utterance when the mind could not have devised a speech for itself. It was evidently composed by David after he had come to the throne,—see Ps 61:6. The second verse leads us to believe that it was written during the psalmist's enforced exile from the tabernacle, which was the visible abode of God: if so, the period of Absalom's rebellion has been most suitably suggested as the date of its authorship, and Delitzsch is correct in entitling it, "Prayer and thanksgiving of an expelled King on his way back to his throne." We might divide the verses according to the sense, but it is preferable to follow the author's own arrangement, and make a break at each SELAH.

EXPOSITION

Verse 1. Hear my cry, O God. He was in terrible earnest; he shouted, he lifted up his voice on high.

Verse 2. From the end of the earth will I cry unto thee. He was banished from the spot which was the center of his delight, and at the same time his mind was in a depressed and melancholy condition; both actually and figuratively he was an outcast, yet he does not therefore restrain prayer, but rather finds therein a reason for the louder and more importunate cries.

Verse 3. For thou hast been a shelter for me. Observe how the psalmist rings the changes on, Thou hast, and I will,—Ps 61:3-6. Experience is the nurse of faith. From the past we gather arguments for present confidence.

Verse 4. I will abide in thy tabernacle for ever. Let me once get back to thy courts, and nothing shall again expel me from them: even now in my banishment my heart is there; and ever will I continue to worship thee in spirit wherever my lot may be cast.

Verse 5. For thou, O God, hast heard my vows. Proofs of divine faithfulness are to be had in remembrance, and to be mentioned to the Lord's honor.

Verse 6. Thou wilt prolong the king's life; or, better, "days to the days of the King thou wilt add." Death threatened, but God preserved his beloved.

Verse 7. He shall abide before God for ever. Though this is true of David in a modified sense, we prefer to view the Lord Jesus as here intended as the lineal descendant of David, and the representative of his royal race. Jesus is enthroned before God to eternity; here is our safety, dignity, and delight.

Verse 8. So will I sing praise unto thy name for ever. Because my prayer is answered, my song shall be perpetual; because Jesus for ever sits at thy right hand, it shall be acceptable; because I am preserved in him, it shall be grateful. David had given vocal utterance to his prayer by a cry; he will now give expression to his praise by a song: there should be a parallel between our supplications and our thanksgivings. We ought not to leap in prayer, and limp in praise. The vow to celebrate the divine name for ever is no hyperbolical piece of extravagance, but such as grace and glory shall enable us to carry out to the letter. That I may daily perform my vows. To God who adds days to our days we will devote all our days.

Psalm 61

1-4
1. Hear my cry, O God! It is not exactly ascertained at what time this psalm was composed; but there seems to be some probability in the conjecture, that David had been for a considerable period in possession of the throne before he fell into the circumstances of distress which are here mentioned. By using the term cry, he would intimate the vehemency of his desire; and it is a word which expresses inward fervency of spirit.
2. There can be no question that, by the ends of the earth, he refers to the place of his banishment, as being cut off from access to the temple and the royal city. Let those who may have been deprived of the hearing of the word, and the dispensation of the sacraments, so as, in a manner, to be banished out of the Church, learn from the example of David to persevere in crying to God, even under these solitary circumstances.
3. For thou hast been my hope. Here we may suppose, either that he calls to his remembrance such benefits as he had formerly received, or that he congratulates himself upon deliverance which he had presently experienced. There is much probability in either supposition. Nothing animates our hopes more than the recollection of the past goodness of God, and, in the midst of his prayers, we frequently find David indulging in reflections of this kind.
4. In the verse which follows, he expresses the confidence which he had that he would dwell from this time forth in the sanctuary of the Lord. By the words which immediately follow, he shows that he did not, like too many uninformed persons, attach a superstitious importance to the mere externals of religion, adding, that he found his safety under the shadow of God's wings.

5-8
5. For thou, O God! hast heard my vows. He here shows the grounds upon which he had spoken of his abiding under the wings of God. The sudden joy which he experienced arose from the circumstance of God's having heard his prayers, and made light to spring out of darkness.
6. Thou shalt add days upon days to the king etc. David cannot be considered as using these words with an exclusive reference to himself. It is true that he lived to an extreme old age, and died full of days, leaving the kingdom in a settled condition, and in the hands of his son, who succeeded him; but he did not exceed the period of one man's life, and the greater part of it was spent in continued dangers and anxieties.
7. He shall abide before the face of God for ever. This is only a simpler way of expressing what he had said before, I will abide in thy tabernacle for ever. He refers to the security and peace which he would enjoy under the protection of God.
8. In the concluding words, he expresses his resolution to persevere in the constant celebration of the praises of God, with a view to fulfilling the vows which he had contracted.

Psalm 61

1-4 Crying to God in distress.
In these verses we may observe,
I. David's close adherence and application to God by prayer in the day of his distress and trouble: "Whatever comes, I will cry unto thee (v. 2),—not cry unto other gods, but to thee only."
II. The particular petition he put up to God when his heart was overwhelmed and he was ready to sink: Lead me to the rock that is higher than I; that is,
III. His desire and expectation of an answer of peace. He begs in faith (v. 1): "Hear my cry, O God! attend unto my prayer; that is, let me have the present comfort of knowing that I am heard (Ps. xx. 6), and in due time let me have that which I pray for."
IV. The ground of this expectation, and the plea he uses to enforce his petition (v. 3): "Thou hast been a shelter for me; I have found in thee a rock higher than I: therefore I trust thou wilt still lead me to that rock."
V. His resolution to continue in the way of duty to God and dependence on him, v. 4. 1. The service of God shall be his constant work and business.

5-8 Mercies recollected.
In these verses we may observe,
I. With what pleasure David looks back upon what God had done for him formerly (v. 5): Thou, O God! hast heard my vows.
II. With what assurance he looks forward to the continuance of his life (v. 6): Thou shalt prolong the king's life.
III. With what importunity he begs of God to take him and keep him always under his protection: O prepare mercy and truth which may preserve him! God's promises and our faith in them are not to supersede, but to quicken and encourage prayer. David is sure that God will prolong his life, and therefore prays that he would preserve it, not that he would prepare him a strong lifeguard.
IV. With what cheerfulness he vows the grateful returns of duty to God (v. 8): So will I sing praise unto thy name for ever. Note, God's preservation of us calls upon us to praise him; and therefore we should desire to live, that we may praise him: Let my soul live, and it shall praise thee. That I may daily perform my vows. His praising God was itself the performance of his vows, and it disposed his heart to the performance of his vows in other instances.
Note, 1. The vows we have made we must conscientiously perform.
2. Praising God and paying our vows to him must be our constant daily work; every day we must be doing something towards it, because it is all but little in comparison with what is due, because we daily receive fresh mercies, and because, if we think much to do it daily, we cannot expect to be doing it eternally.

Psalm 62

Title
To the chief Musician, to Jeduthun, a Psalm of David.

1-6
1 Truly my soul waiteth upon God: from him cometh my salvation.
2 He only is my rock and my salvation; he is my defense; I shall not be greatly moved.
3 How long will ye imagine mischief against a man? ye shall be slain all of you: as a bowing wall shall ye be, and as a tottering fence.
4 They only consult to cast him down from his excellency: they delight in lies: they bless with their mouth, but they curse inwardly. Selah.
5 My soul, wait thou only upon God; for my expectation is from him.
6 He only is my rock and my salvation: he is my defense; I shall not be moved.

Psalm 62

TITLE. To the Chief Musician, to Jeduthun. This is the second Psalm which is dedicated to Jeduthun, or Ethan, the former one being the thirty-ninth, a Psalm which is almost a twin with this in many respects, containing in the original the word translated only four times as this does six. We shall meet with two other Psalms similarly appointed for Jeduthun: namely, Psalms 77 and 89. The sons of Jeduthun were porters or doorkeepers, according to 1Ch 16:42. Those who serve well make the best of singers, and those who occupy the highest posts in the choir must not be ashamed to wait at the posts of the doors of the Lord's house. A PSALM OF DAVID. Even had not the signature of the royal poet been here placed, we should have been sure from internal evidence that he alone penned these stanzas; they are truly Davidic. From the six fold use of the word ac or only, we have been wont to call it THE ONLY PSALM.
DIVISION. The Psalmist has marked his own pauses, by inserting SELAH at the end of Ps 62:4,8. His true and sole confidence in God laughs to scorn all its enemies. When this Psalm was composed it was not necessary for us to know, since true faith is always in season, and is usually under trial. Moreover, the sentiments here uttered are suitable to occasions which are very frequent in a believer's life, and therefore no one historic incident is needful for their explanation.

EXPOSITION
Verse 1. Truly, or verily, or only. The last is probably the most prominent sense here. That faith alone is true which rests on God alone, that confidence which relies but partly on the Lord is vain confidence. If we Anglicized the word by our word verily, as some do, we should have here a striking reminder of our blessed Lord's frequent use of that adverb. My soul waiteth upon God. My inmost self draws near in reverent obedience to God. I am no hypocrite or mere posture maker.
Verse 2. He only is my rock and my salvation. Sometimes a metaphor may be more full of meaning and more suggestive than literal speech: hence the use of the figure of a rock, the very mention of which would awaken grateful memories in the psalmist's mind. David had often lain concealed in rocky caverns, and here he compares his God to such a secure refuge; and, indeed, declares him to be his only real protection, all-sufficient in himself and never failing.
Verse 3. How long will ye imagine mischief against a man? It is always best to begin with God, and then we may confront our enemies. Make all sure with heaven, then may you grapple with earth and hell. David expostulates with his insensate foes; he marvels at their dogged perseverance in malice, after so many failures and with certain defeat before them. He tells them that their design was an imaginary one, which they never could accomplish however deeply they might plot.
Verse 4. They only consult to cast him down from his excellency. The excellencies of the righteous are obnoxious to the wicked, and the main object of their fury. The elevation which God gives to the godly in Providence, or in dispute, is also the envy of the baser sort, and they labor to pull them down to their own level.
Verse 5. My soul, wait thou only upon God. When we have already practiced a virtue, it is yet needful that we bind ourselves to a continuance in it. The soul is apt to be dragged away from its anchorage, or is readily tempted to add a second confidence to the one sole and sure ground of reliance; we must, therefore, stir ourselves up to maintain the holy position which we were at first able to assume.
Verse 6. He only is my rock and my salvation. Alone, and without other help, God is the foundation and completion of my safety. We cannot too often hear the toll of that great bell only; let it ring the death knell of all carnal reliances, and lead us to cast ourselves on the bare arm of God.

JOHN CALVIN

Psalm 62

1-2

1. Nevertheless, my soul is silent towards God. We know that the Lord's people cannot always reach such a measure of composure as to be wholly exempt from distraction. They would wish to receive the word of the Lord with submission, and to be dumb under his correcting hand; but inordinate affections will take possession of their minds, and break in upon that peace which they might otherwise attain to in the exercise of faith and resignation.

2. The believer triumphs in one encounter with temptation only to enter upon another; and here David, who appeared to have emerged from his distress, shows that he had still to struggle with remaining difficulties. We meet with the same particle no fewer than six times throughout the psalm. This, too, may explain the many titles which he applies to God, each of which is to be considered as a foil by which he would ward off the attacks of the tempter.

3-6

3. How long will ye continue mischief? The sense of the passage seems to be, How long will ye meditate evil against a man, and persist in mischievous devices for accomplishing his ruin? He has in view the obstinate malice of his enemies, moving every stone for his destruction, and forming new plans daily for effecting it.

4. Yet they consult to cast him down from his elevation. David, on the one hand, encouraged himself by determining to rest steadfastly upon the promise of divine favor; but, upon the other, he had before him the machinations of his enemies, characterized by cruelty, audacity, pride, and deceit.

5. Nevertheless, my soul, be thou silent before God. His soul was silent before God; and where the necessity of this new silence, as if still under agitation of spirit? Here it is to be remembered, that our minds can never be expected to reach such perfect composure as shall preclude every inward feeling of disquietude, but are, at the best, as the sea before a light breeze, fluctuating sensibly, though not swollen into billows.

7-10

7. In God is my salvation. One expression is here heaped upon another and this apparently because he wished to rein that infirmity of disposition which makes us so prone to slide into wrong exercise. We may throw out a passing and occasional acknowledgement, that our only help is to be found in God, and yet shortly display our distrust in him by busying ourselves in all directions to supplement what we consider defective in his aid. The various terms which he employs to express the sufficiency of God as a deliverer, may thus be considered as so many arguments to constancy, or so many checks which he would apply to the waywardness of the carnal heart, ever disposed to depend for support upon others rather than God.

8.David is here to be considered as exposing that diseased but deeply-rooted principle in our nature, which leads us to hide

MATTHEW HENRY

Psalm 62

1-7 Waiting upon God; confidence in God.

In these verses we have,

I. David's profession of dependence upon God, and upon him only, for all good (v. 1): Truly my soul waiteth upon God. Nevertheless (so some) or "However it be, whatever difficulties or dangers I may meet with, though God frown upon me and I meet with discouragements in my attendance on him, yet still my soul waits upon God" (or is silent to God, as the word is), "Says nothing against what he does, but quietly expects what he will do."

II. The ground and reason of this dependence (v. 2): He only is my rock and my salvation; he is my defense.

III. The improvement he makes of his confidence in God.

1. Trusting in God, his heart is fixed. "If God is my strength and mighty deliverer, I shall not be greatly moved (that is, I shall not be undone and ruined); I may be shocked, but I shall not be sunk." This hope in God will be an anchor of the soul, sure and steadfast.

2. His enemies are slighted, and all their attempts against him looked upon by him with contempt, v. 3, 4. If God be for us, we need not fear what man can do against us, though ever so mighty and malicious. He here,

(1.) Gives a character of his enemies: They imagine mischief, design it with a great deal of the serpent's venom and contrive it with a great deal of the serpent's subtlety, and this against a man, one of their own kind, against one single man, that is not an equal match for them, for they are many; they continued their malicious persecution though Providence had often defeated their mischievous designs.

(2.) He reads their doom, pronounces a sentence of death upon them, not as a king, but as a prophet: You shall be slain all of you, by the righteous judgments of God. Saul and his servants were slain by the Philistines on Mount Gilboa, according to this prediction. Those who seek the ruin of God's chosen are but preparing ruin for themselves.

3. He is himself encouraged to continue waiting upon God (v. 5-7): My soul, wait thou only upon God. Note, The good we do we should stir up ourselves to continue doing, and to do yet more and more, as those that have, through grace, experienced the comfort and benefit of it.

8-12 An exhortation to trust in God.

Here we have David's exhortation to others to trust in God and wait upon him, as he had done. Those that have found the comfort of the ways of God themselves will invite others into those ways; there is enough in God for all the saints to draw from, and we shall have never the less for others sharing with us.

Psalm 62

7-12
7 In God is my salvation and my glory: the rock of my strength, and my refuge, is in God.
8 Trust in him at all times; ye people, pour out your heart before him: God is a refuge for us. Selah.
9 Surely men of low degree are vanity, and men of high degree are a lie: to be laid in the balance, they are altogether lighter than vanity.
10 Trust not in oppression, and become not vain in robbery: if riches increase, set not your heart upon them.
11 God hath spoken once; twice have I heard this; that power belongeth unto God.
12 Also unto thee, O Lord, belongeth mercy: for thou renderest to every man according to his work.

Verse 7. In God is my salvation and my glory. Wherein should we glory but in him who saves us? Our honor may well be left with him who secures our souls. To find all in God, and to glory that it is so, is one of the sure marks of an enlightened soul. The rock of my strength, and my refuge, is in God. He multiplies titles, for he would render much honor to the Lord, whom he had tried, and proved to be a faithful God under so many aspects. Ignorance needs but few words, but when experience brings a wealth of knowledge, we need varied expressions to serve as coffers for our treasure. God who is our rock when we flee for shelter, is also our strong rock when we stand firm and defy the foe; he is to be praised under both characters.
Verse 8. Trust in him at all times. Faith is an abiding duty, a perpetual privilege. We should trust when we can see, as well as when we are utterly in the dark. Adversity is a fit season for faith; but prosperity is not less so. God at all times deserves our confidence. We at all times need to place our confidence in him. A day without trust in God is a day of wrath, even if it be a day of mirth. Lean ever, ye saints, on him, on whom the world leans.
Verse 9. Surely men of low degree are vanity. Here the word is only again; men of low degree are only vanity, nothing more. They are many and enthusiastic, but they are not to be depended on; they are mobile as the waves of the sea, ready to be driven to and fro by any and every wind; they cry "Hosanna" today, and "Crucify him" tomorrow. The instability of popular applause is a proverb; as well build a house with smoke as find comfort in the adulation of the multitude.
Verse 10. Trust not in oppression, and become not vain in robbery. Wealth ill gotten is the trust only of fools, for the deadly pest lies in it; it is full of canker, it reeks with God's curse. To tread down the poor and silence their cries for justice, is the delight of many a braggart bully, who in his arrogance imagines that he may defy both God and man; but he is warned in these words, and it will be well for him if he takes the warning.
Verse 11. God hath spoken once. So immutable is God that he need not speak twice, as though he had changed; so infallible, that one utterance suffices, for he cannot err; so omnipotent, that his solitary word achieves all his designs. We speak often and say nothing; God speaks once and utters eternal verities. All our speaking may yet end in sound; but he speaks, and it is done; he commands, and it stands fast.
Verse 12. Also unto thee, O Lord, belongeth mercy. This tender attribute sweetens the grand thought of his power: the divine strength will not crush us, but will be used for our good. God is so full of mercy that it belongs to him, as if all the mercy in the universe came from God, and still was claimed by him as his possession. His mercy, like his power, endureth for ever, and is ever present in him, ready to be revealed, For thou renderest to every man according to his work. This looks rather like justice than mercy; but if we understand it to mean that God graciously rewards the poor, imperfect works of his people, we see in it a clear display of mercy. May it not also mean that according to the work he allots us is the strength which he renders to us? he is not a hard master; he does not bid us make bricks without straw, but he metes out to us strength equal to our day. In either meaning we have power and mercy blended, and have a double reason for waiting only upon God. Man neither helps us nor rewards us; God will do both. In him power and grace are eternally resident; our faith should therefore patiently hope and quietly wait, for we shall surely see the salvation of God. Deo soli gloria. All glory be to God only.

JOHN CALVIN

our griefs, and ruminate upon them, instead of relieving ourselves at once by pouring out our prayers and complaints before God. The consequence is, that we are distracted more and more with our distresses, and merge into a state of hopeless despondency.

9. Nevertheless, the sons of Adam are vanity. It is only when allied with the knowledge of God that any of the endowments conferred upon us from above can be said to have a real excellency;—apart from this, they are vitiated by that contagion of sin which has not left a vestige in man of his original integrity. With too much justice, then, might David say that all men are vanity and nothingness.

10. Trust not in oppression and robbery. We are here taught that there can be no real trusting in God until we put away all those vain confidences which prove so many means of turning us away from him. The Psalmist bids us remove whatsoever would have this tendency, and purge ourselves of every vicious desire that would usurp the place of God in our hearts.

To set the heart upon riches, means more than simply to covet the possession of them. It implies being carried away by them into a false confidence, or, to use an expression of Paul, "Being high-minded." The admonition here given is one which daily observation teaches us to be necessary. It is uniformly seen that prosperity and abundance engender a haughty spirit, leading men at once to be presumptuous in their carriage before God, and reckless in inflicting injury upon their fellow-creatures. But, indeed, the worst effect to be feared from a blind and ungoverned spirit of this kind is, that, in the intoxication of outward greatness, we be left to forget how frail we are, and proudly and contumeliously to exalt ourselves against God.

11-12

11. God hath spoken once. The Psalmist considered that the only effectual method of abstracting the minds of men from the vain delusions in which they are disposed to trust, was bringing them to acquiesce implicitly and firmly in the judgment of God. Usually they are swayed in different directions, or inclined at least to waver, just as they observe things changing in the world; but he brings under their notice a surer principle for the regulation of their conduct, when he recommends a deferential regard to God's Word. God himself "dwells in the light which is inaccessible," (1 Timothy 6:16;) and as none can come to him except by faith, the Psalmist calls our attention to his word, in which he testifies the truth of his divine and righteous government of the world.

12. The Psalmist adds, Thou wilt certainly render to every man according to his work. Since the Scriptures promise a reward to the saints, with the sole intention of stimulating their minds, and encouraging them in the divine warfare, and not with the remotest design of derogating from the mercy of God, it is absurd to allege that in any sense merit can be bestowed by God on people as a result of them doing good deeds. As regards the wicked, none will dispute that the punishment awarded to them, as violators of the law, is strictly deserved.

MATTHEW HENRY

I. He counsels all to wait upon God, as he did, v. 8. Observe,

1. To whom he gives this good counsel: You people (that is, all people); all shall be welcome to trust in God, for he is the confidence of all the ends of the earth, Ps. lxv. 5.

2. What the good counsel is which he gives.

(1.) To confide in God: "Trust in him; deal with him, and be willing to deal upon trust; depend upon him to perform all things for you, upon his wisdom and goodness, his power and promise, his providence and grace. Do this at all times."

(2.) To converse with God: Pour out your heart before him. The expression seems to allude to the pouring out of the drink-offerings before the Lord. When we make a penitent confession of sin our hearts are therein poured out before God, 1 Sam. vii. 6. But here it is meant of prayer, which, if it be as it should be, is the pouring out of the heart before God. We must lay our grievances before him, offer up our desires to him with all humble freedom, and then entirely refer ourselves to his disposal, patiently submitting our wills to his: this is pouring out our hearts.

3. What encouragement he gives us to take this good counsel: God is a refuge for us, not only my refuge (v. 7), but a refuge for us all, even as many as will flee to him and take shelter in him.

II. He cautions us to take heed of misplacing our confidence, in which, as much as in any thing, the heart is deceitful, Jer. xvii. 5-9. Those that trust in God truly (v. 1) will trust in him only, v. 5.

1. Let us not trust in the men of this world, for they are broken reeds (v. 9): Surely men of low degree are vanity, utterly unable to help us, and men of high degree are a lie, that will deceive us if we trust to them.

2. Let us not trust in the wealth of this world, let not that be made our strong city (v. 10): Trust not in oppression; that is, in riches got by fraud and violence, because where there is a great deal it is commonly got by indirect scraping or saving (our Savior calls it the mammon of unrighteousness, Luke xvi. 9), or in the arts of getting riches.

III. He gives a very good reason why we should make God our confidence, because he is a God of infinite power, mercy, and righteousness, v. 11, 12. This he himself was well assured of and would have us be assured of it: God has spoken once; twice have I heard this; that is, "God has spoken it, and I have heard it, once, yea, twice. He has spoken it, and I have heard it by the light of reason, which easily infers it from the nature of the infinitely perfect Being and from his works both of creation and providence. He has spoken it, and I have heard once, yea, twice (that is, many a time), by the events that have concerned me in particular. He has spoken it and I have heard it by the light of revelation, by dreams and visions (Job xiii. 15), by the glorious manifestation of himself upon Mount Sinai" (to which, some think, it does especially refer), "and by the written word."

Psalm 63

Title
A Psalm of David, when he was in the wilderness of Judah.

1-5
1 O God, thou art my God; early will I seek thee: my soul thirsteth for thee, my flesh longeth for thee in a dry and thirsty land, where no water is;
2 To see thy power and thy glory, so as I have seen thee in the sanctuary.
3 Because thy loving kindness is better than life, my lips shall praise thee.
4 Thus will I bless thee while I live: I will lift up my hands in thy name.
5 My soul shall be satisfied as with marrow and fatness; and my mouth shall praise thee with joyful lips:

Psalm 63

TITLE. A Psalm of David, when he was in the wilderness of Judah. This was probably written while David was fleeing from Absalom; certainly at the time he wrote it he was king (Ps 63:11), and hard pressed by those who sought his life. David did not leave off singing because he was in the wilderness, neither did he in slovenly idleness go on repeating Psalms intended for other occasions; but he carefully made his worship suitable to his circumstances, and presented to his God a wilderness hymn when he was in the wilderness. There was no desert in his heart, though there was a desert around him. We too may expect to be cast into rough places ere we go hence. In such seasons, may the Eternal Comforter abide with us, and cause us to bless the Lord at all times, making even the solitary place to become a temple for Jehovah. The distinguishing word of this Psalm is EARLY. When the bed is the softest we are most tempted to rise at lazy hours; but when comfort is gone, and the couch is hard, if we rise the earlier to seek the Lord, we have much for which to thank the wilderness.
DIVISION. In Ps 63:1-8 verses the writer expresses his holy desires after God, and his confidence in him, and then in Ps 63:9-11 remaining three verses he prophesies the overthrow of all his enemies. This Psalm is peculiarly suitable for the bed of sickness, or in any constrained absence from public worship.

EXPOSITION
Verse 1. O God, thou art my God; or, O God, thou art my Mighty One. The last Psalm left the echo of power ringing in the ear, and it is here remembered. Strong affiance bids the fugitive poet confess his allegiance to the only living God; and firm faith enables him to claim him as his own. He has no doubts about his possession of his God; and why should other believers have any? The straightforward, clear language of this opening sentence would be far more becoming in Christians than the timorous and doubtful expressions so usual among professors. How sweet is such language!
My soul thirsteth for thee. Thirst is an insatiable longing after that which is one of the most essential supports of life; there is no reasoning with it, no forgetting it, no despising it, no overcoming it by stoical indifference. Thirst will be heard; the whole man must yield to its power; even thus is it with that divine desire which the grace of God creates in regenerate men; only God himself can satisfy the craving of a soul really aroused by the Holy Spirit.
My flesh longeth for thee; by the two words soul and flesh, he denotes the whole of his being. The flesh, in the New Testament sense of it, never longs after the Lord, but rather it lusteth against the spirit; David only refers to that sympathy which is sometimes created in our bodily frame by vehement emotions of the soul.
Verse 2. To see thy power and thy glory, so as I have seen thee in the sanctuary. He longed not so much to see the sanctuary as to see his God; he looked through the veil of ceremonies to the invisible One. Often had his heart been gladdened by communion with God in the outward ordinances, and for this great blessing he sighs again; as well he might, for it is the weightiest of all earth's sorrows for a Christian man to lose the conscious presence of his covenant God. He remembers and mentions the two attributes which had most impressed themselves upon his mind when he had been rapt in adoration in the holy place; upon these his mind had dwelt in the preceding Psalm, and the savor of that contemplation is evidently upon his heart when in the wilderness: these he desires to behold again in the place of his banishment. It is a precious thought that the divine power and glory are not confined in their manifestation to any places or localities; they are to be heard above the roaring of the sea, seen amid the glare of the tempest, felt in the forest and the prairie, and enjoyed wherever there is a heart that longs and thirsts to behold them.

JOHN CALVIN

Psalm 63

The following psalm cannot so properly be said to consist of prayers as of a variety of pious meditations, which comforted the mind of David under dangers, anxieties, and troubles of a severe description. It contains the vows too which he made to God in the distress occasioned by the alarming circumstances in which he was placed.

1-4

1. O God! thou art my God. The wilderness of Judah, spoken of in the title, can be no other than that of Ziph, where David wandered so long in a state of concealment. We may rely upon the truth of the record he gives us of his exercise when under his trials; and it is apparent that he never allowed himself to be so far overcome by them, as to cease lifting up his prayers to heaven, and even resting, with a firm and constant faith, upon the divine promises. Apt as we are, when assaulted by the very slightest trials, to lose the comfort of any knowledge of God we may previously have possessed, it is necessary that we should notice this, and learn, by his example, to struggle to maintain our confidence under the worst troubles that can befall us. He does more than simply pray; he sets the Lord before him as his God, that he may throw all his cares unhesitatingly upon him, deserted as he was of man, and a poor outcast in the waste and howling wilderness.

2. Thus in the sanctuary, etc. It is apparent that God was ever in his thoughts, though wandering in the wilderness under such circumstances of destitution. He was well aware that he needed such helps to devotion. But now, when shut out, in the providence of God, from any such privilege, he shows, by the delight which he took in spiritual views of God, that his was not a mind engrossed with the symbols, or mere outward ceremonial of religion. He gives evidence how much he had profited by the devotional exercises enjoined under that dispensation. It is noticeable of ignorant and superstitious persons, that they seem full of zeal and fervor so long as they come in contact with the ceremonies of religion, while their seriousness evaporates immediately upon these being withdrawn. David, on the contrary, when these were removed, continued to retain them in his recollection, and rise, through their assistance, to fervent aspirations after God. We may learn by this, when deprived at any time of the outward means of grace, to direct the eye of our faith to God in the worst circumstances, and not to forget him whenever the symbols of holy things are taken out of our sight. The great truth, for example, of our spiritual regeneration, though but once represented to us in baptism, should remain fixed in our minds through our whole life, (Titus 3:5; Ephesians 5:26.)

3. Because thy mercy is better than life, etc. David would appear to be giving the reason of his earnestness in desiring God. By life is to be understood, in general, everything which men use for their own maintenance and defense. When we think ourselves well provided otherwise, we feel no disposition

MATTHEW HENRY

Psalm 63

1-2 Devout affections.

The title tells us when the psalm was penned, when David was in the wilderness of Judah; that is, in the forest of Hareth (1 Sam. xxii. 5) or in the wilderness of Ziph, 1 Sam. xxiii. 15.

1. Even in Canaan, though a fruitful land and the people numerous, yet there were wildernesses, places less fruitful and less inhabited than other places. It will be so in the world, in the church, but not in heaven; there it is all city, all paradise, and no desert ground; the wilderness there shall blossom as the rose.

2. The best and dearest of God's saints and servants may sometimes have their lot cast in a wilderness, which speaks them lonely and solitary, desolate and afflicted, wanting, wandering, and unsettled, and quite at a loss what to do with themselves.

3. All the straits and difficulties of a wilderness must not put us out of tune for sacred songs; but even then it is our duty and interest to keep up a cheerful communion with God. There are psalms proper for a wilderness, and we have reason to thank God that it is the wilderness of Judah we are in, not the wilderness of Sin.

David, in these verses, stirs up himself to take hold on God,

I. By a lively active faith: O God! thou art my God. Note, In all our addresses to God we must eye him as God, and our God, and this will be our comfort in a wilderness-state. We must acknowledge that God is, that we speak to one that really exists and is present with us, when we say, O God! which is a serious word; pity it should ever be used as a by-word.

II. By pious and devout affections, pursuant to the choice he had made of God and the covenant he had made with him.

1. He resolves to seek God, and his favor and grace: Thou art my God, and therefore I will seek thee; for should not a people seek unto their God? Isa. viii. 19.

2. He longs to enjoy God. What is it that he does so passionately wish for? What is his petition and what is his request? It is this (v. 2), To see thy power and thy glory, so as I have seen thee in the sanctuary.

3-6 Joyful praises.

How soon are David's complaints and prayers turned into praises and thanksgivings! After two verses that express his desire in seeking God, here are some that express his joy and satisfaction in having found him. Observe,

I. What David will praise God for (v. 3): Because thy lovingkindness is better than life, than lives, life and all the comforts of life, life in its best estate, long life and prosperity.

II. How he will praise God, and how long, v. 4. He resolves to live a life of thankfulness to God and dependence on him.

Psalm 63

6-11
6 When I remember thee upon my bed, and meditate on thee in the night watches.
7 Because thou hast been my help, therefore in the shadow of thy wings will I rejoice.
8 My soul followeth hard after thee: thy right hand upholdeth me.
9 But those that seek my soul, to destroy it, shall go into the lower parts of the earth.
10 They shall fall by the sword: they shall be a portion for foxes.
11 But the king shall rejoice in God; every one that sweareth by him shall glory: but the mouth of them that speak lies shall be stopped.

Verse 3. Because thy lovingkindness is better than life. A reason for that which went before, as well as for that which follows. Life is dear, but God's love is dearer. To dwell with God is better than life at its best; life at ease, in a palace, in health, in honor, in wealth, in pleasure; yea, a thousand lives are not equal to the eternal life which abides in Jehovah's smile.
Verse 4. Thus will I bless thee while I live. As I now bless thee so will I ever do; or rather, so as thou shalt reveal thy lovingkindness to me, I will in return continue to extol thee. While we live we will love. If we see no cause to rejoice in our estate, we shall always have reason for rejoicing in the Lord. If none others bless God, yet his people will; his very nature, as being the infinitely good God, is a sufficient argument for our praising him as long as we exist.
Verse 5. My soul shall be satisfied as with marrow and fatness. Though unable to feast on the sacrifice at thine altar, my soul shall even here be filled with spiritual joys, and shall possess a complete, a double contentment. There is in the love of God a richness, a sumptuousness, a fullness of soul filling joy, comparable to the richest food with which the body can be nourished.
Verse 6. When I remember thee upon my bed. Lying awake, the good man betook himself to meditation, and then began to sing. He had a feast in the night, and a song in the night. He turned his bedchamber into an oratory, he consecrated his pillow, his praise anticipated the place of which it is written, "There is no night there." Perhaps the wilderness helped to keep him awake, and if so, all the ages are debtors to it for this delightful hymn.
Verse 7. Because thou hast been my help. Meditation had refreshed his memory and recalled to him his past deliverances. It were well if we oftener read our own diaries, especially noting the hand of the Lord in helping us in suffering, want, labor, or dilemma. This is the grand use of memory, to furnish us with proofs of the Lord's faithfulness, and lead us onward to a growing confidence in him.
Verse 8. My soul followeth hard after thee, or is glued to thee. We follow close at the Lord's heels, because we are one with him. Who shall divide us from his love? If we cannot walk with him with equal footsteps, we will at least follow after with all the strength he lends us, earnestly panting to reach him and abide in his fellowship.
Verse 9. As David earnestly sought for God, so there were men of another order who as eagerly sought after his blood; of these he speaks: But those that seek my soul, to destroy it. At his life they aimed, at his honor, his best welfare; and this they would not merely injure but utterly ruin.
Verse 10. They shall fall by the sword. So David's enemies did. They that take the sword shall perish with the sword; bloody men shall feel their own life gushing forth from them, when their evil day shall at last come, and they shall be given up to feel in their own persons the horrors of death.
Verse 11. But the king shall rejoice in God. Usurpers shall fade, but he shall flourish; and his prosperity shall be publicly acknowledged as the gift of God. The Lord's anointed shall not fail to offer his joyful thanksgiving: his well established throne shall own the superior lordship of the King of kings; his rejoicing shall be alone in God. When his subjects sing, "Io triumphe," he will bid them chant, "Te Deum." Every one that sweareth by him shall glory. His faithful followers shall have occasion for triumph; they shall never need to blush for the oath of their allegiance. Or, "swearing by him," may signify adherence to God, and worship paid to him.

JOHN CALVIN

to have recourse to the mercy of God. That being (to speak so) which we have of our own, prevents us from seeing that we live through the mere grace of God.
4. In the lifting up of hands, in the second clause of the verse, allusion is made to praying and vowing; and he intimates, that besides giving thanks to God, he would acquire additional confidence in supplication, and be diligent in the exercise of it. Any experience we may have of the divine goodness, while it stirs us up to gratitude, should, at the same time, strengthen our hopes of the future, and lead us confidently to expect that God will perfect the grace which he has begun.

5-8
5. My soul shall be satisfied as with marrow, etc. In accordance with what was said in the foregoing verse, David expresses his assured persuasion of obtaining a rich and abundant measure of every blessing that could call for thanksgiving and praise. At the period of composing this psalm, he may have been already in the enjoyment of ease and plenty; but there is reason to believe that he cherished the persuasion referred to, even when wandering in the wilderness in a state of poverty and destitution. If we would evidence a strong faith, we must anticipate the divine favor before it has been actually manifested, and when there is no present appearance of its forthcoming.
6. I shall surely remember thee, etc. He particularly mentions the night watches, as, when retired from the sight of our fellow-creatures, we not only revert to what may have given us anxiety, but feel our thoughts drawn out more freely to different subjects. We have next the reason assigned for the engagement or declaration he has just made, which is, that he owed to God his preservation. The experience of the divine goodness should dispose us to prayer as well as praise. "I will come into thy house," says the Psalmist in another place, "in the multitude of thy mercy," (Psalm 5:7.)
7. The second part of the seventh verse is expressive of the lively hope with which he was animated. He was resolved to rejoice and triumph under the shadow of God's wings, as feeling the same peace and satisfaction in reliance upon his protection as he could have done had no danger existed.
8. My soul has cleaved hard after thee. The Hebrew verb means also to apprehend, or follow, especially when in construction with the preposition which is here joined to it, and therefore we might very properly render the words,—My soul shall press or follow after thee. The sense is, that David's heart was devoted to God with steadfast perseverance. The phrase, after thee, is emphatic, and denotes that he would follow with unwearied constancy, long as the way might be, and full of hardships, and beset with obstacles, and however sovereignly God might himself seem to withdraw his presence. The latter clause of the verse may be taken as referring simply to the deliverance which he had previously mentioned as having been received. He had good reason to persevere, without fainting, in following after God, when he considered that he had been preserved in safety, up to this time, by the divine hand.

MATTHEW HENRY

III. With what pleasure and delight he would praise God, v. 5.
IV. How he would entertain himself with thoughts of God when he was most retired (v. 6): I will praise thee when I remember thee upon my bed. We must praise God upon every remembrance of him.
Observe here,
1. How David employed himself in thinking of God. God was in all his thoughts, which is the reverse of the wicked man's character, Ps. x. 4.
2. When David employed himself thus—upon his bed and in the night-watches. David was now wandering and unsettled, but, wherever he came, he brought his religion along with him. Upon my beds (so some); being hunted by Saul, he seldom lay two nights together in the same bed; but wherever he lay, if, as Jacob, upon the cold ground and with a stone for his pillow, good thoughts of God lay down with him.

7-11 Confidence in God; David triumphing in hope.
David, having expressed his desires towards God and his praises of him, here expresses his confidence in him and his joyful expectations from him (v. 7): In the shadow of thy wings I will rejoice, alluding either to the wings of the cherubim stretched out over the ark of the covenant, between which God is said to dwell. Now let us see further,
I. What were the supports and encouragements of David's confidence in God. Two things were as props to that hope which the word of God was the only foundation of:
1. His former experiences of God's power in relieving him: "Because thou hast been my help when other helps and helpers failed me, therefore I will still rejoice in thy salvation, will trust in thee for the future, and will do it with delight and holy joy."
2. The present sense he had of God's grace carrying him on in these pursuits (v. 8): My soul follows hard after thee, which speaks a very earnest desire and a serious vigorous endeavor to keep up communion with God.
II. What it was that David triumphed in the hopes of.
1. That his enemies should be ruined, v. 9, 10. There were those that sought his soul to destroy it, not only his life, but his soul, which they sought to destroy by banishing him from God's ordinances.
2. That he himself should gain his point at last (v. 11), that he should be advanced to the throne to which he had been anointed: The king shall rejoice in God. He calls himself the king, because he knew himself to be so in the divine purpose and designation; thus Paul, while yet in the conflict, writes himself more than a conqueror, Rom. viii. 37. Believers are made kings, though they are not to have the dominion till the morning of the resurrection.

Psalm 64

Title
To the chief Musician. A Psalm of David.

1-5
1 Hear my voice, O God, in my prayer: preserve my life from fear of the enemy.
2 Hide me from the secret counsel of the wicked; from the insurrection of the workers of iniquity:
3 Who whet their tongue like a sword, and bend their bows to shoot their arrows, even bitter words:
4 That they may shoot in secret at the perfect: suddenly do they shoot at him, and fear not.
5 They encourage themselves in an evil matter: they commune of laying snares privily; they say, Who shall see them?

Psalm 64

TITLE. To the Chief Musician. The leader of the choir, for the time being, is charged with this song. It were well if the chief musicians of all our congregations estimated their duty at its due solemnity, for it is no mean thing to be called to lead the sacred song of God's people, and the responsibility is by no means light. A Psalm of David. His life was one of conflict, and very seldom does he finish a Psalm without mentioning his enemies; in this instance his thoughts are wholly occupied with prayer against them.
DIVISION. From Ps 64:1-6 he describes the cruelty and craftiness of his foes, and from Ps 64:7-10 he prophesies their overthrow.

EXPOSITION
Verse 1. Hear my voice, O God, in my prayer. It often helps devotion if we are able to use the voice and speak audibly; but even mental prayer has a voice with God which he will hear. We do not read that Moses had spoken with his lips at the Red Sea, and yet the Lord said to him, "Why criest thou unto me?" Prayers which are unheard on earth may be among the best heard in heaven. It is our duty to note how constantly David turns to prayer; it is his battle axe and weapon of war; he uses it under every pressure, whether of inward sin or outward wrath, foreign invasion or domestic rebellion. We shall act wisely if we make prayer to God our first and best trusted resource in every hour of need. Preserve my life from fear of the enemy. From harm and dread of harm protect me; or it may be read as an expression of his assurance that it would be so; "from fear of the foe thou wilt preserve me." With all our sacrifices of prayer we should offer the salt of faith.
Verse 2. Hide me from the secret counsel of the wicked. From their hidden snares hide me. Circumvent their counsel; let their secrets be met by thy secret providence, their counsels of malice by thy counsels of love. From the insurrection of the workers of iniquity. When their secret counsels break forth into clamorous tumults, be thou still my preserver. When they think evil, let thy divine thoughts defeat them; and when they do evil, let thy powerful justice overthrow them: in both cases, let me be out of reach of their cruel hand, and even out of sight of their evil eye.
Verse 3. Who whet their tongue like a sword. Slander has ever been the master weapon of the good man's enemies, and great is the care of the malicious to use it effectively. As warriors grind their swords, to give them an edge which will cut deep and wound desperately, so do the unscrupulous invent falsehoods which shall be calculated to inflict pain, to stab the reputation, to kill the honor of the righteous.
Verse 4. That they may shoot in secret at the perfect. They lie in ambush, with bows ready bent to aim a coward's shaft at the upright man. Sincere and upright conduct will not secure us from the assaults of slander. The devil shot at our Lord himself, and we may rest assured he has a fiery dart in reserve for us; He was absolutely perfect, we are only so in a relative sense, hence in us there is fuel for fiery darts to kindle on. Observe the meanness of malicious men; they will not accept fair combat, they shun the open field, and skulk in the bushes, lying in ambush against those who are not so acquainted with deceit as to suspect their treachery, and are to manly to imitate their despicable modes of warfare.
Verse 5. They encourage themselves in an evil matter. Good men are frequently discouraged, and not infrequently discourage one another, but the children of darkness are wise in their generation and keep their spirits up, and each one has a cheering word to say to his fellow villain. Anything by which they can strengthen each other's hands in their one common design they resort to; their hearts are thoroughly in their black work. They commune of laying snares privily. Laying their heads together they count

JOHN CALVIN

Psalm 64

This psalm expresses the language of complaint and prayer. David, in order that he may incline God to compassionate his case, dwells upon the injustice and cruelty, the intrigues and deceitfulness of his enemies. At the close, his eyes are directed to God, in the anticipation of a joyful deliverance from their hands.

1-6

1. Hear my voice, O God! He begins by saying that he prayed earnestly, and with vehemence, stating, at the same time, what rendered this necessary. The voice is heard in prayer, proportionally to the earnestness and ardor which we feel. He condescends upon the circumstances of distress in which he was presently placed, and takes notice of the dangers to which his life was exposed from enemies, with other points fitted to excite the favorable consideration of God. His praying that God would protect his life, proves that it must have been in danger at this time.

2. In the second verse, he intimates that his enemies were numerous; and that, without divine assistance, he would be unable to sustain their attacks. His language implies that he looked upon the protection of heaven as amply sufficient against the greatest combination of adversaries. I may add, that there is an implied plea for strengthening his cause in prayer, in what he says of the malice and wickedness of those who were opposed to him; for the more cruel and unjust the conduct of our enemies may be, we have proportionally the better ground to believe that God will interpose in our behalf.

3. For they have whetted their tongue like a sword. His enemies, in their rage, aimed at nothing less than his life, and yet what he complains of, more than all beside, is the poison with which their words were imbued. It is probable that he refers to the calumnious reports which he knew to be falsely spread to his discredit, and with a view of damaging his reputation with the people. Their tongues he likens to swords; their bitter and venomous words to arrows. And when he adds, that, they shoot against the upright and innocent, he is to be considered as contrasting his integrity with their unprincipled conduct.

4. In mentioning that they shoot secretly and suddenly, he refers to the craft which characterized them. They were not only eagerly bent upon mischief, and intent in watching their opportunities, but so expert and quick in their movements, as to smite their victim before he could suspect danger. When we hear that David, who was a man in every respect so much more holy and upright in his conduct than ourselves, suffered from groundless aspersions upon his character, we have no reason to be surprised that we should be exposed to a similar trial. This comfort, at least, we always have, that we can betake ourselves to God, and obtain his defense of the upright cause.

5. They assure themselves in an evil work. He proceeds to complain of the perverse determination with which they pursued their wickedness, and of their combinations amongst themselves; remarking, at the same time, upon the confidence

MATTHEW HENRY

Psalm 64

1-6 Malice of David's enemies.

David, in these verses, puts in before God a representation of his own danger and of his enemies' character, to enforce his petition that God would protect him and punish them.

I. He earnestly begs of God to preserve him (v. 1, 2): Hear my voice, O God! in my prayer; that is, grant me the thing I pray for, and this is it, Lord, preserve my life from fear of the enemy, that is, from the enemy that I am in fear of. He makes request for his life, which is, in a particular manner, dear to him, because he knows it is designed to be very serviceable to God and his generation.

II. He complains of the great malice and wickedness of his enemies: "Lord, hide me from them, for they are the worst of men, not fit to be connived at; they are dangerous men, that will stick at nothing; so that I am undone if thou do not take my part."

1. They are very spiteful in their calumnies and reproaches, v. 3, 4. They are described as military men, with their sword and bow, archers that take aim exactly, secretly, and suddenly, and shoot at the harmless bird that apprehends not herself in any danger.

2. They are very close and very resolute in their malicious projects, v. 5.

(1.) They strengthen and corroborate themselves and one another in this evil matter, and by joining together in it they make one another the more bitter and the more bold.

(2.) They consult with themselves and one another how to do the most mischief and most effectually: They commune of laying snares privily.

(3.) They please themselves with an atheistic conceit that God himself takes no notice of their wicked practices.

3. They are very industrious in putting their projects in execution (v. 6): "They search out iniquity; they take a great deal of pains to find out some iniquity or other to lay to my charge; they dig deep, and look far back, and put things to the utmost stretch, that they may have something to accuse me of."

7-10 God's judgments on persecutors.

We may observe here,

I. The judgments of God which should certainly come upon these malicious persecutors of David. Though they encouraged themselves in their wickedness, here is that which, if they would believe and consider it, was enough to discourage them. And it is observable how the punishment answers the sin.

1. They shot at David secretly and suddenly, to wound him; but God shall shoot at them, for he ordains his arrows against the persecutors (Ps. vii. 13), against the face of them, Ps. xxi. 12. And God's arrows will hit surer, and fly swifter, and pierce deeper, than theirs do or can. They have many arrows, but they are only

Psalm 64

6-10

6 They search out iniquities; they accomplish a diligent search: both the inward thought of every one of them, and the heart, is deep.

7 But God shall shoot at them with an arrow; suddenly shall they be wounded.

8 So they shall make their own tongue to fall upon themselves: all that see them shall flee away.

9 And all men shall fear, and shall declare the work of God; for they shall wisely consider of his doing.

10 The righteous shall be glad in the LORD, and shall trust in him; and all the upright in heart shall glory.

and recount their various devices, so as to come at some new and masterly device. They know the benefit of cooperation, and are not sparing in it; they pour their experience into one common fund, they teach each other fresh methods.

Verse 6. They search out iniquities. Diligently they consider, invent, devise, and seek for wicked plans to wreak their malice. These are no common villains, but explorers in iniquity, inventors and concoctors of evil. Sad indeed it is that to ruin a good man the evil disposed will often show as much avidity as if they were searching after treasure. The Inquisition could display instruments of torture, revealing as much skill as the machinery of our modern exhibitions. The deep places of history, manifesting most the skill of the human mind, are those in which revenge has arranged diplomacy, and used intrigue to compass its diabolical purposes.

They accomplish a diligent search. Their design is perfected, consummated, and brought into working order. They cry "Eureka;" they have sought and found the sure method of vengeance. Exquisite are the refinements of malice! hell's craft furnishes inspiration to the artistes who fashion deceit. Earth and the places under it are ransacked for the material of war, and profound skill turns all to account. Both the inward thought of every one of them, and the heart, is deep.

Verse 7. But God shall shoot at them with an arrow. They shot, and shall be shot. A greater archer than they are shall take sure aim at their hearts. One of his arrows shall be enough, for he never misses his aim. The Lord turns the tables on his adversaries, and defeats them at their own weapons. Suddenly shall they be wounded. They were looking to surprise the saint, but, lo! they are taken at unawares themselves; they desired to inflict deadly wounds, and are smitten themselves with wounds which none can heal. While they were bending their bows, the great Lord had prepared his bow already, and he let slip the shaft when least they looked for such an unsparing messenger of justice. "Vengeance is mine; I will repay, saith the Lord." The righteous need not learn the arts of self defense or of attack, their avenging is in better hands than their own.

Verse 9. And all men shall fear. They shall be filled with awe by the just judgments of God, as the Canaanites were by the overthrow of Pharaoh at the Red Sea. Those who might have been bold in sin shall be made to tremble and to stand in awe of the righteous Judge. And shall declare the work of God. It shall become the subject of general conversation. So strange, so pointed, so terrible shall be the Lord's overthrow of the malicious, that it shall be spoken of in all companies. They sinned secretly, but their punishment shall be wrought before the face of the sun. For they shall wisely consider of his doing. The judgments of God are frequently so clear and manifest that men cannot misread them, and if they have any thought at all, they must extract the true teaching from them.

Verse 10. The righteous shall be glad in the Lord. Admiring his justice and fully acquiescing in its displays, they shall also rejoice at the rescue of injured innocence yet, their joy shall not be selfish or sensual, but altogether in reference to the Lord. And shall trust in him. Their observation of providence shall increase their faith; since he who fulfils his threatenings will not forget his promises. And all the upright in heart shall glory. The victory of the oppressed shall be the victory of all upright men; the whole host of the elect shall rejoice in the triumph of virtue. While strangers fear, the children are glad in view of their Father's power and justice. That which alarms the evil, cheers the good.

with which they stirred one another up to the most daring acts of iniquity. In this there can be little doubt that they were encouraged by the present state of weakness to which David was reduced in his circumstances, taking occasion, when they found him in poverty and exile, and without means of resistance, to persecute him with the greater freedom.

6. In the verse which follows, he speaks severely against the deceit which they practiced. He speaks of their having exhausted all the arts of mischief, so as to have left nothing in this department to be discovered. The search referred to has relation to the secret methods of doing evil. He adds, that their malice was deep. By the inward part and the heart, which was deep, he means the hidden devices to which the wicked have recourse for concealment.

7-10

7. And God shall shoot an arrow at them. The Psalmist now congratulates himself in the confident persuasion that his prayers have not been without effect, but already answered. Though there was no appearance of God's approaching judgment, he declares that it would suddenly be executed; and in this he affords a remarkable proof of his faith.

8. And they shall make their own tongue to fall upon themselves. Pursuing the same subject, he remarks, that the poison concocted in their secret counsels, and which they revealed with their tongues, would prove to have a deadly effect upon themselves. The sentiment is the same with that expressed elsewhere by another figure, when they are said to be caught in their own snares, and to fall into the pit which they have dug themselves, (Psalm 57:6.) It is just that Heaven should make the mischiefs which they had devised against innocent and upright men to recoil upon their own heads. The judgment is one which we see repeatedly and daily exemplified before our eyes, and yet we find much difficulty in believing that it can take place.

We should feel ourselves bound the more to impress the truth upon our hearts, that God is ever watching, as it were, his opportunity of converting the stratagems of the wicked into means just as completely effective of their destruction, as if they had intentionally employed them for that end. In the close of the verse, to point out the striking severity of their punishment, it is said that all who saw them should flee away. The judgments of God are lifted above out of the sight of an ignorant world, and ere it can be roused to fear and dismay, these must be such as to bear signal marks indeed of a divine hand.

9. And all men shall see, and shall declare the work of God. He insists more fully upon the good effects which would result from the judgment executed in leading such as had formerly overlooked a Divine Providence altogether, to catch a spirit of inquiry from the singularity of the spectacle; and acquaint themselves with, and speak one to another of a subject hitherto entirely new to them.

Those formerly called the righteous are now styled the upright in heart, to teach us, that the only righteousness which proves acceptable is that which proceeds from inward sincerity. This truth I have insisted upon at large elsewhere.

bitter words, and words are but wind: the curse causeless shall not come. But God has one arrow that will be their death, his curse which is never causeless, and therefore shall come; with it they shall be suddenly wounded, that is, their wound by it will be a surprise upon them, because they were secure and not apprehensive of any danger.

2. Their tongues fell upon him, but God shall make their tongues to fall upon themselves. They do it by the desert of their sin; God does it by the justice of his wrath, v. 8. When God deals with men according to the desert of their tongue-sins, and brings those mischiefs upon them which they have passionately and maliciously imprecated upon others, then he makes their own tongues to fall upon them; and it is weight enough to sink a man to the lowest hell, like a talent of lead. Many have cut their own throats, and many more have damned their own souls, with their tongues, and it will be an aggravation of their condemnation.

II. The influence which these judgments should have upon others; for it is done in the open sight of all, Job xxxiv. 26.

1. Their neighbors shall shun them and shift for their own safety. They shall flee away, as the men of Israel did from the tents of Korah, Dathan, and Abiram, Num. xvi. 27. Some think this was fulfilled in the death of Saul, when not only his army was dispersed, but the inhabitants of the neighboring country were so terrified with the fall, not only of their king but of his three sons, that they quitted their cities and fled, 1 Sam. xxxi. 7.

2. Spectators shall reverence the providence of God therein, v. 9.

(1.) They shall understand and observe God's hand in all (and, unless we do so, we are not likely to profit by the dispensations of Providence, Hos. xiv. 9): They shall wisely consider his doing. There is need of consideration and serious thought rightly to apprehend the matter of fact, and need of wisdom to put a true interpretation upon it. God's doing is well worth our considering (Eccl. vii. 13), but it must be considered wisely, that we put not a corrupt gloss upon a pure text.

(2.) They shall be affected with a holy awe of God upon the consideration of it. All men (all that have any thing of the reason of a man in them) shall fear and tremble because of God's judgments, Ps. cxix. 120. They shall fear to do the like, fear being found persecutors of God's people. Smite the scorner and the simple shall beware.

3. Good people shall in a special manner take notice of it, and it shall affect them with a holy pleasure, v. 10.

(1.) It shall increase their joy.

(2.) It shall encourage their faith.

(3.) Their joy and faith shall both express themselves in a holy boasting: All the upright in heart, that keep a good conscience and approve themselves to God, shall glory, not in themselves, but in the favor of God.

Psalm 65

Title
To the chief Musician. A Psalm and song of David.

1-6
1 Praise waiteth for thee, O God, in Sion: and unto thee shall the vow be performed.
2 O thou that hearest prayer, unto thee shall all flesh come.
3 Iniquities prevail against me: as for our transgressions, thou shalt purge them away.
4 Blessed is the man whom thou choosest, and causest to approach unto thee, that he may dwell in thy courts: we shall be satisfied with the goodness of thy house, even of thy holy temple.
5 By terrible things in righteousness wilt thou answer us, O God of our salvation; who art the confidence of all the ends of the earth, and of them that are afar off upon the sea:
6 Which by his strength setteth fast the mountains; being girded with power:

Psalm 65

TITLE. This title is very similar to many we have before studied. To the Chief Musician. It is consigned to the care of the usual overseer of song. When a man does his work well, there is no use in calling in others for novelty's sake. A Psalm and song of David. The Hebrew calls it a Shur and Mizmor, a combination of psalm and song, which may be best described by the term, "A Lyrical Poem." In this case the Psalm may be said or sung, and be equally suitable. We have had two such Psalms before, Psalms 30 and 48, and we have now the first of a little series of four following each other. It was meant that Psalms of pleading and longing should be followed by hymns of praise.
SUBJECT AND DIVISION. David sings of the glory of God in his church, and in the fields of nature: here is the song both of grace and providence. It may be that he intended hereby to commemorate a remarkably plentiful harvest, or to compose a harvest hymn for all ages. It appears to have been written after a violent rebellion had been quelled, Ps 65:7, and foreign enemies had been subdued by signal victory, Ps 65:8. It is one of the most delightful hymns in any language. We shall view in Ps 65:1-4 the way of approach to God, then from Ps 65:5-8 we shall see the Lord in answer to prayer performing wonders for which he is praised, and then from Ps 65:9-13 we shall sing the special harvest song.

EXPOSITION
Verse 1. Praise waiteth for thee, O God, in Sion. Though Babylon adores Antichrist, Zion remains faithful to her King; to him, and to him only, she brings her perpetual oblation of worship. Those who have seen in Zion the blood of sprinkling, and know themselves to belong to the church of the firstborn, can never think of her without presenting humble praise to Zion's God; his mercies are too numerous and precious to be forgotten. The praises of the saints wait for a signal from the divine Lord, and when he shows his face they burst forth at once. Like a company of musicians gathered to welcome and honor a prince, who wait till he makes his appearance, so do we reserve our best praises till the Lord reveals himself in the assembly of his saints; and, indeed, till he shall descend from heaven in the day of his appearing.
Verse 2. O thou that hearest prayer. This is thy name, thy nature, thy glory. God not only has heard, but is now hearing prayer, and always must hear prayer, since he is an immutable being and never changes in his attributes. What a delightful title for the God and Father of our Lord Jesus Christ!
Verse 3. Iniquities prevail against me. Others accuse and slander me, and in addition to my own sins rise up and would beset me to my confusion, were it not for the remembrance of the atonement which covers every one of my iniquities. Our sins would, but for grace, prevail against us in the court of divine justice, in the court of conscience, and in the battle of life.
Verse 4. Blessed is the man whom thou choosest, and causest to approach unto thee. After cleansing comes benediction, and truly this is a very rich one. It comprehends both election, effectual calling, access, acceptance, and sonship.
Verse 5. By terrible things in righteousness wilt thou answer us, O God of our salvation. God's memorial is that he hears prayer, and his glory is that he answers it in a manner fitted to inspire awe in the hearts of his people. The saints, in the commencement of the Psalm, offered praise in reverential silence; and now, in the like awe stricken spirit, they receive answers to their prayers. The direct allusion here is, no doubt, to the Lord's overthrow of the enemies of his people in ways calculated to strike terror into all beholders; his judgments in their severe righteousness were calculated to excite fear both among friends and foes.

JOHN CALVIN

Psalm 65

1-3
1. Praise waiteth for thee, O God! in Zion. Literally it runs, Praise is silent to thee. The meaning of the expression is, that God's goodness to his people is such as to afford constantly new matter of praise. It is diffused over the whole world, but specially shown to the Church. Besides, others who do not belong to the Church of God, however abundantly benefits may be showered upon them, see not whence they come, and riot in the blessings which they have received without any acknowledgement of them. But the main thing meant to be conveyed by the Psalmist is, that thanksgiving is due to the Lord for his goodness shown to his Church and people.
2. The title here given to God carries with it a truth of great importance that the answer of our prayers is secured by the fact, that in rejecting them he would in a certain sense deny his own nature.
3. Words of iniquity have prevailed against me. He does not complain of the people being assailed with calumny, but is to be understood as confessing that their sins were the cause of any interruption which had taken place in the communication of the divine favor to the Jews.

4-8
4. Blessed is the man whom thou hast chosen. Having already acknowledged that the people had separated themselves from God by their sins, and forfeited all right to be heard, he now takes refuge in the free grace of God, which secures the remission of sin amongst other blessings. He thus casts an additional light upon what he had said on the point of guilt being purged away, by pointing to the cause of God, as being favorable to poor sinners, which can only be found in his fatherly love leading him to welcome them into his presence, however undeserving.
5. Terrible things in righteousness wilt thou answer to us. He proceeds to illustrate, although in a somewhat different form, the same point of the blessedness of those who are admitted into the temple of God, and nourished in his house. He declares that God would answer his people by miracles or fearful signs, displaying his power; as if he had said, in deliverances as wonderful as those which he wrought for their fathers when they went out of Egypt.
6. By his strength setting fast the mountains. For the sake of illustration, he instances the power of God seen in the general fabric of the world. In these times it sounded as a new and strange truth to say that the Gentiles should be called to the same hope with the Jews. To prove that it was not so incredible as they were apt to conceive, the Psalmist very properly adverts to the Divine power apparent in all parts of the world.
8. They also that dwell, etc. By the signs referred to, we must evidently understand those signal and memorable works of the Lord which bear the impress of his glorious hand. It is true, that the minutest and meanest objects, whether in the heavens or upon the earth, reflect to some extent the glory of God; but the name mentioned emphatically applies to

MATTHEW HENRY

Psalm 65

1-5 The praises of Zion; motives for devout.
The psalmist here has no particular concern of his own at the throne of grace, but begins with an address to God, as the master of an assembly and the mouth of a congregation; and observe,
I. How he gives glory to God, v. 1.
1. By humble thankfulness: Praise waiteth for thee, O God! in Zion, waits till it arrives, that it may be received with thankfulness at its first approach. When God is coming towards us with his favors we must go forth to meet him with our praises, and wait till the day dawn. "Praise waits, with an entire satisfaction in thy holy will and dependence on thy mercy."
2. By sincere faithfulness: Unto thee shall the vow be performed, that is, the sacrifice shall be offered up which was vowed. We shall not be accepted in our thanksgivings to God for the mercies we have received unless we make conscience of paying the vows which we made when we were in pursuit of the mercy; for better it is not to vow than to vow and not to pay.
II. What he gives him glory for.
1. For hearing prayer (v. 2): Praise waits for thee; and why is it so ready?
(1.) "Because thou art ready to grant our petitions. O thou that hearest prayer! thou canst answer every prayer, for thou art able to do for us more than we are able to ask or think (Eph. iii. 20), and thou wilt answer every prayer of faith, either in kind or kindness."
(2.) Because, for that reason, we are ready to run to him when we are in our straits.
2. For pardoning sin. In this who is a God like unto him? Micah vii. 18. By this he proclaims his name (Exod. xxxiv. 7), and therefore, upon this account, praise waits for him, v. 3.
3. For the kind entertainment he gives to those that attend upon him and the comfort they have in communion with him. Iniquity must first be purged away (v. 3) and then we are welcome to compass God's altars, v. 4. Those that come into communion with God shall certainly find true happiness and full satisfaction in that communion.
4. For the glorious operations of his power on their behalf (v. 5): By terrible things in righteousness wilt thou answer us, O God of our salvation! This may be understood of the rebukes which God in his providence sometimes gives to his own people; he often answers them by terrible things, for the awakening and quickening of them, but always in righteousness; he neither does them any wrong nor means them any hurt, for even then he is the God of their salvation.
5. For the care he takes of all his people, however distressed, and whithersoever dispersed. He is the confidence of all the ends of the earth that is, of all the saints all the world over and not theirs only that were of the seed of Israel; for he is the God of the

Psalm 65

7-13

7 Which stilleth the noise of the seas, the noise of their waves, and the tumult of the people.

8 They also that dwell in the uttermost parts are afraid at thy tokens: thou makest the outgoings of the morning and evening to rejoice.

9 Thou visitest the earth, and waterest it: thou greatly enrichest it with the river of God, which is full of water: thou preparest them corn, when thou hast so provided for it.

10 Thou waterest the ridges thereof abundantly: thou settlest the furrows thereof: thou makest it soft with showers: thou blessest the springing thereof.

11 Thou crownest the year with thy goodness; and thy paths drop fatness.

12 They drop upon the pastures of the wilderness: and the little hills rejoice on every side.

13 The pastures are clothed with flocks; the valleys also are covered over with corn; they shout for joy, they also sing.

Verse 6. Which by his strength setteth fast the mountains. He, as it were, fixed them in their sockets, and preserved them from falling by earthquake or storm. The firmest owe their stability to him. Philosophers of the forget God school are too much engrossed with their laws of upheaval to think of the Upheaver. Their theories of volcanic action and glacier action, etc., etc., are frequently used as bolts and bars to shut the Lord out of his own world. Our poet is of another mind, and sees God's hand settling Alps and Andes on their bases, and therefore he sings in his praise. Let me for ever be just such an unphilosophical simpleton as David was, for he was nearer akin to Solomon than any of our modern theorists.

Verse 7. Which stilleth the noise of the seas. His soft breath smooths the sea into a glass, and the mountainous waves into ripples. God does this. Calms are of the God of peace; it needs not that we look for a hurricane when it is said that he cometh. He walked of old in the garden in the cool of the day; he is resting even now, for his great seventh day is not yet over, and he is always "the Lord and giver of peace." Let mariners magnify the God who rules the waves.

Verse 8. They also that dwell in the uttermost parts are afraid of thy tokens. Signs of God's presence are not few, nor confined to any one region.

Verse 9. Thou visitest the earth, and waterest it. God's visits leave a blessing behind; this is more than can be said of every visitor. When the Lord goes on visitations of mercy, he has abundance of necessary things for all his needy creatures. He is represented here as going round the earth, as a gardener surveys his garden.

Verse 10. Thou waterest the ridges thereof abundantly: thou settlest the furrows thereof. Ridge and furrow are drenched. The ridges beaten down and settled, and the furrows made to stand like gutters flooded to the full. Thou makest it soft with showers. The drought turned the clods into iron, but the plenteous showers dissolve and loosen the soil.

Verse 11. Thou crownest the year with thy goodness. The harvest is the plainest display of the divine bounty, and the crown of the year. The Lord himself conducts the coronation, and sets the golden coronal upon the brow of the year. Or we may understand the expression to mean that God's love encircles the year as with a crown; each month has its gems, each day its pearl. Unceasing kindness girdles all time with a belt of love.

Verse 12. They drop upon the pastures of the wilderness. Not alone where man is found do the showers descend, but away in the lone places, where only wild animals have their haunt, there the bountiful Lord makes the refreshing rain to drop. Ten thousand oases smile while the Lord of mercy passes by.

Verse 13. The pastures are clothed with flocks. The clothing of man first clothes the fields. Pastures appear to be quite covered with numerous flocks when the grass is abundant. The valleys also are covered over with corn. The arable as well as the pasture land is rendered fruitful. God's clouds, like ravens, bring us both bread and flesh. Grazing flocks and waving crops are equally the gifts of the Preserver of men, and for both praise should be rendered.

They also sing. The voice of nature is articulate to God; it is not only a shout, but a song. Well ordered are the sounds of animate creation as they combine with the equally well tuned ripple of the waters, and sighings of the wind. Nature has no discords. Her airs are melodious, her chorus is full of harmony. All, all is for the Lord; the world is a hymn to the Eternal, blessed is he who, hearing, joins in it, and makes one singer in the mighty chorus.

miracles, as affording a better display of the divine majesty. So striking would be the proofs of God's favor to his Church, that, as the Psalmist here intimates to us, they would constrain the homage and wonder of the most distant and barbarous nations.

9-13
9. Thou hast visited the earth, and watered it. This and the verbs which follow denote action continually going forward, and may therefore be rendered in the present tense. There is a force in the form of expression used by the Psalmist when he adds, that corn is provided for man, because the earth has been so prepared by God; which means, that the reason of that abundance with which the earth teems, is its having been expressly formed by God in his fatherly care of the great household of mankind, to supply the wants of his children.
10. Thou dost saturate its furrows. David continues the strain of thanksgiving, and praises God for moistening and saturating the earth with rains that it may be fitted for producing fruit. By this he would signify to us, that the whole order of things in nature shows the fatherly love of God, in condescending to care for our daily sustenance. He multiplies his expressions when speaking of a part of the divine goodness, which many have wickedly and impiously disparaged.
11. Thou crownest the year with thy goodness. Some read—Thou crownest the year of thy goodness; as if the Psalmist meant that the fertile year had a peculiar glory attached to it, and were crowned, so to speak, by God. Thus, if there was a more abundant crop or vintage than usual, this would be the crown of the year. And it must be granted that God does not bless every year alike. Still there is none but what is crowned with some measure of excellency; and for that reason it would seem best to retain the simpler rendering of the words, and view them as meaning that the Divine goodness is apparent in the annual returns of the season.
He amplifies this goodness of God, by adding, that his fatness drops even upon the wilder and more uncultivated districts. The wilderness is not to be taken here for the absolute waste where nothing grows, but for such places as are not so well cultivated, where there are few inhabitants, and where, notwithstanding, the Divine goodness is even more illustrated than elsewhere in dropping down fatness upon the tops of the mountains.
13. Notice is next taken of the valleys and level grounds, to show that there is no part of the earth overlooked by God, and that the riches of his liberality extend over all the world. The variety of its manifestation is commended when it is added, that the valleys and lower grounds are clothed with flocks, as well as with corn. He represents inanimate things as rejoicing, which may be said of them in a certain sense, as when we speak of the fields smiling, when they refresh our eye with their beauty. It may seem strange, that he should first tell us, that they shout for joy, and then add the feebler expression, that they sing. This denotes a continuation of joy, that they would rejoice, not only one year, but through the endless succession of the seasons.

Gentiles as well as of the Jews, the confidence of those that are afar off from his holy temple and its courts, that dwell in the islands of the Gentiles, or that are in distress upon the sea.

6-13 The Almighty power of God; indications of divine power and goodness.
That we may be the more affected with the wonderful condescensions of the God of grace, it is of use to observe his power and sovereignty as the God of nature, the riches and bounty of his providential kingdom.
I. He establishes the earth and it abides, Ps. cxix. 90. By his own strength he setteth fast the mountains (v. 6), did set them fast at first and still keeps them firm, though they are sometimes shaken by earthquakes.
II. He stills the sea, and it is quiet, v. 7. The sea in a storm makes a great noise, which adds to its threatening terror; but, when God pleases, he commands silence among the waves and billows, and lays them to sleep, turns the storm into a calm quickly, Ps. cvii. 29.
III. He renews the morning and evening, and their revolution is constant, v. 8. This regular succession of day and night may be considered, as an instance of God's great power, and as an instance of God's great goodness, and so it brings comfort to all.
IV. He waters the earth and makes it fruitful. On this instance of God's power and goodness he enlarges very much, the psalm being probably penned upon occasion either of a more than ordinarily plentiful harvest or of a seasonable rain after long drought.
1. How much there is in it of the power and goodness of God, which is here set forth by a great variety of lively expressions.
2. How much benefit is derived from it to the earth and to man upon it.
(1.) To the earth itself. The rain in season gives it a new face; nothing is more reviving, more refreshing, than the rain upon the new-mown grass, Ps. lxxii. 6. Even the ridges of the earth, off which the rain seems to slide, are watered abundantly, for they drink in the rain which comes often upon them; the furrows of it, which are turned up by the plough, in order to the seedness, are settled by the rain and made fit to receive the seed (v. 10); they are settled by being made soft.
(2.) To man upon the earth. God, by providing rain for the earth, prepares corn for man, v. 9. As for the earth, out of it comes bread (Job xxviii. 5), for out of it comes corn; but every grain of corn that comes out of it God himself prepared. Corn and cattle are the two staple commodities with which the husbandman, who deals immediately in the fruits of the earth, is enriched; and both are owing to the divine goodness in watering the earth, v. 13. To this it is owing that the pastures are clothed with flocks, v. 13. Let all these common gifts of the divine bounty increase our love to God.

Psalm 66

Title
To the chief Musician. A Song or Psalm.

1-6
1 Make a joyful noise unto God, all ye lands:
2 Sing forth the honor of his name: make his praise glorious.
3 Say unto God, How terrible art thou in thy works! through the greatness of thy power shall thine enemies submit themselves unto thee.
4 All the earth shall worship thee, and shall sing unto thee; they shall sing to thy name. Selah.
5 Come and see the works of God: he is terrible in his doing toward the children of men.
6 He turned the sea into dry land: they went through the flood on foot: there did we rejoice in him.

Psalm 66

TITLE. To the Chief Musician. He had need be a man of great skill, worthily to sing such a Psalm as this: the best music in the world would be honored by marriage with such expressions. A Song or Psalm, or a Song and Psalm. It may be either said or sung; it is a marvelous poem if it be but read; but set to suitable music, it must have been one of the noblest strains ever heard by the Jewish people. We do not know who is its author, but we see no reason to doubt that David wrote it. It is in the Davidic style, and has nothing in it unsuited to his times. It is true the "house" of God is mentioned, but the tabernacle was entitled to that designation as well as the temple.
SUBJECT AND DIVISION. Praise is the topic, and the subjects for song are the Lord's great works, his gracious benefits, his faithful deliverances, and all his dealings with his people, brought to a close by a personal testimony to special kindness received by the prophet bard himself. Ps 66:1-4 are a kind of introductory hymn, calling upon all nations to praise God, and dictating to them the words of a suitable song. Ps 66:5-7 invite the beholder to "Come and see" the works of the Lord, pointing attention to the Red Sea, and perhaps the passage of Jordan. This suggests the similar position of the afflicted people which is described, and its joyful issue predicted, Ps 66:8-12. The singer then becomes personal, and confesses his own obligations to the Lord (Ps 66:13-15); and, bursting forth with a vehement "Come and hear," declares with thanksgiving the special favor of the Lord to himself, Ps 66:16-20.

EXPOSITION
Verse 1. Make a joyful noise unto God. "In Zion," where the more instructed saints were accustomed to profound meditation, the song was silent unto God, and was accepted of him; but in the great popular assemblies a joyful noise was more appropriate and natural, and it would be equally acceptable. If praise is to be wide spread, it must be vocal; exulting sounds stir the soul and cause a sacred contagion of thanksgiving. Composers of tunes for the congregation should see to it that their airs are cheerful; we need not so much noise, as joyful noise.
Verse 2. Sing forth the honor of his name. The noise is to be modulated with tune and time, and fashioned into singing, for we adore the God of order and harmony. The honor of God should be our subject, and to honor him our object when we sing. To give glory to God is but to restore to him his own. It is our glory to be able to give God glory; and all our true glory should be ascribed unto God, for it is his glory.
Verse 3. Say unto God. Turn all your praises to him. Devotion, unless it be resolutely directed to the Lord, is no better than whistling to the wind. How terrible art thou in thy works. The mind is usually first arrested by those attributes which cause fear and trembling; and, even when the heart has come to love God, and rest in him, there is an increase of worship when the soul is awed by an extraordinary display of the more dreadful of the divine characteristics.
Verse 4. All the earth shall worship thee, and shall sing unto thee. All men must even now prostrate themselves before thee, but a time will come when they shall do this cheerfully; to the worship of fear shall be added the singing of love. What a change shall have taken place when singing shall displace sighing, and music shall thrust out misery! They shall sing to thy name. The nature and works of God will be the theme of earth's universal song, and he himself shall be the object of the joyful adoration of our emancipated race.
Verse 5. Come and see the works of God. Such glorious events, as the cleaving of the Red Sea and the overthrow of Pharaoh, are standing wonders, and throughout all time a voice sounds forth concerning them— "Come and see." Even till the close of all things, the marvelous works of

JOHN CALVIN

Psalm 66

1-4

1. Shout unto God, all the earth. The psalm begins with this general declaration, which is afterwards reduced to particulars. He addresses himself to the whole world, and from this it would seem evident, that he predicts the extent to which the kingdom of God should reach at the coming of Christ.

2. In the second verse the call is repeated with increasing vehemency, to stir up to the praises of God, such as might otherwise be remiss in the service. To sing the honor of his name, is an expression sufficiently obvious; meaning, that we should extol his sacred name in a manner suitable to its dignity, so that it may obtain its due and deserved adoration.

3. Say unto God, How terrible art thou in thy works! Here he proceeds to state the grounds why he would have us to praise God. Many content themselves with coldly descanting to others of his praises, but with the view of awakening and more deeply impressing our hearts, he directs us to address ourselves immediately to God. It is when we hold converse with him apart, and with no human eye to witness us, that we feel the vanity of hypocrisy, and will be likely to utter only what we have well and seriously meditated in our hearts.

4. All the earth shall worship thee. The Psalmist had good reason for insisting upon this one point again and again. Though all tongues were tuned to the praise of God, they never could adequately extol it; and yet such are the negligence and the perversity of men, that they will scarcely lift one feeble note in celebration of a theme which should command their united strength and might.

5-9

5. Come and see the works of God. An indirect censure is here passed upon that almost universal thoughtlessness which leads men to neglect the praises of God. Why is it that they so blindly overlook the operations of his hand, but just because they never direct their attention seriously to them? We need to be aroused upon this subject. The words before us may receive some explanation by referring to a parallel passage, Psalm 46:8. But the great scope of them is this, that the Psalmist would withdraw men from the vain or positively sinful and pernicious pursuits in which they are engaged, and direct their thoughts to the works of God. To this he exhorts them, chiding their backwardness and negligence.

7. He ruleth by his power over the world. As an evidence of his care reaching to the different countries round, he takes notice of the judgments which God executed upon the wicked and the ungodly. He proves that there was no part of the human family which God overlooked, by referring to the fact of the punishment of evil-doers. There may be much in the Divine administration of the world calculated to perplex our conclusions; but there are always some tokens to be seen of his judgments, and these sufficiently clear to strike the eye of an acute and attentive observer.

8. Bless our God, O ye people! Although calling upon all, without exception, to praise God, he refers particularly to

MATTHEW HENRY

Psalm 66

1-7 All mankind exhorted to praise God.

I. In these verses the psalmist calls upon all people to praise God, all lands, all the earth, all the inhabitants of the world that are capable of praising God, v. 1.

II. He had called upon all lands to praise God (v. 1), and he foretells (v. 4) that they shall do so: All the earth shall worship thee; some in all parts of the earth, even the remotest regions, for the everlasting gospel shall be preached to every nation and kindred; and this is the purport of it, Worship him that made heaven and earth, Rev. xiv. 6, 7.

III. That we may be furnished with matter for praise, we are here called upon to come and see the works of God; for his own works praise him, whether we do or no; and the reason why we do not praise him more and better is because we do not duly and attentively observe them. Let us therefore see God's works and observe the instances of his wisdom, power, and faithfulness in them (v. 5), and then speak of them, and speak of them to him (v. 3): Say unto God, How terrible art thou in thy works, terrible in thy doings!

1. God's works are wonderful in themselves, and such as, when duly considered, may justly fill us with amazement. God is terrible (that is, admirable) in his works, through the greatness of his power.

2. They are formidable to his enemies, and have many a time forced and frightened them into a feigned submission (v. 3): Through the greatness of thy power, before which none can stand, shall thy enemies submit themselves unto thee; they shall lie unto thee (so the word is), that is, they shall be compelled, sorely against their wills, to make their peace with thee upon any terms.

3. They are comfortable and beneficial to his people, v. 6. When Israel came out of Egypt, he turned the sea into dry land before them, which encouraged them to follow God's guidance through the wilderness; and, when they were to enter Canaan, for their encouragement in their wars Jordan was divided before them, and they went through that flood on foot; and such foot, so signally owned by heaven, might well pass for cavalry, rather than infantry, in the wars of the Lord.

4. They are commanding to all. God by his works keeps up his dominion in the world (v. 7): He rules by his power for ever; his eyes behold the nations.

8-12 The saints exhorted to praise God.

In these verses the psalmist calls upon God's people in a special manner to praise him. Let all lands do it, but Israel's land particularly. Bless our God; bless him as ours, a God in covenant with us, and that takes care of us as his own. Let them make the voice of his praise to be heard (v. 8); for from whom should it be heard but from those who are his peculiar favorites and select attendants? Two things we have reason to bless God for:

Psalm 66

7-12

7 He ruleth by his power for ever; his eyes behold the nations: let not the rebellious exalt themselves. Selah.
8 O bless our God, ye people, and make the voice of his praise to be heard:
9 Which holdeth our soul in life, and suffereth not our feet to be moved.
10 For thou, O God, hast proved us: thou hast tried us, as silver is tried.
11 Thou broughtest us into the net; thou laidst affliction upon our loins.
12 Thou hast caused men to ride over our heads; we went through fire and through water: but thou broughtest us out into a wealthy place.

God at the Red Sea will be the subject of meditation and praise; for, standing on the sea of glass mingled with fire, the triumphal armies of heaven sing the song of Moses, the servant of God, and the song of the Lamb.

Verse 6. He turned the sea into dry land. It was no slight miracle to divide a pathway through such a sea, and to make it fit for the traffic of a whole nation. He who did this can do anything, and must be God, the worthy object of adoration.

Verse 7. He ruleth by his power for ever. He has not deceased, nor abdicated, nor suffered defeat. The prowess displayed at the Red Sea is undiminished: the divine dominion endures throughout eternity. His eyes behold the nations. Even as he looked out of the cloud upon the Egyptians and discomfited them, so does he spy out his enemies, and mark their conspiracies.

Verse 8. O bless our God, ye people. Ye chosen seed, peculiarly beloved, it is yours to bless your covenant God as other nations cannot. Ye should lead the strain, for he is peculiarly your God. First visited by his love, ye should be foremost in his praise. And make the voice of his praise to be heard. Whoever else may sing with bated breath, do you be sure to give full tongue and volume to the song. Compel unwilling ears to hear the praises of your covenant God. Make rocks, and hills, and earth, and sea, and heaven itself to echo with your joyful shouts.

Verse 9. Which holdeth our soul in life. At any time the preservation of life, and especially the soul's life, is a great reason for gratitude but much more when we are called to undergo extreme trials, which of themselves would crush our being. Blessed be God, who, having put our souls into possession of life, has been pleased to preserve that heaven given life from the destroying power of the enemy.

Verse 10. For thou, O God, hast proved us. He proved his Israel with sore trials. David had his temptations. All the saints must go to the proving house; God had one Son without sin, but he never had a son without trial.

Verse 11. Thou broughtest us into the net. The people of God in the olden time were often enclosed by the power of their enemies, like fishes or birds entangled in a net; there seemed no way of escape for them. The only comfort was that God himself had brought them there, but even this was not readily available, since they knew that he had led them there in anger as a punishment for their transgressions; Israel in Egypt was much like a bird in the fowler's net.

Verse 12. Thou hast caused men to ride over our heads. They stormed, and hectored, and treated us like the mire of the street. Riding the high horse, in their arrogance, they, who were in themselves mean men, treated the Lord's people as if they were the meanest of mankind. They even turned their captives into beasts of burden, and rode upon their heads, as some read the Hebrew. Nothing is too bad for the servants of God when they fall into the hands of proud persecutors. We went through fire and through water. Trials many and varied were endured by Israel in Egypt, and are still the portion of the saints. The fires of the brick kiln and the waters of the Nile did their worst to destroy the chosen race; hard labor and child murder were both tried by the tyrant, but Israel went through both ordeals unharmed, and even thus the church of God has outlived, and will outlive, all the artifices and cruelties of man. Fire and water are pitiless and devouring, but a divine fiat stays their fury, and forbids these or any other agents from utterly destroying the chosen seed.

Verse 13. I will. The child of God is so sensible of his own personal indebtedness to grace, that he feels that he must utter a song of his own. He joins in the common thanksgiving, but since the best public form must fail to meet each individual case, he makes sure that the special mercies received by him shall not be forgotten, for he records them with his own pen, and sings of theme with his own lips. I will go into thy house with burnt

JOHN CALVIN

some Divine interposition in behalf of the Church. He would seem to hint that the Gentiles were destined, at a future period, to share the favor now exclusively enjoyed by God's chosen people. In the meantime, he reminds them of the signal and memorable nature of the deliverance granted, by calling upon them to spread abroad the fame of it.

9. Though he speaks of the Jewish people as having been brought unto life, (an expression intended to denote deliverance of a more than ordinary kind,) this means that they had been preserved from approaching danger rather than recovered from a calamity which had actually overtaken them, It is said that their feet had not been suffered to fall, which implies, that, through seasonable help which they had received, they had not fallen, but stood firm.

10-12

10. For thou, O God! hast proved us. When visited with affliction, it is of great importance that we should consider it as coming from God, and as expressly intended for our good. It is in reference to this that the Psalmist speaks of their having been proved and tried. At the same time, while he adverts to God's trying his children with the view of purging away their sin, as dross is expelled from the silver by fire, he would intimate, also, that trial had been made of their patience. The figure implies that their probation had been severe; for silver is cast repeatedly into the furnace.

11. The expression, laying a restraint [or chain] upon their loins, is introduced as being stronger than the one which goes before. It was not a net of thread which had been thrown over them, but rather they had been bound down with hard and insolvable fetters.

12. The expression which follows refers to men who had shamefully tyrannized over them, and ridden them down as cattle. By fire and water are evidently meant complicated afflictions; and it is intimated that God had exercised his people with every form of calamity. They are the two elements which contribute more than any other to sustain human life, but are equally powerful for the destruction of it. It is noticeable, that the Psalmist speaks of all the cruelties which they had most unjustly suffered from the hands of their enemies, as an infliction of Divine punishment; and would guard the Lord's people against imagining that God was ignorant of what they had endured.

13-16

13. I will come into thy house with burnt offerings. Hitherto the Psalmist has spoken in the name of the people at large. Now he emphatically gives expression to his own private feelings, and calls upon them, by his example, to engage individually in the exercises of religion, it being impossible that there should be any hearty common consent unless each entered seriously upon the service of thanksgiving for himself and apart. We are taught that when God at any time succors us in our adversity, we do an injustice to his name if we forget to celebrate our deliverances with solemn acknowledgements. More is spoken of in this passage than thanksgiving. He

MATTHEW HENRY

I. Common protection (v. 9): He holdeth our soul in life, that it may not drop away of itself; for, being continually in our hands, it is apt to slip through our fingers.

II. Special deliverance from great distress. Observe,

1. How grievous the distress and danger were, v. 11, 12. What particular trouble of the church this refers to does not appear; it might be the trouble of some private persons or families only. But, whatever it was, they were surprised with it as a bird with a snare, enclosed and entangled in it as a fish in a net; they were pressed down with it, and kept under as with a load upon their loins, v. 11.

2. How gracious God's design was in bringing them into this distress and danger. See what the meaning of it is (v. 10): Thou, O God! hast proved us, and tried us. Then we are likely to get good by our afflictions, when we look upon them under this notion, for then we may see God's grace and love at the bottom of them and our own honor and benefit in the end of them. By afflictions we are proved as silver in the fire.

3. How glorious the issue was at last. The troubles of the church will certainly end well.

13-20 David resolves to praise God; David declaring what God has done for his soul.

The psalmist, having before stirred up all people, and all God's people in particular, to bless the Lord, here stirs up himself and engages himself to do it.

I. In his devotions to his God, v. 13-15. He had called upon others to sing God's praises and to make a joyful noise with them; but, for himself, his resolutions go further, and he will praise God,

1. By costly sacrifices, which, under the law, were offered to the honor of God. All people had not wherewithal to offer these sacrifices, or wanted zeal to be at such an expense in praising God; but David, for his part, being able, is as willing, in this chargeable way to pay his homage to God (v. 13): I will go into thy house with burnt-offerings. His sacrifices should be public, in the place which God had chosen: "I will go into thy house with them." Christ is our temple, to whom we must bring our spiritual gifts, and by whom they are sanctified.

2. By a conscientious performance of his vows. We do not acceptably praise God for our deliverance out of trouble unless we make conscience of paying the vows we made when we were in trouble. This was the psalmist's resolution (v. 13, 14), I will pay thee my vows, which my lips have uttered when I was in trouble.

II. In his declarations to his friends, v. 16. He calls together a congregation of good people to hear his thankful narrative of God's favors to him: "Come and hear, all you that fear God, for,

1. You will join with me in my praises and help me in giving thanks." And we should be as desirous of the assistance of those that fear God in returning thanks for the mercies we have received as in praying for those we want.

Psalm 66

13-20

13 I will go into thy house with burnt offerings: I will pay thee my vows,
14 Which my lips have uttered, and my mouth hath spoken, when I was in trouble.
15 I will offer unto thee burnt sacrifices of fatlings, with the incense of rams; I will offer bullocks with goats. Selah.
16 Come and hear, all ye that fear God, and I will declare what he hath done for my soul.
17 I cried unto him with my mouth, and he was extolled with my tongue.
18 If I regard iniquity in my heart, the Lord will not hear me:
19 But verily God hath heard me; he hath attended to the voice of my prayer.
20 Blessed be God, which hath not turned away my prayer, nor his mercy from me.

offerings; the usual sacrifices of godly men. Even the thankful heart dares not come to God without a victim of grateful praise; of this as well as of every other form of worship, we may say, "the blood is the life thereof." Reader, never attempt to come before God without Jesus, the divinely promised, given, and accepted burnt offering. I will pay thee my vows. He would not appear before the Lord empty, but at the same time he would not boast of what he offered, seeing it was all due on account of former vows. After all, our largest gifts are but payments; when we have given all, we must confess, "O Lord, of thine own have we given unto thee." We should be slow in making vows, but prompt in discharging them.

Verse 15. I will offer unto thee burnt sacrifices of fatlings. The good man will give his best things to God. No starveling goat upon the hills will he present at the altar, but the well fed bullocks of the luxuriant pastures shall ascend in smoke from the sacred fire. He who is miserly with God is a wretch indeed. Few devise liberal things, but those few find a rich reward in so doing.

Verse 16. Come and hear. Before, they were bidden to come and see. Hearing is faith's seeing. Mercy comes to us by way of ear gate. "Hear, and your soul shall live." They saw how terrible God was, but they heard how gracious he was. All ye that fear God. These are a fit audience when a good man is about to relate his experience; and it is well to select our hearers when inward soul matters are our theme. It is forbidden us to throw pearls before swine. We do not want to furnish wanton minds with subjects for their comedies, and therefore it is wise to speak of personal spiritual matters where they can be understood, and not where they will be burlesqued.

Verse 17. I cried unto him with my mouth, and he was extolled with my tongue. It is well when prayer and praise go together, like the horses in Pharaoh's chariot. Some cry who do not sing, and some sing who do not cry: both together are best. Since the Lord's answers so frequently follow close at the heels of our petitions, and even overtake them, it becomes us to let our grateful praises keep pace with our humble prayers.

Verse 18. If I regard iniquity in my heart. If, having seen it to be there, I continue to gaze upon it without aversion; if I cherish it, have a side glance of love toward it, excuse it, and palliate it; The Lord will not hear me. How can he? Can I desire him to connive at my sin, and accept me while I willfully cling to any evil way? Nothing hinders prayer like iniquity harbored in the breast; as with Cain, so with us, sin lieth at the door, and blocks the passage.

Verse 19. But verily God hath heard me. Sure sign this that the petitioner was no secret lover of sin. The answer to his prayer was a fresh assurance that his heart was sincere before the Lord.

Verse 20. Blessed be God. Be his name honored and loved. Which hath not turned away my prayer, nor his mercy from me. He has neither withdrawn his love nor my liberty to pray. He has neither cast out my prayer nor me. His mercy and my cries still meet each other. The psalm ends on its key note. Praise all through is its spirit and design. Lord enable us to enter into it. Amen.

speaks of vows having been contracted by him in his affliction, and these evidenced the constancy of his faith. The exhortation of the Apostle James is worthy of our special notice—"Is any among you afflicted? let him pray. Is any merry? let him sing psalms." (James 5:13) How many are there who lavish their hypocritical praises upon God in the career of their good fortune, while they are no sooner reduced to straits than the fervor of their love is damped, or gives place to the violence of fretfulness and impatience.

14. The words, which my lips have uttered, are not an unmeaning addition, but imply that he had never allowed himself to be so far overcome by grief as not to throw his desires into the express form of petition, declaring that he cast himself for safety into the hands of God.

15. I will offer unto thee burnt-sacrifices of fatlings. The reason why God ordered victims to be offered as an expression of thanksgiving was, as is well known, to teach the people that their praises were polluted by sin, and needed to be sanctified from without. However we might propose to ourselves to praise the name of God, we could only profane it with our impure lips, had not Christ once offered himself up a sacrifice, to sanctify both us and our services. (Hebrews 10:7).

16. In calling, as he does, upon all the fearers of the Lord, the Psalmist teaches us, that if we duly feel the goodness of God, we will be inflamed with a desire to publish it abroad, that others may have their faith and hope confirmed, by what they hear of it, as well as join with us in a united song of praise.

17-20

17. I cried unto him with my mouth. He proves that he owed his safety to Divine interposition, from the circumstance of his having prayed, and in consequence, having sensibly experienced his kindness. Answers to prayer serve in no small degree to illustrate the goodness of God; and confirm our faith in it.

18. He particularly refers to the heart, intimating that not only were his hands clean, in the sense of his being innocent before men, but that he could appeal to God in proof of his inward integrity. When the heart does not correspond to the outward conduct, and harbors any secret evil intent, the fair exterior appearance may deceive men; but it is an abomination in the sight of God.

19. The Psalmist affirms with emphasis, that his prayers had been answered, and we ought to draw the inference that we shall never be disappointed, if we seek God in sincerity.

20. Blessed be God! who hath not turned away my prayer. He concludes the psalm, as he began it, with thanksgiving, and gives the reason of his not having met with a repulse; or, to take the figurative expression which he employs, of God's not having turned away his prayer. This was, that he had not withdrawn his mercy. For it is entirely of his free grace that he is propitious, and that our prayers are not wholly ineffectual.

2. "You will be edified and encouraged by that which I have to say. The humble shall hear of it and be glad, Ps. xxxiv. 2. Those that fear thee will be glad when they see me (Ps. cxix. 74), and therefore let me have their company, and I will declare to them, not to vain carnal people that will banter it and make a jest of it" (pearls are not to be cast before swine); "but to those that fear God, and will make a good use of it, I will declare what God has done for my soul," not in pride and vain-glory, that he might be thought more a favorite of heaven than other people, but for the honor of God, to which we owe this as a just debt, and for the edification of others.

(1.) He had wrought in him a love to the duty of prayer, and had by his grace enlarged his heart in that duty (v. 17): I cried unto him with my mouth. But if God, among other things done for our souls, had not given us the Spirit of adoption, teaching and enabling us to cry, Abba, Father, we should never have done it. By crying to him we extol him.

(2.) He had wrought in him a dread of sin as an enemy to prayer (v. 18): If I regard iniquity in my heart, I know very well the Lord will not hear me. The Jewish writers, some of them that have the leaven of the Pharisees, which is hypocrisy, put a very corrupt gloss upon these words: If I regard iniquity in my heart, that is (say they), If I allow myself only in heart-sins, and iniquity does not break out in my words and actions, God will not hear me, that is, he will not be offended with me, will take no notice of it, so as to lay it to my charge; as if heart-sins were no sins in God's account.

(3.) He had graciously granted him an answer of peace to his prayers (v. 19). And therefore he concludes (v. 20), Blessed be God. The two foregoing verses are the major and minor propositions of a syllogism: If I regard iniquity in my heart, God will not hear my prayer; that is the proposition: but verily God has heard me; that is the assumption, from which he might have rationally inferred, "Therefore I do not regard iniquity in my heart;" but, instead of taking the comfort to himself, he gives the praise to God: Blessed be God. Whatever are the premises, God's glory must always be the conclusion. God has heard me, and therefore blessed be God.

Note, What we win by prayer we must wear with praise. Mercies in answer to prayer do, in a special manner, oblige us to be thankful. He has not turned away my prayer, nor his mercy. Lest it should be thought that the deliverance was granted for the sake of some worthiness in his prayer, he ascribes it to God's mercy. This he adds by way of correction: "It was not my prayer that fetched the deliverance, but his mercy that sent it."

Psalm 67

Title
To the chief Musician. On Neginoth. A Psalm or Song.

1 God be merciful unto us, and bless us; and cause his face to shine upon us; Selah.
2 That thy way may be known upon earth, thy saving health among all nations.
3 Let the people praise thee, O God; let all the people praise thee.
4 O let the nations be glad and sing for joy: for thou shalt judge the people righteously, and govern the nations upon earth. Selah.
5 Let the people praise thee, O God; let all the people praise thee.
6 Then shall the earth yield her increase; and God, even our own God, shall bless us.
7 God shall bless us; and all the ends of the earth shall fear him.

Psalm 67

TITLE. To the Chief Musician. Who he was matters not, and who we may be is also of small consequence, so long as the Lord is glorified. On Neginoth, or upon stringed instruments. This is the fifth Psalm so entitled, and no doubt like the others was meant to be sung with the accompaniment of "harpers harping with their harps." No author's name is given, but he would be a bold man who should attempt to prove that David did not write it. We will be hard pushed before we will look for any other author upon whom to father these anonymous odes which lie side by side with those ascribed to David, and wear a family likeness to them. A Psalm or Song. Solemnity and vivacity are here united. A Psalm is a song, but all songs are not Psalms: this is both one and the other.

EXPOSITION
Verse 1. God be merciful unto us, and bless us; and cause his face to shine upon us. This is a fit refrain to the benediction of the High Priest in the name of the Lord, as recorded in Nu 6:24-25. "The Lord bless thee, and keep thee: the Lord make his face shine upon thee, and be gracious unto thee." It begins at the beginning with a cry for mercy. Forgiveness of sin is always the first link in the chain of mercies experienced by us. Mercy is a foundation attribute in our salvation.
Verse 2. That thy way may be known upon earth. As showers which first fall upon the hills afterwards run down in streams into the valleys, so the blessing of the Most High comes upon the world through the church. We are blessed for the sake of others as well as ourselves.
Verse 3. Let the people praise thee, O God. Cause them to own thy goodness and thank thee with all their hearts; let nations do this, and do it continually, being instructed in thy gracious way. Let all the people praise thee. May every man bring his music, every citizen his canticle, every peasant his praise, every prince his psalm.
Verse 4. O let the nations be glad and sing for joy, or, they shall joy and triumph. When men know God's way and see his salvation, it brings to their hearts much happiness. Nothing creates gladness so speedily, surely, and abidingly as the salvation of God. Nations never will be glad till they follow the leadership of the great Shepherd.
Verse 5. These words are no vain repetition, but are a chorus worthy to be sung again and again. The great theme of the psalm is the participation of the Gentiles in the worship of Jehovah; the psalmist is full of it, he hardly knows how to contain or express his joy.
Verse 6. Then shall the earth yield her increase. Sin first laid a curse on the soil, and grace alone can remove it. Under tyrannical governments lands become unproductive; even the land which flowed with milk and honey is almost a wilderness under Turkish rule.
Verse 7. God shall bless us. The prayer of the first verse is the song of the last. We have the same phrase twice, and truly the Lord's blessing is manifold; he blesses and blesses and blesses again. How many are his beatitudes! How choice his benedictions! They are the peculiar heritage of his chosen. He is the Savior of all men, but specially of them that believe. In this verse we find a song for all future time. He cannot turn away from doing good to his elect. And all the ends of the earth shall fear him. The far off shall fear. The ends of the earth shall end their idolatry, and adore their God. All tribes, without exception, shall feel a sacred awe of the God of Israel. Ignorance shall be removed, insolence subdued, injustice banished, idolatry abhorred, and the Lord's love, light, life, and liberty, shall be over all, the Lord himself being King of kings and Lord of lords. Amen, and Amen.

JOHN CALVIN

Psalm 67

1. God be merciful unto us, and bless us. The psalm contains a prediction of Christ's kingdom, under which the whole world was to be adopted into a privileged relationship with God; but the Psalmist begins by praying for the Divine blessing, particularly upon the Jews. They were the first-born, (Exodus 4:22,) and the blessing was to terminate upon them first, and then go out to all the surrounding nations.
2. That they may know thy way upon the earth. Here we have a clear prophecy of that extension of the grace of God by which the Gentiles were united into one body with the posterity of Abraham.
The Psalmist prays for some conspicuous proof of favor to be shown his chosen people, which might attract the Gentiles to seek participation in the same blessed hope. By the way of God is meant his covenant, which is the source or spring of salvation, and by which he discovered himself in the character of a Father to his ancient people, and afterwards more clearly under the Gospel, when the Spirit of adoption was shed abroad in greater abundance. Accordingly, we find Christ himself saying, "This is life eternal, that they might know thee the only true God," (John 17:3).
3. Let the people praise thee, O God! Having spoken of all nations participating in the saving knowledge of God, he next tells us that they would proclaim his goodness, and exhorts them to the exercise of gratitude. The repetition used clearly shows of itself that he alludes to an event of a new and unprecedented kind. Had the allusion been to some such manifestation of his favor as he ordinarily made to the Jews, we would not have looked for the same vehemency of expression.
4. The cause assigned for joy plainly in itself points to the event of the calling of the Gentiles. The reference is not to that government of God which is general in its nature, but to that special and spiritual jurisdiction which he exercises over the Church, in which he cannot properly be said to govern any but such as he has gathered under his sway by the doctrine of his law.
The word righteousness is inserted in commendation of his government. Language almost identical is used by Isaiah and Micah when they speak of the times in which the word of salvation would be diffused throughout all the earth, (Isaiah 11:4; Micah 4:3.)
6. The earth has given its increase. Mention having been made of the principal act of the Divine favor, notice is next taken of the temporal blessings which he confers upon his children, that they may have everything necessary to complete their happiness. And here it is to be remembered, that every benefit which God bestowed upon his ancient people was, as it were, a light held out before the eyes of the world, to attract the attention of the nations to him. From this the Psalmist argues, that should God liberally supply the wants of his people, the consequence would be, to increase the fear of his name, since all ends of the earth would submit themselves to his government.

MATTHEW HENRY

Psalm 67

1-7 Prayer for the prosperity and extension of the Church; conversion of the Gentiles.
I. He begins with a prayer for the welfare and prosperity of the church then in being, in the happiness of which he should share, and think himself happy, v. 1. Our Savior, in teaching us to say, Our Father, has intimated that we ought to pray with and for others; so the psalmist here prays not, God be merciful to me, and bless me, but to us, and bless us; for we must make supplication for all saints, and be willing and glad to take our lot with them.
II. He passes from this to a prayer for the conversion of the Gentiles (v. 2): That thy way may be known upon earth. "Lord, I pray not only that thou wilt be merciful to us and bless us, but that thou wilt be merciful to all mankind, that thy way may be known upon earth." Thus public-spirited must we be in our prayers. Father in heaven, hallowed be thy name, thy kingdom come. We shall have never the less of God's mercy, and blessing, and favor, for others coming in to share with us.

1. These verses, which point at the conversion of the Gentiles, may be taken, as a prayer, and as a prophecy that it shall be as he here prays.

2. Three things are here prayed for, with reference to the Gentiles:
(1.) That divine revelation might be sent among them, v. 2.
(2.) That divine worship may be set up among them, as it will be where divine revelation is received and embraced (v. 3): "Let the people praise thee, O God! let them have matter for praise, let them have hearts for praise; yea, let not only some, but all the people, praise thee," all nations in their national capacity, some of all nations. It is again repeated (v. 5) as that which the psalmist's heart was very much upon.
(3.) That the divine government may be acknowledged and cheerfully submitted to (v. 4): O let the nations be glad, and sing for joy! Holy joy, joy in God and in his name, is the heart and soul of thankful praise. That all the people may praise thee, let the nations be glad.
III. He concludes with a joyful prospect of all good when God shall do this, when the nations shall be converted and brought to praise God.
1. The lower world shall smile upon them, and they shall have the fruits of that (v. 6): Then shall the earth yield her increase.
2. The upper world shall smile upon them, and they shall have the favors of that, which is much better: God, even our own God, shall bless us, v. 6. And again (v. 7), God shall bless us.
3. All the world shall be brought to do like them: The ends of the earth shall fear him, that is, worship him. The blessings God bestows upon us call us not only to love him, but to fear him, to keep up high thoughts of him and to be afraid of offending him.

Psalm 68

Title
To the chief Musician. A Psalm or Song of David.

1-7
1 Let God arise, let his enemies be scattered: let them also that hate him flee before him.
2 As smoke is driven away, so drive them away: as wax melteth before the fire, so let the wicked perish at the presence of God.
3 But let the righteous be glad; let them rejoice before God: yea, let them exceedingly rejoice.
4 Sing unto God, sing praises to his name: extol him that rideth upon the heavens by his name JAH, and rejoice before him.
5 A father of the fatherless, and a judge of the widows, is God in his holy habitation.
6 God setteth the solitary in families: he bringeth out those which are bound with chains: but the rebellious dwell in a dry land.
7 O God, when thou wentest forth before thy people, when thou didst march through the wilderness; Selah:

Psalm 68

TITLE. To the Chief Musician, a Psalm or Song of David. We have already said enough upon this title when dealing with Psalms 65 and 66. The present is obviously a song to be sung at the removal of the ark; and in all probability was rehearsed when David conducted it with holy joy from the house of Obededom to the prepared place on Mount Zion. It is a most soul stirring hymn. The first verses were often the battle song of the Covenanters and Ironsides; and the whole Psalm fitly pictures the way of the Lord Jesus among his saints, and his ascent to glory. The Psalm is at once surpassingly excellent and difficult. Its darkness in some stanzas is utterly impenetrable. Well does a German critic speak of it as a Titan very hard to master. Our slender scholarship has utterly failed us and we have had to follow a surer Guide. We trust our thoughts may not however prove unprofitable.
DIVISION. With the words of the first two verses the ark is uplifted, and the procession begins to move. In Ps 68:3-6, the godly in the assembly are exhorted to commence their joyous songs, and arguments are adduced to help their joy. Then the glorious march of Jehovah in the wilderness is sung: Ps 68:7-10, and his victories in war are celebrated in verses Ps 68:11-14. The joyous shouts are louder as Zion comes in sight, and the ark is borne up the hill: Ps 68:15-19. On the summit of the mount the priests sing a hymn concerning the Lord's goodness and justice; the safety of his friends, and ruin of his foes: Ps 68:20-23. Meanwhile the procession is described as it winds up the hill: Ps 68:24-27. The poet anticipates a time of wider conquest, Ps 68:28-31: and concludes with a noble burst of song unto Jehovah.

EXPOSITION
Verse 1. Let God arise. In some such words Moses spake when the cloud moved onward, and the ark was carried forward. The ark would have been a poor leader if the Lord had not been present with the symbol. Before we move, we should always desire to see the Lord lead the way. The words suppose the Lord to have been passive for awhile, suffering his enemies to rage, but restraining his power. Israel beseeches him to "arise," as elsewhere to "awake," "gird on his sword," and other similar expressions. We, also, may thus importunately cry unto the Lord, that he would be pleased to make bare his arm, and plead his own cause. Let his enemies be scattered. Our glorious Captain of the vanguard clears the way readily, however many may seek to obstruct it; he has but to arise, and they flee, he has easily over thrown his foes in days of yore, and will do so all through the ages to come.
Verse 2. As smoke is driven away. Easily the wind chases the smoke, completely it removes it, no trace is left; so, Lord, do thou to the foes of thy people. They fume in pride, they darken the sky with their malice, they mount higher and higher in arrogance, they defile wherever they prevail. Lord, let they breath, thy Spirit, thy Providence, make them to vanish for ever from the march of thy people.
Verse 3. But let the righteous be glad. The presence of God on the throne of grace is an overflowing source of delight to the godly; and let them not fail to drink of the streams which are meant to make them glad. Let them rejoice before God. The courtiers of the happy God should wear the garments of gladness, for in his presence is fullness of joy.
Verse 4. Sing unto God, sing praises to his name. To time and tune, with order and care, celebrate the character and deeds of God, the God of his people. Do it again and again; and let the praise, with resolution of heart, be all directed to him. Sing not for ostentation, but devotion; not to be heard of men, but of the Lord himself.

JOHN CALVIN

Psalm 68

1-6
1. God shall arise: his enemies shall be scattered. In this verse the Psalmist intimates, as it were by way of preface, the subject which he proposed to treat in the psalm, and which related to the truth that God, however long he may seem to connive at the audacity and cruelty of the enemies of his Church, will eventually arise to avenge it, and will prove himself able to protect it by the mere forth-putting of his hand.
2. The Psalmist adds a striking figure to illustrate how easily God can overthrow the machinations of our enemies, comparing them to smoke which vanishes when blown upon by the wind, or wax which melts before the fire. We consider it utterly incredible that such a formidable array of opposition should be made to disappear in a moment.
3. But the righteous shall be glad. It is here intimated by David, that when God shows himself formidable to the wicked, this is with the design of securing the deliverance of his Church. He would seem indirectly to contrast the joy of which he now speaks with the depression and grief felt by well affected men under the reign of Saul—suggesting, that God succeeds a season of temporary trouble with returns of comfort, to prevent his people from being overwhelmed by despondency. He leaves us also to infer, that one reason of that joy which they experience is derived from knowing that God is propitious to them, and interests himself in their safety.
4. Sing unto God, sing praises to his name: exalt him that rideth, etc. He now proceeds to call upon the Lord's people to praise God. And he begins by pointing out the grounds in general which they have for this exercise, because he comprehends the whole world under his power and government, adding, that he condescends to take the poorest and the most wretched of our family under his protection. His infinite power is commended, when it is said that he rides upon the clouds, or the heavens, for this proves that he sits superior over all things.
5. There can be no doubt that orphans and widows are named to indicate in general all such as the world are disposed to overlook as unworthy of their regard. Generally we distribute our attentions where we expect some return. We give the preference to rank and splendor, and despise or neglect the poor. When it is said, God is in the habitation of his holiness, this may refer either to heaven or to the temple, for either sense will suit the connection. God does not dwell in heaven to indulge his own ease, but heaven is, as it were, his throne, from which he judges the world.
6. In the next verse, other instances of the Divine goodness are mentioned—that he gives the bereaved and solitary a numerous offspring, and releases the bonds of the captive.

7-10
7. O God! when thou wentest forth before thy people, etc. The Psalmist now proceeds to show that the Divine goodness

MATTHEW HENRY

Psalm 68

1-6 Prayer for the dispersion of God's enemies.
In these verses,
I. David prays that God would appear in his glory,

1. For the confusion of his enemies (v. 1, 2): "Let God arise, as a judge to pass sentence upon them, as a general to take the field and do execution upon them; and let them be scattered, and flee before him, as unable to keep their ground, much less to make head against him. Let God arise, as the sun when he goes forth in his strength; and the children of darkness shall be scattered, as the shadows of the evening flee before the rising sun.

2. For the comfort and joy of his own people (v. 3): "Let the righteous be glad, that are now in sorrow; let them rejoice before God in his favorable presence. God is the joy of his people; let them rejoice whenever they come before God, yea, let them exceedingly rejoice, let them rejoice with gladness." Note, Those who rejoice in God have reason to rejoice with exceeding joy; and this joy we ought to wish to all the saints, for it belongs to them. Light is sown for the righteous.

II. He praises God for his glorious appearances, and calls upon us to praise him, to sing to his name, and extol him,
1. As a great God, infinitely great (v. 4): He rides upon the heavens, by his name Jah. He is the spring of all the motions of the heavenly bodies, directs and manages them, as he that rides in the chariot sets it a-going, has a supreme command of the influences of heaven; he rides upon the heavens for the help of his people (Deut. xxxiii. 26), so swiftly, so strongly, and so much above the reach of opposition. He rules these by his name Jah, or Jehovah, a self-existent self-sufficient being; the fountain of all being, power, motion, and perfection; this is his name for ever.
2. As a gracious God, a God of mercy and tender compassion. He is great, but he despises not any, no, not the meanest; nay, being a God of great power, he uses his power for the relief of those that are distressed, v. 5, 6. The fatherless, the widows, the solitary, find him a God all-sufficient to them. Observe how much God's goodness is his glory. He that rides on the heavens by his name Jah, one would think should immediately have been adored as King of kings and Lord of lords, and the sovereign director of all the affairs of states and nations; he is so, but this he rather glories in, that he is a Father of the fatherless.

7-14 Thankful praises to God; mercies recollected.
The psalmist here, having occasion to give God thanks for the great things he had done for him and his people of late, takes occasion thence to praise him for what he had done for their fathers in the days of old. Fresh mercies should put us in mind of former mercies and revive our grateful sense of them. Let it never be forgotten,

Psalm 68

8-14

8 The earth shook, the heavens also dropped at the presence of God: even Sinai itself was moved at the presence of God, the God of Israel.
9 Thou, O God, didst send a plentiful rain, whereby thou didst confirm thine inheritance, when it was weary.
10 Thy congregation hath dwelt therein: thou, O God, hast prepared of thy goodness for the poor.
11 The Lord gave the word: great was the company of those that published it.
12 Kings of armies did flee apace: and she that tarried at home divided the spoil.
13 Though ye have lien among the pots, yet shall ye be as the wings of a dove covered with silver, and her feathers with yellow gold.
14 When the Almighty scattered kings in it, it was white as snow in Salmon.

Verse 5. A father of the fatherless, and a judge of the widows, is God in his holy habitation. In the wilderness the people were like an orphan nation, but God was more than a father to them. As the generation which came out of Egypt gradually died away, there were many widows and fatherless ones in the camp, but they suffered no want or wrong, for the righteous laws and the just administrators whom God had appointed, looked well to the interests of the needy.

Verse 6. God setteth the solitary in families. The people had been sundered and scattered over Egypt; family ties had been disregarded, and affections crushed; but when the people escaped from Pharaoh they came together again, and all the fond associations of household life were restored. This was a great joy. He bringeth out those which are bound with chains. The most oppressed in Egypt were chained and imprisoned, but the divine Emancipator brought them all forth into perfect liberty. He who did this of old continues his gracious work.

Verse 7. O God, when thou wentest forth before thy people. What a sweetly suitable association, "thou" and "thy people;"—thou before, and thy people following! The Lord went before, and, therefore, whether the Red Sea or burning sand lay in the way, it mattered not; the pillar of cloud and fire always led them by a right way. When thou didst march through the wilderness. He was the Commander in chief of Israel, from whom they received all orders, and the march was therefore his march.

Verse 8. The earth shook. Beneath the sublime tread the solid ground trembled. The heavens also dropped at the presence of God, as if they bowed before their God, the clouds descended, and "a few dark shower drops stole abroad." Even Sinai itself was moved at the presence of God. Moses tell us, in Exodus 19, that "the whole mountain quaked greatly." That hill, so lone and high, bowed before the manifested God.

Verse 9. Thou, O God, didst send a plentiful rain. The march of God was not signalized solely by displays of terror, for goodness and bounty were also made conspicuous. Such rain as never fell before dropped on the desert sand, bread from heaven and winged fowl fell all around the host; good gifts were poured upon them, rivers leaped forth from rocks.

Verse 10. Thy congregation hath dwelt therein. In the wilderness itself, enclosed as in a wall of fire, thy chosen church has found a home; or, rather, girdled by the shower of free grace which fell all around the camp, thy flock has rested. The congregation of the faithful find the Lord to be their "dwelling place in all generations." Where there were no dwellings of men, God was the dwelling of his people.

Verse 11. In the next verse we do not sing of marching, but of battle and victory. The Lord gave the word. The enemy was near, and the silver trumpet from the tabernacle door was God's mouth to warn the camp: then was there hurrying to and fro, and a general telling of the news; great was the company of those that published it. The women ran from tent to tent and roused their lords to battle. Ready as they always were to chant the victory, they were equally swift to publish the fact that the battle note had been sounded. The ten thousand maids of Israel, like good handmaids of the Lord, aroused the sleepers, called in the wanderers, and bade the valiant men to hasten to the fray. O for the like zeal in the church of today, that, when the gospel is published, both men and women may eagerly spread the glad tidings of great joy.

Verse 12. Kings of armies did flee apace. The lords of hosts fled before the Lord of Hosts. No sooner did the ark advance than the enemy turned his back: even the princely leaders stayed not, but took to flight.

Verse 13. Though ye have lien among the pots. Does he mean that the women at home, who had been meanly clad as they performed their household work, would be so gorgeously arrayed in the spoil, that they would be like doves of silver wing and golden plumage? Or, would he say that Israel, which had been begrimed in the brick kilns of Egypt, should

JOHN CALVIN

is principally displayed in the Church, which God has selected as the great theater where his fatherly care may be manifested. What follows is evidently added with the view of leading the posterity of Abraham, as the Lord's chosen people, to apply the observations which had been just made to themselves.

8. When he speaks of the earth being moved, he would not seem to allude entirely to what occurred upon the promulgation of the law, but to the fact that, throughout all their progress, the course of nature was repeatedly altered, as if the very elements had trembled at the presence of the Lord.

9. Thou, O God! shalt make a liberal rain to fall upon thine inheritance Mention is made here of the continued course of favor which had been extended to the people from the time when they first entered the promised land. It is called the inheritance of God, as having been assigned over to his own children.

11-14

11. The Lord shall give the word, etc. David now adverts to the victories by which God had signally displayed his power in behalf of his people. He had himself been the instrument of restoring peace to the country, by putting down its foes, and he had extended the boundaries of the kingdom; but he ascribes the praise of all that had been done in stratagems and counsels of war to God. In representing God as issuing orders for the song of triumph, he intimates, figuratively, that it is he who determines the successful issue of battles.

12. From the verse which succeeds, we are taught that the mightiest preparations which the enemies of the Church may make for its destruction shall be overthrown. The greatness of the spoil taken is intimated by the circumstance stated, that a share of it would come even to the women who remained at home.

13. Though ye should lie among the pots. Having spoken of God as fighting the battles of his people, he adds, by way of qualification, that they may lie for a time under darkness, though eventually God will appear for their deliverance.

14. When the Almighty scattered kings in it. The country had, as it were, been sullied by the hostile confusions into which it was thrown, and he says that it had now recovered its fair appearance, and resembled Salmon, which is well known to have been ordinarily covered with snows.

15-17

15. The hill of God, the hill of Bashan. Here he adverts to the spring and source of all the kindness which God had shown, this being the circumstance that he had chosen mount Zion as the place of his palace and temple, whence all blessings should go out to the nation. A Divine declaration to that effect had been made to David, and this pre-eminence and dignity conferred upon mount Zion is very properly adduced as a proof of his being king, lawfully and by Divine appointment; for there was an inseparable connection between God's dwelling upon that mountain, and David's sitting upon the throne to govern the people.

MATTHEW HENRY

I. That God himself was the guide of Israel through the wilderness; when he had brought them out of their chains he did not leave them in the dry land, but he himself went before them in a march through the wilderness, v. 7. It was not a journey, but a march, for they went as soldiers, as an army with banners.

II. That he manifested his glorious presence with them at Mount Sinai, v. 8. Never did any people see the glory of God, nor hear his voice, as Israel did, Deut. iv. 32, 33. Never had any people such an excellent law given them, so expounded, so enforced. Then the earth shook, and the neighboring countries, it is likely, felt the shock; terrible thunders there were, accompanied no doubt with thunder-showers, in which the heavens seemed to drop; while the divine doctrine dropped as the rain, Deut. xxxii. 2.

III. That he provided very comfortably for them both in the wilderness and in Canaan (v. 9, 10): Thou didst send a plentiful rain and hast prepared of thy goodness for the poor.

IV. That he often gave them victory over their enemies; armies, and kings of armies, appeared against them, from their first coming into Canaan, and all along in the times of the judges, till David's days, but, first or last, they gained their point against them, v. 11, 12, 14. Observe here,

1. That God was their commander-in-chief: The Lord gave the word, as general of their armies.

2. That they had prophets, as God's messengers, to make known his mind to them.

3. That their enemies were defeated, and put to confusion: Kings of armies did flee, did flee with the greatest terror and precipitation imaginable, did not fight and flee, but flee and flee, retired without striking a stroke; they fled apace, fled and never rallied again.

4. That they were enriched with the plunder of the field: She that tarried at home divided the spoil.

5. That these great things which God did for them were sanctified to them and contributed to their reformation (v. 14).

V. That from a low and despised condition they had been advanced to splendor and prosperity. When they were bond-slaves in Egypt, and afterwards when they were oppressed sometimes by one potent neighbor and sometimes by another, they did, as it were, lie among the pots or rubbish, as despised broken vessels, or as vessels in which there was no pleasure—they were dirty, and discolored. But God, at length, delivered them from the pots (Ps. lxxxi. 6).

15-21 Glory of Zion; the King of Zion.

David, having given God praise for what he had done for Israel in general, as the God of Israel (v. 8), here comes to give him praise as Zion's God in a special manner; compare Ps. ix. 11. Sing praises to the Lord who dwelleth in Zion, for which reason Zion is called the hill of God.

I. He compares it with the hill of Bashan and other high and fruitful hills, and prefers it before them, v. 15,

Psalm 68

15-21
15 The hill of God is as the hill of Bashan; an high hill as the hill of Bashan.
16 Why leap ye, ye high hills? this is the hill which God desireth to dwell in; yea, the LORD will dwell in it for ever.
17 The chariots of God are twenty thousand, even thousands of angels: the Lord is among them, as in Sinai, in the holy place.
18 Thou hast ascended on high, thou hast led captivity captive: thou hast received gifts for men; yea, for the rebellious also, that the LORD God might dwell among them.
19 Blessed be the Lord, who daily loadeth us with benefits, even the God of our salvation. Selah.
20 He that is our God is the God of salvation; and unto GOD the Lord belong the issues from death.
21 But God shall wound the head of his enemies, and the hairy scalp of such an one as goeth on still in his trespasses.

come forth lustrous and happy in triumph and liberty? Or, did the song signify that the ark should be brought from its poor abode with Obededom into a fairer dwelling place? It is a hard passage, a nut for the learned to crack. If we knew all that was known when this ancient hymn was composed, the allusion would no doubt strike us as being beautifully appropriate, but as we do not, we will let it rest among the unriddled things.
Verse 14. When the almighty scattered kings in it, it was white as snow in Salmon. The victory was due to the Almighty arm alone; he scattered the haughty ones who came against his people, and he did it as easily as snow is driven from the bleak sides of Salmon.
Verse 15. Here the priests on the summit of the chosen hill begin to extol the Lord for his choice of Zion as his dwelling place. The hill of God is as the hill of Bashan, or more accurately, "a hill of God is Bashan," that is to say, Bashan is an eminent mountain, far exceeding Zion in height. According to the Hebrew custom, every great or remarkable thing is thus designated. Where we talk of the Devil's Dyke, the Devil's Ditch, the Devil's Punch Bowl, etc., the more commendable idiom of the Hebrews speaks of the hill of God, the trees of the Lord, the river of God, etc.
Verse 16. Why leap ye, ye high hills? Why are ye moved to envy? Envy as ye may, the Lord's choice is fixed. Lift up yourselves, and even leap from your seats, ye cannot reach the sublimity which Jehovah's presence has bestowed on the little hill of Moriah. This is the hill which God desireth to dwell in. Elohim makes Zion his abode, yea, Jehovah resides there. Yea, the Lord will dwell in it for ever. Spiritually the Lord abides eternally in Zion, his chosen church, and it was Zion's glory to be typical thereof.
Verse 17. The chariots of God are twenty thousand. Other countries, which in the former verse were symbolically referred to as "high hills," gloried in their chariots of war; but Zion, though far more lowly, was stronger than they, for the omnipotence of God was to her as two myriads of chariots.
Verse 18. Thou hast ascended on high. The ark was conducted to the summit of Zion; God himself took possession of the high places of the earth, being extolled and very high. The antitype of the ark, the Lord Jesus, has ascended into the heavens with signal marks of triumph.
Verse 19. Blessed be the Lord. At the mention of the presence of God among men the singers utter an earnest acclamation suggested by reverential love, and return blessings to him who so plentifully blesses his people. Who daily loadeth us with benefits. Our version contains a great and precious truth, though probably not the doctrine intended here. God's benefits are not few nor light, they are loads; neither are they intermittent, but they come "daily;" nor are they confined to one or two favorites, for all Israel can say, he loadeth us with benefits.
Verse 20. He that is our God is the God of salvation. The Almighty who has entered into covenant with us is the source of our safety, and the author of our deliverances. As surely as he is our God he will save us. To be his is to be safe. And unto God the Lord belong the issues from death. He has ways and means of rescuing his children from death: when they are at their wit's end, and see no way of escape, he can find a door of deliverance for them.
Verse 21. But God shall wound the head of his enemies. The Preserver is also the Destroyer. He smites his foes on the crown of their pride. The seed of the woman crushes the serpent's head. There is no defense against the Lord, he can in a moment smite with utter destruction the lofty crests of his haughty foes. And the hairy scalp of such an one as goeth on still in his trespasses. He may glory in his outward appearance, and make his hair his pride, as Absalom did; but the Lord's sword shall find him out, and pour out his soul. Headstrong sinners will find that providence overcomes them despite their strong heads.
Verse 22. The powers of evil may flee to the utmost ends of the earth, but the Lord will arrest them, and lead them back in chains to adorn his triumph.

16. Why leap ye, ye high hills? In this verse there is no obscurity or ambiguity. David having said that there was only one mountain in all the world which God had chosen, calls upon the highest hills to yield it the pre-eminency. As he repeats in the plural number what had been said immediately before of Bashan, this leads me to think that he intended first to oppose that mountain, and then all other high mountains generally, to Zion. Mountains are here to be understood figuratively, and the great truth conveyed is, that the kingdom of Christ, which God had begun to shadow forth in the person of David, far excels all that is reckoned glorious by the world.

17. The chariots of God are twenty thousand thousands of angels. For the most part, we are apt to undervalue the Divine presence, and therefore David presents us with a description fitted to exalt our thoughts of it. Owing to our unbelieving hearts, the least danger which occurs in the world weighs more with us than the power of God. We tremble under the slightest trials; for we forget or cherish low views of his omnipotence.

18-24

18. Thou hast ascended on high, thou hast led captivity captive. There can be little doubt that these words are intended to magnify the proofs of Divine favor granted upon the elevation of David to the throne, by contrasting the state of matters with that under Saul. The ascending on high implies the being previously low, and intimates, that under the melancholy confusions which had prevailed in the kingdom, there was no longer the same conspicuous display of the Divine glory as formerly.

19. Blessed be the Lord, etc. David would have us to understand, that in recounting the more particular deliverances which God had wrought, he did not mean to draw our minds away from the fact, that the Church is constantly and at all times indebted for its safety to the Divine care and protection. He adds, Blessed be God daily. And he intimates, that deliverances might be expected from him with great abundance of every blessing.

20. This is a truth particularly worthy of our notice, as teaching us to beware of judging by sense in the matter of Divine deliverances. However deep we may have sunk in trouble, it becomes us to trust the power of God, who claims it as his peculiar work to open up a way where man can see none.

21. Surely God shall wound, etc. The enemies of the Church are fierce and formidable, and it is impossible that she can be preserved from their continued assaults, without a vigorous protection being extended. To persuade us that she enjoys such a defense, David represents God as armed with dreadful power for the overthrow of the ungodly.

22. The Lord said, I will bring back from Bashan. That the Israelites might not be led to take an irreligious and self-glorious view of their victories; that they might look to God as the author of them; and rest assured of his protection in time to come, David sends them back to the first periods of their

16. It is true, Zion was but little and low in comparison with them, and was not covered over with flocks and herds as they were, yet, upon this account, it has the pre-eminence above them all, that it is the hill of God, the hill which he desires to dwell in, and where he chooses to manifest the tokens of his peculiar presence, Ps. cxxxii. 13, 14.

II. He compares it with Mount Sinai, of which he had spoken (v. 8), and shows that it has the Shechinah or divine presence in it as really, though not as sensibly, as Sinai itself had, v. 17. Angels are the chariots of God, his chariots of war, which he make use of against his enemies, his chariots of conveyance, which he sends for his friends, as he did for Elijah (and Lazarus is said to be carried by the angels), his chariots of state, in the midst of which he shows his glory and power.

III. The glory of Mount Zion was the King whom God set on that holy hill (Ps. ii. 6), who came to the daughter of Zion, Matt. xxi. 5. Of his ascension the psalmist here speaks, and to it his language is expressly applied (Eph. iv. 8): Thou hast ascended on high (v. 18); compare Ps. xlvii. 5, 6. Christ's ascending on high is here spoken of as a thing past, so sure was it; and spoken of to his honor, so great was it. It may include his whole exalted state, but points especially at his ascension into heaven to the right hand of the Father, which was as much our advantage as his advancement.

IV. The glory of Zion's King is that he is a Savior and benefactor to all his willing people and a consuming fire to all those that persist in rebellion against him, v. 19-21. We have here good and evil, life and death, the blessing and the curse, set before us, like that (Mark xvi. 16), He that believes shall be saved; he that believes not shall be damned.

1. Those that take God for their God, and so give up themselves to him to be his people, shall be loaded with his benefits, and to them he will be a God of salvation. If in sincerity we avouch God to be our God, and seek to him as such,

(1.) He will continually do us good and furnish us with occasion for praise. Having mentioned the gifts Christ received for us (v. 18), fitly does he subjoin, in the next words, Blessed be the Lord; for it is owing to the mediation of Christ that we live, and live comfortably, and are daily loaded with benefits.

(2.) He will at length be unto us the God of salvation, of everlasting salvation, the salvation of God, which he will show to those that order their conversation aright (Ps. 1. 23), the salvation of the soul.

2. Those that persist in their enmity to him will certainly be ruined (v. 21): God shall wound the head of his enemies,—of Satan the old serpent (of whom it was by the first promise foretold that the seed of the woman should break his head, Gen. iii. 15),—of all the powers of the nations, whether Jews or Gentiles, that oppose him and his kingdom among men (Ps. cx. 6, He shall wound the heads over many countries),—

Psalm 68

22-28

22 The Lord said, I will bring again from Bashan, I will bring my people again from the depths of the sea:
23 That thy foot may be dipped in the blood of thine enemies, and the tongue of thy dogs in the same.
24 They have seen thy goings, O God; even the goings of my God, my King, in the sanctuary.
25 The singers went before, the players on instruments followed after; among them were the damsels playing with timbrels.
26 Bless ye God in the congregations, even the Lord, from the fountain of Israel.
27 There is little Benjamin with their ruler, the princes of Judah and their council, the princes of Zebulun, and the princes of Naphtali.
28 Thy God hath commanded thy strength: strengthen, O God, that which thou hast wrought for us.

Verse 23. That thy foot may be dipped in the blood of thine enemies. Vengeance shall be awarded to the oppressed people, and that most complete and terrible. And the tongue of thy dogs in the same. So overwhelming should be the defeat of the foe that dogs should lick their blood.

Verse 24. They have seen thy goings, O God. In the song the marchings of the Lord had been described; friends and foes had seen his goings forth with the ark and his people. We suppose that the procession was now climbing the hill, and entering the enclosure where the tabernacle of the ark was pitched; it was suitable at this moment to declare with song that the tribes had seen the glorious progress of the Lord as he led forth his people. Even the goings of my God, my King, in the sanctuary. The splendid procession of the ark, which symbolized the throne of the great King, was before the eyes of men and angels as it ascended to the holy place; and the psalmist points to it with exultation before he proceeds to describe it. All nature and providence are, as it were, a procession attending the great Lord, in his visitations of this lower globe.

Verse 25. The singers went before, the players on instruments followed after. This was the order of the march, and God is to be worshipped evermore with due decorum. First the singers, and lastly the musicians, for the song must lead the music, and not the music drown the singing. In the midst of the vocal and instrumental band, or all around them, were the maidens: among them were the damsels playing with timbrels.

Verse 26. Bless ye God in the congregations. Let the assembled company magnify the God whose ark they followed. United praise is like the mingled perfume which Aaron made, it should all be presented unto God. He blesses us; let him be blessed. Even the Lord, from the fountain of Israel. A parallel passage to that in Deborah's song: "They that are delivered from the noise of archers in the places of drawing water, there shall they rehearse the righteous acts of the Lord." The seat of the ark would be the fountain of refreshing for all the tribes, and there they were to celebrate his praises.

Verse 27. There is little Benjamin with their ruler. The tribe was small, having been greatly reduced in numbers, but it had the honor of including Zion within its territory. "And of Benjamin he said, The beloved of the Lord shall dwell in safety by him; and the Lord shall cover him all the day long, and he shall dwell between his shoulders." Little Benjamin had been Jacob's darling, and now the tribe is made to march first in the procession, and to dwell nearest to the holy place.

Verse 28. Thy God hath commanded thy strength. His decree had ordained the nation strong, and his arm had made them so. As a commander in chief, the Lord made the valiant men pass in battle array, and bade them be strong in the day of conflict. This is a very rich though brief sentence, and, whether applied to an individual believer, or to the whole church, it is full of consolation.

Verse 29. Because of thy temple at Jerusalem shall kings bring presents unto thee. The palace of God, which towered above Jerusalem, is prophesied as becoming a wonder to all lands, and when it grew from the tabernacle of David to the temple of Solomon, it was so. So splendid was that edifice that the queen of far off Sheba came with her gifts; and many neighboring princes, overawed by the wealth and power therein displayed, came with tribute to Israel's God. The church of God, when truly spiritual, wins for her God the homage of the nations. In the latter day glory this truth shall be far more literally and largely verified.

Verse 30. Rebuke the company of spearmen; or, the beasts of the reeds, as the margin more correctly renders it. Speak to Egypt, let its growing power and jealousy be kept in order, by a word from thee. Israel remembers her old enemy, already plotting the mischief, which would break out under Jeroboam, and begs for a rebuking word from her Omnipotent Friend.

JOHN CALVIN

history, and reminds them how their fathers had been originally brought by the victorious hand of God out of the lowest depths of trouble.
24. They have seen thy goings, O God! This verse may refer to processions of a warlike kind, or to such as are made in times of peace by those who give thanks for victory. It is customary for the people of God, on occasions of the latter description, to go forth and present peace-offerings in the temple.

25-27
25. The singers went before. It is evident that he does not now speak of an army in battle array, but of a solemn assembly held for offering up thanksgivings to God for victory. God had openly shown that he was their leader in war, and to him the song of triumph is with propriety addressed. Mention is made of distinct choirs employed in his service, and particularly of such as played upon the timbrel; for, absurd as the practice may appear to us, it was then customary for the women to play upon that instrument.
26. By the fountain from which they are called upon to bless God. All are summoned to praise the Lord who could deduce their origin from the patriarch Jacob. Many might not sustain the character which answered to their high vocation; but, as the whole race had been chosen of God, the Psalmist very properly invites them to engage in this devotional exercise.
27. It has caused some surprise that, in a general description of the sacred assemblies of the people, precedence should have been given to the tribe of Benjamin. The inspired writers, in speaking of the tribes, often allude to the patriarchs from whom they respectively took their origin; nor is it surprising that the posterity of Benjamin, who was the youngest of Jacob's children, should receive the designation here given to them; and the truth is, that even antecedently to the heavy stroke which befell them, they were not numerous.

28-30
28. Thy God hath commanded thy strength Men are always disposed to arrogate to themselves the glory of what they may have done instead of tracing their success to God, and David reminds the people once more that they had not triumphed by their own strength, but by power communicated from above.
29. What is said of the temple in the following verse is intended to carry out the same strain of sentiment which has been already expressed. It gives the reason why God had exerted his power in behalf of the Israelites rather than others; which was, that it might be displayed as coming forth from the sanctuary and the ark of the covenant. Hence the emphasis with which David calls him in a previous part of the psalm—the God of Israel.
30. Destroy the company of spearmen. David evidently prays in this passage that God would deliver his chosen people by destroying their cruel and bloody enemies.
When we find David, after all the victories he had gained, still commending himself and his people to the protection of God, it should teach us to abandon the hope of ever seeing

MATTHEW HENRY

of all those, whoever they are, that will not have him to reign over them, for those he accounts his enemies, and they shall be brought forth and slain before him, Luke xix. 27. He will wound the hairy scalp of such a one as goeth on still in his trespasses.

22-31 Redemption of God's people; duties enforced by the discoveries of grace.
In these verses we have three things:
I. The gracious promise which God makes of the redemption of his people, and their victory over his and their enemies (v. 22, 23): The Lord said, in his own gracious purpose and promise, "I will do great things for my people, as the God of their salvation," v. 20. God will not fail the expectations of those who by faith take him for their God. It is promised,
1. That he will set them in safety from their danger, as he had done formerly: "I will again bring them from the depths of the sea," as he did Israel when he brought them out of the slavery of Egypt into the ease and liberty of the wilderness.
2. That he will make them victorious over their enemies (v. 23): That thy feet may be dipped, as thou passest along, in the blood of thy enemies, shed like water in great abundance, and the tongue of thy dogs may lap in the same. Dogs licked the blood of Ahab; and, in the destruction of the anti-Christian generation, we read of blood up to the horses' bridles, Rev. xiv. 20.
II. The welcome entertainment which God's own people shall give to these glorious discoveries of his grace, both in his word and in his works. Has he spoken in his holiness? Has he said he will bring again from Bashan? What then is required of us in return to this?
1. That we observe his motions (v. 24): "They have seen, thy people have seen, thy goings, O God! While others regard not the work of the Lord, nor the operation of his hands, they have seen the goings of my God, my King, in the sanctuary."
2. That we give him glory in the most devout and solemn manner. When we see his goings in his sanctuary let those that are immediately employed in the service of the temple praise him, v. 25. It was expected that the Levites, some of whom were singers and others players on instruments, who had the nearest views of his outgoings in his sanctuary, should lead in his praises.
3. That we seek unto him, and depend upon him, for the perfecting of what he has begun, v. 28. In the former part of the verse the psalmist speaks to Israel: "Thy God has commanded thy strength; that is, whatever is done for thee, or whatever strength thou hast to help thyself, it comes from God, his power and grace, and the word which he has commanded; thou hast no reason to fear while thou hast strength of God's commanding, and no reason to boast while thou hast no strength but what is of his commanding."

Psalm 68

29-25

29 Because of thy temple at Jerusalem shall kings bring presents unto thee.
30 Rebuke the company of spearmen, the multitude of the bulls, with the calves of the people, till every one submit himself with pieces of silver: scatter thou the people that delight in war.
31 Princes shall come out of Egypt; Ethiopia shall soon stretch out her hands unto God.
32 Sing unto God, ye kingdoms of the earth; O sing praises unto the Lord; Selah:
33 To him that rideth upon the heavens of heavens, which were of old; lo, he doth send out his voice, and that a mighty voice.
34 Ascribe ye strength unto God: his excellency is over Israel, and his strength is in the clouds.
35 O God, thou art terrible out of thy holy places: the God of Israel is he that giveth strength and power unto his people. Blessed be God.

Antichrist also, that great red dragon, needs the effectual word of the Lord to rebuke its insolence. The multitude of the bulls, the stronger foes; the proud, headstrong, rampant, fat, and roaring bulls, which sought to gore the chosen nation,—these also need the Lord's rebuke, and they shall have it too. All Egypt's sacred bulls could not avail against a "thus saith Jehovah."
Verse 31. Princes shall come out of Egypt. Old foes shall be new friends. Solomon shall find a spouse in Pharaoh's house. Christ shall gather a people from the realm of sin. Great sinners shall yield themselves to the scepter of grace, and great men shall become good men, by coming to God.
Verse 32. Sing unto God, ye kingdoms of the earth. Glorious shall that song be in which whole empires join. Happy are men that God is one who is consistently the object of joyous worship, for not such are the demons of the heathen. So sweet a thing is song that it ought to be all the Lord's; a secular concert seems almost a sacrilege, a licentious song is treason. O sing praises unto the Lord. Again and again is God to be magnified; we have too much sinning against God, but cannot have too much singing to God. Selah. Well may we rest now that our contemplations have reached the millennial glory. What heart will refuse to be lifted up by such a prospect!
Verse 33. To him that rideth upon the heavens of heavens, which were of old. Before, he was described in his earthly manifestations, as marching through the desert; now, in his celestial glory, as riding in the heavens of the primeval ages. Long ere this heaven and earth were made, the loftier abodes of the Deity stood fast; before men or angels were created, the splendors of the Great King were as great as now, and his triumphs as glorious. Our knowledge reaches but to a small fragment of the life of God, whose "goings forth were of old, even from everlasting."
Verse 34. Ascribe ye strength unto God. When even his voice rends the rocks and uproots the cedars, what cannot his hand do? His finger shakes the earth; who can conceive the power of his arm? Let us never by our doubts or our daring defiances appear to deny power unto God; on the contrary, by yielding to him and trusting in him, let our hearts acknowledge his might. When we are reconciled to God, his omnipotence is an attribute of which we sing with delight. His excellency is over Israel. The favored nation is protracted by his majesty; his greatness is to them goodness, his glory is their defense. And his strength is in the clouds. He does not confine his power to the sons of men, but makes it like a canopy to cover the skies.
Verse 35. O God, thou art terrible out of thy holy places. You inspire awe and fear. Thy saints obey with fear and trembling, and thine enemies flee in dismay. From thy threefold courts, and especially from the holy of holies, thy majesty flashes forth and makes the sons of men prostrate themselves in awe. The God of Israel is he that giveth strength and power unto his people. In this thou, who art Israel's God by covenant, art terrible to thy foes by making thy people strong, so that one shall chase a thousand, and two put ten thousand to flight. All the power of Israel's warriors is derived from the Lord, the fountain of all might. He is strong, and makes strong: blessed are they who draw from his resources, they shall renew their strength. While the self sufficient faint, the All sufficient shall sustain the feeblest believer, Blessed be God. A short but sweet conclusion. Let our souls say Amen to it, and yet again, Amen.

the Church placed in a state of perfect tranquility in this world, exposed, as it is, to a succession of enemies raised up by the malice of Satan, and designed by God for the trial and exercise of our patience.

31-35

31. Princes shall come out of Egypt. He resumes the strain of thanksgiving, and confirms what he had previously asserted, that kings would come and pay tribute unto God. The examples which he brings forward are those of the Egyptians and Ethiopians. This sufficiently proves that the prediction must be extended to Christ, by whom the Egyptians and Ethiopians were brought under the sway of God.

32. In the next verse he goes farther than before, and calls upon the kingdoms of the earth to praise God, language which implies that those who had once been distinguished by their hostility to him would be ranked amongst his willing worshippers. There must be the knowledge of God before men can celebrate the praises of his name; and we have a proof of the calling of the Gentiles, in the fact that Moses and the prophets invite them to offer sacrifices of praise. That it might not seem a strange and incredible thing to speak of the extension of the worship of God from one land, within which it had been hitherto confined, to the whole world, David insists upon God's rightful dominion over all parts of the earth.

33. He rideth upon the heaven of heavens; that is, as we have observed at the beginning of the psalm, he has supreme power over all creatures, and governs the universe at his will. This truth is one which, even in its general application, is well fitted to beget a reverential consideration of the majesty of God; but we must not overlook the more particular reason for which it is here introduced.

34. Give strength unto God over Israel The expression is in allusion to the sentence which went before, and in which God was said to send forth a strong or mighty voice. Not that, properly speaking, we can give anything to Him, but, disposed as we are to withhold that honor which is his due, David subjoins to what he had said of his thundering with a mighty voice, an injunction that we should, on our part, be ready to sound forth his praises. To guard the Gentile nations against those false ideas upon religion in which they were accustomed to indulge, he brings them back to the doctrine of the Law, in which God had specially revealed himself, and intimates that, if they would not lose themselves in error, they must advance by necessary steps from the creation and government of the world, to that doctrine in which God had condescended to make a familiar revelation of himself to men.

35. So much is included when God is spoken of here as the God of Israel. But he does not satisfy himself with enjoining them to celebrate the power of God with praises of the voice. He exhorts them to the exercise of faith, for in reality we cannot better ascribe strength unto God, than by reposing in his protection as all-sufficient. Thus, after having said that his strength is in the clouds; he adds, that he is terrible out of his holy places, by which is meant, that he exerts a power in his temple which is sufficient to confound his enemies.

III. The powerful invitation and inducement which would hereby be given to those that are without to come in and join themselves to the church, v. 29-31. This was in part fulfilled by the accession of many proselytes to the Jewish religion in the days of David and Solomon; but it was to have its full accomplishment in the conversion of the Gentile nations to the faith of Christ, and the making of them fellow-heirs, and of the same body, with the seed of Israel, Eph. iii. 6. 1. Some shall submit for fear (v. 30): "The company of spearmen, that stand it out against Christ and his gospel, that are not willing to be ruled by him, that persecute the preachers and professors of his name, that are furious and outrageous as a multitude of bulls, fat and wanton as the calves of the people" (which is a description of those Jews and Gentiles that opposed the gospel of Christ and did what they could to prevent the setting up of his kingdom in the world).

32-35 Praise to God for His sovereign dominion.

The psalmist, having prayed for and prophesied of the conversion of the Gentiles, here invites them to come in and join with the devout Israelites in praising God, intimating that their accession to the church would be the matter of their joy and praise (v. 32): Let the kingdoms of the earth sing praises to the Lord; they all ought to do it, and, when they become the kingdoms of the Lord and of his Christ, they will do it. God is here proposed to them as the proper object of praise upon several accounts:

I. Because of his supreme and sovereign dominion: He rides upon the heavens of heavens which were of old (v. 33); compare v. 4. He has from the beginning, nay from before all time, prepared his throne; he sits on the circuit of heaven, guides all the motions of the heavenly bodies; and from the highest heavens, which are the residence of his glory, he dispenses the influences of his power and goodness to this lower world.

II. Because of his awful and terrible majesty: He sends out his voice, and that a mighty voice.

III. Because of his mighty power: Ascribe you strength unto God (v. 34); acknowledge him to be a God of such irresistible power that it is folly to contend with him and wisdom to submit to him.

IV. Because of the glory of his sanctuary and the wonders wrought there (v. 35): O God! thou art terrible out of thy holy places.

V. Because of the grace bestowed upon his people: The God of Israel is he that gives strength to his people, which the gods of the nations could not give to their worshippers; how should they help them, when they could not help themselves? All Israel's strength against their enemies came from God; they owned they had no might of their own, 2 Chron. xx. 12. And all our sufficiency for our spiritual work and warfare is from the grace of God.

Psalm 69

Title
To the chief Musician upon Shoshannim. A Psalm of David.

1-7
1 Save me, O God; for the waters are come in unto my soul.
2 I sink in deep mire, where there is no standing: I am come into deep waters, where the floods overflow me.
3 I am weary of my crying: my throat is dried: mine eyes fail while I wait for my God.
4 They that hate me without a cause are more than the hairs of mine head: they that would destroy me, being mine enemies wrongfully, are mighty: then I restored that which I took not away.
5 O God, thou knowest my foolishness; and my sins are not hid from thee.
6 Let not them that wait on thee, O Lord GOD of hosts, be ashamed for my sake: let not those that seek thee be confounded for my sake, O God of Israel.
7 Because for thy sake I have borne reproach; shame hath covered my face.

Psalm 69

TITLE. To the Chief Musician upon Shoshannim. Thus for the second time we have a Psalm entitled "upon the lilies." In the forty-first they were golden lilies, dropping sweet smelling myrrh, and blooming in the fair gardens which skirt the ivory palaces: in this we have the lily among thorns, the lily of the valley, fair and beautiful, blooming in the garden of Gethsemane. A Psalm of David. If any enquire, "of whom speaketh the psalmist this? of himself, or of some other man?" we would reply, "of himself, and of some other man." Who that other is, we need not be long in discovering; it is the Crucified alone who can say, "in my thirst they gave me vinegar to drink." His footprints all through this sorrowful song have been pointed out by the Holy Spirit in the New Testament, and therefore we believe, and are sure, that the Son of Man is here. Yet is seems to be the intention of the Spirit, while he gives us personal types, and so shows the likeness to the firstborn which exists in the heirs of salvation, to set forth the disparities between the best of the sons of men, and the Son of God, for there are verses here which we dare not apply to our Lord; we almost shudder when we see our brethren attempting to do so, as for instance Ps 69:5. Especially do we note the difference between David and the Son of David in the imprecations of the one against his enemies, and the prayers of the other for them. We commence our exposition of this Psalm with much trembling, for we feel that we are entering with our Great High Priest into the most holy place.
DIVISION. This Psalm consists of two portions of 18 verses each. These again may each be sub divided into three parts. Under the first head, from Ps 69:1-4, the sufferer spreads his complaint before God; then he pleads that his zeal for God is the cause of his sufferings, in Ps 69:5-12: and this encourages him to plead for help and deliverance, from Ps 69:13-18. In the second half of the Psalm he details the injurious conduct of his adversaries, from Ps 69:19-21; calls for their punishment, Ps 69:22-28, and then returns to prayer, and to a joyful anticipation of divine interposition and its results, Ps 69:29-36.

EXPOSITION
Verse 1. Save me, O God. "He saved others, himself he cannot save." With strong cries and tears he offered up prayers and supplications unto him that was able to save him from death, and was heard in that he feared (Heb 5:7). Thus David had prayed, and here his Son and Lord utters the same cry. This is the second Psalm which begins with a "Save me, O God," and the former (Psalm 54) is but a short summary of this more lengthened complaint. It is remarkable that such a scene of woe should be presented to us immediately after the jubilant ascension hymn of the last Psalm, but this only shows how interwoven are the glories and the sorrows of our ever blessed Redeemer.
Verse 2. I sink in deep mire. In water one might swim, but in mud and mire all struggling is hopeless; the mire sucks down its victim. Where there is no standing. Everything gave way under the Sufferer; he could not get foothold for support—this is a worse fate than drowning. Here our Lord pictures the close, clinging nature of his heart's woes.
Verse 3. I am weary of my crying. Not of it, but by it, with it. He had prayed till he sweat great drops of blood, and well might physical weariness intervene. My throat is dried, parched, and inflamed. Long pleading with awful fervor had scorched his throat as with flames of fire. Few, very few, of his saints follow their Lord in prayer so far as this.
Verse 4. They that hate me. Surprising sin that men should hate the altogether lovely one, truly is it added, without a cause, for reason there was none for this senseless enmity. He neither blasphemed God, nor injured man. As Samuel said: "Whose ox have I taken? or whose ass have I taken? or whom have I defrauded? Whom have I oppressed?" Even so

JOHN CALVIN

Psalm 69

1-5

1. Save me, O God! for the waters, etc. Under the figure of waters, the Psalmist represents his condition as so extremely distressing that it brought him even to the brink of despair; and yet we know that, so far from being a soft and an effeminate person, he was one who encountered and overcame dreadful temptations with extraordinary courage. Whence we may infer the bitterness of the distress with which he was at that time afflicted.

2. I am sunk in deep mire, where there is no standing place. Here he compares his afflictions to a deep sink of mire, where there is still greater danger; for if a man fixes his feet upon a solid bottom, he may raise himself up, there having been many instances in which persons, placing their feet on the bottom, have by a sudden spring emerged and escaped the peril of the waters; but when a man finds himself once sunk in some slough or muddy river, it is all over with him, he has no means of saving himself.

3. I am weary of crying David, in seeking and calling upon God, when his affairs were in such a confused and desperate condition, exhibited an instance of rare and wonderful patience. He complains of having continued crying until he was exhausted and became hoarse, and all to no purpose. By the word weary, he does not mean that he gave up with prayer, as if he had cast from him all love to and delight in that exercise upon finding that it proved unavailing as a means of deliverance. He rather describes his untiring perseverance; and the same idea is expressed by his hoarse throat and failing eyes.

4. They who hate me without cause are more in number than the hairs of my head. The Psalmist now expresses without figure what he had said under the metaphors of the mire and of the impetuous rushing of the waters. Persecuted as he was by so great a multitude of enemies, he had too good reason to be afraid of death in innumerable ways.

5. O God! thou knowest my foolishness. Let us be always ready to satisfy men; but if they refuse to listen to what we have to say in self-vindication, let us proceed in our course through evil report as well as good report, following the example of Paul where he fearlessly appeals to the judgment of God, "who will bring to light the hidden things of dark," (1 Corinthians 4:5).

6-9

6. O Jehovah, Lord of Hosts! let not them that wait for thee be ashamed in me. David declares that he is set forth as an example from which all the people of God may derive matter either of hope or despair. Although he was held in detestation and execrated by the great body of the people, there yet remained a few who were ready to bear just and impartial testimony to his innocence; knowing as they did that he was unrighteously afflicted by his persecutors, that he constantly reposed on the grace and goodness of God, and that no temptations could discourage or prevent him from continuing steadfast in the practice of true godliness.

MATTHEW HENRY

Psalm 69

1-12 Complaints and petitions.

In these verses David complains of his troubles, intermixing with those complaints some requests for relief.

I. His complaints are very sad, and he pours them out before the Lord, as one that hoped thus to ease himself of a burden that lay very heavy upon him.

1. He complains of the deep impressions that his troubles made upon his spirit (v. 1, 2): "The waters of affliction, those bitter waters, have come unto my soul, not only threaten my life, but disquiet my mind; they fill my head with perplexing cares and my heart with oppressive grief, so that I cannot enjoy God and myself as I used to do." We shall bear up under our troubles if we can but keep them from our hearts; but, when they put us out of the possession of our own souls, our case is bad.

2. He complains of the long continuance of his troubles (v. 3): I am weary of my crying. Though he could not keep his head above water, yet he cried to his God, and the more death was in his view the more life was in his prayers; yet he had not immediately an answer of peace given in, no, nor so much of that support and comfort in praying which God's people used to have; so that he was almost weary of crying, grew hoarse, and his throat so dried that he could cry no more.

3. He complains of the malice and multitude of his enemies, their injustice and cruelty, and the hardships they put upon him, v. 4. They hated him, they would destroy him, for hatred aims at the destruction of the person hated; but what was his iniquity, what was his sin, what provocation had he given them, that they were so spiteful towards him? None at all: "They hate me without a cause; I never did them the least injury, that they should bear me such ill-will." Our Savior applies this to himself (John xv. 25): They hated me without a cause. We are apt to use this in justification of our passion against those that hate us, that we never gave them cause to hate us.

4. He complains of the unkindness of his friends and relations, and this is a grievance which with an ingenuous mind cuts as deeply as any (v. 8): "I have become a stranger to my brethren; they make themselves strange to me and use me as a stranger, are shy of conversing with me and ashamed to own me." This was fulfilled in Christ, whose brethren did not believe on him (John vii. 5), who came to his own and his own received him not (John i. 11), and who was forsaken by his disciples, whom he had been free with as his brethren.

5. He complains of the contempt that was put upon him and the reproach with which he was continually loaded. And in this especially his complaint points at Christ, who for our sakes submitted to the greatest disgrace and made himself

Psalm 69

8-14
8 I am become a stranger unto my brethren, and an alien unto my mother's children.
9 For the zeal of thine house hath eaten me up; and the reproaches of them that reproached thee are fallen upon me.
10 When I wept, and chastened my soul with fasting, that was to my reproach.
11 I made sackcloth also my garment; and I became a proverb to them.
12 They that sit in the gate speak against me; and I was the song of the drunkards.
13 But as for me, my prayer is unto thee, O LORD, in an acceptable time: O God, in the multitude of thy mercy hear me, in the truth of thy salvation.
14 Deliver me out of the mire, and let me not sink: let me be delivered from them that hate me, and out of the deep waters.

might Jesus enquire. Besides, he had not only done us no evil, but he had bestowed countless and priceless benefits. Well might he demand, "For which of these works do ye stone me?" Yet from his cradle to his cross, beginning with Herod and not ending with Judas, he had foes without number; and he justly said, they are more than the hairs of mine head.
Verse 5. O God, thou knowest my foolishness. David might well say this, but not David's Lord; unless it be understood as an appeal to God as to his freedom from the folly which men imputed to him when they said he was mad. That which was foolishness to men was superlative wisdom before God. How often might we use these words in their natural sense, and if we were not such fools as to be blind to our own folly, this confession would be frequently on our lips.
Verse 6. Let not them that wait on thee, O Lord God of hosts, be ashamed for my sake. If he were deserted, others who were walking in the same path of faith would be discouraged and disappointed. Unbelievers are ready enough to catch at anything which may turn humble faith into ridicule, therefore, O God of all the armies of Israel, let not my case cause the enemy to blaspheme—such is the spirit of this verse.
Verse 7. Because for thy sake I have borne reproach. Because he undertook to do the Father's will, and teach his truth, the people were angry; because he declared himself to be the Son of God, the priesthood raved. They could find no real fault in him, but were forced to hatch up a lying accusation before they could commence their sham trial of him.
Verse 8. I am become a stranger unto my brethren. The Jews his brethren in race rejected him, his family his brethren by blood were offended at him, his disciples his brethren in spirit forsook him and fled; one of them sold him, and another denied him with oaths and cursings.
Verse 9. For the zeal of thine house hath eaten me up. His burning ardor, like the flame of a candle, fed on his strength and consumed it. His heart, like a sharp sword, cut through the scabbard. Some men are eaten up with lechery, others with covetousness, and a third class with pride, but the master passion with our great leader was the glory of God, jealousy for his name, and love to the divine family.
Verse 10. When I wept, and chastened my soul with fasting, that was to my reproach. Having resolved to hate him, everything he did was made a fresh reason for reviling. If he ate and drank as others, he was a man gluttonous and a winebibber; if he wept himself away and wore himself out with fasting, then he had a devil and was mad.
Verse 11. I made sackcloth also my garment. This David did literally, but we have no reason to believe that Jesus did. In a spiritual sense he, as one filled with grief, was always a sackcloth wearer. And I became a proverb to them. He was ridiculed as "the man of sorrows," quoted as "the acquaintance of grief." He might have said, "here I and sorrow sit." This which should have won him pity only earned him new and more general scorn. To interweave one's name into a mocking proverb is the highest stretch of malice, and to insult one's acts of devotion is to add profanity to cruelty.
Verse 12. They that sit in the gate speak against me. The ordinary gossips who meet at the city gates for idle talk make me their theme, the business men who there resort for trade forget their merchandise to slander me, and even the beggars who wait at men's doors for alms contribute their share of insult to the heap of infamy. And I was the song of the drunkard. The ungodly know no merrier jest than that in which the name of the holy is traduced. The flavor of slander is piquant, and gives a relish to the revelers' wine.
Verse 13. But as for me, my prayer is unto thee, O Lord. He turned to Jehovah in prayer as being the most natural thing for the godly to do in their distress. To whom should a child turn but to his father. He did not answer them; like a sheep before her shearers he was dumb to them, but he

JOHN CALVIN

7. For on thy account I have suffered reproach. He now expresses more distinctly what he had stated ironically in the fifth verse, where he asserts that his faults were not hidden from God. Nay, he proceeds farther, declaring not only that the evil treatment which he met with from his enemies was unjust and altogether unmerited, but also that his cause was really God's cause, since whatever he had undertaken and engaged in was expressly in obedience to the command of God.
8. The Psalmist farther aggravates his complaint by the additional circumstance, that he was cruelly cast off by his own relations and friends; from which we are taught, that when by our devotedness to the cause of religion we cannot avoid exciting the displeasure of our brethren against us, it is our duty simply to follow God, and not to confer with flesh and blood.
9. For the zeal of thy house hath eaten me up. David's enemies, no doubt, professed that nothing was farther from their mind than to touch the sacred name of God; but he reproves their hypocritical pretences, and affirms that he is fighting in God's quarrel.

10-13
10. And I wept, my soul fasted. David here proves, by the signs or effects, that his efforts to promote the Divine glory proceeded from a pure and well-regulated zeal, inasmuch as he was not impelled or inflamed by the impetuosity of the flesh, but rather humbly abased himself before God, choosing him to be the witness of his sorrow.
11. When he saw things in such a state of confusion, he voluntarily engaged in this sorrowful exercise to testify that nothing was more grievous to him than to witness the sacred name of God exposed to contumely.
12. They who sit in the gate defame me. Had David been molested only by vulgar buffoons and the refuse of the people, it would have been more easily endured; for it is not surprising that mean persons, who have no regard to what is becoming and honorable, degrade themselves by indulging in defamation without shame. But when the very judges, forgetful of what is demanded by the dignity of their office, abandon themselves to the same audacious conduct, the iniquity and baseness of it is greatly aggravated.
13. But as for me, my prayer is to thee, O Jehovah! It was a sign of uncommon virtue in David, that even this hard treatment could not shake his mind, and sink him into despondency.

14-18
14. Deliver me from the mire, that I may not sink. The Psalmist repeats the same similitude which he had used before, but in a different manner. He had previously said that he was sunk in the mire, and now he prays that he may not sink in it. In short, he now prays that those things may not now befall him which he had formerly complained of as having befallen him.
15. This is expressed still more clearly in the last clause of the 15th verse, where he prays, Let not the pit close its mouth

MATTHEW HENRY

of no reputation. We having by sin injured God in his honor, Christ made him satisfaction, not only by divesting himself of the honors due to an incarnate deity, but by submitting to the greatest dishonors that could be done to any man.
II. His confessions of sin are very serious (v. 5): "O God! thou knowest my foolishness, what is and what is not; my sins that I am guilty of are not hidden from thee, and therefore thou knowest how innocent I am of those crimes which they charge upon me."
III. His supplications are very earnest.
1. For himself (v. 1): "Save me, O God! save me from sinking, from despairing." Thus Christ was heard in that he feared, for he was saved from letting fall his undertaking, Heb. v. 7.
2. For his friends (v. 6): Let not those that wait on thee, O Lord God of hosts! and that seek thee, O God of Israel! (under these two characters we ought to seek God, and in seeking him to wait on him, as the God of hosts, who has all power to help, and as the God of Israel in covenant with his people, whom therefore he is engaged in honor and truth to help) be ashamed and confounded for my sake.
IV. His plea is very powerful, v. 7, 9. Reproach was one of the greatest of his burdens: "Lord, roll away the reproach, and plead my cause."

13-21 Complaints and petitions.
David had been speaking before of the spiteful reproaches which his enemies cast upon him; here he adds, But, as for me, my prayer is unto thee. They spoke ill of him for his fasting and praying, and for that he was made the song of the drunkards; but, notwithstanding that, he resolves to continue praying. Now observe,
I. What his requests are.
1. That he might have a gracious audience given to his complaints, the cry of his affliction, and the desire of his heart. Hear me (v. 13), and again, Hear me, O Lord! (v. 16), Hear me speedily (v. 17), not only hear what I say, but grant what I ask. Christ knew that the Father heard him always, John xi. 42.
2. That he might be rescued out of his troubles, might be saved from sinking under the load of grief (Deliver me out of the mire; let me not stick in it, so some, but help me out, and set my feet on a rock, Ps. xl. 2), might be saved from his enemies, that they might not swallow him up, nor have their will against him: "Let me be delivered from those that hate me, as a lamb from the paw of a lion, v. 14. Though I have come into keep waters (v. 2), where I am ready to conclude that the floods will overflow me, yet let my fears be prevented and silenced; let not the waterflood, though it flow upon me, overflow me, v. 15. Let me not fall into the gulf of despair; let not that deep swallow me up; let not that pit shut her mouth upon me, for then I am undone." He gave himself up for lost in the beginning of the psalm; yet now he has his head above water, and is not so weary of crying as he thought himself.

Psalm 69

15-21
15 Let not the waterflood overflow me, neither let the deep swallow me up, and let not the pit shut her mouth upon me.
16 Hear me, O LORD; for thy loving kindness is good: turn unto me according to the multitude of thy tender mercies.
17 And hide not thy face from thy servant; for I am in trouble: hear me speedily.
18 Draw nigh unto my soul, and redeem it: deliver me because of mine enemies.
19 Thou hast known my reproach, and my shame, and my dishonor: mine adversaries are all before thee.
20 Reproach hath broken my heart; and I am full of heaviness: and I looked for some to take pity, but there was none; and for comforters, but I found none.
21 They gave me also gall for my meat; and in my thirst they gave me vinegar to drink.

opened his mouth unto the Lord his God, for he would hear and deliver. In an acceptable time. It was a time of rejection with man, but of acceptance with God. Sin ruled on earth, but grace reigned in heaven.
Verse 14. Deliver me out of the mire and let me not sink. He turns into prayer the very words of his complaint; and it is well, if, when we complain, we neither feel nor say anything which we should fear to utter before the Lord as a prayer.
Verse 15. Let not the waterflood overflow me. He continues to recapitulate the terms of his lament. He is willing to bear suffering, but entreats grace that it may not get the victory over him. He was heard in that he feared. Neither let the deep swallow me up. As Jonah came forth again, so let me also arise from the abyss of woe; here also our Lord was heard, and so shall we be. Death itself must disgorge us. Let not the pit shut her mouth upon me.
Verse 16. Hear me, O Lord. Do not refuse thy suppliant Son. It is to the covenant God, the ever living Jehovah, that he appeals with strong crying. For thy lovingkindness is good. By the greatness of thy love have pity upon thine afflicted. It is always a stay to the soul to dwell upon the preeminence and excellence of the Lord's mercy. It has furnished sad souls much good cheer to take to pieces that grand old Saxon word, which is here used in our version, lovingkindness. Its composition is of two most sweet and fragrant things, fitted to inspire strength into the fainting, and make desolate hearts sing for joy.
Verse 17. And hide not thy face from thy servant. A good servant desires the light of his master's countenance; that servus servorum, who was also rex regium, could not bear to lose the presence of his God. The more he loved his Father, the more severely he felt the hiding of his face. For I am in trouble. Stay thy rough wind in the day of thine east wind; do not add sorrow upon sorrow. If ever a man needs the comforting presence of God it is when he is in distress; and, being in distress, it is a reason to be pleaded with a merciful God why he should not desert us. We may pray that our flight be not in the winter, and that God will not add spiritual desertion to all our other tribulations.
Verse 18. Draw nigh unto my soul. The near approach of God is all the sufferer needs; one smile of heaven will still the rage of hell. And redeem it. It shall be redemption to me if thou wilt appear to comfort me. This is a deeply spiritual prayer, and one very suitable for a deserted soul. It is in renewed communion that we shall find redemption realized.
Verse 19. Thou hast known my reproach, and my shame, and my dishonor. It is no novelty or secret, it has been long continued; thou, O God, hast seen it; and for thee to see the innocent suffer is an assurance of help. Here are three words piled up to express the Redeemer's keen sense of the contempt poured upon him; and his assurance that every form of malicious despite was observed of the Lord.
Verse 20. Reproach hath broken my heart. There is no hammer like it. Our Lord died of a broken heart, and reproach had done the deed. Intense mental suffering arises from slander; and in the case of the sensitive nature of the immaculate Son of Man, it sufficed to lacerate the heart till it broke.
Verse 21. They gave me also gall for my meat. This was the sole refreshment cruelty had prepared for him. Others find pleasure in their food, but his taste was made to be an additional path of pain to him. And in my thirst they gave me vinegar to drink. A criminal's draught was offered to our innocent Lord, a bitter portion to our dying Master. Sorry entertainment had earth for her King and Savior. How often have our sins filled the gall cup for our Redeemer? While we blame the Jews, let us not excuse ourselves. From this point David and our Lord for awhile part company, if we accept the rendering of our version. The severe spirit of the law breathes out imprecations, while the tender heart of Jesus offers prayers for his murderers. The whole of these verses, however, may be viewed as

upon me; which is as if he had said, Let not the great multitude and weight of my afflictions overwhelm me, and let not sorrow swallow me up.

16. Answer me, O Jehovah! for thy mercy is good. The appeal which he here makes to the mercy and compassion of God is an evidence of the distressed condition into which he was brought. There can be no doubt that he sustained a dreadful conflict, when he had recourse to these as the only means of his safety. It is a very difficult matter to believe that God is merciful to us when he is angry with us, and that he is near us when he has withdrawn himself from us.

18. Draw near to my soul, redeem it. David was doubtless fully persuaded by faith that God was near him; but as we are accustomed to measure the presence or absence of God by the effects, David here tacitly complains, judging according to the flesh, that he is far from him. By the expression, Draw near, he means, that in so far as could be gathered from his actual condition, God appeared to have no regard to his welfare. Again, by calling upon God to draw near to his life, which he seemed to have forsaken, he exhibits a striking proof of the strength of his faith.

19-21

19. Thou knowest my reproach, and my confusion. This is a confirmation of the preceding sentence. Whence is it that the greater part of men become dispirited when they see the wicked outrageously rushing upon them, and their wickedness, like a water-flood, carrying all before it, but because they think that heaven is so obscured and overcast with clouds as to prevent God from beholding what is done upon the earth? It becomes us, therefore, in this matter, to call to our remembrance the doctrine of a Divine Providence, that contemplating it we may be assured beyond all doubt, that God will appear for our succor in due season.

20. Reproach hath broken my heart, and I am afflicted. He expresses more distinctly not only that he was confounded, or ashamed at the sad aspect which he presented of having been deserted, but that he was well nigh overwhelmed with sorrow by lying so long under reproach and shame. Whence it is evident that he did not overcome this sorrow without a struggle; and that the reason why he so firmly withstood the waves of temptations was, not because they did not reach his heart, but because, being sorely smitten, he made resistance with a corresponding degree of intrepidity.

21. And they put gall into my meat. Here he again repeats that his enemies carry their cruelty towards him to the utmost extent in their power. He speaks metaphorically when he describes them as mingling gall or poison with his meat, and vinegar with his drink; even as it is said in Jeremiah, "Behold, I will feed them, even this people, with wormwood, and give them water of gall to drink." (Jeremiah 9:15) But still the Apostle John justly declares that this Scripture was fulfilled when the soldiers gave Christ vinegar to drink upon the cross, (John 19:28-30;) for it was requisite that whatever cruelty the reprobate exercise towards the members of Christ, should by a visible sign be represented in Christ himself.

3. That God would turn to him (v. 16), that he would smile upon him, and not hide his face from him, v. 17. The tokens of God's favor to us, and the light of his countenance shining upon us, are enough to keep our spirits from sinking in the deepest mire of outward troubles, nor need we desire any more to make us safe and easy, v. 18. "Draw nigh to my soul, to manifest thyself to it, and that shall redeem it."

II. What his pleas are to enforce these petitions.

1. He pleads God's mercy and truth (v. 13): In the multitude of thy mercy hear me. There is mercy in God, a multitude of mercies, all kinds of mercy, inexhaustible mercy, mercy enough for all, enough for each; and hence we must take our encouragement in praying. The truth also of his salvation (the truth of all those promises of salvation which he has made to those that trust in him) is a further encouragement.

2. He pleads his own distress and affliction: "Hide not thy face from me, for I am in trouble (v. 17), and therefore need thy favor; therefore it will come seasonably, and therefore I shall know how to value it." He pleads particularly the reproach he was under and the indignities that were done him (v. 19): Thou hast known my reproach, my shame, and my dishonor. See what a stress is laid upon this; for, in the sufferings of Christ for us, perhaps nothing contributed more to the satisfaction he made for sin, which had been so injurious to God in his honor, than the reproach, and shame, and dishonor he underwent, which God took notice of, and accepted as more than an equivalent for the everlasting shame and contempt which our sins had deserved, and therefore we must by repentance take shame to ourselves and bear the reproach of our youth. And if at any time we be called out to suffer reproach, and shame, and dishonor, for his sake, this may be our comfort, that he knows it, and, as he is before-hand with us, so he will not be behind-hand with us. The Psalmist speaks the language of an ingenuous nature when he says (v. 20): Reproach has broken my heart; I am full of heaviness; for it bears hard upon one that knows the worth of a good name to be put under a bad character; but when we consider what an honor it is to be dishonored for God, and what a favor to be counted worthy to suffer shame for his name (as they deemed it, Acts v. 41), we shall see there is no reason at all why it should sit so heavily or be any heart-breaking to us.

3. He pleads the insolence and cruelty of his enemies (v. 18): Deliver me because of my enemies, because they were such as he had before described them, v. 4. "My adversaries are all before thee (v. 19); thou knowest what sort of men they are, what danger I am in from them, what enemies they are to thee, and how much thou art reflected upon in what they do and design against me."

4. He pleads the unkindness of his friends and his disappointment in them (v. 20): I looked for some to take pity, but there was none; they all failed him like the brooks in summer. This was fulfilled in Christ, for

Psalm 69

22-28

22 Let their table become a snare before them: and that which should have been for their welfare, let it become a trap.
23 Let their eyes be darkened, that they see not; and make their loins continually to shake.
24 Pour out thine indignation upon them, and let thy wrathful anger take hold of them.
25 Let their habitation be desolate; and let none dwell in their tents.
26 For they persecute him whom thou hast smitten; and they talk to the grief of those whom thou hast wounded.
27 Add iniquity unto their iniquity: and let them not come into thy righteousness.
28 Let them be blotted out of the book of the living, and not be written with the righteous.

predictions, and then they certainly refer to our Lord, for we find portions of them quoted in that manner by the apostle in Ro 11:9-10, and by Christ himself in Mt 23:38.

Verse 22. Let their table become a snare before them. There they laid snares, and there they shall find them. From their feasts they would afford nothing but wormwood for their innocent victim, and now their banquets shall be their ruin. It is very easy for the daily provisions of mercy to become temptations to sin. As birds and beasts are taken in a trap by means of baits for the appetite, so are men snared full often by their meats and drinks. Those who despise the upper springs of grace, shall find the nether springs of worldly comfort prove their poison.

Verse 23. Let their eyes be darkened, that they see not. They shall wander in a darkness that may be felt. They have loved darkness rather than light, and in darkness they shall abide. Judicial blindness fell upon Israel after our Lord's death and their persecution of his apostles; they were blinded by the light which they would not accept. Eyes which see no beauty in the Lord Jesus, but flash wrath upon him, may well grow yet more dim, till death spiritual leads to death eternal. And make their loins continually to shake.

Verse 24. Pour out thine indignation upon them. What can be too severe a penalty for those who reject the incarnate God, and refuse to obey the commands of his mercy? They deserve to be flooded with wrath, and they shall be; for upon all who rebel against the Savior, Christ the Lord, "the wrath is come to the uttermost." 1Th 2:16. God's indignation is no trifle; the anger of a holy, just, omnipotent, and infinite Being, is above all things to be dreaded; even a drop of it consumes, but to have it poured upon us is inconceivably dreadful. O God, who knoweth the power of thine anger? And let thy wrathful anger take hold of them. If they flee, let it overtake and seize them; let it lay them by the heels in the condemned cell, so that they cannot escape from execution.

Verse 25. Let their habitation be desolate; and let none dwell in their tents. This may signify that their posterity shall be cut off, and the abode which they occupy shall be left a ruin; or, as our Lord quoted it, it refers to the temple, which was left by its divine occupant and became a desolation. What occurs on a large scale to families and nations is often fulfilled in individuals, as was conspicuously the case with Judas, to whom Peter referred this prophecy, Ac 1:20, "For it is written in the book of Psalms, let this habitation be desolate, and let no man dwell therein."

Verse 26. For they persecute him whom thou hast smitten. They are cruel where they should be pitiful. When a stroke comes to any in the providence of God, their friends gather around them and condole, but these wretches hunt the wounded and vex the sick. Their merciless hearts invent fresh blows for him who is "smitten of God and afflicted." And they talk to the grief of those whom thou hast wounded. They lay bare his wounds with their rough tongues.

Verse 27. Add iniquity unto their iniquity. Unbelievers will add sin to sin, and so, punishment to punishment. This is the severest imprecation, or prophecy, of all. For men to be let alone to fill up the measure of their iniquity, is most equitable, but yet most awful. And let them not come into thy righteousness. If they refuse it, and resist thy gospel, let them shut themselves out of it.

Verse 28. Let them be blotted out of the book of the living. Though in their conceit they wrote themselves among the people of God, and induced others to regard them under that character, they shall be unmasked and their names removed from the register.

Verse 29. But I am poor and sorrowful. The psalmist was afflicted very much, but his faith was in God. The poor in spirit and mourners are both blessed under the gospel, so that here is a double reason for the Lord to smile on his suppliant. No man was ever poorer or more sorrowful than

JOHN CALVIN

22-29
22. Let their table before them be for a snare. Here we have a series of dire imprecations, with respect to which we must bear in mind, what we have elsewhere observed, that David did not allow himself recklessly to pour out his wrath, even as the greater part of men, when they feel themselves wronged, intemperately give way to their own passion; but, being under the guidance of the Holy Spirit, he was kept from going beyond the bounds of duty, and simply called upon God to exercise just judgment against the reprobate. Farther, it was not on his own account that he pleaded in this manner; but it was a holy zeal for the divine glory which impelled him to summon the wicked to God's judgment-seat. It was also owing to this: that he was not carried away by violence of passion, like those who are actuated by a desire of taking revenge. Since, then, the Spirit of wisdom, uprightness, and moderation, put these imprecations into the mouth of David, his example cannot justly be pleaded in self-vindication by those who pour forth their wrath and spite upon every one that comes in their way, or who are carried away by a foolish impatience to take revenge; never allowing themselves to reflect for a moment what good purpose this can serve, nor making any efforts to keep their passion within due bounds. We need wisdom by which to distinguish between those who are wholly reprobate and those of whose amendment there is still some hope; we have also need of uprightness, that none may devote himself exclusively to his own private interests; and of moderation too, to dispose our minds to calm endurance.
23. Let their eyes be darkened, that they may not see. The Psalmist here refers chiefly to two powers of the body, those of the eyes and of the loins; and I have no hesitation in considering his language as a prayer that God would deprive his enemies of reason and understanding, and at the same time enfeeble their strength, that they might be altogether unfitted for exerting themselves in any way.
24. Pour out thy fury upon them. It is not surprising that David utters a lengthened series of imprecations; for we know well that the frantic enemies of the Church, into whom it was his object to inspire terror, are not easily moved. He therefore lifts up his voice against them in tones of greater vehemence, that they might be led to desist from their wrongful and insolent conduct.
25 Let their habitation be desolate. Here he proceeds farther than in the preceding verse, praying that God would cause his wrath to descend to their posterity; and it is no new thing for the sins of the fathers to be cast into the bosom of the children. As David uttered these imprecations by the inspiration and influence of the Holy Spirit, so he took them out of the law itself, in which God threatens that he will "visit the iniquity of the fathers upon the children unto the third and fourth generation of them that hate him," (Exodus 20:5). In this way he desires that the memorial of them may be cursed, and that thus God would not spare them even after their death.
26. For they have persecuted him whom thou hast smitten. He brings forward the crime with which they were chargeable, to

MATTHEW HENRY

in his sufferings all his disciples forsook him and fled. We cannot expect too little from men (miserable comforters are they all); nor can we expect too much from God, for he is the Father of mercy and the God of all comfort and consolation.

22-29 Pleading with God; prophetic imprecations.
Let us observe here,
I. What the judgments are which should come upon the crucifiers of Christ; not upon all of them, for there were those who had a hand in his death and yet repented and found mercy (Acts ii. 23; iii. 14, 15), but upon those of them and their successors who justified it by an obstinate infidelity and rejection of his gospel, and by an inveterate enmity to his disciples and followers. See 1 Thess. ii. 15, 16. It is here foretold,
1. That their sacrifices and offerings should be a mischief and prejudice to them (v. 22): Let their table become a snare. This may be understood of the altar of the Lord, which is called his table and theirs because in feasting upon the sacrifices they were partakers of the altar. This should have been for their welfare or peace (for they were peace-offerings), but it became a snare and a trap to them; for by their affection and adherence to the altar they were held fast in their infidelity and hardened in their prejudices against Christ, that altar which those had no right to eat of who continued to serve the tabernacle, Heb. xiii. 10.
2. That they should never have the comfort either of that knowledge or of that peace which believers are blessed with in the gospel of Christ (v. 23), that they should be given up.
3. That they should fall and lie under God's anger and fiery indignation (v. 24): Pour out thy indignation upon them.
4. That their place and nation should be utterly taken away, the very thing they were afraid of, and to prevent which, as they pretended, they persecuted Christ (John xi. 48): Let their habitation be desolate (v. 25), which was fulfilled when their country was laid waste by the Romans, and Zion, for their sakes, was ploughed as a field, Mic. iii. 12. The temple was the house which they were in a particular manner proud of, but this was left unto them desolate, Matt. xxiii. 38.
5. That their way to ruin should be downhill, and nothing should stop them, nor interpose to prevent it (v. 27): "Lord, leave them to themselves, to add iniquity to iniquity." Those that are bad, if they be given up to their own hearts' lusts, will certainly be worse; they will add sin to sin, nay, they will add rebellion to their sin, Job xxxiv. 37.
6. That they should be cut off from all hopes of happiness (v. 28): Let them be blotted out of the book of the living; let them not be suffered to live any longer, since, the longer they live, the more mischief they do. Multitudes of the unbelieving Jews fell by sword and famine, and none of those who had

Psalm 69

29-36

29 But I am poor and sorrowful: let thy salvation, O God, set me up on high.

30 I will praise the name of God with a song, and will magnify him with thanksgiving.

31 This also shall please the LORD better than an ox or bullock that hath horns and hoofs.

32 The humble shall see this, and be glad: and your heart shall live that seek God.

33 For the LORD heareth the poor, and despiseth not his prisoners.

34 Let the heaven and earth praise him, the seas, and every thing that moveth therein.

35 For God will save Zion, and will build the cities of Judah: that they may dwell there, and have it in possession.

36 The seed also of his servants shall inherit it: and they that love his name shall dwell therein.

Jesus of Nazareth, yet his cry out of the depths was heard, and he was uplifted to the highest glory.

Verse 30. I will praise the name of God with a song. He who sang after the Passover, sings yet more joyously after the resurrection and ascension. He is, in very truth, "the sweet singer of Israel." He leads the eternal melodies, and all his saints join in chorus.

Verse 31. This also shall please the Lord better than an ox or bullock that hath horns and hoofs. No sacrifice is so acceptable to God, who is a Spirit, as that which is spiritual. He accepted bullocks under a dim and symbolical dispensation; but in such offerings, in themselves considered, he had no pleasure.

Verse 32. The humble shall see this and be glad. Grateful hearts are ever on the look out for recruits, and the rejoicing psalmist discerns with joy the fact, that other oppressed and lowly men observing the Lord's dealings with his servants are encouraged to look for a like issue to their own tribulations.

Verse 33. For the Lord heareth the poor. The examples of David and David's Lord, and tens of thousands of the saints, all go to prove this. Monarchs of the nations are deaf to the poor, but the Sovereign of the Universe has a quick ear for the needy. None can be brought lower than was the Nazarene, but see how highly he is exalted: descend into what depths we may, the prayer hearing God can bring us up again.

Verse 34. Let the heaven and earth praise him, the seas, and every thing that moveth therein. The doxology of a glowing heart. The writer had fathomed the deeps, and had ascended to the heights; and, therefore, calls on the whole range of creation to bless the Lord.

Verse 35. For God will save Zion, and will build the cities of Judah. Poor, fallen Israel shall have a portion in the mercy of the Lord; but, above all, the church, so dear to the heart of her glorious bridegroom, shall be revived and strengthened. Ancient saints so dearly loved Zion, that even in their distresses they did not forget her; with the first gleam of light which visited them, they fell to pleading for the faithful: see notable instances of this which have passed under our eye already. Ps 5:11 14:7 22:23 51:18.

Verse 36. The seed also of his servants shall inherit it. Under this image, which, however, we dare not regard as a mere simile, but as having in itself a literal significance, we have set forth to us the enrichment of the saints, consequent upon the sorrow of their Lord. The termination of this Psalm strongly recalls in us that of the twenty-second. The seed lie near the Savior's heart, and their enjoyment of all promised good is the great concern of his disinterested soul. Because they are his Father's servants, therefore he rejoices in their welfare. And they that love his name shall dwell therein. He has an eye to the Father's glory, for it is to his praise that those who love him should attain, and for ever enjoy, the utmost happiness. Thus a Psalm, which began in the deep waters, ends in the city which hath foundations. How gracious is the change. Hallelujah.

JOHN CALVIN

make it manifest that they richly deserved such dreadful punishments.

27. Add iniquity to their iniquity. It is abundantly evident, from the second clause, that what David prays for is that God, taking his Spirit altogether from the wicked, would give them over to a reprobate mind, that they might never seek or have any desire to be brought to genuine repentance and amendment.

28. Let them be blotted out from the book of the living. This is the last imprecation, and it is the most dreadful of the whole; but it nevertheless uniformly follows the persevered in impenitence and incorrigible obduracy of which the Psalmist has spoken above.

29. As for me, I am poor and sorrowful. From this verse we perceive more distinctly how David cast away from him the swelling and raging passion of those who, with ungovernable fury, pour forth imprecation and vengeance. He here, without doubt, offers himself to God with the sacrifice of a broken and humble heart, that by this meekness of spirit he may obtain favor with him.

30-33

30. I will celebrate the name of God in a song. The Psalmist now elevated with joy, and sustained by the confident hope of deliverance, sings the triumphant strains of victory.

31. And this will please Jehovah more than a young bullock. The more effectually to strengthen himself for this exercise, David affirms that the thanksgiving which he is about to tender, will be to God a sacrifice of a sweet and an acceptable savor.

32. The afflicted have seen it. He here shows that the blessed effects of his deliverance will extend to others as well as to himself, a point which he frequently insists on in the Psalms.

33. The Psalmist immediately after describes the means by which this will be brought about in the children of God, which is, that believing the deliverance of David to be a common token or pledge of the grace of God presented before them, they will confidently come to the conclusion, that God regards the needy, and does not despise the prisoners.

34-36

34. Let the heavens and the earth praise him. From this we may conclude with the greater certainty, that David in the whole of this psalm spake in the name of the whole Church; for he now transfers to the Church what he had spoken in particular concerning himself.

35. He begins at the restoration of a new state of things, which by his means was suddenly brought about upon the death of Saul, when a melancholy devastation threatened at once the utter destruction of the worship of God, and the desolation of the whole country.

36. And the seed of his servants shall inherit it. In this verse he declares that the blessing now mentioned would extend through a continued succession of ages. the enduring possession of all good things depends upon Christ, of whom David was a type.

MATTHEW HENRY

embraced the Christian faith perished among them; the nation, as a nation, was blotted out, and became not a people. Many understand it of their rejection from God's covenant and all the privileges of it; that is the book of the living: "Let the commonwealth of Israel itself, Israel according to the flesh, now become alienated from that covenant of promise which hitherto it has had the monopoly of. Let it appear that they were never written in the Lamb's book of life, but reprobate silver let men call them, because the Lord has rejected them. Let them not be written with the righteous; that is, let them not have a place in the congregation of the saints when they shall all be gathered in the general assembly of those whose names are written in heaven," Ps. i. 5.

II. What the sin is for which these dreadful judgments should be brought upon them (v. 26): They persecute him whom thou hast smitten, and talk to the grief of thy wounded.

III. What the psalmist thinks of himself in the midst of all (v. 29): "But I am poor and sorrowful; that is the worst of my case, under outward afflictions, yet written among the righteous, and not under God's indignation as they are." It is better to be poor and sorrowful, with the blessing of God, than rich and jovial and under his curse.

30-36 Comfort for the persecuted; thanksgiving and praise.

The psalmist here, both as a type of Christ and as an example to Christians, concludes a psalm with holy joy and praise which he began with complaints and remonstrances of his griefs.

I. He resolves to praise God himself, not doubting but that therein he should be accepted of him (v. 30, 31): "I will praise the name of God, not only with my heart, but with my song, and magnify him with thanksgiving;" for he is pleased to reckon himself magnified by the thankful praises of his people.

II. He encourages other good people to rejoice in God and continue seeking him (v. 32, 33): The humble shall see this and be glad.

III. He calls upon all the creatures to praise God, the heaven, and earth, and sea, and the inhabitants of each, v. 34. Heaven and earth, and the hosts of both, were made by him, and therefore let heaven and earth praise him.

For, 1. It shall be peopled and inhabited. There shall be added to it such as shall be saved. The cities of Judah shall be built, particular churches shall be formed and incorporated according to the gospel model, that there may be a remnant to dwell there and to have it in possession, to enjoy the privileges conferred upon it and to pay the tributes and services required from it.

2. It shall be perpetuated and inherited. Christianity was not to be res unius ætatis—a transitory thing. No: The seed of his servants shall inherit it. God will secure and raise up for himself a seed to serve him.

Psalm 70

Title
To the chief Musician. A Psalm of David. To bring to remembrance.

1 Make haste, o god, to deliver me; make haste to help me, O LORD.
2 Let them be ashamed and confounded that seek after my soul: let them be turned backward, and put to confusion, that desire my hurt.
3 Let them be turned back for a reward of their shame that say, Aha, aha.
4 Let all those that seek thee rejoice and be glad in thee: and let such as love thy salvation say continually, Let God be magnified.
5 But I am poor and needy: make haste unto me, O God: thou art my help and my deliverer; O LORD, make no tarrying.

Psalm 70

The title corresponds with Psalm 40, of which this is a copy with variations. David appears to have written the full length Psalm, and also to have made this excerpt from it, and altered it to suit the occasion. See Psalm 40:13-17. This is the second Psalm which is a repetition of another, the former being Psalm 53, which was a rehearsal of Psalm 14.

JOHN CALVIN

Psalm 70

This psalm is merely a part of the fortieth, and the inscription, To call to remembrance, is perhaps designed to indicate this; David having taken these five verses out of that other psalm, and accommodated them for being used

MATTHEW HENRY

Psalm 70

See Psalm 40:13-17.

Psalm 71

1-8

1 In thee, O LORD, do I put my trust: let me never be put to confusion.
2 Deliver me in thy righteousness, and cause me to escape: incline thine ear unto me, and save me.
3 Be thou my strong habitation, whereunto I may continually resort: thou hast given commandment to save me; for thou art my rock and my fortress.
4 Deliver me, O my God, out of the hand of the wicked, out of the hand of the unrighteous and cruel man.
5 For thou art my hope, O Lord GOD: thou art my trust from my youth.
6 By thee have I been holden up from the womb: thou art he that took me out of my mother's bowels: my praise shall be continually of thee.
7 I am as a wonder unto many; but thou art my strong refuge.
8 Let my mouth be filled with thy praise and with thy honor all the day.

Psalm 71

TITLE. There is no title to this Psalm, and hence some conjecture that Psalm 70 is intended to be a prelude to it, and has been broken off from it. Such imaginings have no value with us. We have already met with five Psalms without title, which are, nevertheless, as complete as those which bear them. We have here THE PRAYER OF THE AGED BELIEVER, who, in holy confidence of faith, strengthened by a long and remarkable experience, pleads against his enemies, and asks further blessings for himself. Anticipating a gracious reply, he promises to magnify the Lord exceedingly.

DIVISION. The first four verses are faith's cry for help; the next four are a testimony of experience. From Ps 71:9-13, the aged saint pleads against his foes, and then rejoices in hope, Ps 71:14-16. He returns to prayer again in Ps 71:17-18, repeats the confident hopes which cheered his soul, Ps 71:19-21; and then he closes with the promise of abounding in thanksgiving. Throughout, this Psalm may be regarded as the utterance of struggling, but unstaggering, faith.

EXPOSITION

Verse 2. Deliver me in thy righteousness, and cause me to escape. Be true, O God, to thy word. It is a righteous thing in thee to keep the promises which thou hast made unto thy servants. I have trusted thee, and thou wilt not be unrighteous to forget my faith. I am taken as in a net, but do thou liberate me from the malice of my persecutors. Incline thine ear unto me, and save me. Stoop to my feebleness, and hear my faint whispers; be gracious to my infirmities, and smile upon me: I ask salvation; listen thou to my petitions, and save me. Like one wounded and left for dead by mine enemies, I need that thou bend over me and bind up my wounds. These mercies are asked on the plea of faith, and they cannot, therefore, be denied.

Verse 3. Be thou my strong habitation. Permit me to enter into thee, and be as much at home as a man in his own house, and then suffer me to remain in thee as my settled abode. Whereas foes molest me, I need a dwelling framed and bulwarked, to sustain a siege and resist the attacks of armies; let, then, thine omnipotence secure me, and be as a fortress unto me.

Verse 4. Deliver me, O my God, out of the hand of the wicked. God is on the same side with us, and those who are our enemies are also his, for they are wicked; therefore will the Lord surely rescue his own confederates, and he will not suffer the evil to triumph over the just.

Verse 5. For thou art my hope, O Lord God. God who gives us grace to hope in him, will assuredly fulfill our hope, and, therefore, we may plead it in prayer. His name is "Jehovah, the hope of Israel" (Jer 17:13); and, as he cannot be a false or failing hope, we may expect to see our confidence justified.

Verse 6. By thee have I been holden up from the womb. Before he was able to understand the power which preserved him, he was sustained by it. God knows us before we know anything. The elect of old lay in the bosom of God before they were laid on their mothers' bosoms; and when their infantile weakness had no feet strong enough to carry it, the Lord upheld it. We do well to reflect upon divine goodness to us in childhood, for it is full of food for gratitude.

Verse 7. I am as a wonder unto many. "To thousand eyes a mark and gaze am I." The saints are men wondered at; often their dark side is gloomy even to amazement, while their bright side is glorious even to astonishment. The believer is a riddle, an enigma puzzling the unspiritual; he is a monster warring with those delights of the flesh, which are the all in all of other men; he is a prodigy, unaccountable to the judgments of ungodly men; a wonder gazed at, feared, and, by and by, contemptuously derided. Few understand us, many are surprised at us. But thou art my strong refuge.

Psalm 71

1-4

1. In thee, O Jehovah! do I put my trust. It has been thought that the occasion of the composition of this psalm was the conspiracy of Absalom; and the particular reference which David makes to his old age renders this conjecture not improbable. As when we approach God, it is faith alone which opens the way for us, David, in order to obtain what he sought, protests, according to his usual manner, that he does not pour forth at the throne of grace hypocritical prayers, but betakes himself to God with sincerity of heart, fully persuaded that his salvation is laid up in the Divine hand.

3. In these words of the third verse, Into which I may at all times enter, which are not to be found in the other psalm, David briefly prays that he may have so ready and easy access to God for succor, as to find in him a secure refuge whenever threatened by any immediate danger. Lord! as if he had said, let me always find ready succor in thee, and do thou meet me with a smile of benignity and grace, when I betake myself to thee.

4. O my God! deliver me from the hand of the wicked man. Here he uses the singular number; but he is not to be understood as indicating one man only. It is highly probable that he comprehends the whole host of the enemies who assaulted him.

5-8

5. For thou art my expectation, O Lord Jehovah! The Psalmist here repeats what he had said a little before concerning his trust or confidence. By adverting to what God had done for him, he expresses the real cause of faith, (if I may so speak;) and from this we may easily perceive the powerful influence which the remembrance of God's benefits had in nourishing his hope.

6. Upon thee have I been sustained from the womb. This verse corresponds with the preceding, except that David proceeds farther. He not only celebrates the goodness of God which he had experienced from his childhood, but also those proofs of it which he had received previous to his birth.

7. I have been as a prodigy to the great ones. There is no heart so strong and impervious to outward influences as not to be deeply pierced when those who are considered to excel in wisdom and judgment, and who are invested with authority, treat a suffering and an afflicted man with such indignity, that they shrink with horror from him, as if he were a monster.

8. In the next verse, as if he had obtained the desire of his heart, he expresses it to be his resolution to yield a grateful acknowledgement to God. To encourage himself to hope with the greater confidence for a happy issue to his present troubles, he promises loudly to celebrate the praises of God, and to do this not only on one occasion, but to persevere in the exercise without intermission.

Psalm 71

1-13 David professes His confidence in God; believing prayers.

Two things in general David here prays for—that he might not be confounded and that his enemies and persecutors might be confounded.

I. He prays that he might never be made ashamed of his dependence upon God nor disappointed in his believing expectations from him. With this petition every true believer may come boldly to the throne of grace; for God will never disappoint the hope that is of his own raising. Now observe here,

1. How David professes his confidence in God, and with what pleasure and grateful variety of expression he repeats his profession of that confidence, still presenting the profession of it to God and pleading it with him. We praise God, and so please him, by telling him (if it be indeed true) what an entire confidence we have in him (v. 1): "In thee, O Lord! and in thee only, do I put my trust. Whatever others do, I choose the God of Jacob for my help." Those that are entirely satisfied with God's all-sufficiency and the truth of his promise, and in dependence upon that, as sufficient to make them amends, are freely willing to do and suffer, to lose and venture, for him, may truly say, In thee, O Lord! do I put my trust. Those that will deal with God must deal upon trust; if we are shy of dealing with him, it is a sign we do not trust him. Thou art my rock and my fortress (v. 3); and again, "Thou art my refuge, my strong refuge" (v. 7); that is, "I fly to thee, and am sure to be safe in thee, and under thy protection. If thou secure me, none can hurt me. Thou art my hope and my trust" (v. 5); that is, "thou hast proposed thyself to me in thy word as the proper object of my hope and trust; I have hoped in thee, and never found it in vain to do so."

2. How his confidence in God is supported and encouraged by his experiences (v. 5, 6): "Thou hast been my trust from my youth; ever since I was capable of discerning between my right hand and my left, I stayed myself upon thee, and saw a great deal of reason to do so; for by thee have I been holden up from the womb." Ever since he had the use of his reason he had been a dependent upon God's goodness, because ever since he had had a being he had been a monument of it.

3. What his requests to God are, in this confidence.

(1.) That he might never be put to confusion (v. 1), that he might not be disappointed of the mercy he expected and so made ashamed of his expectation. Thus we may all pray in faith that our confidence in God may not be our confusion. Hope of the glory of God is hope that makes not ashamed.

(2.) That he might be delivered out of the hand of his enemies (v. 2): "Deliver me in thy righteousness. As thou art the righteous Judge of the world, pleading the cause of the injured and punishing the injurious, cause

Psalm 71

9-16

9 Cast me not off in the time of old age; forsake me not when my strength faileth.
10 For mine enemies speak against me; and they that lay wait for my soul take counsel together,
11 Saying, God hath forsaken him: persecute and take him; for there is none to deliver him.
12 O God, be not far from me: O my God, make haste for my help.
13 Let them be confounded and consumed that are adversaries to my soul; let them be covered with reproach and dishonor that seek my hurt.
14 But I will hope continually, and will yet praise thee more and more.
15 My mouth shall shew forth thy righteousness and thy salvation all the day; for I know not the numbers thereof.
16 I will go in the strength of the Lord GOD: I will make mention of thy righteousness, even of thine only.

Verse 8. Let my mouth be filled with thy praise and with thy honor all the day. What a blessed mouthful! A man never grows nauseated though the flavor of it be all day in his mouth. God's bread is always in our mouths, so should his praise be. He fills us with good; let us be also filled with gratitude. This would leave no room for murmuring or backbiting; therefore, may we well join with holy David in this sacred wish.

Verse 9. Cast me not off in the time of old age. David was not tired of his Master, and his only fear was lest his Master should be tired of him. The Amalekite in the Bible history left his Egyptian servant to famish when he grew old and sick, but not so the Lord of saints; even to hoar hairs he bears and carries us. Alas for us, if we were abandoned by our God, as many a courtier has been by his prince! Old age robs us of personal beauty, and deprives us of strength for active service; but it does not lower us in the love and favor of God.

Verse 10. For mine enemies speak against me. Dogs howl over a dying lion. When David's arm was able to chastise his foes, they were yet impudent enough to slander him, and he fears that now they will take fresh license in the hour of his weakness. The text most properly means that his enemies had said that God would forsake him; and, therefore, he is the more earnest that the Lord's faithful dealings may give them the lie.

Verse 11. Saying, God hath forsaken him. O bitter taunt! There is no worse arrow in all the quivers of hell. Our Lord felt this barbed shaft, and it is no marvel if his disciples feel the same. Were this exclamation the truth, it were indeed an ill day for us; but, glory be to God, it is a barefaced lie.

Verse 12. O God, be not far from me. Nearness to God is our conscious security. A child in the dark is comforted by grasping its father's hand. O my God, make haste for my help. To call God ours, as having entered into covenant with us, is a mighty plea in prayer, and a great stay to our faith. The cry of "make haste" has occurred many times in this portion of the Psalms, and it was evoked by the sore pressure of affliction. Sharp sorrows soon put an end to procrastinating prayers.

Verse 13. Let them be confounded and consumed that are adversaries to my soul. It will be all this to them to see thy servant preserved; their envy and malice, when disappointed, will fill them with life consuming bitterness. The defeat of their plans shall nonplus them, they shall be confounded as they enquire the reason for their overthrow; the men they seek to destroy seem so weak, and their cause so contemptible, that they will be filled with amazement as they see them not only survive all opposition, but even surmount it.

Verse 14. The holy faith of the persecuted saint comes to the front in these three verses. But I will hope continually. When I cannot rejoice in what I have, I will look forward to what shall be mine, and will still rejoice. Hope will live on a bare common, and sing on a branch laden down with snow. No date and no place are unsuitable for hope.

Verse 15. My mouth shall shew forth thy righteousness and thy salvation all the day. We are to bear testimony as experience enables us, and not withhold from others that which we have tasted and handled. The faithfulness of God in saving us, in delivering us out of the hand of our enemies, and in fulfilling his promises, is to be everywhere proclaimed by those who have proved it in their own history. How gloriously conspicuous is righteousness in the divine plan of redemption!

Verse 16. I will go in the strength of the Lord God. Our translators give us a good sense, but not the sense in this place, which is on this wise, "I will come with the mighty deeds of the Lord Jehovah." He would enter into those deeds by admiring study, and then, wherever he went, he would continue to rehearse them. He should ever be a welcome guest who can tell us of the mighty acts of the Lord, and help us to put our trust in him.

9-13
9. Cast me not off in the time of my old age. David having just now declared that God had been the protector of his life at his birth, and afterwards his foster-father in his childhood, and the guardian of his welfare during the whole course of his past existence; being now worn out with age, casts himself anew into the fatherly bosom of God.
10, 11. For my enemies have said of me, etc. He pleads, as an argument with God to show him mercy, the additional circumstance, that the wicked took greater license in cruelly persecuting him, from the belief which they entertained that he was rejected and abandoned of God.
12. O God! be not far from me. It is scarcely possible to express how severe and hard a temptation it was to David, when he knew that the wicked entertained the persuasion that he was rejected of God. They did not without consideration circulate this report; but after having seemed wisely to weigh all circumstances, they gave their judgment on the point as of a thing which was placed beyond all dispute.
13. While invoking the aid of God, he at the same time prays that his enemies may be filled with shame until they be consumed.

14-16
14. But I will hope continually. David again, as having obtained the victory, prepares himself for thanksgiving. There is, however, no doubt, that during the time when the wicked derided his simplicity, he struggled manfully amidst his distresses, as may be gathered from the word hope. Although, to outward appearance, there was no prospect of deliverance from his troubles, and although the wicked ceased not proudly to pour contempt upon his trust in God, he nevertheless determined to persevere in the exercise of hope; even as it is a genuine proof of faith, to look exclusively to the Divine promise, in order to be guided by its light alone amidst the thickest darkness of afflictions.
15. My mouth shall recount thy righteousness. Here he expresses more clearly what sacrifice of praise he resolved to present to God, promising to proclaim continually his righteousness and salvation.
16. I will go in the strength of the Lord Jehovah! If David, in regard to his mere external condition in life, could remain stable and secure only by renouncing all other confidences, and casting himself upon the righteousness of God; what stability, I pray you to consider, are we likely to have, when the reference is to the spiritual and everlasting life, if we fall away, let it be never so little, from our dependence upon the grace of God? It is, therefore, undeniable that the doctrine which divides the work of perseverance in holiness between man's free will and God's grace, precipitates wretched souls into destruction.

17-19
17. O God! thou hast taught me from my youth. The Psalmist again declares the great obligations under which he

me in some way or other to escape" (God will, with the temptation, make a way to escape, 1 Cor. x. 13).
(3.) That he might always find rest and safety in God (v. 3): Be thou my strong habitation; by thou to me a rock of repose, whereto I may continually resort. Those that are at home in God, that live a life of communion with him and confidence in him, that continually resort unto him by faith and prayer, having their eyes ever towards him, may promise themselves a strong habitation in him, such as will never fall of itself nor can ever be broken through by any invading power; and they shall be welcome to resort to him continually upon all occasions, and not be upbraided as coming too often.
(4.) That he might have continual matter for thanksgiving to God, and might be continually employed in that pleasant work (v. 8): "Let my mouth be filled with thy praise, as now it is with my complaints, and then I shall not be ashamed of my hope, but my enemies will be ashamed of their insolence."
(5.) That he might not be neglected now in his declining years (v. 9): Cast me not off now in the time of my old gage; forsake me not when my strength fails.
II. He prays that his enemies might be made ashamed of their designs against him. Observe,
1. What it was which they unjustly said against him, v. 10, 11. Their plot was deep and desperate; it was against his life: They lay wait for my soul (v. 10), and are adversaries to that, v. 13. Their powers and policies were combined: They take counsel together. And very insolent they were in their deportment: They say, God has forsaken him; persecute and take him. Here their premises are utterly false, that because a good man was in great trouble and had continued long in it, and was not so soon delivered as perhaps he expected, therefore God had forsaken him and would have no more to do with him.
2. What it was which he justly prayed for, from a spirit of prophecy, not a spirit of passion (v. 13): "Let them be confounded and consumed that are adversaries to my soul. If they will not be confounded by repentance, and so saved, let them be confounded with everlasting dishonor, and so ruined." God will turn into shame the glory of those who turn into shame the glory of God and his people.

14-24 Joyful praises; rejoicing in hope.
Observe, in these verses,
I. How his heart is established in faith and hope; and it is a good thing that the heart be so established. Observe what he hopes in: in the power of God, v. 16; and, in the promise of God: "I will make mention of thy righteousness, that is, thy faithfulness to every word which thou hast spoken."
II. Let us now see how his heart is enlarged in joy and praises, how he rejoices in hope, and sings in hope for we are saved by hope.
1. He will speak of God's righteousness and his salvation, as great things, things which he was well

Psalm 71

17-24

17 O God, thou hast taught me from my youth: and hitherto have I declared thy wondrous works.

18 Now also when I am old and greyheaded, O God, forsake me not; until I have shewed thy strength unto this generation, and thy power to every one that is to come.

19 Thy righteousness also, O God, is very high, who hast done great things: O God, who is like unto thee!

20 Thou, which hast shewed me great and sore troubles, shalt quicken me again, and shalt bring me up again from the depths of the earth.

21 Thou shalt increase my greatness, and comfort me on every side.

22 I will also praise thee with the psaltery, even thy truth, O my God: unto thee will I sing with the harp, O thou Holy One of Israel.

23 My lips shall greatly rejoice when I sing unto thee; and my soul, which thou hast redeemed.

24 My tongue also shall talk of thy righteousness all the day long: for they are confounded, for they are brought unto shame, that seek my hurt.

Verse 17. O God, thou hast taught me from my youth. It was comfortable to the psalmist to remember that from his earliest days he had been the Lord's disciple. None are too young to be taught of God, and they make the most proficient scholars who begin betimes.

Verse 18. Now also when I am old and grey headed, O God, forsake me not. There is something touching in the sight of hair whitened with the snows of many a winter: the old and faithful soldier receives consideration from his king, the venerable servant is beloved by his master.

Verse 19. Thy righteousness also, O God, is very high. Very sublime, unsearchable, exalted, and glorious is the holy character of God, and his way of making men righteous. His plan of righteousness uplifts men from the gates of hell to the mansions of heaven. It is a high doctrine gospel, gives a high experience, leads to high practice, and ends in high felicity.

Verse 20. Thou, which hast shewed me great and sore troubles, shalt quicken me again. Here is faith's inference from the infinite greatness of the Lord. He has been strong to smite; he will be also strong to save. He has shown me many heavy and severe trials, and he will also show me many and precious mercies.

Verse 21. Thou shalt increase my greatness. As a king, David grew in influence and power. God did great things for him, and by him, and this is all the greatness believers want. May we have faith in God, such as these words evince. And comfort me on every side. As we were surrounded with afflictions, so shall we be environed with consolations. From above, and from all around, light shall come to dispel our former gloom; the change shall be great, indeed, when the Lord returns to comfort us. Here is the final vow of praise.

Verse 22. I will also praise thee with the psaltery. Love so amazing calls for sweetest praise. David would give his best music, both vocal and instrumental, to the Best of Masters. His harp should not be silent, nor his voice. Even thy truth, O my God. This is ever a most enchanting attribute—viz., the truth or faithfulness of our covenant God. On this we rest, and from it we draw streams of richest consolation. His promises are sure, his love unalterable, his veracity indisputable.

Verse 23. My lips shall greatly rejoice when I sing unto thee. It shall be no weariness to me to praise thee. It shall be a delightful recreation, a solace, a joy. The essence of song lies in the holy joy of the singer. And my soul, which thou hast redeemed.

Verse 24. My tongue also shall talk of thy righteousness all the day long. I will talk to myself, and to thee, my God, and to my fellow men: my theme shall be thy way of justifying sinners, the glorious display of thy righteousness and grace in thy dear Son; and this most fresh and never to be exhausted subject shall be ever with me, from the rising of the sun to the going down of the same.

lay to God for his goodness, not only with the view of encouraging himself to gratitude, but also of exciting himself to continue cherishing hope for the time to come: which will appear from the following verse.

18. The Psalmist's reasoning is this: Since thou, O God! hast from the commencement of my existence given me such abundant proofs of thy goodness, wilt thou not stretch forth thy hand to succor me, when now thou seest me decaying through the influence of old age? And, indeed, the conclusion is altogether inevitable, that as God vouchsafed to love us when we were infants, and embraced us with his favor when we were children, and has continued without intermission to do us good during the whole course of our life, he cannot but persevere in acting toward us in the same way even to the end.

19. And thy righteousness, O God! is very high. David prosecutes at greater length the subject of which he had previously spoken.

20-24

20, 21. Thou hast made me to see great and sore troubles. We must be brought down even to the gates of death before God can be seen to be our deliverer. As we are born without thought and understanding, our minds, during the earlier part of our life, are not sufficiently impressed with a sense of the Author of our existence; but when God comes to our help, as we are lying in a state of despair, this resurrection is to us a bright mirror from which is seen reflected his grace.

22. I will also, O my God! praise thee. He again breaks forth into thanksgiving; for he was aware that the design of God, in so liberally succoring his servants, is, that his goodness may be celebrated. By the word truth, the Psalmist means that the hope which he reposed in God was rewarded, when God preserved him in the midst of dangers. The promises of God, and his truth in performing them, are inseparably joined together.

23. My lips shall rejoice when I sing to thee. In this verse David expresses more distinctly his resolution not to give thanks to God hypocritically, nor in a superficial manner, but to engage with unfeigned earnestness in this religious exercise. By the figures which he introduces, he briefly teaches us, that to praise God would be the source of his greatest pleasure; and thus he indirectly censures the profane mirth of those who, forgetting God, confine their congratulations to themselves in their prosperity.

24. The scope of the last verse is to the same effect, implying that no joy would be sweet and desirable to him, but such as was connected with the praises of God, and that to celebrate his Redeemer's praises would afford him the greatest satisfaction and delight.

acquainted with, and much affected with, which he desired God might have the glory of and others might have the comfortable knowledge of (v. 15): My mouth shall show forth thy righteousness and thy salvation; and again (v. 24), My tongue shall talk of thy righteousness, and this all the day. God's righteousness, which David seems here to be in a particular manner affected with, includes a great deal: the rectitude of his nature, the equity of his providential disposals, the righteous laws he has given us to be ruled by, the righteous promises he has given us to depend upon, and the everlasting righteousness which his Son has brought in for our justification.

2. He will speak of them with wonder and admiration, as one astonished at the dimensions of divine love and grace, the height and depth, the length and breadth, of it: "I know not the numbers thereof, v. 15. Though I cannot give a particular account of thy favors to me, they are so many, so great (if I would count them, they are more in number than the sand, Ps. xl. 5), yet, knowing them to be numberless, I will be still speaking of them, for in them I shall find new matter," v. 19. The righteousness that is in God is very high; that which is done by him for his people is very great: put both together, and we shall say, O God! who is like unto thee?

3. He will speak of them with all the expressions of joy and exultation, v. 22, 23. Observe, how he would eye God in praising him, as a faithful God, as a God in covenant with him, and, as the Holy One of Israel, Israel's God in a peculiar manner, glorious in his holiness among that people and faithful to his covenant with them.

(2.) How he will express his joy and exultation.

[1.] With his hand, in sacred music—with the psaltery, with the harp; at these David excelled, and the best of his skill shall be employed in setting forth God's praises to such advantage as might affect others.

[2.] With his lips, in sacred songs: "Unto thee will I sing, to thy honor, and with a desire to be accepted of thee. My lips shall greatly rejoice when I sing unto thee, knowing they cannot be better employed."

[3.] In both with his heart: "My soul shall rejoice which thou hast redeemed." Note that redeemed souls ought to be joyful thankful souls. The work of redemption ought, above all God's works, to be celebrated by us in our praises. The Lamb that was slain, and has redeemed us to God, must therefore be counted worthy of all blessing and praise.

Psalm 72

Title
A Psalm for Solomon.

1-7
1 Give the king thy judgments, O God, and thy righteousness unto the king's son.
2 He shall judge thy people with righteousness, and thy poor with judgment.
3 The mountains shall bring peace to the people, and the little hills, by righteousness.
4 He shall judge the poor of the people, he shall save the children of the needy, and shall break in pieces the oppressor.
5 They shall fear thee as long as the sun and moon endure, throughout all generations.
6 He shall come down like rain upon the mown grass: as showers that water the earth.
7 In his days shall the righteous flourish; and abundance of peace so long as the moon endureth.

Psalm 72

TITLE. A Psalm for Solomon. The best linguists affirm that this should be rendered, of or by Solomon. There is not sufficient ground for the rendering for. It is pretty certain that the title declares Solomon to be the author of the Psalm, and yet from Ps 72:20 it would seem that David uttered it in prayer before he died. With some diffidence we suggest that the spirit and matter of the Psalm are David's, but that he was too near his end to pen the words, or cast them into form: Solomon, therefore, caught his dying father's song, fashioned it in goodly verse, and, without robbing his father, made the Psalm his own. It is, we conjecture, the Prayer of David, but the Psalm of Solomon. Jesus is here, beyond all doubt, in the glory of his reign, both as he now is, and as he shall be revealed in the latter day glory.
DIVISION. We shall follow the division suggested by Alexander. "A glowing description of the reign of Messiah as righteous, Ps 72:1-7; universal, Ps 72:8-11; beneficent, Ps 72:12-14; and perpetual, Ps 72:15-17; to which are added a doxology, Ps 72:18-19; and a postscript, Ps 72:20."

EXPOSITION
Verse 1. Give the king thy judgments, O God. The right to reign was transmitted by descent from David to Solomon, but not by that means alone: Israel was a theocracy, and the kings were but the viceroys of the greater King; hence the prayer that the new king might be enthroned by divine right, and then endowed with divine wisdom.
Verse 2. He shall judge thy people with righteousness. Clothed with divine authority, he shall use it on the behalf of the favored nation, for whom he shall show himself strong, that they be not misjudged, slandered, or in any way treated maliciously. His sentence shall put their accusers to silence, and award the saints their true position as the accepted of the Lord. What a consolation to feel that none can suffer wrong in Christ's kingdom: he sits upon the great white throne, unspotted by a single deed of injustice, or even mistake of judgment: reputations are safe enough with him.
Verse 3. The mountains shall bring peace to the people. Thence, aforetime, rushed the robber bands which infested the country; but now the forts there erected are the guardians of the land, and the watchmen publish far and near the tidings that no foe is to be seen. Where Jesus is there is peace, lasting, deep, eternal.
Verse 4. He shall judge the poor of the people. He will do them justice, yea, and blessed be his name, more than justice, for he will delight to do them good. He shall save the children of the needy. Poor, helpless things, they were packhorses for others, and paupers themselves, but their King would be their protector. Happy are God's poor and needy ones; they are safe under the wing of the Prince of Peace, for he will save them from all their enemies.
Verse 5. They shall fear thee as long as the sun and moon endure. And well they may. Such righteousness wins the cheerful homage of the poor and the godly, and strikes dismay into the souls of unrighteous oppressors; so that all through the lands, both good and bad are filled with awe. Where Jesus reigns in power men must render obeisance of some sort. His kingdom, moreover, is no house of cards, or dynasty of days; it is as lasting as the lights of heaven; days and nights will cease before he abdicates his throne.
Verse 6. He shall come down like rain upon the mown grass. Blessings upon his gentle sway! Those great conquerors who have been the scourges of mankind have fallen like the fiery hail of Sodom, transforming fruitful lands into deserts; but he with mild, benignant influence softly refreshes the weary and wounded among men, and makes them spring up into newness of life. Pastures mown with the scythe, or shorn by the teeth of cattle, present, as it were, so many bleeding stems of grass, but when the rain falls

JOHN CALVIN

Psalm 72

72:1-6

1. O God! give thy judgments to the king. While David, to whom the promise had been made, at his death affectionately recommended to God his son, who was to succeed him in his kingdom, he doubtless endited to the Church a common form of prayer, that the faithful, convinced of the impossibility of being prosperous and happy, except under one head, should show all respect, and yield all obedience to this legitimate order of things, and also that from this typical kingdom they might be conducted to Christ. In short, this is a prayer that God would furnish the king whom he had chosen with the spirit of uprightness and wisdom.

2. In the second clause, he expressly mentions the poor, who, on account of their poverty and weakness, have need of the help of others, and for whose sake kings are armed with the sword to grant them redress when unjustly oppressed.

3. Hence, also, proceeds peace, of which mention is made in the third verse. The term peace being employed among the Hebrews to denote not only rest and tranquility, but also prosperity, David teaches us that the people would enjoy prosperity and happiness, when the affairs of the nation were administered according to the principles of righteousness. The bringing forth of peace is a figurative expression taken from the fertility of the earth.

4. He shall judge the poor of the people. The poet continues his description of the end and fruit of a righteous government, and unfolds at greater length what he had briefly touched upon concerning the afflicted among the people. But it is a truth which ought to be borne in mind, that kings can keep themselves within the bounds of justice and equity only by the grace of God; for when they are not governed by the Spirit of righteousness proceeding from heaven, their government is converted into a system of tyranny and robbery.

5. They shall fear thee with the sun. The preservation of mutual equity among men is an inestimable blessing; but the service of God is well worthy of being preferred even to this. David, therefore, very properly commends to us the blessed fruits of a holy and righteous government, by telling us that it will draw in its train true religion and the fear of God.

6. He shall descend as the rain upon the mown grass. This comparison may seem at first sight to be somewhat harsh; but it elegantly and appositely expresses the great advantage which is derived by all from the good and equitable constitution of a kingdom.

7-11

7. In his days shall the righteous flourish. All these sentences depend upon the first verse. David, therefore, prayed that the king might be adorned with righteousness and judgment, that the just might flourish and the people prosper. This prediction receives its highest fulfillment in Christ. It was, indeed, the duty of Solomon to maintain the righteous; but it is the proper office of Christ to make men righteous.

MATTHEW HENRY

Psalm 72

Verse 1 Prayer for Solomon.

I. We may apply it to Solomon: Give him thy judgments, O God! and thy righteousness; make him a man, a king; make him a good man, a good king.

II. We may also apply it to Christ; not that he who intercedes for us needs us to intercede for him; but,

1. It is a prayer of the Old-Testament church for sending the Messiah, as the church's King, King on the holy hill of Zion, of whom the King of kings had said, Thou art my Son, Ps. ii. 6, 7. "Hasten his coming to whom all judgment is committed;" and we must thus hasten the second coming of Christ, when he shall judge the world in righteousness.

2. It is an expression of the satisfaction which all true believers take in the authority which the Lord Jesus has received from the Father: "Let him have all power both in heaven and earth, and be the Lord our righteousness; let him be the great trustee of divine grace for all that are his; give it to him, that he may give it to us."

2-17 The kingdom of Messiah.

This is a prophecy of the prosperity and perpetuity of the kingdom of Christ under the shadow of the reign of Solomon. It comes in,

1. As a plea to enforce the prayer: "Lord, give him thy judgments and thy righteousness, and then he shall judge thy people with righteousness, and so shall answer the end of his elevation, v. 2. Give him thy grace, and then thy people, committed to his charge, will have the benefit of it." Because God loved Israel, he made him king over them to do judgment and justice, 2 Chron. ix. 8. We may in faith wrestle with God for that grace which we have reason to think will be of common advantage to his church.

2. As an answer of peace to the prayer. As by the prayer of faith we return answers to God's promises of mercy, so by the promises of mercy God returns answers to our prayers of faith.

Let us observe the many great and precious promises here made, which were to have their full accomplishment only in the kingdom of Christ; and yet some of them were in part fulfilled in Solomon's reign.

I. That it should be a righteous government (v. 2): He shall judge thy people with righteousness. Compare Isa. xi. 4. All the laws of Christ's kingdom are consonant to the eternal rules of equity; the chancery it erects to relieve against the rigors of the broken law is indeed a court of equity; and against the sentence of his last judgment there will lie no exception. The peace of his kingdom shall be supported by righteousness (v. 3); for then only is the peace like a river, when the righteousness is as the waves of the sea. The world will be judged in righteousness, Acts xvii. 31.

II. That it should be a peaceable government: The mountains shall bring peace, and the little hills (v. 3);

Psalm 72

8-14
8 He shall have dominion also from sea to sea, and from the river unto the ends of the earth.
9 They that dwell in the wilderness shall bow before him; and his enemies shall lick the dust.
10 The kings of Tarshish and of the isles shall bring presents: the kings of Sheba and Seba shall offer gifts.
11 Yea, all kings shall fall down before him: all nations shall serve him.
12 For he shall deliver the needy when he crieth; the poor also, and him that hath no helper.
13 He shall spare the poor and needy, and shall save the souls of the needy.
14 He shall redeem their soul from deceit and violence: and precious shall their blood be in his sight.

it is balm to all these wounds, and it renews the verdure and beauty of the field; fit image of the visits and benedictions of "the consolation of Israel."
Verse 7. In his days shall the righteous flourish. Beneath the deadly Upas of unrighteous rule no honest principles can be developed, and good men can scarcely live; but where truth and uprightness are on the throne, the best of men prosper most. A righteous king is the patron and producer of righteous subjects. None flourish under Nero but those who are monsters like himself: like will to like; and under the gentle Jesus the godly find a happy shelter. And abundance of peace so long as the moon endureth. Where Jesus reigns he is known as the true Melchizedek, king both of righteousness and peace. Peace based upon right is sure to be lasting, but no other will be.
Verse 8. He shall have dominion also from sea to sea. Wide spread shall be the rule of Messiah; only the Land's End shall end his territory: to the Ultima Thule shall his scepter be extended. From Pacific to Atlantic, and from Atlantic to Pacific, he shall be Lord, and the oceans which surround each pole shall be beneath his sway.
Verse 9. They that dwell in the wilderness shall bow before him. Unconquered by arms, they shall be subdued by love. Wild and lawless as they have been, they shall gladly wear his easy yoke; then shall their deserts be made glad, yea, they shall rejoice and blossom as the rose. And his enemies shall lick the dust. If they will not be his friends, they shall be utterly broken and humbled.
Verse 10. The kings of Tarshish and of the isles shall bring presents. Trade shall be made subservient to the purposes of mediatorial rule; merchant princes, both far and near, shall joyfully contribute of their wealth to his throne. Seafaring places are good centers from which to spread the gospel; and seafaring men often make earnest heralds of the cross. Tarshish of old was so far away, that to the eastern mind it was lost in its remoteness, and seemed to be upon the verge of the universe; even so far as imagination itself can travel, shall the Son of David rule; across the blue sea shall his scepter be stretched; the white cliffs of Britain already own him, the gems of the Southern Sea glitter for him, even Iceland's heart is warm with his love.
Verse 11. Yea, all kings shall fall down before him. Personally shall they pay their reverence, however mighty they may be. No matter how high their state, how ancient their dynasty, or far off their realms, they shall willingly accept him as their Imperial Lord. All nations shall serve him. The people shall be as obedient as the governors. The extent of the mediatorial rule is set forth by the two far reaching alls, all kings, and all nations: we see not as yet all things put under him, but since we see Jesus crowned with glory and honor in heaven, we are altogether without doubt as to his universal monarchy on earth. It is not to be imagined that an Alexander or a Caesar shall have wider sway than the Son of God. "Every knee shall bow to him, and every tongue shall confess that Jesus Christ is Lord, to the glory of God the Father." Hasten it, O Lord, in thine own time.
Verse 12. For he shall deliver the needy. Here is an excellent reason for man's submission to the Lord Christ; it is not because they dread his overwhelming power, but because they are won over by his just and condescending rule. Who would not fear so good a Prince, who makes the needy his peculiar care, and pledges himself to be their deliverer in times of need? When he crieth. He permits them to be so needy as to be driven to cry bitterly for help, but then he hears them, and comes to their aid. A child's cry touches a father's heart, and our King is the Father of his people. If we can do no more than cry it will bring omnipotence to our aid.
Verse 13. He shall spare the poor and needy. His pity shall be manifested to them; he will not allow their trials to overwhelm them; his rod of correction shall fall lightly; he will be sparing of his rebukes, and not sparing in his consolations. And shall save the souls of the needy. His is the dominion of

8. He shall have dominion from sea to sea. As the Lord, when he promised his people the land of Canaan for an inheritance, assigned to it these four boundaries, (Genesis 15:18,) David intimates, that so long as the kingdom shall continue to exist, the possession of the promised land will be entire, to teach the faithful that the blessing of God cannot be fully realized, except whilst this kingdom shall flourish.
9. The Prophet immediately adds, that the enemies of the king shall lick the dust in token of their reverence. This, as is well known, was in ancient times a customary ceremony among the nations of the East; and Alexander the Great, after he had conquered the East, wished to compel his subjects to practice it, from which arose great dissatisfaction and contentions, the Macedonians disdainfully refusing to yield such a slavish and degrading mark of subjection. The meaning then is, that the king chosen by God in Judea will obtain so complete a victory over all his enemies, far and wide, that they shall come humbly to pay him homage.
10. The kings of Tarshish and of the isles shall bring presents. The Psalmist still continues, as in the preceding verse, to speak of the extent of the kingdom. The Hebrews apply the appellation of Tarshish to the whole coast, which looks towards Cilicia. By the isles, therefore, is denoted the whole coast of the Mediterranean Sea, from Cilicia to Greece.
11. And all kings shall prostrate themselves before him. This verse contains a more distinct statement of the truth, That the whole world will be brought in subjection to the authority of Christ. The kingdom of Judah was unquestionably never more flourishing than under the reign of Solomon; but even then there were only a small number of kings who paid tribute to him, and what they paid was inconsiderable in amount; and, moreover, it was paid upon condition that they should be allowed to live in the enjoyment of liberty under their own laws. While David then began with his own son, and the posterity of his son, he rose by the Spirit of prophecy to the spiritual kingdom of Christ; a point worthy of our special notice, since it teaches us that we have not been called to the hope of everlasting salvation by chance, but because our heavenly Father had already destined to give us to his Son.

12-15
12-14. For he will deliver the poor when he crieth to him. The Psalmist again affirms that the kingdom which he magnifies so greatly will not be tyrannical or cruel. The majority of kings, neglecting the well-being of the community, have their minds wholly engrossed with their own private interests. The consequence is, that they unmercifully oppress their miserable subjects; and it even happens that the more formidable any of them is, and the more absorbing his rapacity, he is accounted so much the more eminent and illustrious.
15. And he shall live. When he speaks of the common prayers of the people, by which they will commend the prosperity of the king to the care of God, he intimates that so well-pleased will they be with being his subjects, that they will account nothing so desirable as to yield entire submission to his

that is (says Dr. Hammond), both the superior and the inferior courts of judicature in Solomon's kingdom. There shall be abundance of peace, v. 7. Solomon's name signifies peaceable, and such was his reign; for in it Israel enjoyed the victories of the foregoing reign and preserved the tranquility and repose of that reign. But peace is, in a special manner, the glory of Christ's kingdom; for, as far as it prevails, it reconciles men to God, to themselves, and to one another, and slays all enmities; for he is our peace.
III. That the poor and needy should be, in a particular manner, taken under the protection of this government: He shall judge thy poor, v. 2. Those are God's poor that are impoverished by keeping a good conscience, and those shall be provided for with a distinguishing care, shall be judged for with judgment, with a particular cognizance taken of their case and a particular vengeance taken for their wrongs. The poor of the people, and the children of the needy, he will be sure so to judge as to save, v. 4. This is insisted upon again (v. 12, 13), intimating that Christ will be sure to carry his cause on behalf of his injured poor. He will deliver the needy that lie at the mercy of their oppressors.
IV. That religion shall flourish under Christ's government (v. 5): They shall fear thee as long as the sun and moon endure. Solomon indeed built the temple, and the fear and worship of God were well kept up, for some time, under his government, but it did not last long; this therefore must point at Christ's kingdom, all the subjects of which are brought to and kept in the fear of God; for the Christian religion has a direct tendency to, and a powerful influence upon, the support and advancement of natural religion. Faith in Christ will set up, and keep up, the fear of God; and therefore this is the everlasting gospel that is preached, Fear God, and give honor to him, Rev. xiv. 7. And, as Christ's government promotes devotion towards God, so it promotes both justice and charity among men (v. 7): In his days shall the righteous flourish; righteousness shall be practiced, and those that practice righteousness shall be preferred.
V. That Christ's government shall be very comfortable to all his faithful loving subjects (v. 6): He shall, by the graces and comforts of his Spirit, come down like rain upon the mown grass; not on that which is cut down, but that which is left growing, that it may spring again, though it was beheaded. The gospel of Christ distils as the rain, which softens the ground that was hard, moistens that which was dry, and so makes it green and fruitful, Isa. live. 10. Let our hearts drink in the rain, Heb. vi. 7.
VI. That Christ's kingdom shall be extended very far, and greatly enlarged; considering,

1. The extent of his territories (v. 8): He shall have dominion from sea to sea (from the South Sea to the North, or from the Red Sea to the Mediterranean) and from the river Euphrates, or Nile, to the ends of the earth. Solomon's dominion was

Psalm 72

15-20

15 And he shall live, and to him shall be given of the gold of Sheba: prayer also shall be made for him continually; and daily shall he be praised.
16 There shall be an handful of corn in the earth upon the top of the mountains; the fruit thereof shall shake like Lebanon: and they of the city shall flourish like grass of the earth.
17 His name shall endure for ever: his name shall be continued as long as the sun: and men shall be blessed in him: all nations shall call him blessed.
18 Blessed be the LORD God, the God of Israel, who only doeth wondrous things.
19 And blessed be his glorious name for ever: and let the whole earth be filled with his glory; Amen, and Amen.
20 The prayers of David the son of Jesse are ended.

souls, a spiritual and not a worldly empire; and the needy, that is to say, the consciously unworthy and weak, shall find that he will give them his salvation. Jesus calls not the righteous, but sinners to repentance. He does not attempt the superfluous work of aiding proud Pharisees to air their vanity; but he is careful of poor Publicans whose eyes dare not look up to heaven by reason of their sense of sin. We ought to be anxious to be among these needy ones whom the Great King so highly favors.

Verse 14. He shall redeem their soul from deceit and violence. These two things are the weapons with which the poor are assailed: both law and no law are employed to fleece them. The fox and the lion are combined against Christ's lambs, but the Shepherd will defeat them, and rescue the defenseless from their teeth. A soul hunted by the temptations of Satanic craft, and the insinuations of diabolical malice, will do well to fly to the throne of Jesus for shelter. And precious shall their blood be in his sight. He will not throw away his subjects in needless wars as tyrants have done, but will take every means for preserving the humblest of them.

Verse 15. And he shall live. Vive le Roi! O King! live for ever! He was slain, but is risen and ever liveth. And to him shall be given of the gold of Sheba. These are coronation gifts of the richest kind, cheerfully presented at his throne. How gladly would we give him all that we have and are, and count the tribute far too small. We may rejoice that Christ's cause will not stand still for want of funds; the silver and the gold are his, and if they are not to be found at home, far off lands shall hasten to make up the deficit.

Verse 16. There shall be an handful of corn in the earth upon the top of the mountains. From small beginnings great results shall spring. A mere handful in a place naturally ungenial shall produce a matchless harvest. What a blessing that there is a handful; "except the Lord of hosts had left unto us a very small remnant we should have been as Sodom, and we should have been like unto Gomorrah:" but now the faithful are a living seed, and shall multiply in the land. The fruit thereof shall shake like Lebanon. The harvest shall be so great that the wind shall rustle through it, and sound like the cedars upon Lebanon.

Verse 17. His name shall endure for ever. In its saving power, as the rallying point of believers, and as renowned and glorified, his name shall remain for ever the same. His name shall be continued as long as the sun. While time is measured out by days, Jesus shall be glorious among men. And men shall be blessed in him. There shall be cause for all this honor, for he shall really and truly be a benefactor to the race. He himself shall be earth's greatest blessing; when men wish to bless others they shall bless in his name.

Verses 18-19. As Quesnel well observes, these verses explain themselves. They call rather for profound gratitude, and emotion of heart, than for an exercise of the understanding; they are rather to be used for adoration than for exposition. It is, and ever will be, the acme of our desires, and the climax of our prayers, to behold Jesus exalted King of kings and Lord of lords.

Verse 20. The prayers of David the son of Jesse are ended. What more could he ask? He has climbed the summit of the mount of God; he desires nothing more. With this upon his lip, he is content to die. He strips himself of his own royalty and becomes only the "son of Jesse," thrice happy to subside into nothing before the crowned Messiah. Before his believing eye the reign of Jesus, like the sun, filled all around with light, and the holy soul of the man after God's own heart exulted in it, and sung his "Nunc dimittis." We, too, will cease from all petitioning if it be granted to us to see the day of the Lord. Our blissful spirits will then have nothing further to do but for ever to praise the Lord our God.

authority. Many, no doubt, reject his yoke, and hypocrites fret and murmur secretly in their hearts, and would gladly extinguish all remembrance of Christ, were it in their power; but the affectionate interest here predicted is what all true believers are careful to cultivate, not only because to pray for earthly kings is a duty enjoined upon them in the Word of God, but also because they ought to feel a special desire and solicitude for the enlargement of the boundaries of this kingdom, in which both the majesty of God shines forth, and their own welfare and happiness are included.

16-20
16. A handful of corn shall be in the earth upon the top of the mountains. His words may be considered as denoting that so great will be the fertility, so abundant the produce of wheat which the mountain tops shall yield, that it may be reaped with full hand. By this figure is portrayed the large abundance of all good things which, through the blessing of God, would be enjoyed under the reign of Christ.
17. His name shall endure for ever. The inspired writer again repeats what he had previously affirmed concerning the perpetual duration of this kingdom. And he doubtless intended carefully to distinguish it from earthly kingdoms, which either suddenly vanish away, or at length, oppressed with their own greatness, fall into ruin, affording by their destruction incontestible evidence that nothing in this world is stable and of long duration.
18. Blessed be Jehovah God! the God of Israel. David, after having prayed for prosperity to his successors, breaks forth in praising God, because he was assured by the divine oracle that his prayers would not be in vain. Had he not with the eyes of faith beheld those things which we have seen above, his rejoicing would have been less free and lively.
20. The prayers of David the son of Jesse are ended. We have before observed that this was not without cause added by Solomon, (if we may suppose him to have put the matter of this psalm into the form of poetical compositions) not only that he might avoid defrauding his father of the praise which was due to him, but also to stir up the Church the more earnestly to pour forth before God the same prayers which David had continued to offer even with his last breath. Let us then remember that it is our bounden duty to pray to God, both with unfeigned earnestness, and with unwearied perseverance, that he would be pleased to maintain and defend the Church under the government of his Son. The name of Jesse, the father of David, seems to be here introduced to bring to remembrance David's origin, that the grace of God may appear the more illustrious in having raised from the sheepfold a man of mean birth, as well as the youngest and the least esteemed among his brethren, and in having advanced him to so high a degree of honor, as to make him king over the chosen people.

very large (1 Kings iv. 21), according to the promise, Gen. xv. 18.

2. The dignity of his tributaries. He shall not only reign over those that dwell in the wilderness, the peasants and cottagers, but over those that dwell in the palaces (v. 10): The kings of Tarshish, and of the isles, that lie most remote from Israel and are the isles of the Gentiles (Gen. x. 5), shall bring presents to him as their sovereign Lord, by and under whom they hold their crowns and all their crown lands.

VII. That he shall be honored and beloved by all his subjects (v. 15): He shall live; his subjects shall desire his life (O king! live for ever) and with good reason; for he has said, Because I live, you shall live also; and of him it is witnessed that he liveth, ever liveth, making intercession, Heb. vii. 8, 25. He shall live, and live prosperously.

VIII. That under his government there shall be a wonderful increase both of meat and mouths, both of the fruits of the earth in the country and of the people inhabiting the cities, v. 16.

IX. That his government shall be perpetual, both to his honor and to the happiness of his subjects. The Lord Jesus shall reign for ever, and of him only this must be understood, and not at all of Solomon. It is Christ only that shall be feared throughout all generations (v. 5) and as long as the sun and moon endure, v. 7. The honor of the princes is immortal and shall never be sullied (v. 17): His name shall endure for ever, in spite of all the malicious attempts and endeavors of the powers of darkness to eclipse the luster of it and to cut off the line of it; it shall be preserved; it shall be perpetuated; it shall be propagated. As the names of earthly princes are continued in their posterity, so Christ's in himself. His name shall descend to posterity. All nations, while the world stands, shall call him blessed, shall bless God for him, continually speak well of him, and think themselves happy in him.

18-20 Thanksgiving and prayer.
Such an illustrious prophecy as is in the foregoing verses of the Messiah and his kingdom may fitly be concluded, as it is here, with hearty prayers and praises.

I. The psalmist is here enlarged in thanksgivings for the prophecy and promise, v. 18, 19. So sure is every word of God, and with so much satisfaction may we rely upon it, that we have reason enough to give thanks for what he has said, though it be not yet done.

II. He is in prayer for the accomplishment of this prophecy and promise: Let the whole earth be filled with his glory, as it will be when the kings of Tarshish, and the isles, shall bring presents to him. All those that wish well to the honor of God and the welfare of mankind, cannot but desire that the earth may be filled with the discoveries of his glory, suitably returned in thankful acknowledgments of his glory.

Book Three: Psalms 73-89

Psalm 73

Title
A Psalm of Asaph.

1-7
1 Truly God is good to Israel, even to such as are of a clean heart.
2 But as for me, my feet were almost gone; my steps had well nigh slipped.
3 For I was envious at the foolish, when I saw the prosperity of the wicked.
4 For there are no bands in their death: but their strength is firm.
5 They are not in trouble as other men; neither are they plagued like other men.
6 Therefore pride compasseth them about as a chain; violence covereth them as a garment.
7 Their eyes stand out with fatness: they have more than heart could wish.

Book Three: Psalms 73-89

Psalm 73

TITLE. A Psalm of Asaph. This is the second Psalm ascribed to Asaph, and the first of eleven consecutive Psalms bearing the name of this eminent singer. Some writers are not sure that Asaph wrote them, but incline to the belief that David was the author, and Asaph the person to whom they were dedicated, that he might sing them when in his turn he became the chief musician. But though our own heart turns in the same direction, facts must be heard; and we find in 2Ch 29:30, that Hezekiah commanded the Levites to sing "the words of David and of Asaph the seer;" and, moreover, in Ne 12:46, David and Asaph are mentioned together, as distinct from "the chief of the singers," and as it would seem, as joint authors of psalmody. We may, therefore, admit Asaph to be the author of some, if not all, of the twelve Psalms ascribed to him. Often a great star which seems to be but one to the eyes of ordinary observers, turns out upon closer inspection to be of a binary character; so here the Psalms of David are those of Asaph too. The great sun of David has a satellite in the moon of Asaph. By reading our notes on Psalm Fifty, in Volume 2, the reader will glean a little more concerning this man of God.
SUBJECT. Curiously enough this Seventy-third Psalm corresponds in subject with the Thirty-seventh: it will help the memory of the young to notice the reversed figures. The theme is that ancient stumbling block of good men, which Job's friends could not get over; viz.—the present prosperity of wicked men and the sorrows of the godly. Heathen philosophers have puzzled themselves about this, while to believers it has too often been a temptation.
DIVISION. In Ps 73:1 the psalmist declares his confidence in God, and, as it were, plants his foot on a rock while he recounts his inward conflict. From Ps 73:2-14 he states his temptation; then, from Ps 73:15-17 he is embarrassed as how to act, but ultimately finds deliverance from his dilemma. He describes with awe the fate of the ungodly in Ps 73:18-20, condemns his own folly and adores the grace of God, Ps 73:21-24, and concludes by renewing his allegiance to his God, whom he takes afresh to be his portion and delight.

EXPOSITION
Verse 1. Truly, or, more correctly, only, God is good to Israel. He is only good, nothing else but good to his own covenanted ones. He cannot act unjustly, or unkindly to them; his goodness to them is beyond dispute, and without mixture. Even to such as are of a clean heart. These are the true Israel, not the ceremonially clean but the really so; those who are clean in the inward parts, pure in the vital mainspring of action.
Verse 2. Here begins the narrative of a great soul battle, a spiritual Marathon, a hard and well fought field, in which the half defeated became in the end wholly victorious. But as for me. He contrasts himself with his God who is ever good; he owns his personal want of good, and then also compares himself with the clean in heart, and goes on to confess his defilement.
Verse 3. For I was envious at the foolish. "The foolish" is the generic title of all the wicked: they are beyond all others fools, and he must be a fool who envies fools. Some read it, "the proud:" and, indeed, these, by their ostentation, invite envy, and many a mind which is out of gear spiritually, becomes infected with that wasting disease. It is a pitiful thing that an heir of heaven should have to confess "I was envious," but worse still that he should have to put it, "I was envious at the foolish." Yet this acknowledgment is, we fear, due from most of us.

JOHN CALVIN

Book Three: Psalms 73-89

Psalm 73

1-3
1. Yet God is good to Israel. David opens the psalm abruptly; and from this we learn, what is worthy of particular notice, that before he broke forth into this language, his mind had been agitated with many doubts and conflicting suggestions. As a brave and valiant champion, he had been exercised in very painful struggles and temptations; but, after long and arduous exertion, he at length succeeded in shaking off all perverse imaginations, and came to the conclusion that yet God is gracious to his servants, and the faithful guardian of their welfare.
2. As for me, etc. Literally, it is, And I: which ought to be read with emphasis; for David means that those temptations, which cast an affront upon the honor of God, and overwhelm faith, not only assail the common class of men, or those who are endued only with some small measure of the fear of God, but that he himself, who ought to have profited above all others in the school of God, had experienced his own share of them.
3. For I envied the foolish. Here he declares the nature of the temptation with which he was assailed. It consisted in this, that when he saw the present prosperous state of the wicked, and from it judged them to be happy, he had envied their condition. We are certainly under a grievous and a dangerous temptation, when we not only, in our own minds, quarrel with God for not setting matters in due order, but also when we give ourselves loose reins, boldly to commit iniquity, because it seems to us that we may commit it, and yet escape with impunity.

4-9
4. For there are no bands to their death. The Psalmist describes the comforts and advantages of the ungodly, which are as it were so many temptations to shake the faith of the people of God. He begins with the good health which they enjoy, telling us, that they are robust and vigorous, and have not to draw their breath with difficulty through continual sicknesses, as will often be the case with regard to true believers.
5. They are not in the trouble that is common to man. Here it is declared that the wicked enjoy a delightful repose, and are as it were by special privilege exempted from the miseries to which mankind in general are subject.
6. Therefore pride compasseth them as a chain. This complaint proceeds farther than the preceding; for we are here told that although God sees the ungodly shamefully and wickedly abusing his kindness and clemency, he notwithstanding bears with their ingratitude and rebellion. The Psalmist employs a similitude taken from the dress and attire of the body, to show that such persons glory in their evil deeds.
7. Their eye goeth out for fatness. He now adds, that it is not wonderful to see the ungodly breaking forth with such

MATTHEW HENRY

Book Three: Psalms 73-89

Psalm 73

1-14 God's goodness to his people; unsanctified prosperity.
I. The psalmist lays down, in the first place, that great principle which he is resolved to abide by and not to quit while he was parleying with this temptation, v. 1. Job, when he was entering into such a temptation, fixed for his principle the omniscience of God: Times are not hidden from the Almighty, Job xxiv. 1.
II. He comes now to relate the shock that was given to his faith in God's distinguishing goodness to Israel by a strong temptation to envy the prosperity of the wicked, and therefore to think that the Israel of God are no happier than other people and that God is no kinder to them than to others.

1. He speaks of it as a very narrow escape that he had not been quite foiled and overthrown by this temptation (v. 2): "But as for me, though I was so well satisfied in the goodness of God to Israel, yet my feet were almost gone (the tempter had almost tripped up my heels), my steps had well-nigh slipped (I had like to have quitted my religion, and given up all my expectations of benefit by it); for I was envious at the foolish."
2. Let us take notice of the process of the psalmist's temptation, what he was tempted with and tempted to.
(1.) He observed that foolish wicked people have sometimes a very great share of outward prosperity. He saw, with grief, the prosperity of the wicked, v. 3. Wicked people are really foolish people, and act against reason and their true interest, and yet every stander-by sees their prosperity.
(2.) He observed that they made a very bad use of their outward prosperity and were hardened by it in their wickedness, which very much strengthened the temptation he was in to fret at it. If it had done them any good, if it had made them less provoking to God or less oppressive to man, it would never have vexed him; but it had quite a contrary effect upon them.
(3.) He observed that while wicked men thus prospered in their impiety, and were made more impious by their prosperity, good people were in great affliction, and he himself in particular, which very much strengthened the temptation he was in to quarrel with Providence. He looked abroad and saw many of God's people greatly at a loss (v. 10): "Because the wicked are so very daring therefore his people return hither; they are at the same pause, the same plunge, that I am at; they know not what to say to it any more than I do, and the rather because waters of a full cup are wrung out to them; they are not only made to drink, and to drink deeply, of the bitter cup of affliction, but to drink all. Care is taken that they lose not a drop of that unpleasant potion; the waters are wrung out unto them, that they may have

Psalm 73

8-14

8 They are corrupt, and speak wickedly concerning oppression: they speak loftily.
9 They set their mouth against the heavens, and their tongue walketh through the earth.
10 Therefore his people return hither: and waters of a full cup are wrung out to them.
11 And they say, How doth God know? and is there knowledge in the most High?
12 Behold, these are the ungodly, who prosper in the world; they increase in riches.
13 Verily I have cleansed my heart in vain, and washed my hands in innocency.
14 For all the day long have I been plagued, and chastened every morning.

Verse 4. For there are no bands in their death. This is mentioned as the chief wonder, for we usually expect that in the solemn article of death, a difference will appear, and the wicked will become evidently in trouble. The notion is still prevalent that a quiet death means a happy hereafter. The psalmist had observed that the very reverse is true. Careless persons become case hardened, and continue presumptuously secure, even to the last.
Verse 5. They are not in trouble as other men. The prosperous wicked escape the killing toils which afflict the mass of mankind; their bread comes to them without care, their wine without stint.
Verse 6. Therefore pride compasseth them about as a chain. They are as great in their own esteem as if they were aldermen of the New Jerusalem; they want no other ornament than their own pomposity. No jeweler could sufficiently adorn them; they wear their own pride as a better ornament than a gold chain.
Verse 7. Their eyes stand out with fatness. In cases of obesity the eyes usually appear to be enclosed in fat, but sometimes they protrude; in either case the countenance is changed, loses its human form, and is assimilated to that of fatted swine. The face is here the index of the man: the man has more than suffices him; he is glutted and surfeited with wealth, and yet is one of the wicked whom God abhorreth.
Verse 8. They are corrupt. They rot above ground; their heart and life are depraved. And speak wickedly concerning oppression. The reek of the sepulcher rises through their mouths; the nature of the soul is revealed in the speech. They choose oppression as their subject, and they not only defend it, but advocate it, glory in it, and would fain make it the general rule among all nations.
Verse 9. They set their mouth against the heavens. Against God himself they aim their blasphemies. One would think, to hear them, that they were demigods themselves, and held their heads above the clouds, for they speak down upon other men as from a sublime elevation peculiar to themselves. Yet they might let God alone, for their pride will make them enemies enough without their defying him. And their tongue walketh through the earth.
Verse 10. Therefore his people return hither. God's people are driven to fly to his throne for shelter; the doggish tongues fetch home the sheep to the Shepherd. The saints come again, and again, to their Lord, laden with complaints on account of the persecutions which they endure from these proud and graceless men.
Verse 11. And they say, How doth God know? Thus dare the ungodly speak. They flatter themselves that their oppressions and persecutions are unobserved of heaven. If there be a God, is he not too much occupied with other matters to know what is going on upon this world? So they console themselves if judgments be threatened. Boasting of their own knowledge, they yet dare to ask, Is there knowledge in the Most High? Well were they called foolish. A God, and not know? This is a solecism in language, a madness of thought. Such, however, is the acted insanity of the graceless theists of this age; theists in name, because avowed infidelity is disreputable, but atheists in practice beyond all question.
Verse 12. Behold, these are the ungodly, who prosper in the world. Look! See! Consider! Here is the standing enigma! The crux of Providence! The stumbling block of faith! Here are the unjust rewarded and indulged, and that not for a day or an hour, but in perpetuity. From their youth up these men, who deserve perdition, revel in prosperity.
Verse 13. Verily I have cleansed my heart in vain. Poor Asaph! he questions the value of holiness when its wages are paid in the coin of affliction. With no effect has he been sincere; no advantage has come to him through his purity, for the filthy hearted are exalted and fed on the fat of the land. Thus foolishly will the wisest of men argue, when faith is napping. Asaph was a

violence and cruelty, since, by reason of fatness and pampering, their eyes are ready to start out of their heads.
8. They become insolent, and wickedly talk of extortion. "What!" they will say, "is it not in my power to deprive you of all that you possess, and even to cut your throat?" Robbers, it is true, can do the same thing; but then they hide themselves for fear. These giants, or rather inhuman monsters, of whom David speaks, on the contrary not only imagine that they are exempted from subjection to any law, but, unmindful of their own weakness, foam furiously, as if there were no distinction between good and evil, between right and wrong.
9. They have set their mouth against the heavens. Here it is declared that they utter their contumelious speeches as well against God as against men; for they imagine that nothing is too arduous for them to attempt, and flatter themselves that heaven and earth are subject to them.

10-14
10. On this account his people will return hither. Commentators wrest this sentence into a variety of meanings. In the first place, as the relative his is used, without an antecedent indicating whose people are spoken of, some understand it simply of the ungodly, as if it had been said, That the ungodly always fall back upon this reflection: and they view the word people as denoting a great troop or band; for as soon as a wicked man raises his standard, he always succeeds in drawing a multitude of associates after him.
11. And they say, How doth God know? The meaning of this passage is, that not only the wicked, when they see things in the world so full of disorder, conceive only of a blind government, which they attribute to fortune or chance; but that even true believers themselves are shaken, so as to doubt of the Providence of God; and that unless they were wonderfully preserved by his hand, they would be completely swallowed up in this abyss.
12. Behold! these are the ungodly. The Psalmist here shows, as it were by a vivid pictorial representation, the character of that envy which had well nigh overthrown him. Behold! says he, these are wicked men! and yet they happily enjoy their ease and pleasures undisturbed, and are exalted to power and influence; and that not merely for a few days, but their prosperity is of long duration, and has, as it were, an endless course.
13. He tells us that he was scourged daily, and that as often as the sun rose, some affliction or other was prepared for him, so that there was no end to his calamities. In short the amount of his reasoning is this, "Truly I have labored in vain to obtain and preserve a pure heart and clean hands, seeing continued afflictions await me, and, so to speak, are on the watch to meet me at break of day. Such a condition surely shows that there is no reward for innocence before God, else he would certainly deal somewhat more compassionately towards those who serve him."

15-17
15. If I should say, I will speak thus. David, perceiving the sinfulness of the thoughts with which he was tempted, puts a

the dregs of the cup. They pour out abundance of tears when they hear wicked people blaspheme God and speak profanely," as David did, Ps. cxix. 136.
(4.) From all this arose a very strong temptation to cast off his religion. Though the psalmist's feet were not so far gone as to question God's omniscience, yet he was tempted to question the benefit of religion, and to say (v. 13), Verily, I have cleansed my heart in vain, and have, to no purpose, washed my hands in innocency. See here what it is to be religious; it is to cleanse our hearts, in the first place, by repentance and regeneration, and then to wash our hands in innocency by a universal reformation of our lives.

15-20 The end of the wicked.
We have seen what a strong temptation the psalmist was in to envy prospering profaneness; now here we are told how he kept his footing and got the victory.
I. He kept up a respect for God's people, and with that he restrained himself from speaking what he had thought amiss, v. 15. He got the victory by degrees, and this was the first point he gained; he was ready to say, Verily, I have cleansed my heart in vain, and thought he had reason to say it, but he kept his mouth with this consideration, "If I say, I will speak thus, behold, I should myself revolt and apostatize from, and so give the greatest offence imaginable to, the generation of thy children."
II. He foresaw the ruin of wicked people. By this he baffled the temptation, as by the former he gave some check to it. Because he durst not speak what he had thought, for fear of giving offence, he began to consider whether he had any good reason for that thought (v. 16): "I endeavored to understand the meaning of this unaccountable dispensation of Providence; but it was too painful for me. I could not conquer it by the strength of my own reasoning." It is a problem, not to be solved by the mere light of nature, for, if there were not another life after this, we could not fully reconcile the prosperity of the wicked with the justice of God. But (v. 17) he went into the sanctuary of God; he applied to his devotions, meditated upon the attributes of God, and the things revealed, which belong to us and to our children; he consulted the scriptures, and the lips of the priests who attended the sanctuary; he prayed to God to make this matter plain to him and to help him over this difficulty; and, at length, he understood the wretched end of wicked people, which he plainly foresaw to be such that even in the height of their prosperity they were rather to be pitied than envied, for they were but ripening for ruin.
1. The prosperity of the wicked is short and uncertain. The high places in which Providence sets them are slippery places (v. 18), where they cannot long keep footing; but, when they offer to climb higher, that very attempt will be the occasion of their sliding and falling.
2. Their prosperity is therefore not to be envied at all, but despised rather, quod erat demonstrandum—

Psalm 73

15-21

15 If I say, I will speak thus; behold, I should offend against the generation of thy children.
16 When I thought to know this, it was too painful for me;
17 Until I went into the sanctuary of God; then understood I their end.
18 Surely thou didst set them in slippery places: thou castedst them down into destruction.
19 How are they brought into desolation, as in a moment! they are utterly consumed with terrors.
20 As a dream when one awaketh; so, O Lord, when thou awakest, thou shalt despise their image.
21 Thus my heart was grieved, and I was pricked in my reins.

seer, but he could not see when reason left him in the dark; even seers must have the sunlight of revealed truth to see by, or they grope like the blind. In the presence of temporal circumstances, the pure in heart may seem to have cleansed themselves altogether in vain, but we must not judge after the sight of the eyes.

Verse 14. For all the day long have I been plagued. He was smitten from the moment he woke to the time he went to bed. His griefs were not only continued, but renewed with every opening day. And chastened every morning. This was a vivid contrast to the lot of the ungodly. There were crowns for the reprobates and crosses for the elect. Strange that the saints should sigh and the sinners sing. Rest was given to the disturbers, and yet peace was denied to the peace makers. The downcast seer was in a muse and a maze. The affairs of mankind appeared to him to be in a fearful tangle; how could it be permitted by a just ruler that things should be so turned upside down, and the whole course of justice dislocated.

Verse 15. If I say, I will speak thus. It is not always wise to speak one's thoughts; if they remain within, they will only injure ourselves; but once uttered, their mischief may be great. From such a man as the psalmist, the utterance which his discontent suggested would have been a heavy blow and deep discouragement to the whole brotherhood. He dared not, therefore, come to such a resolution, but paused, and would not decide to declare his feelings. It was well, for in his case second thoughts were by far the best. I should offend against the generation of thy children. I should scandalize them, grieve them, and perhaps cause them to offend also. We ought to look at the consequences of our speech to all others, and especially to the church of God.

Verse 16. When I thought to know this, it was too painful for me. The thought of scandalizing the family of God he could not bear, and yet his inward thoughts seethed and fermented, and caused an intolerable anguish within. To speak might have relieved one sorrow, but, as it would have created another, he forbore so dangerous a remedy; yet this did not remove the first pangs, which grew even worse and worse, and threatened utterly to overwhelm him.

Verse 17. Until I went into the sanctuary of God. His mind entered the eternity where God dwells as in a holy place, he left the things of sense for the things invisible, his heart gazed within the veil, he stood where the thrice holy God stands. Thus he shifted his point of view, and apparent disorder resolved itself into harmony.

Verse 18. The Psalmist's sorrow had culminated, not in the fact that the ungodly prospered, but that God had arranged it so: had it happened by mere chance, he would have wondered, but could not have complained; but how the arranger of all things could so dispense his temporal favors, was the vexatious question. Here, to meet the case, he sees that the divine hand purposely placed these men in prosperous and eminent circumstances, not with the intent to bless them but the very reverse.

Verse 19. How are they brought into desolation, as in a moment! This is an exclamation of godly wonder at the suddenness and completeness of the sinners' overthrow. Headlong is their fall; without warning, without escape, without hope of future restoration! Despite their golden chains, and goodly apparel, death stays not for manners but hurries them away; and stern justice unbribed by their wealth hurls them into destruction. They are utterly consumed with terrors.

Verse 20. As a dream when one awaketh; so, O Lord, when thou awakest, thou shalt despise their image. They owe their existence and prosperity to the forbearance of God, which the psalmist compares to a sleep; but as a dream vanishes so soon as a man awakes, so the instant the Lord begins to exercise his justice and call men before him, the pomp and prosperity of proud transgressors shall melt away. When God awakes to judgment, they who despise him shall be despised; they are already "such stuff as dreams are made of," but then the baseless fabric shall not leave a wreck behind.

bridle upon himself, and reproves his inconstancy in allowing his mind to entertain doubts on such a subject.
16. Although I applied my mind to know this. The Psalmist does not speak of unbelievers who are willfully blind, who involve themselves in errors, and are also very glad to find some color or pretext for taking offense, that they may withdraw to a distance from God. It is of himself that he speaks; and although he applied his mind to the investigation of divine subjects, not only earnestly, but with all humility; and although, at the same time, he contemplated, according to his small measure, the high judgments of God, not only with attention, but also with reverence, yet he confesses that he failed of success; for the word trouble here implies unprofitable or lost labor.
17. By the sanctuaries of God some, even among the Hebrews, understand the celestial mansions in which the spirits of the just and angels dwell; as if David had said, This was a painful thing in my sight, until I came to acknowledge in good earnest that men are not created to flourish for a short time in this world, and to luxuriate in pleasures while in it, but that their condition here is that of pilgrims, whose aspirations, during their earthly pilgrimage, should be towards heaven.

18-20
18. Surely thou hast set them in slippery places. David, having now gone through his conflicts, begins, if we may use the expression, to be a new man; and he speaks with a quiet and composed mind, being, as it were, elevated on a watchtower, from which he obtained a clear and distinct view of things which before were hidden from him. It was the prophet Habakkuk's resolution to take such a position, and, by his example, he prescribes this to us as a remedy in the midst of troubles—"I will stand upon my watch," says he, "and set me upon the tower," (Habakkuk 2:1.) David, therefore, shows how much advantage is to be derived from approaching God. I now see, says he, how thou proceedest in thy providence; for, although the ungodly continue to stand for a brief season, yet they are, as it were, perched on slippery places, that they may fall ere long into destruction.
19. How have they been destroyed, as it were in a moment! The language of wonder in which the Psalmist breaks forth serves much to confirm the sentiment of the preceding verse. As the consideration of the prosperity of the ungodly induces a torpor upon our minds, yea, even renders them stupid; so their destruction, being sudden and unlooked for, tends the more effectually to awaken us, each being thus constrained to inquire how such an event came to pass, which all men thought could never happen. The prophet, therefore, speaks of it in the way of interrogation, as of a thing incredible. Yet he, at the same time, thus teaches us that God is daily working in such a manner as that, if we would but open our eyes, there would be presented to us just matter for exciting our astonishment.
20. As it were a dream after a man is awakened. This similitude is often to be met with in the Sacred Writings. Thus, Isaiah, (Isaiah 29:7,) speaking of the enemies of the Church, says, "They shall be as a dream of a night vision." In the passage

which was the point to be established, v. 20. As a dream when one awaketh, so, O Lord! when thou awakest, or when they awake (as some read it), thou shalt despise their image, their shadow, and make it to vanish.

21-28 Devout confidence.
Behold Samson's riddle again unriddled, Out of the eater came forth meat, and out of the strong sweetness; for we have here an account of the good improvement which the psalmist made of that sore temptation with which he had been assaulted and by which he was almost overcome. He that stumbles and does not fall, by recovering himself takes so much the longer steps forward. It was so with the psalmist here; many good lessons he learned from his temptation, his struggles with it, and his victories over it. Nor would God suffer his people to be tempted if his grace were not sufficient for them, not only to save them from harm, but to make them gainers by it; even this shall work for good.
I. He learned to think very humbly of himself and to abase and accuse himself before God (v. 21, 22); he reflects with shame upon the disorder and danger he was in, and the vexation he gave himself by entertaining the temptation and parleying with it: My heart was grieved, and I was pricked in my reins, as one afflicted with the acute pain of the stone in the region of the kidneys. If evil thoughts at any time enter into the mind of a good man, he does not roll them under his tongue as a sweet morsel, but they are grievous and painful to him; temptation was to Paul as a thorn in the flesh, 2 Cor. xii. 7. This particular temptation, the working of envy and discontent, is as painful as any; where it constantly rests it is the rottenness of the bones (Prov. xiv. 30); where it does but occasionally come it is the pricking of the reins. Fretfulness is a corruption that is its own correction.
II. He took occasion hence to own his dependence on and obligations to the grace of God (v. 23): "Nevertheless, foolish as I am, I am continually with thee and in thy favor; thou hast holden me by my right hand." This may refer either,
1. To the care God had taken of him, and the kindness he had shown him, all along from his beginning hitherto. He had said, in the hour of temptation (v. 14), All the day long have I been plagued; but here he corrects himself for that passionate complaint: "Though God has chastened me, he has not cast me off; notwithstanding all the crosses of my life, I have been continually with thee; I have had thy presence with me, and thou hast been nigh unto me in all that which I have called upon thee for; and therefore, though perplexed, yet not in despair. Though God has sometimes written bitter things against me, yet he has still holden me by my right hand, both to keep me, that I should not desert him or fly off from him, and to prevent my sinking and fainting under my burdens, or

Psalm 73

22-28

22 So foolish was I, and ignorant: I was as a beast before thee.
23 Nevertheless I am continually with thee: thou hast holden me by my right hand.
24 Thou shalt guide me with thy counsel, and afterward receive me to glory.
25 Whom have I in heaven but thee? and there is none upon earth that I desire beside thee.
26 My flesh and my heart faileth: but God is the strength of my heart, and my portion for ever.
27 For, lo, they that are far from thee shall perish: thou hast destroyed all them that go a whoring from thee.
28 But it is good for me to draw near to God: I have put my trust in the Lord GOD, that I may declare all thy works.

Verse 21. The holy poet here reviews his inward struggle and awards himself censure for his folly. His pain had been intense; he says, Thus my heart was grieved. It was a deep seated sorrow, and one which penetrated his inmost being.

Verse 22. So foolish was I. He, though a saint of God, had acted as if he had been one of the fools whom God abhorreth. Had he not even envied them?—and what is that but to aspire to be like them? The wisest of men have enough folly in them to ruin them unless grace prevents. And ignorant. He had acted as if he knew nothing, had babbled like an idiot, had uttered the very drivel of a witless loon. He did not know how sufficiently to express his sense of his own fatuity. I was as a beast before thee. Even in God's presence he had been brutish, and worse than a beast.

Verse 23. Nevertheless I am continually with thee. He does not give up his faith, though he confesses his folly. Sin may distress us, and yet we may be in communion with God. It is sin beloved and delighted in which separates us from the Lord, but when we bewail it heartily, the Lord will not withdraw from us.

Verse 24. Thou shalt guide me with thy counsel. I have done with choosing my own way, and trying to pick a path amid the jungle of reason. He yielded not only the point in debate, but all intentions of debating, and he puts his hand into that of the great Father, asking to be led, and agreeing to follow. Our former mistakes are a blessing, when they drive us to this. The end of our own wisdom is the beginning of our being wise.

Verse 25. Whom have I in heaven but thee? Thus, then, he turns away from the glitter which fascinated him to the true gold which was his real treasure. He felt that his God was better to him than all the wealth, health, honor, and peace, which he had so much envied in the worldling; yea, He was not only better than all on earth, but more excellent than all in heaven.

Verse 26. My flesh and my heart faileth. They had failed him already, and he had almost fallen; they would fail him in the hour of death, and, if he relied upon them, they would fail him at once. But God is the strength of my heart, and my portion for ever. His God would not fail him, either as protection or a joy. His heart would be kept up by divine love, and filled eternally with divine glory.

Verse 27. For, lo, they that are far from thee shall perish. We must be near God to live; to be far off by wicked works is death. Thou hast destroyed all them that go a whoring from thee. If we pretend to be the Lord's servants, we must remember that he is a jealous God, and requires spiritual chastity from all his people. Offences against conjugal vows are very offensive, and all sins against God have the same element in them.

Verse 28. But it is good for me to draw near to God. Had he done so at first he would not have been immersed in such affliction; when he did so he escaped from his dilemma, and if he continued to do so he would not fall into the same evil again. The greater our nearness to God, the less we are affected by the attractions and distractions of earth. Access into the most holy place is a great privilege, and a cure for a multitude of ills.

before us the metaphor is very appropriate. How is it to be accounted for, that the prosperity of the wicked is regarded with so much wonder, but because our minds have been lulled into a deep sleep? In short, the pictures which we draw in our imaginations of the happiness of the wicked, and of the desirableness of their condition, are just like the imaginary kingdoms which we construct in our dreams when we are asleep.

21-24

21. For my heart was in a ferment. The Psalmist again returns to the confession which he had previously made, acknowledging that whilst he felt his heart pierced with perverse envy and emulation, he had complained against God, in a peevish or fretful manner. He compares his anger to leaven.

22. And I was foolish and ignorant. David here rebuking himself sharply, as it became him to do, in the first place declares that he was foolish; secondly, he charges himself with ignorance; and, thirdly, he affirms that he resembled the brutes.

23. Nevertheless I was continually with thee. Here the Psalmist declares, in a different sense, that he was with God. He gives him thanks for having kept him from utterly falling, when he was in so great danger of being precipitated into destruction.

24. Thou shalt guide me with thy counsel. As the verbs are put in the future tense, the natural meaning, in my opinion, is, that the Psalmist assured himself that the Lord, since by his leading he had now brought him back into the right way, would continue henceforth to guide him, until at length he received him into His glorious presence in heaven.

25-28

25. Whom have I in heaven but thee? The Psalmist shows more distinctly how much he had profited in the sanctuary of God; for being satisfied with him alone, he rejects every other object, except God, which presented itself to him.

26. My flesh and my heart have failed. Some understand the first part of the verse as meaning that David's heart and flesh failed him through the ardent desire with which he was actuated; and they think that by it he intends to testify the earnestness with which he applied his mind to God.

27. For, lo! they who depart from thee shall perish. Here he proves, by an argument taken from things contrary, that nothing was better for him than simply to repose himself upon God alone; for no sooner does any one depart from God than he inevitably falls into the most dreadful destruction. All depart from him who divide and scatter their hope among a variety of objects. The phrase to go a whoring is of similar import; for it is the worst kind of adultery to divide our heart that it may not continue fixed exclusively upon God.

28. As for me, it is good for me to draw near to God. Literally the reading is, And I, etc. David speaking expressly of himself, affirms that he would study to continue always in a state of nearness to God.

losing my way in the wildernesses through which I have walked."

2. To the late experience he had had of the power of divine grace in carrying him through this strong temptation and bringing him off a conqueror: "I was foolish and ignorant, and yet thou hast had compassion on me and taught me (Heb. v. 2), and kept me under thy protection."

III. He encouraged himself to hope that the same God who had delivered him from this evil work would preserve him to his heavenly kingdom, as St. Paul does (2 Tim. iv. 18): "I am now upheld by thee, therefore thou shalt guide me with thy counsel, leading me, as thou hast done hitherto, many a difficult step; and, since I am now continually with thee, thou shalt afterwards receive me to glory" v. 24. This completes the happiness of the saints, so that they have no reason to envy the worldly prosperity of sinners.

IV. He was hereby quickened to cleave the more closely to God, and very much confirmed and comforted in the choice he had made of him, v. 25, 26. His thoughts here dwell with delight upon his own happiness in God, as much greater than the happiness of the ungodly that prospered in the world. He saw little reason to envy them what they had in the creature when he found how much more and better, surer and sweeter, comforts he had in the Creator, and what cause he had to congratulate himself on this account. He had complained of his afflictions (v. 14); but this makes them very light and easy, All is well if God be mine.

V. He was fully convinced of the miserable condition of all wicked people. This he learned in the sanctuary upon this occasion, and he would never forget it (v. 27): "Lo, those that are far from thee, in a state of distance and estrangement, that desire the Almighty to depart from them, shall certainly perish; so shall their doom be; they choose to be far from God, and they shall be far from him for ever. Thou wilt justly destroy all those that go a whoring from thee, that is, all apostates, that in profession have been betrothed to God, but forsake him, their duty to him, to embrace the bosom of a stranger."

VI. He was greatly encouraged to cleave to God and to confide in him, v. 28. If those that are far from God shall perish, then,

1. Let this constrain us to live in communion with God; "if it fare so ill with those that live at a distance from him, then it is good, very good, the chief good, that good for a man, in this life, which he should most carefully pursue and secure, it is best for me to draw near to God, and to have God draw near to me;" the original may take in both.

2. Let us therefore live in a continual dependence upon him: "I have put my trust in the Lord God, and will never go a whoring from him after any creature confidences."

Psalm 74

Title
Maschil of Asaph.

1-8
1 O God, why hast thou cast us off for ever? why doth thine anger smoke against the sheep of thy pasture?
2 Remember thy congregation, which thou hast purchased of old; the rod of thine inheritance, which thou hast redeemed; this mount Zion, wherein thou hast dwelt.
3 Lift up thy feet unto the perpetual desolations; even all that the enemy hath done wickedly in the sanctuary.
4 Thine enemies roar in the midst of thy congregations; they set up their ensigns for signs.
5 A man was famous according as he had lifted up axes upon the thick trees.
6 But now they break down the carved work thereof at once with axes and hammers.
7 They have cast fire into thy sanctuary, they have defiled by casting down the dwelling place of thy name to the ground.
8 They said in their hearts, Let us destroy them together: they have burned up all the synagogues of God in the land.

Psalm 74

TITLE. Maschil of Asaph. An instructive Psalm by Asaph. The history of the suffering church is always edifying; when we see how the faithful trusted and wrestled with their God in times of dire distress, we are thereby taught how to behave ourselves under similar circumstances; we learn moreover, that when fiery trial befalls us, no strange thing happened unto us, we are following the trail of the host of God.
DIVISION. From Ps 74:1-11 the poet pleads the sorrows of the nation, and the despite done to the assemblies of the Lord; then he urges former displays of divine power as a reason for present deliverance (Ps 74:12-23). Whether it is a prophetic Psalm, intended for use in troubles foreseen, or whether it was written by a later Asaph, after the invasion by Sennacherib or during the Maccabean wars, it would be very hard to determine, but we see no difficulty in the first supposition.

EXPOSITION
Verse 1. O God, why hast thou cast us off for ever? To cast us off at all were hard, but when thou dost for so long a time desert they people it is an evil beyond all endurance—the very chief of woes and abyss of misery. It is our wisdom when under chastisement to enquire, "Show me wherefore thou contendest with me?" and if the affliction be a protracted one, we should more eagerly enquire the purport of it. Sin is usually at the bottom of all the hiding of the Lord's face; let us ask the Lord to reveal the special form of it to us, that we may repent of it, overcome it, and henceforth forsake it.
Verse 2. Remember thy congregation, which thou hast purchased of old. What a mighty plea is redemption. O God, canst thou see the blood mark on thine own sheep, and yet allow grievous wolves to devour them? The church is no new purchase of the Lord; from before the world's foundation the chosen were regarded as redeemed by the Lamb slain; shall ancient love die out, and the eternal purpose become frustrate?
Verse 3. Lift up thy feet unto the perpetual desolations. The ruin made had already long been an eyesore to the suppliant, and there seemed no hope of restoration. Havoc lorded it not only for a day or a year, but with perpetual power. This is another argument with God. Would Jehovah sit still and see his own land made a wilderness, his own palace a desolation? Until he should arise, and draw near, the desolation would remain; only his presence could cure the evil, therefore is he entreated to hasten with uplifted feet for the deliverance of his people.
Verse 4. Thine enemies roar in the midst of thy congregations. Where thy people sang like angels, these barbarians roar like beasts. When thy saints come together for worship, these cruel men attack them with all the fury of lions. They have no respect for the most solemn gatherings, but intrude themselves and their blasphemies into our most hallowed meetings. How often in times of persecution or prevalent heresy has the church learned the meaning of such language.
Verse 5. A man was famous according as he had lifted up axes upon the thick trees. Once men were renowned for felling the cedars and preparing them for building the temple, but now the axe finds other work, and men are as proud of destroying as their fathers were of erecting. Thus in the olden times our sires dealt sturdy blows against the forests of error, and labored hard to lay the axe at the root of the trees; but, alas! their sons appear to be quite as diligent to destroy the truth and to overthrow all that their fathers built up. O for the good old times again! O for an hour of Luther's hatchet, or Calvin's mighty axe!
Verse 6. But now they break down the carved work thereof at once with axes and hammers. The invaders were as industrious to destroy as the ancient builders had been to construct. Such fair carving it was barbarous to hew in pieces, but the Vandals had no mercy and broke down all, with

JOHN CALVIN

Psalm 74

1-8

1. O God! why hast thou east us off for ever? If this complaint was written when the people were captives in Babylon, although Jeremiah had assigned the 70th year of their captivity as the period of their deliverance, it is not wonderful that waiting so long was to them a very bitter affliction, that they daily groaned under it, and that so protracted a period seemed to them like an eternity.

2. Remember thy congregation, which thou hast possessed of old. Here they boast of having been the peculiar people of God, not on account of any merit of their own, but by the grace of adoption. They boast in like manner of their antiquity,—that they are not subjects who have come under the government of God only within a few months ago, but such as had fallen to him by right of inheritance.

3. Lift up thy strokes. Here the people of God, on the other hand, beseech him to inflict a deadly wound upon their enemies, corresponding to the cruelty with which they had raged against his sanctuary. They would intimate, that a moderate degree of punishment was not sufficient for such impious and sacrilegious fury; and that, therefore, those who had shown themselves such violent enemies of the temple and of the worshippers of God should be completely destroyed, their impiety being altogether desperate.

4. Thy adversaries have roared in the midst of thy sanctuaries. Here the people of God compare their enemies to lions, (Amos 3:8,) to point out the cruelty which they exercised even in the very sanctuaries of God. In this passage we are to understand the temple of Jerusalem as spoken of rather than the Jewish synagogues; nor is it any objection to this interpretation that the temple is here called in the plural number sanctuaries, as is frequently the case in other places, it being so called because it was divided into three parts.

5. He who lifted up the axe upon the thick trees was renowned. The prophet again aggravates still more the barbarous and brutal cruelty of the enemies of his countrymen, from the circumstance, that they savagely demolished an edifice which had been built at such vast expense, which was embellished with such beauty and magnificence, and finished with so great labor and art.

7. They have set fire to thy sanctuaries. The Psalmist now complains that the temple was burned, and thus completely razed and destroyed, whereas it was only half demolished by the instruments of war.

The name of God is here employed to teach us that his essence was not confined to or shut up in the temple, but that he dwelt in it by his power and operation, that the people might there call upon him with the greater confidence.

8. They have said in their heart, Let us destroy them all together. To express the more forcibly the atrocious cruelty of the enemies of the Church, the prophet introduces them speaking together, and exciting one another to commit devastation without limit or measure. His language implies, that each of them, as if they had not possessed enough of

MATTHEW HENRY

Psalm 74

1-11 Mournful complaints.

Three things the people of God here complain of:

I. The displeasure of God against them, as that which was the cause and bitterness of all their calamities.

II. They complain of the outrage and cruelty of their enemies.

III. The great aggravation of all these calamities was that they had no prospect at all of relief, nor could they foresee an end of them (v. 9): "We see our enemy's sign set up in the sanctuary, but we see not our signs, none of the tokens of God's presence, no hopeful indications of approaching deliverance. There is no more any prophet to tell us how long the trouble will last and when things concerning us shall have an end, that the hope of an issue at last may support us under our troubles."

12-17 Acknowledgments of divine power.

The lamenting church fastens upon something here which she calls to mind, and therefore hath she hope (as Lam. iii. 21), with which she encourages herself and silences her own complaints. Two things quiet the minds of those that are here sorrowing for the solemn assembly:

I. That God is the God of Israel, a God in covenant with his people (v. 12): God is my King of old. This comes in both as a plea in prayer to God (Ps. xliv. 4, thou art my King, O God!) and as a prop to their own faith and hope, to encourage themselves to expect deliverance, considering the days of old, Ps. lxxvii. 5.

II. That the God of Israel is the God of nature, v. 16, 17. It is he that orders the regular successions and revolutions,

1. Of day and night. He is the Lord of all time. The evening and the morning are of his ordaining. It is he that opens the eyelids of the morning light, and draws the curtains of the evening shadow. He has prepared the moon and the sun (so some read it), the two great lights, to rule by day and by night alternately. The preparing of them denotes their constant readiness and exact observance of their time, which they never miss a moment.

2. Of summer and winter: "Thou hast appointed all the bounds of the earth, and the different climates of its several regions, for thou hast made summer and winter, the frigid and the torrid zones; or, rather, the constant revolutions of the year and its several seasons." Herein we are to acknowledge God, from whom all the laws and powers of nature are derived.

18-23 Earnest supplications; pleading with God.

The psalmist here, in the name of the church, most earnestly begs that God would appear for them against their enemies, and put an end to their present troubles. To encourage his own faith, he interests God in this matter (v. 22): Arise, O God! plead thy own cause. This we may be sure he will do, for he is

Psalm 74

9-16

9 We see not our signs: there is no more any prophet: neither is there among us any that knoweth how long.

10 O God, how long shall the adversary reproach? shall the enemy blaspheme thy name for ever?

11 Why withdrawest thou thy hand, even thy right hand? pluck it out of thy bosom.

12 For God is my King of old, working salvation in the midst of the earth.

13 Thou didst divide the sea by thy strength: thou brakest the heads of the dragons in the waters.

14 Thou brakest the heads of leviathan in pieces, and gavest him to be meat to the people inhabiting the wilderness.

15 Thou didst cleave the fountain and the flood: thou driedst up mighty rivers.

16 The day is thine, the night also is thine: thou hast prepared the light and the sun.

any weapon which came to hand. In these days men are using axes and sledgehammers against the gospel and the church. Glorious truths, far more exquisite than the goodliest carving, are caviled over and smashed by the blows of modern criticism.

Verse 7. They have cast fire into thy sanctuary. Axes and hammers were not sufficient for the purpose of the destroyers, they must needs try fire. Malice knows no bounds. Those who hate God are never sparing of the most cruel weapons. To this day the enmity of the human heart is quite as great as ever; and, if providence did not restrain, the saints would still be as fuel for the flames. They have defiled by casting down the dwelling place of thy name to the ground. They made a heap of the temple, and left not one stone upon another. When the Lord left Mount Zion, and the Roman gained entrance, the military fury led the soldiers to burn out and root up the memorial of the famous House of the Lord. Could the powers of darkness have their way, a like fate would befall the church of Christ.

Verse 8. They said in their hearts, Let us destroy them together. It was no idle wish, their cruelty was sincere, deep seated, a matter of their inmost heart. Extirpation was the desire of Haman, and the aim of many another tyrant; not a remnant of the people of God would have been left if oppressors could have had their way. Pharaoh's policy to stamp out the nation has been a precedent for others, yet the Jews survive, and will: the bush though burning has not been consumed. Even thus the church of Christ has gone through baptism of blood and fire, but it is all the brighter for them. They have burned up all the synagogues of God in the land. Here is no allusion to places called synagogues, but to assemblies; and as no assemblies for worship here held in but one place, the ruin of the temple was the destruction of all the holy gatherings, and so in effect all the meeting places were destroyed.

Verse 9. We see not our signs. Alas, poor Israel! No Urim and Thummim blazed on the High Priest's bosom, and no Shechaniah shone from between the cherubim. The smoke of sacrifice and cloud of incense no more arose from the holy hill; solemn feasts were suspended, and even circumcision, the covenant sign, was forbidden by the tyrant. We, too, as believers, know what it is to lose our evidences and grope in darkness; and too often do our churches also miss the tokens of the Redeemer's presence, and their lamps remain untrimmed. Sad complaint of a people under a cloud! There is no more any prophet. Prophecy was suspended. No inspiring psalm or consoling promise fell from bard or seer. It is ill with the people of God when the voice of the preacher of the gospel fails, and a famine of the word of life falls on the people.

Verse 10. O God, how long shall the adversary reproach? Though we know not how long yet thou dost. The times and seasons are with thee. When God is reproached, there is hope for us, for it may be he will hearken and avenge his dishonored name. Wickedness has great license allowed it, and justice lingers on the road; God has his reasons for delay, and his seasons for action, and in the end it shall be seen that he is not slack concerning his promise as some men count slackness.

Verse 11. Why withdrawest thou thy hand, even thy right hand? Wherefore this inaction, this indifference for thine own honor and thy people's safety? How bold is the suppliant! Does he err? Nay, verily, we who are so chill, and distant, and listless in prayer are the erring ones. The kingdom of heaven suffereth violence, and he who learns the art shall surely prevail with God by its means. It is fit that we should enquire why the work of grace goes on so slowly, and the enemy has so much power over men: the inquiry may suggest practical reflections of unbounded value.

Verses 12-23. Having spread the sad case before the Lord, the pleader now urges another series of arguments for divine help. He reasons from the Lord's former wonders of grace, and his deeds of power, imploring a repetition of the same divine works.

courage to do mischief, stirred up and stimulated his fellow to waste and destroy the whole of God's people, without leaving so much as one of them.

9-12

9. We see not our signs. Here the pious Jews show that their calamities were aggravated from the circumstance that they had no consolation by which to alleviate them. It is a powerful means of encouraging the children of God, when he enables them to cherish the hope of his being reconciled to them, by promising, that even in the midst of his wrath he will remember his mercy.

10. How long, O God! shall the adversary reproach? Here it is intimated that nothing inflicted upon them greater anguish than when they saw the name of God blasphemed by the ungodly. By this manner of praying, the object of the inspired writer was to kindle in our hearts a zeal for maintaining the Divine glory. We are naturally too delicate and tender for bearing calamities; but it is a decided proof of genuine godliness, when the contumely which is cast upon God grieves and disquiets our minds more than all our own personal sufferings.

11. How long wilt thou withdraw thy hand? It is easy to see what the prophet here intends, and yet interpreters are not agreed as to the words. Some by the word hand, in the first part of the verse, understand the left hand, to distinguish it from the right hand, mentioned in the last clause of the verse. But this is mere trifling; for when he uses the term right hand, he simply repeats the same thing according to his usual manner.

12. But God is my King from the beginning. In this verse, as we have often seen to be the case in other places, the people of God intermingle meditations with their prayers, thereby to acquire renewed vigor to their faith, and to stir up themselves to greater earnestness in the duty of prayer. We know how difficult it is to rise above all doubts, and boldly to persevere in a free and unrestrained course of prayer.

13-17

13. Thou hast divided the sea by thy power. The prophet now collects together certain kinds of deliverances highly worthy of remembrance; all of them, however, belonging to the first deliverance by which God emancipated his people from the tyranny of Egypt. We will find him afterwards descending to the general commendation of the goodness of God which is diffused through the whole world.

14. When he says that leviathan was given for food to the Israelites, and that even in the wilderness, there is a beautiful allusion to the destruction of Pharaoh and his host. It is as if he had said, that then a bountiful provision of victuals was laid up for the nourishment of the people; for when their enemies were destroyed, the quiet and security which the people in consequence enjoyed served, so to speak, as food to prolong their life. By the wilderness, is not meant the countries lying on the sea coast, though they are dry and barren, but the deserts at a great distance from the sea.

jealous for his own honor; whatever is his own cause he will plead it with a strong hand, will appear against those that oppose it and with and for those that cordially espouse it. He will arise and plead it, though for a time he seems to neglect it; he will stir up himself, will manifest himself, will do his own work in his own time. Note, The cause of religion is God's own cause and he will certainly plead it. Now, to make it out that the cause is God's, he pleads,

I. That the persecutors are God's sworn enemies: "Lord, they have not only abused us, but they have been, and are, abusive to thee; what is done against us, for thy sake, does, by consequence, reflect upon thee. But that is not all; they have directly and immediately reproached thee, and blasphemed thy name," v. 18. This was that which they roared in the sanctuary; they triumphed as if they had now got the mastery of the God of Israel, of whom they had heard such great things. As nothing grieves the saints more than to hear God's name blasphemed, so nothing encourages them more to hope that God will appear against their enemies than when they have arrived at such a pitch of wickedness as to reproach God himself; this fills the measure of their sins apace and hastens their ruin. The psalmist insists much upon this: "We dare not answer their reproaches; Lord, do thou answer them. Remember that the foolish people have blasphemed thy name (v. 18) and that still the foolish man reproaches thee daily." Observe the character of those that reproach God; they are foolish. As atheism is folly (Ps. xiv. 1), profaneness and blasphemy are no less so. Perhaps those are cried up as the wits of the age that ridicule religion and sacred things; but really they are the greatest fools, and will shortly be made to appear so before all the world. And yet see their malice. They reproach God daily, as constantly as his faithful worshippers pray to him and praise him; see their impudence. They do not hide their blasphemous thoughts in their own bosoms, but proclaim them with a loud voice (forget not the voice of thy enemies, v. 23), and this with a daring defiance of divine justice; they rise up against thee, and by their blasphemies even wage war with heaven and take up arms against the Almighty. Their noise and tumult ascend continually (so some), as the cry of Sodom came up before God, calling for vengeance, Gen. xviii. 21. It increases continually (so we read it); they grow worse and worse, and are hardened in their impieties by their successes. Now, Lord, remember this; do not forget it. God needs not to be put in remembrance by us of what he has to do, but thus we must show our concern for his honor and believe that he will vindicate us.

II. That the persecuted are his covenant-people.

1. See what distress they are in. They have fallen into the hands of the multitude of the wicked, v. 19. How are those increased that trouble them! There is no standing before an enraged multitude, especially like

Psalm 74

17-23

17 Thou hast set all the borders of the earth: thou hast made summer and winter.
18 Remember this, that the enemy hath reproached, O LORD, and that the foolish people have blasphemed thy name.
19 O deliver not the soul of thy turtledove unto the multitude of the wicked: forget not the congregation of thy poor for ever.
20 Have respect unto the covenant: for the dark places of the earth are full of the habitations of cruelty.
21 O let not the oppressed return ashamed: let the poor and needy praise thy name.
22 Arise, O God, plead thine own cause: remember how the foolish man reproacheth thee daily.
23 Forget not the voice of thine enemies: the tumult of those that rise up against thee increaseth continually.

Verse 12. For God is my King of old. How consoling is this avowal! Israel in holy loyalty acknowledges her King, and claims to have been his possession from of old, and thence she derives a plea for defense and deliverance. If the Lord be indeed the sole monarch of our bosoms, he will in his love put forth his strength on our behalf; if from eternity he has claimed us as his own, he will preserve us from the insulting foe. Working salvation in the midst of the earth. From the most remote period of Israel's history the Lord had worked out for her many salvations; especially at the Red Sea, the very heart of the world was astonished by his wonders of deliverance. Now, every believer may plead at this day the ancient deeds of the Lord, the work of Calvary, the overthrow of sin, death, and hell. He who wrought out our salvation of old will not, cannot desert us now.

Verse 21. O let not the oppressed return ashamed. Though broken and crushed they come to thee with confidence; suffer them not to be disappointed, for then they will be ashamed of their hope. Let the poor and needy praise thy name. By thy speedy answer to their cries make their hearts glad, and they will render to thee their gladdest songs. It is not the way of the Lord to allow any of those who trust in him to be put to shame; for his word is, "He shall call upon me, and I will deliver him, and he shall glorify me."

Verse 22. Arise, O God, plead thine own cause. Answer thou the taunts of the profane by arguments which shall annihilate both the blasphemy and the blasphemer. God's judgments are awful replies to the defiance of his foes. When he makes empires crumble, and smites persecutors to the heart, his cause is pleaded by himself as none other could have advocated it. O that the Lord himself would come into the battle field. Long has the fight been trembling in the balance; one glance of his eyes, one word from his lip, and the banners of victory shall be borne on the breeze. Remember how the foolish man reproacheth thee daily. The Lord is begged to remember that he is himself reproached, and that by a mere man—that man a fool, and he is also reminded that these foul reproaches are incessant and repeated with every revolving day. It is bravely done when faith can pluck pleas out of the dragon's mouth and out of the blasphemies of fools find arguments with God.

Verse 23. Forget not the voice of thine enemies. Great warrior let the enemy's taunt provoke thee to the fray. They challenge thee; accept thou the gage of battle, and smite them with thy terrible hand. If the cries of thy children are too feeble to be heard, be pleased to note the loud voices of thy foes and silence their profanities for ever. The tumult of those that rise up against thee increaseth continually. The ungodly clamor against thee and thy people, their blasphemies are loud and incessant, they defy thee, even thee, and because thou repliest not they laugh thee to scorn. They go from bad to worse, from worse to worst; their fury swells like the thunders of an advancing tempest. What will it come too? O Lord, how long shall it be ere thou wilt ease thyself of those profane wretches, the priests, and cast the harlot of Babylon into the ditch of corruption? May the church never cease to plead with thee till judgment shall be executed, and the Lord avenged upon Antichrist.

JOHN CALVIN

15. The same subject is prosecuted in the following verse, where it is declared, that the fountain was cleaved or divided, that is, it was so when God caused a stream of water to gush from the rock to supply the wants of the people. Finally, it is added, that mighty rivers were dried up, an event which happened when God caused the waters of the Jordan to turn back to make a way for his people to pass over.
16. The day is thine, the night also is thine. The prophet now descends to the consideration of the divine benefits which are extended in common to all mankind. Having commenced with the special blessings by which God manifested himself to be the Father of his chosen people, he now aptly declares that God exercises his beneficence towards the whole human family.
17. Thou hast fixed all the boundaries of the earth. What is here stated concerning the boundaries or limits assigned to the earth, and concerning the regular and successive recurrence of summer and winter every year, is to the same effect as the preceding verse.

18-23
18. Remember this. The prophet having encouraged the hearts of the godly by magnifying the divine power and goodness, now returns to the prosecution of his prayer. He first complains that the enemies of his people revile God, and yet continue unpunished. When he says, Remember this, the manner of expression is emphatic; and the occasion demanded it, for it is not a crime of small magnitude to treat with contumely the sacred name of God.
19. Give not to the beast the soul of thy turtle dove. This form of expression will contain a very apposite comparison between the life of a weak and timorous bird, and a powerful army of men, or a cruel beast.
20. Have regard to thy covenant. That God may be the more inclined to show mercy, the prophet brings to his remembrance the Divine covenant; even as the refuge of the saints, when they have found themselves involved in extreme dangers, has always been to hope for deliverance, because God had promised, in the covenant which he made with them, to be a father to them. From this we learn, that the only firm support on which our prayers can rest is, that God has adopted us to be his people by his free choice.
21. Let not him who is oppressed return with shame. The word return, as it has a reference to God, is equivalent to the expression, to go away empty. The faithful, then, beseech Him that they may not be put to shame by suffering a repulse at his hands. They call themselves afflicted, poor, and needy, as an argument to obtain the Divine favor and mercy.
22. Arise, O God! plead thy cause. The pious Jews again supplicate God to ascend into his judgment-seat. He is then said to arise, when, after having long exercised forbearance, he shows, in very deed, that he has not forgotten his office as judge.
23. The faithful conclude by invoking God that he would not forget such heaven-daring conduct in men who fiercely poured forth their blasphemies against him.

MATTHEW HENRY

these, armed with power; and, as they are numerous, so they are barbarous: The dark places of the earth are full of the habitations of cruelty. The land of the Chaldeans, where there was none of the light of the knowledge of the true God (though otherwise it was famed for learning and arts), was indeed a dark place; the inhabitants of it were alienated from the life of God through the ignorance that was in them, and therefore they were cruel: where there was no true divinity there was scarcely to be found common humanity. They were especially cruel to the people of God; certainly those have no knowledge who eat them up, Ps. xiv. 4. They are oppressed (v. 21) because they are poor and unable to help themselves; they are oppressed, and so impoverished and made poor.
2. See what reason they had to hope that God would appear for their relief and not suffer them to be always thus trampled upon. Observe how the psalmist pleads with God for them.
(1.) "It is thy turtle-dove that is ready to be swallowed up by the multitude of the wicked," v. 19. The church is a dove for harmlessness and mildness, innocency and inoffensiveness, purity and fruitfulness, a dove for mournfulness in a day of distress, a turtle-dove for fidelity and the constancy of love: turtle-doves and pigeons were the only fowls that were offered in sacrifice to God. "Shall thy turtle-dove, that is true to thee and devoted to thy honor, be delivered, its life and soul and all, into the hand of the multitude of the wicked, to whom it will soon become an easy and acceptable prey? Lord, it will be thy honor to help the weak, especially to help thy own."
(2.) "It is the congregation of thy poor, and they are not the less thine for their being poor (for God has chosen the poor of this world, Jam. ii. 5), but they have the more reason to expect thou wilt appear for them because they are many: it is the congregation of thy poor; let them not be abandoned and forgotten for ever."
(3.) "They are in covenant with thee; and wilt thou not have respect unto the covenant? v. 20. Wilt thou not perform the promises thou hast, in thy covenant, made to them? Wilt thou not own those whom thou hast brought into the bond of the covenant?" When God delivers his people it is in remembrance of his covenant, Lev. xxvi. 42.
(4.) "They trust in thee, and boast of their relation to thee and expectations from thee. O let not them return ashamed of their hope (v. 21), as they will be if they be disappointed."
(5.) "If thou deliver them, they will praise thy name and give thee the glory of their deliverance. Appear, Lord, for those that will praise thy name, against those that blaspheme it."

Psalm 75

Title
To the chief Musician. Al-taschith. A Psalm or Song of Asaph.

1-5
1 Unto thee, O God, do we give thanks, unto thee do we give thanks: for that thy name is near thy wondrous works declare.
2 When I shall receive the congregation I will judge uprightly.
3 The earth and all the inhabitants thereof are dissolved: I bear up the pillars of it. Selah.
4 I said unto the fools, Deal not foolishly: and to the wicked, Lift not up the horn:
5 Lift not up your horn on high: speak not with a stiff neck.

Psalm 75

TITLE. To the Chief Musician. Here is noble work for him, for the cry of the last Psalm is about to be heard, and the challenge of the foes of Israel taken up by God himself. Here the virgin daughter of Zion despises her foe, and laughs him to scorn. The destruction of Sennacherib's army is a notable illustration of this sacred song. Al-taschith. Here is another of the "destroy not" Psalms, and the title may be intended as a check upon the natural fierceness of the oppressed, or a taunt for the savage foe, who is here bitterly bidden to destroy not, because the nation is well aware that he cannot. Here, in holy faith, the sucking child plays at the hole of the asp, and the weaned child puts his hand on the cockatrice den. A Psalm or Song of Asaph. For reading or singing. A hymn to God and a song for his saints. Happy were the people who having found a Milton in David had an almost equal songster in Asaph: happiest of all, because these poets were not inspired by earth's Castalian fount, but drank of "the fount of every blessing."
DIVISION. The people's song of gratitude and adoration begins the hymn in Ps 75:1. In the next four Ps 75:2-5, the Lord reveals himself as ruling the world in righteousness. Then follows a warning voice from the church to her enemies, Ps 75:6-8, and a closing song anticipatory of the glory due to God and the utter defeat of the foe.

EXPOSITION
Verse 1. Unto thee, O God, do we give thanks. Not to ourselves, for we were helpless, but to Elohim who heard our cry, and replied to the taunt of our foes. Never let us neglect thanksgiving, or we may fear that another time our prayers will remain unanswered. As the smiling flowers gratefully reflect in their lovely colors the various constituents of the solar ray, so should gratitude spring up in our hearts after the smiles of God's providence. Unto thee do we give thanks. We should praise God again and again. Stinted gratitude is ingratitude. For infinite goodness there should be measureless thanks. Faith promises redoubled praise for greatly needed and signal deliverances. For that thy name is near thy wondrous works declare. God is at hand to answer and do wonders—adore we then the present Deity. We sing not of a hidden God, who sleeps and leaves the church to her fate, but of one who ever in our darkest days is most near, a very present help in trouble. "Near is his name." Baal is on a journey, but Jehovah dwells in his church. Glory be unto the Lord, whose perpetual deeds of grace and majesty are the sure tokens of his being with us always, even unto the ends of the world.
Verse 2. When I shall receive the congregation I will judge uprightly. This is generally believed to be the voice of God, who will, when he accepts his people, mount his judgment seat and avenge their cause in righteousness. He determines the period of interposition, and when that arrives swift are his blows and sure are his deliverances. God sends no delegated judge, but sits himself upon the throne. O Lord, let thy set time come for grace. Tarry no longer, but for the truth and the throne of Jesus be thou speedily at work. Let the appointed assize come, O Jesus, and sit thou on thy throne to judge the world in equity.
Verse 3. The earth and all the inhabitants thereof are dissolved. When anarchy is abroad, and tyrants are in power, everything is unloosed, dissolution threatens all things, the solid mountains of government melt as wax; but even then the Lord upholds and sustains the right. I bear up the pillars of it. Hence, there is no real cause for fear. While the pillars stand, and stand they must for God upholds them, the house will brave out the storm. In the day of the Lord's appearing a general melting will take place, but in that day our covenant God will be the sure support of our confidence.
Verse 4. I said unto the fools, Deal not foolishly. The Lord bids the boasters boast not, and commands the mad oppressors to stay their folly. How calm

JOHN CALVIN

Psalm 75

It affords matter of rejoicing and thanksgiving to the whole Church, to reflect that the world is governed exclusively according to the will of God, and that she herself is sustained by his grace and power alone. Encouraged by this consideration, she triumphs over the proud despisers of God, who, by their infatuated presumption, are driven headlong into all manner of excess.

1-7

1. We will praise thee, O God! The author, whoever he was, whether David or some other prophet, breaks forth at the very commencement into the language of joy and thanksgiving: We will praise thee, O God! we will praise thee. The repetition serves the more forcibly to express his strong affection and his ardent zeal in singing the praises of God. The verbs in the Hebrew are in the past tense; but the subject of the psalm requires that they should be translated into the future; which may be done in perfect consistency with the idiom of the Hebrew language. The inspired writer, however, may declare that God had been praised among his people for the benefits which he had bestowed in the times of old, the design being thereby to induce God to persevere in acting in the same manner, that thus continuing like himself, he might from time to time afford his people new matter for celebrating his praises.

2. When I shall have taken the congregation. In abandoning his people for a season to the will of their enemies, God seems to forsake them and to exercise no care about them; so that they are like a flock of sheep which is scattered, and wanders hither and thither without a shepherd. It being his object, then, to convey in these words a promise that he would remedy such a confused state of things, he very properly commences with the gathering together of his Church.

3. The earth is dissolved, and all its inhabitants. This verse is connected with the preceding; for it confirms the truth that God in due time will manifest himself to be an impartial and righteous judge; it being an easy matter for him, although the whole fabric of the world were fallen into ruins, to rebuild it from its decayed materials.

4. I said to the fools, Act not foolishly. After he has set the office of God full in his own view and in the view of the faithful, he now triumphs over all the ungodly, whom he impeaches of madness and blind rage, the effect of their despising God, which leads them to indulge to excess in pride and self-glorification.

5. Lift not up your horn on high is repeated once and again. They are next enjoined not to speak with a fat or a stiff neck; by which is meant that they should not speak harshly and injuriously; for it is usual with proud persons to erect the neck and raise the head when they pour forth their menaces.

6. For exaltations come neither from the east nor from the west. The prophet here furnishes an admirable remedy for correcting pride, when he teaches us that promotion or advancement proceeds not from the earth but from God

MATTHEW HENRY

Psalm 75

1-5 The magistrate's resolution.

In these verses,

I. The psalmist gives to God the praise of his advancement to honor and power, and the other great things he had done for him and for his people Israel (v. 1): Unto thee, O God! do we give thanks for all the favors thou hast bestowed upon us; and again, unto thee do we give thanks; for our thanksgivings must be often repeated. Did not we often pray for mercy when we were in pursuit of it; and shall we think it will suffice once or twice to give thanks when we have obtained it? Not only I do give thanks, but we do, and I and all my friends. If we share with others in their mercies, we must join with them in their praises. "Unto thee, O God! the author of our mercies (and we will not give that glory to the instruments which is due to thee only), we give thanks; for that thy name is near (that the complete accomplishment of thy promise made to David is not far off) thy wondrous works, which thou hast already done for him, declare."

II. He lays himself under an obligation to use his power well, pursuant to the great trust reposed in him (v. 2): When I shall receive the congregation I will judge uprightly. Here he takes it for granted that God would, in due time, perfect that which concerned him, that though the congregation was very slow in gathering to him, and great opposition was made to it, yet, at length, he should receive it; for what God has spoken in his holiness he will perform by his wisdom and power. Being thus in expectation of the mercy, he promises to make conscience of his duty: "When I am a judge I will judge, and judge uprightly; not as those that went before me, who either neglected judgment or, which was worse, perverted it, either did no good with their power or did hurt."

III. He promises himself that his government would be a public blessing to Israel, v. 3. The present state of the kingdom was very bad: The earth and all the inhabitants thereof are dissolved; and no marvel, when the former reign was so dissolute that all went to wrack and ruin. There was a general corruption of manners, for want of putting the laws in execution against vice and profaneness. They were divided one from another for want of centering, as they ought to have done, in the government God had appointed. They were all to pieces, two against three and three against two, crumbled into factions and parties, which was likely to issue in their ruin; but I bear up the pillars of it. Even in Saul's time David did what he could for the public welfare; but he hoped that when he had himself received the congregation he should do much more, and should not only prevent the public ruin, but recover the public strength and beauty.

IV. He checks those that opposed his government, that were against his accession to it and obstructed the administration of it, striving to keep up that vice and profaneness which he had made it his business

Psalm 75

6-10
6 For promotion cometh
neither from the east, nor
from the west, nor from the
south.
7 But God is the judge:
he putteth down one, and
setteth up another.
8 For in the hand of the
LORD there is a cup, and the
wine is red; it is full of mix-
ture; and he poureth out of
the same: but the dregs
thereof, all the wicked of
the earth shall wring them
out, and drink them.
9 But I will declare for
ever; I will sing praises to
the God of Jacob.
10 All the horns of the
wicked also will I cut off;
but the horns of the right-
eous shall be exalted.

is he, how quiet are his words, yet how divine the rebuke. If the wicked were not insane, they would even now hear in their consciences the still small voice bidding them cease from evil, and forbear their pride. And to the wicked, Lift not up the horn. He bids the ungodly stay their haughtiness. The horn was the emblem of boastful power; only the foolish, like wild and savage beasts, will lift it high; but they assail heaven itself with it, as if they would gore the Almighty himself. In dignified majesty he rebukes the inane glories of the wicked, who beyond measure exalt themselves in the day of their fancied power.

Verse 5. Lift not up your horn on high. For their abounding pride there is a double rebuke. A word from God soon abases the lofty. Would to God that all proud men would obey the word here given them; for, if they do not, he will take effectual means to secure obedience, and then woe will come upon them, such as shall break their horns and roll their glory in the mire for ever. Speak not with a stiff neck. Impudence before God is madness. The outstretched neck of insolent pride is sure to provoke his axe.

Verse 6. For promotion cometh neither from the east, nor from the west, nor from the south. There is a God, and a providence, and things happen not by chance. Though deliverance be hopeless from all points of the compass, yet God can work it for his people; and though judgment come neither from the rising or the setting of the sun, nor from the wilderness of mountains, yet come it will, for the Lord reigneth. Men forget that all things are ordained in heaven; they see but the human force, and the carnal passion, but the unseen Lord is more real far than these. He is at work behind and within the cloud.

Verse 7. But God is the judge. Even now he is actually judging. His seat is not vacant; his authority is not abdicated; the Lord reigneth evermore. He putteth down one, and setteth up another. Empires rise and fall at his bidding. A dungeon here, and there a throne, his will assigns. Assyria yields to Babylon, and Babylon to the Medes. Kings are but puppets in his hand; they serve his purpose when they rise and when they fall. A certain author has issued a work called "Historic Ninepins," (Timbs), a fit name of scorn for all the great ones of the earth. God only is; all power belongs to him; all else is shadow, coming and going, unsubstantial, misty, dream like.

Verse 8. For in the hand of the Lord there is a cup. The punishment of the wicked is prepared, God himself holds it in readiness; he has collected and concocted woes most dread, and in the chalice of his wrath he holds it. They scoffed his feast of love; they shall be dragged to his table of justice, and made to drink their due deserts. And the wine is red. The retribution is terrible, it is blood for blood, foaming vengeance for foaming malice. The very color of divine wrath is terrible; what must the taste be? It is full of mixture. Spices of anger, justice, and incensed mercy are there.

Verse 9. But I will declare for ever. Thus will the saints occupy themselves with rehearsing Jehovah's praises, while their foes are drunken with the wine of wrath. They shall chant while the others roar in anguish, and justly so, for the former Psalm informed us that such had been the case on earth,—"thine enemies roar in the sanctuary,"—the place where the chosen praised the Lord.

Verse 10. All the horns of the wicked also will I cut off. Power and liberty being restored to Israel, she begins again to execute justice, by abasing the godless who had gloried in the reign of oppression. Their power and pomp are to be smitten down. Men wore horns in those days as a part of their state, and these, both literally and figuratively, were to be lopped off.

alone. That which most frequently blinds the eyes of men is, their gazing about on the right hand and on the left, and their gathering together from all quarters riches and other resources, that, strengthened with these, they may be able to gratify their desires and lusts. The prophet, therefore, affirms, that in not rising above the world, they are laboring under a great mistake, since it is God alone who has the power to exalt and to abase.

7. Although God has in his own hand sovereign power and authority, so that he can do whatever he pleases, yet he, is styled judge, to teach us that he governs the affairs of mankind with the most perfect equity. Whence it follows, that every man who abstains from inflicting injuries and committing deeds of mischief, may, when he is injured and treated unjustly, betake himself to the judgment-seat of God.

8-10

8. For in the hand of Jehovah there is a cup. The Psalmist here applies more directly to the use of the godly that judgment of which he has just now spoken. He affirms, that the object for which God reigns is, that no iniquity may remain unpunished; but that when wicked men have broken through all restraint and abandoned themselves to wickedness, he may drag them to deserved punishment. From this we again learn what estimate we ought to form of the providence of God—that we ought to regard it as exercising its control by an ever-present energy over every part of our life. It is therefore asserted that God has in his hand a cup with which to make the wicked drunk. As red wine among the Jews was the strongest and sharpest, we may suppose that it is here referred to; and the similitude is very appropriate, which represents God as having in his hand wine of a highly intoxicating character, with which to make the ungodly drunk even to death. It is implied, that the swiftness of divine vengeance is incredible, resembling the rapidity and power with which strong wine penetrates to the brain, and either produces madness or kindles a fever. It is on this account said, that the wine in God's cup is of a red color; as it is said in Proverbs 23:31, "Look not upon the wine when it is red in the cup."

The expression, it is full of mixture, was added to give additional force to the statement of the prophet; his object being to compare the vehemence and fury of God's wrath to spiced wine. By these figures he intimates that it will be impossible for the ungodly to escape drinking the cup which God will put into their hands, and that they will be compelled to drain it to the last drop.

9, 10. But I will publish for ever. This conclusion of the psalm evinces the joy which God's people felt from having experienced that He was their deliverer in adversity; for it seems to be their own experience which they engage to publish, and on account of which they resolve to sing praise to God. Whence also they gather, that by the divine aid they will overcome all the power of the reprobate; and that being themselves possessed of righteousness and equity, they will be sufficiently armed for their own preservation and defense.

to suppress (v. 4, 5): I said unto the fools, Deal not foolishly. He had said so to them in Saul's time. When he had not power to restrain them, yet he had wisdom and grace to reprove them, and to give them good counsel; though they bore themselves high, upon the favor of that unhappy prince, he cautioned them not to be too presumptuous. Or, rather, he does now say so to them. As soon as he came to the crown he issued out a proclamation against vice and profaneness, and here we have the contents of it.

6-10 God's government of the world.

In these verses we have two great doctrines laid down and two good inferences drawn from them, for the confirmation of what he had before said.

I. Here are two great truths laid down concerning God's government of the world, which we ought to mix faith with, both pertinent to the occasion:

1. That from God alone kings receive their power (v. 6, 7), and therefore to God alone David would give the praise of his advancement; having his power from God he would use it for him, and therefore those were fools that lifted up the horn against him. We see strange revolutions in states and kingdoms, and are surprised at the sudden disgrace of some and elevation of others; we are all full of such changes, when they happen; but here we are directed to look at the author of them, and are taught where the original of power is, and whence promotion comes. Whence comes preferment to kingdoms, to the sovereignty of them? And whence come preferments in kingdoms, to places of power and trust in them? The former depends not upon the will of the people, nor the latter on the will of the prince, but both on the will of God, who has all hearts in his hands; to him therefore those must look who are in pursuit of preferment, and then they begin aright.

2. That from God alone all must receive their doom (v. 8): In the hand of the Lord there is a cup, which he puts into the hands of the children of men, a cup of providence, mixed up (as he thinks fit) of many ingredients, a cup of affliction. The sufferings of Christ are called a cup, Matt. xx. 22; John xviii. 11.

II. Here are two good practical inferences drawn from these great truths, and they are the same purposes of duty that he began the psalm with. This being so, he will praise God, and give him glory, for the power to which he has advanced him (v. 9): I will declare for ever that which thy wondrous works declare, v. 1. He will praise God for his elevation, not only at first, while the mercy was fresh, but for ever, so long as he lives. The exaltation of the Son of David will be the subject of the saints' everlasting praises. He will give glory to God, not only as his God, but as the God of Jacob, knowing it was for Jacob his servant's sake, and because he loved his people Israel, that he made him king over them.

Psalm 76

Title
To the chief Musician on Neginoth. A Psalm or Song of Asaph.

1-6
1 In Judah is God known: his name is great in Israel.
2 In Salem also is his tabernacle, and his dwelling place in Zion.
3 There brake he the arrows of the bow, the shield, and the sword, and the battle. Selah.
4 Thou art more glorious and excellent than the mountains of prey.
5 The stouthearted are spoiled, they have slept their sleep: and none of the men of might have found their hands.
6 At thy rebuke, O God of Jacob, both the chariot and horse are cast into a dead sleep.

Psalm 76

TITLE. To the Chief Musician on Neginoth. The Precentor is here instructed to perform this song to the music of stringed instruments. The master of the harpers was called for his most skilful minstrelsy, and truly the song is worthy of the sweetest sounds that strings can yield.
A Psalm or Song of Asaph. The style and matter indicate the same hand as that which wrote the preceding; and it is an admirable arrangement which placed the two in juxtaposition. Faith in the 75th Psalm sung of victories to come, and here it sings of triumphs achieved. The present Psalm is a most jubilant war song, a paean to the King of kings, the hymn of a theocratic nation to its divine ruler. We have no need to mark divisions in a song where the unity is so well preserved.

EXPOSITION
Verse 1. In Judah is God known. If unknown in all the world beside, he has so revealed himself to his people by his deeds of grace, that he is no unknown God to them. His name is great in Israel. To be known, in the Lord's case, is to be honored: those who know his name admire the greatness of it. Although Judah and Israel were unhappily divided politically, yet the godly of both nations were agreed concerning Jehovah their God; and truly whatever schisms may mar the visible church, the saints always "appear as one" in magnifying the Lord their God. Dark is the outer world, but within the favored circle Jehovah is revealed, and is the adoration of all who behold him. The world knows him not, and therefore blasphemes him, but his church is full of ardor to proclaim his fame unto the ends of the earth.
Verse 2. In Salem also is his tabernacle. In the peaceful city he dwells, and the peace is perpetuated, because there his sacred tent is pitched. The church of God is the place where the Lord abides and he is to her the Lord and giver of peace.
Verse 3. There brake he the arrows of the bow. Without leaving his tranquil abode, he sent forth his word and snapped the arrows of his enemies before they could shoot them. The idea is sublime, and marks the ease, completeness, and rapidity of the divine action. The shield, and the sword, and the battle. Every weapon, offensive and defensive, the Lord dashed in pieces; death bearing bolts and life preserving armor were alike of no avail when the Breaker sent forth his word of power. In the spiritual conflicts of this and every age, the like will be seen; no weapon that is formed against the church shall prosper, and every tongue that rises against her in judgment, she shall condemn. Selah. It is meet that we should dwell on so soul stirring a theme, and give the Lord our grateful adoration,—hence a pause is inserted.
Verse 4. Thou art more glorious and excellent than the mountains of prey. Far more is Jehovah to be extolled than all the invading powers which sought to oppress his people, though they were for power and greatness comparable to mountains. Assyria had pillaged the nations till it had become rich with mountains of spoil, this was talked of among men as glory, but the psalmist despised such renown, and declares that the Lord was far more illustrious.
Verse 5. The stouthearted are spoiled. They came to spoil, and lo! they are spoiled themselves. Their stout hearts are cold in death, the angel of the pestilence has dried up their life blood, their very heart is taken from them. They have slept their sleep. Their last sleep—the sleep of death. And none of the men of might have found their hands. Their arms are palsied, they cannot lift a finger, for the rigor of death has stiffened them. What a scene was that when Sennacherib's host was utterly destroyed in one night. The hands which were furious to pull down Jerusalem, could not even be raised from the sod, the most valiant warriors were as weak as the palsied cripples

JOHN CALVIN

Psalm 76

1-6
1. God is known in Judah. In the outset, we are taught that it was not by human means that the enemies of Israel were compelled to retire without accomplishing any thing, but by the ever-to-be-remembered aid of Jehovah. Whence came that knowledge of God and the greatness of his name which are spoken of, but because He stretched forth his hand in an extraordinary manner, to make it openly manifest that both the chosen people and the city were under his defense and protection? It is therefore asserted, that the glory of God was conspicuously displayed when the enemies of Israel were discomfited by such a miraculous interposition.
2. And his tabernacle was in Salem. Here the reason is assigned why God, putting the Assyrians to flight, vouchsafed to deliver the city of Jerusalem, and to take it under his protection. The reason is, because he had there chosen for himself a dwelling-place, in which his name was to be called upon.
3. There he broke the arrows of the bow. We have here stated the particular way in which God was known in Judah. He was known by the wonderful proofs of his power, which he exhibited in preserving the city. Under these figures is described the destruction of the enemies of the chosen people.
4. It is farther added that God is more glorious and terrible than the mountains of prey. By the mountains of prey, is meant kingdoms distinguished for their violence and extortion. We know that from the beginning, he who exercised himself most in robbery and pillage, was the man who most enlarged his borders and became greatest. The Psalmist, therefore, here compares those great kings, who had acquired large dominions by violence and the shedding of human blood, to savage beasts, who live only upon prey.
5. The stout-hearted were spoiled, The power of God in destroying his enemies is here exalted by another form of expression.
What is added in the second clause is to the same purpose, All the men of might have not found their hands, that is to say, they were as incapable of fighting as if their hands had been maimed or cut off. In short, their strength, of which they boasted, was utterly overthrown.
6. The same subject is farther confirmed from the statement, that the chariot and the horse were cast into a deep sleep at the rebuke of God. This implies, that whatever activity characterized these enemies, it was rendered powerless, simply by the nod of God. Although, therefore, we may be deprived of all created means of help, let us rest contented with the favor of God alone, accounting it all-sufficient, since he has no need of great armies to repel the assaults of the whole world, but is able, by the mere breath of his mouth, to subdue and dissipate all assailants.

7-12
7. Thou, even thou, art terrible. The repetition of the pronoun Thou, is intended to exclude all others from what is here

MATTHEW HENRY

Psalm 76

1-6 Triumph in God.
The church is here triumphant even in the midst of its militant state. The psalmist, in the church's name, triumphs here in God, the center of all our triumphs.
I. In the revelation God had made of himself to them, v. 1. It is the honor and privilege of Judah and Israel that among them God is known, and where he is known his name will be great. God is known as he is pleased to make himself known; and those are happy to whom he discovers himself—happy people that have their land filled with the knowledge of God, happy persons that have their hearts filled with that knowledge. In Judah God was known as he was not known in other nations, which made the favor the greater, inasmuch as it was distinguishing, Ps. cxlvii. 19, 20.
II. In the tokens of God's special presence with them in his ordinances, v. 2. In the whole land of Judah and Israel God was known and his name was great; but in Salem, in Zion, were his tabernacle and his dwelling-place. There he kept court; there he received the homage of his people by their sacrifices and entertained them by the feasts upon the sacrifices; thither they came to address themselves to him, and thence by his oracles he issued out his orders; there he recorded his name, and of that place he said, Here will I dwell, for I have desired it. It is the glory and happiness of a people to have God among them by his ordinances; but his dwelling-place is a tabernacle, a movable dwelling. Yet a little while is that light with us.
III. In the victories they had obtained over their enemies (v. 3): There broke he the arrows of the bow. Observe how threatening the danger was. Though Judah and Israel, Salem and Zion, were thus privileged, yet war is raised against them, and the weapons of war are furbished.

7-12 The defense and glory of Israel.
This glorious victory with which God had graced and blessed his church is here made to speak three things:
I. Terror to God's enemies (v. 7-9): "Thou, even thou, art to be feared; thy majesty is to be reverenced, thy sovereignty to be submitted to, and thy justice to be dreaded by those that have offended thee." Let all the world learn by this event to stand in awe of the great God.
II. Comfort to God's people, v. 10. We live in a very angry provoking world; we often feel much, and are apt to fear more, from the wrath of man, which seems boundless. But this is a great comfort to us,
1. That as far as God permits the wrath of man to break forth at any time he will make it turn to his praise, will bring honor to himself and serve his own purposes by it: Surely the wrath of man shall praise thee, not only by the checks given to it, when it shall

Psalm 76

7-12

7 Thou, even thou, art to be feared: and who may stand in thy sight when once thou art angry?
8 Thou didst cause judgment to be heard from heaven; the earth feared, and was still,
9 When God arose to judgment, to save all the meek of the earth. Selah.
10 Surely the wrath of man shall praise thee: the remainder of wrath shalt thou restrain.
11 Vow, and pay unto the LORD your God: let all that be round about him bring presents unto him that ought to be feared.
12 He shall cut off the spirit of princes: he is terrible to the kings of the earth.

at the temple gate, yea, their eyes they could not open, a deep sleep sealed their vision in everlasting darkness.

Verse 6. At thy rebuke. A word accomplished all, there was no need of a single blow. O God of Jacob. God of thy wrestling people, who again like their father supplant their enemy; God of the covenant and the promise, thou hast in this gracious character fought for thine elect nation.

Verse 7. Thou, even thou, art to be feared. Not Sennacherib, nor Nisroch his god, but Jehovah alone, who with a silent rebuke had withered all the monarch's host.

Verse 8. Thou didst cause judgment to be heard from heaven. So complete an overthrow was evidently a judgment from heaven; those who saw it not, yet heard the report of it, and said, "This is the finger of God." Man will not hear God's voice if he can help it, but God takes care to cause it to be heard. The echoes of that judgment executed on the haughty Assyrian are heard still, and will ring on down all the ages, to the praise of divine justice. The earth feared and was still. All nations trembled at the tidings, and sat in humbled awe. Repose followed the former turmoils of war, when the oppressor's power was broken, and God was reverenced for having given quiet to the peoples.

Verse 9. When God arose to judgment. Men were hushed when he ascended the judgment seat and actively carried out the decrees of justice. When God is still the people are in tumult; when he arises they are still as a stone. To save all the meek of the earth. The Ruler of men has a special eye towards the poor and despised; he makes it his first point to right all their wrongs.

Verse 10. Surely the wrath of man shall praise thee. It shall not only be overcome but rendered subservient to thy glory. Man with his breath of threatening is but blowing the trumpet of the Lord's eternal fame. Furious winds often drive vessels the more swiftly into port. The devil blows the fire and melts the iron, and then the Lord fashions it for his own purposes. Let men and devils rage as they may, they cannot do otherwise than subserve the divine purposes. The remainder of wrath shalt thou restrain. Malice is tethered and cannot break its bounds. The fire which cannot be utilized shall be damped. Some read it "thou shalt gird," as if the Lord girded on the wrath of man as a sword to be used for his own designs, and certainly men of the world are often a sword in the hand of God, to scourge others.

Verse 11. Vow, and pay unto the Lord your God. Well may we do so in memory of such mercies and judgments. To vow or not is a matter of choice, but to discharge our vows is our bounden duty. He who would defraud God, his own God, is a wretch indeed. He keeps his promises, let not his people fail in theirs. He is their faithful God and deserves to have a faithful people. Let all that be round about him bring presents unto him that ought to be feared. Let surrounding nations submit to the only living God, let his own people with alacrity present their offerings, and let his priests and Levites be leaders in the sacred sacrifice.

Verse 12. He shall cut off the spirit of princes. Their courage, skill, and life are in his hands, and he can remove them as a gardener cuts off a slip from a plant. None are great in his hand. Caesars and Napoleons fall under his power as the boughs of the tree beneath the woodman's axe. He is terrible to the kings of the earth. While they are terrible to others, he is terrible to them. If they oppose themselves to his people, he will make short work of them; they shall perish before the terror of his arm, "for the Lord is a man of war, the Lord is his name." Rejoice before him all ye who adore the God of Jacob.

predicated of God, as if it had been said, Whatever power there is in the world, it at once vanishes away, and is reduced to nothing, when He comes forth and manifests himself; and, therefore, He alone is terrible. This is confirmed by the comparison added immediately after, which intimates that, although the wicked are so filled with pride as to be ready to burst with it, yet they are unable to abide the look and presence of God.

8. From heaven thou hast made thy judgment to be heard. By the name of heaven, the Psalmist forcibly intimates that the judgment of God was too manifest to admit of the possibility of its being ascribed either to fortune or to the policy of men. Sometimes God executes his judgments obscurely, so that they seem to proceed out of the earth.

9. When God arose to judgment. The great object which God had in view in executing this judgment is now declared; which was, that he might furnish a proof of his fatherly love towards all his people. He is, therefore, introduced as speaking, not with his mouth, but with his hand, that he may show to all how precious in his sight is the salvation of all who fear and love him. Under the word arise, there is a reference to the inactivity and indolence ascribed by wicked men to God, an opinion which had led them to take so much liberty to themselves.

10. Surely the wrath of men shall praise thee. I consider the meaning simply to be that although at first the rage of the enemies of God and his Church may throw all things into confusion, and, as it were, envelop them in darkness, yet all will at length redound to his praise; for the issue will make it manifest, that, whatever they may contrive and attempt, they cannot in any degree prevail against him.

11. Vow and pay to Jehovah your God. The faithful are now exhorted to the exercise of gratitude. As under the law the custom prevailed among the Jews of vowing sacrifices for singular blessings which God had conferred upon them, by which they solemnly acknowledged that their safety depended solely upon him, and that to him they were entirely indebted for it, they are called anew to engage in this exercise of religion; and by the word pay it is intended to inculcate steadfastness,—to teach them that they should not make merely a sudden and inconsiderate acknowledgement, but that they should also testify at all times that the remembrance of their deliverance was deeply fixed in their hearts.

Their most important business, no doubt, was seriously to reflect with themselves that God was the author of their salvation; but still it is to be observed, that the solemn profession of religion, by which every man stimulates not only himself but also others to the performance of their duty, is far from being superfluous.

12. He will cut off the spirit of princes. The majority of princes being enemies to the Church of God, it is expressly affirmed, that He is sufficiently terrible to subdue all the kings of the earth. When it is said, that their spirit is cut off, or taken away from them, it is to be limited to tyrants and robbers whom God infatuates, because he sees that they apply all their ingenuity and counsels to do mischief.

be forced to confess its own impotency, but even by the liberty given to it for a time. The hardships which God's people suffer by the wrath of their enemies are made to redound to the glory of God and his grace; and the more the heathen rage and plot against the Lord and his anointed the more will God be praised for setting his King upon his holy hill of Zion in spite of them, Ps. ii. 1, 6. When the heavenly hosts make this the matter of their thanksgiving-song that God has taken to himself his great power and has reigned, though the nations were angry (Rev. xi. 17, 18), then the wrath of man adds luster to the praises of God.

2. That what will not turn to his praise shall not be suffered to break out: The remainder of wrath shalt thou restrain. Men must never permit sin, because they cannot check it when they will; but God can. He can set bounds to the wrath of man, as he does to the raging sea. Hitherto it shall come and no further; here shall its proud waves be stayed. God restrained the remainder of Sennacherib's rage, for he put a hook in his nose and a bridle in his jaws (Isa. xxxvii. 29); and, though he permitted him to talk big, he restrained him from doing what he designed.

III. Duty to all, v. 11, 12. Let all submit themselves to this great God and become his loyal subjects. Observe,

1. The duty required of us all, all that are about him, that have any dependence upon him or any occasion to approach to him; and who is there that has not? We are therefore every one of us commanded to do our homage to the King of kings: Vow and pay; that is, take an oath of allegiance to him and make conscience of keeping it. Vow to be his, and pay what you vow. Our prayers and praises, and especially our hearts, are the presents we should bring to the Lord our God.

2. The reasons to enforce this duty: Render to all their due, fear to whom fear is due; and is it not due to God? Yes;

(1.) He ought to be feared: He is the fear (so the word is); his name is glorious and fearful; and he is the proper object of our fear; with him is terrible majesty. The God of Abraham is called the fear of Isaac (Gen. xxxi. 42), and we are commanded to make him our fear, Isa. viii. 13. When we bring presents to him we must have an eye to him as greatly to be feared; for he is terrible in his holy places.

(2.) He will be feared, even by those who think it their own sole prerogative to be feared (v. 12): He shall cut off the spirit of princes; he shall slip it off as easily as we slip off a flower from the stalk or a bunch of grapes from the vine; so the word signifies. He can dispirit those that are most daring and make them heartless; for he is, or will be, terrible to the kings of the earth; and sooner or later, if they be not so wise as to submit themselves to him, he will force them to call in vain to rocks and mountains to fall on them and hide them from his wrath, Rev. vi. 16. Since there is no contending with God, it is as much our wisdom as it is our duty to submit to him.

Psalm 77

Title
To the chief Musician to Jeduthun. A Psalm of Asaph.

1-7
1 I cried unto God with my voice, even unto God with my voice; and he gave ear unto me.
2 In the day of my trouble I sought the Lord: my sore ran in the night, and ceased not: my soul refused to be comforted.
3 I remembered God, and was troubled: I complained, and my spirit was overwhelmed. Selah.
4 Thou holdest mine eyes waking: I am so troubled that I cannot speak.
5 I have considered the days of old, the years of ancient times.
6 I call to remembrance my song in the night: I commune with mine own heart: and my spirit made diligent search.
7 Will the Lord cast off for ever? and will he be favorable no more?

Psalm 77

TITLE. To the Chief Musician, to Jeduthun. It was meet that another leader of the psalmody should take his turn. No harp should be silent in the courts of the Lord's house. A Psalm of Asaph. Asaph was a man of exercised mind, and often touched the minor key; he was thoughtful, contemplative, believing, but withal there was a dash of sadness about him, and this imparted a tonic flavor to his songs. To follow him with understanding, it is needful to have done business on the great waters, and weathered many an Atlantic gale.
DIVISION. If we follow the poetical arrangement, and divide at the Selahs, we shall find the troubled man of God pleading in Ps 77:1-3, and then we shall hear him lamenting and arguing within himself, Ps 77:4-9. From Ps 77:10-15 his meditations run toward God, and in the close he seems as in a vision to behold the wonders of the Red Sea and the wilderness. At this point, as if lost in an ecstasy, he hurriedly closes the Psalm with an abruptness, the effect of which is quite startling. The Spirit of God knows when to cease speaking, which is more than those do who, for the sake of making a methodical conclusion, prolong their words even to weariness. Perhaps this Psalm was meant to be a prelude to the next, and, if so, its sudden close is accounted for. The hymn now before us is for experienced saints only, but to them it will be of rare value as a transcript of their own inner conflicts.

EXPOSITION
Verse 1. I cried unto God with my voice. This Psalm has much sadness in it, but we may be sure it will end well, for it begins with prayer, and prayer never has an ill issue. Asaph did not run to man but to the Lord, and to him he went, not with studied, stately, stilted words, but with a cry, the natural, unaffected, unfeigned expression of pain. He used his voice also, for though vocal utterance is not necessary to the life of prayer, it often seems forced upon us by the energy of our desires. Sometimes the soul feels compelled to use the voice, for thus it finds a freer vent for its agony. It is a comfort to hear the alarm bell ringing when the house is invaded by thieves. Even unto God with my voice. He returned to his pleading. If once sufficed not, he cried again. He needed an answer, he expected one, he was eager to have it soon, therefore he cried again and again, and with his voice too, for the sound helped his earnestness. And he gave ear unto me. Importunity prevailed. The gate opened to the steady knock. It shall be so with us in our hour of trial, the God of grace will hear us in due season.
Verse 2. In the day of my trouble I sought the Lord. All day long his distress drove him to his God, so that when night came he continued still in the same search. God had hidden his face from his servant, therefore the first care of the troubled saint was to seek his Lord again. This was going to the root of the matter and removing the main impediment first. Diseases and tribulations are easily enough endured when God is found of us, but without him they crush us to the earth.
Verse 3. I remembered God, and was troubled. He who is the wellspring of delight to faith becomes an object of dread to the psalmist's distracted heart. The justice, holiness, power, and truth of God have all a dark side, and indeed all the attributed may be made to look black upon us if our eye be evil; even the brightness of divine love blinds us, and fills us with a horrible suspicion that we have neither part nor lot in it. He is wretched indeed whose memories of the Ever Blessed prove distressing to him; yet the best of men know the depth of this abyss.
Verse 4. Thou holdest mine eyes waking. The fears which thy strokes excite in me forbid my eyelids to fall, my eyes continue to watch as sentinels forbidden to rest. Sleep is a great comforter, but it forsakes the sorrowful, and then their sorrow deepens and eats into the soul. If God holds the eyes

JOHN CALVIN

Psalm 77

1-6

1. My voice came to God, and I cried. This is not a mere complaint, as some interpreters explain it, denoting the surprise which the people of God felt in finding that he who hitherto had been accustomed to grant their requests shut his ears to them, and was called upon in vain. It appears more probable that the prophet either speaks of the present feeling of his mind, or else calls to remembrance how he had experienced that God was inclined and ready to hear his prayers. There can be no doubt that he describes the greatness of the sorrow with which he was afflicted; and, in my opinion, he denotes a continued act both by the past and the future tenses of the verbs.

2. I sought the Lord in the day of my trouble. In this verse he expresses more distinctly the grievous and hard oppression to which the Church was at that time subjected.

3. I will remember God, and will be troubled. The Psalmist here employs a variety of expressions to set forth the vehemence of his grief, and, at the same time, the greatness of his affliction. He complains that what constituted the only remedy for allaying his sorrow became to him a source of disquietude. It may, indeed, seem strange that the minds of true believers should be troubled by remembering God. But the meaning of the inspired writer simply is, that although he thought upon God his distress of mind was not removed.

4. Thou hast held the watches of my eyes. This verse is to the same effect with the preceding. The Psalmist affirms that he spent whole nights in watching, because God granted him no relief. The night in ancient times was usually divided into many watches; and, accordingly, he describes his continued grief, which prevented him from sleeping, by the metaphorical term watches.

5. I have recounted the days of old. There is no doubt that he endeavored to assuage his grief by the remembrance of his former joy; but he informs us that relief was not so easily nor so speedily obtained. By the days of old, and the years of ancient times, he seems not only to refer to the brief course of his own life, but to comprehend many ages.

6. I will call to remembrance my song in the night. By his song he denotes the exercise of thanksgiving in which he had engaged during the time of his prosperity. There is no remedy better adapted for healing our sorrows than this; but Satan often craftily suggests to our thoughts the benefits of God, that the very feeling of the want of them may inflict upon our minds a deeper wound. It is, therefore, highly probable, that the prophet was pierced with bitter pangs when he compared the joy experienced by him in time past with the calamities which he was presently suffering. He expressly mentions the night; because, when we are then alone by ourselves, and withdrawn from the society and presence of men, it engenders in the mind more cares and thoughts than are experienced during the day.

MATTHEW HENRY

Psalm 77

1-10 Prevailing melancholy; mournful supplications.

We have here the lively portraiture of a good man under prevailing melancholy, fallen into and sinking in that horrible pit and that miry clay, but struggling to get out. Drooping saints, that are of a sorrowful spirit, may here as in a glass see their own faces. The conflict which the psalmist had with his griefs and fears seems to have been over when he penned this record of it; for he says (v. 1), I cried unto God, and he gave ear unto me, which, while the struggle lasted, he had not the comfortable sense of, as he had afterwards; but he inserts it in the beginning of his narrative as an intimation that his trouble did not end in despair; for God heard him, and, at length, he knew that he heard him. Observe,

I. His melancholy prayers. Being afflicted, he prayed (Jam. v. 13), and, being in an agony, he prayed more earnestly (v. 1): My voice was unto God, and I cried, even with my voice unto God. He was full of complaints, loud complaints, but he directed them to God, and turned them all into prayers, vocal prayers, very earnest and importunate. Thus he gave vent to his grief and gained some ease; and thus he took the right way in order to relief (v. 2): In the day of my trouble I sought the Lord.

Note, Days of trouble must be days of prayer, days of inward trouble especially, when God seems to have withdrawn from us; we must seek him and seek till we find him. In the day of his trouble he did not seek for the diversion of business or recreation, to shake off his trouble that way, but he sought God, and his favor and grace. Those that are under trouble of mind must not think to drink it away, or laugh it away, but must pray it away. My hand was stretched out in the night and ceased not; so Dr. Hammond reads the following words, as speaking the incessant importunity of his prayers. Compare Ps. cxliii. 5, 6.

II. His melancholy grief. Grief may then be called melancholy indeed,

1. When it admits of no intermission; such was his: My sore, or wound, ran in the night, and bled inwardly, and it ceased not, no, not in the time appointed for rest and sleep.

2. When it admits of no consolation; and that also as his case: My soul refused to be comforted; he had no mind to hearken to those that would be his comforters. As vinegar upon nitre, so is he that sings songs to a heavy heart, Prov. xxv. 20. Nor had he any mind to think of those things that would be his comforts; he put them far from him, as one that indulged himself in sorrow. Those that are in sorrow, upon any account, do not only prejudice themselves, but affront God, if they refuse to be comforted.

III. His melancholy musings. He pored so much upon the trouble, whatever it was, personal or public, that,

1. The methods that should have relieved him did but increase his grief, v. 3.

Psalm 77

8-14
8 Is his mercy clean gone for ever? doth his promise fail for evermore?
9 Hath God forgotten to be gracious? hath he in anger shut up his tender mercies? Selah.
10 And I said, This is my infirmity: but I will remember the years of the right hand of the most High.
11 I will remember the works of the LORD: surely I will remember thy wonders of old.
12 I will meditate also of all thy work, and talk of thy doings.
13 Thy way, O God, is in the sanctuary: who is so great a God as our God?
14 Thou art the God that doest wonders: thou hast declared thy strength among the people.

waking, what anodyne shall give us rest? How much we owe to him who giveth his beloved sleep! I am so troubled that I cannot speak. Great griefs are dumb. Deep streams brawl not among the pebbles like the shallow brooklets which live on passing showers. Words fail the man whose heart fails him.

Verse 5. I have considered the days of old, the years of ancient times. If no good was in the present, memory ransacked the past to find consolation. She fain would borrow a light from the altars of yesterday to light the gloom of today. It is our duty to search for comfort, and not in sullen indolence yield to despair; in quiet contemplation topics may occur to us which will prove the means of raising our spirits, and there is scarcely any theme more likely to prove consolatory than that which deals with the days of yore, the years of the olden time, when the Lord's faithfulness was tried and proven by hosts of his people.

Verse 6. I call to remembrance my song in the night. At other times his spirit had a song for the darkest hour, but now he could only recall the strain as a departed memory. Where is the harp which once thrilled sympathetically to the touch of those joyful fingers? My tongue, hast thou forgotten to praise? Hast thou no skill except in mournful ditties? Ah me, how sadly fallen am I!

Verse 7. Wilt the Lord cast off forever? This was one of the matters he enquired into. He painfully knew that the Lord might leave his people for a season, but his fear was that the time might be prolonged and have no close; eagerly, therefore, he asked, will the Lord utterly and finally reject those who are his own, and suffer them to be the objects of his contemptuous reprobation, his everlasting cast offs? This he was persuaded could not be. No instance in the years of ancient times led him to fear that such could be the case.

Verse 8. Is his mercy clean gone for ever? If he has no love for his elect, has he not still his mercy left? Has that dried up? Has he no pity for the sorrowful? Doth his promise fail for evermore? His word is pledged to those who plead with him; is that become of none effect? Shall it be said that from one generation to another the Lord's word has fallen to the ground; whereas aforetime he kept his covenant to all generations of them that fear him? It is a wise thing thus to put unbelief through the catechism.

Verse 9. Hath God forgotten to be gracious? Has El, the Mighty One, become great in everything but grace? Does he know how to afflict, but not how to uphold? Can he forget anything? Above all, can he forget to exercise that attribute which lies nearest to his essence, for he is love? Hath he in anger shut up his tender mercies? Are the pipes of goodness choked up so that love can no more flow through them? Do the bowels of Jehovah no longer yearn towards his own beloved children? Thus with cord after cord unbelief is smitten and driven out of the soul; it raises questions and we will meet it with questions.

Verse 10. And I said, This is my infirmity. He has won the day, he talks reasonably now, and surveys the field with a cooler mind. He confesses that unbelief is an infirmity, a weakness, a folly, a sin. He may also be understood to mean, "this is my appointed sorrow," I will bear it without complaint. When we perceive that our affliction is meted out by the Lord, and is the ordained portion of our cup, we become reconciled to it, and no longer rebel against the inevitable.

Verse 11. I will remember the works of the Lord. Fly back my soul, away from present turmoil, to the grandeurs of history, the sublime deeds of Jehovah, the Lord of Hosts; for he is the same and is ready even now to defend his servants as in days of yore. Surely I will remember thy wonders of old. Whatever else may glide into oblivion, the marvelous works of the Lord in the ancient days must not be suffered to be forgotten. Memory is a fit handmaid for faith. When faith has its seven years of famine, memory like Joseph in Egypt opens her granaries.

JOHN CALVIN

7-10
7, 8. Will the Lord cast off for ever? The statements here made undoubtedly form a part of the searchings which engaged the Psalmist's mind. He intimates that he was almost overwhelmed by a long succession of calamities; for he did not break forth into this language until he had endured affliction for so long a period as hardly to venture to entertain the hope that God would in future be favorable to him. He might well argue with himself whether God would continue to be gracious; for when God embraces us with his favor, it is on the principle that he will continue to extend it towards us even to the end.
9. Hath God forgotten to be merciful? The prophet still continues debating with himself the same subject. His object, however, is not to overthrow his faith, but rather to raise it up. He does not put this question, as if the point to which it refers were a doubtful matter. It is as if he had said, Hath God forgotten himself? or, hath he changed his nature? for he cannot be God unless he is merciful.
10. And I said, My death, the years of the right hand, etc. I have no doubt that the prophet here unburdens himself by cherishing the confident persuasion, that although he was at present cast down, it was only for a season, and that therefore it behoved him patiently to endure this sickness or disease, since it was not mortal.

11-14
11. I will remember the works of God. The prophet now, inspired with new courage, vigorously resists the temptations, which had so far prevailed against him as well nigh to overwhelm his faith. This remembering of the works of God differs from the remembering of which he had previously spoken. Then he contemplated from a distance the divine benefits, and he found the contemplation of them inadequate to assuage or mitigate his grief.
12. The Psalmist repeats in the 12th verse, that he will meditate continually upon these works, until, in due time, he receive the full advantage which this meditation is calculated to afford. The reason why so many examples of the grace of God contribute nothing to our profit, and fail in edifying our faith, is, that as soon as we have begun to make them the subjects of our consideration, our inconstancy draws us away to something else, and thus, at the very commencement, our minds soon lose sight of them.
13. Thy ways, O God! are in the sanctuary. The temple, in which God manifested himself was, as it were, a heaven on earth. The meaning of the inspired writer is that as at the commencement he had uttered distressing complaints, so now, having attained to a calm and settled state of mind, he admires and adores the high ways of God, and conscious of his own weakness, quietly and modestly keeps himself within the bounds prescribed to him, not permitting himself to judge or pass sentence upon the secret judgments of God according to the dictates of his carnal understanding.
14. Thou art the God that doest wonders. The Psalmist confirms the preceding sentence, proving the greatness of God from the

MATTHEW HENRY

2. The means of his present relief were denied him, v. 4. He could not enjoy sleep, which, if it be quiet and refreshing, is a parenthesis to our griefs and cares: "Thou holdest my eyes waking with thy terrors, which make me full of tossings to and fro until the dawning of the day."
IV. His melancholy reflections (v. 5, 6): "I have considered the days of old, and compared them with the present days; and our former prosperity does but aggravate our present calamities: for we see not the wonders that our fathers told us off."
V. His melancholy fears and apprehensions: "I communed with my own heart, v. 6. Come, my soul, what will be the issue of these things? What can I think of them and what can I expect they will come to at last? I made diligent search into the causes of my trouble, enquiring wherefore God contended with me and what would be the consequences of it. And thus I began to reason, Will the Lord cast off for ever, as he does for the present? He is not now favorable; and will he be favorable no more? His mercy is now gone; and is it clean gone for ever? His promise now fails; and does it fail for evermore? God is not now gracious; but has he forgotten to be gracious? His tender mercies have been withheld, perhaps in wisdom; but are they shut up, shut up in anger?" v. 7-9. This is the language of a disconsolate deserted soul, walking in darkness and having no light, a case not uncommon even with those that fear the Lord and obey the voice of his servant, Isa. 1. 10.

11-20 Acknowledgments of the divine majesty, of God's wonders wrought for Israel.
The psalmist here recovers himself out of the great distress and plague he was in, and silences his own fears of God's casting off his people by the remembrance of the great things he had done for them formerly, which though he had in vain tried to quiet himself with (v. 5, 6) yet he tried again, and, upon this second trial, found it not in vain. It is good to persevere in the proper means for the strengthening of faith, though they do not prove effectual at first: "I will remember, surely I will, what God has done for his people of old, till I can thence infer a happy issue of the present dark dispensation," v. 11, 12.

Two things, in general, satisfied him very much:
I. That God's way is in the sanctuary, v. 13. It is in holiness, so some. When we cannot solve the particular difficulties that may arise in our constructions of the divine providence, this we are sure of, in general, that God is holy in all his works, that they are all worthy of himself and consonant to the eternal purity and rectitude of his nature.
II. That God's way is in the sea. Though God is holy, just, and good, in all he does, yet we cannot give an account of the reasons of his proceedings, nor make any certain judgment of his designs: His path is in the great waters and his footsteps are not known, v. 19.

Psalm 77

15-20
15 Thou hast with thine arm redeemed thy people, the sons of Jacob and Joseph. Selah.
16 The waters saw thee, O God, the waters saw thee; they were afraid: the depths also were troubled.
17 The clouds poured out water: the skies sent out a sound: thine arrows also went abroad.
18 The voice of thy thunder was in the heaven: the lightnings lightened the world: the earth trembled and shook.
19 Thy way is in the sea, and thy path in the great waters, and thy footsteps are not known.
20 Thou leddest thy people like a flock by the hand of Moses and Aaron.

Verse 12. I will meditate also of all thy work. Sweet work to enter into Jehovah's work of grace, and there to lie down and ruminate, every thought being absorbed in the one precious subject. And talk of thy doings. It is well that the overflow of the mouth should indicate the good matter which fills the heart. Meditation makes rich talking; it is to be lamented that so much of the conversation of professors is utterly barren, because they take no time for contemplation.
Verse 13. Thy way, O God, is in the sanctuary, or in holiness. In the holy place we understand our God, and rest assured that all his ways are just and right. When we cannot trace his way, because it is "in the sea," it is a rich consolation that we can trust it, for it is in holiness. We must have fellowship with holiness if we would understand "the ways of God to man." He who would be wise must worship.
Verse 14. Thou art the God that doest wonders. Thou alone art Almighty. The false gods are surrounded with the pretence of wonders, but you really work them. It is thy peculiar prerogative to work marvels; it is no new or strange thing with thee, it is according to thy wont and use. Herein is renewed reason for holy confidence. It would be a great wonder if we did not trust the wonder working God.
Verse 15. Thou hast with thine arm redeemed thy people, the sons of Jacob and Joseph. All Israel, the two tribes of Joseph as well as those which sprang from the other sons of Jacob, were brought out of Egypt by a display of divine power, which is here ascribed not to the hand but to the arm of the Lord, because it was the fullness of his might.
Verse 16. The waters saw thee, O God, the waters saw thee; they were afraid. As if conscious of its Maker's presence, the sea was ready to flee from before his face. The conception is highly poetical, the psalmist has the scene before his mind's eye, and describes it gloriously.
Verse 17. The clouds poured out water. Obedient to the Lord, the lower region of the atmosphere yielded its aid to overthrow the Egyptian host.
Verse 18. The voice of thy thunder was in the heaven, or in the whirlwind. Rushing on with terrific swiftness and bearing all before it, the storm was as a chariot driven furiously, and a voice was heard (even thy voice, O Lord!) out of the fiery car, even as when a mighty man in battle urges forward his charger, and shouts to it aloud.
Verse 19. Thy way is in the sea. Far down in secret channels of the deep is thy roadway; when thou wilt thou canst make a sea a highway for thy glorious march. And thy path in the great waters. There, where the billows surge and swell, thou still dost walk; Lord of each crested wave.
Verse 20. Thou leddest thy people like a flock by the hand of Moses and Aaron. What a transition from tempest to peace, from wrath to love. Quietly as a flock Israel was guided on, by human agency which veiled the excessive glory of the divine presence. The smiter of Egypt was the shepherd of Israel. He drove his foes before him, but went before his people. Heaven and earth fought on his side against the sons of Ham, but they were equally subservient to the interests of the sons of Jacob. Therefore, with devout joy and full of consolation, we close this Psalm; the song of one who forgot how to speak and yet learned to sing far more sweetly than his fellows.

wonderful character of his works. He does not speak of the hidden and mysterious essence of God which fills heaven and earth, but of the manifestations of his power, wisdom, goodness, and righteousness, which are clearly exhibited, although they are too vast for our limited understandings to comprehend.

15-20

15. Thou hast redeemed thy people by thy arm. The Psalmist here celebrates, above all the other wonderful works of God, the redemption of the chosen people, to which the Holy Spirit everywhere throughout the Scriptures invites the attention of true believers, in order to encourage them to cherish the hope of their salvation. It is well known that the power of God was at that time manifested to the Gentiles.

16. The waters saw thee, O God! Some of the miracles in which God had displayed the power of his arm are here briefly adverted to. When it is said that the waters saw God, the language is figurative, implying that they were moved, as it were, by a secret instinct and impulse to obey the divine command in opening up a passage for the chosen people.

17. The clouds poured out waters. The meaning obviously is, that not only the sea and the river Jordan, but also the waters which were suspended in the clouds, yielded to God the honor to which he is entitled, the air, by the concussion of the thunder, having poured forth copious showers.

18. With this verse we are to connect the following, in which it is said, that the voice of the thunder was heard in the air, and that the lightnings illumined the world, so that the earth trembled. The amount is, that at the departure of the people from Egypt, ample testimony was borne to the power of God, both to the eyes and the ears of men; peals of thunder having been heard in every quarter of the heavens, and the whole sky having shone with flashes of lightning, while at the same time the earth was made to tremble.

19. Thy ways are in the sea. The miracle which was wrought in drying up the Red Sea is here again described in different phraseology. What, properly speaking, refers to the Israelites is applied to God, under whose protection and guidance they passed dry-shod through the midst of the Red Sea. It is declared that a path had been opened up for them in a very strange and unusual manner; for the sea was not drained by the skill of man, nor was the river Jordan turned aside from its ordinary course into a different channel, but the people walked through the midst of the waters in which Pharaoh and his whole army were soon after drowned. On this account, it is said, that the footsteps of God were not known, for no sooner had God made the people to pass over than he caused the waters to return to their accustomed course.

20. The purpose for which this was effected is now added,—the deliverance of the Church: Thou didst lead thy people like a flock. And this deliverance should be regarded by all the godly as affording them the best encouragement to cherish the hope of safety and salvation. The comparison of the people to sheep, tacitly intimates that they were in themselves entirely destitute of wisdom, power, and courage, and that God, in his great goodness, condescended to perform the office of a shepherd in leading through the sea.

God's ways are like the deep waters which cannot be fathomed (Ps. xxxvi. 6), like the way of a ship in the sea, which cannot be tracked, Prov. xxx. 18, 19. God's proceedings are always to be acquiesced in, but cannot always be accounted for. He specifies some particulars, for which he goes as far back as the infancy of the Jewish church, and from which he gathers,

1. That there is no God to be compared with the God of Israel (v. 13): Who is so great a God as our God? Let us first give to God the glory of the great things he has done for his people, and acknowledge him, therein, great above all comparison; and then we may take to ourselves the comfort of what he has done and encourage ourselves with it.

2. That he is a God of almighty power (v. 14): "Thou art the God that alone doest wonders, above the power of any creature; thou hast visibly, and beyond any contradiction, declared thy strength among the people." What God has done for his church has been a standing declaration of his almighty power, for therein he has made bare his everlasting arm.

(1.) God brought Israel out of Egypt, v. 15.

(2.) He divided the Red Sea before them (v. 16).

(3.) He destroyed the Egyptians (v. 17): The clouds poured out water upon them, while the pillar of fire, like an umbrella over the camp of Israel, sheltered it from the shower, in which, as in the deluge, the waters that were above the firmament concurred with those that were beneath the firmament to destroy the rebels. Then the skies sent out a sound; thy arrows also went abroad, which is explained (v. 18): The voice of thy thunder was heard in the heaven (that was the sound which the skies sent forth); the lightnings lightened the world—those were the arrows which went abroad, by which the host of the Egyptians was discomfited, with so much terror that the earth of the adjacent coast trembled and shook. Thus God's way was in the sea, for the destruction of his enemies, as well as for the salvation of his people; and yet when the waters returned to their place his footsteps were not known (v. 19); there was no mark set upon the place, as there was, afterwards, in Jordan, Josh. iv. 9.

(4.) He took his people Israel under his own guidance and protection (v. 20): Thou leddest thy people like a flock. They being weak and helpless, and apt to wander like a flock of sheep, and lying exposed to the beasts of prey, God went before them with all the care and tenderness of a shepherd, that they might not fail.

The psalm concludes abruptly, and does not apply those ancient instances of God's power to the present distresses of the church, as one might have expected. But as soon as the good man began to meditate on these things he found he had gained his point; his very entrance upon this matter gave him light and joy (Ps. cxix. 130); his fears suddenly and strangely vanished, so that he needed to go no further; he went his way, and did eat, and his countenance was no more sad, like Hannah, 1 Sam. i. 18.

Psalm 78

Title
Maschil of Asaph.

1-8

1 Give ear, O my people, to my law: incline your ears to the words of my mouth.
2 I will open my mouth in a parable: I will utter dark sayings of old:
3 Which we have heard and known, and our fathers have told us.
4 We will not hide them from their children, shewing to the generation to come the praises of the LORD, and his strength, and his wonderful works that he hath done.
5 For he established a testimony in Jacob, and appointed a law in Israel, which he commanded our fathers, that they should make them known to their children:
6 That the generation to come might know them, even the children which should be born; who should arise and declare them to their children:
7 That they might set their hope in God, and not forget the works of God, but keep his commandments:
8 And might not be as their fathers, a stubborn and rebellious generation; a generation that set not their heart aright, and whose spirit was not steadfast with God.

Psalm 78

TITLE. Maschil of Asaph. This is rightly entitled an instructive Psalm. It is not a mere recapitulation of important events in Israelitish history, but is intended to be viewed as a parable setting forth the conduct and experience of believers in all ages. It is a singular proof of the obtuseness of mind of many professors that they will object to sermons and expositions upon the historical parts of Scripture, as if they contained no instruction in spiritual matters: were such persons truly enlightened by the Spirit of God, they would perceive that all Scripture is profitable, and would blush at their own folly in undervaluing any portion of the inspired volume.

DIVISION. The unity is well maintained throughout, but for the sake of the reader's convenience, we may note that Ps 78:1-8 may be viewed as a preface, setting forth the psalmist's object in the epic which he is composing. From Ps 78:9-41 the theme is Israel in the wilderness; then intervenes an account of the Lord's preceding goodness towards his people in bringing them out of Egypt by plagues and wonders, Ps 78:42-52. The history of the tribes is resumed at Ps 78:53, and continued to Ps 78:66, where we reach the time of the removal of the ark to Zion and the transference of the leadership of Israel from Ephraim to Judah, which is rehearsed in song from Ps 78:67-72.

EXPOSITION

Verse 1. Give ear, O my people, to my law. The inspired bard calls on his countrymen to give heed to his patriotic teaching. We naturally expect God's chosen nation to be first in hearkening to his voice. When God gives his truth a tongue, and sends forth his messengers trained to declare his word with power, it is the least we can do to give them our ears and the earnest obedience of our hearts. Shall God speak, and his children refuse to hear? His teaching has the force of law, let us yield both ear and heart to it. Incline your ears to the words of my mouth. Give earnest attention, bow your stiff necks, lean forward to catch every syllable. We are at this day, as readers of the sacred records, bound to study them deeply, exploring their meaning, and laboring to practice their teaching. As the officer of an army commences his drill by calling for "Attention," even so every trained soldier of Christ is called upon to give ear to his words. Men lend their ears to music, how much more then should they listen to the harmonies of the gospel; they sit enthralled in the presence of an orator, how much rather should they yield to the eloquence of heaven.

Verse 2. I will open my mouth in a parable. Analogies are not only to be imagined, but are intended by God to be traced between the story of Israel and the lives of believers. Israel was ordained to be a type; the tribes and their marchings are living allegories traced by the hand of an all wise providence. Unspiritual persons may sneer about fancies and mysticisms, but Paul spake well when he said "which things are an allegory," and Asaph in the present case spake to the point when he called his narrative "a parable."

Verse 3. Which we have heard and known, and our fathers have told us. Tradition was of the utmost service to the people of God in the olden time, before the more sure word of prophecy had become complete and generally accessible. The receipt of truth from the lips of others laid the instructed believer under solemn obligation to pass on the truth to the next generation. Truth, endeared to us by its fond associations with godly parents and venerable friends, deserves of us our best exertions to preserve and propagate it. Our fathers told us, we hear them, and we know personally what they taught; it remains for us in our turn to hand it on.

Verse 4. We will not hide them from their children. Our negligent silence shall not deprive our own and our father's offspring of the precious truth of God, it would be shameful indeed if we did so. Shewing to the generation

JOHN CALVIN

Psalm 78

1-6

1. Give ear, O my people! to my law. From the close of the psalm, it may with probability be conjectured, that it was written long after the death of David; for there we have celebrated the kingdom erected by God in the family of David. There also the tribe of Ephraim, which is said to have been rejected, is contrasted with, and set in opposition to, the house of David. From this it is evident, that the ten tribes were at that time in a state of separation from the rest of the chosen people; for there must be some good reason why the kingdom of Ephraim is branded with a mark of dishonor as being illegitimate and bastard.

2. This passage is quoted by Matthew, (Matthew 13:35,) and applied to the person of Christ, when he held the minds of the people in suspense by parables which they could not understand. Christ's object in doing so, was to prove that he was a distinguished prophet of God, and that thus he might be received with the greater reverence.

3. What we have heard and known. It is the design of the prophet to remove from the mind all doubt respecting his sayings, and for this purpose, he determines to bring forward nothing new, but such subjects as had been long well known, and received without dispute in the Church.

4. We will not conceal them from their children in the generation to come. All pretense of ignorance is removed; for it was the will of God that these things should be published from age to age without interruption; so that being transmitted from father to child in each family, they might reach even the last family of man.

5. He established a testimony in Jacob. As the reception or approbation of any doctrine by men would not be a sufficient reason for yielding a firm assent to its truth, the prophet proceeds farther, and represents God as the author of what he brings forward. He declares, that the father's were not led to instruct their children in these truths under the mere impulse of their own minds, but by the commandment of God.

6. That the generation to come might know them. In this verse, the Psalmist confirms what he had said concerning the continued transmission of divine truth. It greatly concerns us to know, that the law was given not for one age only; but that the fathers should transmit it to their children, as if it were their rightful inheritance, in order that it might never be lost, but be preserved to the end of the world.

7-11

7. That they might set their hope in God. Here the Psalmist points out the use to which the doctrine which he had stated should be applied. In the first place, the fathers, when they find that on the one hand they are instrumental in maintaining the pure worship of God, and that on the other, they are the means of providing for the salvation of their children, should, by such a precious result of their labors, be the more powerfully stirred up to instruct their children. In the second place, the children on their part, being inflamed

MATTHEW HENRY

Psalm 78

1-8 The importance of religious instruction.

These verses, which contain the preface to this history, show that the psalm answers the title; it is indeed Maschil—a psalm to give instruction; if we receive not the instruction it gives, it is our own fault. Here,

I. The psalmist demands attention to what he wrote (v. 1): Give ear, O my people! to my law. Every good truth, received in the light and love of it, will have the power of a law upon the conscience.

II. Several reasons are given why we should diligently attend to that which is here related.

1. The things here discoursed of are weighty, and deserve consideration, strange, and need it (v. 2): I will open my mouth in a parable, in that which is sublime and uncommon, but very excellent and well worthy your attention; I will utter dark sayings, which challenge your most serious regards as much as the enigmas with which the eastern princes and learned men used to try one another. These are called dark sayings, not because they are hard to be understood, but because they are greatly to be admired and carefully to be looked into.

2. They are the monuments of antiquity—dark sayings of old which our fathers have told us, v. 3. They are things of undoubted certainty; we have heard them and known them, and there is no room left to question the truth of them. The gospel of Luke is called a declaration of those things which are most surely believed among us (Luke i. 1), so were the things here related. The honor we owe to our parents and ancestors obliges us to attend to that which our fathers have told us, and, as far as it appears to be true and good, to receive it with so much the more reverence and regard.

3. They are to be transmitted to posterity, and it lies as a charge upon us carefully to hand them down (v. 4); because our fathers told them to us we will not hide them from their children.

9-39 Wonders wrought in behalf of Israel; the crimes of the Israelites; judgments brought on the Israelites.

In these verses,

I. The psalmist observes the late rebukes of Providence that the people of Israel had been under, which they had brought upon themselves by their dealing treacherously with God, v. 9-11. The children of Ephraim, in which tribe Shiloh was, though they were well armed and shot with bows, yet turned back in the day of battle. This seems to refer to that shameful defeat which the Philistines gave them in Eli's time, when they took the ark prisoner, 1 Sam. iv. 10, 11. Of this the psalmist here begins to speak, and, after a long digression, returns to it again, v. 61. Well might that event be thus fresh in mind in David's time, above forty years after, for the ark, which in that memorable battle was seized by the Philistines,

Psalm 78

9-16

9 The children of Ephraim, being armed, and carrying bows, turned back in the day of battle.
10 They kept not the covenant of God, and refused to walk in his law;
11 And forgat his works, and his wonders that he had shewed them.
12 Marvelous things did he in the sight of their fathers, in the land of Egypt, in the field of Zoan.
13 He divided the sea, and caused them to pass through; and he made the waters to stand as an heap.
14 In the daytime also he led them with a cloud, and all the night with a light of fire.
15 He clave the rocks in the wilderness, and gave them drink as out of the great depths.
16 He brought streams also out of the rock, and caused waters to run down like rivers.

to come the praises of the Lord. We will look forward to future generations, and endeavor to provide for their godly education.

Verse 5. For he established a testimony in Jacob. The favored nation existed for the very purpose of maintaining God's truth in the midst of surrounding idolatry. Theirs were the oracles, they were the conservators and guardians of the truth. And appointed a law in Israel, which he commanded our fathers, that they should make them known to their children. The testimony for the true God was to be transmitted from generation to generation by the careful instruction of succeeding families.

Verse 6. That the generation to come might know them, even the children which should be born. As far on as our brief life allows us to arrange, we must industriously provide for the godly nurture of youth. The narratives, commands, and doctrines of the word of God are not worn out; they are calculated to exert an influence as long as our race shall exist. Who should arise and declare them to their children. The one object aimed at is transmission; the testimony is only given that it may be passed on to succeeding generations.

Verse 7. That they might set their hope in God. Faith cometh by hearing. Those who know the name of the Lord will set their hope in him, and that they may be led to do so is the main end of all spiritual teaching. And not forget the works of God. Grace cures bad memories; those who soon forget the merciful works of the Lord have need of teaching; they require to learn the divine art of holy memory.

Verse 8. And might not be as their fathers, a stubborn and rebellious generation. There was room for improvement. Fathers stubborn in their own way, and rebellious against God's way, are sorry examples for their children; and it is earnestly desired that better instruction may bring forth a better race. It is common in some regions for men to count their family custom as the very best rule; but disobedience is not to be excused because it is hereditary.

Verse 9. The children of Ephraim, being armed, and carrying bows, turned back in the day of battle. Well equipped and furnished with the best weapons of the times, the leading tribe failed in faith and courage and retreated before the foe. There were several particular instances of this, but probably the psalmist refers to the general failure of Ephraim to lead the tribes to the conquest of Canaan.

Verse 10. They kept not the covenant of God. Vows and promises were broken, idols were set up, and the living God was forsaken. They were brought out of Egypt in order to be a people separated unto the Lord, but they fell into the sins of other nations, and did not maintain a pure testimony for the one only true God.

Verse 11. And forgat his works, and his wonders that he had shewed them. Had they remembered them they would have been filled with gratitude and inspired with holy awe: but the memory of God's mercies to them was as soon effaced as if written upon water.

Verse 12. Egypt, here called the field of Zoan, was the scene of marvelous things which were done in open day in the sight of Israel. These were extraordinary, upon a vast scale, astounding, indisputable, and such as ought to have rendered it impossible for an Israelite to be disloyal to Jehovah, Israel's God.

Verse 13. He divided the sea, and caused them to pass through. A double wonder, for when the waters were divided the bottom of the sea would naturally be in a very unfit state for the passage of so vast a host as that of Israel; it would in fact have been impassable, had not the Lord made the road for his people. Who else has ever led a nation through a sea? Yet the Lord has done this full often for his saints in providential deliverances, making a highway for them where nothing short of an almighty arm could have done so.

Verse 14. In the daytime also he led them with a cloud. HE did it all. He alone. He brought them into the wilderness, and he led them through it; it is

with greater zeal, should eagerly press forward in the acquisition of divine knowledge, and not suffer their minds to wander in vain speculations, but should aim at, or keep their eyes directed to, the right mark.
8. And that they might not be as their fathers, a rebellious and provoking generation. The Psalmist here shows still more distinctly how necessary this sermon was, from the circumstance that the Jews were exceedingly prone to revolt from God, if they were not kept in subjection by powerful restraints.
9. The children of Ephraim being armed, and shooting with the bow. The sacred writer sets before us an example of this unfaithfulness in the children of Ephraim. As those who are pertinaciously set upon doing evil are not easily led to repentance and reformation by simple instruction, the punishments with which God visited the children of Ephraim are brought forward, and by these it is proved that they were reprobates.
10. They kept not the covenant of God. This is the reason assigned for the Ephraimites turning their backs in the day of battle; and it explains why the divine assistance was withheld from them. Others, it is true, were guilty in this respect as well as they, but the vengeance of God executed on that tribe, which by its influence had corrupted almost the whole kingdom, is purposely brought forward as a general warning.
11. And they forgat his works. This shameful impiety is here represented as having originated in ingratitude, inasmuch as they wickedly buried, and made no account of the deliverance wrought for them, which was worthy of everlasting remembrance.

12-16
12. He wrought marvelously in the sight of their fathers. The Psalmist is still to be regarded as condemning the posterity of the Israelites for their guilt; but he very properly, at the same time, begins to speak of the first ancestors of the nation, intimating, that the whole race of them, even from their first original, were of a perverse and rebellious disposition. But having remarked that the children of Ephraim had fallen into apostasy, because they had forgotten the wonderful works of God, he continues to prosecute the same subject.
In the first place, he adverts to the miracles which were wrought in the midst of the land of Egypt, previous to the departure of the people from it.
13. He next comes to speak of the passage through the sea, where he repeats what was brought under our notice in the previous psalm, that the order of nature was reversed when the waters stopped in their course, and were even raised up into solid heaps like mountains.
14. In the third place, he declares, that after the people had passed through the Red Sea, God still continued to be their guide in their journey; and that this might not be a mere temporary deliverance, he graciously continued to stretch forth his hand to bestow upon them new testimonies of his goodness.

though it was quickly brought out of captivity, was never brought out of obscurity till David fetched it from Kirjath-jearim to his own city. Observe,
1. The shameful cowardice of the children of Ephraim, that warlike tribe, so famed for valiant men, Joshua's tribe; the children of that tribe, though as well armed as ever, turned back when they came to face the enemy. Note, Weapons of war stand men in little stead without a martial spirit, and that is gone if God be gone. Sin dispirits men and takes away the heart.
2. The causes of their cowardice, which were no less shameful; and these were,
(1.) A shameful violation of God's law and their covenant with him (v. 10); they were basely treacherous and perfidious, for they kept not the covenant of God, and basely stubborn and rebellious (as they were described, v. 8), for they peremptorily refused to walk in his law, and, in effect, told him to his face they would not be ruled by him.
(2.) A shameful ingratitude to God for the favors he had bestowed upon them: They forgot his works and his wonders, his works of wonder which they ought to have admired, v. 11.
II. He takes occasion hence to consult precedents and to compare this with the case of their fathers, who were in like manner unmindful of God's mercies to them and ungrateful to their founder and great benefactor, and were therefore often brought under his displeasure. The narrative in these verses is very remarkable, for it relates a kind of struggle between God's goodness and man's badness, and mercy, at length, rejoices against judgment.
1. God did great things for his people Israel when he first incorporated them and formed them into a people: Marvelous things did he in the sight of their fathers, and not only in their sight, but in their cause, and for their benefit, so strange, so kind, that one would think they should never be forgotten. What he did for them in the land of Egypt is only just mentioned here (v. 12), but afterwards resumed, v. 43. He proceeds here to show,
(1.) How he made a lane for them through the Red Sea, and caused them, gave them courage, to pass through, though the waters stood over their heads as a heap, v. 13. See Isa. lxiii. 12, 13, where God is said to lead them by the hand, as it were, through the deep that they should not stumble.
(2.) How he provided a guide for them through the untrodden paths of the wilderness (v. 14); he led them step by step, in the day time by a cloud, which also sheltered them from the heat, and all the night with a light of fire, which perhaps warmed the air; at least it made the darkness of night less frightful, and perhaps kept off wild beasts, Zech. ii. 5.
(3.) How he furnished their camp with fresh water in a dry and thirsty land where no water was, not by opening the bottles of heaven (that would have been a common way), but by broaching a rock (v. 15, 16): He clave the rocks in the wilderness, which yielded

Psalm 78

17-24

17 And they sinned yet more against him by provoking the most High in the wilderness.
18 And they tempted God in their heart by asking meat for their lust.
19 Yea, they spake against God; they said, Can God furnish a table in the wilderness?
20 Behold, he smote the rock, that the waters gushed out, and the streams overflowed; can he give bread also? can he provide flesh for his people?
21 Therefore the LORD heard this, and was wroth: so a fire was kindled against Jacob, and anger also came up against Israel;
22 Because they believed not in God, and trusted not in his salvation:
23 Though he had commanded the clouds from above, and opened the doors of heaven,
24 And had rained down manna upon them to eat, and had given them of the corn of heaven.

not the Lord's manner to begin a work, and then cease from it while it is incomplete. The cloud both led and shadowed the tribes. It was by day a vast sun screen, rendering the fierce heat of the sun and the glare of the desert sand bearable.

Verse 15. He clave the rocks in the wilderness. Moses was the instrument, but the Lord did it all. Twice he made the flint a gushing rill. What can he not do? And gave them drink as out of the great depths,—as though it gushed from earth's innermost reservoirs. The streams were so fresh, so copious, so constant, that they seemed to well up from the earth's primeval fountains, and to leap at once from "the deep which coucheth beneath."

Verse 16. The supply of water was as plenteous in quantity as it was miraculous in origin. Torrents, not driblets came from the rocks. Streams followed the camp; the supply was not for an hour or a day. This was a marvel of goodness.

Verse 17. And they sinned yet more against him. Outdoing their former sins, going into greater deeps of evil: the more they had the more loudly they clamored for more, and murmured because they had not every luxury that pampered appetites could desire. It was bad enough to mistrust their God for necessaries, but to revolt against him in a greedy rage for superfluities was far worse.

Verse 18. And they tempted God in their heart. He was not tempted, for he cannot be tempted by any, but they acted in a manner calculated to tempt him, and it always just to charge that upon men which is the obvious tendency of their conduct. Christ cannot die again, and yet many crucify him afresh, because such would be the legitimate result of their behavior if its effects were not prevented by other forces.

Verse 19. From this verse we learn that unbelief of God is a slander against him. Yea, they spake against God. But how? The answer is, They said, Can God furnish a table in the wilderness? To question the ability of one who is manifestly Almighty, is to speak against him.

Verse 20. Behold, he smote the rock, that the waters gushed out, and the streams overflowed. They admit what he had done, and yet, with superabundant folly and insolence, demand further proofs of his omnipotence.

Verse 21. Therefore the Lord heard this, and was wroth. He was not indifferent to what they said. He dwelt among them in the holy place, and, therefore, they insulted him to his face. He did not hear a report of it, but the language itself came into his ears.

Verse 22. Because they believed not in God, and trusted not in his salvation. This is the master sin, the crying sin. Like Jeroboam, the son of Nebat, it sins and makes Israel to sin; it is in itself evil and the parent of evils.

Verse 23. Though he had commanded the clouds from above. Such a marvel ought to have rendered unbelief impossible: when clouds become granaries, seeing should be believing, and doubts should dissolve.

Verse 24. And had rained down manna upon them to eat. There was so much of it, the skies poured with food, the clouds burst with provender. It was fit food, proper not for looking at but for eating; they could eat it as they gathered it. Mysterious though it was, so that they called it manna, or "what is it?" yet it was eminently adapted for human nourishment; and it was both abundant and adapted, so also was it available! They had not far to fetch it, it was nigh them, and they had only to gather it up. O Lord Jesus, thou blessed manna of heaven, how all this agrees with Thee! We will even now feed on Thee as our spiritual meat, and will pray Thee to chase away all wicked unbelief from us. Our fathers ate manna and doubted; we feed upon Thee and are filled with assurance.

Verse 25. Man did eat angel's food. The delicacies of kings were outdone, for the dainties of angels were supplied. Bread of the mighty ones fell on feeble man. Those who are lower than the angels fared as well. It was not

JOHN CALVIN

15. He clave the rocks in the wilderness. The Psalmist produces another evidence of the fatherly love by which God testified the greatness of the care which he exercised about the welfare of this people. It is not simply said that God gave them drink, but that he did this in a miraculous manner.
16. Now it is stated that where there had not been a single drop of water before there was a large and mighty river. Had there only sprung out of the rock a small rivulet, ungodly men might have had some apparent ground for caviling at, and underrating the goodness of God, but when the water gushed out in such copious abundance all on a sudden, who does not see that the ordinary course of nature was changed, rather than that some vein or spring which lay hidden in the earth was opened?

17-22
17. Yet they continued still to sin against him. The prophet, having briefly declared how God, by a continual succession of benefits, had clearly manifested the greatness of his love towards the children of Abraham, now adds, that after having been laid under such deep and solemn obligations to him, they, as was natural to them, and according to their customary way, wickedly rebelled against him.
18. And they tempted God in their heart. This is the provocation of which mention is made in the preceding verse. Not that it was unlawful for them simply to ask food, when constrained to do so by the cravings of hunger. Who can impute blame to persons, when being hungry, they implore God to supply their necessities? The sin with which the Israelites were chargeable consisted in this, that not content with the food which He had appointed them, they gave loose reins to their lusts.
19. And they spake against God. The prophet had said that they tempted God in their heart; and now he adds, that they were not ashamed openly to utter with their impure and blasphemous tongues, the impiety which they had inwardly conceived. From this, it is the more abundantly manifest that malignity and wickedness had taken entire possession of their hearts. Thus we see how lust conceives sin, when it is admitted into the soul with unhallowed consent.
20. When it is said in the following verse, Behold! God smote the rock, and the waters gushed out, etc., this, I have no doubt, is the language of bitter irony, with which the prophet taunts their unblushing insolence. It is not very likely that they spake in this manner; but he relates, as it were, with their mouth, or in their person, the things which took place before their eyes.
21, 22. Therefore Jehovah heard, and was wroth. This hearing of God implies full and perfect knowledge; and it is a figure taken from earthly judges, who cannot punish criminals until they have become thoroughly acquainted with the cause. He is said to hear his own people, when he shows his favor and mercy towards them by granting their requests; and, on the other hand, he is said to hear those blasphemies which he does not allow to pass unpunished. To remove all ground for thinking that the divine wrath was unduly severe, the enormity of the guilt of the Israelites is again described as manifested in this, that they believed not

MATTHEW HENRY

water, though they were not capable of receiving it either from the clouds above or the springs beneath. Out of the dry and hard rock he gave them drink. And that rock was Christ.

2. When God began thus to bless them they began to affront him (v. 17): They sinned yet more against him, more than they had done in Egypt, though there they were bad enough, Ezek. xx. 8. They bore the miseries of their servitude better than the difficulties of their deliverance, and never murmured at their taskmasters so much as they did at Moses and Aaron; as if they were delivered to do all these abominations, Jer. vii. 10. As sin sometimes takes occasion by the commandment, so at other times it takes occasion by the deliverance, to become more exceedingly sinful. They provoked the Most High. Though he is most high, and they knew themselves an unequal match for him, yet they provoked him and even bade defiance to his justice; and this in the wilderness, where he had them at his mercy and therefore they were bound in interest to please him, and where he showed them so much mercy and therefore they were bound in gratitude to please him; yet there they said and did that which they knew would provoke him: They tempted God in their heart, v. 18. Their sin began in their heart, and thence it took its malignity. They do always err in their heart, Heb. iii. 10. Thus they tempted God, tried his patience to the utmost, whether he would bear with them or no, and, in effect, bade him do his worst.

3. God justly resented the provocation and was much displeased with them (v. 21): The Lord heard this, and was wroth. Note, God is a witness to all our murmurings and distrusts; he hears them and is much displeased with them. A fire was kindled for this against Jacob; the fire of the Lord burnt among them, Num. xi. 1. Or it may be understood of the fire of God's anger which came up against Israel. To unbelievers our God is himself a consuming fire. Those that will not believe the power of God's mercy shall feel the power of his indignation, and be made to confess that it is a fearful thing to fall into his hands. Now here we are told,
(1.) Why God thus resented the provocation (v. 22): Because by this it appeared that they believed not in God; they did not give credit to the revelation he had made of himself to them, for they durst not commit themselves to him, nor venture themselves with him: They trusted not in the salvation he had begun to work for them; for then they would not thus have questioned its progress. Those cannot be said to trust in God's salvation as their felicity at last who cannot find in their hearts to trust in his providence for food convenient in the way to it. That which aggravated their unbelief was the experience they had had of the power and goodness of God, v. 23-25. He had given them undeniable proofs of his power.
(2.) How he expressed his resentment of the provocation, not in denying them what they so inordinately lusted after, but in granting it to them.

Psalm 78

25-32

25 Man did eat angels' food: he sent them meat to the full.
26 He caused an east wind to blow in the heaven: and by his power he brought in the south wind.
27 He rained flesh also upon them as dust, and feathered fowls like as the sand of the sea:
28 And he let it fall in the midst of their camp, round about their habitations.
29 So they did eat, and were well filled: for he gave them their own desire;
30 They were not estranged from their lust. But while their meat was yet in their mouths,
31 The wrath of God came upon them, and slew the fattest of them, and smote down the chosen men of Israel.
32 For all this they sinned still, and believed not for his wondrous works.

for the priests, or the princes, that the manna fell; but for all the nation, for every man, woman, and child in the camp: and there was sufficient for them all, for he sent them meat to the full. God's banquets are never stinted; he gives the best diet, and plenty of it.

Verse 26. He caused an east wind to blow in the heaven. He is Lord Paramount, above the prince of the power of the air: storms arise and tempests blow at his command. Winds sleep till God arouses them, and then, like Samuel, each one answers, "Here am I, for thou didst call me."

Verse 27. He rained flesh also upon them as dust. First he rained bread and then flesh, when he might have rained fire and brimstone. The words indicate the speed, and the abundance of the descending quails. And feathered fowls like as the sand of the sea; there was no counting them. By a remarkable providence, if not by miracle, enormous numbers of migratory birds were caused to alight around the tents of the tribes. It was, however, a doubtful blessing, as easily acquired and super abounding riches generally are. The Lord save us from meat which is seasoned with divine wrath.

Verse 28. And he let it fall in the midst of their camp. They had no journey to make; they had clamored for flesh, and it almost flew into their mouths, round about their habitations. This made them glad for the moment, but they knew not that mercies can be sent in anger, else they had trembled at sight of the good things which they had lusted after.

Verse 29. So they did eat, and were well filled. They greedily devoured the birds, even to repletion. The Lord shewed them that he could "provide flesh for his people," even enough and to spare. He also shewed them that when lust wins its desire it is disappointed, and by the way of satiety arrive at distaste. First the food satiates, then it nauseates. For he gave them their own desire. They were filled with their own ways. The flesh meat was unhealthy for them, but as they cried for it they had it, and a curse with it. O my God, deny me my most urgent prayers sooner than answer them in displeasure. Better hunger and thirst after righteousness than to be well filled with sin's dainties.

Verses 30-31. They were not estranged from their lust. Lust grows upon that which it feeds on. If sick of too much flesh, yet men grow not weary of lust, they change the object, and go on lusting still. When one sin is proved to be a bitterness, men do not desist, but pursue another iniquity. If, like Jehu, they turn from Baal, they fall to worshipping the calves of Bethel. But while their meat was yet in their mouths, before they could digest their coveted meat, it turned to their destruction. The wrath of God came upon them before they could swallow their first meal of flesh. Short was the pleasure, sudden was the doom.

Verse 32. For all this they sinned still. Judgments moved them no more than mercies. They defied the wrath of God. Though death was in the cup of their iniquity, yet they would not put it away, but continued to quaff it as if it were a healthful potion. How truly might these words be applied to ungodly men who have been often afflicted, laid upon a sick bed, broken in spirit, and impoverished in estate, and yet have persevered in their evil ways, unmoved by terrors, unswayed by threatenings. And believed not for his wondrous works. Their unbelief was chronic and incurable. Miracles both of mercy and judgment were unavailing. They might be made to wonder, but they could not be taught to believe.

Verse 33. Therefore their days did he consume in vanity. Apart from faith life is vanity. To wander up and down in the wilderness was a vain thing indeed, when unbelief had shut them out of the promised land. It was meet that those who would not live to answer the divine purpose by believing and obeying their God should be made to live to no purpose, and to die before their time, unsatisfied, unblessed. Those who wasted their days in sin had little cause to wonder when the Lord cut short their lives, and sware that they should never enter the rest which they had despised.

God, nor trusted in his salvation. It is here taken as an indisputable point, that promises were made to them to which they ought to have yielded an assent, which, however, they were prevented from yielding by the extreme infatuation with which they were carried away. To trust in the salvation of God, is to lean upon his fatherly providence, and to regard him as sufficient for the supply of all our wants. From this we learn not only how hateful unbelief is in the sight of God, but also, what is the true nature of faith, and what are the fruits which it produces.

23-25

23-25. But he had commanded the clouds from above. It is a mistake to suppose that this miracle is related merely in the way of history. The prophet rather censures the Israelites the more severely from the consideration, that although fed to the full with manna, they ceased not to lust after the dainties which they knew God had denied them. It was the basest ingratitude to scorn and reject the heavenly food, which, so to speak, associated them with angels. Were a man who dwells in France or Italy to grieve and fret that he has not the bread of Egypt to eat, nor the wine of Asia to drink, would he not make war against God and nature, after the manner of the giants of old? Much less excusable was the inordinate lust of the Israelites, whom God not only furnished with earthly provision in rich abundance, but to whom he also gave the bread of heaven for their support.

26-31

26-29. He caused an east wind to blow in the heavens. We have here related how God granted the request of his people. This does not imply that he favorably regarded their fretful desires, but that he showed by the effect that it was in his power to do what they believed it to be impossible for him to accomplish. From this, we may perceive how injudiciously some expositors here join together the flesh and the manna. The reason why the flesh was given was altogether different from that for which the manna was given. God, in giving the manna, performed the office of a father; but by the flesh, he satisfied their gluttonous desires, that their very greediness in devouring it might choke them. It would not have been a difficult matter for God to have created quails in the midst of the wilderness; but he chose rather to bring them by the force of the winds, to teach the Israelites that all the elements are obedient to his command, and that the distance of places cannot prevent his power from immediately penetrating from the east even to the west.

30, 31. The Psalmist expresses this still more clearly, by adding immediately after, that this pampering proved fatal to them, as if with the meat they had swallowed the flame of the divine wrath. When he says that they were not estranged from their lust, this implies, that they were still burning with their lust.

32-37

32. For all this they still sinned. It is a common proverb, that fools become wise when the rod is applied to them. Hence it

[1.] Did they question his power? He soon gave them a sensible conviction that he could furnish a table in the wilderness. Though the winds seem to blow where they list, yet, when he pleased, he could make them his caterers to fetch in provisions, v. 26. He caused an east wind to blow and a south wind, either a south-east wind, or an east wind first to bring in the quails from that quarter and then a south wind to bring in more from that quarter; so that he rained flesh upon them, and that of the most delicate sort, not butchers' meat, but wild-fowl, and abundance of it, as dust, as the sand of the sea (v. 27), so that the meanest Israelite might have sufficient; and it cost them nothing, no, not the pains of fetching it from the mountains, for he let it fall in the midst of their camp, round about their habitation, v. 28. We have the account Num. xi. 31, 32. See how good God is even to the evil and unthankful, and wonder that his goodness does not overcome their badness. See what little reason we have to judge of God's love by such gifts of his bounty as these; dainty bits are no tokens of his peculiar favor. Christ gave dry bread to the disciples that he loved, but a sop dipped in the sauce to Judas that betrayed him.

[2.] Did they defy his justice and boast that they had gained their point? He made them pay dearly for their quails; for, though he gave them their own desire, they were not estranged from their lust (v. 29, 30); their appetite was insatiable; they were well filled and yet they were not satisfied; for they knew not what they would have. Such is the nature of lust; it is content with nothing, and the more it is humored the more humorsome it grows. Those that indulge their lust will never be estranged from it. Or it intimates that God's liberality did not make them ashamed of their ungrateful lustings, as it would have done if they had had any sense of honor. But what came of it? While the meat was yet in their mouth, rolled under the tongue as a sweet morsel, the wrath of God came upon them and slew the fattest of them (v. 31), those that were most luxurious and most daring. See Num. xi. 33, 34. They were fed as sheep for the slaughter: the butcher takes the fattest first. We may suppose there were some pious and contented Israelites, that did eat moderately of the quails and were never the worse; for it was not the meat that poisoned them, but their own lust. Let epicures and sensualists here read their doom. The end of those who make a god of their belly is destruction, Phil. iii. 19. The prosperity of fools shall destroy them, and their ruin will be the greater.

4. The judgments of God upon them did not reform them, nor attain the end, any more than his mercies (v. 32): For all this, they sinned still; they murmured and quarreled with God and Moses as much as ever. Though God was wroth and smote them, yet they went on frowardly in the way of their heart (Isa. live. 17); they believed not for his wondrous works. Though his works of justice were as wondrous and as great proofs of his power as his works of

Psalm 78

33-40
33 Therefore their days did he consume in vanity, and their years in trouble.
34 When he slew them, then they sought him: and they returned and enquired early after God.
35 And they remembered that God was their rock, and the high God their redeemer.
36 Nevertheless they did flatter him with their mouth, and they lied unto him with their tongues.
37 For their heart was not right with him, neither were they steadfast in his covenant.
38 But he, being full of compassion, forgave their iniquity, and destroyed them not: yea, many a time turned he his anger away, and did not stir up all his wrath.
39 For he remembered that they were but flesh; a wind that passeth away, and cometh not again.
40 How oft did they provoke him in the wilderness, and grieve him in the desert!

Verse 34. When he slew them, then they sought him. Like whipped curs, they licked their Master's feet. They obeyed only so long as they felt the whip about their loins. Hard are the hearts which only death can move. While thousands died around them, the people of Israel became suddenly religious, and repaired to the tabernacle door, like sheep who run in a mass while the black dog drives them, but scatter and wander when the shepherd whistles him off.
Verse 35. And they remember that God was their rock. Sharp strokes awoke their sleepy memories. Reflection followed infliction. They were led to see that all their dependence must be placed upon their God; for he alone had been their shelter, their foundation, their fountain of supply, and their unchangeable friend. What could have made them forget this? Was it that their stomachs were so full of flesh that thy had no space for ruminating upon spiritual things? And the high God their redeemer. They had forgotten this also.
Verse 36. Nevertheless they did flatter him with their mouth. Bad were they at their best. False on their knees, liars in their prayers. Mouth worship must be very detestable to God when dissociated from the heart: other kings love flattery, but the King of kings abhors it. Since the sharpest afflictions only extort from carnal men a feigned submission to God, there is proof positive that the heart is desperately set on mischief, and that sin is ingrained in our very nature. If you beat a tiger with many stripes you cannot turn him into a sheep. The devil cannot be whipped out of human nature, though another devil, namely, hypocrisy may be whipped into it.
Verse 37. For their heart was not right with him. There was no depth in their repentance, it was not heart work. They were fickle as a weathercock, every wind turned them, their mind was not settled upon God. Neither were they steadfast in his covenant. Their promises were no sooner made than broken, as if only made in mockery. Good resolutions called at their hearts as men do at inns; they tarried awhile, and then took their leave. They were hot today for holiness, but cold towards it tomorrow.
Verse 38. But he, being full of compassion, forgave their iniquity, and destroyed them not. Though they were full of flattery, he was full of mercy, and for this cause he had pity on them. Not because of their pitiful and hypocritical pretensions to penitence, but because of his own real compassion for them he overlooked their provocations.
Verse 39. For he remembered that they were but flesh. They were forgetful of God, but he was mindful of them. He knew that they were made of earthy, frail, corruptible material, and therefore he dealt leniently with them. Though in this he saw no excuse for their sin, yet he constrained it into a reason for mercy; the Lord is ever ready to discover some plea or other upon which he may have compassion.
Verse 40. How oft did they provoke him in the wilderness. Times enough did they rebel: they were as constant in provocation as he was in his patience. In our own case, who can count his errors? In what book could all our perverse rebellions be recorded? The wilderness was a place of manifest dependence, where the tribes were helpless without divine supplies, yet they wounded the hand which fed them while it was in the act of feeding them. Is there no likeness between us and them? Does it bring no tears into our eyes, while as in a glass, we see our own selves? And grieve him in the desert. Their provocations had an effect; God was not insensible to them, he is said to have been grieved. His holiness could not find pleasure in their sin, his justice in their unjust treatment, or his truth in their falsehood.
Verses 41. Yea, they turned back. Their hearts sighed for Egypt and its fleshpots. They turned to their old ways again and again, after they had been scourged out of them. Full of twists and turns, they never kept the straight path.
Verse 42. They remembered not his hand. Yet it must have been difficult to forget it. Such displays of divine power as those which smote Egypt with

follows, that those who have often been chastised of God, and yet are not thereby brought to repentance and amendment, are utterly to be despaired of. Such was the obstinacy of the Israelites here described. They could not be reformed by any of the afflictions which were sent upon them. It was a dreadful manifestation of the vengeance of God to see so many bodies of strong and vigorous men stretched dead on the ground. It was therefore a proof of monstrous obduracy, when they were not moved at such an appalling spectacle.

33. And he consumed their days in vanity. As the Psalmist here speaks of the whole people, as if he had said, that all without exception were speedily consumed, from the least even to the greatest, this might with probability be referred to that most grievous punishment which was confirmed and ratified by the wrath of God.

34. When he slew them, then they sought him. By the circumstance here recorded, it is intended to aggravate their guilt. When under a conviction of their wickedness they acknowledged that they were justly punished, and yet did not with sincerity of heart humble themselves before God, but rather mocked him, intending to put him off with false pretences, their impiety was the less excusable.

35. We are informed not only that they were convinced of wickedness, but also that they were affected with a sense and a remembrance of the redemption from which they were fallen. By this means they are the more effectually deprived of all excuse on the ground of ignorance. The language implies that they were not carried away inadvertently, or deceived through ignorance, but that they had provoked the wrath of God, by dealing treacherously, as it were with deliberate purpose. And, indeed, God opened their eyes with the view of more openly discovering their desperate wickedness, as if, shaking off their hypocrisy and flatteries, he drew them from their lurking-places into the light.

36. And they flattered him with their mouth, and lied to him with their tongue. Here they are charged with perfidiousness, because they neither confessed their guilt with sincerity of heart, nor truly ascribed to God the glory of their deliverance. We are not to suppose that they made no acknowledgement at all; but it is intimated that the confession of the mouth, as it did not proceed from the heart, was constrained and not voluntary.

37. The Psalmist points out the cause and source of this dissimulation to be, that they were not steadfast and faithful. By this he intimates, that whatever does not proceed from unfeigned purity of heart is accounted lying and deceit in the sight of God. Since this uprightness is every where required in the law, he accuses the people with being covenant-breakers, because they had not kept the covenant of God with that fidelity which became them.

38-41

38. Yet he, being merciful, expiated their iniquity. To show the more fully that no means had succeeded in bending the Israelites, and causing them to return to a sound state of mind, we are now informed that, although God bare with their multiplied transgressions, and exercised his mercy in

mercy, yet they were not wrought upon by them to fear God, nor convinced how much it was their interest to make him their friend. Those hearts are hard indeed that will neither be melted by the mercies of God nor broken by his judgments.

5. They persisting in their sins, God proceeded in his judgments, but they were judgments of another nature, which wrought not suddenly, but slowly. He punished them not now with such acute diseases as that was which slew the fattest of them, but a lingering chronicle distemper (v. 33): Therefore their days did he consume in vanity in the wilderness and their years in trouble.

6. Under these rebukes they professed repentance, but they were not cordial and sincere in this profession.

(1.) Their profession was plausible enough (v. 34, 35): When he slew them, or condemned them to be slain, then they sought him; they confessed their fault, and begged his pardon. When some were slain others in a fright cried to God for mercy, and promised they would reform and be very good; then they returned to God, and enquired early after him.

(2.) They were not sincere in this profession (v. 36, 37): They did but flatter him with their mouth, as if they thought by fair speeches to prevail with him to revoke the sentence and remove the judgment, with a secret intention to break their word when the danger was over; they did not return to God with their whole heart, but feignedly, Jer. iii. 10.

7. God hereupon, in pity to them, put a stop to the judgments which were threatened and in part executed (v. 38, 39): But he, being full of compassion, forgave their iniquity. One would think this counterfeit repentance should have filled up the measure of their iniquity. What could be more provoking than to lie thus to the holy God, than thus to keep back part of the price, the chief part? Acts v. 3. And yet he, being full of compassion, forgave their iniquity thus far, that he did not destroy them and cut them off from being a people, as he justly might have done, but spared their lives till they had reared another generation which should enter into the promised land. Destroy it not, for a blessing is in it, Isa. lxv. 8. Many a time he turned his anger away (for he is Lord of his anger) and did not stir up all his wrath, to deal with them as they deserved.

40-72 Judgments and mercies; wonders wrought for Israel; renewed mercies to Israel.

The matter and scope of this paragraph are the same with the former, showing what great mercies God had bestowed upon Israel, how provoking they had been, what judgments he had brought upon them for their sins, and yet how, in judgment, he remembered mercy at last. Observe,

I. The sins of Israel in the wilderness again reflected on, because written for our admonition (v. 40, 41): How often did they provoke him in the wilderness!

Psalm 78

41-48

41 Yea, they turned back and tempted God, and limited the Holy One of Israel.
42 They remembered not his hand, nor the day when he delivered them from the enemy.
43 How he had wrought his signs in Egypt, and his wonders in the field of Zoan.
44 And had turned their rivers into blood; and their floods, that they could not drink.
45 He sent divers sorts of flies among them, which devoured them; and frogs, which destroyed them.
46 He gave also their increase unto the caterpillar, and their labor unto the locust.
47 He destroyed their vines with hail, and their sycamore trees with frost.
48 He gave up their cattle also to the hail, and their flocks to hot thunderbolts.

astonishment, it must have needed some more than usual effort to blot it from the tablets of memory. It is probably meant that they practically, rather than actually, forgot. He who forgets the natural returns of gratitude, may justly be charged with not remembering the obligation.

Verse 43. How he had wrought his signs in Egypt. The plagues were ensigns of Jehovah's presence and proofs of his hatred of idols; these instructive acts of power were wrought in the open view of all, as signals are set up to be observed by those far and near.

Verse 44. And had turned their rivers into blood. The waters had been made the means of the destruction of Israel's newborn infants, and now they do as it were betray the crime—they blush for it, they avenge it on the murderers. The Nile was the vitality of Egypt, its true life blood, but at God's command it became a flowing curse; every drop of it was a horror, poison to drink, and terror to gaze on.

Verse 45. He sent diverse sorts of flies among them, which devoured them. Small creatures become great tormentors. When they swarm they can sting a man till they threaten to eat him up. In this case, various orders of insects fought under the same banner; lice and beetles, gnats and hornets, wasps and gadflies dashed forward in fierce battalions, and worried the sinners of Egypt without mercy. The tiniest plagues are the greatest. What sword or spear could fight with these innumerable bands? Vain were the monarch's armor and robes of majesty, the little cannibals were no more lenient towards royal flesh than any other; it had the same blood in it, and the same sin upon it. How great is that God who thus by the minute can crush the magnificent.

Verse 46. He gave also their increase unto the caterpillar, and their labor unto the locust. Different sorts of devourers ate up every green herb and tree. What one would not eat another did. What they expected from the natural fertility of the soil, and what they looked for from their own toil, they saw devoured before their eyes by an insatiable multitude against whose depredation no defense could be found.

Verse 47. He destroyed their vines with hail. No more shall thy butler press the clusters into thy cup, O Pharaoh! The young fruit bearing shoots were broken off, the vintage failed. And their sycamore trees with frost. Frost was not usual, but Jehovah regards no laws of nature when men regard not his moral laws.

Verse 48. He gave up their cattle also to the hail. What hail it must have been to have force enough to batter down bullocks and other great beasts. God usually protects animals from such destruction, but here he withdraws his safeguards and gave them up: may the Lord never give us up. Some read, "shut up," and the idea of being abandoned to destructive influences is then before us in another shape. And their flocks to hot thunderbolts. Fire was mingled with the hail, the fire ran along upon the ground, it smote the smaller cattle. What a storm must that have been: its effects were terrible enough upon plants, but to see the poor dumb creatures stricken must have been heartbreaking. Adamantine was that heart which quailed not under such plagues as these, harder than adamant those hearts which in after years forgot all that the Lord had done, and broke off from their allegiance to him.

Verse 49. He cast upon them the fierceness of his anger, wrath, and indignation, and trouble. His last arrow was the sharpest. He reserved the strong wine of his indignation to the last. Note how the psalmist piles up the words, and well he might; for blow followed blow, each one more staggering than its predecessor, and then the crushing stroke was reserved for the end.

Verse 50. He made a way to his anger, coming to the point with them by slow degrees; assailing their outworks first by destroying their property, and then coming in upon their persons as through an open breach in the walls. He broke down all the comforts of their life, and then advanced against their

JOHN CALVIN

forgiving them, they had no less manifested their wickedness in abusing his benignity in every instance in which it was displayed, than they had shown themselves refractory and obstinate when he treated them with severity.
39. And he remembered that they were flesh. Another reason is now brought forward why God had compassion on the people, which is, his unwillingness to try his strength against men who are so constituted as to live only for a short period in this world, and who then quickly pass away; for the forms of expression here used denote the frailty by which the condition of men is made miserable.
40. How often did they provoke him in the desert? Here the preceding sentence is confirmed, it being declared that, as they had in so many instances provoked God in the wilderness, by the vast accumulation of their sins, they must of necessity have perished a thousand times, had not God as often shown himself favorable and merciful towards them.
41. In the same sense it is added immediately after, that they returned to their former ways, and tempted God. The word return does not here signify change, but a continued course of sinning. The heinous indignity which is done to God when men tempt him, is expressed by a beautiful metaphor.

42-51
42. They remembered not his hand. The sacred writer still continues to upbraid the Israelites; for the simple remembrance of God's benefits might have restrained them, had they not willfully and perversely forgotten whatever they had experienced. From this impious forgetfulness proceed waywardness and all rebellion.
43. Farther, he recounts certain examples of the power of God, which he calls first signs, and then miracles, that, by the recital of these, he may again rebuke the shameful stupidity of the people. By both these words he expresses the same thing; but in the second clause of the verse, the word miracles gives additional emphasis, implying that, by such strange and unheard-of events, the Egyptians had at that time been stricken with such terror as ought not to have vanished so speedily from the minds of the Israelites.
44-46. When he turned their rivers into blood. The Psalmist does not enumerate in their order the miracles by which God gave evidence of his power in the deliverance of his people. He considered it enough to bring to their remembrance the well-known histories of these events, which would be sufficient to lay open the wickedness and ingratitude with which they were chargeable; nor is it necessary for us to stay long on these things, since the narrative of Moses gives a more distinct and fuller account of what is here briefly stated.
49. In the last place, it is added that God executed these judgments by angels. Although God has, according as it has pleased him, established certain laws, both in heaven and on earth, and governs the whole order of nature in such a manner as that each creature has assigned to it its own peculiar office; yet whenever it seems good to him he makes use of the ministration of angels for executing his commands, not by ordinary or natural means, but by his secret power,

MATTHEW HENRY

Note once, nor twice, but many a time; and the repetition of the provocation was a great aggravation of it, as well as the place, v. 17. God kept an account how often they provoked him, though they did not. Num. xiv. 22, They have tempted me these ten times. By provoking him they did not so much anger him as grieve him, for he looked upon them as his children (Israel is my son, my first-born), and the undutiful disrespectful behavior of children does more grieve than anger the tender parents; they lay it to heart, and take it unkindly, Isa. i. 2. They grieved him because they put him under a necessity of afflicting them, which he did not willingly. After they had humbled themselves before him they turned back and tempted God, as before, and limited the Holy One of Israel, prescribing to him what proofs he should give of his power and presence with them and what methods he should take in leading them and providing for them.
II. The mercies of God to Israel, which they were unmindful of when they tempted God and limited him; and this catalogue of the works of wonder which God wrought for them begins higher, and is carried down further, than that before, v. 12, &c.

1. This begins with their deliverance out of Egypt, and the plagues with which God compelled the Egyptians to let them go: these were the signs God wrought in Egypt (v. 43), the wonders he wrought in the field of Zoan, that is, in the country of Zoan, as we say, in Agro N., meaning in such a country.
(1.) Several of the plagues of Egypt are here specified, which speak aloud the power of God and his favor to Israel, as well as terror to his and their enemies. As,
[1.] The turning of the waters into blood; they had made themselves drunk with the bloods of God's people, even the infants, and now God gave them blood to drink, for they were worthy, v. 44.
[2.] The flies and frogs which infested them, mixtures of insects in swarms, in shoals, which devoured them, which destroyed them, v. 45. For God can make the weakest and most despicable animals instruments of his wrath when he pleases; what they want in strength may be made up in number.
[3.] The plague of locusts, which devoured their increase, and that which they had labored for, v. 46. They are called God's great army, Joel ii. 25.
[4.] The hail, which destroyed their trees, especially their vines, the weakest of trees (v. 47), and their cattle, especially their flocks of sheep, the weakest of their cattle, which were killed with hot thunder-bolts (v. 48), and the frost, or congealed rain (as the word signifies), was so violent that it destroyed even the sycamore-trees.
[5.] The death of the first-born was the last and sorest of the plagues of Egypt, and that which perfected the deliverance of Israel; it was first in intention (Exod. iv. 23), but last in execution; for, if gentler methods would have done the work, this would have been prevented: but it is here largely described, v. 49-51.

Psalm 78

49-56

49 He cast upon them the fierceness of his anger, wrath, and indignation, and trouble, by sending evil angels among them.

50 He made a way to his anger; he spared not their soul from death, but gave their life over to the pestilence;

51 And smote all the firstborn in Egypt; the chief of their strength in the tabernacles of Ham:

52 But made his own people to go forth like sheep, and guided them in the wilderness like a flock.

53 And he led them on safely, so that they feared not: but the sea overwhelmed their enemies.

54 And he brought them to the border of his sanctuary, even to this mountain, which his right hand had purchased.

55 He cast out the heathen also before them, and divided them an inheritance by line, and made the tribes of Israel to dwell in their tents.

56 Yet they tempted and provoked the most high God, and kept not his testimonies:

life itself. Nothing could stand in his way; he cleared a space in which to do execution upon his adversaries.

Verse 51. And smote all the firstborn in Egypt. No exceptions were made, the monarch bewailed his heir as did the menial at the mill. They smote the Lord's firstborn, even Israel, and he smites theirs. The chief of their strength in the tabernacles of Ham. Swinging his scythe over the field, death topped off the highest flowers. The tents of Ham knew each one its own peculiar sorrow, and were made to sympathies with the sorrows which had been ruthlessly inflicted upon the habitations of Israel. Thus curses come home to roost. Oppressors are repaid in their own coin, without the discount of a penny.

Verse 52. But made his own people to go forth like sheep. The contrast is striking, and ought never to have been forgotten by the people. The wolves were slain in heaps, the sheep were carefully gathered, and triumphantly delivered. The tables were turned, and the poor serfs became the honored people, while their oppressors were humbled before them.

Verse 53. And he led them on safely, so that they feared not. After the first little alarm, natural enough when they found themselves pursued by their old taskmasters, they plucked up courage and ventured forth boldly into the sea, and afterwards into the desert where no man dwelt. But the sea overwhelmed their enemies. They were gone, gone for ever, never to disturb the fugitives again. That tremendous blow effectually defended the tribes for forty years from any further attempt to drive them back.

Verse 54. And he brought them to the border of his sanctuary. He conducted them to the frontier of the Holy Land, where he intended the tabernacle to become the permanent symbol of his abode among his people. He did not leave them halfway upon their journey to their heritage; his power and wisdom preserved the nation till the palm trees of Jericho were within sight on the other side of the river.

Verse 55. He cast out the heathen also before them, or "he drove out the nations." Not only were armies routed, but whole peoples displaced. The iniquity of the Canaanites was full; their vices made them rot above ground; therefore, the land ate up its inhabitants, the hornets vexed them, the pestilence destroyed them, and the sword of the tribes completed the execution to which the justice of long provoked heaven had at length appointed them.

Verse 56. Yet they tempted and provoked the most high God. Change of condition had not altered their manners. They left their nomadic habits, but not their tendencies to wander from their God. Though every divine promise had been fulfilled to the letter, and the land flowing with milk and honey was actually their own, yet they tried the Lord again with unbelief, and provoked him with other sins.

Verse 57. But turned back. Turned over the old leaf, repeated the same offences, started aside like an ill made bow, were false and faithless to their best promises. And dealt unfaithfully like their fathers, proving themselves legitimate by manifesting the treachery of their sires. They were a new generation, but not a new nation—another race yet not another.

Verse 58. For they provoked him to anger with their high places. This was their first error—will worship, or the worship of God, otherwise than according to his command. Many think lightly of this, but it was no mean sin; and its tendencies to further offence are very powerful. The Lord would have his holy place remain as the only spot for sacrifice; and Israel, in willful rebellion, (no doubt glossed over by the plea of great devotion,) determined to have many altars upon many hills.

Verse 59. When God heard this, he was wroth. The mere report of it filled him with indignation; he could not bear it, he was incensed to the uttermost, and most justly so. And greatly abhorred Israel. He cast his idolatrous people from his favor, and left them to themselves, and their own devices. How could he have fellowship with idols? What concord hath Christ with which to us is incomprehensible. Both the heavenly and elect angels, and the fallen angels, are justly accounted the ministers or executors of calamity; but they are to be regarded as such in different senses. The former yield a prompt and willing obedience to God; but the latter, as they are always eagerly intent upon doing mischief, and would, if they could, turn the whole world upside down, are fit instruments for inflicting calamities upon men.

50, 51. He made a way to his anger. To take away all excuse from this ungrateful people, whom the most evident and striking proofs of the goodness of God which were presented before their eyes could not keep in their obedience to him, it is here again repeated that the wrath of God overflowed Egypt like an impetuous torrent. The miracle adverted to is the last which was there wrought, when God, by the powerful hand of his angel, slew, in one night, all the first-born of Egypt.

52-58

52. And he made his people to go forth like sheep. The Psalmist again celebrates God's fatherly love towards the chosen people, whom, as we have elsewhere remarked, he compares to a flock of sheep. They had no wisdom or power of their own to preserve and defend themselves; but God graciously condescended to perform towards them the office of a shepherd. It is a singular token of the love which he bore towards them, that he did not disdain to humble himself so far as to feed them as his own sheep. What could a multitude who had never been trained up to the art of war do against powerful and warlike enemies? So far from having learned the art of war, the people, as is well known, had been employed, when in Egypt, in mean and servile occupations, as if they had been condemned to toil under the earth in mines or in quarries.

53, 54. And he conducted them in safety, and they were not afraid. This does not imply that they relied on God confidently, and with tranquil minds, but that, having God for their guide and the guardian of their welfare, they had no just cause to be afraid. When at any time they were thrown into consternation, this was owing to their own unbelief.

55. He expelled the heathen from before them; and made them to fall into their part of the inheritance. These words are an explanation of the concluding sentence of the preceding verse: they describe the manner in which the land of Canaan was acquired, plainly intimating that the Israelites were not such a warlike race, nor those heathen nations so cowardly, as to render it an easy matter for the former to vanquish the latter, and that it would have been impossible for the former to have expelled the latter from the country, had they not been led on to victory under the conduct of God, and been aided by his power. Besides, it would have been unlawful for them to have taken possession of the country, had it not been the will of God that the first inhabitants should be deprived of it, and that strangers should be established in it in their room.

56. And they tempted and provoked the Most High God. Here they are upbraided for having, notwithstanding the many tokens of the divine favor by which they were

(2.) By these plagues on the Egyptians God made a way for his own people to go forth like sheep, distinguishing between them and the Egyptians, as the shepherd divides between the sheep and the goats, having set his own mark on these sheep by the blood of the lamb sprinkled on their door-posts. He made them go forth like sheep, not knowing whither they went, and guided them in the wilderness, as a shepherd guides his flock, with all possible care and tenderness, v. 52. He led them on safely, though in dangerous paths, so that they feared not, that is, they needed not to fear; they were indeed frightened at the Red Sea (Exod. xiv. 10), but that was said to them, and done for them, which effectually silenced their fears. But the sea overwhelmed their enemies that ventured to pursue them into it, v. 63. It was a lane to them, but a grave to their persecutors.

2. It is carried down as far as their settlement in Canaan (v. 54): He brought them to the border of his sanctuary, to that land in the midst of which he set up his sanctuary, which was, as it were, the center and metropolis, the crown and glory, of it. That is a happy land which is the border of God's sanctuary. It was the happiness of that land that there God was known, and there were his sanctuary and dwelling-place, Ps. lxxvi. 1, 2.

III. The sins of Israel after they were settled in Canaan, v. 56-58. The children were like their fathers, and brought their old corruptions into their new habitations. Though God had done so much for them, yet they tempted and provoked the most high God still. He gave them his testimonies, but they did not keep them; they began very promisingly, but they turned back, gave God good words, but dealt unfaithfully, and were like a deceitful bow, which seemed likely to send the arrow to the mark, but, when it is drawn, breaks, and drops the arrow at the archer's foot, or perhaps makes it recoil in his face. There was no hold of them, nor any confidence to be put in their promises or professions. They seemed sometimes devoted to God, but they presently turned aside, and provoked him to anger with their high places and their graven images. Idolatry was the sin that did most easily beset them, and which, though they often professed their repentance for, they as often relapsed into. It was spiritual adultery either to worship idols or to worship God by images, as if he had been an idol, and therefore by it they are said to move him to jealousy, Deut. xxxii. 16, 21.

IV. The judgments God brought upon them for these sins. Their place in Canaan would no more secure them in a sinful way than their descent from Israel. You only have I known of all the families of the earth, therefore I will punish you, Amos iii. 2. Idolatry is winked at among the Gentiles, but not in Israel,

1. God was displeased with them (v. 59): When God heard this, when he heard the cry of their iniquity, which came up before him, he was wroth, he took it very heinously, as well he might, and he greatly

Psalm 78

57-64
57 But turned back, and dealt unfaithfully like their fathers: they were turned aside like a deceitful bow.
58 For they provoked him to anger with their high places, and moved him to jealousy with their graven images.
59 When God heard this, he was wroth, and greatly abhorred Israel:
60 So that he forsook the tabernacle of Shiloh, the tent which he placed among men;
61 And delivered his strength into captivity, and his glory into the enemy's hand.
62 He gave his people over also unto the sword; and was wroth with his inheritance.
63 The fire consumed their young men; and their maidens were not given to marriage.
64 Their priests fell by the sword; and their widows made no lamentation.

Belial? Sin is in itself so offensive that it makes the sinner offensive too. Idols of any sort are highly abhorrent to God, and we must see to it that we keep ourselves from them through divine grace, for rest assured idolatry is not consistent with true grace in the heart.

Verse 60. So that he forsook the tabernacle of Shiloh, the tent which he placed among men. His glory would no more reveal itself there, he left Shiloh to become a complete ruin. At the door of that tent shameless sin had been perpetrated, and all around it idols had been adored, and therefore the glory departed and Ichabod was sounded as a word of dread concerning Shiloh and the tribe of Ephraim. Thus may the candlestick be removed though the candle is not quenched.

Verse 61. And delivered his strength into captivity. The ark was captured by the Philistines in battle, only because the Lord for the punishment of Israel chose to deliver it into their hands, otherwise they could have had no power at all against it. The token of the divine presence is here poetically called "his strength", and, indeed, the presence of the Lord is his strength among his people.

Verse 62. He gave his people over also unto the sword. They fell in battle because they were no longer aided by the divine strength. Sharp was the sword, but sharper still the cause of its being unsheathed. And was wroth with his inheritance. They were his still, and twice in this verse they are called so; yet his regard for them did not prevent his chastening them, even with a rod of steel.

Verse 63. The fire consumed their young men. As fire slew Nadab and Abihu literally, so the fire of divine wrath fell on the sons of Eli, who defiled the sanctuary of the Lord, and the like fire, in the form of war, consumed the flower of the people. And their maidens were not given to marriage. No nuptial hymn were sung, the bride lacked her bridegroom, the edge of the sword had cut the bands of their espousals, and left unmarried those who else had been extolled in hymns and congratulations.

Verse 64. Their priests fell by the sword. Hophni and Phineas were slain; they were among the chief in sin, and, therefore, they perished with the rest. Priesthood is no shelter for transgressors; the jeweled breastplate cannot turn aside the arrows of judgment. And their widows made no lamentation. Their private griefs were swallowed up in the greater national agony, because the ark of God was taken. As the maidens had no heart for the marriage song, so the widows had no spirit, even to utter the funeral wail. The dead were buried too often and too hurriedly to allow of the usual rites of lamentation.

Verse 65. The Lord awaked as one out of sleep. Justly inactive, he had suffered the enemy to triumph, his ark to be captured, and his people to be slain; but now he arouses himself, his heart is full of pity for his chosen, and anger against the insulting foe.

Verse 66. He smote his enemies in the hinder parts. The emerods rendered them ridiculous, and their numerous defeats made them yet more so. They fled but were overtaken and wounded in the back to their eternal disgrace. He put them to a perpetual reproach. Orientals are not very refined, and we can well believe that the haemorrhoids were the subject of many a taunt against the Philistines, as also were their frequent defeats by Israel until at last they were crushed under, never to exist again as a distinct nation.

Verse 67. Moreover he refused the tabernacle of Joseph. God had honored Ephraim, for to that tribe belonged Joshua the great conqueror, and Gideon the great judge, and within its borders was Shiloh the place of the ark and the sanctuary; but now the Lord would change all this and set up other rulers.

Verse 68. But chose the tribe of Judah. To give the nation another trial this tribe was elected to supremacy. This was according to Jacob's dying prophecy. Our Lord sprang out of Judah, and he it is whom his brethren shall praise. The Mount Zion which he loved. The tabernacle and ark were

JOHN CALVIN

distinguished, persevered in acting perfidiously: yea, even although God from time to time conferred upon them new benefits, to recover them to their allegiance to him, they, notwithstanding, by their rebellion, shook off his yoke.
57. The instability of the people is next expressed by a very apposite figure, which Hosea also employs in Hosea 7:16. As archers are deceived when they have a bow which is too weak, or ill bent, or crooked and flexible, so it is stated, that this people turned back, and slipped away by their deceitful and tortuous craftiness, that they might not be governed by the hand of God.
58. And they provoked him to anger with their high places. We have here adduced the species of defection by which the Israelites afforded incontestable evidence that they refused to be faithful to God, and to yield allegiance to him. They had been sufficiently, and more than sufficiently warned, that the service of God would be perverted and contaminated, unless they were regulated in every part of it by the Divine Word; and now, disregarding his whole law, they recklessly follow their own inventions.

59-66
59. God heard it, and was wroth. The prophet again shows that God, when he found that no good resulted from his long-suffering, which the people abused, yea, even treated with mockery, and perverted as an encouragement to greater excess in sinning, at length proceeded to inflict severe punishments upon them. The metaphor, which he borrows from earthly judges, is frequently to be met with in the Scriptures.
60. After it is said that Israel, whom God had loved so much, was become an abomination in his sight, it is added, that they were bereft of the presence of God, which is the only source of true felicity and comfort under calamities of every kind. God, then, is said to have abhorred Israel, when he permitted the ark of the covenant to be carried into another country, as if he intended by this to indicate that he had departed from Judea, and bidden the people farewell.
61. And he delivered his strength into captivity. In this verse, the same subject is prosecuted: it is declared, that the strength of God, by which the Israelites had been shielded and defended, was at that time in captivity.
62. And he shut up his people to the sword. Other parts of the calamity which befell Israel in the time of the high priest Eli are here mentioned. God, in permitting the ark to be carried away, showed that he had withdrawn his favor from them. This was also demonstrated from the fact, that all the flower of the people—those who were in the prime and blush of manhood—were consumed by the wrath of God: which is expressed by the fire devouring them.
63, 64. The great extent of this slaughter is heightened by another figure, which is, that for want of men, the maidens continued unmarried. This is the meaning of the clause, Their virgins were not applauded; the reference being to the nuptial songs which were wont to be sung at marriages in praise of the bride. To aggravate still more the unwonted and appalling nature of the calamity, it is added, that even the priests, whom

MATTHEW HENRY

abhorred Israel, whom he had greatly loved and delighted in. Those that had been the people of his choice became the generation of his wrath.
2. He deserted his tabernacle among them, and removed the defense which was upon that glory, v. 60. God never leaves us till we leave him, never withdraws till we have driven him from us. His name is Jealous, and he is a jealous God; and therefore no marvel if a people whom he had betrothed to himself be loathed and rejected, and he refuse to cohabit with them any longer, when they have embraced the bosom of a stranger. The tabernacle at Shiloh was the tent God had placed among men, in which God would in very deed dwell with men upon the earth; but, when his people treacherously forsook it, he justly forsook it, and then all its glory departed. Israel has small joy of the tabernacle without the presence of God in it.
3. He gave up all into the hands of the enemy. Those whom God forsakes become an easy prey to the destroyer. The Philistines are sworn enemies to the Israel of God, and no less so to the God of Israel, and yet God will make use of them to be a scourge to his people.
(1.) God permits them to take the ark prisoner, and carry it off as a trophy of their victory, to show that he had not only forsaken the tabernacle, but even the ark itself, which shall now be no longer a token of his presence (v. 61): He delivered his strength into captivity, as if it had been weakened and overcome, and his glory fell under the disgrace of being abandoned into the enemy's hand.
(2.) He suffers the armies of Israel to be routed by the Philistines (v. 62, 63): He gave his people over unto the sword, to the sword of his own justice and of the enemy's rage, for he was wroth with his inheritance; and that wrath of his was the fire which consumed their young men, in the prime of their time, by the sword or sickness, and made such a devastation of them that their maidens were not praised, that is, were not given in marriage (which is honorable in all), because there were no young men for them to be given to, and because the distresses and calamities of Israel were so many and great that the joys of marriage-solemnities were judged unseasonable, and it was said, Blessed is the womb that beareth not.
(3.) Even their priests, who attended the ark, fell by the sword, Hophni and Phinehas. Justly they fell, for they made themselves vile, and were sinners before the Lord exceedingly; and their priesthood was so far from being their protection that it aggravated their sin and hastened their fall. Justly did they fall by the sword, because they exposed themselves in the field of battle, without call or warrant. We throw ourselves out of God's protection when we go out of our place and out of the way of our duty. When the priests fell their widows made no lamentation, v. 64.
V. God's return, in mercy, to them, and his gracious appearances for them after this. We read not of their

Psalm 78

65-72

65 Then the LORD awaked as one out of sleep, and like a mighty man that shouteth by reason of wine.
66 And he smote his enemies in the hinder parts: he put them to a perpetual reproach.
67 Moreover he refused the tabernacle of Joseph, and chose not the tribe of Ephraim:
68 But chose the tribe of Judah, the mount Zion which he loved.
69 And he built his sanctuary like high palaces, like the earth which he hath established for ever.
70 He chose David also his servant, and took him from the sheepfolds:
71 From following the ewes great with young he brought him to feed Jacob his people, and Israel his inheritance.
72 So he fed them according to the integrity of his heart; and guided them by the skillfulness of his hands.

removed to Zion during the reign of David; no honor was left to the wayward Ephraimites. Hard by this mountain the Father of the Faithful had offered up his only son, and there in future days the great gatherings of his chosen seed would be, and therefore Zion is said to be lovely unto God.

Verse 69. And he built his sanctuary like high palaces. The tabernacle was placed on high, literally and spiritually it was a mountain of beauty. True religion was exalted in the land.

Verse 70. He chose David also his servant. It was an election of a sovereignly gracious kind, and it operated practically by making the chosen man a willing servant of the Lord. He was not chosen because he was a servant, but in order that he might be so. David always esteemed it to be a high honor that he was both elect of God, and a servant of God.

Verse 71. From following the ewes great with young he brought him to feed Jacob his people, and Israel his inheritance. Exercising the care and art of those who watch for the young lambs, David followed the ewes in their wanderings; the tenderness and patience thus acquired would tend to the development of characteristics most becoming in a king. To the man thus prepared, the office and dignity which God had appointed for him, came in due season, and he was enabled worthily to wear them.

Verse 72. So he fed them according to the integrity of his heart. David was upright before God, and never swerved in heart from the obedient worship of Jehovah. Whatever faults he had, he was unfeignedly sincere in his allegiance to Israel's superior king; he shepherded for God with honest heart. And guided them by the skillfulness of his hands. He was a sagacious ruler, and the psalmist magnifies the Lord for having appointed him. Under David, the Jewish kingdom rose to an honorable position among the nations, and exercised an influence over its neighbors. In closing the Psalm which has described the varying conditions of the chosen nation, we are glad to end so peacefully; with all noise of tumult or of sinful rites hushed into silence. After a long voyage over a stormy sea, the ark of the Jewish state rested on its Ararat, beneath a wise and gentle reign, to be wafted no more hither and thither by floods and gales. The psalmist had all along intended to make this his last stanza, and we too may be content to finish all our songs of love with the reign of the Lord's anointed.

God had taken under his special protection, perished indiscriminately with others. When it is said, that the widows made no lamentation, I would explain it as denoting, either that they themselves died first for sorrow, so that they had no opportunity of mourning for others, or else, that when led captive by their enemies, they were prohibited to mourn.
65. The figure of a drunken man may seem somewhat harsh; but the propriety of using it will appear, when we consider that it is employed in accommodation to the stupidity of the people. Had they been of a pure and clear understanding, God would not have thus transformed himself, and assumed a character foreign to his own.

67-72
67. And he rejected the tabernacle of Joseph. The meaning of the text is that when the ark was taken by the Philistines, God was, so to speak, asleep, having been made drunk by the sins of his people, so that he could no longer keep watch for their defense as he had been accustomed to do; and yet, that he did not continue long sunk in sleep, but that, whenever he saw the ungodly Philistines treating with mockery the glory of his majesty, this heinous insult awoke and provoked him, just as if a giant, having well supped, had awoke from his first sleep before he had recovered from the exciting effects of his wine; and that, at the same time, his anger had not been so provoked against this heathen and uncircumcised nation as to prevent him from exhibiting some signs of the chastisement which he had inflicted upon the wicked and ungrateful Israelites even to the end.
68. But he chose the tribe of Judah. The meaning is, that God preferred the tribe of Judah to all the rest of the people, and chose from it a king, whom he might set over all the Israelites as well as the Jews. And he chose the mountain of Zion, appointing a certain spot upon it to be the seat of his sanctuary.
69. And built his sanctuary like high places. In this verse, what is intimated is simply this, that Mount Zion was singularly beautified; which, however, ought to be referred to the heavenly pattern. It was not the will of God that the minds of his people should be entirely engrossed with the magnificence of the building, or with the pomp of outward ceremonies; but that they should be elevated to Christ.
70. And he chose David his servant. After having made mention of the temple, the prophet now proceeds to speak of the kingdom; for these two things were the chief signs of God's choice of his ancient people, and of his favor towards them; and Christ also hath appeared as our king and priest to bring a full and perfect salvation to us.
71. He took him from following the suckling ewes, etc. The grace of God is farther commended from the circumstance, that David, who was a keeper of sheep, was made the shepherd of the chosen people and heritage of God.
72. David had faithfully performed the duties of the trust committed to him. By this the prophet indirectly rebukes the ingratitude and perverseness of the people, who not only overturned the holy and inviolable order which God had established, but who had also, in shaking off his salutary yoke, thrown themselves into a state of miserable dispersion.

repentance and return to God, but God was grieved for the miseries of Israel (Judg. x. 16) and concerned for his own honor, fearing the wrath of the enemy, lest they should behave themselves strangely, Deut. xxxii. 27. And therefore then the Lord awaked as one out of sleep (v. 65), and like a mighty man that shouteth by reason of wine, not only like one that is raised out of sleep and recovers himself from the slumber which by drinking he was overcome with, who then regards that which before he seemed wholly to neglect, but like one that is refreshed with sleep, and whose heart is made glad by the sober and moderate use of wine, and is therefore the more lively and vigorous, and fit for business. When God had delivered the ark of his strength into captivity, as one jealous of his honor, he soon put forth the arm of his strength to rescue it, stirred up his strength to do great things for his people.
1. He plagued the Philistines who held the ark in captivity, v. 66. He smote them with emerods in the hinder parts, wounded them behind, as if they were fleeing from him, even when they thought themselves more than conquerors. He put them to reproach, and they themselves helped to make it a perpetual reproach by the golden images of their emerods, which they returned with the ark for a trespass-offering (1 Sam. vi. 5), to remain in perpetuam rei memoriam—as a perpetual memorial. Note, Sooner or later God will glorify himself by putting disgrace upon his enemies, even when they are most elevated with their successes.
2. He provided a new settlement for his ark after it had been some months in captivity and some years in obscurity. He did indeed refuse the tabernacle of Joseph; he never sent it back to Shiloh, in the tribe of Ephraim, v. 67. The ruins of that place were standing monuments of divine justice. God, see what I did to Shiloh, Jer. vii. 12. But he did not wholly take away the glory from Israel; the moving of the ark is not the removing of it. Shiloh has lost it, but Israel has not. God will have a church in the world, and a kingdom among men, though this or that place may have its candlestick removed; nay, the rejection of Shiloh is the election of Zion, as, long after, the fall of the Jews was the riches of the Gentiles, Rom. xi. 12. When God chose not the tribe of Ephraim, of which tribe Joshua was, he chose the tribe of Judah (v. 68), because of that tribe Jesus was to be, who is greater than Joshua. Kirjath-jearim, the place to which the ark was brought after its rescue out of the hands of the Philistines, was in the tribe of Judah. There it took possession of that tribe; but thence it was removed to Zion, the Mount Zion which he loved (v. 68), which was beautiful for situation, the joy of the whole earth; there it was that he built his sanctuary like high palaces and like the earth, v. 69. David indeed erected only a tent for the ark, but a temple was then designed and prepared for, and finished by his son.

Psalm 79

Title
A Psalm of Asaph.

1-6
1 O God, the heathen are
come into thine inheri-
tance; thy holy temple have
they defiled; they have laid
Jerusalem on heaps.
2 The dead bodies of thy
servants have they given to
be meat unto the fowls of
the heaven, the flesh of thy
saints unto the beasts of the
earth.
3 Their blood have they
shed like water round
about Jerusalem; and there
was none to bury them.
4 We are become a
reproach to our neighbors,
a scorn and derision to
them that are round about
us.
5 How long, LORD? wilt
thou be angry for ever?
shall thy jealousy burn like
fire?
6 Pour out thy wrath
upon the heathen that have
not known thee, and upon
the kingdoms that have not
called upon thy name.

Psalm 79

TITLE AND SUBJECT. A Psalm of Asaph. A Psalm of complaint such as Jeremiah might have written amid the ruins of the beloved city. It evidently treats of times of invasion, oppression, and national overthrow. Asaph was a patriotic poet, and was never more at home than when he rehearsed the history of his nation. Would to God that we had national poets whose song should be of the Lord.
DIVISION. From Ps 79:1-4 the complaint is poured out, from Ps 79:5-12 prayer is presented, and, in the closing verse, praise is promised.

EXPOSITION
Verse 1. O God, the heathen are come into thine inheritance. It is the cry of amazement at sacrilegious intrusion; as if the poet were struck with horror. The stranger pollutes thine hallowed courts with his tread. All Canaan is thy land, but thy foes have ravaged it. Thy holy temple have they defiled. Into the inmost sanctuary they have profanely forced their way, and there behaved themselves arrogantly. Thus, the holy land, the holy house, and the holy city, were all polluted by the uncircumcised.
Verse 2. "The dead bodies of thy servants have they given to be meat unto the fowls of the heaven, the flesh of thy saints unto the beasts of the earth." The enemy cared not to bury the dead, and there was not a sufficient number of Israel left alive to perform the funeral rites; therefore, the precious relics of the departed were left to be devoured of vultures and torn by wolves. Beasts on which man could not feed fed on him. The flesh of creation's Lord became meat for carrion crows and hungry dogs. Dire are the calamities of war, yet have they happened to God's saints and servants.
Verse 3. "Their blood have they shed like water round about Jerusalem." The invaders slew men as if their blood was of no more value than so much water; they poured it forth as lavishly as when the floods deluge the plains. The city of holy peace became a field of blood. "And there was none to bury them." The few who survived were afraid to engage in the task. This was a serious trial and grievous horror to the Jews, who evinced much care concerning their burials.
Verse 4. "We are become a reproach to our neighbors." Those who have escaped the common foe make a mockery of us, they fling our disasters into our face, and ask us, "Where is your God?" Pity should be shown to the afflicted, but in too many cases it is not so, for a hard logic argues that those who suffer more than ordinary calamities must have been extraordinary sinners. Neighbors especially are often the reverse of neighborly; the nearer they dwell the less they sympathize. It is most pitiable it should be so.
Verse 5. "How long, Lord?" Will there be no end to these chastisements? They are most sharp and overwhelming; wilt thou much longer continue them? "Wilt thou be angry for ever?" Is thy mercy gone so that thou wilt for ever smite? "Shall thy jealousy burn like fire?" There was great cause for the Lord to be jealous, since idols had been set up, and Israel had gone aside from his worship, but the psalmist begs the Lord not to consume his people utterly as with fire, but to abate their woes.
Verse 6. "Pour out thy wrath upon the heathen that have not known thee." If thou must smite look further afield; spare thy children and strike thy foes. There are lands where thou art in no measure acknowledged; be pleased to visit these first with thy judgments, and let thine erring Israel have a respite. "And upon the kingdoms that have not called upon thy name." Hear us the prayerful, and avenge thyself upon the prayerless. Sometimes providence appears to deal much more severely with the righteous than with the wicked, and this verse is a bold appeal founded upon such an appearance. It in effect says—Lord, if thou must empty out the vials of thy wrath, begin with those who have no measure of regard for thee, but are

JOHN CALVIN

Psalm 79

1-4

1-3. O God! the heathen have come into thy inheritance. Here the prophet, in the person of the faithful, complains that the temple was defiled, and the city destroyed. In the second and third verses, he complains that the saints were murdered indiscriminately, and that their dead bodies were cast forth upon the face of the earth, and deprived of the honor of burial. Almost every word expresses the cruelty of these enemies of the Church. When it is considered that God had chosen the land of Judea to be a possession to his own people, it seemed inconsistent with this choice to abandon it to the heathen nations, that they might ignominiously trample it under foot, and lay it waste at their pleasure. The prophet, therefore, complains that when the heathen came into the heritage of God, the order of nature was, as it were, inverted.

4. We have been a reproach to our neighbors. Here another complaint is uttered, to excite the mercy of God. The more proudly the ungodly mock and triumph over us, the more confidently may we expect that our deliverance is near; for God will not bear with their insolence when it breaks forth so audaciously; especially when it redounds to the reproach of his holy name.

5-9

5 How long, O Jehovah! wilt thou be wroth for ever? I have already observed that these two expressions, how long and for ever, when joined together, denote a lengthened and an uninterrupted continuance of calamities; and that there is no appearance, when looking to the future, of their coming to a termination. We may, therefore, conclude that this complaint was not ended within a month or two after persecution against the Church commenced, but at a time when the hearts of the faithful were almost broken through the weariness produced by prolonged suffering.

6. Pour out thy fury upon the heathen, who have not known thee. This prayer is apparently inconsistent with the rule of charity; for, while we feel anxious about our own calamities, and desire to be delivered from them, we ought to desire that others may be relieved as well as ourselves. It would seem, therefore, that the faithful are to be blamed in here wishing the destruction of unbelievers, for whose salvation they ought rather to have been solicitous.

8. Remember not against us the iniquities of former times. The godly Jews here confirm the sentiment which they had before briefly and obscurely touched upon, namely, that they had justly deserved the chastisements which had been inflicted upon them. And they present this prayer, because they could only get relief from their calamities by obtaining reconciliation with God. This is the sovereign remedy for every kind of adversity; for so long as he is angry with even our prosperity turns out to be unproductive of advantage and happiness.

The contrast between the expressions, make haste, and the iniquities of former times, is worthy of notice. Had God called the Israelites to a strict account for all the sins which they had

MATTHEW HENRY

Psalm 79

1-5 Mournful complaints.

I. They complain here of the anger of their enemies and the outrageous fury of the oppressor, exerted,

1. Against places, v. 1. They did all the mischief they could,

(1.) To the holy land; they invaded that, and made inroads into it: "The heathen have come into thy inheritance, to plunder that, and lay it waste."

(2.) To the holy city: They have laid Jerusalem on heaps, heaps of rubbish, such heaps as are raised over graves, so some. The inhabitants were buried in the ruins of their own houses, and their dwelling places became their sepulchers, their long homes.

2. Against persons, against the bodies of God's people; and further their malice could not reach.

(1.) They were prodigal of their blood, and killed them without mercy; their eye did not spare, nor did they give any quarter (v. 3): Their blood have they shed like water, wherever they met with them, round about Jerusalem, in all the avenues to the city; whoever went out or came in was waited for of the sword. Abundance of human blood was shed, so that the channels of water ran with blood. And they shed it with no more reluctancy or regret than if they had spilt so much water, little thinking that every drop of it will be reckoned for in the day when God shall make inquisition for blood.

(2.) They were abusive to their dead bodies. When they had killed them they would let none bury them. Nay, those that were buried, even the dead bodies of God's servants, the flesh of his saints, whose names and memories they had a particular spite at, they dug up again, and gave them to be meat to the fowls of the heaven and to the beasts of the earth; or, at least, they left those so exposed whom they slew; they hung them in chains, which was in a particular manner grievous to the Jews to see, because God had given them an express law against this, as a barbarous thing, Deut. xxi. 23. This inhuman usage of Christ's witnesses is foretold (Rev. xi. 9), and thus even the dead bodies were witnesses against their persecutors.

3. Against their names (v. 4): "We that survive have become a reproach to our neighbors; they all study to abuse us and load us with contempt, and represent us as ridiculous, or odious, or both, upbraiding us with our sins and with our sufferings, or giving the lie to our relation to God and expectations from him; so that we have become a scorn and derision to those that are round about us."

II. They wonder more at God's anger, v. 5. This they discern in the anger of their neighbors, and this they complain most of: How long, Lord, wilt thou be angry? Shall it be for ever? This intimates that they desired no more than that God would be reconciled to them, that his anger might be turned away, and then the remainder of men's wrath would be restrained. Note,

Psalm 79

7-13

7 For they have devoured Jacob, and laid waste his dwelling place.

8 O remember not against us former iniquities: let thy tender mercies speedily prevent us: for we are brought very low.

9 Help us, O God of our salvation, for the glory of thy name: and deliver us, and purge away our sins, for thy name's sake.

10 Wherefore should the heathen say, Where is their God? let him be known among the heathen in our sight by the revenging of the blood of thy servants which is shed.

11 Let the sighing of the prisoner come before thee; according to the greatness of thy power preserve thou those that are appointed to die;

12 And render unto our neighbors sevenfold into their bosom their reproach, wherewith they have reproached thee, O Lord.

13 So we thy people and sheep of thy pasture will give thee thanks for ever: we will shew forth thy praise to all generations.

openly up in arms against thee; and be pleased to spare thy people, who are thine notwithstanding all their sins.

Verse 7. "For they have devoured Jacob." The oppressor would quite eat up the saints if he could. If these lions do not swallow us, it is because the Lord has sent his angel and shut the lions' mouths. "And laid waste his dwelling place," or his pasture. The invader left no food for man or beast, but devoured all as the locust. The tender mercies of the wicked are cruel.

Verse 8. "O remember not against us former iniquities." Sins accumulate against nations. Generations lay up stores of transgressions to be visited upon their successors; hence this urgent prayer. In Josiah's days the most earnest repentance was not able to avert the doom which former long years of idolatry had sealed against Judah. Every man has reason to ask for an act of oblivion for his past sins, and every nation should make this a continual prayer.

Verse 9. "Help us O God of our salvation, for the glory of thy name." This is masterly pleading. No argument has such force as this. God's glory was tarnished in the eyes of the heathen by the defeat of his people, and the profanation of his temple; therefore, his distressed servants implore his aid, that his great name may no more be the scorn of blaspheming enemies.

Verse 10. "Wherefore should the heathen say, Where is their God?" Why should those impious mouths be filled with food so sweet to them, but so bitter to us? When the afflictions of God's people become the derision of sinners, and cause them to ridicule religion, we have good ground for expostulation with the Lord.

Verse 11. "Let the sighing of the prisoner come before thee." When thy people cannot sing, and dare not shout aloud, then let their silent sigh ascend into thine ear, and secure for them deliverance. These words are suitable for the afflicted in a great variety of conditions; men of experience will know how to adapt them to their own position and to use them in reference to others.

"According to the greatness of thy power preserve thou those that are appointed to die." Faith grows while it prays; the appeal to the Lord's tender mercy is here supplemented by another addressed to the divine power, and the petitioner rises from a request for those who are brought low, to a prayer for those who are on the verge of death, set apart as victims for the slaughter. How consoling is it to desponding believers to reflect that God can preserve even those who bear the sentence of death in themselves.

Verse 12. "And render unto our neighbors sevenfold into their bosom their reproach, wherewith they have reproached thee, O Lord." They denied thine existence, mocked thy power, insulted thy worship, and destroyed thy house; up, therefore, O Lord, and make them feel to the full that thou art not to be mocked with impunity. Pour into their laps good store of shame because they dared insult the God of Israel. Recompense them fully, till they have received the perfect number of punishments. It will be so. The wish of the text will become matter of fact. The Lord will avenge his own elect though he bear long with them.

Verse 13. "So we thy people and sheep of thy pasture will give thee thanks for ever: we will shew forth thy praise to all generations." The gratitude of the church is lasting as well as deep. On her tablets are memorials of great deliverances, and, as long as she shall exist, her sons will rehearse them with delight. We have a history which will survive all other records, and it is bright in every line with the glory of the Lord. From the direst calamities God's glory springs, and the dark days of his people become the prelude to unusual displays of the Lord's love and power.

committed during three or four hundred years before, the time of their deliverance would have been long delayed. The faithful, therefore, beseech him to forget their former offenses, and to make haste to succor them.

9. Help O God of our salvation! They again repeat in this verse, that whatever afflictions they endured were to be traced to the anger of God, and that they could have no comfort under them unless He were reconciled to them. Being deeply sensible that they had committed many transgressions, to strengthen their hope of obtaining pardon, they employ a variety of expressions.

10-13

10. Why should the heathen say, Where is their God? Here the people of God, in urging his name as a plea at the throne of grace: do so in a different sense from that in which they had urged it before. He extends his compassion towards us for his own name's sake; for, as he is merciful, and will have our mouths stopped, that he alone may be accounted righteous, he freely pardons our sins. But here, the faithful beseech him that he would not allow his sacred name to be exposed to the blasphemies and insults of the wicked. From this we are taught that we do not pray in a right manner, unless a concern about our own salvation, and zeal for the glory of God, are inseparably joined together in our exercise.

From the second clause of the verse, the same question may be raised which we have just now answered. Although God declares that he will execute vengeance upon our enemies, we are not warranted to thirst for revenge when we are injured. Let us remember that this form of prayer was not dictated for all men indiscriminately, but that, under the guidance and instruction of the Holy Spirit, they might plead the cause of the whole Church, in common, against the wicked.

11. Let the sighing of the prisoner come before thee. The people of God, I have no doubt, were in captivity when the Holy Spirit endited this prayer; and, therefore, the name of prisoners is applied to them all in general, because they were so shut up within the bounds of Assyria and Chaldea.

12. And render to our neighbors sevenfold. The faithful show clearly that they are not so much moved by the injuries done to themselves personally, as inflamed with a holy zeal when they see the sacred name of God blasphemed, and, as it were, torn in pieces by the wicked. If this affection reign in our hearts, it will easily moderate the ungovernableness of our flesh, and if the wisdom of the Spirit is added to it, our prayers will be in strict accordance with the just judgment of God.

13. In the last verse, the pious Jews declare that the fruit of their deliverance will be, that the name of God will be celebrated; and we ought not to desire our preservation or welfare for any other end. When he freely bestows upon us all things, the design for which he does this is, that his goodness may be made known and exalted. Now, these sufferers engage to make a grateful acknowledgement of their deliverance, and declare that this will not be done merely for a short time, but that the remembrance of it will be transmitted to their posterity, and pass, in continued succession, from age to age to the end of the world.

Those who desire God's favor as better than life cannot but dread and deprecate his wrath as worse than death.

6-13 Petitions for succor and relief; petitions for deliverance.

The petitions here put up to God are very suitable to the present distresses of the church, and they have pleas to enforce them, interwoven with them, taken mostly from God's honor.

I. They pray that God would so turn away his anger from them as to turn it upon those that persecuted and abused them (v. 6): "Pour out thy wrath, the full vials of it, upon the heathen; let them wring out the dregs of it, and drink them." This prayer is in effect a prophecy, in which the wrath of God is revealed from heaven against all ungodliness and unrighteousness of men.

II. They pray for the pardon of sin, which they own to be the procuring cause of all their calamities. How unrighteous soever men were, God was righteous in permitting them to do what they did.

III. They pray that God would work deliverance for them, and bring their troubles to a good end and that speedily: Let thy tender mercies speedily prevent us, v. 8. They had no hopes but from God's mercies, his tender mercies; their case was so deplorable that they looked upon themselves as the proper objects of divine compassion, and so near to desperate that, unless divine mercy did speedily interpose to prevent their ruin, they were undone. This whets their importunity: "Lord, help us; Lord, deliver us; help us under our troubles, that we may bear them well; help us out of our troubles, that the spirit may not fail. Deliver us from sin, from sinking."

IV. They pray that God would avenge them on their adversaries for their cruelty and barbarity (v. 10): "Let the avenging of our blood" (according to the ancient law, Gen. ix. 6) "be known among the heathen; let them be made sensible that what judgments are brought upon them are punishments of the wrong they have done to us; let this be in our sight, and by this means let God be known among the heathen as the God to whom vengeance belongs (Ps. xciv. 1) and the God that espouses his people's cause."

V. They pray that God would find out a way for the rescue of his poor prisoners, especially the condemned prisoners, v. 11.

Lastly, They promise the returns of praise for the answers of prayer (v. 13): So we will give thee thanks for ever. Observe how they plead this with God: "Lord, appear for us against our enemies; for, if they get the better, they will blaspheme thee (v. 12); but, if we be delivered, we will praise thee."

Note, Those lives that are entirely devoted to God's praise are assuredly taken under his protection.

Psalm 80

Title
To the chief Musician upon Shoshannim Eduth. A Psalm of Asaph.

1-6
1 Give ear, O Shepherd of Israel, thou that leadest Joseph like a flock; thou that dwellest between the cherubims, shine forth.
2 Before Ephraim and Benjamin and Manasseh stir up thy strength, and come and save us.
3 Turn us again, O God, and cause thy face to shine; and we shall be saved.
4 O LORD God of hosts, how long wilt thou be angry against the prayer of thy people?
5 Thou feedest them with the bread of tears; and givest them tears to drink in great measure.
6 Thou makest us a strife unto our neighbors: and our enemies laugh among themselves.

Psalm 80

TITLE. To the Chief Musician upon Shoshannim Eduth. For the fourth time we have a song upon Shoshannim, or the lilies; the former ones being Psalms 45, 60, and 69. Why this title is given it would be difficult to say in every case, but the delightfully poetical form of the present Psalm may well justify the charming title. Eduth signifies testimony. The Psalm is a testimony of the church as a "lily among thorns." Some interpreters understand the present title to refer to an instrument of six strings, and Schleusner translates the two words, "the hexachord of testimony." It may be that further research will open up to us these "dark sayings upon a harp." We shall be content to accept them as evidence that sacred song was not lightly esteemed in the days of old. A Psalm of Asaph. A latter Asaph we should suppose, who had the unhappiness to live, like the "last minstrel," in evil times. If by the Asaph of David's day, this Psalm was written in the spirit of prophecy, for it sings of times unknown to David.
DIVISION. The Psalm divides itself naturally at the refrain which occurs three times: "Turn us again, O God," etc. Ps 80:1-3 is an opening address to the Lord God of Israel; from Ps 80:4-7 is a lamentation over the national woe, and from Ps 80:8-19 the same complaint is repeated, the nation being represented in a beautiful allegory as a vine. It is a mournful Psalm, and its lilies are lilies of the valley.

EXPOSITION
Verse 1. "Give ear, O Shepherd of Israel." Hear thou the bleatings of thy suffering flock. The name is full of tenderness, and hence is selected by the troubled psalmist: broken hearts delight in names of grace. Good old Jacob delighted to think of God as the Shepherd of Israel, and this verse may refer to his dying expression: "From thence is the Shepherd, the stone of Israel."
Verse 2. "Before Ephraim and Benjamin and Manasseh stir up thy strength, and come and save us." It is wise to mention the names of the Lord's people in prayer, for they are precious to him. Jesus bears the names of his people on his breastplate. Just as the mention of the names of his children has power with a father, so it is with the Lord.
Verse 3. "Turn us again, O God." It is not so much said, "turn our captivity," but "turn us." All will come right if we are right. The best turn is not that of circumstances but of character. When the Lord turns his people he will soon turn their condition. It needs the Lord himself to do this, for conversion is as divine a work as creation; and those who have been once turned unto God, if they at any time backslide, as much need the Lord to turn them again as to turn them at the first.
Verse 4. "O Lord God of Hosts, how long wilt thou be angry against the prayer of thy people?" How long shall the smoke of thy wrath drown the smoking incense of our prayers? Prayer would fain enter thy holy place, but they wrath battles with it, and prevents its entrance. That God should be angry with us when sinning seems natural enough, but that he should be angry even with our prayers is a bitter grief.
Verse 5. "Thou feedest them with the bread of tears." Their meat is seasoned with brine distilled from weeping eyes. Their meals, which were once such pleasant seasons of social merriment, are now like funeral feasts to which each man contributes his bitter morsel. Thy people ate bread of wheat before, but now they receive from thine own hand no better diet than bread of tears.
Verse 6. "Thou makest us a strife unto our neighbors." Always jealous and malicious, Edom and Moab exulted over Israel's troubles, and then fell to disputing about their share of the spoil. A neighbor's jeer is ever most cutting, especially if a man has been superior to them, and claimed to possess more grace. None are neighborly as envious neighbors. "And our enemies laugh among themselves." They find mirth in our misery, comedy

JOHN CALVIN

Psalm 80

1-3
1. Hearken, O Shepherd of Israel! The prophet, previous to his naming Manasseh and Ephraim, makes mention of Joseph; and why does he speak of Joseph rather than of Judah, but because it was his design to treat separately of the kingdom of Israel, the government of which was in the family and posterity of Joseph? Nor, since God sent special prophets among them, after he had stricken them with his rods, is there any inconsistency when, at the same time, the prayer is added, That God would gather together the remnant to himself. Moreover, that they might not delude themselves by trusting in their spurious worship, the prophet, by applying to God the appellation of Him who sitteth between the Cherubim, calls them back to the pure doctrine of the law.
3. Turn us again, O God! The meaning of this prayer is, Restore us to our former state. They had petitioned, in the preceding verse, that God would stir up his strength in the sight of Ephraim and Manasseh; and now they complain that they are but castaways until God succor them, and remedy their miserable dispersion.

4-7
4. O Jehovah, God of Hosts! God having in the Scriptures freely promised, and so often assured us, that the prayers of his people will not be disappointed, it may excite our surprise to find the faithful here alleging before him, that he continues unpacified, although they betake themselves to him. They complain not only that they are not heard, but also that he is angry, when they call upon him; as if he purposely rejected this religious service.
5. Thou hast fed us with bread of tears, etc. By these forms of expression, they depict the greatness of their grief, and the long continuance of their calamities; as if they had said, We are so filled with sorrow, that we can contain no more.
6. They add, in the following verse that they were made a strife to their neighbors This admits of being explained in two ways. It means either that their neighbors had taken up a quarrel against them; or that, having obtained the victory over them, they were contending about the spoil, as is usually the case in such circumstances, each being eager to drag it to himself.
7. The seventh verse is a repetition of the third; and this repetition is undoubtedly intended as a means of surmounting every obstacle. God did not here intend to endite for his people a vain repetition of words: his object was to encourage them, when bowed down under the load of their calamities, boldly to rise up, heavy though the load might be. This ground of support was often presented to them; and it is repeated the third time in the concluding verse of the psalm.

8-13
8. Thou hast brought a vine out of Egypt. Under the figure of a vine, the singular grace which God was graciously

MATTHEW HENRY

Psalm 80

1-7 Mournful complaints.
The psalmist here, in the name of the church, applies to God by prayer, with reference to the present afflicted state of Israel.
I. He entreats God's favor for them (v. 1, 2); that is all in all to the sanctuary when it is desolate, and is to be sought in the first place. Observe,
1. How he eyes God in his address as the Shepherd of Israel, whom he had called the sheep of his pasture (Ps. lxxix. 13), under whose guidance and care Israel was, as the sheep are under the care and conduct of the shepherd.
2. What he expects and desires from God, that he would give ear to the cry of their miseries and of their prayers, that he would shine forth both in his own glory and in favor and kindness to his people, that he would show himself and smile on them, that he would sir up his strength, that he would excite it and exert it.
II. He complains of God's displeasure against them. God was angry, and he dreads that more than any thing, v. 4.
1. It was great anger. He apprehended that God was angry against the prayer of his people, not only that he was angry notwithstanding their prayers, by which they hoped to turn away his wrath from them, but that he was angry with their prayers, though they were his own people that prayed.
2. It was anger that had continued a great while: "How long wilt thou be angry? We have still continued praying and yet are still under thy frowns." Now the tokens of God's displeasure which they had been long under were both their sorrow and shame.
III. He prays earnestly for converting grace in order to their acceptance with God, and their salvation: Turn us again, O God! v. 3. Turn us again, O God of hosts! (v. 7) and then cause thy face to shine and we shall be saved. It is the burden of the song, for we have it again, v. 19. They are conscious to themselves that they have gone astray from God and their duty, and have turned aside into sinful ways, and that it was this that provoked God to hide his face from them and to give them up into the hand of their enemies; and therefore they desire to begin their work at the right end: "Lord, turn us to thee in a way of repentance and reformation, and then, no doubt, thou wilt return to us in a way of mercy and deliverance."

8-19 The desolated vine.
The psalmist is here presenting his suit for the Israel of God, and pressing it home at the throne of grace, pleading with God for mercy and grace for them. The church is here represented as a vine (v. 8, 14) and a vineyard, v. 15. The root of this vine is Christ, Rom. xi. 18. The branches are believers, John xv. 5. The church is like a vine, weak and needing support, unsightly and having an unpromising outside, but spreading and fruitful, and its fruit most excellent. The

Psalm 80

7-12
7 Turn us again, O God of hosts, and cause thy face to shine; and we shall be saved.
8 Thou hast brought a vine out of Egypt: thou hast cast out the heathen, and planted it.
9 Thou preparedst room before it, and didst cause it to take deep root, and it filled the land.
10 The hills were covered with the shadow of it, and the boughs thereof were like the goodly cedars.
11 She sent out her boughs unto the sea, and her branches unto the river.
12 Why hast thou then broken down her hedges, so that all they which pass by the way do pluck her?

in our tragedy, salt for their wit in the brine of our tears, amusement in our amazement. It is devilish to sport with another's griefs; but it is the constant habit of the world which lieth in the wicked one to make merry with the saints' tribulations; the seed of the serpent follow their progenitor and rejoice in evil.
Verse 7. "Turn us again, O God of hosts." The prayer rises in the form of its address to God. He is here the God of Hosts. The more we approach the Lord in prayer and contemplation the higher will our ideas of him become.
Verse 8. "Thou hast brought a vine out of Egypt." There it was in unfriendly soil: the waters of the Nile watered it not, but were as death to its shoots, while the inhabitants of the land despised it and trampled it down. Glorious was the right hand of the Lord when with power and great wonders he removed his pleasant plant in the teeth of those who sought its destruction.
Verse 9. "Thou preparedst room before it." The weeds, brambles, and huge stones were cleared; the Amorites, and their brethren in iniquity, were made to quit the scene, their forces were routed, their kings slain, their cities captures, and Canaan became like a plot of land, made ready for a vineyard.
Verse 10. "The hills were covered with the shadow of it." Israel dwelt up the mountains' summits, cultivating every foot of soil. The nation multiplied and became so great that other lands felt its influence, or were shadowed by it.
Verse 11. "She sent out her boughs unto the sea." Along the Mediterranean and, perhaps, across its waters, Israel's power was felt. "And her branches unto the river." On her Eastern side she pushed her commerce even to the Euphrates. Those were brave days for Israel, and would have continued, had not sin cut them short. When the church pleases the Lord, her influence becomes immense, far beyond the proportion which her numbers or her power would lead us to expect; but, alas! when the Lord leaves her she becomes as worthless, useless, and despised as an untended vine, which is of all plants the most valueless.
Verse 12. "Why hast thou then broken down her hedges?" Thou hast withdrawn protection from her after caring for her with all this care; wherefore is this, O Lord? A vine unprotected is exposed to every form of injury; none regard it, all prey upon it: such was Israel when given over to her enemies; such has the church full often been. "So that all they which pass by the way do pluck her." Her cruel neighbors have a pluck at her, and marauding bands, like roaming beasts, must needs pick at her. With God no enemy can harm us, without him none are so weak as to be unable to do us damage.
Verse 13. The boar out of the wood doth waste it. Such creatures are famous for rending and devouring vines. Babylon, like a beast from the marshes of the Euphrates, came up and wasted Judah and Israel. Fierce peoples, comparable to wild swine of the forest, warred with the Jewish nation, until it was gored and torn like a vine destroyed by greedy hogs. And the wild beast of the field doth devour it. First one foe and then another wreaked vengeance on the nation, neither did God interpose to chase them away. Ruin followed ruin; the fox devoured the young shoots which had been saved from the damage wrought by the boar. Alas, poor land. How low wast thou brought! An oak or cedar might have been crushed by such ravages, but how canst thou endure it, O weak and tender vine? See what evils follow in the train of sin, and how terrible a thing it is for a people to be forsaken of their God.
Verse 14. Return, we beseech thee, O God of hosts. Turn thyself to us as well as us to thee. Thou hast gone from us because of our sins, come back to us, for we sigh and cry after thee. Or, if it be too much to ask thee to come then do at least give us some consideration and cast an eye upon our griefs. Look down from heaven, and behold, and visit this vine. Do not close thine eyes; it is thy vine, do not utterly turn away from it as though it were quite gone from thy mind. Great Husbandman, at least note the mischief

pleased to exercise towards his people after he had redeemed them is celebrated; and this powerfully contributed to inspire them with the hope of being heard. For which of us can be so presumptuous as to dare to come into the presence of God until he himself has previously invited us? Now, he allures us to himself both by his benefits and by his word. The object in view in now presenting his liberality before him is, that he should not leave unfinished the work of his hands which he had commenced. It is indeed true that, without his word, the benefits which he has conferred upon us would make a faint impression upon our hearts; but when experience is added to the testimony of his word, it greatly encourages us. Now, the redemption of which mention is here made was inseparably connected with the covenant of God; for he had, even four hundred years before, entered into covenant with Abraham, in which he promised the deliverance of his seed. What is stated amounts in short to this, that it is unbecoming that God should now suffer the vine which he had planted and cultivated so carefully with his own hand to be wasted by wild beasts. God's covenant was not made to last only for a few days, or for a short time: when he adopted the children of Abraham, he took them under his keeping for ever.

12. Why then hast thou broken down its hedges? This is the application of the similitude; for nothing seems more inconsistent than that God should abandon the vine which he had planted with his own hand, to be rooted up by wild beasts. It is true that he often threatened and forewarned the people by his prophets that he would do this; but what constrained him to inflict upon them so strange and dreadful a species of punishment was, that he might render their ingratitude the more detestable. At the same time, it is not without reason that true believers are enjoined to take encouragement from such distinguished liberality on the part of God; that, even in the midst of this rooting up, they might at least hope that He, who never forsakes the work of his own hands, would graciously extend his care towards them, (Psalm 138:8.) The people were brought to desolation, on account of their own incurable obstinacy; but God did not fail to save a small number of shoots, by means of which he afterwards restored his vine. This form of supplicating pardon was, indeed, set forth for the use of the whole people, with the view of preventing a horrible destruction. But as very few sought to appease the wrath of God by truly humbling themselves before him, it was enough that these few were delivered from destruction, that from them a new vine might afterwards spring up and flourish. The indignity which was done to the Church is aggravated from the contrast contained in the words, when God, on the one hand, is exhibited to us as a vine-keeper, and when the destroyers of this vine, on the other, are represented to be not only all that pass by, but also the wild boars and other savage beasts

14-19

14. Return, I beseech thee, O God of Hosts! In these words it is intended to teach, that we ought not to yield to

church is a choice and noble vine; we have reason to acknowledge the goodness of God that he has planted such a vine in the wilderness of this world, and preserved it to this day. Now observe here,

I. How the vine of the Old-Testament church was planted at first. It was brought out of Egypt with a high hand; the heathen were cast out of Canaan to make room for it, seven nations to make room for that one. Thou didst sweep before it (so some read v. 9), to make clear work; the nations were swept away as dirt with the besom of destruction. God, having made room for it, and planted it, cause it to take deep root by a happy establishment of their government both in church and state, which was so firm that, though their neighbors about them often attempted it, they could not prevail to pluck it up.

II. How it spread and flourished.

1. The land of Canaan itself was fully peopled. At first they were not so numerous as to replenish it, Exod. xxiii. 29. But in Solomon's time Judah and Israel were many as the sand of the sea; the land was filled with them, and yet such a fruitful land that it was not over-stocked, v. 10. The hills of Canaan were covered with their shadow, and the branches, though they extended themselves far, like those of the vine, yet were not weak like them, but as strong as those of the goodly cedars. Israel not only had abundance of men, but those mighty men of velour.

2. They extended their conquests and dominion to the neighboring countries (v. 11): She sent out her boughs to the sea, the great sea westward, and her branches to the river, to the river of Egypt southward, the river of Damascus northward, or rather the river Euphrates eastward, Gen. xv. 18.

III. How it was wasted and ruined: "Lord, thou hast done great things for this vine, and why shall it be all undone again? If it were a plant not of God's planting, it were not strange to see it rooted up; but will God desert and abandon that which he himself gave being to?" v. 12. Why hast thou then broken down her hedges? There was a good reason for this change in God's way towards them. This noble vine had become the degenerate plant of a strange vine (Jer. ii. 21), to the reproach of its great owner, and then no marvel if he took away its hedge (Isa. v. 5); yet God's former favors to this vine are urged as pleas in prayer to God, and improved as encouragements to faith, that, notwithstanding all this, God would not wholly cast them off. Observe,

1. The malice and enmity of the Gentile nations against Israel. As soon as ever God broke down their hedges and left them exposed troops of enemies presently broke in upon them, that waited for an opportunity to destroy them. Those that passed by the way plucked at them; the board out of the wood and the wild beast of the field were ready to ravage it, v. 13. But,

2. See also the restraint which these cruel enemies were under; for till God had broken down their hedges

Psalm 80

13-19
13 The boar out of the wood doth waste it, and the wild beast of the field doth devour it.
14 Return, we beseech thee, O God of hosts: look down from heaven, and behold, and visit this vine;
15 And the vineyard which thy right hand hath planted, and the branch that thou madest strong for thyself.
16 It is burned with fire, it is cut down: they perish at the rebuke of thy countenance.
17 Let thy hand be upon the man of thy right hand, upon the son of man whom thou madest strong for thyself.
18 So will not we go back from thee: quicken us, and we will call upon thy name.
19 Turn us again, O LORD God of hosts, cause thy face to shine; and we shall be saved.

which the beasts have done, for then it may be thy heart will pity, and thy hand will be outstretched to deliver.
Verse 15. And the vineyard which thy right hand hath planted. Shall all thy care be lost? Thou has done so much, wilt thou lose thy labor? With thy power and wisdom thou didst great things for thy people, wilt thou now utterly give them up, and suffer thine enemies to exult in the evil which they delight in? And the branch that thou madest strong for thyself. A prayer for the leader whom the Lord had raised up, or for the Messiah whom they expected. Though the vine had been left, yet one branch had been regarded of the Lord, as if to furnish a scion for another vine; therefore, is the prayer made in this form. Let us pray the Lord, if he will not in the first place look upon his church, to look upon the Lord Jesus, and then behold her in mercy for his sake. This is the true art of prayer, to put Christ forward and cry, "Him and then the sinner see, Look through Jesus' wounds on me."
Verse 16. It is burned with fire. In broken utterances the sorrowful singer utters his distress. The vineyard was like a forest which has been set on fire; the choice vines were charred and dead. It is cut down. The cruel axe had hacked after its murderous fashion, the branches were lopped, the trunk was wounded, desolation reigned supreme. They perish at the rebuke of thy countenance. God's rebuke was to Israel what fire would be to a vine. His favor is life, and his wrath is as messengers of death. One angry glance from Jehovah's eye is sufficient to lay all the vineyards of Ephraim desolate. O Lord, look not thus upon our churches. Rebuke us, but not in anger.
Verse 17. Let thy hand be upon the man of thy right hand. Let thy power rest on thy true Benjamin, son of thy right hand; give a commission to some chosen man by whom thou wilt deliver. Honor him, save us, and glorify thyself. There is no doubt here an outlook to the Messiah, for whom believing Jews had learned to look as the Savior in time of trouble. Upon the son of man whom thou madest strong for thyself. Send forth thy power with him whom thou shalt strengthen to accomplish thy purposes of grace. It pleases God to work for the sons of men by sons of men. "By man came death, by man came also the resurrection from the dead." Nations rise or fall largely through the instrumentality of individuals: by a Napoleon the kingdoms are scourged, and by a Wellington nations are saved from the tyrant. It is by the man Christ Jesus that fallen Israel is yet to rise, and indeed through him, who deigns to call himself the Son of Man, the world is to be delivered from the dominion of Satan and the curse of sin.
Verse 18. So will not we go back from thee. Under the leadership of one whom God had chosen the nation would be kept faithful, grace would work gratitude, and so cement them to their allegiance. It is in Christ that we abide faithful; because he lives we live also. There is no hope of our perseverance apart from him.
Verse 19. Turn us again, O Lord God of Hosts. Here we have another advance in the title and the incommunicable name of Jehovah, the I AM is introduced. Faith's day grows brighter as the hours roll on; and her prayers grow more full and mighty. Cause thy face to shine; and we shall be saved. Even we who were so destroyed. No extremity is too great for the power of God. He is able to save at the last point, and that too by simply turning his smiling face upon his afflicted. Men can do little with their arm, but God can do all things with a glance. Oh, to live for ever in the light of Jehovah's countenance.

temptation although God should hide his face from us for a time, yea even although to the eye of sense and reason he should seem to be alienated from us. For, provided he is sought in the confident expectation of his showing mercy, he will become reconciled, and receive into his favor those whom he seemed to have cast off. It was a distinguished honor for the seed of Abraham to be accounted the vineyard of God; but while the faithful adduce this consideration as an argument for obtaining the favor of God, instead of bringing forward any claims of their own, they only beseech him not to cease to exercise his accustomed liberality towards them. The words, from heaven, have, no doubt, been introduced, that the faithful might find no difficulty in extending their faith to a distance, although God, from whom they had departed, was far from them; and, farther that if they saw no prospect of deliverance upon earth, they might lift up their eyes to heaven.

16. It is burnt with fire. The calamities of the people are now more clearly expressed. It had been said that the Lord's vine was abandoned to the wild beasts, that they might lay it waste. But it was a greater calamity for it to be consumed with fire, rooted up and utterly destroyed. The Israelites had perfidiously apostatized from the true religion; but, as has been previously observed, they were still a part of the Church. We are accordingly warned by this melancholy example, of the severity of the punishment due to our ingratitude.

17. Let that hand be upon the Man of thy right hand. Here the Psalmist repeats in plain words the prayer which he had expressed under the figure of a vineyard, pleading that God would defend, under his hand, the Man of his right hand, and the Son of man whom he hath strengthened for himself. I have no hesitation in considering the whole body of the Church as comprehended under the expressions, the Man of God's right hand, and the Son of man. The similar number is very properly made use of, it having been the Divine will that the chosen people should be as one man. For the same reason, the Apostle Paul also, in Galatians 3:16, lays great stress upon the words, one seed; for Ishmael, Esau, and others, were separated and scattered when God redeemed arm gathered together the seed of Abraham. Thus, by the Son of man is to be understood the people whom God had adopted to himself, that they might be as one man.

18. In the 18th verse, the faithful engage, upon God's hearing them, gratefully to acknowledge his goodness, not only by rendering to him the sacrifice of praise, but also by their whole life. Calling upon God's name, is here to be understood of "the calves of the lips," (Hosea 45:3;) but when it is said, We will not go back from thee, this means the uniform and continued course of the whole life. The verse, however, may be interpreted thus: O Lord! we will continue in our obedience to thee, even when our circumstances, so far as we can perceive, are hopeless; never shall the sharpness of our calamities have the effect of driving us to apostasy from thee: and when we are restored by thy grace and power, we will magnify thy name.

they could not pluck a leaf of this vine. The devil could not hurt Job so long as God continued the hedge round about him, Job i. 10. See how much it is the interest of any people to keep themselves in the favor of God and then they need not fear any wild beast of the field, Job v. 23. If we provoke God to withdraw, our defense has departed from us, and we are undone. The deplorable state of Israel is described (v. 16): It is burnt with fire; it is cut down; the people are treated like thorns and briers, that are nigh unto cursing and whose end is to be burned, and no longer like vines that are protected and cherished. They perish not through the rage of the wild beast and the boar, but at the rebuke of thy countenance; that was it which they dreaded and to which they attributed all their calamities. It is well or ill with us according as we are under God's smiles or frowns.

IV. What their requests were to God hereupon.

1. That God would help the vine (v. 14, 15), that he would graciously take cognizance of its case and do for it as he thought fit: "Return, we beseech thee, O Lord of hosts! for thou hast seemed to go away from us. Look down from heaven, to which thou hast retired,—from heaven, that place of prospect, whence thou seest all the wrongs that are done us, that place of power, whence thou canst send effectual relief,—from heaven, where thou hast prepared thy throne of judgment, to which we appeal, and where thou hast prepared a better country for those that are Israelites indeed,—thence give a gracious look, thence make a gracious visit, to this vine.

2. That he would help the vine-dresser (v. 17, 18): "Let thy hand be upon the man of thy right hand," that king (whoever it was) of the house of David that was now to go in and out before them; "let thy hand be upon him, not only to protect and cover him, but to own him, and strengthen him, and give him success." We have this phrase, Ezra vii. 28, And I was strengthened as the hand of the Lord my God was upon me. Their king is called the man of God's right hand as he was the representative of their state, which was dear to God, as his Benjamin, the son of his right hand, as he was president in their affairs and an instrument in God's right hand of much good to them, defending them from themselves and from their enemies and directing them in the right way, and as he was under-shepherd under him who was the great shepherd of Israel.

Lastly, The psalm concludes with the same petition that had been put up twice before, and yet it is no vain repetition (v. 19): Turn us again. The title given to God rises, v. 3, O God! v. 7, O God of hosts! v. 19, O Lord (Jehovah) God of hosts! When we come to God for his grace, his good-will towards us and his good work in us, we should pray earnestly, continue instant in prayer, and pray more earnestly.

Psalm 81

Title
To the chief Musician upon Gittith. A Psalm of Asaph.

1-8
1 Sing aloud unto God our strength: make a joyful noise unto the God of Jacob.
2 Take a psalm, and bring hither the timbrel, the pleasant harp with the psaltery.
3 Blow up the trumpet in the new moon, in the time appointed, on our solemn feast day.
4 For this was a statute for Israel, and a law of the God of Jacob.
5 This he ordained in Joseph for a testimony, when he went out through the land of Egypt: where I heard a language that I understood not.
6 I removed his shoulder from the burden: his hands were delivered from the pots.
7 Thou calledst in trouble, and I delivered thee; I answered thee in the secret place of thunder: I proved thee at the waters of Meribah. Selah.
8 Hear, O my people, and I will testify unto thee: O Israel, if thou wilt hearken unto me;

Psalm 81

TITLE. To the Chief Musician upon Gittith. Very little is known of the meaning of this title. We have given the best explanation known to us in connection with Psalm 8 in Vol. 1 of this work. If it be intended to indicate a vintage song, it speaks well for the piety of the people for whom it was written; it is to be feared that in few places even in Christian countries would holy hymns be thought suitable to be sung in connection with the winepress. When the bells upon the horses shall be holiness unto the Lord, then shall the juice of the grape gush forth to the accompaniment of sacred song. A Psalm of Asaph. This poet here again dwells upon the history of his country; his great forte seems to be rehearsing the past in admonitory psalmody. He is the poet of the history and politics of Israel. A truly national songster, at once pious and patriotic.
DIVISION. Praise is called for to celebrate some memorable day, perhaps the Passover; whereupon the deliverance out of Egypt is described, Ps 81:1-7. Then the Lord gently chides his people for their ingratitude, and pictures their happy estate had they but been obedient to his commands.

EXPOSITION
Verse 1. Sing, in tune and measure, so that the public praise may be in harmony; sing with joyful notes, and sounds melodious. Aloud. For the heartiest praise is due to our good Lord. His acts of love to us speak more loudly than any of our words of gratitude can do. No dullness should ever stupefy our psalmody, or half heartedness cause is to limp along. Sing aloud, ye debtors to sovereign grace, your hearts are profoundly grateful: let your voices express your thankfulness.
Verse 2. Take a psalm. Select a sacred song, and then raise it with your hearty voices. And bring hither the timbrel. Beat on your tambourines, ye damsels, let the sound be loud and inspiriting. "Sound the trumpets, beat the drums." God is not to be served with misery but with mirthful music, sound ye then the loud timbrel, as of old ye smote it by "Egypt's dark sea."
Verse 3. Blow up the trumpet in the new moon. Announce the sacred month, the beginning of months, when the Lord brought his people out of the house of bondage. Clear and shrill let the summons be which calls all Israel to adore the Redeeming Lord. In the time appointed, on our solemn feast day. Obedience is to direct our worship, not whim and sentiment: God's appointment gives a solemnity to rites and times which no ceremonial pomp or hierarchical ordinance could confer. The Jews not only observed the ordained month, but that part of the month which had been divinely set apart.
Verse 4. For this was a statute for Israel, and a law of the God of Jacob. It was a precept binding upon all the tribes that a sacred season should be set apart to commemorate the Lord's mercy; and truly it was but the Lord's due, he had a right and a claim to such special homage.
Verse 5. This he ordained in Joseph for a testimony. The nation is called Joseph, because in Egypt it would probably be known and spoken of as Joseph's family, and indeed Joseph was the foster father of the people. The Passover, which is probably here alluded to, was to be a standing memorial of the redemption from Egypt; and everything about it was intended to testify to all ages, and all peoples, the glory of the Lord in the deliverance of his chosen nation.
Verse 6. I removed his shoulder from the burden. Israel was the drudge and slave of Egypt, but God gave him liberty. It was by God alone that the nation was set free. Other peoples owe their liberties to their own efforts and courage, but Israel received its Magna Charta as a free gift of divine power. Truly may the Lord say of everyone of his freed men, I removed his shoulder from the burden. His hands were delivered from the pots. He was no longer compelled to carry earth, and mould it, and bake it; the earth basket was

JOHN CALVIN

Psalm 81

1-3

1. Sing joyfully to God our strength. This psalm, it is probable, was appointed to be sung on the festival days on which the Jews kept their solemn assemblies. In the exordium, there is set forth the order of worship which God had enjoined. They were not to stand deaf and dumb at the tabernacle; for the service of God does not consist in indolence, nor in cold and empty ceremonies; but they were, by such exercises as are here prescribed, to cherish among themselves the unity of faith; to make an open profession of their piety; to stir up themselves to continual progress therein; to endeavor to join, with one accord, in praising God; and, in short, to continue steadfast in the sacred covenant by which God had adopted them to himself.

3. Under the new moon, by the figure synecdoche, is comprehended all the other high feasts. Sacrifices were daily offered; but the days on which the faithful met together at the tabernacle, according to the express appointment of the law, are called, by way of eminence, the days of sacrifice.

4. For this is a statute to Israel. To give the more effect to the preceding exhortation, it is here taught that this law or ordinance had been prescribed to God's ancient people, for the purpose of ratifying the everlasting covenant. And as in covenants there is a mutual agreement between the parties, it is declared that this statute was given to Israel, and that God, in contracting, reserved this for himself, as a right to which he was justly entitled.

5 The words when he went forth will apply equally to God and to the people. It is a common form of expression to speak of God as going forth before his people, as a shepherd goes before his flock, or as a general before his army.

6. I have removed his shoulder from the burden. Here God begins to recount the benefits which he had bestowed upon the Israelites, and the many ways in which he had laid them under obligations to him. The more galling the bondage was from which they had been delivered, the more desirable and precious was their liberty. When, therefore, it is affirmed that their burdens were so heavy that they stooped under them, and that they were doomed to the labor of making bricks, and to other slavish and toilsome occupations, the comparison of this their first state with their condition afterwards is introduced to illustrate the more strikingly the greatness of the blessing of their deliverance.

7. Thou didst cry in trouble, and I delivered thee. Here the same subject is prosecuted. By their crying when they were in distress, I understand the prayers which they then offered to God.

8-12

8. Hear, O my people! The more effectually to touch the hearts of the people, God is here invested with the character of a teacher, and introduced as speaking familiarly in the midst of the congregation; and this is done for the purpose of instructing them, that all assemblies are unprofitable and

MATTHEW HENRY

Psalm 81

1-7 An invitation to praise.

When the people of God were gathered together in the solemn day, the day of the feast of the Lord, they must be told that they had business to do, for we do not go to church to sleep nor to be idle; no, there is that which the duty of every day requires, work of the day, which is to be done in its day. And here,

I. The worshippers of God are excited to their work, and are taught, by singing this psalm, to stir up both themselves and one another to it, v. 1-3. Our errand is, to give unto God the glory due unto his name, and in all our religious assemblies we must mind this as our business.

1. In doing this we must eye God as our strength, and as the God of Jacob, v. 1.

2. We must do this by all the expressions of holy joy and triumph. It was then to be done by musical instruments, the timbrel, harp, and psaltery; and by blowing the trumpet, some think in remembrance of the sound of the trumpet on Mount Sinai, which waxed louder and louder. It was then and is now to be done by singing psalms, singing aloud, and making a joyful noise.

3. This must be done in the time appointed. No time is amiss for praising God (Seven times a day will I praise thee; nay, at midnight will I rise and give thanks unto thee); but some are times appointed, not for God to meet us (he is always ready), but for us to meet one another, that we may join together in praising Do. The solemn feast-day must be a day of praise; when we are receiving the gifts of God's bounty, and rejoicing in them, then it is proper to sing his praises.

II. They are here directed in their work.

1. They must look up to the divine institution which it is the observation of. In all religious worship we must have an eye to the command (v. 4): This was a statute for Israel, for the keeping up of a face of religion among them; it was a law of the God of Jacob, which all the seed of Jacob are bound by, and must be subject to. Note, Praising God is not only a good thing, which we do well to do, but it is our indispensable duty, which we are obliged to do; it is at our peril if we neglect it; and in all religious exercises we must have an eye to the institution as our warrant and rule: "This I do because God has commanded me; and therefore I hope he will accept me;" then it is done in faith.

2. They must look back upon those operations of divine Providence which it is the memorial of. This solemn service was ordained for a testimony (v. 5), a standing traditional evidence, for the attesting of the matters of fact. It was a testimony to Israel, that they might know and remember what God had done for their fathers, and would be a testimony against them if they should be ignorant of them and forget them.

Psalm 81

9-16

9 There shall no strange god be in thee; neither shalt thou worship any strange god.
10 I am the LORD thy God, which brought thee out of the land of Egypt: open thy mouth wide, and I will fill it.
11 But my people would not hearken to my voice; and Israel would none of me.
12 So I gave them up unto their own hearts' lust: and they walked in their own counsels.
13 Oh that my people had hearkened unto me, and Israel had walked in my ways!
14 I should soon have subdued their enemies, and turned my hand against their adversaries.
15 The haters of the LORD should have submitted themselves unto him: but their time should have endured for ever.
16 He should have fed them also with the finest of the wheat: and with honey out of the rock should I have satisfied thee.

no more imposed upon the people, nor the tale of bricks exacted, for they came out into the open country where none could exact upon them.
Verse 7. Thou calledst in trouble, and I delivered thee. God heard his people's cries in Egypt, and at the Red Sea: this ought to have bound them to him. Since God does not forsake us in our need, we ought never to forsake him at any time. When our hearts wander from God, our answered prayers cry "shame" upon us. I answered thee in the secret place of thunder. Out of the cloud the Lord sent forth tempest upon the foes of his chosen. That cloud was his secret pavilion, within it he hung up his weapons of war, his javelins of lightning his trumpet of thunder; forth from that pavilion he came and overthrew the foe that his own elect might be secure.
Verse 8. Hear, O my people, and I will testify unto thee. What? Are the people so insensible as to be deaf to their God? So it would seem, for he earnestly asks a hearing.
Verse 9. There shall no strange god be in thee. No alien god is to be tolerated in Israel's tents. Neither shalt thou worship any strange god. Where false gods are, their worship is sure to follow. Man is so desperate an idolater that the image is always a strong temptation: while the nests are there the birds will be eager to return. No other god had done anything for the Jews, and therefore they had no reason for paying homage to any other.
Verse 10. I am the Lord thy God, which brought thee out of the land of Egypt. Thus did Jehovah usually introduce himself to his people. The great deliverance out of Egypt was that claim upon his people's allegiance which he most usually pleaded. If ever people were morally bound to their God, certainly Israel was a thousand times pledged unto Jehovah, by his marvelous deeds on their behalf in connection with the Exodus.
Verse 11. But my people would not hearken to my voice. His warnings were rejected, his promises forgotten, his precepts disregarded. Though the divine voice proposed nothing but good to them, and that upon an unparalleled scale of liberality, yet they turned aside.
Verse 12. So I gave them up unto their own hearts' lust. No punishment is more just or more severe than this. If men will not be checked, but madly take the bit between their teeth and refuse obedience, who shall wonder if the reins are thrown upon their necks, and they are let alone to work out their own destruction.
Verse 13. O that my people had hearkened unto me, and Israel had walked in my ways! The condescending love of God expresses itself in painful regrets for Israel's sin and punishment. Such were the laments of Jesus over Jerusalem. Certain doctrinalists find a stumbling stone in such passages, and set themselves to explain them away, but to men in sympathy with the divine nature the words and the emotions are plain enough.
Verse 14. I should soon have subdued their enemies. As he did in Egypt overthrow Pharaoh, so would he have baffled every enemy.
Verse 15. The haters of the Lord should have submitted themselves unto him. Though the submission would have been false and flattering, yet the enemies of Israel would have been so humiliated that they would have hastened to make terms with the favored tribes.
Verse 16. He should have fed them also with the finest of the wheat. Famine would have been an unknown word, they would have been fed on the best of the best food, and have had abundance of it as their every day diet. And with honey out of the rock should I have satisfied thee. Luxuries as well as necessaries would be forthcoming. The Lord can do great things for an obedient people.

trifling in which the voice of God stirring up men to faith and true godliness is not uttered.

9. Let there be no strange god in thee. Here there is propounded the leading article of the covenant, and almost the whole sum of it, which is, that God alone must have the pre-eminence.

10. I am Jehovah thy God, who brought thee out of the land of Egypt: open thy mouth wide. God, by making mention of the deliverance which he had wrought for the people, put a bridle upon those whom he had taken under his protection, by which he might hold them bound to his service; and now he assures them, that with respect to the time to come, he had an abundant supply of all blessings with which to fill and satisfy their desires.

11. But my people hearkened not to my voice. God now complains, that the Israelites, whom he endeavored gently to allure to him, despised his friendly invitation; yea, that although he had for a long time continued to exhort them, they always shut their ears against his voice.

12. This is the reason why, as is stated in the following verse, he gave them up to the hardness of their own heart, or, as others translate it, to the thoughts of their own heart. By these words, God testifies, that he justly punished his people, when he deprived them of good and wholesome doctrine, and gave them over to a reprobate mind.

13-16

13. O if my people had hearkened to me! By the honorable designation which God gives to the people of Israel, He exposes the more effectually their shameful and disgraceful conduct. Their wickedness was doubly aggravated, as will appear from the consideration, that although God called them to be his people, they differed nothing from those who were the greatest strangers to him.

14. I would soon have brought their enemies low. Here the Israelites are taught, that all the calamities which had befallen them were to be imputed to their own sins; for their enemies did not fight against them with any other strength than that with which they were supplied from above..

15. The haters of Jehovah would have lied to him. Here the Israelites are informed that their enemies would have humbly submitted to their authority had not their impiety emboldened them to run to excess, when they shook off the yoke of God, and waxed wanton against him.

16. By the fat of corn is meant, metaphorically, pure grain, unless it may be thought preferable to understand it of the finest wheat. Some are of opinion that the expression, honey out of the rock, is hyperbolical, implying that honey would have flowed from the very rocks rather than that God would have failed to satisfy his people. But as it is evident from sacred history that honey was found everywhere in the hollows of the rocks so long as they enjoyed the blessing of God, the meaning simply is, that the grace of God would have continued to flow in an unbroken and uniform course, had it not been interrupted by the perverseness and wickedness of the people.

8-16 Expostulation with Israel.

God, by the psalmist, here speaks to Israel, and in them to us, on whom the ends of the world are come.

I. He demands their diligent and serious attention to what he was about to say (v. 8): "Hear, O my people! and who should hear me if my people will not? I have heard and answered thee; now wilt thou hear me? Hear what is said with the greatest solemnity and the most unquestionable certainty, for it is what I will testify unto thee. Do not only give me the hearing, but hearken unto me, that is, be advised by me, be ruled by me."

II. He puts them in mind of their obligation to him as the Lord their God and Redeemer (v. 10): I am the Lord thy God, who brought thee out of the land of Egypt; this is the preface to the ten commandments, and a powerful reason for the keeping of them, showing that we are bound to it in duty, interest, and gratitude, all which bonds we break asunder if we be disobedient.

III. He gives them an abstract both of the precepts and of the promises which he gave them, as the Lord and their God, upon their coming out of Egypt.

IV. He charges them with a high contempt of his authority as their lawgiver and his grace and favor as their benefactor, v. 11. He had done much for them, and designed to do more; but all in vain: "My people would not hearken to my voice, but turned a deaf ear to all I said."

V. He justifies himself with this in the spiritual judgments he had brought upon them (v. 12): So I gave them up unto their own hearts' lusts, which would be more dangerous enemies and more mischievous oppressors to them than any of the neighboring nations ever were. God withdrew his Spirit from them, took off the bridle of restraining grace, left them to themselves, and justly.

VI. He testifies his good-will to them in wishing they had done well for themselves. He saw how sad their case was, and how sure their ruin, when they were delivered up to their own lusts; that is worse than being given up to Satan, which may be in order to reformation (1 Tim. i. 20) and to salvation (1 Cor. v. 5); but to be delivered up to their own hearts' lusts is to be sealed under condemnation. Observe here,

1. The great mercy God had in store for his people, and which he would have wrought for them if they had been obedient.

2. The duty God required from them as the condition of all this mercy.

3. Observe how the reason of the withholding of the mercy is laid in their neglect of the duty: If they had hearkened to me, I would soon have subdued their enemies. National sin or disobedience is the great and only thing that retards and obstructs national deliverance. Note, Therefore God would have us do our duty to him, that we may be qualified to receive favor from him. He delights in our serving him, not because he is the better for it, but because we shall be.

Psalm 82

Title
A Psalm of Asaph.

1 God standeth in the congregation of the mighty; he judgeth among the gods.
2 How long will ye judge unjustly, and accept the persons of the wicked? Selah.
3 Defend the poor and fatherless: do justice to the afflicted and needy.
4 Deliver the poor and needy: rid them out of the hand of the wicked.
5 They know not, neither will they understand; they walk on in darkness: all the foundations of the earth are out of course.
6 I have said, Ye are gods; and all of you are children of the most High.
7 But ye shall die like men, and fall like one of the princes.
8 Arise, O God, judge the earth: for thou shalt inherit all nations.

Psalm 82

TITLE AND SUBJECT. A Psalm of Asaph. This poet of the temple here acts as a preacher to the court and to the magistracy. Men who do one thing well are generally equal to another; he who writes good verse is not unlikely to be able to preach. What preaching it would have been had Milton entered the pulpit, or had Virgil been an apostle.

Asaph's sermon before the judges is now before us. He speaks very plainly, and his song is rather characterized by strength than by sweetness. We have here a clear proof that all psalms and hymns need not be direct expressions of praise to God; we may, according to the example of this psalm, admonish one another in our songs. Asaph no doubt saw around him much bribery and corruption, and while David punished it with the sword, he resolved to scourge it with a prophetic psalm. In so doing, the sweet singer was not forsaking his profession as a musician for the Lord, but rather was practically carrying it out in another department. He was praising God when he rebuked the sin which dishonored him, and if he was not making music, he was hushing discord when he bade rulers dispense justice with impartiality.

DIVISION. The Psalm is a whole and needs no formal division.

EXPOSITION

Verse 1. God standeth in the congregation of the mighty. He is the overlooker, who, from his own point of view, sees all that is done by the great ones of the earth. When they sit in state he stands over them, ready to deal with them if they pervert judgment. Judges shall be judged, and to justices justice shall be meted out.

Verse 2. How long will ye judge unjustly and accept the persons of the wicked? It is indirectly stated that the magistrates had been unjust and corrupt. They not only excused the wicked, but even decided in their favor against the righteous.

Verse 3. Defend the poor and fatherless. Cease to do evil, learn to do well. Look not to the interests of the wealthy whose hands proffer you bribes, but protect the rights of the needy, and especially uphold the claims of orphans whose property too often becomes a prey. Do not hunt down the peasant for gathering a few sticks, and allow the gentlemanly swindler to break through the meshes of the law.

Verse 4. Deliver the poor and needy: rid them out of the hand of the wicked. Break the nets of the man catchers, the legal toils, the bonds, the securities, with which cunning men capture and continue to hold in bondage the poor and the embarrassed.

Verse 5. They know not, neither will they understand. A wretched plight for a nation to be in when its justices know no justice, and its judges are devoid of judgment. Neither to know his duty nor to wish to know it is rather the mark of an incorrigible criminal than of a magistrate, yet such a stigma was justly set upon the rulers of Israel.

Verse 6. I have said, ye are gods. The greatest honor was thus put upon them; they were delegated gods, clothed for a while with a little of that authority by which the Lord judges among the sons of men.

Verse 7. But ye shall die like men. What sarcasm it seems! Great as the office made the men, they were still but men, and must die.

Verse 8. Arise, O God, and judge the earth. Come thou Judge of all mankind, put the bad judges to thy bar and end their corruption and baseness. Here is the world's true hope of rescue from the fangs of tyranny. The second advent is still earth's brightest hope. Come quickly, even so, come, Lord Jesus.

JOHN CALVIN

Psalm 82

1-4

1. God sitteth in the assembly of God. It is unquestionably a very unbecoming thing for those whom God has been pleased to invest with the government of mankind for the common good, not to acknowledge the end for which they have been exalted above others, nor yet by whose blessing they have been placed in so elevated a station; but instead of doing this, contemning every principle of equity, to rule just as their own unbridled passions dictate.
2. How long will ye judge unjustly? Many suppose that God is here introduced speaking, and that these are the words which he utters from his throne of judgment. But I would rather consider the prophet himself as the speaker, who, in order to prepare the way for administering a rebuke, had spoken in the manner in which he did in the first verse.
3. Determine the cause of the poor and the orphan. We are here briefly taught that a just and well-regulated government will be distinguished for maintaining the rights of the poor and afflicted. By the figure synecdoche, one part of equitable administration is put for the whole; for it cannot be doubted that rulers are bound to observe justice towards all men without distinction.

5-8

5 They know not, neither do they understand. After having reminded princes of their duty, the Psalmist complains that his admonition from their infatuation is ineffectual, and that they refuse to receive wholesome instruction; yea, that although the whole world is shaken to its foundations, they, notwithstanding, continue thoughtless and secure in the neglect of their duty.
6. I have said, ye are gods. God has invested judges with a sacred character and title. This the prophet concedes; but he, at the same time, shows that this will afford no support and protection to wicked judges. He does not introduce them as speaking of the dignity of their office; but anticipating the style of reasoning which they would be disposed to adopt, he replies, "If you appeal to your dignity as an argument to shield you, this boasting will avail you nothing; yea, rather you are deceiving yourselves by your foolish confidence; for God, in appointing you his substitutes, has not divested himself of his own sovereignty as supreme ruler. Again, he would have you to remember your own frailty as a means of stirring you up to execute with fear and trembling the office intrusted to you."
8. Arise, O God! judge the earth. The reason why this psalm concludes with a prayer has been already stated at the commencement. The prophet, finding that his admonitions and remonstrances were ineffectual, and that princes, inflated with pride, treated with contempt all instruction on the principles of equity, addresses himself to God, and calls upon Him to repress their insolence. By this means, the Holy Spirit furnishes us with ground of comfort whenever we are cruelly treated by tyrants. It is therefore our bounden duty to beseech him to restore to order what is embroiled in confusion.

MATTHEW HENRY

Psalm 82

1-5 The duty of magistrates.
We have here,
I. God's supreme presidency in all councils and courts asserted and laid down, as a great truth necessary to be believed both by princes and subjects (v. 1).
II. A charge given to all magistrates to do good with their power, as they will answer it to him by whom they are entrusted with it, v. 3, 4. They are to be the protectors of those who lie exposed to injury and the patrons of those who want advice and assistance: Defend the poor, who have no money wherewith to make friends or fee counsel, and the fatherless, who, while they are young and unable to help themselves, have lost those who would have been the guides of their youth. Magistrates, as they must be fathers to their country in general, so particularly to those in it who are fatherless.
III. A charge drawn up against bad magistrates, who neglect their duty and abuse their power, forgetting that God standeth among them, v. 2, 5. Observe,
1. What the sin is they are here charged with; they judge unjustly, contrary to the rules of equity and the dictates of their consciences, giving judgment against those who have right on their side, out of malice and ill-will, or for those who have an unrighteous cause, out of favor and partial affection.
2. What was the cause of this sin. They were told plainly enough that it was their office and duty to protect and deliver the poor; it was many a time given them in charge; yet they judge unjustly, for they know not, neither will they understand. They do not care to hear their duty; they will not take pains to study it; they have no desire to take things right, but are governed by interest, not by reason or justice. A gift in secret blinds their eyes.

6-8 The duty of magistrates.
We have here,
I. Earthly gods abased and brought down, v. 6, 7. The dignity of their character is acknowledged (v. 6).
II. The God of heaven exalted and raised high, v. 8. The psalmist finds it to little purpose to reason with these proud oppressors; they turned a deaf ear to all he said and walked on in darkness; and therefore he looks up to God, appeals to him, and begs of him to take unto himself his great power: Arise, O God! judge the earth; and, when he prays that he would do it, he believes that he will do it: Thou shalt inherit all nations. This has respect,
1. To the kingdom of providence. God governs the world, sets up and puts down whom he pleases.
2. To the kingdom of the Messiah. It is a prayer for the hastening of that, that Christ would come, who is to judge the earth, and that promise is pleaded, that God shall give him the heathen for his inheritance.

Psalm 83

Title
A Song or Psalm of Asaph.

1-6
1 Keep not thou silence, O God: hold not thy peace, and be not still, O God.
2 For, lo, thine enemies make a tumult: and they that hate thee have lifted up the head.
3 They have taken crafty counsel against thy people, and consulted against thy hidden ones.
4 They have said, Come, and let us cut them off from being a nation; that the name of Israel may be no more in remembrance.
5 For they have consulted together with one consent: they are confederate against thee:
6 The tabernacles of Edom, and the Ishmaelites; of Moab, and the Hagarenes;

Psalm 83

TITLE. A Psalm or Song of Asaph. This is the last occasion upon which we shall meet with this eloquent writer. The patriotic poet sings again of wars and dangers imminent, but it is no godless song of a thoughtless nation entering upon war with a light heart. Asaph the seer is well aware of the serious dangers arising from the powerful confederate nations, but his soul in faith stays itself upon Jehovah, while as a poet preacher he excites his countrymen to prayer by means of this sacred lyric. The Asaph who penned this song was in all probability the person referred to in 2Ch 20:14, for the internal evidence referring the subject of the Psalm to the times of Jehoshaphat is overwhelming. The division in the camp of the confederate peoples in the wilderness of Tekoa not only broke up their league, but led to a mutual slaughter, which crippled the power of some of the nations for many years after. They thought to destroy Israel and destroyed each other.
DIVISION. An appeal to God in a general manner fills Ps 83:1-4; and then the psalmist enters into details of the league, Ps 83:5-8. This leads to an earnest entreaty for the overthrow of the enemy, Ps 83:9-15, with an expression of desire that God's glory may be promoted thereby.

EXPOSITION
Verse 1. Keep not thou silence, O God. Man is clamorous, be not thou speechless. He rails and reviles, wilt not thou reply? On word of thine can deliver thy people; therefore, O Lord, break thy quiet and let thy voice be heard. Hold not thy peace, and be not still, O God. Here the appeal is to El., the Mighty One.
Verse 2. For, lo, thine enemies make a tumult. They are by no means sparing of their words, they are like a hungry pack of dogs, all giving tongue at once. So sure are they of devouring thy people that they already shout over the feast. And they that hate thee have lifted up the head. Confident of conquest, they carry themselves proudly and exalt themselves as if their anticipated victories were already obtained.
Verse 3. They have taken crafty counsel against thy people. Whatever we may do, our enemies use their wits and lay their heads together; in united conclave they discourse upon the demands and plans of the campaign, using much treachery and serpentine cunning in arranging their schemes. Malice is cold blooded enough to plot with deliberation; and pride, though it be never wise, is often allied with craft.
Verse 4. They have said, Come, and let us cut them off from being a nation. Easier said than done. Yet it shows how thorough going are the foes of the church. Theirs was the policy of extermination. They laid the axe at the root of the matter.
Verse 5. For they have consulted together with one consent. They are hearty and unanimous in their designs. They seem to have but one heart, and that a fierce one, against the chosen people and their God. They are confederate against thee. At the Lord himself they aim through the sides of his saints. They make a covenant, and ratify it with blood, resolutely banding themselves together to war with the Mighty God.
Verse 6. The tabernacles of Edom. Nearest of kin, yet first in enmity. Their sire despised the birthright, and they despise the possessors of it. Leaving their rock built mansions for the tents of war, the Edomites invaded the land of Israel. And the Ishmaelites. A persecuting spirit ran in their blood, they perpetuated the old grudge between the child of the bondwoman and the son of the freewoman. Of Moab. Born of incest, but yet a near kinsman, the feud of Moab against Israel was very bitter. Little could righteous Lot have dreamed that his unhallowed seed would be such unrelenting enemies of his uncle Abraham's posterity. And the Hagarenes—perhaps descendants of Hagar by a second husband. Whoever they may have been, they cast their power into the wrong scale, and with all their might sought the ruin of Israel.

JOHN CALVIN

Psalm 83

1-4

1. O God! hold not thy peace. It is very generally agreed among commentators, that this psalm was composed during the reign of king Jehoshaphat; and in this opinion I readily concur. That godly king, as is well known, had to engage in dreadful wars against multiplied hosts of enemies. Although the Ammonites and Moabites were the originators of the principal war in which he was engaged, yet they mustered forces not only from Syria, but also from distant countries, and the troops thus brought together well nigh overwhelmed Judea with their multitude. It would then appear, from the long list of enemies, here enumerated, who had conspired together to destroy the people of God, that the conjecture is well-founded which refers the composition of this psalm to that occasion; and sacred history informs us, that one of the Levites, under the influence of the Spirit of prophecy, gave the king assurance of victory, and that the Levites sang before the Lord.

2. For, behold! thy enemies are tumultuous. As an argument for enforcing the prayer of the preceding verse, it is affirmed that the faithful are oppressed both by the impetuous violence and the crafty policy of their enemies, which, to all human appearance, rendered their escape from death utterly hopeless. When it is said that they are tumultuous and lift up the head, the meaning is, that relying upon their own power, they behave themselves insolently and proudly.

3. To keep us from thinking that we are abandoned to the snares and traps of our enemies, the prophet here seasonably sets before us a consideration calculated to administer the highest consolation and hope, when he calls us God's hidden ones We are hidden under the shadow of God's wings; for although to outward appearance we lie open, and are exposed to the will of the wicked and the proud, we are preserved by the hidden power of God.

4. They have said, Come and let us cut them off from being a nation. The wickedness of these hostile powers is aggravated from the circumstance, that it was their determined purpose utterly to exterminate the Church. The prime agent in exciting such cruel hatred was doubtless Satan, who has all along from the beginning been exerting himself to extinguish the Church of God, and who, for this purpose, has never ceased to stir up his own children to outrage. The phrase, to cut them off from being a nation, signifies to exterminate them root and branch, and thus to put an end to them as a nation or people.

5-8

5. For they have consulted with the heart together. The multiplied hosts which united their powers together to oppose the Church of God and to effect her overthrow, are here enumerated. As so many nations, formed into one powerful confederacy, were bent on the destruction of a kingdom not greatly distinguished by its power, the miraculous aid of God was indispensably necessary for the deliverance of a people

MATTHEW HENRY

Psalm 83

1-8 Complaints against enemies.

The Israel of God were now in danger, and fear, and great distress, and yet their prayer is called, A song or psalm; for singing psalms is not unseasonable, no, not when the harps are hung upon the willow-trees.

I. The psalmist here begs of God to appear on the behalf of his injured threatened people (v. 1): "Keep not thou silence, O God! but give judgment for us against those that do us an apparent wrong."

II. He here gives an account of the grand alliance of the neighboring nations against Israel, which he begs of God to break, and blast the projects of. Now observe here,

1. Against whom this confederacy is formed; it is against the Israel of God, and so, in effect, against the God of Israel. Thus the psalmist takes care to interest God in their cause, not doubting but that, if it appeared that they were for God, God would make it to appear that he was for them, and then they might set all their enemies at defiance; for whom then could be against them? "Lord," says he, "they are thy enemies, and they hate thee." All wicked people are God's enemies (the carnal mind is enmity against God), but especially wicked persecutors; they hated the religious worshippers of God, because they hated God's holy religion and the worship of him. This was that which made God's people so zealous against them—that they fought against God: They are confederate against thee, v. 5. Were our interest only concerned, we could the better bear it; but, when God himself is struck at, it is time to cry, Help, Lord. Keep not thou silence, O God! He proves that they are confederate against God, for they are so against the people of God, who are near and dear to him, his son, his first-born, his portion, and the lot of his inheritance; he may truly be said to fight against me that endeavors to destroy my children, to root out my family, and to ruin my estate. "Lord," says the psalmist, "they are thy enemies, for they consult against thy hidden ones."

2. How this confederacy is managed. The devil is at the bottom of it, and therefore it is carried on,

(1.) With a great deal of heat and violence: Thy enemies make a tumult, v. 2. The heathen rage, Ps. ii. 1. The nations are angry, Rev. xi. 18. They are noisy in their clamors against the people whom they hope to run down with their loud calumnies. This comes in as a reason why God should not keep silence: "The enemies talk big and talk much; Lord, let them not talk all, but do thou speak to them in thy wrath," Ps. ii. 5.

(2.) With a great deal of art and policy: They have taken crafty counsel, v. 3. The subtlety of the old serpent appears in their management, and they contrive by all possible means, though ever so base, ever so bad, to gain their point. They are profound to make slaughter (Hos. v. 2), as if they could outwit Infinite Wisdom.

Psalm 83

7-12
7 Gebal, and Ammon, and Amalek; the Philistines with the inhabitants of Tyre;
8 Assur also is joined with them: they have holpen the children of Lot. Selah.
9 Do unto them as unto the Midianites; as to Sisera, as to Jabin, at the brook of Kison:
10 Which perished at Endor: they became as dung for the earth.
11 Make their nobles like Oreb, and like Zeeb: yea, all their princes as Zebah, and as Zalmunna:
12 Who said, Let us take to ourselves the houses of God in possession.

Verse 7. Gebal was probably a near neighbor of Edom, though there was a Gebal in the region of Tyre and Sidon. And Ammon, and Amalek. Two other hereditary foes of Israel, fierce and remorseless as ravening wolves. In the roll of infamy let these names remain detestably immortalized.
Verse 8. Assur is also joined with them. It was then a rising power, anxious for growth, and it thus early distinguished itself for evil. What a motley group they were; a league against Israel is always attractive, and gathers whole nations within its bonds. Herod and Pilate are friends, if Jesus is to be crucified. Romanism and Ritualism make common cause against the gospel. They have holpen the children of Lot. All these have come to the aid of Moab and Ammon, which two nations were among the fiercest in the conspiracy. There were ten to one against Israel, and yet she overcame all her enemies. Her name is not blotted out; but many, nay, most of her adversaries are now a name only, their power and their excellence are alike gone. Selah. There was good reason for a pause when the nation was in such jeopardy: and yet it needs faith to make a pause, for unbelief is always in a hurry.
Verse 9. Do unto them as unto the Midianites. Faith delights to light upon precedents, and quote them before the Lord; in the present instance, Asaph found a very appropriate one, for the nations in both cases were very much the same, and the plight of the Israelites very similar. Yet Midian perished, and the psalmist trusted that Israel's present foes would meet with the like overthrow from the hand of the Lord. As to Sisera, as to Jabin, at the brook of Kison. The hosts were swept away by the suddenly swollen torrent, and utterly perished; which was a second instance of divine vengeance upon confederated enemies of Israel. When God wills it, a brook can be as deadly as a sea. Kishon was as terrible to Jabin as was the Red Sea to Pharaoh. How easily can the Lord smite the enemies of his people. God of Gideon and of Barak, wilt thou not again avenge thine heritage of their bloodthirsty foes?
Verse 10. Which perished at Endor. There was the center of the carnage, where the heaps of the slain lay thickest. They became as dung for the earth, manuring it with man; making the earth, like Saturn, feed on its own children. War is cruel, butt in this case it avengements were most just,—those who would not give Israel a place above ground are themselves denied a hiding place under the ground; they counted God's people to be as dung, and they became dung themselves. Asaph would have the same fate befell other enemies of Israel; and his prayer was a prophecy, for so it happened to them.
Verse 11. Make their nobles like Oreb, and like Zeeb. Smite the great ones as well as the common ruck. Suffer not the ringleaders to escape. As Oreb fell at the rock and Zeeb at the winepress, so do thou mete out vengeance to Zion's foes wherever thou mayest overtake them. They boastfully compare themselves to ravens and wolves; let them receive the fate which is due to such wild beasts. Yea, all their princes as Zebah, and as Zalmunnua. These were captured and slain by Gideon, despite their claiming to have been anointed to the kingdom. Zebah became a sacrifice, and Zalmunna was sent to those shadowy images from which his name is derived. The psalmist seeing these four culprits hanging in history upon a lofty gallows, earnestly asks that others of a like character may, for truth's sake, share their fate.
Verse 12. Who said, Let us take to ourselves the houses of God in possession. Viewing the temple, and also the dwellings of the tribes, as all belonging to God, these greedy plunderers determined to push out the inhabitants, slay them, and become themselves landlords and tenants of the whole. These were large words and dark designs, but God could bring them all to nothing. It is in vain for men to say "Let us take," if God does not give. He who robs God's house will find that he has a property reeking with a curse; it will plague him and his seed for ever. "Will a man rob God?" Let him try it, and he will find it hot and heavy work.

who, in such extremity, were altogether unable to defend themselves.
6, 7. Some interpreters refer the tents of Edom to warlike furniture, and understand the words as meaning, that these enemies came well equipped and provided with tents for prolonging the war; but the allusion seems rather to be to the custom which prevailed among those nations of dwelling in tents. It is, however, a hyperbolical form of expression; as if it had been said, So great was their eagerness to engage in this war, that they might be said even to pluck their tents from the places where they were pitched.
8. When it is said that Assur and the rest were an arm to the sons of Lot, this is evidently an additional aggravation of the wickedness of the sons of Lot. It would have been an act of unnatural cruelty for them to have aided foreign nations against their own kindred. But when they themselves are the first to sound the trumpet, and when of their own suggestion they invite the aid of the Assyrians and other nations to destroy their own brethren, ought not such barbarous inhumanity to call forth the deepest detestation?

9-12
9. Do to them as to the Midianites. The faithful, having complained of the very grievous oppressions to which they were subjected, with the view of inducing God the more readily to succor them, now call to their remembrance the many occasions on which he had afforded relief to his people, when brought into the most desperate circumstances. From this, it is an obvious inference, that God wisely delays his aid to his servants under oppression, that when they seem to be reduced to the last extremity, he may appear in a miraculous manner for their succor.
10. The reason why it is said, They perished at Endor, it is somewhat difficult to ascertain. The name, Endor, is to be found in Joshua 17:11; and it is probable, that the army of king Jabin was destroyed there.
12. Who have said, Let us take in possession for ourselves the habitations of God. These heathen enemies are again accused of treason against the King of heaven, in seizing upon his heritage like lawless robbers. They would not, we may be sure, avow in so many words that it was their intention to commit such a crime; but as they despised God, who, as they well knew, was worshipped by the people of Israel, they are here justly charged with the guilt of endeavoring to dispossess Him of his own inheritance.

13-18
13. O my God! make them like a whirling ball. As the ungodly, when they gird and prepare themselves for destroying the Church, are usually inflated with intolerable pride, the inspired bard beseeches God to put them to shame, it being impossible to abate their pride until they are laid prostrate, confounded, and shamefully disappointed.
16. When he declares (verse 16) that, as the result of this, they will seek the name of God, he is not to be understood as speaking of their being brought to true repentance, or of their

(3.) With a great deal of unanimity. Whatever separate clashing interest they have among themselves, against the people of God they consult with one consent (v. 5), nor is Satan's kingdom divided against itself.

3. What it is that is aimed at in this confederacy. They consult not like the Gibeonites to make a league with Israel, that they might strengthen themselves by such a desirable alliance, which would have been their wisdom. They consult, not only to clip the wings of Israel, to recover their new conquests, and check the progress of their victorious arms, not only to keep the balance even between them and Israel, and to prevent their power from growing exorbitant; this will not serve. It is no less than the utter ruin and extirpation of Israel that they design (v. 4): "Come, let us cut them off from being a nation, as they cut off the seven nations of Canaan; let us leave them neither root nor branch, but lay their country so perfectly waste that the name of Israel may be no more in remembrance, no, not in history;" for with them they would destroy their Bibles and burn all their records.

4. Who they are that are drawn into this confederacy. The nations that entered into this alliance are here mentioned (v. 6-8); the Edomites and Ishmaelites, both descendants from Abraham, lead the van; for apostates from the church have been its most bitter and spiteful enemies, witness Julian. These were allied to Israel in blood and yet in alliance against Israel. There are no bonds of nature so strong but the spirit of persecution has broken through them. The brother shall betray the brother to death. Moab and Ammon were the children of righteous Lot; but, as an incestuous, so a degenerate race. The Philistines were long a thorn in Israel's side, and very vexatious. How the inhabitants of Tyre, who in David's time were Israel's firm allies, come in among their enemies, I know not; but that Assur (that is, the Assyrian) also is joined with them is not strange, or that (as the word is) they were an arm to the children of Lot. See how numerous the enemies of God's church have always been. Lord, how are those increased that trouble it! God's heritage was as a speckled bird; all the birds round about were against her (Jer. xii. 9), which highly magnifies the power of God in preserving to himself a church in the world, in spite of the combined force of earth and hell.

9-18 Prophetic imprecations.
The psalmist here, in the name of the church, prays for the destruction of those confederate forces, and, in God's name, foretells it; for this prayer that it might be so amounts to a prophecy that it shall be so, and this prophecy reaches to all the enemies of the gospel-church; whoever they be that oppose the kingdom of Christ, here they may read their doom. The prayer is, in short, that these enemies, who were confederate against Israel, might be defeated in all their attempts, and that they might prove their own

Psalm 83

13-18
13 O my God, make them like a wheel; as the stubble before the wind.
14 As the fire burneth a wood, and as the flame setteth the mountains on fire;
15 So persecute them with thy tempest, and make them afraid with thy storm.
16 Fill their faces with shame; that they may seek thy name, O LORD.
17 Let them be confounded and troubled for ever; yea, let them be put to shame, and perish:
18 That men may know that thou, whose name alone is JEHOVAH, art the most high over all the earth.

Verse 13. O my God, make them like a wheel; like a rolling thing which cannot rest, but is made to move with every breath. Let them have no quiet. May their minds eternally revolve and never come to peace. Blow them away like thistle down, as the stubble before the wind. Scatter them, chase them, drive them to destruction. Every patriot prays thus against the enemies of his country, he would be no better than a traitor if he did not.
Verse 14. As the fire burneth a wood. Long years have strewn the ground with deep deposits of leaves; these being dried in the sun are very apt to take fire, and when they do so the burning in terrific. The underwood and the ferns blaze, the bushes crackle, the great trees kindle and to their very tops are wrapped in fire, while the ground is all red as a furnace. In this way, O Lord, mete out destruction to thy foes, and bring all of them to an end. The flame setteth the mountains on fire. Up the hill sides the hanging woods glow like a great sacrifice, and the forests on the mountain's crown smoke towards heaven. Even thus, O Lord, do thou conspicuously and terribly overthrow the enemies of thine Israel.
Verse 15. So persecute them with thy tempest, and make them afraid with thy storm. The Lord will follow up his enemies, alarm them, and chase them till they are put to a hopeless rout. He did this, according to the prayer of the present Psalm, for his servant Jehoshaphat; and in like manner will he come to the rescue of any or all of his chosen.
Verse 16. Fill their faces with shame; that they may seek thy name, O Lord. Shame has often weaned men from their idols, and set them upon seeking the Lord. If this was not the happy result, in the present instance, with the Lord's enemies, yet it would be so with his people who were so prone to err. They would be humbled by his mercy, and ashamed of themselves because of his grace; and then they would with sincerity return to the earnest worship of Jehovah their God, who had delivered them.
Verse 17. Where no good result followed, and the men remained as fierce and obstinate as ever, justice was invoked to carry out the capital sentence. Let them be confounded and troubled for ever; yea, let them be put to shame, and perish. What else could be done with them? It was better that they perished than that Israel should be rooted up. What a terrible doom it will be to the enemies of God to be "confounded, and troubled for ever," to see all their schemes defeated, and their bodies and souls full of anguish without end: from such a shameful perishing may our souls be delivered.
Verse 18. That men may know that thou, whose name alone is JEHOVAH, art the most high over all the earth. Hearing of the Lord's marvelous deeds in defeating such a numerous confederacy, the very heathen would be compelled to acknowledge the greatness of Jehovah. We read in 2Ch 20:30, that the fear of God was on all the neighboring kingdoms when they heard that Jehovah fought against the enemies of Israel. Jehovah is essentially the Most High. He who is self existent is infinitely above all creatures, all the earth is but his footstool. The godless race of man disregards this, and yet at times the wonderful works of the Lord compel the most unwilling to adore his majesty. Thus has this soul stirring lyric risen from the words of complaint to those of adoration; let us in our worship always seek to do the same. National trouble called out the nation's poet laureate, and well did he discourse at once of her sorrows, and prayers, and hopes. Sacred literature thus owes much to sorrow and distress.

genuine conversion. I indeed admit that the first step to genuine repentance is when men, brought low by affliction, willingly humble themselves. But what is here meant is nothing more than a forced and slavish submission like that of Pharaoh, king of Egypt. It is a case of frequent occurrence for the wicked, when subdued by adversity, to give glory to God, for a short period. But they are soon again carried away with a frantic madness, which clearly discovers their hypocrisy, and brings to light the pride and rebellion which lurked in their hearts.

17. This is more clearly apparent from the 17th verse, where he distinctly prays that they may be destroyed for ever; which would not at all correspond with his previous statement, were it regarded as a prayer for their being brought to repentance.

18. And let them know that thou art, thy name Jehovah. It is not the saving knowledge of God which is here spoken of, but that acknowledgement of him which his irresistible power extorts from the wicked. It is not simply said that they will know that there is a God; but a special kind of knowledge is laid down, it being intimated that the heathen who before held the true religion in contempt, would at length perceive that the God who made himself known in the Law, and who was worshipped in Judea, was the only true God. Still, however, it must be remembered, that the knowledge spoken of is only that which is of an evanescent character, having neither root nor the living juice to nourish it; for the wicked will not submit to God willingly and cordially, but are drawn by compulsion to yield a counterfeit obedience, or, being restrained by him, dare not break forth into open outrage. This, then, is an experimental recognition of God which penetrates not to the heart, but is extorted from them by force and necessity. The prayer amounts to this: Lord, make them to know that the idols which they have fabricated for themselves are no gods, and in fact are nothing. The despisers of God may indeed shun the light, and at one time may overcast themselves with clouds, while at another their may plunge into the deep and thick shades of darkness; but He pursues them, and draws them forth to the knowledge of himself, which they would fain bury in ignorance. And as the world indiscriminately and disgracefully applies his sacred name to its own trifling inventions, this profanation is corrected when it is added, thy name Jehovah. This implies that being, or really to be, is in the strict sense applicable to God alone; for although unbelievers may attempt to tear his glory to pieces, he continues perfect and unchanged. The contrast of which I have spoken, must be kept in mind by the reader. A nation has never existed so barbarous as not to have worshipped some deity; but every country forged particular gods for itself. And although the Moabites, the Edomites, and the rest of these nations, admitted that some power and authority belonged to the God of Israel, yet they conceived that this power and authority did not extend beyond the boundaries of Judea. Thus the king of Syria called him, "the God of the hills," (1 Kings 20:23.) This preposterous and absurd division of God's glory, which men make, is disproved by one word, and all the superstitions which at that time prevailed in the world are overthrown, when the Prophet attributes to the God of Israel, as well the essence of Deity as the name.

ruin, and so God's Israel might be preserved and perpetuated. Now this is here illustrated,

I. By some precedents. Let that be their punishment which has been the fate of others who have formerly set themselves against God's Israel. The defeat and discomfiture of former combinations may be pleaded in prayer to God and improved for the encouragement of our own faith and hope, because God is the same still that ever he was, the same to his people and the same against his and their enemies; with him is no variableness.

II. He illustrates it by some similitudes, and prays,

1. That God would make them like a wheel (v. 13), that they might be in continual motion, unquiet, unsettled, and giddy in all their counsels and resolves, that they might roll down easily and speedily to their own ruin.

2. That they might be chased as stubble, or chaff, before the fierce wind. "The wheel, though it continually turn round, is fixed on its own axis; but let them have no more fixation than the light stubble has, which the wind hurries away, and nobody desires to save it, but is willing it should go," Ps. i. 4.

III. He illustrates it by the good consequences of their confusion, v. 16-18. He prays here that God, having filled their hearts with terror, would thereby fill their faces with shame, that they might be ashamed of their enmity to the people of God (Isa. xxvi. 11), ashamed of their folly in acting both against Omnipotence itself and their own true interest. Now,

1. The beginning of this shame might be a means of their conversion: "Let them be broken and baffled in their attempts, that they may seek thy name, O Lord! Let them be put to a stand, that they may have both leisure and reason to pause a little, and consider who it is that they are fighting against and what an unequal match they are for him, and may therefore humble and submit themselves and desire conditions of peace. Let them be made to fear thy name, and perhaps that will bring them to seek thy name."

2. If it did not prove a means of their conversion, the perfecting of it would redound greatly to the honor of God. If they will not be ashamed and repent, let them be put to shame and perish; if they will not be troubled and turned, which would soon put an end to all their trouble, a happy end, let them be troubled for ever, and never have peace: this will be for God's glory (v. 18), that other men may know and own, if they themselves will not, that thou, whose name alone is JEHOVAH (that incommunicable, though not ineffable name) art the Most High over all the earth. God's triumphs over his and his church's enemies will be incontestable proofs,

(1.) That he is, a self-existent self-sufficient Being.

(2.) That he is the most high God, Lord of all.

(3.) That he is so, not only over the land of Israel, but over all the earth, even those nations of the earth that do not know him or own him; for his kingdom rules over all.

Psalm 84

Title
To the chief Musician upon Gittith. A Psalm for the sons of Korah.

1-6
1 How amiable are thy tabernacles, O LORD of hosts!
2 My soul longeth, yea, even fainteth for the courts of the LORD: my heart and my flesh crieth out for the living God.
3 Yea, the sparrow hath found an house, and the swallow a nest for herself, where she may lay her young, even thine altars, O LORD of hosts, my King, and my God.
4 Blessed are they that dwell in thy house: they will be still praising thee. Selah.
5 Blessed is the man whose strength is in thee; in whose heart are the ways of them.
6 Who passing through the valley of Baca make it a well; the rain also filleth the pools.

Psalm 84

TITLE AND SUBJECT. To the Chief Musician upon Gittith. A Psalm for the sons of Korah. This Psalm well deserved to be committed to the noblest of the sons of song. No music could be too sweet for its theme, or too exquisite in sound to match the beauty of its language. Sweeter than the joy of the wine press, (for that is said to be the meaning of the word rendered upon Gittith), is the joy of the holy assemblies of the Lord's house; not even the favored children of grace, who are like the sons of Korah, can have a richer subject for song than Zion's sacred festivals. It matters little when this Psalm was written, or by whom; for our part it exhales to us a Davidic perfume, it smells of the mountain heather and the lone places of the wilderness, where King David must have often lodged during his many wars. This sacred ode is one of the choicest of the collection; it has a mild radiance about it, entitling it to be called The Pearl of Psalms. If the twenty-third be the most popular, the one-hundred-and-third the most joyful, the one-hundred-and-nineteenth the most deeply experimental, the fifty-first the most plaintive, this is one of the most sweet of the Psalms of peace. Pilgrimages to the tabernacle were a grand feature of Jewish life. In our country, pilgrimages to the shrine of Thomas of Canterbury, and our Lady of Walsingham, were so general as to affect the entire population, cause the formation of roads, the erection and maintenance of hostelries, and the creation of a special literature; this may help us to understand the influence of pilgrimage upon the ancient Israelites. Families journeyed together, making bands which grew at each halting place; they camped in sunny glades, sang in unison along the roads, toiled together over the hill and through the slough, and as they went along, stored up happy memories which would never be forgotten. One who was debarred the holy company of the pilgrims, and the devout worship of the congregation, would find in this Psalm fit expression for his mournful spirit.
DIVISION. We will make our pauses where the poet or the musician placed them, namely, of the Selahs.

EXPOSITION
Verse 2. My soul longeth, it pines, and faints to meet with the saints in the Lord's house. The desire was deep and insatiable—the very soul of the man was yearning for his God. Yea, even fainteth; as though it could not long hold out, but was exhausted with delay. He had a holy lovesickness upon him, and was wasted with an inward consumption because he was debarred the worship of the Lord in the appointed place.
Verse 3. Yea, the sparrow hath found an house. He envied the sparrows which lived around the house of God, and picked up the stray crumbs in the courts thereof; he only wished that he, too, could frequent the solemn assemblies and bear away a little of the heavenly food. And the swallow a nest for herself, where she may lay her young. He envied also the swallows whose nests were built under the eaves of the priest's houses, who there found a place for their young, as well as for themselves. We rejoice not only in our personal religious opportunities, but in the great blessing of taking our children with us to the sanctuary.
Verse 4. Blessed are they that dwell in thy house. Those he esteems to be highly favored who are constantly engaged in divine worship—the canons residentiary, yea, the pew openers, the menials who sweep and dust. To come and go is refreshing, but to abide in the place of prayer must be heaven below.
Verse 5. Blessed is the man whose strength is in thee. Having spoken of the blessedness of those who reside in the house of God, he now speaks of those who are favored to visit it at appointed seasons, going upon pilgrimage with their devout brethren: he is not, however, indiscriminate in his eulogy, but speaks only of those who heartily attend to the sacred

JOHN CALVIN

Psalm 84

1-4
1. How amiable are thy tabernacles, O Jehovah of Hosts! David complains of his being deprived of liberty of access to the Church of God, there to make a profession of his faith, to improve in godliness, and to engage in the divine worship. Some would understand by the tabernacles of God, the kingdom of heaven, as if David mourned over his continuance in this state of earthly pilgrimage; but they do not sufficiently consider the nature of his present afflicted circumstances—that he was debarred from the sanctuary. He knew that God had not in vain appointed the holy assemblies, and that the godly have need of such helps so long as they are sojourners in this world.
2. I have observed, that in the second verse a more than ordinary ardor of desire is expressed. David states that his soul fainteth after the courts of the Lord, which is equivalent to our pining away, when, under the influence of extreme mental emotion, we are in a manner transported out of ourselves. He speaks only of the courts of the tabernacle, because, not being a priest, it was not lawful for him to go beyond the outer court. None but the priests, as is well known, were permitted to enter into the inner sanctuary. In the close of the verse, he declares, that this longing extended itself even to his body, that is, it manifested itself in the utterance of the mouth, the languor of the eyes, and the action of the hands. The reason why he longed so intensely to have access to the tabernacle was, to enjoy the living God; not that he conceived of God as shut up in so narrow a place as was the tent of the ark, but he was convinced of the need he had of steps, by which to rise up to heaven, and knew that the visible sanctuary served the purpose of a ladder, because, by it the minds of the godly were directed and conducted to the heavenly model.
3. The sparrow also hath found a house for herself, and the swallow a nest for herself. David, with the view of aggravating the misery of his condition, compares himself with the sparrows and swallows, showing how hard a case it was for the children of Abraham to be driven out of the heritage which had been promised them, whilst the little birds found some place or other for building their nests.
4. Blessed are they who dwell in thy house. Here the Psalmist expresses more distinctly the proper and legitimate use of the sanctuary; and thus he distinguishes himself from hypocrites, who are sedulously attentive to the observance of outward ceremonies, but destitute of genuine heart godliness. David, on the contrary, testifies, that the true worshippers of God offer to him the sacrifice of praise, which can never be dissociated from faith.

5-7
5. Blessed is the man whose strength is in thee. David again informs us, that the purpose for which he desired liberty of access to the sanctuary was, not merely to gratify his eyes with what was to be seen there, but to make progress in faith. To lean with the whole heart upon God, is to attain to no

MATTHEW HENRY

Psalm 84

1-7 The pleasures of public worship; benefit of public worship.
The psalmist here, being by force restrained from waiting upon God in public ordinances, by the want of them is brought under a more sensible conviction than ever of the worth of them. Observe,
I. The wonderful beauty he saw in holy institutions (v. 1): How amiable are thy tabernacles, O Lord of hosts! Some think that he here calls God the Lord of hosts (that is, in a special manner of the angels, the heavenly hosts) because of the presence of the angels in God's sanctuary; they attended the Shechinah, and were (as some think) signified by the cherubim. God is the Lord of these hosts, and his the tabernacle is: it is spoken of as more than one (thy tabernacles) because there were several courts in which the people attended, and because the tabernacle itself consisted of a holy place and a most holy.
II. The longing desire he had to return to the enjoyment of public ordinances, or rather of God in them, v. 2. It was an entire desire; body, soul, and spirit concurred in it. He was not conscious to himself of any rising thought to the contrary.
III. His grudging the happiness of the little birds that made their nests in the buildings that were adjoining to God's altars, v. 3. This is an elegant and surprising expression of his affection to God's altars: The sparrow has found a house and the swallow a nest for herself. These little birds, by the instinct and direction of nature, provide habitations for themselves in houses, as other birds do in the woods, both for their own repose and in which to lay their young; some such David supposes there were in the buildings about the courts of God's house, and wishes himself with them. He would rather live in a bird's nest nigh God's altars than in a palace at a distance from them.
IV. His acknowledgment of the happiness both of the ministers and of the people that had liberty of attendance on God's altars: "Blessed are they. O when shall I return to the enjoyment of that blessedness?"
1. Blessed are the ministers, the priests and Levites, who have their residence about the tabernacle and are in their courses employed in the service of it (v. 4): Blessed are those that dwell in thy house, that are at home there, and whose business lies there.
2. Blessed are the people, the inhabitants of the country, who, though they do not constantly dwell in God's house as the priests do, yet have liberty of access to it at the times appointed for their solemn feasts, the three great feasts, at which all the males were obliged to give their attendance, Deut. xvi. 16. David was so far from reckoning this an imposition, and a hardship put upon them, that he envies the happiness of those who might thus attend, v. 5-7.

Psalm 84

7-12
7 They go from strength to strength, every one of them in Zion appeareth before God.
8 O LORD God of hosts, hear my prayer: give ear, O God of Jacob. Selah.
9 Behold, O God our shield, and look upon the face of thine anointed.
10 For a day in thy courts is better than a thousand. I had rather be a doorkeeper in the house of my God, than to dwell in the tents of wickedness.
11 For the LORD God is a sun and shield: the LORD will give grace and glory: no good thing will he withhold from them that walk uprightly.
12 O LORD of hosts, blessed is the man that trusteth in thee.

festivals. The blessedness of sacred worship belongs not to half hearted, listless worshippers, but to those who throw all their energies into it. Neither prayer, nor praise, nor the hearing of the word will be pleasant or profitable to persons who have left their hearts behind them.

Verse 6. Who passing through the valley of Baca make it a well. Traversing joyfully the road to the great assembly, the happy pilgrims found refreshment even in the dreariest part of the road. As around a well men meet and converse cheerfully, being refreshed after their journey, so even in the vale of tears, or any other dreary glen, the pilgrims to the skies find sweet solace in brotherly communion and in anticipation of the general assembly above, with its joys unspeakable. Probably there is here a local allusion, which will never now be deciphered, but the general meaning is clear enough. There are joys of pilgrimage which make men forget the discomforts of the road.

Verse 7. They go from strength to strength. So far from being wearied they gather strength as they proceed. Each individual becomes happier, each company becomes more numerous, each holy song more sweet and full. We grow as we advance if heaven be our goal. If we spend our strength in God's ways we shall find it increase.

Verse 8. O Lord God of hosts, hear my prayer. Give me to go up to thy house, or if I may not do so, yet let my cry be heard. Thou listenest to the united supplications of thy saints, but do not shut out my solitary petition, unworthy though I be. Give ear, O God of Jacob. Though Jehovah of hosts, thou art also the covenant God of solitary pleaders like Jacob; regard thou, then, my plaintive supplication.

Verse 9. Behold, O God our shield, and look upon the face of thine anointed. Here we have the nation's prayer for David; and the believer's prayer for the Son of David. Let but the Lord look upon our Lord Jesus, and we shall be shielded from all harm; let him behold the face of his Anointed, and we shall be able to behold his face with joy. We also are anointed by the Lord's grace, and our desire is that he will look upon us with an eye of love in Christ Jesus.

Verse 10. For a day in thy courts is better than a thousand. Of course the psalmist means a thousand days spent elsewhere. Under the most favorable circumstances in which earth's pleasures can be enjoyed, they are not comparable by so much as one in a thousand to the delights of the service of God. To feel his love, to rejoice in the person of the anointed Savior, to survey the promises and feel the power of the Holy Ghost in applying precious truth to the soul, is a joy which worldlings cannot understand, but which true believers are ravished with. Even a glimpse at the love of God is better than ages spent in the pleasures of sense.

Verse 11. For the Lord God is a sun and shield. Pilgrims need both as the weather may be, for the cold would smite them were it not for the sun, and foes are apt to waylay the sacred caravan, and would haply destroy it if it were without a shield. Heavenly pilgrims are not left uncomforted or unprotected.

Verse 12. O Lord of hosts, blessed is the man that trusteth in thee. Here is the key of the Psalm. The worship is that of faith, and the blessedness is peculiar to believers. No formal worshipper can enter into this secret. A man must know the Lord by the life of real faith, or he can have no true rejoicing in the Lord's worship, his house, his Son, or his ways. Dear reader, how fares it with thy soul?

ordinary degree of advancement: and this cannot be attained by any man, unless all his pride is laid prostrate in the dust, and his heart truly humbled.
6. They passing through the valley of weeping, will together make it a well. The meaning of the Psalmist is, that no impediments can prevent the enlightened and courageous worshippers of God from making conscience of waiting upon the sanctuary. By this manner of speaking, he confirms the statement which he had previously made, That nothing is more desirable than to be daily engaged in the worship of God; showing, as he does, that no difficulties can put a stop to the ardent longings of the godly, and prevent them from hastening with alacrity, yea, even though their way should be through dry and barren deserts, to meet together to solemnize the holy assemblies.
7. They will go from strength to strength. In this verse the same sentiment is repeated. Mount Zion being the place where, according to the appointment of the law, the holy assemblies were observed, after the ark of the covenant was removed thither, it is said, that the people of God will come to Zion in great numbers, provoking one another to this good work.

8-11
8. O Jehovah, God of Hosts! hear my prayer. David, instead of acting like worldly men, who foolishly and unprofitably distress and torment themselves by inwardly cherishing their desires, very wisely directs his wishes and prayers to God. From this it is also evident, that he was not accustomed to indulge in ostentatious boasting, as is the case with many hypocrites.
9. He next anticipates a temptation which might very readily arise from his being at present apparently cut off from the Church, and wards it off, by associating and ranking himself with all true believers, under the protection of God.
10. For better is one day in thy courts than a thousand elsewhere. Unlike the greater part of mankind, who desire to live without knowing why, wishing simply that their life may be prolonged, David here testifies, not only that the end which he proposed to himself in living was to serve God, but that in addition to this, he set a higher value on one day which he could spend in the divine service, than upon a long time passed among the men of the world, from whose society true religion is banished.
11. Jehovah God is our sun and shield. The idea conveyed by the comparison derived from the sun is, that as the sun by his light vivifies, nourishes, and rejoices the world, so the benign countenance of God fills with joy the hearts of his people, or rather, that they neither live nor breathe except in so far as he shines upon them.
12. The exclamation with which David concludes the psalm, Blessed is the man who trusteth in thee, seems to refer to the season of his banishment. So long as we are deprived of God's benefits, we must necessarily groan and be sad in heart. But, that the sense of our distresses may not overwhelm us, we ought to impress it upon our minds, that even in the midst of our calamities we do not cease to be happy, when faith and patience are in exercise.

8-12 Delight in God's ordinances.
Here,
I. The psalmist prays for audience and acceptance with God, not mentioning particularly what he desired God would do for him. He needed to say no more when he had professed such an affectionate esteem for the ordinances of God, which now he was restrained and banished from. All his desire was, in that profession, plainly before God, and his longing, his groaning, was not hidden from him; therefore he prays (v. 8, 9) only that God would hear his prayer and give ear, that he would behold his condition, behold his good affection, and look upon his face, which way it was set, and how his countenance discovered the longing desire he had towards God's courts. He calls himself (as many think) God's anointed, for David was anointed by him and anointed for him. In this petition.
II. He pleads his love to God's ordinances and his dependence upon God himself.
1. God's courts were his choice, v. 10. A very great regard he had for holy ordinances: he valued them above any thing else, and he expresses his value for them,
(1.) By preferring the time of God's worship before all other time.
(2.) By preferring the place of worship before any other place.
2. God himself was his hope, and joy, and all. Therefore he loved the house of his God, because his expectation was from his God, and there he used to communicate himself, v. 11. See,
(1.) What God is, and will be, to his people: The Lord God is a sun and shield. We are here in darkness, but, if God be our God, he will be to us a sun, to enlighten and enliven us, to guide and direct us. We are here in danger, but he will be to us a shield to secure us from the fiery darts that fly thickly about us. With his favor he will compass us as with a shield.
(2.) What he does, and will, bestow upon them: The Lord will give grace and glory. Grace signifies both the good-will of God towards us and the good work of God in us; glory signifies both the honor which he now puts upon us, in giving us the adoption of sons, and that which he has prepared for us in the inheritance of sons. God will give them grace in this world as a preparation for glory, and glory in the other world as the perfection of grace; both are God's gift, his free gift. And if God will give grace and glory, which are the two great things that concur to make us happy in both worlds, we may be sure that no good thing will be withheld from those that walk uprightly. It is the character of all good people that they walk uprightly, that they worship God in spirit and in truth, and have their conversation in the world in simplicity and godly sincerity; and such may be sure that God will withhold no good thing from them.
Lastly, He pronounces those blessed who put their confidence in God, as he did, v. 12. Those are blessed who have the liberty of ordinances and the privileges of God's house.

Psalm 85

Title
To the chief Musician. A Psalm for the sons of Korah.

1-6
1 Lord, thou hast been favorable unto thy land: thou hast brought back the captivity of Jacob.
2 Thou hast forgiven the iniquity of thy people, thou hast covered all their sin. Selah.
3 Thou hast taken away all thy wrath: thou hast turned thyself from the fierceness of thine anger.
4 Turn us, O God of our salvation, and cause thine anger toward us to cease.
5 Wilt thou be angry with us for ever? wilt thou draw out thine anger to all generations?
6 Wilt thou not revive us again: that thy people may rejoice in thee?

Psalm 85

TITLE. To the Chief Musician, A Psalm for the sons of Korah. There is no need to repeat our observations upon a title which is of so frequent occurrence; the reader is referred to notes placed in the headings of preceding psalms. Yet it may not be out of place to quote Ne 12:46. In the days of David and Asaph of old there were chief of the singers, and songs of praise and thanksgiving unto God.

OBJECT AND OCCASION. It is the prayer of a patriot for his afflicted country, in which he pleads the Lord's former mercies, and by faith foresees brighter days. We believe that David wrote it, but many question that assertion. Certain interpreters appear to grudge the psalmist David the authorship of any of the psalms, and refer the sacred songs by wholesale to the times of Hezekiah, Josiah, the Captivity, and the Maccabees. It is remarkable that, as a rule, the more skeptical a writer is, the more resolute is he to have done with David; while the purely evangelic annotators are for the most part content to leave the royal poet in the chair of authorship. The charms of a new theory also operate greatly upon writers who would have nothing at all to say if they did not invent a novel hypothesis, and twist the language of the psalm in order to justify it. The present psalm has of course been referred to the Captivity, the critics could not resist the temptation to do that, though, for our part we see no need to do so: it is true a captivity is mentioned in Ps 85:1, but that does not necessitate the nation's having been carried away into exile, since Job's captivity was turned, and yet he had never left his native land: moreover, the text speaks of the captivity of Jacob as brought back, but had it referred to the Babylonian emigration, it would have spoken of Judah; for Jacob or Israel, as such, did not return. The first verse in speaking of "the land" proves that the author was not an exile. Our own belief is that David penned this national hymn when the land was oppressed by the Philistines, and in the spirit of prophecy he foretold the peaceful years of his own reign and the repose of the rule of Solomon, the psalm having all along an inner sense of which Jesus and his salvation are the key. The presence of Jesus the Savior reconciles earth and heaven, and secures to us the golden age, the balmy days of universal peace.

DIVISION. In Ps 85:1-4 the poet sings of the Lord's former mercies and begs him to remember his people; from Ps 85:5-7 he pleads the cause of afflicted Israel; and then, having listened to the sacred oracle in Ps 85:8, he publishes joyfully the tidings of future good, Ps 85:9-13.

EXPOSITION

Verse 1. LORD, thou hast been favorable unto thy land. The self existent, all sufficient JEHOVAH is addressed: by that name he revealed himself to Moses when his people were in bondage, by that name he is here pleaded with. It is wise to dwell upon that view of the divine character which arouses the sweetest memories of his love. Sweeter still is that dear name of "Our Father," with which Christians have learned to commence their prayers.

Verse 2. Thou hast forgiven the iniquity of thy people. Often and often had he done this, pausing to pardon even when his sword was bared to punish. Who is a pardoning God like thee, O Jehovah? Who is so slow to anger, so ready for forgive? Every believer in Jesus enjoys the blessing of pardoned sin, and he should regard this priceless boon as the pledge of all other needful mercies.

Verse 3. Thou hast taken away all thy wrath. Having removed the sin, the anger is removed also. How often did the longsuffering of God take away from Israel the punishments which had been justly laid upon them! How often also has the Lord's chastising hand been removed from us when our waywardness called for heavier strokes! Thou hast turned thyself from the fierceness of thine anger. Even when judgments had been most severe, the

JOHN CALVIN

Psalm 85

1-4

1. O Jehovah! thou hast been favorable to thy land. Those who translate these words in the future tense, in my opinion, mar their meaning. This psalm, it is probable, was endited to be sung by the people when they were persecuted by the cruel tyranny of Antiochus; and from the deliverance wrought for them in the past, they were encouraged to expect in the future, fresh and continued tokens of the divine favor,—God having thereby testified, that their sins, however numerous and aggravated, could not efface from his memory the remembrance of his covenant, so as to render him inexorable towards the children of Abraham, and deaf to their prayers.

2. Thou hast taken away the iniquity of thy people. It was very natural for the faithful to feel alarmed and perplexed on account of their sins, and therefore the prophet removes all ground for overwhelming apprehension, by showing them, that God, in delivering his people, had given an irrefragable proof of free forgiveness. He had before traced this deliverance to the mere good pleasure and free grace of God as its source; but after it was wrought, the iniquities of the people having separated between them and their God, and estranged them from him, it was necessary that the remedy of pardon should be brought to their aid.

4. Turn us, O God of our salvation! The faithful now make a practical application to themselves, in their present circumstances, of what they had rehearsed before concerning God's paternal tenderness towards his people whom he had redeemed. And they attribute to him, by whom they desire to be restored to their former state, the appellation, O God of our salvation! to encourage themselves, even in the most desperate circumstances, in the hope of being delivered by the power of God.

5-8

5 Wilt thou be wroth against us for ever? Here the godly bewail the long continuance of their afflictions, and derive an argument in prayer from the nature of God. This truth has also been brought to our notice in Psalm 30:5, "For his anger endureth but a moment; in his favor is life: weeping may endure for a night, but joy cometh in the morning." It thus becomes us, when we engage in prayer, to meditate upon the Divine promises that we may be furnished with suitable expressions.

6. The godly, still dwelling on the same theme, ask, in the 6th verse, whether God will not turn again and quicken them Being fully convinced of the truth of this principle, That the punishments with which God chastises his children are only temporary; they thereby encourage themselves in the confident expectation, that although he may be now justly displeased, and may have turned away his face from them, yet, when they implore his mercy, he will be entreated, and raising the dead to life again, will turn their mourning into gladness.

7. Show us thy mercy, O Jehovah! In these words there is the same contrast as in the preceding sentence. In supplicating

MATTHEW HENRY

Psalm 85

1-7 Prayer in time of trouble.

The church, in affliction and distress, is here, by direction from God, making her application to God. So ready is God to hear and answer the prayers of his people that by his Spirit in the word, and in the heart, he indites their petitions and puts words into their mouths. The people of God, in a very low and weak condition, are here taught how to address themselves to God.

I. They are to acknowledge with thankfulness the great things God had done for them (v. 1-3): "Thou has done so and so for us and our fathers." Note, The sense of present afflictions should not drown the remembrance of former mercies; but, even when we are brought very low, we must call to remembrance past experiences of God's goodness, which we must take notice of with thankfulness, to his praise. They speak of it here with pleasure,

1. That God had shown himself propitious to their land, and had smiled upon it as his own: "Thou hast been favorable to thy land, as thine, with distinguishing favors."

2. That he had rescued them out of the hands of their enemies and restored them to their liberty: "Thou hast brought back the captivity of Jacob, and settled those in their own land again that had been driven out and were strangers in a strange land, prisoners in the land of their oppressors." The captivity of Jacob, though it may continue long, will be brought back in due time.

3. That he had not dealt with them according to the desert of their provocations (v. 2): "Thou hast forgiven the iniquity of thy people, and not punished them as in justice thou mightest. Thou hast covered all their sin." When God forgives sin he covers it; and, when he covers the sin of his people, he covers it all. The bringing back of their captivity was then an instance of God's favor to them, when it was accompanied with the pardon of their iniquity.

4. That he had not continued his anger against them so far, and so long, as they had reason to fear (v. 3): "Having covered all their sin, thou hast taken away all thy wrath;" for when sin is set aside God's anger ceases; God is pacified if we are purified. See what the pardon of sin is: Thou hast forgiven the iniquity of thy people, that is, "Thou hast turned thy anger from waxing hot, so as to consume us in the flame of it. In compassion to us thou hast not stirred up all thy wrath, but, when an intercessor has stood before thee in the gap, thou hast turned away thy anger."

II. They are taught to pray to God for grace and mercy, in reference to their present distress; this is inferred from the former: "Thou hast done well for our fathers; do well for us, for we are the children of the same covenant." They pray for the manifestation of God's good-will to them (v. 7): "Show us thy mercy, O Lord! show thyself merciful to us; not only have mercy on

Psalm 85

7-13
7 Shew us thy mercy, O LORD, and grant us thy salvation.
8 I will hear what God the LORD will speak: for he will speak peace unto his people, and to his saints: but let them not turn again to folly.
9 Surely his salvation is nigh them that fear him; that glory may dwell in our land.
10 Mercy and truth are met together; righteousness and peace have kissed each other.
11 Truth shall spring out of the earth; and righteousness shall look down from heaven.
12 Yea, the LORD shall give that which is good; and our land shall yield her increase.
13 Righteousness shall go before him; and shall set us in the way of his steps.

Lord had in mercy stayed his hand. In mid volley he had restrained his thunder.
Verse 4. Turn us, O God of our salvation. This was the main business. Could the erring tribes be rendered penitent all would be well. It is not that God needs turning from his anger so much as that we need turning from our sin; here is the hinge of the whole matter. Our trials frequently arise out of our sins, they will not go till the sins go.
Verse 5. Wilt thou be angry with us for ever? See how the psalmist makes bold to plead. We are in time as yet and not in eternity, and does not time come to an end, and therefore thy wrath!
Verse 6. Wilt thou not revive us again? Hope here grows almost confident. She feels sure that the Lord will return in all his power to save. We are dead or dying, faint and feeble, God alone can revive us, he has in other times refreshed his people, he is still the same, he will repeat his love. Will he not? Why should he not? We appeal to him—Wilt thou not? That thy people may rejoice in thee. Thou lovest to see thy children happy with that best of happiness which centers in thyself, therefore revive us, for revival will bring us the utmost joy.
Verse 7. Shew us thy mercy, O LORD. Reveal it to our poor half blinded eyes. We cannot see it or believe it by reason of our woes, but thou canst make it plain to us. Others have beheld it, Lord shew it to us. We have seen thine anger, Lord let us see thy mercy. Thy prophets have told us of it, but O Lord, do thou thyself display it in this our hour of need.
Verse 8. I will hear what God the LORD will speak. When we believe that God hears us, it is but natural that we should be eager to hear him. Only from him can come the word which can speak peace to troubled spirits; the voices of men are feeble in such a case.
Verse 9. Surely his salvation is nigh them that fear him. Faith knows that a saving God is always near at hand, but only (for such is the true rendering) to those who fear the Lord, and worship him with holy awe. In the gospel dispensation this truth is conspicuously illustrated. If to seeking sinners salvation is nigh, it is assuredly very nigh to those who have once enjoyed it, and have lost its present enjoyment by their folly; they have but to turn unto the Lord and they shall enjoy it again.
Verse 10. Mercy and truth are met together. In answer to prayer, the exulting psalmist sees the attributes of God confederating to bless the once afflicted nation. Mercy comes hand in hand with truth to fulfill the faithful promise of their gracious God.
Verse 11. Truth shall spring out of the earth. Promises which lie unfulfilled, like buried seeds, shall spring up and yield harvests of joy; and men renewed by grace shall learn to be true to one another and their God, and abhor the falsehood which they loved before.
Verse 12. Yea, the LORD shall give that which is good. Being himself pure goodness, he will readily return from his wrath, and deal out good things to his repenting people. Our evil brings evil upon us, but when we are brought back to follow that which is good, the Lord abundantly enriches us with good things.
Verse 13. Righteousness shall go before him; and shall set us in the way of his steps. God's march of right will leave a track wherein his people will joyfully follow. He who smote in justice will also bless in justice, and in both will make his righteousness manifest, so as to affect the hearts and lives of all his people. Such are the blessings of our Lord's first advent, and such shall be yet more conspicuously the result of his second coming. Even so, come Lord Jesus.

that mercy may be extended to them, and deliverance granted them, they confess that they are deprived of all sense of both these blessings. Such having been the state of the saints in old time, let us learn, even when we are so oppressed with calamities as to be reduced to extremity, and on the brink of despair, to betake ourselves notwithstanding to God. Mercy is appropriately put in the first place; and then there is added salvation, which is the work and fruit of mercy; for no other reason can be assigned why God is induced to show himself our Savior, but that he is merciful.

8. I will hear what God Jehovah will speak. The prophet, by his own example, here exhorts the whole body of the Church to quiet and calm endurance. As he had burst forth under the influence of strong emotion into a degree of vehemence, he now restrains himself as it were with a bridle; and in all our desires, be they never so devout and holy, we must always beware of their running to excess. When a man gives indulgence to his own infirmity, he is easily carried beyond the bounds of moderation by an undue ardor.

9-13

9. Surely his salvation is near to them that fear him. Here the Psalmist confirms the statement made in the preceding verse. He encourages both himself and other servants of God in the hope, that although to outward appearance God was far off from his people, yet deliverance was near at hand; because it is certain, that God secretly regards those whom he seems openly to neglect.

10. Mercy and truth shall meet together. Here the verbs are in the past tense; but it is evident from the scope of the passage, that they should be translated into the future. I cordially embrace the opinion which is held by many, that we have here a prophecy concerning the kingdom of Christ. There is no doubt, that the faithful lifted up their eyes to Him, when their faith had need of encouragement and support in reference to the restoration of the Church; and especially after their return from Babylon.

12. Likewise, Jehovah will grant prosperity. Let it be observed, that the faithful generally have only granted to them a limited portion of the comforts of this transitory life: that they may not be lulled asleep by the allurements of earth. I have therefore said, that, while on earth, they only taste of God's fatherly love, and are not filled with an overflowing abundance of the good things of this world. 13. Righteousness shall go before him. The word righteousness is taken by some for a righteous person; but this is unnatural. Viewed in this light, the passage, indeed, contains the useful and important truth, That the righteous man will walk before God, and will make it his object to regulate all his actions according to the principles of moral rectitude. But there being no necessity for wresting the word righteousness so violently, it will be better to adopt the more correct and simple view, which is, that under the reign of Christ order will be so well established, that righteousness will walk before God, and occupy every path.

us, but let us have the comfortable evidences of that mercy; let us know that thou hast mercy on us and mercy in store for us."

III. They are taught humbly to expostulate with God concerning their present troubles, v. 5, 6. Here observe,

1. What they dread and deprecate: "Wilt thou be angry with us for ever? We are undone if thou art, but we hope thou wilt not. Wilt thou draw out thy anger unto all generations? No; thou art gracious, slow to anger, and swift to show mercy, and wilt not contend for ever. Thou wast not angry with our fathers for ever, but didst soon turn thyself from the fierceness of thy wrath; why then wilt thou be angry with us for ever? Are not thy mercies and compassions as plentiful and powerful as ever they were? Impenitent sinners God will be angry with for ever; for what is hell but the wrath of God drawn out unto endless generations? But shall a hell upon earth be the lot of thy people?"

2. What they desire and hope for: "Wilt thou not revive us again (v. 6), revive us with comforts spoken to us, revive us with deliverances wrought for us? Thou hast been favorable to thy land formerly, and that revived it; wilt thou not again be favorable, and so revive it again?"

8-13 Divine answer to prayer; blessings given in answer to prayer.

We have here an answer to the prayers and expostulations in the foregoing verses.

I. In general, it is an answer of peace. This the psalmist is soon aware of (v. 8), for he stands upon his watch-tower to hear what God will say unto him, as the prophet, Hab. ii. 1, 2. I will hear what God the Lord will speak.

II. Here are the particulars of this answer of peace. He doubts not but all will be well in a little time, and therefore gives us the pleasing prospect of the flourishing estate of the church in the last five verses of the psalm, which describe the peace and prosperity that God, at length, blessed the children of the captivity with, when, after a great deal of toil and agitation, at length they gained a settlement in their own land. Here is,

1. Help at hand (v. 9).

2. Graces meeting, and happily embracing (v. 10, 11): Mercy and truth, righteousness and peace, kiss each other.

3. Great plenty of every thing desirable (v. 12).

4. A sure guidance in the good way (v. 13): The righteousness of his promise which he has made to us, assuring us of happiness, and the righteousness of sanctification, that good work which he has wrought in us, these shall go before him to prepare his way, both to raise our expectations of his favor and to qualify us for it; and these shall go before us also, and be our guide to set us in the way of his steps.

Psalm 86

Title
A Prayer of David.

1-8
1 Bow down thine ear, O LORD, hear me: for I am poor and needy.
2 Preserve my soul; for I am holy: O thou my God, save thy servant that trusteth in thee.
3 Be merciful unto me, O Lord: for I cry unto thee daily.
4 Rejoice the soul of thy servant: for unto thee, O Lord, do I lift up my soul.
5 For thou, Lord, art good, and ready to forgive; and plenteous in mercy unto all them that call upon thee.
6 Give ear, O LORD, unto my prayer; and attend to the voice of my supplications.
7 In the day of my trouble I will call upon thee: for thou wilt answer me.
8 Among the gods there is none like unto thee, O Lord; neither are there any works like unto thy works.

Psalm 86

TITLE. A Prayer of David. We have here one of the five psalms entitled Tephillahs or prayers. This psalm consists of praise as well as prayer, but it is in all parts so directly addressed to God that it is most fitly called "a prayer." A prayer is none the less but all the more a prayer because veins of praise run through it. This psalm would seem to have been specially known as David's prayer; even as the ninetieth is "the prayer of Moses." David composed it, and no doubt often expressed himself in similar language; both the matter and the wording are suitable to his varied circumstances and expressive of the different characteristics of his mind. In many respects it resembles Ps 17:1-15, which bears the same title, but in other aspects it is very different; the prayers of a good man have a family likeness, but they vary as much as they agree. We may learn from the present psalm that the great saints of old were accustomed to pray very much in the same fashion as we do; believers in all ages are of one genus. The name of God occurs very frequently in this psalm, sometimes it is Jehovah, but more commonly Adonai, which it is believed by many learned scholars was written by the Jewish transcribers instead of the sublimer title, because their superstitious dread led them to do so: we, laboring under no such tormenting fear, rejoice in Jehovah, our God. It is singular that those who were so afraid of their God, that they dared not write his name, had yet so little godly fear, that they dared to alter his word.
DIVISION. The psalm is irregular in its construction but may be divided into three portions, each ending with a note of gratitude or of confidence: we shall therefore read from Ps 86:1-7, and then, (after another pause at the end of Ps 86:13), we will continue to the end.

EXPOSITION
Verse 1. Bow down thine ear, O Lord, hear me. In condescension to my littleness, and in pity to my weakness, "bow down thine ear, O Lord." When our prayers are lowly by reason of our humility, or feeble by reason of our sickness, or without wing by reason of our despondency, the Lord will bow down to them, the infinitely exalted Jehovah will have respect unto them.
Verse 2. Preserve my soul. Let my life be safe from my enemies, and my spiritual nature be secure from their temptations. He feels himself unsafe except he be covered by the divine protection.
Verse 3. Be merciful unto me, O Lord. The best of men need mercy, and appeal to mercy, yea to nothing else but mercy; they need it for themselves, and crave it eagerly of their God as a personal requisite. For I cry unto thee daily. Is there not a promise that importunity shall prevail? May we not, then, plead our importunity as an argument with God? He who prays every day, and all the day, for so the word may mean, may rest assured that the Lord will hear him in the day of his need.
Verse 4. Rejoice the soul of thy servant. Make my heart glad, O my Maker, for I count it my honor to call myself again and again thy servant, and I reckon thy favor to be all the wages I could desire. I look for all my happiness in thee only, and therefore unto thee, O Lord, do I lift up my soul.
Verse 5. For thou, Lord, art good, and ready to forgive. Good at giving and forgiving; supplying us with his good, and removing our evil. Here was the great reason why the Psalmist looked to the Lord alone for his joy, because every joy creating attribute is to be found in perfection in Jehovah alone.
Verse 6. Give ear, O LORD, unto my prayer. Even the glory which his spirit had beheld did not withdraw him from his prayer, but rather urged him to be more fervent in it; hence he implores the Lord to hear his requests.
Verse 7. In the day of my trouble I will call upon thee: for thou wilt answer me. A pious resolve backed by a judicious reason. It is useless to cry to those who cannot or will not hear; once convince men that prayer has no effect upon God, and they will have no more of it. In these busy days and

JOHN CALVIN

Psalm 86

1-7

1. Incline thy ear, O Jehovah! Neither the inscription nor the contents of this psalm enable us to conclude with certainty what dangers David here complains of; but the psalm in all probability refers to that period of his life when he was persecuted by Saul, and describes the train of thought which then occupied his mind, although it may not have been written until after his restoration to a state of outward peace and tranquility, when he enjoyed greater leisure. He does not without cause allege before God the oppressions which he endured as a plea for obtaining the divine favor; for nothing is more suitable to the nature of God than to succor the afflicted: and the more severely any one is oppressed, and the more destitute he is of the resources of human aid, the more inclined is God graciously to help him.

2. Preserve my soul, for I am meek. Here the Psalmist adduces two other arguments by which to stir up God to grant him succor,—his own gentleness towards his neighbors, and the trust which he reposed in God.

3. Have mercy upon me, O Jehovah! The Psalmist again betakes himself to the mercy of God. It is as if he had said, I bring no merit of my own, but humbly pray for deliverance solely on the ground of thy mercy. When he speaks of crying daily, it is a proof of his hope and confidence, of which we have spoken a little before. By the word cry, as I have already had occasion frequently to remark, is denoted vehemence and earnestness of soul.

5 For thou, O Lord! art good and propitious. We have here a confirmation of the whole preceding doctrine, derived from the nature of God. It would avail the afflicted nothing to have recourse to him, and to lift up their desires and prayers to heaven, were they not persuaded that he is a faithful rewarder of all who call upon him. The point upon which David now insists is, that God is bountiful and inclined to compassion, and that his mercy is so great, as to render it impossible for him to reject any who implore his aid.

6. Listen, O Jehovah! to my prayer. From the earnest repetition of his former requests in this and the subsequent verse, it is evident that he was oppressed with no ordinary degree of grief, and also agitated with extreme anxiety, From this example, we are taught that those who, having engaged in prayer once, allow themselves immediately to give over that exercise, provided God does not at once grant them their desire, betray the coldness and inconstancy of their hearts.

8-11

8. Among the gods there is none like unto thee, O Lord! Here the Psalmist may be considered either as bursting forth into thanksgivings, after having obtained what he desired, or else as gathering courage and new strength for prayer. The latter opinion I am most inclined to adopt; but perhaps it may be preferable to regard both views as included.

9. All nations which thou hast made shall come. This may refer to the universal power of God; but whether he speaks of

MATTHEW HENRY

Psalm 86

1-7 Humble petitions.

This psalm was published under the title of a prayer of David; not as if David sung all his prayers, but into some of his songs he inserted prayers; for a psalm will admit the expressions of any pious and devout affections. But it is observable how very plain the language of this psalm is, and how little there is in it of poetic flights or figures, in comparison with some other psalms; for the flourishes of wit are not the proper ornaments of prayer. Now here we may observe,

I. The petitions he puts up to God. It is true, prayer accidentally may preach, but it is most fit that (as it is in this prayer) every passage should be directed to God, for such is the nature of prayer as it is here described (v. 4): Unto thee, O Lord! do I lift up my soul, as he had said Ps. xxv. 1. In all the parts of prayer the soul must ascend upon the wings of faith and holy desire, and be lifted up to God, to meet the communications of his grace, and in an expectation raised very high of great things from him.

1. He begs that God would give a gracious audience to his prayers (v. 1): Bow down thy ear, O Lord! hear me. When God hears our prayers it is fitly said that he bows down his ear to them, for it is admirable condescension in God that he is pleased to take notice of such mean creatures as we are and such defective prayers as ours are. He repeats this again (v. 6): "Give ear, O Lord! unto my prayer, a favorable ear, though it be whispered, though it be stammered; attend to the voice of my supplications."

2. He begs that God would take him under his special protection, and so be the author of his salvation (v. 2): Preserve my soul; save thy servant.

3. He begs that God would look upon him with an eye of pity and compassion (v. 3): Be merciful to me, O Lord! It is mercy in God to pardon our sins and to help us out of our distresses; both these are included in this prayer, God be merciful to me. "Men show no mercy; we ourselves deserve no mercy, but, Lord, for mercy-sake, be merciful unto me." 4. He begs that God would fill him with inward comfort (v. 4): Rejoice the soul of thy servant. It is God only that can put gladness into the heart.

II. The pleas with which he enforces these petitions.

1. He pleads his relation to God and interest in him: "Thou art my God, to whom I have devoted myself, and on whom I depend, and I am thy servant (v. 2), in subjection to thee, and therefore looking for protection from thee."

2. He pleads his distress: "Hear me, for I am poor and needy, therefore I want thy help, therefore none else will hear me." God is the poor man's King, whose glory it is to save the souls of the needy; those who are poor in spirit, who see themselves empty and necessitous, are most welcome to the God of all grace.

3. He pleads God's good will towards all that seek him (v. 5): "To thee do I lift up my soul in desire and

Psalm 86

9-17

9 All nations whom thou hast made shall come and worship before thee, O Lord; and shall glorify thy name.
10 For thou art great, and doest wondrous things: thou art God alone.
11 Teach me thy way, O LORD; I will walk in thy truth: unite my heart to fear thy name.
12 I will praise thee, O Lord my God, with all my heart: and I will glorify thy name for evermore.
13 For great is thy mercy toward me: and thou hast delivered my soul from the lowest hell.
14 O God, the proud are risen against me, and the assemblies of violent men have sought after my soul; and have not set thee before them.
15 But thou, O Lord, art a God full of compassion, and gracious, long suffering, and plenteous in mercy and truth.
16 O turn unto me, and have mercy upon me; give thy strength unto thy servant, and save the son of thine handmaid.
17 Shew me a token for good; that they which hate me may see it, and be ashamed: because thou, LORD, hast holpen me, and comforted me.

especially in troublous times, men cannot afford to waste time in entreaties which must be unavailing.

Verse 8. Among the gods there is none like unto thee, O Lord. There are gods by delegated office, such as kings and magistrates, but they are as nothing in the presence of Jehovah; there are also gods by the nomination of superstition, but these are vanity itself, and cannot be compared with the living and true God.

Verse 9. All nations whom thou hast made, and these include all mankind, since they all come of the first Adam—thy creature, and their lives are all distinct creations of thine omnipotence. All these shall come with penitent hearts, in thine own way, to thine own self, and worship before thee, O Lord.

Verse 10. For thou art great. He had before said, "thou art good"; it is a grand thing when greatness and goodness are united; it is only in the Divine Being that either of them exists absolutely, and essentially. Happy is it for us that they both exist in the Lord to an equal degree.

Verse 11. Teach me thy way, O LORD. Instruct me thus at all times, let me live in thy school; but teach me now especially since I am in trouble and perplexity. Be pleased to shew me the way which thy wisdom and mercy have prepared for my escape; behold I lay aside all willfulness, and only desire to be informed as to thy holy and gracious mind.

Verse 12. I will praise thee, O Lord my God, with all my heart. When my heart is one, I will give thee all of it. Praise should never be rendered with less than all our heart, and soul, and strength, or it will be both unreal and unacceptable.

Verse 13. For great is thy mercy toward me. Personal experience is ever the master singer. Whatever thou art to others, to me thy mercy is most notable. The psalmist claims to sing among the loudest, because his debt to divine mercy is among the greatest. And thou hast delivered my soul from the lowest hell. From the direst death and the deepest dishonor David had been kept by God.

Verse 14. O God, the proud are risen against me. They could not let God's poor servant alone, his walk with God was as smoke to their eyes, and therefore they determined to destroy him. None hate good men so fiercely as do the high minded and domineering. And the assemblies of violent men have sought after my soul. Unitedly oppressors sought the good man's life; they hunted in packs, with keen scent, and eager foot.

Verse 15. But thou, O Lord. What a contrast! We get away from the hectorings and blusterings of proud but puny men to the glory and goodness of the Lord. We turn from the boisterous foam of chafing waves to the sea of glass mingled with fire, calm and serene.

Verse 16. O turn unto me. As though the face of God had been before averted in anger, the suppliant pleads for a return of conscious favor. One turn of God's face will turn all our darkness into day. And have mercy upon me, that is all he asks, for he is lowly in heart; that is all he wants, for mercy answereth all a sinner's needs. Give thy strength unto thy servant.

Verse 17. Shew to me a token for good. Let me be assured of thy mercy by being delivered out of trouble. What bodes good to me shall make them quail and blush. Disappointed and defeated, the foes of the good man would feel ashamed of what they had designed. "Because thou, LORD, hast holpen me, and comforted me." God doth nothing by halves, those whom he helps he also consoles, and so makes them not merely safe but joyful.

the grace that was bestowed upon himself alone, or treats, in general, of the works of God, we must bear in mind that whenever he celebrates the prevalence of true godliness among the heathen, he has an eye to the kingdom of Christ, prior to whose coming God gave only the initial or dawning manifestation of his glory, which at length was diffused through the whole world by the preaching of the Gospel.

10. For thou art great, and thou alone, O God! doest wondrous things. In this verse there is again repeated the cause which will bring all nations to worship before the Lord, namely, the discovery made of his glory by the greatness of his works. The contemplation of God's glory in his works is the true way of acquiring genuine godliness.

11. Show me thy ways, O Jehovah! David now rises higher, praying that he may be governed by the spirit of sound understanding, in order to his living a holy life, and that he may be strengthened in his endeavors thereto by the spirit of fortitude. He tacitly contrasts the ways of God with all the counsels which he could derive from carnal reason.

12-17

12. I will praise thee, O Lord my God! David engages, when he shall have experienced God to be in all respects a beneficent father, to yield to him the tribute of gratitude. He expressed in the preceding verse a desire to have his heart united to God, that he might fear him; and now he affirms it to be his resolution to publish or celebrate his praises.

13. In the 13th verse, he sets forth the reason of this, which is, because, in delivering him, God had given a singular and remarkable proof of his mercy.

14. O God! the proud are risen up against me. In representing his enemies as having no regard to God, he means to set forth the extreme excess of their cruelty. The fury of our lusts, unless we are restrained by the fear of God and the sense of his judgment, will become so great as to dare any thing, however atrocious.

15. And thou, O Lord! art God, merciful, ready to forgive. By immediately passing on to the celebration of these divine attributes, he would intimate, that we have adequate strength and protection against the audacity and rage of the wicked, in the divine goodness, mercy, and faithfulness.

16. Look to me, and have pity upon me. Here the Psalmist makes a more distinct application to himself of what he had said concerning the divine mercy and goodness. As God is merciful, he assures himself that his welfare will be the object of the divine care.

17. The last verse contains an additional confirmation of the statement, that he was in a manner forsaken of God. He would not have desired to be favored with some token of the divine favor, had he not been on all sides driven to despair, and had not the divine favor been hidden from him to try his patience. He desires that his enemies may be put to shame, because they assailed his simplicity with mockery and scoffing, as if he had acted a foolish part by trusting in God.

expectation; for thou, Lord, art good;" and whither should beggars go but to the door of the good housekeeper? The goodness of God's nature is a great encouragement to us in all our addresses to him.

8-17 Petitions and praises; prayer for mercy and grace.

David is here going on in his prayer.

I. He gives glory to God; for we ought in our prayers to praise him, ascribing kingdom, power, and glory, to him, with the most humble and reverent adorations.

1. As a being of unparalleled perfection, such a one that there is none like him nor any to be compared with him, v. 8. Among the gods, the false gods, whom the heathens worshipped, the angels, the kings of the earth, among them all, there is none like unto thee, O Lord!

2. As the fountain of all being and the center of all praise (v. 9): "Thou hast made all nations, made them all of one blood; they all derive their being from thee, and have a constant dependence on thee, and therefore they shall come and worship before thee and glorify thy name."

3. As a being infinitely great (v. 10).

4. As a being infinitely good. Man is bad, very wicked and vile (v. 14); no mercy is to be expected from him; but thou, O Lord! art a God full of compassion, and gracious, v. 15. This is that attribute by which he proclaims his name, and by which we are therefore to proclaim it, Exod. xxxiv. 6, 7. It is his goodness that is over all his works.

5. As a kind friend and bountiful benefactor to him. We ought to praise God as good in himself, but we do it most feelingly when we observe how good he has been to us. This therefore the psalmist dwells upon with most pleasure, v. 12, 13. He had said (v. 9), All nations shall praise thee, O Lord!

II. He prays earnestly for mercy and grace from God. He complains of the restless and implacable malice of his enemies against him (v. 14): "Lord, be thou for me; for there are many against me." He then takes notice of their character; they were proud men that looked with disdain upon poor David. His petitions are,

1. For the operations of God's grace in him, v. 11.

2. For the tokens of God's favor to him, v. 16, 17.

Three things he here prays for:

(1.) That God would speak peace and comfort to him: "O turn unto me, as to one thou lovest and hast a kind and tender concern for. My enemies turn against me, my friends turn from me; Lord, do thou turn to me and have mercy upon me; it will be a comfort to me to know that thou pitiest me."

(2.) That God would work deliverance for him, and set him in safety: "Give me thy strength; put strength into me, that I may help myself, and put forth thy strength for me, that I may be saved out of the hands of those that seek my ruin."

(3.) That God would put a reputation on him.

Psalm 87

Title
A Psalm or Song for the sons of Korah.

1 His foundation is in the holy mountains.
2 The LORD loveth the gates of Zion more than all the dwellings of Jacob.
3 Glorious things are spoken of thee, O city of God. Selah.
4 I will make mention of Rahab and Babylon to them that know me: behold Philistia, and Tyre, with Ethiopia; this man was born there.
5 And of Zion it shall be said, This and that man was born in her: and the highest himself shall establish her.
6 The LORD shall count, when he writeth up the people, that this man was born there. Selah.
7 As well the singers as the players on instruments shall be there: all my springs are in thee.

Psalm 87

TITLE. A Psalm or Song for the sons of Korah. A sacred hymn and a national lyric. A theocracy blends the religious and the patriotic ideas in one; and in proportion as nations become Christianized, their popular songs will become deeply imbued with pious sentiments. Judged by this standard, our own land is far in arrears. This "Psalm or song" was either composed by the sons of Korah, or dedicated to them: as they kept the doors of the house of the Lord, they could use this beautiful composition as a Psalm within the doors, and as a song outside.
SUBJECT AND DIVISION. The song is in honor of Zion, or Jerusalem, and it treats of God's favor to that city among the mountains, the prophecies which made it illustrious, and the honor of being a native of it. Many conceive that it was written at the founding of David's city of Zion, but does not the mention of Babylon imply a later date? It would seem to have been written after Jerusalem and the Temple had been built, and had enjoyed a history, of which glorious things could be spoken. Among other marvels of God's love in its later history, it had been untouched by Sennacherib when other cities of Israel and Judah had fallen victims to his cruelty.

EXPOSITION
Verse 1. His foundation is in the holy mountains. The Psalm begins abruptly, the poet's heart was full, and it gained vent on a sudden. Sudden passion is evil, but bursts of holy joy are most precious. God has chosen to found his earthly temple upon the mountains; he might have selected other spots, but it was his pleasure to have his chosen abode upon Zion.
Verse 2. The Lord loveth the gates of Zion more than all the dwellings of Jacob. The gates are put for the city itself. The love of God is greatest to his own elect nation, descended from his servant Jacob, yet the central seat of his worship is dearer still; no other supposable comparison could have so fully displayed the favor which Jehovah bore to Jerusalem,—he loves Jacob best and Zion better than the best.
Verse 3. Glorious things are spoken of thee, O city of God. This is true of Jerusalem. Her history, which is the story of the nation of which she is the capital, is full of glorious incidents, and her use and end as the abode of the true God, and of his worship, was preeminently glorious.
Verse 4. I will make mention of Rahab and Babylon to them that know me. This shall be a glorious subject to speak of concerning Zion, that her old foes are new born and have become her friends, worshipping in the temple of her God.
Verse 5. And of Zion it shall be said, This and that man was born in her. Not as nations only, but one by one, as individuals, the citizens of the New Jerusalem shall be counted, and their names publicly declared.
Verse 6. The Lord shall count, when he writeth up the people, that this man was born there. At the great census which the Lord himself shall take, he will number the nations without exception and make an exact registry of them, whether they were by their natural descent Babylonians or Tyrians, or other far off heathen. May it be our happy lot to be numbered with the Lord's chosen both in life and death.
Verse 7. In vision the Psalmist sees the citizens of Zion rejoicing at some sacred festival, and marching in triumphant procession with vocal and instrumental music:—As well the singers as the players on instruments shall be there. Where God is there must be joy, and where the church is increased by numerous conversions the joy becomes exuberant and finds out ways of displaying itself.

JOHN CALVIN

Psalm 87

1-3
1. His foundations are in the holy mountains. There is this difference, which is always to be remembered, that while other cities were founded and built by the guidance and power of God, merely for the sake of civil government, Jerusalem was his peculiar sanctuary, and his royal seat. Isaiah also uses a similar form of expression, (Isaiah 14:32,) "The Lord hath founded Zion, and the poor of his people shall trust in it." Besides, although the whole country of Judea was consecrated to God, yet he is said to have rejected all the other cities, and to have chosen this one for himself in which to reign.
2. Jehovah loveth the gates of Zion above all the dwellings of Jacob. Here we are taught that all the excellence of the holy city depended on the free choice which God had made of it. With this agrees what is stated in Psalm 78:60, 67, that God rejected Shiloh, the tribe of Ephraim, and the tabernacle of Joseph, that he might dwell in Zion which he loved.
3. Glorious things are spoken of thee, O city of God! The reading literally is, That which is spoken in thee are glorious things. We must consider the design of the prophet, or rather the object of the Spirit of God, speaking by the mouth of the prophet. From the low and despised condition of the whole people, it was difficult to cherish the hope that the holy city would be restored.

4-6
4. I will make mention of Rahab and Babel. The name of Rahab is put for Egypt in many other parts of Scripture; and this signification is very suitable to the present passage, the object of which is to portray the magnificent amplitude of the Church, which as yet was only matter of hope.
5. And it shall be said of Zion, Man and man is born in her. It is asserted, in the 4th verse, that new citizens shall be gathered into the Church of God from different parts of the world; and here the same subject is prosecuted. Another figure is however employed, which is, that strangers by birth shall be accounted among the holy people, just as if they were descended from Abraham.
6. The Lord will recount, when he writeth the peoples. The meaning is, that Zion will acquire such renown as to excite all men with the greatest earnestness to desire to be admitted into the number and rank of her citizens. It is a highly honorable condition which is spoken of, the language implying, that when God shall take a census of the people on whom he will be graciously pleased to confer the highest honor, he will write them as belonging to Zion, rather than to Babylon; for to be one of the common people among the citizens of Zion, will be a greater distinction than to be invested with the highest rank anywhere else.
7. The singers as the players upon instruments. The sense here is that so great will be the ground for rejoicing, that the praises of God will resound in Zion continually, with the energy of the living voice, as well as with musical instruments.

MATTHEW HENRY

Psalm 87

1-3 The glory of Zion.
Three things are here observed, in praise of the temple:
1. That it was founded on the holy mountains, v. 1. The church has a foundation, so that it cannot sink or totter; Christ himself is the foundation of it, which God has laid. The Jerusalem above is a city that has foundations. The foundation is upon the mountains. It is built high; the mountain of the Lord's house is established upon the top of the mountains, Isa. ii. 2. It is built firmly; the mountains are rocky, and on a rock the church is built.
2. That God had expressed a particular affection for it (v. 2): The Lord loveth the gates of Zion, of the temple, of the houses of doctrine (so the Chaldee), more than all the dwellings of Jacob, whether in Jerusalem or any where else in the country. God had said concerning Zion, This is my rest for ever; here will I dwell. There he met his people, and conversed with them, received their homage, and showed them the tokens of his favor, and therefore we may conclude how well he loves those gates.
3. That there was much said concerning it in the word of God (v. 3): Glorious things are spoken of thee, O city of God! We are to judge of things and persons by the figure they make and the estimate put upon them in and by the scripture.

4-7 The glory of Zion.
Zion is here compared with other places, and preferred before them; the church of Christ is more glorious and excellent than the nations of the earth.
1. It is owned that other places have their glories (v. 4): "I will make mention of Rahab" (that is, Egypt) "and Babylon, to those that know me and are about me, and with whom I discourse about public affairs; behold Philistia and Tyre, with Ethiopia" (or rather Arabia), "we will observe that this man was born there; here and there one famous man, eminent for knowledge and virtue, may be produced, that was a native of these countries; here and there one that becomes a proselyte and worshipper of the true God."
2. It is proved that the glory of Zion outshines them all, upon many accounts; for Zion shall produce many great and good men that shall be famous in their generation, v. 5. Of Zion it shall be said by all her neighbors that this and that man were born in her, many men of renown for wisdom and piety, and especially for acquaintance with the words of God and the visions of the Almighty—many prophets and kings, who should be greater favorites of heaven, and greater blessings to the earth, than ever were bred in Egypt or Babylon. The worthies of the church far exceed those of heathen nations, and their names will shine brighter than in perpetual records.

Psalm 88

Title

A Song or Psalm for the sons of Korah. To the chief Musician upon Mahalath Leannoth, Maschil of Heman the Ezrahite.

1-6

1 O lord God of my salvation, I have cried day and night before thee:
2 Let my prayer come before thee: incline thine ear unto my cry;
3 For my soul is full of troubles: and my life draweth nigh unto the grave.
4 I am counted with them that go down into the pit: I am as a man that hath no strength:
5 Free among the dead, like the slain that lie in the grave, whom thou rememberest no more: and they are cut off from thy hand.
6 Thou hast laid me in the lowest pit, in darkness, in the deeps.

Psalm 88

TITLE. A Song or Psalm for the sons of Korah. This sad complaint reads very little like a Song, nor can we conceive how it could be called by a name which denotes a song of praise or triumph; yet perhaps it was intentionally so called to show how faith "glories in tribulations also." Assuredly, if ever there was a song of sorrow and a Psalm of sadness, this is one. The sons of Korah, who had often united in chanting jubilant odes, are now bidden to take charge of this mournful dirge like hymn. Servants and singers must not be choosers. To the chief Musician. He must superintend the singers and see that they do their duty well, for holy sorrow ought to be expressed with quite as much care as the most joyful praise; nothing should be slovenly in the Lord's house. It is more difficult to express sorrow fitly than it is to pour forth notes of gladness. Upon Mahalath Leannoth. This is translated by Alexander, "concerning afflictive sickness", and if this be correct, it indicates the mental malady which occasioned this plaintive song. Maschil. This term has occurred many times before, and the reader will remember that it indicates an instructive or didactic Psalm:—the sorrows of one saint are lessons to others; experimental teaching is exceedingly valuable. Of Heman the Ezrahite. This, probably, informs us as to its authorship; it was written by Heman, but which Heman it would not be easy to determine, though it will not be a very serious mistake if we suppose it to be the man alluded to in 1Ki 4:31, as the brother of Ethan, and one of the five sons of Zerah (1Ch 2:6), the son of Judah, and hence called "the Ezrahite": if this be the man, he was famous for his wisdom, and his being in Egypt during the time of Pharaoh's oppression may help to account for the deep bass of his song, and for the antique form of many of the expressions, which are more after the manner of Job than David. There was, however, a Heman in David's day who was one of the grand trio of chief musicians, "Heman, Asaph, and Ethan" (1Ch 15:19), and no one can prove that this was not the composer. The point is of no consequence; whoever wrote the Psalm most have been a man of deep experience, who had done business on the great waters of soul trouble.

SUBJECT AND DIVISION. This Psalm is fragmentary, and the only division of any service to us would be that suggested by Albert Barnes, viz.—A description of the sick man's sufferings (Ps 88:1-9), and a prayer for mercy and deliverance (Ps 88:10-18). We shall, however, consider each verse separately, and so exhibit the better the incoherence of the author's grief. The reader had better first peruse the Psalm as a whole.

EXPOSITION

Verse 1. O Lord God of my salvation. This is a hopeful title by which to address the Lord, and it has about it the only ray of comfortable light which shines throughout the Psalm. The writer has salvation, he is sure of that, and God is the sole author of it. While a man can see God as his Savior, it is not altogether midnight with him.

Verse 2. Let my prayer come before thee. Admit it to an audience; let it speak with thee. Though it be my prayer, and therefore very imperfect, yet deny it not thy gracious consideration. Incline thine ear unto my cry. It is not music save to the ear of mercy, yet be not vexed with its discord, though it be but a cry, for it is the most natural expression of my soul's anguish. When my heart speaks, let thine ear hear.

Verse 3. For my soul is full of troubles. I am satiated and nauseated with them. Like a vessel full to the brim with vinegar, my heart is filled up with adversity till it can hold no more. He had his house full and his hands full of sorrow; but, worse than that, he had his heart full of it. Trouble in the soul is the soul of trouble.

Verse 4. I am counted with them that go down into the pit. My weakness is so great that both by myself and others I am considered as good as dead.

JOHN CALVIN

Psalm 88

1-5
1. O Jehovah! God of my salvation! Let me call upon you particularly to notice what I have just now stated, that although the prophet simply, and without hyperbole, recites the agony which he suffered from the greatness of his sorrows, yet his purpose was at the same time to supply the afflicted with a form of prayer that they might not faint under any adversities, however severe, which might befall them. We will hear him by and by bursting out into vehement complaints on account of the grievousness of his calamities; but he seasonably fortifies himself by this brief exordium, lest, carried away with the heat of his feelings, he might become chargeable with complaining and murmuring against God, instead of humbly supplicating Him for pardon.
3-4. For my soul is filled with troubles. These words contain the excuse which the prophet pleads for the excess of his grief. They imply that his continued crying did not proceed from softness or effeminacy of spirit, but that from a due consideration of his condition, it would be found that the immense accumulation of miseries with which he was oppressed was such as might justly extort from him these lamentations. Nor does he speak of one kind of calamity only; but of calamities so heaped one upon another that his heart was filled with sorrow, till it could contain no more. He next particularly affirms that his life was not far from the grave. This idea he pursues and expresses in terms more significant in the following verse, where he complains that he was, as it were, dead.
5. Free among the dead, lie the slain who lie in the grave. The prophet intended to express something more distressing and grievous than common death. First, he says, that he was free among the dead, because he was rendered unfit for all the business which engages human life, and, as it were, cut off from the world. In the next place, comparing himself with those who have been wounded, he bewails his condition as worse than if, enfeebled by calamities, he were going down to death by little and little; for we are naturally inspired with horror at the prospect of a violent death.

6-9
6. Thou hast laid me in the lowest pit. The Psalmist now acknowledges more distinctly, that whatever adversities he endured proceeded from the Divine hand. Nor indeed will any man sincerely betake himself to God to seek relief without a previous persuasion that it is the Divine hand which smites him, and that nothing happens by chance. It is observable that the nearer the prophet approaches God the more is his grief embittered; for nothing is more dreadful to the saints than the judgment of God.
7. This verse views the prophet as declaring that he sustained the whole burden of God's wrath; seeing he was afflicted with His waves. Farther, as so dreadful a flood did not prevent him from lifting up his heart and prayers to God, we may learn

MATTHEW HENRY

Psalm 88

1-9 Sorrowful complaints; complaining to God.
Now here we have the psalmist,
I. A man of prayer, one that gave himself to prayer at all times, but especially now that he was in affliction; for is any afflicted? let him pray. It is his comfort that he had prayed; it is his complaint that, notwithstanding his prayer, he was still in affliction. He was,
1. Very earnest in prayer: "I have cried unto thee (v. 1), and have stretched out my hands unto thee (v. 9), as one that would take hold on thee, and even catch at the mercy, with a holy fear of coming short and missing of it."
2. He was very frequent and constant in prayer: I have called upon thee daily (v. 9), nay, day and night, v. 1. For thus men ought always to pray, and not to faint; God's own elect cry day and night to him, not only morning and evening, beginning every day and every night with prayer, but spending the day and night in prayer. This is indeed praying always; and then we shall speed in prayer, when we continue instant in prayer.
3. He directed his prayer to God, and from him expected and desired an answer (v. 2): "Let my prayer come before thee, to be accepted of thee, not before men, to be seen of them, as the Pharisees' prayers." He does not desire that men should hear them, but, "Lord, incline thy ear unto my cry, for to that I refer myself; give what answer to it thou pleasest."
II. He was a man of sorrows, and therefore some make him, in this psalm, a type of Christ, whose complaints on the cross, and sometimes before, were much to the same purport with this psalm. He cries out (v. 3): My soul is full of troubles; so Christ said, Now is my soul troubled; and, in his agony, My soul is exceedingly sorrowful even unto death, like the psalmist's here, for he says, My life draws nigh unto the grave. Heman was a very wise man, and a very good man, a man of God, and a singer too.
III. He looked upon himself as a dying man, whose heart was ready to break with sorrow (v. 5): "Free among the dead (one of that ghastly corporation), like the slain that lie in the grave, whose rotting and perishing nobody takes notice of or is concerned for, nay, whom thou rememberest no more, to protect or provide for the dead bodies, but they become an easy prey to corruption and the worms; they are cut off from thy hand, which used to be employed in supporting them and reaching out to them; but, now there is no more occasion for this, they are cut off from it and cut off by it" (for God will not stretch out his hand to the grave, Job xxx. 24); "thou hast laid me in the lowest pit, as low as possible, my condition low, my spirits low, in darkness, in the deep (v. 6), sinking, and seeing no way open of escape, brought to the last extremity, and ready to give up all for gone." Thus greatly may good men be afflicted, such dismal apprehensions may they

Psalm 88

7-12

7 Thy wrath lieth hard upon me, and thou hast afflicted me with all thy waves. Selah.
8 Thou hast put away mine acquaintance far from me; thou hast made me an abomination unto them: I am shut up, and I cannot come forth.
9 Mine eye mourneth by reason of affliction: LORD, I have called daily upon thee, I have stretched out my hands unto thee.
10 Wilt thou shew wonders to the dead? shall the dead arise and praise thee? Selah.
11 Shall thy loving kindness be declared in the grave? or thy faithfulness in destruction?
12 Shall thy wonders be known in the dark? and thy righteousness in the land of forgetfulness?

If those about me have not ordered my coffin they have at least conversed about my sepulcher, discussed my estate, and reckoned their share of it. Many a man has been buried before he was dead, and the only mourning over him has been because he refused to fulfill the greedy expectations of his hypocritical relatives by going down to the pit at once. It has come to this with some afflicted believers, that their hungry heirs think they have lived too long.

Verse 5. Free among the dead. Unbound from all that links a man with life, familiar with death's door, a freeman of the city of the sepulcher, I seem no more one of earth's drudges, but begin to anticipate the rest of the tomb. It is a sad case when our only hope lies in the direction of death, our only liberty of spirit amid the congenial horrors of corruption.

Verse 6. Thou hast laid me in the lowest pit, in darkness, in the deeps. What a collection of forcible metaphors, each one expressive of the utmost grief. Heman compared his forlorn condition to an imprisonment in a subterranean dungeon, to confinement in the realms of the dead, and to a plunge into the abyss. None of the similes are strained. The mind can descend far lower than the body, for it there are bottomless pits.

Verse 7. Thy wrath lieth hard upon me. Dreadful plight this, the worst in which a man can be found. Wrath is heavy in itself; God's wrath is crushing beyond conception, and when that presses hard the soul is oppressed indeed. The wrath of God is the very hell of hell, and when it weighs upon the conscience a man feels a torment such as only that of damned spirits can exceed. Joy or peace, or even numbness of indifference, there can be none to one who is loaded with this most tremendous of burdens.

Verse 8. Thou hast put away mine acquaintance far from me. If ever we need friends it is in the dreary hour of despondency and the weary time of bodily sickness; therefore does the sufferer complain because divine providence had removed his friends. Perhaps his disease was infectious or defiling, so that he was legally separated from his fellow men, perhaps their fears kept them away from his plague stricken house, or else his good name had become so injured that they naturally avoided him. Lost friends require but small excuse for turning their backs on the afflicted.

Verse 9. Mine eye mourneth by reason of affliction. He wept his eyes out. He exhausted the lachrymal glands, he wore away the sight itself. Tears in showers are a blessing, and work our good; but in floods they become destructive and injurious.

Verse 10. Wilt thou shew wonders to the dead? Wherefore then suffer me to die? While I live thou canst in me display the glories of thy grace, but when I have passed into the unknown land, how canst thou illustrate in me thy love? If I perish thou wilt lose a worshipper who both reverenced, and in his own experience illustrated, the wonders of thy character and acts. This is good pleading, and therefore he repeats it.

Verse 11. Shall thy lovingkindness be declared in the grave? Thy tender goodness—who shall testify concerning it in that cold abode where the worm and corruption hold their riot? The living may indite "meditations among the Tombs", but the dead know nothing, and therefore can declare nothing. Or thy faithfulness in destruction? If the Lord suffered his servant to die before the divine promise was fulfilled, it would be quite impossible for his faithfulness to be proclaimed.

Verse 12. Shall thy wonders be known in the dark? If not here permitted to prove their goodness of Jehovah, how could the singer do so in the land of darkness and death shade? Could his tongue, when turned into a clod, alarm the dull cold ear of death? Is not a living dog better than a dead lion, and a living believer of more value to the cause of God on earth than all the departed put together?

Verse 13. But unto thee have I cried, O LORD; I have continued to pray for help to thee, O Jehovah, the living God, even though thou hast so long delayed to answer. A true born child of God may be known by his continuing

from his example to cast the anchor of our faith and prayers direct into heaven in all the perils of shipwreck to which we may be exposed.
8. Thou hast removed my acquaintances from me. He was now destitute of all human aid, and that also he attributes to the anger of God, in whose power it is either to bend the hearts of men to humanity, or to harden them, and render them cruel.
9. My eye mourneth because of my affliction. To prevent it from being supposed that he was iron-hearted, he again repeats that his afflictions were so severe and painful as to produce manifest traces of his sorrow, even in his countenance and eyes—a plain indication of the low condition to which he was reduced. But he, notwithstanding, testifies that he was not drawn away from God, like many who, secretly murmuring in their hearts, and, to use a proverbial expression, chafing upon the bit, have nothing farther from their thoughts than to disburden their cares into the bosom of God, in order to derive comfort from Him.

10-13
10. Wilt thou perform a miracle for the dead? By these words the prophet intimates, that God, if he did not make haste to succor him, would be too late, there being scarce anything betwixt him and death; and that therefore this was the critical juncture, if God was inclined to help him, for should the present opportunity not be embraced another would not occur. He asks how long God meant to delay,—if he meant to do so till death intervened, that he might raise the dead by a miracle? He does not speak of the resurrection at the last day, which will surpass all other miracles, as if he called it in question; yet he cannot be vindicated from the charge of going to excess, for it does not belong to us to prescribe to God the season of succoring us. We impeach his power if we believe not that it is as easy for him to restore life to the dead as to prevent, in proper season, the extreme danger which may threaten us from actually lighting upon us. Great as has been the constancy of the saints, it has always had some mixture of the infirmity of the flesh, which has rendered it necessary for God, in the exercise of his fatherly clemency, to bear with the sin with which even their very virtues have been to a degree contaminated. When the Psalmist asks, Shall thy loving-kindness be declared in the grave? he does not mean that the dead are devoid of consciousness; but he pursues the same sentiment which he had previously stated, That it is a more seasonable time to succor men, whilst in the midst of danger they are as yet crying, than to raise them up from their graves when they are dead. He reasons from what ordinarily happens; it not being God's usual way to bring the dead out of their graves to be witnesses and publishers of his goodness.
13. But to thee have I cried, O Jehovah! There may have been a degree of intemperateness in the language of the prophet, which, as I have granted, cannot be altogether vindicated; but still it was a sign of rare faith and piety to persevere as he did with never-failing earnestness in prayer. This is what is meant when he says, that he made haste in the morning; by which

have concerning their afflictions, and such dark conclusions may they sometimes be ready to make concerning the issue of them, through the power of melancholy and the weakness of faith.
IV. He complained most of God's displeasure against him, which infused the wormwood and the gall into the affliction and the misery (v. 7): Thy wrath lies hard upon me. Could he have discerned the favor and love of God in his affliction, it would have lain light upon him; but it lay hard, very hard, upon him, so that he was ready to sink and faint under it. The impressions of this wrath upon his spirits were God's waves with which he afflicted him, which rolled upon him, one on the neck of another, so that he scarcely recovered from one dark thought before he was oppressed with another; these waves beat against him with noise and fury; not some, but all, of God's waves were made use of in afflicting him and bearing him down. Even the children of God's love may sometimes apprehend themselves children of wrath, and no outward trouble can lie so hard upon them as that apprehension.
V. It added to his affliction that his friends deserted him and made themselves strange to him. When we are in trouble it is some comfort to have those about us that love us, and sympathize with us; but this good man had none such, which gives him occasion, not to accuse them, or charge them with treachery, ingratitude, and inhumanity, but to complain to God, with an eye to his hand in this part of the affliction (v. 8): Thou hast put away my acquaintance far from me. Providence had removed them, or rendered them incapable of being serviceable to him, or alienated their affections from him; for every creature is that to us (and no more) that God makes it to be.
VI. He looked upon his case as helpless and deplorable: "I am shut up, and I cannot come forth, a close prisoner, under the arrests of divine wrath, and no way open of escape." He therefore lies down and sinks under his troubles, because he sees not any probability of getting out of them. For thus he bemoans himself (v. 9): My eye mourneth by reason of affliction.

10-18 Pleading with God.
In these verses,
I. The psalmist expostulates with God concerning the present deplorable condition he was in (v. 10-12): "Wilt thou do a miraculous work to the dead, and raise them to life again? Shall those that are dead and buried rise up to praise thee? No; they leave it to their children to rise up in their room to praise God; none expects that they should do it; and wherefore should they rise, wherefore should they live, but to praise God? The life we are born to at first, and the life we hope to rise to at last, must thus be spent. But shall thy lovingkindness to thy people be declared in the grave, either by those or to those that lie buried there? And thy faithfulness to thy promise, shall that be told in destruction? shall thy wonders be wrought in the dark, or known there, and

Psalm 88

13-18
13 But unto thee have I cried, O LORD; and in the morning shall my prayer prevent thee.
14 LORD, why castest thou off my soul? why hidest thou thy face from me?
15 I am afflicted and ready to die from my youth up: while I suffer thy terrors I am distracted.
16 Thy fierce wrath goeth over me; thy terrors have cut me off.
17 They came round about me daily like water; they compassed me about together.
18 Lover and friend hast thou put far from me, and mine acquaintance into darkness.

to cry; a hypocrite is great at a spurt, but the genuine believer holds on till he wins his suit.

Verse 14. LORD, why castest thou oft my soul? Hast thou not aforetime chosen me, wilt thou now reject me? Shall thine elect ones become thy reprobates? Dost thou, like changeable men, give a writing of divorcement to those whom thy love has espoused? Can thy beloveds become thy cast offs? Why hidest thou thy face from me? Wilt thou not so much as look upon me? Canst thou not afford me a solitary smile? Why this severity to one who has in brighter days basked in the light of thy favor? We may put these questions to the Lord, nay, we ought to do so. It is not undue familiarity, but holy boldness.

Verse 15. I am afflicted and ready to die from my youth up. His affliction had now lasted so long that he could hardly remember when it commenced; it seemed to him as if he had been at death's door ever since he was a child. This was no doubt an exaggeration of a depressed spirit.

Verse 16. Thy fierce wrath goeth over me. What an expression, "fierce wrath", and it is a man of God who feels it! Do we seek an explanation? It seemed so to him, but "tidings are not what they seem." No punitive anger ever falls upon the saved one, for Jesus shields him from it all; but a father's anger may fall upon his dearest child, none the less but all the more, because he loves it. Since Jesus bore my guilt as my substitute, my Judge cannot punish me, but my Father can and will correct me. In this sense the Father may even manifest "fierce wrath" to his erring child, and under a sense of it that dear broken down one may be laid in the dust and covered with wretchedness, and yet for all that he may be accepted and beloved of the Lord all the while.

Verse 17. They came round about me daily like water. My troubles, and thy chastisement poured in upon me, penetrating everywhere, and drowning all. Such is the permeating and pervading power of spiritual distress, there is no shutting it out; it soaks into the soul like the dew into Gideon's fleece; it sucks the spirit down as the quicksand swallows the ship; it overwhelms it as the deluge submerged the green earth.

Verse 18. Lover and friend: hast thou put far from me. Even when they are near me bodily, they are so unable to swim with me in such deep waters, that they stand like men far away on the shore while I am buffeted with the billows; but, alas, they shun me, the dearest lover of all is afraid of such a distracted one, and those who took counsel with me avoid me now! The Lord Jesus knew the meaning of this in all its wormwood and gall when in his passion. In dreadful loneliness he trod the wine press, and all his garments were distained with the red blood of those sour grapes. Lonely sorrow falls to the lot of not a few; let them not repine, but enter herein into close communion with that dearest lover and friend who is never far from his tried ones. And mine acquaintance into darkness, or better still, my acquaintance is darkness. I am familiar only with sadness, all else has vanished. I am a child crying alone in the dark. Will the heavenly Father leave his child there? Here he breaks off, and anything more from us would only spoil the abruptness of the unexpected FINIS.

he would have us not to imagine that he slowly and coldly lingered till he was constrained by dire necessity. At the same time, he modestly intimates by these words, that his pining away in long continued miseries was not owing to his own sluggishness, as if he had not sought God. This is an example particularly worthy of notice, that we may not become discouraged if it happen sometimes that our prayers are for a time unsuccessful, although they may proceed from the heart, and may be assiduously persevered in.

14-18

14. Wherefore, O Jehovah! wilt thou reject my soul? These lamentations at first sight would seem to indicate a state of mind in which sorrow without any consolation prevailed; but they contain in them tacit prayers. The Psalmist does not proudly enter into debate with God, but mournfully desires some remedy to his calamities. This kind of complaint justly deserves to be reckoned among the unutterable groanings of which Paul makes mention in Romans 8:26. Had the prophet thought himself rejected and abhorred by God, he certainly would not have persevered in prayer. But here he sets forth the judgment of the flesh, against which he strenuously and magnanimously struggled, that it might at length be manifest from the result that he had not prayed in vain. Although, therefore, this psalm does not end with thanksgiving, but with a mournful complaint, as if there remained no place for mercy, yet it is so much the more useful as a means of keeping us in the duty of prayer. The prophet, in heaving these sighs, and discharging them, as it were, into the bosom of God, doubtless ceased not to hope for the salvation of which he could see no signs by the eye of sense. He did not call God, at the opening of the psalm, the God of his salvation, and then bid farewell to all hope of succor from him.

15-17. The reason why he says that he was ready to die from his youth, is uncertain, unless it may be considered a probable conjecture that he was severely tried in a variety of ways, so that his life, as it were, hung by a thread amidst various tremblings and fears. Whence also we gather that God's wraths and terrors, of which he speaks in the 16th verse, were not of short continuance. He expresses them in the 17th verse as having encompassed him daily. Since nothing is more dreadful than to conceive of God as angry with us, he not improperly compares his distress to a flood. Hence also proceeded his doubting. For a sense of the divine anger must necessarily have agitated his mind with sore disquietude. When the heart is in perplexity and doubt, or rather is tossed hither and thither, faith seems to be swallowed up. But experience teaches us, that faith, while it fluctuates amidst these agitations, continues to rise again from time to time, so as not to be overwhelmed; and if at any time it is at the point of being stifled, it is nevertheless sheltered and cherished, for though the tempests may become never so violent, it shields itself from them by reflecting that God continues faithful, and never disappoints or forsakes his own children.

thy righteousness in the grave, which is the land of forgetfulness, where men remember nothing, nor are themselves remembered? Departed souls may indeed know God's wonders and declare his faithfulness, justice, and lovingkindness; but deceased bodies cannot; they can neither receive God's favors in comfort nor return them in praise."

II. He resolves to continue instant in prayer, and the more so because the deliverance was deferred (v. 13): "Unto thee have I cried many a time, and found comfort in so doing, and therefore I will continue to do so; in the morning shall my prayer prevent thee."

III. He sets down what he will say to God in prayer.

1. He will humbly reason with God concerning the abject afflicted condition he was now in (v. 14): "Lord, why castest thou off my soul? What is it that provokes thee to treat me as one abandoned? Show me wherefore thou contendest with me." He speaks it with wonder that God should cast off an old servant, should cast off one that was resolved not to cast him off: "No wonder men cast me off; but, Lord, why dost thou, whose gifts and callings are without repentance? Why hidest thou thy face, as one angry at me, that either hast no favor for me or wilt not let me know that thou hast?"

2. He will humbly repeat the same complaints he had before made, until God have mercy on him. Two things he represents to God as his grievances:

(1.) That God was a terror to him: I suffer thy terrors, v. 15. He had continual frightful apprehensions of the wrath of God against him for his sins and the consequences of that wrath.

Note, Even those that are designed for God's favors may yet, for a time, suffer his terrors. The spirit of adoption is first a spirit of bondage to fear.

[1.] They had almost taken away his life: "I am so afflicted with them that I am ready to die, and" (as the word is) "to give up the ghost. Thy terrors have cut me off," v. 16. What is hell, that eternal excision, by which damned sinners are for ever cut off from God and all happiness, but God's terrors fastening and preying upon their guilty consciences?

[2.] They had almost taken away the use of his reason: When I suffer thy terrors I am distracted.

(2.) That no friend he had in the world was a comfort to him (v. 18): Lover and friend hast thou put far from me; some are dead, others at a distance, and perhaps many unkind. Next to the comforts of religion are those of friendship and society; therefore to be friendless is (as to this life) almost to be comfortless; and to those who have had friends, but have lost them, the calamity is the more grievous. With this the psalmist here closes his complaint, as if this were that which completed his woe and gave the finishing stroke to the melancholy piece. If our friends are put far from us by scattering providences, nay, if by death our acquaintance are removed into darkness, we have reason to look upon it as a sore affliction, but must acknowledge and submit to the hand of God in it.

Psalm 89

Title
Maschil of Heman the Ezrahite.

1-8
1 I will sing of the mercies of the LORD for ever: with my mouth will I make known thy faithfulness to all generations.
2 For I have said, Mercy shall be built up for ever: thy faithfulness shalt thou establish in the very heavens.
3 I have made a covenant with my chosen, I have sworn unto David my servant,
4 Thy seed will I establish for ever, and build up thy throne to all generations. Selah.
5 And the heavens shall praise thy wonders, O LORD: thy faithfulness also in the congregation of the saints.
6 For who in the heaven can be compared unto the LORD? who among the sons of the mighty can be likened unto the LORD?
7 God is greatly to be feared in the assembly of the saints, and to be had in reverence of all them that are about him.
8 O LORD God of hosts, who is a strong LORD like unto thee? or to thy faithfulness round about thee?

Psalm 89

We have now reached the majestic Covenant Psalm, which, according to the Jewish arrangement closes the third book of the Psalms. It is the utterance of a believer, in presence of great national disaster, pleading with his God, urging the grand argument of covenant engagements, and expecting deliverance and help, because of the faithfulness of Jehovah.
TITLE. Maschil. This is most fitly called a Maschil, for it is most instructive. No subject is more important or is so fully the key to all theology as that of the covenant. He who is taught by the Holy Spirit to be clear upon the covenant of grace will be a scribe well instructed in the things of the kingdom; he whose doctrinal theory is a mingle mangle of works and grace is scarcely fit to be teacher of babes. Of Ethan the Ezrahite: perhaps the same person as Jeduthun, who was a musician in David's reign; was noted for his wisdom in Solomon's days, and probably survived till the troubles of Rehoboam's period. If this be the man, he must have written this Psalm in his old age, when troubles were coming thick and heavy upon the dynasty of David and the land of Judah; this is not at all improbable, and there is much in the Psalm which looks that way.
DIVISION. The sacred poet commences by affirming his belief in the faithfulness of the Lord to his covenant with the house of David, and makes his first pause at Ps 89:4. He then praises and magnifies the name of the Lord for his power, justice, and mercy, Ps 89:5-14. This leads him to sing of the happiness of the people who have such a God to be their glory and defense, Ps 89:15-18. He rehearses the terms if the covenant at full length with evident delight, Ps 89:19-37, and then mournfully pours out his complaint and petition, Ps 89:38-51, closing the whole with a hearty benediction and a double Amen. May the Holy Spirit greatly bless to us the reading of this most precious Psalm of instruction.

EXPOSITION
Verse 1. I will sing of the mercies of the Lord for ever. A devout resolve, and very commendable when a man is exercised with great trouble on account of an apparent departure of the Lord from his covenant and promise. Whatever we may observe abroad or experience in our own persons, we ought still to praise God for his mercies, since they most certainly remain the same, whether we can perceive them or not.
Verse 2. For I have said, Mercy shall be built up for ever. His heart was persuaded of it, and he had affirmed it as an indisputable truth. He was certain that upon a sure foundation the Lord intended to pile up a glorious palace of goodness—a house of refuge for all people, wherein the Son of David should for ever be glorified as the dispenser of heavenly grace.
Verse 3. I have made a covenant with my chosen, I have sworn unto David my servant. This was the ground of the Psalmist's confidence in God's mercy and truth, for he knew that the Lord had made a covenant of grace with David and his seed, and confirmed it by an oath. Here he quotes the very words of God, which were revealed to him by the Holy Spirit, and are a condensation of the original covenant in 2Sa 7:1-29.
Verse 4. Thy seed will I establish for ever. David must always have a seed, and truly in Jesus this is fulfilled beyond his hopes. What a seed David has in the multitude which have sprung from him who was both his Son and his Lord. The Son of David is the Great Progenitor, the second Adam, the Everlasting Father, he sees his seed, and in them beholds of the travail of his soul.
Verse 5. And the heavens shall praise thy wonders, O Lord. Looking down upon what God had done, and was about to do, in connection with his covenant of grace, all heaven would be filled with adoring wonder. The sun and moon, which had been made tokens of the covenant, would praise God for such an extraordinary display of mercy, and the angels and redeemed spirits would sing, "as it were, a new song."

JOHN CALVIN

Psalm 89

1-4
1. I will sing of the mercies of Jehovah for ever. It must be borne in mind that the Psalmist opens with the praises of God, and with calling to mind the Divine covenant, to encourage the faithful to strengthen their faith against the formidable assaults of temptation. If when we set about the duty of prayer some despairing thought, at the very outset, presents itself to us, we must forcibly and resolutely break through it, lest our hearts faint and utterly fail. The design of the prophet, therefore, was to fortify the minds of the godly at the very commencement, with stable and substantial supports, that, relying on the Divine promise, which, to outward appearance, had almost fallen to the ground, and repelling all the assaults of temptation with which their faith was severely shaken, they might with confidence hope for the re-establishment of the kingdom, and continue perseveringly to pray for this blessing.
2. For I have said, Mercy shall be built up for ever. He assigns the reason why he perseveres in singing the Divine praises in the midst of adversities; which is, that he does not despair of the manifestation of God's loving-kindness towards his people, although at present they were under severe chastisement. Never will a man freely open his mouth to praise God, unless he is fully persuaded that God, even when he is angry with his people, never lays aside his fatherly affection towards them.
3. I have made a covenant with my chosen. The more effectually to confirm himself and all the godly in the faith of the Divine promise, he introduces God himself as speaking and sanctioning, by his authority, what had been said in the preceding verse. As faith ought to depend on the Divine promise, this manner of speaking, by which God is represented as coming forward and alluring us to himself by his own voice, is more forcible than if the prophet himself had simply stated the fact.

5-8
5. And the heavens shall praise thy wondrous work. The prophet, having spoken of God's covenant, even as faith ought to begin at the word, now descends to a general commendation of his works. It is, however, to be observed, that when he treats of the wonderful power of God, he has no other end in view than to exalt and magnify more highly the holiness of the covenant. He exclaims, that this is the God who has rightful claims to be served and feared, who ought to be believed, and upon whose power the most unhesitating confidence may be reposed.
6. For who in the clouds can be compared to Jehovah? The prophet now proceeds to illustrate farther what he had said respecting God's wonders, and exclaims emphatically, Who in the clouds can be compared to God? The reason why he speaks of the clouds, or heaven, is because, what is not surprising, nothing is to be found upon the earth which can at all approach the glory of God.

MATTHEW HENRY

Psalm 89

1-4 The divine mercy and faithfulness.
The psalmist has a very sad complaint to make of the deplorable condition of the family of David at this time, and yet he begins the psalm with songs of praise; for we must, in every thing, in every state, give thanks; thus we must glorify the Lord in the fire. We think, when we are in trouble, that we get ease by complaining; but we do more—we get joy, by praising. Let our complaints therefore be turned into thanksgivings; and in these verses we find that which will be matter of praise and thanksgiving for us in the worst of times, whether upon a personal or a public account,
1. However it be, the everlasting God is good and true, v. 1. Though we may find it hard to reconcile present dark providences with the goodness and truth of God, yet we must abide by this principle, That God's mercies are inexhaustible and his truth is inviolable; and these must be the matter of our joy and praise: "I will sing of the mercies of the Lord for ever, sing a praising song to God's honor, a pleasant song for my own solace, and Maschil, an instructive song, for the edification of others."
2. However it be, the everlasting covenant is firm and sure, v. 2-4. Here we have,
(1.) The psalmist's faith and hope: "Things now look black, and threaten the utter extirpation of the house of David; but I have said, and I have warrant from the word of God to say it, that mercy shall be built up for ever." As the goodness of God's nature is to be the matter of our song (v. 1), so much more the mercy that is built for us in the covenant; it is still increasing, like a house in the building up, and shall still continue our rest for ever, like a house built up. It shall be built up for ever; for the everlasting habitations we hope for in the new Jerusalem are of this building.
(2.) An abstract of the covenant upon which this faith and hope are built: I have said it, says the psalmist, for God hath sworn it, that the heirs of promise might be entirely satisfied of the immutability of his counsel. He brings in God speaking (v. 3), owning, to the comfort of his people, "I have made a covenant, and therefore will make it good."

5-14 The divine power and justice; the glory of God celebrated.
These verses are full of the praises of God. Observe,
I. Where, and by whom, God is to be praised.
1. God is praised by the angels above: The heavens shall praise thy wonders, O Lord! v. 5; that is, "the glorious inhabitants of the upper world continually celebrate thy praises." Bless the Lord, you his angels, Ps. ciii. 20.
2. God is praised by the assemblies of his saints on earth (praise waits for him in Zion); and, though their praises fall so far short of the praises of angels, yet God is pleased to take notice of them, and accept of

Psalm 89

9-16

9 Thou rulest the raging of the sea: when the waves thereof arise, thou stillest them.

10 Thou hast broken Rahab in pieces, as one that is slain; thou hast scattered thine enemies with thy strong arm.

11 The heavens are thine, the earth also is thine: as for the world and the fullness thereof, thou hast founded them.

12 The north and the south thou hast created them: Tabor and Hermon shall rejoice in thy name.

13 Thou hast a mighty arm: strong is thy hand, and high is thy right hand.

14 Justice and judgment are the habitation of thy throne: mercy and truth shall go before thy face.

15 Blessed is the people that know the joyful sound: they shall walk, O LORD, in the light of thy countenance.

16 In thy name shall they rejoice all the day: and in thy righteousness shall they be exalted.

Verse 6. For who in the heaven can be compared unto the Lord—therefore all heaven worships him, seeing none can equal him. Who among the sons of the mighty can be likened unto the Lord?—therefore the assemblies of the saints on earth adore him, seeing none can rival him.

Verse 7. God is greatly to be feared in the assembly of the saints. The holiest tremble in the presence of the thrice Holy One: their familiarity is seasoned with the profoundest awe. Perfect love casts out the fear which hath torment, and works in lieu thereof that other fear which is akin to joy unutterable.

Verse 8. O Lord God of hosts, who is a strong Lord like unto thee? Or Jehovah, God of Hosts, who is like thee, Mighty Jah. Alexander remarks, that the infinite superiority of God to men and angels is here expressed, or rather indicated, by an accumulation of descriptive titles. Here we have the name which displays his self existence, the title which denotes his dominion over all his creatures, and an adjective which sets forth the power with which he exercises his sovereignty.

Verse 9. Thou rulest the raging of the sea. Always, even in the hour of ocean's maddest fury, the Lord controls it. At the Red Sea the foaming billows saw their God and stood upright in awe. When the waves thereof arise, thou stillest them. None else can do this; to attempt it would be madness, but the Lord's "hush" silences the boisterous storm.

Verse 10. Thou hast broken Rahab in pieces as one that is slain. Egypt was crushed like a corpse beneath the chariot wheels of the destroyer: its pomp and glory were broken like the limbs of the dead in battle. Egypt was Israel's ancient foe, and its overthrow wits a theme to which devout minds constantly reverted, as to a subject fit for their most exulting songs.

Verse 11. The heavens are thine, the earth also is thine. All things are alike God's—rebellious earth as well as adoring heaven. Let us not despair of the kingdom of truth; the Lord has not abdicated the throne of earth or handed it over to the sway of Satan. As for the world and the fullness thereof, thou hast founded them. The habitable and cultivated earth, with all its produce, owns the Lord to be both its Creator and Sustainer, builder and upholder.

Verse 12. The north and the south thou hast created them. North and south, opposite poles, agree in this—that Jehovah fashioned them. Tabor and Hermon shall rejoice in thy name, that is to say, east and west are equally formed by thee, and therefore give thee praise. Turn to all points of the compass, and behold the Lord is there.

Verse 13. Thou hast a mighty arm, omnipotence is thine in smiting or uplifting; strong is thy hand, thy power to create and grasp is beyond conception great; and high is thy right hand—thy skill is incomparable, thy favor ennobling, thy working glorious. The power of God so impressed the Psalmist that in many ways he repeated the same thought: and indeed the truth of God's omnipotence is so full of refreshment to gracious hearts that it cannot be too much dwelt upon, especially when viewed in connection with his mercy and truth, as in the following verse.

Verse 14. Justice and judgment are the habitation of thy throne. They are the basis of the divine government, the sphere within which his sovereignty moves. God as a sovereign is never unjust or unwise. He is too holy to be unrighteous, too wise to be mistaken; this is constant matter for joy to the upright in heart.

Verse 15. Blessed is the people that know the joyful sound. It is a blessed God of whom the Psalmist has been singing, and therefore they are a blessed people who partake of his bounty, and know how to exult in his favor. Praise is a peculiarly joyful sound, and blessed are those who are familiar with its strains.

Verse 16. In thy name shall they rejoice all the day. And good cause they have for so doing, for to the soul which, in Christ Jesus, has entered into covenant with God, every attribute is a fountain of delight. There is no hour in the day, and no day in our life, in which we may not rejoice in the name, person, and character of the Lord. We need no other reason for rejoicing.

7-8. God is very terrible in the assembly of the saints. In these words is censured that devilish superstition, to which almost all men are prone, of exalting angels beyond measure, and without reason. But if the angels themselves tremble, and are afraid before the Divine Majesty, why should they not be regarded as subjects, and kept in their own rank, that God alone may have the sovereignty entirely to himself? Farther, when they are represented as around God, the meaning is, that they surround his royal throne like body-guards, and are always ready to execute his behests.

9-14

9. Thou governest the pride of the sea. The prophet has spoken generally concerning the power of God, referring to the miracle of the deliverance of the Israelites from Egypt, which he now celebrates in express terms.

11. The heavens are thine, the earth also is thine. He again repeats, the third time, that the same God who had been the deliverer of the chosen people exercises supreme dominion over the whole world. From the fact that God created all things, he concludes, that it is He who actually presides over, and controls whatever takes place in heaven and in earth.

14. Righteousness and judgement are the place of thy throne. These encomiums serve more effectually to confirm the hope of true believers than if the Divine power alone had been presented to our view. Whenever mention is made of God, it behoves us to apply our minds principally to those attributes of his nature which are specially fitted for establishing our faith, that we may not lose ourselves by vainly indulging in subtle speculations, by which foolish men, although they may minister to their own mental recreation, make no advances to the right understanding of what God really is.

15-18

15. Blessed is the people that know the joyful sound. Here the same train of reflection concerning the Church is pursued, not only because unbelievers are blind to the consideration of God's works, but also because the prophet has no other purpose in view than to inspire the godly with good hope, that they may with confidence rely upon God, and not be discouraged by any adversities from boldly calling upon him.

17. For thou art the glory of their strength. The same sentiment is confirmed when it is declared, that God never leaves his faithful servants destitute of strength. By the appellation the glory of their strength, which is ascribed to him, is meant that they are always so sustained by his present aid as to have just ground to glory in him; or which amounts to the same thing, that his power appears always glorious in aiding and sustaining them.

18. For to Jehovah is our buckler. As the chief protection of the people was in the person of their king, it is here expressly shown, that the maintenance of the welfare of the faithful by his instrumentality is the gift of God.

them, and reckon himself honored by them. "Thy faithfulness and the truth of thy promise, that rock on which the church is built, shall be praised in the congregation of the saints, who owe their all to that faithfulness, and whose constant comfort it is that there is a promise, and that he is faithful who has promised." It is expected from God's saints on earth that they praise him; who should, if they do not? Let every saint praise him, but especially the congregation of saints; when they come together, let them join in praising God. The more the better; it is the more like heaven. Of the honor done to God by the assembly of the saints he speaks again (v. 7): God is greatly to be feared in the assembly of the saints. Saints should assemble for religious worship, that they may publicly own their relation to God and may stir up one another to give honor to him, and, in keeping up communion with God, may likewise maintain the communion of saints.

II. What it is to praise God; it is to acknowledge him to be a being of unparalleled perfection, such a one that there is none like him, nor any to be compared with him, v. 6. If there be any beings that can pretend to vie with God, surely they must be found among the angels; but they are all infinitely short of him: Who in the heaven can be compared with the Lord, so as to challenge any share of the reverence and adoration which are due to him only, or to set up in rivalship with him for the homage of the children of men? They are sons of the mighty, but which of them can be likened unto the Lord? Nobles are princes' peers; some parity there is between them. But there is none between God and the angels; they are not his peers. To whom will you liken me, or shall I be equal? saith the Holy One, Isa. xl. 25. This is insisted on again (v. 8): Who is a strong Lord like unto thee? No angel, no earthly potentate, whatsoever, is comparable to God, or has an arm like him, or can thunder with a voice like him.

III. What we ought, in our praises, to give God the glory of. Several things are here mentioned.

1. The command God has of the most ungovernable creatures (v. 9): Thou rulest the raging of the sea, than which nothing is more frightful or threatening, nor more out of the power of man to give check to; it can swell no higher, roll no further, beat no harder, continue no longer, nor do any more hurt, than God suffers it.

2. The victories God has obtained over the enemies of his church. His ruling the raging of the sea and quelling its billows was an emblem of this (v. 10): Thou hast broken Rahab, many a proud enemy (so it signifies), Egypt in particular, which is sometimes called Rahab, broken it in pieces, as one that is slain and utterly unable to make head again.

3. The incontestable property he has in all the creatures of the upper and lower world (v. 11, 12): "Men are honored for their large possessions; but the heavens are thine, O Lord! the earth also is thine; therefore we praise thee, therefore we trust in thee,

Psalm 89

17-24

17 For thou art the glory of their strength: and in thy favor our horn shall be exalted.
18 For the LORD is our defense; and the Holy One of Israel is our king.
19 Then thou spakest in vision to thy holy one, and saidst, I have laid help upon one that is mighty; I have exalted one chosen out of the people.
20 I have found David my servant; with my holy oil have I anointed him:
21 With whom my hand shall be established: mine arm also shall strengthen him.
22 The enemy shall not exact upon him; nor the son of wickedness afflict him.
23 And I will beat down his foes before his face, and plague them that hate him.
24 But my faithfulness and my mercy shall be with him: and in my name shall his horn be exalted.

Verse 17. For thou art the glory of their strength. Surely in the Lord Jehovah have we both righteousness and strength. He is our beauty and glory when we are strong in him, as well as our comfort and sustenance when we tremble because of conscious weakness in ourselves. No man whom the Lord makes strong may dare to glory in himself, he must ascribe all honor to the Lord alone; we have neither strength nor beauty apart from him.

Verse 18. For the Lord is our defense. Whoever else may defend us, he is our ultimate Defender and Shield. And the Holy one of Israel is our king. He who protects should govern, our defender should be acknowledged as our king. Kings are called the shields of nations, and the God of Israel is both our Ruler and our Defense.

Verse 19. Then thou spakest in vision to thy holy one. The Psalmist returns to a consideration of the covenant made with David. The holy one here meant may be either David or Nathan the prophet, but most probably the latter, for it was to him that the word of the Lord came by night.

Verse 20. I have found David my servant. David was discovered by the Lord among the sheepfolds and recognized as a man of gracious spirit, full of faith and courage, and therefore fit to be leader in Israel. With my holy oil have I anointed him. By the hand of Samuel, David was anointed to be king long before he ascended the throne. The verse must also be expounded of the Prince Emmanuel; he became the servant of the Lord for our sakes, the Father having found for us in his person a mighty deliverer, therefore upon him rested the Spirit without measure, to qualify him for all the offices of love to which he was set apart.

Verse 21. With whom my hand shall be established, or, "with whom my hand shall ever be present." The almightiness of God abides permanently with Jesus in his work as Redeemer and Ruler of his people. Mine arm also shall strengthen him. The fullness of divine power shall attend him.

Verse 22. The enemy shall not exact upon him; he shall not be vexed and persecuted as a helpless debtor by an extortionate creditor. Nor the son of wickedness afflict him. Graceless men shall no longer make his life a burden.

Verse 23. And I will beat down his foes before his face—crushing them and their plans. God himself thus fights the battles of his Son, and effectually overturns his foes. And plague them that hate him, or smite his haters. May none of us learn the terror of this threatening, which is surely being fulfilled upon all those unbelievers who have rejected the Son of God, and died in the hardness of their hearts. The prophecy is also having another fulfillment in the overthrow of systems of error, and the vexation caused to their promoters. There is no such plague to bad men as the prosperity of the cause of Jesus.

Verse 24. But my faithfulness and my mercy shall be with him. These were the two attributes of which the Psalmist began to sing in Ps 89:1, doubtless because he saw them to be most prominent in the covenant which he was about to plead with God. To David and his seed, God was gracious and faithful, and though through their sin the literal kingdom lost all its glory and the dynasty became obscure, yet the line remained unbroken and more than all its former glory was restored by the enthronisation of Him who is Prince of the kings of the earth, with whom the Lord's mercy and faithfulness remain for ever. All who are in Jesus should rejoice, for they shall prove in their own experience the faithful mercy of the Lord.

Verse 25. I will set his hand also in the sea, and his right hand in the rivers. He shall reach far beyond the little rivers which stand for boundaries in Palestine; he shall by his power embrace all lands from sea to sea. He shall have his hand in the ocean and his right hand in earth's mightiest streams. As monarchs hold in their hands a globe to set forth their dominion over the earth, he shall grasp the far more unconquerable sea, and be Lord of all. This power is to be given him of the Lord, and is to be abiding; so we understand the words "I will set." The verse has in it a voice of good cheer

JOHN CALVIN

19-23
19. Then thou spakest in vision to thy meek ones. The Psalmist now declares at greater length why he said that the king, set over the chosen people for the preservation of the public good, was given them from heaven; namely, because he was not chosen by the suffrages of men, nor usurped at his own hand the supreme power, nor insinuated himself into it by corrupt arts, but was elected by God to be the instrument of maintaining the public good, and performed the duties of his office under the auspices and conduct of God.
20. I have found David my servant. The prophet confirms the same proposition, That there was nothing of royalty in David, who owed all to the sovereignty of God in preventing him by his grace. Such is the import of the word found, as if God had said, When I took him to elevate him, this proceeded entirely from my free goodness. The name servant, therefore, does not denote any merit, but is to be referred to the divine call.
22. The enemy shall not exact upon him. Here it is declared in express terms, that although David may not be without enemies, the power of God will be always ready to maintain and defend him, that he may not be oppressed with unrighteous violence. It is accordingly affirmed, that David will not be tributary to his enemies, as he who is vanquished in battle is constrained to grant such conditions of peace as his conqueror may dictate, however injurious to himself these may be.

24-29
24. My truth and my mercy shall be with him. God shows that he will continue to exercise without intermission that grace which he had manifested towards David at first. These words are as if he had said, that to prove himself faithful to his word, he would be always gracious and bountiful. Thus we see that God, not only at the outset, furnished David with testimonies of his goodness, but that he always continued to deal with him in the same merciful way. This has a reference to the whole Church of Christ, so that the divine goodness is manifested in the whole course of our salvation, and not only at our first entrance upon it. The horn of David denotes here, as it often does in other places, his glory, dignity, and power. The meaning therefore is, that by the grace of God, this kingdom shall always flourish and prosper.
25. And I will set his hand in the sea. The vast extent of the kingdom is here adverted to. As the people by their wickedness had, as it were, blocked up the way, and intercepted the blessing of God, their inheritance was more limited than the promise implied. But now God declares, that during the reign of David, it will be again enlarged, so that the people shall possess the whole country, from the sea even to the river Euphrates. From this we gather, that what God had promised by Moses was fulfilled only in the person of David, that is to say, from his time. By the rivers may be understood, either the Euphrates alone, which is cut into many channels, or the other neighboring rivers on the coast of Syria.
26. He shall cry to me, Thou art my Father. In this verse it is declared, that the chief excellence of this king will consist in this, that he will be accounted the Son of God. This indeed

MATTHEW HENRY

therefore we will not fear what man can do against us."
4. The power and justice, the mercy and truth, with which he governs the world and rules in the affairs of the children of men, v. 13, 14.

15-18 The blessedness of Israel declared.
The psalmist, having largely shown the blessedness of the God of Israel, here shows the blessedness of the Israel of God. As there is none like unto the God of Jeshurun, so, happy art thou, O Israel! there is none like unto thee, O people! especially as a type of the gospel—Israel, consisting of all true believers, whose happiness is here described.
I. Glorious discoveries are made to them, and glad tidings of good brought to them; they hear, they know, the joyful sound, v. 15.
II. Special tokens of God's favor are granted them: "They shall walk, O Lord! in the light of thy countenance; they shall govern themselves by thy directions, shall be guided by the eye; and they shall delight themselves in thy consolations. They shall have the favor of God; they shall know that they have it, and it shall be continual matter of joy and rejoicing to them. They shall go through all the exercises of a holy life under the powerful influences of God's lovingkindness, which shall make their duty pleasant to them and make them sincere in it, aiming at this, as their end, to be accepted of the Lord." We then walk in the light of the Lord when we fetch all our comforts from God's favor and are very careful to keep ourselves in his love.
III. They never want matter for joy: Blessed are God's people, for in his name, in all that whereby he has made himself known, if it be not their own fault, they shall rejoice all the day. Those that rejoice in Christ Jesus, and make God their exceeding joy, have enough to counterbalance their grievances and silence their griefs; and therefore their joy is full (1 John i. 4) and constant; it is their duty to rejoice evermore.
IV. Their relation to God is their honor and dignity. They are happy, for they are high. Surely in the Lord, in the Lord Christ, they have righteousness and strength, and so are recommended by him to the divine acceptance; and therefore in him shall all the seed of Israel glory, Isa. xlv. 24, 25. So it is here, v. 16, 17.
V. Their relation to God is their protection and safety (v. 18): "For our shield is of the Lord" (so the margin) "and our king is from the Holy One of Israel. If God be our ruler, he will be our defender; and who is he then that can harm us?" It was the happiness of Israel that God himself had the erecting of their bulwarks and the nominating of their king (so some take it); or, rather, that he was himself a wall of fire round about them, and, as a Holy One, the author and center of their holy religion; he was their King, and so their glory in the midst of them. Christ is the Holy One of Israel, that holy thing; and in nothing was that peculiar people more blessed than in this, that he was born King of the

Psalm 89

25-32

25 I will set his hand also in the sea, and his right hand in the rivers.

26 He shall cry unto me, Thou art my father, my God, and the rock of my salvation.

27 Also I will make him my firstborn, higher than the kings of the earth.

28 My mercy will I keep for him for evermore, and my covenant shall stand fast with him.

29 His seed also will I make to endure for ever, and his throne as the days of heaven.

30 If his children forsake my law, and walk not in my judgments;

31 If they break my statutes, and keep not my commandments;

32 Then will I visit their transgression with the rod, and their iniquity with stripes.

concerning sailors, and all dwellers on the waters; the hand of Jesus is over them, and as he found his first apostles by the sea, so we trust he still finds earnest disciples there.

Verse 27. Also I will make him my firstborn. Among the kings the seed of David were to be most favored and indulged with most love and paternal regard from God: but in Jesus we see this in the highest degree verified, for he has preeminence in all things, inasmuch as by inheritance he has a more glorious name than any other, and is higher than the kings of the earth. Who can rival heaven's Firstborn? The double portion and the government belong to him. Kings are honored when they honor him, and those who honor him are kings!

Verse 28. My mercy will I keep for him for evermore. The kings of David's line needed mercy, and mercy prevented their house from utterly perishing until the Son of Mary came. He needs no mercy for himself, but he is a representative man, and the mercy of God is required for those who are in him: for such mercy is kept for ever. And my covenant shall stand fast with him. With Jesus the covenant is ratified both by blood of sacrifice and by oath of God, it cannot be cancelled or altered, but is an eternal verity, resting upon the veracity of one who cannot lie. What exultation fills our hearts as we see that the covenant of grace is sure to all the seed, because it stands fast with him with whom we are indissolubly united.

Verse 29. His seed also will I make to endure for ever. David's seed lives on in the person of the Lord Jesus, and the seed of Jesus in the persons of believers. Saints are a race that neither death nor life can kill. Rome and its priests, with their inquisition and other infernal cruelties, have labored to exterminate the covenant seed, but "vain is their rage, their efforts vain." As long as God lives, his people must live.

Verse 30. If his children forsake my law, and walk not in my judgments. It was possible, terribly possible, that David's posterity might wander from the Lord; indeed they did so, but what then? Was the mercy of God to pass away from David's seed?—far from it. So, too, the seed of the Son of David are apt to start aside, but are they therefore cast away? Not a single word gives liberty for such an idea, but the very reverse. Expositors in their fear of Calvinistic doctrine shake off the fear of adding to the word of God, or else they would not have spent their time in talking about "the conditions" of this absolutely unconditional covenant.

Verse 31. If they break my statutes, and keep not my commandments. The dreadful "if" is suggested again, and the sad case is stated in other forms. But if it should be so, what then? Death and rejection? Ah, no; Blessed be God, No! If their sin be negative or positive, if it be forsaking or profanation; if either judgments or commandments or both be violated, yet there is not a word as to final destruction, but the very reverse. Legalism will import its ifs, but the Lord slays the ifs as fast as they rise. Eternal shalls and wills make glorious havoc among the ifs and buts.

Verse 32. Then will I visit their transgressions with the rod. Not with the sword, not with death and destruction; but still with a smarting, tingling, painful rod. Saints must smart if they sin: God will see to that. He hates sin too much not to visit it, and he loves his saints too well not to chasten them. God never plays with his rod, he lays it well home to his children, he visits them with it in their houses, bodies, and hearts, and makes them know that he is grieved with their ways. He smites home and chastens their iniquity with stripes, which are either many or few in proportion as the heart is properly affected by them. The rod is a covenant blessing, and is meant to be used. As sin is so frequent, the rod never rests long together; in God's family the rod is not spared, or the children would be spoiled.

Verse 33. Nevertheless. And a glorious nevertheless too! Nevertheless my lovingkindness will I not utterly take from him. O glorious fear killing sentence! This crowns the covenant with exceeding glory. Mercy may seem to depart from the Lord's chosen, but it shall never altogether do so. Jesus is a title of honor, which is applied to all whom God ordains to be kings, as we have seen in a previous psalm, "I have said, Ye are gods; and all of you are children of the Most High:" (Psalm 82:6), but in the passage before us, something special is expressed of the holy king whom God had chosen, and it is intended to say, that he will be the son of God in a different sense.

28. And I will keep my mercy to him for ever. We see how God frequently repeats, that he had set up the kingdom of David with the express design of establishing it for ever. By placing his mercy first in order, and then adding his covenant, he points out the cause of this covenant, intimating in one word, that it is gratuitous, and that his grace is not only the foundation on which it rests, but also the cause why it is preserved inviolate. The amount is, that God will be always merciful to David, in order that his covenant may never fail.

30-37

30. If his children shall forsake my law. The prophet proceeds yet farther, declaring, that although the posterity of David should fall into sin, yet God had promised to show himself merciful towards them, and that he would not punish their transgressions to the full extent of their desert. Moreover, to give the promise the greater efficacy, he always introduces God speaking, as if he presented to him a request corresponding with the precise words and express articles of his covenant. It was very necessary that this should be added; for so easily do we slide into evil, and so prone are we to continual falls, that unless God, in the exercise of his infinite mercy, pardoned us, there would not be a single article of his covenant which would continue steadfast. God, therefore, seeing that it could not be otherwise, but that the posterity of David, in so far as it depended upon themselves, would frequently fall from the covenant, by their own fault, has provided a remedy for such cases, in his pardoning grace.

This passage teaches us, that when God adopts men into his family, they do not forthwith completely lay aside the flesh with its corruptions, as is held by some enthusiasts, who dream, that as soon as we are grafted into the body of Christ, all the corruption that is in us must be destroyed. Would to God that we could all on a sudden change our nature, and thus exhibit that angelic perfection which they require! But as it is quite apparent, that we are far from such an attainment, so long as we carry about with us this tabernacle of flesh, let us bid adieu to that devilish figment, and let us all betake ourselves to the sanctuary of forgiveness, which is at all times open for us. God, unquestionably, is speaking of the household of his Church; and yet it is declared, with sufficient plainness, in the promise which he makes of pardoning their offenses, that they will transgress and be guilty of revolting from him.

34. My covenant will I not break. As the true knowledge of God's mercy can only be obtained from his word, he enjoins us to keep our eyes intently fixed upon his covenant. The more excellent and invaluable a blessing it is, "Never to be rejected after having been once adopted by him," the more

Jews. Now this account of the blessedness of God's Israel comes in here as that to which it was hard to reconcile their present calamitous state.

19-37 God's covenant with David.

The covenant God made with David and his seed was mentioned before (v. 3, 4); but in these verses it is enlarged upon, and pleaded with God, for favor to the royal family, now almost sunk and ruined; yet certainly it looks at Christ, and has its accomplishment in him much more than in David; nay, some passages here are scarcely applicable at all to David, but must be understood of Christ only (who is therefore called David our king, Hos. iii. 5), and very great and precious promises they are which are here made to the Redeemer, which are strong foundations for the faith and hope of the redeemed to build upon. The comforts of our redemption flow from the covenant of redemption; all our springs are in that, Isa. live. 3. I will make an everlasting covenant with you, even the sure mercies of David, Acts xiii. 34. Now here we have an account of those sure mercies. Observe,

I. What assurance we have of the truth of the promise, which may encourage us to build upon it. We are here told,

1. How it was spoken (v. 19): Thou didst speak in vision to thy Holy One. God's promise to David, which is especially referred to here, was spoken in vision to Nathan the prophet, 2 Sam. vii. 12-17. Then, when the Holy One of Israel was their king (v. 18), he appointed David to be his viceroy. But to all the prophets, those holy ones, he spoke in vision concerning Christ, and to him himself especially, who had lain in his bosom from eternity, and was made perfectly acquainted with the whole design of redemption, Matt. xi. 27.

2. How it was sworn to and ratified (v. 35): Once have I sworn by my holiness, that darling attribute. In swearing by his holiness, he swore by himself; for he will as soon cease to be as be otherwise than holy. His swearing once is enough; he needs not swear again, as David did (1 Sam. xx. 17); for his word and oath are two immutable things. As Christ was made a priest, so he was made a king, by an oath (Heb. vii. 21); for his kingdom and priesthood are both unchangeable.

II. The choice made of the person to whom the promise is given, v. 19, 20. David was a king of God's own choosing, so is Christ, and therefore both are called God's kings, Ps. ii. 6. David was mighty, a man of courage and fit for business; he was chosen out of the people, not out of the princes, but the shepherds. God found him out, exalted him, laid help upon him, and ordered Samuel to anoint him. But this is especially to be applied to Christ.

III. The promises made to this chosen one, to David in the type and the Son of David in the antitype, in which not only gracious, but glorious things are spoken of him.

Psalm 89

33-40
33 Nevertheless my loving kindness will I not utterly take from him, nor suffer my faithfulness to fail.
34 My covenant will I not break, nor alter the thing that is gone out of my lips.
35 Once have I sworn by my holiness that I will not lie unto David.
36 His seed shall endure for ever, and his throne as the sun before me.
37 It shall be established for ever as the moon, and as a faithful witness in heaven. Selah.
38 But thou hast cast off and abhorred, thou hast been wroth with thine anointed.
39 Thou hast made void the covenant of thy servant: thou hast profaned his crown by casting it to the ground.
40 Thou hast broken down all his hedges; thou hast brought his strong holds to ruin.

still enjoys the divine favor, and we are in him, and therefore under the most trying circumstances the Lord's lovingkindness to each one of his chosen will endure the strain.
Verse 34. My covenant will I not break. It is his own covenant. He devised it, drew up the draft of it, and voluntarily entered into it: he therefore thinks much of it. It is not a man's covenant, but the Lord claims it as his own. It is an evil thing among men for one to be a "covenant breaker", and such an opprobrious epithet shall never be applicable to the Most High.
Verse 35. Once have I sworn by my holiness that I will not lie unto David. Because he could swear by no greater he swore by himself, and by that peculiar attribute which is his highest glory, being the subject of threefold adoration by all the hosts of heaven. God here pledges the crown of his kingdom, the excellent beauty of his person, the essence of his nature. He does as good as say that if he ceases to be true to his covenant he will have forfeited his holy character.
Verse 36. His seed shall endure for ever. David's line in the person of Jesus is an endless one, and the race of Jesus, as represented in successive generations of believers, shows no sign of failure. No power, human or Satanic, can break the Christian succession; as saints die others shall rise up to fill their places, so that till the last day, the day of doom, Jesus shall have a seed to serve him. And his throne as the sun before me. In our Lord Jesus the dynasty of David remains upon the throne. Jesus has never abdicated, nor gone into banishment. He reigns, and must reign so long as the sun continues to shine upon the earth.
Verse 37. It shall be established for ever as the moon. The kingdom may wax and wane to mortal eyes, but it shall still abide as long as the moon walks in her silver beauty. And as a faithful witness in heavens. The most stable part of the universe is selected as a type of Messiah's kingdom, and both sun and moon are made to be symbols of its long endurance. Whatever else there is in the sky which faithfully witnesses to the unbending course of nature is also called upon to be a sign of the Lord's truth.
Verse 38. But thou hast cast off and abhorred. The Lord had promised not to cast off the seed of David, and yet it looked as if he had done so, and that too in the most angry manner, as if he loathed the person of the king. God's actions may appear to us to be the reverse of his promises, and then our best course is to come before him in prayer and put the matter before him just as it strikes our apprehension.
Verse 39. Thou hast made void the covenant of thy servant. The dispensations of providence looked as if there had been a disannulling of the sacred compact, though indeed it was not so.
Verse 40. Thou hast broken down all his hedges. He was no longer sheltered from the slanderous assaults of contemptuous tongues; the awe which should guard the royal name had ceased to separate him from his fellows. The "divinity which doth hedge a king" had departed. Hitherto, the royal family had been like a vine within an enclosure, but the wall was now laid low, and the vine was unprotected. It is sorrowfully true that in many places the enclosures of the church have been destroyed, the line of demarcation between the church and the world has almost vanished, and godless men fill the sacred offices.
Verse 41. All that pass by the way spoil him. Idle passers by, who have nothing else to do, must needs have a pluck at this vine, and they do it without difficulty, since the hedges are gone. Woe is the day when every petty reasoner has an argument against religion, and men in their cups are fluent with objections against the gospel of Jesus. Although Jesus on the cross is nothing to them, and they pass him by without inquiring into what he has done for them, yet they can loiter as long as you will, if there be but the hope of driving another nail into his hands and helping to crucify the Lord afresh. They will not touch him with the finger of faith, but they pluck

difficult it is for us to believe its truth. And we know how many thoughts from time to time present themselves to our minds, tempting us to call it in question. That the faithful, therefore, may not harass themselves beyond measure in debating in their own minds whether or no they are in favor with God, they are enjoined to look to the covenant, and to embrace the salvation which is offered to them in it. God here commends to us his own faithfulness, that we may account his promise sufficient, and that we may not seek the certainty of our salvation any where else.

35. Once have I sworn by my holiness. God now confirms by an oath what he previously stated he had promised to David; from which it appears that it was not a matter of small importance; it being certain that God would not interpose his holy name in reference to what was of no consequence. It is a token of singular loving-kindness for him, upon seeing us prone to distrust, to provide a remedy for it so compassionately. We have, therefore, so much the less excuse if we do not embrace, with true and unwavering faith, his promise which is so strongly ratified, since in his deep interest about our salvation, he does not withhold his oath, that we may yield entire credence to his word. If we do not reckon his simple promise sufficient, he adds his oath, as it were, for a pledge.

36. His seed shall endure for ever. There now follows the promise that the right of sovereignty shall always remain with the posterity of David. These two things—his offspring and his throne, are conjoined; and by these words the everlasting duration of the kingdom is promised, so that it should never pass to those who were of a strange and different race. The sun and the moon are produced as witnesses; for although they are creatures subject to corruption, they yet possess more stability than the earth or air; the elements, as we see, being subject to continual changes. As the whole of this lower world is subject to unceasing agitation and change, there is presented to us a more steadfast state of things in the sun and moon, that the kingdom of David might not be estimated according to the common order of nature. Since, however, this royal throne was shaken in the time of Rehoboam, as we have before had occasion to remark, and afterwards broken down and overthrown, it follows that this prophecy cannot be limited to David. For although at length the outward majesty of this kingdom was put an end to without hope of being re-established, the sun ceased not to shine by day, nor the moon by night. Accordingly, until we come to Christ, God might seem to be unfaithful to his promises. But in the branch which sprung from the root of Jesse, these words were fulfilled in their fullest sense.

38-45

38. But thou hast abhorred and rejected him. Here the prophet complains that in consequence of the decayed state of the kingdom, the prophecy appeared to have failed of its accomplishment. Not that he accuses God of falsehood; but he speaks in this manner, that he may with all freedom cast his cares and griefs into the bosom of God, who permits us to deal thus familiarly with him. It doubtless becomes us to

1. With reference to himself, as king and God's servant: and what makes for him makes for all his loving subjects. It is here promised,

(1.) That God would stand by him and strengthen him in his undertaking (v. 21): With him my hand not only shall be, but shall be established, by promise, shall be so established that he shall by it be established and confirmed in all his offices, so that none of them shall be undermined and overthrown, though by the man of sin they shall all be usurped and fought against.

(2.) That he should be victorious over his enemies, that they should not encroach upon him (v. 22): The son of wickedness shall not exact upon him, nor afflict him. He that at first broke the peace would set himself against him that undertook to make peace, and do what he could to blast his design: but he could only reach to bruise his heel; further he could not exact upon him nor afflict him. Christ became a surety for our debt, and thereby Satan and death thought to gain advantage against him; but he satisfied the demands of God's justice, and then they could not exact upon him.

(3.) That he should be the great trustee of the covenant between God and men, that God would be gracious and true to us (v. 24): My faithfulness and my mercy shall be with him. They were with David; God continued merciful to him, and so approved himself faithful. They were with Christ; God made good all his promises to him. But that is not all; God's mercy to us, and his faithfulness to us, are with Christ; he is not only pleased with him, but with us in him; and it is in him that all the promises of God are yea and amen. So that if any poor sinners hope for benefit by the faithfulness and mercy of God, let them know it is with Christ; it is lodged in his hand, and to him they must apply for it (v. 28): My mercy will I keep for him, to be disposed of by him, for evermore; in the channel of Christ's mediation all the streams of divine goodness will for ever run. Therefore it is the mercy of our Lord Jesus Christ which we look for unto eternal life, Jude 21; John xvii. 2.

(4.) That his kingdom should be greatly enlarged (v. 25): I will set his hand in the sea (he shall have the dominion of the seas, and the isles of the sea), and his right hand in the rivers, the inland countries that are watered with rivers.

(5.) That he should own God as his Father, and God would own him as his Son, his firstborn, v. 26, 27. This is a comment upon these words in Nathan's message concerning Solomon (for he also was a type of Christ as well as David), I will be his Father and he shall be my Son (2 Sam. vii. 14), and the relation shall be owned on both sides.

2. With reference to his seed. God's covenants always took in the seed of the covenanters; this does so (v. 29, 36): His seed shall endure for ever, and with it his throne. Now this will be differently understood according as we apply it to Christ or David.

Psalm 89

41-46
41 All that pass by the way spoil him: he is a reproach to his neighbors.
42 Thou hast set up the right hand of his adversaries; thou hast made all his enemies to rejoice.
43 Thou hast also turned the edge of his sword, and hast not made him to stand in the battle.
44 Thou hast made his glory to cease, and cast his throne down to the ground.
45 The days of his youth hast thou shortened: thou hast covered him with shame. Selah.
46 How long, LORD? wilt thou hide thyself for ever? shall thy wrath burn like fire?

at him with the hand of malice. He is a reproach to his neighbors. David's successors had neighborly neighbors, who were a reproach to good fellowship, because they were so ready to reproach their neighbor. The Jews were much taunted by the surrounding Gentiles when at any time they fell into trouble.

Verse 42. Thou hast set up the right hand of thy adversaries. Thou hast done it, thou, who hast sworn to give him help and victory, thou hast, instead thereof, sided with his enemies, and lent them thy strength, so that they have gained the supremacy. Thou hast made all his enemies to rejoice. They are boasting over him, and are glorying in his defeat, and this is done by thyself. O God,—how is this? Where is the covenant? Hast thou forgotten thine own pledges and promises?

Verse 43. Also turned the edge of his sword. When he goes to war he is as unsuccessful as though his sword refused to cut, and gave way like a sword of lead. His weapons fail him. And hast not made him to stand in the battle. His heart fails him as well as his sword—he wavers, he falls. This has happened even to naturally brave men—a terrible dread has unmanned them. At this present the church has few swords of true Jerusalem metal; her sons are pliable, her ministers yield to pressure. We need men whose edge cannot be turned, firm for truth, keen against error, sharp towards sin, cutting their way into men's hearts. Courage and decision are more needed now than ever, for charity towards heresy is the fashionable vice, and indifference to all truth, under the name of liberal mindedness, is the crowning virtue of the age. The Lord send us men of the school of Elias, or, at least, of Luther and Knox.

Verse 44. Thou hast made his glory to cease. The brightness of his reign and the prosperity of his house are gone, his fame is tarnished, his honor disgraced. And cast his throne down to the ground. He has lost his power to govern at home or to conquer abroad. This happened to kings of David's line, and, more grievous to tell, it is happening in these days to the visible kingdom of the Lord Jesus. Where are the glories of Pentecost? Where is the majesty of the Reformation? Where does his kingdom come among the sons of men? Woe is unto us, for the glory has departed, and the gospel throne of Jesus is hidden from our eyes!

Verse 45. The days of his youth hast thou shortened. The time of the king's energy was brief, he grew feeble before his time. Thou hast covered him with shame. Shame was heaped upon him because of his premature decay and his failure in arms. This was very grievous to the writer of this Psalm, who was evidently a most loyal adherent of the house of David. In this our day we have to bemoan the lack of vigor in religion—the heroic days of Christianity are over, her raven locks are sprinkled with untimely grey. Is this according to the covenant? Can this be as the Lord has promised?

Verse 46. How long, Lord? The appeal is to Jehovah, and the argument is the length of the affliction endured. Chastisement with a rod is not a lengthened matter, therefore he appeals to God to cut short the time of tribulation. Wilt thou hide thyself for ever? Hast thou not promised to appear for thy servant—wilt thou then for ever forsake him? Shall thy wrath burn like fire? Shall it go on and on evermore till it utterly consume its object? Be pleased to set a bound! How far wilt thou go? Wilt thou burn up the throne which thou hast sworn to perpetuate? Even thus we would entreat the Lord to remember the cause of Christ in these days. Can he be so angry with his church as to leave her much longer? How far will he suffer things to go?

Verse 47. Remember how short my time is. If so brief, do not make it altogether bitter. If thine anger burn on it will outlast this mortal life, and then there will be no time for thy mercy to restore me. Some expositors ascribe these words, and all the preceding verses, to the state of the Lord Jesus in the days of his humiliation, and this gives an instructive meaning; but we prefer to continue our reference all through to the church, which is the seed of the Lord Jesus, even as the succeeding kings were the seed of David.

frame our desires according to the divine will; but that person cannot be said to pass beyond due bounds who humbly laments that he is deprived of the tokens of the divine favor, provided be does not despair, or rebelliously murmur against God; and we shall afterwards see that the prophet, when he blesses God at the close of the psalm, affords a proof of tranquil submission, by which he corrects or qualifies his complaints.

40. Thou hast broken down all his walls. The prophet, although he might easily have found another cause to which to impute the breaking down and razing of the fortifications, yet under the influence of devout and sanctified feeling acknowledges God to be the author of this calamity; being fully convinced that men could not at their pleasure have destroyed the kingdom which God had set up had not the Divine anger been kindled. Afterwards speaking metaphorically, he complains that the kingdom was exposed as a prey to all passers-by, resembling a field or garden, of which the walls were broken down, and the ground laid open to depredation.

42. Thou hast exalted the right hand of his oppressors. Here he states that God took part with the enemies of the king; for he was well aware that these enemies could not have prevailed but by the will of God, who inspires some with courage, and renders others faint-hearted. In short, in proportion to the number of the calamities which had befallen the chosen people, was the number of the evidences of their having been forsaken by God; for, so long as he continued his favor, the whole world, by all their machinations, were unable to impair the stability of that kingdom.

45. Thou hast shortened the days of his youth. This similitude is highly appropriate; for the kingdom, if we compare the state of it at that period with the Divine promise, had scarce yet fully unfolded its blossom, when, amidst its first advances, suddenly smitten with a grievous decay, its freshness and beauty were defaced, while at length it vanished away. Moreover, what we have previously stated must be borne in mind, that when the prophet complains that the issue does not correspond with the promise, or is not such as the promise led the chosen people to expect, he does not, on that account, charge God with falsehood, but brings forward this apparent discrepancy for another purpose—to encourage himself, from the consideration of the Divine promises, to come to the throne of grace with the greater confidence and boldness; and, while he urged this difficulty before God, he was fully persuaded that it was impossible for Him not to show himself faithful to his word.

46-48

46. How long, O Jehovah? wilt thou hide thyself for ever? After having poured forth his complaints respecting the sad and calamitous condition of the Church, the Psalmist now turns himself to prayer. Whence it follows that the language of lamentation to which he had hitherto given utterance, although it emanated from carnal sense, was nevertheless conjoined with faith. Unbelievers, in the agitation of trouble, may sometimes engage in prayer, yet whatever they ask proceeds from feigned

(1.) If we apply it to David, by his seed we are to understand his successors, Solomon and the following kings of Judah, who descended from the loins of David. It is supposed that they might degenerate, and not walk in the spirit and steps of their father David; in such a case they must expect to come under divine rebukes, such as the house of David was at this time under, v. 38.

(2.) If we apply it to Christ, by his seed we are to understand his subjects, all believers, his spiritual seed, the children which God has given him, Heb. ii. 13. This is that seed which shall be made to endure for ever, and his throne in the midst of them, in the church in the heart, as the days of heaven.

[1.] The continuance of Christ's kingdom is here made doubtful by the sins and afflictions of his subjects; their iniquities and calamities threaten the ruin of it. This case is here put, that we may not be offended when it comes to be a case in fact, but that we may reconcile it with the stability of the covenant and be assured of that notwithstanding.

First, It is here supposed that there will be much amiss in the subjects of Christ's kingdom. His children may forsake God's law (v. 30) by omissions, and break his statutes (v. 31) by commissions. There are spots which are the spots of God's children, Deut. xxxii. 5. Many corruptions there are in the bowels of the church, as well as in the hearts of those who are the members of it, and these corruptions break out.

Secondly, They are here told that they must smart for it (v. 32): I will visit their transgression with a rod, their transgression sooner than that of others. You only have I known, and therefore I will punish you, Amos iii. 2. Their being related to Christ shall not excuse them from being called to an account.

[2.] The continuance of Christ's kingdom is made certain by the inviolable promise and oath of God, notwithstanding all this (v. 33): Nevertheless, my kindness will I not totally and finally take from him.

38-52 Complaints and expostulations; David's expostulation with God.

In these verses we have,

I. A very melancholy complaint of the present deplorable state of David's family, which the psalmist thinks hard to be reconciled to the covenant God made with David. "Thou saidst thou wouldst not take away thy lovingkindness, but thou hast cast off." Sometimes, it is no easy thing to reconcile God's providences with his promises, and yet we are sure they are reconcilable; for God's works fulfill his word and never contradict it.

1. David's house seemed to have lost its interest in God, which was the greatest strength and beauty of it. God had been pleased with his anointed, but now he was wroth with him (v. 38), had entered into covenant with the family, but now, for aught he could perceive, he had made void the covenant, not broken some of the articles of it, but cancelled it, v. 39. We

Psalm 89

47-52

47 Remember how short my time is: wherefore hast thou made all men in vain?
48 What man is he that liveth, and shall not see death? shall he deliver his soul from the hand of the grave? Selah.
49 Lord, where are thy former loving kindnesses, which thou swarest unto David in thy truth?
50 Remember, Lord, the reproach of thy servants; how I do bear in my bosom the reproach of all the mighty people;
51 Wherewith thine enemies have reproached, O LORD; wherewith they have reproached the footsteps of thine anointed.
52 Blessed be the LORD for evermore. Amen, and Amen.

Verse 48. What man is he that liveth, and shall not see death? All must die. None of our race can answer to the question here propounded except in the negative; there is none that can claim to elude the arrows of death. Shall he deliver his soul from the hand of the grave? Neither by strength, wisdom, nor virtue can any man escape the common doom, for to the dust return we must. Since then we must all die, do not make this life all wretchedness, by smiting us so long, O Lord.

Verse 49. Lord, where are thy former loving kindnesses, which thou swarest unto David in thy truth? Here he comes to grand pleading, hand to hand work with the covenant angel. We may remind the Lord of his first deeds of love, his former love to his church, his former favor to ourselves. Then may we plead his oath, and beg him to remember that he has sworn to bless his chosen: and we may wrestle hard also, by urging upon him his own character, and laying hold upon his inviolable truth.

Verse 50. Remember, Lord, the reproach of thy servants. By reason of their great troubles they were made a mock of by ungodly men, and hence the Lord's pity is entreated. Will a father stand by and see his children insulted? The Psalmist entreats the Lord to compassionate the wretchedness brought upon his servants by the taunts of their adversaries, who jested at them on account of their sufferings. How I do bear in my bosom the reproach of all the mighty people. The Psalmist himself laid the scorn of the great and the proud to heart.

Verse 51. Wherewith thine enemies have reproached, O Lord. Here is another forcible point; the scoffers are the Lord's enemies as well as ours, and their reproach falls upon him as well as upon us; therefore we cry for the Lord's interposition.

Verse 52. Blessed be the Lord for evermore. He ends where he began; he has sailed round the world and reached port again. Let us bless God before we pray, and while we pray, and when we have done praying, for he always deserves it of us. If we cannot understand him, we will not distrust him. When his ways are beyond our judgment we will not be so foolish as to judge; yet we shall do so if we consider his dealings to be unkind or unfaithful. He is, he must be, he shall be, for ever, our blessed God. Amen, and Amen. All our hearts say so. So be it, Lord, we wish it over and over again. Be thou blessed evermore.

JOHN CALVIN

lips. But the prophet, by connecting prayer with his complaints, bears testimony that he had never lost his confidence in the truth of the Divine promises.
47. Remember how short my time is. After having confessed that the severe and deplorable afflictions which had befallen the Church were to be traced to her own sins as the procuring cause, the prophet, the more effectually to move God to commiseration, lays before him the brevity of human life, in which, if we receive no taste of the Divine goodness, it will seem that we have been created in vain. 48. What man shall live, and shall not see death? This verse contains a confirmation of what has been already stated concerning the brevity of human life. The amount is, that unless God speedily hasten to show himself a father to men, the opportunity of causing them to experience his grace will no longer exist.

49-52
49. O Lord! where are thy former mercies? The prophet encourages himself, by calling to remembrance God's former benefits, as if his reasoning were, That God can never be unlike himself, and that therefore the goodness which he manifested in old time to the fathers cannot come to an end. This comparison might indeed make the godly despond, when they find that they are not dealt with by him so gently as he dealt with the fathers, did not another consideration at the same time present itself to their minds—the consideration that he never changes, and never wearies in the course of his beneficence.
50. O Lord! remember the reproach of thy servants. They again allege, that they are held in derision by the ungodly,—a consideration which had no small influence in moving God to compassion: for the more grievous and troublesome a temptation it is, to have the wicked deriding our patience, that, after having made us believe that God is not true in what he has promised, they may precipitate us into despair; the more ready is he to aid us, that our feeble minds may not yield to the temptation. The prophet does not simply mean that the reproaches of his enemies are to him intolerable, but that God must repress their insolence in deriding the faith and patience of the godly.
51. With which thy enemies, O Jehovah! have reproached thee. What the Psalmist now affirms is, not that the wicked torment the saints with their contumelious language, but that they revile even God himself. And he makes this statement to beseech him to maintain his own cause, because all the reproaches by which the simplicity of our faith is held up to scorn recoil upon himself, than to beseech him to do this, because he is wounded in the person of his Church.
52. Blessed be Jehovah for ever! I am surprised why some interpreters should imagine, that this verse was added by some transcriber in copying the book, affirming, that it does not correspond with the context: as if the language of praise and thanksgiving to God were not as suitable at the close of a psalm as at the opening of it. I have therefore no doubt, that the prophet, after having freely bewailed the calamities of the Church, now, with the view of allaying the bitterness of his grief, purposely breaks forth into the language of praise.

MATTHEW HENRY

misconstrue the rebukes of Providence if we think they make void the covenant.
2. The honor of the house of David was lost and laid in the dust: Thou hast profaned his crown (which was always looked upon as sacred) by casting it to the ground, to be trampled on, v. 39. Thou hast made his glory to cease (so uncertain is all earthly glory, and so soon does it wither) and thou hast cast his throne down to the ground, not only dethroned the king, but put a period to the kingdom, v. 44. If it was penned in Rehoboam's time, it was true as to the greatest part of the kingdom, five parts of six; if in Zedekiah's time, it was more remarkably true of the poor remainder.
3. It was exposed and made a prey to all the neighbors, who insulted over that ancient and honorable family (v. 40): Thou hast broken down all his hedges (all those things that were a defense to them, and particularly that hedge of protection which they thought God's covenant and promise had made about them) and thou hast made even his strong-holds a ruin, so that they were rather a reproach to them than any shelter; and then, All that pass by the way spoil him (v. 41) and make an easy prey of him; see Ps. lxxx. 12, 13. The enemies talk insolently: He is a reproach to his neighbors, who triumph in his fall from so great a degree of honor. Nay, every one helps forward the calamity (v. 42): "Thou hast set up the right hand of his adversaries, not only given them power, but inclined them to turn their power this way."
4. It was disabled to help itself (v. 43): "Thou hast turned the edge of his sword, and made it blunt, that it cannot do execution as it has done; and (which is worse) thou hast turned the edge of his spirit, and taken off his courage, and hast not made him to stand as he used to do in the battle."
5. It was upon the brink of an inglorious exit (v. 45).
II. A very pathetic expostulation with God upon this. Four things they plead with God for mercy:
1. The long continuance of the trouble (v. 46): How long, O Lord! wilt thou hide thyself? For ever?
2. The shortness of life, and the certainty of death.
3. The next plea is taken from the kindness God had for and the covenant he made with his servant David (v. 49).
4. The last plea is taken from the insolence of the enemies and the indignity done to God's anointed (v. 50, 51).
III. The psalm concludes with praise, even after this sad complaint (v. 52): Blessed be the Lord for evermore, Amen, and amen. Thus he confronts the reproaches of his enemies. The more others blaspheme God the more we should bless him. Here is a double Amen, according to the double signification. Amen—so it is, God is blessed for ever. Amen—be it so, let God be blessed for ever. He began the psalm with thanksgiving, before he made his complaint (v. 1); and now he concludes it with a doxology.

Book Four: Psalms 90-106

Psalm 90

Title
A Prayer of Moses the man of God.

1-5
1 Lord, thou hast been our dwelling place in all generations.
2 Before the mountains were brought forth, or ever thou hadst formed the earth and the world, even from everlasting to everlasting, thou art God.
3 Thou turnest man to destruction; and sayest, Return, ye children of men.
4 For a thousand years in thy sight are but as yesterday when it is past, and as a watch in the night.
5 Thou carriest them away as with a flood; they are as a sleep: in the morning they are like grass which groweth up.

Book Four: Psalms 90-106

Psalm 90

TITLE. A Prayer of Moses the man of God. Many attempts have been made to prove that Moses did not write this Psalm, but we remain unmoved in the conviction that he did so. The condition of Israel in the wilderness is so preeminently illustrative of each verse, and the turns, expressions, and words are so similar to many in the Pentateuch, that the difficulties suggested are, to our mind, light as air in comparison with the internal evidence in favor of its Mosaic origin. Moses was mighty in word as well as deed, and this Psalm we believe to be one of his weighty utterances, worthy to stand side by side with his glorious oration recorded in Deuteronomy. Moses was peculiarly a man of God and God's man; chosen of God, inspired of God, honored of God, and faithful to God in all his house, he well deserved the name which is here given him. The Psalm is called a prayer, for the closing petitions enter into its essence, and the preceding verses are a meditation preparatory to the supplication. Men of God are sure to be men of prayer. This was not the only prayer of Moses, indeed it is but a specimen of the manner in which the seer of Horeb was leant to commune with heaven, and intercede for the good of Israel. This is the oldest of the Psalms, and stands between two books of Psalms as a composition unique in its grandeur, and alone in its sublime antiquity. Many generations of mourners have listened to this Psalm when standing around the open grave, and have been consoled thereby, even when they have not perceived its special application to Israel in the wilderness and have failed to remember the far higher ground upon which believers now stand.
SUBJECT AND DIVISION. Moses sings of the frailty of man, and the shortness of life, contrasting therewith the eternity of God, and founding thereon earnest appeals for compassion. The only division which will be useful separates the contemplation Ps 90:1-11 from the Ps 90:12-17 there is indeed no need to make even this break, for the unity is well preserved throughout.

EXPOSITION
Verse 1. Lord, thou hast been our dwelling place in all generations. We must consider the whole Psalm as written for the tribes in the desert, and then we shall see the primary meaning of each verse. Moses, in effect, says, wanderers though we be in the howling wilderness, yet we find a home in thee, even as our forefathers did when they came out of Ur of the Chaldees and dwelt in tents among the Canaanites. To the saints the Lord Jehovah, the self existent God, stands instead of mansion and rooftree; he shelters, comforts, protects, preserves, and cherishes all his own. Foxes have holes and the birds of the air have nests, but the saints dwell in their God, and have always done so in all ages. Not in the tabernacle or the temple do we dwell, but in God himself; and this we have always done since there was a church in the world.
Verse 2. Before the mountains were brought forth. Before those elder giants had struggled forth from nature's womb, as her dread firstborn, the Lord was glorious and self sufficient. Mountains to him, though hoar with the snows of ages, are but new born babes, young things whose birth was but yesterday, mere novelties of an hour. Or ever thou hadst formed the earth and the world. Here too the allusion is to a birth. Earth was born but the other day, and her solid land was delivered from the flood but a short while ago. Even from everlasting to everlasting, thou art God, or, "thou art, O God." God was, when nothing else was. He was God when the earth was not a world but a chaos, when mountains were not upheaved, and the generation of the heavens and the earth had not commenced. In this Eternal One there is a safe abode for the successive generations of men.

JOHN CALVIN

Book Four: Psalms 90-106

Psalm 90

As Moses is about to treat as well of the brevity and miseries of human life, as of the punishments inflicted upon the people of Israel, in order to minister some consolation for assuaging the grief and fear which the faithful might have entertained upon observing the operation of the common law, to which all mankind are subject, and especially, upon considering their own afflictions, he opens the psalm by speaking of the peculiar grace which God had vouchsafed to his chosen tribes. He next briefly recites, how wretched the condition of men is, if they allow their hearts to rest in this world, especially when God summons them as guilty sinners to his judgment seat. And after he has bewailed, that even the children of Abraham had experienced for a time such severity, that they were almost consumed with sorrow, confiding in God's free favor, by which He had adopted them to himself, he prays that He would deal towards them in a merciful and gracious manner, as he had done in times past, and that he would continue even to the end the ordinary course of his grace.

1-2
1. O Lord! thou hast been our dwelling-place. In separating the seed of Abraham by special privilege from the rest of the human family, the Psalmist magnifies the grace of adoption, by which God had embraced them as his children. The object which he has in view in this exordium is, that God would now renew the grace which he had displayed in old time towards the holy patriarchs, and continue it towards their offspring. Some commentators think that he alludes to the tabernacle, because in it the majesty of God was not less conspicuous than if he had dwelt in the midst of the people; but this seems to me to be altogether out of place. He rather comprehends the whole time in which the Fathers sojourned in the land of Canaan. As the tabernacle had not yet continued for the space of forty years, the long duration here mentioned—our dwelling-place from generation to generation—would not at all be applicable to it. It is not then intended to recount what God showed himself to be towards the Israelites from the time that he delivered them from Egypt; but what their fathers had experienced him to be in all ages, even from the beginning. Now it is declared that as they had always been pilgrims and wanderers, so God was to them instead of a dwelling-place. No doubt, the condition of all men is unstable upon earth; but we know that Abraham and his posterity were, above all others, sojourners, and as it were exiles.
2. Before the mountains were brought forth. Moses designs to set forth some high and hidden mystery, and yet he seems to speak feebly, and, as it were, in a puerile manner. For who does not know that God existed before the world? This we grant is a truth which all men admit; but we will scarcely find one in a hundred who is thoroughly persuaded that God remains unchangeably the same. God is here contrasted with created beings, who, as all know, are subject to continual changes, so that there is nothing stable under heaven.

MATTHEW HENRY

Book Four: Psalms 90-106

Psalm 90

1-6 God's care of His people; frailty of human life.
This psalm is entitled a prayer of Moses. Where, and in what volume, it was preserved from Moses's time till the collection of psalms was begun to be made, is uncertain; but, being divinely inspired, it was under a special protection: perhaps it was written in the book of Jasher, or the book of the wars of the Lord. Moses taught the people of Israel to pray, and put words into their mouths which they might make use of in turning to the Lord. Moses is here called the man of God, because he was a prophet, the father of prophets, and an eminent type of the great prophet. In these verses we are taught,

I. To give God the praise of his care concerning his people at all times, and concerning us in our days (v. 1): Lord, thou hast been to us a habitation, or dwelling-place, a refuge or help, in all generations. Now that they had fallen under God's displeasure, and he threatened to abandon them, they plead his former kindnesses to their ancestors. Canaan was a land of pilgrimage to their fathers the patriarchs, who dwelt there in tabernacles; but then God was their habitation, and, wherever they went, they were at home, at rest, in him.

II. To give God the glory of his eternity (v. 2): Before the mountains were brought forth, before he made the highest part of the dust of the world (as it is expressed, Prov. viii. 26), before the earth fell in travail, or, as we may read it, before thou hadst formed the earth and the world (that is, before the beginning of time) thou hadst a being; even from everlasting to everlasting thou art God, an eternal God, whose existence has neither its commencement nor its period with time, nor is measured by the successions and revolutions of it, but who art the same yesterday, to-day, and for ever, without beginning of days, or end of life, or change of time.

III. To own God's absolute sovereign dominion over man, and his irresistible incontestable power to dispose of him as he pleases (v. 3): Thou turnest man to destruction, with a word's speaking, when thou pleasest, to the destruction of the body, of the earthly house; and thou sayest, Return, you children of men.

1. When God is, by sickness or other afflictions, turning men to destruction, he does thereby call men to return unto him, that is, to repent of their sins and live a new life.

2. When God is threatening to turn men to destruction, to bring them to death, and they have received a sentence of death within themselves, sometimes he wonderfully restores them, and says, as the old translation reads it, Again thou sayest, Return to life and health again. For God kills and makes alive again, brings down to the grave and brings up.

Psalm 90

6-11

6 In the morning it flourisheth, and groweth up; in the evening it is cut down, and withereth.

7 For we are consumed by thine anger, and by thy wrath are we troubled.

8 Thou hast set our iniquities before thee, our secret sins in the light of thy countenance.

9 For all our days are passed away in thy wrath: we spend our years as a tale that is told.

10 The days of our years are threescore years and ten; and if by reason of strength they be fourscore years, yet is their strength labor and sorrow; for it is soon cut off, and we fly away.

11 Who knoweth the power of thine anger? even according to thy fear, so is thy wrath.

Verse 3. Thou turnest man to destruction, or "to dust." Man's body is resolved into its elements, and is as though it had been crushed and ground to powder. And sayest, Return, ye children of men, i.e., return even to the dust out of which ye were taken. The frailty of man is thus forcibly set forth; God creates him out of the dust, and back to dust he goes at the word of his Creator. God resolves and man dissolves. A word created and a word destroys.

Verse 4. For a thousand years in thy sight are but as yesterday when it is past. A thousand years! This is a long stretch of time. How much may be crowded into it,—the rise and fall of empires, the glory and obliteration of dynasties, the beginning and the end of elaborate systems of human philosophy, and countless events, all important to household and individual, which elude the pens of historians. Yet this period, which might even be called the limit of modern history, and is in human language almost identical with an indefinite length of time, is to the Lord as nothing, even as time already gone.

Verse 5. Thou carriest them away as with a flood. As when a torrent rushes down the river bed and bears all before it, so does the Lord bear away by death the succeeding generations of men. As the hurricane sweeps the clouds from the sky, so time removes the children of men. They are as a sleep. Before God men must appear as unreal as the dreams of the night, the phantoms of sleep. Not only are our plans and devices like a sleep, but we ourselves are such.

Verse 6. In the morning it flourisheth, and groweth up. Blooming with abounding beauty till the meadows are all besprent with gems, the grass has a golden hour, even as man in his youth has a heyday of flowery glory. In the evening it is cut down, and withereth. The scythe ends the blossoming of the field flowers, and the dews at flight weep their fall. Here is the history of the grass—sown, grown, blown, mown, gone; and the history of man is not much more. Natural decay would put an end both to us and the grass in due time; few, however, are left to experience the full result of age, for death comes with his scythe, and removes our life in the midst of its verdure. How great a change in how short a time! The morning saw the blooming, and the evening sees the withering.

Verse 7. This mortality is not accidental, neither was it inevitable in the original of our nature, but sin has provoked the Lord to anger, and therefore thus we die. For we are consumed by thine anger. This is the scythe which mows and the scorching heat which withers. This was specially the case in reference to the people in the wilderness, whose lives were cut short by justice on account of their waywardness; they failed, not by a natural decline, but through the blast of the well deserved judgments of God.

Verse 8. Thou hast set our iniquities before thee. Hence these tears! Sin seen by God must work death; it is only by the covering blood of atonement that life comes to any of us. When God was overthrowing the tribes in the wilderness he had their iniquities before him, and therefore dealt with them in severity. He could not have their iniquities before him and not smite them.

Verse 9. For all our days are passed away in thy wrath. Justice shortened the days of rebellious Israel; each halting place became a graveyard; they marked their march by the tombs they left behind them. Because of the penal sentence their days were dried up, and their lives wasted away. We spend our years as a tale that is told. Yea, not their days only, but their years flew by them like a thought, swift as a meditation, rapid and idle as a gossip's story. Sin had cast a shadow over all things, and made the lives of the dying wanderers to be both vain and brief.

Verse 10. The days of our years are threescore years and ten. Moses himself lived longer than this, but his was the exception not the rule: in his day life had come to be very much the same in duration as it is with us. This is brevity itself compared with the men of the elder time; it is nothing when contrasted with eternity. Yet is life long enough for virtue and piety, and all too long for vice and blasphemy.

JOHN CALVIN

3-8
3. Thou shalt turn man to destruction. Moses mentions how frail and transitory is the life of man, and bewails its miseries. This he does, not for the purpose of quarrelling with God, but as an argument to induce him the more readily to exercise his mercy, even as he is elsewhere said to pardon mortal men, when he considers of what they are made, and remembers that they are but dust and grass, (Psalm 103:14.) he compares the course of our life to a ring or circle, because God, placing us upon the earth, turns us about within a narrow circuit, and when we have reached the last point, draws us back to himself in a moment.
5. Thou carriest them away as with a flood. Moses confirms what he had previously said, that men, so long as they are sojourners in this world, perform, as it were, a revolution which lasts only for a moment. I do not limit the expression to carry away as with a flood to calamities of a more grievous kind, but consider that death is simply compared in general to a flood; for when we have staid a little while in the world, we forthwith fall into the grave and are covered with earth. Thus death, which is common to all, is with propriety called an inundation. While we are breathing the breath of life, the Lord overflows us by death, just as those who perish in a shipwreck are engulfed in the ocean; so that death may be fitly called an invisible deluge.
7. For we fail by thy anger. Moses makes mention of the anger of God advisedly; for it is necessary that men be touched with the feeling of this, in order to their considering in good earnest, what experience constrains them to acknowledge, how soon they finish their course and pass away. He had, however, still another reason for joining together the brevity of human life and the anger of God. Whilst men are by nature so transitory, and, as it were, shadowy, the Israelites were afflicted by the hostile hand of God; and his anger is less supportable by our frail natures, which speedily vanish away, than it would be were we furnished with some tolerable degree of strength.
8. Thou hast set our iniquities before thee. To show that by this complaint he is far from intending to murmur against God, he asserts that the Divine anger, however terrible it had been, was just, inasmuch as the people had provoked it by their iniquities; for those who, when stricken by the Divine hand, are not brought to genuine humiliation, harden themselves more and more. The true way to profit, and also to subdue our pride, is to feel that He is a righteous judge.

9-10
9. For all our days are passed away in thy indignation. This might be viewed as a general confirmation of the preceding sentence, that the whole course of man's life is suddenly brought to an end, as soon as God shows himself displeased. But in my opinion Moses rather amplifies what he has said above concerning the rigor of God's wrath, and his strict examination of every case in which he punishes sin. He asserts that this terror which God brought upon his people was not only for a short time, but that it was extended without

MATTHEW HENRY

3. When God turns men to destruction, it is according to the general sentence passed upon all, which is this, "Return, you children of men, one, as well as another, return to your first principles; let the body return to the earth as it was (dust to dust, Gen. iii. 19) and let the soul return to God who gave it," Eccl. xii. 7. 4.
IV. To acknowledge the infinite disproportion there is between God and men, v. 4. Some of the patriarchs lived nearly a thousand years; Moses knew this very well, and had recorded it: but what is their long life to God's eternal life? "A thousand years, to us, are a long period, which we cannot expect to survive; or, if we could, it is what we could not retain the remembrance of; but it is, in thy sight, as yesterday, as one day, as that which is freshest in mind; nay, it is but as a watch of the night," which was but three hours.
V. To see the frailty of man, and his vanity even at his best estate (v. 5, 6): look upon all the children of men, and we shall see that their life is a dying life: Thou carriest them away as with a flood, that is, they are continually gliding down the stream of time into the ocean of eternity.

7-11 Penitent submission.
Moses had, in the foregoing verses, lamented the frailty of human life in general; the children of men are as a sleep and as the grass. But here he teaches the people of Israel to confess before God that righteous sentence of death which they were under in a special manner, and which by their sins they had brought upon themselves.
I. They are here taught to acknowledge the wrath of God to be the cause of all their miseries. We are consumed, we are troubled, and it is by thy anger, by thy wrath (v. 7); our days have passed away in thy wrath, v. 9. The afflictions of the saints often come purely from God's love, as Job's; but the rebukes of sinners, and of good men for their sins, must be seen coming from the anger of God, who takes notice of, and is much displeased with, the sins of Israel. We are too apt to look upon death as no more than a debt owing to nature; whereas it is not so; if the nature of man had continued in its primitive purity and rectitude, there would have been no such debt owing to it. It is a debt to the justice of God, a debt to the law.
II. They are taught to confess their sins, which had provoked the wrath of God against them (v. 8): Thou hast set our iniquities before thee, even our secret sins. It was not without cause that God was angry with them. He had said, Provoke me not, and I will do you no hurt; but they had provoked him, and will own that, in passing this severe sentence upon them, he justly punished them.
III. They are taught to look upon themselves as dying and passing away, and not to think either of a long life or of a pleasant one; for the decree gone forth against them was irreversible (v. 9): All our days are likely to be passed away in thy wrath, under the tokens of thy

Psalm 90

12-17

12 So teach us to number our days, that we may apply our hearts unto wisdom.
13 Return, O LORD, how long? and let it repent thee concerning thy servants.
14 O satisfy us early with thy mercy; that we may rejoice and be glad all our days.
15 Make us glad according to the days wherein thou hast afflicted us, and the years wherein we have seen evil.
16 Let thy work appear unto thy servants, and thy glory unto their children.
17 And let the beauty of the LORD our God be upon us: and establish thou the work of our hands upon us; yea, the work of our hands establish thou it.

Verse 11. Who knoweth the power of thine anger? Moses saw men dying all around him: he lived among funerals, and was overwhelmed at the terrible results of the divine displeasure. He felt that none could measure the might of the Lord's wrath. Even according to thy fear, so is thy wrath. Good men dread that wrath beyond conception, but they never ascribe too much terror to it: bad men are dreadfully convulsed when they awake to a sense of it, but their horror is not greater than it had need be, for it is a fearful thing to fall into the hands of an angry God. Holy Scripture when it depicts God's wrath against sin never uses an hyperbole; it would be impossible to exaggerate it.
Verse 12. So teach us to number our days. Instruct us to set store by time, mourning for that time past wherein we have wrought the will of the flesh, using diligently the time present, which is the accepted hour and the day of salvation, and reckoning the time which lieth in the future to be too uncertain to allow us safely to delay any gracious work or prayer. Numeration is a child's exercise in arithmetic, but in order to number their days aright the best of men need the Lord's teaching. We are more anxious to count the stars than our days, and yet the latter is by far more practical.
Verse 13. Return, O Lord, how long? Come in mercy, to us again. Do not leave us to perish. Suffer not our lives to be both brief and bitter. Thou hast said to us, "Return, ye children of men", and now we humbly cry to thee, "Return, thou preserver of men." Thy presence alone can reconcile us to this transient existence; turn thou unto us. As sin drives God from us, so repentance cries to the Lord to return to us.
Verse 14. O satisfy us early with thy mercy. Since they must die, and die so soon, the psalmist pleads for speedy mercy upon himself and his brethren. Good men know how to turn the darkest trials into arguments at the throne of grace. He who has but the heart to pray need never be without pleas in prayer.
Verse 15. Make us glad according to the days wherein thou hast afflicted us, and the years wherein we have seen evil. None can gladden the heart as thou canst, O Lord, therefore as thou hast made us sad be pleased to make us glad. Fill the other scale. Proportion thy dispensations. Give us the lamb, since thou has sent us the bitter herbs. Make our days as long as our nights. The prayer is original, childlike, and full of meaning; it is moreover based upon a great principle in providential goodness, by which the Lord puts the good over against the evil in due measure.
Verse 16. Let thy work appear unto thy servants. See how he dwells upon that word servants. It is as far as the law can go, and Moses goes to the full length permitted him henceforth Jesus calls us not servants but friends, and if we are wise we shall make full use of our wider liberty. Moses asks for displays of divine power and providence conspicuously wrought, that all the people might be cheered thereby.
Verse 17. And let the beauty of the Lord our God be upon us. Even upon us who must not see thy glory in the land of Canaan; it shall suffice us if in our characters the holiness of God is reflected, and if over all our camp the lovely excellences of our God shall cast a sacred beauty. Sanctification should be the daily object of our petitions.

intermission even to death. He complains that the Jews had almost wasted away by continual miseries; because God neither remitted nor mitigated his anger. It is therefore not surprising to find him declaring that their years passed away like a tale, when God's anger rested upon them so unremittingly.
10. In the days of our years there are threescore years and ten. He again returns to the general doctrine respecting the precariousness of the condition of men, although God may not openly display his wrath to terrify them. "What," says he, "is the duration of life? Truly, if we reckon all our years, we will at length come to threescore and ten, or, if there be some who are stronger and more vigorous, they will bring us even to fourscore."

11-13
11. Who knoweth, the power of thy anger? Moses again returns to speak of the peculiar afflictions of the Israelites; for he had also on this occasion complained before of the common frailty and miseries of mankind. He justly exclaims that the power of God's wrath is immeasurably great.
12. Teach us so to number our days. Some translate to the number of our days, which gives the same sense. As Moses perceived that what he had hitherto taught is not comprehended by the understandings of men until God shine upon them by his Spirit, he now sets himself to prayer. It indeed seems at first sight absurd to pray that we may know the number of our years. Since even the strongest scarcely reach the age of fourscore years, is there any difficulty in reckoning up so small a sum? It is surely a monstrous thing that men can measure all distances without themselves, that they know how many feet the moon is distant from the center of the earth, what space there is between the different planets; and, in short, that they can measure all the dimensions both of heaven and earth; while yet they cannot number threescore and ten years in their own case. It is therefore evident that Moses had good reason to beseech God for ability to perform what requires a wisdom which is very rare among mankind.
13. Return, O Jehovah! how long? After having spoken in the language of complaint, Moses adds a prayer, That God, who had not ceased for a long time to punish his people, would at length be inclined to deal gently with them.

14-17
16. Let thy work appear towards thy servants. As God, when he forsakes his Church, puts on as it were a character different from his own, Moses, with much propriety, calls the blessing of protection which had been divinely promised to the children of Abraham God's proper work. Although, therefore, God's work was manifest in all the instances in which he had punished the ingratitude, and unhallowed desires of his people, yet Moses, by way of eminence, prefers before all other proofs of God's power, that care which he exercised in maintaining the welfare of the people.

displeasure; and, though we are not quite deprived of the residue of our years, yet we are likely to spend them as a tale that is told.
IV. They are taught by all this to stand in awe of the wrath of God (v. 11): Who knows the power of thy anger? None can perfectly comprehend it. The psalmist speaks as one afraid of God's anger, and amazed at the greatness of the power of it.

12-17 Prayers for mercy.
These are the petitions of this prayer, grounded upon the foregoing meditations and acknowledgments. Is any afflicted? Let him learn thus to pray. Four things they are here directed to pray for:
I. For a sanctified use of the sad dispensation they were now under. Being condemned to have our days shortened, "Lord, teach us to number our days (v. 12); Lord, give us grace duly to consider how few they are, and how little a while we have to live in this world."
II. For the turning away of God's anger from them, that though the decree had gone forth, and was past revocation, there was no remedy, but they must die in the wilderness: "Yet return, O Lord! be thou reconciled to us, and let it repent thee concerning thy servants (v. 13); send us tidings of peace to comfort us again after these heavy tidings. How long must we look upon ourselves as under thy wrath, and when shall we have some token given us of our restoration to thy favor? We are thy servants, thy people (Isa. lxiv. 9); when wilt thou change thy way toward us?" In answer to this prayer, and upon their profession of repentance (Num. xiv. 39, 40), God, in the next chapter, proceeding with the laws concerning sacrifices (Num. xv. 1, &c.), which was a token that it repented him concerning his servants; for, if the Lord had been pleased to kill them, he would not have shown them such things as these.
III. For comfort and joy in the returns of God's favor to them, v. 14, 15. They pray for the mercy of God; for they pretend not to plead any merit of their own. Have mercy upon us, O God! is a prayer we are all concerned to say Amen to. Let us pray for early mercy, the seasonable communications of divine mercy, that God's tender mercies may speedily prevent us, early in the morning of our days, when we are young and flourishing, v. 6. Let us pray for the true satisfaction and happiness which are to be had only in the favor and mercy of God, Ps. iv. 6, 7. A gracious soul, if it may but be satisfied of God's lovingkindness, will be satisfied with it, abundantly satisfied, will take up with that, and will take up with nothing short of it.
IV. For the progress of the work of God among them notwithstanding, v. 16, 17, it is necessary for God Himself to be manifest in carrying it on: "Let thy work appear upon thy servants; let it appear that thou hast wrought upon us, to bring us home to thyself and to fit us for thyself."

Psalm 91

1-8

1 He that dwelleth in the secret place of the most High shall abide under the shadow of the Almighty.

2 I will say of the LORD, He is my refuge and my fortress: my God; in him will I trust.

3 Surely he shall deliver thee from the snare of the fowler, and from the noisome pestilence.

4 He shall cover thee with his feathers, and under his wings shalt thou trust: his truth shall be thy shield and buckler.

5 Thou shalt not be afraid for the terror by night; nor for the arrow that flieth by day;

6 Nor for the pestilence that walketh in darkness; nor for the destruction that wasteth at noonday.

7 A thousand shall fall at thy side, and ten thousand at thy right hand; but it shall not come nigh thee.

8 Only with thine eyes shalt thou behold and see the reward of the wicked.

Psalm 91

TITLE. This Psalm is without a title, and we have no means of ascertaining either the name of its writer, or the date of its composition, with certainly. The Jewish doctors consider that when the author's name is not mentioned we may assign the Psalm to the last named writer; and, if so, this is another Psalm of Moses, the man of God. Many expressions here used are similar to those of Moses in Deuteronomy, and the internal evidence, from the peculiar idioms, would point towards him as the composer. The continued lives of Joshua and Caleb, who followed the Lord fully, make remarkably apt illustrations of this Psalm, for they, as a reward for abiding in continued nearness to the Lord, lived on "amongst the dead, amid their graves." For these reasons it is by no means improbable that this Psalm may have been written by Moses, but we dare not dogmatize. If David's pen was used in giving us this matchless ode, we cannot believe as some do that he this commemorated the plague which devastated Jerusalem on account of his numbering the people. For him, then, to sing of himself as seeing "the reward of the wicked" would be clean contrary to his declaration, "I have sinned, but these sheep, what have they done?"; and the absence of any allusion to the sacrifice upon Zion could not be in any way accounted for, since David's repentance would inevitably have led him to dwell upon the atoning sacrifice and the sprinkling of blood by the hyssop.

In the whole collection there is not a more cheering Psalm, its tone is elevated and sustained throughout, faith is at its best, and speaks nobly. A German physician was wont to speak of it as the best preservative in times of cholera, and in truth, it is a heavenly medicine against plague and pest. He who can live in its spirit will be fearless, even if once again London should become a lazar-house, and the grave be gorged with carcases.

DIVISION. On this occasion we shall follow the divisions which our translators have placed at the head of the Psalm, for they are pithy and suggestive.

Ps 91:1-2—The state of the godly.

Ps 91:3-8—Their safety.

Ps 91:9-10—Their habitation.

Ps 91:11-13—Their servants.

Ps 91:14-16—Their friend; with the effects of them all.

EXPOSITION

Verse 1. He that dwelleth in the secret place of the most High. The blessings here promised are not for all believers, but for those who live in close fellowship with God. Every child of God looks towards the inner sanctuary and the mercy seat, yet all do not dwell in the most holy place; they run to it at times, and enjoy occasional approaches, but they do not habitually reside in the mysterious presence. Those who through rich grace obtain unusual and continuous communion with God, so as to abide in Christ and Christ in them, become possessors of rare and special benefits, which are missed by those who follow afar off, and grieve the Holy Spirit of God.

Verse 2. I will say of the Lord, He is my refuge and my fortress. To take up a general truth and make it our own by personal faith is the highest wisdom. It is but poor comfort to say "the Lord is a refuge," but to say he is my refuge, is the essence of consolation.

Verse 3. Surely he shall deliver thee from the snare of the fowler. Assuredly no subtle plot shall succeed against one who has the eyes of God watching for his defense, We are foolish and weak as poor little birds, and are very apt to be lured to our destruction by cunning foes, but if we dwell near to God, he will see to it that the most skilful deceiver shall not entrap us.

Verse 4. He shall cover thee with thy feathers, and under his wings shalt thou trust. A wonderful expression! Had it been invented by an uninspired man it would have verged upon blasphemy, for who should dare to apply

JOHN CALVIN

Psalm 91

1-4
1. He that dwelleth in the secret place of the High One. Those who dwell in the secret place of God are here said by the Psalmist to dwell under his shadow, in the sense that they experience to what a rich extent his protection reaches. Men generally seek out a great-variety of hiding-places, having recourse to one or another, according as the calamities are different which threaten to overtake them; but here we are taught that the only safe and impregnable fortress to which we can betake ourselves is the protection of God. He contrasts the security of those who trust in God with the vanity of all other confidences by which we are apt to delude ourselves.
2. In the second verse he repeats the truth which he had already inculcated, showing at the same time that he speaks from his personal feeling and experience as a believer. This is very necessary in one who would be a teacher; for we cannot communicate true knowledge unless we deliver it not merely with the lips, but as something which God has revealed to our own hearts.
3. In verse third the Psalmist expresses his assurance that the trust of which he had spoken would not be vain and delusory, but that God would prove at all times the deliverer of his people. He is evidently to be considered as addressing himself, and in this way encouraging his own heart to hope in the Lord.
4. He shall protect thee with his wings. This figure, which is employed in other parts of Scripture, is one which beautifully expresses the singularly tender care with which God watches over our safety. When we consider the majesty of God, there is nothing which would suggest a likeness such as is here drawn between him and the hen or other birds, who spread their wings over their young ones to cherish and protect them. But, in accommodation to our infirmity, he does not scruple to descend, as it were, from the heavenly glory which belongs to him, and to encourage us to approach him under so humble a similitude.

5-8
5. Thou shalt not fear for the terror of the night. The Psalmist continues to insist upon the truth which I have just adverted to, that, if we confide with implicit reliance upon the protection of God, we will be secure from every temptation and assault of Satan. It is of importance to remember, that those whom God has taken under his care are in a state of the most absolute safety.
7. A thousand shall fall at thy side. He proceeds to show that, though the state of all men may to appearance be alike, the believer has the special privilege of being exempted from evils of an imminent and impending nature; for it might be objected that he was but man, and, as such, exposed with others to death in its thousand different forms. To correct this mistake, the Psalmist does not hesitate to assert that, when universal ruin prevails around, the Lord's children are the objects of his distinguishing care, and are preserved amidst the general destruction.

MATTHEW HENRY

Psalm 91

1-8 The security of believers.
In these verses we have,
I. A great truth laid down in general, That all those who live a life of communion with God are constantly safe under his protection, and may therefore preserve a holy serenity and security of mind at all times (v. 1): He that dwells, that sits down, in the secret place of the Most High, shall abide under the shadow of the Almighty; he that by faith chooses God for his guardian shall find all that in him which he needs or can desire.
II. The psalmist's comfortable application of this to himself (v. 2): I will say of the Lord, whatever others say of him, "He is my refuge; I choose him as such, and confide in him. Others make idols their refuge, but I will say of Jehovah, the true and living God, He is my refuge: any other is a refuge of lies. He is a refuge that will not fail me; for he is my fortress and strong-hold."
III. The great encouragement he gives to others to do likewise, not only from his own experience of the comfort of it (for in that there might possibly be a fallacy), but from the truth of God's promise, in which there neither is nor can be any deceit (v. 3, 4, &c.): Surely he shall deliver thee. Those who have themselves found the comfort of making God their refuge cannot but desire that others may do so. Now here it is promised,
1. That believers shall be kept from those mischiefs which they are in imminent danger of, and which would be fatal to them (v. 3), from the snare of the fowler, which is laid unseen and catches the unwary prey on a sudden, and from the noisome pestilence, which seizes men unawares and against which there is no guard.
2. That God himself will be their protector; those must needs be safe who have him for their keeper, and successful for whom he undertakes (v. 4): He shall cover thee, shall keep thee secret (Ps. xxxi. 20), and so keep thee safe, Ps. xxvii. 5.
3. That he will not only keep them from evil, but from the fear of evil, v. 5, 6.
4. That they shall be preserved in common calamities, in a distinguishing way (v. 7): "When death rides in triumph, and diseases rage, so that thousands and ten thousands fall, fall by sickness, or fall by the sword in battle, fall at thy side, at thy right hand, and the sight of their fall is enough to frighten thee, and if they fall by the pestilence their falling so near thee may be likely to infect thee, yet it shall not come nigh thee, the death shall not, the fear of death shall not." Those that preserve their purity in times of general corruption may trust God with their safety in times of general desolation. The sprinkling of blood secured the first-born of Israel when thousands fell. Nay, it is promised to God's people that they shall have the satisfaction of seeing, not only God's promises

Psalm 91

9-16

9 Because thou hast made the LORD, which is my refuge, even the most High, thy habitation;
10 There shall no evil befall thee, neither shall any plague come nigh thy dwelling.
11 For he shall give his angels charge over thee, to keep thee in all thy ways.
12 They shall bear thee up in their hands, lest thou dash thy foot against a stone.
13 Thou shalt tread upon the lion and adder: the young lion and the dragon shalt thou trample under feet.
14 Because he hath set his love upon me, therefore will I deliver him: I will set him on high, because he hath known my name.
15 He shall call upon me, and I will answer him: I will be with him in trouble; I will deliver him, and honor him.
16 With long life will I satisfy him, and shew him my salvation.

such words to the Infinite Jehovah? But as he himself authorized, yea, dictated the language, we have here a transcendent condescension, such as it becomes us to admire and adore.

Verse 5. Thou shalt not be afraid for the terror by night. Such frail creatures are we that both by night and by day we are in danger, and so sinful are we that in either season we may be readily carried away by fear; the promise before us secures the favorite of heaven both from danger and from the fear of it.

Verse 6. Nor for the pestilence that walketh in darkness. It is shrouded in mystery as to its cause and cure, it marches on, unseen of men, slaying with hidden weapons, like an enemy stabbing in the dark, yet those who dwell in God are not afraid of it.

Verse 7. A thousand shall fall at thy side and ten thousand at thy right hand. So terribly may the plague rage among men that the bills of mortality may become very heavy and continue to grow ten times heavier still, yet shall such as this Psalm speaks of survive the scythe of death.

Verse 8. Only with thine eyes shalt thou behold and see the reward of the wicked. The sight shall reveal both the justice and the mercy of God; in them that perish the severity of God will be manifest, and in the believer's escape the richness of divine goodness will be apparent. Joshua and Caleb verified this promise.

Verses 9-10. The psalmist in these verses assures the man who dwells in God that he shall be secure. Though faith claims no merit of its own, yet the Lord rewards it wherever he sees it. He who makes God his refuge shall find him a refuge; he who dwells in God shall find his dwelling protected.

Verse 11. For he shall give his angels charge over thee. Not one guardian angel, as some fondly dream, but all the angels are here alluded to. They are the bodyguard of the princes of the blood imperial of heaven, and they have received commission from their Lord and ours to watch carefully over all the interests of the faithful.

Verse 12. They, that is the angels, God's own angels, shall cheerfully become our servants. They shall bear thee up in their hands; as nurses carry little children, with careful love, so shall those glorious spirits bear up each individual believer.

Verse 13. Thou shalt tread upon the lion and adder. Over force and fraud shalt thou march victoriously; bold opponents and treacherous adversaries shall alike be trodden down.

Verse 14. Here we have the Lord himself speaking of his own chosen one. Because he hath set his love upon me, therefore will I deliver him. Not because he deserves to be thus kept, but because with all his imperfections he does love his God; therefore not the angels of God only, but the God of angels himself will come to his rescue in all perilous times, and will effectually deliver him.

Verse 15. He shall call upon me, and I will answer him. He will have need to pray, he will be led to pray aright and the answer shall surely come. Saints are first called of God and then they call upon God; such calls as theirs always obtain answers. Not without prayer will the blessing come to the most favored, but by means of prayer they shall receive all good things.

Verse 16. With long life will I satisfy him. The man described in this Psalm fills out the measure of his days, and whether he dies young or old he is quite satisfied with life, and is content to leave it. And shew him my salvation. The full sight of divine grace shall be his closing vision.

JOHN CALVIN

8. In the verse succeeding more is meant than merely that the believer will have personal experience of the truth which the Psalmist had stated, actually feeling and seeing with his own eyes that God manages his defense; a new argument is brought forward in support of the truth, which is this, that God, as the righteous judge of the world, cannot but punish the wicked according to their sins, and extend protection to his own children.

9-12

9. Because thou, Jehovah, art my protection. He dwells at this length in commendation of the providence of God, as knowing how slow men naturally are to resort to God in a right manner; and how much they need to be stimulated to this duty, and to be driven from those false and worldly refuges in which they confide.
10. This verse may be considered as connected with that which follows, and as stating the cause or reason of what is there asserted; for it is added, There shall no evil befall thee. And how are coming evils averted, but just by our resting with confidence in the protection of God? Troubles, it is true, of various kinds assail the believer as well as others, but the Psalmist means that God stands between him and the violence of every assault, so as to preserve him from being overwhelmed.
11. For he has given his angels charge concerning thee. This is added by the Psalmist expressly with the view of obviating any fears which might arise from our infirmity; so that we cannot fail to be struck with the benignant condescension of God in thus not only forgiving our diffidence, but proposing the means by which it may be best removed.
12. They shall bear thee upon their hands. He gives us a still higher idea of the guardianship of the angels, informing us, that they not only watch lest any evil should befall us, and are on the alert to extend assistance, but bear up our steps with their hands, so as to prevent us from stumbling in our course.

13-16

13. Thou shalt walk over the lion and asp. The same truth is here expressed in different words.
14. Because he hath trusted in me, I will deliver him. It may prevent any feeling of disgust or weariness under the repetition and enlargement of the Psalmist upon his present subject, to remember, that, as I have already observed, he is influenced in this by a due consideration of our weakness, ever indisposed, as we are upon the approach of danger, to exercise a due reliance upon the providence of God.
15. He shall call upon me. He now shows more clearly what was meant by trusting in God, or placing our love and delight in him. For that affection and desire which is produced by faith, prompts us to call upon his name. This is another proof in support of the truth that prayer is properly grounded upon the word of God. We are not at liberty in this matter, to follow the suggestions of our own mind or will, but must seek God only in so far as he has in the first place invited us to approach him.

MATTHEW HENRY

fulfilled to them, but his threatenings fulfilled upon those that hate them (v. 8): Only with thy eyes shalt thou behold and see the just reward of the wicked, which perhaps refers to the destruction of the first-born of Egypt by the pestilence.

9-16 The security of believers.
Here are more promises to the same purport with those in the foregoing verses, and they are exceedingly great and precious, and sure to all the seed.
I. The psalmist assures believers of divine protection, from his own experience; and that which he says is the word of God, and what we may rely upon.
Observe, 1. The character of those who shall have the benefit and comfort of these promises; it is much the same with that, v. 1. They are such as make the Most High their habitation (v. 9), as are continually with God and rest in him, as make his name both their temple and their strong tower, as dwell in love and so dwell in God.
2. The promises that are sure to all those who have thus made the Most High their habitation. That, whatever happens to them, nothing shall hurt them (v. 10).
II. He brings in God himself speaking words of comfort to the saints, and declaring the mercy he had in store for them, v. 14-16. Some make this to be spoken to the angels as the reason of the charge given them concerning the saints, as if he had said, "Take care of them, for they are dear to me, and I have a tender concern for them." And now, as before, we must observe,
1. To whom these promises do belong; they are described by three characters:
(1.) They are such as know God's name. His nature we cannot fully know; but by his name he has made himself known, and with that we must acquaint ourselves.
(2.) They are such as have set their love upon him; and those who rightly know him will love him, will place their love upon him as the only adequate object of it.
(3.) They are such as call upon him, as by prayer keep up a constant correspondence with him, and in every difficult case refer themselves to him.
2. What the promises are which God makes to the saints.
(1.) That he will, in due time, deliver them out of trouble: I will deliver him (v. 14 and again v. 15).
(2.) That he will, in the mean time, be with them in trouble, v. 15.
(3.) That herein he will answer their prayers.
(4.) That he will exalt and dignify them.
(5.) That they shall have a sufficiency of life in this world (v. 16).
(6.) That they shall have an eternal life in the other world. All these promises, some think, point primarily at Christ, and had their accomplishment in his resurrection and exaltation.

Psalm 92

Title
A Psalm or Song for the sabbath day.

1-7
1 It is a good thing to give thanks unto the LORD, and to sing praises unto thy name, o most High:
2 To shew forth thy loving kindness in the morning, and thy faithfulness every night,
3 Upon an instrument of ten strings, and upon the psaltery; upon the harp with a solemn sound.
4 For thou, LORD, hast made me glad through thy work: I will triumph in the works of thy hands.
5 O LORD, how great are thy works! and thy thoughts are very deep.
6 A brutish man knoweth not; neither doth a fool understand this.
7 When the wicked spring as the grass, and when all the workers of iniquity do flourish; it is that they shall be destroyed for ever:

Psalm 92

TITLE. A Psalm or Song for the Sabbath day. This admirable composition is both a Psalm and a Song, full of equal measures of solemnity and joy; and it was intended to be sung upon the day of rest. The subject is the praise of God; praise is Sabbatic work, the joyful occupation of resting hearts. Since a true Sabbath can only be found in God, it is wise to meditate upon him on the Sabbath day. The style is worthy of the theme and of the day, its inspiration is from the "fount of every blessing"; David spake as the Spirit gave him utterance. In the church of Christ, at this hour, no Psalm is more frequently sung upon the Lord's day than the present.
The Sabbath was set apart for adoring the Lord in his finished work of creation, hence the suitableness of this Psalm; Christians may take even a higher flight, for they celebrate complete redemption. No one acquainted with David's style will hesitate to ascribe to him the authorship of this divine hymn; the ravings of the Rabbis who speak of its being composed by Adam, only need to be mentioned to be dismissed. Adam in Paradise had neither harps to play upon, nor wicked men to contend with.

EXPOSITION
Verse 1. It is a good thing to give thanks unto the Lord, or JEHOVAH. It is good ethically, for it is the Lord's right; it is good emotionally, for it is pleasant to the heart; it is good practically, for it leads others to render the same homage.
Verse 2. To shew forth thy loving kindness in the morning. The day should begin with praise: no hour is too early for holy song. Loving kindness is a most appropriate theme for those dewy hours when morn is sowing all the earth with orient pearl. Eagerly and promptly should we magnify the Lord.
Verse 3. Upon an instrument of ten strings; with the fullest range of music, uttering before God with the full compass of melody the richest emotions of his soul.
Verse 5. O Lord, how great are thy works! He is lost in wonder. He utters an exclamation of amazement. How vast! How stupendous are the doings of Jehovah! Great for number, extent, and glory and design are all the creations of the Infinite One.
Verse 6. A brutish man knoweth not; neither doth a fool understand this. In this and the following verses the effect of the psalm is heightened by contrast; the shadows are thrown in to bring out the lights more prominently. What a stoop from the preceding verse; from the saint to the brute, from the worshipper to the boor, from the psalmist to the fool! Yet, alas, the character described here is no uncommon one. The boorish or boorish man, for such is almost the very Hebrew word, sees nothing in nature; and if it be pointed out to him, his foolish mind will not comprehend it.
Verse 7. When the wicked spring as the grass, in abundance, and apparent strength, hastening on their progress like verdant plants, which come to perfection in a day, and when all the workers of iniquity do flourish; flowering in their prime and pride, their pomp and their prosperity; it is that they shall be destroyed for ever. They grow to die, they blossom to be blasted. They flower for a short space to wither without end. Greatness and glory are to them but the prelude of their overthrow.
Verse 8. But thou, Lord, art most high for evermore. This is the middle verse of the Psalm, and the great fact which this Sabbath song is meant to illustrate. God is at once the highest and most enduring of all beings. Others rise to fall, but he is the Most High to eternity.
Verse 9. For, lo, thine enemies, O Lord. It is a wonder full of instruction and warning, observe it, O ye sons of men; for, lo, thine enemies shall parish; they shall cease from among men, they shall be known no more. In that the thing is spoken twice it is confirmed by the Lord, it shall surely be, and that speedily.

JOHN CALVIN

Psalm 92

1-4
1. It is good to give thanks unto Jehovah. There is no reason to doubt that the Jews were in the habit of singing this psalm, as the inscription bears, upon the Sabbath-day, and it is apparent, from different passages, that other psalms were applied to this use. The reason why the Psalmist appropriated this psalm to the Sabbath is sufficiently obvious. That day is not to be holy, in the sense of being devoted to idleness, as if this could be an acceptable worship to God, but in the sense of our separating ourselves from all other occupations, to engage in meditating upon the Divine works.
2. In the succeeding verse, he adverts to the grounds which we have for praising God, that we may not imagine that God calls upon us to engage in this service without reason, or simply in consideration of his greatness and power, but in remembrance of his goodness and faithfulness, which should inflame our hearts to such exercise, if we had any proper sense and experience of them. He would have us consider, in mentioning these, that not only is God worthy of praise, but that we ourselves are chargeable with ingratitude and perversity should we refuse it. We are the proper objects of his faithfulness and goodness, and it would argue inexcusable indifference if they did not elicit our cordial praises.
3. He more immediately addresses the Levites, who were appointed to the office of singers, and calls upon them to employ their instruments of music—not as if this were in itself necessary, only it was useful as an elementary aid to the people of God in these ancient times. The intention of them was to stimulate the worshippers, and stir them up more actively to the celebration of the praise of God with the heart.
4. Because thou, Jehovah, hast made me glad. The Psalmist repeats the truth that the Sabbath was not prescribed as a day of idleness, but a season when we should collect our whole energies for meditation upon the works of God. He intimates, at the same time, that those are best qualified for celebrating the praises of God who recognize and feel his fatherly goodness, and can undertake this service with willing and joyful minds.

5-8
5. O Jehovah! how highly exalted are thy works! The Psalmist, having spoken of the works of God in general, proceeds to speak more particularly of his justice in the government of the world. Though God may postpone the punishment of the wicked, he shows, in due time, that in conniving at their sins, he did not overlook or fail to perceive them; and though he exercises his own children with the cross, he proves in the issue, that he was not indifferent to their welfare.
6. The foolish man shall not know them. This is added with propriety, to let us know that the fault lies with ourselves, in not praising the Divine judgments as we ought. For although the Psalmist had spoken of them as deep and mysterious, he

MATTHEW HENRY

Psalm 92

1-6 Incitements to praise of God.
In these verses,
I. We are called upon and encouraged to praise God (v. 1-3): It is a good thing to give thanks unto the Lord. Praising God is good work: it is good in itself and good for us. It is our duty, the rent, the tribute, we are to pay to our great Lord; we are unjust if we withhold it. It is our privilege that we are admitted to praise God, and have hope to be accepted in it. It is good, for it is pleasant and profitable, work that is its own wages; it is the work of angels, the work of heaven. It is good to give thanks for the mercies we have received, for that is the way of fetching in further mercy: it is fit to sing to his name who is Most High, exalted above all blessing and praise.
II. We have an example set before us in the psalmist himself, both to move us to and to direct us in this work (v. 4): Thou, Lord, hast made me glad through thy work. Note,
1. Those can best recommend to others the duty of praise who have themselves experienced the pleasantness of it. "God's works are to be praised, for they have many a time rejoiced my heart; and therefore, whatever others may think of them, I must think well and speak well of them."
2. If God has given us the joy of his works, there is all the reason in the world why we should give him the honor of them. Has he made our hearts glad? Let us then make his praises glorious. Has God made us glad through the works of his providence for us, and of his grace in us, and both through the great work of redemption?
(1.) Let us thence fetch encouragement for our faith and hope; so the psalmist does: I will triumph in the works of thy hands.
(2.) Let us thence fetch matter for holy adorings and admirings of God (v. 5): O Lord! how great are thy works—great beyond conception, beyond expression, the products of great power and wisdom, of great consequence and importance!
III. We are admonished not to neglect the works of God, by the character of those who do so, v. 6. Those are fools, they are brutish, who do not know, who do not understand, how great God's works are, who will not acquaint themselves with them, nor give him the glory of them; they regard not the work of the Lord nor consider the operation of his hands (Ps. xxviii. 5); particularly, they understand not the meaning of their own prosperity (which is spoken of v. 7); they take it as a pledge of their happiness, whereas it is a preparative for their ruin. If there are so many who know not the designs of Providence, nor care to know them, those who through grace are acquainted with them, and love to be so, have the more reason to be thankful.

Psalm 92

8-15
8 But thou, LORD, art most high for evermore.
9 For, lo, thine enemies, O LORD, for, lo, thine enemies shall perish; all the workers of iniquity shall be scattered.
10 But my horn shalt thou exalt like the horn of an unicorn: I shall be anointed with fresh oil.
11 Mine eye also shall see my desire on mine enemies, and mine ears shall hear my desire of the wicked that rise up against me.
12 The righteous shall flourish like the palm tree: he shall grow like a cedar in Lebanon.
13 Those that be planted in the house of the LORD shall flourish in the courts of our God.
14 They shall still bring forth fruit in old age; they shall be fat and flourishing;
15 To shew that the LORD is upright: he is my rock, and there is no unrighteousness in him.

Verse 10. But my horn shalt thou exalt like the horn of an unicorn. The believer rejoices that he shall not be suffered to perish, but shall be strengthened and enabled to triumph over his enemies, by the divine aid. The unicorn may have been some gigantic ox or buffalo now unknown, and perhaps extinct—among the ancients it was the favorite symbol of unconquerable power; the psalmist adopts it as his emblem. Faith takes delight in foreseeing the mercy of the Lord, and sings of what he will do as well as of what he has done.

Verse 11. The good man is quite silent as to what he expected to hear; he knew that what he should hear would vindicate his faith in his God, and he was content to leave his cruel foes in God's hands, without an expression concerning his own desire one way or the other.

Verse 12. The song now contrasts the condition of the righteous with that of the graceless. The wicked "spring as the grass", but The righteous shall flourish like a palm tree, whose growth may not be so rapid, but whose endurance for centuries is in fine contrast with the transitory verdure of the meadow. When we see a noble palm standing erect, sending all its strength upward in one bold column, and growing amid the dearth and drought of the desert, we have a fine picture of the godly man, who in his uprightness aims alone at the glory of God; and, independent of outward circumstances, is made by divine grace to live and thrive where all things else perish.

Verse 13. Those that be planted in the house of the Lord shall flourish in the courts of our God. In the courtyards of Oriental houses trees were planted, and being thoroughly screened, they would be likely to bring forth their fruit to perfection in trying seasons; even so, those who by grace are brought into communion with the Lord, shall be likened to trees planted in the Lord's house, and shall find it good to their souls. No heart has so much joy as that which abides in the Lord Jesus. Fellowship with the stem begets fertility in the branches. If a man abide in Christ he brings forth much fruit.

Verse 14. They shall still bring forth fruit in old age. Nature decays but grace thrives. Fruit, as far as nature is concerned, belongs to days of vigor; but in the garden of grace, when plants are weak in themselves, they become strong in the Lord, and abound in fruit acceptable with God. Happy they who can sing this Sabbath Psalm, enjoying the rest which breathes through every verse of it; no fear as to the future can distress them.

Verse 15. This mercy to the aged proves the faithfulness of their God, and leads them to shew that the Lord is upright, by their cheerful testimony to his ceaseless goodness. We do not serve a Master who will run back from his promise. Whoever else may defraud us, he never will. Every aged Christian is a letter of commendation to the immutable fidelity of Jehovah. He is my rock, and there is no unrighteousness in him. Here is the psalmist's own seal and sign manual; still was he building upon his God, and still was the Lord a firm foundation for his trust. For shelter, for defense, for indwelling, for foundation, God is our rock; hitherto he has been to us all that he said he would be, and we may be doubly sure that he will abide the same even unto the end. He has delayed our reward, but he has never been unrighteous to forget our work of faith and labor of love. He is a friend without fault, a helper without fail. Whatever he may do with us, he is always in the right; his dispensations have no flaw in them, no, not the most minute. He is true and righteous altogether, and so we weave the end of the psalm with its beginning, and make a coronet of it, for the head of our Beloved. It is a good thing to sing praises unto the Lord, for "he is my rock, and there is no unrighteousness in him."

here informs us that they would be discerned without difficulty, were it not for our stupidity and indifference.
7. When the wicked flourish as the grass. He points out, and exposes, by a striking and appropriate figure, the folly of imagining that the wicked obtain a triumph over God, when he does not, it may be, immediately bring them under restraint.

9-11
9. For, lo! thine enemies, O Jehovah! The Psalmist concludes it to be impossible that God should not overthrow his enemies. This clearly shows that it was his design to establish our faith under the strong temptations to which it is subjected, and, more especially, to remove that offense out of the way, which has disturbed the minds of many, and led them astray;—we refer to the prosperity of the wicked, and its effect in attaching a certain perplexity to the judgments of God.

12-13
12. The righteous shall flourish like the palm-tree. He now passes to the consideration of another general truth, That though God may exercise his people with many trials, subject them to hardships, and visit them with privations, he will eventually show that he had not forgotten them. We need not be surprised that he insists so explicitly and carefully upon this point, as nothing is more difficult than for the saints of God to entertain expectations of being raised up and delivered when they have been reduced almost to the state of the dead, and it does not appear how they can live.
13. The expression which is employed—planted in the house of the Lord—gives the reason of their vigorous growth; nor is it meant that they have merely a place there, (which can be said even of hypocrites,) but that they are firmly fixed, and deeply rooted in it, so as to be united to God. The Psalmist speaks of the courts of the Lord, because none but the priests were allowed to enter the holy place; the people worshipped in the court. By those who are planted in the Church he means such as are united to God in real and sincere attachment, and insinuates that their prosperity cannot be of a changeable and fluctuating nature, because it is not founded upon anything that is in the world.
15. That they may show that Jehovah is upright. It is evident from this verse that the great object of the Psalmist is, to allay that disquietude of mind which we are apt to feel under the disorder which reigns apparently in the affairs of this world; and to make us cherish the expectation, that God will bring light and order eventually out of confusion. That they may show, it is said particularly, that the Lord is upright; for through the influence of our corruption we are apt to conclude, when things do not proceed as we would wish in the world, that God is chargeable not only with neglect but with unrighteousness, in abandoning his people, and tolerating the commission of sin.

7-15 The triumph of the righteous; the happiness of the righteous.
The psalmist had said (v. 4) that from the works of God he would take occasion to triumph; and here he does so.
I. He triumphs over God's enemies (v. 7, 9, 11), triumphs in the foresight of their destruction, not as it would be the misery of his fellow-creatures, but as it would redound to the honor of God's justice and holiness. He is confident of the ruin of sinners, although they are flourishing (v. 7), and although they are daring, v. 9.
II. He triumphs in God, and his glory and grace.
1. In the glory of God (v. 8): "But thou, O Lord! art most high for evermore. The workers of iniquity who fight against us may be high for a time, and think to carry all before them with a high hand, but thou art high, most high, for evermore. Their height will be humbled and brought down, but thine is everlasting."
2. In the grace of God, his favor and the fruits of it,
(1.) To himself (v. 10): "Thou, O Lord! that art thyself most high, shalt exalt my horn." The great God is the fountain of honor, and he, being high for evermore, himself will exalt his people for ever, for he is the praise of all his saints, Ps. cxlviii. 14.
(2.) To all the saints. They are here represented as trees of righteousness, Isa. lxi. 3; Ps. i. 3. Observe,
[1.] The good place they are fixed in; they are planted in the house of the Lord, v. 13. The trees of righteousness do not grow of themselves; they are planted, not in common soil, but in paradise, in the house of the Lord. Trees are not usually planted in a house; but God's trees are said to be planted in his house because it is from his grace, by his word and Spirit, that they receive all the sap and virtue that keep them alive and make them fruitful.
[2.] The good plight they shall be kept in. It is here promised, First, That they shall grow, v. 12. Where God gives true grace he will give more grace. God's trees shall grow higher, like the cedars, the tall cedars in Lebanon; they shall grow nearer heaven, and with a holy ambition shall aspire towards the upper world; they shall grow stronger, like the cedars, and fitter for use. He that has clean hands shall be stronger and stronger. Secondly, That they shall flourish, both in the credit of their profession and in the comfort and joy of their own souls. They shall be cheerful themselves and respected by all about them. The wicked flourish as the grass (v. 7), which is soon withered, but the righteous as the palm-tree, which is long-lived and which the winter does not change. It has been said of the palm-tree, Sub pondere crescit—The more it is pressed down the more it grows; so the righteous flourish under their burdens; the more they are afflicted the more they multiply.

Psalm 93

1 The LORD reigneth, he is clothed with majesty; the LORD is clothed with strength, wherewith he hath girded himself: the world also is stablished, that it cannot be moved.
2 Thy throne is established of old: thou art from everlasting.
3 The floods have lifted up, O LORD, the floods have lifted up their voice; the floods lift up their waves.
4 The LORD on high is mightier than the noise of many waters, yea, than the mighty waves of the sea.
5 Thy testimonies are very sure: holiness becometh thine house, O LORD, for ever.

Psalm 93

This brief Psalm is without title or name of author, but its subject is obvious enough, being stated in the very first line. It is the Psalm of Omnipotent Sovereignty: Jehovah, despite all opposition, reigns supreme. Possibly at the time this sacred ode was written, the nation was in danger from its enemies, and the hopes of the people of God were encouraged by remembering that the Lord was still King. What sweeter and surer consolation could they desire?

EXPOSITION
Verse 1. The LORD reigneth, or Jehovah reigns. Whatever opposition may arise, his throne is unmoved; he has reigned, does reign, and will reign for ever and ever. Whatever turmoil and rebellion there may be beneath the clouds, the eternal King sits above all in supreme serenity; and everywhere he is really Master, let his foes rage as they may. All things are ordered according to his eternal purposes, and his will is done. In the verse before us it would seem as if the Lord had for a while appeared to vacate the throne, but on a sudden he puts on his regal apparel and ascends his lofty seat, while his happy people proclaim him with new joy, shouting "The Lord reigneth."
Verse 2. Thy throne is established of old. Though thou mayest just now appear in more conspicuous sovereignty, yet thine is no upstart sovereignty: in the most ancient times thy dominion was secure, yea, before time was thy throne was set up. We often hear of ancient dynasties, but what are they when compared with the Lord? Are they not as the bubble on the breaker, born an instant ago and gone as soon as seen? Thou art from everlasting. The Lord himself is eternal.
Verse 3. The floods have lifted up, 0 LORD. Men have raged like angry waves of the sea, but vain has been their tumult. Observe that the psalmist turns to the Lord when he sees the billows foam, and hears the breakers roar; he does not waste his breath by talking to the waves, or to violent men; but like Hezekiah he spreads the blasphemies of the wicked before the Lord. The floods have lifted up their voice; the floods lift up their waves. These repetitions are needed for the sake both of the poetry and the music, but they also suggest the frequency and the violence of wicked assaults upon the government of God, and the repeated defeats which they sustain. Sometimes men are furious in words—they lift up their voice, and at other times they rise to acts of violence—they lift up their waves; but the Lord has control over them in either case.
Verse 4. The Lord on high is mightier than the noise of many waters. The utmost of their power is to him but a sound and he can readily master it, therefore he calls it a noise by way of contempt. When men combine to overthrow the kingdom of Jesus, plot secretly, and by and by rage openly, the Lord thinks no more of it than of so much noise upon the sea beach. Jehovah, the self existent and omnipotent, cares not for the opposition of dying men, however many or mighty they may be.
Verse 5. Thy testimonies are very sure. As in providence the throne of God is fixed beyond all risk, so in revelation his truth is beyond all question. Other teachings are uncertain, but the revelations of heaven are infallible. As the rocks remain unmoved amid the tumult of the sea, so does divine truth resist all the currents of man's opinion and the storms of human controversy; they are not only sure, but very sure. Glory be to God, we have not been deluded by a cunningly devised fable: our faith is grounded upon the eternal truth of the Most High. Holiness becometh thine house, O Lord, for ever. Truth changes not in its doctrines, which are very sure, nor holiness in its precepts, which are incorruptible.

JOHN CALVIN

Psalm 93

The psalm commences with the celebration of the infinite glory of God. It is then declared that such is his faithfulness that he never deceives his own people, who, embracing his promises, wait with tranquil minds for their salvation amidst all the tempests and agitations of the world.

1-2

1. Jehovah hath reigned. We here see that in the power of God there is exhibited to us matter of confidence; for our not investing God with the power which belongs to him, as we ought to do, and thus wickedly despoiling him of his authority, is the source of that fear and trembling which we very often experience. This, it is true, we dare not do openly, but were we well persuaded of his invincible power, that would be to us an invincible support against all the assaults of temptation. All admit in word what the prophet here teaches, That God reigns; but how few are there who oppose this shield to the hostile powers of the world, as it becomes them to do, that they may fear nothing however terrible? In this then consists the glory of God, that he governs mankind according to his will. It is said that he clothes himself with majesty and strength; not that we ought to imagine that there is any thing in him which is derived from another, but it is intended by the effect and indubitable experience to show his wisdom and righteousness in the government of mankind.

2. Thy throne is stable. The term throne signifies, by the figure synecdoche, righteousness, and office or power of government; it being customary to transfer such images taken from men to God, in accommodation to our infirmity. By this ascription of praise the Psalmist effectually disposes of all the absurd ideas which have been broached, tending to deny or disparage the power of God, and declares, upon the matter, that God may sooner cease to be, than to sit upon his throne in the government of this world.

3-5

3. The floods have lifted up, O Jehovah! I have no doubt the Psalmist sets forth the power of God by adducing one brief illustration out of many which might have been given. We need not go farther for a striking instance of Divine power—one that may impress us with an idea of his tremendous majesty—than to the floods of waters, and agitations of the ocean; as in Psalm 29:4, the mighty voice of God is said to be in the thunder. God manifests his power in the sound of the floods, and in the tempestuous waves of the sea, in a way calculated to excite our reverential awe.

5. Thy testimonies are singularly true. As yet the Psalmist has insisted upon the excellency of God in the work of creation, and the providential government of the world. Now he speaks of his distinguishing goodness to his chosen people, in making known to them the doctrine which bringeth salvation. He begins by commending the absolute trustworthiness and truthfulness of the law of God.

MATTHEW HENRY

Psalm 93

1-5 The glory and majesty of God.

Next to the being of God there is nothing that we are more concerned to believe and consider than God's dominion, that Jehovah is God, and that this God reigns (v. 1), not only that he is King of right, and is the owner and proprietor of all persons and things, but that he is King in fact, and does direct and dispose of all the creatures and all their actions according to the counsel of his own will. This is celebrated here, and in many other psalms: The Lord reigns.

I. The Lord reigns gloriously: He is clothed with majesty. The majesty of earthly princes, compared with God's terrible majesty, is but like the glimmerings of a glow-worm compared with the brightness of the sun when he goes forth in his strength.

II. He reigns powerfully. He is not only clothed with majesty, as a prince in his court, but he is clothed with strength, as a general in the camp.

III. He reigns eternally (v. 2): Thy throne is established of old. God's right to rule the world is founded in his making it; he that gave being to it, no doubt, may give law to it, and so his title to the government is incontestable: Thy throne is established; it is a title without a flaw in it.

IV. He reigns triumphantly, v. 3, 4. We have here,

1. A threatening storm supposed: The floods have lifted up, O Lord! (to God himself the remonstrance is made) the floods have lifted up their voice, which speaks terror; nay, they have lifted up their waves, which speaks real danger.

2. An immovable anchor cast in this storm (v. 4): The Lord himself is mightier. Let this keep our minds fixed,

(1.) That God is on high, above them, which denotes his safety (they cannot reach him, Ps. xxix. 10) and his sovereignty; they are ruled by him, they are overruled, and, wherein they rebel, overcome, Exod. xviii. 11.

(2.) That he is mightier, does more wondrous things than the noise of many waters; they cannot disturb his rest or rule; they cannot defeat his designs and purposes.

V. He reigns in truth and holiness, v. 5.

1. All his promises are inviolably faithful: Thy testimonies are very sure. As God is able to protect his church, so he is true to the promises he has made of its safety and victory. His word is passed, and all the saints may rely upon it.

2. All his people ought to be conscientiously pure: Holiness becomes thy house, O Lord! for ever. God's church is his house; it is a holy house, cleansed from sin, consecrated by God, and employed in his service. The holiness of it is its beauty (nothing better becomes the saints than conformity to God's image and an entire devotedness to his honor), and it is its strength and safety; it is the holiness of God's house that secures it against the many waters and their noise.

Psalm 94

1-8
1 O Lord God, to whom vengeance belongeth; O God, to whom vengeance belongeth, shew thyself.
2 Lift up thyself, thou judge of the earth: render a reward to the proud.
3 LORD, how long shall the wicked, how long shall the wicked triumph?
4 How long shall they utter and speak hard things? and all the workers of iniquity boast themselves?
5 They break in pieces thy people, O LORD, and afflict thine heritage.
6 They slay the widow and the stranger, and murder the fatherless.
7 Yet they say, The LORD shall not see, neither shall the God of Jacob regard it.
8 Understand, ye brutish among the people: and ye fools, when will ye be wise?

Psalm 94

SUBJECT. The writer sees evil doers in power, and smarts under their oppressions. His sense of the divine sovereignty, of which he had been singing in the previous Psalm, leads him to appeal to God as the great Judge of the earth; this he does with much vehemence and importunity, evidently tingling under the lash of the oppressor. Confident in God's existence, and assured of his personal observation of the doings of men, the psalmist rebukes his atheistic adversaries, and proclaims his triumph in his God: he also interprets the severe dispensation of Providence to be in very deed most instructive chastisements, and so he counts those happy who endure them. The Psalm is another pathetic form of the old enigma—"Wherefore do the wicked prosper?" It is another instance of a good man perplexed by the prosperity of the ungodly, cheering his heart by remembering that there is, after all, a King in heaven, by whom all things are overruled for good.
DIVISION. In Ps 94:1-7 the psalmist utters his complaint against wicked oppressors. From Ps 94:8-11 he reasons against their skeptical notion that God did not notice the actions of men. He then shows that the Lord does bless his people and will deliver them, though for a while they may be chastened, Ps 94:12-15. He again pleads for help in Ps 94:16, and declares his entire dependence upon God for preservation, Ps 94:17-19; yet a third time urges his complaint, Ps 94:20-21; and then concludes with the confident assurance that his enemies, and all other wicked men, would certainly be made to reap the due reward of their deeds,—"yea, the Lord our God shall cut them off."

EXPOSITION
Verse 1. O LORD God, to whom vengeance belongeth; O God, to whom vengeance belongeth, shew thyself: or, God of retribution, Jehovah, God of retribution, shine forth! A very natural prayer when innocence is trampled down, and wickedness exalted on high. If the execution of justice be a right thing,—and who can deny the fact?—then it must be a very proper thing to desire it; not out of private revenge, in which case a man would hardly dare to appeal to God, but out of sympathy with right, and pity for those who are made wrongfully to suffer, Who can see a nation enslaved, or even an individual downtrodden, without crying to the Lord to arise and vindicate the righteous cause? The toleration of injustice is here attributed to the Lord's being hidden, and it is implied that the bare sight of him will suffice to alarm the tyrants into ceasing their oppressions.
Verse 2. Lift up thyself, thou judge of the earth. Ascend thy judgment seat and be acknowledged as the ruler of men: and, moreover, raise thyself as men do who are about to strike with all their might; for the abounding sin of mankind requires a heavy blow from thy hand.
Verse 3. LORD, how long shall the wicked, how long shall the wicked triumph? Shall wrong for ever rule? Are slavery, robbery, tyranny, never to cease? Since there is certainly a just God in heaven, armed with almighty power, surely there must be sooner or later an end to the ascendancy of evil, innocence must one day find a defender.
Verse 4. How long shall they utter and speak hard things? The ungodly are not content with deeds of injustice, but they add hard speeches, boasting, threatening, and insulting over the saints. Will the Lord for ever endure this? Will he leave his own children much longer to be the prey of their enemies?
Verse 5. They break in pieces thy people, O LORD, grinding them with oppression, crushing them with contempt. Yet the men they break in pieces are God's own people, and they are persecuted because they are so; this is a strong plea for the divine interposition. And afflict thine heritage, causing them sorrowful humiliation and deep depression of heart.

JOHN CALVIN

Psalm 94

1-6
1. O Jehovah! God of vengeances. We know that the Jews were surrounded by many neighbors who were not well affected towards them, and were thus incessantly subject to the assaults and oppression of bitter enemies. As this persecution was even more severe than the unrestrained violence of the wicked, we need not wonder that the Psalmist should earnestly beseech God for deliverance from it. The expressions which he uses, calling upon God to shine forth conspicuously, and lift himself up on high, amount in common language to this, that God would give some actual manifestation of his character as judge or avenger; for in that case he is seen ascending his tribunal to exact the punishment due to sin, and demonstrate his power in preserving order and government in the world.
3. O Jehovah! how long shall the wicked? The Psalmist justifies himself in this verse for the fervent importunity which he showed in prayer. There was need of immediate help, when the wicked had proceeded to such an extent of audacity. The necessity of our case may justly embolden us in our requests, which must be all the more readily heard as they are reasonable; and here the Psalmist insists that his complaints were not without cause, nor originated in trifling reasons, but were extorted by injuries of the most flagrant description.
4. They pour forth, they speak hard things. He shows in still clearer terms, how their fierceness in persecution was such that they did not scruple to glory in their guilt. We see how wicked men are instigated by pride and vain-glory, to demean and disgrace themselves so far as to boast vain-gloriously of their power, breathing forth threatenings of bloodshed, violence, and monstrous cruelty. It is to such ebullitions that the Psalmist refers, when men who are lost to all sense of shame and modesty boast of the wickedness which they can perpetrate at will.
5. They break in pieces thy people, O Jehovah! Having spoken of their discourse or language as vain-glorious and shameless, he proceeds to speak of their deeds, in cruelly persecuting the Church. It is hard that even the subjects of heathen princes should be subjected to unjust persecution, but a more intolerable thing still, that those who are God's own people, his peculiar inheritance, should be trampled under the foot of tyranny.
6. It is farther added—that they spare not the widow, and the orphan, and murder the stranger God, while he has commanded us in general to cultivate equity and justice in our common intercourse, has commended the orphan, widow, and stranger, to our peculiar care, as being more exposed to injury, and therefore more entitled to humanity and compassion. To treat such objects with cruelty argues a singular degree of impiety, and contempt of divine authority, and is not only an outrage of common justice, but the infraction of a privilege of special protection which God has condescended to cast around them.

MATTHEW HENRY

Psalm 94

1-11 Appeal to God against persecutors; the folly of atheists and oppressors.
In these verses we have,
I. A solemn appeal to God against the cruel oppressors of his people, v. 1, 2. This speaks terror enough to them, that they have the prayers of God's people against them, who cry day and night to him to avenge them of their adversaries; and shall he not avenge them speedily? Luke xviii. 3, 7. Observe here,
1. The titles they give to God for the encouraging of their faith in this appeal: O God! to whom vengeance belongeth; and thou Judge of the earth. We may with boldness appeal to him; for He is judge, supreme judge, judge alone, from whom every man's judgment proceeds. He that gives law gives sentence upon every man according to his works, by the rule of that law. He has prepared his throne for judgment.
2. What it is they ask of God.
(1.) That he would glorify himself, and get honor to his own name.
(2.) That he would mortify the oppressors: Render a reward to the proud; that is, "Reckon with them for all their insolence, and the injuries they have done to thy people."
II. A humble complaint to God of the pride and cruelty of the oppressors, and an expostulation with him concerning it, v. 3-6. Here observe,
1. The character of the enemies they complain against. They are wicked; they are workers of iniquity; they are bad, very bad, themselves, and therefore they hate and persecute those whose goodness shames and condemns them. Those are wicked indeed, and workers of the worst iniquity, lost to all honor and virtue, who are cruel to the innocent and hate the righteous.
2. Their haughty barbarous carriage which they complain of.
3. A modest pleading with God concerning the continuance of the persecution: "Lord, how long shall they do thus?" And again, How long? When shall this wickedness of the wicked come to an end?
III. A charge of atheism exhibited against the persecutors, and an expostulation with them upon that charge.
1. Their atheistic thoughts are here discovered (v. 7): Yet they say, The Lord shall not see. Though the cry of their wickedness is very great and loud, though they rebel against the light of nature and the dictates of their own consciences, yet they have the confidence to say, "The Lord shall not see; he will not only wink at small faults, but shut his eyes at great ones too."
2. They are here convicted of folly and absurdity. He that says either that Jehovah the living God shall not see or that the God of Jacob shall not regard the injuries done to his people, Nabal is his name and folly is with him; and yet here he is fairly reasoned

Psalm 94

9-16

9 He that planted the ear, shall he not hear? he that formed the eye, shall he not see?

10 He that chastiseth the heathen, shall not he correct? he that teacheth man knowledge, shall not he know?

11 The LORD knoweth the thoughts of man, that they are vanity.

12 Blessed is the man whom thou chastenest, O LORD, and teachest him out of thy law;

13 That thou mayest give him rest from the days of adversity, until the pit be digged for the wicked.

14 For the LORD will not cast off his people, neither will he forsake his inheritance.

15 But judgment shall return unto righteousness: and all the upright in heart shall follow it.

16 Who will rise up for me against the evildoers? or who will stand up for me against the workers of iniquity?

Verse 6. They slay the widow and the stranger, and murder the fatherless. They deal most arrogantly with those who are the most evident objects of compassion. The law of God especially commends these poor ones to the kindness of good men, and it is peculiar wickedness which singles them out to be the victims not only of fraud but of murder. Must not such inhuman conduct as this provoke the Lord?

Verse 7. Yet they say, the Lord shall not see. This was the reason of their arrogance, and the climax of their wickedness: they were blindly wicked because they dreamed of a blind God. When men believe that the eyes of God are dim, there is no reason to wonder that they give full license to their brutal passions. The persons mentioned above not only cherished an infidel unbelief, but dared to avow it, uttering the monstrous doctrine that God is too far away to take notice of the actions of men. Neither shall the God of Jacob regard it.

Verse 8. Understand, ye brutish among the people. They said that God did not note, and now, using the same word in the original, the psalmist calls on the wicked to note, and have regard to the truth. He designates them as boors, boorish, swinish men, and well was the term deserved; and he bids them understand or consider, if they can.

Verse 9. He that planted the ear, shall he not hear? He fashioned that marvelous organ, and fixed it in the most convenient place near to the brain, and is he deaf himself? Is he capable of such design and invention, and yet can he not discern what is done in the world which he made? He made you hear, can he not himself hear? Unanswerable question! It overwhelms the skeptic, and covers him with confusion.

Verse 10. He that chastiseth the heathen, shall not he correct? He reproves whole nations, can he not reprove individuals? All history shows that he visits national sin with national judgment, and can he not deal with single persons? The question which follows is equally full of force, and is asked with a degree of warmth which checks the speaker, and causes the inquiry to remain incomplete. It begins, He that teacheth man knowledge, and then it comes to a pause, which the translators have supplied with the words, shall not he know? but no such words are in the original, where the sentence comes to an abrupt end, as if the inference were too natural to need to be stated, and the writer had lost patience with the brutish men with whom he had argued.

Verse 11. Whether men admit or deny that God knows, one thing is here declared, namely, that the Lord knoweth the thoughts of man, that they are vanity. Not their words alone are heard, and their works seen, but he reads the secret motions of their minds, for men themselves are not hard to be discerned of him, before his glance they themselves are but vanity. It is in the Lord's esteem no great matter to know the thoughts of such transparent pieces of vanity as mankind are, he sums them up in a moment as poor vain things.

Verse 12. Blessed is the man whom thou chastenest, O LORD. The psalmist's mind is growing quiet. He no longer complains to God or argues with men, but tunes his harp to softer melodies, for his faith perceives that with the most afflicted believer all is well. Though he may not feel blessed while smarting under the rod of chastisement, yet blessed he is; he is precious in God's sight, or the Lord would not take the trouble to correct him, and right happy will the results of his correction be.

Verse 13. That thou mayest give him rest from the days of adversity, until the pit be digged for the wicked. The chastening hand and instructive book are sanctified to us, so that we learn to rest in the Lord. We see that his end is our everlasting benefit, and therefore abide quiet under all trying providences and bitter persecutions, waiting our time.

Verse 14. For the LORD will not cast off his people. He may cast them down, but he never can cast them off. During fierce persecutions the saints have been apt to think that the Lord had left his own sheep, and given them

JOHN CALVIN

7-10
7. And they have said, God shall not see. When the Psalmist speaks of the wicked as taunting God with blindness and ignorance, we are not to conceive of them as just exactly entertaining this imagination of him in their hearts, but they despise his judgments as much as if he took no cognizance of human affairs. Were the truth graven upon men's hearts that they cannot elude the eye of God, this would serve as a check and restraint upon their conduct. When they proceed to such audacity in wickedness as to lay the hand of violence upon their fellow-creatures, to rob, and to destroy, it shows that they have fallen into a state of brutish security in which they virtually consider themselves as concealed from the view of the Almighty.
8. Understand, ye stupid among the people. As it was execrable impiety to deny God to be Judge of the earth, the Psalmist severely reprimands their folly in thinking to elude his government, and even succeed by artifices in escaping his view. The expression, stupid among the people, is stronger than had he simply condemned them as foolish. It rendered their folly more inexcusable because they belonged to the posterity of Abraham.
10. He that chastiseth the nations, shall not he correct? He would have them argue from the greater to the less, that if God did not spare even whole nations, but visits their iniquity with punishment, they could not imagine that he would suffer a mere handful of individuals to escape with impunity.

11-13
11. Jehovah knoweth the thoughts of men, etc. He again insists upon the folly of men in seeking to wrap themselves up in darkness, and hide themselves from the view of God. To prevent them from flattering themselves with vain pretexts, he reminds them that the mists of delusion will be scattered at once when they come to stand in God's presence. Nothing can avail them, so long as God from heaven stamps vanity upon their deepest counsels.
12. Blessed is the man whom thou hast instructed, O God! The Psalmist now passes from the language of censure to that of consolation, comforting himself and others of the Lord's people with the truth, that though God might afflict them for a time, he consulted their true interests and safety. At no period of life is this a truth which it is unnecessary to remember, called as we are to a continued warfare. God may allow us intervals of ease, in consideration of our weakness, but would always have us exposed to calamities of various kinds.

14-15
14. Surely Jehovah will not cast off his people. He enforces the same truth which he had stated above in still clearer terms, denying it to be possible that God should cast off his people, whom he had chosen in a manner to be his inheritance. When assailed by afflictions, we should fly to this consideration, as a sanctuary of refuge, that we are God's people, gratuitously adopted into his family, and that he must necessarily have a most intimate and tender regard for our safety, having promised to watch as carefully over his

MATTHEW HENRY

with, for his conviction and conversion, to prevent his confusion (v. 8): "Understand, you brutish among the people, and let reason guide you."
(1.) From the works of creation (v. 9).
(2.) From the works of providence (v. 10).
(3.) From the works of grace: He that teaches man knowledge, shall he not know? He not only, as the God of nature, has given the light of reason, but, as the God of grace, has given the light of revelation, has shown man what is true wisdom and understanding; and he that does this, shall he not know? Job xxviii. 23, 28. The flowing of the streams is a certain sign of the fullness of the fountain. If all knowledge is from God, no doubt all knowledge is in God. From this general doctrine of God's omniscience, the psalmist not only confutes the atheists, who said, "The Lord shall not see (v. 7), he will not take cognizance of what we do;" but awakens us all to consider that God will take cognizance even of what we think (v. 11): The Lord knows the thoughts of man, that they are vanity.

12-23 Comfort to suffering saints; God the defense of his people.
The psalmist, having denounced tribulation to those that trouble God's people, here assures those that are troubled of rest. See 2 Thess. i. 6, 7. He speaks comfort to suffering saints from God's promises and his own experience.
I. From God's promises, which are such as not only save them from being miserable, but secure a happiness to them (v. 12): Blessed is the man whom thou chastenest. Here he looks above the instruments of trouble, and eyes the hand of God, which gives it another name and puts quite another color upon it. The enemies break in pieces God's people (v. 5); they aim at no less; but the truth of the matter is that God by them chastens his people, as the father the son in whom he delights, and the persecutors are only the rod he makes use of. Howbeit they mean not so, neither doth their heart think so, Isa. x. 5-7. Now it is here promised,
1. That God's people shall get good by their sufferings. When he chastens them he will teach them, and blessed is the man who is thus taken under a divine discipline, for none teaches like God.
2. That they shall see through their sufferings (v. 13): That thou mayest give him rest from the days of adversity.
3. That they shall see the ruin of those that are the instruments of their sufferings, which is the matter of a promise, not as gratifying any passion of theirs, but as redounding to the glory of God: Until the pit is digged (or rather while the pit is digging) for the wicked, God is ordering peace for them at the same time that he is ordaining his arrows against the persecutors.
4. That, though they may be cast down, yet certainly they shall not be cast off, v. 14. Let God's suffering people assure themselves of this, that, whatever their

Psalm 94

17-23

17 Unless the LORD had been my help, my soul had almost dwelt in silence.
18 When I said, My foot slippeth; thy mercy, O LORD, held me up.
19 In the multitude of my thoughts within me thy comforts delight my soul.
20 Shall the throne of iniquity have fellowship with thee, which frameth mischief by a law?
21 They gather themselves together against the soul of the righteous, and condemn the innocent blood.
22 But the LORD is my defense; and my God is the rock of my refuge.
23 And he shall bring upon them their own iniquity, and shall cut them off in their own wickedness; yea, the LORD our God shall cut them off.

over to the wolf; but it has never been so, nor shall it ever be, for the Lord will not withdraw his love, neither will he forsake his inheritance.

Verse 15. But judgment shall return unto righteousness. The great Judge will come, the reign of righteousness will commence, the course of affairs will yet be turned into the right channel, and then all the godly will rejoice. The chariot of right will be drawn in triumph through our streets, and all the upright in heart shall follow it, as in happy procession.

Verse 16. Notwithstanding the psalmist's persuasion that all would be well eventually, he could not at the time perceive any one who would stand side by side with him in opposing evil; no champion of the right was forthcoming, the faithful failed from among men. This also is a bitter trial, and a sore evil under the sun; yet it has its purpose, for it drives the heart still more completely to the Lord, compelling it to rest alone in him.

Verse 17. Unless the Lord had been my help, my soul had almost dwelt in silence. Without Jehovah's help, the psalmist declares that he should have died outright, and gone into the silent land, where no more testimonies can be borne for the living God. Or he may mean that he would not have had a word to speak against his enemies, but would have been wrapped in speechless shame.

Verse 18. When I said, My foot slippeth—is slipping even now: I perceived my danger, and cried out in horror, and then, at the very moment of my extremity, came the needed help, thy mercy, O LORD, held me up. Often enough is this the case, we feel our weakness, and see our danger, and in fear and trembling we cry out. At such times nothing can help us but mercy.

Verse 19. In the multitude of my thoughts within me. When I am tossed to and fro with various reasonings, distractions, questions, and forebodings, I will fly to my true rest, for thy comforts delight my soul.

Verse 20. Shall the throne of iniquity have fellowship with thee? Such thrones there are, and they plead a right divine, but their claim is groundless, a fraud upon mankind and a blasphemy of heaven. God enters into no alliance with unjust authority, he gives no sanction to unrighteous legislation.

Verse 21. They gather themselves together against the soul of the righteous, so many are there of them that they crowd their assemblies, and carry their hard measures with enthusiasm; they are the popular party, and are eager to put down the saints. In counsel, and in action, they are unanimous; their one resolve is to hold their own tyrannical position, and put down the godly party.

Verse 22. Let the wicked gather as they may, the psalmist is not afraid, but sweetly sings, The Lord is my defense, and my God is the rock of my refuge. Firm as a rock is Jehovah's love, and there do we betake ourselves for shelter. In him we find safety, let the world rage as it may; we ask not aid from man, but are content to flee into the bosom of omnipotence.

Verse 23. The natural result of oppression is the destruction of the despot; his own iniquities crush him ere long. Providence arranges retaliations as remarkable as they are just. High crimes in the end bring on heavy judgments, to sweep away evil men from off the face of the earth. Wicked men are often arrested by the pursuivants of divine justice red handed, with the evidences of their guilt upon them. He shall bring upon them their own iniquity, and shall cut them off in their own wickedness.

Church as if it were his own heritage. We are thus again taught that our patience will soon give way and fail, unless the tumult of carnal suggestions be allayed by a knowledge of the Divine favor shining in upon our souls.
15. But judgment will return unto righteousness. In the dark season of affliction, it is not easy to recognize the secret love which God even then bears to his own children, and the Psalmist adduces another ground of comfort, in the consideration that God will eventually put an end to the confusions which perplex them, and reduce matters to order.

16-19
16. Who will rise up for me against my adversaries? Here the Psalmist points out, in a lively and graphic manner, how destitute he was of all human aid. As if at the moment in danger, he cries out—Who will stand up for me? Who will oppose himself to my enemies? And immediately afterwards he replies, that had not God helped him, he must have despaired of safety. In declaring that he had been thus miraculously rescued from death, when deserted by all the world, he commends the more God's kindness and grace.
17. He speaks of his life dwelling in silence, for the dead lie in the grave without feeling or strength. Thus the Psalmist owns that there was no means by which his life could have been preserved, had not God interposed without delay.
18. If I said, My foot has fallen. What is said in this verse confirms the preceding statement. The more to commend God's kindness and power, he declares that it was no common danger from which he had been rescued, but in a manner from present death. The import of the language is, that death stared him so full in view, that he despaired of himself; as Paul speaks of having had the message of death in himself, when his condition was desperate, and he had given up hope of life, (2 Corinthians 1:9.)

20-23
20. Shall the throne of iniquities have fellowship with thee? He again derives an argument for confidence from the nature of God, it being impossible that he should show favor to the wicked, or sanction their evil devices. With God for their enemy, how could they escape being destroyed? The words have greater force from being thrown into the form of a question, to show how completely opposed all sin is to the divine nature.
21. They will gather together against the soul of the righteous. The Psalmist evidently intimates that he had to do with leading persons of influence, and not with those merely in private station. The term implies too, that it was not merely one or two private individuals who persecuted him, and others of the Lord's people, but a public convention.
22. But Jehovah has been my fortress. The Psalmist does more than say that God was a fortress, where he might hide with safety, and from the top of which he could bid defiance to every assault. Having congratulated himself upon the divine protection, he proceeds to denounce destruction upon his enemies.

friends do, God will not cast them off, nor throw them out of his covenant or out of his care; he will not forsake them, because they are his inheritance, which he will not quit his title to nor suffer himself to be diseased of. St. Paul comforted himself with this, Rom. xi. 1.
5. That, bad as things are, they shall mend, and, though they are now out of course, yet they shall return to their due and ancient channel (v. 15): Judgment shall return unto righteousness; the seeming disorders of Providence (for real ones there never were) shall be rectified.
II. From his own experiences and observations.
1. He and his friends had been oppressed by cruel and imperious men, that had power in their hands and abused it by abusing all good people with it. They were themselves evil-doers and workers of iniquity (v. 16); they abandoned themselves to all manner of impiety and immorality, and then their throne was a throne of iniquity, v. 20.
2. The oppression they were under bore very hard upon them, and oppressed their spirits too. Let not suffering saints despair, though, when they are persecuted, they find themselves perplexed and cast down; it was so with the psalmist here: His soul had almost dwelt in silence (v. 17).
3. In this distress they sought for help, and succor, and some relief. They looked about for it and were disappointed (v. 16): "Who will rise up for me against the evil-doers? Have I any friend who, in love to me, will appear for me? Has justice any friend who, in a pious indignation at unrighteousness, will plead my injured cause?" He looked, but there was none to save, there was none to uphold.
4. They found succor and relief in God, and in him only. When other friends failed, in him they had a faithful and powerful friend; and it is recommended to all God's suffering saints to trust in him.
(1.) God helps at a dead lift (v. 17).
(2.) God's goodness is the great support of sinking spirits (v. 18).
(3.) Divine consolations are the effectual relief of troubled spirits (v. 19).
5. God is, and will be, as a righteous Judge, the patron and protector of right and the punisher and avenger of wrong; this the psalmist had both the assurance of and the experience of.
(1.) He will give redress to the injured (v. 22).
(2.) He will reckon with the injurious (v. 23): He shall render to them their own iniquity; he shall deal with them according to their deserts.
This the psalm concludes with the triumphant assurance of: Yea, the Lord our God, who takes our part and owns us for his, shall cut them off from any fellowship with him, and so shall make them completely miserable and their pomp and power shall stand them in no stead.

Psalm 95

1-5
1 O come, let us sing unto the LORD: let us make a joyful noise to the rock of our salvation.
2 Let us come before his presence with thanksgiving, and make a joyful noise unto him with psalms.
3 For the LORD is a great God, and a great King above all gods.
4 In his hand are the deep places of the earth: the strength of the hills is his also.
5 The sea is his, and he made it: and his hands formed the dry land.

Psalm 95

TITLE. This Psalm has no title, and all we know of its authorship is that Paul quotes it as "in David." (Heb 4:7.) It is true that this may merely signify that it is to be found in the collection known as David's Psalms; but if such were the Apostle's meaning it would have been more natural for him to have written, "saying in the Psalms;" we therefore incline to the belief that David was the actual author of this poem. It is in its original a truly Hebrew song, directed both in its exhortation and warning to the Jewish people, but we have the warrant of the Holy Spirit in the epistle to the Hebrews for using its appeals and entreaties when pleading with Gentile believers. It is a psalm of invitation to worship. It has about it a ring like that or church bells, and like the bells it sounds both merrily and solemnly, at first ringing out a lively peal, and then dropping into a funeral knell as if tolling at the funeral of the generation which perished in the wilderness. We will call it THE PSALM OF THE PROVOCATION.
DIVISION. It would be correct as to the sense to divide this psalm into an invitation and a warning so as to commence the second part with the last clause of Ps 95:7: but upon the whole it may be more convenient to regard Ps 95:6 as "the beating heart of the psalm," as Hengstenberg calls it, and make the division at the end of Ps 95:5. Thus it will form (1) an invitation with reasons, and (2) an invitation with warnings.

EXPOSITION
Verse 1. O come, let us sing unto the LORD. Other nations sing unto their gods, let us sing unto Jehovah. We love him, we admire him, we reverence him, let us express our feelings with the choicest sounds, using our noblest faculty for its noblest end. It is well thus to urge others to magnify the Lord, but we must be careful to set a worthy example ourselves, so that we may be able not only to cry "Come", but also to add "let us sing", because we are singing ourselves. It is to be feared that very much even of religious singing is not unto the Lord but unto the car of the congregation: above all things we must in our service of song take care that all we offer is with the heart's sincerest and most fervent intent directed toward the Lord himself.
Verse 2. Let us come before his presence with thanksgiving. Here is probably a reference to the peculiar presence of God in the Holy of Holies above the mercy seat, and also to the glory which shone forth out of the cloud which rested above the tabernacle. Everywhere God is present, but there is a peculiar presence of grace and glory into which men should never come without the profoundest reverence. We may make bold to come before the immediate presence of the Lord—for the voice of the Holy Ghost in this psalm invites us, and when we do draw near to him we should remember his great goodness to us and cheerfully confess it.
Verse 3. For the LORD is a great God, and a great King above all gods. No doubt the surrounding nations imagined Jehovah to be a merely local deity, the god of a small nation, and therefore one of the inferior deities; the psalmist utterly repudiates such an idea. Idolaters tolerated gods many and lords many, giving to each a certain measure of respect; the monotheism of the Jews was not content with this concession, it rightly claimed for Jehovah the chief place, and the supreme power.
Verse 4. In his hand are the deep places of the earth. He is the God of the valleys and the hills, the caverns, and the peaks. Far down where the miners sink their shafts, deeper yet where lie the secret oceans by which springs are fed, and deepest of all in the unknown abyss where rage and flame the huge central fires of earth, there Jehovah's power is felt, and all things are under the dominion of his hand. As princes hold the mimic globe in their hands, so does the Lord in very deed hold the earth. When Israel drank of the crystal fount which welled up from the great deep, below the smitten rock, the people knew that in the Lord's hands were the deep

JOHN CALVIN

Psalm 95

The inspired penman of this psalm, whoever he was, in exhorting the Jews to praise God in solemn assembly, states two grounds why God should be praised; the one, that he sustains by his power the world which he created, the other, that he had of his free grace adopted the Church into a gracious relationship with himself. As many take God's praises into their lips in a hypocritical manner, he exhorts the people at the same time to be sincere, serious, and devoted in the service, and to show by the tenor of their life that they had not been chosen in vain. The more effectually to guard them against hypocrisy, he mentions that their fathers from the beginning had been of a stubborn spirit, and chargeable with ingratitude to God; and he takes notice of the dreadful punishment which fell upon them, and which might well deter their children from following in the footsteps of their rebelliousness.

1-5
1. Come, let us rejoice before Jehovah. This psalm is suited for the Sabbath, when we know that the religious assemblies were more particularly convened for the worship of God. It is not individuals among the godly whom he exhorts to celebrate the divine praises in private; he enjoins these to be offered up in the public meeting. By this he showed that the outward worship of God principally consisted in the sacrifice of praise, and not in dead ceremonies. He enjoins haste upon them; by which they might testify their alacrity in this service.
3. For Jehovah is a great God. By these words the Psalmist reminds us what abundant grounds we have for praising God, and how far we are from needing to employ the lying panegyric with which rhetoricians flatter earthly princes. He extols the greatness of God, drawing a tacit contrast between him and such false gods as men have invented for themselves.

6-7
6. Come ye, let us worship. Now that the Psalmist exhorts God's chosen people to gratitude, for that pre-eminency among the nations which he had conferred upon them in the exercise of his free favor, his language grows more vehement. God supplies us with ample grounds of praise when he invests us with spiritual distinction, and advances us to a pre-eminency above the rest of mankind which rests upon no merits of our own. In three successive terms he expresses the one duty incumbent upon the children of Abraham, that of an entire devotement of themselves to God. The worship of God, which the Psalmist here speaks of, is assuredly a matter of such importance as to demand our whole strength; but we are to notice, that he particularly condescends upon one point, the paternal favor of God, evidenced in his exclusive adoption of the posterity of Abraham unto the hope of eternal life. We are also to observe, that mention is made not only of inward gratitude, but the necessity of an outward profession of godliness.
7. Because he is our God. While it is true that all men were created to praise God, there are reasons why the Church is

MATTHEW HENRY

Psalm 95

1-7 Invitation to praise God; motives to praise.
The psalmist here, as often elsewhere, stirs up himself and others to praise God; for it is a duty which ought to be performed with the most lively affections, and which we have great need to be excited to, being very often backward to it and cold in it. Observe,
I. How God is to be praised.
1. With holy joy and delight in him. The praising song must be a joyful noise, v. 1 and again v. 2. Spiritual joy is the heart and soul of thankful praise.
2. With humble reverence, and a holy awe of him (v. 6): "Let us worship, and bow down, and kneel before him, as becomes those who know what an infinite distance there is between us and God, how much we are in danger of his wrath and in need of his mercy."
II. Why God is to be praised and what must be the matter of our praise. We do not want matter; it were well if we did not want a heart. We must praise God,

1. Because he is a great God, and sovereign Lord of all, v. 3. He is great, and therefore greatly to be praised. He is infinite and immense, and has all perfection in himself.

2. Because he is our God, not only has a dominion over us, as he has over all the creatures, but stands in special relation to us (v. 7): He is our God, and therefore it is expected we should praise him; who will, if we do not? What else did he make us for but that we should be to him for a name and a praise?
(1.) He is our Creator, and the author of our being; we must kneel before the Lord our Maker, v. 6. Idolaters kneel before gods which they themselves made; we kneel before a God who made us and all the world and who is therefore our rightful proprietor; for his we are, and not our own.
(2.) He is our Savior, and the author of our blessedness. He is here called the rock of our salvation (v. 1), not only the founder, but the very foundation, of that work of wonder, on whom it is built. That rock is Christ; to him therefore we must sing our songs of praises, to him that sits upon the throne and to the Lamb.
(3.) We are therefore his, under all possible obligations: We are the people of his pasture and the sheep of his hand. All the children of men are so; they are fed and led by his Providence, which cares for them, and conducts them, as the shepherd the sheep.

7-11 Warning against hardness of heart.
The latter part of this psalm, which begins in the middle of a verse, is an exhortation to those who sing gospel psalms to live gospel lives, and to hear the voice of God's word; otherwise, how can they expect that he should hear the voice of their prayers and praises? Observe,
I. The duty required of all those that are the people of Christ's pasture and the sheep of his hand. He

Psalm 95

6-11

6 O come, let us worship and bow down: let us kneel before the LORD our maker.
7 For he is our God; and we are the people of his pasture, and the sheep of his hand. To day if ye will hear his voice,
8 Harden not your heart, as in the provocation, and as in the day of temptation in the wilderness:
9 When your fathers tempted me, proved me, and saw my work.
10 Forty years long was I grieved with this generation, and said, It is a people that do err in their heart, and they have not known my ways:
11 Unto whom I sware in my wrath that they should not enter into my rest.

places of the earth. The strength of the hills is his also. When Sinai was altogether on a smoke the tribes learned that Jehovah was God of the hills as well as of the valleys. Everywhere and at all times is this true; the Lord rules upon the high places of the earth in lonely majesty. The vast foundations, the gigantic spurs, the incalculable masses, the untrodden heights of the mountains are all the Lord's.

Verse 5. The sea is his. This was seen to be true at the Red Sea when the waters saw their God, and obediently stood aside to open a pathway for his people. It was not Edom's sea though it was red, nor Egypt's sea though it washed her shores. The Lord on high reigned supreme over the flood, as King far ever and ever. So is it with the broad ocean, whether known as Atlantic or Pacific, Mediterranean or Arctic; no man can map it out and say "It is mine"; the illimitable acreage of waters knows no other lord but God alone. Jehovah rules the waves.

Verse 6. Here the exhortation to worship is renewed and backed with a motive which, to Israel of old and to Christians now, is especially powerful; for both the Israel after the flesh and the Israel of faith may be described as the people of his pasture, and by both he is called "our God." O come, let us worship and bow down. The adoration is to be humble.

Verse 7. For he is our God. Here is the master reason for worship. Jehovah has entered into covenant with us, and from all the world beside has chosen us to be his own elect. If others refuse him homage, we at least will render it cheerfully. He is ours, and our God; ours, therefore will we love him; our God, therefore will we worship him. Happy is that man who can sincerely believe that this sentence is true in reference to himself.

Verse 8. Harden not your heart. If ye will hear, learn to fear also. The sea and the land obey him, do not prove more obstinate than they! We cannot soften our hearts, but we can harden them, and the consequences will be fatal. Today is too good a day to be profaned by the hardening of our hearts against our own mercies. While mercy reigns let not obduracy rebel.

Verse 9. When your fathers tempted me. As far as they could do so they tempted God to change his usual way, and to do their sinful bidding, and though he cannot be tempted of evil, and will never yield to wicked requests, yet their intent was the same, and their guilt was none the less. God's way is perfect, and when we would have him alter it to please us, we are guilty of tempting him; and the fact that we do so in vain, while it magnifies the Lord's holiness, by no means excuses our guilt.

Verse 10. Forty years long was I grieved with this generation. The impression upon the divine mind is most vivid; he sees them before him now, and calls them "this generation." He does not leave his prophets to upbraid the sin, but himself utters the complaint and declares that he was grieved, nauseated, and disgusted.

Verse 11. Unto whom I sware in my wrath that they should not enter into my rest. There can be no rest to an unbelieving heart. If manna and miracles could not satisfy Israel, neither would they have been content with the land which flowed with milk and honey. Canaan was to be the typical resting place of God, where his ark should abide, and the ordinances of religion should be established; the Lord had for forty years borne with the ill manners of the generation which came out of Egypt, and it was but right that he should resolve to have no more of them. Was it not enough that they had revolted all along that marvelous wilderness march? Jehovah would not have it so. He not only said but swore that into his rest they should not come, and that oath excluded every one of them.

specially said to have been formed for that end, (Isaiah 61:3.) The Psalmist was entitled to require this service more particularly from the hands of his chosen people. This is the reason why he impresses upon the children of Abraham the invaluable privilege which God had conferred upon them in taking them under his protection. God may indeed be said in a sense to have done so much for all mankind. But when asserted to be the Shepherd of the Church, more is meant than that he favors her with the common nourishment, support, and government which he extends promiscuously to the whole human family; he is so called because he separates her from the rest of the world, and cherishes her with a peculiar and fatherly regard.

8-11

8. Harden not your heart, as in Meribah The Psalmist, having extolled and commended the kindness of God their Shepherd, takes occasion, as they were stiff-necked and disobedient, to remind them of their duty, as his flock, which was to yield a pliable and meek submission; and the more to impress their minds, he upbraids them with the obstinacy of their fathers.

9. When your fathers tempted me, they proved me. The Psalmist insinuates that the Jews had been from the first of a perverse and almost intractable spirit. Had their fathers not manifested a rebellions spirit, they might have retorted by asking the question, Upon what ground he warned them against hardness of heart, their nation having hitherto maintained a character for docility and tractableness? The fact being otherwise—their fathers having from the first been perverse and stubborn, the Psalmist had a plain reason for insisting upon the correction of this particular vice.

10. Forty years I strove with this generation. The Psalmist brings it forward as an aggravation of their perverse obstinacy, that God strove with them for so long a time without effect. Occasionally it will happen that there is a violent manifestation of perversity which soon subsides; but God complains that he had constant grounds of contention with his people, throughout the whole forty years. And this proves to us the incurable waywardness of that people. The word generation is used with the same view.

11. Wherefore I have sworn in my wrath. The Greek version, taking it for a mark of similitude, reads, As I have sworn. But I think that it may be properly considered as expressing an inference or conclusion; not as if they were then at last deprived of the promised inheritance when they tempted God, but the Psalmist, having spoken, in the name of God, of that obstinacy which they displayed, takes occasion to draw the inference that there was good reason for their being prohibited, with an oath, from entering the land. Proportionally as they multiplied their provocations, it became the more evident that, being incorrigible, they had been justly cut off from God's rest. The meaning would be more clear by reading in the pluperfect tense—I had sworn; for God had already shut them out from the promised inheritance, having foreseen their misconduct; before he thus strove with them.

expects that they hear his voice, for he has said, My sheep hear my voice, John x. 27. We are his people, say they. Are you so? Then hear his voice. If you call him Master, or Lord, then do the things which he says, and be his willing obedient people. Hear the voice of his doctrine, of his law, and, in both, of his Spirit; hear and heed; hear and yield.

II. The sin they are warned against, as inconsistent with the believing obedient ear required, and that is hardness of heart. If you will hear his voice, and profit by what you hear, then do not harden your hearts; for the seed sown on the rock never brought any fruit to perfection.

III. The example they are warned by, which is that of the Israelites in the wilderness.

1. "Take heed of sinning as they did, lest you be shut out of the everlasting rest as they were out of Canaan." Be not, as your fathers, a stubborn and rebellious generation, Ps. lxxxviii. 8. Thus here, Harden not your heart as you did (that is, your ancestors) in the provocation, or in Meribah, the place where they quarreled with God and Moses (Exod. xvii. 2-7), and in the day of temptation in the wilderness, v. 8.

2. Now here observe,

(1.) The charge drawn up, in God's name, against the unbelieving Israelites, v. 9, 10. God here, many ages after, complains of their ill conduct towards him, with the expressions of high resentment.

[1.] Their sin was unbelief: they tempted God and proved him.

[2.] The aggravation of this sin was that they saw God's work; they saw what he had done for them in bringing them out of Egypt, nay, what he was now doing for them every day, this day, in the bread he rained from heaven for them and the water out of the rock that followed them.

[3.] The causes of their sin. See what God imputed it to: It is a people that do err in their hearts, and they have not known my ways. Men's unbelief and distrust of God, their murmurings and quarrels with him, are the effect of their ignorance and mistake.

(2.) The sentence passed upon them for their sin (v. 11): "Unto whom I swore in my wrath, If they shall enter into my rest, then say I am changeable and untrue:" see the sentence at large, Num. xiv. 21, &c.

Now this case of Israel may be applied to those of their posterity that lived in David's time, when this psalm was penned; let them hear God's voice, and not harden their hearts as their fathers did, lest, if they were stiff-necked like them, God should be provoked to forbid them the privileges of his temple at Jerusalem, of which he had said, This is my rest. But it must be applied to us Christians, because so the apostle applies it. There is a spiritual and eternal rest set before us, and promised to us, of which Canaan was a type; we are all (in profession, at least) bound for this rest; yet many that seem to be so come short and shall never enter into it.

Psalm 96

1-6
1 O sing unto the LORD a new song: sing unto the LORD, all the earth.
2 Sing unto the LORD, bless his name; shew forth his salvation from day to day.
3 Declare his glory among the heathen, his wonders among all people.
4 For the LORD is great, and greatly to be praised: he is to be feared above all gods.
5 For all the gods of the nations are idols: but the LORD made the heavens.
6 Honor and majesty are before him: strength and beauty are in his sanctuary.

Psalm 96

SUBJECT. This Psalm is evidently taken from that sacred song which was composed by David at the time when "the ark of God was set in the midst of the tent which David had prepared for it, and they offered burnt sacrifices and peace offerings before God." See the sixteenth chapter of the first book of the Chronicles. The former part of that sacred song was probably omitted in this place because it referred to Israel, and the design of the Holy Ghost in this psalm was to give forth a song for the Gentiles, a triumphant hymn wherewith to celebrate the conversion of the nations to Jehovah in gospel times. It follows fitly upon the last Psalm, which describes the obstinacy of Israel, and the consequent taking of the gospel from them that it might be preached among the nations who would receive it, and in due time be fully won to Christ by its power. It thus makes a pair with the Ninety-fifth Psalm. It is a grand MISSIONARY HYMN, and it is a wonder that Jeers can read it and yet remain exclusive. If blindness in part had not happened unto Israel, they might have seen long ago, and would now see, that their God always had designs of love for all the families of men, and never intended that his grace and his covenant should relate only to the seed of Abraham after the flesh. We do not wonder that the large hearted David rejoiced and danced before the ark, while he saw in vision all the earth turning from idols to the one living and true God. Had Michal, Saul's daughter, only been able to enter into his delight, she would not have reproached him, and if the Jews at this day could only be enlarged in heart to feel sympathy with all mankind, they also would sing for joy at the great prophecy that all the earth shall be fitted with the glory of the Lord.
DIVISION. We will make none, for the song is one and indivisible, a garment of praise without seam, woven from the top throughout.

EXPOSITION
Verse 1. O sing unto the Lord a new song. New joys are filling the hearts of men, for the glad tidings of blessing to all people are proclaimed, therefore let them sing a new song. Angels inaugurated the new dispensation with new songs, and shall not we take up the strain?
Verse 2. Sing unto the Lord, bless his name. Thrice is the name of the Lord repeated, and not without meaning. Is it not unto the Three One Lord that the enlightened nations will sing? Unitarianism is the religion of units; it is too cold to warm the world to worship; the sacred fire of adoration only burns with vehement flame where the Trinity is believed in and beloved.
Verse 3. Declare his glory among the heathen. His salvation is his glory, the word of the gospel glorifies him; and this should be published far and wide, till the remotest nations of the earth have known it.
Verse 4. For the LORD is great and greatly to be praised. He is no petty deity, presiding, as the heathen imagined their gods to do, over some one nation, or one department of nature. Jehovah is great in power and dominion, great in mind and act; nothing mean or narrow can be found in him or his acts, in all things he is infinite. Praise should be proportionate to its object, therefore let it be infinite when rendered unto the Lord. We cannot praise him too much, too often, too zealously, too carefully, too joyfully.
Verse 5. For all the gods of the nations are idols. Mere images of wood and stone, vanities, nothings. But the Lord made the heavens. The reality of his Godhead is proved by his works, and foremost among these the psalmist mentions that matchless piece of architecture which casts its arch over every man's head, whose lamps are the light of all mankind, whose rains and dew fall upon the fields of every people, and whence the Lord in voice of thunder is heard speaking to every creature. The idol gods have no existence, but our God is the author of all existences; they are mere earthly vanities, while he is not only heavenly, but made the heavens. This is mentioned as an argument for Jehovah's universal praise. Who can be worshipped but he? Since none can rival him, let him be adored alone.

JOHN CALVIN

Psalm 96

1-3

1. Sing unto Jehovah a new song. This commencement shows that the Psalmist is exhorting the whole world, and not the Israelites merely, to the exercise of devotion. Nor could this be done, unless the gospel were universally diffused as the means of conveying the knowledge of God.

3. Declare his glory among the heathen. Additional terms are adduced to commend the salvation spoken of. It is called his glory and his wonders; which is equivalent to saying that it was glorious and admirable. By such titles the Psalmist would distinguish it from any deliverances which had formerly been granted, as indeed there can be but one opinion, that when God appeared as Redeemer of all the world, he gave a display of his mercy and of his favor, such as he never vouchsafed before.

4-6

4. For Jehovah is great, and greatly to be praised. He particularly describes that God, whom he would have men to celebrate, and this because the Gentile nations were prone to merge into error upon this subject. That the whole world might abjure its superstitions, and unite in the true religion, he points out the one only God who is worthy of universal praise. This is a point of the greatest importance. Unless men are restrained by a due respect to it, they can only dishonor him the more that they attempt to worship him. We must observe this order if we would not profane the name of God, and rank ourselves amongst unbelieving men, who set forth gods of their own invention.

6. Strength and honor are before him. It is evident that the next member of the verse is a repetition, and there it reads, Power and Glory are in his sanctuary. The Psalmist means that we cannot be said to know God if we have not discovered that there is in him an incomparable glory and majesty. He first takes notice of his power and strength, as that in which his glory consists. There, as God is invisible, he directs the thoughts of his people to the sanctuary, which we have already seen to be the symbol of his presence. Such is the weakness of our minds that we rise with difficulty to the contemplation of his glory in the heavens.

7-9

7. Give to Jehovah, etc. Since praise waited for God in Zion, (Psalm 65:1,) and that was the place devoted to the celebration of his worship, and the posterity of Abraham were alone invested with the privilege of priesthood, we cannot doubt that the Psalmist refers here to that great change which was to take place in the Church upon the advent of Christ. An opposition or distinction is intended between God's ancient people and the Gentile tribes, which were to be afterwards adopted into the same fellowship. To declare his glory and strength, is the same with declaring the glory of his strength.

9. Worship before Jehovah. The Psalmist prosecutes the same train of sentiment. In requiring oblations of his people, God

MATTHEW HENRY

Psalm 96

1-9 An invitation to praise and honor God; a call to glorify God.

These verses will be best expounded by pious and devout affections working in our souls towards God, with a high veneration for his majesty and transcendent excellency. The call here given us to praise God is very lively, the expressions are raised and repeated, to all which the echo of a thankful heart should make agreeable returns.

I. We are here required to honor God,

1. With songs, v. 1, 2. Three times we are here called to sing unto the Lord; sing to the Father, to the Son, to the Holy Ghost, as it was in the beginning, when the morning stars sang together, is now, in the church militant, and ever shall be, in the church triumphant. We have reason to do it often, and we have need to be often reminded of it, and stirred up to it. Sing unto the Lord, that is, "Bless his name, speak well of him, that you may bring others to think well of him."

2. With sermons (v. 3): Declare his glory among the heathen, even his wonders among all people.

3. With religious services, v. 7-9. Hitherto, though in every nation those that feared God and wrought righteousness were accepted of him, yet instituted ordinances were the peculiarities of the Jewish religion; but, in gospel-times, the kindreds of the people shall be invited and admitted into the service of God and be as welcome as ever the Jews were. The court of the Gentiles shall no longer be an outward court, but shall be laid in common with the court of Israel. All the earth is here summoned to fear before the Lord, to worship him according to his appointment. In every place incense shall be offered to his name, Mal. i. 11; Zech. xiv. 17; Isa. lxvi. 23.

II. In the midst of these calls to praise God and give glory to him glorious things are here said of him, both as motives to praise and matter of praise: The Lord is great, and therefore greatly to be praised (v. 4) and to be feared, great and honorable to his attendants, great and terrible to his adversaries. Even the new song proclaims God great as well as good; for his goodness is his glory; and, when the everlasting gospel is preached, it is this, Fear God, and give glory to him, Rev. xiv. 6, 7.

1. He is great in his sovereignty over all that pretend to be deities; none dare vie with him: He is to be feared above all gods—all princes, who were often deified after their deaths, and even while they lived were adored as petty gods—or rather all idols, the gods of the nations v. 5.

2. He is great in his right, even to the noblest part of the creation; for it is his own work and derives its being from him: The Lord made the heavens and all their hosts; they are the work of his fingers (Ps. viii. 3), so nicely, so curiously, are they made.

Psalm 96

7-13

7 Give unto the LORD, O ye kindreds of the people, give unto the LORD glory and strength.
8 Give unto the LORD the glory due unto his name: bring an offering, and come into his courts.
9 O worship the LORD in the beauty of holiness: fear before him, all the earth.
10 Say among the heathen that the LORD reigneth: the world also shall be established that it shall not be moved: he shall judge the people righteously.
11 Let the heavens rejoice, and let the earth be glad; let the sea roar, and the fullness thereof.
12 Let the field be joyful, and all that is therein: then shall all the trees of the wood rejoice
13 Before the LORD: for he cometh, for he cometh to judge the earth: he shall judge the world with righteousness, and the people with his truth.

Verse 6. Honor and majesty are before him. Men can but mimic these things; their pompous pageants are but the pretence of greatness. Honor and majesty are with him and with him alone. In the presence of Jehovah real glory and sovereignty abide, as constant attendants. Strength and beauty are in his sanctuary. In him are combined all that is mighty and lovely, powerful and resplendent.

Verse 7. The first six verses commenced with an exhortation to sing, three times repeated, with the name of the Lord thrice mentioned; here we meet with the expression, Give unto the Lord, used in the same triple manner. This is after the manner of those poets whose flaming sonnets have best won the ear of, the people, they reiterate choice words till they penetrate the soul and fire the heart.

Verse 8. Give unto the LORD the glory due unto his name. But who can do that to the full? Can all the nations of the earth put together discharge the mighty debt? All conceivable honor is due to our Creator, Preserver, Benefactor, and Redeemer, and however much of zealous homage we may offer to him, we cannot give him more than his due.

Verse 9. O worship the Lord in the beauty of holiness. This is the only beauty which he cares for in our public services, and it is one for which no other can compensate. Beauty of architecture and apparel he does not regard; moral and spiritual beauty is that in which his soul delighteth. Worship must not be rendered to God in a slovenly, sinful, superficial manner; we must be reverent, sincere, earnest, and pure in heart both in our prayers and praises.

Verse 10. Say among the heathen that the LORD reigneth. This is the gladdest news which can be carried to them,—the Lord Jehovah, in the person of his Son has assumed the throne, and taken to himself his great power. Tell this out among the heathen, and let the heathen themselves, being converted, repeat the same rejoicing.

Verse 11. Let the heavens rejoice, and let the earth be glad. Above and below let the joy be manifested. Let the angels who have stood in amaze at the wickedness of men, now rejoice over their repentance and restoration to favor, and let men themselves express their pleasure in seeing their true prince set upon his throne. The book of creation has two covers, and on each of these let the glory of the Lord be emblazoned in letters of joy.

Verse 12. Let the field be joyful, and all that is therein. Let the cultivated plains praise the Lord. Peace enables their owners to plough and sow and reap, without fear of the rapine of invaders, and therefore in glad notes they applaud him whose empire is peace.

Verse 13. Before the LORD: for he cometh. Even now he is near, his advent should, therefore, be the cause of immediate rejoicing: already are we in his presence, let us worship him with delight. For he cometh to judge the earth, to rule it with discretion; not to tax it, and control it by force, as kings often do, but to preside as magistrates do whose business it is to see justice carried out between man and man. All the world will be under the jurisdiction of this great Judge, and before his bar all will be summoned to appear. At this moment he is on the road, and the hour of his coming draweth nigh. His great assize is proclaimed. Hear ye not the trumpets? His foot is on the threshold. He shall judge the world with righteousness. His essential rectitude will determine all causes and cases, there will be no bribery and corruption there, neither can error or failure be found in his decisions.

was not to be considered as standing in need of the services of the creature, but as giving them an opportunity of professing their faith. The true reason, therefore, is here mentioned why the oblation was enjoined, That his people might prostrate themselves before him, and acknowledge that they and all belonging to them were his. Mention is made of the beauty of the temple, referring to the fact that the Gentiles should be raised to a new honor, in being associated into one body with God's chosen people.

10-13

10. Say among the heathen, Jehovah reigneth. His language again implies that it is only where God rules and presides that he can be worshipped. The Gentiles could not possibly profess the worship of God, so long as his throne was only in the small corner of Judea, and they were not acknowledging his government. Accordingly, the Psalmist speaks of his extending his kingdom to all parts of the world, with the view of gathering unto himself in one, those who had formerly been divided and scattered. The expression, Say among the heathen, signifies that God would enlarge the boundaries of his kingdom by his word and doctrine.

11. Let the heavens rejoice, and let the earth be glad. With the view of giving us a more exalted conception of the display of God's goodness in condescending to take all men under his government, the Psalmist calls upon the irrational things themselves, the trees, the earth, the seas, and the heavens, to join in the general joy. Nor are we to understand that by the heavens he means the angels, and by the earth men; for he calls even upon the dumb fishes of the deep to shout for joy. The language must therefore be hyperbolical, designed to express the desirableness and the blessedness of being brought unto the faith of God. At the same time, it denotes to us that God does not reign with terror, or as a tyrant, but that his power is exercised sweetly, and so as to diffuse joy amongst his subjects. The wicked may tremble when his kingdom is introduced, but the erection of it is only the cause of their fear indirectly.

We might notice also, that the hyperbole here employed does not want a certain foundation of a more literal kind. As all elements in the creation groan and travail together with us, according to Paul's declaration, (Romans 8:22) they may reasonably rejoice in the restoration of all things according to their earnest desire. The words teach us how infatuated that joy is, which is wantonly indulged in by men who are without God. From the close of the psalm, we learn that it is impossible to experience the slightest measure of true joy, as long as we have not seen the face of God, Rejoice before the Lord, because he cometh And if the very sea and land mourn so long as God is absent, may we not ask what shall become of us, who are properly the subjects of God's dreadful curse? The Psalmist, to remove all doubt regarding an event which might seem incredible, repeats his assertion of it, and states, at the same time, in what that rectitude consists, which he had formerly mentioned, when he adds, that God shall govern the world with righteousness and truth.

3. He is great in the manifestation of his glory both in the upper and lower world, among his angels in heaven and his saints on earth (v. 6).

10-13 The kingdom of Christ.
We have here instructions given to those who were to preach the gospel to the nations what to preach, or to those who had themselves received the gospel what account to give of it to their neighbors, what to say among the heathen; and it is an illustrious prophecy of the setting up of the kingdom of Christ upon the ruins of the devil's kingdom.

I. Let it be told that the Lord reigns, the Lord Christ reigns, that King whom God determined to set upon his holy hill of Zion. See how this was first said among the heathen by Peter, Acts x. 42.

II. Let it be told that Christ's government will be the world's happy settlement. The world also shall be established, that it shall not be moved.

III. Let them be told that Christ's government will be incontestably just and righteous: He shall judge the people righteously (v. 10), judge the world with righteousness, and with his truth, v. 13.

IV. Let them be told that his coming draws nigh, that this King, this Judge, standeth before the door; for he cometh, for he cometh. Enoch, the seventh from Adam, said so. Behold, the Lord cometh, Jude 14.

V. Let them be called upon to rejoice in this honor that is put upon the Messiah, and this great trust that is to be lodged in his hand (v. 11, 12): Let heaven and earth rejoice, the sea, the field, and all the trees of the wood. The dialect here is poetical; the meaning is,

1. That the days of the Messiah will be joyful days, and, as far as his grace and government are submitted to, will bring joy along with them. We have reason to give that place, that soul, joy into which Christ is admitted.

2. That it is the duty of every one of us to bid Christ and his kingdom welcome; for, though he comes conquering and to conquer, yet he comes peaceably. Hosanna, Blessed is he that cometh; and again, Hosanna, Blessed be the kingdom of our father David (Mark xi. 9, 10).

3. That the whole creation will have reason to rejoice in the setting up of Christ's kingdom, even the sea and the field.

4. That there will, in the first place, be joy in heaven, joy in the presence of the angels of God; for, when the First-begotten was brought into the world, they sang their anthems to his praise, Luke ii. 14.

5. That God will graciously accept the holy joy and praises of all the hearty well-wishers to the kingdom of Christ, be their capacity ever so mean. The sea can but roar, and how the trees of the wood can show that they rejoice I know not; but he that searches the heart knows what is the mind of the Spirit, and understands the language, the broken language, of the weakest.

KING JAMES VERSION

Psalm 97

1-6
1 The LORD reigneth; let the earth rejoice; let the multitude of isles be glad thereof.
2 Clouds and darkness are round about him: righteousness and judgment are the habitation of his throne.
3 A fire goeth before him, and burneth up his enemies round about.
4 His lightnings enlightened the world: the earth saw, and trembled.
5 The hills melted like wax at the presence of the LORD, at the presence of the Lord of the whole earth.
6 The heavens declare his righteousness, and all the people see his glory.

CHARLES H. SPURGEON

Psalm 97

SUBJECT. As the fast Psalm sung the praises of the Lord in connection with the proclamation of the gospel among the Gentiles, so this appears to foreshadow the mighty working of the Holy Ghost in subduing the colossal systems of error, and casting down the idol gods. Across the sea to maritime regions a voice cries for rejoicing at the reign of Jesus (Ps 97:1), the sacred fire descends (Ps 97:3), like lightning the gospel flames forth (Ps 97:4), difficulties vanish (Ps 97:5), and all the nations see the glory of God (Ps 97:6). The idols are confounded (Ps 97:7), the church rejoices (Ps 98:8), the Lord is exalted (Ps 98:9). The Psalm closes with an exhortation to holy steadfastness under the persecution which would follow, and bids the saints rejoice that their path is bright, and their reward glorious and certain. Modern critics, always intent upon ascribing the psalms to anybody rather than to David, count themselves successful in dating this song further on than the captivity, because it contains passages similar to those which occur in the later prophets; but we venture to assert theft it is quite as probable that the prophets adopted the language of David as that some unknown writer borrowed from them. One psalm in this series is said to be "in David", and we believe that the rest are in the same place, and by the same author. The matter is not important, and we only mention it because it seems to be the pride of certain critics to set up new theories; and there are readers who imagine this to be a sure proof of prodigious learning. We do not believe that their theories are worth the paper they are written upon.
DIVISION. The psalm divides itself into four portions, each containing three verses. The coming of the Lord is described (Ps 97:1-3); its effect upon the earth is declared (Ps 97:4-6); and then its influence upon the heathen and the people of God (Ps 97:7-9). The last part contains both exhortation and encouragement, urging to holiness and inculcating happiness (Ps 97:10-12).

EXPOSITION
Verse 1. The Lord reigneth. This is the watchword of the psalm—Jehovah reigns. It is also the essence of the gospel proclamation, and the foundation of the gospel kingdom. Jesus has come, and all power is given unto him in heaven and in earth, therefore men are bidden to yield him their obedient faith. Saints draw comfort from these words, and only rebels cavil at them.
Verse 2. Clouds and darkness are round about him. So the Lord revealed himself at Sinai, so must he ever surround his essential Deity when he shows himself to the sons of men, or his excessive glory would destroy them. Every revelation of God must also be an obvelation; there must be a veiling of his infinite splendor if anything is to be seen by finite beings. It is often thus with the Lord in providence; when working out designs of unmingled love he conceals the purpose of his grace that it may be the more clearly discovered at the end.
Verse 3. A fire goeth before him. Like an advance guard clearing the way. So was it at Sinai, so must it be: the very Being of God is power, consuming all opposition; omnipotence is a devouring flame which burneth up his enemies round about. God is longsuffering, but when he comes forth to judgment he will make short work with the unrighteous, they will be as chaff before the flame. Reading this verse in reference to the coming of Jesus, and the descent of the Spirit, we are reminded of the tongues of fire, and of the power which attended the gospel, so that all opposition was speedily overcome.
Verse 4. His lightnings enlightened the world. In times of tempest the whole of nature is lighted up with a lurid glare, even the light of the sun itself seems dim compared with the blaze of lightning. If such are the common lights of nature what must be the glories of the Godhead itself? When God draws aside the curtain for a moment how astonished are the nations, the

JOHN CALVIN

Psalm 97

1-5
1. Jehovah reigns. His inviting men to rejoice, is a proof that the reign of God is inseparably connected with the salvation and best happiness of mankind. And, the joy he speaks of being common to the whole world and to the regions beyond the seas, it is evident that he predicts the enlargement of God's kingdom, which had been confined within the narrow boundaries of Judea, to a far wider extent. The Psalmist, in setting forth the various particulars of the Divine glory in the four verses which follow, would seek to impress all men with a reverential fear of him. Thus he gives us a representation of the formidable majesty attaching to God, that he may dash and humble vain confidence and carnal pride. A cloudy sky overawes us more than a clear one, as the darkness produces a peculiar effect upon the senses. The Psalmist makes use of this symbol, no doubt, to impress the world with the greater reverence of God. Others refine more upon the words, and think that clouds are said to be round about God, to check human rashness and presumption, and restrain that excessive curiosity which would pry more than is fit into the mysteries of Godhead. This is an interpretation of the words which makes them convey a very useful lesson; but I am against all refined renderings, and think that the Psalmist intended in associating darkness with God, to impress the hearts of men with a fear of him in general. The same meaning is brought out in the remaining context, when fire is said to go before him, and burn up his enemies, his lightnings to shake the earth, and the mountains to flow down. Should any object that this does not agree with what was said of the joy which his kingdom diffuses, I might answer, first, that although God is ready on his part to diffuse blessedness wherever he reigns, all are not capable of appreciating it. Besides, the truth is one of use to believers, humbling the pride of the flesh, and deepening their adoration of God. God's throne is represented as founded in justice and judgment, to denote the benefit which we derive from it.

6-8
6. The heavens have declared his righteousness. Here he states that there would be such an illustrious display of the righteousness of God, that the heavens themselves would herald it. The meaning is not the same as in the beginning of the nineteenth psalm, "The heavens declare the glory of God," etc. In that psalm David means no more than that the wisdom and power of God are as conspicuous in the fabric of the heavens, as if God should assert them with an audible voice. The meaning of the passage before us is, that the spiritual righteousness of God should be so signally manifested under the reign of Christ as to fill both heaven and earth.
7. Confounded be all those who serve graven images. The Psalmist draws a broad distinction here, as in the psalm next to this, between the true God and the false gods which men form for themselves. This he does that the praise which he

MATTHEW HENRY

Psalm 97

1-7 Righteousness and glory of the divine government; establishment of Christ's kingdom.
What was to be said among the heathen in the foregoing psalm (v. 10) is here said again (v. 1) and is made the subject of this psalm, and of psalm xcix. The Lord reigns; that is the great truth here laid down. The Lord Jehovah reigns, he that made the world governs it; he that gave being gives motion and power, gives law and commission, gives success and event. Every man's judgment proceeds from the Lord, from his counsel and providence, and in all affairs, both public and private, he performs the thing which he himself has appointed. The Lord Jesus reigns; the providential kingdom is twisted in with the mediatorial and the administration of both is in the hand of Christ, who therefore is both the head of the church and head over all things to the church. The kingdom of Christ is so constituted that,
I. It may be matter of joy to all; and it will be so if it be not their own fault. Let the earth rejoice, for hereby it is established (Ps. xcvi. 10); it is honored and enriched, and, in part, rescued from the vanity which by sin it is made subject to. Not only let the people of Israel rejoice in him as King of the Jews, and the daughter of Zion as her King, but let all the earth rejoice in his elevation; for the kingdoms of the world shall, more or less, sooner or later, become his kingdoms: Let the multitude of isles, the many or great isles, be glad thereof. This is applicable to our country, which is a great isle, and has many belonging to it; at least, it speaks comfort in general to the Gentiles, whose countries are called the isles of the Gentiles, Gen. x. 5. There is enough in Christ for the multitude of the isles to rejoice in; for, though many have been made happy in him, yet still there is room. All have reason to rejoice in Christ's government.
II. Christ's government, though it may be matter of joy to all, will yet be matter of terror to some, and it is their own fault that it is so, v. 3-5, 7. Observe,
1. When the kingdom of Christ was to be set up in the world, after his ascension, it would meet with many enemies, and much opposition would be given to it. He that reigns, to the joy of the whole earth, yet, as he has his subjects, so he has his enemies (v. 3), that not only will not have him to reign over them, but would not have him to reign at all, that not only will not enter into the kingdom of heaven themselves, but do all they can to hinder those that are entering, Matt. xxiii. 13. This was fulfilled in the enmity of the unbelieving Jews to the gospel of Christ, and the violent persecution which in all places they stirred up against the preachers and professors of it. These enemies are here called hills (v. 5), for their height, and strength, and immovable obstinacy. It was the princes of this world that crucified the Lord of glory, 1 Cor. ii. 8; Ps. ii. 2.

Psalm 97

7-12
7 Confounded be all they that serve graven images, that boast themselves of idols: worship him, all ye gods.
8 Zion heard, and was glad; and the daughters of Judah rejoiced because of thy judgments, O LORD.
9 For thou, LORD, art high above all the earth: thou art exalted far above all gods.
10 Ye that love the LORD, hate evil: he preserveth the souls of his saints; he delivereth them out of the hand of the wicked.
11 Light is sown for the righteous, and gladness for the upright in heart.
12 Rejoice in the LORD, ye righteous; and give thanks at the remembrance of his holiness.

light compels them to cover their eyes and bow their heads in solemn awe. Jesus in the gospel lights up the earth with such a blaze of truth and grace as was never seen or even imagined before.

Verse 5. The hills melted like wax at the presence of the LORD. Inanimate nature knows its Creator, and worships him in its own fashion. States and kingdoms which stand out upon the world like mountains are utterly dissolved when he decrees their end.

Verse 6. The heavens declare his righteousness. It is as conspicuous as if written across the skies, both the celestial and the terrestrial globes shine in its light. It is the manner of the inspired poets to picture the whole creation as in sympathy with the glory of God, and indeed it is not mere poetry, for a great truth underlies it, the whole creation has been made to groan through man's sin, and it is yet to share in the joy of his restoration.

Verse 7. Confounded be all they that serve graven images, that boast themselves of idols. They shall be so; shame shall cover their faces, they shall blush to think of their former besotted boastings. When a man gravely worships what has been engraved by a man's hand, and puts his trust in a mere nothing and nonentity, he is indeed brutish, and when he is converted from such absurdity, he may well be ashamed.

Verse 8. Zion heard, and was glad. While the heathen are confounded the people of God are made to triumph, for they love to see their God exalted. The day shall come when the literal Zion, so long forsaken, shall joy in the common salvation. It did so at the first when the apostles dwelt at Jerusalem, and the good days will come back again.

Verse 9. For thou, Lord, art high above all the earth. And therefore do we rejoice to see the idols abolished and to see all mankind bending at thy throne. There is but one God, there cannot be another, and he is and ever must be over all.

Verse 10. Ye that love the Lord, hate evil. For He hates it, his fire consumes it, his lightnings blast it, his presence shakes it out of its place, and his glory confounds all the lovers of it. We cannot love God without hating that which he hates. We are not only to avoid evil, and to refuse to countenance it, but we must be in arms against it, and bear towards it a hearty indignation.

Verse 11. Light is sown for the righteous. All along their pathway it is strewn. Their night is almost over, their day is coming, the morning already advancing with rosy steps is sowing the earth with orient pearls. The full harvest of delight is not yet ours, but it is sown for us; it is springing, it will yet appear in fullness. This is only for those who are light before the Lord in his own righteousness, for all others the blackness of darkness is reserved.

Verse 12. Rejoice in the LORD, ye righteous. The psalmist had bidden the earth rejoice, and here he turns to the excellent of the earth and bids them lead the song. If all others fail to praise the Lord, the godly must not. To them God is peculiarly revealed, by them he should be specially adored. And give thanks at the remembrance of his holiness—which is the harmony of all his attributes, the superlative wholeness of his character. This is a terror to the wicked, and a cause of thankfulness to the gracious. To remember that Jehovah is holy is becoming in those who dwell in his courts, to give thanks in consequence of that remembrance is the sure index of their fitness to abide in his presence. In reference to the triumphs of the gospel, this text teaches us to rejoice greatly in its purifying effect; it is the death of sin and the life of virtue. An unholy gospel is no gospel. The holiness of the religion of Jesus is its glory, it is that which makes it glad tidings, since while man is left in his sins no bliss can be his portion. Salvation from sin is the priceless gift of our thrice holy God

had ascribed might not be applied to any but the true God. Men are all ready to admit that they ought to celebrate the praises of God, but, naturally prone as they are to superstition, few indeed will be bound down to worship God in the manner which is right.

8. Zion heard, and was glad. In the former part of the psalm he had spoken of that joy which should be common to all the world. Now he makes special mention of God's chosen nation; and this partly, because they were to enjoy the first-fruits of this joy, and partly, because he would remove all occasion for rivalry or envy. Accordingly, having said that the Gentile nations should be brought to equal privileges with the posterity of Abraham, he adds, that the Jews would not suffer any diminution of honor by this co-partnership of privilege, but might rather reasonably rejoice in being chosen of God to be the fountain out of which the world was to be watered and refreshed. Those of whom the Psalmist speaks were the true children of Abraham and them only.

9-12

9. For thou, Jehovah, art high above all the earth Having already, in another place, explained these words, I shall not say more at present upon them. Only it is to be noticed, that there is a comparison drawn between God and the angels, and whatever has any claim to eminence. The Psalmist limits all other excellency in such a manner, as to leave no room for questioning that all majesty is comprehended in God only. This was the case more eminently when God manifested himself in his only-begotten Son, who is the express image of himself. Before that period his greatness was less apparent, because he was less known.

10. Ye that love Jehovah, hate evil. Those that fear God are here enjoined to practice righteousness, as Paul says, "Let every one that nameth the name of Christ depart from iniquity," (2 Timothy 2:19). He shows from the very nature of God, that we cannot be judged and acknowledged to be his servants unless we depart from sin, and practice holiness.

11. Light has been sown for the righteous He confirms the truth just advanced, and anticipates an objection which might be brought against it. We have seen that the Lord's people are often treated with the utmost cruelty and injustice, and would seem to be abandoned to the fury of their enemies. The Psalmist reminds us for our encouragement that God, even when he does not immediately deliver his children, upholds them by his secret power. In the first clause of the verse there is a double metaphor. By light is meant joy, or a prosperous issue, (according to a phraseology which is common in Scripture,) as darkness denotes adversity. The latter metaphor of sowing is rather more difficult to understand. Some think that gladness is sown for the just, as seed which, when cast into the ground, dies or lies buried in the earth a considerable time before it germinates.

12. In the concluding verse he exhorts the Lord's people to gratitude, that looking upon God as their Redeemer, they should lead a life corresponding to the mercy they have received.

2. The opposition which the Jews gave to the setting up of Christ's kingdom turned to their own ruin. Their persecuting the apostles, and forbidding them to speak to the Gentiles, filled up their sin, and brought wrath upon them to the uttermost, 1 Thess. ii. 15, 16.

3. Idolaters also would be put to confusion by the setting up of Christ's kingdom (v. 7).

8-12 Zion rejoicing in the reign of Christ.

The kingdom of the Messiah, like the pillar of cloud and fire, as it has a dark side towards the Egyptians, so it has a bright side towards the Israel of God. It is set up in spite of opposition; and then the earth saw and trembled (v. 4), but Zion heard and was glad, very glad, to hear of the conversion of some and of the confusion of others, that is, the conquest of all that stood it out against Christ. Now here observe,

I. The reasons that are given for Zion's joy in the government of the Redeemer. The faithful servants of God may well rejoice and be glad,

1. Because God is glorified, and whatever redounds to his honor is very much his people's pleasure. They rejoice because of thy judgments, O Lord! which may take in both the judgments of his mouth and the judgments of his hand, the word of his gospel and his works wrought for the propagating of it, miracles and marvelous providences; for in these we must own, "Thou, Lord, art high above all the earth (v. 9); thou hast manifested thy sovereignty in the kingdom of nature, and thy command of all its powers, and thy dominion over all nations, over all hearts; thou art exalted far above all gods."

2. Because care is taken for their safety. Those that pay allegiance to Christ as a King shall be sure of his protection. Princes are the shields of the earth; Christ is so to his subjects; they may put their trust under his shadow and rejoice in it, for (v. 10) He preserves the souls of the saints.

3. Because provision is made for their comfort. Those that rejoice in Christ Jesus, and in his exaltation, have fountains of joy treasured up for them, which will be opened sooner or later (v. 11): Light is sown for the righteous, that is, gladness for the upright in heart.

II. The rules that are given for Zion's joy.

1. Let it be a pure and holy joy.

2. Let the joy terminate in God (v. 12): Rejoice in the Lord, you righteous. Let all the streams of comfort, which flow to us in the channel of Christ's kingdom, lead us to the fountain, and oblige us to rejoice in the Lord.

3. Let it express itself in praise and thanksgiving: Give thanks at the remembrance of his holiness. Whatever is the matter of our rejoicing ought to be the matter of our thanksgiving, and particularly the holiness of God. Those that hate sin themselves are glad that God does so, in hopes that therefore he will not suffer it to have dominion over them.

Psalm 98

Title
A Psalm.

1-4
1 O sing unto the LORD a new song; for he hath done marvelous things: his right hand, and his holy arm, hath gotten him the victory.
2 The LORD hath made known his salvation: his righteousness hath he openly shewed in the sight of the heathen.
3 He hath remembered his mercy and his truth toward the house of Israel: all the ends of the earth have seen the salvation of our God.
4 Make a joyful noise unto the LORD, all the earth: make a loud noise, and rejoice, and sing praise.

Psalm 98

TITLE AND SUBJECT. This sacred ode, which bears simply the title of "A Psalm," follows fitly upon the last, and is evidently an integral part of the series of royal psalms. If Ps 97:1-12 described the publication of the gospel, and so the setting up of the kingdom of heaven, the present Psalm is a sort of Coronation Hymn, officially proclaiming the conquering Messiah as Monarch over the nations, with blast of trumpets, clapping of hands, and celebration of triumphs. It is a singularly bold and lively song. The critics have fully established the fact that similar expressions occur in Isaiah, but we see no force in the inference that therefore it was written by him; on this principle half the books in the English language might be attributed to Shakespeare. The fact is that these associated Psalms make up a mosaic, in which each one of them has an appropriate place, and is necessary to the completeness of the whole, and therefore we believe them, to be each and all the work of one and the same mind. Paul, if we understand him aright, ascribes Ps 95:1-11 to David, and as we believe that the same writer must have written the whole group, we ascribe this also to the son of Jesse. Whoever that may be, the song is worthy to rank among the most devout and soul stirring of sacred lyrics.
DIVISION. We have here three stanzas of three verses each. In the first, Ps 98:1-3, the subject of praise is announced, in the second, Ps 98:4-6, the manner of that praise is prescribed; and in the third, Ps 98:7-9, the universal extent of it is proclaimed.

EXPOSITION
Verse 1. O sing unto the LORD a new song; for he hath done marvelous things. We had a new song before (Ps 96:1-13) because the Lord was coming, but now we have another new song because he has come, and seen and conquered. Jesus, our King, has lived a marvelous life, died a marvelous death, risen by a marvelous resurrection, and ascended marvelously into heaven. By his divine power he has sent forth the Holy Spirit doing marvels, and by that sacred energy his disciples have also wrought marvelous things and astonished all the earth. Idols have fallen, superstitions have withered, systems of error have fled, and empires of cruelty have perished. For all this he deserves the highest praise.
Verse 2. The LORD hath made known his salvation,—by the coming of Jesus and by the outpouring of the Holy Ghost, by whose power the gospel was preached among the Gentiles. The Lord is to be praised not only for effecting human salvation, but also for making it known, for man would never have discovered it for himself; nay, not so much as one single soul would ever have found out for himself the way of mercy through a Mediator; in every case it is a divine revelation to the mind and heart. In God's own light his light is seen.
Verse 3. He hath remembered his mercy and his truth toward the house of Israel. To them Jesus came in the flesh, and to them was the gospel first preached; and though they counted themselves unworthy of eternal life, yet the covenant was not broken, for the true Israel were called into fellowship and still remain so. The mercy which endureth for ever, and the fidelity which cannot forget a promise, secure to the chosen seed the salvation long ago guaranteed by the covenant of grace. All the ends of the earth have seen the salvation of our God. Not to Abraham's seed alone after the flesh, but to the elect among all nations, has grace been given; therefore, let the whole church of God sing unto him a new song. It was no small blessing, or little miracle, that throughout all lands the gospel should be published in so short a time, with such singular success and such abiding results.
Verse 4. Make a joyful noise unto the LORD, all the earth. Every tongue must applaud, and that with the rigor which joy of heart alone can arouse

JOHN CALVIN

Psalm 98

This psalm has a great resemblance to the ninety-sixth, not only in matter, but language.
The great scope of it is to show that the glory of God would be illustriously displayed in the spread of the knowledge of his name throughout the world, both from the more ample fulfillment which would be given upon the manifestation of the Savior, to the promises made to the posterity of Abraham, and from the sudden extension of salvation to all parts of the earth. He calls upon men to magnify the name of God on this account.

1-3
1. Sing unto Jehovah a new song I have already remarked, that the expression here used denotes an extraordinary, not a common, ascription of praise. This appears from the reason assigned for it, That God had manifested his salvation in a singular and incredible manner. For having spoken of marvelous things, he represents this as the sum of all, that God had procured salvation with his own right hand; that is, not by human means, or in an ordinary way, but delivering his Church in an unprecedented manner.
Isaiah enlarges upon this miracle of God's power:
"The Lord looked if there were any to help, and wondered that there was no intercessor: therefore his own arm brought salvation, and his righteousness sustained him,"
(Isaiah 59:16).

In both passages the arm of God stands opposed to ordinary means, which although when employed they derogate nothing from the glory of God, yet prevent us from so fully discovering his presence as we might otherwise do.
The language of the Psalmist amounts to a declaration that God would not save the world by means of an ordinary kind, but would come forth himself and show that he was the author of a salvation in every respect so singular. He reasonably infers that mercy of such a wonderful, and, to us, incomprehensible kind, should be celebrated by no ordinary measures of praise.

This is brought out still more clearly in the verse which follows, where it is said that his salvation and righteousness are shown to the nations. What could have been less looked for than that light should have arisen upon these dark and benighted places, and that righteousness should have appeared in the habitations of desperate wickedness?

Salvation is mentioned first, although it is, properly speaking, the effect of righteousness. Such an inversion of the natural order is often observed in stating divine benefits; nor is it surprising that what is the means, and should be mentioned first, is sometimes set last, and follows by way of explanation. I may add, that the righteousness of God, which is the source of salvation, does not consist in his recompensing men according to their works, but is just the illustration of his mercy, grace, and faithfulness.
3. He hath remembered his goodness Having spoken of the general manifestation of his salvation, he now celebrates his

MATTHEW HENRY

Psalm 98

1-3 An invitation to praise.
We are here called upon again to sing unto the Lord a new song, as before, Ps. xcvi. 1. "Sing a most excellent song, the best song you have." Let the song of Christ's love be like Solomon's on that subject, a song of songs. A song of praise for redeeming love is a new song, such a song as had not been sung before; for this is a mystery which was hidden from ages and generations. Converts sing a new song, very different from what they had sung; they change their wonder and change their joy, and therefore change their note. If the grace of God put a new heart into our breasts, it will therewith put a new song into our mouths. In the new Jerusalem there will be new songs sung, that will be new to eternity, and never wax old. Let this new song be sung to the praise of God, in consideration of these four things:
I. The wonders he has wrought: He has done marvelous things, v. 1.
II. The conquests he has won: His right hand and his holy arm have gotten him the victory. Our Redeemer has surmounted all the difficulties that lay in the way of our redemption, has broken through them all, and was not discouraged by the services or sufferings appointed him. He has subdued all the enemies that opposed it, has gotten the victory over Satan, disarmed him, and cast him out of his strong-holds, has spoiled principalities and powers (Col. ii. 15), has taken the prey from the mighty (Isa. xlix. 24), and given death his death's wound.
III. The discoveries he has made to the world of the work of redemption. What he has wrought for us he has revealed to us, and both by his Son; the gospel-revelation is that on which the gospel-kingdom is founded—the word which God sent, Acts x. 36.
IV. The accomplishment of the prophecies and promises of the Old Testament, in this (v. 3): He has remembered his mercy and his truth towards the house of Israel. God had mercy in store for the seed of Abraham, and had given them many and great assurances of the kindness he designed them in the latter days; and it was in pursuance of all those that he raised up his Son Jesus to be not only a light to lighten the Gentiles, but the glory of his people Israel; for he sent him, in the first place, to bless them. God is said, in sending Christ, to perform the mercy promised to our fathers, and to remember the holy covenant, Luke i. 72. It was in consideration of that, and not of their merit.

4-9 An invitation to praise.
The setting up of the kingdom of Christ is here represented as a matter of joy and praise.
I. Let all the children of men rejoice in it, for they all have, or may have, benefit by it. Again and again we are here called upon by all ways and means possible to express our joy in it and give God praise for it:

Psalm 98

5-9
5 Sing unto the LORD with the harp; with the harp, and the voice of a psalm.
6 With trumpets and sound of cornet make a joyful noise before the LORD, the King.
7 Let the sea roar, and the fullness thereof; the world, and they that dwell therein.
8 Let the floods clap their hands: let the hills be joyful together
9 Before the LORD; for he cometh to judge the earth: with righteousness shall he judge the world, and the people with equity.

to action. As men shout when they welcome a king, so must we. Loud hosannas, full of happiness, must be lifted up. If ever men shout for joy it should be when the Lord comes among them in the proclamation of his gospel reign. John Wesley said to his people, "Sing lustily, and with a good courage. Beware of singing as if you were half dead or half asleep; but lift up your voice with strength. Be no more afraid of your voice now, nor more ashamed of its being heard, than when you sung the songs of Satan." Make a loud noise, and rejoice, and sing praise; or Burst forth, and sing, and play.
Verse 5. Sing unto the LORD with the harp. Skill in music should not be desecrated to the world's evil mirth, it should aid the private devotions of the saint, and then, like George Herbert, he will sing,
"My God, my God,
My music shall find thee,
And every string
Shall have his attribute to sing."
Martin Luther was thus wont to praise the Lord, whom he loved so well. God's praises should be performed in the best possible manner, but their sweetness mainly lies in spiritual qualities. The concords of faith and repentance, the harmonies of obedience and love are true music in the ear of the Most High.
Verses 5-6. The song and the stringed instruments belonged to the Levites, and the trumpets to the priests alone. Kitto says the trumpets did not join in the concert, but were sounded during certain regulated pauses in the vocal and instrumental music. The harps and voices made the sweetness, while the trumpets and horns added the strength; melody and energy should combine in the worship of God.
Verse 6. With trumpets and sound of cornet make a joyful noise. God's worship should be heartily loud. The far resounding trump and horn well symbolize the power which should be put forth in praise.
Verse 7. Let the sea roar, and the fullness thereof. Even its thunders will not be too grand for such a theme. Handel, in some of his sublime choruses, would have been glad of its aid to express his lofty conceptions, and assuredly the inspired psalmist did well to call in such infinite uproar. The sea is his, let it praise its Maker. Within and upon its bosom it bears a wealth of goodness, why should it be denied a place in the orchestra of nature? Its deep bass will excellently suit the mystery of the divine glory. The world, and they that dwell therein. The land should be in harmony with the ocean. Its mountains and plains, cities and villages, should prolong the voice of jubilee which welcomes the Lord of all.
Verse 8. Let the floods clap their hands. The rolling rivers, the tidal estuaries, the roaring cataracts, are here summoned to pay their homage, and to clap their hands, as men do when they greet their sovereigns with acclamation. Let the hills be joyful together, or in concert with the floods. Silent as are the mighty mountains, let them forget themselves, and burst forth into a sublime uproariousness of mirth.
Verse 9. Before the Lord; for he cometh to judge the earth. Stiller music such as made the stars twinkle with their soft kind eyes suited his first coming at Bethlehem, but his second advent calls for trumpets, for he is a judge; and for all earth's acclamations, for he has put on his royal splendor. The rule of Christ is the joy of nature. All things bless his throne, yea, and the very coming of it. As the dawn sets the earth weeping for joy at the rising of the sun, till the dewdrops stand in her eyes, so should the approach
of Jesus' universal reign make all creation glad.

goodness more particularly to his own chosen people. God exhibited himself as a Father to Gentiles as well as Jews; but to the Jews first, who were, so to speak, the first-born. The glory of the Gentiles lay in their being adopted and in-grafted into the holy family of Abraham, and the salvation of the whole world sprung from the promise made to Abraham, as Christ said, "Salvation is of the Jews," (John 4:22).

The Psalmist therefore very properly observes, that God in redeeming the world remembered his truth, which he had given to Israel his people—language, too, which implies that he was influenced by no other motive than that of faithfully performing what he had himself promised. The more clearly to show that the promise was not grounded at all on the merit or righteousness of man, he mentions the goodness of God first, and afterwards his faithfulness, which stood connected with it.

The cause, in short, was not to be found out of God himself, (to use a common expression,) but in his mere good pleasure, which had been testified long before to Abraham and his posterity.

The word remembered is used in accommodation to man's apprehension; for what has been long suspended seems to have been forgotten. Upwards of two thousand years elapsed from the time of giving the promise to the appearance of Christ, and as the people of God were subjected to many afflictions and calamities, we need not wonder that they should have sighed, and given way to ominous fears regarding the fulfillment of this redemption.

When it is added, all the ends of the earth have seen the salvation of God, this is not merely commendatory of the greatness of the salvation, meaning that it should be so illustrious that the report of it would reach the ends of the earth; but it signifies that the nations formerly immersed in delusions and superstitions would participate in it.

4-9

4. Exult before Jehovah all the earth. Here he repeats the exhortation with which he had begun, and by addressing it to the nations at large, he indicates that when God should break down the middle wall of partition all would be gathered to the common faith, and one Church formed throughout the whole world. When he speaks of musical instruments the allusion is evidently to the practice of the Church at that time, without any intention of binding down the Gentiles to the observance of the ceremonies of the law.

The repetition made use of is emphatic, and implies that the most ardent attempts men might make to celebrate the great work of the world's redemption would fall short of the riches of the grace of God. This is brought out still more forcibly in what follows, where feeling is ascribed to things inanimate.

Make a joyful noise, as before, Ps. xcv. 1, 2. Make a loud noise, as those that are affected with those glad tidings and are desirous to affect others with them. Rejoice and sing praise, sing Hosannas (Matt. xxi. 9), sing Hallelujahs, Rev. xix. 6. Let him be welcomed to the throne, as new kings are, with acclamations of joy and loud shouts, till the earth ring again, as when Solomon was proclaimed, 1 Kings i. 40. And let the shouts of the crowd be accompanied with the singers and players on instruments (Ps. lxxvii. 7; lxvi. 25), as is usual in such solemnities.

1. Let sacred songs attend the new King: "Sing praise, sing with the voice of a psalm. Express your joy; thus proclaim it, thus excite it yet more, and thus propagate it among others."

2. Let these be assisted with sacred music, not only with the soft and gentle melody of the harp, but since it is a victorious King whose glory is to be celebrated, who goes forth conquering and to conquer, let him be proclaimed with the martial sound of the trumpet and cornet, v. 6. Let all this joy be directed to God, and expressed in a solemn religious manner: Make a joyful noise to the Lord, v. 4. Sing to the Lord, (v. 5); do it before the Lord, the King, v. 6. Carnal mirth is an enemy to this holy joy. When David danced before the ark he pleaded that it was before the Lord; and the piety and devotion of the intention not only vindicated what he did, but commended it. We must rejoice before the Lord whenever we draw near to him (Deut. xii. 12), before the Lord Jesus, and before him, not only as the Savior, but as the King, the King of kings, the church's King, and our King.

II. Let the inferior creatures rejoice in it, v. 7-9. This is to the same purport with what we had before (Ps. xcvi. 11-13): Let the sea roar, and let that be called, not as it used to be, a dreadful noise, but a joyful noise; for the coming of Christ, and the salvation wrought out by him, have quite altered the property of the troubles and terrors of this world, so that when the floods lift up their voice, lift up their waves, we must not construe that to be the sea roaring against us, but rather rejoicing with us. Let the floods express their joy, as men do when they clap their hands; and let the hills, that trembled for fear before God when he came down to give the law at Mount Sinai, dance for joy before him when his gospel is preached and that word of the Lord goes forth from Zion in a still small voice: Let the hills be joyful together before the Lord. This intimates that the kingdom of Christ would be a blessing to the whole creation; but that, as the inferior creatures declare the glory of the Creator (Ps. xix. 1), so they declare the glory of the Redeemer, for by him all things not only subsist in their being, but consist in their order. It intimates likewise that the children of men would be wanting in paying their due respects to the Redeemer, and therefore that he must look for his honor from the sea and the floods, which would shame the stupidity and ingratitude of mankind.

Psalm 99

1-4
1 The LORD reigneth; let the people tremble: he sitteth between the cherubims; let the earth be moved.
2 The LORD is great in Zion; and he is high above all the people.
3 Let them praise thy great and terrible name; for it is holy.
4 The king's strength also loveth judgment; thou dost establish equity, thou executest judgment and righteousness in Jacob.

Psalm 99

This may be called THE SANCTUS, or, THE HOLY, HOLY, HOLY PSALM, for the word "holy" is the conclusion and the refrain of its three main divisions. Its subject is the holiness of the divine government, the sanctity of the mediatorial reign. It seems to us to declare the holiness of Jehovah himself in Ps 99:1-3; it mentions the equity of the king whom the Lord had appointed, as an illustration of the Lord's love of holiness, or more probably it describes the Lord as himself the king, in Ps 99:4-5, and it then sets forth the severely righteous character of God's dealings with those favored persons whom in former times he had selected to approach him on behalf of the people, Ps 99:6-9. It is a hymn fitted for the cherubim who surround the throne, who are mentioned in Ps 99:1; it is a Psalm most fitting for saints who dwell in Zion, the holy city, and especially worthy to be reverently sung by all who, like David the king, Moses the lawgiver, Aaron the priest, or Samuel the seer, are honored to lead the church of God, and plead for her with her Lord.

EXPOSITION
Verse 1. The Lord reigneth. One of the most joyous utterances which ever leaped from mortal lip. The overthrow of the reign of evil and the setting up of Jehovah's kingdom of goodness, justice, and truth, is worthy to be hymned again and again, as we have it here for the third time in the psalms. Let the people tremble. Let the chosen people feel a solemn yet joyful awe, which shall thrill their whole manhood. Saints quiver with devout emotion, and sinners quiver with terror when the rule of Jehovah is fully perceived and felt. It is not a light or trifling matter, it is a truth which, above all others, should stir the depths of our nature. He sitteth between the cherubims. In grandeur of sublime glory, yet in nearness of mediatorial condescension, Jehovah revealed himself above the mercy seat, whereon stood the likeness of those flaming ones who gaze upon his glory, and for ever cry, "Holy, Holy, Holy, Lord God of hosts."
Verse 2. The Lord is great in Zion. Of old the temple's sacred hill was the center of the worship of the great King, and the place where his grandeur was most clearly beheld: his church is now his favored palace, where his greatness is displayed, acknowledged, and adored. He there unveils his attributes and commands the lowliest homage; the ignorant forget him, the wicked despise him, the atheistical oppose him, but among his own chosen he is great beyond comparison.
Verse 3. Let them praise thy great and terrible name: let all the dwellers in Zion and all the nations upon the earth praise the Lord, or "acknowledge thankfully" the goodness of his divine nature, albeit that there is so much in it which must inspire their awe. Under the most terrible aspect the Lord is still to be praised. Many profess to admire the milder beams of the sun of righteousness, but burn with rebellion against its more flaming radiance: so it ought not to be: we are bound to praise a terrible, God and worship him who casts the wicked down to hell. Did not Israel praise him "who overthrew Pharaoh and his hosts in tile Red Sea, for his mercy endureth for ever." The terrible Avenger is to be praised, as well as the loving Redeemer.
Verse 4. The king's strength also loveth judgment. God is the king, the mercy-seat is his throne, and the scepter which he sways is holy like himself. His power never exerts itself tyrannically; he is a sovereign, and he is absolute in his government, but his might delights in right, his force is used for just purposes only. Men in these days are continually arranging the Lord's government, and setting up to judge whether he does right or not; but saintly men in the olden time were of another mind, they were sure that what the Lord did was just, and instead of calling him to account they humbly submitted themselves to his will, rejoicing in the firm persuasion that with his whole omnipotence God was pledged to promote righteousness, and work justice among all his creatures.

JOHN CALVIN

Psalm 99

This psalm differs from those which precede it in one respect, that it speaks of the kingdom of God, and the blessings consequent upon it, as confined within Judea; and rather calls upon the posterity of Abraham, in distinction from the surrounding nations, to praise God for the privilege of their adoption.

1-4
1. Jehovah reigns. The people, who were formerly called upon to rejoice, are now commanded to tremble. For as the Jews were encompassed by enemies, it was of the utmost importance that God's power should be magnified among them, that they might know that, while under his guardianship, they would be constantly and completely safe from the hatred and fury of every foe.
2. Jehovah in Zion. It is proper that we should not forget the antithesis that God is great in Zion to destroy and annihilate all the enemies of his Church; and that, when the Psalmist goes on to say, he is high above all nations, his meaning is, not that he presides over them to promote their welfare, but to disconcert their counsels, to baffle their designs, and to subvert all their power. That which immediately follows about the praising of God's name, refers not to the nations at large, but in my opinion to the faithful, from whom alone the prophet demands a tribute of gratitude. For although God compels his vanquished enemies to acknowledge him, yet as they do not cease from speaking against his glory, and blaspheming his holy name, it cannot be to them that the exhortation is addressed, Praise the name of God, for it is holy; but to the faithful, who, from their knowledge of God's holy name, very cordially engage in the celebration of its praises.
4. The king's strength also loves judgment. This may be viewed as a threatening designed to fill his enemies with dismay; as if he should say, such is God's regard for righteousness and equity, that he hath clothed himself with power to avenge the injuries which his enemies have done to him. I think it preferable, however, to apply it to the Church, because she is under the government of God for the express purpose of practicing righteousness and holiness.

5-9
5. Exalt Jehovah our God. This exhortation is properly addressed to the Church alone, because having been made a partaker of the grace of God, she ought the more zealously to devote herself to his service, and to the love of godliness. The Psalmist, therefore, calls upon the Jews to exalt that God from whom they had received such manifest help, and enjoins them to render that worship appointed in his Law. The temple indeed is frequently in other places denominated God's seat, or house, or rest, or dwelling-place; here it is called his footstool, and for the use of this metaphor, there is the best of all reasons. For God desired to dwell in the midst of his people in such a manner, as not only to direct their

MATTHEW HENRY

Psalm 99

1-5 The dominion of God.
The foundation of all religion is laid in this truth, That the Lord reigns. God governs the world by his providence, governs the church by his grace, and both by his Son. We are to believe not only that the Lord lives, but that the Lord reigns. This is the triumph of the Christian church, and here it was the triumph of the Jewish church, that Jehovah was their King; and hence it is inferred, Let the people tremble, that is,
1. Let even the subjects of this kingdom tremble; for the Old-Testament dispensation had much of terror in it. At Mount Sinai Israel, and even Moses himself, did exceedingly fear and quake; and then God was terrible in his holy places. Even when he appeared in his people's behalf, he did terrible things. But we are not now come to that mount that burned with fire, Heb. xii. 18. Now that the Lord reigns let the earth rejoice. Then he ruled more by the power of holy fear; now he rules by the power of holy love.
2. Much more let the enemies of this kingdom tremble; for he will either bring them into obedience to his golden scepter or crush them with his iron rod. The Lord reigns, though the people be stirred with indignation at it; though they fret away all their spirits, their rage is all in vain.
God's kingdom, set up in Israel, is here made the subject of the psalmist's praise.
I. Two things the psalmist affirms:
1. God presided in the affairs of religion: He sitteth between the cherubim (v. 1), as on his throne, to give law by the oracles thence delivered—as on the mercy-seat, to receive petitions. This was the honor of Israel, that they had among them the Shechinah, or special presence of God, attended by the holy angels; the temple was the royal palace, and the Holy of holies was the presence-chamber. The Lord is great in Zion (v. 2); there he is known and praised (Ps. lxxvi. 1, 2); there he is served as great, more than any where else. He is high there above all people; as that which is high is exposed to view, and looked up to, so in Zion the perfections of the divine nature appear more conspicuous and more illustrious than any where else. Therefore let those that dwell in Zion, and worship there, praise thy great and terrible name, and give thee the glory due unto it, for it is holy. The holiness of God's name makes it truly great to his friends and terrible to his enemies, v. 3. This is that which those above adore—Holy, holy, holy.
2. He was all in all in their civil government, v. 4. As in Jerusalem was the testimony of Israel, whither the tribes went up, so there were set thrones of judgment, Ps. cxxii. 4, 5. Their government was a theocracy. God raised up David to rule over them (and some think this psalm was penned upon occasion of his quiet and happy settlement in the throne) and he is the king whose strength loves judgment.

Psalm 99

5-9

5 Exalt ye the LORD our God, and worship at his footstool; for he is holy.
6 Moses and Aaron among his priests, and Samuel among them that call upon his name; they called upon the LORD, and he answered them.
7 He spake unto them in the cloudy pillar: they kept his testimonies, and the ordinance that he gave them.
8 Thou answeredst them, O LORD our God: thou wast a God that forgavest them, though thou tookest vengeance of their inventions.
9 Exalt the LORD our God, and worship at his holy hill; for the LORD our God is holy.

Verse 5. Exalt ye the LORD our God. If no others adore him, let his own people render to him the most ardent worship. Infinite condescension makes him stoop to be called our God, and truth and faithfulness bind him to maintain that covenant relationship; and surely we, to whom by grace he so lovingly gives himself, should exalt him with all our hearts. He shines upon us from under the veiling wings of cherubim, and above the seat of mercy, therefore let us come and worship at his footstool. When he reveals himself in Christ Jesus, as our reconciled God, who allows us to approach even to his throne, it becomes us to unite earnestness and humility, joy and adoration, and, while we exalt him, prostrate ourselves in the dust before him.

Verse 6. Moses and Aaron among his priests, and Samuel among them that call upon his name. Though not ordained to the typical priesthood, Moses was a true priest, even as Melchizedek had been before him. God has ever had a priesthood beside and above that of the law. The three holy men here mentioned all stood in his courts, and saw his holiness, each one after his own order. Moses saw the Lord in flaming fire revealing each perfect law, Aaron full often watched the sacred fire devour the sin-offering, and Samuel witnessed the judgment of the Lord on Eli's house, because of the error of his way. These each one stood in the gap when the wrath of God broke forth, because his holiness had been insulted; and acting as intercessors, they screened the nation from the great and terrible God, who otherwise would in a dreadful manner have executed judgment in Jacob. Let these men, or such as these, lead us in our worship, and let us approach the Lord at the mercy-seat as they did, for he is as accessible to us as to them.

Verse 7. He spake unto them in the cloudy pillar. We have had mention of the ark and the shekinah, and now of the fiery cloudy pillar, which was another visible token of the presence of God in the midst of Israel. Responses came to Moses and Aaron out of that glorious overshadowing cloud, and though Samuel saw it not, yet to him also came the mystic voice which was wont to thunder forth from that divine canopy. Men have had converse with God, let men therefore speak to God in return. He has told us things to come, let us in return confess the sins which are past; he has revealed his mind to us, let us then pour out our hearts before him. They kept his testimonies. When others turned aside they were faithful; in their hearts they laid up his word, and in their lives they obeyed it.

Verse 8. Thou answeredst them, O LORD our God. A sweet title and a cheering fact. Our covenant God in a very special manner heard his three servants when they pleaded for the people. Thou wast a God that forgavest them, though thou tookest vengeance of their inventions. He forgave the sinners, but he slew their sins.

Verse 9. Exalt the LORD our God. A second time the delightful title of Jehovah our God is used, and it is quickly followed by a third. The Psalm is Trinitarian in its whole structure. In each of his sacred persons the Lord is the God of his people; the Father is ours, the Son is ours, and the Holy Spirit is ours: let us exalt him with all our ransomed powers. And worship at his holy hill. Where he appoints his temple let us resort. No spot of ground is now fenced about as peculiarly holy; yet his visible church is his chosen hill, and there would we be found and unite with them in worship. For the LORD our God is holy. Again this devout description is repeated, and made the climax of the song. Oh for hearts made pure within, so that we may rightly perceive and worthily praise the infinite perfection of the Triune Lord.

thoughts to the outward temple and to the ark of the covenant, but rather to elevate them to things above. Hence the term house or dwelling-place tended to impart courage and confidence to them, that all the faithful might have boldness to draw near unto God freely, whom they beheld coming to meet them of his own accord.
6. Moses and Aaron. The Psalmist magnifies the special grace which God in a very remarkable manner vouchsafed to the seed of Abraham, that thence he chose for himself prophets and priests to be, as it were, mediators between him and the people, to ratify the covenant of salvation. And he mentions three persons who were famous in former times. For Moses was, as it were, a mediator to reconcile the people unto God. Aaron was invested with the same office; and, subsequently, Samuel sustained the same character. There is no doubt, however, that under these three persons he included all the people with whom God had made a covenant. But he mentions the names of those who were the depositaries and guardians of this invaluable treasure.
They called upon Jehovah. The Psalmist explains that God from the very first, and with a special reference to his gracious covenant, bestowed great benefits upon the descendants of Abraham—the Jews. And, therefore, as often as they experienced the loving-kindness of God, it behooved them to call to mind his former loving-kindness. The prophet, too, makes particular mention of the visible symbol of the cloudy pillar, by which God designed to testify in all ages that his presence was ever with his people. Not that God always showed a cloudy pillar to his ancient people, but considering that the dullness of men is so great, that they do not perceive the presence of God unless they are put in mind by external signs, the prophet very properly reminds the Jews of this memorable token. And as God had appeared openly in the desert to their fathers, so their posterity might be well assured that he would also be near to them. He adds, that they had kept God's testimonies, for the purpose of enforcing the duty of like obedience upon succeeding generations.
8. O Jehovah our God. The prophet here reminds them that God had heard their prayers because his grace and their piety harmonized. Consequently, encouraged by their exemplary success in prayer, their posterity ought to call upon God, not merely pronouncing his name with their lips, but keeping his covenant with all their heart. He farther reminds us that if God does not display his glory so bountifully, and so profusely in every age, the fault is with men themselves, whose posterity have either utterly forsaken, or greatly declined from the faith of the fathers. It is not to be wondered at that God should withdraw his hand, or at least not stretch it forth in any remarkable way, when he beholds piety waxing cold on the earth.
9. In the close of the psalm he repeats the same sentence which we had in the fifth verse, only substituting his holy mountain instead of his footstool. He now says more plainly, Jehovah our God is holy. His intention is to show that God is not to be worshipped by the Israelites at random, but that his worship is founded upon the assurance of faith.

II. Putting these two things together, we see what was the happiness of Israel above any other people, as Moses had described it (Deut. iv. 7, 8), that they had God so night unto them, sitting between the cherubim, and that they had statutes and judgments so righteous, by which equity was established, and God himself ruled in Jacob, from which he infers this command to that happy people (v. 5): "Exalt you the Lord our God, and worship at his footstool; give him the glory of the good government you are under, as it is now established, both in church and state."

6-9 Divine justice and mercy.
The happiness of Israel in God's government is here further made out by some particular instances of his administration, especially with reference to those that were, in their day, the prime leaders and most active useful governors of that people—Moses, Aaron, and Samuel, in the two former of whom the theocracy or divine government began (for they were employed to form Israel into a people) and in the last of whom that form of government, in a great measure, ended; for when the people rejected Samuel, and urged him to resign, they are said to reject God himself, that he should not be so immediately their king as he had been (1 Sam. viii. 7), for now they would have a king, like all the nations. Moses, as well as Aaron, is said to be among his priests, for he executed the priest's office till Aaron was settled in it and he consecrated Aaron and his sons; therefore the Jews call him the priest of the priests. Now concerning these three chief rulers observe,
I. The intimate communion they had with God, and the wonderful favor to which he admitted them. None of all the nations of the earth could produce three such men as these, that had such an intercourse with Heaven, and whom God knew by name, Exod. xxxiii. 17.
II. The good offices they did to Israel. They interceded for the people, and for them also they obtained many an answer of peace. Moses stood in the gap, and Aaron between the living and the dead; and, when Israel was in distress, Samuel cried unto the Lord for them, 1 Sam. vii. 9. This is here referred to (v. 8): "Thou answeredst them, O Lord our God! and, at their prayer, thou wast a God that forgavest the people they prayed for; and, though thou tookest vengeance of their inventions, yet thou didst not cut them off from being a people, as their sin deserved." "Thou wast a God that wast propitious for them (so Dr. Hammond), for their sakes, and sparedst the people at their request, even when thou wast about to take vengeance of their inventions, that is, when thy wrath was so highly provoked against them that it was just ready to break in upon them, to their utter overthrow." These were some of the many remarkable instances of God's dominion in Israel, more than in any other nation, for which the people are again called upon to praise God (v. 9).

Psalm 100

Title
A Psalm of praise.

1 Make a joyful noise unto the LORD, all ye lands.
2 Serve the LORD with gladness: come before his presence with singing.
3 Know ye that the LORD he is God: it is he that hath made us, and not we ourselves; we are his people, and the sheep of his pasture.
4 Enter into his gates with thanksgiving, and into his courts with praise: be thankful unto him, and bless his name.
5 For the LORD is good; his mercy is everlasting; and his truth endureth to all generations.

Psalm 100

TITLE. A Psalm of Praise; or rather of thanksgiving. This is the only psalm bearing this precise inscription. It is all ablaze with grateful adoration, and has for this reason been a great favorite with the people of God ever since it was written. "Let us sing the Old Hundredth" is one of the every-day expressions of the Christian church, and will be so while men, exist whose hearts are loyal to the Great King. Nothing can be more sublime this side heaven than the singing of this noble psalm by a vast congregation. Watts' paraphrase, beginning "Before Jehovah's awful throne," and the Scotch "All people that on earth do dwell." In this divine lyric we sing with gladness the creating power and goodness of the Lord, even as before with trembling we adored his holiness.

EXPOSITION
Verse 1. Make a joyful noise unto the LORD, all ye lands. This is a repetition of Ps 98:4. The original word signifies a glad shout, such as loyal subjects give when their king appears among them. Our happy God should be worshipped by a happy people; a cheerful spirit is in keeping with his nature, his acts, and the gratitude which we should cherish for his mercies. In every land Jehovah's goodness is seen, therefore in every land should he be praised. Nearer will the world be in its proper condition till with one unanimous shout it adores the only God. O ye nations, how long will ye blindly reject him? Your golden age will never arrive till ye with all your hearts revere him.
Verse 2. Serve the LORD with gladness. "Glad homage pay with awful mirth." He is our Lord, and therefore he is to be served; he is our gracious Lord, and therefore to be served with joy. The invitation to worship here given is not a melancholy one, as though adoration were a funeral solemnity, but a cheery gladsome exhortation, as though we were bidden to a marriage feast.
Verse 3. Know ye that the Lord, he is God. Our worship must be intelligent. We ought to know whom we worship and why. "Man, know thyself," is a wise aphorism, yet to know our God is truer wisdom; and it is very questionable whether a man can know himself until he knows his God. Jehovah is God in the fullest, most absolute, and most exclusive sense, he is God alone; to know him in that character and prove our knowledge by obedience, trust, submission, zeal, and love is an attainment which only grace can bestow.
Verse 4. Enter into his gates with thanksgiving. To the occurrence of the word thanksgiving in this place the Psalm probably owes its title. In all our public service the rendering of thanks must abound; it is like the incense of the temple, which filled the whole house with smoke. Expiatory sacrifices are ended, but those of gratitude will never be out of date. So long as we are receivers of mercy we must be givers of thanks. Mercy permits us to enter his gates; let us praise that mercy.
Verse 5. For the Lord is good. This sums up his character and contains a mass of reasons for praise. He is good, gracious, kind, bountiful, loving; yea, God is love. He who does not praise the good is not good himself. The kind of praise inculcated in the Psalm, viz., that of joy and gladness, is most fitly urged upon us by an argument from the goodness of God. His mercy is everlasting. God is not mere justice, stern and cold; he has bowels of compassion, and wills not the sinner's death. Towards his own people mercy is still more conspicuously displayed; it has been theirs from all eternity, and shall be theirs world without end. Everlasting mercy is a glorious theme for sacred song.

JOHN CALVIN

Psalm 100

The title of this psalm may serve for a summary of its contents Moreover, its brevity renders a lengthened discourse unnecessary. The Psalmist, in an especial manner, invites believers to praise God, because he has chosen them to be his people, and has taken them under his care.

1-3

1. Make a joyful noise. The Psalmist refers only to that part of the service of God which consists in recounting his benefits and giving thanks. And since he invites the whole of the inhabitants of the earth indiscriminately to praise Jehovah, he seems, in the spirit of prophecy, to refer to the period when the Church would be gathered out of different nations. Hence he commands (verse 2) that God should be served with gladness, intimating that his kindness towards his own people is so great as to furnish them with abundant ground for rejoicing. This is better expressed in the third verse, in which he first reprehends the presumption of those men who had wickedly revolted from the true God, both in fashioning for themselves gods many, and in devising various forms of worshipping them. And as a multitude of gods destroys and suppresses the true knowledge of one God only, and tarnishes his glory, the prophet, with great propriety, calls upon all men to bethink themselves, and to cease from robbing God of the honor due to his name; and, at the same time, inveighs against their folly in that, not content with the one God, they were become vain in their imaginations.

The prophet next makes mention of the great benefits received from God, and, in an especial manner, desires the faithful to meditate upon them. To say God made us is a very generally acknowledged truth; but not to advert to the ingratitude so usual among men, that scarcely one among a hundred seriously acknowledges that he holds his existence from God, although, when hardly put to it, they do not deny that they were created out of nothing; yet every man makes a god of himself, and virtually worships himself, when he ascribes to his own power what God declares belongs to him alone.

4-5

4. Enter his gates. The conclusion of the psalm is almost the same as the beginning of it, excepting that he adopts a mode of speech which relates to the worship of God which obtained under the law; in which, however, he merely reminds us that believers, in rendering thanks to God, do not discharge their duty aright, unless they also continue in the practice of a steady profession of piety. Meanwhile, under the name of the temple, he signifies that God cannot be otherwise worshipped than in strict accordance with the manner prescribed in his law. And, besides, he adds, that God's mercy endureth for ever, and that his truth also is everlasting, to point out to us that we can never be at a loss for constant cause of praising him.

MATTHEW HENRY

Psalm 100

1-5 Importunate exhortations to praise God; motives for praising God.
Here,
I. The exhortations to praise are very importunate. The psalm does indeed answer to the title, A psalm of praise; it begins with that call which of late we have several times met with (v. 1), Make a joyful noise unto the Lord, all you lands, or all the earth, all the inhabitants of the earth. When all nations shall be discipled, and the gospel preached to every creature, then this summons will be fully answered to. But, if we take the foregoing psalm to be a call to the Jewish church to rejoice in the administration of God's kingdom, which they were under this psalm, perhaps, was intended for proselytes. However, we have here,
1. A strong invitation to worship God; not that God needs us, or any thing we have or can do, but it is his will that we should serve the Lord, should devote ourselves to his service and employ ourselves in it; and that we should not only serve him in all instances of obedience to his law, but that we should come before his presence in the ordinances which he has appointed and in which he has promised to manifest himself (v. 2), that we should enter into his gates and into his courts (v. 4), that we should attend upon him among his servants, and keep there where he keeps court.
2. Great encouragement given us, in worshipping God, to do it cheerfully (v. 2): Serve the Lord with gladness. This intimates a prediction that in gospel-times there should be special occasion for joy; and it prescribes this as a rule of worship: Let God be served with gladness.
II. The matter of praise, and motives to it, are very important, v. 3, 5. Know you what God is in himself and what he is to you. Note, Knowledge is the mother of devotion and of all obedience: blind sacrifices will never please a seeing God. "Know it; consider and apply it, and then you will be more close and constant, more inward and serious, in the worship of him." Let us know then these seven things concerning the Lord Jehovah, with whom we have to do in all the acts of religious worship:
1. That the Lord he is God, the only living and true God.
2. That he is our Creator: It is he that has made us, and not we ourselves.
3. That therefore he is our rightful owner.
4. That he is our sovereign ruler.
5. That he is our bountiful benefactor.
6. That he is a God of infinite mercy and goodness (v. 5).
7. That he is a God of inviolable truth and faithfulness: His truth endures to all generations, and no word of his shall fall to the ground as revoked. The promise is sure to all the seed, from age to age.

Psalm 101

Title
A Psalm of David.

1-8
1 I will sing of mercy and judgment: unto thee, O LORD, will I sing.
2 I will behave myself wisely in a perfect way. O when wilt thou come unto me? I will walk within my house with a perfect heart.
3 I will set no wicked thing before mine eyes: I hate the work of them that turn aside; it shall not cleave to me.
4 A froward heart shall depart from me: I will not know a wicked person.
5 Whoso privily slandereth his neighbor, him will I cut off: him that hath an high look and a proud heart will not I suffer.
6 Mine eyes shall be upon the faithful of the land, that they may dwell with me: he that walketh in a perfect way, he shall serve me.
7 He that worketh deceit shall not dwell within my house: he that telleth lies shall not tarry in my sight.
8 I will early destroy all the wicked of the land; that I may cut off all wicked doers from the city of the LORD.

Psalm 101

TITLE. A Psalm of David. This is just such a psalm as the man after God's own heart would compose when he was about to become king in Israel. It is David all over, straight forward, resolute, devout; there is no trace of policy or vacillation, the Lord has appointed him to be king, and he knows it, therefore he purposes in all things to behave as becomes a monarch who me the Lord himself has chosen. If we call this THE PSALM or PIOUS RESOLUTIONS, we shall perhaps remember it all the more readily. After songs of praise a psalm of practice not only makes variety, but comes in most fittingly. We never praise the Lord better than when we do those things which are pleasing in his sight.

EXPOSITION
Verse 1. I will sing of mercy and judgment. He would extol both the love and the severity, the sweets and the bitters, which the Lord had mingled in Iris experience; he would admire the justice and the goodness of the Lord. Such a song would fitly lead up to godly resolutions as to his own conduct, for that which we admire in our superiors we naturally endeavor to imitate.
Verse 2. I will behave myself wisely in a perfect way. To be holy is to be wise; a perfect way is a wise way. David's resolve was excellent, but his practice did not fully tally with it. Alas! he was not always wise or perfect, but it was well that it was in his heart.
Verse 3. I will set no wicked thing before mine eyes. I will neither delight in it, aim at it or endure it. If I have wickedness brought before me by others I will turn away from it, I will not gaze upon it with pleasure. The psalmist is very sweeping in his resolve.
Verse 4. A froward heart shall depart from me. He refers both to himself and to those round about him; he would neither be crooked in heart himself, nor employ persons of evil character in his house; if he found such in his court he would chase them away. He who begins with his own heart begins at the fountain head, and is not likely to tolerate evil companions.
Verse 5. Whose privily slandereth his neighbor, him will I cut off. He had known so bitterly the miseries caused by slanderers that he intended to deal severely with such vipers when he came into power, not to revenge his own ills, but to prevent others from suffering as he had done.
Verse 6. Mine eyes shall be upon the faithful of the land, that they may dwell with me. He would seek them out, engage their services, take care of them, and promote them to honor: this is a noble occupation for a king, and one which will repay him infinitely better than listening to the soft nothings of flatterers.
Verse 7. He that worketh deceit shall not dwell within my house. He had power to choose his courtiers, and he meant to exercise it. Deceit among most orientals is reckoned to be a virtue, and is only censured when it is not sufficiently cunning, and therefore comes to be found out; it was therefore all the more remarkable that David should have so determinedly set his face against it.
Verse 8. I will early destroy all the wicked of the land. At the very outset of his government he would promptly deal out justice to the worthless, he would leave them no rest, but make them leave their wickedness or feel the lash of the law. The righteous magistrate "beareth not the sword in vain." To favor sin is to discourage virtue; undue leniency to the bad is unkindness to the good. When our Lord comes in judgment, this verse will be fulfilled on a large scale; till then he sinks the judge in the Savior, and bids men leave their sins and find pardon. Under the gospel we also are bidden to suffer long, and to be kind, even to the unthankful and the evil.

Psalm 101

1-5

1. I will sing of mercy and of judgment. What David here says concerning singing must be understood by the reader as intimating that this psalm contains the substance of his meditations with himself, as to what kind of king he would be whenever he should be put in possession of the sovereign power which had been promised him. To sing therefore of mercy and of judgment, is equivalent to declaring in solemn terms, that he would be a just and an upright king.
2. I will behave myself prudently in a perfect way. David here shows that he carefully considered how weighty a charge was laid upon him when he was made king. We know, and it is a truth taught us by experience, that almost all kings are intoxicated with the splendors of royalty.
3. I will not set a wicked thing before my eyes. After having protested, that in leading a private life, he would practice virtue and righteousness, even as it becomes good princes to begin with this, he now adds, that in executing the office of prince, he will be the enemy of all injustice and wickedness. To set a wicked thing before one's eyes, is equivalent to purposing to do something that is wicked.
4. The perverse heart shall depart from me. As David has added in the second clause by way of exposition, I will not know evil, he doubtless in the first protests that he will be free from all perfidiousness and wickedness.
5. Whoso slandereth his neighbor in secret, him will I destroy. In this verse he speaks more distinctly of the duty of a king who is armed with the sword, for the purpose of restraining evil-doers. Detraction, pride, and vices of every description, are justly offensive to all good men; but all men have not the power or right to cut off the proud or detractors, because they are not invested with public authority, and consequently have their hands bound.

6-8

6. My eyes are towards the faithful of the land. David here lays down another virtue of a wise prince, when he affirms that it will be his care to make all the faithful of the land his intimate friends,—that he will avail himself of their good offices, and have as domestic servants such only as are distinguished for personal worth.
7. He who worketh deceit shall not dwell in the midst of my house This verse may be explained of all magistrates to whose charge the exercise of public judgments is committed, as well as of household servants. But as David has just now spoken in general of all officers, he seems now to speak properly of those who are near the person of the king.
8. Early will I destroy all the wicked of the land. The Psalmist at length concludes by asserting, that he will endeavor to the utmost of his power to purge the land from infamous and wicked persons. He affirms that he will do this early; for if princes are supine and slothful, they will never seasonably remedy the evils which exist. They must therefore oppose the beginnings of evil.

Psalm 101

1-8 Mercy and judgment; David's pious resolution. Observe,
I. The chosen subject of the psalm (v. 1): I will sing of mercy and judgment, that is,

1. Of God's mercy and judgment, and then it looks back upon the dispensations of Providence concerning David since he was first anointed to be king, during which time he had met with many a rebuke and much hardship on the one hand, and yet, on the other hand, had had many wonderful deliverances wrought for him and favors bestowed upon him; of these he will sing unto God.

2. It may be understood of David's mercy and judgment; he would, in this psalm, promise to be merciful, and just, or wise, for judgment is often put for discretion. To do justly and love mercy is the sum of our duty; these he would covenant to make conscience of in that place and relation to which God had called him and this in consideration of the various providences of God that had occurred to him.

II. The general resolution David took up to conduct himself carefully and conscientiously in his court, v. 2.
III. His particular resolution to practice no evil himself (v. 3): "I will set no wicked thing before my eyes; I will not design nor aim at any thing but what is for the glory of God and the public welfare."
IV. His further resolution not to keep bad servants, nor to employ those about him that were vicious. He will have nothing to do,
1. With spiteful malicious people, who are ill-natured, and will bear a grudge a great while, and care not what mischief they do to those they have a pique against (v. 4).
2. With slanderers, and those who take a pleasure in wounding their neighbor's reputation secretly (v. 5).
3. With haughty, conceited, ambitious people; none do more mischief in a family, in a court, in a church, for only by pride comes contention.
4. With false deceitful people, that scruple not to tell lies, or commit frauds (v. 7).
V. His resolution to put those in trust under him that were honest and good (v. 6): My eyes shall be upon the faithful in the land.
VI. His resolution to extend his zeal to the reformation of the city and country, as well as of the court (v. 8): "I will early destroy all the wicked of the land, all that are discovered and convicted; the law shall have its course against them." He would do his utmost to destroy all the wicked. He would do it early; he would lose no time and spare no pains; he would be forward and zealous in promoting the reformation of manners and suppression of vice; and those must rise betimes that will do anything to purpose in the work. The day is coming when the Son of David shall cut off all wicked doers from the new Jerusalem, for there shall not enter into it any that do iniquity.

Psalm 102

Title
A prayer of the afflicted, when he is overwhelmed, and poureth out his complaint before the Lord.

1-7
1 Hear my prayer, O LORD, and let my cry come unto thee.
2 Hide not thy face from me in the day when I am in trouble; incline thine ear unto me: in the day when I call answer me speedily.
3 For my days are consumed like smoke, and my bones are burned as an hearth.
4 My heart is smitten, and withered like grass; so that I forget to eat my bread.
5 By reason of the voice of my groaning my bones cleave to my skin.
6 I am like a pelican of the wilderness: I am like an owl of the desert.
7 I watch, and am as a sparrow alone upon the house top.

Psalm 102

TITLE. A prayer of the afflicted, when he is overwhelmed, and poureth out his complaint before the Lord. This Psalm is a prayer far more in spirit than in words. The formal petitions are few, but a strong stream of supplication runs from beginning to end, and like an under-current, finds its way heavenward through the moanings of grief and confessions of faith which make up the major part of the Psalm. It is a prayer of the afflicted, or of "a sufferer." It is scarcely correct to call it a penitential Psalm, for the sorrow of it is rather of one suffering than sinning. It has its own bitterness, and it is not the same as that of the Fifty-first. The sufferer is afflicted more for others than for himself, more for Zion and the house of the Lord, than for his own house. When he is overwhelmed, or sorely troubled, and depressed. The best of men are not always able to stem the torrent of sorrow. Even when Jesus is on board, the vessel may fill with water and begin to sink. And poureth out his complaint before the LORD. When a cup is overwhelmed or turned bottom over, all that is in it is naturally poured out; great trouble removes the heart from all reserve and causes the soul to flow out without restraint; it is well when that which is in the soul is such as may be poured out in the presence of God, and this is only the case where the heart has been renewed by divine grace. The word rendered "complaint" has in it none of the idea of fault-finding or repining, but should rather be rendered "moaning,"—the expression of pain, not of rebellion. To help the memory we will call this Psalm THE PATRIOT'S PLAINT.
SUBJECT. This is a patriot's lament over his country's distress. He arrays himself in the griefs of his nation as in a garment of sackcloth, and casts her dust and ashes upon his head as the ensigns and causes of his sorrow. It is in vain to enquire into the precise point of Israel's history which thus stirred a patriot's soul, for many a time was the land oppressed, and at any of her sad seasons this song and prayer would have been a most natural and appropriate utterance.
DIVISION. In the first part of the Psalm, Ps 102:1-11, the moaning monopolizes every verse, the lamentation is unceasing, sorrow rules the hour. The second portion, from Ps 102:12-28, has a vision of better things, a view of the gracious Lord, and his eternal existence, and care for his people, and therefore it is interspersed with sunlight as well as shaded by the cloud, and it ends up right gloriously with calm confidence for the future, and sweet restfulness in the Lord. The whole composition may be compared to a day which, opening with wind and rain, clears up at noon and is warm with the sun, continues fine, with intervening showers, and finally closes with a brilliant sunset.

EXPOSITION
Verse 1. Hear my prayer, O LORD. Or O Jehovah. Sincere supplicants are not content with praying for praying's sake, they desire really to reach the ear and heart of the great God. It is a great relief in time of distress to acquaint others with our trouble.
Verse 2. Hide not thy face from me in the day when I am in trouble. Do not seem as if thou didst not see me, or wouldst not own me. Smile now at any rate. Reserve thy frowns for other times when I can bear them better, if, indeed, I can ever bear them; but now in my heavy distress, favor me with looks of compassion.
Verse 3. For my days are consumed like smoke. My grief has made life unsubstantial to me, I seem to be but a puff of vapor which has nothing in it, and is soon dissipated. The metaphor is very admirably chosen, for, to the unhappy, life seems not merely to be frail, but to be surrounded by so much that is darkening, and depressing, that, sitting down in despair, they compare themselves to men wandering in a dense fog, and themselves so dried up thereby that they are little better than pillars of smoke.

JOHN CALVIN

Psalm 102

1-2
1. O Jehovah! hear my prayer. This earnestness shows, again, that these words were not dictated to be pronounced by the careless and light-hearted, which could not have been done without grossly insulting God. In speaking thus, the captive Jews bear testimony to the severe and excruciating distress which they endured, and to the ardent desire to obtain some alleviation with which they were inflamed. No person could utter these words with the mouth without profaning the name of God, unless he were, at the same time, actuated by a sincere and earnest affection of heart.
2. Hide not thy face from me in the day of my affliction. The prayer, that God would not hide his face, is far from being superfluous. As the people had been languishing in captivity for the space of nearly seventy years, it might seem that God had for ever turned away his favor from them. But they are, notwithstanding, commanded, in their extreme affliction, to have recourse to prayer as their only remedy.

3-7
3. For my days are consumed like smoke. These expressions are hyperbolical, but still they show how deeply the desolation of the Church ought to wound the hearts of the people of God. Let every man, therefore, carefully examine himself on this head. If we do not prefer the Church to all the other objects of our solicitude, we are unworthy of being accounted among her members. Whenever we meet with such forms of expression as these, let us remember that they reproach our slothfulness in not being affected with the afflictions of the Church as we ought.
4. My heart is smitten, and dried up like grass. Here he employs a third similitude, declaring that his heart is withered, and wholly dried up like mown grass. But he intends to express something more than that his heart was withered, and his bones reduced to a state of dryness. His language implies, that as the grass, when it is cut down, can no longer receive juice from the earth, nor retain the life and rigor which it derived from the root, so his heart being, as it were, torn and cut off from its root, was deprived of its natural nourishment. The meaning of the last clause, I have forgotten to eat my bread, is, My sorrow has been so great, that I have neglected my ordinary food.
6. I have become like a pelican of the wilderness. It is as if he had said: I am removed from the society of men, and am become almost like a wild beast of the forest. Although the people of God dwelt in a well cultivated and fertile region, yet the whole country of Chaldea and Assyria was to them like a wilderness, since their hearts were bound by the strongest ties of affection to the temple, and to their native country from which they had been expelled.

8-11
8. My enemies have reviled me daily. The faithful, to excite the compassion of God towards them, tell him that they are

MATTHEW HENRY

Psalm 102

1-11 Complaints in affliction.
I. The psalmist humbly begs of God to take notice of his affliction, and of his prayer in his affliction, v. 1, 2. When we pray in our affliction,
1. It should be our care that God would graciously hear us; for, if our prayers be not pleasing to God, they will be to no purpose to ourselves. Let this therefore be in our eye that our prayer may come unto God, even to his ears (Ps. xviii. 6); and, in order to that, let us lift up the prayer, and our souls with it.
2. It may be our hope that God will graciously hear us, because he has appointed us to seek him and has promised we shall not seek him in vain. If we put up a prayer in faith, we may in faith say, Hear my prayer, O Lord! "Hear me."
II. He makes a lamentable complaint of the low condition to which he was reduced by his afflictions.
1. His body was macerated and emaciated, and he had become a perfect skeleton, nothing but skin and bones. As prosperity and joy are represented by making fat the bones, and the bones flourishing like a herb, so great trouble and grief are here represented by the contrary: My bones are burnt as a hearth (v. 3); they cleave to my skin (v. 5); nay, my heart is smitten, and withered like grass (v. 4); it touches the vitals, and there is a sensible decay there. I am withered like grass (v. 11), scorched with the burning heat of my troubles. If we be thus brought low by bodily distempers, let us not think it strange; the body is like grass, weak and of the earth, no wonder then that it withers.
2. He was very melancholy and of a sorrowful spirit. He was so taken up with the thoughts of his troubles that he forgot to eat his bread (v. 4); he had no appetite to his necessary food nor could he relish it. When God hides his face from a soul the delights of sense will be sapless things. He was always sighing and groaning, as one pressed above measure (v. 5), and this wasted him and exhausted his spirits. He affected solitude, as melancholy people do. His friends deserted him and were shy of him, and he cared as little for their company (v. 6, 7): "I am like a pelican of the wilderness, or a bittern (so some) that make a doleful noise; I am like an owl, that affects to lodge in deserted ruined buildings; I watch, and am as a sparrow upon the house-top. I live in a garret, and there spend my hours in poring on my troubles and bemoaning myself."
3. He was evil-spoken of by his enemies, and all manner of evil was said against him. When his friends went off from him his foes set themselves against him (v. 8): My enemies reproach me all the day, designing thereby both to create vexation to him (for an ingenuous mind regrets reproach) and to bring an odium upon him before men. When they could not otherwise reach him they shot these arrows at him, even bitter words. In this they were unwearied; they

Psalm 102

8-14

8 Mine enemies reproach me all the day; and they that are mad against me are sworn against me.
9 For I have eaten ashes like bread, and mingled my drink with weeping.
10 Because of thine indignation and thy wrath: for thou hast lifted me up, and cast me down.
11 My days are like a shadow that declineth; and I am withered like grass.
12 But thou, O LORD, shall endure for ever; and thy remembrance unto all generations.
13 Thou shalt arise, and have mercy upon Zion: for the time to favor her, yea, the set time, is come.
14 For thy servants take pleasure in her stones, and favor the dust thereof.

Verse 4. My heart is smitten, like a plant parched by the fierce heat of a tropical sun, and withered like grass, which dries up when once the scythe has laid it low. The psalmist's heart was as a wilted, withered flower, a burned up mass of what once was verdure. His energy, beauty, freshness, and joy, were utterly gone, through the wasting influence of his anguish.
Verse 5. By reason of the voice of my groaning my bones cleave to my skin. He became emaciated with sorrow. He had groaned himself down to a living skeleton, and so in his bodily appearance was the more like the smoke-dried, withered, burnt-up things to which he had previously compared himself.
Verse 6. I am like a pelican of the wilderness, a mournful and even hideous object, the very image of desolation. I am like an owl of the desert; loving solitude, moping among ruins, hooting discordantly. The Psalmist likens himself to two birds which were commonly used as emblems of gloom and wretchedness; on other occasions he had been as the eagle, but the griefs of his people had pulled him down, the brightness was gone from his eye, and the beauty from his person; he seemed to himself to be as a melancholy bird sitting among the fallen palaces and prostrate temples of his native land.
Verse 7. I watch, and am like a sparrow alone upon the house top: I keep a solitary vigil as the lone sentry of my nation; my fellows are too selfish, too careless to care for the beloved land, and so like a bird which sits alone on the housetop, I keep up a sad watch over my country. The Psalmist compared himself to a bird,—a bird when it has lost its mate or its young, or is for some other reason made to mope alone in a solitary place.
Verse 8. Mine enemies reproach me all the day. Their rage was unrelenting and unceasing, and vented itself in taunts and insults, the Psalmist's patriotism and his griefs were both made the subjects of their sport.
Verse 9. For I have eaten ashes like bread. He had so frequently cast ashes upon his head in token of mourning, that they had mixed with his ordinary food, and grated between his teeth when he ate his daily bread. One while he forgot to eat, and then the fit changed, and he ate with such a hunger that even ashes were devoured. Grief has strange moods and tenses.
Verse 10. Because of thine indignation and thy wrath: for thou hast lifted me up and cast me down. A sense of the divine wrath which had been manifested in the overthrow of the chosen nation and their sad captivity led the Psalmist into the greatest distress.
Verse 11. My days are like a shadow that declineth. His days were but a shadow at best, but now they seem to be like a shadow which was passing away. A shadow is unsubstantial enough, how feeble a thing must a declining shadow be? No expression could more forcibly set forth his extreme feebleness.
Verse 12. Now the writer's mind is turned away from his personal and relative troubles to the true source of all consolation, namely, the Lord himself, and his gracious purposes towards his own people. But thou, O Lord, shalt endure for ever. I perish, but thou wilt not, my nation has become almost extinct, but thou art altogether unchanged.
Verse 13. Thou shalt arise, and have mercy upon Zion. He firmly believed and boldly prophesied that apparent inaction on God's part would turn to effective working. Others might remain sluggish in the matter, but the Lord would most surely bestir himself. Zion had been chosen of old, highly favored, gloriously inhabited, and wondrously preserved, and therefore by the memory of her past mercies it was certain that mercy would again be showed to her.
Verse 14. For thy servants take pleasure in her stones, and favor the dust thereof. They delight in her so greatly that even her rubbish is dear to them. It was a good omen for Jerusalem when the captives began to feel a homesickness, and began to sigh after her. We may expect the modern Jews to be restored to their own land when the love of their country begins to sway them, and casts out the love of gain.

JOHN CALVIN

not only objects of mockery to their enemies, but also that they swore by them. The indignity complained of is, that the ungodly so shamefully triumphed over God's chosen people, as even to borrow from their calamities a form of swearing and imprecation. This was to regard the fate of the Jews as a signal pattern in uttering the language of imprecation.

9. For I have eaten ashes like bread. The prophet intended to intimate that when he partook of his meals, there was no table set before him, but his bread was thrown upon the ground to him in a foul and disgusting manner. Speaking, therefore, in the person of the faithful, he asserts that he was so fixed to the ground that he did not even rise from it to take his food.

10. On account of thy anger and thy wrath. He now declares that the greatness of his grief proceeded not only from outward troubles and calamities, but from a sense that these were a punishment inflicted upon him by God. And surely there is nothing which ought to wound our hearts more deeply, than when we feel that God is angry with us. The meaning then amounts to this—O Lord! I do not confine my attention to those things which would engage the mind of worldly men; but I rather turn my thoughts to thy wrath; for were it not that thou art angry with us, we would have been still enjoying the inheritance given us by thee, from which we have justly been expelled by thy displeasure.

11. My days are like the shadow which declineth. When the sun is directly over our heads, that is to say, at mid-day, we do not observe such sudden changes of the shadows which his light produces; but when he begins to decline towards the west the shadows vary almost every moment, This is the reason why the sacred writer expressly makes mention of the shadow which declineth. What he attributes to the afflicted Church seems indeed to be equally applicable to all men; but he had a special reason for employing this comparison to illustrate the condition of the Church when subjected to the calamity of exile.

12-14

12. And thou, O Jehovah! shalt dwell for ever. When the prophet, for his own encouragement, sets before himself the eternity of God, it seems, at first sight, to be a far-fetched consolation; for what benefit will accrue to us from the fact that God sits immutable on his heavenly throne, when, at the same time, our frail and perishing condition does not permit us to continue unmoved for a single moment? And, what is more, this knowledge of the blessed repose enjoyed by God enables us the better to perceive that our life is a mere illusion. But the inspired writer, calling to remembrance the promises by which God had declared that he would make the Church the object of his special care, and particularly that remarkable article of the covenant, "I will dwell in the midst of you," (Exodus 25:8) and, trusting to that sacred and indissoluble bond, has no hesitation in representing all the godly languishing, though they were in a state of suffering and wretchedness, as partakers of this celestial glory in which God dwells.

MATTHEW HENRY

did it all the day; it was a continual dropping. His enemies were very outrageous: They are mad against me, and very obstinate and implacable. They are sworn against me; as the Jews that bound themselves with an oath that they would kill Paul; or, They have sworn against me as accusers, to take away my life.

4. He fasted and wept under the tokens of God's displeasure (v. 9, 10): "I have eaten ashes like bread; instead of eating my bread, I have lain down in dust and ashes, and I have mingled my drink with weeping; when I should have refreshed myself with drinking I have only eased myself with weeping."

5. He looked upon himself as a dying man: My days are consumed like smoke (v. 3), which vanishes away quickly. Or, They are consumed in smoke, of which nothing remains; they are like a shadow that declines (v. 11), like the evening-shadow, or a forerunner of approaching night.

12-22 The future glory of Zion.

I. We are dying creatures, and our interests and comforts are dying, but God is an ever living everlasting God (v. 12): "My days are like a shadow; there is no remedy; night is coming upon me; but, thou, O Lord! shalt endure for ever. Our life is transient, but thine is permanent; our friends die, but thou our God diest not; what threatened us cannot touch thee; our names will be written in the dust and buried in oblivion, but thy remembrance shall be unto all generations; to the end of time, nay, to eternity, thou shalt be known and honored."

II. Poor Zion is now in distress, but there will come a time for her relief and succor (v. 13): Thou shalt arise and have mercy upon Zion. The hope of deliverance is built upon the goodness of God—"Thou wilt have mercy upon Zion, for she has become an object of thy pity;" and upon the power of God—"Thou shalt arise and have mercy, shalt stir up thyself to do it, shalt do it in contempt of all the opposition made by the church's enemies." The zeal of the Lord of hosts shall do this. That which is very encouraging is that there is a time set for the deliverance of the church, which not only will come some time, but will come at the time appointed, the time which Infinite Wisdom has appointed (and therefore it is the best time) and which Eternal Truth has fixed it to, and therefore it is a certain time, and shall not be forgotten nor further adjourned. At the end of seventy years, the time to favor Zion, by delivering her from the daughter of Babylon, was to come, and at length it did come. Zion was now in ruins, that is, the temple that was built in the city of David: the favoring of Zion is the building of the temple up again, as it is explained, v. 16. This is expected from the favor of God; that will set all to rights, and nothing but that, and therefore Daniel prays (Dan. ix. 17), Cause thy face to shine upon thy sanctuary, which is desolate. The building up of Zion is as great a favor to any people as they can desire.

Psalm 102

15-21
15 So the heathen shall fear the name of the LORD, and all the kings of the earth thy glory.
16 When the LORD shall build up Zion, he shall appear in his glory.
17 He will regard the prayer of the destitute, and not despise their prayer.
18 This shall be written for the generation to come: and the people which shall be created shall praise the LORD.
19 For he hath looked down from the height of his sanctuary; from heaven did the LORD behold the earth;
20 To hear the groaning of the prisoner; to loose those that are appointed to death;
21 To declare the name of the LORD in Zion, and his praise in Jerusalem;

Verse 15. So the heathen shall fear the name of the LORD. Mercy within the church is soon perceived by those without. When a candle is lit in the house, it shines through the window. When Zion rejoices in her God, the heathen been to reverence his name, for they hear of the wonders of his power, and are impressed thereby. And all the kings of the earth thy glory. The restoration of Jerusalem was a marvel among the princes who heard of it, and its ultimate resurrection in days yet to come will be one of the prodigies of history. A church quickened by divine power is so striking an object in current history that it cannot escape notice, rulers cannot ignore it, it affects the Legislature, and forces from the great ones of the earth a recognition of the divine working.
Verse 16. When the LORD shall build up Zion, he shall appear in his glory. As kings display their skill and power and wealth in the erection of their capitals, so would the Lord reveal the splendor of his attributes in the restoration of Zion, and so will he now glorify himself in the edification of his church. Never is the Lord more honorable in the eyes of his saints than when he prospers the church.
Verse 17. He will regard the prayer of the destitute. Only the poorest of the people were left to sigh and cry among the ruins of the beloved city; as for the rest, they were strangers in a strange land, and far away from the holy place, yet the prayers of the captives and the forlorn offscourings of the land would be heard of the Lord, who does not hear men because of the amount of money they possess, or the breadth of the acres which they call their own, but in mercy listens most readily to the cry of the greatest need. And not despise their prayer.
Verse 18. This shall be written for the generation to come. A note shall be made of it, for there will be destitute ones in future generations,—"the poor shall never cease out of the land,"—and it will make glad their eyes to read the story of the Lord's mercy to the needy in former times. Registers of divine kindness ought to be made and preserved; we write down in history the calamities of nations,—wars, famines, pestilences, and earthquakes are recorded; how much rather then should we set up memorials of the Lord's lovingkindness!
Verses 19-20. For he hath looked down from the heights of his sanctuary, or "leaned from the high place of his holiness," from heaven did the LORD behold the earth, looking out like a watcher from his tower. What was the object of this leaning from the battlements of heaven? Why this intent gaze upon the race of men? The answer is full of astounding mercy; the Lord does not look upon mankind to note their grandees, and observe the doings of their nobles, but to hear the groaning of the prisoner; to loose those that are appointed to death. Now the groans of those in prison so far from being musical are very horrible to hear, yet God bends to hear them: those who are bound for death are usually ill company, yet Jehovah deigns to stoop from his greatness to relieve their extreme distress and break their chains.
Verse 21. To declare the name of the LORD in Zion, and his praise in Jerusalem. Great mercy displayed to those greatly in need of it, is the plainest method of revealing the attributes of the Most High. Actions speak more loudly than words; deeds of grace are a revelation even more impressive than the most tender promises.
Verse 22. When the people are gathered together, and the kingdoms, to serve the Lord. The great work of restoring ruined Zion is to be spoken of in those golden ages when the heathen nations shall be converted unto God; even those glorious times will not be able to despise that grand event, which, like the passage of Israel through the Red Sea, will never be eclipsed and never cease to awaken the enthusiasm of the chosen people.
Verse 23. He weakened my strength in the way. Here the Psalmist comes down again to the mournful string, and pours forth his personal complaint. His sorrow had cast down his spirit, and even caused weakness in his

13. Thou shalt arise, and have mercy upon Zion. We have here the conclusion drawn from the truth stated in the preceding verse—God is eternal, and therefore he will have compassion upon Zion. God's eternity is to be considered as impressed upon the memorial, or word, by which he has brought himself under obligation to maintain our welfare.
14. For thy servants take pleasure in her stones. The prophet, I have no doubt, speaks in general of the whole Church, intimating that this was not the wish entertained merely by one man, but was shared by the whole body of the Church. The more effectually to induce God to listen to his prayer, he calls upon all the godly, who were then in the world, to join with him in the same request.

15-18
15. And the nations shall fear the name of Jehovah. The prophet here describes the fruit which would result from the deliverance of the ancient tribes; which is, that thereby God's glory would be rendered illustrious among nations and kings. He tacitly intimates, that when the Church is oppressed, the Divine glory is at the same time debased; even as the God of Israel was, no doubt, at the period referred to, derided by the ungodly, as if he had been destitute of the power to succor his people. It is therefore declared, that if he redeem them, it will afford such a remarkable proof of his power as to constrain the Gentiles to reverence him whom they contemned.
16. The concluding part of the 16th verse, He hath appeared in his glory, refers to the manifestation which God made of himself when he brought forth his Church from the darkness of death; even as it is said in another place concerning her first deliverance, "Judah was his sanctuary, and Israel his dominions" (Psalm 114:2) In like manner in the present passage, by again gathering to himself his people who were dispersed, and by raising his Church, as it were, from death to life, he appeared in his glory.
17. He hath regarded the prayer of the solitary. It is worthy of notice, that the deliverance of the chosen tribes is ascribed to the prayers of the faithful. God's mercy was indeed the sole cause which led him to deliver his Church, according as he had graciously promised this blessing to her; but to stir up true believers to greater earnestness in prayer, he promises that what he has purposed to do of his own good pleasure, he will grant in answer to their requests.
18. This shall be registered for the generation that is to come. The Psalmist magnifies still more the fruit of the deliverance of his people, for the purpose of encouraging himself and others in the hope of obtaining the object of their prayers. He intimates, that this will be a memorable work of God, the praise of which shall be handed down to succeeding ages.

19-22
19. For he hath looked down from the high place of his holiness. Now the prophet contemplates the deliverance after which he breathes with anxious desire, as if it had been already accomplished. That the malignity of men might not attempt to obscure such a signal blessing of Heaven, he

No blessing more desirable to a ruined state than the restoring and re-establishing of their church-privileges.
III. The prayers of God's people now seem to be slighted and no notice taken of them, but they will be reviewed and greatly encouraged (v. 17): He will regard the prayer of the destitute. It was said (v. 16) that God will appear in his glory, such a glory as kings themselves shall stand in awe of, v. 15. When great men appear in their glory they are apt to look with disdain upon the poor that apply to them; but the great God will not do so.
IV. The prisoners under condemnation unjustly seem as sheep appointed for the slaughter, but care shall be taken for their discharge (v. 19, 20): God has looked down from the height of his sanctuary, from heaven, where he has prepared his throne, that high place, that holy place; thence did the Lord behold the earth, for it is a place of prospect, and nothing on this earth is or can be hidden from his all-seeing eye; he looks down, not to take a view of the kingdoms of the world and the glory of them, but to do acts of grace, to hear the groaning of the prisoners (which we desire to be out of the hearing of), and not only to hear them, but to help them, to loose those that are appointed to death, then when there is but a step between them and it. See the divine pity in hearing the prisoner's groans, and the divine power in loosing the prisoner's bonds, even when they are appointed to death and are pinioned and double-shackled. We have an instance in Peter, Acts xii. 6.

23-28 Hoping in God's compassion.
We may here observe,
I. The imminent danger that the Jewish church was in of being quite extirpated and cut off by the captivity in Babylon (v. 23): He weakened my strength in the way. They were for many ages in the way to the performance of the great promise made to their fathers concerning the Messiah, longing as much for it as ever a traveler did to be at his journey's end. The legal institutions led them in the way; but when the ten tribes were lost in Assyria, and the two almost lost in Babylon, the strength of that nation was weakened, and, in all appearance, its day shortened; for they said, Our hope is lost; we are cut off for our parts, Ezek. xxxvii. 11. And then what becomes of the promise that Shiloh should arise out of Judah, the star out of Jacob, and the Messiah out of the family of David? If these fail, the promise fails.
II. A prayer for the continuance of it (v. 24): "O my God! take me not away in the midst of my days; let not this poor church be cut off in the midst of the days assigned it by the promise; let it not be cut off till the Messiah shall come. Destroy it not, for that blessing is in it," Isa. lxv. 8. She is a criminal, but, for the sake of that blessing which is in her, she pleads for a reprieve. This is a prayer for the afflicted, and which, with submission to the will of God, we may in faith put

Psalm 102

22-28

22 When the people are gathered together, and the kingdoms, to serve the LORD.
23 He weakened my strength in the way; he shortened my days.
24 I said, O my God, take me not away in the midst of my days: thy years are throughout all generations.
25 Of old hast thou laid the foundation of the earth: and the heavens are the work of thy hands.
26 They shall perish, but thou shalt endure: yea, all of them shall wax old like a garment; as a vesture shalt thou change them, and they shall be changed:
27 But thou art the same, and thy years shall have no end.
28 The children of thy servants shall continue, and their seed shall be established before thee.

bodily frame, so that he was like a pilgrim who limped along the road, and was ready to lie down and die.

Verse 24. I said, O my God, take me not away in the midst of my days. He betook himself to prayer. What better remedy is there for heart-sickness and depression? We may lawfully ask for recovery from sickness and may hope to be heard. Good men should not dread death, but they are not forbidden to love life: for many reasons the man who has the best hope of heaven may nevertheless think it desirable to continue here a little longer, for the sake of his family, his work, the church of God, and even the glory of God itself.

Verse 25. Of old hast thou laid the foundation of the earth. Creation is no new work with God, and therefore to "create Jerusalem a praise in the earth" will not be difficult to him. Long ere the holy city was laid in ruins the Lord made a world out of nothing, and it will be no labor to him to raise the walls from their heaps and replace the stones in their courses.

Verse 26. They shall perish, but thou shalt endure. The power which made them shall dissolve them, even as the city of thy love was destroyed at thy command; yet neither the ruined city nor the ruined earth can make a change in thee, reverse thy purpose, or diminish thy glory. Thou standest when all things fall. Yea, all of them shall wax old like a garment; as a vesture shalt thou change them, and they shall be changed. Time impairs all things, the fashion becomes obsolete and passes away. The visible creation, which is like the garment of the invisible God, is waxing old and wearing out, and our great King is not so poor that he must always wear the same robes; he will ere long fold up the worlds and put them aside as worn out vestures, and he will array himself in new attire, making a new heaven and a new earth wherein dwelleth righteousness.

Verse 27. But thou art the same, or, "thou art he." As a man remains the same when he has changed his clothing, so is the Lord evermore the unchanging One, though his works in creation may be changed, and the operations of his providence may vary. When heaven and earth shall flee away from the dread presence of the great Judge, he will be unaltered by the terrible confusion, and the world in conflagration will effect no change in him; even so, the Psalmist remembered that when Israel was vanquished, her capital destroyed, and her temple leveled with the ground, her God remained the same self-existent, all-sufficient being.

Verse 28. The children of thy servants shall continue. The Psalmist had early in the psalm looked forward to a future generation, and here he speaks with confidence that such a race would arise and be preserved and blessed of God. Some read it as a prayer, "let the sons of thy servants abide." Any way, it is full of good cheer to us; we may plead for the Lord's favor to our seed, and we may expect that the cause of God and truth will revive in future generations. Let us hope that those who are to succeed us will not be so stubborn, unbelieving and erring as we have been. If the church has been minished and brought low by the lukewarmness of the present race, let us entreat the Lord to raise up a better order of men, whose zeal and obedience shall win and hold a long prosperity.

JOHN CALVIN

openly and in express terms claims for God his rightful praise; and the people were constrained in many ways to acknowledge therein the divine hand.

20. To hear the groaning of the prisoner Here the prophet repeats once more what he had previously touched upon concerning prayer, in order again to stir up the hearts of the godly to engage in that exercise, and that after their deliverance they might know it to have been granted to their faith, because, depending on the divine promises, they had sent up their groanings to heaven.

21. That the name of Jehovah may be declared in Zion. Here is celebrated a still more ample and richer fruit of this deliverance than has been previously mentioned, which is, that the Jews would not only be united into one body to give thanks to God, but that, when brought back to their own country, they would also gather kings and nations into the same unity of faith, and into the same divine worship with themselves.

23-28

23. He hath afflicted my strength in the way. As the manifestation of Christ was the goal of the race which God's ancient people were running, they justly complain that they are afflicted and weakened in the midst of their course. Thus they set before God his promise, telling him, that although they had not run at random, but had confided in his protection, they were nevertheless broken and crushed by his hand in the midst of their journey. They do not indeed find fault with him, as if he had disappointed their hope; but fully persuaded, that he does not deal deceitfully with those who serve him, by this complaint they strengthen themselves in the hope of a favorable issue.

25. Thou hast aforetime founded the earth. Here the sacred writer amplifies what he had previously stated, declaring, that compared with God the whole world is a form which quickly vanishes away; and yet a little after he represents the Church as exempted from this the common lot of all sublunary things, because she has for her foundation the word of God, while her safety is secured by the same word.

28. The children of thy servants shall dwell. By these words the prophet intimates that he does not ask the preservation of the Church, because it is a part of the human race, but because God has raised it above the revolutions of the world. And undoubtedly, when He adopted us as his children, his design was to cherish us as it were in his own bosom. The inference of the inspired bard is not, therefore, far-fetched, when, amidst innumerable storms, each of which might carry us away, he hopes that the Church will have a permanent existence. It is true, that when through our own fault we become estranged from God, we are also as it were cut off from the fountain of life; but no sooner are we reconciled to Him than he begins again to pour down his blessings upon us. Whence it follows that true believers, as they are regenerated by the incorruptible seed, shall continue to live after death, because God continues unchangeably the same.

MATTHEW HENRY

up, that God would not take us away in the midst of our days, but that, if it be his will, he would spare us to do him further service and to be made riper for heaven.

III. A plea to enforce this prayer taken from the eternity of the Messiah promised, v. 25-27. The apostle quotes these verses (Heb. i. 10-12) and tells us, He saith this to the Son, and in that exposition we must acquiesce. It is very comfortable, in reference to all the changes that pass over the church, and all the dangers it is in, that Jesus Christ is the same yesterday, to-day, and for ever. Thy years are throughout all generations, and cannot be shortened. It is likewise comfortable in reference to the decay and death of our own bodies, and the removal of our friends from us, that God is an ever living God, and that therefore, if he be ours, in him we may have everlasting consolation. In this plea observe how, to illustrate the eternity of the Creator, he compares it with the mutability of the creature; for it is God's sole prerogative to be unchangeable.

1. God made the world, and therefore had a being before it from eternity. The Son of God, the eternal Word, made the world. It is expressly said, All things were made by him, and without him was not any thing made that was made; and therefore the same was in the beginning from eternity with God, and was God, John i. 1-3; Col. i. 16; Eph. iii. 9; Heb. i. 2.

2. God will unmake the world again, and therefore shall have a being to eternity (v. 26, 27): They shall perish, for thou shalt change them by the same almighty power that made them, and therefore, no doubt, thou shalt endure; thou art the same. God and the world, Christ and the creature, are rivals for the innermost and uppermost place in the soul of man, the immortal soul; now what is here said, one would think, were enough to decide the controversy immediately and to determine us for God and Christ.

IV. A comfortable assurance of an answer to this prayer (v. 28): The children of thy servants shall continue; since Christ is the same, the church shall continue from one generation to another; from the eternity of the head we may infer the perpetuity of the body, though often weak and distempered, and even at death's door. Those that hope to wear out the saints of the Most High will be mistaken. Christ's servants shall have children; those children shall have a seed, a succession, of professing people; the church, as well as the world, is under the influence of that blessing, Be fruitful and multiply. These children shall continue, not in their own persons, by reason of death, but in their seed, which shall be established before God (that is, in his service, and by his grace); the entail of religion shall not be cut off while the world stands, but, as one generation of good people passes away, another shall come, and thus the throne of Christ shall endure.

Psalm 103

Title
A Psalm of David.

1-7
1 Bless the LORD, O my soul: and all that is within me, bless his holy name.
2 Bless the LORD, O my soul, and forget not all his benefits:
3 Who forgiveth all thine iniquities; who healeth all thy diseases;
4 Who redeemeth thy life from destruction; who crowneth thee with loving kindness and tender mercies;
5 Who satisfieth thy mouth with good things; so that thy youth is renewed like the eagle's.
6 The LORD executeth righteousness and judgment for all that are oppressed.
7 He made known his ways unto Moses, his acts unto the children of Israel.

Psalm 103

TITLE. A Psalm of David.—Doubtless by David; it is in his own style when at its best, and we should attribute it to his later years when he had a higher sense of the preciousness of pardon, because a keener sense of sin, than in his younger days. His clear sense of the frailty of life indicates his weaker years. As in the lofty Alps some peaks rise above all others so among even the inspired Psalms there are heights of song which overtop the rest. This one hundred and third Psalm has ever seemed to us to be the Monte Rosa of the divine chain of mountains of praise, glowing with a ruddier light than any of the rest. It is as the apple tree among the trees of the wood, and its golden fruit has a flavor such as no fruit ever bears unless it has been ripened in the full sunshine of mercy. It is man's reply to the benedictions of his God, his Song on the Mount answering to his Redeemer's Sermon on the Mount. Nebuchadnezzar adored his idol with flute, harp, psaltery, dulcimer and all kinds of music; and David, in far nobler style awakens all the melodies of heaven and earth in honor of the one only living and true God. Our attempt at exposition is commenced under an impressive sense of the utter impossibility of doing justice to so sublime a composition; we call upon our soul and all that is within us to aid in the pleasurable task; but, alas, our soul is finite, and our all of mental faculty far too little for the enterprise. There is too much in the Psalm, for a thousand pens to write, it is one of those all-comprehending Scriptures which is a Bible in itself, and it might alone almost suffice for the hymn-book of the church.
DIVISION. First the Psalmist sings of personal mercies which he had himself received Ps 103:1-5; then he magnifies the attributes of Jehovah as displayed in his dealings with his people, Ps 103:6-19; and he closes by calling upon all the creatures in the universe to adore the Lord and join with himself in blessing Jehovah, the ever gracious.

EXPOSITION
Verse 1. Bless the Lord O my soul. Soul music is the very soul of music. The Psalmist strikes the best keynote when he begins with stirring up his inmost self to magnify the Lord. He soliloquizes, holds self-communion and exhorts himself, as though he felt that dullness would all too soon steal over his faculties, as, indeed, it will over us all, unless we are diligently on the watch.
Verse 2. Bless the LORD, O my soul. He is in real earnest, and again calls upon himself to arise. Had he been very sleepy before? Or was he now doubly sensible of the importance, the imperative necessity of adoration? Certainly, he uses no vain repetitions, for the Holy Spirit guides his pen; and thus he shews us that we have need, again and again, to bestir ourselves when we are about to worship God, for it would be shameful to offer him anything less than the utmost our souls can render. These first verses are a tuning of the harp, a screwing up of the loosened strings that not a note may fail in the sacred harmony.
Verse 3. Who forgiveth all thine iniquities. Here David begins his list of blessings received, which he rehearses as themes and arguments for praise. He selects a few of the choicest pearls from the casket of divine love, threads them on the string of memory, and hangs them about the neck of gratitude. Pardoned sin is, in our experience, one of the choicest boons of grace, one of the earliest gifts of mercy,—in fact, the needful preparation for enjoying all that follows it.
Verse 4. Who redeemeth thy life from destruction. By purchase and by power the Lord redeems us from the spiritual death into which we had fallen, and from the eternal death which would have been its consequence. Had not the death penalty of sin been removed, our forgiveness and healing would have been incomplete portions of salvation, fragments only, and but of small value, but the removal of the guilt and power of sin is fitly attended by the reversal of the sentence of death which had been passed

JOHN CALVIN

Psalm 103

1-5
1. Bless Jehovah, O my soul! The prophet, by stirring up himself to gratitude, gives by his own example a lesson to every man of the duty incumbent upon him. And doubtless our slothfulness in this matter has need of continual incitement. If even the prophet, who was inflamed with a more intense and fervent zeal than other men, was not free from this malady, of which his earnestness in stimulating himself is a plain confession, how much more necessary is it for us, who have abundant experience of our own torpor, to apply the same means for our quickening? The Holy Spirit, by his mouth, indirectly upbraids us on account of our not being more diligent in praising God, and at the same time points out the remedy, that every man may descend into himself and correct his own sluggishness.
2. And forget not any of his benefits. Here, he instructs us that God is not deficient on his part in furnishing us with abundant matter for praising him. It is our own ingratitude which hinders us from engaging in this exercise.
3. Who forgiveth all thy iniquities. He now enumerates the different kinds of the divine benefits, in considering which he has told us that we are too forgetful and slothful. It is not without cause that he begins with God's pardoning mercy, for reconciliation with him is the fountain from which all other blessings flow. God's goodness extends even to the ungodly; but they are, notwithstanding, so far from having the enjoyment of it, that they do not even taste it.
4. Who redeemeth thy life from the grave. The Psalmist expresses more plainly what our condition is previous to God's curing our maladies—that we are dead and adjudged to the grave. The consideration that the mercy of God delivers us from death and destruction ought, therefore, to lead us to prize it the more highly. If the resurrection of the soul from the grave is the first step of spiritual life, what room for self-glorification is left to man? The prophet next teaches us that the incomparable grace of God shines forth in the very commencement of our salvation, as well as in its whole progress; and the more to enhance the commendation of this grace, he adds the word compassions in the plural number.

6-8
6. Jehovah executeth righteousness. David having recounted the Divine benefits bestowed upon himself, now passes from this personal consideration to take a wider view of the subject. There is, however, no doubt that when he declares God to be the succorer of the oppressed, he includes himself among the number, for he had enjoyed the Divine help under many persecutions; and, from his own experience, he describes the character in which God is accustomed to manifest himself towards all who are unrighteously afflicted.
7. He hath made known his ways to Moses. David now speaks in the name of the chosen people; and this he does very suitably, being led to it by the consideration of the benefits which God had bestowed upon himself. Convinced that it

MATTHEW HENRY

Psalm 103

1-5 Cheerful praise.
David is here communing with his own heart, and he is no fool that thus talks to himself and excites his own soul to that which is good. Observe,
I. How he stirs up himself to the duty of praise, v. 1, 2.
1. It is the Lord that is to be blessed and spoken well of; for he is the fountain of all good, whatever are the channels or cisterns; it is to his name, his holy name, that we are to consecrate our praise, giving thanks at the remembrance of his holiness.
2. It is the soul that is to be employed in blessing God, and all that is within us. We make nothing of our religious performances if we do not make heart-work of them, if that which is within us, nay, if all that is within us, be not engaged in them. The work requires the inward man, the whole man, and all little enough.
3. In order to our return of praises to God, there must be a grateful remembrance of the mercies we have received from him: Forget not all his benefits.
1. "He has pardoned thy sins (v. 3); he has forgiven, and does forgive, all thy iniquities." This is mentioned first because by the pardon of sin that is taken away which kept good things from us, and we are restored to the favor of God, which bestows good things on us. Think what the provocation was; it was iniquity, and yet pardoned; how many the provocations were, and yet all pardoned. He has forgiven all our trespasses. It is a continued act; he is still forgiving, as we are still sinning and repenting.
2. "He has cured thy sickness." The corruption of nature is the sickness of the soul; it is its disorder, and threatens its death. This is cured in sanctification; when sin is mortified, the disease is healed; though complicated, it is all healed.
3. "He has rescued thee from danger." A man may be in peril of life, not only by his crimes, or his diseases, but by the power of his enemies; and therefore here also we experience the divine goodness: Who redeemed thy life from destruction (v. 4), from the destroyer, from hell (so the Chaldee), from the second death. The redemption of the soul is precious; we cannot compass it, and therefore are the more indebted to divine grace that has wrought it out, to him who has obtained eternal redemption for us. See Job xxxiii. 24, 28.
4. "He has not only saved thee from death and ruin, but has made thee truly and completely happy, with honor, pleasure, and long life."
(1.) "He has given thee true honor and great honor, no less than a crown: He crowns thee with his lovingkindness and tender mercies."
(2.) "He has given thee true pleasure: He satisfies thy mouth with good things" (v. 5).
(3.) "He has given thee a prospect and pledge of long life: Thy youth is renewed like the eagle's."

Psalm 103

8-14

8 The LORD is merciful and gracious, slow to anger, and plenteous in mercy.
9 He will not always chide: neither will he keep his anger for ever.
10 He hath not dealt with us after our sins; nor rewarded us according to our iniquities.
11 For as the heaven is high above the earth, so great is his mercy toward them that fear him.
12 As far as the east is from the west, so far hath he removed our transgressions from us.
13 Like as a father pitieth his children, so the LORD pitieth them that fear him.
14 For he knoweth our frame; he remembereth that we are dust.

upon us. Glory be to our great Substitute, who delivered us from going down into the pit, by giving himself to be our ransom.
Verse 5. Who satisfieth thy mouth with good things, or rather "filling with good thy soul." No man is ever filled to satisfaction but a believer, and only God himself can satisfy even him. Many a worldling is satiated, but not one is satisfied. God satisfies the very soul of man, his noblest part, his ornament and glory; and of consequence he satisfies his mouth, however hungry and craving it might otherwise be.
Verse 6. The LORD executeth righteousness and judgment for all that are of oppressed. Our own personal obligations must not absorb our song; we must also magnify the Lord for his goodness to others. He does not leave the poor and needy to perish at the hands of their enemies, but interposes on their behalf, for he is the executor of the poor and the executioner of the cruel.
Verse 7. He made known his ways unto Moses. Moses was made to see the manner in which the Lord deals with men; he saw this at each of the three periods of his life, in the court, in retirement, and at the head of the tribes of Israel. To him the Lord gave specially clear manifestations of his dispensations and modes of ruling among mankind, granting to him to see more of God than had before been seen by mortal man, while he communed with him upon the mount.
Verse 8. The Lord is merciful and gracious. Those with whom he deals are sinners. However much he favors them they are guilty and need mercy at his hands, nor is he slow to compassionate their lost estate, or reluctant by his grace to lift them out of it.
Verse 9. He will not always chide. He will sometimes, for he cannot endure that his people should harbor sin in their hearts, but not for ever will he chasten them; as soon as they turn to him and forsake their evil ways he will end the quarrel. He might find constant cause for striving with us, for we have always something in us which is contrary to his holy mind, but he refrains himself lest our spirits should fail before him.
Verse 10. He hath not dealt with us after our sins; nor rewarded us according to our iniquities. Else had Israel perished outright, and we also had long ago been consigned to the lowest hell. We ought to praise the Lord for what he has not done as well as for what he has wrought for us; even the negative side deserves our adoring gratitude.
Verse 11. For as the heaven is high above the earth, so great is his mercy toward them that fear him. Boundless in extent towards his chosen is the mercy of the Lord; it is no more to be measured than the height of heaven or the heaven of heavens. "Like the height of the heavens" is the original language, which implies other points of comparison besides extent, and suggests sublimity, grandeur, and glory.
Verse 12. As far as the east is from the west, so far hath he removed our transgressions from us. O glorious verse, no word even upon the inspired page can excel it! Sin is removed from us by a miracle of love! What a load to move, and yet is it removed so far that the distance is incalculable. Fly as far as the wing of imagination can bear you, and if you journey through space eastward, you are further from the west at every beat of your wing.
Verse 13. Like as a father pitieth his children, so the Lord pitieth them that fear him. To those who truly reverence his holy name, the Lord is a father and acts as such. These he pities, for in the very best of men the Lord sees much to pity, and when they are at their best state they still need his compassion. This should check every propensity to pride, though at the same time it should yield us the richest comfort. Fathers feel for their children, especially when they are in pain, they would like to suffer in their stead, their sighs and groans cut them to the quick: thus sensitive towards us is our heavenly Father.
Verse 14. For he knoweth our frame. He knows how we are made, for he made us. Our make and build, our constitution and temperament, our

was only as a member of the Church that he had been enriched with so many blessings, he immediately carries back his contemplations to the common covenant made with the people of Israel. He, however, continues the same train of thought as in the preceding verse; for these ways, which he says had been shown to Moses, were nothing else than the deliverance wrought for the people until they entered the promised land.
8. Jehovah is merciful and gracious. David seems to allude to the exclamation of Moses, recorded in Exodus 34:6, where the nature of God, revealed in a remarkable way, is more clearly described than in other places. When Moses was admitted to take a nearer view of the Divine glory than was usually obtained, he exclaimed upon beholding it, "O God! merciful and gracious, forgiving iniquity, slow to wrath, and abundant in goodness." As, therefore, he has summarily comprehended in that passage all that is important for us to know concerning the Divine character, David happily applies these terms, by which God is there described, to his present purpose.

9-12
9. He will not always chide. David, from the attributes ascribed to God in the preceding verse, draws the conclusion, that when God has been offended, he will not be irreconcilable, since, from his nature, he is always inclined to forgive. It was necessary to add this statement; for our sins would be continually shutting the gate against his goodness were there not some way of appeasing his anger. David tacitly intimates that God institutes an action against sinners to lay them low under a true sense of their guilt; and that yet he recedes from it whenever he sees them subdued and humbled.
10. He hath not dealt with us after our sins. The Psalmist here proves from experience, or from the effect, what he has stated concerning the Divine character; for it was entirely owing to the wonderful forbearance of God that the Israelites had hitherto continued to exist. Let each of us, as if he had said, examine his own life; let us inquire in how many ways we have provoked the wrath of God? or, rather, do we not continually provoke it? and yet he not only forbears to punish us, but bountifully maintains those whom he might justly destroy.
11. For in proportion to the height of the heavens above the earth. The Psalmist here confirms by a comparison the truth that God does not punish the faithful as they have deserved, but, by his mercy, strives against their sins. The form of expression is equivalent to saying that God's mercy towards us is infinite.

13-16
13. As a father is compassionate towards his children. The Psalmist not only explains by a comparison what he has already stated, but he at the same time assigns the cause why God so graciously forgives us, which is, because he is a father. It is then in consequence of God's having freely and sovereignly adopted us as his children that he continually pardons our sins, and accordingly we are to draw from that fountain the hope of forgiveness. And as no man has been

6-18 Goodness and compassion of God.
Hitherto the psalmist had only looked back upon his own experiences and thence fetched matter for praise; here he looks abroad and takes notice of his favor to others also; for in them we should rejoice and give thanks for them, all the saints being fed at a common table and sharing in the same blessings.
I. Truly God is good to all (v. 6): He executes righteousness and judgment, not only for his own people, but for all that are oppressed; for even in common providence he is the patron of wronged innocency, and, one way or other, will plead the cause of those that are injured against their oppressors. It is his honor to humble the proud and help the helpless.
II. He is in a special manner good to Israel, to every Israelite indeed, that is of a clean and upright heart.
1. He has revealed himself and his grace to us (v. 7): He made known his ways unto Moses, and by him his acts to the children of Israel, not only by his rod to those who then lived, but by his pen to succeeding ages.
2. He has never been rigorous and severe with us, but always tender, full of compassion, and ready to forgive.
(1.) It is in his nature to be so (v. 8): The Lord is merciful and gracious; this was his way which he made known unto Moses at Mount Horeb, when he thus proclaimed his name (Exod. xxxiv. 6, 7), in answer to Moses's request (chi. xxxiii. 13), I beseech thee, show me thy way, that I may know thee. It is my way, says God, to pardon sin.
(2.) We have found him so; we, for our parts, must own that he has not dealt with us after our sins, v. 10. The scripture says a great deal of the mercy of God, and we may all set to our seal that it is true, that we have experienced it.
3. He has pardoned our sins, not only my iniquity (v. 3), but our transgressions, v. 12. Though it is of our own benefit, by the pardoning mercy of God, that we are to take the comfort, yet of the benefit others have by it we must give him the glory. Observe,
(1.) The transcendent riches of God's mercy (v. 11): As the heaven is high above the earth (so high that the earth is but a point to the vast expanse), so God's mercy is above the merits of those that fear him most.
(2.) The fullness of his pardons, an evidence of the riches of his mercy (v. 12): As far as the east is from the west so far has he removed our transgressions from us, so that they shall never be laid to our charge, nor rise up in judgment against us.
4. He has pitied our sorrows, v. 13, 14.
5. He has perpetuated his covenant-mercy and thereby provided relief for our frailty, v. 15-18. See here,
(1.) How short man's life is and of what uncertain continuance. The lives even of great men and good men are so, and neither their greatness nor their goodness can alter the property of them.

Psalm 103

15-22

15 As for man, his days are as grass: as a flower of the field, so he flourisheth.
16 For the wind passeth over it, and it is gone; and the place thereof shall know it no more.
17 But the mercy of the LORD is from everlasting to everlasting upon them that fear him, and his righteousness unto children's children;
18 To such as keep his covenant, and to those that remember his commandments to do them.
19 The LORD hath prepared his throne in the heavens; and his kingdom ruleth over all.
20 Bless the LORD, ye his angels, that excel in strength, that do his commandments, hearkening unto the voice of his word.
21 Bless ye the LORD, all ye his hosts; ye ministers of his, that do his pleasure.
22 Bless the LORD, all his works in all places of his dominion: bless the Lord, O my soul.

prevailing infirmity and most besetting temptation he well perceives, for he searches our inmost nature.

Verse 15. As for man, his days are as grass. He lives on the grass, and lives like the grass. Corn is but educated grass, and man, who feeds on it, partakes of its nature. The grass lives, grows, flowers, falls beneath the scythe, dries up, and is removed from the field: read this sentence over again, and you will find it the history of man. If he lives out his little day, he is cut down at last, and it is far more likely that he will wither before he comes to maturity, or be plucked away on a sudden, long before he has fulfilled his time.

Verse 16. For the wind passeth over it, and it is gone. Only a little wind is needed, not even a scythe is demanded, a breath can do it, for the flower is so frail. How small a portion of deleterious gas suffices to create a deadly fever, which no art of man can stay. No need of sword or bullet, a puff of foul air is deadlier far, and fails not to lay low the healthiest and most stalwart son of man. And the place thereof shall know it no more. The flower blooms no more.

Verse 17. But the mercy of the LORD is from everlasting to everlasting upon them that fear him. Blessed but! How vast the contrast between the fading flower and the everlasting God! How wonderful that his mercy should link our frailty with his eternity, and make us everlasting too!

Verse 18. Children of the righteous are not, however, promised the Lord's mercy without stipulation, and this verse completes the statement of the last by adding: To such as keep his covenant, and to those that remember his commandments to do them. The parents must be obedient and the children too. We are here bidden to abide by the covenant, and those who run off to any other confidence than the finished work of Jesus are not among those who obey this precept; those with whom the covenant is really made stand firm to it, and having begun in the Spirit, they do not seek to be made perfect in the flesh.

Verse 19. The LORD has prepared his throne in the heavens. Here is a grand burst of song produced by a view of the boundless power, and glorious sovereignty of Jehovah. His throne is fixed, for that is the word; it is established, settled, immovable.

Verse 20. Bless the Lord, ye his angels, that excel in strength. Finding his work of praise growing upon his hands, he calls upon "the firstborn sons of light" to speak the praises of the Lord, as well they may, for as Milton says, they best can tell. Dwelling nearer to that prepared throne than we as yet have leave to climb, they see in nearer vision the glory which we would adore.

Verse 21. Bless ye the Lord, all ye his hosts; to whatever race of creatures ye may belong, for ye are all his troops, and he is the Generallissimo of all your armies. The fowl of the air and the fish of the sea, and whatsoever passeth through the paths of the sea, should all unite in praising their Creator, after the best of their ability.

Verse 22. Bless the Lord, all his works in all places of his dominion. Here is a trinity of blessing for the thrice blessed God, and each one of the three blessings is an enlargement upon that which went before. This is the most comprehensive of all, for what can be a wider call than to all in all places? See how finite man can awaken unbounded praise!

adopted on the ground of his own merit, it follows that sins are freely pardoned.
14. For he knoweth. David here annihilates all the worth which men would arrogate to themselves, and asserts that it is the consideration of our misery, and that alone, which moves God to exercise patience towards us.

17-18
17. But the goodness of Jehovah, etc. The Psalmist leaves nothing to men to rely upon but the mercy of God; for it would be egregious folly to seek a ground of confidence in themselves. After having shown the utter emptiness of men, he adds the seasonable consolation, that, although they have no intrinsic excellence, which does not vanish into smoke, yet God is an inexhaustible fountain of life, to supply their wants.

19-22
19. Jehovah hath established his throne in the heavens. David having recounted the benefits by which God lays each of us in particular, and also the whole Church, under obligation to him, now extols in general his infinite glory. The amount is, that whenever God is mentioned, men should learn to ascend in their contemplations above the whole world, because his majesty transcends the heavens; and they should farther learn not to measure his power by that of man, since it has under its control all kingdoms and dominions. That none may think that earthly creatures only are here put in subjection to God, the Psalmist chiefly addresses the angels. In calling upon them to join in praising God, he teaches both himself and all the godly, that there is not a better nor a more desirable exercise than to praise God, since there is not a more excellent service in which even the angels are employed. The angels are doubtless too willing and prompt in the discharge of this duty, to stand in need of incitement from us.
21. Bless Jehovah, all ye his hosts. By hosts is not to be understood the stars, as some explain it. The subject of the preceding verse is still continued. Nor is the repetition superfluous; for the word hosts teaches us that there are myriads of myriads who stand before the throne of God, ready to receive every intimation of his will.
22. Bless Jehovah, all ye his works. The Psalmist in conclusion addresses all creatures; for although they may be without speech and understanding, yet they ought in a manner to re-echo the praises of their Creator. This he does on our account, that we may learn that there is not a corner in heaven or on earth where God is not praised. We have less excuse, if, when all the works of God by praising their Maker reproach us for our sloth we do not at least follow their example. The express mention of all places of his dominion, seems to be intended to stir up the faithful to greater ardor in this exercise; for if even those countries where his voice is unheard ought not to be mute in his praise, how can we lawfully remain silent to whom he opens his mouth, anticipating us by his own sacred voice? In short, David shows that his design in recounting God's benefits, and magnifying the extent of his empire, was to animate himself the more to the exercise of praising him.

(2.) How long and lasting God's mercy is to his people (v. 17, 18): it will continue longer than their lives, and will survive their present state.

19-22 Cheerful praise.
Here is,
I. The doctrine of universal providence laid down, v. 19. He has secured the happiness of his peculiar people by promise and covenant, but the order of mankind, and the world in general, he secures by common providence. The Lord has a throne of his own, a throne of glory, a throne of government. He that made all rules all, and both by a word of power: He has prepared his throne, has fixed and established it that it cannot be shaken; he has afore-ordained all the measures of his government and does all according to the counsel of his own will. He has prepared it in the heavens, above us, and out of sight; for he holds back the face of his throne, and spreads a cloud upon it (Job xxvi. 9); yet he can himself judge through the dark cloud, Job xxiii. 13. Hence the heavens are said to rule (Dan. iv. 26), and we are led to consider this by the influence which even the visible heavens have upon this earth, their dominion, Job xxxviii. 33; Gen. i. 16. But though God's throne is in heaven, and there he keeps his court, and thither we are to direct to him (Our Father who art in heaven), yet his kingdom rules over all. He takes cognizance of all the inhabitants, and all the affairs, of this lower world, and disposes all persons and things according to the counsel of his will, to his own glory (Dan. iv. 35): His kingdom rules over all kings and all kingdoms, and from it there is no exempt jurisdiction.
II. The duty of universal praise inferred from it: if all are under God's dominion, all must do him homage.
1. Let the holy angels praise him (v. 20, 21): Bless the Lord, you his angels; and again, Bless the Lord, all you his hosts, you ministers of his. David had been stirring up himself and others to praise God, and here, in the close, he calls upon the angels to do it; not as if they needed any excitement of ours to praise God, they do it continually; but thus he expresses his high thoughts of God as worthy of the adorations of the holy angels, thus he quickens himself and others to the duty with this consideration.
2. Let all his works praise him (v. 22), all in all places of his dominion; for, because they are his works, they are under his dominion, and they were made and are ruled that they may be unto him for a name and a praise. All his works, that is, all the children of men, in all parts of the world, let them all praise God. Yet all this shall not excuse David from praising God, but rather excite him to do it the more cheerfully, that he may bear a part in this concert; for he concludes, Bless the Lord, O my soul! as he began, v. 1. Blessing God and giving him glory must be the alpha and the omega of all our services.

Psalm 104

1-7

1 Bless the LORD, O my soul. O LORD my God, thou art very great; thou art clothed with honor and majesty.

2 Who coverest thyself with light as with a garment: who stretchest out the heavens like a curtain:

3 Who layeth the beams of his chambers in the waters: who maketh the clouds his chariot: who walketh upon the wings of the wind:

4 Who maketh his angels spirits; his ministers a flaming fire:

5 Who laid the foundations of the earth, that it should not be removed for ever.

6 Thou coveredst it with the deep as with a garment: the waters stood above the mountains.

7 At thy rebuke they fled; at the voice of thy thunder they hasted away.

Psalm 104

GENERAL REMARKS. Here we have one of the loftiest and longest sustained flights of the inspired muse. The psalm gives an interpretation to the many voices of nature, and sings sweetly both of creation and providence. The poem contains a complete cosmos sea and land, cloud and sunlight, plant and animal, light and darkness, life and death, are all proved to be expressive of the presence of the Lord. Traces of the six days of creation are very evident, and though the creation of man, which was the crowning work of the sixth day, is not mentioned, this is accounted for from the fact that man is himself the singer: some have ever, discerned marks of the divine rest upon the seventh day in Ps 104:31. It is a poet's version of Genesis. Nor is it alone the present condition of the earth which is here the subject of song; but a hint is given of those holier times when we shall see "a new earth wherein dwelleth righteousness," out of which the sinner shall be consumed, Ps 104:35. The spirit of ardent praise to God runs through the whole, and with it a distinct realization of the divine Being as a personal existence, loved and trusted as well as adored.

We have no information as to the author, but the Septuagint assigns it to David, and we see no reason for ascribing it to any one else. His spirit, style, and manner of writing are very manifest therein, and if the psalm must be ascribed to another, it must be to a mind remarkably similar, and we could only suggest the wise son of David—Solomon, the poet preacher, to whose notes upon natural history in the Proverbs some of the verses bear a striking likeness. Whoever the human penman may have been, the exceeding glory and perfection of the Holy Spirit's own divine authorship are plain to every spiritual mind.

DIVISION. After ascribing blessedness to the Lord the devout psalmist sings of the light and the firmament, which were the work of the first and second days Ps 104:1-6. By an easy transition he describes the separation of the waters from the dry land, the formation of rain, brooks and rivers, and the uprising of green herbs, which were the produce of the third day Ps 104:7-18. Then the appointment of the sun and moon to be the guardians of day and night commands the poet's admiration Ps 104:19-23, and so he sings the work of the fourth day. Having already alluded to many varieties of living creatures, the psalmist proceeds from Ps 104:24-30 to sing of the life with which the Lord was pleased to fill the air, the sea, and the land; these forms of existence were the peculiar produce of the fifth and sixth days. We may regard the closing verses Ps 104:31-35 as a Sabbath meditation, hymn, and prayer. The whole lies before us as a panorama of the universe viewed by the eye of devotion. O for grace to render due praise unto the Lord while reading it.

EXPOSITION

Verse 1. Bless the LORD, O my soul. This psalm begins and ends like the Hundred and Third, and it could not do better: when the model is perfect it deserves to exist in duplicate. True praise begins at home. It is idle to stir up others to praise if we are ungratefully silent ourselves.

Verse 2. Who coverest thyself with light as with a garment: wrapping the light about him as a monarch puts on his robe. The conception is sublime: but it makes us feel how altogether inconceivable the personal glory of the Lord must be; if light itself is but his garment and veil, what must be the blazing splendor of his own essential being! We are lost in astonishment, and dare not pry into the mystery lest we be blinded by its insufferable glory.

Verse 3. Who layeth the beams of his chambers in the water's. His lofty halls are framed with the waters which are above the firmament. The upper rooms of God's great house, the secret stories far above our ken, the palatial chambers wherein he resides, are based upon the floods which form the upper ocean. To the unsubstantial he lends stability; he needs no

JOHN CALVIN

Psalm 104

1-4
1. Bless Jehovah, O my soul! After having exhorted himself to praise God, the Psalmist adds, that there is abundant matter for such an exercise; thus indirectly condemning himself and others of ingratitude, if the praises of God, than which nothing ought to be better known, or more celebrated, are buried by silence. In comparing the light with which he represents God as arrayed to a garment, he intimates, that although God is invisible, yet his glory is conspicuous enough. In respect of his essence, God undoubtedly dwells in light that is inaccessible; but as he irradiates the whole world by his splendor, this is the garment in which He, who is hidden in himself, appears in a manner visible to us. The knowledge of this truth is of the greatest importance. If men attempt to reach the infinite height to which God is exalted, although they fly above the clouds, they must fail in the midst of their course.
3. Laying the beams of his chambers in the waters. David now proceeds to explain at greater length what he had briefly stated under the figure of God's raiment. The scope of the passage is shortly this, that we need not pierce our way above the clouds for the purpose of finding God, since he meets us in the fabric of the world, and is everywhere exhibiting to our view scenes of the most vivid description.

5-9
5. He hath founded the earth upon its foundations. Here the prophet celebrates the glory of God, as manifested in the stability of the earth. Since it is suspended in the midst of the air, and is supported only by pillars of water, how does it keep its place so steadfastly that it cannot be moved? This I indeed grant may be explained on natural principles; for the earth, as it occupies the lowest place, being the center of the world, naturally settles down there.
6. He hath covered it with the deep as with a garment. This may be understood in two ways, either as implying that now the sea covers the earth as a garment, or that at the beginning, before God by his omnipotent word held gathered the waters together into one place, the earth was covered with the deep. But the more suitable sense appears to be, that the sea is now the covering of the earth. At the first creation the deep was not so much a garment as a grave, inasmuch as nothing bears less resemblance to the adorning of apparel than the state of confused desolation and shapeless chaos in which the earth then was. Accordingly, in my judgment, there is here celebrated that wonderful arrangement by which the deep, although without form, is yet the garment of the earth.
9. Thou hast set a bound which they shall not pass. The miracle spoken of is in this verse amplified, from its perpetuity. Natural philosophers are compelled to admit, and it is even one of their first principles, that the water is circular, and occupies the region intermediate between the earth and the air. It is entirely owing to the providence of God, that part of the earth remains dry and fit for the habitation of

MATTHEW HENRY

Psalm 104

1-9 The divine majesty.
In these verses,
I. The psalmist looks up to the divine glory shining in the upper world, of which, though it is one of the things not seen, faith is the evidence. With what reverence and holy awe does he begin his meditation with that acknowledgment: O Lord my God! thou art very great! It is the joy of the saints that he who is their God is a great God. The grandeur of the prince is the pride and pleasure of all his good subjects. The majesty of God is here set forth by various instances, alluding to the figure which great princes in their public appearances covet to make.
II. He looks down, and looks about, to the power of God shining in this lower world. He is not so taken up with the glories of his court as to neglect even the remotest of his territories; no, not the sea and dry land.
1. He has founded the earth, v. 5. Though he has hung it upon nothing (Job xxvi. 7), ponderibus librata suis—balanced by its own weight, yet it is as immovable as if it had been laid upon the surest foundations.
2. He has set bounds to the sea; for that also is his. He brought it within bounds in the creation. At first the earth, which, being the more ponderous body, would subside of course, was covered with the deep (v. 6).

10-18 The divine bounty.
Having given glory to God as the powerful protector of this earth, in saving it from being deluged, here he comes to acknowledge him as its bountiful benefactor, who provides conveniences for all the creatures.
I. He provides fresh water for their drink: He sends the springs into the valleys, v. 10. There is water enough indeed in the sea, that is, enough to drown us, but not one drop to refresh us, be we ever so thirsty—it is all so salt; and therefore God has graciously provided water fit to drink. Naturalists dispute about the origin of fountains; but, whatever are their second causes, here is their first cause; it is God that sends the springs into the brooks, which walk by easy steps between the hills, and receive increase from the rain-water that descends from them. These give drink, not only to man, and those creatures that are immediately useful to him, but to every beast of the field (v. 11); for where God has given life he provides a livelihood and takes care of all the creatures.
II. He provides food convenient for them, both for man and beast: The heavens drop fatness; they hear the earth, but God hears them, Hos. ii. 21. He waters the hills from his chambers (v. 13), from those chambers spoken of (v. 3), the beams of which he lays in the waters, those store-chambers, the clouds that distil fruitful showers. The hills that are not watered by the rivers, as Egypt was by the Nile, are watered by the

Psalm 104

8-14
8 They go up by the mountains; they go down by the valleys unto the place which thou hast founded for them.
9 Thou hast set a bound that they may not pass over; that they turn not again to cover the earth.
10 He sendeth the springs into the valleys, which run among the hills.
11 They give drink to every beast of the field: the wild asses quench their thirst.
12 By them shall the fowls of the heaven have their habitation, which sing among the branches.
13 He watereth the hills from his chambers: the earth is satisfied with the fruit of thy works.
14 He causeth the grass to grow for the cattle, and herb for the service of man: that he may bring forth food out of the earth;

joists and rafters, for his palace is sustained by his own power. We are not to interpret literally where the language is poetical, it would be simple absurdity to do so.
Verse 4. Who maketh his angels spirits; or wields, for the word means either. Angels are pure spirits, though they are permitted to assume a visible form when God desires us to see them. God is a spirit, and he is waited upon by spirits in his royal courts. Angels are like winds for mystery, force, and invisibility, and no doubt the winds themselves are often the angels or messengers of God.
Verse 5. Who laid the foundations of the earth. Thus the commencement of creation is described, in almost the very words employed by the Lord himself in Job 38:4. "Where wast thou when I laid the foundations of the earth? Whereupon are the foundations thereof fastened, and who laid the corner stone thereof?" And the words are found in the same connection too, for the Lord proceeds to say, "When the morning stars sang together and all the sons of God shouted for joy."
Verse 6. Thou coveredst it with the deep as with a garment. The new born earth was wrapped in aqueous swaddling bands. In the first ages, ere man appeared, the proud waters ruled the whole earth. The waters stood above the mountains, no dry land was visible, vapor as from a steaming cauldron covered all. Geologists inform us of this as a discovery, but the Holy Spirit had revealed the fact long before. The passage before us shows us the Creator commencing his work, and laying the foundation for future order and beauty: to think of this reverently will fill us with adoration; to conceive of it grossly and carnally would be highly blasphemous.
Verse 7. At thy rebuke they fled; at the voice of thy thunder they hasted away. When the waters and vapors covered all, the Lord had but to speak and they disappeared at once. As though they had been intelligent agents the waves hurried to their appointed deeps and left the land to itself; then the mountains lifted their heads, the high lands rose from the main, and at length continents and islands, slopes and plains were left to form the habitable earth. The voice of the Lord effected this great marvel.
Verse 8. The vanquished waters are henceforth obedient. They go up by the mountains, climbing in the form of clouds even to the summits of the Alps. They go down by the valleys unto the place which thou hast founded for them: they are as willing to descend in rain, and brooks, and torrents as they were eager to ascend in mists. The loyalty of the mighty waters to the laws of their God is most notable; the fierce flood, the boisterous rapid; the tremendous torrent, are only forms of that gentle dew which trembles on the tiny blade of grass, and in those ruder shapes they are equally obedient to the laws which their Maker has impressed upon them.
Verse 9. Thou hast set a bound that they may not pass over; that they turn not again to cover the earth. That bound has once been passed, but it shall never be so again. The deluge was caused by the suspension of the divine mandate which held the floods in check: they knew their old supremacy, and hastened to reassert it, but now the covenant promise for ever prevents a return of that carnival of waters, that revolt of the waves.
Verse 10. He sendeth the springs into the valleys, which run among the hills. This is a beautiful part of the Lord's arrangement of the subject waters: they find vents through which they leap into liberty where their presence will be beneficial in the highest degree.
Verse 11. They give drink to every beast of the field. Who else would water them if the Lord did not? They are his cattle, and therefore he leads them forth to watering. Not one of them is forgotten of him. The wild asses quench their thirst. The good Lord gives them enough and to spare.
Verse 12. By them shall the fowls of the heaven have their habitation, which sing among the branches. How refreshing are these words! What happy memories they arouse of splashing waterfalls and entangled boughs, where the merry din of the falling and rushing water forms a sort of solid

men. This is a fact of which mariners have the most satisfactory evidence. Yea, were even the rudest and most stupid of our race only to open their eyes, they would behold in the sea mountains of water elevated far above the level of the land.

10-15
10. Sending out springs by the valleys The Psalmist here describes another instance both of the power and goodness of God, which is, that he makes fountains to gush out in the mountains, and to run down through the midst of the valleys. Although it is necessary for the earth to be dry, to render it a fit habitation for us, yet, unless we had water to drink, and unless the earth opened her veins, all kinds of living creatures would perish. The prophet, therefore, speaks in commendation of that arrangement by which the earth, though dry, yet supplies us with water by its moisture.
13. In the 13th verse, it is said that God watereth the mountains from his chambers. It is no ordinary miracle that the mountains, which seem to be condemned to perpetual drought, and which, in a manner, are suspended in the air, nevertheless abound in pastures. The prophet, therefore, justly concludes that this fruitfulness proceeds from nothing else but the agency of God, who is their secret cultivator.
14. Making grass to grow for cattle. The Psalmist now comes to men, of whom God vouchsafes to take a special care as his children. After having spoken of the brute creation, he declares, that corn is produced, and bread made of it, for the nourishment of the human race; and he mentions in addition to this, wine and oil, two things which not only supply the need of mankind, but also contribute to their cheerful enjoyment of life.
15. And wine that cheereth the heart of man. In these words we are taught, that God not only provides for men's necessity, and bestows upon them as much as is sufficient for the ordinary purposes of life, but that in his goodness he deals still more bountifully with them by cheering their hearts with wine and oil. Nature would certainly be satisfied with water to drink; and therefore the addition of wine is owing to God's superabundant liberality.

16-18
16. The trees of Jehovah shall be satiated. The Psalmist again treats of God's general providence in cherishing all the parts of the world. In the first place, he asserts, that by the watering of which he had spoken the trees are satiated, or filled with sap, that thus flourishing they may be a place of abode to the birds. He next declares, that the wild deer and conies have also their places of shelter, to show that no part of the world is forgotten by Him, who is the best of fathers, and that no creature is excluded from his care. The transition which the prophet makes from men to trees is as if he had said, It is not to be wondered at, if God so bountifully nourishes men who are created after his own image, since he does not grudge to extend his care even to trees. By the trees of the Lord, is meant those which are high and of surpassing beauty; for

rain from heaven, which is called the river of God (Ps. lxv. 9), as Canaan was, Deut. xi. 11, 12. Thus the earth is satisfied with the fruit of his works, either with the rain it drinks in (the earth knows when it has enough; it is a pity that any man should not) or with the products it brings forth. It is a satisfaction to the earth to bear the fruit of God's works for the benefit of man, for thus it answers the end of its creation. The food which God brings forth out of the earth (v. 14) is the fruit of his works, which the earth is satisfied with.
2. The divine providence not only furnishes animals with their proper food, but vegetables also with theirs (v. 16): The trees of the Lord are full of sap, not only men's trees, which they take care of and have an eye to, in their orchards, and parks, and other enclosures, but God's trees, which grow in the wildernesses, and are taken care of only by his providence; they are full of sap and want no nourishment.
III. He takes care that they shall have suitable habitations to dwell in. To men God has given discretion to build for themselves and for the cattle that are serviceable to them; but there are some creatures which God more immediately provides a settlement for, such as the birds, and the smaller sort of beasts (v. 18).

19-30 The divine bounty.
We are here taught to praise and magnify God,
I. For the constant revolutions and succession of day and night, and the dominion of sun and moon over them. The heathen were so affected with the light and influence of the sun and moon, and their serviceableness to the earth, that they worshipped them as deities; and therefore the scripture takes all occasions to show that the gods they worshipped are the creatures and servants of the true God (v. 19): He appointed the moon for seasons, for the measuring of the months, the directing of the seasons for the business of the husbandman, and the governing of the tides. God herein consults the comfort of man.
1. The shadows of the evening befriend the repose of the night (v. 20): Thou makes darkness and it is night, which, though black, contributes to the beauty of nature, and is as a foil to the light of the day; and under the protection of the night all the beasts of the forest creep forth to feed, which they are afraid to do in the day, God having put the fear and dread of man upon every beast of the earth (Gen. ix. 2), which contributes as much to man's safety as to his honor.
2. The light of the morning befriends the business of the day (v. 22, 23): The sun arises (for, as he knows his going down, so, thanks be to God, he knows his rising again), and then the wild beasts betake themselves to their rest; even they have some society among them, for they gather themselves together and lay down in their dens, which is a great mercy to the children of men, that while they are abroad, as becomes honest travelers, between sun and sun, care is taken that they shall not be set upon by wild

Psalm 104

15-21

15 And wine that maketh glad the heart of man, and oil to make his face to shine, and bread which strengtheneth man's heart.
16 The trees of the LORD are full of sap; the cedars of Lebanon, which he hath planted;
17 Where the birds make their nests: as for the stork, the fir trees are her house.
18 The high hills are a refuge for the wild goats; and the rocks for the conies.
19 He appointed the moon for seasons: the sun knoweth his going down.
20 Thou makest darkness, and it is night: wherein all the beasts of the forest do creep forth.
21 The young lions roar after their prey, and seek their meat from God.

background of music, and the sweet tuneful notes of the birds are the brighter and more flashing lights in the harmony.

Verse 13. He watereth the hills from his chambers. As the mountains are too high to be watered by rivers and brooks, the Lord himself refreshes them from those waters above the firmament which the poet had in a former verse described as the upper chambers of heaven. Clouds are detained among the mountain crags, and deluge the hill sides with fertilizing rain.

Verse 14. He causeth the grass to grow for the cattle, and herb for the service of man. Grass grows as well as herbs, for cattle must be fed as well as men. God appoints to the lowliest creature its portion and takes care that it has it.

Verse 15. And wine that maketh glad the heart of man. By the aid of genial showers the earth produces not merely necessaries but luxuries, that which furnishes a feast as well as that which makes a meal. O that man were wise enough to know how to use this gladdening product of the vine.

Verse 16. The watering of the hills not only produces the grass and the cultivated herbs, but also the nobler species of vegetation, which come not within the range of human culture. The trees of the Lord—the greatest, noblest, and most royal of trees; those too which are unowned of man, and untouched by his hand.

Verse 17. Where the birds make their nests: as for the stork, the fir trees are her house. So far from being in need, these trees of God afford shelter to others, birds small and great make their nests in the branches. Thus what they receive from the great Lord they endeavor to return to his weaker creatures.

Verse 18. The high hills are a refuge for the wild goats; and the rocks for the conics. All places teem with life. We call our cities populous, but are not the forests and the high hills more densely peopled with life? We speak of uninhabitable places, but where are they?

Verse 19. The appointed rule of the great lights is now the theme for praise. The moon is mentioned first, because in the Jewish day the night leads the way. He appointed the moon for seasons. By the waxing and waning of the moon the year is divided into months, and weeks, and by this means the exact dates of the holy days were arranged. Never let us regard the moon's motions as the inevitable result of inanimate impersonal law, but as the appointment of our God.

Verse 20. Thou, makest darkness, and it is night. Drawing down the blinds for us, he prepares our bedchamber that we may sleep. Were there no darkness we should sigh for it, since we should find repose so much more difficult, if the weary day were never calmed into night. Let us see God's hand in the veiling of the sun, and never fear either natural or providential darkness, since both are of the Lord's own making.

Verse 21. The young lions roar after their prey, and seek their meat from God. This is the poetic interpretation of a roar. To whom do the lions roar? Certainly not to their prey, for the terrible sound tends to alarm their victims, and drive them away. They after their own fashion express their desires for food, and the expression of desire is a kind of prayer.

Verse 22. The sun ariseth. Every evening has its morning to make the day. Were it not that we have seen the sun rise so often we should think it the greatest of miracles, and the most amazing of blessings. They gather themselves together, and lay them down in their dens. Thus they are out of man's way, and he seldom encounters them unless he desires to do so. The forest's warriors retire to their quarters when the morning's drum is heard, finding in the recesses of their dens a darkness suitable for their slumbers; there they lay them down and digest their food, for God has allotted even to them their portion of rest and enjoyment. There was one who in this respect was poorer than lions and foxes, for he had not where to lay his head: all were provided for except their incarnate Provider. Blessed Lord, thou hast

JOHN CALVIN

God's blessing is more conspicuous in them. It seems scarcely possible for any juice of the earth to reach so great a height, and yet they renew their foliage every year.

19-22

19. He hath appointed the moon to distinguish seasons. The Psalmist now comes to another commendation of God's providence as manifested in the beautiful arrangement by which the course of the sun and moon alternately succeeds each other; for the diversity in their mutual changes is so far from producing confusion, that all must easily perceive the impossibility of finding any better method of distinguishing time. When it is said, that the moon was appointed to distinguish seasons, interpreters agree that this is to be understood of the ordinary and appointed feasts. The Hebrews having been accustomed to compute their months by the moon, this served for regulating their festival days and assemblies, both sacred and political.

21. The lions roar after their prey. Although lions, if hunger compels them, go forth from their dens and roar even at noon-day, yet the prophet describes what is most usually the case. He therefore says, that lions do not venture to go abroad during the daytime, but that, trusting to the darkness of the night, they then sally forth in quest of their prey. Herein is manifested the wonderful providence of God, that a beast so dreadful confines itself within its den, that men may walk abroad with the greater freedom. And if lions sometimes range with greater liberty, this is to be imputed to the fall of Adam, which has deprived men of their dominion over the wild beasts. There are, however, still some remains of the original blessing conferred by God on men, inasmuch as he holds in check so many wild beasts by the light of day, as if by iron cages or chains.

22. The sun shall rise. The Psalmist continues to prosecute the same subject, showing that God so distributes the successions of time, as that the day belongs properly to man. Did not God put a restraint upon so many wild beasts which are hostile to us, the human race would soon become extinct. As wild beasts since the fall of man may seem to be born to do us hurt, and to rend and tear in pieces all whom they meet with, this savage cruelty must be kept under check by the providence of God. And in order to keep them shut up within their dens, the only means which he employs is to inspire them with terror, simply by the light of the sun. This instance of divine goodness, the prophet commends the more on account of its necessity; for were it otherwise, men would have no liberty to go forth to engage in the labors and business of life. Man being thus protected by the light against the violence and injuries of wild beasts, in this is to be seen the unparalleled goodness of God, who in so fatherly a manner has provided for his convenience and welfare.

24-26

24. O Jehovah! how magnificent are thy works. The prophet does not make a full enumeration of the works of God, which would be an endless task, but only touches upon certain

MATTHEW HENRY

beasts, for they are then drawn out of the field, and the sluggard shall have no ground to excuse himself from the business of the day with this.

II. For the replenishing of the ocean (v. 25, 26): As the earth is full of God's riches, well stocked with animals, and those well provided for, so that it is seldom that any creature dies merely for want of food, so is this great and wide sea which seems a useless part of the globe, at least not to answer the room it takes up; yet God has appointed it its place and made it serviceable to man both for navigation and also to be his storehouse for fish.

III. For the seasonable and plentiful provision which is made for all the creatures, v. 27, 28.

1. God is a bountiful benefactor to them: He gives them their meat; he opens his hand and they are filled with good. He supports the armies both of heaven and earth. Even the meanest creatures are not below his cognizance. He is open-handed in the gifts of his bounty, and is a great and good housekeeper that provides for so large a family.

2. They are patient expectants from him: They all wait upon him. They seek their food, according to the natural instinct God has put into them and in the proper season for it, and affect not any other food, or at any other time, than nature has ordained. They do their part for the obtaining of it: what God gives them they gather, and expect not that Providence should put it into their mouths; and what they gather they are satisfied with—they are filled with good. They desire no more than what God sees fit for them, which may shame our murmurings, and discontent, and dissatisfaction with our lot.

IV. For the absolute power and sovereign dominion which he has over all the creatures, by which every species is still continued, though the individuals of each are daily dying and dropping off. See here,

1. All the creatures perishing (v. 29): Thou hidest thy face, withdrawest thy supporting power, thy supplying bounty, and they are troubled immediately. Every creature has as necessary a dependence upon God's favors as every saint is sensible he has and therefore says with David (Ps. xxx. 7), Thou didst hide thy face and I was troubled. God's displeasure against this lower world for the sin of man is the cause of all the vanity and burden which the whole creation groans under. Thou takest away their breath, which is in thy hand, and then, and not till then, they die and return to their dust, to their first principles. The spirit of the beast, which goes downward, is at God's command, as well as the spirit of a man, which goes upward. The death of cattle was one of the plagues of Egypt, and is particularly taken notice of in the drowning of the world.

2. All preserved notwithstanding, in a succession (v. 30): Thou sendest forth thy spirit, they are created. The same spirit (that is, the same divine will and power) by which they were all created at first still preserves the several sorts of creatures in their

Psalm 104

22-28
22 The sun ariseth, they gather themselves together, and lay them down in their dens.
23 Man goeth forth unto his work and to his labor until the evening.
24 O LORD, how manifold are thy works! in wisdom hast thou made them all: the earth is full of thy riches.
25 So is this great and wide sea, wherein are things creeping innumerable, both small and great beasts.
26 There go the ships: there is that leviathan, whom thou hast made to play therein.
27 These wait all upon thee; that thou mayest give them their meat in due season.
28 That thou givest them they gather: thou openest thine hand, they are filled with good.

stooped beneath the conditions of the brutes to lift up worse than brutish men!
Verse 23. Man goeth forth. It is his turn now, and the sunrise has made things ready for him. His warm couch he forsakes and the comforts of home, to find his daily food; this work is good for him, both keeping him out of mischief, and exercising his faculties.
Verse 24. O Lord, how manifold are thy works. They are not only many for number but manifold for variety. Mineral, vegetable, animal—what a range of works is suggested by these three names! No two even of the same class are exactly alike, and the classes are more numerous than science can number. Works in the heavens above and in the earth beneath, and in the waters under the earth, works which abide the ages, works which come to perfection and pass away in a year, works which with all their beauty do not outlive a day, works within works, and works within these—who can number one of a thousand? God is the great worker, and ordainer of variety.
Verse 25. So is this great and wide sea. He gives an instance of the immense number and variety of Jehovah's works by pointing to the sea. "Look," saith he, "at yonder ocean, stretching itself on both hands and embracing so many lands, it too swarms with animal life, and in its deeps lie treasures beyond all counting. The heathen made the sea a different province from the land, and gave the command thereof to Neptune, but we know of a surety that Jehovah rules the waves." Wherein, are things creeping innumerable, both small and great beasts; read moving things and animals small arid great, and you have the true sense.
Verse 26. There go the ships. So that ocean is not altogether deserted of mankind. It is the highway of nations, and unites, rather than divides, distant lands. There is that leviathan, whom thou hast made to play therein. Them huge whale turns the sea into his recreation ground, and disports himself as God designed that he should do.
Verse 27. These wait all upon thee. They come around thee as fowls around the farmer's door at the time for feeding, and look up with expectation. Men or marmots, whales or minnows, they alike rely upon thy care. That thou mayest give them meat in due season; that is to say, when they need it and when it is ready for them. God has a time for all things, and does not feed his creatures by fits and starts; he gives them daily bread, and a quantity proportioned to their needs.
Verse 28. That thou givest them they gather. God gives it, but they must gather it, and they are glad that he does so, for otherwise their gathering would be in vain. We often forget that animals and birds in their free life have to work to obtain food even as we do; and yet it is true with them as with us that our heavenly Father feeds all.
Verse 29. Thou hidest thy face, they are troubled. So dependent are all living things upon God's smile, that a frown fills them with terror, as though convulsed with anguish. This is so in the natural world, and certainly not less so in the spiritual: saints when the Lord hides his face are in terrible perplexity. Thou takest away their breath, they die, and return to their dust. The breath appears to be a trifling matter, and the air an impalpable substance of but small importance, yet, once withdrawn, the body loses all vitality, and crumbles back to the earth from which it was originally taken.
Verse 30. Thou sendest forth thy spirit, they are created: and thou renewest the face of the earth. The loss of their breath destroys them, and by Jehovah's breath a new race is created. The works of the Lord are majestically simple, and are performed with royal ease—a breath creates, and its withdrawal destroys.
Verse 31. The glory of the LORD shall endure forever. His works may pass away, but not his glory. Were it only for what he has already done, the Lord deserves to be praised without ceasing. His personal being and character ensure that he would be glorious even were all the creatures dead.

particulars, that every one may be led from the consideration of them to reflect the more attentively on that wisdom by which God governs the whole world, and every particular part of it. Accordingly, breaking off his description, he exclaims with admiration,—How greatly to be praised are thy works! even as we then only ascribe to God due honor when seized with astonishment, we acknowledge that our tongues and all our senses fail us in doing justice to so great a subject. If a small portion of the works of God make us amazed, how inadequate are our feeble minds to comprehend the whole extent of them! In the first place, it is said, that God has made all things in wisdom, and then it is added, that the earth is full of his riches.

The mention of wisdom only is not intended to exclude the divine power, but the meaning is, that there is nothing in the world confused,—that, so far from this, the vast variety of things mixed together in it are arranged with the greatest wisdom, so as to render it impossible for any thing to be added, abstracted, or improved. This commendation is set in opposition to the unhallowed imaginations, which often creep upon us when we are unable to discover the designs of God in his works, as if indeed he were subject to folly like ourselves, so as to be forced to bear the reprehension of those who are blind in the consideration of his works. The prophet here bids us attend more carefully to the wisdom of God, and to that wonderful skill which shines forth in the whole government of the world.

Under riches are comprehended the goodness and beneficence of God; for it is not on his own account that he has so richly replenished the earth but on ours, that nothing which contributes to our advantage may be wanting. We ought to know that the earth does not possess such fruitfulness and riches of itself, but solely by the blessing of God, who makes it the means of administering to us his bounty.

25. Great is this sea, and wide in extent. After having treated of the evidences which the earth affords of the glory of God, the prophet goes down into the sea, and teaches us that it is a new mirror in which may be beheld the divine power and wisdom. Although the sea were not inhabited by fishes, yet the mere view of its vastness would excite our wonder, especially when at one time it swells with the winds and tempests, while at another it is calm and unruffled.

27-30

27. All these wait upon thee. The prophet here again describes God as acting the part of the master of a household, and a foster-father towards all sorts of living creatures, by providing liberally for them. He had said before, that God made food to grow on the mountains for the support of cattle, and that sustenance is ministered to the very lions by the hand of the same God, although they live upon prey. Now he amplifies this wonder of the divine beneficence by an additional circumstance. While the different species of living creatures are almost innumerable, and the number in each species is so great, there is yet not one of them which does not

being, and place, and usefulness; so that, though one generation of them passes away, another comes, and from time to time they are created; new ones rise up instead of the old ones, and this is a continual creation. Thus the face of the earth is renewed from day to day by the light of the sun (which beautifies it anew every morning), from year to year by the products of it, which enrich it anew every spring and put quite another face upon it from what it had all winter. The world is as full of creatures as if none died, for the place of those that die is filled up. This (the Jews say) is to be applied to the resurrection, which every spring is an emblem of, when a new world rises out of the ashes of the old one.

In the midst of this discourse the psalmist breaks out into wonder at the works of God (v. 24): O Lord! how manifold are thy works! They are numerous, they are various, of many kinds, and many of every kind; and yet in wisdom hast thou made them all. When men undertake many works, and of different kinds, commonly some of them are neglected and not done with due care; but God's works, though many and of very different kinds, are all made in wisdom and with the greatest exactness; there is not the least flaw nor defect in them. The works of art, the more closely they are looked upon with the help of microscopes, the more rough they appear; the works of nature through these glasses appear more fine and exact. They are all made in wisdom, for they are all made to answer the end they were designed to serve, the good of the universe, in order to the glory of the universal Monarch.

31-35 The divine bounty.

The psalmist concludes this meditation with speaking,

I. Praise to God, which is chiefly intended in the psalm.

1. He is to be praised,

(1.) As a great God, and a God of matchless perfection: The glory of the Lord shall endure for ever, v. 31. It shall endure to the end of time in his works of creation and providence; it shall endure to eternity in the felicity and adorations of saints and angels.

(2.) As a gracious God: The Lord shall rejoice in his works. He continues that complacency in the products of his own wisdom and goodness which he had when he saw every thing that he had made, and behold it was very good, and rested the seventh day. We often do that which, upon the review, we cannot rejoice in, but are displeased at, and wish undone again, blaming our own management. But God always rejoices in his works, because they are all done in wisdom.

(3.) As a God of almighty power (v. 32): He looks on the earth, and it trembles, as unable to bear his frowns—trembles, as Sinai did, at the presence of the Lord. He touches the hills, and they smoke. The volcanoes are emblems of the power of God's wrath

Psalm 104

29-25

29 Thou hidest thy face, they are troubled: thou takest away their breath, they die, and return to their dust.

30 Thou sendest forth thy spirit, they are created: and thou renewest the face of the earth.

31 The glory of the LORD shall endure for ever: the LORD shall rejoice in his works.

32 He looketh on the earth, and it trembleth: he toucheth the hills, and they smoke.

33 I will sing unto the LORD as long as I live: I will sing praise to my God while I have my being.

34 My meditation of him shall be sweet: I will be glad in the LORD.

35 Let the sinners be consumed out of the earth, and let the wicked be no more. Bless thou the LORD, O my soul. Praise ye the LORD.

Verse 32. He looketh on the earth, and it trembleth. The Lord who has graciously displayed his power in acts and works of goodness might, if he had seen fit, have overwhelmed us with the terrors of destruction, for even at a glance of his eye the solid earth rocks with fear. He toucheth the hills, and they smoke. Sinai was altogether on a smoke when the Lord descended upon it. It was but a touch, but it sufficed to make the mountain dissolve in flame. Even our God is a consuming fire. Woe unto those who shall provoke him to frown upon them, they shall perish at the touch of his hand. If sinners were not altogether insensible a glance of the Lord's eye would make them tremble, and the touches of his hand in affliction would set their hearts on fire with repentance.

Verse 33. I will sing unto the LORD as long as I live, or, literally, in my lives. Here and hereafter the psalmist would continue to praise the Lord, for the theme is an endless one, and remains for ever fresh and new. The birds sang God's praises before men were created, but redeemed men will sing his glories when the birds are no more. Jehovah, who ever lives and makes us to live shall be for ever exalted, and extolled in the songs of redeemed men. I will sing praise to my God while I have my being. A resolve both happy for himself and glorifying to the Lord. Note the sweet title—my God. We never sing so well as when we know that we have an interest in the good things of which we sing, and a relationship to the God whom we praise.

Verse 34. My meditation of him shall be sweet. Sweet both to him and to me. I shall be delighted thus to survey his works and think of his person, and he will graciously accept my notes of praise. Meditation is the soul of religion. It is the tree of life in the midst of the garden of piety, and refreshing is its fruit to the soul. And as it is good towards man, so is it towards God. As the fat of the sacrifice was the Lord's portion, so are our best meditations due to the Most High and are most acceptable to him. We ought, therefore, both for our own good and for the Lord's honor to be much occupied with meditation, and that meditation should chiefly dwell upon the Lord himself: it should be "meditation of him."

Verse 35. Let the sinners be consumed out of the earth, and let the wicked be no more. They are the only blot upon creation. In holy indignation the psalmist would fain rid the world of beings so base as not to love their gracious Creator, so blind as to rebel against their Benefactor. He does but ask for that which just men look forward to as the end of history: for the day is eminently to be desired when in all God's kingdom there shall not remain a single traitor or rebel. The Christian way of putting it will be to ask that grace may turn sinners into saints, and win the wicked to the ways of truth. Bless thou the LORD, O my soul. Here is the end of the matter—whatever sinners may do, do thou, my soul, stand to thy colors, and be true to thy calling. Their silence must not silence thee, but rather provoke thee to redoubled praise to make up for their failures.

stand in need of daily food. The meaning then of the expression, All things wait upon thee, is, that they could not continue in existence even for a few days, unless God were to supply their daily need, and to nourish each of them in particular. We thus see why there is so great a diversity of fruits; for God assigns and appoints to each species of living creatures the food suitable and proper for them.
29. Thou shalt hide thy face, and they shall be afraid. In these words, the Psalmist declares, that we stand or fall according to the will of God. We continue to live, so long as he sustains us by his power; but no sooner does he withdraw his life-giving spirit than we die. Even Plato knew this, who so often teaches that, properly speaking, there is but one God, and that all things subsist, or have their being only in him. Nor do I doubt, that it was the will of God, by means of that heathen writer, to awaken all men to the knowledge, that they derive their life from another source than from themselves.

31-35
31. Glory be to Jehovah for ever. The inspired writer shows for what purpose he has celebrated in the preceding part of the psalm the power, wisdom, and goodness of God in his works, namely, to stir up men to praise him. It is no small honor that God for our sake has so magnificently adorned the world, in order that we may not only be spectators of this beauteous theater, but also enjoy the multiplied abundance and variety of good things which are presented to us in it. Our gratitude in yielding to God the praise which is his due, is regarded by him as a singular recompense. What the Psalmist adds, Let Jehovah rejoice in his works, is not superfluous; for he desires that the order which God has established from the beginning may be continued in the lawful use of his gifts. As we read in Genesis 6:6, that "it repented the Lord that he had made man on the earth," so when he sees that the good things which he bestows are polluted by our corruptions, he ceases to take delight in bestowing them.
33. I will sing to Jehovah whilst I live. Here the Psalmist points out to others their duty by his own example, declaring, that throughout the whole course of his life he will proclaim the praises of God without ever growing weary of that exercise. The only boundary which he fixes to the celebration of God's praises is death; not that the saints, when they pass from this world into another state of existence, desist from this religious duty, but because the end for which we are created is, that the divine name may be celebrated by us on the earth. Conscious of his unworthiness to offer to God so precious a sacrifice, he humbly prays, (verse 34,) that the praises which he will sing to God may be acceptable to him, although they proceed from polluted lips.
35. Let sinners perish from the earth. This imprecation depends on the last clause of the 31st verse, Let Jehovah rejoice in his works As the wicked infect the world with their pollutions, the consequence is, that God has less delight in his own workmanship, and is even almost displeased with it. Men not only forget their Maker, but turn to a perverse end, whatever good things he has bestowed upon them.

fastening upon proud unhumbled sinners. God rejoices in his works because they are all so observant of him; and he will in like manner take pleasure in those that fear him and that tremble at his word.
2. The psalmist will himself be much in praising him (v. 33): "I will sing unto the Lord, unto my God, will praise him as Jehovah, the Creator, and as my God, a God in covenant with me, and this not now only, but as long as I live, and while I have my being." Because we have our being from God, and depend upon him for the support and continuance of it, as long as we live and have our being we must continue to praise God.
II. Joy to himself (v. 34): My meditation of him shall be sweet; it shall be fixed and close; it shall be affecting and influencing; and therefore it shall be sweet. Thoughts of God will then be most pleasing, when they are most powerful. Note, Divine meditation is a very sweet duty to all that are sanctified: "I will be glad in the Lord; it shall be a pleasure to me to praise him; I will be glad of all opportunities to set forth his glory; and I will rejoice in the Lord always and in him only." All my joys shall center in him, and in him they shall be full.

III. Terror to the wicked (v. 35): Let the sinners be consumed out of the earth; and let the wicked be no more.
1. Those that oppose the God of power, and fight against him, will certainly be consumed; none can prosper that harden themselves against the Almighty.
2. Those that rebel against the light of such convincing evidence of God's being, and refuse to serve him whom all the creatures serve, will justly be consumed. Those that make that earth to groan under the burden of their impieties which God thus fills with his riches deserve to be consumed out of it, and that it should spew them out.
3. Those that heartily desire to praise God themselves cannot but have a holy indignation at those that blaspheme and dishonor him, and a holy satisfaction in the prospect of their destruction and the honor that God will get to himself upon them. Even this ought to be the matter of their praise: "While sinners are consumed out of the earth, let my soul bless the Lord that I am not cast away with the workers of iniquity, but distinguished from them by the special grace of God. When the wicked are no more I hope to be praising God world without end; and therefore, Praise you the Lord; let all about me join with me in praising God. Hallelujah; sing praise to Jehovah." This is the first time that we meet with Hallelujah; and it comes in here upon occasion of the destruction of the wicked; and the last time we meet with it is upon a similar occasion. When the New-Testament Babylon is consumed, this is the burden of the song, Hallelujah, Rev. xix. 1, 3, 4, 6.

Psalm 105

1-8
1 O give thanks unto the LORD; call upon his name: make known his deeds among the people.
2 Sing unto him, sing psalms unto him: talk ye of all his wondrous works.
3 Glory ye in his holy name: let the heart of them rejoice that seek the LORD.
4 Seek the LORD, and his strength: seek his face evermore.
5 Remember his marvelous works that he hath done; his wonders, and the judgments of his mouth;
6 O ye seed of Abraham his servant, ye children of Jacob his chosen.
7 He is the LORD our God: his judgments are in all the earth.
8 He hath remembered his covenant for ever, the word which he commanded to a thousand generations.

Psalm 105

GENERAL REMARKS. This historical psalm was evidently composed by King David, for the first fifteen verses of it were used as a hymn at the carrying up of the ark from the house of Obededom, and we read in 1Ch 16:7, "Then on that day David delivered first this psalm to thank the Lord, into the hand of Asaph and his brethren." Such a song was suitable for the occasion, for it describes the movements of the Lord's people and his guardian care over them in every place, and all this on account of the covenant of which the ark, then removing, was a symbol. Our last psalm sang the opening chapters of Genesis, and this takes up its closing chapters and conducts us into Exodus and Numbers.

DIVISION. The first verses are full of joyful praise, and call upon the people to extol Jehovah, Ps 105:1-7; then the earliest days of the infant nation, are described, Ps 105:8-15; the going into Egypt, Ps 105:16-23, the coming forth from it with the Lord's outstretched arm, Ps 105:24-38, the journeying through the wilderness and the entrance into Canaan.
We are now among the long Psalms, as at other times we have been among the short ones. These varying lengths of the sacred poems should teach us not to lay down any law either of brevity or prolixity in either prayer or praise. Short petitions and single verses of hymns are often the best for public occasions, but there are seasons when a whole night of wrestling or an entire day of psalm slinging will be none too long. The Spirit is ever free in his operations, and is not to be confined with, the rules of conventional propriety. The wind bloweth as it listeth, and at one time rushes in short and rapid sweep, while at another it continues to refresh the earth hour after hour with its reviving breath.

EXPOSITION
Verse 1. O give thanks unto the Lord. Jehovah is the author of all our benefits, therefore let him have all our gratitude. Call upon his name, or call him by his name; proclaim his titles and fill the world with his renown. Make known his deeds among the people, or among the nations. Let the heathen hear of our God, that they may forsake their idols and learn to worship him.
Verse 2. Sing unto him. Bring your best thoughts and express them in the best language to the sweetest sounds. Take care that your singing is "unto him, "and not merely for the sake of the music or to delight the ears of others. Singing is so delightful an exercise that it is a pity so much or it should be wasted upon trifles or worse than trifles.
Verse 3. Glory ye in his holy name. Make it a matter of joy that you have such a God. His character and attributes are such as will never make you blush to call him your God. Idolaters may well be ashamed of the actions attributed to their fancied deities, their names are foul with lust and red with blood, but Jehovah is wholly glorious; every deed of his will bear the strictest scrutiny; his name is holy, his character is holy, his law is holy, his government is holy, his influence is holy. In all this we may make our boast, nor can any deny our right to do so.
Verse 4. Seek the Loan and his strength. Put yourselves under his protection. Regard him not as a puny God, but look unto his omnipotence, and seek to know the power of his grace.
Verse 5. Remember his marvelous works that he hath done. Memory is never better employed than upon such topics. Alas, we are far more ready to recollect foolish and evil things than to retain in our minds the glorious deeds of Jehovah. If we would keep these in remembrance our faith would be stronger, our gratitude warmer, our devotion more fervent, and our love more intense. Shame upon us that we should let slip what it would seem impossible to forget.

JOHN CALVIN

Psalm 105

1-5

1. Praise ye Jehovah, etc. The object of these opening words simply is, that the offspring of Abraham should place all their blessedness in the free adoption of God. It was indeed a blessing not to be despised that they had been created men, that they had been cherished in the world by God's fatherly care, and that they had received sustenance at his hand; but it was a far more distinguished privilege to have been chosen to be his peculiar people. While the whole human race are condemned in Adam, the condition of the Israelites was so different from all other nations, as to give them ground to boast, that they were consecrated to God. This is the reason why the prophet heaps together so many words in commendation of this grace.

4. Seek ye Jehovah, and his strength. Although he had in the preceding verse characterized the faithful by the honorable designation, those who seek God, yet he again exhorts them to earnestness in seeking him, which is not an unnecessary exhortation. Seeking God, it is true, is the mark by which all genuine saints are particularly distinguished from the men of the world; but they come far short of seeking him with due ardor; and, accordingly, they have always need of incitements, to urge them on to this exercise, although they run of their own accord.

6-11

6. Ye seed of Abraham his servant. The Psalmist addresses himself by name to his own countrymen, whom, as has been stated, God had bound to himself by a special adoption. It was a bond of union still more sacred, that by the mere good pleasure of God they were preferred to all other nations. By calling them the seed of Abraham, and the sons of Jacob, he reminds them that they had not attained so great dignity by their own power, but because they were descended from the holy fathers. He, however, affirms at the same time, that the holiness of their fathers flowed exclusively from God's election, and not from their own nature. He expressly states both these truths, first, that before they were born children of Abraham, they were already heirs of the covenant, because they derived their origin from the holy fathers; and, secondly, that the fathers themselves had not acquired this prerogative by their own merit or worth, but had been freely chosen; for this is the reason why Jacob is called God's chosen.

8. He hath remembered his covenant for ever. The Psalmist now celebrates the effect and actual fulfillment of the covenant, and proves from the deliverance wrought for the Israelites what he had stated before, namely, That God, while he reigned alike over all nations, extended his peculiar favor to the offspring of Abraham alone. How comes it to pass that God, in delivering his people, displayed the might of his arm by so many miracles, if it was not that he might faithfully perform the promise which he had made to his servants in time past?

11. Saying, I will give thee the land of Canaan. As this was only a small portion of the blessings offered to the fathers, the

MATTHEW HENRY

Psalm 105

1-7 An invitation to praise.

Our devotion is here warmly excited; and we are stirred up, that we may stir up ourselves to praise God. Observe,

I. The duties to which we are here called, and they are many, but the tendency of them all is to give unto God the glory due unto his name.

1. We must give thanks to him, as one who has always been our bountiful benefactor and requires only that we give him thanks for his favors—poor returns for rich receivings.

2. Call upon his name, as one whom you depend upon for further favors. Praying for further mercies is accepted as an acknowledgment of former mercies. Because he has inclined his ear unto me, therefore will I call upon him.

3. Make known his deeds (v. 1), that others may join with you in praising him. Talk of all his wondrous works (v. 2), as we talk of things that we are full of, and much affected with, and desire to fill others with.

4. Let the hearts of those rejoice that do seek him (v. 3); for they have chosen well, are well fixed, and well employed, and they may be sure that their labor will not be in vain, for he will not only be found, but he will be found the rewarder of those that diligently seek him. If those have reason to rejoice that seek the Lord, much more those that have found him.

II. Some arguments to quicken us to these duties.

1. "Consider both what he has said and what he has done to engage us for ever to him. You will see yourselves under all possible obligations to give thanks to him, and call upon his name, if you remember the wonders which should make deep and durable impressions upon you,—the wonders of his providence which he has wrought for you and those who are gone before you, the marvelous works that he has done, which will be had in everlasting remembrance with the thoughtful and with the grateful,—the wonders of his law, which he has written to you, and entrusted you with, the judgments of his mouth, as well as the judgments of his hand," v. 5.

2. "Consider the relation you stand in to him (v. 6): You are the seed of Abraham his servant; you are born in his house, and being thereby entitled to the privilege of his servants, protection and provision, you are also bound to do the duty of servants, to attend your Master, consult his honor, obey his commands, and do what you can to advance his interests. You are the children of Jacob his chosen, and are chosen and beloved for the fathers' sake, and therefore ought to tread in the steps of those whose honors you inherit. You are the children of godly parents; do not degenerate. You are God's church upon earth, and, if you do not praise him, who should?"

3. Consider your interest in him: He is the Lord our God, v. 7. We depend upon him, are devoted to him, and from him our expectation is.

Psalm 105

9-16

9 Which covenant he made with Abraham, and his oath unto Isaac;
10 And confirmed the same unto Jacob for a law, and to Israel for an everlasting covenant:
11 Saying, Unto thee will I give the land of Canaan, the lot of your inheritance:
12 When they were but a few men in number; yea, very few, and strangers in it.
13 When they went from one nation to another, from one kingdom to another people;
14 He suffered no man to do them wrong: yea, he reproved kings for their sakes;
15 Saying, Touch not mine anointed, and do my prophets no harm.
16 Moreover he called for a famine upon the land: he brake the whole staff of bread.

Verse 6. O ye seed of Abraham his servant, ye children of Jacob his chosen. Should all the world forget, ye are bound to remember. Your father Abraham saw his wonders and judgments upon Sodom, and upon the kings who came from far, and Jacob also saw the Lord's marvelous works in visiting the nations with famine, yet providing for his chosen a choice inheritance in a goodly land; therefore let the children praise their father's God.

Verse 7. He is the Lord our God. Blessed be his name. Jehovah condescends to be our God. This sentence contains a greater wealth of meaning than all the eloquence of orators can compass, and there is more joy in it than in all the sonnets of them that make merry. His judgments are in all the earth, or in all the land, for the whole of the country was instructed by his law, ruled by his statutes, and protected by his authority.

Verse 8. He hath remembered his covenant for ever. Here is the basis of all his dealings with his people: he had entered into covenant with them in their father Abraham, and to this covenant he remained faithful. The exhortation to remember (Ps 105:5) receives great force from the fact that God has remembered.

Verse 9. Which covenant he made with Abraham. When the victims were divided and the burning lamp passed between the pieces (Gen. 15.) then the Lord made, or ratified, the covenant with the patriarch. This was a solemn deed, performed not without blood, and the cutting in pieces of the sacrifice; it points us to the greater covenant which in Christ Jesus is signed, sealed, and ratified, that it may stand fast for ever and ever.

Verse 10. And confirmed the same unto Jacob for a law. Jacob in his wondrous dream (Ge 28:10-15) received a pledge that the Lord's mode of procedure with him would be in accordance with covenant relations: for said Jehovah, "I will not leave thee till I have done that which I have spoken to thee of." Thus, if we may so speak with all reverence, the covenant became a law unto the Lord himself by which he bound himself to act.

Verse 11. Saying, Unto thee will I give the land of Canaan, the lot of your inheritance. This repetition of the great covenant promise is recorded in Ge 35:9-12 in connection with the change of Jacob's name, and very soon after that slaughter of the Shechemites, which had put the patriarch into such great alarm and caused him to use language almost identical with that of the next verse.

Verse 12. When they were but a few men in number. Literally, men of number; so few as easily to be numbered: in opposition to what their posterity afterwards were, as the sand of the sea, without number.

Verse 13. When they went from one nation, to another, from one Kingdom to another people. Migrating as the patriarchs did from the region of one tribe to the country of another they were singularly preserved. The little wandering family might have been cut off root and branch had not a special mandate been issued from the throne for their protection.

Verse 14. He suffered no man to do them wrong. Men cannot wrong us unless he suffers them to do so; the greatest of them must wait his permission before they can place a finger upon us. The wicked would devour us if they could, but they cannot even cheat us of a farthing without divine sufferance.

Verse 15. Saying, touch not mine anointed, and do my prophets no harm. Abraham and his seed were in the midst of the world a generation of priests anointed to present sacrifice unto the most High God; since to them the oracles were committed, they were also the prophets of mankind; and they were kings too—a royal priesthood; hence they had received a threefold anointing. Their holy office surrounded them with a sacredness which rendered it sacrilege to molest them. The Lord was pleased to impress the wild tribes of Canaan with a respectful awe of the pious strangers who had come to abide with them, so that they came not near them to do them ill. The words here mentioned may not have been actually spoken, but the impression of awe which fell upon the nations is thus poetically described.

prophet seems at first view too much to limit the covenant of God, which extended even to the hope of an eternal inheritance. But he considered it enough to show, by the figure synecdoche, that a part of what God had promised to the fathers had received its complete accomplishment. His drift is to intimate that they did not possess the land of Canaan by any other right than because it was the legitimate inheritance of Abraham according to the covenant which God had made with him. If man exhibit the promised earnest of a contract, he does not violate the contract. When, therefore, the prophet proves by a visible symbol that God did not make a covenant with his servants in vain, and that he did not disappoint their hope, he does not take away or abolish the other blessings included in it.

12-15

12. When they were but very few in number. The prophet here recounts the benefits which God had conferred upon the holy fathers from the commencement, to manifest that even long before the deliverance from Egypt, the covenant was not ineffectual. The great object aimed at in this recital, is to show that ever since God took Abraham under his protection, he cherished him in a wonderful manner, and also that his fatherly love and care were displayed in maintaining and defending the other two patriarchs. When it is said, that they were but very few in number, the power of God by this circumstance is not only magnified, but the cause why he was so beneficent towards them is also pointed out. We must then attend to this, that the prophet, lest the Jews should arrogate anything to themselves, expressly declares, that their fathers had experienced the divine favor, even when they were feeble and despised, wandering from place to place, in every respect poor and miserable according to the flesh. Thus also Moses reproaches them, "The Lord did not set his love upon you, nor choose you, because ye were more in number than any people; for ye were the fewest of all people; but because the Lord loved you." Deuteronomy 7:7, 8. In short, in the choosing of this people, no regard was had either to number, or to any excellence whatever.

14. He did not suffer men to hurt them. Abraham and his children had not merely two or three enemies: they were harassed by whole nations. As then many rose up one after another in troops against them, the Psalmist says indefinitely, that men were withheld from hurting them.

15. Saying, Touch not my anointed ones. The Psalmist proceeds farther, affirming, that when God made war against kings for the sake of his servants, they were defended by him, not only as he is accustomed to succor the miserable and the unjustly oppressed, but because he had taken them under his special guardianship. God protects his people, not only upon a general ground, but because he has declared on account of his free adoption, that he will maintain them. This is the reason why these holy patriarchs are here honored with two designations, his prophets and his anointed ones.

8-24 The divine promise to the patriarchs; providences concerning the patriarchs.

Two things are here made the subject of praise:

I. God's promise to the patriarchs, that great promise that he would give to their seed the land of Canaan for an inheritance, which was a type of the promise of eternal life made in Christ to all believers. In all the marvelous works which God did for Israel he remembered his covenant (v. 8) and he will remember it for ever; it is the word which he commanded to a thousand generations.

II. His providences concerning the patriarchs while they were waiting for the accomplishment of this promise, which represent to us the care God takes of his people in this world, while they are yet on this side the heavenly Canaan; for these things happened unto them for examples and encouragements to all the heirs of promise, that life by faith as they did.

1. They were wonderfully protected and sheltered, and (as the Jewish masters express it) gathered under the wings of the divine Majesty. This is accounted for, v. 12-15. Here we may observe,

(1.) How they were exposed to injuries from men. To the three renowned patriarchs, Abraham, and Isaac, and Jacob, God's promises were very rich; again and again he told them he would be their God; but his performances in this world were so little proportionable that, if he had not prepared for them a city in the other world, he would have been ashamed to be called their God (see Heb. xi. 16), because he was always generous; and yet even in this world he was not wanting to them, but that he might appear, to do uncommon things for them, he exercised them with uncommon trials.

(2.) How they were guarded by the special providence of God, the wisdom and power of which were the more magnified by their being so many ways exposed, v. 14, 15. They were not able to help themselves and yet, no men were suffered to wrong them, but even those that hated them, and would gladly have done them a mischief, had their hands tied, and could not do what they would. This may refer to Gen. xxxv. 5, where we find that the terror of God (an unaccountable restraint) was upon the cities that were round about them, so that, though provoked, they did not pursue after the sons of Jacob.

2. They were wonderfully provided for and supplied. And here also,

(1.) They were reduced to great extremity. Even in Canaan, the land of promise, he called for a famine, v. 16.

(2.) God graciously took care for their relief. It was in obedience to his precept, and in dependence upon his promise, that they were now sojourners in Canaan, and therefore he could not in honor suffer any evil to befall them or any good thing to be wanting to them. As he restrained one Pharaoh from doing them wrong, so he raised up another to do them a kindness, by preferring and entrusting Joseph, of

Psalm 105

17-24
17 He sent a man before them, even Joseph, who was sold for a servant:
18 Whose feet they hurt with fetters: he was laid in iron:
19 Until the time that his word came: the word of the LORD tried him.
20 The king sent and loosed him; even the ruler of the people, and let him go free.
21 He made him lord of his house, and ruler of all his substance:
22 To bind his princes at his pleasure; and teach his senators wisdom.
23 Israel also came into Egypt; and Jacob sojourned in the land of Ham.
24 And he increased his people greatly; and made them stronger than their enemies.

Verse 16. Moreover he called for a famine upon the land. He had only to call for it as a man calls for his servant, and it came at once. How grateful ought we to be that he does not often call in that terrible servant of his, so meager and gaunt, and grim, so pitiless to the women and the children, so bitter to the strong men, who utterly fail before it.
Verse 17. He sent a man before them, even Joseph. He was the advance guard and pioneer for the whole clan. His brethren sold him, but God sent him. Where the hand of the wicked is visible God's hand may be invisibly at work, overruling their malice. No one was more of a man, or more fit to lead the van than Joseph: an interpreter of dreams was wanted, and his brethren had said of him, "Behold, this dreamer cometh." Who was sold for a servant, or rather for a slave. Joseph's journey into Egypt was not so costly as Jonah's voyage when he paid his own fare: his free passage was provided by the Midianites, who also secured his introduction to a great officer of state by handing him over as a Slave. His way to a position in which he could feed his family lay through the pit, the slaver's caravan, the slave market and the prison, and who shall deny but what it was the right way, the surest way, the wisest way, and perhaps the shortest way.
Verse 18. Whose feet they hurt with fetters. From this we learn a little more of Joseph's sufferings than we find in the book of Genesis: inspiration had not ceased, and David was as accurate an historian as Moses, for the same Spirit guided his pen. He was laid in iron, or "into iron came his soul." The prayer book version, "the iron entered into his soul," is ungrammatical, but probably expresses much the same truth. His fetters hurt his mind as well as his body, and well did Jacob say, "The archers shot at him, and sorely grieved him." Under the cruelly false accusation, which he could not disprove, his mind was, as it were, belted and bolted around with iron, and had not the Lord been with him he might have sunk under his sufferings.
Verse 19. Until the time that his word came. God has his times, and his children must wait till his "until" is fulfilled. Joseph was tried as in a furnace, until the Lord's assaying work was fully accomplished. The word of the chief butler was nothing, he had to wait until God's word came, and meanwhile the word of the Lord tried him.
Verse 20. The king sent and loosed him. He was thrust into the roundhouse by an officer, but he was released by the monarch himself. Even the ruler of the people, and let him go free. The tide had turned, so that Egypt's haughty potentate gave him a call from the prison to the palace. He had interpreted the dreams of captives, himself a captive; he must now interpret for a ruler and become a ruler himself. When God means to enlarge his prisoners, kings become his turnkeys.
Verse 21. He made him lord of his house. Reserving no power, but saying "only in the throne will I be greater than thou." The servitor of slaves becomes lord over nobles. How soon the Lord lifteth his chosen from the dunghill to set them among princes.
Verse 22. To bind his princes at his pleasure. He who was bound obtains authority to bind. He is no longer kept in prison, but keeps all the prisons, and casts into them the greatest nobles when justice demands it. And teach his senators wisdom. The heads of the various peoples, the elders of the nations, learned from him the science of government, the art of providing for the people. Joseph was a great instructor in political economy, and we doubt not that he mingled with it the purest morals, the most upright jurisprudence, and something of that divine wisdom without which the most able senators remain in darkness.
Verse 23. Israel also came into Egypt. The aged patriarch came, and with him that increasing company which bore his name. He was hard to bring there. Perhaps nothing short of the hope of seeing Joseph could have drawn him to take so long a journey from the tombs of his forefathers; but the divine will was accomplished and the church of God was removed into an enemy's country, where for a while it was nourished.

16-19

16. And he called a famine upon the land. Here the inspired writer recounts a most illustrious proof of divine providence towards the chosen people, at the time when the covenant might seem to be void and disannulled. The inheritance of the land of Canaan was added, as an earnest or pledge for confirmation. The descent of Jacob into Egypt, which deprived his house of the sight of the land, could not make the covenant to perish. In this the constancy of God shone forth the brighter; yea, by this trial he manifested more plainly how provident a father he was in preserving the seed of Abraham.

17. He sent a man before them. This whole passage graphically teaches us, that whatever befell that people was by the hand and counsel of God. The simple recital would have been to say, that the famine came upon the land, after Joseph had been sold by his brethren, and carried into Egypt. But the prophet speaks emphatically, declaring that Joseph by the divine counsel had been sent before into Egypt, to support his father's house, that afterwards the famine was called, and that then, by God's providence, a remedy was presented beyond all hope. This, indeed, is generally true in human affairs; but there is here commemorated a special care which God took in governing and nourishing his Church.

18. They afflicted his feet in the fetters. It is not without cause that the Psalmist prosecutes the winding course of Jacob's early history, which might so confuse the minds of men as to prevent them from directing their attention to the counsel of God. What seemed less likely than to believe that God, by so directly opposite and circuitous a path, meant to accomplish what he had purposed? But his providence, by surmounting so many obstacles, is brought out more conspicuously, than if he had dispatched the whole matter by a short and easy road. Had Joseph, as soon as he arrived in Egypt, been presented to the king, and made its governor, the way to what followed would have been easy.

19. Until the time that his word came. Here the prophet teaches, that although, according to the judgment of the flesh, God seems to be too tardy in his steps, yet he holds supreme rule over all things, that he may at length accomplish in due time what he has determined.

20-24

20. The king sent and loosed him. The Psalmist celebrates in high terms the deliverance of Joseph; for God's singular power was conspicuously displayed in a matter so incredible. What is of more rare occurrence than for a most powerful monarch to bring a stranger out of prison to constitute him ruler over his whole kingdom, and to raise him to a rank of honor, second only to himself?

23. And Israel came into Egypt. The prophet does not rehearse the whole history, nor was this necessary. He only presents to our view how divine providence was concerned in it, which very few consider in reading the narrative of Moses. He accordingly declares, that after Joseph had been sent before into Egypt, to be the means of supporting his father and the whole family, Jacob then came into Egypt, that is, he did so

whose story we have here an abstract. He was to be the shepherd and stone of Israel and to save that holy seed alive, Gen. xlix. 24; 1. 20. In order to this,

[1.] He was humbled, greatly humbled (v. 17, 18).

[2.] He was exalted, highly exalted. He continued a prisoner, neither tried nor bailed, until the time appointed of God for his release (v. 19), when his word came, that is, his interpretations of the dreams came to pass, and the report thereof came to Pharaoh's ears by the chief butler. And then the word of the Lord cleared him; that is, the power God gave him to foretell things to come rolled away the reproach his mistress had loaded him with; for it could not be thought that God would give such a power to so bad a man as he was represented to be.

3. They were wonderfully multiplied, according to the promise made to Abraham that his seed should be as the sand of the sea for multitude, v. 24. In Egypt he increased his people greatly; they multiplied like fishes, so that in a little time they became stronger than their enemies and formidable to them. Pharaoh took notice of it. Exod. i. 9, The children of Israel are more and mightier than we. When God pleases a little one shall become a thousand; and God's promises, though they work slowly, work surely.

25-45 Israel's deliverance out of Egypt.

After the history of the patriarchs follows here the history of the people of Israel, when they grew into a nation.

I. Their affliction in Egypt (v. 25): He turned the heart of the Egyptians, who had protected them, to hate them and deal subtilely with them. God's goodness to his people exasperated the Egyptians against them; and, though their old antipathy to the Hebrews (which we read of Gen. xliii. 32; xlvi. 34) was laid asleep for a while, yet now it revived with more violence than ever: formerly they hated them because they despised them, now because they feared them. They dealt subtilely with them, set all their politics on work to find out ways and means to weaken them, and waste them, and prevent their growth; they made their burdens heavy and their lives bitter, and slew their male children as soon as they were born. Malice is crafty to destroy: Satan has the serpent's subtlety, with his venom. It was God that turned the hearts of the Egyptians against them; for every creature is that to us that he makes it to be, a friend or an enemy. Though God is not the author of the sins of men, yet he serves his own purposes by them.

II. Their deliverance out of Egypt, that work of wonder, which, that it might never be forgotten, is put into the preface to the ten commandments. Observe,

1. The instruments employed in that deliverance (v. 26): He sent Moses his servant on this errand and joined Aaron in commission with him. Moses was designed to be their lawgiver and chief magistrate, Aaron to be their chief priest; and therefore, that they might respect them the more and submit to them the

Psalm 105

25-32

25 He turned their heart to hate his people, to deal subtilly with his servants.
26 He sent Moses his servant; and Aaron whom he had chosen.
27 They shewed his signs among them, and wonders in the land of Ham.
28 He sent darkness, and made it dark; and they rebelled not against his word.
29 He turned their waters into blood, and slew their fish.
30 Their land brought forth frogs in abundance, in the chambers of their kings.
31 He spake, and there came divers sorts of flies, and lice in all their coasts.
32 He gave them hail for rain, and flaming fire in their land.

Verse 24. And he increased his people greatly. In Goshen they seem to have increased rapidly from the first, and this excited the fears of the Egypt, inns, so that they tried to retard their increase by oppression, but the Lord continued to bless them.

Verse 25. He turned their hearts to hate his people. It was his goodness to Israel which called forth the ill will of the Egyptian court, and so far the Lord caused it, and moreover he made use of this feeling to lead on to the discomfort of his people, and so to their readiness to leave the land to which they had evidently become greatly attached. Thus far but no further did the Lord turn the hearts of the Egyptians. God cannot in any sense be the author of sin so far as to be morally responsible for its existence, but it often happens through the evil which is inherent in human nature that the acts of the Lord arouse the ill feelings of ungodly men.

Verse 26. He sent Moses his servant; and Aaron whom he had chosen. When the oppression was at the worst, Moses came. For the second time we have here the expression, "he sent"; he who sent Joseph sent also Moses and his eloquent brother. The Lord had the men in readiness and all he had to do was to commission them and thrust them forward.

Verse 27. They showed his signs among them, and wonders in the land of Ham. The miracles which were wrought by Moses were the Lord's, not his own: signs, as being the marks of Jehovah's presence hence they are here called "his" and power. The plagues were "words of his signs" (see margin), that is to say, they were speaking marvels, which testified more plainly than words to the omnipotence of Jehovah, to his determination to be obeyed, to his anger at the obstinacy of Pharaoh. Never were discourses more plain, pointed, personal, or powerful, and yet it took ten of them to accomplish the end designed.

Verse 28. He sent darkness, and made it dark. It was no natural or common darkness to be accounted for by the blinding dust, it was beyond all precedent and out of the range of ordinary events. It was a horrible palpable obscurity which men felt clinging about them as though it were a robe of death. It was a thick darkness, a total darkness, a darkness which lasted three days, a darkness in which no one dared to stir. What a condition to be in! This plague is first mentioned, thought it is not first in order, because it fitly describes all the period of the plagues: the land was in the darkness of sorrow, and in the darkness of sin all the time. If we shudder as we think of that long and terrible gloom, let us reflect upon the gross darkness which still covers heathen lands as the result of sin, for it is one of the chief plagues which iniquity creates for itself. May the day soon come when the people which sit in darkness shall see a great light.

Verse 29. He turned their waters into blood, and slew their fish. So that the plague was not a mere coloring of the water with red earth, as some suppose, but the river was offensive and fatal to the fish. The beloved Nile and other streams were all equally tainted and ensanguined. Their commonest mercy became their greatest curse.

Verse 30. Their land brought forth frogs in abundance. If fish could not live frogs might, yea, they multiplied both on land and in the water till they swarmed beyond all count. In the chambers of their kings. They penetrated the choicest rooms of the palace, and were found upon the couches of state.

Verse 31. He spake. See the power of the divine word. He had only to say it and it was done: and there came divers sorts of flies. Insects of various annoying kinds came up in infinite hordes, a mixture of biting, stinging, buzzing gnats, mosquitoes, files, beetles, and other vermin such as make men's flesh their prey, the place of deposit for their eggs, and the seat of peculiar torments.

Verse 32. He gave them hail for rain. They seldom had rain, but now the showers assumed the form of heavy, destructive hail storms, and being accompanied with a hurricane and thunderstorm, they were overwhelming, terrible, and destructive.

when all things were admirably arranged, that he might find abundance of bread among a people, the proudest of the whole world, when all others were perishing for want of food. From this it appears, that what is accounted to be slowness in God, tends to no other end than to accomplish his work on the best possible occasion.

24. And he greatly increased his people. The singular favor of God towards his Church is now commended by the additional circumstance, that within a short space of time, the chosen people increased beyond the common proportion. In this matter the wonderful blessing of God was strikingly displayed. So much the more offensive then is the barking of some dogs, who insolently scoff at the account given by Moses of the multiplying of the people, because it goes far beyond what takes place in the ordinary course of things. Had the people increased only at the common rate, these persons would have immediately objected, that therein no work of God was to be seen.

25-30

25. He turned their heart, so that they hated his people. The Egyptians, though at first kind and courteous hosts to the Israelites, became afterwards cruel enemies; and this also the prophet ascribes to the counsel of God. They were undoubtedly driven to this by a perverse and malignant spirit, by pride and covetousness; but still such a thing did not happen without the providence of God, who in an incomprehensible manner so accomplishes his work in the reprobate, as that he brings forth light even out of darkness.

26. He sent Moses his servant. Here the prophet briefly adverts to such things regarding the deliverance of the people as were worthy of particular notice. Had the Egyptians of their own accord suffered the people to depart, neither the service of Moses nor miracles would have been required. God then appointed that their deliverance should take place in such a way, as would render the denial of his being its author impossible. Moses is called the servant of the Lord, to teach us that he was not self-elected to his office, and that he attempted nothing by his own authority, but, being the minister of God, executed the office with which he had been intrusted.

27. They set among them the words of his signs. The prophet briefly glances at those things which Moses has detailed at greater length. Nor does he follow the order of the events observed in the history; for he contents himself with showing, that the deliverance of the chosen people was the work of God. He again distinguishes between the power of God, and the ministry of Moses and Aaron. He indeed asserts that these men performed miracles, but these miracles proceeded from God, so that celestial power was not obscurely displayed by their instrumentality.

28. In the 28th verse he specifics one of these miracles, which yet was not the first in order, but from which it is easy to gather that God was the author of the deliverance of Israel, and in which the course of nature was entirely changed; for nothing is more astonishing than to see the light turned into darkness. In the second clause, he commends the faithfulness

more cheerfully, God made use of them as their deliverers.

2. The means of accomplishing that deliverance; these were the plagues of Egypt. Moses and Aaron observed their orders, in summoning them just as God appointed them, and they rebelled not against his word (v. 28) as Jonah did, who, when he was sent to denounce God's judgments against Nineveh, went to Tarshish. Moses and Aaron were not moved, either with a foolish fear of Pharaoh's wrath or a foolish pity of Egypt's misery, to relax or retard any of the plagues which God ordered them to inflict on the Egyptians, but stretched forth their hand to inflict them as God appointed. Those that are instructed to execute judgment will find their remissness construed as a rebellion against God's word. The plagues of Egypt are here called God's signs, and his wonders (v. 27); they were not only proofs of his power, but tokens of his wrath, and to be looked upon with admiration and holy awe. They showed the words of his signs (so it is in the original), for every plague had an exposition going along with it; they were not, as the common works of creation and providence, silent signs, but speaking ones, and they spoke aloud. They are all or most of them here specified, though not in the order in which they were inflicted.

(1.) The plague of darkness, v. 28.

(2.) The turning of the river Nilus (which they idolized) into blood, and all their other waters, which slew their fish (v. 29), and so they were deprived, not only of their drink, but of the daintiest of their meat, Num. xi. 5.

(3.) The frogs, shoals of which their land brought forth, which poured in upon them, not only in such numbers, but with such fury, that they could not keep them out of the chambers of their kings and great men, whose hearts had been full of vermin, more nauseous and more noxious-contempt of, and enmity to, both God and his Israel.

(4.) Flies of divers sorts swarmed in their air, and lice in their clothes, v. 31.

(5.) Hail-stones shattered their trees, even the strongest timber-trees in their coasts, and killed their vines, and their other fruit-trees, v. 32, 33.

(6.) Locusts and caterpillars destroyed all the herbs which were made for the service of man and ate the bread out of their mouths, v. 34, 35.

(7.) Having mentioned all the plagues but those of the murrain and boils, he concludes with that which gave the conquering stroke, and that was the death of the first-born, v. 36.

3. The mercies that accompanied this deliverance. In their bondage,

(1.) They had been impoverished, and yet they came out rich and wealthy. God not only brought them forth, but he brought them forth with silver and gold, v. 37. God empowered them to ask and collect the contributions of their neighbors (which were indeed but part of payment for the service they had done

Psalm 105

33-38
33 He smote their vines also and their fig trees; and brake the trees of their coasts.
34 He spake, and the locusts came, and caterpillars, and that without number,
35 And did eat up all the herbs in their land, and devoured the fruit of their ground.
36 He smote also all the firstborn in their land, the chief of all their strength.
37 He brought them forth also with silver and gold: and there was not one feeble person among their tribes.
38 Egypt was glad when they departed: for the fear of them fell upon them.

Verse 33. He smote their vines also and their fig trees. So that all hope of gathering their best fruits was gone, and the trees were injured for future bearing. All the crops were destroyed, and these are mentioned as being the more prominent forms of their produce, used by them both at festivals and in common meals. And brake the trees of their coasts. From end to end of Egypt the trees were battered and broken by the terrible hailstorm. God is in earnest when he deals with proud spirits, he will either end them or mend them.

Verse 34. He spoke, and the locusts came, and caterpillars, and that without number. One word from the Captain and the armies leap forward. The expression is very striking, and sets forth the immediate result of the divine word.

Verse 35. Did eat up all the herbs. The locusts had devoured every green herb and every blade of grass; and had it not been for the reeds, on which our cattle entirely subsisted while we skirted the banks of the river, the journey must have been discontinued, at least in the line that had been proposed.

Verse 36. Are smote also all the firstborn in their land, the chief of all their strength. Now came the master blow. The Lord spoke before, but now he smites; before he only smote vines, but now he strikes men themselves.

Verse 37. He brought them forth also with silver and gold. This they asked of the Egyptians, perhaps even demanded, and well they might, for they had been robbed and spoiled for many a day, and it was not meet that they should go forth empty handed. Glad were the Egyptians to hand over their jewels to propitiate a people who had such a terrible friend above; they needed no undue pressure, they feared them too much to deny them their requests. The Israelites were compelled to leave their houses and lands behind them, and it was but justice that they should be able to turn these into portable property.

Verse 38. Egypt was glad when they departed, which would not have been the case had the gold and silver been borrowed by the Israelites, for men do not carry their goods into a far country. The awe of God like to see borrowers lad to nay them to be was on Egypt, and they feared his people and were glad to pay them to be gone. What a change from the time when the sons of Jacob were the drudges of the land, the offscouring of all things, the brick makers whose toil was only requited by the lash or the stick. Now they were reverenced as prophets and priests; for the fear of them fell upon them, the people proceeded even to a superstitious terror them. Thus with cheers and good wishes their former taskmasters sent them on their way: Pharaoh was foiled and the chosen people were once more on the move, journeying to the place which the Lord had given to them by a covenant of salt. "O give thanks unto Jehovah; call upon his name, make known his deeds among the people."

Verse 39. He spread a cloud for a covering. Never people were so favored. What would not travelers in the desert now give for such a canopy? The sun could not scorch them with its burning ray; their whole camp was screened like a king in his pavilion. Nothing seemed to be too good for God to give his chosen nation, their comfort was studied in every way. And fire to give light in the night. While cities were swathed in darkness, their town of tents enjoyed a light which modern art with all its appliances cannot equal. God himself was their sun and shield, their glory and their defense.

Verse 40. The people asked. But how badly, how wickedly! And yet his grace forgave the sin of their murmuring and heard its meaning: or perhaps we may consider that while the multitude murmured there were a few, who were really gracious people, who prayed, and therefore the blessing came. He brought quails, and satisfied them with the bread of heaven. He gave them what they asked amiss as well as what was good for them, mingling judgment with goodness, for their discipline.

Verse 41. He opened the rock, and the waters gushed out. With Moses' rod and his own word he cleft the rock in the desert, and forth leaped abundant

of Moses and Aaron, in courageously executing whatever God had commanded them: And they were not rebellious against his words. There was, as if it had been said, the most perfect harmony between the command of God and the obedience of both his servants.
29. He turned their waters into blood. How grievous this plague was to the Egyptians may be conjectured from the consideration, that the element of water is one of the two great means of supporting life. And the power of God shines forth the brighter, from the fact, that although the land of Egypt is well irrigated, yet the Egyptians were parched with drought amidst abundance of water. It is afterwards said, that frogs were brought forth, and entered even into the chambers of the kings; by which God manifestly evinced that he was the author of the miracle; for although all Egypt swarmed with frogs, the courts of the kings ought to have been exempt from this nuisance.
31. He spake, and there came a swarm of flies. By the word spake the Psalmist intimates that the flies and lice came not forth by chance. The command, we know, was uttered by the mouth of Moses; for although God could have given the command himself, he interposed Moses as his herald. God, however, gave no less efficacy to his word, when he commanded it to be uttered by a man, than if he himself had thundered from heaven.
34. He spake, and the grasshopper came. This calamity, which was brought upon the fields, could not be attributed to Fortune; for the grasshoppers made their appearance suddenly and in countless multitudes, so that they covered all the land of Egypt. The miracle was very evident from the word spoken, by which it was introduced. Its being announced as to happen, removed all doubt of its being the work of the Most High.
37. And he brought them forth with silver and gold. The prophet celebrates the grace of God which preserved the chosen people untouched and safe from all these plagues. If both parties had been indiscriminately afflicted with them, the hand of God would not have been so signally manifest. But now when the Israelites, amidst so many calamities, experienced an entire exemption from harm, this difference exhibits to us, as in a picture, God's fatherly care about his own people. For this reason, it is stated, Nor was there a feeble person, or one who stumbled. But I prefer taking it simply in this sense, That whilst Egypt was hastening to destruction, the people of God were vigorous, and free from every malady. When it is said, He brought them forth, and when it is afterwards added, in his tribes, there is a change of the number, which is quite common in the Hebrew language.
38. Egypt rejoiced at their departure. The Psalmist sets forth the power of God from the additional circumstance that the Egyptians willingly allowed the chosen people to depart, when yet nothing was farther from their intention. Although they wished them destroyed a hundred times, yet they thought that they had the wolf by the ears, as we say; and thus the fear of revenge made them more determined to blot out the memory of that people.
39-43
39. He spread out a cloud for a covering. The Psalmist enumerates certain miracles by which God continued his grace

them) and inclined the Egyptians to furnish them with what they asked. Their wealth was his, and therefore he might, their hearts were in his hand, and therefore he could, give it to the Israelites.
(2.) Their lives had been made bitter to them, and their bodies and spirits broken by their bondage; and yet, when God brought them forth, there was not one feeble person, none sick, none so much as sickly, among their tribes. They went out that very night that the plague swept away all the first-born of Egypt, and yet they went out all in good health, and brought not with them any of the diseases of Egypt. Surely never was the like, that among so many thousands there was not one sick! So false was the representation which the enemies of the Jews, in after-ages, gave of this matter, that they were all sick of a leprosy, or some loathsome disease, and that therefore the Egyptians thrust them out of their land.
(3.) They had been trampled upon and insulted over; and yet they were brought out with honor (v. 38): Egypt was glad when they departed; for God had so wonderfully owned them, and pleaded their cause, that the fear of Israel fell upon them, and they owned themselves baffled and overcome. God can and will make his church a burdensome stone to all that heave at it and seek to displace it, so that those shall think themselves happy that get out of its way, Zech. xii. 3. When God judges, he will overcome.
(4.) They had spent their days in sorrow and in sighing, by reason of their bondage; but now he brought them forth with joy and gladness, v. 43. When Egypt's cry for grief was loud, their first-born being all slain, Israel's shouts for joy were as loud, both when they looked back upon the land of slavery out of which they were rescued and when they looked forward to the pleasant land to which they were hastening. God now put a new song into their mouth.

4. The special care God took of them in the wilderness.
(1.) For their shelter. Besides the canopy of heaven, he provided them another heavenly canopy: He spread a cloud for a covering (v. 39), which was to them not only a screen and umbrella, but a cloth of state. A cloud was often God's pavilion (Ps. xviii. 11) and now it was Israel's; for they also were his hidden ones.
(2.) For their guidance and refreshment in the dark. He appointed a pillar of fire to give light in the night, that they might never be at a loss. Note, God graciously provides against all the grievances of his people, and furnishes them with convenient succors for every condition, for day and night, till they come to heaven, where it will be all day to eternity.
(3.) He fed them both with necessaries and dainties. Sometimes he furnished their tables with wild fowl (v. 40): The people asked, and he brought quails; and, when they were not thus feasted, yet they were abundantly satisfied with the bread of heaven. And, as every bit they ate had miracle in it, so had every

Psalm 105

39-45
39 He spread a cloud for a covering; and fire to give light in the night.
40 The people asked, and he brought quails, and satisfied them with the bread of heaven.
41 He opened the rock, and the waters gushed out; they ran in the dry places like a river.
42 For he remembered his holy promise, and Abraham his servant.
43 And he brought forth his people with joy, and his chosen with gladness:
44 And gave them the lands of the heathen: and they inherited the labor of the people;
45 That they might observe his statutes, and keep his laws. Praise ye the LORD.

floods for their drinking where they had feared to die of thirst. From most unlikely sources the all sufficient God can supply his people's needs; hard rocks become springing fountains at the Lord's command. They ran in the dry places like a river: so that those at a distance from the rock could stoop down and refresh themselves, and the stream flowed on, so that in future journeyings they were supplied. The desert sand would naturally swallow up the streams, and yet it did not so, the refreshing river ran "in the dry places." We know that the rock set forth our Lord Jesus Christ, from whom there flows a fountain of living waters which shall never be exhausted till the last pilgrim has crossed the Jordan and entered Canaan.

Verse 42. For he remembered his holy promise, and Abraham his servant. Here is the secret reason for all this grace. The covenant and he for whose sake it was made are ever on the heart of the Most High. He remembered his people because he remembered his covenant. He could not violate that gracious compact for it was sacred to him,—"his holy promise." A holy God must keep his promise holy. In our case the Lord's eye is upon his beloved Son, and his engagements with him.

Verse 43. And he brought forth his people with joy, and his chosen with gladness. Up from the wilderness he led them, rejoicing over them himself and making them rejoice too. They were his people, his chosen, and hence in them he rejoiced, and upon them he showered his favors, that they might rejoice in him as their God, and their portion.

Verse 44. And gave them the lands of the heathen. He drove out the Canaanites and allotted the lands to the tribes. They were called on to fight, but the Lord wrought so wonderfully that the conquest was not effected by their bow or spear—the Lord gave them the land. And they inherited the labor of the people, they dwelt in houses which they had not built, and gathered fruit front vines and olives which they had not planted.

Verse 45. That they might observe his statutes, and keep his laws. This was the practical design of it all. The chosen nation was to be the conservator of truth, the exemplar of morality, the pattern of devotion: everything was so ordered as to place them in advantageous circumstances for fulfilling this trust. Theirs was a high calling and a glorious election. It involved great responsibilities, but it was in itself a distinguished blessing, and one for which the nation was bound to give thanks. Most justly then did the music close with the jubilant but solemn shout of HALLELUJAH. Praise ye the Lord. If this history did trot make Israel praise God, what would?

towards his people in the wilderness. This order is worthy of notice; for it was no small confirmation which was added to that incomparable work of redemption, when God ceased not to show himself the guide of their journey. Accordingly, after they had passed through the Red Sea, he spread a cloud over them by day to protect them from the heat of the sun; and during the night, he gave them light by a pillar of fire, that even in the midst of the darkness they might have a bright token of his presence. This continued display of his goodness was surely an unquestionable proof of his perpetual love, an open demonstration that he had adopted the children of Abraham, to foster them under his protection even to the end.
42. For he remembered his holy promise. The Psalmist again mentions the cause why God dealt so graciously with that people, and sustained them so tenderly, namely, that he might fulfill his promise; for he had entered into a covenant with Abraham, engaging to be the God of his seed. Nor did the prophets without cause teach so carefully as we find them doing, that the free covenant is the fountain whence the deliverance, and the continual welfare of the people flowed.
43. And he brought forth his people with joy. The prophet makes mention of joy and gladness, the more highly to magnify the greatness of God's grace. It was no small matter, that at the very time when the Egyptians were afflicted by a severe and dreadful plague,—when the whole kingdom was full of weeping and howling,—and when in almost every house there was a dead body,—the people who a little before were groaning in great distress, or rather lay almost dead, went forth with joyful hearts. By the appellation the chosen of God, they are reminded, that his favor was not thus exercised towards them on account of their own merits, but because he had adopted them, that men having nothing left them in which to vaunt themselves might learn to glory in God alone.

44-45
44. And he gave them the countries of the nations. The Psalmist sets forth the final cause why God in so many ways displayed his wonderful power in redeeming the people, why he did not cease to cherish and defend them in the deserts—why he gave them the possession of the land as he had promised; and this was, that they might dedicate and devote themselves wholly to his service. And, in fact, the end which God proposed in our election was, that he might have on the earth a people by whom he should be called upon and served. The more effectually to stir up the Jews to gratitude, the prophet magnifies the greatness of the divine goodness, by declaring, that they occupied far and wide the countries of the nations, and that all the property which many states had acquired with great labor, they now possessed as it were by right of inheritance. The plural number, both as to the word countries and nations, serves to exhibit in a still more striking light the divine goodness in this matter. The psalm concludes with briefly defining the manner of glorifying God, That they might keep his law It would not be enough to celebrate his grace only with the tongue.

drop they drank: He opened the rock, and the waters gushed out, v. 41. Common providence fetches waters from heaven, and bread out of the earth; but for Israel the divine power brings bread from the clouds and water from the rocks: so far is the God of nature from being tied to the laws and courses of nature. The water did not only gush out once, but it ran like a river, plentifully and constantly, and attended their camp in all their removes; hence they are said to have the rock follow them (1 Cor. x. 4), and, which increased the miracle, this river of God (so it might be truly called) ran in dry places, and yet was not drunk in and lost, as one would have expected it to be, by the sands of the desert of Arabia. To this that promise alludes, I will give rivers in the desert, to give drink to my chosen, Isa. xliii. 19, 20.

5. Their entrance, at length, into Canaan (v. 44): He gave them the lands of the heathen, put them in possession of that which they had long been put in hopes of; and what the Canaanites had taken pains for God's Israel had the enjoyment of: They inherited the labor of the people; and the wealth of the sinner is laid up for the just. The Egyptians had long inherited their labors, and now they inherited the labors of the Canaanites. Thus sometimes one enemy of the church is made to pay another's scores.

6. The reasons why God did all this for them.
(1.) Because he would himself perform the promises of the word, v. 42. They were unworthy and unthankful, yet he did those great things in their favor because he remembered the word of his holiness (that is, his covenant) with Abraham his servant, and he would not suffer one iota or tittle of that to fall to the ground. See Deut. vii. 8.
(2.) Because he would have them to perform the precepts of the word, to bind them to which was the greatest kindness he could put upon them. He put them in possession of Canaan, not that they might live in plenty and pleasure, in ease and honor, and might make a figure among the nations, but that they might observe his statutes and keep his laws and that, God having thus done them good, they might the more cheerfully receive his law, concluding that also designed for their good, and might be sensible of their obligations in gratitude to live in obedience to him. We are therefore made, maintained, and redeemed, that we may live in obedience to the will of God; and the hallelujah with which the psalm concludes may be taken both as a thankful acknowledgment of God's favors and as a cheerful concurrence with this great intention of them. Has God done so much for us, and yet does he expect so little from us? Praise you the Lord.

Psalm 106

1-8
1 Praise ye the LORD. O give thanks unto the LORD; for he is good: for his mercy endureth for ever.
2 Who can utter the mighty acts of the LORD? who can shew forth all his praise?
3 Blessed are they that keep judgment, and he that doeth righteousness at all times.
4 Remember me, O LORD, with the favor that thou bearest unto thy people: O visit me with thy salvation;
5 That I may see the good of thy chosen, that I may rejoice in the gladness of thy nation, that I may glory with thine inheritance.
6 We have sinned with our fathers, we have committed iniquity, we have done wickedly.
7 Our fathers understood not thy wonders in Egypt; they remembered not the multitude of thy mercies; but provoked him at the sea, even at the Red sea.
8 Nevertheless he saved them for his name's sake, that he might make his mighty power to be known.

Psalm 106

GENERAL REMARKS. This Psalm begins and ends with Hallelujah—"Praise ye the Lord." The space between these two descriptions of praise is filled up with the mournful details of Israel's sin, and the extraordinary patience of God; and truly we do well to bless the Lord both at the beginning and the end of our meditations when sin and grace are the themes. This sacred song is occupied with the historical part of the Old Testament, and is one of many which are thus composed: surely this should be a sufficient rebuke to those who speak slightingly of the historical Scriptures; it in becomes a child of God to think lightly of that which the Holy Spirit so frequently uses for our instruction. What other Scriptures had David beside those very histories which are so depreciated, and yet he esteemed them beyond his necessary food, and made them his songs in the house of his pilgrimage?

Israel's history is here written with the view of showing human sin, even as the preceding psalm was composed to magnify divine goodness. It is, in fact, a national confession, and includes an acknowledgment of the transgressions of Israel in Egypt, in the wilderness, and in Canaan, with devout petitions for forgiveness such as rendered the Psalm suitable for use in all succeeding generations, and especially in times of national captivity. It was probably written by David,—at any rate its first and last two verses are to be found in that sacred song which David delivered to Asaph when he brought up the ark of the Lord (1Ch 16:34,35,36). While we are studying this holy Psalm, let us all along see ourselves in the Lord's ancient people, and bemoan our own provocations of the Most High, at the same time admiring his infinite patience, and adoring him because of it. May the Holy Spirit sanctify it to the promotion of humility and gratitude.

DIVISION. Praise and prayer are blended in the introduction (Ps 106:1-5). Then comes the story of the nation's sins, which continues till the closing prayer and praise of the last two verses. While making confession the Psalmist acknowledges the sins committed in Egypt and at the Red Sea (Ps 106:6-12), the lusting in the wilderness (Ps 106:13-15), the envying of Moses and Aaron (Ps 106:16-18), the worship of the golden calf (Ps 106:19-23) the despising of the promised land (Ps 106:24-27), the iniquity of Baal Peor (Ps 106:28-30), and the waters of Meribah (Ps 106:28-33). Then he owns the failure of Israel when settled in Canaan, and mentions their consequent chastisement (Ps 106:34-44), together with the quick compassion which came to their relief when they were brought low (Ps 106:44-46). The closing prayer and doxology fill up the remaining verses.

EXPOSITION

Verse 1. Praise ye the Lord. Hallelujah. Praise ye Jah. This song is for the assembled people, and they are all exhorted to join in praise to Jehovah. It is not meet for a few to praise and the rest to be silent; but all should join. If David were present in churches where quartets and choirs carry on all the singing, he would turn to the congregation and say, "Praise ye the Lord."

Verse 2. Who can utter the mighty acts of the LORD? What tongue of men or angels can duly describe the great displays of divine power? They are unutterable. Even those who saw them could not fully tell them. Who can shew forth all his praise? To declare his works is the same thing as to praise him, for his own doings are his best commendation.

Verse 3. Since the Lord is so good and so worthy to be praised, it must be for our happiness to obey him. Blessed are they that keep judgment, and he that doeth righteousness at all times. Multiplied are the blessings which must descend upon the whole company of the keepers of the way of justice, and especially upon that one rare man who at all times follows that which is right. Holiness is happiness.

Verse 4. Remember me, O Lord, with the favor which thou bearest unto thy people. Insignificant as I am, do not forget me. Think of me with kindness,

JOHN CALVIN

Psalm 106

1-5

1. Praise ye Jehovah. This exhortation supplies the want of a title; not that the psalm contains nothing else than thanksgiving and praise to God, but that the people, from the experience of past favors, may obtain the assurance of reconciliation; and thus entertain the hope that God, although at present offended, would soon be pacified towards them. In celebrating the praises of God, therefore, he orders them to call to mind such things as would have a tendency to assuage their grief on account of present ills, and to animate their spirits, and prevent them from sinking into despair.

2. Who shall express. This verse is capable of two interpretations; for if you read it in connection with the one immediately following, the sense will be, that all men are not alike equal to the task of praising God, because the ungodly and the wicked do nothing else than profane his holy name with their unclean lips; as it is said in the fiftieth psalm: "But unto the wicked God saith, What hast thou to do to declare my statutes, or that thou shouldest take my covenant in thy mouth?" And hence to this sentence the following clause should have been annexed, in the form of a reply, Blessed are they that keep judgment I am of opinion, however, that the prophet had another design, namely, that there is no man who has ever endeavored to concentrate all his energies, both physical and mental, in the praising of God, but will find himself inadequate for so lofty a subject, the transcendent grandeur of which overpowers all our senses.

3. Blessed are they that keep judgment. I make a distinction between this and the preceding verse, and yet so as to preserve the connection between them. For the prophet, having declared the magnitude of God's power to be such that no tongue could utter all its praises, now says, that the praises of the lip merely are not acceptable to God, but that the concurrence of the heart is indispensable, nay, that even the whole of our deportment must be in unison with this exercise.

4. Remember me. By these words the prophet declares it to be his chief desire, that God would extend to him that love which he bore towards the Church, that he might thus become a participator of all the blessings which, from the very first, he bestows upon his chosen, and which day by day he continues with them. Nor does he desire this for himself alone, but in name of the universal Church, offers up a prayer alike for all, that, by his example, he might stimulate the faithful to present similar petitions.

6-11

6. We have sinned with our fathers. It is quite plain from these words, that although the prophet may have spoken in the person of one man, he yet dictates a form of prayer for the common use of the whole Church, seeing that he now identifies himself with the whole body. And from this to the end of the psalm, he gleans from ancient histories that their fathers had always been of a malign and perverse spirit, of

MATTHEW HENRY

Psalm 106

1-5 Praise for divine goodness.

We are here taught,

I. To bless God (v. 1, 2): Praise you the Lord, that is,

1. Give him thanks for his goodness, the manifestation of it to us, and the many instances of it.

2. Give him the glory of his greatness, his mighty acts, proofs of his almighty power, wherein he has done great things, and such as would be opposed.

II. To bless the people of God, to call and account them happy (v. 3): Those that keep judgment are blessed, for they are fit to be employed in praising God.

III. To bless ourselves in the favor of God, to place our happiness in it, and to seek it, accordingly, with all seriousness, as the psalmist here, v. 4, 5.

1. He has an eye to the lovingkindness of God, as the fountain of all happiness: "Remember me, O Lord! to give me that mercy and grace which I stand in need of, with the favor which thou bearest to thy people."

2. He has an eye to the salvation of God, the great salvation, that of the soul, as the foundation of happiness: O visit me with thy salvation. "Afford me (says Dr. Hammond) that pardon and that grace which I stand in need of, and can hope for from none but thee." Let that salvation be my portion for ever, and the pledges of it my present comfort.

3. He has an eye to the blessedness of the righteous, as that which includes all good (v. 5): "That I may see the good of thy chosen and be as happy as the saints are; and happier I do not desire to be." God's people are here called his chosen, his nation, his inheritance; for he has set them apart for himself, incorporated them under his own government, is served by them and glorified in them.

6-12 The sins of Israelites.

Here begins a penitential confession of sin, which was in a special manner seasonable now that the church was in distress; for thus we must justify God in all that he brings upon us, acknowledging that therefore he has done right, because we have done wickedly; and the remembrance of former sins, notwithstanding which God did not cast off his people, is an encouragement to us to hope that, though we are justly corrected for our sins, yet we shall not be utterly abandoned.

I. God's afflicted people here own themselves guilty before God (v. 6): "We have sinned with our fathers, that is, like our fathers, after the similitude of their transgression. We have added to the stock of hereditary guilt, and filled up the measure of our fathers' iniquity, to augment yet the fierce anger of the Lord," Num. xxxii. 14; Matt. xxiii. 32. And see how they lay a load upon themselves, as becomes penitents: "We have committed iniquity, that which is in its own nature sinful, and we have done wickedly; we have sinned with a high hand presumptuously." Or this is a

Psalm 106

9-16

9 He rebuked the Red sea also, and it was dried up: so he led them through the depths, as through the wilderness.
10 And he saved them from the hand of him that hated them, and redeemed them from the hand of the enemy.
11 And the waters covered their enemies: there was not one of them left.
12 Then believed they his words; they sang his praise.
13 They soon forgat his works; they waited not for his counsel:
14 But lusted exceedingly in the wilderness, and tempted God in the desert.
15 And he gave them their request; but sent leanness into their soul.
16 They envied Moses also in the camp, and Aaron the saint of the LORD.

even as thou thinkest of thine own elect. I cannot ask more, nor would I seek less. Treat me as the least of thy saints are treated and I am content. It should be enough for us if we fare as the rest of the family.

Verse 5. That I may see the good of thy chosen. His desire for the divine favor was excited by the hope that he might participate in all the good things which flow to the people of God through their election. The Father has blessed us with all spiritual blessings in Christ Jesus, according as he has chosen us in him, and in these precious gifts we desire to share through the saving visitation of the Lord. No other good do we wish to see, perceive, and apprehend, but that which is the peculiar treasure of the saints.

Verse 6. We have sinned with our fathers. Here begins a long and particular confession. Confession of sin is the readiest way to secure an answer to the prayer of verse 4; God visits with his salvation the soul which acknowledges its need of a Savior.

Verse 7. Our fathers understood not thy wonders in Egypt. The Israelites saw the miraculous plagues and ignorantly wondered at them: their design of love, their deep moral and spiritual lessons, and their revelation of the divine power and justice they were unable to perceive. A long sojourn among idolaters had blunted the perceptions of the chosen family, and cruel slavery had ground them down into mental sluggishness. Alas, how many of God's wonders are not understood, or misunderstood by us still.

Verse 8. Nevertheless he saved them for his name's sake, that he might make his mighty power to be known. When he could find no other reason for his mercy he found it in his own glory, and seized the opportunity to display his power. If Israel does not deserve to be saved, yet Pharaoh's pride needs to be crushed, and therefore Israel shall be delivered.

Verse 9. He rebuked the Red sea also, and it was dried up. A word did it. The sea heard his voice and obeyed. How many rebukes of God are lost upon us! Are we not more unmanageable than the ocean? God did, as it were, chide the sea, and say, "Wherefore dost thou stop the way of my people? Their path to Canaan lies through thy channel, how dare you hinder them?" The sea perceived its Master and his seed royal, and made way at once. So he led them through the depths, as through the wilderness.

Verse 10. And he saved them from the hand of them that hated them. Pharaoh was drowned, and the power of Egypt so crippled that throughout the forty years' wanderings of Israel they were never threatened by their old masters. And redeemed them from the hand of the enemy. This was a redemption by power, and one of the most instructive types of the redemption of the Lord's people from sin and hell by the power which worketh in them.

Verse 11. And the waters covered their enemies: there was not one of them left. The Lord does nothing by halves. What he begins he carries through to the end. This, again, made Israel's sin the greater, because they saw the thoroughness of the divine justice, and the perfection of the divine faithfulness.

Verse 12. Then believed they his words. That is to say, they believed the promise when they saw it fulfilled, but not till then. This is mentioned, not to their credit, but to their shame. Those who do not believe the Lord's word till they see it performed are not believers at all. Who would not believe when the fact stares them in the face? The Egyptians would have done as much as this.

Verse 13. They soon forgat his works. They seemed in a hurry to get the Lord's mercies out of their memories; they hasted to be ungrateful. They waited not for his counsel, neither waiting for the word of command or promise; eager to have their own way, and prone to trust in themselves. This is a common fault in the Lord's family to this day; we are long in learning to wait for the Lord, and upon the Lord.

Verse 14. But lusted exceedingly in the wilderness. Though they would not wait God's will, they are hot to have their own. When the most suitable and corrupt practice, rebellious, ungrateful and perfidious towards God; and confesses that their descendants were not better; and having made this confession, they come and ask the remission of their sins. And as we are unable to obtain the pardon of our sins until we have first confessed ourselves to be guilty of sin, and as our hardness of heart shuts out the grace of God from us, the prophet, therefore, with great propriety, humbly acknowledges the guilt of the people in this their severe and sore chastisement, and that God might justly inflict upon them a yet harder punishment.

7. Our fathers understood not thy wonders in Egypt. Here he relates how the people immediately, from the very commencement of their emancipation from bondage, were ungrateful to God, and conducted themselves in a rebellious manner.

8. And saved them. The prophet here teaches what any one could easily learn from the preceding sentence, that the Israelites were saved, not on account of their deserving to be so, but because God had a regard to his own glory. That obstacle being removed, God went on to accomplish that deliverance which he had commenced, in order that his holy name might not become a reproach among the heathen.

Besides, we must not overlook the antithesis between the name of God and the merits of men, because God, out of a regard to his own glory, can find in us no cause wherefore he should be moved to save us. The inestimable kindness of God, which, for the sake of a people so perverse, altered the usual order of nature, is more illustriously displayed by the account which is afterwards given of the means by which they were preserved. When he says that the sea was rebuked, he extols the power of God, at whose command and will the sea was dried up—the waters receded, so that a free passage was opened up between the opposite heaps of waters.

12-15

12. Then they believed his words. In stating that they believed God's word, and sang his praise, the prophet does not say this to their commendation, but rather to increase, in a twofold manner, their guilt; because, being convinced by such indubitable testimony, they yet instantly resumed their wonted disposition of mind, and began to rebel against God, as if they had never beheld his wonderful works. How very inexcusable was that impiety which in a moment could forget the remarkable benefits which they had been constrained to admit! Overpowered by the grandeur of God's works, they were, he says, in spite of themselves, compelled to believe in God, and give glory to him, and thus the criminality of their rebellion was increased; because, although their stubbornness was overcome, yet they immediately relapsed into their former state of unbelief.

14. And they lusted. He goes on, according to the history, to mention the sin which, agreeably to the duty of his office as a teacher, he had briefly noticed. Should any one inquire in what way they did not attend to God's counsel, he answers, because they had indulged in the gratification of their lusts; for the only way of acting with proper moderation is, when

confession, not only of their imitation of, but their interest in, their fathers' sins: We have sinned with our fathers, for we were in their loins and we bear their iniquity, Lam. v. 7.

II. They bewail the sins of their fathers when they were first formed into a people, which, since children often smart for, they are concerned to sorrow for, even further than to the third and fourth generation. Even we now ought to take occasion from the history of Israel's rebellions to lament the depravity and perverseness of man's nature and its unaptness to be amended by the most probable means. Observe here,

1. The strange stupidity of Israel in the midst of the favors God bestowed upon them (v. 7): They understood not thy wonders in Egypt. They saw them, but they did not rightly apprehend the meaning and design of them.

2. Their perverseness arising from this stupidity: They provoked him at the sea, even at the Red Sea. The provocation was, despair of deliverance (because the danger was great) and wishing they had been left in Egypt still, Exod. xiv. 11, 12. Quarrelling with God's providence, and questioning his power, goodness, and faithfulness, are as great provocations to him as any whatsoever.

3. The great salvation God wrought for them notwithstanding their provocations, v. 8-11.

(1.) He forced a passage for them through the sea: He rebuked the Red Sea for standing in their way and retarding their march, and it was dried up immediately; as, in the creation, at God's rebuke the waters fled, Ps. civ. 7.

(2.) He interposed between them and their pursuers, and prevented them from cutting them off, as they designed. From the hand of his enemy, who was just ready to seize them, God redeemed them (v. 10), interposing himself, as it were, in the pillar of fire, between the persecuted and the persecutors.

(3.) To complete the mercy, and turn the deliverance into a victory, the Red Sea, which was a lane to them, was a grave to the Egyptians (v. 11): The waters covered their enemies, so as to slay them, but not so as to conceal their shame; for, the next tide, they were thrown up dead upon the shore, Exod. xiv. 30. There was not one of them left alive, to bring tidings of what had become of the rest. And why did God do this for them? Nay, why did he not cover them, as he did their enemies, for their unbelief and murmuring? He tells us (v. 8): it was for his name's sake.

4. The good impression this made upon them for the present (v. 12): Then believed they his words, and acknowledged that God was with them of a truth, and had, in mercy to them, brought them out of Egypt, and not with any design to slay them in the wilderness; then they feared the Lord and his servant Moses, Exod. xiv. 31.

Psalm 106

17-24
17 The earth opened and swallowed up Dathan and covered the company of Abiram.
18 And a fire was kindled in their company; the flame burned up the wicked.
19 They made a calf in Horeb, and worshipped the molten image.
20 Thus they changed their glory into the similitude of an ox that eateth grass.
21 They forgat God their savior, which had done great things in Egypt;
22 Wondrous works in the land of Ham, and terrible things by the Red sea.
23 Therefore he said that he would destroy them, had not Moses his chosen stood before him in the breach, to turn away his wrath, lest he should destroy them.
24 Yea, they despised the pleasant land, they believed not his word:

pleasant food was found them in abundance, it did not please them long, but they grew dainty and sniffed at angel's food, and must needs have flesh to eat, which was unhealthy diet for that warm climate, and for their easy life.

Verse 15. And he gave them their request. Prayer may be answered in anger and denied in love. That God gives a man his desire is no proof that he is the object of divine favor, everything depends upon what that desire is. But sent leanness into their soul. Ah, that "but!" It embittered all. The meat was poison to them when it came without a blessing; whatever it might do in fattening the body, it was poor stuff when it made the soul lean. If we must know scantiness, may God grant it may not be scantiness of soul: yet this is a common attendant upon worldly prosperity.

Verse 16. They envied Moses also in the camp. Though to him as the Lord's chosen instrument they owed everything, they grudged him the authority which it was needful that he should exercise for their good. Some were more openly rebellious than others, and became leaders of the mutiny, but a spirit of dissatisfaction was general, and therefore the whole nation is charged with it.

Verse 17. The earth opened and swallowed up Dathan, and covered the company of Abiram. Korah is not mentioned, for mercy was extended to his household, though he himself perished. The earth could no longer bear up under the weight of these rebels and ingrates: God's patience was exhausted when they began to assail his servants, for his children are very dear to him, and he that toucheth them touches the apple of his eye.

Verse 18. And a fire was kindled in their company; the flame burned up the wicked. The Levites who were with Korah perished by fire, which was a most fitting death for those who intruded into the priesthood, and so offered strange fire. God has more than one arrow in his quiver, the fire can consume those whom the earthquake spares.

Verse 19. They made a calf in Horeb. In the very place where they had solemnly pledged themselves to obey the Lord they broke the second, if not the first, of his commandments, and set up the Egyptian symbol of the ox, and bowed before it. The ox image is here sarcastically called "a calf"; idols are worthy of no respect, scorn is never more legitimately used than when it is poured upon all attempts to set forth the Invisible God.

Verse 20. Thus they changed their glory into the similitude of an ox that eateth grass. They said that they only meant to worship the one God under a fitting and suggestive similitude by which his great power would be set forth to the multitude; they pleaded the great Catholic revival which followed upon this return to a more ornate ceremonial, for the people thronged around Aaron, and danced before the calf with all their might. But in very deed they had given up the true God, whom it had been their glory to adore, and had set up a rival to him, not a representation of him; for how should he be likened to a bullock? The psalmist is very contemptuous, and justly so: irreverence towards idols is an indirect reverence to God.

Verse 21. They forgat God their savior. Remembering the calf involved forgetting God. He had commanded them to make no image, and in daring to disobey they forgot his commands. Moreover, it is clear that they must altogether have forgotten the nature and character of Jehovah, or they could never have likened him to a grass eating animal.

Verse 23. Therefore he said that he would destroy them. The threatening of destruction came at last. For the first wilderness sin he chastened them, sending leanness into their soul; for the second he weeded out the offenders, the flame burned up the wicked; for the third he threatened to destroy them; for the fourth he lifted up his hand and almost came to blows (Ps 106:26); for the fifth he actually smote them, "and the plague brake in among them"; and so the punishment increased with their perseverance in sin.

Verse 24. Yea, they despised the pleasant land. They spoke lightly of it, though it was the joy of all lands: they did not think it worth the trouble of

God rules and presides over our affections. It is therefore the more necessary to bridle that strong tendency to fleshly lusts which naturally rage within us. For whoever allows himself to desire more than is needful, openly sets himself in direct opposition to God, inasmuch as all fleshly lusts are directly opposed to him.
15. He gave them their desire. God withheld his blessing from the food which they had so immoderately longed for, in order that this their punishment for their transgression might humble them.

16-22
16. And they envied. He refers here very shortly to another transgression, and that, too, in such a way as to furnish both to himself and others ample grounds for deep consideration. For, as the people, in devising from time to time new modes of sinning, displayed so much cunning in their attempts to provoke God's anger, so we ought the more to be filled with fear on that account.
17. The earth opened. The heinousness of their sin may be seen in the magnitude of the punishment by which it was visited. But the design of the prophet was to accuse and reprove publicly the obstinacy of the people, who, so far from being bettered by their corrections, conducted themselves the more perversely.
19. They made a calf. Here he represents their rebellion as exceedingly base, in that they abandoned the true worship of God, and made to themselves a calf. For although it was their intention to worship God in this manner, yet the prophet reprehends their brutal stupidity, because they worshipped before the molten image, and represented God by the figure of an ox which eateth grass. From this the prophet infers, that God had been robbed of his honor, and that all his glory had been tarnished.
21. They forgot God. The prophet again repeats that the people had sinned not simply through ignorance, but also willfully, inasmuch as God had already given a very palpable manifestation of his power and glory. And as he makes himself known in the creation of the heavens and of the earth, the blindness of men is totally inexcusable. But far more aggravating is the sin of the children of Israel, who, after God had made himself known to them, in the most condescending manner, cast him off altogether, and gave themselves up to the practice of brutish idolatry.

23-27
23. And he said. The prophet informs us, by these words, that the people had a feeling sense of their remarkable deliverance from impending destruction, by means of prayer alone, which, for a season, restrained God's vengeance from bursting forth against them. In a very short time, however, they return to their wonted disposition of mind, a striking proof of the awful perversity of their hearts. To represent how highly God was offended, the prophet says that he had purposed to destroy the transgressors: not that God is subject to human passions, to be very angry for a little, and then

13-33 Provocation of Israel in the wilderness.
This is an abridgment of the history of Israel's provocations in the wilderness, and of the wrath of God against them for those provocations: and this abridgment is abridged by the apostle, with application to us Christians (1 Cor. x. 5, &c.); for these things were written for our admonition, that we sin not like them, lest we suffer like them.

I. The cause of their sin was disregard to the works and word of God, v. 13. They minded not what he had done for them: They soon forgot his works, and lost the impressions they had made upon them. This is mentioned again (v. 21, 22): They forgot God their Savior; that is, they forgot that he had been their Savior. Those that forget the works of God forget God himself, who makes himself known by his works.
II. Many of their sins are here mentioned, together with the tokens of God's displeasure which they fell under for those sins.
1. They would have flesh, and yet would not believe that God could give it to them (v. 14): They lusted a lust (so the word is) in the wilderness; there, where they had bread enough and to spare, yet nothing would serve them but they must have flesh to eat. Now how did God show his displeasure against them for this. We are told how (v. 15): He gave them their request, but gave it them in anger, and with a curse, for he sent leanness into their soul; he filled them with uneasiness of mind, and terror of conscience, and a self-reproach, occasioned by their bodies being sick with the surfeit, such as sometimes drunkards experience after a great debauch. Or this is put for that great plague with which the Lord smote them, while the flesh was yet between their teeth, as we read, Num. xi. 33. It was the consumption of the life.
2. They quarreled with the government which God had set over them both in church and state (v. 16): They envied Moses his authority in the camp, as general of the armies of Israel and chief justice in all their courts; they envied Aaron his power, as saint of the Lord, consecrated to the office of high priest, and Korah would needs put in for the pontificate, while Dathan and Abiram, as princes of the tribe of Reuben, Jacob's eldest son, would claim to be chief magistrates, by the so-much-admired right of primogeniture.

3. They made and worshipped the golden calf, and this in Horeb, where the law was given, and where God had expressly said, Thou shalt neither make any graven image nor bow down to it; they did both: They made a calf and worshipped it, v. 19.
(1.) Herein they bade defiance to, and put an affront upon, the two great lights which God has made to rule the moral world:
[1.] That of human reason; for they changed their glory, their God, at least the manifestation of him, which always had been in a cloud (either a dark cloud or a bright one), without any manner of visible similitude, into the similitude of Apis, one of the Egyptian idols, an ox that eateth grass, than which

Psalm 106

25-32

25 But murmured in their tents, and hearkened not unto the voice of the LORD.
26 Therefore he lifted up his hand against them, to overthrow them in the wilderness:
27 To overthrow their seed also among the nations, and to scatter them in the lands.
28 They joined themselves also unto Baalpeor, and ate the sacrifices of the dead.
29 Thus they provoked him to anger with their inventions: and the plague brake in upon them.
30 Then stood up Phinehas, and executed judgment: and so the plague was stayed.
31 And that was counted unto him for righteousness unto all generations for evermore.
32 They angered him also at the waters of strife, so that it went ill with Moses for their sakes:

seeking and conquering; they even spoke of Egypt, the land of their iron bondage, as though they preferred it to Canaan, the land which floweth with milk and honey. It is an ill sign with a Christian when he begins to think lightly of heaven and heavenly things; it indicates a perverted mind, and it is, moreover, a high offence to the Lord to despise that which he esteems so highly that he in infinite love reserves it for his own chosen.

Verse 25. But murmured in their tents. From unbelief to murmuring is a short and natural step; they even fell to weeping when they had the best ground for rejoicing. Murmuring is a great sin and not a mere weakness; it contains within itself unbelief, pride, rebellion, and a whole host of sins.

Verse 26. Therefore he lifted up his hand against them, to overthrow them in the wilderness. He swore in his wrath that they should not enter into his rest; he commenced his work of judgment upon them, and they began to die. Only let God lift his hand against a man and his day has come; he falls terribly whom Jehovah overthrows.

Verse 28. They joined themselves also unto Baalpeor. Ritualism led on to the adoration of false gods. If we choose a false way of worship we shall, ere long, choose to worship a false god. This abomination of the Moabites was an idol in whose worship women gave up their bodies to the most shameless lust. Think of the people of a holy God coming down to this.

Verse 29. Thus they provoked him to anger with their inventions: and the plague brake in upon them. Open licentiousness and avowed idolatry were too gross to be winked at. This time the offences clamored for judgment, and the judgment came at once. Twenty-four thousand persons fell before a sudden and deadly disease which threatened to run through the whole camp. Their new sins brought on them a disease new to their tribes. When men invent sins God will not be slow to invent punishments.

Verse 30. Then stood up Phinehas, and executed judgment: and so the plague was stayed. God has his champions left in the worst times, and they will stand up when the time comes for them to come forth to battle. This righteous indignation moved him to a quick execution of two open offenders. His honest spirit could not endure that lewdness should be publicly practiced at a time when a fast had been proclaimed. Such daring defiance of God and of all law he could not brook, and so with his sharp javelin he transfixed the two guilty ones in the very act.

Verse 31. And that was counted unto him for righteousness unto all generations for evermore. Down to the moment when this psalm was penned the house of Phinehas was honored in Israel. His faith had performed a valorous deed, and his righteousness was testified of the Lord, and honored by the continuance of his family in the priesthood. He was impelled by motives that what would otherwise have been a deed of blood was justified in the sight of God; nay, more, was made the evidence that Phinehas was righteous. No personal ambition, or private revenge, or selfish passion, or even fanatical bigotry, inspired the man of God, but zeal for God, indignation at open filthiness, and true patriotism urged him on. Once again we have cause to note the mercy of God that even when his warrant was out, and actual execution was proceeding, he stayed his hand at the suit of one man: finding, as it were, an apology for his grace when justice seemed to demand immediate vengeance.

Verse 32. They angered him also at the waters of strife. Will they never have done? The scene changes, but the sin continues. Aforetime they had mutinied about water when prayer would soon have turned the desert into a standing pool, but now they do it again after their former experience of the divine goodness. This made the sin a double, yea a sevenfold offence, and caused the anger of the Lord to be the more intense.

Verse 33. Because they provoked his spirit, so that he spake unadvisedly with his lips. Which seems a small sin compared with that of others, but then it was the sin of Moses, the Lord's chosen servant, who had seen and known so much of the Lord, and therefore it could not be passed by. He did immediately afterwards, on being appeased, changes his purpose; for God, in his secret counsel, had resolved upon their forgiveness, even as he actually did pardon them. But the prophet makes mention of another purpose, by which God designed to strike the people with terror, that coming to know and acknowledge the greatness of their sin, they might be humbled on account of it. This is that repentance so frequently referred to in the Scriptures.

24. And they despised. It was an evident demonstration of the unconquerable wickedness of the Jews, that, after they had been in the jaws of destruction, and while they had scarcely escaped from danger so great and so imminent, they rose up in rebellion against God.

26. And he lifted up. He describes another example of the vengeance of God, the recollection of which ought to have been deeply seated in their hearts, so that cherishing a constant fear of him, they might watch over themselves with the utmost solicitude. No good having ensued from all this, it is obvious that the madness of that people was incurable. At that time God did restrain his anger, in that he did not disperse their offspring throughout various parts of the earth; but his threatening of itself ought to have sufficed for the subduing of their pride, had they not been incorrigible.

28-31

28. And they joined themselves to Baal-peor. The prophet tells us that the Jews, after they had been threatened with very awful punishment, very soon fell into a new species of apostasy.

As the idolatry here mentioned originated from carnal intrigues, some expositors are of opinion, that on this account the prophet charges the people with the commission of a twofold trespass, in their not only being inveigled by the Midianitish women, but also in binding themselves by another bond to Baal-peor, (Numbers 25). Be that as it may, the prophet exclaims against the perfidy of his own nation, because in forsaking the true worship of God, they had broken that holy union by which they had been betrothed to him. For we know, that as God adopts the Church as his spouse, when she gives herself up to idolatry, she no less shamefully violates her fidelity, than when a wife leaves her husband, and becomes an adulteress.

29. And they provoked God to anger. The prophet once more informs us, that they had been put upon their guard by another plague, in order that it might appear that God had always a strict regard for his own glory, in chastising the people; but as they were not bettered by these plagues, these chastisements were fruitless. Having formerly stated, that God's wrath had been appeased by the prayers of Moses, he now says, that the plague had been arrested or ceased by means of the kind interposition of Phinehas.

31. And that deed was imputed. The prophet, in thus praising one individual, heaps reproach upon the whole body of the people. For we infer from this token of approbation with which the Holy Spirit condescended to stamp the excellent action of Phinehas, how very base their conduct must have been. Neither

nothing could be more grossly and scandalously absurd, v. 20.

[2.] That of divine revelation, which was afforded to them, not only in the words God spoke to them, but in the works he wrought for them, wondrous works, which declared aloud that the Lord Jehovah is the only true and living God and is alone to be worshipped, v. 21, 22.

(2.) For this God showed his displeasure by declaring the decree that he would cut them off from being a people, as they had, as far as lay in their power, in effect cut him off from being a God; he spoke of destroying them (v. 23), and certainly he would have done it if Moses, his chosen, had not stood before him in the breach (v. 23), if he had not seasonably interposed to deal with God as an advocate about the breach or ruin God was about to devote them to and wonderfully prevailed to turn away his wrath. See here the mercy of God, and how easily his anger is turned away, even from a provoking people. See the power of prayer, and the interest which God's chosen have in heaven. See a type of Christ, God's chosen, his elect, in whom his soul delights, who stood before him in the breach to turn away his wrath from a provoking world, and ever lives, for this end, making intercession.

4. They gave credit to the report of the evil spies concerning the land of Canaan, in contradiction to the promise of God (v. 24): They despised the pleasant land.

5. They were guilty of a great sin in the matter of Peor; and this was the sin of the new generation, when they were within a step of Canaan (v. 28): They joined themselves to Baal-peor, and so were entangled both in idolatry and in adultery, in corporeal and in spiritual whoredom, Num. xxv. 1-3. Those that did often partake of the altar of the living God now ate the sacrifices of the dead, of the idols of Moab (that were dead images, or dead men canonized or deified), or sacrifices to the infernal deities on the behalf of their dead friends. Thus they provoked God to anger with their inventions (v. 29), in contempt of him and his institutions, his commands, and his threatenings. The iniquity of Peor was so great that, long after, it is said, They were not cleansed from it, Josh. xxii. 17.

6. They continued their murmurings to the very last of their wanderings; for in the fortieth year they angered God at the waters of strife (v. 32), which refers to that story, Num. xx. 3-5. And that which aggravated it now was that it went ill with Moses for their sakes; for, though he was the meekest of all the men in the earth, yet their clamors at that time were so peevish and provoking that they put him into a passion, and, having now grown very old and off his guard, he spoke unadvisedly with his lips (v. 33), and not as became him on that occasion; for he said in a heat, Hear now, you rebels, must we fetch water out of this rock for you? This was Moses's infirmity, and is

Psalm 106

33-40

33 Because they provoked his spirit, so that he spake unadvisedly with his lips.
34 They did not destroy the nations, concerning whom the LORD commanded them:
35 But were mingled among the heathen, and learned their works.
36 And they served their idols: which were a snare unto them.
37 Yea, they sacrificed their sons and their daughters unto devils,
38 And shed innocent blood, even the blood of their sons and of their daughters, whom they sacrificed unto the idols of Canaan: and the land was polluted with blood.
39 Thus were they defiled with their own works, and went a whoring with their own inventions.
40 Therefore was the wrath of the LORD kindled against his people, insomuch that he abhorred his own inheritance.

not speak blasphemously, or falsely, but only hastily and without care; but this is a serious fault in a lawgiver, and especially in one who speaks for God. This passage is to our mind one of the most terrible in the Bible. Truly we serve a jealous God. Yet he is not a hard master, or austere; we must not think so, but we must then rather be jealous of ourselves, and watch that we live the more carefully, and speak the more advisedly, because we serve such a Lord.

Verse 34. They did not destroy the nations, concerning whom the LORD commanded them. They were commissioned to act as executioners upon races condemned for their unnatural crimes, and through sloth, cowardice, or Sinful complacency they sheathed the sword too soon, very much to their own danger and disquietude.

Verse 35. But were mingled among the heathen, and learned their works. It was not the wilderness which caused Israel's sins; they were just as disobedient when settled in the land of promise. They found evil company, and delighted in it. Those whom they should have destroyed they made their friends.

Verse 36. And they served their idols: which were a snare unto them. They were fascinated by the charms of idolatry, though it brings misery upon its votaries. A man cannot serve sin without being ensnared by it. It is like birdlime, and to touch it is to be taken by it. Samson laid his head in the Philistine woman's lap, but ere long he woke up shorn of his strength. Dalliance with sin is fatal to spiritual liberty.

Verse 37. Yea, they sacrificed their sons and their daughters unto devils. This was being snared indeed; they were spell bound by the cruel superstition, and were carried so far as even to become murderers of their own children, in honor of the most detestable deities, which were rather devils than gods.

Verse 39. Thus were they defiled with their own works, and went a whoring with their own inventions. Not only the land but the inhabitants of it were polluted. They broke the marriage bond between them and the Lord, and fell into spiritual adultery. The language is strong, but the offence could not be fitly described in less forcible words. As a husband is deeply dishonored and sorely wounded should his wife become unchaste and run riot with many paramours in his own house, so was the Lord incensed at his people for setting up gods many and lords many in his own land. They made and invented new gods, and then worshipped what they had made. What a folly! Their novel deities were loathsome monsters and cruel demons, and yet they paid them homage. What wickedness! And to commit this folly and wickedness they cast off the true God, whose miracles they had seen, and whose people they were. This was provocation of the severest sort.

Verses 40. Therefore was the wrath of the LORD kindled against his people, in so much that he abhorred his own inheritance. Not that even then he broke his covenant or utterly cast off his offending people, but he felt the deepest indignation, and even looked upon them with abhorrence. The feeling described is like to that of a husband who still loves his guilty wife, and yet when he thinks of her lewdness feels his whole nature rising in righteous anger at her, so that the very sight of her afflicts his soul.

Verse 42. Their enemies also oppressed them. This was according to their nature; an Israelite always fares ill at the hands of the heathen. Leniency to Canaan turned out to be cruelty to themselves. And they were brought into subjection under their hand. They were bowed down by laborious bondage, and made to lie low under tyranny. In their God they had found a kind master, but in those with whom they had perversely sought fellowship they found despots of the most barbarous sort. He who leaves his God leaves happiness for misery.

Verse 43. Many times did he deliver them. By reading the book of Judges we shall see how truthful is this sentence: again and again their foes were routed, and they were set free again, only to return with rigor to their former was this honor reserved for him alone, but his posterity were to enjoy it throughout their succeeding generations. In order, therefore, to cast the greater reproach upon the people, Phinehas alone is contrasted with them.

32-39
32. And they provoked him. The prophet mentions another offense of which they were guilty, in that, they contended with God at the waters of strife, from which circumstance that place derived its name. The clamor was, it is true, raised directly against Moses, but if we examine the matter properly, we will find that they virtually murmured against God himself. And to point out the aggravation of their offense, he says that Moses was hardly dealt with on their account. From this it may be inferred that their transgression was very heinous, in that God did not spare even his own servant, whom he had chosen in preference to all others.
33. For they grieved his spirit. The prime movers of the rebellion must have committed a very heinous offense, seeing that Moses, who had been pushed on by the impetuosity of the people to sin, was so severely dealt with by God. But while the prophet informs us that Moses was punished on the people's account, he is not to be understood as saying that he was altogether blameless. For even admitting that his spirit was ruffled in consequence of the tumult of the people, this ought to have made him the more careful to continue steadfast in his adherence to the Law of God.
34. They did not destroy the nations. They had been remiss in driving out the heathen, or more probably that they had not obeyed the Divine command to root them out of the land. Now that the cup of the iniquity of the Amorites was full, it was the purpose of God that they should be exterminated, lest their society might prove injurious to the holy people. For God, having chosen that land for a habitation to himself, intended that it should be holy and purified from all defilement.
35. But were mingled. He describes what was the result of this foolish humanity; namely, that they were defiled with the pollutions of the nations whom they had spared. Had they exclusively inhabited the land of Canaan, they would have more easily retained the pure worship of God. Allured by the influence of such neighbors, it is not wonderful that they soon degenerated from the footsteps of their fathers, for we are more inclined to follow the example of the bad than of the good.
37. And they sacrificed. The prophet here mentions one species of superstition which demonstrates the awful blindness of the people; their not hesitating to sacrifice their sons and daughters to devils. In applying such an abominable designation to the sin of the people, he means to exhibit it in more hateful colors. From this we learn that inconsiderate zeal is a flimsy pretext in favor of any act of devotion.
38. And they shed. He inveighs with still greater indignation against that religious phrensy which led them to sacrifice their own children, and thus to pollute the land by the shedding of innocent blood.

written for our admonition, that we may learn, when we are in the midst of provocation, to keep our mouth as with a bridle (Ps. xxxix. 1-3), and to take heed to our spirits, that they admit not resentments too much.

34-48 Provocation of Israel in the wilderness; the divine compassion.

Here,

I. The narrative concludes with an account of Israel's conduct in Canaan, which was of a piece with that in the wilderness, and God's dealings with them, wherein, as all along, both justice and mercy appeared.

1. They were very provoking to God. The miracles and mercies which settled them in Canaan made no more deep and durable impressions upon them than those which fetched them out of Egypt; for by the time they were just settled in Canaan they corrupted themselves, and forsook God. Observe,

(1.) The steps of their apostasy.

[1.] They spared the nations which God had doomed to destruction (v. 34).

[2.] When they spared them they promised themselves that, notwithstanding this, they would not join in any dangerous affinity with them. But the way of sin is down-hill; omissions make way for commissions; when they neglect to destroy the heathen the next news we hear is, They were mingled among the heathen, made leagues with them and contracted an intimacy with them, so that they learned their works, v. 35. That which is rotten will sooner corrupt that which is sound than be cured or made sound by it.

[3.] When they mingled with them, and learned some of their works that seemed innocent diversions and entertainments, yet they thought they would never join with them in their worship; but by degrees they learned that too (v. 36): They served their idols in the same manner, and with the same rites, that they served them; and they became a snare to them.

[4.] When they joined with them in some of their idolatrous services, which they thought had least harm in them, they little thought that ever they should be guilty of that barbarous and inhuman piece of idolatry the sacrificing of their living children to their dead gods; but they came to that at last (v. 37, 38), in which Satan triumphed over his worshippers, and regaled himself in blood and slaughter.

(2.) Their sin was, in part, their own punishment; for by it,

[1.] They wronged their country: The land was polluted with blood, v. 38. That pleasant land, that holy land, was rendered uncomfortable to themselves, and unfit to receive those kind tokens of God's favor and presence in it which were designed to be its honor.

[2.] They wronged their consciences (v. 39): They went a whoring with their own inventions, and so debauched their own minds, and were defiled with their own works, and rendered odious in the eyes of the holy God, and perhaps of their own consciences.

Psalm 106

41-48

41 And he gave them into the hand of the heathen; and they that hated them ruled over them.

42 Their enemies also oppressed them, and they were brought into subjection under their hand.

43 Many times did he deliver them; but they provoked him with their counsel, and were brought low for their iniquity.

44 Nevertheless he regarded their affliction, when he heard their cry:

45 And he remembered for them his covenant, and repented according to the multitude of his mercies.

46 He made them also to be pitied of all those that carried them captives.

47 Save us, O LORD our God, and gather us from among the heathen, to give thanks unto thy holy name, and to triumph in thy praise.

48 Blessed be the LORD God of Israel from everlasting to everlasting: and let all the people say, Amen. Praise ye the LORD.

evil ways. But they provoked him with their counsel. With deliberation they agreed to transgress anew; self will was their counselor, and they followed it to their own destruction. And were brought low for their iniquity.

Verse 44. Nevertheless he regarded their affliction, when he heard their cry. Notwithstanding all these provoking rebellions and detestable enormities the Lord still heard their prayer and pitied them. This is very wonderful, very godlike. One would have thought that the Lord would have shut out their prayer, seeing they had shut their ears against his admonitions; but no, he had a father's heart, and a sight of their sorrows touched his soul, the sound of their cries overcame his heart, and he looked upon them with compassion. Verse 45. And he remembered for them his covenant. The covenant is the sure foundation of mercy, and when the whole fabric of outward grace manifested in the saints lies in ruins this is the fundamental basis of love which is never moved, and upon it the Lord proceeds to build again a new structure of grace. Covenant mercy is sure as the throne of God.

Verse 46. He made them also to be pitied of all those that carried them captives. Having the hearts of all men in his hands he produced compassion even in heathen bosoms. Even as he found Joseph friends in Egypt, so did he raise up sympathizers for his captive servants. In our very worst condition our God has ways and means for allaying the severity of our sorrows: he can find us helpers among those who have been our oppressors, and he will do so if we be indeed his people.

Verse 47. This is the closing prayer, arranged by prophecy for those who would in future time be captives, and suitable for all who before David's days had been driven from home by the tyranny of the various scatterings by famine and distress which had happened in the iron age of the judges. Save us, O Lord our God. The mention of the covenant encouraged the afflicted to call the Lord their God, and this enabled them with greater boldness to entreat him to interpose on their behalf and rescue them.

Verse 48. Blessed be the LORD God of Israel from everlasting to everlasting. Has not his mercy endured for ever, and should not his praise be of like duration? Jehovah, the God of Israel, has blessed his people, should they not also bless him? And let all the people say, Amen. They have all seen spared by his grace, let them all join in the adoration with loud unanimous voice. What a thunder of praise would thus be caused! Yet should a nation thus magnify him, yea, should all the nations past and present unite in the solemn acclaim, it would fall far short of his deserts. O for the happy day when all flesh shall see the glory of God, and all shall aloud proclaim his praise.

39. And they were polluted with their own works. He now concludes by stating generally, that the Jews, in adopting the abominable practices of the heathen, were become wholly filthy; because in all the devices of men there is nothing else than impurity.

40-46
40. And the wrath of Jehovah waxed hot. The severity of the punishment inflicted upon the people confirms the truth of what we formerly said, that they had been guilty of no trivial offense, in presuming to corrupt the worship of God. And they themselves showed how hopeless their reformation was, in that all this as yet failed to bring them truly to repent of their sin.
43. Many times. As the wicked perversity of the people was manifested in that God's severe chastisements failed to produce their reformation, so now, on the other hand, the prophet deduces the detestable hardness of their hearts from the fact, that all the benefits which they had received from God could not bend them into obedience.
45. And he remembered. God's being mindful of his covenant is here assigned as the cause of his great mercy and long-suffering. In that covenant, he not only declares that there is a gracious pardon for transgressions, but he also adverts to the perverse blindness of those who were not brought back by such remedies to the covenant, in which they were well aware that their safety was placed. But above all, he charges them with ingratitude; because, when deserving to perish, they did not acknowledge that they were indebted to the mercy of God alone for their preservation.
46. And he made them to find pity. As he had above said, that the Jews had been delivered into the hands of their enemies, because God's anger was, as it were, arms to their adversaries to subdue them; so now he says, that the same God had softened the hearts of these very enemies, who, by terrible means, and with great cruelty, had executed his vengeance upon them.

47-48
47. Save us, Jehovah our God! From the conclusion of the psalm, it is evident, that it was composed during the sad and calamitous dispersion of the people. And although subsequent to the times of Haggai and Malachi, no famous prophets appeared among the people, it is nevertheless probable that some of the priests were endued with the spirit of prophecy that they might direct them to the source whence they might receive all needful consolation.
48. Blessed be Jehovah, the God of Israel. The prophet here regulates the prayers of the people in such a way that the dejected captives may not cease to render thanks to God. When borne down by adversity, there is scarcely one among a hundred, who, with composure of spirit, draws near to God; but, on the contrary, he betrays the pride of his heart by the careless and insipid manner in which he prays, or in pouring out complaints about his afflicted condition. But the only way in which we can expect God to lend a favorable ear to the voice of our supplications is, in the spirit of meekness to submit to his corrections.

2. God brought his judgments upon them; and what else could be expected? For his name is Jealous, and he is a jealous God.
(1.) He fell out with them for it, v. 40. He was angry with them: The wrath of God, that consuming fire, was kindled against his people; for from them he took it as more insulting and ungrateful than from the heathen that never knew him.
(2.) Their enemies then fell upon them, and, their defense having departed, made an easy prey of them (v. 41, 42): He gave them into the hands of the heathen. The heathen hated them. Apostates lose all the love on God's side, and get none on Satan's; and when those that hated them ruled over them, and they were brought into subjection under them, no marvel that they oppressed them and ruled them with rigor; and thus God made them know the difference between his service and the service of the kings of the countries, 2 Chron. xii. 8.
(3.) When God granted them some relief, yet they went on in their sins, and their troubles also were continued, v. 43. This refers to the days of the Judges, when God often raised up deliverers and wrought deliverances for them, and yet they relapsed to idolatry and provoked God with their counsel, their idolatrous inventions, to deliver them up to some other oppressor, so that at last they were brought very low for their iniquity. Those that by sin disparage themselves, and will not by repentance humble themselves, are justly debased, and humbled, and brought low, by the judgments of God.
(4.) At length they cried unto God, and God returned in favor to them, v. 44-46. They were chastened for their sins, but not destroyed, cast down, but not cast off.
II. The psalm concludes with prayer and praise.
1. Prayer for the completing of his people's deliverance. Even when the Lord brought back the captivity of his people still there was occasion to pray, Lord, turn again our captivity (Ps. cxxvi. 1, 4); so here (v. 47), Save us, O Lord our God! and gather us from among the heathen.
2. Praise for the beginning and progress of it (v. 48): Blessed be the Lord God of Israel from everlasting to everlasting. He is a blessed God from eternity, and will be so to eternity, and so let him be praised by all his worshippers. Let the priests say this, and then let all the people say, Amen, Hallelujah, in token of their cheerful concurrence in all these prayers, praises, and confessions. According to this rubric, or directory, we find that when this psalm (or at least the closing verses of it) was sung all the people said Amen, and praised the Lord by saying, Hallelujah. By these two comprehensive words it is very proper, in religious assemblies, to testify their joining with their ministers in the prayers and praises which, as their mouth, they offer up to God, according to his will, saying Amen to the prayers and Hallelujah to the praises.

Book Five: Psalms 107-150

Psalm 107

1-7
1 O give thanks unto the LORD, for he is good: for his mercy endureth for ever.
2 Let the redeemed of the LORD say so, whom he hath redeemed from the hand of the enemy;
3 And gathered them out of the lands, from the east, and from the west, from the north, and from the south.
4 They wandered in the wilderness in a solitary way; they found no city to dwell in.
5 Hungry and thirsty, their soul fainted in them.
6 Then they cried unto the LORD in their trouble, and he delivered them out of their distresses.
7 And he led them forth by the right way, that they might go to a city of habitation.

Book Five: Psalms 107-150

Psalm 107

SUBJECT. This is a choice song for the redeemed of the Lord (Ps 107:2). Although it celebrates providential deliverances, and therefore may be sung by any man whose life has been preserved in time of danger; yet under cover of this, it mainly magnifies the Lord for spiritual blessings, of which temporal favors are but types arid shadows. The theme is thanksgiving, and the motives for it. The construction of the psalm is highly poetical, and merely as a composition it would be hard to find its compeer among human productions. The bards of the Bible hold no second place among the sons of song.
DIVISION. The psalmist commences by dedicating his poem to the redeemed who have been gathered from captivity, Ps 107:1-3; he then likens their history to that of travelers lost in the desert, Ps 107:4-9; to that of prisoners in iron bondage, Ps 107:10-16; to that of sick men, Ps 107:17-22; and to that of mariners tossed with tempest, Ps 107:23-32. In the closing verses the judgment of God on the rebellious, and the mercies of God to his own afflicted people are made the burden of the song, Ps 107:33-42; and then the psalm closes with a sort of summing up, in Ps 107:43, which declares that those who study the works and ways of the Lord shall be sure to see and praise his goodness.

EXPOSITION
Verse 1. O give thanks unto the Lord, for he is good. It is all we can give him, and the least we can give; therefore let us diligently render to him our thanksgiving. The psalmist is in earnest in the exhortation, hence the use of the interjection "O", to intensity his words: let us be at all times thoroughly fervent in the praises of the Lord, both with our lips and with our lives, by thanksgiving and thanks living.
Verse 2. Let the redeemed of the LORD say so. Whatever others may think or say, the redeemed have overwhelming reasons for declaring the goodness of the Lord. Theirs is a peculiar redemption, and for it they ought to render peculiar praise.
Verse 3. And gathered them out of the lands, from the east, and from the west, from the north, and from the south. Gathering follows upon redeeming. The captives of old were restored to their own land from every quarter of the earth, and even from beyond the sea; for the word translated south is really the sea. No matter what divides, the Lord will gather his own into one body, and first on earth by "one Lord, one faith, and one baptism", and then in heaven by one common bliss they shall be known to be the one people of the One God.
Verse 4. They wandered in the wilderness. They wandered, for the track was lost, no vestige of a road remained; worse still, they wandered in a wilderness, where all around was burning sand. They were lost in the worst possible place, even as the sinner is who is lost in sin; they wandered up and down in vain searches and researches as a sinner does when he is awakened and sees his lost estate; but it ended in nothing, for they still continued in the wilderness, though they had hoped to escape from it. In a solitary way. No dwelling of man was near, and no other company of travelers passed within hail. Solitude is a great intensifier of misery.
Verse 5. Hungry and thirsty, their soul fainted in them. The spirits sink when the bodily frame becomes exhausted by long privations. Who can keep his courage up when he is ready to fall to the ground at every step through utter exhaustion? The supply of food is all eaten, the water is spent in the bottles, and there are neither fields nor streams in the desert, the heart therefore sinks in dire despair.

JOHN CALVIN

Book Five: Psalms 107-150

Psalm 107

1-9
1. Praise Jehovah. The penman of this psalm, whoever he was, has, instead of the ordinary preface, inserted this beautiful sentiment, in which praise and thanksgiving to God were so frequently expressed by the Israelite Church. Immediately he proceeds to speak more particularly. And first, he exhorts those to offer up a tribute of gratitude to God; who, after having been delivered from slavery and imprisonment, and after a long and painful journey, arrived in safety at their place of abode. These he calls the redeemed of God; because, in wandering through the trackless desert, and howling wilderness, they many a time would have been prevented from returning home, had not God, as it were, with his outstretched hand, appeared as their guard and their guide.
2. But the second verse might be joined with the first, as if the prophet were commanding the persons whom he was addressing to sing this celebrated ode. It may with equal propriety be read by itself thus: Let the redeemed of Jehovah, who have returned from captivity to their own land, come forth now, and take part in the celebration of God's praises, and let them publish his loving-kindness which they have experienced in their deliverance. Among the Jews, who had occasion to undertake extensive journeys, such occurrences as these were very common; because they could hardly leave their own land, without from all quarters encountering ways rugged, and difficult, and perilous; and the same observation is equally applicable to mankind in general.
6. In their straits they called upon Jehovah. The verbs are here in the past tense, and according to grammarians, represent a continued action. The meaning therefore is, that those who are wandering in desert places are often pinched with hunger and thirst in consequence of finding no place in which to lodge; and who, when all hope of deliverance fails them, then cry unto God. Doubtless, God grants deliverance to many when in straits, even though they do not present their supplications to Him for aid; and hence it was not so much the design of the prophet in this passage to extol the faith of the pious, who call upon God with all their heart, as to describe the common feelings of humanity. There may be not a few whose hope does not center on God, who, nevertheless, are constrained, by some invisible disposition of mind, to come to Him, when under the pressure of dire necessity.

10-16
10. They who dwell in darkness. The Spirit of God makes mention here of another species of danger in which God manifestly discovers his power and grace in the protecting and delivering of men. The world calls these vicissitudes the sport of fortune; and hardly one among a hundred can be found who ascribes them to the superintending providence of God. It is a very different kind of practical wisdom which God expects at our hands; namely, that we ought to meditate on

MATTHEW HENRY

Book Five: Psalms 107-150

Psalm 107

1-9 Exhortation to celebrate God's praises.
Here is,
I. A general call to all to give thanks to God, v. 1. Let all that sing this psalm, or pray over it, set themselves herein to give thanks to the Lord; and those that have not any special matter for praise may furnish themselves with matter enough from God's universal goodness. In the fountain he is good; in the streams his mercy endures for ever and never fails.
II. A particular demand hereof from the redeemed of the Lord, which may well be applied spiritually to those that have an interest in the great Redeemer and are saved by him from sin and hell. They have, of all people, most reason to say that God is good, and his mercy everlasting; these are the children of God that were scattered abroad, whom Christ died to gather together in one, out of all lands, John xi. 52; Matt. xxiv. 31. But it seems here to be meant of a temporal deliverance, wrought for them when in their distress they cried unto the Lord, v. 6. Is any afflicted? Let him pray. Does any pray? God will certainly hear and help. When troubles become extreme that is man's time to cry; those who but whispered prayer before then cry aloud, and then it is God's time to succor. In the mount he will be seen.
1. They were in an enemy's country, but God wrought out their rescue: He redeemed them from the hand of the enemy (v. 2), not by might or power, it may be (Zech. iv. 6), nor by price or reward (Isa. xlv. 13), but by the Spirit of God working on the spirits of men.
2. They were dispersed as out-casts, but God gathered them out of all the countries whither they were scattered in the cloudy and dark day, that they might again be incorporated, v. 3. See Deut. xxx. 4; Ezek. xxxiv. 12. God knows those that are his, and where to find them.
3. They were bewildered, had no road to travel in, no dwelling place to rest in, v. 4. When they were redeemed out of the hand of the enemy, and gathered out of the lands, they were in danger of perishing in their return home through the dry and barren deserts. They wandered in the wilderness, where there was no trodden path, no company, but a solitary way, no lodging, no conveniences, no accommodations, no inhabited city where they might have quarters or refreshment. But God led them forth by the right way (v. 7), directed them to an inn, nay, directed them to a home, that they might go to a city of habitation, which was inhabited, nay which them themselves should inhabit.
4. They were ready to perish for hunger (v. 5): Their soul even fainted in them. They were spent with the fatigues of their journey and ready to drop down for want of refreshment. Those that have constant plenty,

Psalm 107

8-14

8 Oh that men would praise the LORD for his goodness, and for his wonderful works to the children of men!
9 For he satisfieth the longing soul, and filleth the hungry soul with goodness.
10 Such as sit in darkness and in the shadow of death, being bound in affliction and iron;
11 Because they rebelled against the words of God, and contemned the counsel of the most High:
12 Therefore he brought down their heart with labor; they fell down, and there was none to help.
13 Then they cried unto the LORD in their trouble, and he saved them out of their distresses.
14 He brought them out of darkness and the shadow of death, and brake their bands in sunder.

Verse 6. Then they cried unto the LORD in their trouble. Not till they were in extremities did they pray, but the mercy is that they prayed then, and prayed in the right manner, with a cry, and to the right person, even to the Lord. Nothing else remained for them to do; they could not help themselves, or find help in others, and therefore they cried to God.

Verse 7. And he led them forth by the right way. There are many wrong ways, but only one right one, and into this none can lead us but God himself. When the Lord is leader the way is sure to be right; we never need question that. Forth from the pathless mazes of the desert he conducted the lost ones; he found the way, made the way, and enabled them to walk along it, faint and hungry as they were.

Verse 8. Oh that men would praise the LORD for his goodness. Men are not mentioned here in the original, but the word is fitly supplied by the translators; the psalmist would have all things in existence magnify Jehovah's name. Surely men will do this without being exhorted to it when the deliverance is fresh in their memories. They must be horrible ingrates who will not honor such a deliverer for so happy a rescue from the most cruel death. It is well that the redeemed should be stirred up to bless the Lord again and again, for preserved life deserves life long thankfulness.

Verse 9. For he satisfieth the longing soul. This is the summary of the lost traveler's experience. He who in a natural sense has been rescued from perishing in a howling wilderness ought to bless the Lord who brings hint again to eat bread among men. The spiritual sense is, however, the more rich in instruction. The Lord sets us longing and then completely satisfies us.

Verse 10. Such as sit in darkness and in the shadow of death. The cell is dark of itself, and the fear of execution casts a still denser gloom over the prison. Such is the cruelty of man to man that tens of thousands have been made to linger in places only fit to be tombs; unhealthy, suffocating, filthy sepulchers, where they have sickened and died of broken hearts. Meanwhile the dread of sudden death has been the most hideous part of the punishment; the prisoners have felt as if the chill shade of death himself froze them to the very marrow.

Verse 11. Because they rebelled against the words of God. This was the general cause of bondage among the ancient people of God, they were given over to their adversaries because they were not loyal to the Lord. God's words are not to be trifled with, and those who venture on such rebellion will bring themselves into bondage.

Verse 12. Therefore he brought down their heart with labor. In eastern prisons men are frequently made to labor like beasts of the field. As they have no liberty, so they have no rest. This soon subdues the stoutest heart, and makes the proud boaster sing another tune. Trouble and hard toil are enough to tame a lion. God has methods of abating the loftiness of rebellious looks; the cell and the mill make even giants tremble. They fell down, and there was none to help.

Verse 13. Then they cried unto the Lord in their trouble. Not a prayer till then. While there was any to help below they would not look above. No cries till their hearts were brought down and their hopes were all dead—then they cried, but not before. So many a man offers what he calls prayer when he is in good case and thinks well of himself, but in very deed the only real cry to God is that which is forced out of him by a sense of utter helplessness and misery.

Verse 14. He brought them out of darkness and the shadow of death. The Lord in providence fetches out prisoners from their cells and bids them breathe the sweet fresh air again, and then he takes off their fetters, and gives liberty to their aching limbs. So also he frees men from care and trouble, and especially from the misery and slavery of sin. This he does with his own hand, for in the experience of all the saints it is certified that there is no jail delivery unless by the Judge himself.

his judgments in the time of adversity, and on his goodness in delivering us from it. For surely it is not by mere chance that a person falls into the hands of enemies or robbers; neither is it by chance that he is rescued from them. But this is what we must constantly keep in view, that all afflictions are God's rod, and that therefore there is no remedy for them elsewhere than in his grace. If a person fall into the hands of robbers or pirates, and be not instantly murdered, but, giving up all hope of life, expects death every moment; surely the deliverance of such a one is a striking proof of the grace of God, which shines the more illustriously in proportion to the fewness of the number who make their escape. Thus, then, should a great number perish, this circumstance ought by no means to diminish the praises of God.

11. Because they rebelled In assigning the cause of their afflictions he corrects the false impressions of those persons who imagine that these happen by chance. Were they to reflect on the judgments of God, they would at once perceive that there was nothing like chance or fortune in the government of the world. Moreover, until men are persuaded that all their troubles come upon them by the appointment of God, it will never come into their minds to supplicate him for deliverance. Farther, when the prophet assigns the reason for their afflictions, he is not to be regarded as speaking of those persons as if they were notoriously wicked, but he is to be considered as calling upon the afflicted carefully to examine some particular parts of their life, and although no one accuse them, to look into their hearts, where they will always discover the true origin of all the miseries which overtake them.

17-22

17. Fools are afflicted on account of the way of their transgression. He comes to another species of chastisement. For as he observed above, that those were given over to captivity who refused to yield obedience to God, so now he teaches that others have been visited by God with disease, as the fruit of their transgressions. And when the transgressor shall find that it is God who is administering correction to him, this will pave the way for his arriving at the knowledge of his grace.

He denominates those fools, who, thoughtlessly giving themselves up to sensuality, bring destruction upon themselves. The sin which they commit is not the result of ignorance and error only, but of their carnal affections, which depriving them of proper understanding, cause them to devise things detrimental to themselves. The maxim, that the fear of God is wisdom, must never be lost sight of. Hence it plainly follows, that they who shake off the yoke of God, and surrender themselves to Satan and sin, are the victims of their own folly and fury. And as constituting a principal ingredient of this madness, the prophet employs the term deletion or transgression; and subsequently he adds iniquities; because it happens that when once a man departs from God, from that moment he loses all self-control, and falls from one sin into another. But it is not of the distempers which commonly

and are every day fed to the full, know not what a miserable case it is to be hungry and thirsty, and to have no supply. This was sometimes the case of Israel in the wilderness, and perhaps of other poor travelers; but God's providence finds out ways to satisfy the longing soul and fill the hungry soul with goodness, v. 9. Israel's wants were seasonably supplied, and many have been wonderfully relieved when they were ready to perish. The same God that has led us has fed us all our life long unto this day, has fed us with food convenient, has provided food for the soul, and filled the hungry soul with goodness. Those that hunger and thirst after righteousness, after God, the living God, and communion with him, shall be abundantly replenished with the goodness of his house, both in grace and glory. Now for all this those who receive mercy are called upon to return thanks (v. 8): Oh that men (it is meant especially of those men whom God has graciously relieved) would praise the Lord for his goodness to them in particular, and for his wonderful works to others of the children of men!

10-16 The divine goodness towards prisoners.

We are to take notice of the goodness of God towards prisoners and captives. Observe,

1. A description of this affliction. Prisoners are said to sit in darkness (v. 10), in dark dungeons, close prisons, which intimates that they are desolate and disconsolate; they sit in the shadow of death, which intimates not only great distress and trouble, but great danger.

2. The cause of this affliction, v. 11. It is because they rebelled against the words of God. Willful sin is rebellion against the words of God; it is a contradiction to his truths and a violation of his laws.

3. The design of this affliction, and that is to bring down their heart (v. 12), to humble them for sin, to make them low in their own eyes, to cast down every high, proud, aspiring thought. Afflicting providences must be improved as humbling providences; and we not only lose the benefit of them, but thwart God's designs and walk contrary to him in them if our hearts be unhumbled and unbroken, as high and hard as ever under them.

4. The duty of this afflicted state, and that is to pray (v. 13): Then they cried unto the Lord in their trouble, though before perhaps they had neglected him. Prisoners have time to pray, who, when they were at liberty, could not find time; they see they have need of God's help, though formerly they thought they could do well enough without him.

5. Their deliverance out of the affliction: They cried unto the Lord, and he saved them, v. 13. He brought them out of darkness into light, welcome light, and then doubly sweet and pleasant, brought them out of the shadow of death to the comforts of life, and their liberty was to them life from the dead, v. 14. Were they fettered? He broke their bands asunder. Were they

Psalm 107

15-21

15 Oh that men would praise the LORD for his goodness, and for his wonderful works to the children of men!
16 For he hath broken the gates of brass, and cut the bars of iron in sunder.
17 Fools because of their transgression, and because of their iniquities, are afflicted.
18 Their soul abhorreth all manner of meat; and they draw near unto the gates of death.
19 Then they cry unto the LORD in their trouble, and he saveth them out of their distresses.
20 He sent his word, and healed them, and delivered them from their destructions.
21 Oh that men would praise the LORD for his goodness, and for his wonderful works to the children of men!

Verse 15. Oh that men would praise the LORD for his goodness, and for his wonderful works to the children of men. The sight of such goodness makes a right minded man long to see the Lord duly honored for his amazing mercy. When dungeon doors fly open, and chains are snapped, who can refuse to adore the glorious goodness of the Lord? It makes the heart sick to think of such gracious mercies remaining unsung: we cannot but plead with men to remember their obligations and extol the Lord their God.

Verse 16. For he hath broken the gates of brass, and cut the bars of Zion in sunder. This verse belongs to that which precedes it, and Sums up the mercy experienced by captives. The Lord breaks the strongest gates and bars when the time comes to set free his prisoners: and spiritually the Lord Jesus has broken the most powerful of spiritual bonds and made us free indeed. Brass and iron are as tow before the flame of Jesus' love. The gates of hell shall not prevail against us, neither shall the bars of the grave detain us. Those of us who have experienced his redeeming power must and will praise the Lord for the wonders of his grace displayed on our behalf.

Verse 17. Fools because of their transgression, and because of their iniquities, are afflicted. Many sicknesses are the direct result of foolish acts. Thoughtless and lustful men by drunkenness, gluttony, and the indulgence of their passions fill their bodies with diseases of the worst kind. Sin is at the bottom of all sorrow, but some sorrows are the immediate results of wickedness: men by a course of transgression afflict themselves and are fools for their pains. Worse still, even when they are in affliction they are fools still; and if they were brayed in a mortar among wheat with a pestle, yet would not their folly depart from them. From one transgression they go on to many iniquities, and while under the rod they add sin to sin. Alas, even the Lord's own people sometimes play the fool in this sad manner.

Verse 18. Their soul abhorreth all manner of meat. Appetite departs from men when they are sick: the best of food is nauseous to them, their stomach turns against it. And they draw near unto the gates of death. From want of food, and from the destructive power of their malady, they slide gradually down till they lie at the door of the grave; neither does the skill of the physician suffice to stay their downward progress.

Verse 19. Then they cry unto the LORD in their trouble. They join the praying legion at last. Saul also is among the prophets. The fool lays aside his motley in prospect of the shroud, and betakes himself to his knees. What a cure for the soul sickness of body is often made to be by the Lord's grace! And he saveth them out of their distresses. Prayer is as effectual on a sick bed as in the wilderness or in prison; it may be tried in all places and circumstances with certain result. We may pray about our bodily pains and weaknesses, and we may look for answers too. When we have no appetite for meat we may have an appetite for prayer. He who cannot feed on the word of God may yet turn to God himself and find mercy.

Verse 20. He sent his word and healed them. Man is not healed by medicine alone, but by the word which proceedeth out of the mouth of God is man restored from going down to the grave. A word will do it, a word has done it thousands of times. And delivered them from their destructions. They escape though dangers had surrounded them, dangers many and deadly. The word of the Lord has a great delivering power; he has but to speak and the armies of death flee in an instant.

Verse 21. Oh that men would praise the Lord for his goodness, and for his wonderful works to the children of men. It is marvelous that men can be restored from sickness and yet refuse to bless the Lord. It would seem impossible that they should forget such great mercy, for we should expect to see both themselves and the friends to whom they are restored uniting in a lifelong act of thanksgiving. Yet when ten are healed it is seldom that more than one returns to give glory to God. Alas, where are the nine? When a spiritual cure is wrought by the great Physician, praise is one of the surest signs of renewed health. A mind rescued from the disease of sin and the prevail in the world to which a reference is made in this passage, but to those which are deemed fatal, and in which all hope of life is abandoned, so that the grace of God becomes the more conspicuous when deliverance from them is obtained. When a man recovers from a slight indisposition, he does not so plainly discern the effects of God's power, as when it is put forth in a wonderful and notable manner to bring back some from the gates of death, and restores them to their wonted health and rigor. He says, therefore, that they are preserved from many corruptions, which is equivalent to his saying, that they are delivered from as many deaths. To this purport are the following words of the prophet, in which he says, that they approach the gates of death, and that they loathe all food We have already adverted to their calling upon God, namely, that when men are reduced to the greatest straits, they, by thus calling upon God for aid, acknowledge that they would be undone unless he wonderfully interposed for their deliverance.

20. He sendeth his word. Again, in saying that they are delivered from destruction, the prophet shows that he is here alluding to those diseases which, in the opinion of men, are incurable, and from which few are delivered. Besides, he contrasts God's assistance with all the remedies which are in the power of man to apply; as if he should say, that their disease having baffled the skill of earthly physicians, their recovery has been entirely owing to the exertion of God's power. It is proper also to notice the manner in which their recovery is effected; God has but to will it, or to speak the word, and instantly all diseases, and even death itself, are expelled. I do not regard this as exclusively referring to the faithful, as many expositors do. I own, indeed, that it is of comparatively little consequence to us to be the subjects of bodily care, if our souls still remain unsanctified by the word of God; and hence it is the intention of the prophet that we consider the mercy of God as extending to the evil and unthankful. The meaning of the passage, therefore, is, that diseases neither come upon us by chance, nor are to be ascribed to natural causes alone, but are to be viewed as God's messengers executing his commands; so that we must believe that the same person that sent them can easily remove them, and for this purpose he has only to speak the word. And since we now perceive the drift of the passage, we ought to attend to the very appropriate analogy contained in it. Corporeal maladies are not removed except by the word or command of God, much less are men's souls restored to the enjoyment of spiritual life, except this word be apprehended by faith.

22. And let them sacrifice. This clause is subjoined by way of explanation, the more strongly to express how God is robbed of his due, if in the matter of sacrifice his providence be not recognized. Even nature itself teaches that some kind of homage and reverence is due to God; this is acknowledged by the heathens themselves, who have no other instructor than nature. We know too, that the practice of offering sacrifices has obtained among all nations; and doubtless it was by the observance of this ritual, that God designed to preserve in the human family some sense of piety and religion. To

imprisoned in strong castles? He broke the gates of brass and the bars of iron wherewith those gates were made fast; he did not put back, but cut in sunder.

6. The return that is required from those whose bands God has loosed (v. 15): Let them praise the Lord for his goodness, and take occasion from their own experience of it, and share in it, to bless him for that goodness which the earth is full of, the world and those that dwell therein.

17-22 The divine goodness towards the afflicted.

Bodily sickness is another of the calamities of this life which gives us an opportunity of experiencing the goodness of God in recovering us, and of that the psalmist speaks in these verses, where we may observe,

I. That we, by our sins, bring sickness upon ourselves and then it is our duty to pray, v. 17-19.

1. It is the sin of the soul that is the cause of sickness; we bring it upon ourselves both meritoriously and efficiently: Fools, because of their transgression, are thus afflicted; they are thus corrected for the sins they have committed and thus cured of their evil inclinations to sin.

2. The weakness of the body is the effect of sickness, v. 18. When people are sick their soul abhors all manner of meat; they not only have no desire to eat nor power to digest it, but they nauseate it, and their stomach is turned against it.

3. Then is a proper time for prayer: Then they cry unto the Lord, v. 19. Is any sick? Let him pray; let him be prayed for. Prayer is a salve for every sore.

II. That it is by the power and mercy of God that we are recovered from sickness, and then it is our duty to be thankful. Compare with this Job xxxiii. 18, 28.

1. When those that are sick call upon God he returns them an answer of peace. They cry unto him and he saves them out of their distresses (v. 19); he removes their griefs and prevents their fears. He does it easily: He sent his word and healed them, v. 20. This may be applied to the miraculous cures which Christ wrought when he was upon earth, by a word's speaking; he said, Be clean, Be whole, and the work was done.

2. When those that have been sick are restored they must return to God an answer of praise (v. 21, 22): Let all men praise the Lord for his goodness, and let those, particularly, to whom God has thus granted a new life, spend it in his service; let them sacrifice with thanksgiving, not only bring a thank-offering to the altar, but a thankful heart to God.

23-32 The divine goodness to mariners.

The psalmist here calls upon those to give glory to God who are delivered from dangers at sea. Though the Israelites dealt not much in merchandise, yet their neighbors the Tyrians and Zidonians did, and for them perhaps this part of the psalm was especially calculated.

Psalm 107

22-28

22 And let them sacrifice the sacrifices of thanksgiving, and declare his works with rejoicing.
23 They that go down to the sea in ships, that do business in great waters;
24 These see the works of the LORD, and his wonders in the deep.
25 For he commandeth, and raiseth the stormy wind, which lifteth up the waves thereof.
26 They mount up to the heaven, they go down again to the depths: their soul is melted because of trouble.
27 They reel to and fro, and stagger like a drunken man, and are at their wit's end.
28 Then they cry unto the LORD in their trouble, and he bringeth them out of their distresses.

weary pains of conviction, must and will adore Jehovah Rophi, the healing God: yet it were well if there were a thousand times as much even of this.

Verse 22. And let them sacrifice the sacrifices of thanksgiving. In such a case let there be gifts and oblations as well as words. Let the good Physician have his fee of gratitude. Let life become a sacrifice to him who has prolonged it, let the deed of self denying gratitude be repeated again and again: there must be many cheerful sacrifices to celebrate the marvelous boon.

Verse 23. They that go down to the sea in ships. Navigation was so little practiced among the Israelites that mariners were invested with a high mystery, and their craft was looked upon as one of singular daring degree of and peril.

Verse 24. These see the works of the LORD. Beyond the dwellers on the land they see the Lord's greatest works, or at least such as stayers at home judge to be so when they hear the report thereof. Instead of the ocean proving to be a watery wilderness, it is full of God's creatures, and if we were to attempt to escape from his presence by flying to the uttermost parts of it, we should only rush into Jehovah's arms, and find ourselves in the very center of his workshop. And his wonders in the deep. They see wonders in it and on it. It is in itself a wonder and it swarms with wonders. Seamen, because they have fewer objects around them, are more observant of those they have than landsmen are, and hence they are said to see the wonders in the deep.

Verse 25. For he commandeth: his word is enough for anything, he has but to will it and the tempest rages. And raiseth the stormy wiled. It seemed to he asleep before, but it knows its Master's bidding, and is up at once in all its fury. Which lifteth up the waves thereof. The glassy surface of the sea is broken, and myriads of white heads appear and rage and toss themselves to and fro as the wind blows upon them. Whereas they were lying down in quiet before, the waves rise in their might and leap towards the sky as soon as the howling of the wind awakens them. Thus it needs but a word from God and the soul is in troubled waters, tossed to and fro with a thousand afflictions.

Verse 26. They mount up to the heaven. Borne aloft on the crest of the wave, the sailors and their vessels appear to climb the skies, but it is only for a moment, for very soon in the trough of the sea they go down again to the depths. As if their vessel were but a sea bird, the mariners are tossed "up and down, up and down, from the base of the wave to the billow's crown." Their soul is melted because of trouble.

Verse 27. They reel to and fro, and stagger like a drunken man. The violent motion of the vessel prevents their keeping their legs, and their fears drive them out of all power to use their brains, and therefore they look like intoxicated men. And are at their wit's end. What more can they do? They have used every expedient known to navigation, but the ship is so strained and beaten about that they know not how to keep her afloat. Here too the spiritual mariner's log agrees with that of the sailor on the sea. We have staggered frightfully! We could stand to nothing and hold by nothing. We knew not what to do, and could have done nothing if we had known it. We were as men distracted, and felt as if destruction itself would be better than our horrible state of suspense. As for wit and wisdom, they were clean washed out of us, we felt ourselves to be at a nonplus altogether.

Verse 28. Then they cry unto the LORD in their trouble. Though at their wit's end, they had wit enough to pray; their heart was melted, and it ran out in cries for help.

Verse 29. He maketh the storm a calm. He reveals his power in the sudden and marvelous transformations which occur at his bidding. He commanded the storm and now he ordains a calm: God is in all natural phenomena, and we do well to recognize his working.

Verse 30. Then are they glad because they be quiet. No one can appreciate this verse unless he has been in a storm at sea. No music can be sweeter

JOHN CALVIN

acknowledge the bounty and beneficence of God, is the most acceptable sacrifice which can be presented to him; to this subject, therefore, the prophet intends to recall the attention of the insensate and indifferent portion of men. I do not deny that there may be also an allusion to the ceremonial law; but inasmuch as in the world at large sacrifices formed part of the religious exercises, he charges those with ingratitude, who, after having escaped from some imminent peril, forget to celebrate the praises of their Great Deliverer.

23-32

23. They that go down to the sea in ships Here we have another instance of God's superintending care towards mankind pointed out to us by the prophet, exemplified in the bringing of those who are shipwrecked to the harbor, and this, too, as if he had raised them from the depth and darkness of the tomb, and brought them to live in the light of day. I do not understand what is here said about those who are accustomed to navigate the ocean seeing the wonders of God, as referring generally to the many wonderful things with which it abounds. Such persons are well fitted to bear testimony regarding the works of God, because they there behold more vast and various wonders than are to be seen upon earth. But it appears to me preferable to connect this with the subsequent context, where the prophet is his own interpreter, and where he shows how suddenly God raises and calms the tempest.

The sum of the matter is, that the scope of the passage is to point out that the lives of those who navigate the seas are often in great jeopardy by the storms which they encounter; because, as often as the ocean heaves and is agitated, and the billows rise and rage, so often does death stare them in the face. But he furnishes us with a still more vivid picture of the providence of God; for in telling us, that the sea does not of its own accord rise into a tempest, he makes use of the verb, he speaks, intimating that the word and providence of God make the winds blow, to agitate the sea. True, indeed, the mariners imagine from certain phenomena, that a storm is approaching, but sudden changes proceed only from the secret appointment of God. Therefore, he gives not merely a historical narrative of the manner in which squalls and storms arise, but, assuming the character of a teacher, begins with the cause itself, and then directs to the imminent danger with which the tempest is fraught; or rather, portrays, as in a picture, the image of death, in order that the goodness of God may appear the more conspicuous when the tempest happily ceases without any loss of life. They mount up, says he, to the heavens, they descend into the deeps; as if he should say, they mount up into the air, so that their life may be destroyed, and then they tumble down towards the caverns of the ocean, where they may be drowned.

Next, he mentions the fears which torment them, or rather which may deprive them of understanding; intimating by these words, that however skillfully mariners may steer their vessels, they may happen to be deprived of their senses; and being thus paralyzed, they could not avail themselves of aid,

MATTHEW HENRY

I. Much of the power of God appears at all times in the sea, v. 23, 24. It appears to those that go down to the sea in ships, as mariners, merchants, fishermen, or passengers, that do business in great waters. And surely none will expose themselves there but those that have business (among all Solomon's pleasant things we do not read of any pleasure-boat he had), but those that go on business, lawful business, may, in faith, put themselves under the divine protection. These see the works of the Lord, and his wonders, which are the more surprising, because most are born and bred upon land, and what passes at sea is new to them. The deep itself is a wonder, its vastness, its saltiness, its ebbing and flowing. The great variety of living creatures in the sea is wonderful. Let those that go to sea be led, by all the wonders they observe there, to consider and adore the infinite perfections of that God whose the sea is, for he made it and manages it.

II. It especially appears in storms at sea, which are much more terrible than at land. Observe here,

1. How dangerous and dreadful a tempest at sea is. Then wonders begin to appear in the deep, when God commands and raises the strong wind, which fulfils his word, Ps. cxlviii. 8. He raises the winds, as a prince by his commission raises forces. Satan pretends to be the prince of the power of the air; but he is a pretender; the powers of the air are at God's command, not at his. When the wind becomes stormy it lifts up the waves of the sea, v. 25. Then the ships are kicked like tennis-balls on the tops of the waves; they seem to mount up to the heavens, and then they couch again, as if they would go down to the depths, v. 26. A stranger, who had never seen it, would not think it possible for a ship to live at sea, as it will in a storm, and ride it out, but would expect that the next wave would bury it and it would never come up again; and yet God, who taught man discretion to make ships that should so strangely keep above water, does by his special providence preserve them, that they answer the end to admiration. When the ships are thus tossed the soul of the seaman melts because of trouble; and, when the storm is very high, even those that are used to the sea can neither shake off nor dissemble their fears, but they reel to and fro, and tossing makes them giddy, and they stagger and are sick, it may be, like a drunken man; the whole ship's crew are in confusion and quite at their wits' end (v. 27), not knowing what to do more for their preservation; all their wisdom is swallowed up, and they are ready to give up themselves for gone, Jonah i. 5, &c.

2. How seasonable it is at such a time to pray. Those that go to sea must expect such perils as are here described, and the best preparation they can make for them is to make sure a liberty of access to God by prayer, for then they will cry unto the Lord, v. 28. We have a saying, "Let those that would learn to pray go to sea;" I say, Let those that will go to sea learn to

Psalm 107

29-35
29 He maketh the storm a calm, so that the waves thereof are still.
30 Then are they glad because they be quiet; so he bringeth them unto their desired haven.
31 Oh that men would praise the LORD for his goodness, and for his wonderful works to the children of men!
32 Let them exalt him also in the congregation of the people, and praise him in the assembly of the elders.
33 He turneth rivers into a wilderness, and the water springs into dry ground;
34 A fruitful land into barrenness, for the wickedness of them that dwell therein.
35 He turneth the wilderness into a standing water, and dry ground into water springs.

than the rattling of the chain as the shipmen let down the anchor; and no place seems more desirable than the little cove, or the wide bay, in which the ship rests in peace. So he bringeth them unto their desired haven. The rougher the voyage the more the mariners long for port, and heaven becomes more and more "a desired haven", as our trials multiply. By storms and by favorable breezes, though tempest and fair weather, the great Pilot and Ruler of the sea brings mariners to port, and his people to heaven.
Verse 31. Oh that men would praise the Loud for his goodness, and for his wonderful works to the children of men! Let the sea sound forth Jehovah's praises because of his delivering grace. As the sailor touches the shore let him lift the solemn hymn to heaven, and let others who see him rescued from the jaws of death unite in his thanksgiving.
Verse 32. Let them exalt him also in the congregation of the people. Thanks for such mercies should be given in public in the place where men congregate for worship. And praise him in the assembly of the elders. The praise should be presented with great solemnity in the presence of men of years, experience, and influence. High and weighty service should be rendered for great and distinguished favors, and therefore let the sacrifice be presented with due decorum and with grave seriousness. Often when men hear of a narrow escape from shipwreck they pass over the matter with a careless remark about good luck, but it should never be thus jested with. When a heart has been in great spiritual storms and has at last found peace, there will follow as a duty and a privilege the acknowledgment of the Lord's mercy before his people, and it is well that this should be done in the presence of those who hold office in the church, and who from their riper years are better able to appreciate the testimony.
Verse 33. He turneth rivers into a wilderness, and the water springs into dry ground. When the Lord deals with rebellious men he can soon deprive them of those blessings of which they feel most assured: their rivers and perennial springs they look upon as certain never to be taken from them, but the Lord at a word can deprive them even of these.
Verse 34. A fruitful land into barrenness. This has been done in many instances, and notably in the case of the psalmist's own country, which was once the glory of all lands and is now almost a desert. For the wickedness of them that dwell therein. Sin is at the bottom of sorrow. It first made the ground sterile in father Adam's day, and it continues to have a blighting effect upon all that it touches. If we have not the salt of holiness we shall soon receive the salt of barrenness, for the text in the Hebrew is—"a fruitful land into saltness." If we will not yield the Lord a harvest of obedience he may forbid the soil to yield us a harvest of bread, and what then?
Verse 35. He turneth the wilderness into a standing water. With another turn of his hand he more than restores that which in judgment he took away. He does his work of mercy on a royal scale, for a deep lake is seen where before there was only a sandy waste. It is not by natural laws, working by some innate force, that this wonder is wrought, but by himself—HE TURNETH.
Verse 36. And there he maketh the hungry to dwell, where none could dwell before. They will appreciate the change and prize his grace; as the barrenness of the land caused their hunger so will its fertility banish it for ever, and they will settle down a happy and thankful people to bless God for every handful of corn which the land yields to them. None are so ready to return a revenue of praise to God for great mercies as those who have known the lack of them. Hungry souls make sweet music when the Lord fills them with his gracious gifts.
Verse 37. And sow the fields, and plant vineyards, which may yield fruits of increase. Men work when God works. His blessing encourages the sower, cheers the planter, and rewards the laborer. Not only necessaries but luxuries are enjoyed, wine as well as corn, when the heavens are caused to yield the needed rain to fill the watercourses. Divine visitations bring

were it even at hand. For though they collect all their tackling, cast their sounding line into the deep, and unfurl their sails to all points, yet after making every attempt, and all human skill is baffled, they give themselves up to the mercy of wind and wave. All hope of safety being cut off, no farther means are employed by them. And now that all human aid fails, they cry unto God for deliverance, which is a convincing evidence that they had been as it were dead.

29. He maketh the storm a calm. A profane author, in narrating the history of such an event, would have said, that the winds were hushed, and the raging billows were calmed; but the Spirit of God, by this change of the storm into a calm, places the providence of God as presiding over all; thereby meaning, that it was not by human agency that this violent commotion of the sea and wind, which threatened to subvert the frame of the world, was so suddenly stilled. When, therefore, the sea is agitated, and boils up in terrific fury, as if wave were contending with wave, whence is it that instantly it is calm and peaceful, but that God restrains the raging of the billows, the contention of which was so awful, and makes the bosom of the deep as smooth as a mirror?

33-41

33. He turneth rivers into a wilderness Here then is an account of changes which it would be the height of folly to attribute to chance. Fruitful lands become unfruitful, and barren lands assume the new aspect of freshness and fruitfulness. And how happens it that one district becomes sterile, and another becomes fat and fertile, contrary to what they were wont to be, but because that God pours out his wrath upon the inhabitants of the one, by taking his blessing from them, and renders the other fruitful to feed the hungry? It may be ascribed to the thinness of the population, that many parts of Asia and Greece, once exceedingly fruitful, now lie uncultivated and unproductive; but we must ascribe to the providence of God, which the prophet praises, the well authenticated fact, that in some places the earth that was fruitful has now become barren and parched, while others are beginning to be fertile.

35. He turneth the desert into a pool of water. This change, in contrast with the former, places the miraculous power of God in a more luminous position. Because, were the fields ceasing to be so productive as in former times, men of the world, as was common of old, would attribute this to the frequent crops which exhausted their productive power. But whence is it that parched grounds become so fruitful, that one would almost say that the atmosphere, as well as the nature of the soil, had undergone a change, unless it be that God hath there put forth a wonderful display of his power and goodness? Wherefore, the prophet very justly says, that the deserts were turned into pools of water, so that populous cities may rise up in waste and uncultivated places, where once there was not a single cottage.

39. Afterwards they are lessened. As we had formerly a description of the changes which these districts underwent in relation to the nature of the soil, so now we are informed that

pray, and accustom themselves to pray, that they may come with the more boldness to the throne of grace when they are in trouble. Even heathen mariners, in a storm, cried every man to his god; but those that have the Lord for their God have a present and powerful help in that and every other time of need, so that when they are at their wits' end they are not at their faith's end.

3. How wonderfully God sometimes appears for those that are in distress at sea, in answer to their prayers: He brings them out of the danger; and the sea is still: He makes the storm a calm, v. 29. The winds fall, and only by their soft and gentle murmurs serve to lull the waves asleep again, so that the surface of the sea becomes smooth and smiling.

33-43 Wonders of divine providence.

The psalmist, having given God the glory of the providential reliefs granted to persons in distress, here gives him the glory of the revolutions of providence, and the surprising changes it sometimes makes in the affairs of the children of men.

I. He gives some instances of these revolutions.

1. Fruitful countries are made barren and barren countries are made fruitful. Much of the comfort of this life depends upon the soil in which our lot is cast. Now,

(1.) The sin of man has often marred the fruitfulness of the soil and made it unserviceable, v. 33, 34. Land watered with rivers is sometimes turned into a wilderness, and that which had been full of water-springs now has not so much as water-streams; it is turned into dry and sandy ground, that has not consistency and moisture enough to produce any thing valuable.

(2.) The goodness of God has often mended the barrenness of the soil, and turned a wilderness, a land o drought, into water-springs, v. 35.

2. Necessitous families are raised and enriched, while prosperous families are impoverished and go to decay. If we look broad in the world,

(1.) We see many greatly increasing whose beginning was small, and whose ancestors were mean and made no figure, v. 36-38. Those that were hungry are made to dwell in fruitful lands; there they take root, and gain a settlement, and prepare a city for habitation for themselves and theirs after them.

(2.) We see many that have thus suddenly risen as suddenly sunk and brought to nothing (v. 39): Again they are diminished and brought low by adverse providences, and end their days as low as they began them; or their families after them lose as fast as they got, and scatter what they heaped together.

3. Those that were high and great in the world are abased, and those that were mean and despicable are advanced to honor, v. 40, 41. We have seen,

(1.) Princes dethroned and reduced to straits. He pours contempt upon them, even among those that

Psalm 107

36-43
36 And there he maketh the hungry to dwell, that they may prepare a city for habitation;
37 And sow the fields, and plant vineyards, which may yield fruits of increase.
38 He blesseth them also, so that they are multiplied greatly; and suffereth not their cattle to decrease.
39 Again, they are minished and brought low through oppression, affliction, and sorrow.
40 He poureth contempt upon princes, and causeth them to wander in the wilderness, where there is no way.
41 Yet setteth he the poor on high from affliction, and maketh him families like a flock.
42 The righteous shall see it, and rejoice: and all iniquity shall stop her mouth.
43 Whoso is wise, and will observe these things, even they shall understand the loving kindness of the LORD.

great spiritual riches, foster varied works of faith and labors of love, and cause every good fruit to abound to our comfort and to God's praise. When God sends the blessing it does not supersede, but encourages and develops human exertion. Paul plants, Apollos waters, and God gives the increase.

Verse 38. He blesseth them also, so that they are multiplied greatly; and suffereth not their cattle to decrease. God's blessing is everything. It not only makes men happy, but it makes men themselves, by causing men to be multiplied upon the earth. When the Lord made the first pair he blessed them and said "be fruitful and multiply", and here he restores the primeval blessing.

Verse 39. Again they are minished and brought low through oppression, affliction, and sorrow. As they change in character, so do their circumstances alter. Under the old dispensation, this was very clearly to be observed; Israel's ups and downs were the direct consequences of her sins and repentance.

Verses 40-41. In these two verses we see how the Lord at will turns the wheel of providence. Paying no respect to man's imaginary grandeur, he puts princes down and makes them wander in banishment as they had made their captives wander when they drove them from land to land: at the same time, having ever a tender regard for the poor and needy, the Lord delivers the distressed and sets them in a position of comfort and happiness. This is to be seen upon the roll of history again and again, and in spiritual experience we remark its counterpart: the self sufficient are made to despise themselves and search in vain for help in the wilderness of their nature, while poor convicted souls are added to the Lord's family and dwell in safety as the sheep of his fold.

Verse 42. The righteous shall see it, and rejoice. Divine providence causes joy to God's true people; they see the hand of the Lord in all things, and delight to study the ways of his justice and of his grace. And all iniquity shall stop her mouth. What can she say? God's providence is often so conclusive in its arguments of fact, that there is no replying or questioning. It is not long that the impudence of ungodliness can be quiet, but when God's judgments are abroad it is driven to hold its tongue.

Verse 43. Those who notice providence shall never be long without a providence notice. It is wise to observe what the Lord doth, for he is wonderful in counsel; has given us eyes to see with, and it is foolish to close them when there is most to observe; but we must observe wisely, otherwise we may soon confuse ourselves and others with hasty reflections upon the dealings of the Lord. In a thousand ways the lovingkindness of the Lord is shown, and if we will prudently watch, we shall come to a better understanding of it. To understand the delightful attribute of lovingkindness is an attainment as pleasant it is profitable: those who are proficient scholars in this art will be among sweetest singers to the glory of Jehovah.

mankind do not for ever continue in the same condition; because they both decrease in number, and lose their place and property by being reduced by wars or by civil commotions, or by other casualties. Therefore, whether they are wasted by the pestilence, or are defeated in battle, or are cut off by intestine broils, it is manifest that both their rank and condition undergo alteration. And what is the occasion of this change, but that God withdraws his grace, which hitherto formed the hidden spring from which all their prosperity issued? And as there are a thousand casualties by which cities may be ruined, the prophet brings forward one species of change of all others the most palpable and remarkable. And since God's hand is not observed in that which relates to persons living in comparative obscurity, he brings into view princes themselves, whose name and fame will not permit any memorable event which befalls them to remain in obscurity. For it seems that the world is made on their account. When God, therefore, hurls them from their lofty estate, then men, aroused as it were from their slumber, are prepared to regard his judgments.

42-43

42. The righteous shall see that, and shall rejoice. The prophet now draws the conclusion, that so many evident tokens of God's superintending and overruling providence could not transpire before the righteous without attracting their notice, and that their vision being illuminated by faith, these scenes are contemplated by them with unfeigned delight; while the wicked remain perplexed and mute. For he very judiciously makes a distinction between these two classes of persons. In whatever manner the wicked may be constrained to recognize God as the supreme ruler of the universe, nevertheless, in seeing they see not, and derive nothing from the sight, except that their conduct is rendered the more inexcusable.

43. Whosoever is wise, so as to observe these things. We are now informed that men begin to be wise when they turn their whole attention to the contemplation of the works of God, and that all others besides are fools. For however much they may pique themselves upon their superior acuteness and subtlety, all this is of no avail so long as they shut their eyes against the light which is presented to them. In employing this interrogatory form of address, he indirectly adverts to that false persuasion which prevails in the world, at the very time when the most daring heaven-despiser esteems himself to be the wisest of men; as if he should say, that all those who do not properly observe the providence of God, will be found to be nothing but fools. This caution is the more necessary, since we find that some of the greatest of philosophers were so mischievous as to devote their talents to obscure and conceal the providence of God, and, entirely overlooking his agency, ascribed all to secondary causes.

By the term, observe, he informs us, that the bare apprehension of the works of God is not enough,—they must be carefully considered in order that the knowledge of them may be deliberately and maturely digested. And, therefore, that it may be engraven upon our hearts, we must make these works the theme of our attentive and constant meditation.

have idolized them. Those that exalt themselves God will abase, and, in order thereunto, will infatuate: He makes them to wander in the wilderness, where there is no way. He baffles those counsels by which they thought to support themselves, and their own power and pomp, and drives them headlong, so that they know not what course to steer, nor what measures to take. We met with this before, Job xii. 24, 25.

(2.) Those of low degree advanced to the posts of honor (v. 41): Yet setteth he the poor on high, raiseth from the dust to the throne of glory, 1 Sam. ii. 8; Ps. cxiii. 7, 8. Those that were afflicted and trampled on are not only delivered, but set on high out of the reach of their troubles, above their enemies, and have dominion over those to whom they had been in subjection. That which adds to their honor, and strengthens them in their elevation, is the multitude of their children: He maketh him families like a flock of sheep, so numerous, so useful, so sociable with one another, and so meek and peaceable. He that sent them meat sent them mouths. Happy is the man that has his quiver filled with arrows, for he shall boldly speak with the enemy in the gate, Ps. cxxvii. 5. God is to be acknowledged both in setting up families and in building them up. Let not princes be envied, nor the poor despised, for God has many ways of changing the condition of both.

II. He makes some improvement of these remarks; such surprising turns as these are of use,

1. For the solacing of saints. They observe these dispensations with pleasure (v. 42): The righteous shall see it and rejoice in the glorifying of God's attributes and the manifesting of his dominion over the children of men.

2. For the silencing of sinners: All iniquity shall stop her mouth; it shall be a full conviction of the folly of atheists, and of those that deny the divine providence; and, forasmuch as practical atheism is at the bottom of all sin, it shall in effect stop the mouth of all iniquity. When sinners see how their punishment answers to their sin, and how justly God deals with them in taking away from them those gifts of his which they had abused, they shall not have one word to say for themselves; for God will be justified, he will be clear.

3. For the satisfying of all concerning the divine goodness (v. 43): Whoso is wise, and will observe these things, these various dispensations of divine providence, even they shall understand the lovingkindness of the Lord. Here is,

(1.) A desirable end proposed, and that is, rightly to understand the loving kindness of the Lord. It is of great use to us, in religion, to be fully assured of God's goodness, to be experimentally acquainted and duly affected with it, that his lovingkindness may be before our eyes, Ps. xxvi. 3.

(2.) A proper means prescribed for attaining this end, and that is a due observance of God's providence. We must lay up these things, mind them, and keep them in mind, Luke ii. 19.

Psalm 108

Title
A Song or Psalm of David.

1 O God, my heart is fixed; I will sing and give praise, even with my glory.
2 Awake, psaltery and harp: I myself will awake early.
3 I will praise thee, O LORD, among the people: and I will sing praises unto thee among the nations.
4 For thy mercy is great above the heavens: and thy truth reacheth unto the clouds.
5 Be thou exalted, O God, above the heavens: and thy glory above all the earth;
6 That thy beloved may be delivered: save with thy right hand, and answer me.
7 God hath spoken in his holiness; I will rejoice, I will divide Shechem, and mete out the valley of Succoth.
8 Gilead is mine; Manasseh is mine; Ephraim also is the strength of mine head; Judah is my lawgiver;
9 Moab is my washpot; over Edom will I cast out my shoe; over Philistia will I triumph.
10 Who will bring me into the strong city? who will lead me into Edom?
11 Wilt not thou, O God, who hast cast us off? and wilt not thou, O God, go forth with our hosts?
12 Give us help from trouble: for vain is the help of man.
13 Through God we shall do valiantly: for he it is that shall tread down our enemies.

Psalm 108

For Psalm 108:1-5 see Psalm 57:7-11, for Psalm 108:6-13 see Psalm 60:5-12. It will be at once seen that those two portions of Scripture, Ps 57:7-11 and Ps 60:5-12) are almost identical with the verses from Psalm before us.

Psalm 108

Because this psalm is composed of parts taken from the fifty-seventh and sixtieth psalms, it would be superfluous to repeat, in this place, what we have already said by way of exposition in those psalms.

For Psalm 108:1-5, see Psalm 57:7-11; Psalm 108:6-13, see Psalm 60:5-12.

Psalm 108

For Psalm 108:1-5 see Psalm 57:7-11, for Psalm 108:6-13 see Psalm 60:5-12.

Psalm 109

Title
To the chief Musician. A Psalm of David.

1-7
1 Hold not thy peace, O God of my praise;
2 For the mouth of the wicked and the mouth of the deceitful are opened against me: they have spoken against me with a lying tongue.
3 They compassed me about also with words of hatred; and fought against me without a cause.
4 For my love they are my adversaries: but I give myself unto prayer.
5 And they have rewarded me evil for good, and hatred for my love.
6 Set thou a wicked man over him: and let Satan stand at his right hand.
7 When he shall be judged, let him be condemned: and let his prayer become sin.

Psalm 109

To The Chief Musician. Intended therefore to be sung, and sung in the temple service! Yet is it by no means easy to imagine the whole nation singing such dreadful imprecations. We ourselves, at any rate, under the gospel dispensation, find it very difficult to infuse into the Psalm a gospel sense, or a sense at all compatible with the Christian spirit; and therefore one would think the Jews must have found it hard to chant such strong language without feeling the spirit of revenge excited; and the arousal of that spirit could never have been the object of divine worship in any period of time—under law or under gospel. At the very outset this title shows that the Psalm has a meaning with which it is fitting for men of God to have fellowship before the throne of the Most High: but what is that meaning? This is a question of no small difficulty, and only a very childlike spirit will ever be able to answer it.

A Psalm of David. Not therefore the ravings of a vicious misanthrope, or the execrations of a hot, revengeful spirit. David would not smite the man who sought his blood, he frequently forgave those who treated him shamefully; and therefore these words cannot be read in a bitter, revengeful sense, for that would be foreign to the character of the son of Jesse. The imprecatory sentences before us were penned by one who with all his courage in battle was a man of music and of tender heart, and they were meant to be addressed to God in the form of a Psalm, and therefore they cannot possibly have been meant to be mere angry cursing.

DIVISION. In the first five verses (Ps 109:1-5) David humbly pleads with God that he may be delivered from his remorseless and false hearted enemies. From Ps 109:6-20, filled with a prophetic fervor, which carries him entirely beyond himself, he denounces judgment upon his foes, and then from Ps 109:21-31 he returns to his communion with God in prayer and praise. The central portion of the Psalm in which the difficulty lies must be regarded not as the personal wish of the psalmist in cool blood, but as his prophetic denunciation of such persons as he describes, and emphatically of one special "son of perdition" whom he sees with prescient eye. We would all pray for the conversion of our worst enemy, and David would have done the same; but viewing the adversaries of the Lord, and doers of iniquity, As Such, and as incorrigible we cannot wish them well; on the contrary, we desire their overthrow, and destruction. The gentlest hearts burn with indignation when they hear of barbarities to women and children, of crafty plots for ruining the innocent, of cruel oppression of helpless orphans, and gratuitous ingratitude to the good and gentle. A curse upon the perpetrators of the atrocities in Turkey may not be less virtuous than a blessing upon the righteous. We wish well to all mankind, and for that very reason we sometimes blaze with indignation against the inhuman wretches by whom every law which protects our fellow creatures is trampled down, and every dictate of humanity is set at nought.

EXPOSITION

Verse 1. Hold not thy peace. Mine enemies speak, be thou pleased to speak too. Break thy solemn silence, and silence those who slander me. It is the cry of a man whose confidence in God is deep, and whose communion with him is very close and bold. Note, that he only asks the Lord to speak: a word from God is all a believer needs.

Verse 2. For the mouth of the wicked and the mouth of the deceitful are opened against me. Wicked men must needs say wicked things, and these we have reason to dread; but in addition they utter false and deceitful things, and these are worst of all.

Verse 3. They compassed me about also with words of hatred. Turn which way he would they hedged him in with falsehood, misrepresentation,

JOHN CALVIN

Psalm 109

109:1-5

1. O God of my praise! be not silent. In these words, which may be considered as an introduction to the psalm, David declares that he neither could find nor would desire any other than God to stand forward in vindication of the integrity of his heart. For in denominating him the God of his praise, he intrusts to him the vindication of his innocence, in the face of the calumnies by which he was all but universally assailed. Some are of opinion that this clause is to be understood as referring to David's having actually declared that he himself was the publisher of God's praises; but the scope of the passage is opposed to such an interpretation; for we find David appealing to the judgment of God against the unjust and cruel hatred to which he was subjected in the world. There is in the words an implied contrast, because, when calumny is rampant, innocence is duly and properly estimated by none but God only. The meaning of the passage is this: Lord, although I may be regarded as the vilest of the vile, and exposed to the reproach of the world, yet thou wilt maintain the uprightness of my character, and on this account thou wilt also set forth my praise.

2. Because the mouth of the wicked. David here very plainly declares, that he was the more solicitous to obtain help from God, in consequence of justice not being found among men. And though it is probable that he was rashly and furiously assailed, nevertheless, he complains that the mouth of deceit and fraud had been opened against him, and that he was surrounded with false tongues.

3. And they have encompassed me. He complains, that from all quarters he was assailed with the most hostile and abusive epithets, and that, too, most undeservedly. And, under a beautiful similitude, he shows that the tongues of his enemies were so full of deadly poison, that it was harder for him to endure their attacks than that of a great army, and the more so that he merited no such treatment at their hands.

4. On account of my love they have been opposed to me. The Psalmist had already solemnly declared, that his adversaries, unprovoked by any injury inflicted upon them by him, and without any just cause, became, through mere diabolical rage, his most implacable foes. Here he confirms the truth of that declaration by saying, that he had been their friend. For there is far more merit in showing kindness to an enemy than simply abstaining from doing that which is evil.

6-11

6. Set thou over him a wicked person. Hitherto he poured out his complaint against a vast number of persons; now he seems to direct it against a single individual. Probably he speaks of each of them individually. It is, however, equally probable that he refers in very marked terms to some one in particular among these wicked persons, the most notorious transgressor of any of them. Some conjecture, and not without reason, that Doeg is the person here aimed at, who, by his treason and revolt, sought to bring ruin, not only upon

MATTHEW HENRY

Psalm 109

1-5 Appeal to God against enemies.

It is the unspeakable comfort of all good people that, whoever is against them, God is for them, and to him they may apply as to one that is pleased to concern himself for them. Thus David here.

I. He refers himself to God's judgment (v. 1): "Hold not thy peace, but let my sentence come forth from thy presence, Ps. xvii. 2. Delay not to give judgment upon the appeal made to thee." God saw what his enemies did against him, but seemed to connive at it, and to keep silence: "Lord," says he, "do not always do so."

II. He complains of his enemies, showing that they were such as it was fit for the righteous God to appear against.

1. They were very spiteful and malicious: They are wicked; they delight in doing mischief (v. 2); their words are words of hatred, v. 3. They had an implacable enmity to a good man because of his goodness. "They open their mouths against me to swallow me up, and fight against me to cut me off if they could."

2. They were notorious liars; and lying comprehends two of the seven things which the Lord hates. "They are deceitful in their protestations and professions of kindness, while at the same time they speak against me behind my back, with a lying tongue."

3. They were both public and restless in their designs; "They compassed me about on all sides, so that, which way soever I looked, I could see nothing but what made against me."

4. They were unjust; their accusations of him, and sentence against him, were all groundless: "They have fought against me without a cause; I never gave them any provocation." Nay, which was worst of all,

5. They were very ungrateful, and rewarded him evil for good, v. 5. Many a kindness he had done them, and was upon all occasions ready to do them, and yet he could not work upon them to abate their malice against him, but, on the contrary, they were the more exasperated because they could not provoke him to give them some occasion against him (v. 4): For my love they are my adversaries. The more he endeavored to gratify them the more they hated him.

III. He resolves to keep close to his duty and take the comfort of that: But I give myself unto prayer (v. 4), I prayer (so it is in the original); "I am for prayer, I am a man of prayer, I love prayer, and prize prayer, and practice prayer, and make a business of prayer, and am in my element when I am at prayer."

6-20 Prophetic imprecations.

I. The imprecations here are very terrible-woe, and a thousand woes, to that man against whom God says Amen to them; and they are all in full force against the implacable enemies and persecutors of God's church and people, that will not repent, to give him glory. It is here foretold concerning this bad man,

Psalm 109

8-15

8 Let his days be few; and let another take his office.
9 Let his children be fatherless, and his wife a widow.
10 Let his children be continually vagabonds, and beg: let them seek their bread also out of their desolate places.
11 Let the extortioner catch all that he hath; and let the strangers spoil his labor.
12 Let there be none to extend mercy unto him: neither let there be any to favor his fatherless children.
13 Let his posterity be cut off; and in the generation following let their name be blotted out.
14 Let the iniquity of his fathers be remembered with the LORD; and let not the sin of his mother be blotted out.
15 Let them be before the LORD continually, that he may cut off the memory of them from the earth.

accusation, and scorn. Whispers, sneers, insinuations, satires, and open charges filled his ear with a perpetual buzz, and all for no reason, but sheer hate. Each word was as full of venom as an egg is full of meat: they could not speak without showing their teeth.

Verse 4. For my love they are my adversaries. They hate me because I love them. One of our poets says of the Lord Jesus—"Found guilty of excess of love." Surely it was his only fault. Our Lord might have used all the language of this complaint most emphatically—they hated him without a cause and returned him hatred for love.

Verse 5. And they have rewarded me evil for good, and hatred for my love. Evil for good is devil like. This is Satan's line of action, and his children upon earth follow it greedily; it is cruel, and wounds to the quick. The revenge which pays a man back in his own coin has a kind of natural justice in it; but what shall be said of that baseness which returns to goodness the very opposite of what it has a right to expect? Our Lord endured such base treatment all his days, and, alas, in his members, endures it still.

Verse 6. Set thou a wicked man over him. What worse punishment could a man have? The proud man cannot endure the proud, nor the oppressor brook the rule of another like himself.

Verse 7. When he shall be judged, let him be condemned. He judged and condemned others in the vilest manner, he suffered not the innocent to escape; and it would be a great shame if in his time of trial, being really guilty, he should be allowed to go free.

Verse 8. Let his days be few. Who would desire a persecuting tyrant to live long? As well might we wish length of days to a mad dog. If he will do nothing but mischief the shortening of his life will be the lengthening of the world's tranquility.

Verse 9. Let his children be fatherless, and his wife a widow. This would inevitably be the case when the man died, but the psalmist uses the words in an emphatic sense, he would have his widow "a widow indeed", and his children so friendless as to be orphaned in the bitterest sense. He sees the result of the bad man's decease, and includes it in the punishment.

Verse 10. Let his children be continually vagabonds, and beg. May they have neither house nor home, settlement nor substance; and while they thus wander and beg may it ever be on their memory that their father's house lies in ruins,—let them seek their bread also out of their desolate places. It has often been so: a race of tyrants has become a generation of beggars.

Verse 11. Let the extortioner catch all that he hath. A doom indeed. Those who have once fallen into the hands of the usurer can tell you what this means: it were better to be a fly in the web of a spider. In the most subtle, worrying, and sweeping manner the extortioner takes away, piece by piece, his victim's estate, till not a fraction remains to form a pittance for old age.

Verse 12. Let there be none to extend mercy unto him. He had no mercy, but on the contrary, he crushed down all who appealed to him. Loath to smite him with his own weapon, stern justice can do no otherwise, she lifts her scales and sees that this, too, must be in the sentence.

Verse 13. Let his posterity be cut off; and in the generation following let their name be blotted out. Both from existence and from memory let them pass away till none shall know that such a vile brood ever existed.

Verse 14. This verse is, perhaps, the most terrible of all, but yet as a matter of fact children do procure punishment upon their parents' sins, and are often themselves the means of such punishment. A bad son brings to mind his father's bad points of character; people say, "Ah, he is like the old man. He takes after his father." A mother's sins also will be sure to be called to mind if her daughter becomes grossly wicked.

Verse 15. Again, he wishes that his father's sins may follow up the transgressor and assist to fill the measure of his own iniquities, so that for the whole accumulated load the family may be smitten with utter extinction.

David, but also upon all the holy priests; and we know that this psalm is applied by Peter to Judas, (Acts 1:20) But with equal propriety, and certainly not less forcibly, may this complaint be considered as applicable to some most intimate and particular friend of the Psalmist.

Respecting the imprecations contained in this psalm David forms such maledictions, or expresses his desires for them, he is not instigated by any immoderate carnal propensity, nor is he actuated by zeal without knowledge, nor is he influenced by any private personal considerations.

7. When he is judged, let him depart guilty. Another imprecation is, that, being summoned to judgment, he might be punished without mercy, and that, though he humbly crave forgiveness, the judge should remain inexorable. This might with propriety be understood to relate not merely to his being judged at the bar of men, but also at the tribunal of God. But as it accords very well with the decisions awarded by an earthly judge, and as this is the commonly received interpretation, I have no wish to depart from it.

8. Let his days be few. Although this world is the scene of much toil and trouble, yet we know that these are pledges and proofs of God's loving-kindness, inasmuch as he frequently, and as a token of his love, promises to prolong the lives of men; not that it is absolutely necessary for us to remain long here, but that we may have an opportunity of sharing of God's fatherly love which he bears towards us, by which we may be led to cherish the hope of immortality.

In the two succeeding verses the malediction is extended both to the wife and children; and the desire, that she may be left a widow and they become fatherless, depends upon the brevity of that life to which the prophet formerly adverted.

12-16

12. Let there be none prolonging mercy to him. To continue to show humanity and mercy is, according to the Hebrew idiom, equivalent to constant and successive acts of kindness; and it also sometimes denotes pity, or the being moved to sympathy, when, through the lapse of years, anger is appeased, and even one's calamity melts the heart of the man who bore hatred towards him.

13. Let his posterity be cut off. This is a continuation of the same subject that God would visit the iniquities of the fathers upon their children. And as he had to deal with the whole court of Saul, and not with any single individual, he here employs the plural number. But as in deeds of wickedness, there are always some who are the prime movers, and act as the ringleaders of others, we need not be surprised that having spoken of one person, he next addresses the many, and then returns to the same person.

16. Because he forgot to show mercy. The prophet comes now to show that he had good reason for desiring such awful and direful calamities to be inflicted upon his enemies, whose thirst for cruelty was insatiable, and who were transported with rage, no less cruel than obstinate, against the afflicted and poor man, persecuting him with as little scruple as if they were attacking a dead dog. Even philosophers look upon

1. That he should be cast and sentenced as a criminal, with all the dreadful pomp of a trial, conviction, and condemnation (v. 6, 7): Set thou a wicked man over him, to be as cruel and oppressive to him as he has been to others; for God often makes one wicked man a scourge to another, to spoil the spoilers and to deal treacherously with those that have dealt treacherously.

2. That, being condemned, he should be executed as a most notorious malefactor.

(1.) That he should lose his life, and the number of his months be cut off in the midst, by the sword of justice: Let his days be few, or shortened, as a condemned criminal has but a few days to live (v. 8); such bloody and deceitful men shall not live out half their days.

(2.) That consequently all his places should be disposed of to others, and they should enjoy his preferments and employments: Let another take his office. This Peter applies to the filling up of Judas's place in the truly sacred college of the apostles, by the choice of Matthias, Acts i. 20. Those that mismanage their trusts will justly have their office taken from them and given to those that will approve themselves faithful.

(3.) That his family should be beheaded and beggared, that his wife should be made a widow and his children fatherless, by his untimely death, v. 9. Wicked men, by their wicked courses, bring ruin upon their wives and children, whom they ought to take care of and provide for. Yet his children, if, when they lost their father, they had a competency to live upon, might still subsist in comfort; but they shall be vagabonds and shall beg; they shall not have a house of their own to live in, but shall creep out of their desolate places with fear and trembling, like beasts out of their dens, to seek their bread (v. 10), because they are conscious to themselves that all mankind have reason to hate them for their father's sake.

(4.) That his estate should be ruined, as the estates of malefactors are confiscated (v. 11): Let the extortioner, the officer, seize all that he has and let the stranger, who was nothing akin to his estate, spoil his labor, either for his crimes or for his debts, Job v. 4, 5.

(5.) That his posterity should be miserable. Fatherless children, though they have nothing of their own, yet sometimes are well provided for by the kindness of those whom God inclines to pity them; but this wicked man having never shown mercy there shall be none to extend mercy to him, by favoring his fatherless children when he is gone, v. 12.

(6.) That his memory should be infamous, and buried in oblivion and disgrace (v. 13): Let his posterity be cut off; let his end be to destruction (so Dr. Hammond).

II. The ground of these imprecations bespeaks them very just, though they sound very severe.

1. To justify the imprecations of vengeance upon the sinner's posterity, the sin of his ancestors is here

Psalm 109

16-23

16 Because that he remembered not to shew mercy, but persecuted the poor and needy man, that he might even slay the broken in heart.
17 As he loved cursing, so let it come unto him: as he delighted not in blessing, so let it be far from him.
18 As he clothed himself with cursing like as with his garment, so let it come into his bowels like water, and like oil into his bones.
19 Let it be unto him as the garment which covereth him, and for a girdle wherewith he is girded continually.
20 Let this be the reward of mine adversaries from the LORD, and of them that speak evil against my soul.
21 But do thou for me, O GOD the Lord, for thy name's sake: because thy mercy is good, deliver thou me.
22 For I am poor and needy, and my heart is wounded within me.
23 I am gone like the shadow when it declineth: I am tossed up and down as the locust.

A king might justly wish for such an end to fall upon an incorrigible brood of rebels; and of persecutors, continuing in the same mind, the saints might well pray for their extinction; but the passage is dark; and we must leave it so. It must be right or it would not be here, but how we cannot see. Why should we expect to understand all things? Perhaps it is more for our benefit to exercise humility, and reverently worship God over a hard text, than it would be to comprehend all mysteries.

Verse 16. Because that he remembered not to shew mercy. Because he had no memory to show mercy the Judge of all will have a strong memory of his sins. So little mercy had he ever shown that he had forgotten how to do it, he was without common humanity, devoid of compassion, and therefore only worthy to be dealt with after the bare rule of justice.

Verse 17. As he loved cursing, so let it come unto him. Deep down in every man's soul the justice of the lex talionis is established. Retaliation, not for private revenge, but as a measure of public justice, is demanded by the psalmist and deserved by the crime.

Verses 18-19. He was so openly in the habit of wishing ill to others that he seemed to wear robes of cursing, therefore let it be as his raiment girded and belted about him, yea, let it enter as water into his bowels, and search the very marrow of his bones like a penetrating oil. It is but common justice that he should receive a return for his malice, and receive it in kind, too.

Verse 20. This is the summing up of the entire imprecation, and fixes it upon the persons who had so maliciously assailed the inoffensive man of God. David was a man of gentle mould, and remarkably free from the spirit of revenge, and therefore we may here conceive him to be speaking as a judge or as a representative man, in whose person great principles needed to be vindicated and great injuries redressed.

Verse 21. But do thou for me, O God the Lord, for thy name's sake. How eagerly he turns from his enemies to his God! He sets the great THOU in opposition to all his adversaries, and you see at once that his heart is at rest.

Verse 22. For I am poor and needy. When he does plead anything about himself he urges not his riches or his merits, but his poverty and his necessities: this is gospel supplication, such as only the Spirit of God can indite upon the heart.

Verse 23. I am gone like the shadow when it declineth. I am a mere shadow, a shadow at the vanishing point, when it stretches far, but is almost lost in the universal gloom of evening which settles over all, and so obliterates the shadows cast by the setting sun. Lord, there is next to nothing left of me, wilt thou not come in before I am quite gone? I am tossed up and down as the locust, which is the sport of the winds, and must go up or down as the breeze carries it. The psalmist felt as powerless in his distress as a poor insect, which a child may toss up and down at its pleasure. He entreats the divine pity, because he had been brought to this forlorn and feeble condition by the long persecution which his tender heart had endured. Slander and malice are apt to produce nervous disorders and to lead on to pining diseases. Those who use these poisoned arrows are not always aware of the consequences; they scatter fire brands and death and say it is sport.

Verse 24. My knees are weak through fasting; either religious fasting, to which he resorted in the dire extremity of his grief, or else through loss of appetite occasioned by distress of mind. Who can eat when every morsel is soured by envy? This is the advantage of the slanderer, that he feels nothing himself, while his sensitive victim can scarcely eat a morsel of bread because of his sensitiveness. However, the good God knoweth all this, and will succor his afflicted.

Verse 25. I became also a reproach unto them. They made him the theme of ridicule, the butt of their ribald jests: his emaciation by fasting made him a tempting subject for their caricatures and lampoons. When they looked upon me they shaked their heads. Words were not a sufficient expression cruelty, directed against the helpless and miserable, as an act worthy only of a cowardly and groveling nature; for it is between equals that envy is cherished. For this reason the prophet represents the malignity of his enemies as being bitter in persecuting him when he was in affliction and poverty. The expression, the sorrowful in heart, is still more emphatic. For there are persons who, notwithstanding of their afflictions, are puffed up with pride; and as this conduct is unreasonable and unnatural, these individuals incur the displeasure of the powerful.

17-20
17. As he loved cursing. David still continues to enumerate the sins of his adversaries, and is thus severe in his treatment of them, in order to render it more apparent, that he is strictly conforming to the judgment of God. For as often as we draw near to the tribunal of God, we must take care that the equity of our cause may be so sure and evident as to secure for it and us a favorable reception from him. Fortified by the testimony of an approving conscience, David here declares his readiness to commit the matter between him and his enemies to the judgment of God. The words, which are expressive of cursing and blessing, are in the past tense, cursing came upon him, and blessing was far from him, but it is necessary to translate them as expressive of a wish or desire; for David continues to pray that his enemy may be visited with the same unparalleled ills which he had inflicted upon others. A stranger to every act of kindness, and taking pleasure in doing evil, it is the wish of the Psalmist that he may now be subjected to every species of calamity.
20. Let this be the work from Jehovah. That is, let the gain or reward of the work be from God. In pointing out the work as proceeding immediately from God, he intends to show that, though deprived of all human aid, he yet entertained the hope that God would grant him deliverance, and avenge the injuries of his servant. From this verse we learn that David did not rashly, or unadvisedly, utter curses against his enemies, but strictly adhered to what the Spirit dictated.

21-27
21. And thou, O Jehovah my Lord! From the pouring out of complaints and imprecations against his enemies, the Psalmist passes to prayers; or rather, after having betaken himself to God as his guardian and deliverer, he appears to take occasion, from this circumstance, to encourage himself in prayer; even as all the pious reflections by which the faithful exercise and strengthen their faith, stimulate them to call upon the name of God. At the same time, he does not pique himself upon any service which he has rendered to God, as deserving of his help, nor does he rely upon his own worthiness, but he places all his confidence in the free grace and mercy of God.
23. I walk about as a shadow. These are two very appropriate similitudes: the first of them also comes in Psalm 102:12; namely, that the afflicted person, and he who is almost lifeless, is very fitly compared to the shadow of the evening.

brought into the account (v. 14, 15), the iniquity of his fathers and the sin of his mother. These God often visits even upon the children's children, and is not unrighteous therein: when wickedness has long run in the blood justly does the curse run along with it.
2. To justify the imprecations of vengeance upon the sinner himself, his own sin is here charged upon him, which called aloud for it.
(1.) He had loved cruelty, and therefore give him blood to drink (v. 16): He remembered not to show mercy, remembered not those considerations which should have induced him to show mercy, remembered not the objects of compassion that had been presented to him, but persecuted the poor, whom he should have protected and relieved, and slew the broken in heart, whom he should have comforted and healed. Here is a barbarous man indeed, not it to live.
(2.) He had loved cursing, and therefore let the curse come upon his head, v. 17-19. Those that were out of the reach of his cruelty he let fly at with his curses, which were impotent and ridiculous; but they shall return upon him. The word of the curse is quick and powerful, and divides between the joints and the marrow; it works powerfully and effectually; it fastens on the soul; it is a piercing thing, and there is no antidote against it. Let it compass him on every side as a garment, v. 19. Let God's cursing him be his shame, as his cursing his neighbor was his pride; let it cleave to him as a girdle, and let him never be able to get clear of it. Let it be to him like the waters of jealousy, which caused the belly to swell and the thigh to rot. This points at the utter ruin of Judas, and the spiritual judgments which fell on the Jews for crucifying Christ. The psalmist concludes his imprecations with a terrible Amen, which signifies not only, "I wish it may be so," but "I know it shall be so." Let this be the reward of my adversaries from the Lord, v. 20. And this will be the reward of all the adversaries of the Lord Jesus; his enemies that will not have him to reign over them shall be brought forth and slain before him. And he will one day recompense tribulation to those that trouble his people.

21-31 Humble petitions; triumphing in God.
David, having denounced God's wrath against his enemies, here takes God's comforts to himself, but in a very humble manner, and without boasting.
I. He pours out his complaint before God concerning the low condition he was in, which, probably, gave advantage to his enemies to insult over him: "I am poor and needy, and therefore a proper object of pity, and one that needs and craves thy help."
1. He was troubled in mind (v. 22): My heart is wounded within me.
2. He apprehended himself drawing near to his end: I am gone like the shadow when it declines.
3. His body was wasted, and almost worn away (v. 24): My knees are weak through fasting.

Psalm 109

24-31

24 My knees are weak through fasting; and my flesh faileth of fatness.
25 I became also a reproach unto them: when they looked upon me they shaked their heads.
26 Help me, O LORD my God: O save me according to thy mercy:
27 That they may know that this is thy hand; that thou, LORD, hast done it.
28 Let them curse, but bless thou: when they arise, let them be ashamed; but let thy servant rejoice.
29 Let mine adversaries be clothed with shame, and let them cover themselves with their own confusion, as with a mantle.
30 I will greatly praise the LORD with my mouth; yea, I will praise him among the multitude.
31 For he shall stand at the right hand of the poor, to save him from those that condemn his soul.

of their scorn, they resorted to gestures which were meant both to show their derision and to irritate his mind.

Verse 26. Help me, O LORD my God. Laying hold of Jehovah by the appropriating word my, he implores his aid both to help him to bear his heavy load and to enable him to rise superior to it. He has described his own weakness, and the strength and fury of his foes, and by these two arguments he urges his appeal with double force. This is a very rich, short, and suitable prayer for believers in any situation of peril, difficulty, or sorrow.

Verse 27. That they may know that this is thy hand. Dolts as they are, let the mercy shown to me be so conspicuous that they shall be forced to see the Lord's agency in it. Ungodly men will not see God's hand in anything if they can help it, and when they see good men delivered into their power they become more confirmed than ever in their atheism; but all in good time God will arise and so effectually punish their malice.

Verse 28. Let them curse, but bless thou, or, they will curse and thou wilt bless. Their cursing will then be of such little consequence that it will not matter a straw. One blessing from the Lord will take the poison out of ten thousand curses of men.

Verse 29. Let mine adversaries be clothed with shame. It is a prophecy as well as a wish, and may be read both in the indicative and the imperative. Where sin is the underclothing, shame will soon be the outer vesture. He who would clothe good men with contempt shall himself be clothed with dishonor.

Verse 30. I will greatly praise the LORD with my mouth. Enthusiastically, abundantly, and loudly will he extol the righteous Lord, who redeemed him from all evil; and that not only in his own chamber or among his own family, but in the most public manner. Yea, I will praise him among the multitude. Remarkable and public providence demand public recognition, for otherwise men of the world will judge us to be ungrateful.

Verse 31. For he shall stand at the right hand of the poor. God will not be absent when his people are on their trial; he will hold a brief for them and stand in court as their advocate. How different is this from the doom of the ungodly who has Satan at his right hand (Ps 109:6). To save him from those that condemn his soul. The court only met as a matter of form, the malicious had made up their minds to the verdict, they judged him guilty, for their hate condemned him, yea, they pronounced sentence of damnation upon the very soul of their victim: but what mattered it? The great King was in court, and their sentence was turned against themselves. Nothing can more sweetly sustain the heart of a slandered believer than the firm conviction that God is near to all who are wronged, and is sure to work out their salvation.

At sunrise, or when he is shining in noon-day brightness, the constant shifting of the shadow is not so perceptible; but, towards sunset, the shadow flits before us during every moment that passes.

24. My knees are become feeble. Though David had the necessaries of life, yet he emaciated himself by voluntary abstinence, to which, as well as to prayer, he gave himself, and therefore we may regard this verse as expressive of his sorrow and sadness. We may also understand it as expressive of his having no relish for meat or drink, knowing, as we do, that persons who are in sorrow and sadness have no appetite for food; even life itself is burdensome to them.

26. Help me, O Jehovah! The prophet repeats his prayer, because the more we are assailed by the subtlety and deceit of Satan, the more necessary is it for us to strive more ardently, and display the greater boldness. We may, indeed, have the full assurance of God being propitious towards us, yet when he delays to manifest it, and when the ungodly slander us, it must be that various doubts which keep intruding themselves upon us arise in our minds. Hence, it is not without reason that David, in order that he might withstand such attacks, places himself under the protection of that God who, according to his mercy and goodness, helps his people in their time of need.

28-31

28. They shall curse. Those who view the words as a prayer, misinterpret them; because David, having already presented his petitions to God, and being secure in his favor, seems now rather to boast that their cursing will do him no harm; for Thou, says he, wilt bless me. By this means, he proves how little and how lightly he regarded the menaces of his enemies, though they might assail him by the poison of the tongue, and the power of the sword.

30. I will praise Jehovah greatly with my mouth. These words clearly establish the truth that David does not pray God to curse his enemies, but, by the holy boldness of his faith, sets them at defiance; for he prepares to offer up a tribute of gratitude to God, as if he had already realized the object of his desire. The phrase, with my mouth, is not, as some erroneously suppose, superfluous, but is to be considered as a public acknowledgement, on his part, of his thanksgiving to God for the deliverance vouchsafed to him; as if he should say, I will, not only when alone, and in the inward recesses of my heart, meditate upon the great goodness which I have received from God, but also in the appointed sacrifice of praise will I declare publicly, how much I am indebted to his grace.

4. He was ridiculed and reproached by his enemies (v. 25).

II. He prays for mercy for himself. In general (v. 21): "Do thou for me, O God the Lord! appear for me, act for me." If God be for us, he will do for us, will do more abundantly for us than we are able either to ask or think. He does not prescribe to God what he should do for him, but refers himself to his wisdom: "Lord, do for me what seems good in thy eyes. Do that which thou knowest will be for me, really for me, in the issue for me, though for the present it may seem to make against me." More particularly, he prays (v. 26): "Help me, O Lord my God! O save me! Help me under my trouble, save me out of my trouble; save me from sin, help me to do my duty." He prays (v. 28), Though they curse, bless thou. Here he despises the causeless curses of his enemies: Let them curse.

III. He prays that his enemies might be ashamed (v. 28), clothed with shame (v. 29), that they might cover themselves with their own confusion, that they might be left to themselves, to do that which would expose them and manifest their folly before all men, or rather that they might be disappointed in their designs and enterprises against David, and thereby might be filled with shame, as the adversaries of the Jews were, Neh. vi. 16.

IV. He pleads God's glory, the honor of his name. Do for me, for thy name's sake (v. 21), especially the honor of his goodness, by which he has proclaimed his name: "Deliver me, because thy mercy is good; it is what thou thyself dost delight in, and it is what I do depend upon. Save me, not according to my merit, for I have none to pretend to, but according to thy mercy; let that be the fountain, the reason, the measure, of my salvation."

Lastly, He concludes the psalm with joy, the joy of faith, joy in assurance that his present conflicts would end in triumphs.

1. He promises God that he will praise him (v. 30): "I will greatly praise the Lord, not only with my heart, but with my mouth; I will praise him, not in secret only, but among the multitude."

2. He promises himself that he shall have cause to praise God (v. 31): He shall stand at the right hand of the poor, nigh to him, a present help; he shall stand at his right hand as his patron and advocate to plead his cause against his accusers and to bring him off, to save him from those that condemn his soul and would execute their sentence if they could. God was David's protector in his sufferings, and was present also with the Lord Jesus in his, stood at his right hand, so that he was not moved (Ps. xvi. 8).

Psalm 110

Title
A Psalm of David.

1 The LORD said unto my Lord, Sit thou at my right hand, until I make thine enemies thy footstool.
2 The LORD shall send the rod of thy strength out of Zion: rule thou in the midst of thine enemies.
3 Thy people shall be willing in the day of thy power, in the beauties of holiness from the womb of the morning: thou hast the dew of thy youth.
4 The LORD hath sworn, and will not repent, Thou art a priest for ever after the order of Melchizedek.
5 The Lord at thy right hand shall strike through kings in the day of his wrath.
6 He shall judge among the heathen, he shall fill the places with the dead bodies; he shall wound the heads over many countries.
7 He shall drink of the brook in the way: therefore shall he lift up the head.

Psalm 110

TITLE. A Psalm of David. Of the correctness of this title there can be no doubt, since our Lord in Mt 22:1 says, "How then doth David in spirit call him Lord." Yet some critics are so fond of finding new authors for the psalms that they dare to fly in the face of the Lord Jesus himself. To escape from finding Jesus here, they read the title, "Psalm of (or concerning) David," as though it teas not so much written by him as of him, but he that reads with understanding will see little enough of David here except as the writer. He is not the subject of it even in the smallest degree, but Christ is all. How much was revealed to the patriarch David! How blind are some modern wise men, even amid the present blaze of light, as compared with this poet prophet of the darker dispensation. May the Spirit who spoke by the man after God's own heart give us eyes to see the hidden mysteries of this marvelous Psalm, in which every word has an infinity of meaning.
SUBJECT AND DIVISION. The subject is THE PRIEST KING. None of the kings of Israel united these two offices, though some endeavored to do so. Although David performed some acts which appeared to verge upon the priestly, yet he was no priest, but of the tribe of Judah, "of which tribe Moses spake nothing concerning the priesthood"; and he was far too devout a man to thrust himself into that office uncalled. The Priest King here spoken of is David's Lord, a mysterious personage typified by Melchizedek, and looked for by the Jews as the Messiah. He is none other than the apostle and high priest of our profession, Jesus of Nazareth, the King of the Jews. The Psalm describes the appointment of the kingly priest, his followers, his battles, and his victory. Its center is verse 4, and so it may be divided, as Alexander suggests, into the introduction, verses Ps 106:1-3; the central thought, verse 4; and the supplementary verses, Ps 106:5-7.

EXPOSITION
Verse 2. The LORD shall send the rod of thy strength out of Zion. It is in and through the church that for the present the power of the Messiah is known. Jehovah has given to Jesus all authority in the midst of his people, whom he rules with his royal scepter, and this power goes forth with divine energy from the church for the ingathering of the elect, and the subduing of all evil.
Verse 3. Thy people shall be willing in the day of thy power, in the beauties of holiness from the womb of the morning: thou hast the dew of thy youth. In consequence of the sending forth of the rod of strength, namely, the power of the gospel, out of Zion, converts will come forward in great numbers to enlist under the banner of the Priest King.
Verse 4. We have now reached the heart of the psalm, which is also the very center and soul of our faith. Our Lord Jesus is a Priest King by the ancient oath of Jehovah: "he glorified not himself to be made an high priest," but was ordained there unto from of old, and was called of God an high priest after the order of Melchizedek.
Verse 5. The Lord at thy right hand shall strike through kings in the day of his wrath. Now that he has come into the field of action, the infinite Jehovah comes with him as the strength of his right hand.
Verse 6. He shall judge among the heathen, or, among the nations. All nations shall feel his power, and either yield to it joyfully or be crushed before it.
Verse 7. He shall drink of the brook in the way. So swiftly shall he march to conquest that he shall not stay for refreshment, but drink as he hastens on. Like Gideon's men that lapped, he shall throw his heart into the fray and cut it short in righteousness Long has Jesus borne with our rebellious race, but he wilt rise to end the warfare of longsuffering, by the blows of justice.

JOHN CALVIN

Psalm 110

1-4
1. Jehovah said to my Lord. What is here stated might to some extent be applied to the person of David, inasmuch as he neither ascended the royal throne illegally, nor did he find his way to it by nefarious artifices, nor was he raised to it by the fickle suffrages of the people, but it was by the direct authority of God that he reigned over Israel.
2. Jehovah shall send out of Zion the scepter of thy power. The Psalmist not only confirms, in different terms, what he stated above, but also adds, that Christ's kingdom shall be vastly extended, because God would make his scepter stretch far and wide. David did indeed render not a few of the surrounding nations tributaries to him, but still his kingdom, when contrasted with other monarchies, was always confined within narrow limits. There is in the words an implied contrast, as if he had said, that Christ should not reign as King upon mount Zion only, because God would cause his power to extend to the remotest regions of the earth.
3. Thy people shall come. In this verse the Psalmist sets forth the honors of Christ's kingdom in relation to the number of his subjects, and their prompt and cheerful obedience to his commands.
4. Jehovah hath sworn. This verse is a satisfactory proof that the person here spoken of is none other than Christ. There can be no question that the Holy Ghost here refers to something specific and peculiar, as distinguishing and separating this king from all other kings. This, too, is the well known title with which Melchizedek was honored by Moses, (Genesis 14:18).

5-7
5. The Lord at thy right hand. In these words David celebrates the dreadful nature of that power which Christ possesses for the dispersion and destruction of his enemies; and by this means he affirms, that though encompassed by bands of deadly foes, yet their malignant attempts would not prevent God from upholding the King whom he has set up. The expression, in the day of his wrath, instructs us to patiently endure the cross.
7. He shall drink. The similitude seems to be drawn from the conduct of brave and powerful generals, who, when in hot pursuit of the enemy, do not suffer themselves to be diverted from their purpose by attending to luxuries; but, without kneeling down, are content to quench their thirst by drinking of the stream which they are passing. It was in this way that Gideon found out the brave and warlike soldiers; regarding such as kneeled down to drink as destitute of courage, he sent them back to their homes, Judges 7:5. It therefore appears to me that David figuratively attributes military prowess to Christ, declaring that he would not take time to refresh himself, but would hastily drink of the river which might come in his way. This is designed to strike his enemies with terror, intimating to them the rapid approach of impending destruction.

MATTHEW HENRY

Psalm 110

1-4 The Messiah's dominion.
Some have called this psalm David's creed, almost all the articles of the Christian faith being found in it. Glorious things are here spoken of Christ, and such as oblige us to consider how great he is.
I. That he is David's Lord. We must take special notice of this because he himself does. Matt. xxii. 43, David, in spirit, calls him Lord. And as the apostle proves the dignity of Melchizedek, and in him of Christ, by this, that so great a man as Abraham was paid him tithes (Heb. vii. 4), so we may by this prove the dignity of the Lord Jesus that David called him his Lord; by him that king acknowledges himself to reign, and to him to be acceptable as a servant to his lord.
II. That he is constituted a sovereign Lord by the counsel and decree of God himself: The Lord, Jehovah, said unto him, Sit as a king.
III. That he was to be advanced to the highest honor, and entrusted with an absolute sovereign power both in heaven and in earth: Sit thou at my right hand.
IV. That all his enemies were in due time to be made his footstool.
V. That he should have a kingdom set up in the world, beginning at Jerusalem (v. 2): "The Lord shall send the rod or scepter of thy strength out of Zion, by which thy kingdom shall be erected, maintained, and administered."
VI. That his kingdom, being set up, should be maintained and kept up in the world, in spite of all the oppositions of the power of darkness.
VII. That he should have a great number of subjects, who should be to him for a name and a praise, v. 3.

5-7 The Messiah's dominion.
Here we have our great Redeemer,
I. Conquering his enemies (v. 5, 6) in order to the making of them his footstool, v. 1. Observe here,
1. The conqueror: The Lord-Adonai, the Lord Jesus, he to whom all judgment is committed, he shall make his own part good against his enemies.
2. The time fixed for this victory: In the day of his wrath, that is, the time appointed for it.
3. The extent of this victory. It shall reach very high: He shall strike through kings.
4. The equity of this victory: He shall judge among them.
5. The effect of this victory; it shall be the complete and utter ruin of all his enemies.
II. We have here the Redeemer saving his friends and comforting them (v. 7); for their benefit,
1. He shall be humbled: He shall drink of the brook in the way, that bitter cup which the Father put into his hand.
2. He shall be exalted: Therefore shall he lift up the head. David spoke as a type of him in this (Ps. xxvii. 6), Now shall my head be lifted up above my enemies.

Psalm 111

1-5

1 Praise ye the LORD. I will praise the LORD with my whole heart, in the assembly of the upright, and in the congregation.
2 The works of the LORD are great, sought out of all them that have pleasure therein.
3 His work is honorable and glorious: and his righteousness endureth for ever.
4 He hath made his wonderful works to be remembered: the LORD is gracious and full of compassion.
5 He hath given meat unto them that fear him: he will ever be mindful of his covenant.

Psalm 111

TITLE. There is no title to this psalm, but it is an alphabetical hymn of praise, having for its subject the works of the Lord in creation, providence, and grace. The sweet singer dwells upon the one idea that God should be known by his people, and that this knowledge when turned into practical piety is man's true wisdom, and the certain cause of lasting adoration. Many are ignorant of what their Creator has done, and hence they are foolish in heart, and silent as to the praises of God: this evil can only be removed by a remembrance of God's works, and a diligent study of them; to this, therefore, the psalm is meant to arouse us. It may be called The Psalm of God's Works intended to excite us to the work of praise.
DIVISION. The psalmist begins with an invitation to praise, Ps 111:1; and then proceeds to furnish us with matter for adoration in God's works and his dealings with his people, Ps 111:2-9. He closes his song with a commendation of the worship of the Lord, and of the men who practice it.

EXPOSITION
Verse 1. Praise ye the LORD, or, Hallelujah! All ye his saints unite in adoring Jehovah, who worketh so gloriously. Do it now, do it always: do it heartily, do it unanimously, do it eternally. Even if others refuse, take care that ye have always a song for your God. Put away all doubt, question, murmuring, and rebellion, and give yourselves up to the praising of Jehovah, both with your lips and in your lives. I will praise the Load with my whole heart. The sweet singer commences the song, for his heart is all on flame: whether others will follow him or not, he will at once begin and long continue. What we preach we should practice. The best way to enforce an exhortation is to set an example; but we must let that example be of the best kind, or we may lead others to do the work in a limping manner. David brought nothing less than his whole heart to the duty; all his love went out towards God, and all his zeal, his skill, and his ardor went with it.
Verse 2. The works of the LORD are great. In design, in size, in number, in excellence, all the works of the Lord are great. Even the little things of God are great. In some point of view or other each one of the productions of his power, or the deeds of his wisdom, will appear to be great to the wise in heart. Sought out of all them that have pleasure therein. Those who love their Maker delight in his handiwork, they perceive that there is more in them than appears upon the surface, and therefore they bend their minds to study and understand them.
Verse 3. His work is honorable and glorious. His one special work, the salvation of his people, is here mentioned as distinguished from his many other works. This reflects honor and glory upon him. It is deservedly the theme of the highest praise, and compels those who understand it and experience it to ascribe all honor and glory unto the Lord. Its conception, its sure foundations, its gracious purpose, its wise arrangements, its gift of Jesus as Redeemer, its application of redemption by the Holy Ghost in regeneration and sanctification, and all else which make up the one glorious whole, all redound to the infinite honor of Him who contrived and carried out so astounding a method of salvation.
Verse 4. He hath made his wonderful works to be remembered. He meant them to remain in the recollection of his people, and they do so: partly because they are in themselves memorable, and because also he has taken care to record them by the pen of inspiration, and has written them upon the hearts of his people by his Holy Spirit. By the ordinances of the Mosaic law, the coming out of Egypt, the sojourn in the wilderness, and other memorabilia of Israel's history were constantly brought before the minds of the people, and their children were by such means instructed in the wonders which God had wrought in old time. Deeds such as God has wrought are not to be admired for an hour and then forgotten, they are

Psalm 111

The title to this psalm supplies the place of an argument; and, that others may be induced to engage in the praises of God, the Psalmist points out the manner of doing so by his own example. Then he gives a short account of the manifold benefits which, in olden times, he conferred upon the faithful, and is daily conferring upon them. The psalm is composed in alphabetical order, each verse containing two letters. The first verse begins with a, aleph, while the letter b, beth, is placed at the commencement of the next half of the verse. The last two verses only are not divided in this way; but each of these has three letters.

1-4

1. I will praise Jehovah. The best and most efficient method of inculcating the performance of any duty is to be exemplary; and, accordingly, we find that the prophet, in the present instance, sets himself for an example, to lead others to engage in the celebration of God's praises. His resolution to praise God consists of two parts; that he would celebrate God's praises unfeignedly, with all his heart, and that he would do it publicly, in the assembly of the faithful. He very properly begins with heart-praise, because it is much better to praise in secret, and when no one is conscious of it, than to lift up our voice, and shout forth his praises with feigned lips. At the same time, the person who, in secret, pours out his heart in grateful emotions towards God, will also set forth his praises in swelling strains, otherwise God would be deprived of one half of the honor which is due to him. The prophet then determines to praise God with the whole heart, that is, with an upright and honest heart; not that he engages to come up to the full measure of his duty, but he declares that he would not be like the hypocrites, who, coldly and with a double heart, or rather guilefully and perfidiously, employ their lips only in the praises of God.

2. The works of Jehovah are great. He now proceeds to inform us that there are abundant materials for praising God, supplied by his works, to which at present he makes only a general reference, and which he, subsequently, defines more explicitly in relation to the government of the Church. The magnitude of God's works is a subject which, generally, eludes the observation of men, and, therefore, few of them are acquainted with it. This ignorance the prophet ascribes to the indifference and ingratitude of men, comparatively few of whom condescend to notice the great wisdom, goodness, justice, and power, which shine forth in these works.

3. His work is beautiful. Others render it splendor. The meaning of the clause is this, That every act of God is replete with glorious majesty. In the following part of the verse he specifies more clearly in what this beauty and magnificence consist, by stating that the justice of God is everywhere conspicuous.

In the next verse, he more especially extols the wonderful works in which God has principally set forth his power. To cause his marvelous works to be remembered, is equivalent to the doing of works worthy of being remembered, or the

Psalm 111

1-5 The excellence of the divine works.

The title of the psalm being Hallelujah, the psalmist (as every author ought to have) has an eye to his title, and keeps to his text.

I. He resolves to praise God himself, v. 1. What duty we call others to we must oblige and excite ourselves to; nay, whatever others do, whether they will praise God or no, we and our houses must determine to do it, we and our hearts; for such is the psalmist's resolution here: I will praise the Lord with my whole heart. My heart, my whole heart, being devoted to his honor, shall be employed in this work; and this in the assembly, or secret, of the upright, in the cabinet-council, and in the congregation of Israelites. Note, We must praise God both in private and in public, in less and greater assemblies, in our own families and in the courts of the Lord's house; but in both it is most comfortable to do it in concert with the upright, who will heartily join in it. Private meetings for devotion should be kept up as well as more public and promiscuous assemblies.

II. He recommends to us the works of the Lord as the proper subject of our meditations when we are praising him—the dispensations of his providence towards the world, towards the church, and towards particular persons. 1. God's works are very magnificent, great like himself; there is nothing in them that is mean or trifling: they are the products of infinite wisdom and power, and we must say this upon the first view of them, before we come to enquire more particularly into them, that the works of the Lord are great, v. 2. There is something in them surprising, and that strikes an awe upon us. All the works of the Lord are spoken of as one (v. 3); it is his work, such is the beauty and harmony of Providence.

6-10 The happiness of the righteous.

We are here taught to give glory to God,

I. For the great things he has done for his people, for his people Israel, of old and of late: He has shown his people the power of his works (v. 6), in what he has wrought for them; many a time he has given proofs of his omnipotence, and shown them what he can do, and that there is nothing too hard for him to do. Two things are specified to show the power of his works:

1. The possession God gave to Israel in the land of Canaan, that he might give them, or in giving them, the heritage of the heathen. This he did in Joshua's time, when the seven nations were subdued, and in David's time, when the neighboring nations were many of them brought into subjection to Israel and became tributaries to David. Herein God showed his sovereignty, in disposing of kingdoms as he pleases, and his might, in making good his disposals. If God will make the heritage of the heathen to be the heritage of Israel, who can either arraign his counsel or stay his hand?

Psalm 111

6-10
6 He hath shewed his people the power of his works, that he may give them the heritage of the heathen.
7 The works of his hands are verity and judgment; all his commandments are sure.
8 They stand fast for ever and ever, and are done in truth and uprightness.
9 He sent redemption unto his people: he hath commanded his covenant for ever: holy and reverend is his name.
10 The fear of the LORD is the beginning of wisdom: a good understanding have all they that do his commandments: his praise endureth for ever.

meant to be perpetual signs and instructive tokens to all coming generations; and especially are they designed to confirm the faith of his people in the divine love, and to make them know that the Lord is gracious and full of compassion. They need not fear to trust his grace for the future, for they remember it in the past. Grace is as conspicuous as righteousness in the great work of God, yea, a fullness of tender love is seen in all that he has done.

Verse 5. He hath given meat unto them that fear him. Or spoil, as some read it, for the Lord's people both in coming out of Egypt and at other times have been enriched from their enemies. Not only in the wilderness with manna, but everywhere else by his providence he has supplied the necessities of his believing people. Somewhere or other they have had food convenient for them, and that in times of great scarcity. As for spiritual meat, that has been plentifully furnished them in Christ Jesus; they have been fed with the finest of the wheat, and made to feast on royal dainties. His word is as nourishing to the soul as bread to the body, and there is such an abundance of it that no heir of heaven shall ever be famished. Truly the fear of the Lord is wisdom, since it secures to a man the supply of all that he needs for soul and body.

Verse 6. He hath shewed his people the power of his works. They have seen what he is able to do and what force he is prepared to put forth on their behalf. This power Israel saw in physical works, and we in spiritual wonders, for we behold the matchless energy of the Holy Ghost and feel it in our own souls. In times of dire distress the Lord has put forth such energy of grace that we have been astonished at his power; and this was part of his intent in bringing us into such conditions that he might reveal to us the arm of his strength.

Verse 7. The works of his hands are verity and judgment. Truth and justice are conspicuous in all that Jehovah does. Nothing like artifice or crooked policy can ever be seen in his proceedings; he acts faithfully and righteously towards his people, and with justice and impartiality to all mankind. This also should lead us to praise him, since it is of the utmost advantage to us to live under a sovereign whose laws, decrees, acts, and deeds are the essence of truth and justice.

Verse 8. They stand fast for ever and ever. That is to say, his purposes, commands, and courses of action. The Lord is not swayed by transient motives, or moved by the circumstances of the hour; immutable principles rule in the courts of Jehovah, and he pursues his eternal purposes without the shadow of a turning. Our works are too often as wood, hay, and stubble, but his doings are as gold, silver, and precious stones. We take up a purpose for a while and then exchange it for another, but he is of one mind, and none can turn him: he acts in eternity and for eternity, and hence what he works abides for ever.

Verse 9. He sent redemption unto his people. When they were in Egypt he sent not only a deliverer, but an actual deliverance; not only a redeemer, but complete redemption. He has done the like spiritually for all his people, having first by blood purchased them out of the hand of the enemy, and then by power rescued them from the bondage of their sins.

Verse 10. The fear of the LORD is the beginning of wisdom. It is its first principle, but it is also its head and chief attainment. The word "beginning" in Scripture sometimes means the chief; and true religion is at once the first element of wisdom, and its chief fruit. To know God so as to walk aright before him is the greatest of all the applied sciences. Holy reverence of God leads us to praise him, and this is the point which the psalm drives at, for it is a wise act on the part of a creature towards his Creator.

JOHN CALVIN

renown of which shall continue for ever. And having above called upon us to contemplate his justice, now, in like manner, and almost in like terms, he celebrates the grace and mercy of God, principally in relation to his works, because that justice which he displays in the preservation and protection of his people, issues from the source of his unmerited favor which he bears towards them.

5-8

5. He hath given a portion to them that fear him. The Church being a mirror of the grace and justice of God, what the prophet said respecting them is here expressly applied to her; not that he designs to treat of the justice of God, in general, but only of that which he peculiarly displays towards his own people. Hence he adds, that God's care of his people is such as to lead him to make ample provision for the supply of all their wants.

The next verse is subjoined, by way of exposition, for the purpose of showing that God, in bestowing upon his people the heritage of the heathen, had manifested to them the power of his works. He does indeed employ the term show, but he means a true showing; because the possession of the Holy Land was not acquired by mere human power, but it was given to them by Divine power, and through the working of many miracles; and thus God, as it were, openly testified to the descendants of Abraham with what incomparable power he is invested. It is on this account that he sets up the people of Israel as a match for so many other nations, who would assuredly never have vanquished so many enemies, unless they had been sustained from on high.

7. The works of his hands. In the first clause of the verse he exclaims that God is known to be faithful and upright in his works, and then he goes on to extol the same truth and rectitude as pervading the doctrine of the law; the amount of which is, that a beautiful harmony characterizes all the sayings and doings of God, because every where he shows himself to be just and faithful. We have a memorable proof of this fact in the redemption of his ancient people. Yet I doubt not, that, under the term, works, the prophet comprehends the constant government of the Church;.

9-10

9. He sent redemption to his people. What he had already stated is here repeated in different words.

10. The fear of Jehovah. Having treated of the kindness of God, and paid a well-merited tribute to the law, the prophet goes on to exhort the faithful to reverence God, and be zealous in the keeping of the law. In calling the fear of God, The beginning or source of wisdom, he charges with folly those who do not render implicit obedience unto God. As if he should say, They who fear not God, and do not regulate their lives according to his law, are brute beasts: and are ignorant of the first elements of true wisdom.

The psalm concludes by saying that nothing is more profitable for them, than to spend their lives in the celebration of the praises of God.

MATTHEW HENRY

2. The many deliverances which he wrought for his people when by their iniquities they had sold themselves into the hand of their enemies (v. 9): He sent redemption unto his people, not only out of Egypt at first, but often afterwards; and these redemptions were typical of the great redemption which in the fullness of time was to be wrought out by the Lord Jesus, that redemption in Jerusalem which so many waited for.

II. For the stability both of his word and of his works, which assure us of the great things he will do for them.

1. What God has done shall never be undone. He will not undo it himself, and men and devils cannot (v. 7): The works of his hand are verity and judgment (v. 8), that is, they are done in truth and uprightness; all he does is consonant to the eternal rules and reasons of equity, all according to the counsel of his wisdom and the purpose of his will, all well done and therefore there is nothing to be altered or amended, but his works are firm and unchangeable. Upon the beginning of his works we may depend for the perfecting of them; work that is done properly will last, will neither go to decay nor sink under the stress that is laid upon it.

2. What God has said shall never be unsaid: All his commandments are sure, all straight and therefore all steady. His purposes, the rule of his actions, shall all have their accomplishment: Has he spoken, and will he not make it good? No doubt he will; whether he commands light or darkness, it is done as he commands.

III. For the setting up and establishing of religion among men. Because holy and reverend is his name, and the fear of him is the beginning of wisdom, therefore his praise endureth for ever, that is, he is to be everlastingly praised.

1. Because the discoveries of religion tend so much to his honor. Review what he has made known of himself in his word and in his works, and you will see, and say, that God is great and greatly to be feared.

2. Because the dictates of religion tend so much to man's happiness. We have reason to praise God that the matter is so well contrived that our reverence of him and obedience to him are as much our interest as they are our duty.

(1.) Our reverence of him is so: The fear of the Lord is the beginning of wisdom. It is not only reasonable that we should fear God, because his name is reverend and his nature is holy, but it is advantageous to us.

(2.) Our obedience to him is so: A good understanding have all those that do his commandments. Where the fear of the Lord rules in the heart there will be a constant conscientious care to keep his commandments, not to talk of them, but to do them; and such have a good understanding.

Psalm 112

1-5

1 Praise ye the LORD. Blessed is the man that feareth the LORD, that delighteth greatly in his commandments.
2 His seed shall be mighty upon earth: the generation of the upright shall be blessed.
3 Wealth and riches shall be in his house: and his righteousness endureth for ever.
4 Unto the upright there ariseth light in the darkness: he is gracious, and full of compassion, and righteous.
5 A good man sheweth favor, and lendeth: he will guide his affairs with discretion.

Psalm 112

TITLE AND SUBJECT. There is no title to this psalm, but it is evidently a companion to the hundred and eleventh, and, like it, it is an alphabetical psalm. Even in the number of verses, and clauses of each verse, it coincides with its predecessor, as also in many of its words and phrases. The reader should carefully compare the two psalms line by line. The subject of the poem before us is—the blessedness of the righteous man, and so it bears the same relation to the preceding which the moon does to the sun; for, while the first declares the glory of God, the second speaks of the reflection of the divine brightness in men born from above. God is here praised for the manifestation of his glory which is seen in his people, just as in the preceding psalm he was magnified for his own personal acts. The hundred and eleventh speaks of the great Father, and this describes his children renewed after his image. The psalm cannot be viewed as the extolling of man, for it commences with "Praise ye the Lord;" and it is intended to give to God all the honor of his grace which is manifested in the sons of God.
DIVISION. The subject is stated in the first verse, and enlarged upon under several heads from 2 to 9. The blessedness of the righteousness is set forth by contrast with the fate of the ungodly in verse 10.

EXPOSITION
Verse 1. Praise ye the LORD. This exhortation is never given too often; the Lord always deserves praise, we ought always to render it, we are frequently forgetful of it, and it is always well to be stirred up to it. The exhortation is addressed to all thoughtful persons who observe the way and manner of life of men that fear the Lord. If there be any virtue, if there be any praise, the Lord should have all the glory of it, for we are his workmanship. Blessed is the man that feareth the Lord. According to the last verse of Psalm 111, the fear of the Lord is the beginning of wisdom; this man, therefore, has begun to be wise, and wisdom has brought him present happiness, and secured him eternal felicity. Jehovah is so great that he is to be feared and had in reverence of all them that are round about him, and he is at the same time so infinitely good that the fear is sweetened into filial love, and becomes a delightful emotion, by no means engendering bondage.
Verse 2. His seed shall be mighty upon earth, that is to say, successive generations of God fearing men shall be strong and influential in society, and in the latter days they shall have dominion. The true seed of the righteous are those who follow them in their virtues, even as believers are the seed of Abraham, because they imitate his faith; and these are the real heroes of their era, the truly great men among the sons of Adam; their lives are sublime, and their power upon their age is far greater than at first sight appears.
Verse 3. Wealth and riches shall be in his house. Understood literally this is rather a promise of the old covenant than of the new, for many of the best of the people of God are very poor; yet it has been found true that uprightness is the road to success, and, all other things being equal, the honest man is the rising man. Many are kept poor through knavery and profligacy; but godliness hath the promise of the life that now is. If we understand the passage spiritually it is abundantly true.
Verse 4. Unto the upright there ariseth light in the darkness. He does not lean to injustice in order to ease himself, but like a pillar stands erect, and he shall be found so standing when the ungodly, who are as a bowing wall and a tottering fence, shall lie in ruins. He will have his days of darkness, he may be sick and sorry, poor and pining, as well as others; his former riches may take to themselves wings and fly away, while even his righteousness may be cruelly suspected; thus the clouds may lower around

JOHN CALVIN

Psalm 112

As the majority of mankind expect to prosper by evil deeds, and as they generally endeavor to enrich themselves by plunder, fraud, and every species of injustice, the prophet enumerates the blessings of God which attend those who worship him in purity, in order that we may know that, in aiming at a life of piety and morality, we shall not lose our reward.

1-3

1. Blessed is the man that feareth Jehovah. Although the prophet begins with an exhortation, he has something farther in view, than simply the calling upon the faithful to praise God. To practice wickedness, and perpetrate injustice, is, in all quarters, accounted a great happiness; and, although integrity may be occasionally praised, nevertheless, there is scarcely one among a hundred who pursues it, because all imagine that they will be miserable unless, by one means or another, they seize as booty every thing which comes in their way. In opposition to this, the prophet tells us that more advantage is to be expected from God's paternal regard, than from the inflicting of every species of injury, and the perpetrating of every kind of injustice in our power; and by setting before us the certain hope of reward, he calls us back to the practice of equity and beneficence.

The following is the analysis which I give of the verse: Blessed is the man that feareth the Lord, and delighteth himself in his commandments; and thus, by the second clause of the verse, the prophet specifies in what the fear of God consists.

2. His seed shall be powerful. For the purpose of confirming the statement which he advanced respecting the happiness of the man that fears Jehovah and takes delight in his commandments, the prophet enumerates the tokens of God's loving-kindness, which he is wont to bestow upon his worshippers. He says that God's fatherly kindness is not confined to their own persons, it also extends to their posterity.

4-8

4. Light ariseth. When the whole world is overwhelmed with troubles, God's grace shines upon the faithful, who feel comfortable and happy, because he is propitious towards them. It is thus that their condition is properly distinguished from that which forms the common lot of other men. For the ungodly, however they may exult in prosperity, are, nevertheless, blind in the midst of light, because they are strangers to God's paternal kindness; and, in adversity, they are plunged into the darkness of death; and, consequently, they never enjoy a season of calm repose.

5. A good man. This is the commonly received interpretation of the passage. I am disposed, however, to prefer another, That it shall be well with those who are gracious and communicative; because this is more in accordance with the purport of the prophet's language. It is his intention to show how greatly the ungodly are deceived, when they aspire after

MATTHEW HENRY

Psalm 112

1-5 The character of the righteous.

The psalmist begins with a call to us to praise God, but immediately applies himself to praise the people of God; for whatever glory is acknowledged to be on them it comes from God, and must return to him; as he is their praise, so they are his. We have reason to praise the Lord that there are a people in the world who fear him and serve him, and that they are a happy people, both which are owing entirely to the grace of God. Now here we have,

I. A description of those who are here pronounced blessed, and to whom these promises are made.

1. They are well-principled with pious and devout affections. Those have the privileges of God's subjects, not who cry, Lord, Lord, but who are indeed well affected to his government.

(1.) They are such as stand in awe of God and have a constant reverence for his majesty and deference to his will. The happy man is he that fears the Lord, v. 1.

(2.) They are such as take a pleasure in their duty. He that fears the Lord, as a Father, with the disposition of a child, not of a slave, delights greatly in his commandments, is well pleased with them and with the equity and goodness of them; they are written in his heart; it is his choice to be under them, and he calls them an easy, a pleasant, yoke; it is his delight to be searching into and conversing with God's commandments, by reading, hearing, and meditation, Ps. i. 2.

2. They are honest and sincere in their professions and intentions. They are called the upright (v. 2, 4), who are really as good as they seem to be, and deal faithfully both with God and man. There is no true religion without sincerity; that is gospel-perfection.

3. They are both just and kind in all their dealings: He is gracious, full of compassion, and righteous (v. 4), dares not do any wrong to any man, but does to every man all the good he can, and that from a principle of compassion and kindness. It was said of God, in the foregoing psalm (v. 4), He is gracious, and full of compassion; and here it is said of the good man that he is so; for herein we must be followers of God as dear children; be merciful as he is. He is full of compassion, and yet righteous; what he does good with is what he came honestly by. God hates robbery for burnt-offerings, and so does he. One instance is given of his beneficence (v. 5): He shows favor and lends.

II. The blessedness that is here entailed upon those that answer to these characters. Happiness, all happiness, to the man that feareth the Lord. Whatever men think or say of them, God says that they are blessed; and his saying so makes them so.

1. The posterity of good men shall fare the better for his goodness (v. 2): His seed shall be mighty on earth. Perhaps he himself shall not be so great in the

Psalm 112

6-10

6 Surely he shall not be moved for ever: the righteous shall be in everlasting remembrance.

7 He shall not be afraid of evil tidings: his heart is fixed, trusting in the LORD.

8 His heart is established, he shall not be afraid, until he see his desire upon his enemies.

9 He hath dispersed, he hath given to the poor; his righteousness endureth for ever; his horn shall be exalted with honor.

10 The wicked shall see it, and be grieved; he shall gnash with his teeth, and melt away: the desire of the wicked shall perish.

him, but his gloom shall not last for ever, the Lord will bring him light in due season, for as surely as a good man's sun goes down it shall rise again. If the darkness be caused by depression of spirit, the Holy Ghost will comfort him; if by pecuniary loss or personal bereavement, the presence of Christ shall be his solace; and if by the cruelty and malignity of men, the sympathy of his Lord shall be his support. It is as ordinary for the righteous to be comforted as for the day to dawn. Wait for the light and it will surely come; for even if our heavenly Father should in our last hours put us to bed in the dark, we shall find it morning when we awake.

Verse 5. A good man sheweth favor, and lendeth. Having passed beyond stern integrity into open handed benevolence he looks kindly upon all around him, and finding himself in circumstances which enable him to spare a little of his wealth he lends judiciously where a loan will be of permanent service. Providence has made him able to lend, and grace makes him willing to lend. He is not a borrower, for God has lifted him above that necessity; neither is he a hoarder, for his new nature saves him from that temptation; but he wisely uses the talents committed to him.

Verse 6. Surely he shall not be moved for ever. God has rooted and established him so that neither men nor devils shall sweep him from his place. His prosperity shall be permanent, and not like that of the gambler and the cheat, whose gains are evanescent: his reputation shall be bright and lustrous from year to year, for it is not a mere pretence; his home shall be permanent, and he shall not need to wander from place to place as a bird that wanders from her nest; and even his memory shall be abiding, for a good man is not soon forgotten, and the righteous shall be in everlasting remembrance.

Verse 7. He shall not be afraid of evil tidings. He shall have no dread that evil tidings will come, and he shall not be alarmed when they do come. Rumors and reports he despises; prophecies of evil, vented by fanatical mouths, he ridicules; actual and verified information of loss and distress he bears with equanimity, resigning everything into the hands of God.

Verse 8. His heart is established. His love to God is deep and true, his confidence in God is firm and unmoved; his courage has a firm foundation, and is supported by Omnipotence. He has become settled by experience, and confirmed by years. He is not a rolling stone, but a pillar in the house of the Lord. He shall not be afraid. He is ready to face any adversary—a holy heart gives a brave face.

Verse 9. He hath dispersed, he hath given, to the poor. What he received, he distributed; and distributed to those who most needed it. He was God's reservoir, and forth from his abundance flowed streams of liberality to supply the needy. If this be one of the marks of a man who feareth the Lord, there are some who are strangely destitute of it. They are great at gathering, but very slow at dispersing; they enjoy the blessedness of receiving, but seldom taste the greater joy of giving.

Verse 10. The tenth and last verse sets forth very forcibly the contrast between the righteous and the ungodly, thus making the blessedness of the godly appear all the more remarkable. Usually we see Ebal and Gerizim, the blessing and the curse, set the one over against the other, to invest both with the greater solemnity. The wicked shall see it, and be grieved. The ungodly shall first see the example of the saints to their own condemnation, and shall at last behold the happiness of the godly and to the increase of their eternal misery. The child of wrath shall be obliged to witness the blessedness of the righteous, though the sight shall make him gnaw his own heart. He shall fret and fume, lament and wax angry, but he shall not be able to prevent it, for God's blessing is sure and effectual.

happiness by nefarious and unlawful practices; seeing that the favor of God is the source and cause of all good things. Hence it becomes necessary to supply the relative who. He proceeds, therefore, to put us on our guard as to the deception which those practice upon themselves, who hasten to enrich themselves by sordid parsimony and oppressive extortion; inasmuch as the faithful, by their clemency and kindness, open up a channel, through which the favor of God flows to them.

6. Surely he shall not be moved. He refers in more explicit terms to that happiness of which he spake, that God sustains the compassionate and humane, so that amid all the vicissitudes of life they remain unmoved; that he makes their innocence appear, and protects them from unjust calumny. It is said they are never moved. They are indeed liable to the incidents common to humanity, and even may often appear as if they were about to sink under the weight of their calamities; but their confidence remains unshaken, and by invincible patience they surmount all their adversities.

7. He shall not be afraid when he hears evil tidings. Genuine stability is that which the prophet here describes, and which consists in reposing with unshaken confidence in God. On the other hand, that presumptuous confidence with which the ungodly are intoxicated exposes them the more, to the indignation of God, inasmuch as they overlook the frailty of human life, and in their pride of heart madly set themselves in opposition to him. Therefore, when "they shall say, Peace and safety, then shall sudden destruction come upon them," (1 Thessalonians 5:3.) But a sense of calamities, while it alarms and disconcerts the faithful, does not make them faint-hearted, because it does not shake their faith, by which they are rendered bold and steadfast. In a word, they are not insensible to their trials, but the confidence which they place in God enables them to rise above all the cares of the present life. Thus they preserve calmness and composedness of mind, and wait patiently till the fit season arrives for taking vengeance upon the reprobate.

9-10

9. He has distributed, he hath given to the poor. Once more he affirms that the righteous never lose the fruit and the reward of their liberality.

10. The wicked shall see it. Here follows a contrast similar to that which we met with in Psalm 2:5, which renders the grace of God towards the faithful the more illustrious. His meaning is, that though the wicked may cast off all regard to piety, and banish from their minds all thoughts of human affairs being under the superintending providence of God, they shall yet be made to feel, whether they will or no, that the righteous, in compliance with God's command, do not vainly devote themselves to the cultivation of charity and mercy. Let them harden themselves as they choose, yet he declares that the honor, which God confers upon his children, shall be exhibited to them, the sight of which shall make them gnash with their teeth, and shall excite an envy that shall consume them by inches. In conclusion, he adds, that the wicked shall be disappointed of their desires.

world, nor make such a figure, as his seed after him shall for his sake.

2. They shall prosper in the world, and especially their souls shall prosper, v. 3. They shall be blessed with outward prosperity as far as is good for them: Wealth and riches shall be in the upright man's house, not in his heart (for he is none of those in whom the love of money reigns), perhaps not so much in his hand (for he only begins to raise the estate), but in his house; his family shall grow rich when he is gone.

3. They shall have comfort in affliction (v. 4): Unto the upright there arises light in the darkness. It is here implied that good men may be in affliction; the promise does not exempt them from that.

4. They shall have wisdom for the management of all their concerns, v. 5. He that does good with his estate shall, through the providence of God, increase it, not by miracle, but by his prudence: He shall guide his affairs with discretion, and his God instructs him to discretion and teaches him, Isa. xxviii. 26.

6-10 The blessedness of the righteous; the misery of the wicked.

In these verses we have,

I. The satisfaction of saints, and their stability. It is the happiness of a good man that he shall not be moved for ever, v. 6. Satan and his instruments endeavor to move him, but his foundation is firm and he shall never be moved, at least not moved for ever; if he be shaken for a time, yet he settles again quickly.

1. A good man will have a settled reputation, and that is a great satisfaction. A good man shall have a good name, a name for good things, with God and good people: The righteous shall be in everlasting remembrance (v. 6); in this sense his righteousness (the memorial of it) endures for ever, v. 9.

2. A good man shall have a settled spirit, and that is a much greater satisfaction than the former; for so shall a man have rejoicing in himself alone, and not in another. Surely he shall not be moved, whatever happens, not moved either from his duty or from his comfort; for he shall not be afraid; his heart is established, v. 7, 8. This is a part both of the character and of the comfort of good people

II. The vexation of sinners, v. 10. Two things shall fret them:

1. The felicity of the righteous: The wicked shall see the righteous in prosperity and honor and shall be grieved. It will vex them to see their innocency cleared and their low estate regarded.

2. Their own disappointment: The desire of the wicked shall perish. Their desire was wholly to the world and the flesh, and they ruled over them; and therefore, when these perish, their joy is gone, and their expectations from them are cut off, to their everlasting confusion; their hope is as a spider's web.

Psalm 113

1-4
1 Praise ye the LORD. Praise, O ye servants of the LORD, praise the name of the LORD.
2 Blessed be the name of the LORD from this time forth and for evermore.
3 From the rising of the sun unto the going down of the same the LORD's name is to be praised.
4 The LORD is high above all nations, and his glory above the heavens.

Psalm 113

TITLE AND SUBJECT. This Psalm is one of pure praise, and contains but little which requires exposition; a warm heart full of admiring adoration of the Most High will best of all comprehend this sacred hymn. Its subject is the greatness and condescending goodness of the God of Israel, as exhibited in lifting up the needy from their low estate. It may fitly be sung by the church during a period of revival after it has long been minished and brought low. With this Psalm begins the Hallel, or Hallelujah of the Jews, which was sung at their solemn feasts: we will therefore call it THE COMMENCEMENT OF THE HALLEL. Dr. Edersheim tells us that the Talmud dwells upon the peculiar suitableness of the Hallel to the Passover, "since it not only recorded the goodness of God towards Israel, but especially their deliverance from Egypt, and therefore appropriately opened with Praise ye Jehovah, ye servants of Jehovah,—and no longer servants of Pharaoh." Its allusions to the poor in the dust and the needy upon the dunghill are all in keeping with Israel in Egypt, and so also is the reference to the birth of numerous children where they were least expected.
DIVISION. No division need be made in the exposition of this Psalm, except it be that which is suggested by the always instructive headings supplied by the excellent authors of our common version: an exhortation to praise God, for his excellency, 1-5; for his mercy.

EXPOSITION
Verse 1. Praise ye the LORD, or Hallelujah, praise to JAH, Jehovah. Praise is an essential offering at all the solemn feasts of the people of God. Prayer is the myrrh, and praise is the frankincense, and both of these must be presented unto the Lord. How can we pray for mercy for the future if we do not bless God for his love in the past? The Lord hath wrought all good things for us, let us therefore adore him. All other praise is to be excluded, the entire devotion of the soul must be poured out unto Jehovah only.
Verse 2. Blessed be the name of the LORD. While praising him aloud, the people were also to bless him in the silence of their hearts, wishing glory to his name, success to his cause, and triumph to his truth. By mentioning the name, the Psalmist would teach us to bless each of the attributes of the Most High, which are as it were the letters of his name; not quarrelling with his justice or his severity, nor servilely dreading his power, but accepting him as we find him revealed in the inspired word and by his own acts, and loving him and praising him as such. We must not give the Lord a new name nor invent a new nature, for that would be the setting up of a false god.
Verse 3. From the rising of the sun unto the going down of the same the LORD'S name is to be praised. From early morn till eve the ceaseless hymn should rise unto Jehovah's throne, and from east to west over the whole round earth pure worship should be rendered unto his glory. So ought it to be; and blessed be God, we are not without faith that so it shall be. We trust that ere the world's dread evening comes, the glorious name of the Lord will be proclaimed among all nations, and all people shall call him blessed.
Verse 4. The Lord is high above all nations. Though the Gentiles knew him not, yet was Jehovah their ruler: their false gods were no gods, and their kings were puppets in his hands. The Lord is high above all the learning, judgment, and imagination of heathen sages, and far beyond the pomp and might of the monarchs of the nations. Like the great arch of the firmament, the presence of the Lord spans all the lands where dwell the varied tribes of men, for his providence is universal: this may well excite our confidence and praise.
Verse 5. Who is like unto the LORD our God? The challenge will never be answered. None can be compared with him for an instant; Israel's God is without parallel; our own God in covenant stands alone, and none can be likened unto him. Even those whom he has made like himself in some

JOHN CALVIN

Psalm 113

In this psalm the providence of God furnishes matter for praising him, because, though his excellency is far above the heavens, nevertheless, he deigns to cast his eyes upon the earth to take notice of mankind. And as not a few are disconcerted by the vicissitudes which they behold occurring in the world, the prophet takes occasion, from these sudden and unlooked for changes, to warn us to attend expressly to God's providence, that we may entertain no doubt that all things are governed according to his will and pleasure.

1-4

1. Praise, ye servants of Jehovah! This psalm contains abundant reasons for all men without exception to praise God. The faithful alone being endued with spiritual perception to recognize the hand of God, the prophet addresses them in particular. And if we consider how cold and callous men are in this religious exercise, we will not deem the repetition of the call to praise God superfluous. We all acknowledge that we are created to praise God's name, while, at the same time, his glory is disregarded by us.

2. Blessed be the name of Jehovah. The prophet confirms that the praises of God must be continued throughout the whole course of our life. If his name is to be continually praised, it ought, at least, to be our earnest endeavor, during our brief pilgrimage here, that the remembrance of it may flourish after we are dead.

In the next verse, he extends the glory of God's name to all parts of the earth; wherefore our apathy will be totally inexcusable, if we do not make its praises resound among ourselves. Under the law, God could not be praised aright, excepting in Judea by his own people, to whom the knowledge of him was confined. His works, however, which are visible to all nations, are worthy of the admiration of the whole world. To the same effect is the following clause respecting the loftiness of God's glory; for can there be any thing more base, than for us to magnify it but seldom and tardily, considering it ought to fill our thoughts with enrapturing admiration? In extolling the name of God so highly, the prophet intends to show us that there is no ground for indifference; that silence would savor of impiety were we not to exert ourselves to the utmost of our ability to celebrate his praises, in order that our affections may, as it were, rise above the heavens.

When he adds, that God is high above all nations, there is an implied reproach, by which he fastens upon the chosen people the charge of apathy in the exercise of praise. For can there be any thing more preposterous, than for those who are eye-witnesses of God's glory, which shines forth even among the blind, to refrain from making it the theme of their praises? At the very time when God conferred upon the Jews the exclusive honor of being the depositaries of the knowledge of his heavenly doctrine, he was nevertheless, according to Paul, not without a witness, (Acts 14:17; Romans 1:20) After the promulgation of the Gospel, his

MATTHEW HENRY

Psalm 113

1-9 A call to praise God; God's greatness and condescension.

In this psalm,

I. We are extorted to give glory to God, to give him the glory due to his name.

1. The invitation is very pressing: praise you the Lord, and again and again, Praise him, praise him; blessed be his name, for it is to be praised, v. 1-3. This intimates,

(1.) That it is a necessary and most excellent duty, greatly pleasing to God, and has a large room in religion.

(2.) That it is a duty we should much abound in, in which we should be frequently employed and greatly enlarged.

(3.) That it is work which we are very backward to, and which we need to be engaged and excited to by precept upon precept and line upon line.

(4.) That those who are much in praising God themselves will court others to it, both because they find the weight of the work, and that there is need of all the help they can fetch in (there is employment for all hearts, all hands, and all little enough), and because they find the pleasure of it, which they wish all their friends may share in.

2. The invitation is very extensive. Observe,

(1.) From whom God has praise—from his own people; they are here called upon to praise God, as those that will answer the call: Praise, O you servants of the Lord!

(2.) From all places—from the rising of the sun to the going down of the same, that is, throughout the habitable world.

II. We are here directed what to give him the glory of.

1. Let us look up with an eye of faith, and see how high his glory is in the upper world, and mention that to his praise, v. 4, 5. We are, in our praises, to exalt his name, for he is high, his glory is high.

2. Let us look around with an eye of observation, and see how extensive his goodness is in the lower world, and mention that to his praise. He is a God who exalts himself to dwell, who humbles himself in heaven, and in earth. Some think there is a transposition, He exalts himself to dwell in heaven, he humbles himself to behold on earth; but the sense is plain enough as we take it, only observe, God is said to exalt himself and to humble himself, both are his own act and deed; as he is self-existent, so he is both the fountain of his own honor and the spring of his own grace; God's condescending goodness appears,

(1.) In the cognizance he takes of the world below him. His glory is above the nations and above the heavens, and yet neither is neglected by him. God is great, yet he despises not any, Job xxxvi. 5. He humbles himself to behold all his creatures, all his subjects, though he is infinitely above them. Considering the infinite perfection, sufficiency, and

Psalm 113

5-9

5 Who is like unto the LORD our God, who dwelleth on high,
6 Who humbleth himself to behold the things that are in heaven, and in the earth!
7 He raiseth up the poor out of the dust, and lifteth the needy out of the dunghill;
8 That he may set him with princes, even with the princes of his people.
9 He maketh the barren woman to keep house, and to be a joyful mother of children. Praise ye the LORD.

respects are not like him in godhead, for his divine attributes are many of them incommunicable and inimitable. None of the metaphors and figures by which the Lord is set forth in the Scriptures can give us a complete idea of him; his full resemblance is borne by nothing in earth or in heaven. Only in Jesus is the Godhead seen, but he unhesitatingly declared "he that hath seen me hath seen the Father."

Verse 6. Who humbleth himself to behold the things that are in heaven, and in the earth! He dwells so far on high that even to observe heavenly things he must humble himself. He must stoop to view the skies, and bow to see what angels do. What, then, must be his condescension, seeing that he observes the humblest of his servants upon earth, and makes them sing for joy like Mary when she said, "Thou hast regarded the low estate of thine handmaiden." How wonderful are those words of Isaiah, "For thus saith the high and lofty One that inhabiteth eternity, whose name is Holy; I dwell in the high and holy place, with him also that is of a contrite and humble spirit, to revive the spirit of the humble, and to revive the heart of the contrite ones." Heathen philosophers could not believe that the great God was observant of the small events of human history; they pictured him as abiding in serene indifference to all the wants and woes of his creatures.

Verse 7. He raiseth up the poor out of the dust. This is an instance of his gracious stoop of love: he frequently lifts the lowest of mankind out of their poverty and degradation and places them in positions of power and honor. His good Spirit is continually visiting the down trodden, giving beauty for ashes to those who are cast down, and elevating the hearts of his mourners till they shout for joy. These up liftings of grace are here ascribed directly to the divine hand, and truly those who have experienced them will not doubt the fact that it is the Lord alone who brings his people up from the dust of sorrow and death. When no hand but his can help he interposes, and the work is done. It is worth while to be cast down to be so divinely raised from the dust.

Verse 8. That he may set him with princes. The Lord does nothing by halves: when he raises men from the dust he is not content till he places them among the peers of his kingdom. We are made kings and priests unto God, and we shall reign for ever and ever. Instead of poverty, he gives us the wealth of princes; and instead of dishonor, he gives us a more exalted rank than that of the great ones of the earth.

Verse 9. He maketh the barren woman to keep house, and to be a joyful mother of children. The strong desire of the easterns to have children caused the birth of offspring to be hailed as the choicest of favors, while barrenness was regarded as a curse; hence this verse is placed last as if to crown the whole, and to serve as a climax to the story of God's mercy. The glorious Lord displays his condescending grace in regarding those who are despised on account of their barrenness, whether it be of body or of soul. Sarah, Rachel, the wife of Manoah, Hannah, Elizabeth, and others were all instances of the miraculous power of God in literally fulfilling the statement of the psalmist. Women were not supposed to have a house till they had children; but in certain cases where childless women pined in secret the Lord visited them in mercy, and made them not only to have a house, but to keep it. The Gentile church is a spiritual example upon a large scale of the gift of fruitfulness after long years of hopeless barrenness; and the Jewish church in the latter days will be another amazing display of the same quickening power.

JOHN CALVIN

exaltation above the nations was more evident, for then the whole world was placed under his sway.

5-9

5. Who is like unto Jehovah our God. The prophet strengthens his position for the celebration of God's praises, by contrasting the height of his glory and power with his unbounded goodness. Not that his goodness can be separated from his glory; but this distinction is made out of regard to men, who would not be able to endure his majesty, were he not kindly to humble himself, and gently and kindly draw us towards him. The amount is, that God's dwelling above the heavens, at such a distance from us, does not prevent him from showing himself to be near at hand, and plainly providing for our welfare; and, in saying that God is exalted above the heavens, he magnifies his mercy towards men, whose condition is mean and despicable, and informs us that he might righteously hold even angels in contempt, were it not that, moved by paternal regard, he condescends to take them under his care.

7. Who raiseth the poor from the dust. In this passage, he speaks in terms of commendation of God's providential care in relation to those diversified changes which men are disposed to regard as accidental. He declares that it is solely by the appointment of God that things undergo changes far surpassing our anticipations. If the course of events were always uniform, men would ascribe it merely to natural causes, whereas, the vicissitudes which take place teach us that all things are regulated in accordance with the secret counsel of God.

On the other hand, struck with astonishment at the events which have happened contrary to our expectation, we instantly ascribe them to chance. And as we are so apt to view things from a point the very reverse from that of recognizing God's superintending care, the prophet enjoins us to admire his providence in matters of marvelous, or of unusual occurrence; for since cowherds, and men of the lowest and most abject condition, have been elevated to the summit of power, it is most reasonable that our attention should be arrested by a change so unexpected. We now perceive the prophet's design. In this passage, as well as in others, he might have set before us the structure of the heavens and the earth; but, as our minds are unaffected by the ordinary course of things, he declares that the hand of God is most apparent in his marvelous works.

9. Who maketh the barren woman to dwell in the family. He relates another work of God, which if, apparently, not so notable, ought not, on that account, the less to engage our thoughts. Unimpressed as we are by the ordinary works of God, we are constrained to express our astonishment when a woman who has been for a long period barren, unexpectedly becomes the mother of a numerous family. The woman who was formerly barren is blessed with fruitfulness, and fills the house with children. He attributes joy to mothers, because, though the hearts of all are prone to aspire after wealth, or honor, or pleasures, or any other advantages, yet is progeny preferred to every thing else.

MATTHEW HENRY

felicity of the divine nature, it must be acknowledged as an act of wonderful condescension that God is pleased to take into the thoughts of his eternal counsel, and into the hand of his universal Providence, both the armies of heaven and the inhabitants of the earth (Dan. iv. 35); even in this dominion he humbles himself.

(2.) In the particular favor he sometimes shows to the least and lowest of the inhabitants of this meaner lower world. He not only beholds the great things in the earth, but the meanest, and those things which great men commonly overlook. Not does he merely behold them, but does wonders for them, and things that are very surprising, out of the common road of providence and chain of causes, which shows that the world is governed, not by a course of nature, for that would always run in the same channel, but by a God of nature, who delights in doing things we looked not for.

[1.] Those that have been long despicable are sometimes, on a sudden, made honorable (v. 7, 8): He raises up the poor out of the dust, that he may set him with princes. First, Thus God does sometimes magnify himself, and his own wisdom, power, and sovereignty. When he has some great work to do he chooses to employ those in it that were least likely, and least thought of for it by themselves or others, to the highest post of honor: Gideon is fetched from threshing, Saul from seeking the asses, and David from keeping the sheep; the apostles are sent from fishing to be fishers of men.

[2.] Those that have been long barren are sometimes, on a sudden, made fruitful, v. 9. This may look back to Sarah and Rebecca, Rachel, Hannah, and Samson's mother, or forward to Elizabeth; and many such instances there have been, in which God has looked on the affliction of his handmaids and taken away their reproach. He makes the barren woman to keep house, not only builds up the family, but thereby finds the heads of the family something to do. Note, Those that have the comfort of a family must take the care of it; bearing children and guiding the house are put together, 1 Tim. v. 14. When God sets the barren in a family he expects that she should look well to the ways of her household, Prov. xxxi. 27. She is said to be a joyful mother of children, not only because, even in common cases, the pain is forgotten, for joy that a man-child is born into the world, but there is particular joy when a child is born to those that have been long childless (as Luke i. 14) and therefore there ought to be particular thanksgiving. Praise you the Lord. Yet, in this case, rejoice with trembling; for, though the sorrowful mother be made joyful, the joyful mother may be made sorrowful again, if the children be either removed from her or embittered to her. This, therefore, may be applied to the gospel-church among the Gentiles, for which we, who, being sinners of the Gentiles, are children of the desolate, have reason to say, Praise you the Lord.

Psalm 114

1 When Israel went out of Egypt, the house of Jacob from a people of strange language;
2 Judah was his sanctuary, and Israel his dominion.
3 The sea saw it, and fled: Jordan was driven back.
4 The mountains skipped like rams, and the little hills like lambs.
5 What ailed thee, O thou sea, that thou fleddest? thou Jordan, that thou wast driven back?
6 Ye mountains, that ye skipped like rams; and ye little hills, like lambs?
7 Tremble, thou earth, at the presence of the Lord, at the presence of the God of Jacob;
8 Which turned the rock into a standing water, the flint into a fountain of waters.

Psalm 114

SUBJECT AND DIVISION. This sublime SONG OF THE EXODUS is one and indivisible. True poetry has here reached its climax: no human mind has ever been able to equal, much less to excel, the grandeur of this Psalm. God is spoken of as leading forth his people from Egypt to Canaan, and causing the whole earth to be moved at his coming. Things inanimate are represented as imitating the actions of living creatures when the Lord passes by. They are apostrophized and questioned with marvelous force of language, till one seems to look upon the actual scene. The God of Jacob is exalted as having command over river, sea, and mountain, and causing all nature to pay homage and tribute before his glorious majesty.

EXPOSITION

Verse 1. When Israel went out of Egypt. The song begins with a burst, as if the poetic fury could not be restrained, but overleaped all bounds. The soul elevated and filled with a sense of divine glory cannot wait to fashion a preface, but springs at once into the middle of its theme. Israel emphatically came out of Egypt, out of the population among whom they had been scattered, from under the yoke of bondage, and from under the personal grasp of the king who had made the people into national slaves.

Verse 2. Judah was his sanctuary, and Israel his dominion. The meaning of the passage is that the whole people at the coming out of Egypt were separated unto the Lord to be a peculiar people, a nation of priests whose motto should be, "Holiness unto the Lord."

Verse 4. The mountains skipped like rams, and the little hills like lambs. At the coming of the Lord to Mount Sinai, the hills moved; either leaping for joy in the presence of their Creator like young lambs; or, if you will, springing from their places in affright at the terrible majesty of Jehovah, and flying like a flock of sheep when alarmed.

Verse 5. What ailed thee, O thou sea? Wert thou terribly afraid? Did thy strength fail thee? Did thy very heart dry up? What ailed thee, O thou sea, that thou fleddest? Thou wert neighbor to the power of Pharaoh, but thou didst never fear his hosts; stormy wind could never prevail against thee so as to divide thee in twain; but when the way of the Lord was in thy great waters thou was seized with affright, and thou becamest a fugitive from before him.

Verse 6. Ye mountains, that ye skipped like rams; and ye little hills, like lambs? What ailed ye, that ye were thus moved? There is but one reply: the majesty of God made you to leap.

Verse 7. Tremble, thou earth, at the presence of the Lord, at the presence of the God of Jacob. Or "from before the Lord, the Adonai, the Master and King." Very fitly does the Psalm call upon all nature again to feel a holy awe because its Ruler is still in its midst.

Verse 8. Which turned the rock into a standing water, causing a mere or lake to stand at its foot, making the wilderness a pool: so abundant was the supply of water from the rock that it remained like water in a reservoir. The flint into a fountain of waters, which flowed freely in streams, following the tribes in their devious marches. Behold what God can do! It seemed impossible that the flinty rock should become a fountain; but he speaks, and it is done. Not only do mountains move, but rocks yield rivers when the God of Israel wills that it should be so. "O magnify the Lord with me, and let us exalt his name together," for he it is and he alone who doeth such wonders as these. He supplies our temporal needs from sources of the most unlikely kind, and never suffers the stream of his liberality to fail. As for our spiritual necessities they are all met by the water and the blood which gushed of old from the riven rock, Christ Jesus.

JOHN CALVIN

Psalm 114

1-4
1. When Israel went out from Egypt. That exodus being a remarkable pledge and symbol of God's love for the children of Abraham, it is not surprising that it should be so frequently called to remembrance. In the beginning of the psalm, the prophet informs us that the people whom God purchased at so great a price are no more their own.
When God is said to be sanctified, it must be understood that the prophet is speaking after the manner of men, because, in himself, God is incapable of increase or diminution. Judah is called his holiness, and Israel his dominion, because his holy majesty, which hitherto had been little known, secured the veneration of all who had witnessed the displays of his incredible power.
3. The sea saw, and fled. He does not enumerate in succession all the miracles which were wrought at that time, but briefly alludes to the sea, which, though a lifeless and senseless element, is yet struck with terror at the power of God. Jordan did the same, and the very mountains shook. It is in a poetical strain that the Psalmist describes the receding of the sea and of the Jordan.

5-8
5. What ailed thee, O sea! The prophet interrogates the sea, Jordan, and the mountains, in a familiar and poetical strain, as lately he ascribed to them a sense and reverence for God's power. And, by these similitudes, he very sharply reproves the insensibility of those persons, who do not employ the intelligence which God has given them in the contemplation of his works.
The figure drawn from the lambs and rams would appear to be inferior to the magnitude of the subject. But it was the prophet's intention to express in the homeliest way the incredible manner in which God, on these occasions, displayed his power. The stability of the earth being, as it were, founded on the mountains, what connection can they have with rams and lambs, that they should be agitated, skipping hither and thither? In speaking in this homely style, he does not mean to detract from the greatness of the miracle, but more forcibly to engrave these extraordinary tokens of God's power on the illiterate.
7. At the presence of the Lord. Having aroused the senses of men by interrogations, he now furnishes a reply. It must be that the earth quake at the presence of her King. He then introduces the name of the God of Jacob, for the purpose of banishing from men all notions of false gods.
Another miracle is mentioned, in which God, after the passage of the people through the Red Sea, gave an additional splendid manifestation of his power in the wilderness. The glory of God, as he informs us, did not appear for one day only, on the departure of the people; it constantly shone in his other works, as when a stream suddenly issued out of the dry rock, Exodus 17:6. Waters may be found trickling out from among rocks, but to make them flow out of a dry rock, was unquestionably above the ordinary course of nature, or miraculous.

MATTHEW HENRY

Psalm 114

1-8 The deliverance of Israel celebrated.
The psalmist is here remembering the days of old, the years of the right hand of the Most High, and the wonders which their fathers told them of (Judg. vi. 13), for time, as it does not wear out the guilt of sin, so it should not wear out the sense of mercy. Let it never be forgotten,
I. That God brought Israel out of the house of bondage with a high hand and a stretched-out arm: Israel went out of Egypt, v. 1. They did not steal out clandestinely, nor were they driven out, but fairly went out, marched out with all the marks of honor; they went out from a barbarous people, that had used them barbarously, from a people of a strange language, Ps. lxxxi. 5.
II. That he himself framed their civil and sacred constitution (v. 2): Judah and Israel were his sanctuary, his dominion.
III. That the Red Sea was divided before them at their coming out of Egypt, both for their rescue and the ruin of their enemies; and the river Jordan, when they entered into Canaan, for their honor, and the confusion and terror of their enemies (v. 3): The sea saw it, saw there that Judah was God's sanctuary, and Israel his dominion, and therefore fled; for nothing could be more awful. To illustrate this the psalmist asks, in a poetical strain (v. 5), What ailed thee, O thou sea! that thou fleddest? And furnishes the sea with an answer (v. 7); it was at the presence of the Lord. This is designed to express,
1. The reality of the miracle, that it was not by any power of nature, or from any natural cause, but it was at the presence of the Lord, who gave the word.
2. The mercy of the miracle: What ailed thee? Was it in a frolic? Was it only to amuse men? No; it was at the presence of the God of Jacob; it was in kindness to the Israel of God.
3. The wonder and surprise of the miracle. Who would have thought of such a thing? Shall the course of nature be changed, and its fundamental laws dispensed with, to serve a turn for God's Israel?
4. The honor hereby put upon Israel, who are taught to triumph over the sea, and Jordan, as unable to stand before them.
IV. That the earth shook and trembled when God came down on Mount Sinai to give the law (v. 4): The mountains skipped like rams, and then the little hills might well be excused if they skipped like lambs, either when they are frightened or when they sport themselves.
V. That God supplied them with water out of the rock, which followed them through the dry and sandy deserts. Well may the earth and all its inhabitants tremble before that God who turned the rock into a standing water (v. 8), and what cannot he do who did that? The same almighty power that turned waters into a rock to be a wall to Israel (Exod. xiv. 22) turned the rock into waters to be a well to Israel.

Psalm 115

1-6

1 Not unto us, O LORD, not unto us, but unto thy name give glory, for thy mercy, and for thy truth's sake.

2 Wherefore should the heathen say, Where is now their God?

3 But our God is in the heavens: he hath done whatsoever he hath pleased.

4 Their idols are silver and gold, the work of men's hands.

5 They have mouths, but they speak not: eyes have they, but they see not:

6 They have ears, but they hear not: noses have they, but they smell not:

Psalm 115

SUBJECT. In the former psalm the past wonders which God had wrought were recounted to his honor, and in the present psalm he is entreated to glorify himself again, because the heathen were presuming upon the absence of miracles, were altogether denying the miracles of former ages, and insulting the people of God with the question, "Where is now their God?" It grieved the heart of the godly that Jehovah should be thus dishonored, and treating their own condition of reproach as unworthy of notice, they beseech the Lord at least to vindicate his own name. The Psalmist is evidently indignant that the worshippers of foolish idols should be able to put such a taunting question to the people who worshipped the only living and true God; and having spent his indignation in sarcasm upon the images and their makers, he proceeds to exhort the house of Israel to trust in God and bless his name. As those who were dead and gone could no longer sing psalms unto the Lord among the sons of men, he exhorts the faithful who were then living to take care that God is not robbed of his praise, and then he closes with an exulting Hallelujah. Should not living men extol the living God?

DIVISION. For the better expounding of it, the psalm may be divided into an entreaty of God to vindicate his own honor, verses 1, 2; a contemptuous description of the false gods and their worshippers, 3-8; an exhortation to the faithful to trust in God and to expect great blessings from him, 9-15; an explanation of God's relationship to their present condition of things, verse 16; and a reminder, that, not the dead, but the living, must continually praise God here below.

EXPOSITION

Verse 1. It will be well to remember that this psalm was sung at the Passover, and therefore it bears relationship to the deliverance from Egypt. The burden of it, seems to be a prayer that the living God, who had been so glorious at the Red Sea and at the Jordan, should again for his own name's sake display the wonders of his power.

Verse 2. Wherefore should the heathen say, Where is now their God? Or, more literally, "Where, pray, is their God?" Why should the nations be allowed with a sneer of contempt to question the existence, and mercy, and faithfulness of Jehovah? They are always ready to blaspheme; we may well pray that they may not derive a reason for so doing from the course of providence, or the decline of the church.

Verse 3. But our God is in the heavens—where he should be; above the reach of mortal sneers, over hearing all the vain jangling of men, but looking down with silent scorn upon the makers of the babel. Supreme above all opposing powers, the Lord reigneth upon a throne high and lifted up. Incomprehensible in essence, he rises above the loftiest thought of the wise; absolute in will and infinite in power, he is superior to the limitations which belong to earth and time.

Verse 4. Their idols are silver and gold, mere dead inert matter; at the best only made of precious metal, but that metal quite as powerless as the commonest wood or clay. The value of the idol shows the folly of the maker in wasting his substance, but certainly does not increase the power of the image, since there is no more life in silver and gold than in brass or iron.

Verse 5. They have mouths, but they speak not. The idols cannot utter even the faintest sound, they cannot communicate with their worshippers, they can neither promise nor threaten, command nor console, explain the past nor prophesy the future.

Verse 6. They have ears, but they hear not. The Psalmist might have pointed to the monstrous ears with which some heathen deities are disfigured,—truly they have ears; but no prayer of their rotaries, though shouted by a million voices, can ever be heard by them. How can gold and

JOHN CALVIN

Psalm 115

1-3

1. Not unto us, O Jehovah! It is not certain by whom, or at what time, this psalm was composed. We learn from the first part of it, that the faithful betake themselves to God, in circumstances of extreme distress. They do not make known their desires in plain words, but indirectly hint at the nature of their request. They openly disclaim all merit, and all hope of obtaining deliverance otherwise than God's doing it from a sole regard to his own glory, for these things are inseparably connected. Deserving, therefore, to meet with a repulse, they yet beseech God not to expose his name to the derision of the heathen. In their distress they desire to obtain consolation and support; but, finding nothing in themselves meritorious of God's favor, they call upon him to grant their requests, that his glory may be maintained.

2. Why should the heathen say, Where is now their God? They here express how God would maintain his glory in the preservation of the Church, which, if he permitted to be destroyed, would expose his name to the impious reproaches of the heathen, who would blaspheme the God of Israel, as being destitute of power, because he forsook his servants in the time of need. This is not done from the persuasion that God requires any such representation, but rather that the faithful may direct their thoughts back to that holy zeal contained in the words, "The railings of those that railed against thee have fallen upon me," Psalm 69:10.

3. Surely our God is in heaven. The faithful, with holy boldness, encourage themselves the more to prayer. Our prayers, we know, are worthless when we are agitated with doubts. Had that blasphemy penetrated their hearts, it would have inflicted a mortal wound. And hence they very opportunely guard against it, by discontinuing the train of their supplications.

4-8

4. Their idols. This contrast is introduced for the purpose of confirming the faith of the godly, by which they repose upon God alone; because, excepting him, all that the minds of men imagine of divinity is the invention of folly and delusion. To know the error and the madness of the world certainly contributes in no small degree to the confirmation of true godliness; while, on the other hand, a God is presented to us, whom we know assuredly to be the maker of heaven and earth, and whom we are to worship, not without reason or at random.

8. They who make them shall be like unto them. In a word, were they possessed of a particle of common sense, they would not attribute the properties of deity to the works of their own hands, to which they could impart no sensation or motion. And surely this consideration alone should suffice to remove the plea of ignorance, their making false gods for themselves in opposition to the plain dictates of natural reason.

MATTHEW HENRY

Psalm 115

1-8 The absurdity of idolatry.

Sufficient care is here taken to answer both the pretensions of self and the reproaches of idolaters.

I. Boasting is here for ever excluded, v. 1. Let no opinion of our own merits have any room either in our prayers or in our praises, but let both center in God's glory.

1. Have we received any mercy, gone through any service, or gained any success? We must not assume the glory of it to ourselves, but ascribe it wholly to God. We must not imagine that we do any thing for God by our own strength, or deserve any thing from God by our own righteousness; but all the good we do is done by the power of his grace, and all the good we have is the gift of his mere mercy, and therefore he must have all the praise.

2. Are we in pursuit of any mercy and wrestling with God for it? We must take our encouragement, in prayer, from God only, and have an eye to his glory more than to our own benefit in it. "Lord, do so and so for us, not that we may have the credit and comfort of it, but that thy mercy and truth may have the glory of it."

II. The reproach of the heathen is here for ever silenced and justly retorted.

1. The psalmist complains of the reproach of the heathen (v. 2): Wherefore should they say, Where is now their God?

(1.) "Why do they say so? Do they not know that our God is every where by his providence, and always nigh to us by his promise and grace?"

(2.) "Why does God permit them to say so? Nay, why is Israel brought so low that they have some color for saying so? Lord, appear for our relief, that thou mayest vindicate thyself, and glorify thy own name."

2. He gives a direct answer to their question, v. 3. "Do they ask where is our God? We can tell where he is."

(1.) "In the upper world is the presence of his glory: Our God is in the heavens, where the gods of the heathen never were, in the heavens, and therefore out of sight; but, though his majesty be unapproachable, it does not therefore follow that his being is questionable."

(2.) "In the lower world are the products of his power: He has done whatsoever he pleased, according to the counsel of his will; he has a sovereign dominion and a universal uncontrollable influence. Do you ask where he is? He is at the beginning and end of every thing, and not far from any of us."

3. He returns their question upon themselves. They asked, Where is the God of Israel? because he is not seen. He does in effect ask, What are the gods of the heathen? because they are seen.

(1.) He shows that their gods, though they are not shapeless things, are senseless things. Idolaters, at first, worshipped the sun and moon (Job xxxi. 26), which was bad enough, but not so bad as that which

Psalm 115

7-12

7 They have hands, but they handle not: feet have they, but they walk not: neither speak they through their throat.

8 They that make them are like unto them; so is every one that trusteth in them.

9 O Israel, trust thou in the LORD: he is their help and their shield.

10 O house of Aaron, trust in the LORD: he is their help and their shield.

11 Ye that fear the LORD, trust in the LORD: he is their help and their shield.

12 The LORD hath been mindful of us: he will bless us; he will bless the house of Israel; he will bless the house of Aaron.

silver hear, and how can a rational being address petitions to one who cannot even hear his words?

Verse 7. They have hands, but they handle not. Looking lower down upon the images, the Psalmist says, "They have hands, but they handle not, "they cannot receive that which is handed to them, they cannot grasp the scepter of power or the sword of vengeance, they can neither distribute benefits nor dispense judgments, and the most trifling act they are utterly unable to perform. An infant's hand excels them in power. Feet have they, but they walk not. They must be lifted into their places or they would never reach their shrines; they must be fastened in their shrines or they would fall; they must be carried or they could never move; they cannot come to the rescue of their friends, nor escape the iconoclasm of their foes. The meanest insect has more power of locomotion than the greatest heathen god.

Verse 8. They that make them are like unto them. Those who make such things for worship are as stupid, senseless, and irrational as the figures they construct. So far as any spiritual life, thought, and judgment are concerned, they are rather the images of men than rational beings. The censure is by no means too severe. Who has not found the words leaping to his lips when he has seen the idols of the Romans? So is every one that trusteth in them. Those who have sunk so low as to be capable of confiding in idols have reached the extreme of folly, and are worthy of as much contempt as their detestable deities.

Verse 9. O Israel, trust thou in the LORD. Whatever others do, let the elect of heaven keep fast to the God who chose them. Jehovah is the God of Jacob, let his children prove their loyalty to their God by their confidence in him. Whatever our trouble may be, and however fierce the blasphemous language of our enemies, let us not fear nor falter, but confidently rest in him who is able to vindicate his own honor, and protect his own servants. He is their help and their shield. He is the friend of his servants, both actively and passively, giving them both aid in labor and defense in danger. In the use of the pronoun "their," the Psalmist may have spoken to himself, in a sort of soliloquy: he had given the exhortation, "trust in Jehovah," and then he whispers to himself, "They may well do so, for he is at all times the strength and security of his servants."

Verse 10. O house of Aaron, trust in the LORD. You who are nearest to him, trust him most; your very calling is connected with his truth and is meant to declare his glory, therefore never entertain a doubt concerning him, but lead the way in holy confidence. The priests were the leaders, teachers, and exemplars of the people, and therefore above all others they should place an unreserved reliance upon Israel's God. The Psalmist is glad to add that they did so, for he says, He is their help and their shield. It is good to exhort those to faith who have faith: "These things have I written unto you that believe on the name of the Son of God; ...that ye may believe on the name of the Son of God." We may stir up pure minds by way of remembrance, and exhort men to trust in the Lord because we know that they are trusting already.

Verse 11. The next verse is of the same tenor—Ye that fear the LORD, trust in the LORD, whether belonging to Israel, or to the house of Aaron, or not, all those who reverence Jehovah are permitted and commanded to confide in him. He is their help and their shield. He does aid and protect all those who worship him in filial fear, to whatever nation they may belong. No doubt these repeated exhortations were rendered necessary by the trying condition in which the children of Israel were found: the sneers of the adversary would assail all the people, they would most bitterly be felt by the priests and ministers, and those who were secret proselytes would groan in secret under the contempt forced upon their religion and their God.

Verse 12. The Lord hath been mindful of us, or "Jehovah hath remembered us." His past mercies prove that we are on his heart, and though for the present he may afflict us, yet he does not forget us. We have not to put him

9-15
9. O Israel! trust thou in Jehovah. The prophet again resumes the doctrinal point, that the genuine worshippers of God have no cause to fear that he will forsake or frustrate them in the time of need; because he is as much disposed to provide for their safety as he is furnished with power to do it. He proceeds, in the first place, to exhort all the Israelites generally to place their confidence in God; and, secondly, he addresses the house of Aaron in particular; and, thirdly, he sets down all who fear God.
11. Ye who fear Jehovah! He does not speak of strangers, as some erroneously suppose, as if this were a prediction respecting the calling of the Gentiles. Connecting them with the children of Israel and with the sons of Aaron, they are of opinion that he refers to the heathens and to the uncircumcised who were not yet gathered into the sheepfold. By parity of reason one might infer, that the priests are not of the seed of Abraham, because they are separately mentioned. It is more probable that there is in these words a tacit correction of what he had said before, by which he makes a distinction between the genuine worshippers of God and those hypocrites who were the degenerate sons of Abraham. Not a few of the seed of Abraham according to the flesh having departed from the faith of their father, the prophet here restricts the promise to those who, having received it by faith, were worshipping God in purity.
12. Jehovah hath remembered us. The meaning is that God, mindful of his covenant, has hitherto been attentive to us; therefore, as he has begun to favor us, he will continue to do so for ever. In pronouncing these blessings, he observes the same order as above, assigning to the children of Aaron a superior place in God's benediction, excluding from it those among the Israelites who were hypocrites.
15. Ye are blessed of Jehovah In the preceding verse the prophet had given them the hope of uninterrupted happiness, arising from God's infinite resources never failing, however liberally and largely he bestows, and from his never ceasing to enrich those whom he hath admitted as sharers of his bounty. In confirmation of this doctrine, he declares that the children of Abraham were separated from other nations; so that, relying upon this privilege, they might unhesitatingly and unreservedly surrender themselves to a father so benignant and bountiful. And as the flesh, in consequence of its stupidity, cannot perceive the power of God, the understanding of which preserves us in a state of peace and security under his protection, the prophet, in designating him the maker of heaven and earth, reminds us that there is no ground to fear that he is unable to defend us; for, having created the heaven and the earth, he does not now remain unconcerned in heaven, but all creation is under his sovereign control.

16-18
16. The heavens, the heavens are Jehovah's. In this passage the prophet extols the bounty of God, and his paternal regard for the human race, in that, though he stood in need of nothing himself, he yet created the world, with all its fullness,

they were now come to (for evil men grow worse and worse), which was the worshipping of images, v. 4.
(2.) He thence infers the sottishness of their worshippers (v. 8): Those that make them images show their ingenuity, and doubtless are sensible men; but those that make them gods show their stupidity and folly, and are like unto them, as senseless blockish things; they see not the invisible things of the true and living God in the works of creation; they hear not the voice of the day and the night, which in every speech and language declare his glory, Ps. xix. 2, 3.

9-18 Confidence in God.
In these verses,
I. We are earnestly exhorted, all of us, to repose our confidence in God, and not suffer our confidence in him to be shaken by the heathens' insulting over us upon the account of our present distresses. It is folly to trust in dead images, but it is wisdom to trust in the living God, for he is a help and a shield to those that do trust in them, a help to furnish them with and forward them in that which is good, and a shield to fortify them against and protect them from every thing that is evil. Therefore,
1. Let Israel trust in the Lord; the body of the people, as to their public interests, and every particular Israelite, as to his own private concerns, let them leave it to God to dispose of all for them, and believe it will dispose of all for the best and will be their help and shield.
2. Let the priests, the Lord's ministers, and all the families of the house of Aaron, trust in the Lord, (v. 10); they are most maligned and struck at by the enemies and therefore of them God takes particular care. They ought to be examples to others of a cheerful confidence in God, and a faithful adherence to him in the worst of times.
3. Let the proselytes, who are not of the seed of Israel, but fear the Lord, who worship him and make conscience of their duty to him, let them trust in him, for he will not fail nor forsake them, v. 11.
II. We are greatly encouraged to trust in God, and good reason is given us why we should stay ourselves upon him with an entire satisfaction. Consider,
1. What we have experienced (v. 12): The Lord has been mindful of us, and never unmindful, has been so constantly, has been so remarkably upon special occasions. He has been mindful of our case, our wants and burdens, mindful of our prayers to him, his promises to us, and the covenant-relation between him and us.
2. What we may expect. From what he has done for us we may infer, He will bless us; he that has been our help and our shield will be so; he that has remembered us in our low estate will not forget us; for he is still the same, his power and goodness the same, and his promise inviolable; so that we have reason to hope that he who has delivered, and does,

Psalm 115

13-18
13 He will bless them that fear the LORD, both small and great.
14 The LORD shall increase you more and more, you and your children.
15 Ye are blessed of the LORD which made heaven and earth.
16 The heaven, even the heavens, are the LORD's: but the earth hath he given to the children of men.
17 The dead praise not the LORD, neither any that go down into silence.
18 But we will bless the LORD from this time forth and for evermore. Praise the LORD.

in remembrance as though he found it hard to recollect his children, but he hath remembered us and therefore he will in future deal well with us.
Verse 13. He will bless them that fear the LORD, both small and great. So long as a man fears the Lord it matters nothing whether he be prince or peasant, patriarch or pauper, God will assuredly bless him. He supplies the want of every living thing, from the leviathan of the sea to the insect upon a leaf, and he will suffer none of the godly to be forgotten, however small their abilities, or mean their position. This is a sweet cordial for those who are little in faith, and own themselves to be mere babes in the family of grace.
Verse 14. The LORD shall increase you more and more, you and your children. Just as in Egypt he multiplied the people exceedingly, so will he increase the number of his saints upon the earth; not only shall the faithful be blessed with converts, and so with a spiritual seed; but those who are their spiritual children shall become fruitful also, and thus the multitude of the elect shall be accomplished; God shall increase the people, and shall increase the joy.
Verse 15. Ye are blessed of the LORD which made heaven and earth. This is another form of the blessing of Melchizedek: "Blessed be Abram of the Most High God, possessor of heaven and earth"; and upon us through our great Melchizedek this same benediction rests. It is an omnipotent blessing, conveying to us all that an Almighty God can do, whether in heaven or on earth. This fullness is infinite, and the consolation which it brings is unfailing: he that made heaven and earth can give us all things while we dwell below, and bring us safely to his palace above.
Verse 16. The heaven, even the heavens, are the Lord's. There he specially reigns, and manifests his greatness and his glory: but the earth hath he given to the children of men. He hath left the world during the present dispensation in a great measure under the power and will of men, so that things are not here below in the same perfect order as the things which are above.
Verse 17. The dead praise not the LORD—So far as this world is concerned. They cannot unite in the Psalms and hymns and spiritual songs with which the church delights to adore her Lord. The preacher cannot magnify the Lord from his coffin, nor the Christian worker further manifest the power of divine grace by daily activity while he lies in the grave.
Verse 18. But we will bless the LORD from this time forth and for evermore. We who are still living will take care that the praises of God shall not fail among the sons of men. The spiritually dead cannot praise God, but the life within us constrains us to do so. The ungodly may abide in silence, but we will lift up our voices to the praise of Jehovah. Even though for a time he may work no miracle, and we may see no peculiar interposition of his power, yet on the strength of what he has done in ages past we will continue to laud his name "until the day break, and the shadows flee away," when he shall once more shine forth as the sun to gladden the faces of his children. The present time is auspicious for commencing a life of praise, since today he bids us hear his voice of mercy. "From this time forth" is the suggestion of wisdom. It is the dictate of gratitude, for there are pressing reasons for prompt thankfulness.

for their use. How comes it to pass that the earth is every where covered with such a great variety of good things, meeting our eye in all directions, unless that God, as a provident father of a family, had designed to make provision for our wants? In proportion, therefore, to the comforts which we here enjoy, are the tokens of his fatherly care. This is the prophet's meaning, which I am astonished is so little attended to by the most of interpreters. The amount is, that God, satisfied with his own glory, has enriched the earth with abundance of good things, that mankind may not lack any thing. At the same time he demonstrates, that, as God has his dwelling-place in the heavens, he must be independent of all worldly riches; for, assuredly, neither wine, nor corn, nor any thing requisite for the support of the present life is produced there. Consequently, God has every resource in himself. To this circumstance the repetition of the, term heavens refers, The heavens, the heavens are enough for God; and as he is superior to all aid, he is to himself instead of a hundred worlds. It remains, therefore, as another consequence from this, that all the riches with which the world abounds proclaim aloud what a beneficent father God is to mankind. It is indeed surprising that there should be no relish for this doctrine, considering that the Holy Spirit spoke of the inestimable goodness of God. Under the papacy, they chanted this psalm in their churches, and they continue the practice still; but is there one among a hundred of them who reflects that God, in bestowing all good things upon us, reserves nothing for himself, except a grateful acknowledgment of them? And not only in this matter does the ingratitude of the world appear, but the wicked wretches have conducted themselves most vilely, in open and infamous blasphemy; perverting this verse, and making a jest of it, saying that God remains unconcerned in heaven, and pays no regard to the affairs of men. The prophet here expressly declares that the world is employed by God, for the sole purpose of testifying his paternal solicitude towards mankind; and yet these swine and dogs have made these words a laughing-stock, as if God, by reason of his vast distance from men, totally disregarded them.

17. O God! the dead shall not praise thee. In these words the prophet goes on to beseech God to show himself propitious towards his Church, were there no other object to be gained than the preventing mankind from being utterly cut off, and the preserving a people, not only to enjoy his kindness, but also to invoke and praise his name.

In fine, the prophet concludes that the whole course of nature would be subverted, unless God saved his Church. The creation of the world would serve no good purpose, if there were no people to call upon God. He not only promises that the Church shall be preserved, but also calls upon all who are thus preserved to offer a tribute of gratitude to their deliverer. He does not speak merely of the persons who belong to one age, but of the whole body of the Church which God upholds from one generation after another, that he may never leave himself without some to testify and declare his justice, goodness, and mercy.

will yet deliver. The greatest need his blessing, and it shall not be denied to the meanest that fear him. Both the weak in grace and the strong shall be blessed of God, the lambs and the sheep of his flock. It is promised (v. 14), The Lord shall increase you. Whom God blesses he increases; that was one of the earliest and most ancient blessings, Be fruitful and multiply. God's blessing gives an increase—increase in number, building up the family—increase in wealth, adding to the estate and honor—especially an increase in spiritual blessings, with the increasings of God. He will bless you with the increase of knowledge and wisdom, of grace, holiness, and joy. There is a blessing entailed upon the seed of those that fear God even in their infancy. For (v. 15), You are blessed of the Lord, you and your children are so; all that see them shall acknowledge them, that they are the seed which the Lord has blessed, Isa. lax. 9.

III. We are stirred up to praise God by the psalmist's example, who concludes the psalm with a resolution to persevere in his praises.

1. God is to be praised, v. 16. He is greatly to be praised; for,

(1.) His glory is high. See how stately his palace is, and the throne he has prepared in the heavens: The heaven, even the heavens are the Lord's; he is the rightful owner of all the treasures of light and bliss in the upper and better world, and is in the full possession of them, for he is himself infinitely bright and happy.

(2.) His goodness is large, for the earth he has given to the children of men, having designed it, when he made it, for their use, to find them with meat, drink, and lodging.

3. Therefore it concerns us to praise him (v. 18): "But we, we that are alive, will bless the Lord; we and those that shall come after us, will do it, from this time forth and for evermore, to the end of time; we and those we shall remove to, from this time forth and to eternity. The dead praise not the Lord, therefore we will do it the more diligently."

(1.) Others are dead, and an end is thereby put to their service, and therefore we will lay out ourselves to do so much the more for God, that we may fill up the gap. Moses my servant is dead, now therefore, Joshua, arise.

(2.) We ourselves must shortly go to the land of silence; but, while we do live, we will bless the Lord, will improve our time and work that work of him that sent us into the world to praise him before the night comes, and because the night comes, wherein no man can work. The Lord will bless us (v. 12); he will do well for us, and therefore we will bless him, we will speak well of him. Poor returns for such receivings! Nay, we will not only do it ourselves, but will engage others to do it. Praise the Lord; praise him with us; praise him in your places, as we in ours; praise him when we are gone, that he may be praised for evermore. Hallelujah.

Psalm 116

1-6
1 I love the LORD, because he hath heard my voice and my supplications.
2 Because he hath inclined his ear unto me, therefore will I call upon him as long as I live.
3 The sorrows of death compassed me, and the pains of hell gat hold upon me: I found trouble and sorrow.
4 Then called I upon the name of the LORD; O LORD, I beseech thee, deliver my soul.
5 Gracious is the LORD, and righteous; yea, our God is merciful.
6 The LORD preserveth the simple: I was brought low, and he helped me.

Psalm 116

SUBJECT. This is a continuation of the Paschal Hallel, and therefore must in some measure be interpreted in connection with the coming out of Egypt. It has all the appearance of being a personal song in which the believing soul, reminded by the Passover of its own bondage and deliverance, speaks thereof with gratitude, and praises the Lord accordingly. We can conceive the Israelite with a staff in his hand singing, "Return unto thy rest, O my soul," as he remembered the going back of the house of Jacob to the land of their fathers; and then drinking the cup at the feast using the words of Ps 116:13, "I will take the cup of salvation." The pious man evidently remembers both his own deliverance and that of his people as he sings in the language of Ps 116:16, "Thou hast loosed my bonds"; but he rises into sympathy with his nation as he thinks of the courts of the Lord's house and of the glorious city, and pledges himself to sing "in the midst of thee, O Jerusalem." Personal love fostered by a personal experience of redemption is the theme of this Psalm, and in it we see the redeemed answered when they pray, preserved in time of trouble, resting in their God, walking at large, sensible of their obligations, conscious that they are not their own but bought with a price, and joining with all the ransomed company to sing hallelujahs unto God.

Since our divine Master sang this hymn, we can hardly err in seeing here words to which he could set his seal,—words in a measure descriptive of his own experience; but upon this we will not enlarge, as in the notes we have indicated how the Psalm has been understood by those who love to find their Lord in every line.

DIVISION. David Dickson has a somewhat singular division of this Psalm, which strikes us as being exceedingly suggestive. He says, "This Psalm is a threefold engagement of the Psalmist unto thanksgiving unto God, for his mercy unto him, and in particular for some notable delivery of him from death, both bodily and spiritual. The first engagement is, that he shall out of love have recourse unto God by prayer, Ps 116:1-2; the reasons and motives whereof are set down, because of his former deliverances, Ps 116:3-8, the second engagement is to a holy conversation, Ps 116:9, and the motives and reasons are given in Ps 116:10-13; the third engagement is to continual praise and service, and specially to pay those vows before the church, which he had made in days of sorrow, the reasons whereof are given in Ps 116:14-19."

EXPOSITION

Verse 1. I love the LORD. A blessed declaration: every believer ought to be able to declare without the slightest hesitation, "I love the Lord." It was required under the law, but was never produced in the heart of man except by the grace of God, and upon gospel principles. It is a great thing to say "I love the Lord"; for the sweetest of all graces and the surest of all evidences of salvation is love.

Verse 2. Because he hath inclined his ear unto me:—bowing down from his grandeur to attend to my prayer; the figure seems to be that of a tender physician or loving friend leaning over a sick man whose voice is faint and scarcely audible, so as to catch every accent and whisper.

Verse 3. The Psalmist now goes on to describe his condition at the time when he prayed unto God. The sorrows of death compassed me. As hunters surround a stag with dogs and men, so that no way of escape is left, so was David enclosed in a ring of deadly griefs. The bands of sorrow, weakness, and terror with which death is accustomed to bind men ere he drags them away to their long captivity were all around him.

Verse 4. Then I called upon the name of the LORD. Prayer is never out of season, he prayed then, when things were at their worst. When the good man could not run to God, he called to him. In his extremity his faith came

JOHN CALVIN

Psalm 116

1-4

1. I have loved, because Jehovah will hear the voice of my supplication. At the very commencement of this psalm David avows that he was attracted with the sweetness of God's goodness, to place his hope and confidence in him alone. This abrupt mode of speaking, I have loved, is the more emphatic, intimating that he could receive joy and repose nowhere but in God. We know that our hearts will be always wandering after fruitless pleasures, and harassed with care, until God knit them to himself.

The second verse also refers to the same subject, excepting that the latter clause admits of a very appropriate meaning, which expositors overlook. The phrase, during my days I will call upon him, is uniformly understood by them to mean, I, who hitherto have been so successful in addressing God, will pursue the same course all my life long. But it should be considered whether it may not be equally appropriate that the days of David be regarded as denoting a fit season of asking assistance, the season when he was hard pressed by necessity. The scope of the passage will run very well thus: Because he has bowed his ear to me when I called upon him in the time of my adversity, and even at the season, too, when I was reduced to the greatest straits.

5-9

5. Jehovah is gracious. He comes now to point out the fruits of that love of which he spoke, setting before him God's titles, in order that they might serve to preserve his faith in him. First, he denominates him gracious, because he is so ready graciously to render assistance. From this source springs that justice which he displays for the protection of his own people. To this is subjoined mercy, without which we would not deserve God's aid. And as the afflictions which overtake us frequently appear to preclude the exercise of his justice, hence it follows that there is nothing better than to repose upon him alone; so that his fatherly kindness may engross our thoughts, and that no voluptuous pleasure may steal them away to any thing else.

7. Return, O my soul! unto thy rest. He now exhorts himself to be of good courage; or rather, addressing his soul, tells it to be tranquil, because God was propitious towards him. By the term rest, some commentators understand God himself, but this is an unnatural interpretation. It is rather to be regarded as expressive of a calm and composed state of mind. For it is to be noticed, that David confesses himself to have been sorely agitated and perplexed amid an accumulation of ills, in the same way as each of us is conscious of his own inquietude, when the terrors of death encompass us.

9. I will walk in the presence of Jehovah. To wall in the presence of God is, in my opinion, equivalent to living under his charge. And thus David expects to enjoy his safety continually. For nothing is more desirable than that God should be upon the watch for us, that our life may be surrounded by his protecting care. The wicked, indeed, regard

MATTHEW HENRY

Psalm 116

1-9 Grateful acknowledgments.

In this part of the psalm we have,

I. A general account of David's experience, and his pious resolutions (v. 1, 2), which are as the contents of the whole psalm, and give an idea of it.

1. He had experienced God's goodness to him in answer to prayer: He has heard my voice and my supplications. David, in straits, had humbly and earnestly begged mercy of God, and God had heard him, that is, had graciously accepted his prayer, taken cognizance of his case, and granted him an answer of peace. He has inclined his ear to me. This intimates his readiness and willingness to hear prayer; he lays his ear, as it were, to the mouth of prayer, to hear it, though it be but whispered in groanings that cannot be uttered.

2. He resolved, in consideration thereof, to devote himself entirely to God and to his honor.

II. A more particular narrative of God's gracious dealings with him and the good impressions thereby made upon him.

1. God, in his dealings with him, showed himself a good God, and therefore he bears this testimony to him, and leaves it upon record (v. 5): "Gracious is the Lord, and righteous. He is righteous, and did me no wrong in afflicting me; he is gracious, and was very kind in supporting and delivering me."

(1.) Let us review David's experiences.

[1.] He was in great distress and trouble (v. 3): The sorrows of death compassed me, that is, such sorrows as were likely to be his death, such as were thought to be the very pangs of death.

[2.] In his trouble he had recourse to God by faithful and fervent prayer, v. 4. He tells us that he prayed: Then called I upon the name of the Lord; then, when he was brought to the last extremity, then he made use of this, not as the last remedy, but as the old and only remedy, which he had found a salve for every sore. The following words (v. 5), Gracious is the Lord, may be taken as part of his prayer, as a plea to enforce his request and encourage his faith and hope: "Lord deliver my soul, for thou art gracious and merciful, and that only I depend upon for relief."

[3.] God, in answer to his prayer, came in with seasonable and effectual relief. He found by experience that God is gracious and merciful, and in his compassion preserves the simple, v. 6. Because they are simple (that is, sincere, and upright, and without guile) therefore God preserves them, as he preserved Paul, who had his conversation in the world not with fleshly wisdom, but in simplicity and godly sincerity.

(2.) Let David speak his own experience.

[1.] God supported him under his troubles: "I was brought low, was plunged into the depth of misery, and then he helped me."

Psalm 116

7-12
7 Return unto thy rest, O my soul; for the LORD hath dealt bountifully with thee.
8 For thou hast delivered my soul from death, mine eyes from tears, and my feet from falling.
9 I will walk before the LORD in the land of the living.
10 I believed, therefore have I spoken: I was greatly afflicted:
11 I said in my haste, All men are liars.
12 What shall I render unto the LORD for all his benefits toward me?

to the front: it was useless to call on man, and it may have seemed almost as useless to appeal to the Lord; but yet he did with his whole soul invoke all the attributes which make up the sacred name of Jehovah, and thus he proved the truth of his confidence.
Verse 5. Gracious is the Lord, and righteous. In hearing prayer the grace and righteousness of Jehovah are both conspicuous. It is a great favor to hear a sinner's prayer, and yet since the Lord has promised to do so, he is not unrighteous to forget his promise and disregard the cries of his people. The combination of grace and righteousness in the dealings of God with his servants can only be explained by remembering the atoning sacrifice of our Lord Jesus Christ. At the cross we see how gracious is the Lord and righteous.
Verse 6. The LORD preserveth the simple. Those who have a great deal of wit may take care of themselves. Those who have no worldly craft and subtlety and guile, but simply trust in God, and do the right, may depend upon it that God's care shall be over them.
Verse 7. Return, unto thy rest, O my soul. He calls the rest still his own, and feels full liberty to return to it. What a mercy it is that even if our soul has left its rest for a while we can tell it—"it is thy rest still." The Psalmist had evidently been somewhat disturbed in mind, his troubles had ruffled his spirit but now with a sense of answered prayer upon him he quiets his soul. He had rested before, for he knew the blessed repose of faith, and therefore he returns to the God who had been the refuge of his soul in former days.
Verse 8. For thou hast delivered my soul from death, mine eyes from tears, and my feet from falling. The triune God has given us a trinity of deliverances: our life has been spared from the grave, our heart has been uplifted from its griefs, and our course in life has been preserved from dishonor.
Verse 9. I will walk before the Lord in the land of the living. This is the Psalmist's second resolution, to live as in the sight of God in the midst of the sons of men. By a man's walk is understood his way of life: some men live only as in the sight of their fellow men, having regard to human judgment and opinion; but the truly gracious man considers the presence of God, and acts under the influence of his all observing eye.
Verse 10. I believed, therefore have I spoken. I could not have spoken thus if it had not been for my faith: I should never have spoken unto God in prayer, nor have been able now to speak to my fellow men in testimony if it had not been that faith kept me alive, and brought me a deliverance, whereof I have good reason to boast.
Verse 11. I said in my haste, All men are liars. In a modified sense the expression will bear justification, even though hastily uttered, for all men will prove to be liars if we unduly trust in them; some from want of truthfulness, and others from want of power. But from the expression, "I said in my haste," it is clear that the Psalmist did not justify his own language, but considered it as the ebullition of a hasty temper.
Verse 12. What shall I render unto the LORD for all his benefits toward me? He wisely leaves off fretting about man's falsehood and his own ill humor, and directs himself to his God. It is of little use to be harping on the string of man's imperfection and deceitfulness; it is infinitely better to praise the perfection and faithfulness of God. The question of the verse is a very proper one: the Lord has rendered so much mercy to us that we ought to look about us, and look within us, and see what can be done by us to manifest our gratitude. We ought not only to do what is plainly before us, but also with holy ingenuity to search out various ways by which we may render fresh praises unto our God.
Verse 13. I will take the cup of salvation. "I will take" is a strange answer to the question, "What shall I render?" and yet it is the wisest reply that could possibly be given. To take the cup of salvation was in itself an act of worship, and it was accompanied with other forms of adoration, hence the

themselves as secure, the farther they are from God; but the godly consider themselves happy in this one thing, that he directs the whole tenor of their life. God adding, in the land of the living, he means to point out to us the course that we are expected to pursue; and that, almost every moment of time, fresh destructions press upon us, if he overlook us.

10-11

10. I have believed. That his wonderful deliverance may appear the more conspicuous, he again relates the imminent danger in which he had been placed. He begins by declaring that he spake in the true sincerity of his heart, and that nothing proceeded from his lips but what was the fruit of long reflection, and mature deliberation. Such is the import of the clause, I have believed, therefore I will speak; words which proceed from the full affection of the heart. In 2 Corinthians 4:13, Paul, quoting this passage, follows the Greek version, "I believed, therefore I have spoken." I have elsewhere remarked that it was not the design of the apostles to repeat every word and syllable; it is enough for us that the words of David are appropriately applied in their proper and natural sense to the subject to which Paul there refers. Having referred indirectly to the Corinthians, who were exalting themselves above the clouds, as if they had been exempted from the common lot of mankind, "I believed" says he, "and therefore I have spoken, that he who hath once raised Christ from the dead, will also extend Christ's life to us;" that is, I believe, and therefore I speak. Thus he charges the Corinthians with being inflated with foolish pride, because they do not humbly submit to the cross of Christ; especially as they ought to speak in the exercise of the same spirit of faith with himself.

11. I said in my fear. As it figuratively signifies fear, I have no doubt that David here declares that he felt astonished and dejected in spirit, as if he were upon the brink of a precipice, ready to tumble into the abyss. He acknowledges that, when he was so dreadfully harassed in mind, his heart had almost sunk within him.

12-14

12. What shall I render unto Jehovah? He now exclaims with devout admiration, that the multitude of God's benefits was greater than he could find language to give expression to the grateful emotions of his heart. The question is emphatic, What shall I render? and imports, that it was not the desire, but the means, of which he was destitute, to enable him to render thanks to God. Acknowledging his inability, he adopts the only means in his power, by extolling the grace of God as highly as he could. "I am exceedingly wishful to discharge my duty, but when I look around me, I find nothing which will prove an adequate recompense."

13. The cup of salvation. He refers to a custom which was prevalent under the Law. For when they rendered solemn thanks to God, a feast was also appointed, at which, in token of their gladness, there was an holy libation. This being a symbol of their deliverance from Egyptian thralldom, is for that reason here called the cup of salvation.

[2.] God saved him out of his troubles (v. 8): Thou hast delivered, which means either the preventing of the distress he was ready to fall into or the recovering of him from the distress he was already in.

2. David, in his returns of gratitude to God, showed himself a good man. God had done all this for him, and therefore,

(1.) He will live a life of delight in God (v. 7): Return unto thy rest, O my soul!

[1.] "Repose thyself and be easy, and do not agitate thyself with distrustful disquieting fears as thou hast sometimes done. "

[2.] "Repose thyself in God. Return to him as thy rest, and seek not for that rest in the creature which is to be had in him only."

(2.) He will live a life of devotedness to God (v. 9): I will walk before the Lord in the land of the living, that is, in this world, as long as I continue to live in it.

10-19 Grateful acknowledgments; devout resolutions. Three things David here makes confession of:

I. His faith (v. 10): I believed, therefore have I spoken. This is quoted by the apostle (2 Cor. iv. 13) with application to himself and his fellow-ministers, who, though they suffered for Christ, were not ashamed to own him. David believed the being, providence, and promise of God, particularly the assurance God had given him by Samuel that he should exchange his crook for a scepter: a great deal of hardship he went through in the belief of this, and therefore he spoke, spoke to God by prayer (v. 4), by praise, v. 12.

II. His fear (v. 11): I was greatly afflicted, and then I said in my haste, All men are liars, all with whom he had to do, Saul and all his courtiers; his friends, who he thought would stand by him, deserted him and disowned him when he fell into disgrace at court.

III. His gratitude, v. 12, &c. God had been better to him than his fears, and had graciously delivered him out of his distresses; and, in consideration hereof,

1. He enquires what returns he shall make (v. 12): What shall I render unto the Lord for all his benefits towards me? Here he speaks,

(1.) As one sensible of many mercies received from God—all his benefits. This psalm seems to have been penned upon occasion of some one particular benefit (v. 6, 7), but in that one he saw many and that one brought many to mind, and therefore now he thinks of all God's benefits towards him.

(2.) As one solicitous and studious how to express his gratitude: What shall I render unto the Lord? Not as if he thought he could render any thing proportionable, or as a valuable consideration for what he had received; we can no more pretend to give a recompense to God than we can to merit any favor from him; but he desired to render something acceptable, something that God would be pleased with as the acknowledgment of a grateful mind.

Psalm 116

13-19
13 I will take the cup of salvation, and call upon the name of the LORD.
14 I will pay my vows unto the LORD now in the presence of all his people.
15 Precious in the sight of the LORD is the death of his saints.
16 O LORD, truly I am thy servant; I am thy servant, and the son of thine handmaid: thou hast loosed my bonds.
17 I will offer to thee the sacrifice of thanksgiving, and will call upon the name of the LORD.
18 I will pay my vows unto the LORD now in the presence of all his people.
19 In the courts of the LORD's house, in the midst of thee, O Jerusalem. Praise ye the LORD.

Psalmist says, and call upon the name of the Lord. He means that he will utter blessings and thanksgivings and prayers, and then drink of the cup which the Lord had filled with his saving grace. What a cup this is!

Verse 14. I will pay my vows unto the Lord now in the presence of all his people. The Psalmist has already stated his third resolution, to devote himself to the worship of God evermore, and here he commences the performance of that resolve. The vows which he had made in anguish, he now determines to fulfill: "I will pay my vows unto the Lord." He does so at once, "now," and that publicly, "in the presence of all his people." Good resolutions cannot be carried out too speedily; vows become debts, and debts should be paid. It is well to have witnesses to the payment of just debts, and we need not be ashamed to have witnesses to the fulfilling of holy vows, for this will show that we are not ashamed of our Lord, and it may be a great benefit to those who look on and hear us publicly sounding forth the praises of our prayer hearing God.

Verse 15. Precious in the sight of the LORD is the death of his saints, and therefore he did not suffer the Psalmist to die, but delivered his soul from death. This seems to indicate that the song was meant to remind Jewish families of the mercies received by any one of the household, supposing him to have been sore sick and to have been restored to health, for the Lord values the lives of his saints, and often spares them where others perish.

Verse 16. The man of God in paying his vows rededicates himself unto God; the offering which he brings is himself, as he cries, O LORD, truly I am thy servant, rightfully, really, heartily, constantly, I own that I am thine, for thou hast delivered and redeemed me. I am thy servant, and the son of thine handmaid, a servant born in thy house, born of a servant and so born a servant, and therefore doubly thine. My mother was thine handmaid, and I, her son, confess that I am altogether thine by claims arising out of my birth.

Verse 17. I will offer to thee the sacrifice of thanksgiving. Being thy servant, I am bound to sacrifice to thee, and having received spiritual blessings at thy hands I will not bring bullock or goat, but I will bring that which is more suitable, namely, the thanksgiving of my heart.

Verse 18. I will pay my vows unto the Lord now in the presence of all his people. He repeats the declaration. A good thing is worth saying twice. He thus stirs himself up to greater heartiness, earnestness, and diligence in keeping his vow,—really paying it at the very moment that he is declaring his resolution to do so. The mercy came in secret, but the praise is rendered in public; the company was, however, select; he did not cast his pearls before swine, but delivered his testimony before those who could understand and appreciate it.

Verse 19. In the courts of the LORD'S house: in the proper place, where God had ordained that he should be worshipped. See how he is stirred up at the remembrance of the house of the Lord, and must needs speak of the holy city with a note of joyful exclamation—In the midst of thee, O Jerusalem. The very thought of the beloved Zion touched his heart, and he writes as if he were actually addressing Jerusalem, whose name was dear to him. There would he pay his vows, in the abode of fellowship, in the very heart of Judea, in the place to which the tribes went up, the tribes of the Lord. There is nothing like witnessing for Jesus, where the report thereof will be carried into a thousand homes.

The term to call upon, signifies to celebrate the name of God; and this he expresses more plainly, subsequently, by saying that he would pay his vows in the assembly of the faithful, the sanctuary alone being the place where sacrifices could be offered. The amount is, that the faithful need not be greatly perplexed about the way of performing their duties, God not demanding from them a return which he knows they are unable to give, but being satisfied with a bare and simple acknowledgment.

14. I will pay my vows unto Jehovah. The steadfastness of his piety shines forth in this, that, in the midst of his dangers, he had vowed unto God. And now he proves that he by no means forgot these engagements, as most men do, who, when the hand of God lies heavy upon them, implore his help for a short time, but soon bury in oblivion the deliverance which they have received. The Holy Spirit, speaking of the true worship of God, very properly connects, by an indissoluble bond, these two parts of worship, "Call upon me in the day of trouble;" and, "after thy deliverance glorify me," Psalm 50:15.

15-19

15. Precious in the eyes of Jehovah is the death of his meek ones. He goes on now to the general doctrine of God's providential care for the godly, in that he renders them assistance in time of need; their lives being precious in his sight. With this shield he desires to defend himself from the terrors of death, which often pressed upon him, by which he imagined he would instantly be swallowed up. When we are in danger and God apparently overlooks us, we then consider ourselves to be contemned as poor slaves, and that our life is regarded as a thing of nought.

16. Come, O Jehovah! because I am thy servant. As, in the former verse, he gloried that in him God had given an example of the paternal regard which he has for the faithful, so here he applies, in an especial manner, to himself the general doctrine, by declaring that his fetters had been broken, in consequence of his being included among the number of God's servants. He employs the term fetters, as if one, with hands and feet bound, were dragged by the executioner. In assigning, as the reason of his deliverance, that he was God's servant, he by no means vaunts of his services, but rather refers to God's unconditional election.

17. I will sacrifice the sacrifices of praise to thee. He once more repeats what he had said about gratitude, and that publicly; for we must manifest our piety, not only by our secret affection before God, but also by an open profession in the sight of men. David, along with the people, observed the rites of the law, knowing that these, at that time, were not unmeaning services; but while he did this, he had a particular reference to the purpose for which they were appointed, and offered principally the sacrifices of praise and the calves of his lips. He speaks of the courts of God's house, because at that time there was but one altar from which it was unlawful to depart, and it was the will of God that the holy assemblies should be held there, that the faithful might mutually stimulate one another to the cultivation of godliness.

2. He resolves what returns he will make.

(1.) He will in the most devout and solemn manner offer up his praises and prayers to God, v. 13, 17.

[1.] "I will take the cup of salvation, that is, I will offer the drink-offerings appointed by the law, in token of my thankfulness to God, and rejoice with my friends in God's goodness to me;" this is called the cup of deliverance because drunk in memory of his deliverance.

[2.] I will offer to thee the sacrifice of thanksgiving, the thank-offerings which God required, Lev. vii. 11, 12, &c. Note, Those whose hearts are truly thankful will express their gratitude in thank-offerings. We must first give our ownselves to God as living sacrifices (Rom. xii. 1, 2 Cor. viii. 5), and then lay out of what we have for his honor in works of piety and charity.

[3.] I will call upon the name of the Lord. This he had promised (v. 2) and here he repeats it, v. 13 and again v. 17. If we have received kindness from a man like ourselves, we tell him that we hope we shall never trouble him again; but God is pleased to reckon the prayers of his people an honor to him, and a delight, and no trouble; and therefore, in gratitude for former mercies, we must seek to him for further mercies, and continue to call upon him.

(2.) He will always entertain good thoughts of God, as very tender of the lives and comforts of his people (v. 15): Precious in the sight of the Lord is the death of his saints, so precious that he will not gratify Saul, nor Absalom, nor any of David's enemies, with his death, how earnestly soever they desire it. This truth David had comforted himself with in the depth of his distress and danger.

(3.) He will oblige himself to be God's servant all his days. Having asked, What shall I render? here he surrenders himself, which was more than all burnt-offerings and sacrifice (v. 16): O Lord! truly I am thy servant.

(4.) He will make conscience of paying his vows and making good what he had promised, not only that he would offer the sacrifices of praise, which he had vowed to bring, but perform all his other engagements to God, which he had laid himself under in the day of his affliction (v. 14): I will pay my vows; and again, (v. 18), now in the presence of all his people. Note, Vows are debts that must be paid, for it is better not to vow than to vow and not pay. He will pay his vows,

[1.] Presently; he will not, like sorry debtors, delay the payment of them, or beg a day; but, "I will pay them now," Eccl. v. 4.

[2.] Publicly; he will not huddle up his praises in a corner, but what service he has to do for God he will do it in the presence of all his people; nor for ostentation, but to show that he was not ashamed of the service of God, and that others might be invited to join with him. He will pay his vows in the courts of the tabernacle, where there was a crowd of Israelites attending, in the midst of Jerusalem, that he might bring devotion into more reputation.

Psalm 117

1 O praise the LORD, all ye nations: praise him, all ye people.
2 For his merciful kindness is great toward us: and the truth of the LORD endureth for ever. Praise ye the LORD.

Psalm 117

SUBJECT. This Psalm, which is very little in its letter, is exceedingly large in its spirit; for, bursting beyond all bounds of race or nationality, it calls upon all mankind to praise the name of the Lord. In all probability it was frequently used as a brief hymn suitable for almost every occasion, and especially when the time for worship was short. Perhaps it was also sung at the commencement or at the close of other Psalms, just as we now use the doxology. It would have served either to open a service or to conclude it. It is both short and sweet. The same divine Spirit which expatiates in the 119th, here condenses his utterances into two short verses, but yet the same infinite fullness is present and perceptible. It may be worth noting that this is at once the shortest chapter of the Scriptures and the central portion of the whole Bible.

EXPOSITION
Verse 1. O praise the LORD, all ye nations. This is an exhortation to the Gentiles to glorify Jehovah, and a clear proof that the Old Testament spirit differed widely from that narrow and contracted national bigotry with which the Jews of our Lord's day became so inveterately diseased. The nations could not be expected to join in the praise of Jehovah unless they were also to be partakers of the benefits which Israel enjoyed; and hence the Psalm was an intimation to Israel that the grace and mercy of their God were not to be confined to one nation, but would in happier days be extended to all the race of man, even as Moses had prophesied when he said, "Rejoice. O ye nations, his people" (De 32:43), for so the Hebrew has it. The nations were to be his people. He would call them a people that were not a people, and her beloved that was not beloved. We know and believe that no one tribe of men shall be unrepresented in the universal song which shall ascend unto the Lord of all. Individuals have already been gathered out of every kindred and people and tongue by the preaching of the gospel, and these have right heartily joined in magnifying the grace which sought them out, and brought them to know the Savior. These are but the advance guard of a number which no man can number who will come ere long to worship the all glorious One. Praise him, all ye people. Having done it once, do it again, and do it still more fervently, daily increasing in the reverence and zeal with which you extol the Most High. The multitude of the common folk shall bless the Lord. Inasmuch as the matter is spoken of twice, its certainty is confirmed, and the Gentiles must and shall extol Jehovah—all of them, without exception. Under the gospel dispensation we worship no new god, but the God of Abraham is our God for ever and ever; the God of the whole earth shall he be called.
Verse 2. For his merciful kindness is great toward us. By which is meant not only his great love toward the Jewish people, but towards the whole family of man. The Lord is kind to us as his creatures, and merciful to us as sinners, hence his merciful kindness to us as sinful creatures. This mercy has been very great, or powerful. The mighty grace of God has prevailed even as the waters of the flood prevailed over the earth: breaking over all bounds, it has flowed towards all portions of the multiplied race of man. In Christ Jesus, God has shown mercy mixed with kindness, and that to the very highest degree. We can all join in this grateful acknowledgment, and in the praise which is therefore due. And the truth of the Lord endureth for ever. He has kept his covenant that in the seed of Abraham should all nations of the earth be blessed. This should be a cause of constant and grateful praise, wherefore the Psalm concludes as it began, with another Hallelujah, Praise ye the LORD.

JOHN CALVIN

Psalm 117

1-2
1. Praise Jehovah, all ye nations. The Holy Spirit having, by the mouth of the prophet, exhorted all nations to celebrate the praises of God's mercy and faithfulness, Paul, in his Epistle to the Romans, very justly considers this as a prediction respecting the calling of the whole world, (Romans 15:11.)

How can unbelievers be qualified for praising God, who, though not entirely destitute of his mercy, yet are insensible of it, and are ignorant of his truth? It would therefore serve no purpose for the prophet to address the heathen nations, unless they were to be gathered together in the unity of the faith with the children of Abraham. There is no ground for the censorious attempting, by their sophistical arguments, to refute the reasoning of Paul. I grant that the Holy Spirit elsewhere calls upon the mountains, rivers, trees, rain, winds, and thunder, to resound the praises of God, because all creation silently proclaims him to be its Maker. It is in a different manner that he is praised by his rational creatures. The reason assigned is, that God's mercy and truth furnish materials for celebrating his praises. Besides, the prophet does not mean that God shall be praised everywhere by the Gentiles, because the knowledge of his character is confined to a small portion of the land of Judea, but because it was to be spread over the whole world.

First, he enjoins God to be praised, because his goodness is increased, or strengthened, for the Hebrew term admits of both meanings.

Secondly, because his truth remains steadfast for ever How, then, are those qualified to celebrate his praises, who, with brutal insensibility, pass over his goodness, and shut their ears against his heavenly doctrine?

The truth of God, in this passage, is properly introduced as an attestation of his grace. For he can be true even when he menaces the whole world with perdition and ruin. The prophet, however, has placed his mercy first in order that his faithfulness and truth, comprising an assurance of his paternal kindness, might encourage the hearts of the godly. His power and justice are equally praiseworthy; but as men will never cordially praise God until they are drawn by a foretaste of his goodness, the prophet very justly selects God's mercy and truth, which alone open the mouths of those who are mute to engage in this exercise. When his truth is said to be everlasting, it is not set in opposition to his mercy, as if it, after flourishing for a season, then instantly passed away. The same reason would go to prove, that it was small compared with his mercy, which is said to be abundant. The meaning is, that God's mercy is rich towards us, flowing in a perennial stream, because united to his eternal truth. If we read, his mercy is confirmed, all difficulty will be removed, for then both constancy and stability will alike adorn his mercy and his truth.

MATTHEW HENRY

Psalm 117

1-2 All nations admonished to praise God.

There is a great deal of gospel in this psalm. The apostle has furnished us with a key to it (Rom. xv. 11), where he quotes it as a proof that the gospel was to be preached to, and would be entertained by, the Gentile nations, which yet was so great a stumbling-block to the Jews. Why should that offend them when it is said, and they themselves had often sung it, Praise the Lord, all you Gentiles, and laud him, all you people. Some of the Jewish writers confess that this psalm refers to the kingdom of the Messiah; nay, one of them has a fancy that it consists of two verses to signify that in the days of the Messiah God should be glorified by two sorts of people, by the Jews, according to the law of Moses, and by the Gentiles, according to the seven precepts of the sons of Noah, which yet should make one church, as these two verses make one psalm. We have here,

I. The vast extent of the gospel church, v. 1. For many ages in Judah only was God known and his name praised. The sons of Levi and the seed of Israel praised him, but the rest of the nations praised gods of wood and stone (Dan. v. 4), while there was no devotion at all paid, at least none openly, that we know of, to the living and true God. But here all nations are called to praise the Lord, which could not be applied to the Old-Testament times, both because this call was not then given to any of the Gentile nations, much less to all, in a language they understood, and because, unless the people of the land became Jews and were circumcised, they were not admitted to praise God with them. But the gospel of Christ is ordered to be preached to all nations, and by him the partition-wall is taken down, and those that were afar off are made nigh. This was the mystery which was hidden in prophecy for many ages, but was at length revealed in the accomplishment.

II. The unsearchable riches of gospel-grace, which are to be the matter or our praise, v. 2. In the gospel, those celebrated attributes of God, his mercy and his truth, shine most brightly in themselves and most comfortably to us; and the apostle, where he quotes this psalm, takes notice of these as the two great things for which the Gentiles should glorify God (Rom. xv. 8, 9), for the truth of God and for his mercy. We that enjoy the gospel have reason to praise the Lord,

1. For the power of his mercy: His merciful kindness is great towards us; it is strong (so the word signifies); it is mighty for the pardon of mighty sins (Amos v. 12) and for the working out of a mighty salvation.

2. For the perpetuity of his truth: The truth of the Lord endures for ever God's mercy is the fountain of all our comforts and his truth the foundation of all our hopes, and therefore for both we must praise the Lord.

Psalm 118

1-7

1 O give thanks unto the LORD; for he is good: because his mercy endureth for ever.
2 Let Israel now say, that his mercy endureth for ever.
3 Let the house of Aaron now say, that his mercy endureth for ever.
4 Let them now that fear the LORD say, that his mercy endureth for ever.
5 I called upon the LORD in distress: the LORD answered me, and set me in a large place.
6 The LORD is on my side; I will not fear: what can man do unto me?
7 The LORD taketh my part with them that help me: therefore shall I see my desire upon them that hate me.

Psalm 118

AUTHOR AND SUBJECT. In the book Ezr 3:10-11, we read that "when the builders laid the foundation of the temple of the Lord, they set the priests in their apparel with trumpets, and the Levites the sons of Asaph with cymbals, to praise he Lord, after the ordinance of David king of Israel. And they sang together by course in praising and giving thanks unto the Lord; because he is good, for his mercy endureth for ever toward Israel. And all the people shouted with a great shout, when they praised the Lord, because the foundation of the house of the Lord was laid." Now the words mentioned in Ezra are the first and last sentences of this Psalm, and we therefore conclude that the people chanted the whole of this sublime song; and, moreover, that the use of this composition on such occasions was ordained by David, whom we conceive to be its author. The next step leads us to believe that he is its subject, at least in some degree; for it is clear that the writer is speaking concerning himself in the first place, though he may not have strictly confined himself to all the details of his our personal experience. That the Psalmist had a prophetic view of our Lord Jesus is very manifest; the frequent quotations from this song in the New Testament prove this beyond all questions; but at the same time it could not have been intended that every particular line and sentence should be read in reference to the Messiah, for this requires very great ingenuity, and ingenious interpretations are seldom true.

The Psalm, seems to us to describe either David or some other man of God who was appointed by the divine choice to a high and honorable office in Israel. This elect champion found himself rejected by his friends and fellow countrymen, and at the same time violently opposed by his enemies. In faith in God he battles for his appointed place, and in due time he obtains it in such a way as greatly to display the power and goodness of the Lord. He then goes up to the house of the Lord to offer sacrifice, and to express his gratitude for the divine interposition, all the people blessing him, and wishing him abundant prosperity. This heroic personage, whom we cannot help thinking to be David himself, broadly typified our Lord, but not in such a manner that in all the minutiae of his struggles and prayers we are to hunt for parallels. The suggestion of Alexander that the speaker is a typical individual representing the nation, is exceedingly well worthy of attention, but it is not inconsistent with the idea that a personal leader may be intended, since that which describes the leader will be in a great measure true of his followers. The experience of the Head is that of the members, and both may be spoken of in much the same terms. Alexander thinks that the deliverance celebrated cannot be identified with any one so exactly as with that from the Babylonian exile; but we judge it best to refer it to no one incident in particular, but to regard it as a national song, adapted alike for the rise of a chosen here, and the building of a temple. Whether a nation is founded again by a conquering prince, or a temple founded by the laying of its cornerstone in joyful state, the Psalm is equally applicable.

DIVISION. We propose to divide this Psalm thus, from Ps 118:1-4 the faithful are called upon to magnify the everlasting mercy of the Lord; from Ps 118:5-18 the Psalmist gives forth a narrative of his experience, and an expression of his faith; in Ps 118:19-21 he asks admittance into the house of the Lord, and begins the acknowledgment of the divine salvation. In Ps 118:22-27 the priests and people recognize their ruler, magnify the Lord for him, declare him blessed, and bid him approach the altar with his sacrifice. In Ps 118:28-29 the grateful hero himself exalts God the ever merciful.

EXPOSITION

Verse 1. O give thanks unto the LORD. The grateful hero feels that he cannot himself alone sufficiently express his thankfulness, and therefore he

JOHN CALVIN

Psalm 118

1-4
1. Praise ye Jehovah. In this passage we see that David does not merely in a private capacity render thanks to God, but that he loudly summons the people to engage in the common exercises of piety. This he does, not simply from his having been divinely appointed to be the captain and teacher of others; but, God having invested him with royal power, had manifested his sympathy with his distressed Church. Hence he exhorts the Israelites to magnify the grace of God, under whose kind protection he appears to re-establish them in safety. In the beginning of the psalm he alludes generally to the goodness and mercy of God, but he shortly instances himself as an evidence of his goodness, as will be seen in its proper place.

5-9
5. I called upon God in my distress. We have here a particular application of the doctrine we formerly mentioned, to the person of David; with which also is conjoined the rejoicing of the whole Church, for whose public welfare God made provision by upholding him. By his own example he establishes the faithful, showing them that they ought not to faint in the day of adversity. He seems designedly to anticipate an objection, which is apt to arise in the minds of men the moment that the goodness of God is proclaimed, "Why does he permit his servants to be so sore oppressed and afflicted?" David therefore reminds them, notwithstanding, that God's mercy never fails, for we have in prayer, consolation and an antidote for all our ills.
6. Jehovah is with me among those who help me Confiding solely in God's help, he sets at defiance not a few enemies merely, but the whole world. "Defended by God's hand, I may boldly and safely set at nought all the machinations of men." When all the power of the universe is deemed as nothing, in comparison of God, then, indeed, is due honor attributed to him. Thus he tacitly reproves the unbelief of almost all men, who spontaneously alarm themselves with groundless fears.
8. It is better to trust in Jehovah. He appears to state nothing but what is common-place, it being unanimously admitted, that when God and men come into comparison, he must be viewed as infinitely exalted above them, and therefore it is best to trust in him for the aid which he has promised to his own people.

10-14
10. All nations compassed me. In these verses he relates the wonderful deliverance which he had received, that all might know that it was not of human but divine origin. Once and again he declares, that he was compassed not by a few persons, but by a vast multitude. The people, being all inflamed with anger and fury against him, compassed him so that there were no means for his escape, and he could procure help from no quarter but from heaven. His meaning, in my opinion, is, that

MATTHEW HENRY

Psalm 118

1-18 Goodness of God celebrated; grateful acknowledgments.
In these verses,
I. He celebrates God's mercy in general, and calls upon others to acknowledge it, from their own experience of it (v. 1): O give thanks unto the Lord, for he is not only good in himself, but good to you, and his mercy endures for ever, not only in the everlasting fountain, God himself, but in the never-failing streams of that mercy, which shall run parallel with the longest line of eternity, and in the chosen vessels of mercy, who will be everlasting monuments of it. Israel, and the house of Aaron, and all that fear God, were called upon to trust in God (Ps. cxv. 9-11); here they are called upon to confess that his mercy endures for ever, and so to encourage themselves to trust in him, v. 2-4.
II. He preserves an account of God's gracious dealings with him in particular, which he communicates to others, that they might thence fetch both songs of praise and supports of faith, and both ways God would have the glory. David had, in his time, waded through a great deal of difficulty, which gave him great experience of God's goodness. Let us therefore observe here,

1. The great distress and danger that he had been in, which he reflects upon for the magnifying of God's goodness to him in his present advancement. There are many who, when they are lifted up, care not for hearing or speaking of their former depressions; but David takes all occasions to remember his own low estate. He was in distress (v. 5), greatly straitened and at a loss; there were many that hated him (v. 7), and this could not but be a great grief to one of an ingenuous spirit, that strove to gain the good affections of all. All nations compassed me about, v. 10. All the nations adjacent to Israel set themselves to give disturbance to David, when he had newly come to the throne, Philistines, Moabites, Syrians, Ammonites, &c. We read of his enemies round about; they were confederate against him, and thought to cut off all succors from him. This endeavor of his enemies to surround him is repeated (v. 11): They compassed me about, yea, they compassed me about, which intimates that they were virulent and violent, and, for a time, prevalent, in their attempts against him, and when put into disorder they rallied again and pushed on their design.

2. The favor God vouchsafed to him in his distress.
(1.) God heard his prayer (v. 5): "He answered me with enlargements; he did more for me than I was able to ask; he enlarged my heart in prayer and yet gave more largely than I desired."
(2.) God baffled the designs of his enemies against him: They are quenched as the fire of thorns (v. 12),

Psalm 118

8-14

8 It is better to trust in the LORD than to put confidence in man.
9 It is better to trust in the LORD than to put confidence in princes.
10 All nations compassed me about: but in the name of the LORD will I destroy them.
11 They compassed me about; yea, they compassed me about: but in the name of the LORD I will destroy them.
12 They compassed me about like bees: they are quenched as the fire of thorns: for in the name of the LORD I will destroy them.
13 Thou hast thrust sore at me that I might fall: but the LORD helped me.
14 The LORD is my strength and song, and is become my salvation.

calls in the aid of others. Grateful hearts are greedy of men's tongues, and would monopolize them all for God's glory. The whole nation was concerned in David's triumphant accession, and therefore it was right that they should unite in his adoring song of praise.

Verse 2. Let Israel now say, that his mercy endureth for ever. God had made a covenant with their forefathers, a covenant of mercy and love, and to that covenant he was faithful evermore. Israel sinned in Egypt, provoked the Lord in the wilderness, went astray again and again under the judges, and transgressed at all times; and yet the Lord continued to regard them as his people, to favor them with his oracles, and to forgive their sins.

Verse 3. Let the house of Aaron now say, that his mercy endureth for ever. The sons of Aaron were specially set apart to come nearest to God, and it was only because of his mercy that they were enabled to live in the presence of the thrice holy Jehovah, who is a consuming fire.

Verse 4. Let them now that fear the LORD say, that his mercy endureth for ever. If there were any throughout the world who did not belong to Israel after the flesh, but nevertheless had a holy fear and lowly reverence of God, the Psalmist calls upon them to unite with him in his thanksgiving, and to do it especially on the occasion of his exaltation to the throne; and this is no more than they would cheerfully agree to do, since every good man in the world is benefited when a true servant of God is placed in a position of honor and influence.

Verse 5. I called upon the LORD in distress, or, "out of anguish I invoked Jah." Nothing was left him but prayer, his agony was too great for aught beside; but having the heart and the privilege to pray he possessed all things.

Verse 6. The LORD is on my side, or, he is "for me." Once his justice was against me, but now he is my reconciled God, and engaged on my behalf. The Psalmist naturally rejoiced in the divine help; all men turned against him, but God was his defender and advocate, accomplishing the divine purposes of his grace.

Verse 7. The LORD taketh my part with them that help me. Jehovah condescended to be in alliance with the good man and his comrades; his God was not content to look on, but he took part in the struggle.

Verse 8. It is better to trust in the LORD than to put confidence in man. It is better in all ways, for first of all it is wiser: God is infinitely more able to help, and more likely to help, than man, and therefore prudence suggests that we put our confidence in him above all others.

Verse 9. It is better to trust in the LORD than to put confidence in princes. These should be the noblest of men, chivalrous in character, and true to the core. The royal word should be unquestionable. They are noblest in rank and mightiest in power, and yet as a rule princes are not one whit more reliable than the rest of mankind.

Verse 10. All nations compassed me about. The hero of the Psalm, while he had no earthly friend upon whom he could thoroughly rely, was surrounded by innumerable enemies, who heartily hated him. He was hemmed in by his adversaries, and scarce could find a loophole of escape from the bands which made a ring around him. As if by common consent all sorts of people set themselves against him, and yet he was more than a match for them all, because he was trusting in the name of the Lord.

Verse 11. They compassed me about; yea, they compassed me about. He had such a vivid recollection of his danger that his enemies seem to live again in his verses. We see their fierce array, and their cruel combination of forces. They made a double ring, they surrounded him in a circle of many ranks, they not only talked of doing so, but they actually shut him up and enclosed him as within a wall. His heart had vividly realized his position of peril at the time, and now he delights to call it again to mind in order that he may the more ardently adore the mercy which made him strong in the hour of conflict, so that he broke through a troop, yea, swept a host to destruction.

the whole world was adverse to him; because he places God's help alone in opposition to the deadly and furious hatred both of his own countrymen and of the neighboring nations towards him, so that there was not a spot upon the earth where he could be safe. There was, it is true, no army, collected from several nations, besieging him; still he had no peaceable retreat except among the haunts of wild beasts, from which also he was driven by terror. And in proportion to the number of persons he encountered were the snares laid to entrap him. It is, therefore, not wonderful that he said he was compassed by all nations. Besides, this elliptical mode of speaking is more forcible than if he had merely said that he trusted in God, by reason of which he had become victorious. By publicly mentioning the name of God alone, he maintains that no other means of deliverance were within his reach, and that but for his interposition he must have perished.

13. Thou hast sorely thrust at me. He either now changes the person, or directs his discourse to Saul, his principal enemy. In the person of one, he sets at defiance all his enemies together. In saying that he had been thrust at, he admits that he did not withstand the onset by his own bravery, as those who are powerful enough to encounter opposition, sustain the assaults of their enemies without flinching. The power of God is more illustriously displayed in raising him up even from ruin itself.

15-21

15. The voice of shouting and salvation is in the tabernacles of the just. He affirms that the kindness which God had conferred upon him was so extensive, that it would not do to render thanks to him privately. In the benefits which he had received, God's power appeared both remarkable and memorable, and the fruit of it also was extended to the whole Church. Therefore, as David's deliverance was wonderful and advantageous generally to all the godly, he promises that he would make a public thanksgiving; and invites them to join him in this holy exercise. By this circumstance, he chiefly aims at magnifying the grace of God, and also by its effects to demonstrate, that not merely his individual preservation, but that of the whole Church, in his person, was accomplished.

17. I shall not die. David speaks like one emerging from the sepulcher. The very same person who says, I shall not die, acknowledges that he was rescued from death, to which he was near as one condemned to it. For a series of years his life was in imminent danger, exposed every moment to a thousand deaths, and no sooner was he delivered from one than he entered into another. Thus he declares that he would not die, because he regained life, all hope of which he had entirely abandoned. We, whose life is hid with Christ in God, ought to mediate upon this song all our days, Colossians 3:3.

18. In chastising God has chastised me. In these words David owns that his enemies assailed him unjustly, that they were employed by God to correct him, that this was fatherly chastisement, God not inflicting a deadly wound, but correcting him in measure and in mercy. He seems to anticipate the perverse decisions of perverse men which grievously pressed upon him, as if all the ills which he had

which burns furiously for a while, makes a great noise and a great blaze, but is presently out, and cannot do the mischief that it threatened. Such was the fury of David's enemies; such is the laughter of the fool, like the crackling of thorns under a pot (Eccl. vii. 6), and such is the anger of the fool, which therefore is not to be feared, any more than his laughter is to be envied, but both to be pitied. They thrust sorely at him, but the Lord helped him (v. 13), helped him to keep his feet and maintain his ground. Our spiritual enemies would, long before this, have been our ruin if God had not been our helper.

(3.) God preserved his life when there was but a step between him and death (v. 18): "He has chastened me, but he has not given me over unto death, for he has not given me over to the will of my enemies."

3. The improvement he made of this favor.

(1.) It encouraged him to trust in God; from his own experience he can say, It is better, more wise, more comfortable, and more safe, there is more reason for it, and it will speed better, to trust in the Lord, than to put confidence in man, yea, though it be in princes, v. 8, 9. He that devotes himself to God's guidance and government, with an entire dependence upon God's wisdom, power, and goodness, has a better security to make him easy than if all the kings and potentates of the earth should undertake to protect him.

(2.) It enabled him to triumph in that trust. He triumphs in God, and in his relation to him and interest in him (v. 6): "The Lord is on my side. He is a righteous God, and therefore espouses my righteous cause and will plead it." If we are on God's side, he is on ours; if we be for him and with him, he will be for us and with us (v. 7): "The Lord takes my part, and stands up for me, with those that help me. He is to me among my helpers, and so one of them that he is all in all both to them and me, and without him I could not help myself nor could any friend I have in the world help me." Thus (v. 14), "The Lord is my strength and my song; that is, I make him so (without him I am weak and sad, but on him I stay myself as my strength, both for doing and suffering, and in him I solace myself as my song, by which I both express my joy and ease my grief), and, making him so, I find him so: he strengthens my heart with his graces and gladdens my heart with his comforts."

19-29 David triumphs in God; the humiliation and exaltation of the Messiah.

We have here an illustrious prophecy of the humiliation and exaltation of our Lord Jesus, his sufferings, and the glory that should follow. Peter thus applies it directly to the chief priests and scribes, and none of them could charge him with misapplying it, Acts iv. 11. Now observe here,

I. The preface with which this precious prophecy is introduced, v. 19-21.

1. The psalmist desires admission into the sanctuary of God, there to celebrate the glory of him that

Psalm 118

15-21

15 The voice of rejoicing and salvation is in the tabernacles of the righteous: the right hand of the LORD doeth valiantly.

16 The right hand of the LORD is exalted: the right hand of the LORD doeth valiantly.

17 I shall not die, but live, and declare the works of the LORD.

18 The LORD hath chastened me sore: but he hath not given me over unto death.

19 Open to me the gates of righteousness: I will go into them, and I will praise the LORD:

20 This gate of the LORD, into which the righteous shall enter.

21 I will praise thee: for thou hast heard me, and art become my salvation.

Verse 12. They compassed me about like bees. They seemed to be everywhere, like a swarm of bees, attacking him at every point; nimbly flying from place to place, stinging him meanwhile, and inflicting grievous pain.

Verse 13. Thou hast thrust sore at me, "Thrusting, thou hast thrust at me." It is a vigorous apostrophe, in which the enemy is described as concentrating all his thrusting power into the thrusts which he gave to the man of God. He thrust again and again with the keenest point, even as bees thrust their stings into their victim. The foe had exhibited intense exasperation, and fearful determination, nor had he been without a measure of success; wounds had been given and received, and these smarted much, and were exceeding sore.

Verse 14. The LORD my strength and song, my strength while I was in the conflict, my song now that it is ended; my strength against the strong, and my song over their defeat.

Verse 15. The voice of rejoicing and salvation is in the tabernacles of the righteous. They sympathized in the delight of their leader and they abode in their tents in peace, rejoicing that one had been raised up who, in the name of the Lord, would protect them from their adversaries. The families of believers are happy, and they should take pains to give their happiness a voice by their family devotion.

Verse 16. The right hand of the LORD is exalted, lifted up to smite the enemy, or extolled and magnified in the eyes of his people. It is the Lord's right hand, the hand of his skill, the hand of his greatest power, the hand which is accustomed to defend his saints. When that is lifted up, it lifts up all who trust in him, and it casts down all who resist him.

Verse 17. I shall not die, but live. His enemies hoped that he would die, and perhaps he himself feared he should perish at their hand: the news of his death may have been spread among his people, as the tongue of rumor is ever ready with ill news, the false intelligence would naturally cause great sorrow and despondency, but he proclaims himself as yet alive and as confident that he shall not fall by the hand of the destroyer.

Verse 18. The LORD hath chastened me sore. This is faith's version of the former passage, "Thou hast thrust sore at me;" for the attacks of the enemy are chastisements from the hand of God.

Verse 20. This gate of the LORD, into which the righteous shall enter. Psalmist loves the house of God so well that he admires the very gate thereof, and pauses beneath its arch to express his affection for it. He loved it because it was the gate of the Lord.

Verse 21. Having entered, the champion exclaims, I will praise thee, not "I will praise the Lord," for now he vividly realizes the divine presence, and addresses himself directly to Jehovah, whom his faith sensibly discerns. How well it is in all our songs of praise to let the heart have direct and distinct communion with God himself!

Verse 22. The stone which the builders refused is become the head stone of the corner. Here the people magnify God for bringing his chosen servant into the honorable office, which had been allotted to him by divine decree. A wise king and valiant leader is a stone by which the national fabric is built up. David had been rejected by those in authority, but God had placed him in a position of the highest honor and the greatest usefulness, making him the chief cornerstone of the state.

Verse 23. This is the LORD'S doing. The exalted position of Christ in his church is not the work of man, and does not depend for its continuation upon any builders or ministers; God himself has wrought the exaltation of our Lord Jesus.

Verse 24. This is the day which the LORD hath made. A new era has commenced. The day of David's enthronement was the beginning of better times for Israel; and in a far higher sense the day of our Lord's resurrection is a new day of God's own making, for it is the dawn of a blessed dispensation.

endured were so many evidences of his being cast off by God. These calumnies which the reprobate cast upon him he applies very differently, by declaring that his correction was mild and paternal. The main thing in adversity is to know that we are laid low by the hand of God, and that this is the way which he takes to prove our allegiance, to arouse us from our torpidity, to crucify our old man, to purge us from our filthiness, to bring us into submission and subjection to God, and to excite us to meditate on the heavenly life.

19. Open unto me the gates of righteousness. Under the influence of ardent zeal, David here sets himself to testify his gratitude, commanding the temple to be opened to him, as if the oblations were all already prepared. He now confirms what he said formerly, That he would render thanks to God publicly in the properly constituted assembly of the faithful. It was the practice of the priests to open the doors of the temple to the people; it appears, however, that David here alludes to his long exile, which supposition is corroborated by the following verse. Having been for a long period prevented from having access to the sanctuary, and even from coming within sight of it, he now rejoices and exults at being again admitted to offer sacrifice unto God. And he declares that he will not approach as the hypocrites were wont to do, whom God, by the prophet Isaiah, reproaches with treading his courts in vain, but that he will come with the sacrifice of praise, (Isaiah 1:12) Fully persuaded that he drew near in the spirit of genuine devotion, he says it is proper that the doors of the temple, which lately he durst not enter, should be opened to him and such as he. It is, says he, the gate of Jehovah, and, therefore, he will open it for the just. The meaning is, that banished as David had been from the temple and from his country, now that the kingdom is in a better condition, both he and all the true worshippers of God regained their right to approach his sanctuary.

22-26

22. The stone which the builders rejected. In these words David boldly pours contempt on the calumnies with which he was unjustly and undeservedly assailed. As there was something ominous in his being condemned by the entire assemblage of the nobles, and all those who were invested with authority, and as the opinion was prevalent, that he was a wicked and rejected man; this error he deliberately refutes, and vindicates his innocence in the face of the principal men among them. "It is of little importance to me that I am abandoned by the chief men, seeing I have been visibly chosen by the judgment of God to be king over Israel." The similitude which he employs is appropriate, comparing himself to a stone, and the principal rulers of the Church to master-builders It might, indeed, appear most irrational on his part to assert that the heads of the realm, to whom the government of the Church was intrusted, should be deprived of the Spirit of God, and divested of a sound judgment.

24. This is the day which Jehovah made. He now speaks of that as a happy and pleasant day, on which he was at last established king over Israel, and the anointing of him by

cometh in the name of the Lord: Open to me the gates of righteousness.

2. He sees admission granted him (v. 20): This is the gate of the Lord, the gate of his appointing, into which the righteous shall enter; as if he had said, "The gate you knocked at is opened, and you are welcome. Knock, and it shall be opened unto you."

3. He promises to give thanks to God for this favor (v. 21): I will praise thee. Those that saw Christ's day at so great a distance saw cause to praise God for the prospect; for in him they saw that God had heard them, had heard the prayers of the Old-Testament saints for the coming of the Messiah, and would be their salvation.

II. The prophecy itself, v. 22, 23. This may have some reference to David's preferment; he was the stone which Saul and his courtiers rejected, but was by the wonderful providence of God advanced to be the headstone of the building. But its principal reference is to Christ; and here we have,

1. His humiliation. He is the stone which the builders refused; he is the stone cut out of the mountain without hands, Dan. ii. 34. He is a stone, not only for strength, and firmness, and duration, but for life, in the building of the spiritual temple.

2. His exaltation. He has become the headstone of the corner; he is advanced to the highest degree both of honor and usefulness, to be above all, and all in all. He is the chief corner-stone in the foundation, in whom Jew and Gentile are united, that they may be built up one holy house.

3. The hand of God in all this: This is the Lord's doing; it is from the Lord; it is with the Lord; it is the product of his counsel; it is his contrivance. Both the humiliation and the exaltation of the Lord Jesus were his work, Acts ii. 23; iv. 27, 28. He sent him, sealed him; his hand went with him throughout his whole undertaking, and from first to last he did his Father's will; and this ought to be marvelous in our eyes.

III. The joy wherewith it is entertained and the acclamations which attend this prediction.

1. Let the day be solemnized to the honor of God with great joy (v. 24): This is the day the Lord has made. The whole time of the gospel-dispensation, that accepted time, that day of salvation, is what the Lord has made so; it is a continual feast, which ought to be kept with joy.

2. Let the exalted Redeemer be met, and attended, with joyful hosannas, v. 25, 26.

(1.) Let him have the acclamations of the people, as is usual at the inauguration of a prince. Let every one of his loyal subjects shout for joy, Save now, I beseech thee, O Lord!

(2.) Let the priests, the Lord's ministers, do their part in this great solemnity, v. 26.

[1.] Let them bless the prince with their praises: Blessed is he that cometh in the name of the Lord.

[2.] Let them bless the people with their prayers: We have blessed you out of the house of the Lord.

Psalm 118

22-29
22 The stone which the builders refused is become the head stone of the corner.
23 This is the LORD's doing; it is marvelous in our eyes.
24 This is the day which the LORD hath made; we will rejoice and be glad in it.
25 Save now, I beseech thee, O LORD: O LORD, I beseech thee, send now prosperity.
26 Blessed be he that cometh in the name of the LORD: we have blessed you out of the house of the LORD.
27 God is the LORD, which hath shewed us light: bind the sacrifice with cords, even unto the horns of the altar.
28 Thou art my God, and I will praise thee: thou art my God, I will exalt thee.
29 O give thanks unto the LORD; for he is good: for his mercy endureth for ever.

Verse 25. Save now, I beseech thee, O LORD. Hosanna! God save our king! Let David reign! Or as we who live in these latter days interpret it,—Let the Son of David live for ever, let his saving help go forth throughout all nations. This was the peculiar shout of the feast of tabernacles; and so long as we dwell here below in these tabernacles of clay we cannot do better than use the same cry. Perpetually let us pray that our glorious King may work salvation in the midst of the earth.

Verse 26. Blessed is he that cometh in the name of the LORD. The champion had done everything "in the name of the Lord": in that name he had routed all his adversaries, and had risen to the throne, and in that name he had now entered the temple to pay his vows.

Verse 27. God is the LORD, which hath shewed us light, or "God is Jehovah," the only living and true God. There is none other God but he. The words may also be rendered, "Mighty is Jehovah." Only the power of God could have brought us such light and joy as spring from the work of our Champion and King. We have received light, by which we have known the rejected stone to be the head of the corner, and this light has led us to enlist beneath the banner of the once despised Nazarene, who is now the Prince of the kings of the earth. With the light of knowledge has come the light of joy; for we are delivered from the powers of darkness and translated into the kingdom of God's dear Son. Our knowledge of the glory of God in the face of Jesus Christ came not by the light of nature, nor by reason, nor did it arise from the sparks which we ourselves had kindled, nor did we receive it of men; but the mighty God alone hath showed it to us.

Verse 28. Thou art my God, and I will praise thee, my mighty God who hath done this mighty and marvelous thing. Thou shalt be mine, and all the praise my soul is capable of shall be poured forth at thy feet. Thou art my God, I will exalt thee. Thou hast exalted me, and as far as my praises can do it, I will exalt thy name. Jesus is magnified, and he magnifies the Father according to his prayer, "Father, the hour is come; glorify thy Son, that thy Son also may glorify thee." God hath given us grace and promised us glory, and we are constrained to ascribe all grace to him, and all the glory of it also.

Verse 29. O give thanks unto the LORD; for he is good: for his mercy endureth for ever. The Psalm concludes as it began, making a complete circle of joyful adoration. We can well suppose that the notes at the close of the loud hallelujah were more swift, more sweet, more loud than at the beginning. To the sound of trumpet and harp, Israel, the house of Aaron, and all that feared the Lord, forgetting their distinctions, joined in one common hymn, testifying again to their deep gratitude to the Lord's goodness, and to the mercy which is unto eternity. What better close could there be to this right royal song? The Psalmist would have risen to something higher, so as to end with a climax, but nothing loftier remained. He had reached the height of his grandest argument, and there he paused. The music ceased, the song was suspended, the great hallel was all chanted, and the people went every one to his own home, quietly and happily musing upon the goodness of the Lord, whose mercy fills eternity.

Samuel ratified by this event. Doubtless, all days were created alike by God, nevertheless David, by way of eminence, calls that the day of God which, after a long period of darkness, had dawned for the weal of the Church, because it was signalized by a notable event, deserving of being remembered by succeeding generations; and because the Church had thus emerged from a state of deep obscurity, he exhorts the faithful to mirth and joy, and that, too, by reason of the ignorance which many still displayed of the grace of God, or of their treating it with contempt, and of others being so lettered by their perverse attachment to Saul, that they could scarcely be brought to yield allegiance to David.

25. I beseech thee, O Jehovah! save me. This is often used in the form of asking, and this is the meaning I attach to it, and which accords very well with this passage; for I am persuaded that the Holy Spirit, in repeating the same phrase, designed, by the mouth of the prophet, to stir up and stimulate the faithful to great earnestness and ardor in prayer. One thing is plain, that there is here a form of prayer prescribed to the chosen people, to seek for prosperity to the kingdom of David, upon which the common safety of all depended. In these words, too, he protested that he held his kingdom by Divine legation, and, therefore, they who would not agree to wish prosperity to his reign were unworthy of occupying a place in the Church.

27-29

27. Jehovah is God. Here the prophet establishes what he said formerly, that God, out of compassion to his Church, dissipated the darkness, and introduced the light of his grace, when David mounted the throne, for that was the harbinger of the redemption which was anticipated to be effected in due time by Christ.

He also asserts that God was the author of that deliverance, so wonderful and unlooked for, and he declares that, by the result, he plainly showed himself to be truly God. These words, Jehovah himself is a strong God, because he has restored the light of life to us, are tacitly emphatic. For as the faithful, in consequence of the confused state of the Church, were reduced almost to the brink of despair; the ungodly imagined that all this had happened regarding the children of Abraham, by reason of God himself having, as it were, forsaken them. Wherefore he returns to offer up anew his thankful acknowledgments for the divine grace. He commands the faithful to bind the victim to the horns of the altar, because, according to the legal institute, they could not render solemn thanks unto God without sacrifices. As David was a strict observer of the Law, he would not omit the ceremonial observances which God had enjoined. He would, however, always keep his attention steadily fixed on their grand design.

Now that the shadowy dispensation has passed away, it remains that we offer unto God our thanksgivings through Christ, who sanctifies them by his own immaculate offering, lest we should be debarred from this exercise of godliness, by the corruptions of our flesh.

Christ's ministers are not only warranted, but appointed to pronounce a blessing, in his name, upon all his loyal subjects that love him and his government in sincerity, Eph. vi. 24. We assure you that in and through Jesus Christ you are blessed; for he came to bless you. "You are blessed out of the house of the Lord, that is, with spiritual blessings in heavenly places (Eph. i. 3), and therefore have reason to bless him who has thus blessed you."

3. Let sacrifices of thanksgiving be offered to his honor who offered for us the great atoning sacrifice, v. 27. Here is,

(1.) The privilege we enjoy by Jesus Christ: God is the Lord who has shown us light. God is Jehovah, is known by that name, a God performing what he has promised and perfecting what he has begun, Exod. vi. 3. He has shown us light, that is, he has given us the knowledge of himself and his will. He has shined upon us (so some); he has favored us, and lifted up upon us the light of his countenance; he has given us occasion for joy and rejoicing, which is light to the soul, by giving us a prospect of everlasting light in heaven. The day which the Lord has made brings light with it, true light.

(2.) The duty which this privilege calls for: Bind the sacrifice with cords, that, being killed, the blood of it may be sprinkled upon the horns of the altar, according to the law; or perhaps it was the custom (though we read not of it elsewhere) to bind the sacrifice to the horns of the altar while things were getting ready for the slaying of it.

4. The psalmist concludes with his own thankful acknowledgments of divine grace, in which he calls upon others to join with him, v. 28, 29.

(1.) He will praise God himself, and endeavor to exalt him in his own heart and in the hearts of others, and this because of his covenant-relation to him and interest in him: "Thou art my God, on whom I depend, and to whom I am devoted, who ownest me and art owned by me; and therefore I will praise thee."

(2.) He will have all about him to give thanks to God for these glad tidings of great joy to all people, that there is a Redeemer, even Christ the Lord. In him it is that God is good to man and that his mercy endures for ever; in him the covenant of grace is made, and in him it is made sure, made good, and made an everlasting covenant. He concludes this psalm as he began it (v. 1), for God's glory must be the Alpha and Omega, the beginning and the end, of all our addresses to him. Hallowed by thy name, and thine is the glory. And this fitly closes a prophecy of Christ. The angels give thanks for man's redemption. Glory to God in the highest (Luke ii. 14), for there is on earth peace, to which we must echo with our hosannas, as they did, Luke xix. 38. Peace in heaven to us through Christ, and therefore glory in the highest.

Psalm 119

Aleph

1-4
1 Blessed are the undefiled in the way, who walk in the law of the LORD.
2 Blessed are they that keep his testimonies, and that seek him with the whole heart.
3 They also do no iniquity: they walk in his ways.
4 Thou hast commanded us to keep thy precepts diligently.

Psalm 119

TITLE. There is no title to this Psalm, neither is any author's name mentioned. It is THE LONGEST PSALM, and this is a sufficiently distinctive name for it. It equals in bulk twenty-two psalms of the average length of the Songs of Degrees. Nor is it long only; for it equally excels in breadth of thought, depth of meaning, and height of fervor. It is like the celestial city which lieth four square, and the height and the breadth of it are equal. Many superficial readers have imagined that it harps upon one string, and abounds in pious repetitions and redundancies; but this arises from the shallowness of the reader's own mind: those who have studied this divine hymn, and carefully noted each line of it, are amazed at the variety and profundity of the thought. Using only a few words, the writer has produced permutations and combinations of meaning which display his holy familiarity with his subject, and the sanctified ingenuity of his mind. He never repeats himself; for if the same sentiment recurs it is placed in a fresh connection, and so exhibits another interesting shade of meaning. The more one studies it the fresher it becomes. As those who drink the Nile water like it better every time they take a draught, so does this Psalm become the more full and fascinating the oftener you turn to it. It contains no idle word; the grapes of this cluster are almost to bursting full with the new wine of the kingdom. The more you look into this mirror of a gracious heart the more you will see in it. Placid on the surface as the sea of glass before the eternal throne, it yet contains within its depths an ocean of fire, and those who devoutly gaze into it shall not only see the brightness, but feel the glow of the sacred flame. It is loaded with holy sense, and is as weighty as it is bulky. Again and again have we cried while studying it, "Oh the depths!" Yet these depths are hidden beneath an apparent simplicity, as Augustine has well and wisely said, and this makes the exposition all the more difficult. Its obscurity is hidden beneath a veil of light, and hence only those discover it who are in thorough earnest, not only to look on the word, but, like the angels, to look into it.

The Psalm is alphabetical. Eight stanzas commence with one letter, and then another eight with the next letter, and so the whole Psalm proceeds by octonaries quite through the twenty-two letters of the Hebrew alphabet. Besides which, there are multitudes of appositions of sense, and others of those structural formalities with which the oriental mind is pleased,—formalities very similar to those in which our older poets indulged. The Holy Spirit thus deigned to speak to men in forms which were attractive to the attention and helpful to the memory. He is often plain or elegant in his manner, but he does not disdain to be quaint or formal if thereby his design of instruction can be the more surely reached. He does not despise even contracted and artificial modes of speech, if by their use he can fix his teaching upon the mind. Isaac Taylor has worthily set forth the lesson of this fact:—"In the strictest sense this composition is conditioned; nevertheless in the highest sense is it an utterance of spiritual life; and in thus finding these seemingly opposed elements, intimated commingled as they are throughout this Psalm, a lesson full of meaning is silently conveyed lo those who shall receive it—that the conveyance of the things of God to the human spirit is in no way damaged or impeded, much less is it deflected or ciliated by its subjugation to loose modes of utterance which most of all bespeak their adaptation to the infancy and the childlike capacity of the recipient."

AUTHOR. The fashion among modern writers is, as far as possible, to take ever? Psalm from David. As the critics of this school are usually unsound in doctrine and unspiritual in tone, we gravitate in the opposite direction, from a natural suspicion of everything which comes from so unsatisfactory a quarter. We believe that David wrote this Psalm. It is

JOHN CALVIN

Psalm 119

As this psalm treats of various matters, it is difficult to give an epitome of its contents. There are, however, two things which the prophet mainly aims at; the exhorting of the children of God to follow godliness and a holy life; and the prescribing of the rule, and pointing out the form of the true worship of God, so that the faithful may devote themselves wholly to the study of the Law. Along with these he frequently blends promises for the purpose of animating the worshippers of God to live more justly and piously; and, at the same time, he introduces complaints respecting the impious contempt of the Law, lest they should become tainted by bad examples. In short, he frequently passes from one topic to another, and prosecutes no one particular subject continuously; and therefore it will be best to discuss each subject in its proper place.

Psalm 119:1-8

1. Blessed are they who are upright. In these words the prophet sets forth the same paradox which we met with at the commencement of the Book of Psalms. All men naturally aspire after happiness, but instead of searching for it in the right path, they designedly prefer wandering up and down through endless by-paths, to their ruin and destruction. The Holy Spirit deservedly condemns this apathy and blindness. And but for man's cupidity, which, with brutish impetuosity, hurries him in the opposite direction, the meaning of the words would appear quite plain to him. And the further a man wanders from God, the happier does he imagine himself to be; and hence all treat, as a fable, what the Holy Spirit declares about true piety and the service of God. This is a doctrine which scarcely one among a hundred receives.

In the second verse, the same doctrine is confirmed more fully. He tells us that God is by no means satisfied with mere external service, for he demands the sincere and honest affection of the heart.

3. Surely they do not work iniquity. The statement, that they who follow God as their guide do not work iniquity, may seem to be a mere common-place, and universally admitted truth. The prophet has two reasons for making it; first, to teach us that our life must be entirely under the direction of God; and, secondly, that we may more diligently and carefully attend to his doctrine. It is acknowledged by every one, that those who render obedience to God are in no danger of going astray, and yet every one is found turning aside to his own ways. Does not such licentiousness or presumption palpably demonstrate that they have a greater regard for their own devices than for the unerring law of God? And after all, as often as a man happens to fall, is not the plea of inadvertence instantly alleged, as if none ever sinned knowingly and voluntarily; or as if the law of God, which is an antidote to all delinquencies, because it keeps all our vicious propensities in check, did not furnish us with sufficient wisdom to put us upon our guard? The prophet, therefore, very justly declares, that those who are instructed in the law of God, cannot set up the plea of ignorance when they fall into sin, seeing they are

MATTHEW HENRY

Psalm 119

1. ALEPH.

1-3

The psalmist here shows that godly people are happy people; they are, and shall be, blessed indeed. Felicity is the thing we all pretend to aim at and pursue. He does not say here wherein it consists; it is enough for us to know what we must do and be that we may attain to it, and that we are here told. All men would be happy, but few take the right way; God has here laid before us the right way, which we may be sure will end in happiness. Blessednesses are to the righteous; all manner of blessedness. Now observe the characters of the happy people. Those are happy,

1. Who make the will of God the rule of all their actions, and govern themselves, in their whole conversation, by that rule: They walk in the law of the Lord, v. 1. God's word is a law to them, not only in this or that instance, but in the whole course of their conversation; they walk within the hedges of that law, which they dare not break through by doing any thing it forbids; and they walk in the paths of that law, which they will not trifle in, but press forward in them towards the mark, taking every step by rule and never walking at all adventures. This is walking in God's ways (v. 3), the ways which he has marked out to us and has appointed us to walk in. It will not serve us to make religion the subject of our discourse, but we must make it the rule of our walk; we must walk in his ways, not in the way of the world, or of our own hearts, Job xxiii. 10, 11; xxxi. 7.

2. Who are upright and honest in their religion—undefiled in the way, not only who keep themselves pure from the pollutions of actual sin, unspotted from the world, but who are habitually sincere in their intentions, in whose spirit there is no guile, who are really as good as they seem to be and row the same way as they look.

3. Who are true to the trust reposed in them as God's professing people.

4. Who have a single eye to God as their chief good and highest end in all they do in religion (v. 2): They seek him with their whole heart. They do not seek themselves and their own things, but God only; this is that which they aim at, that God may be glorified in their obedience and that they may be happy in God's acceptance.

5. Who carefully avoid all sin (v. 3): They do no iniquity; they do not allow themselves in any sin; they do not commit it as those do who are the servants of sin; they do not make a practice of it, do not make a trade of it.

4-6

We are here taught,

1. To own ourselves under the highest obligations to walk in God's law. The tempter would possess men

Psalm 119

5-8
5 O that my ways were directed to keep thy statutes!
6 Then shall I not be ashamed, when I have respect unto all thy commandments.
7 I will praise thee with uprightness of heart, when I shall have learned thy righteous judgments.
8 I will keep thy statutes: O forsake me not utterly.

Davidic in tone and expression, and it tallies with David's experience in many interesting points. In our youth our teacher called it "David's pocket book", and we incline to the opinion then expressed that here we have the royal diary written at various times throughout a long life. No, we cannot give up this Psalm to the enemy. "This is David's spoil". After long reading an author one gets to know his style, and a measure of discernment is acquired by which his composition is detected even if his name be concealed; we feel a kind of critical certainty that the hand of David is in this thing, yea, that it is altogether his own.

SUBJECT. The one theme is the word of the Lord. The Psalmist sets his subject in many lights, and treats of it in divers ways, but he seldom omits to mention the word of the Lord in each verse under some one or other of the many names by which he knows it; and even if the name be not there, the subject is still heartily pursued in every stanza. He who wrote this wonderful song was saturated with those books of Scripture which he possessed. Andrew Bonar tells of a simple Christian in a farmhouse who had meditated the Bible through three times. This is precisely what this Psalmist had done,—he had gone past reading into meditation. Like Luther, David had shaken every fruit tree in God's garden, and gathered golden fruit therefrom. "The most, "says Martin Boos," read their Bibles like cows that stand in the thick grass, and trample under their feet the finest flowers and herbs." It is to be feared that we too often do the like. This is a miserable way of treating the pages of inspiration. May the Lord prevent us from repeating that sin while reading this priceless Psalm.

There is an evident growth in the subject matter. The earlier verses are of such a character as to lend themselves to the hypothesis that the author was a young man, while many of the later passages could only have suggested themselves to age and wisdom. In every portion, however, it is the fruit of deep experience, careful observation, and earnest meditation. If David did not write in there must have lived another believer of exactly the same order of mind as David, and he must have addicted himself to Psalmody with equal ardor, and have been an equally hearty lover of Holy Writ.

Our best improvement of this sacred composition will come through getting our minds into intense sympathy with its subject. In order to this, we might do well to commit it to memory. Philip Henry's daughter wrote in her diary, "I have of late taken some pains to learn by heart Psalm 119, and have made some progress therein." She was a sensible, godly woman. Having done this, we should consider the fullness, certainty, clearness, and sweetness of the word of God, since by such reflections we are likely to be stirred up to a warm affection for it. What favored beings are those to whom the Eternal God has written a letter in his own hand and style. What ardor of devotion, what diligence of composition can produce a worthy eulogium for the divine testimonies? If ever one such has fallen from the pen of man it is this 119th Psalm, which might well be called the holy soul's soliloquy before an open Bible.

This sacred ode is a little Bible, the Scriptures condensed, a mass of Bibline, Holy Writ rewritten in holy emotions and actions. Blessed are they who can read and understand these saintly aphorisms; they shall find golden apples in this true Hesperides, and come to reckon that this Psalm, like the whole Scripture which it praises, is a pearl island, or, better still, a garden of sweet flowers.

EXPOSITION

Verse 2. Blessed are they that keep his testimonies. What! A second blessing? Yes, they are doubly blessed whose outward life is supported by an inward zeal for God's glory. In the first verse we had an undefiled way, and it was taken for granted that the purity in the way was not mere

JOHN CALVIN

willfully blind. Were they to attend carefully to God's voice, they would be well fortified against all the snares of Satan. To strike them with terror, he informs them in the fourth verse, that God demands a rigid observance of the law; from which it may be gathered, that he will not suffer the contemners of it to escape with impunity. Besides, by speaking to God in the second person, he places him before our eyes as a Judge.

5. I wish that my ways may be directed. Our main desire ought to be for an understanding wisely regulated by the law of God, and also for a docile and obedient heart. Next, he adds, if a man carefully observe the law of God, he need be under no apprehension that he will ever regret what he has done or undertaken to do. The word respect intimates, that we must not be influenced by our own designs, nor decide, according to carnal reason, what we are to do, but must at once come to the determination, that they who turn not aside, either to the right hand or the left, from the observance of God's commandments, are indeed in the right path. They who reverently respect his law, may not escape the censure of the great bulk of mankind, yet the prophet declares, that They shall not be ashamed, because they have a good conscience in the presence of God and the angels, and, with the approval of this celestial assembly, they are well satisfied and contented; for if they depended upon the opinion of the world, their courage would presently fail. He says, all thy precepts, intimating, that among the snares of Satan, amid such thick darkness and so great insensibility as ours, the utmost vigilance and caution are necessary, if we would aim at being entirely exempted from blame. Wherefore, in all that we do, we must endeavor to have the law before us, to keep us from falling.

7. I will praise thee. He affirms it to be a singular instance of the loving-kindness of God, if a person has made considerable proficiency in his law. As a token and testimony of this, he here puts the giving of thanks to God; as if he should say, Lord, thou wilt confer upon me an inestimable blessing, if thou instruct me in thy law. It follows, therefore, that nothing in this life is more to be desired than this; and my fervent prayer is, that we may be fairly and fully convinced of the truth of it.

8. I will observe thy statutes. In these words he avers it to be his intention to observe the law of God, but, conscious of his own weakness, he utters a prayer that God would not deprive him of his grace. The term forsake is susceptible of two interpretations, either that God withdraws his Spirit, or that he permits his people to be brought low by adversity, as if he had forsaken them. The latter interpretation agrees best with the context, and is most in accordance with the phrase immediately subjoined, very far The prophet is not altogether averse to the trial of his faith, only he is apprehensive lest it might fail were the trial to be too long protracted, and therefore he desires to be treated with tenderness in his infirmity. "O God! thou sees my frame of mind, and, as I am but a man, do not conceal too long from me the tokens of thy favor, or defer helping me longer than is proper for me, lest, imagining myself to be forsaken of thee, I turn aside from the direct pursuit of godliness."

MATTHEW HENRY

with an opinion that they are at their liberty whether they will make the word of God their rule or no, that, though it may be good, yet it is not so necessary as they are made to believe it is. He taught our first parents to question the command: Hath God said, You shall not eat? And therefore we are concerned to be well established in this (v. 4): Thou hast commanded us to keep thy precepts, to make religion our rule; and to keep them diligently, to make religion our business and to mind it carefully and constantly. We are bound, and must obey at our peril.

2. To look up to God for wisdom and grace to do so (v. 5): O that my ways were directed accordingly!

3. To encourage ourselves in the way of our duty with a prospect of the comfort we shall find in it, v. 6.

7-8

Here is,

1. David's endeavor to perfect himself in his religion, and to make himself (as we say) master of his business. He hopes to learn God's righteous judgments. He knew much, but he was still pressing forward and desired to know more, as knowing this, that he had not yet attained; but as far as perfection is attainable in this life he reached towards it, and would not take up short of it. As long as we live we must be scholars in Christ's school, and sit at his feet; but we should aim to be head-scholars, and to get into the highest form. God's judgments are all righteous, and therefore it is desirable not only to learn them, but to be learned in them, mighty in the scriptures.

2. The use he would make of his divine learning. He coveted to be learned in the laws of God, not that he might make himself a name and interest among men, or fill his own head with entertaining speculations, but that he might give God the glory of his learning: I will praise thee when I have learned thy judgments, intimating that he could not learn unless God taught him, and that divine instructions are special blessings, which we have reason to be thankful for. Though Christ keeps a free-school, and teaches without money and without price, yet he expects his scholars should give him thanks both for his word and for his Spirit. Those have learned a good lesson who have learned to praise God, for that is the work of angels, the work of heaven.

3. His prayer to God not to leave him: "O forsake me not! that is, leave me not to myself, withdraw not thy Spirit and grace from me, for then I shall not keep thy statutes." Good men see themselves undone if God forsakes them; for then the tempter will be too hard for them. "Though thou seem to forsake me, and threaten to forsake me, and dost, for a time, withdraw from me, yet let not the desertion be total and final; for that is hell. O forsake me not utterly! for woe unto me if God departs from me."

Psalm 119

Beth

9-12

9 Wherewithal shall a young man cleanse his way? by taking heed thereto according to thy word.
10 With my whole heart have I sought thee: O let me not wander from thy commandments.
11 Thy word have I hid in mine heart, that I might not sin against thee.
12 Blessed art thou, O LORD: teach me thy statutes.

surface work, but was attended by the inward truth and life which comes of divine grace. Here that which was implied is expressed. Blessedness is ascribed to those who treasure up the testimonies of the Lord: in which is implied that they search the Scriptures, that they come to an understanding of them, that they love them, and then that they continue in the practice of them.

Verse 3. They also do no iniquity. Blessed indeed would those men be of whom this could be asserted without reserve and without explanation: we shall have reached the region of pure blessedness when we altogether cease from sin. Those who follow the word of God do no iniquity, the rule is perfect, and if it be constantly followed no fault will arise.

Verse 4. Thou hast commanded us to keep thy precepts diligently. So that when we have done all we are unprofitable servants, we have done only that which it was our duty to have done, seeing we have our Lord's command for it. God's precepts require careful obedience: there is no keeping them by accident. Some give to God a careless service, a sort of hit or miss obedience, but the Lord has not commanded such service, nor will he accept it. His law demands the love of all our heart, soul, mind, and strength; and a careless religion has none of these. We are also called to zealous obedience.

Verse 5. O that my ways were directed to keep thy statutes! Divine commands should direct us in the subject of our prayers. We cannot of ourselves keep God's statutes as he would have them kept, and yet we long to do so: what resort have we but prayer? We must ask the Lord to work our works in us, or we shall never work out his commandments. This verse is a sigh of regret because the Psalmist feels that he has not kept the precepts diligently, it is a cry of weakness appealing for help to one who can aid, it is a request of bewilderment from one who has lost his way and would fain be directed in it, and it is a petition of faith from one who loves God and trusts in him for grace.

Verse 6. Then shall I not be ashamed. He had known shame, and here he rejoices in the prospect of being freed from it. Sin brings shame, and when sin is gone, the reason for being ashamed is banished. What a deliverance this is, for to some men death is preferable to shame! When I have respect unto all thy commandments. When he respects God he shall respect himself and be respected. Whenever we err we prepare ourselves for confusion of face and sinking of heart: if no one else is ashamed of me I shall be ashamed of myself if I do iniquity.

Verse 7. I will praise thee. From prayer to praise is here, a long or a difficult journey. Be sure that he who prays for holiness will one day praise for happiness. Shame having vanished, silence is broken, and the formerly silent man declares, "I will praise thee." He cannot but promise praise while he seeks sanctification. Mark how well he knows upon what head to set the crown. "I will praise thee." He would himself be praiseworthy, but he counts God alone worthy of praise.

Verse 8. I will keep thy statutes. A calm resolve. When praise calms down into solid resolution it is well with the soul. Zeal which spends itself in singing, and leaves no practical residuum of holy living, is little worth: "I will praise" should be coupled with "I will keep." This firm resolve is by no means boastful, like Peter's "though I should die with thee, yet will I not forsake thee," for it is followed by a humble prayer for divine help, O forsake me not utterly. Feeling his own incapacity, he trembles lest he should be left to himself, and this fear is increased by the horror which he has of falling into sin. The "I will keep" sounds lightly enough now that the humble cry is heard with it. This is a happy amalgam: resolution and dependence. We meet with those who to all appearance humbly pray, but there is no force of character, no decision in them, and consequently the pleading of the closet is not embodied in the life: on the other band,

JOHN CALVIN

Psalm 119:9-16

9. Wherewith shall a young man cleanse his way? In this place he repeats, in different words, the same truth which he formerly advanced, That, however much men may pique themselves upon their own works, there is nothing pure in their life until they have made a complete surrender of themselves to the word of the Lord. The more effectually to excite them to this, he produces, in an especial manner, the example of children or youths. In mentioning these, he by no means gives an unbridled license to those who have arrived at mature years, or who are aged, as if they were competent to regulate their own life, and as if their own prudence served as a law to them; but because youth puts men where two ways meet, and renders it imperative for them to select the course of life which they mean to follow, he declares that, when a person sets about the regulation of his life, no advice will prove of any advantage, unless he adopts the law of God as his rule and guide.
10. With my whole heart. Conscious of the integrity of his heart, the prophet still implores the help of God, that he might not stumble by reason of his infirmity. He makes no boast of self-preparation, as if he had spontaneously begun to inquire after God, but in praising the grace which he had experienced, he at the same time aspires after steadfastness to persevere in walking in his ways. It is folly on the part of the Papists to seize upon this and similar passages, as if the saints, of their own free will, anticipated the grace of the Holy Spirit, and afterwards were favored with his aid. The prophet does not make a division between God and himself, but rather prays God to continue his work till it is completed, agreeably with what we are generally taught, to keep God mindful of his benefits until he accomplish them.
11. I have hid thy word in my heart. This psalm not being composed for the personal and peculiar use of the author only, we may therefore understand, that as frequently as David sets before us his own example, under this model he points out the course we ought to pursue. Here we are informed that we are well fortified against the stratagems of Satan when God's law is deeply seated in our hearts. For unless it have a fast and firm hold there, we will readily fall into sin.
12. Blessed art thou, O Jehovah! Such had been the prophet's proficiency, that he was not only one of 'God's disciples, but also a public teacher of the Church. Nevertheless, acknowledging himself and all the upright to be only one their journey till they arrive at the close of life, he fails not to ask for the spirit of understanding. This passage informs us generally, that if God do not enlighten us with the spirit of discernment, we are not competent to behold the light which shines forth from his law, though it be constantly before us. And thus it happens, that not a few are blind even when surrounded with the clear revelation of this doctrine, because, confident in their own perspicacity, they contemn the internal illumination of the Holy Spirit. Farther, let us learn from this passage, that none are possessed of such superiority of intellect as not to admit of constant increase. If the prophet, upon whom God had conferred so honorable an office as a teacher

MATTHEW HENRY

2. BETH.

9
Here is,
1. A weighty question asked. By what means may the next generation be made better than this? Wherewithal shall a young man cleanse his way? Cleansing implies that it is polluted. Besides the original corruption we all brought into the world with us (from which we are not cleansed unto this day), there are many particular sins which young people are subject to, by which they defile their way, youthful lusts (2 Tim. ii. 22); these render their way offensive to God and disgraceful to themselves. Young men are concerned to cleanse their way—to get their hearts renewed and their lives reformed; and therefore David asks the question for them.
2. A satisfactory answer given to this question. Young men may effectually cleanse their way by taking heed thereto according to the word of God.
(1.) Young men must make the word of God their rule, must acquaint themselves with it and resolve to conform themselves to it; that will do more towards the cleansing of young men than the laws of princes or the morals of philosophers.
(2.) They must carefully apply that rule and make use of it; they must take heed to their way, must examine it by the word of God, as a touchstone and standard.

10
Here is,
1. David's experience of a good work God had wrought in him, which he takes the comfort of and pleads with God: "I have sought thee, sought to thee as my oracle, sought after thee as my happiness, sought thee as my God; for should not a people seek unto their God? If I have not yet found thee, I have sought thee, and thou never saidst, Seek in vain, nor wilt say so to me, for I have sought thee with my heart, with my whole heart, sought thee only, sought thee diligently."
2. His prayer for the preservation of that work: "Thou that hast inclined me to seek thy precepts, never suffer me to wander from them."

11
Here is,
1. The close application which David made of the word of God to himself: He hid it in his heart, laid it up there, that it might be ready to him whenever he had occasion to use it; he laid it up as that which he valued highly, and had a warm regard for, and which he was afraid of losing and being robbed of.
2. The good uses he designed to make of it: That I might not sin against thee. Good men are afraid of sin, and are in care to prevent it.

Psalm 119

13-16

13 With my lips have I declared all the judgments of thy mouth.
14 I have rejoiced in the way of thy testimonies, as much as in all riches.
15 I will meditate in thy precepts, and have respect unto thy ways.
16 I will delight myself in thy statutes: I will not forget thy word.

we meet with abundance of resolve attended with an entire absence of dependence upon God, and this makes as poor a character as the former. The Lord grant us to have such a blending of excellences that we may be "perfect and entire, wanting nothing."

Verse 9. Wherewithal shall a young man cleanse his way? How shall he become and remain practically holy? He is but a young man, full of hot passions, and poor in knowledge and experience; how shall he get right, and keep right? Never was there a more important question for any man; never was there a fitter time for asking it than at the commencement of life. It is by no means an easy task which the prudent young man sets before him. He wishes to choose a clean way, to be himself clean in it, to cleanse it of any foulness which may arise in the future, and to end by showing a clear course from the first step to the last; but, alas, his way is already unclean by actual sin which he has already committed, and he himself has within his nature a tendency towards that which defileth.

Verse 10. With my whole heart have I sought thee. His heart had gone after God himself: he had not only desired to obey his laws, but to commune with his person. This is a right royal search and pursuit, and well may it be followed with the whole heart. The surest mode of cleansing the way of our life is to seek after God himself, and to endeavor to abide in fellowship with him. Up to the good hour in which he was speaking to his Lord, the Psalmist had been an eager seeker after the Lord, and if faint, he was still pursuing.

Verse 11. When a godly man sues for a favor from God he should carefully use every means for obtaining it, and accordingly, as the Psalmist had asked to be preserved from wandering, he here shows us the holy precaution which he had taken to prevent his falling into sin.

Verse 12. Blessed art thou, O LORD. These are words of adoration arising out of an intense admiration of the divine character, which the writer is humbly aiming to imitate. He blesses God for all that he has revealed to him, and wrought in him; he praises him with warmth of reverent love, and depth of holy wonder. These are also words of perception uttered from a remembrance of the great Jehovah's infinite happiness within himself.

Verse 13. With my lips have I declared all the judgments of thy mouth. The taught one of Ps 119:12 is here a teacher himself. What we learn in secret we are to proclaim upon the housetops. So had the Psalmist done. As much as he had known he had spoken. God has revealed many of his judgments by his mouth, that is to say, by a plain and open revelation; these it is out duty to repeat, becoming, as it were, so many exact echoes of his one infallible voice.

Verse 14. I have rejoiced in the way of thy testimonies. Delight in the word of God is a sure proof that it has taken effect upon the heart, and so is cleansing the life. The Psalmist not only says that he does rejoice, but that he has rejoiced. For years it had been his joy and bliss to give his soul to the teaching of the word. His rejoicing had not only arisen out of the word of God, but out of the practical characteristics of it.

Verse 15. I will meditate in thy precepts. He who has an inward delight in anything will not long withdraw his mind from it. As the miser often returns to look upon his treasure, so does the devout believer by frequent meditation turn over the priceless wealth which he has discovered in the book of the Lord. To some men meditation is a task; to the man of cleansed way it is a joy.

Verse 16. I will delight myself in thy statutes. In this verse delight follows meditation, of which it is the true flower and outgrowth. When we have no other solace, but are quite alone, it will be a glad thing for the heart to turn upon itself, and sweetly whisper, "I will delight myself. What if no minstrel sings in the hall, I will delight myself. If the time of the singing of

JOHN CALVIN

of the Church, confesses himself to be only a disciple or scholar, what madness is it for those who are, greatly behind him in point of attainments not to strain every nerve to rise to higher excellence? Nor does he depend upon his own merits for obtaining his requests; he beseeches God to grant them from a regard to his own glory. This appears from the phraseology by which he introduces his request, Blessed art thou, O Jehovah! intimating, that his confidence of success originated in God's being fully entitled to all praise on account of his unbounded goodness, justice, and mercy.
13. With my lips. In this verse he declares that the law of God was not only deeply engraven on his own heart, but that it was his earnest and strenuous endeavor to gain over many of his fellow-disciples into subjection to God. It is indeed a heartless matter to speak of the law of God abstractly, as we see hypocrites do, who talk very fluently about the whole doctrine of godliness, to which they are entire strangers. What the prophet noticed above, respecting the affection of the heart for God's law, he now likewise applies to the lips. And, immediately afterwards, he again establishes the truth of what he had asserted about his cordial and unfeigned endeavors to instruct others; by saying, that he derived no less pleasure from the doctrine of God than from all the riches of the world. He indirectly contrasts his holy love for the law, with which he was inflamed, with the unholy avarice which has taken possession of almost all the world. "As wealth attracts to itself the hearts of mankind, so I have taken more exquisite delight in the progress which I make in the doctrine of godliness, than if I abounded in all manner of riches."
15. In thy precepts. That to which I formerly adverted must not be forgotten—the prophet's not making a boast of his own acquirements, but setting before others an example for their imitation. We are aware that the majority of mankind are so much involved in the cares of the world, as to leave no time or leisure for meditating upon the doctrine of God. To meet this callous indifference, he very seasonably commends diligence and attention. And even were we not so ensnared by the world, we know how readily we lose sight of the law of God, in the daily temptations which suddenly overtake us.
It is not therefore without reason that the prophet exhorts us to constant exercise, and enjoins us to direct all our energies to the subject of meditation on God's precepts. And as the life of men is unstable, being continually distracted by the carnality of their minds, he declares that he will consider attentively the ways of God. Subsequently, he repeats the exquisite pleasure he took in this pursuit. For our proficiency in the law of God will be small, until we cheerfully and heartily set our minds upon it. And, in fact, the commencement of a good life consists in God's law attracting us to him by its sweetness. By the same means the lusts of the flesh, too, are subdued or mitigated. In our natural state, what is more agreeable to us than that which is sinful? This will be the constant tendency of our minds, unless the delight which we feel in the law carry us in the opposite direction.

MATTHEW HENRY

12
Here,
1. David gives glory to God: "Blessed art thou, O Lord! Thou art infinitely happy in the enjoyment of thyself and hast no need of me or my services; yet thou art pleased to reckon thyself honored by them; assist me therefore, and then accept me."
2. He asks grace from God: "Teach me thy statutes; give me to know and do my duty in every thing. Thou art the fountain of all blessedness; O let me have this drop from that fountain, this blessing from that blessedness: Teach me thy statutes, that I may know how to bless thee, who art a blessed God, and that I may be blessed in thee."

13-16
Here,
I. David looks back with comfort upon the respect he had paid to the word of God. He had the testimony of his conscience for him,
1. That he had edified others with what he had been taught out of the word of God (v. 13): With my lips have I declared all the judgments of thy mouth. He had prayed (v. 12) that God would teach him; and here he pleads, "Lord, I have endeavored to make a good use of the knowledge thou hast given me, therefore increase it;" for to him that has shall be given.
2. That he had entertained himself with it: "Lord, teach me thy statutes; for I desire no greater pleasure than to know and do them (v. 14): I have rejoiced in the way of thy commandments, in a constant even course of obedience to thee; not only in the speculations and histories of thy word, but in the precepts of it, and in that path of serious godliness."
II. He looks forward with a holy resolution never to cool in his affection to the word of God; what he does that he will do, 2 Cor. xi. 12. Those that have found pleasure in the ways of God are likely to proceed and persevere in them.
1. He will dwell much upon them in his thoughts (v. 15): I will meditate in thy precepts. He not only discoursed of them to others (many do that only to show their knowledge and authority), but he communed with his own heart about them, and took pains to digest in his own thoughts what he had declared, or had to declare, to others.
2. He will have them always in his eye: I will have respect unto thy ways, as the traveler has to his road, which he is in care not to miss and always aims and endeavors to hit.
3. He will take a constant pleasure in communion with God and obedience to him. It is not for a season that he rejoices in this light, but "I will still, I will for ever, delight myself in thy statutes, not only think of them, but do them with delight," v. 16.
4. He will never forget what he has learned of the things of God: "I will not forget thy word, not only I will not quite forget it, but I will be mindful of it when I have occasion to use it." Those that meditate in God's word, and delight in it, are in no great danger of forgetting it.

Psalm 119

Gimel

17-20
17 Deal bountifully with thy servant, that I may live, and keep thy word.
18 Open thou mine eyes, that I may behold wondrous things out of thy law.
19 I am a stranger in the earth: hide not thy commandments from me.
20 My soul breaketh for the longing that it hath unto thy judgments at all times.

birds has not yet arrived, and the voice of the turtle is not heard in our land, yet I will delight myself." This is the choicest and noblest of all rejoicing; in fact, it is the good part which can never be taken from us; but there is no delighting ourselves with anything below that which God intended to be the soul's eternal satisfaction.

Verses 17-24. In this section the trials of the way appear to be manifest to the Psalmist's mind, and he prays accordingly for the help which will meet his case. As in the last eight verses he prayed as a youth newly come into the world, so here he pleads as a servant and a pilgrim, who growingly finds himself to be a stranger in an enemy's country. His appeal is to God alone, and his prayer is specially direct and personal. He speaks with the Lord as a man speaketh with his friend.

Verse 17. Deal bountifully with thy servant. He takes pleasure in owning his duty to God, and counts it the joy of his heart to be in the service of his God. Out of his condition he makes a plea, for a servant has some hold upon a master; but in this case the wording of the plea shuts out the idea of legal claim, since he seeks bounty rather than reward. Let my wage be according to thy goodness, and not according to my merit. Reward me according to the largeness of thy liberality, and not according to the scantiness of my service. The hired servants of our Father have all of them bread enough and to spare, and he will not leave one of his household to perish with hunger, .If the Lord will only treat us as he treats the least of his servants we may be well content, for all his true servants are sons, princes of the blood, heirs of life eternal. David felt that his great needs required a bountiful provision, and that his little desert would never earn such a supply; hence he must throw himself upon God's grace, and look for the great things he needed from the great goodness of the Lord. He begs for a liberality of grace, after the fashion of one who prayed, "O Lord, thou must give me great mercy or no mercy, for little mercy will not serve my turn."

Verse 18. Open thou mine eyes. This is a part of the bountiful dealing which he has asked for; no bounty is greater than that which benefits our person, our soul, our mind, and benefits it in so important an organ as the eye. It is far better to have the eyes opened than to be placed in the midst of the noblest prospects and remain blind to their beauty. That I may behold wondrous things out of thy law. Some men can perceive no wonders in the gospel, but David felt sure that there were glorious things in the law: he had not half the Bible, but he prized it more than some men prize the whole

Verse 19. I am a stranger in the earth. This is meant for a plea. By divine command men are bound to be kind to strangers, and what God commands in others he will exemplify in himself. The Psalmist was a stranger for God's sake, else had he been as much at home as worldlings are: he was not a stranger to God, but a stranger to the world, a banished man so long as he was out of heaven.

Verse 20. My soul breaketh for the longing that it hath unto thy judgments at all times. True godliness lies very much in desires. As we are not what we shall be, so also we are not what we would be. The desires of gracious men after holiness are intense,—they cause a wear of heart, a straining of the mind, till it feels ready to snap with the heavenly pull. A high value of the Lord's commandment leads to a pressing desire to know and to do it, and this so weighs upon the soul that it is ready to break in pieces under the crush of its own longings.

Verse 21. Thou hast rebuked the proud that are cursed. This is one of God's judgments: he is sure to deal out a terrible portion to men of lofty looks. God rebuked Pharaoh with sore plagues, and at the Red Sea "In the foundations of the world were discovered at thy rebuke, O Lord." In the person of the naughty Egyptian he taught all the proud that he will certainly abase them. Proud men are cursed men: nobody blesses

JOHN CALVIN

Psalm 119:17-24

17. Do good to thy servant. The prophet asks as a principal favor, that, while he lives, he may devote himself entirely to God; being fully persuaded that the grand object of his existence consists in his exercising himself in his service, an object which he firmly resolves to pursue. For this reason these two clauses are connected together, that I may live, and keep thy word. "I desire no other mode of living than that of approving myself to be a true and faithful servant of God." All wish God to grant them a prolongation of their life; a wish after which the whole world ardently aspire, and yet there is scarcely one among a hundred who reflects upon the purpose for which he ought to live. To withdraw us from cherishing such irrational propensities, the prophet here describes the main object of our existence. He declares it to be owing to the peculiar grace of the Holy Spirit, that any person keeps the law of God. Had he imagined that the preparing oneself for the observance of his law depended on his own free will, then this prayer would have been nothing else than downright hypocrisy.

Very similar is the doctrine contained in the next verse. Having acknowledged, that power to keep the law is imparted to men by God, he, at the same time, adds, that every man is blind, until he also enlighten the eyes of his understanding. Admitting that God gives light to us by his word, the prophet here means that we are blind amid the clearest light, until he remove the veil from our eyes. When he confesses that his eyes are veiled and shut, rendering him unable to discern the light of the heavenly doctrine, until God, by the invisible grace of his Spirit, open them, he speaks as if he were deploring his own blindness, and that of the whole human race.

19. I am a stranger on the earth. It is proper to inquire into the reason for his calling himself a sojourner and stranger in the world. The great concern of the unholy and worldly is to spend their life here easily and quietly; but those who know that they have their journey to pursue, and have their inheritance reserved for them in heaven, are not engrossed nor entangled with these perishable things, but aspire after that place to which they are invited. The meaning may be thus summed up: "Lord, since I must pass quickly through the earth, what will become of me if I am deprived of the doctrine of thy law?" We learn from these words from what point we must commence our journey, if we would go on our way cheerfully unto God.

Besides, God is said to conceal his commandments from those whose eyes he does not open, because, not being endued with spiritual vision, in seeing they see not, so that what is before their eyes is hid from them. And, to demonstrate that he does not present his request in a careless manner, the prophet adds, that his affection for the law is most intense; for it is no common ardor which is expressed by him in the following language, My soul is rent with the desire it hath at all times unto thy judgments. As the man who may concentrate all his thoughts on one point with such intensity as almost to deprive him of the power of perception, may be

MATTHEW HENRY

3. GIMEL.

17

We are here taught,

1. That we owe our lives to God's mercy. David prays, Deal bountifully with me, that I may live. It was God's bounty that gave us life, that gave us this life; and the same bounty that gave it continues it, and gives all the supports and comforts of it; if these be withheld, we die, or, which is equivalent, our lives are embittered and we become weary of them. If God deals in strict justice with us, we die, we perish, we all perish; if these forfeited lives be preserved and prolonged, it is because God deals bountifully with us, according to his mercy, not according to our deserts. The continuance of the most useful life is owing to God's bounty, and on that we must have a continual dependence.

2. That therefore we ought to spend our lives in God's service. Life is therefore a choice mercy, because it is an opportunity of obeying God in this world, where there are so few that do glorify him; and this David had in his eye: "Not that I may live and grow rich, live and be merry, but that I may live and keep thy word, may observe it myself and transmit it to those that shall come after, which the longer I live the better I shall do."

18

Observe here, that there are wondrous things in God's law, which we are all concerned, and should covet, to behold, not only strange things, which are very surprising and unexpected, but excellent things, which are to be highly esteemed and valued, and things which were long hidden from the wise and prudent, but are now revealed unto babes.

19

Here we have,

1. The acknowledgment which David makes of his own condition: I am a stranger in the earth. We all are so, and all good people confess themselves to be so; for heaven is their home, and the world is but their inn, the land of their pilgrimage.

2. The request he makes to God thereupon: Hide not thy commandments from me. He means more: "Lord, show thy commandments to me; let me never know the want of the word of God, but, as long as I live, give me to be growing in my acquaintance with it. I am a stranger; let me have thy commandments always in view, for they will be all this to me, all that a poor stranger can desire. I am a stranger here, and must be gone shortly; by thy commandments let me be prepared for my removal hence."

20

David had prayed that God would open his eyes (v. 18) and open the law (v. 19); now here he pleads the earnestness of his desire for knowledge and grace, for it is the fervent prayer that avails much.

Psalm 119

21-24
21 Thou hast rebuked the proud that are cursed, which do err from thy commandments.
22 Remove from me reproach and contempt; for I have kept thy testimonies.
23 Princes also did sit and speak against me: but thy servant did meditate in thy statutes.
24 Thy testimonies also are my delight and my counselors.

them, and they soon become a burden to themselves. In itself, pride is a plague and torment. Even if no curse came from the law of God, there seems to be a law of nature that proud men should be unhappy men. This led David to abhor pride; he dreaded the rebuke of God and the curse of the law. The proud sinners of his day were his enemies, and he felt happy that God was in the quarrel as well as he. Which do err from thy commandments. Only humble hearts are obedient, for they alone will yield to rule and government. Proud men's looks are high, too high to mark their own feet and keep the Lord's way. Pride lies at the root of all sin: if men were not arrogant they would not be disobedient.
Verse 22. Remove from me reproach and contempt. These are painful things to tender minds. David could bear them for righteousness sake, but they were a heavy yoke, and he longed to be free from them. To be slandered, and then to be despised in consequence of the vile accusation, is a grievous affliction. No one likes to be traduced, or even to be despised. He who says, "I care nothing for my reputation," is not a wise man, for in Solomon's esteem, "a good name is better than precious ointment." The best way to deal with slander is to pray about it: God will either remove it, or remove the sting from it. Our own attempts at clearing ourselves are usually failures; we are like the boy who wished to remove the blot from his copy, and by his bungling made it ten times worse. When we suffer from a libel it is better to pray about it than go to law over it, or even to demand an apology from the inventor. O ye who are reproached, take your matters before the highest court, and leave them with the Judge of all the earth. God will rebuke your proud accuser; be ye quiet and let your advocate plead your cause. For I have kept thy testimonies. Innocence may justly ask to be cleared from reproach. If there be truth in the charges alleged against us what can we urge with God? If, however, we are wrongfully accused our appeal has a locus standi in the court and cannot be refused. If through fear of reproach we forsake the divine testimony we shall deserve the coward's doom; our safety lies in sticking close to the true and to the right. God will keep those who keep his testimonies. A good conscience is the best security for a good name; reproach will not abide with those who abide with Christ, neither will contempt remain upon those who remain faithful to the ways of the Lord. This verse stands as a parallel both in sense and position to Ps 119:6, and it has the catchword of "testimonies," by which it chimes with Ps 119:14.
Verse 23. Princes also did sit and speak against me. David was high game, and the great ones of the earth went a hawking after him. Princes saw in him a greatness which they envied, and therefore they abused him. On their thrones they might have found something better to consider and speak about, but they turned the seat of judgment into the seat of the scorner. Most men covet a prince's good word, and to be spoken ill of by a great man is a great discouragement to them, but the Psalmist bore his trial with holy calmness.
Verse 24. Thy testimonies also are my delight and my counselors. They were not only themes for meditation, but "also" sources of delight and means of guidance. While his enemies took counsel with each other the holy man took counsel with the testimonies of God. The fowlers could not drive the bird from its nest with all their noise. It was their delight to slander and his delight to meditate. The words of the Lord serve us for many purposes; in our sorrows they are our delight, and in our difficulties they are our guide; we derive joy from them and discover wisdom in them. If we desire to find comfort in the Scriptures we must submit ourselves to their counsel, and when we follow their counsel it must not be with reluctance but with delight. This is the safest way of dealing with those who plot for our ruin; let us give more heed to the true testimonies of the Lord than to the false witness of our foes. The best

said to be the victim of his intemperate zeal, so the prophet declares the energy of his mind to be paralyzed and exhausted by his ardent love for the law.

21. Thou hast destroyed the proud. The intention of the prophet is to inform us that God's judgments instructed him to apply his mind to the study of the law; and certainly this is an exercise which we ought on no account to defer till God visit us with chastisement. But when we behold him taking vengeance upon the wicked, and the despisers of his word, we must be stupid, indeed, if his rod do not teach us wisdom; and, doubtless, it is an instance of special kindness on God's part, to spare us, and only to terrify us from afar, that he may bring us to himself without injuring or chastising us at all.

22. Remove from me reproach. The following meaning may not inappropriately be given to the passage: O Lord, since I am conscious to myself, and thou art a witness of my unfeigned integrity, do not permit the unrighteous to sully my reputation, by laying unfounded accusations to my charge. But the meaning will be more complete if we read it as forming one continued sentence: O God, permit not the ungodly to mock me for endeavoring to keep thy law. For this impiety has been rampant in the world even from the beginning, that the sincerity of God's worshippers has been matter of reproach and derision; even as, at this day, the same reproaches are still cast upon God's children, as if not satisfied with the common mode of living, they aspired being wiser than others.

In the following verse, he states more plainly that it was not in vain he besought God to vindicate him from such calumnies; for he was held in derision, not only by the common people, and by the most abandoned of mankind, but also by the chief men, who sat as judges. The term, to sit, imports that they had spoken injuriously and unjustly of him, not merely in their houses and at their tables, but publicly and on the very judgment-seat, where it behooved them to execute justice, and render to every one his due.

24. Also thy testimonies are my delight. To adhere unflinchingly to our purpose, when the world takes up an unjust opinion of us, and, at the same time, constantly to mediate on God's law, is an example of Christian fortitude seldom to be met with. The prophet now informs us how he overcame this temptation. Thy testimonies, says he, are my delight: "Although the cruel injustice of men, in charging me falsely, grieves and annoys me, yet the pleasurable delight which I take in thy law is a sufficient recompense for it all." He adds, that God's testimonies are his counselors, by which we are to understand he did not rely on his own judgment simply, but took counsel from the word of God. This point ought to be carefully considered, inasmuch as we see how blind affection predominates in directing the lives of men. Whence does the avaricious man ask council, but from the erroneous principle which he has assumed, that riches are superior to every thing? Why does the ambitious man aspire after nothing so much as power, but because he regards nothing equal to the holding of honorable rank in the world? It is not surprising, therefore, that men are so grievously

1. His desire was importunate: My soul breaketh for the longing it hath to thy judgments, or (as some read it) "It is taken up, and wholly employed, in longing for thy judgments; the whole stream of its desires runs in this channel. I shall think myself quite broken and undone if I want the word of God, the direction, converse, and comfort of it."

2. It was constant—at all times. It was not now and then, in a good humor, that he was so fond of the word of God; but it is the habitual temper of every sanctified soul to hunger after the word of God as its necessary food, which there is no living without.

21

Here is,

1. The wretched character of wicked people. The temper of their minds is bad. They are proud; they magnify themselves above others. And yet that is not all: they magnify themselves against God, and set up their wills in competition with and opposition to the will of God, as if their hearts, and tongues, and all, were their own.

2. The wretched case of such. They are certainly cursed, for God resists the proud; and those that throw off the commands of the law lay themselves under its curse (Gal. iii. 10), and he that now beholds them afar off will shortly say to them, Go, you cursed. The proud sinners bless themselves; God curses them; and, though the most direful effects of this curse are reserved for the other world, yet they are often severely rebuked in this world.

22

Here,

1. David prays against the reproach and contempt of men, that they might be removed, or (as the word is) rolled, from off him. This intimates that they lay upon him, and that neither his greatness nor his goodness could secure him from being libeled and lampooned.

2. He pleads his constant adherence to the word and way of God: For I have kept thy testimonies. He not only pleads his innocency, that he was unjustly censured, but that he was jeered for well-doing.

23

David was abused even by great men, who should have known better his character and his case, and have been more generous: Princes did sit, sit in council, sit in judgment, and speak against me.

24

Here David explains his meditating in God's statutes (v. 23), which was of such use to him when princes sat and spoke against him. The word of God comforted him, and was his delight, more his delight than any of the pleasures either of court or camp, of city or country.

Psalm 119

Daleth

25-28

25 My soul cleaveth unto the dust: quicken thou me according to thy word.

26 I have declared my ways, and thou heardest me: teach me thy statutes.

27 Make me to understand the way of thy precepts: so shall I talk of thy wondrous works.

28 My soul melteth for heaviness: strengthen thou me according unto thy word.

answer to accusing princes is the word of the justifying King. In Ps 119:16 David said, "I will delight in thy statutes," and here he says "they are my delight": thus resolutions formed in God's strength come to fruit, and spiritual desires ripen into actual attainments. O that it might be so with all the readers of these lines.

Verse 25-32. Here, it seems to me, we have the Psalmist in trouble bewailing the bondage to earthly things in which he finds his mind to be held. His soul cleaves to the dust, melts for heaviness, and cries for enlargement from its spiritual prison. In these verses we shall see the influence of the divine word upon a heart which laments its downward tendencies, and is filled with mourning because of its deadening surroundings. The word of the Lord evidently arouses prayer (Ps 119:25-29), confirms choice (Ps 119:30), and inspires renewed resolve (Ps 119:32): it is in all tribulation whether of body: or mind the surest source of help. This portion has 'D' for its alphabetical letter: it sings of Depression, in the spirit of Devotion, Determination, and Dependence.

Verse 25. My soul cleaveth unto the dust. He means in part that he was full of sorrow; for mourners in the east cast dust on their heads, and sat in ashes, and the Psalmist felt as if these ensigns of woe were glued to him, and his very soul was made to cleave to them because of his powerlessness to rise above his grief. Does he not also mean that he felt ready to die? Did he not feel his life absorbed and fast held by the grave's mould, half choked by the death dust? It may not be straining the language if we conceive that he also felt and bemoaned his earthly mindedness and spiritual deadness.

Verse 26. I have declared my ways. Open confession is good for the soul. Nothing brings more ease and more life to a man than a frank acknowledgment of the evil which has caused the sorrow and the lethargy. Such a declaration proves that the man knows his own condition, and is no longer blinded by pride. Our confessions are not meant to make God know our sins, but to make us know them. And thou heardest me. His confession had been accepted; it was not lost labor; God had drawn near to him in it. We ought never to go from a duty till we have been accepted in it. Pardon follows upon penitent confession, and David felt that he had obtained it. It is God's way to forgive our sinful way when we from our hearts confess the wrong. Teach me thy statutes. Being truly sorry for his fault, and having obtained full forgiveness, he is anxious to avoid offending again, and hence he begs to be taught obedience. He was not willing to sin through ignorance, he wished to know all the mind of God by being taught it by the best of teachers. He pined after holiness.

Verse 27. Make me to understand the way of thy precepts. Give me a deep insight into the practical meaning of thy word; let me get a clear idea of the tone and tenor of thy law. Blind obedience has but small beauty; God would have us follow him with our eyes open. To obey the letter of the word is all that the ignorant can hope for; if we wish to keep God's precepts in their spirit we must come to an understanding of them, and that can be gained nowhere but at the Lord's hands. Our understanding needs enlightenment and direction: he who made our understanding must also make us understand.

Verse 28. My soul melteth for heaviness. He was dissolving away in tears. The solid strength of his constitution was turning to liquid as if molten by the furnace heat of his afflictions. Heaviness of heart is a killing thing, and when it abounds it threatens to turn life into a long death, in which a man seems to drop away in a perpetual drip of grief. Tears are the distillation of the heart; when a man weeps he wastes away his soul. Some of us know what great heaviness means, for we have been brought under its power again and again, and often have we felt ourselves to be poured out like water, and near to being like water misled, seeing they give themselves up to the direction of such evil counselors.

Psalm 119:25-32

25. My soul cleaveth to the dust. He means that he had no more hope of life than if he had been shut up in the tomb; and this must be carefully attended to, that we my not become impatient and grieved, whenever it may please God to make us endure various kinds of death. And, by his own example, he instructs us, when death stares us in the face, and all hope of escape fails, to present our petitions to God, in whose hand, as we have elsewhere seen, are the issues of death, and whose peculiar prerogative it is to restore life to those that are dead, (Psalm 68:21) As the combat is hard, he betakes himself to the promises of God, and invites others to do the same. The expression, according to thy word, is an acknowledgment, that should he depart from God's word, no hope would be left for him; but as God has affirmed that the life of the faithful is in his hand, and under his protection, shut up as he was in the grave, he yet comforted himself with the expectation of life.
26. I have declared my ways. In the first part of this verse he affirms he had prayed sincerely, and had not imitated the proud, who, trusting to their own wisdom, fortitude, and opulence, make not God their refuge. That man is said to declare his ways to God, who presumes neither to attempt nor undertake any thing unless with His assistance, and, depending wholly on His providence, commits all his plans to His sovereign pleasure, and centers all his affections in Him; doing all this honestly, and not as the hypocrites, who profess one thing with their lips, and conceal another within their hearts. He adds, that he was heard, which was of great importance in making him cherish good hope for the future.
28. My soul droppeth away for grief. As a little before he said that his soul cleaved to the dust, so now, almost in the same manner, he complains that it melted away with grief. Some are of opinion that he alludes to tears, as if he had said that his soul was dissolved in tears. But the simpler meaning is, that his strength was poured out like water. The verb is in the future tense, yet it denotes a continued action. The prophet assures himself of a remedy for this his extreme sorrow, provided God stretch out his hand towards him. Formerly, when almost lifeless, he entertained the expectation of a revival through the grace of God; now also, by the same means, he cherishes the hope of being restored to renovated and complete vigor, notwithstanding he was nearly consumed. He repeats the expression, according to thy word, because, apart from his word, God's power would afford us little comfort. But when he comes to our aid, even should our courage and strength fail, his promise is abundantly efficacious to fortify us.
29. Take away from me the way of falsehood. Knowing how prone the nature of man is to vanity and falsehood, he first asks the sanctification of his thoughts, lest, being entangled by the snares of Satan, he fall into error. Next, that he may be kept from falsehood, he prays to be fortified with the doctrine

4. DALETH.

25
Here is,
I. David's complaint. We should have thought his soul soaring to heaven; but he says himself, My soul not only rolls in the dust, but cleaves to the dust, which is a complaint either,
1. Of his corruptions, his inclination to the world and the body (both which are dust), and that which follows upon it, a deadness to holy duties. When he would do good evil was present with him. God intimated that Adam was not only mortal, but sinful, when he said, Dust thou art, Gen. iii. 19.
Or, 2. Of his afflictions, either trouble of mind or outward trouble. Without were fightings, within were fears, and both together brought him even to the dust of death (Ps. xxii. 15), and his soul clave inseparably to it.
II. His petition for relief, and his plea to enforce that petition: "Quicken thou me according to thy word. By thy providence put life into my affairs, by thy grace put life into my affections; cure me of my spiritual deadness and make me lively in my devotion."

26-27
We have here,
1. The great intimacy and freedom that had been between David and his God. David had opened his case, opened his very heart to God: "I have declared my ways, and acknowledged thee in them all, have taken thee along with me in all my designs and enterprises." Thus Jephthah uttered all his words, and Hezekiah spread his letters, before the Lord. "I have declared my ways, my wants, and burdens, and troubles, that I meet with in my way."

28-29
Here is,
1. David's representation of his own griefs: My soul melteth for heaviness, which is to the same purport with v. 25, My soul cleaveth to the dust. Heaviness in the heart of man makes it to melt, to drop away like a candle that wastes. The penitent soul melts in sorrow for sin, and even the patient soul may melt in the sense of affliction, and it is then its interest to pour out its supplication before God.
2. His request for God's grace.
(1.) That God would enable him to bear his affliction well and graciously support him under it: "Strengthen thou me with strength in my soul, according to thy word, which, as the bread of life, strengthens man's heart to undergo whatever God is pleased to inflict. Strengthen me to do the duties, resist the temptations, and bear up under the burdens, of an afflicted state, that the spirit may not fail. Strengthen me according to that word (Deut. xxxiii. 25), As thy days so shall thy strength be."

Psalm 119

29-32
29 Remove from me the way of lying: and grant me thy law graciously.
30 I have chosen the way of truth: thy judgments have I laid before me.
31 I have stuck unto thy testimonies: O LORD, put me not to shame.
32 I will run the way of thy commandments, when thou shalt enlarge my heart.

spilt upon the ground, never again to be gathered up. There is one good point in this downcast state, for it is better to be melted with grief than to be hardened by impenitence.

Verse 29. Remove from me the way of lying. This is the way of sin, error, idolatry, folly, self righteousness, formalism, hypocrisy. David would not only be kept from that way, but have it kept from him; he cannot endure to have it near him, he would have it swept away from his sight. He desired to be right and upright, true and in the truth; but he feared that a measure of falsehood would cling to him unless the Lord took it away, and therefore he earnestly cried for its removal. False motives may at times sway us, and we may fall into mistaken notions of our own spiritual condition before God, which erroneous conceits may be kept up by a natural prejudice in our own layout, and so we may be confirmed in a delusion, and abide under error unless grace comes to the rescue. No true heart can rest in a false view of itself; it finds no anchorage, but is tossed to and fro till it gets into the truth and the truth into it. The true born child of heaven sighs out and cries against a lie, desiring to have it taken away as much as a man desires to be set at a distance from a venomous serpent or a raging lion.

Verse 30. I have chosen the way of truth. As he abhorred the way of lying, so he chose the way of truth: a man must choose one or the other, for there cannot be any neutrality in the case. Men do not drop into the right way by chance; they must choose it, and continue to choose it, or they will soon wander from it. Those whom God has chosen in due time choose his way. There is a doctrinal way of truth which we ought to choose, rejecting every dogma of man's devising; there is a ceremonial way of truth which we should follow, detesting all the forms which apostate churches have invented; and then there is a practical way of truth, the way of holiness, to which we must adhere whatever may be our temptation to forsake it. Let our election be made, and made irrevocably. Let us answer to all seducers, "I have chosen, and what I have chosen I have chosen." O Lord, by thy grace lead us with a hearty free will to choose to do thy will; thus shall thine eternal choice of us bring forth the end which it designs.

Verse 31. I have stuck unto thy testimonies,—or I have cleaved, for the word is the same as in Ps 119:25. Though cleaving to the dust of sorrow and of death, yet he kept fast hold of the divine word. This was his comfort, and his faith stuck to it, his love and his obedience held on to it, his heart and his mind abode in meditation upon it. His choice was so heartily and deliberately made that he stuck to it for life, and could not be removed from it by the reproaches of those who despised the way of the Lord. What could he have gained by quitting the sacred testimony? Say rather, what would he not have lost if he had ceased to cleave to the divine word? It is pleasant to look back upon past perseverance and to expect grace to continue equally steadfast in the future. He who has enabled us to stick to him will surely stick to us.

Verse 32. I will run the way of thy commandments. With energy, promptitude, and zeal he would perform the will of God, but he needed more life and liberty from the hand of God. When thou shalt enlarge my heart. Yes, the heart is the master; the feet soon run when the heart is free and energetic. Let the affections be aroused and eagerly set on divine things, and our actions will be full of force, swiftness, and delight. God must work in us first, and then we shall will and do according to his good pleasure. He must change the heart, unite the heart, encourage the heart, strengthen the heart, and enlarge the heart, and then the course of the life will be gracious, sincere, happy, and earnest; so that from our lowest up to our highest state in grace we must attribute all to the free favor of our God. We must run; for grace is not an overwhelming force which compels unwilling minds to move contrary to their will: our

JOHN CALVIN

of the law. The second clause of the verse is interpreted variously. Some render it, make thy law pleasant to me. And as the law is disagreeable to the flesh, which it subdues and keeps under, there is good cause why God should be asked to render it acceptable and pleasant to us. Some expound it, have mercy upon me according to thy law as if the prophet should draw pity from the fountain-head itself, because God in his law promised it to the faithful. Both of these meanings appear to me forced; and, therefore, I am more disposed to adopt another, freely grant to me thy law. The amount is, that being full of blindness, nothing is more easy than for us to be greatly deceived by error. And, therefore unless God teach us by the Spirit of wisdom, we will presently be hurried away into various errors. The means of our being preserved from error are stated to consist in his instructing us in his law. He makes use of the term to gratify. "It is indeed an incomparable kindness that men are directed by thy law, but in consequence of thy kindness being unmerited, I have no hesitation in asking of thee to admit me as a participator of this thy kindness." If the prophet, who for some time previous served God, in now aspiring after farther attainments, does not ask for a larger measure of grace to be communicated to him meritoriously, but confesses it to be the free gift of God, then that impious tenet, which obtains in the papacy, that an increase of grace is awarded to merit as deserving of it, must fall to the ground.

30. I have chosen the way of truth. In this and the following verse he affirms that he was so disposed as to desire nothing more than to follow righteousness and truth. It is, therefore, with great propriety he employs the term to choose. The old adage, that man's life is as it were at the point where two ways meet, refers not simply to the general tenor of human life, but to every particular action of it. For no sooner do we undertake any thing, no matter how small, than we are grievously perplexed, and as if hurried off by a tempest, are confounded by conflicting counsels. Hence the prophet declares, that in order constantly to pursue the right path, he had resolved and fully determined not to relinquish the truth. And thus he intimates that he was not entirely exempted from temptations, yet that he had surmounted them by giving himself up to the conscientious observance of the law.

32. I will run the way of thy commandments. The meaning of the prophet is, that when God shall inspire him with love for his la he will be vigorous and ready, nay, even steady, so as not to faint in the middle of his course. His words contain an implied admission of the supineness inability of men to make any advancement in well-doing until God enlarge their hearts. No sooner does God expand their hearts, than they are fitted not only for walking, but also for running in the way of his commandments. He reminds us that the proper observance of the law consists not merely in external works,—that it demands willing obedience, so that the heart must, to some extent, and in some way, enlarge itself. Not that it has the self-determining power of doing this, but when once its hardness and obstinacy are subdued, it moves freely without being any longer contracted by its own narrowness. Finally, this passage

MATTHEW HENRY

(2.) That God would keep him from using any unlawful indirect means for the extricating of himself out of his troubles (v. 29): Remove from me the way of lying. David was conscious to himself of a proneness to this sin.

(3.) That he might always be under the guidance and protection of God's government: Grant me thy law graciously; grant me that to keep me from the way of lying. David had the law written with his own hand, for the king was obliged to transcribe a copy of it for his own use (Deut. xvii. 18); but he prays that he might have it written in his heart; for then, and then only, we have it indeed, and to good purpose.

30-32

Observe,

I. That those who will make anything to purpose of their religion must first make it their serious and deliberate choice; so David did: I have chosen the way of truth. The way of serious godliness is the way of truth; the principles it is founded on are principles of eternal truth, and it is the only true way to happiness.

II. That those who have chosen the way of truth must have a constant regard to the word of God as the rule of their walking: Thy judgments have I laid before me, as he who learns to write lays his copy before him, that he may write according to it, as the workman lays his model and platform before him, that he may do his work exactly. As we must have the word in our heart by an habitual conformity to it, so we must have it in our eye by an actual regard to it upon all occasions, that we may walk accurately and by rule.

III. That those who make religion their choice and rule are likely to adhere to it faithfully: "I have stuck to thy testimonies with unchanged affection and an unshaken resolution, stuck to them at all times, through all trials. I have chosen them, and therefore I have stuck to them." Note, The choosing Christian is likely to be the steady Christian; while those that are Christians by chance tack about if the wind turn.

IV. That those who stick to the word of God may in faith expect and pray for acceptance with God; for David means this when he begs, "Lord, put me not to shame; that is, never leave me to do that by which I shall shame myself, and do thou not reject my services, which will put me to the greatest confusion."

V. That the more comfort God gives us the more duty he expects from us, v. 32. Here we have,

1. His resolution to go on vigorously in religion: I will run the way of thy commandments.

2. His dependence upon God for grace to do so: "I shall then abound in thy work, when thou shalt enlarge my heart." God, by his Spirit, enlarges the hearts of his people when he gives them wisdom (for that is called largeness of heart, 1 Kings iv. 29), when he sheds abroad the love of God in the heart, and puts gladness there. The joy of our Lord should be wheels to our obedience.

Psalm 119

He

33-36

33 Teach me, O LORD, the way of thy statutes; and I shall keep it unto the end.
34 Give me understanding, and I shall keep thy law; yea, I shall observe it with my whole heart.
35 Make me to go in the path of thy commandments; for therein do I delight.
36 Incline my heart unto thy testimonies, and not to covetousness.

running is the spontaneous leaping forward of a mind which has been set free by the hand of God, and delights to show its freedom by its bounding speed.

Verse 33. Teach me, O LORD, the way of thy statutes. Child like, blessed words, from the lips of an old, experienced believer, and he a king, and a man inspired of God. Alas, for those who will never be taught. They dote upon their own wisdom; but their folly is apparent to all who rightly judge. The Psalmist will have the Lord for his teacher; for he feels that his heart will not learn of any less effectual instructor. A sense of great slowness to learn drives us to seek a great teacher. What condescension it is on our great Jehovah's part that he deigns to teach those who seek him. The lesson which is desired is thoroughly practical; the holy man would not only learn the statutes, but the way of them, the daily use of them, their tenor, spirit, direction, habit, tendency. He would know that path of holiness which is hedged in by divine law, along which the commands of the Lord stand as sign posts of direction and mile stones of information, guiding and marking our progress. The very desire to learn this way is in itself an assurance that we shall be taught therein, for he who made us long to learn will be sure to gratify the desire.

Verse 34. Give me understanding, and I shall keep thy law. This is the same prayer enlarged, or rather it is a supplement which intensifies it. He not only needs teaching, but the power to learn: he requires not only to understand, but to obtain an understanding. How low has sin brought us; for we even lack the faculty to understand spiritual things, and are quite unable to know them till we are endowed with spiritual discernment. Will God in very deed give us understanding? This is a miracle of grace.

Verse 35. Make me to go in the path of thy commandments; for therein do I delight. "To will is present with me; but how to perform that which good I find not." Thou hast made me to love the way, now make me to move in it. It is a plain path, which others are treading through thy grace; I see it and admire it; cause me to travel in it. This is the cry of a child that longs to walk, but is too feeble; of a pilgrim who is exhausted, yet pants to be on the march; of a lame man who pines to be able to run. It is a blessed thing to delight in holiness, and surely he who gave us this delight will work in us the yet higher joy of possessing and practicing it. Here is our only hope; for we shall not go in the narrow path till we are made to do so by the Maker's own power. O thou who didst once make me, I pray thee make me again: thou hast made me to know; now make me to go. Certainly I shall never be happy till I do, for my sole delight lies in walking according to thy bidding.

Verse 36. Incline my heart unto thy testimonies. Does not this prayer appear to be superfluous, since it is evident that the Psalmist's heart was set upon obedience? We are sure that there is never a word to spare in Scripture. After asking for active virtue it was meet that the man of God should beg that his heart might be in all that he did. What would his goings be if his heart did not go? It may be that David felt a wandering desire, an inordinate leaning of his soul to worldly gain,—possibly it even intruded into his most devout meditations, and at once he cried out for more grace. The only way to cure a wrong leaning is to have the soul bent in the opposite direction. Holiness of heart is the cure for covetousness. What a blessing it is that we may ask the Lord even for an inclination. Our wills are free, and yet without violating their liberty, grace can incline us in the right direction. This can be done by enlightening the understanding as to the excellence of obedience, by strengthening our habits of virtue, by giving us an experience of the sweetness of piety, and by many other ways. If any one duty is irksome to us it behooves us to offer this player with special reference thereto:

JOHN CALVIN

tells us, when God has once enlarged our hearts, there will be no lack of power, because, along with proper affection, he will furnish ability, so that our feet will be ready to run.

Psalm 119:33-40

33. Teach me, O Jehovah, the way of thy statutes. He again presents the same prayer which he has already frequently done in this psalm, it being of the last importance for us to know that the main thing in our life consists in having God for our governor. The majority of mankind think of anything rather than this, as that which they ought to ask from God. The Holy Spirit, therefore, often inculcates this desire, and we ought always to keep it in mind, that not only the inexperienced and unlearned, but those who have made great progress, may not cease to aspire after farther advancement. And as the Spirit of understanding comes from above, they should seek to be guided by his invisible agency to the proper knowledge of the law.
34. Make me to understand. We are here informed that true wisdom consists in being wise according to the law of God, that it may preserve us in fear and obedience to him. In asking God to confer this wisdom upon him, he owns that men, in consequence of their natural blindness, aim at anything rather than this. And, indeed, it is quite foreign to the notions usually prevalent among mankind to strain every nerve to keep God's law. The world esteems as wise those only who look well to their own interests, are acute and politic in temporal matters, and who even excel in the art of beguiling the simple. In opposition to such a sentiment, the prophet pronounces men to be void of true understanding as long as the fear of God does not predominate among them. For himself he asks no other prudence than the surrendering of himself entirely to God's direction. At the same Lime, he acknowledges this to be the special gift of God, which none can procure by his own power or policy; for were each adequate to be his own teacher in this matter, then this petition would be superfluous.
35. Direct me in the path. The frequent repetition of this phraseology by the prophet is not to be considered as redundant. Seeing that the end of man's existence ought to consist in profiting in God's school, we nevertheless perceive how the world distracts him by its allurements, and how he also forms for himself a thousand avocations calculated to withdraw his thoughts from the main business of his life.
The next clause of the verse, in it I take pleasure, must be carefully attended to. For it is an indication of rare excellence when a person so arranges his sentiments and affections as to renounce all the enticements pleasant to the flesh, and take delight in nothing so much as in the service of God. The prophet had already attained to this virtue but he still perceives that he is not yet perfect. Therefore, that his desire may be fully accomplished, he solicits fresh assistance from God, according to the saying of Paul, "It is God that worketh in you, both to will and to do of his good pleasures" Philippians 2:13. Let it be remembered, that he does not boast

MATTHEW HENRY

5. HE.

33-34
Here,
I. David prays earnestly that God himself would be his teacher; he had prophets, and wise men, and priests, about him, and was himself well instructed in the law of God, yet he begs to be taught of God, as knowing that none teaches like him, Job xxxvi. 22. Observe here,
1. What he desires to be taught, not the notions or language of God's statutes, but the way of them—"the way of applying them to myself and governing myself by them. "
2. How he desires to be taught, in such a way as no man could teach him: Lord, give me understanding. As the God of nature, he has given us intellectual powers and faculties; but here we are taught to pray that, as the God of grace, he would give us understanding to use those powers and faculties about the great things which belong to our peace.
II. He promises faithfully that he would be a good scholar. If God would teach him, he was sure he should learn to good purpose: "I shall keep thy law, which I shall never do unless I be taught of God, and therefore I earnestly desire that I may be taught."

35-36
He had before prayed to God to enlighten his understanding, that he might know his duty, and not mistake concerning it; here he prays to God to bow his will, and quicken the active powers of his soul, that he might do his duty. Observe here,
I. The grace he prays for.
1. That God would make him able to do his duty: "Make me to go; strengthen me for every good work."
2. That God would make him willing to do it, and would, by his grace, subdue the aversion he naturally had to it: "Incline my heart to thy testimonies, to those things which thy testimonies prescribe; not only make me willing to do my duty, as that which I must do and therefore am concerned to make the best of, but make me desirous to do my duty as that which is agreeable to the new nature and really advantageous to me."
II. The sin he prays against, and that is covetousness: "Incline my heart to keep thy testimonies, and restrain and mortify the inclination there is in me to covetousness." That is a sin which stands opposed to all God's testimonies; for the love of money is such a sin as is the root of much sin, of all sin.
III. His plea to enforce this prayer: "Lord, bring me to, and keep me in, the way of thy commandments, for therein do I delight; and therefore I pray thus earnestly for grace to walk in that way. Thou hast wrought in me this delight in the way of thy commandments; wilt thou not work in me an ability to walk in them, and so crown thy own work?"

Psalm 119

37-40
37 Turn away mine eyes from beholding vanity; and quicken thou me in thy way.
38 Stablish thy word unto thy servant, who is devoted to thy fear.
39 Turn away my reproach which I fear: for thy judgments are good.
40 Behold, I have longed after thy precepts: quicken me in thy righteousness.

we are to love all the Lord's testimonies, and if we fail in any one point we must pay double attention to it. The learning of the heart is the way in which the life will lean: hence the force of the petition, "Incline my heart." Happy shall we be when we feel habitually inclined to all that is good. This is not the way in which a carnal heart ever leans; all its inclinations are in opposition to the divine testimonies.
Verse 37. Turn away mine eyes from beholding vanity. He had prayed about his heart, and one would have thought that the eyes would so surely have been influenced by the heart that there was no need to make them the objects of a special petition; but our author is resolved to make assurance doubly sure. If the eyes do not see, perhaps the heart may not desire: at any rate, one door of temptation is closed when we do not even look at the painted bauble. Sin first entered man's mind by the eye, and it is still a favorite gate for the incoming of Satan's allurements: hence the need of a double watch upon that portal. The prayer is not so much that the eyes may be shut as "turned away"; for we need to have them open, but directed to right objects.
Verse 38. Stablish thy word unto thy servant. Make me sure of thy sure word: make it sure to me and make me sure of it. If we possess the spirit of service, and yet are troubled with skeptical thoughts we cannot do better than pray to be established in the truth. Times will arise when every doctrine and promise seems to be shaken, and our mind gets no rest: then we must appeal to God for establishment in the faith, for he would have all his servants to be well instructed and confirmed in his word. But we must mind that we are the Lord's servants, for else we shall not long be sound in his truth. Practical holiness is a great help towards doctrinal certainty: if we are God's servants he will confirm his word in our experience.
Verse 39. Turn away my reproach which I fear. He feared just reproach, trembling lest he should cause the enemy to blaspheme through any glaring inconsistency. We ought to fear this, and watch that we may avoid it. Persecution in the form of calumny may also be prayed against, for it is a sore trial, perhaps the sorest of trials to men of sensitive minds. Many would sooner bear burning at the stake than the trial of cruel mockings. David was quick tempered, and he probably had all the greater dread of slander because it raised his anger, and he could hardly tell what he might not do under great provocation. If God turns away our eyes from falsehood, we may also expect that he will turn away falsehood from injuring our good name. We shall be kept from lies if we keep from lies.
Verse 40. Behold, I have longed after thy precepts. He can at least claim sincerity. He is deeply bowed down by a sense of his weakness and need of grace; but he does desire to be in all things conformed to the divine will. Where our longings are, there are we in the sight of God. If we have not attained perfection, it is something to have hungered after it. He who has given us to desire, will also grant us to obtain. The precepts are grievous to the ungodly, and therefore when we are so changed as to long for them we have clear evidence of conversion, and we may safely conclude that he who has begun the good work will carry it on.
Quicken me in thy righteousness. Give me more life wherewith to follow thy righteous law; or give me more life because thou hast promised to hear prayer, and it is according to thy righteousness to keep thy word. How often does David plead for quickening! But never once too often. We need quickening every hour of the day, for we are so sadly apt to become slow and languid in the ways of God. It is the Holy Spirit who can pour new life into us; let us not cease crying to him. Let the life we already possess show itself by longing for more. The last verses of the octaves have generally exhibited an onward look of resolve, hope, and

of the inherent working of his nature, but sets forth the grace he has received, that God may complete the work he has begun. "Lord, thou hast given me courage, grant me also strength." Hence in the term pleasure there is an implied opposition to the lusts of the flesh, which keep the hearts of mankind lettered by their enticements.

36. Incline my heart. In this verse he confesses the human heart to be so far from yielding to the justice of God, that it is more inclined to follow an opposite course. Were we naturally and spontaneously inclined to the righteousness of the law, there would be no occasion for the petition of the Psalmist, Incline my heart. It remains, therefore, that our hearts are full of sinful thoughts, and wholly rebellious, until God by his grace change them.

37. Turn away mine eyes. By these words we are taught that all our senses are so filled with vanity, that, until refined and rectified, their alienation from the pursuit of righteousness is no matter of surprise. In the former verse he informed us of the reigning of that depravity in the hearts of men, which he now says reaches also to the outward senses. "The disease of covetousness not only lurks in our hearts, but spreads over every part, so that neither eyes, ears, feet, nor hands, have escaped its baneful influence; in a word, nothing is exempted from corruption." And we know, assuredly, that the guilt of original sin is not confined to one faculty of man only; it pervades his whole constitution. If our eyes must be turned away from vanity by the special grace of God, it follows, that, as soon as they are opened, they are eagerly set on the impostures of Satan, by which they are beset on all sides.

38. Confirm thy word unto thy servant. Here we have briefly set forth the sole end and legitimate use of prayer, which is, that we may reap the fruits of God's promises. Whence it comes to pass, that they commit sin who utter vague and incoherent desires. For we perceive the prophet allows not himself to petition or wish any thing but what God hath condescended to promise. And certainly their presumption is great, who rush into the presence of God without any call from his word; as if they would make him subservient to their humor and caprice. The argument by which the Psalmist enforces his plea deserves to be noticed; because I am devoted to thy fear.

39. Take away my reproach. It is not certain to what reproach he alludes. Knowing that many calumniators were on the watch to find occasion for reviling him, should they happen to detect him in any offense, it is not without reason he dreaded lest he might fall into such disgrace, and that by his own fault.

40. Behold, I have a desire to thy precepts This is a repetition of what he declared a little before, with regard to his pious affection, and his love of righteousness; and that nothing was wanting but God to complete the work which he had commenced. If this interpretation be admitted, then, to be quickened in the righteousness of God, will be tantamount to being quickened in the way. The term righteousness is often put in this psalm for the law of God, or the rule of a righteous life. This view tends to make the two parts of the verse accord

37

Here,

1. David prays for restraining grace, that he might be prevented and kept back from that which would hinder him in the way of his duty: Turn away my eyes from beholding vanity. The honors, pleasures, and profits of the world are the vanities, the aspect and prospect of which draw multitudes away from the paths of religion and godliness.

2. He prays for constraining grace, that he might not only be kept from every thing that would obstruct his progress heaven-ward, but might have that grace which was necessary to forward him in that progress: "Quicken thou me in thy way; quicken me to redeem time, to improve opportunity, to press forward, and to do every duty with liveliness and fervency of spirit."

38

Here is

1. The character of a good man, which is the work of God's grace in him; he is God's servant, subject to his law and employed in his work, that is, devoted to his fear, given up to his direction and disposal, and taken up with high thoughts of him and all those acts of devotion which have a tendency to his glory.

2. The confidence that a good man has towards God, in dependence upon the word of his grace to him. Those that are God's servants may, in faith and with humble boldness, pray that God would establish his word to them, that is, that he would fulfill his promises to them in due time, and in the mean time give them an assurance that they shall be fulfilled.

39

Here,

1. David prays against reproach, as before, v. 22. David prays that God would deliver him from all his transgressions, that he might not be the reproach of the foolish, which he feared (Ps. xxxix. 8); or he means that reproach which his enemies unjustly loaded him with. Let their lying lips be put to silence.

2. He pleads the goodness of God's judgments: "Lord, thou sittest in the throne, and thy judgments are right and good, just and kind, to those that are wronged, and therefore to thee I appeal from the unjust and unkind censures of men."

40

Here,

1. David professes the ardent affection he had to the word of God.

2. He prays for grace to enable him to answer this profession. "Thou hast wrought in me this languishing desire, put life into me, that I may prosecute it; quicken me in thy righteousness, in thy righteous ways, according to thy righteous promise." Where God has wrought to will he will work to do, and where he has wrought to desire he will satisfy the desire.

Psalm 119

Waw

41-44
41 Let thy mercies come also unto me, O LORD, even thy salvation, according to thy word.
42 So shall I have wherewith to answer him that reproacheth me: for I trust in thy word.
43 And take not the word of truth utterly out of my mouth; for I have hoped in thy judgments.
44 So shall I keep thy law continually for ever and ever.

prayer. Here past fruits of grace are made the plea for further blessing. Onward in the heavenly life is the cry of this verse. In these verses holy fear is apparent and prominent. The man of God trembles lest in any way or degree the Lord should remove his favor from him. The eight verses are one continued pleading for the abiding of grace in his soul, and it is supported by such holy arguments as would only suggest themselves to a spirit burning with love to God.

Verse 41. Let thy mercies come also unto me, O LORD. He desires mercy as well as teaching, for he was guilty as well as ignorant. He needed much mercy and varied mercy, hence the request is in the plural. He needed mercy from God rather than from man, and so he asks for "thy mercies." The way sometimes seemed blocked, and therefore he begs that the mercies may have their way cleared by God, and may "come" to him. He who said, "Let there be light," can also say, "Let there be mercy." It may be that under a sense of unworthiness the writer feared lest mercy should be given to others, and not to himself; he therefore cries, "Bless me, even me also, O my Father."

Verse 42. So shall I have wherewith to answer him that reproacheth me. This is an unanswerable answer. When God, by granting us salvation, gives to our prayers an answer of peace, we are ready at once to answer the objections of the infidel, the quibbles of the skeptical, and the sneers of the contemptuous. It is most desirable that revilers should be answered, and hence we may expect the Lord to save his people in order that a weapon may be put into their hands with which to rout his adversaries. When those who reproach us are also reproaching God, we may ask him to help us to silence them by sure proofs of his mercy and faithfulness.

Verse 43. And take not the word of truth utterly out of my mouth. Do not prevent my pleading for thee by leaving me without deliverance; for how could I continue to proclaim thy word if I found it fail me? such would seem to be the run of the meaning. The word of truth cannot be a joy to our mouths unless we have an experience of it in our lives, and it may be wise for us to be silent if We cannot support our testimonies by the verdict of our consciousness. This prayer may also refer to other modes by which we may be disabled from speaking in the name of the Lord: as, for instance, by our falling into open sin, by our becoming depressed and despairing, by our laboring under sickness or mental aberration, by our finding no door of utterance, or meeting with no willing audience. He who has once preached the gospel from his heart is filled with horror at the idea of being put out of the ministry; he will crave to be allowed a little share in the holy testimony, and will reckon his dumb Sabbaths to be days of banishment and punishment.

Verse 44. So shall I keep thy law continually for ever and ever. Nothing more effectually binds a man to the way of the Lord than an experience of the truth of his word, embodied in the form of mercies and deliverances. Not only does the Lord's faithfulness open our mouths against his adversaries, but it also knits our hearts to his fear, and makes our union with him more and more intense. Great mercies lead us to feel an inexpressible gratitude which, falling to utter itself in time, promises to engross eternity with praises.

Verse 45. And I will walk at liberty: for I seek thy precepts. Saints find no bondage in sanctity. The Spirit of holiness is a free spirit; he sets men at liberty and enables them to resist every effort to bring them under subjection. The way of holiness is not a track for slaves, but the King's highway for freemen, who are joyfully journeying from the Egypt of bandage to the Canaan of rest. God's mercies and his salvation, by teaching us to love the precepts of the word, set us at a happy rest; and the more we seek after the perfection of our obedience the more shall we enjoy complete emancipation from every form of spiritual slavery.

JOHN CALVIN

with one another. "Lord, this is now a remarkable kindness thou hast done me, in having inspired me with a holy desire to keep thy law; one thing is still necessary, that this same virtue pervade my whole life."

Psalm 119:41-48

41. Let thy mercies come to me. There can be no doubt, that, in mentioning the mercy of God first, and afterwards his salvation, the Psalmist, according to the natural order, puts the cause before the effect. By adopting this arrangement, he acknowledges that there is no salvation for him but in the pure mercy of God. And while he desires a gracious salvation, he, at the same time, relies on the promise, as we have already elsewhere seen.

In the second verse he boasts that he is furnished with the best defense against the calumnies of his enemies, arising from his trust in the word of God. We are taught that there will always be evil-speakers, who will not cease to defame the children of God, though they be entirely undeserving of such treatment.

43. Take not the word of truth too long out of my mouth. It may be asked, why he demands rather to have his tongue filled with, than his heart fortified by, the word of truth; inasmuch as the latter takes the precedence, both in point of order and of excellence. What will it profit us to be fluent and eloquent in speech, if our hearts are destitute of faith? On the other hand, wherever there is firm faith, there to speech will flow ultroneously. My reply is, that David was not so concerned about outward confession as not to give the preference to the faith of the heart; but considering that he is making his address to God, there is nothing strange in his making mention only of the former, under which, however, he includes also the latter. "Lord, support not only my heart by faith, lest I be overwhelmed with temptation, but grant me also freedom of speech, that I may fearlessly sound forth thy praises among men." We observe, when he asks to be endued with boldness of speech, that he begins with the heart.

44. I will keep thy law continually. He resolves to devote himself to the study of the law, not for a short time only, but even to the termination of his life.

45. The next verse may be read as expressing a desire that he might walk. Be this as it may, we retain the commonly received reading, That David exults at the thought of his path becoming plain and easy, in consequence of his seeking diligently after God's precepts; that is, to walk at ease The ways of men are frequently rugged and obstructed, because they themselves lay various stumbling blocks in them, or entangle themselves in many inextricable windings. Hence it comes to pass, that while none will submit to the word of God as their rule, every man endures the punishment legitimately due to such arrogance. On all sides God lays snares for us, puts pitfalls in our way, causes us to fall in with paths broken and rugged, and at last shuts us up in a bottomless pit: and by how much the more politic a mart is, by so much the more will he meet with obstructions in his path.

MATTHEW HENRY

6. VAU.

41-42
Here is,
1. David's prayer for the salvation of the Lord. "Lord, thou art my Savior; I am miserable in myself, and thou only canst make me happy; let thy salvation come to me. Hasten temporal salvation to me from my present distresses, and hasten me to the eternal salvation, by giving me the necessary qualifications for it and the comfortable pledges and foretastes of it."
2. David's dependence upon the grace and promise of God for that salvation.
3. David's expectation of the good assurance which that grace and promise of God would give him: "So shall I have wherewith to answer him that reproaches me for my confidence in God, as if it would deceive me." When God saves those out of their troubles who trusted in him he effectually silences those who would have shamed that counsel of the poor (Ps. xiv. 6).

43-44
Here is,
1. David's humble petition for the tongue of the learned, that he might know how to speak a word in season for the glory of God: Take not the word of truth utterly out of my mouth. He means, "Lord, let the word of truth be always in my mouth; let me have the wisdom and courage which are necessary to enable me both to use my knowledge for the instruction of others, and, like the good householder, to bring out of my treasury things new and old, and to make profession of my faith whenever I am called to it."
2. His humble profession of the heart of the upright, without which the tongue of the learned, however it may be serviceable to others, will stand us in no stead.
(1.) David professes his confidence in God: "Lord, make me ready and mighty in the scriptures, for I have hoped in those judgments of thy mouth, and, if they be not at hand, my support and defense have departed from me."
(2.) He professes his resolution to adhere to his duty in the strength of God's grace: "So shall I keep thy law continually. If I have thy word not only in my heart, but in my mouth, I shall do all I should do, stand complete in thy whole will." Thus shall the man of God be perfect, thoroughly furnished for every good word and work, 2 Tim. iii. 17; Col. iii. 16.

45-48
We may observe in these verses,
1. What David experienced of an affection to the law of God: "I seek thy precepts, v. 45. I desire to know and do my duty, and consult thy word accordingly; I do all I can to understand what the will of the Lord is and to discover the intimations of his mind. I seek thy precepts, for I have loved them, v. 47, 48. I not only give consent to them as good, but take complacency

Psalm 119

45-48
45 And I will walk at liberty: for I seek thy precepts.
46 I will speak of thy testimonies also before kings, and will not be ashamed.
47 And I will delight myself in thy commandments, which I have loved.
48 My hands also will I lift up unto thy commandments, which I have loved; and I will meditate in thy statutes.

David at one time of his life was in great bondage through having followed a crooked policy. He deceived Achish so persistently that he was driven to acts of ferocity to conceal it, and must have felt very unhappy in his unnatural position as an ally of Philistines, and captain of the body guard of their king. He must have feared lest through his falling into the crooked ways of falsehood the truth would no longer be on his tongue, and he therefore prayed God in some way to work his deliverance, and set him at liberty from such slavery. By terrible things in righteousness did the Lord answer him at Ziklag: the snare was broken, and he escaped.

Verse 46. I will speak of thy testimonies also before kings, and will not be ashamed. This is part of his liberty; he is free from fear of the greatest, proudest, and most tyrannical of men. David was called to stand before kings when he was an exile; and afterwards, when he was himself a monarch, he knew the tendency of men to sacrifice their religion to pomp and statecraft; but it was his resolve to do nothing of the kind. He would sanctify politics, and make cabinets know that the Lord alone is governor among the nations.

Verse 47. And I will delight myself in thy commandments, which I have loved. Next to liberty and courage comes delight. When we have done our duty, we find a great reward in it. If David had not spoken for his Master before kings, he would have been afraid to think of the law which he had neglected; but after speaking up for his Lord he feels a sweet serenity of heart when musing upon the word. Obey the command, and you will love it; carry the yoke, and it will be easy, and rest will come by it. After speaking of the law the Psalmist was not wearied of his theme, but he retired to meditate upon it; he discoursed and then he delighted, he preached and then repaired to his study to renew his strength by feeding yet again upon the precious truth. Whether he delighted others or not when he was speaking, he never failed to delight himself when he was musing on the word of the Lord. He declares that he loved the Lord's commands, and by this avowal he unveils the reason for his delight in them: where our love is, there is our delight. David did not delight in the courts of kings, for there he found places of temptation to shame, but in the Scriptures he found himself at home; his heart was in them, and they yielded him supreme pleasure. No wonder that he spoke of keeping the law, which he loved; Jesus says, "If a man love me, he will keep my words." No wonder that he spoke of walking at liberty, and speaking boldly, for true love is ever free and fearless. Love is the fulfilling of the law; where love to the law of God reigns in the heart the life must be full of blessedness. Lord, let thy mercies come to us that we may love thy word and way, and find our whole delight therein.

Verse 48. My hands also will I lift up unto thy commandments, which I have loved. He will stretch out towards perfection as far as he can, hoping to reach it one day; when his hands hang down he will cheer himself out of languor by the prospect of glorifying God by obedience; and he will give solemn sign of his hearty assent and consent to all that his God commands. The phrase "lift up my hands" is very full of meaning, and doubtless the sweet singer meant all that we can see in it, and a great deal more. Again he declares his love; for a true heart loves to express itself; it is a kind of fire which must send forth its flames. It was natural that he should reach out towards a law which he delighted in, even as a child holds out its hands to receive a gift which it longs for. When such a lovely object as holiness is set before us, we are bound to rise towards it with our whole nature, and till that is fully accomplished we should at least lift up our hands in prayer towards it. Where holy hands and holy hearts go, the whole man will one day follow.

And I will meditate in thy statutes. He can never have enough of meditation upon the mind of God. Loving subjects wish to be familiar

JOHN CALVIN

This verse teaches us that, if any man yield implicit obedience to God, he will receive this as his reward, that he shall walk with a calm and composed mind; and should he meet with difficulties, he will find the means of surmounting them. The faithful, however readily and submissively they give themselves up to God, may happen to find themselves involved in perplexity; nevertheless, the end contemplated by Paul is accomplished, that though they be in trouble and toil, yet they do not continue in irremediable distress, because it is the duty (so to speak) of God to point out a way for them where there seems to be no way, (2 Corinthians 4:8.) Moreover, when grievously oppressed, even then they walk at ease, for they commit the doubtful issue of events to God in such a manner, that, having him for their guide, they have no doubt they will come out boldly from the depths of distress.

46. And I will steal, of thy testimonies before kings. In these words he seems to believe that he is in possession of that which he formerly prayed for. Having said, "Take not away the word out of my mouths" and now, as if he had obtained what he requested, he rises up, and maintains he will not be dumb, even were he called upon to speak in the presence of kings. There can be no question that he affirms he would willingly stand forward in vindication of the glory of God in the face of the whole world. He selects kings, who are generally more to be dreaded than other men, and haughtily shut the mouths of God's witnesses. Sometimes, indeed, it happens we will not hold out even in the presence of men in the humblest ranks of life. The moment a man sets himself in opposition to the word of God, we instinctively shrink back from fear; and that boldness of speech, of which we boasted at first, instantly disappears: but our want of courage is most palpable when we are summoned before the thrones of kings. And this is the reason why David asserts, that he will not only hold out against enemies among the meanest of men, but also will remain firm and fearless before kings. These words inform us that we have profited well and truly by God's word, when our hearts are so completely fortified against the fear of man, that we do not dread the presence of kings, even though all the world attempts; to fill us with dejection and dismay. It is most unbecoming that God's glory should be obscured by their empty splendor.

47. And I will delight myself. The sentiment contained in this verse is similar to that which he had previously mentioned. The amount is, he held the commandments of God in such high esteem, that he experienced nothing more pleasant to him than the making of them his constant theme of meditation. By the term delight, he expresses the intensity of his love. The phrase I will lift up my hands, refers, to the same thing. It is a sure indication that we eagerly desire a thing when we stretch out the hands to grasp and enjoy it. This simile, therefore denotes the ardor of his desire. If a man, by his mien and gait pretend any such affection for the law of God, and yet pay no regard to it in the affairs of life, he would be justly chargeable with the basest hypocrisy. Again, he affirms, that that affection, so earnest and so ardent, springs from the sweetness of the law of God having knit our hearts

MATTHEW HENRY

in them as good for me." All that love God love his government and therefore love all his commandments.

2. What he expected from this. Five things he promises himself here in the strength of God's grace:

(1.) That he should be free and easy in his duty: "I will walk at liberty, freed from that which is evil, not hampered with the fetters of my own corruptions, and free to that which is good, doing it not by constraint, but willingly." The service of sin is perfect slavery; the service of God is perfect liberty. Licentiousness is bondage to the greatest of tyrants; conscientiousness is freedom to the meanest of prisoners, John viii. 32, 36; Luke i. 74, 75.

(2.) That he should be bold and courageous in his duty: I will speak of thy testimonies also before kings. Before David came to the crown kings were sometimes his judges, as Saul, and Achish; but, if he were called before them to give a reason of the hope that was in him, he would speak of God's testimonies, and profess to build his hope upon them and make them his council, his guards, his crown, his all. We must never be afraid to own our religion, though it should expose us to the wrath of kings, Acts iv. 20. After David came to the crown kings were sometimes his companions; they visited him and he returned their visits; but he did not, in complaisance to them, talk of every thing but religion, for fear of affronting them and making his conversation uneasy to them. No; God's testimonies shall be the principal subject of his discourse with the kings. It is good for kings to hear of God's testimonies, and it will adorn the conversation of princes themselves to speak of them.

(3.) That he should be cheerful and pleasant in his duty (v. 47): "I will delight myself in thy commandments, in conversing with them, in conforming to them. I will never be so well pleased with myself as when I do that which is pleasing to God." The more delight we take in the service of God the nearer we come to the perfection we aim at.

(4.) That he should be diligent and vigorous in his duty: I will lift up my hands to thy commandments, which denotes not only a vehement desire towards them (Ps. cxliii. 6)—"I will lay hold of them as one afraid of missing them, or letting them go;" but a close application of mind to the observance of them—"I will lay my hands to the command, not only to praise it, but practice it; nay, I will lift up my hands to it, that is, I will put forth all the strength I have to do it." The hands that hang down, through sloth and discouragement, shall be lifted up, Heb. xii. 12.

(5.) That he should be thoughtful and considerate in his duty (v. 48): "I will meditate in thy statutes, not only entertain myself with thinking of them as matters of speculation, but contrive how I may observe them in the best manner." By this it will appear that we truly love God's commandments, if we apply both our minds and our hands to them.

Psalm 119

Zayin

49-52
49 Remember the word unto thy servant, upon which thou hast caused me to hope.
50 This is my comfort in my affliction: for thy word hath quickened me.
51 The proud have had me greatly in derision: yet have I not declined from thy law.
52 I remembered thy judgments of old, O LORD; and have comforted myself.

with their sovereign's statutes, for they are anxious that they may not offend through ignorance. Prayer with lifted hands, and meditation with upward glancing eyes will in happy union work out the best inward results.
Verse 49. Remember the word unto thy servant. He asks for no new promise, but to have the old word fulfilled. He is grateful that he has received so good a word, he embraces it with all his heart, and now entreats the Lord to deal with him according to it. He does not say, "remember my service to thee," but "thy word to me." The words of masters to servants are not always such that servants wish their lords to remember them; for they usually observe the faults and failings of the work done, in as much as it does not tally with the word of command. But we who serve the best of masters are not anxious to have one of his words fall to the ground, since the Lord will so kindly remember his word of command as to give us grace wherewith we may obey, and he will couple with it a remembrance of his word of promise, so that our hearts shall be comforted. If God's word to us as his servants is so precious, what shall we say of his word to us as his sons?
Verse 50. This is my comfort in my affliction: for thy word hath quickened me. He means,—Thy word is my comfort, or the fact that thy word has brought quickening to me is my comfort. Or he means that the hope which had given him was his comfort, for God had quickened him thereby ever may be the exact sense, it is clear that the Psalmist had affliction—affliction peculiar to himself, which he calls "my affliction"; that he had comfort in it,—comfort specially his own, for he styles it "my comfort"; and that he knew what the comfort was, and where it came from, for exclaims—"this is my comfort". The worldling clutches his money bag and says, "this is my comfort"; the spendthrift points to his gaiety, shouts, "this is my comfort"; the drunkard lifts his glass, and sings, "this is my comfort"; but the man whose hope comes from God feels the giving power of the word of the Lord, and he testifies, "this is my fort." Paul said, "I know whom I have believed." Comfort is desirable all times; but comfort in affliction is like a lamp in a dark place. Some unable to find comfort at such times; but it is not so with believers, their Savor has said to them, "I will not leave you comfortless." have comfort and no affliction, others have affliction and no comfort; the saints have comfort in their affliction.
Verse 51. The proud have had me greatly in derision. Proud men never love gracious men, and as they fear them they veil their fear under a pretended contempt. In this case their hatred revealed itself in ridicule, and that ridicule was loud and long. When they wanted sport they made sport of David because he was God's servant. Men must have strange eyes to be able to see a farce in faith, and a comedy in holiness; yet it is sadly the case that men who are short of wit can generally provoke a broad grin by jesting at a saint.
Verse 52. I remembered thy judgments of old, O Lord; and have comforted myself. He had asked the Lord to remember, and here he remembers God and his judgments. When we see no present display of the divine power it is wise to fall back upon the records of former ages, since they are just as available as if the transactions were of yesterday, seeing the Lord is always the same. Our true comfort must be found in what our God works on behalf of truth and right, and as the histories of the olden times are full of divine interpositions it is well to be thoroughly acquainted with them. Moreover, if we are advanced in years we have the providence of our early days to review, and these should by no means be forgotten or left out of our thoughts. The argument is good and solid: he who has shown himself strong on behalf of his believing people is the immutable God, and therefore we may expect deliverance at his hands. The grinning of the proud will not trouble us when we remember

to it. Finally, he says, he would meditate on God's testimonies. Along with the majority of commentators, I have no doubt that this refers to the silent and secret musing in which the children of God exercise themselves.

Psalm 119:49-56

49. Remember thy word. He prays that God would really perform what he promised; for the event proves that he does not forget his word. That he is speaking of the promises we infer from the end of the verse, in which he declares, that cause was given him to hope, for which there would be no place unless grace had been presented to him.
In the second verse he asserts, that though God still kept him in suspense, yet he reposed with confidence in his word. At the same time he informs us, that during his troubles and anxieties, he did not search after vain consolation as the world is wont to d who look around them in all quarters to find something to mitigate their miseries; and if any allurements tickle their fancy, they make use of these as a remedy for alleviating their sorrows. On the contrary, the prophet says he was satisfied with the word of God itself; and that when all other refuges failed him, there he found life full and perfect; nevertheless, he covertly confesses, that if he do not acquire courage from the word of God, he will become like a dead man.
51. The proud have greatly scorned me. This example is eminently useful, as it serves to inform us, that though our honesty may render us obnoxious to the insults of the ungodly, we ought, by our unflinching constancy, to repel their pride, lest we should take a dislike to the law of God. Many who, in other respects, would be disposed to fear God, yield to this temptation. The earth has always been filled with the impious contemners of God, and at this day it is almost overrun with them. Wherefore, if we do not disregard their reviling, there will be no stability in our faith. In calling unbelievers proud, he applies to them a very appropriate designation: for their wisdom consists in despising God, lightly esteeming his judgments, trampling all piety under foot, and, in short, pouring contempt upon the celestial kingdom.
52. I called to mind thy judgments of old, O Jehovah! In this psalm, the judgments of God are generally taken for his statutes and decrees, that is, his righteousness. In this place, in consequence of the qualifying phrase, of old, it is more probable that they refer to the examples by which God has made himself known as the righteous Judge of the world. Why does he say that the law of God has been from everlasting? This may to some extent be accounted for from the righteousness here mentioned not being of recent growth, but truly everlasting, because the written law is just an attestation of the law of nature, through means of which God recalls to our memory that which he has previously engraved on our hearts.
53. Terror seized me. By the term fear, I think his ardent zeal is pointed out, in that he was not only deeply grieved at the transgressions of the law, but held in the utmost detestation the impious boldness of those who lightly esteemed the law of God. At the same time, it is worthy of notice, that it is no new

7. ZAIN.

49
Two things David here pleads with God in prayer for that mercy and grace which he hoped for, according to the word, by which his requests were guided:
1. That God had given him the promise on which he hoped: "Lord, I desire no more than that thou wouldst remember thy word unto thy servant, and do as thou hast said;" see 1 Chron. xvii. 23. "Thou art wise, and therefore wilt perfect what thou hast purposed, and not change thy counsel. Thou art faithful, and therefore wilt perform what thou hast promised, and not break thy word." Those that make God's promises their portion may with humble boldness make them their plea.
2. That God, who had given him the promise in the word, had by his grace wrought in him a hope in that promise and enabled him to depend upon it, and had raised his expectations of great things from it.

50
Here is David's experience of benefit by the word.
1. As a means of his sanctification: "Thy word has quickened me. It made me alive when I was dead in sin; it has many a time made me lively when I was dead in duty; it has quickened me to that which is good when I was backward and averse to it, and it has quickened me in that which is good when I was cold and indifferent."
2. Therefore as a means of his consolation when he was in affliction and needed something to support him: "Because thy word has quickened me at other times, it has comforted me then." The word of God has much in it that speaks comfort in affliction.

51
David here tells us, and it will be of use to us to know it,
1. That he had been jeered for his religion. Though he was a man of honor, a man of great prudence, and had done eminent services to his country, yet, because he was a devout conscientious man, the proud had him greatly in derision; they ridiculed him, bantered him, and did all they could to expose him to contempt.
2. That yet he had not been jeered out of his religion: "They have done all they could to make me quit it for shame, but none of these things move me: I have not declined from thy law for all this; but, if this be to be vile I will be yet more vile." He not only had not quite forsaken the law, but had not so much as declined from it.

52
When David was derided for his godliness he not only held fast his integrity, but,

Psalm 119

53-56
53 Horror hath taken hold upon me because of the wicked that forsake thy law.
54 Thy statutes have been my songs in the house of my pilgrimage.
55 I have remembered thy name, O LORD, in the night, and have kept thy law.
56 This I had, because I kept thy precepts.

how the Lord dealt with their predecessors in by gone periods; he destroyed them at the deluge, he confounded them at Babel, he drowned them at the Red Sea, he drove them out of Canaan: he has in all ages bared his arm against the haughty, and broken them as potters' vessels. While in our own hearts we humbly drink of the mercy of God in quietude, we are not without comfort in seasons of turmoil and derision; for then we resort to God's justice, and remember how he scoffs at the scoffers: "He that sitteth in the heavens doth laugh, the Lord doth have them in derision."

Verse 53. Horror hath taken hold upon me because of the wicked that forsake thy law. He was horrified at their action, at the pride which led them to it, and at the punishment which would be sure to fall upon them for it. When he thought upon the ancient judgments of God he was filled with terror at the fate of the godless; as well he might be. Their laughter had not distressed him, but he was distressed by a foresight of their overthrow. Truths which were amusement to them caused amazement to him. He saw them utterly turning away from the law of God, and leaving it as a path forsaken and over grown from want of traffic, and this forsaking of the law filled him with the most painful emotions: he was astonished at their wickedness, stunned by their presumption, alarmed by the expectation of their sudden overthrow, amazed by the terror of their certain doom. See Ps 119:106,158, and note the tenderness which combined with all this.

Verse 54. Thy statutes have been my songs in the house of my pilgrimage. Like others of God's servants, David knew that he was not at home in this world, but a pilgrim through it, seeking a better country. He did not, however, sigh over this fact, but he sang about it. He tells us nothing about his pilgrim sighs, but speaks of his pilgrim songs. Even the palace in which he dwelt was but "the house of his pilgrimage," the inn at which he rested, the station at which he halted for a little while. Men are wont to sing when they come to their inn, and so did this godly sojourner; he sang the songs of Zion, the statutes of the great King. The commands of God were as well known to him as the ballads of his country, and they were pleasant to his taste and musical to his ear. Happy is the heart which finds its joy in the commands of God, and makes obedience its recreation. When religion is set to music it goes well. When we sing in the ways of the Lord it shows that our hearts are in them. Ours are pilgrim psalms, songs of degrees; but they are such as we may sing throughout eternity; for the statutes of the Lord are the psalmody of heaven itself.

Verse 55. I have remembered thy name, O LORD, in the night. When others slept I woke to think of thee, thy person, thy actions, thy covenant, thy name, under which last term he comprehends the divine character as far as it is revealed. He was so earnest after the living God that he woke up at dead of night to think upon him. These were David's Night Thoughts. If they were not Sunny Memories they were memories of the Sun of Righteousness. It is well when our memory furnishes us with consolation, so that we can say with the Psalmist,—Having early been taught to know thee, I had only to remember the lessons of thy grace, and my heart was comforted. This verse shows not only that the man of God had remembered, but that he still remembered the Lord his God.

Verse 56. This I had, because I kept thy precepts. He had this comfort, this remembrance of God, this power to sing, this courage to face the enemy, this hope in the promise, because he had earnestly observed the commands of God, and striven to walk in them. We are not rewarded for our works, but there is a reward in them. Many a comfort is obtainable only by careful living: we can surely say of such consolations, "This I had because I kept thy precepts." How can we defy ridicule if we are living inconsistently? how can we comfortably remember the name of the Lord

ground of offense to the faithful, if numbers throw off God's yoke, and set up the standard of rebellion against him. This, I repeat, must be attended to, because many derive flimsy and frivolous pretexts for it, from the degeneracy of the age, as if they must needs howl while they live among wolves. In the days of David, we see there were many who apostatized from the faith, and yet, so far was he from being discouraged or dismayed by these things, that the fear of God rather kindled a holy indignation in his bosom. What is to be done, then, when surrounded by bad examples, but that we should vie with each other in holding them up to detestation? And here a contrast, if not directly stated, is implied, between the flattering unction which we apply to ourselves, believing that all is lawful which is common, and the horror with which the prophet tells us he was seized. If the wicked, haughtily and without restraint, set themselves in opposition to God, in consequence of our not being alive to his judgments, we convert that into an occasion of perverse confidence and insensibility. On the contrary, the prophet asserts that he was seized with horror, because, though he considered the long-suffering of God, on the one hand, yet, on the other, he was fully persuaded that he must, sooner or later, call for condign punishment.
54. Thy statutes have been my songs. He repeats in different words what he had formerly mentioned, that the law of God was his sole or special delight during all his life. Singing is an indication of joy. The saints are pilgrims in this world, and must be regarded as God's children and heirs of heaven, from the fact that they are sojourners on earth. By the house of their pilgrimage, then, may be understood their journey through life.
55. By night I remembered thy name, O Jehovah! As the second clause of the verse depends on the first, I consider the whole verse as setting forth one and the same truth; and, therefore, the prophet means that he was induced, by the remembrance he had of God, to keep the law. Contempt of the law originates in this, that few have any regard for God; and hence, the Scripture, in condemning the impiety of men, declares that they have forgotten God, (Psalm 50:22; 78:11; 106:21). To rectify this, David exhorts that the remembrance of God is the only remedy for preserving us hi his fear, and in the observance of his law; and assuredly, as often as his majesty occurs to our minds, it will tend to humble us, and the very thought of it will provoke us to the cultivation of godliness.
56. This was done to me. I doubt not that the prophet comprehends all God's benefits; but as he comes before God in relation to blessings then being enjoyed by him, he speaks as if he were pointing to them. Hence, under this term is included an acknowledgment of all the benefits with which he had been crowned; or, at all events, he declares that God had borne testimony, by some signal deliverance, to the integrity of his conduct. He does not boast of meriting any thing, as the Pharisees in our day do, who, when they meet with any such matter in Scripture, pervert it to prove the merit of works. He therefore calls upon himself to return to God, and invites others to follow his example, and exhorts them, that as God is an impartial judge, he will always reserve a recompense for piety. Probably, too, by this holy boasting he repels the base

1. He comforted himself. He not only bore reproach, but bore it cheerfully. It did not disturb his peace, nor break in upon the repose of his spirit in God.
2. That which he comforted himself with was the remembrance of God's judgments of old, the providences of God concerning his people formerly, both in mercy to them and in justice against their persecutors.

53
Here is,
1. The character of wicked people; he means those that are openly and grossly wicked: They forsake thy law. Every sin is a transgression of the law, but a course and way of willful and avowed sin is downright forsaking it and throwing it off.
2. The impression which the wickedness of the wicked made upon David; it frightened him, it put him into an amazement. He trembled to think of the dishonor thereby done to God, the gratification thereby given to Satan, and the mischiefs thereby done to the souls of men.

54
Here is,
1. David's state and condition; he was in the house of his pilgrimage, which may be understood either as his peculiar trouble (he was often tossed and hurried, and forced to fly) or as his lot in common with all. This world is the house of our pilgrimage, the house in which we are pilgrims; it is our tabernacle; it is our inn.
2. His comfort in this state: "Thy statutes have been my songs, with which I here entertain myself," as travelers are wont to divert the thoughts of their weariness, and take off something of the tediousness of their journey, by singing a pleasant song now and then.

55
Here is,
1. The converse David had with the word of God; he kept it in mind, and upon every occasion he called it to mind. God's name is the discovery he has made of himself to us in and by his word.
2. The conscience be made of conforming to it. The due remembrance of God's name, which is prefixed to his law, will have a great influence upon our observance of the law: I remembered thy name in the night, and therefore was careful to keep thy law all day.
3. The advantage he got by it (v. 56): This I had because I kept thy precepts. Some understand this indefinitely: This I had (that is I had that which satisfied me; I had every thing that is comfortable) because I kept thy precepts. Note, God's work is its own wages. A heart to obey the will of God is a most valuable reward of obedience; and the more we do the more we may do, and shall do, in the service of God; the branch that bears fruit is made more fruitful, John xv. 2.

Psalm 119

Heth

57-60

57 Thou art my portion, O LORD: I have said that I would keep thy words.
58 I intreated thy favor with my whole heart: be merciful unto me according to thy word.
59 I thought on my ways, and turned my feet unto thy testimonies.
60 I made haste, and delayed not to keep thy commandments.

if we live carelessly? It may be that David means that he had been enabled to keep the law because he had attended to the separate precepts: he had taken the commands in detail, and so had reached to holiness of life.
Verse 57. Thou art my portion, O LORD. A broken sentence. The translators have mended it by insertions, but perhaps it had been better to have left it alone, and then it would have appeared as an exclamation,—"My portion, O Lord!" The poet is lost in wonder while he sees that the great and glorious God is all his own! Well might he be so, for there is no possession like Jehovah himself. The form of the sentence expresses joyous recognition and appropriation,—"My portion, O Jehovah!" David had often seen the prey divided, and heard the victors shouting over it; here he rejoices as one who seizes his share of the spoil; he chooses the Lord to be his part of the treasure. Like the Levites, he took God to be his portion, and left other matters to those who coveted them. This is a large and lasting heritage, for it includes all, and more than all, and it outlasts all; and yet no man chooses it for himself until God has chosen and renewed him. Who that is truly wise could hesitate for a moment when the infinitely blessed God is set before him to be the object of his choice? David leaped at the opportunity, and grasped the priceless boon. Our author here dares exhibit the title deeds of his portion before the eye of the Lord himself, for he addresses his joyful utterance directly to God whom he boldly calls his own. With much else to choose from, for he was a king, and a man of great resources, Ire deliberately turns from all the treasures of the world, and declares that the Lord, even Jehovah, is his portion.

Verse 58. I intreated thy favor with my whole heart. A fully assured possession of God does not set aside prayer, but rather urges us to it; he who knows God to be his God will seek his face, longing for his presence. Seeking God's presence is the idea conveyed by the marginal reading, "thy face," and this is true to the Hebrew. The presence of God is the highest form of his favor, and therefore it is the most urgent desire of gracious souls: the light of his countenance gives us an antepast of heaven. O that we always enjoyed it! The good man entreated God's smile as one who begged for his life, and the entire strength of his desire went with the entreaty. Such eager pleadings are sure of success; that which comes from our heart will certainly go to God's heart. The whole of God's favors are ready for those who seek them with their whole hearts.
Verse 59. I thought on my ways, and turned my feet unto thy testimonies. While studying the word he was led to study his own life, and this caused a mighty revolution. He came to the word, and then he came to himself, and this made him arise and go to his Father. Consideration is the commencement of conversion: first we think and then we turn. When the mind repents of ill ways the feet are soon led into good ways; but there will be no repenting until there is deep, earnest thought. Many men are averse to thought of any kind, and as to thought upon their ways, they cannot endure it, for their ways will not bear thinking of.
Verse 60. I made haste, and delayed not to keep thy commandments. He made all speed to get back into the royal road from which he had wandered, and to run in that road upon the King's errands. Speed in repentance and speed in obedience are two excellent things. We are too often in haste to sin; O that we may be in a greater hurry to obey. Delay in sin is increase of sin. To be slow to keep the commands is really to break them. There is much evil in a lagging pace when God's command is to be followed. A holy alacrity in service is much to be cultivated. It is wrought in us by the Spirit of God, and the preceding verses describe the method of it: we are made to perceive and mourn our errors, we are

JOHN CALVIN

slanders of the ungodly, by which we lately saw he was grievously assailed.

Psalm 119:57-64

57. David here draws a comparison between the keeping of the law, and the imaginary good which captivates the ambition of mankind. "Let every one covet what seems to him good, and revel in his own pleasures; I have no ground to envy them, provided I retain this as my portion, the complete surrender of myself to the word of God."
58. I have earnestly besought thy face. In this verse David asserts, that he still persevered in the exercise of prayer; for without prayer faith would become languid and lifeless. The manner in which he expresses himself, which, in other languages, might be unpolished, among the Hebrews, expresses that familiar communication to which God admits, and even invites his servants when they come into his presence. The substance of his prayers, and the sum of his desires, he comprehends in a single sentence; namely, that he implored the mercy of God, the sure hope of which he had formed from his word.
59. I thought upon my ways. The amount is, that after the prophet had paid due regard to his manner of life, his only aim then was to follow the teaching of the law. In these words he intimates indirectly, that if it be inquired why men go astray, and are miserably distracted amidst conflicting impulses, the reason is, their thoughtlessly indulging themselves in the gratification of their passions. Every man watches most carefully, and applies all his energy to whatever his inclination may lead him, but all are blind in choosing the object which they ought to pursue; or rather, as if their eyes were sealed, they are either hurried away inconsiderately, or else, through carelessness, wander imperceptibly from one object to another. One thing is certain, that there is no one who carefully considers his ways; and, therefore, it is not without reason the prophet exhorts us, that the commencement of a godly life consists in men awaking from their lethargy, examining their ways, and, at last, wisely considering what it is to regulate their conduct properly.
60. I made haste. Though the words are in the past tense, they denote a continued act. The prophet declares with what promptitude he dedicated himself to the service of God. Diligence and dispatch demonstrate the favor of his zeal.
Next, in saying that he delayed not, this, according to the Hebrew idiom, gives intensity to the idea conveyed by the phrase, I made haste As among the Hebrews, to speak and not to keep silence is equivalent to speaking freely, unreservedly, and without dissimulation, as the occasion demands, so to make haste and not delay is to run quickly without doubt or delay. If we reflect on our own listlessness, and on the snares which Satan never fails to put in our way, we will at once perceive that these words are not added in vain. For let a man be ever so desirous of applying himself truly and heartily to the righteousness of God, yet, according to Paul, we know that "he does not the thing that he would," (Romans 7:15, 18,

MATTHEW HENRY

8. CHETH.

57
We may hence gather the character of a godly man.
1. He makes the favor of God his felicity: Thou art my portion, O Lord! Others place their happiness in the wealth and honors of this world. Their portion is in this life; they look no further; they desire no more; these are their good things, Luke xvi. 25.
2. He makes the law of God his rule: "I have said that I would keep thy words; and what I have said by thy grace I will do, and will abide by it to the end."

58
David, having in the foregoing verse reflected upon his covenants with God, here reflects upon his prayers to God, and renews his petition. Observe,
1. What he prayed for. Having taken God for his portion, he entreated his favor, as one that knew he had forfeited it, was unworthy of it, and yet undone without it, but for ever happy if he could obtain it.
2. How he prayed—with his whole heart, as one that knew how to value the blessing he prayed for. The gracious soul is entirely set upon the favor of God, and is therefore importunate for it. I will not let thee go except thou bless me.
3. What he pleaded—the promise of God: "Be merciful to me, according to thy word. I desire the mercy promised, and depend upon the promise for it." Those that are governed by the precepts of the word and are resolved to keep them (v. 57) may plead the promises of the word and take the comfort of them.

59-60
David had said he would keep God's word (v. 57), and it was well said; now here he tells us how and in what method he pursued that resolution.
1. He thought on his ways. He thought beforehand what he should do, pondering the path of his feet (Prov. iv. 26), that he might walk surely, and not at all adventures. He thought after what he had done, reflected upon his life past, and recollected the paths he had walked in and the steps he had taken.
2. He turned his feet to God's testimonies. He determined to make the word of God his rule, and to walk by that rule. He turned from the by-paths to which he had turned aside, and returned to God's testimonies. Penitent reflections must produce pious resolutions.
3. He did this immediately and without demur (v. 60): I made haste and delayed not. When we are under convictions of sin we must strike while the iron is hot, and not think to defer the prosecution of them, as Felix did, to a more convenient season.

61
Here is,
1. The malice of David's enemies against him. They were wicked men, who hated him for his godliness.

Psalm 119

61-64

61 The bands of the wicked have robbed me: but I have not forgotten thy law.
62 At midnight I will rise to give thanks unto thee because of thy righteous judgments.
63 I am a companion of all them that fear thee, and of them that keep thy precepts.
64 The earth, O LORD, is full of thy mercy: teach me thy statutes.

led to return to the right path, and then we are eager to make up for lost time by dashing forward to fulfill the precept.

Verse 61. The bands of the wicked have robbed me. Aforetime they derided him, and now they have defrauded him. Ungodly men grow worse, aria become more and more daring, so that they go from ridicule to robbery. Much of this bold opposition arose from their being banded together: men will dare to do in company what they durst not have thought of alone. When firebrands are laid together there is no telling what a flame they will create. It seems that whole bands of men assailed this one child of God, they are cowardly enough for anything; though they could not kill him, they robbed him; the dogs of Satan will worry saints if they cannot devour them. David's enemies did their utmost: first the serpents hissed, and then they stung. Since words availed not, the wicked fell to blows. How much the ungodly have plundered the saints in all ages, and how often have the righteous borne gladly the spoiling of their goods!

Verse 62. At midnight I will rise to give thanks unto thee because of thy righteous judgments. He was not afraid of the robbers; he rose, not to watch his house, but to praise his God. Midnight is the hour for burglars, and there were bands of them around David, but they did not occupy his thoughts; these were all up and away with the Lord his God. He thought not of thieves, but of thanks; not of what they would steal, but of what he would give to his God. A thankful heart is such a blessing that it drives out fear and makes room for praise. Thanksgiving turns night into day, and consecrates all hours to the worship of God. Every hour is canonical to a saint.

Verse 64. The earth, O LORD, is full of thy mercy. David had been exiled, but he had never been driven beyond the range of mercy, for he found the world to be everywhere filled with it. He had wandered in deserts and hidden in caves, and there he had seen and felt the lovingkindness of the Lord. He had learned that far beyond the bounds of the land of promise and She race of Israel the love of Jehovah extended, and in this verse he expressed that large hearted idea of God which is so seldom seen in the modern Jew. How sweet it is to us to know that not only is there mercy all over the world, but there is such an abundance of it that the earth is "full" of it. It is little wonder that the Psalmist, since he knew the Lord to be his portion, hoped to obtain a measure of this mercy for himself, and so was encouraged to pray, teach me thy statutes. It was to him the beau ideal of mercy to be taught of God, and taught in God's own law. He could not think of a greater mercy than this. Surely he who fills the universe with his grace will grant such a request as this to his own child. Let us breathe the desire to the All-merciful Jehovah, and we may be assured of its fulfillment.

65-72

In this ninth section the verses all begin with the letter Teth. They are the witness of experience, testifying to the goodness of God, the graciousness of his dealings, and the preciousness of his word. Especially the Psalmist proclaims the excellent uses of adversity, and the goodness of God in afflicting him. The sixty-fifth verse is the text of the entire octave.

Verse 65. Thou hast dealt well with thy servant, O Lord, according unto thy word. This is the summary of his life, and assuredly it is the sum of ours. The Psalmist tells the Lord the verdict of his heart; he cannot be silent, he must speak his gratitude in the, presence of Jehovah, his God. From the universal goodness of God in nature, in Ps 119:64, it is an easy and pleasant step to a confession of the Lord's uniform goodness to ourselves personally. It is something that God has dealt at all with such insignificant and under serving beings as we are, and it is far more

19). Although no outward obstacle may stand in our way, yet we are so retarded by impediments within, that nothing is more difficult than to make haste to keep the law of God. At the same time we must remember, that the prophet is here speaking comparatively in reference to those who are chargeable with procrastination during the greater part of their life, and who draw near to God, not only hesitatingly and tardily, but also purposely loiter in their course, or else prevent themselves from coming by their tortuous ways.

61. The cords of the wicked have caught hold of me. The prophet intends to declare that when Satan assailed the principles of piety in his soul, by grievous temptations, he continued with undeviating steadfastness in the love and practice of God's law.

62. I will rise at midnight to praise thee. In this verse he shows not only that he approved and embraced with his whole heart whatever the Divine law contains, but that he also gave evidence of his gratitude to God for having made him partaker of so great a blessing. It seems to be quite a common thing professedly to assent to God when he teaches us by his law; for who would dare to lift up his voice against Him? But still the world is very far from acknowledging that the truth which he has revealed is in all respects reasonable. In the first place, such is the rebellion of our corrupt nature, that every man would have somewhat either altered or taken away. Again, if men had their choice, they would rather be governed by their own will than by the word of God. In short, human reason, as well as human passions, is widely at variance with the Divine law. He then has profited not little, who both obediently embraces revealed truth, and, taking sweet delight in it, gives thanks to God for it. The prophet, however, does not simply declare that he magnifies God's righteous judgments; he also affirms that he rose at midnight to do so, by which he expresses the earnestness of his desire; for the studies and cares which break our sleep necessarily imply great earnestness of soul. He also, at the same time, intimates, that in bearing his testimony in behalf of the Divine law, he was far from being influenced by ostentation, since in his secret retirement, when no human eye was upon him, he pronounced the highest encomiums on God's righteous judgments.

63. I am a companion to all those who fear thee. He does not simply speak of the brotherly love and concord which true believers cultivate among themselves, but intimates that, whenever he met with any individual who feared God, he gave him his hand in token of fellowship, and that he was not only one of the number of God's servants, but also their helper. Such concord is undoubtedly required in all the godly, that they may contribute to each other's advancement in the fear of God.

64. O Jehovah! the earth is full of thy mercy. It behooves us to remember that it is an evidence that we have given ourselves up to the most shameful sloth, when, contented with a superficial knowledge of Divine truth, we are, in a great measure, indifferent about making further progress, seeing so renowned a teacher of the Church labored with the greatest ardor to become more and more acquainted with God's statutes. Besides, it is certain that he does not here treat of

There were bands or troops of them confederate against him. They did him all the mischief they could; they robbed him; having endeavored to take away his good name (v. 51), they set upon his goods, and spoiled him of them, either by plunder in time of war or by fines and confiscations under color of law.

2. The testimony of David's conscience for him that he had held fast his religion when he was stripped of every thing else, as Job did when the bands of the Chaldeans and Sabeans had robbed him: But I have not forgotten thy law. No care nor grief should drive God's word out of our minds.

62

Though David is, in this psalm, much in prayer, yet he did not neglect the duty of thanksgiving; for those that pray much will have much to give thanks for. See,

1. How much God's hand was eyed in his thanksgivings.

2. How much David's heart was set upon his thanksgivings. He would rise at midnight to give thanks to God. Great and good thoughts kept him awake, and refreshed him, instead of sleep; and so zealous was he for the honor of God that when others were in their beds he was upon his knees at his devotions.

63

David had often expressed the great love he had to God; here he expresses the great love he had to the people of God; and observe,

1. Why he loved them; not so much because they were his best friends, most firm to his interest and most forward to serve him, but because they were such as feared God and kept his precepts.

2. How he showed his love to them: He was a companion of them. He had not only a spiritual communion with them in the same faith and hope, but he joined with them in holy ordinances in the courts of the Lord, where rich and poor, prince and peasant, meet together.

64

Here,

1. David pleads that God is good to all the creatures according to their necessities and capacities; as the heaven is full of God's glory, so the earth is full of his mercy, full of the instances of his pity and bounty.

2. He therefore prays that God would be good to him according to his necessity and capacity: "Teach me thy statutes. Thou feedest the young ravens that cry, with food proper for them; and wilt thou not feed me with spiritual food, the bread of life, which my soul needs and craves, and cannot subsist without? The earth is full of thy mercy; and is not heaven too? Wilt thou not then give me spiritual blessings in heavenly places?"

Psalm 119

Teth
65-68

65 Thou hast dealt well with thy servant, O LORD, according unto thy word.
66 Teach me good judgment and knowledge: for I have believed thy commandments.
67 Before I was afflicted I went astray: but now have I kept thy word.
68 Thou art good, and doest good; teach me thy statutes.

that he has dealt well with us, and so well, so wondrously well. He hath done all things well: the rule has no exception. In providence and in grace, in giving prosperity and sending adversity, in everything Jehovah hath dealt well with us. It is dealing well on our part to tell the Lord that we feel that he hath dealt well with us; for praise of this kind is specially fitting and comely. This kindness of the Lord is, however, no chance matter: he promised to do so, and he has done it according to his word. It is very precious to see the word of the Lord fulfilled in our happy experience; it endears the Scripture to us, and makes us love the Lord of the Scripture.

Verse 66. Teach me good judgment and knowledge. Again he begs for teaching, as in verse 64, and again he uses God's mercy as an argument. Since God had dealt well with him, he is encouraged to pray for judgment to appreciate the Lord's goodness. Good judgment is the form of goodness which the godly man most needs and most desires, and it is one which the Lord is most ready to bestow. David felt that he had frequently failed in judgment in the matter of the Lord's dealings with him: from want of knowledge he had misjudged the chastening hand of the heavenly Father, and therefore he now asks to be better instructed, since he perceives the injustice which he had done to the Lord by his hasty conclusions. He means to say—Lord, thou didst deal well with me when I thought thee hard and stern, be pleased to give me more wit, that I may not a second time think so ill of my Lord. A sight of our errors and a sense of our ignorance should make us teachable. We are not able to judge, for our knowledge is so sadly inaccurate and imperfect; if the Lord teaches us knowledge we shall attain to good judgment, but not otherwise. The Holy Ghost alone can fill us with light, and set the understanding upon a proper balance: let us ardently long for his teachings, since it is most desirable that we should be no longer mere children in knowledge and understanding.

Verse 67. Before I was afflicted I went astray. Partly, perhaps, through the absence of trial. Often our trials act as a thorn hedge to keep us in the good pasture, but our prosperity is a gap through which we go astray. If any of us remember a time in which we had no trouble, we also probably recollect that then grace was low and temptation was strong. It may be that some believer cries, "O that it were with me as in those summer days before I was afflicted." Such a sigh is most unwise, and arises from a carnal love of ease: the spiritual man who prizes growth in grace will bless God that those dangerous days are over, and that if the weather be more stormy it is also more healthy. It is well when the mind is open and candid, as in this instance: perhaps David would never have known and confessed his own straying if he had not smarted under the rod. Let us join in his humble acknowledgments, for doubtless we have imitated him in his straying. Why is it that a little ease works in us so much disease? Can we never rest without rusting? Never be filled without waxing fat? Never rise as to one world without going down as to another! What weak creatures we are to be unable to bear a little pleasure! What base hearts are those which turn the abundance of God's goodness into an occasion for sin.

Verse 68. Thou art good, and doest good. Even in affliction God is good, and does good. This is the confession of experience. God is essential goodness in himself, and in every attribute of his nature he is good in the fullest sense of the term; indeed, he has a monopoly of goodness, for there is none good but one, that is God. His acts are according to his nature: from a pure source flow pure streams. God is not latent and ill active goodness; he displays himself by his doings, he is actively beneficent, he does good. How much good he does no tongue can tell! How good he is no heart can conceive! It is well to worship the Lord as the poet here does by describing him. Facts about God are the best external teaching, but of the inward illumination of the mind, which is the gift of the Holy Spirit.

Psalm 119: 65-72

65. O Jehovah! thou hast done good to thy servant. As express mention is made of the Divine word or promise, the prophet celebrates the faithfulness of God in performing the grace which he had promised. I have really experienced (as if he had said) that Thou art true, and dost not delude thy servants with empty words. Special reference is therefore here made to God's promises, because thence all his benefits flow to us, not, indeed, as from the original fountain-head, but, as it were, by conduit pipes. Although his free goodness is the only cause which induces him to deal bountifully with us, yet we can hope for nothing at his hand until he first bring himself under obligation to us by his word.
66. Teach me goodness of taste and acknowledge. After having confessed that he had found, by experience, the faithfulness of God to his promises, David here adds a request similar to what is contained in the 64th verse, namely, that he may grow in right understanding; although the phraseology is somewhat different; for instead of thy statutes, as in that verse, he here uses goodness of taste and knowledge.
67. Before I was brought low I went astray. David in his own person describes either that wantonness or rebellion, common to all mankind, which is displayed in this, that we never yield obedience to God until we are compelled by his chastisements. It is indeed a monstrous thing obstinately to refuse to submit ourselves to Him; and yet experience demonstrates, that so long as he deals gently with us, we are always breaking forth into insolence. Since even a prophet of God required to have his rebellion corrected by forcible means, this kind of discipline is assuredly most needful for us. The first step in obedience being the mortifying of the flesh, to which all men are naturally disinclined, it is not surprising if God bring us to a sense of our duty by manifold afflictions. Yea, rather as the flesh is from time to time obstreperous, even when it seems to be tamed, it is no wonder to find him repeatedly subjecting us anew to the rod. This is done in different ways. He humbles some by poverty, some by shame, some by diseases, some by domestic distresses, some by hard and painful labors; and thus, according to the diversity of vices to which we are prone, he applies to each its appropriate remedy.

The next verse needs no explanation, being nearly of the same import as the last verse of the former eight. He beseeches God to exercise his goodness towards him, not by causing him to increase in riches and honors, or to abound in pleasures, but by enabling him to make progress in the knowledge of the law.
69. The proud have weaved lies against me. He declares that, notwithstanding the malignant interpretation which the wicked put upon all that he did, and their attempts, by this artifice, to turn him aside from following after and loving uprightness, the state of his mind remained unaltered. It is a severe temptation, when, although innocent, we are loaded with reproach and infamy, and are not only assailed by

9. TETH.

65-66
Here,
1. David makes a thankful acknowledgment of God's gracious dealings with him all along: Thou hast dealt well with thy servant. However God has dealt with us, we must own he has dealt well with us, better than we deserve, and all in love and with design to work for our good. In many instances God has done well for us beyond our expectations.
2. Upon these experiences he grounds a petition for divine instruction: "Teach me good judgment and knowledge, that, by thy grace, I may render again, in some measure, according to the benefit done unto me." Teach me a good taste (so the word signifies), a good relish, to discern things that differ, to distinguish between truth and falsehood, good and evil; for the ear tries words, as the mouth tastes meat.
3. This petition is backed with a plea: "For I have believed thy commandments, received them, and consented to them that they are good, and submitted to their government; therefore, Lord, teach me." Where God has given a good heart a good head too many in faith be prayed for.

67
David here tells us what he had experienced,
1. Of the temptations of a prosperous condition: "Before I was afflicted, while I lived in peace and plenty, and knew no sorrow, I went astray from God and my duty." Sin is going astray; and we are most apt to wander from God when we are easy and think ourselves at home in the world. Prosperity is the unhappy occasion of much iniquity; it makes people conceited of themselves, indulgent of the flesh, forgetful of God, in love with the world, and deaf to the reproofs of the word. See Ps. xxx. 6.
2. Of the benefit of an afflicted state: "Now have I kept thy word, and so have been recovered from my wanderings." God often makes use of afflictions as a means to reduce those to himself who have wandered from him.

68
Here,
1. David praises God's goodness and gives him the glory of it: Thou art good and doest good. All who have any knowledge of God and dealings with him wilt own that he does good, and therefore will conclude that he is good. The streams of God's goodness are so numerous, and run so full, so strong, to all the creatures, that we must conclude the fountain that is in himself to be inexhaustible.
2. He prays for God's grace, and begs to be under the guidance and influence of it: Teach me thy statutes. "Lord, thou doest good to all, art the bountiful benefactor of all the creatures; this is the good I beg thou wilt do to me,—Instruct me in my duty, incline me

Psalm 119

69-72
69 The proud have forged a lie against me: but I will keep thy precepts with my whole heart.
70 Their heart is as fat as grease; but I delight in thy law.
71 It is good for me that I have been afflicted; that I might learn thy statutes.
72 The law of thy mouth is better unto me than thousands of gold and silver.

praise of God. All the glory we can give to God is to reflect his own glory upon himself. We can say no more good of God than God is and does.
Verse 69. The proud have forged a lie against me. They first derided him (Ps 119:51), then defrauded him (Ps 119:61), and now they have defamed him. To injure his character they resorted to falsehood, for they could find nothing against him if they spoke the truth. They forged a lie as a blacksmith beats out a weapon of iron, or they counterfeited the truth as men forge false coin. The original may suggest a common expression—"They have patched up a lie against me." They were not too proud to lie. Pride is a lie, and when a proud man utters lies "he speaketh of his own." Proud men are usually the bitterest opponents of the righteous: they are envious of their good fame and are eager to ruin it. Slander is a cheap and handy weapon if the object is the destruction of a gracious reputation; and when many proud ones conspire to concoct, exaggerate, and spread abroad a malicious falsehood, they generally succeed in wounding their victim, and it is no fault of theirs if they do not kill him outright. O the venom which lies under the tongue of a liar!
Verse 70. Their heart is as fat as grease. They delight in fatness, but I delight in thee. Their hearts, through sensual indulgence, have grown insensible, coarse, and groveling; but thou hast saved me from such a fate through thy chastening hand. Proud men grow fat through carnal luxuries, and this makes them prouder still. They riot in their prosperity, and fill their hearts therewith till they become insensible, effeminate, and self indulgent. A greasy heart is something horrible; it is a fatness which makes a man fatuous, a fatty degeneration of the heart which leads to feebleness and death.
Verse 71. It is good for me that I have been afflicted. Even though the affliction came from bad men, it was overruled for good ends: though it was bad as it came from them, it was good for David. It benefited him in many ways, and he knew it. Whatever he may have thought while under the trial, he perceived himself to be the better for it when it was over. It was not good to the proud to be prosperous, for their hearts grew sensual and insensible; but affliction was good for the Psalmist. Our worst is better for us than the sinner's best. It is bad for sinners to rejoice, and good for saints to sorrow. A thousand benefits have come to us through our pains and griefs, and among the rest is this—that we have thus been schooled in the law.
Verse 72. The law of thy mouth. A sweetly expressive name for the word of God. It comes from God's own mouth with freshness and power to our souls. Things written are as dried herbs; but speech has a liveliness and dew about it. We do well to look upon the word of the Lord as though it were newly spoken into our ear; for in very truth it is not decayed by years, but is as forcible and sure as though newly uttered. Precepts are prized when it is seen that they come forth from the lips of our Father who is in heaven. The same lips which spoke us into existence have spoken the law by which we are to govern that existence. Whence could a law so sweetly proceed as from the mouth of our covenant God? Well may we prize beyond all price that which comes from such a source.
Is better unto me than thousands of gold and silver. If a poor man had said this, the world's witlings would have hinted that the grapes are sour, and that men who have no wealth are the first to despise it; but this is the verdict of a man who owned his thousands, and could judge by actual experience of the value of money and the value of truth. He speaks of great riches, he heaps it up by thousands, he mentions the varieties of its forms,—"gold and silver"; and then he sets the word of God before it all, as better to him, even if others did not think it better to them. Wealth is good in some respects, but obedience is better in all respects. It is well to keep the treasures of this life; but far more commendable to keep the law of the Lord.

injurious words, but also held up to the odium of the world by wicked persons, under some specious pretense or other. We see many who otherwise are good people, and inclined to live uprightly, either become discouraged, or are greatly shaken, when they find themselves so unworthily rewarded. On this account the prophet's example is the more to be attended t that we may not be appalled by the malignity of men; that we may not cease to nourish within us the fear of God, even when they may have succeeded in destroying our reputation in the sight of our fellow-creatures; and that we may be contented to have our piety shining at the judgment-scat of God, although it may be defaced by the calumnies of men. So long as we depend upon the judgment of men, we will always be in a state of fluctuation, as has been already observed.

With this corresponds the statement in the subsequent verse (70th) that their heart is fat as grease,—a vice too common among the despisers of God. Whence is it that wicked men, whom their own conscience gnaws within, vaunt themselves so insolently against the most eminent servants of God, but because a certain grossness overgrows their hearts, so that they are stupefied, and even frenzied by their own obstinacy?

But wonderful and worthy of the highest praise is the magnanimity of the prophet, who found all his delight in the law of God: it is as if he declared that this was the food on which he fed, and with which he was refreshed in the highest degree; which could not have been the case had not his heart been freed, and thoroughly cleansed from all unhallowed pleasures.

71. It has been good for me that I was afflicted. He here confirms the sentiment which we have previously considered—that it was profitable to him to be subdued by God's chastisements, that he might more and more be brought back and softened to obedience.

By these words he confesses that he was not exempt from the perverse obstinacy with which all mankind are infected; for, had it been otherwise with him, the profit of which he speaks, when he says that his docility was owing to his being brought low, would have been merely pretended; even as none of us willingly submits his neck to God, until He soften our natural hardness by the strokes of a hammer. It is good for us to taste continually the fruit which comes to us from God's corrections, that they may become sweet to us; and that, in this way, we, who are so rebellious and wayward, may suffer ourselves to be brought into subjection.

72. The last verse also requires no exposition, as it contains a sentiment of very frequent occurrence in this psalm, and, in itself, sufficiently plain,—That he preferred God's law to all the riches of the world, the immoderate desire of which so deplorably infatuates the great bulk of mankind. He does not compare the law of God with the riches he himself possessed; but he affirms, that it was more precious in his estimation than a vast inheritance.

to it, and enable me to do it. Thou art good, and doest good; Lord, teach me thy statutes, that I may be good and do good, may have a good heart and live a good life."

69-70

David here tells us how he was affected as to the proud and wicked people that were about him.

1. He did not fear their malice, nor was he by it deterred from his duty: They have forged a lie against me. Thus they aimed to take away his good name.

But he will go on in his duty with constancy and resolution: "Let them say what they will, I will keep thy precepts, and not dread their reproach."

2. He did not envy their prosperity, nor was he by it allured from his duty. Their heart is as fat as grease. The proud are at ease (Ps. cxxiii. 4); they are full of the world, and the wealth and pleasures of it; and this makes them senseless, secure, and stupid; they are past feeling: thus the phrase is used, Isa. vi. 10. Make the heart of this people fat. They are not sensible of the touch of the word of God or his rod.

71

See here,

1. That it has been the lot of the best saints to be afflicted. The proud and the wicked lived in pomp and pleasure, while David, though he kept close to God and his duty, was still in affliction. Waters of a full cup are wrung out to God's people, Ps. lxxiii. 10.

2. That it has been the advantage of God's people to be afflicted. David could speak experimentally: It was good for me; many a good lesson he had learnt by his afflictions.

72

This is a reason why David reckoned that when by his afflictions he learned God's statutes, and the profit did so much counterbalance the loss, he was really a gainer by them; for God's law, which he got acquaintance with by his affliction, was better to him than all the gold and silver which he lost by his affliction.

1. David had but a little of the word of God in comparison with what we have, yet see how highly he valued it; how inexcusable then are we, who have both the Old and New Testament complete, and yet account them as a strange thing!

2. He had a great deal of gold and silver in comparison with what we have, yet see how little he valued it. His riches increased, and yet he did not set his heart upon them, but upon the word of God. That was better to him, yielded him better pleasures, and better maintenance, and a better inheritance, than all the treasures he was master of. Those that have read, and believe, David's Psalms and Solomon's Ecclesiastes, cannot but prefer the word of God far before the wealth of this world.

Psalm 119

Yodh

73-76

73 Thy hands have made me and fashioned me: give me understanding, that I may learn thy commandments.
74 They that fear thee will be glad when they see me; because I have hoped in thy word.
75 I know, O LORD, that thy judgments are right, and that thou in faithfulness hast afflicted me.
76 Let, I pray thee, thy merciful kindness be for my comfort, according to thy word unto thy servant.

Verse 73. Thy hands have made me and fashioned me. It is profitable to remember our creation, it is pleasant to see that the divine hand has had much to do with us, for it never moves apart from the divine thought. It excites reverence, gratitude, and affection towards God when we view him as our Maker, putting forth the careful skill and power of his hands in our forming and fashioning. He took a personal interest in us, making us with his own hands; he was doubly thoughtful, for he is represented both as making and molding us. In both giving existence and arranging existence he manifested love and wisdom; and therefore we find reasons for praise, confidence, and expectation in our being and well being.

Verse 74. They that fear thee will be glad when they see me: because I have hoped in thy word. When a man of God obtains grace for himself he becomes a blessing to others, especially if that grace has made him a man of sound understanding and holy knowledge. God fearing men are encouraged when they meet with experienced believers. A hopeful man is a God send when things are declining or in danger. When the hopes of one believer are fulfilled his companions are cheered and established, and led to hope also. It is good for the eyes to see a man whose witness is that the Lord is true; it is one of the joys of saints to hold converse with their more advanced brethren. The fear of God is not a left handed grace, as some have called it; it is quite consistent with gladness; for if even the sight of a comrade gladdens the God fearing, how glad must they be in the presence of the Lord himself! We do not only meet to share each others' burdens, but to partake in each others' joys, and some men contribute largely to the stock of mutual gladness. Hopeful men bring gladness with them. Despondent spirits spread the infection of depression, and hence few are glad to see them, while those whose hopes are grounded upon God's word carry sunshine in their faces, and are welcomed by their fellows. There are professors whose presence scatters sadness, and the godly quietly steal out of their company: may this never be the case with us.

Verse 75. I know, O LORD, that thy judgments are right. He who would learn most must be thankful for what he already knows, and be willing to confess it to the glory of God. The Psalmist had been sorely tried, but he had continued to hope in God under his trial, and now he avows his conviction that be had been justly and wisely chastened. This he not only thought but knew, so that he was positive about it, and spoke without a moment's hesitation. Saints are sure about the rightness of their troubles, even when they cannot see the intent of them. It made the godly glad to hear David say this, And that thou in faithfulness hast afflicted me. Because love required severity, therefore the Lord exercised it. It was not because God was unfaithful that the believer found himself in a sore strait, but for just the opposite reason: it was the faithfulness of God to his covenant which brought the chosen one under the rod. It might not be needful that others should be tried just then; but it was necessary to the Psalmist, and therefore the Lord did not withhold the blessing. Our heavenly Father is no Eli: he will not suffer his children to sin without rebuke, his love is too intense for that. The man who makes the confession of this verse is already progressing in the school of grace, and is learning the commandments. This third verse of the section corresponds to the third of Teth (67), and in a degree to several other verses which make the thirds in their octaves.

Verse 76. Let, I pray thee, thy merciful kindness be for my comfort, according to thy word unto thy servant. Having confessed the righteousness of the Lord, he now appeals to his mercy, and while he does not ask that the rod may be removed, he earnestly begs for comfort under it. Righteousness and faithfulness afford us no consolation if we cannot also taste of mercy, and, blessed be God, this

JOHN CALVIN

Psalm 119:73-80

73. Thy hands have made and fashioned me. The avowal of the prophet, that he had been created by the hand of God, greatly contributed to inspire him with the hope of obtaining the favor which he supplicates. As we are the creatures and the workmanship of God, and as he has not only bestowed upon us vital motion, in common with the lower animals, but has, in addition thereto, given us the light of understanding and reasons—this encourages us to pray that he would direct us to the obedience of his law. And yet the prophet does not call upon God, as if He were under any obligations to him; but, knowing that God never forsakes the work which he has begun, he simply asks for new grace, by which God may carry on to perfection what he has commenced. We have need of the assistance of the law, since all that is sound in our understandings is corrupted; so that we cannot perceive what is right, unless we are taught from some other source. But our blindness and stupidity are still more strikingly manifest, from the fact that teaching will avail us nothing, until our souls are renewed by Divine grace.

74. They who fear thee shall see me and be glad. This verse is either connected with the preceding, or it includes other benefits of God, besides the blessing mentioned in that verse. As God invites all his servants in common to trust in him, it follows, that, whenever he exhibits a token of his grace towards any one of them, he testifies to all that he is faithful to his promises, and that they have no reason to be afraid of his disappointing those who trust in him.

75. I have known, O Jehovah, that thy judgments are justice. By judgments, in this psalm, we are to understand the precepts of the law; but as the prophet immediately adds, that he was justly chastised, he seems to use the word in this verse, for the punishments by which God stirs up men to repentance.

76. I beseech thee let thy goodness be for my consolation. Although he has acknowledged that he had been justly humbled, yet he desires that his sorrow may be alleviated by some consolation. He implores God's mercy, as what was essentially necessary to relieve and cure his miseries. He thus shows that nothing can remove sorrow from the faithful, until they feel that God is reconciled to them. In the Word in which God offers his mercy, there is to be found no small comfort for healing all the grief to which men are liable. But the Psalmist is now speaking of actual mercy, if I may use that term, when God by the very deed declares the favor which he has promised. Confiding in the Divine promise, he already cherished in his heart a joy, proceeding from the hope of receiving the communications of Divine grace. But as all our hope would end in mere disappointment, did not God at length appear as our deliverer, he requests the performance of that which God had promised him. Lord, as if he had said, since thou hast graciously promised to be ready to succor me, be pleased to make good thy word in effect.

77. Let thy companions come unto me. In this verse, the Psalmist repeats and confirms almost the same request as in

MATTHEW HENRY

10. JOD.

73

Here,

1. David adores God as the God of nature and the author of his being: Thy hands have made me and fashioned me, Job x. 8. Every man is as truly the work of God's hands as the first man was, Ps. cxxxix. 15, 16.

2. He addresses himself to God as the God of grace, and begs he will be the author of his new and better being. God made us to serve him and enjoy him; but by sin we have made ourselves unable for his service and indisposed for the enjoyment of him; and we must have a new and divine nature, otherwise we had the human nature in vain; therefore David prays, "Lord, since thou hast made me by thy power for thy glory, make me anew by thy grace, that I may answer the ends of my creation and live to some purpose: Give me understanding, that I may learn thy commandments."

74

Here is,

1. The confidence of this good man in the hope of God's salvation: "I have hoped in thy word; and I have not found it in vain to do so; it has not failed me, nor have I been disappointed in my expectations from it. It is a hope that maketh not ashamed; but is present satisfaction, and fruition at last."

2. The concurrence of other good men with him in the joy of that salvation: "Those that fear thee will be glad when they see me relieved by my hope in thy word and delivered according to my hope." The comforts which some of God's children have in God, and the favors they have received from him, should be matter of joy to others of them.

75

Still David is in affliction, and being so he owns,

1. That his sin was justly corrected: I know, O Lord! that thy judgments are right, are righteousness itself. However God is pleased to afflict us, he does us no wrong, nor can we charge him with any iniquity, but most acknowledge that it is less than we have deserved.

2. That God's promise was graciously performed. The former may silence us under our afflictions, and forbid us to repine, but this may satisfy us, and enable us to rejoice; for afflictions are in the covenant, and therefore they are not only not meant for our hurt, but they are really intended for our good:.

76-77

Here is,

1. An earnest petition to God for his favor. Those that own the justice of God in their afflictions (as David had done, v. 75) may, in faith, and with humble boldness, be earnest for the mercy of God, and the

Psalm 119

77-80
77 Let thy tender mercies come unto me, that I may live: for thy law is my delight.
78 Let the proud be ashamed; for they dealt perversely with me without a cause: but I will meditate in thy precepts.
79 Let those that fear thee turn unto me, and those that have known thy testimonies.
80 Let my heart be sound in thy statutes; that I be not ashamed.

is promised us in the word, and therefore we may expect it. The words "merciful kindness," are a happy combination, and express exactly what we need in affliction: mercy to forgive the sin, and kindness to sustain under the sorrow.
Verse 77. Let thy tender mercies come unto me, that I may live. He was so hard pressed that he was at death's door if God did not succor him. He needed not only mercy, but "mercies," and these must be of a very gracious and considerate kind, even "tender mercies," for he was sore with his wounds. These gentle favors must be of the Lord's giving, for nothing less would suffice; and they must "come" all the way to the sufferer's heart, for he was not able to journey after them; all he could do was to sigh out, "Oh that they would come." If deliverance did not soon come, he felt ready to expire, and yet he told us but a verse or so ago that he hoped in God's word: how true it is that hope lives on when death seems written on all besides.
Verse 78. Let the proud be ashamed. He begged that the judgments of God might no longer fall upon himself, but upon his cruel adversaries. God will not suffer those who hope in his word to be put to shame, for he reserves that reward for haughty spirits: they shall yet be overtaken with confusion, and become the subjects of contempt, while God's afflicted ones shall again lift up their heads. Shame is for the proud, for it is a shameful thing to be proud. Shame is not for the holy, for there is nothing in holiness to be ashamed of.
Verse 79. Let those that fear thee turn unto me, and those that have known thy testimonies. Perhaps the tongue of slander had alienated some of the godly, and probably the actual faults of David had grieved many more. He begs God to turn to him, and then to turn his people towards him. Those who are right with God are also anxious to be right with his children.
Verse 80. Let my heart be sound in thy statutes; that I be not ashamed. This is even more important than to be held in esteem by good men. This is the root of the matter. If the heart be sound in obedience to God, all is well, or will be well. If right at heart we are right in the main. If we be not sound before God, our name for piety is an empty sound. Mere profession will fail, and undeserved esteem will disappear like a bubble when it bursts; only sincerity and truth will endure in the evil day. He who is right at heart has no reason for shame, and he never shall have any; hypocrites ought to be ashamed now, and they shall one day be put to shame without end; their hearts are rotten, and their names shall rot. This eightieth verse is a variation of the prayer of the seventy-third verse; there be sought sound understanding, here he goes deeper, and begs for a sound heart. Those who have learned their own frailty by sad experience, are led to dive beneath the surface, and cry to the Lord for truth in the inward parts. In closing the consideration of these eight verses, let us join with the writer in the prayer, "Let my heart be sound in thy statutes." This portion of the gigantic psalm sees the Psalmist in extremis. His enemies have brought him to the lowest condition of anguish and depression; yet he is faithful to the law and trustful in his God. This octave is the midnight of the psalm, and very dark and black it is. Stars, however, shine out, and the last verse gives promise of the dawn. The strain will after this become more cheerful; but meanwhile it should minister comfort to us to see so eminent a servant of God so hardly used by the ungodly: evidently in our own persecutions, no strange thing has happened unto us.
Verse 81. My soul fainteth for thy salvation. He wished for no deliverance but that which came from God: his one desire was for "thy salvation." But for that divine deliverance he was eager to the last degree,—up to the full measure of his strength, yea, and beyond it till he fainted. So strong was his desire that it produced prostration of spirit. He grew weary with

the preceding verse, although in phraseology somewhat different. As he had just now said, that his sorrow could not be removed, nor his joy restored, in any other way than by God's mercy being exercised towards him; so now he affirms that he cannot have without being reconciled to God. He thus distinguishes himself from worldly men, who are very little affected with a concern about having God reconciled to them; or, rather, who do not cease securely to enjoy themselves, although God is angry with them. He distinctly affirms, that, until he know that God is reconciled to him, he is a dead man even while living; but that, on the other hand, whenever God shall cause his mercy to shine upon him, he will be restored from death to life. By the way, he intimates that he was deprived for a time of the tokens of God's fatherly favor; for it would have been needless for him to have wished that it might come to him, had it not been removed from him.

78. Let the proud be put to shame. It is important to attend to the reason why the Psalmist hopes that God will be an enemy to his enemies; namely, because they wickedly and maliciously assaulted him.

79. Let such as fear thee turn unto me. In this verse, which is connected with the preceding, the Psalmist affirms, that the deliverance which he obtained would afford common instruction to all the godly. My condition, as if he had said, may, for a time, have disheartened the righteous, as well as increased the insolence of my enemies; but now, taking courage, they will turn their eyes to this joyful spectacle.

80. Let my heart be sound in thy statutes. Having, a little before, desired to be endued with a sound understanding, he now prays, in a similar manner, for sincere affection of heart. The understanding and affections, as is well known, are the two principal faculties of the human soul, both of which he clearly shows to be depraved and perverse, when he requests that his understanding may be illuminated, and, at the same time, that his heart may be framed to the obedience of the law. This plainly refutes all that the Papists babble about free will. The prophet not only here prays that God would help him, because his will was weak; but he testifies, without qualification, that uprightness of heart is. the gift of the Holy Spirit. We are, moreover, taught by these words, in what the true keeping of the law consists. A great part of mankind, after having carelessly framed their life according to the Divine law, by outward obedience, think that they want nothing. But the Holy Spirit here declares that no service is acceptable to God, except that which proceeds from integrity of heart. It is as if the prophet had said, that those who are without dissimulation, and who offer to God a pure heart, yield themselves truly to Him. When it is added, that I may not be put to shame, it is intimated, that such shall be the undoubted issue as to all the proud, who, disdaining the grace of God, lean upon their own strength; and as to all hypocrites, who, for a time, parade themselves in gay colors. The amount, then, is, that unless God govern us by his Spirit, and keep us in the performance of our duty, so that our hearts may be sound in his statutes, although our shame may be hidden for a time, yea, although all men should praise us, and hold us in

tokens and fruits of that mercy, in their affliction. He prays for God's merciful kindness (v. 76), his tender mercies, v. 77.

2. The benefit he promised himself from God's lovingkindness: "Let it come to me for my comfort (v. 76); that will comfort me when nothing else will; that will comfort me whatever grieves me." Gracious souls fetch all their comfort from a gracious God, as the fountain of all happiness and joy.

3. His pleas for the benefits of God's favor. He pleads God's promise and his own confidence and complacency in that promise: "Thy law is my delight; I hope in thy word and rejoice in that hope."

78-79

Here David shows,

I. How little he valued the will—will of sinners. There were those that dealt perversely with him, that were peevish and ill-conditioned towards him, that sought advantages against him, and misconstrued all he said and did. Even those that deal most fairly may meet with those that deal perversely. But David regarded it not, for,

1. He knew it was without cause, and that for his love they were his adversaries. The causeless reproach, like the curse causeless, may be easily slighted; it does not hurt us, and therefore should not move us.

2. He could pray, in faith, that they might be ashamed of it; God's dealing favorably with him might make them ashamed to think that they had dealt perversely with him.

II. How much he valued the good-will of saints, and how desirous he was to stand right in their opinion, and keep up his interest in them and communion with them: Let those that fear thee turn to me.

80

Here is,

1. David's prayer for sincerity, that his heart might be brought to God's statutes, and that it might be sound in them, not rotten and deceitful, that he might not rest in the form of godliness, but be acquainted with the subject to the power of it,—that he might be hearty and constant in religion, and that his soul might be in health.

2. His dread of the consequences of hypocrisy: That I be not ashamed. Shame is the portion of hypocrites, either here, if it be repented of, or hereafter, if it be not: "Let my heart be sound, that I fall not into scandalous sin, that I fall not quite off from the ways of God, and so shame myself. Let my heart be sound, that I may come boldly to the throne of grace, and may lift up my face without spot at the great day."

Psalm 119

Kaph

81-84
81 My soul fainteth for thy salvation: but I hope in thy word.
82 Mine eyes fail for thy word, saying, When wilt thou comfort me?
83 For I am become like a bottle in the smoke; yet do I not forget thy statutes.
84 How many are the days of thy servant? when wilt thou execute judgment on them that persecute me?

waiting, faint with watching, sick with urgent need. Thus the sincerity and the eagerness of his desires were proved. Nothing else could satisfy him but deliverance wrought out by the hand of God, his inmost mature yearned and pined for salvation from the God of all grace, and he must have it or utterly fail. But I hope in thy word. Therefore he felt that salvation would come, for God cannot break his promise, nor disappoint the hope which his own word has excited: yea, the fulfillment of his word is near at hand when our hope is firm and our desire fervent. Hope alone can keep the soul from fainting by using the smelling bottle of the promise. Yet hope does not quench desire for a speedy answer to prayer; it increases our importunity, for it both stimulates ardor and sustains the heart under delays. To faint for salvation, and to be kept from utterly failing by the hope of it, is the frequent experience of the Christian man. We are "faint yet pursuing" hope sustains when desire exhausts. While the grace of desire throws us down, the grace of hope lifts us up again.

Verse 82. Mine eyes fail for thy word, saying, When wilt thou comfort me? His eyes gave out with eagerly gazing for the kind appearance of the Lord, while his heart in weariness cried out for speedy comfort. To read the word till the eyes can no longer see is but a small thing compared with watching for the fulfillment of the promise till the inner eyes of expectancy begin to grow dim with hope deferred. We may not set times to God, for this is to limit the Holy One of Israel; yet we may urge our suit with importunity, and make fervent enquiry as to why the promise tarries.

Verse 83. For I am become like a bottle in the smoke. The skins used for containing wine, when emptied, were hung up in the tent, and when the place reeked with smoke the skins grew black and sooty, and in the heat they became wrinkled and worn. The Psalmist's face through sorrow had become dark and dismal, furrowed and lined; indeed, his whole body had so sympathized with his sorrowing mind as to have lost its natural moisture, and to have become like a skin dried and tanned. His character had been smoked with slander, and his mind parched with persecution; he was half afraid that he would become useless and incapable through so much mental suffering, and that men would look upon him as an old worn out skin bottle, which could hold nothing and answer no purpose. What a metaphor for a man to use who was certainly a poet, a divine, and a master in Israel, if not a king, and a man after God's own heart! It is little wonder if we, commoner folk, are made to think very little of ourselves, and are filled with distress of mind. Some of us know the inner meaning of this simile, for we, too, have felt dinghy, mean, and worthless, only fit to be cast away. Very black and hot has been the smoke which has enveloped us; it seemed to come not alone from the Egyptian furnace, but from the bottomless pit; and it had a clinging power which made the soot of it fasten upon us and blacken us with miserable thoughts.

Verse 84. No one knows the appointed number of our days except the Lord, and therefore to him the appeal is made that he would not prolong them beyond his servant's strength. It cannot be the Lord's mind that his own servant should always be treated so unjustly; there must be an end to it; when would it be? When wilt thou execute judgment on them that persecute me? He had placed his case in the Lord's hands, and he prayed that sentence might be given and put into execution. He desired nothing but justice, that his character might be cleared and his persecutors silenced. He knew that God would certainly avenge Iris own elect, but the day of rescue tarried, the hours dragged heavily along, and the persecuted one cried day and night for deliverance.

Verse 85. The proud have digged pits for me, which are not after thy law. As men who hunt wild beasts are wont to make pitfalls and snares, so did David's foes endeavor to entrap him. They went laboriously and

JOHN CALVIN

admiration, yet we cannot avoid falling, at length, into dishonor and ignominy.

Psalm 119:81-88

81. My soul hath fainted for thy salvation. The Psalmist intimates that, although worn out with continual grief, and perceiving no issue to his calamities, yet trouble and weariness had not produced such a discouraging effect upon his mind, as to prevent him from always reposing with confidence in God. To bring out the meaning the more distinctly, we must begin at the second clause, which is obviously added by way of exposition. There he affirms that he trusts in God; and this is the foundation of all. But, intending to express the invincible constancy of his trust, he tells us that he patiently endured all the distresses, under which others succumb. We see some embracing with great eagerness the promises of God; but their ardor, within a short time, vanishes; or, at least, is quenched by adversity.
82. My eyes have waxed dim in looking for thy word. This verse is very similar to the preceding,—transforming to the eyes what had been said before concerning the soul. The only difference is, that, instead of longing after salvation or help, the expression, longing after God's word compromise, is here used; for salvation is an act, as it is termed; that is to say, it consists in effect, whereas a promise keeps us suspended in expectation.
83. For I have been as a bottle in the smoke. We might read the verse in one connected sentence, thus, When I was like a dried bottle, I, nevertheless, did not forget thy law. The obvious design of the Psalmist is to teach us, that, although he had been proved by severe trials, and wounded to the quick, he yet had not been withdrawn from the fear of God. In comparing himself to a bottle or bladder, he intimates that he was, as it were, parched by the continual heat of adversities. Whence we learn, that that sorrow must have been intense which reduced him to such a state of wretchedness and emaciation, that like a shriveled bottle he was almost dried up.
84. How many are the days of thy servant? etc. The Scriptures often use the word days in this sense; as, for example, "the days of Egypt," Ezekiel 30:9; "the days of Babylon," and "the days of Jerusalem," Psalm 137:7; a word which, in other places, is called "the day of visitation," Isaiah 10:3. The Psalmist does not bewail in general the transitory life of man, but he complains that the time of his state of warfare in this world had been too long protracted; and, therefore, he naturally desires that it might be brought to a termination. In expostulating with God about his trouble, he does not do so obstinately, or with a murmuring spirit; but still, in asking how long it will be necessary for him to suffer, he humbly prays that God would not delay to succor him. As to the point of his stirring him up by prayer to execute vengeance, we have elsewhere seen in what sense it was lawful for him to make such a request; namely, because the vengeance which he desired to see was such as is properly suitable to God. It is certain that he had divested himself of all the corrupt

MATTHEW HENRY

11. CAPH.

81-82
Here we have the psalmist,
I. Longing for help from heaven: My soul faints; my eyes fail. He longs for the salvation of the Lord and for his word, that is, salvation according to the word. He is not thus eager for the creatures of fancy, but for the objects of faith, salvation from the present calamities under which he was groaning and the doubts and fears which he was oppressed with. It may be understood of the coming of the Messiah, and so he speaks in the name of the Old-Testament church; the souls of the faithful even fainted to see that salvation of which the prophets testified. (1 Pet. i. 10); their eyes failed for it. Abraham saw it at a distance, and so did others, but at such a distance that it put their eyes to the stretch and they could not steadfastly see it. David was now under prevailing dejections, and, having been long so, his eyes cried our, "When wilt thou comfort me? Comfort me with thy salvation, comfort me with thy word."
II. Waiting for that help, assured that it will come, and tarrying till it come: But I hope in thy word; and but for hope the heart would break. When the eyes fail yet the faith must not; for the vision is for an appointed time, and at the end it shall speak and shall not lie.

83
David begs God would make haste to comfort him,
1. Because his affliction was great, and therefore he was an object of God's pity: Lord, make haste to help me, for I have become like a bottle in the smoke, a leathern bottle, which, if it hung any while in the smoke, was not only blackened with soot, but dried, and parched, and shriveled up. David was thus wasted by age, and sickness, and sorrow. See how affliction will mortify the strongest and stoutest of men!
2. Because, though his affliction was great, yet it had not driven him from his duty, and therefore he was within the reach of God's promise: Yet do I not forget thy statutes. Whatever our outward condition is we must not cool in our affection to the word of God, nor let that slip out of our minds; no care, no grief, must crowd that out.

84
Here,
1. David prays against the instruments of his troubles, that God would make haste to execute judgment on those that persecuted him. He prays not for power to avenge himself (he bore no malice to any), but that God would take to himself the vengeance that belonged to him, and would repay (Rom. xii. 19), as the God that sits in the throne judging right.
2. He pleads the long continuance of his trouble: "How many are the days of thy servant? The days of my life are but few therefore let them not all be miserable, and therefore make haste to appear for me against my enemies, before I go hence and shall be seen no more."

Psalm 119

85-89
85 The proud have digged pits for me, which are not after thy law.
86 All thy commandments are faithful: they persecute me wrongfully; help thou me.
87 They had almost consumed me upon earth; but I forsook not thy precepts.
88 Quicken me after thy loving kindness; so shall I keep the testimony of thy mouth.

cunningly to work to ruin him, "they digged pits"; not one, but many. If one would not take him, perhaps another would, and so they digged again and again. One would think that such haughty people would not have soiled their fingers with digging; but they swallowed their pride in hopes of swallowing their victim. Whereas they ought to have been ashamed of such meanness, they were conscious of no shame, but, on the contrary, were proud of their cleverness; proud of setting a trap for a godly man. "Which are not after thy law." Neither the men nor their pits were according to the divine law: they were cruel and crafty deceivers, and their pits were contrary to the Levitical law, and contrary to the command which bids us love our neighbor. If men would keep to the statutes of the Lord, they would lift the fallen out of the pit, or fill up the pit so that none might stumble into it; but they would never spend a moment in working injury to others.
Verse 86. All thy commandments are faithful. He had no fault to find with God's law, even though he had fallen into sad trouble through obedience to it. Whatever the command might cost him it was worth it; he felt that God's way might be rough, but it was right; it might make him enemies, but still it was his best friend. He believed that in the end God's command would turn out to his own profit, and that he should be no loser by obeying it. They persecute me wrongfully. The fault lay with his persecutors, and neither with his God nor with himself. He had done no injury to anyone, nor acted otherwise than according to truth and justice; therefore he confidently appeals to his God, and cries, "Help thou me." This is a golden prayer, as precious as it is short. The words are few, but the meaning is full. Help was needed that the persecuted one might avoid the snare, might bear up under reproach, and might act so prudently as to baffle his foes. God's help is our hope.
Verse 87. They had almost consumed me upon earth. His foes had almost destroyed him so as to make him altogether fail. If they could they would have eaten him, or burned him alive; anything so that they could have made a full end of the good man. Evidently he had fallen under their power to a large extent, and they had so used that power that he was well nigh consumed. He was almost gone from off the earth; but almost is not altogether, and so he escaped by the skin of his teeth. The lions are chained: they can rage no further than our God permits. The Psalmist perceives the limit of their power: they could only touch his earthly life and earthly goods. Upon earth they almost ate him up, but he had an eternal portion which they could not even nibble at. "But I forsook not thy precepts." Nothing could drive him from obeying the Lord. If we stick to the precepts we shall be rescued by the promises. If ill usage could have driven the oppressed saint from the way of right the purpose of the wicked would have been answered, and we should have heard no more of David. If we are resolved to die sooner than forsake the Lord, we may depend upon it that we shall not die, but shall live to see the overthrow of them that hate us.
Verse 88. Quicken me after thy loving kindness. Most wise, most blessed prayer! If we are revived in our own personal piety we shall be out of reach of our assailants. Our best protection from tempters and persecutors is more life. Lovingkindness itself cannot do us greater service than by making us to have life more abundantly. When we are quickened we are able to bear affliction, to baffle cunning, and to conquer sin. We look to the lovingkindness of God as the source of spiritual revival, and we entreat the Lord to quicken us, not according to our deserts, but after the boundless energy of his grace. What a blessed word is this "loving kindness." Take it to pieces, and admire its double force of love. "So shall I keep the testimony of thy mouth." If quickened by the Holy Ghost we shall be sure to exhibit a holy character.
Verse 89. For ever, O LORD, thy word is settled in heaven. The strain is more joyful, for experience has given the sweet singer a comfortable

affections of the flesh, that he might, with a pure and undisturbed zeal, desire God's judgment. He, however, in this passage, only wishes in general to be delivered by the hand of God from the wrongs which were inflicted upon him, without adjudging to perdition his adversaries; for he was quite contented, provided God appeared to defend him.

85. The proud have digged pits for me. He complains that he had been circumvented by the frauds and artifices of his enemies; as if he had said, They have not only endeavored to injure me by open force and the violence of the sword, but have also maliciously sought to destroy me by snares and secret arts. The additional clause, which thing is not according to thy Law, is introduced as an argument, to excite God to exercise his mercy; for he is the more inclined to succor his servants, when he sees that the attempts made upon their welfare involve the violation of his own Law.

86. All thy commandments are truth. In this verse he again confirms the statement, That, in whatever ways he was afflicted, his mind had not been distracted by various devices, because, trusting in the word of God, he never doubted of his assistance.

In the first place, he tells us, that the consideration, by which he was armed for repelling all assaults, was this, That the faithful, under the conduct of God, engage in a prosperous warfare, the salvation which they hope for from his word being absolutely certain. For this reason he declares, that the commandments of God are true; by which encomium he teaches us, that those who rely upon the word of God are out of all danger; and he lays down this truth, that such a support may always sustain our courage.

In the second place, he complains of the treachery of his enemies, as he declared before.

87. They have almost consumed me upon the earth. He repeats, in somewhat different words, what he had spoken a little before, that, although he had been sorely tempted, he had nevertheless kept his footing, because he had not given up with true religion. A single declaration of this fact would have been enough for those who are perfect; but if we call to mind our own weakness, we will readily confess that it was not unworthy of being repeatedly stated. We not only forget the law of God when we are shaken by extreme conflicts, but the greater part lose their courage even before they engage in the conflict.

88. Quicken me according to thy goodness. This verse contains nothing new. In the beginning of it David represents his life as depending on God's mercy, not only because he was conscious of human frailty, but because he saw himself daily exposed to death in multiplied forms, or rather because he was convinced, that were God's power withdrawn from him, he would be laid prostrate as if he were dead. He next promises, that when he shall be again restored to life, he will not be ungrateful, but will duly acknowledge this as a blessing from God, and that not only with the tongue, but also in his whole life. As the various instances in which God succors us and delivers us from dangers are so many new lives, it is reasonable that we should dedicate to his service whatever additional

85-87

David's state was herein a type and figure of the state both of Christ and Christians that he was grievously persecuted; as there are many of his psalms, so there are many of the verses of this psalm, which complain of this, as those here. Here observe,

I. The account he gives of his persecutors and their malice against him.

1. They were proud, and in their pride they persecuted him, glorying in this, that they could trample upon one who was so much cried up, and hoping to raise themselves on his ruins.

2. They were unjust: They persecuted him wrongfully; so far was he from giving them any provocation that he had studied to oblige them; but for his love they were his adversaries.

3. They were spiteful: They dug pits for him, which intimates that they were deliberate in their designs against him.

4. They carried on their designs against him so far that they had almost consumed him upon earth; they went near to ruin him and all his interests.

II. His application to God in his persecuted state.

1. He acknowledges the truth and goodness of his religion, though he suffered: "However it be, all thy commandments are faithful, and therefore, whatever I lose for my observance of them, I know I shall not lose by it."

2. He begs that God would stand by him, and succor him: "They persecute me; help thou me; help me under my troubles, that I may bear them patiently, and as becomes me, and may still hold fast my integrity, and in due time help me out of my troubles."

III. His adherence to his duty notwithstanding all the malice of his persecutors (v. 87): But I forsook not thy precepts. That which they aimed at was to frighten him from the ways of God, but they could not prevail; he would sooner forsake all that was dear to him in this world than forsake the word of God, would sooner lose his life than lose the comfort of doing his duty.

88

Here is,

1. David in care to be found in the way of his duty. His constant desire and design are to keep the testimony of God's mouth, to keep to it as his rule and to keep hold of it as his confidence and portion for ever. This we must keep, whatever we lose.

2. David at prayer for divine grace to assist him therein: "Quicken me after thy lovingkindness (make me alive and make me lively), so shall I keep thy testimonies," implying that otherwise he should not keep them. He had prayed before, Quicken me in thy righteousness (v. 40); but here, Quicken me after thy lovingkindness. The surest token of God's good-will toward us is his good work in us.

Psalm 119

Lamedh

89-92
89 For ever, O LORD, thy word is settled in heaven.
90 Thy faithfulness is unto all generations: thou hast established the earth, and it abideth.
91 They continue this day according to thine ordinances: for all are thy servants.
92 Unless thy law had been my delights, I should then have perished in mine affliction.

knowledge of the word of the Lord, and this makes a glad theme. After tossing about on a sea of trouble the Psalmist here leaps to shore and stands upon a rock. Jehovah's word is not fickle nor uncertain; it is settled, determined, fixed, sure, immovable. Man's teachings change so often that there is never time for them to be settled; but the Lord's word is from of old the same, and will remain unchanged eternally. Some men are never happier than when they are unsettling everything and everybody; but God's mind is not with them. The power and glory of heaven have confirmed each sentence which the mouth of the Lord has spoken, and so confirmed it that to all eternity it must stand the same,—settled in heaven, where nothing can reach it. In the former section David's soul fainted, but here the good man looks out of self and perceives that the Lord fainteth not, neither is weary, neither is there any failure in his word.

Verse 90. Thy faithfulness is unto all generations. This is an additional glory: God is not affected by the lapse of ages; he is not only faithful to one man throughout his lifetime, but to his children's children after him, yea, and to all generations so long as they keep his covenant and remember his commandments to do them. The promises are ancient things, yet they are not worn out by centuries of use, for the divine faithfulness endureth for ever. He who succored his servants thousands of years ago still shows himself strong on the behalf of all them that trust in him.

Verse 91. They continue this day according to thine ordinances. Because the Lord has bid the universe abide, therefore it stands, and all its laws continue to operate with precision and power. Because the might of God is ever present to maintain them, therefore do all things continue. The word which spake all things into existence has supported them till now, and still supports them both in being and in well being. God's ordinance is the reason for the continued existence of creation. What important forces these ordinances are!

Verse 92. Unless thy law had been my delights, I should then have perished in mine affliction. That word which has preserved the heavens and the earth also preserves the people of God in their time of trial. With that word we are charmed; it is a mine of delight to us. We take a double and treble delight in it, and derive a multiplied delight from it, and this stands us in good stead when all other delights are taken from us. We should have felt ready to lie down and die of our griefs if the spiritual comforts of God's word had not uplifted us; but by their sustaining influence we have been borne above all the depressions and despairs which naturally grow out of severe affliction. Some of us can set our seal to this statement. Our affliction, if it had not been for divine grace, would have crushed us out of existence, so that we should have perished. In our darkest seasons nothing has kept us from desperation but the promise of the Lord: yea, at times nothing has stood between us and self destruction save faith in the eternal word of God. When worn with pain until the brain has become dazed and the reason well nigh extinguished, a sweet text has whispered to us its heart cheering assurance, and our poor struggling mind has reposed upon the bosom of God. That which was our delight in prosperity has been our light in adversity; that which in the day kept us from presuming has in the night kept us from perishing. This verse contains a mournful supposition "unless"; describes a horrible condition—"perished in mine affliction"; and implies a glorious deliverance, for he did not die, but live to proclaim the honors of the word of God.

Verse 93. I will never forget thy precepts: for with them thou hast quickened me. When we have felt the quickening power of a precept we never can forget it. We may read it, learn it, repeat it, and think we have it, and yet it may slip out of our minds; but if it has once given us life or

JOHN CALVIN

time is allotted to us in this world. When the law is called the testimony of God's mouth, by this eulogium its authority is very plainly asserted.

Psalm 119:89-96

89. Thy word, O Jehovah I endure for ever. As we see nothing constant or of long continuance upon earth, he elevates our minds to heaven, that they may fix their anchor there. David, no doubt, might have said, as he has done in many other places, that the whole order of the world bears testimony to the steadfastness of God's word—that word which is most true. But as there is reason to fear that the minds of the godly would hang in uncertainty if they rested the proof of God's truth upon the state of the world, in which such manifold disorders prevail; by placing God's truth in the heavens, he allots to it a habitation subject to no changes. That no person then may estimate God's word from the various vicissitudes which meet his eye in this world, heaven is tacitly set in opposition to the earth. Our salvation, as if it had been said, being shut up in God's word, is not subject to change, as all earthly things are, but is anchored in a safe and peaceful haven.
90. Thy truth is from generation to generation. In this verse the Psalmist repeats and confirms the same sentiment. He expressly teaches, that although the faithful live for a short time as strangers upon earth, and soon pass away, yet their life is not perishable, since they are begotten again of an incorruptible seed. He, however, proceeds still farther. He had before enjoined us to pierce by faith into heaven, because we will find nothing in the world on which we can assuredly rest; and now he again teaches us, by experience, that though the world is subject to revolutions, yet in it bright and signal testimonies to the truth of God shine forth, so that the steadfastness of his word is not exclusively confined to heaven, but comes down even to us who dwell upon the earth. For this reason, it is added, that the earth continues steadfast, even as it was established by God at the beginning. Lord, as if it had been said, even in the earth we see thy truth reflected as it were in a mirror; for though it is suspended in the midst of the sea, yet it continues to remain in the same state.
91. By thy judgments they continue to this day. In using the term judgments, he makes an allusion to the law, intimating, that the same regard to rectitude which is exhibited in the law is brightly displayed in every part; of God's procedure. From this it follows, that men are very perverse, when, by their unbelief, they do what they can to shake and impair the faithfulness of God, upon which all creatures repose; and, moreover, when by their rebellion they impeach his righteousness, and deny the authority of his commands, upon which the stability of the whole world depends.
92. Had not thy law been my delight. The prophet continues to prosecute almost the same theme; affirming, that he would have been undone, had he not in his calamities sought consolation from the law of God. The prophet declares that he was grievously oppressed by a weight of afflictions enough to overwhelm him; but that the consolation which he derived

MATTHEW HENRY

12. LAMED.

89-91
Here,
1. The psalmist acknowledges the unchangeableness of the word of God and of all his counsels: "For ever, O Lord! thy word is settled. Thou art for ever thyself (so some read it); thou art the same, and with thee there is no variableness, and this is a proof of it. Thy word, by which the heavens were made, is settled there in the abiding products of it;" or the settling of God's word in heaven is opposed to the changes and revolutions that are here upon earth.
2. He produces, for proof of it, the constancy of the course of nature: Thou hast established the earth for ever and it abides; it is what it was at first made, and where it was at first placed, poised with its own weight, and notwithstanding the convulsions in its own bowels, the agitations of the sea that is interwoven with it, and the violent concussions of the atmosphere that surrounds it, it remains unmoved. "They" (the heavens and the earth and all the hosts of both) "continue to this day according to thy ordinances; they remain in the posts wherein thou hast set them; they fill up the place assigned them, and answer the purposes for which they were intended."

92
Here is,
1. The great distress that David was in. He was in affliction, and ready to perish in his affliction, not likely to die, so much as likely to despair; he was ready to give up all for gone, and to look upon himself as cut off from God's sight; he therefore admires the goodness of God to him, that he had not perished.
2. His support in this distress. God's law was his delight. It had been so formerly, and the remembrance of that was a comfort to him, as it afforded him a good evidence of his integrity.

93
Here is,
1. A very good resolution: "I will never forget thy precepts, but will always retain a remembrance of and regard to thy word as my rule." It is a resolution for perpetuity, never to be altered.
2. A very good reason for it: "For by them thou hast quickened me; not only they are quickening, but they have been so to me; I have found them so." Those speak best of the things of God who speak by experience, who can say that by the word the spiritual life has been begun in them, maintained and strengthened in them, excited and comforted in them.

94
Here,
1. David claims relation to God: "I am thine, devoted to thee and owned by thee, thine in covenant." He

Psalm 119

93-96
93 I will never forget thy precepts: for with them thou hast quickened me.
94 I am thine, save me: for I have sought thy precepts.
95 The wicked have waited for me to destroy me: but I will consider thy testimonies.
96 I have seen an end of all perfection: but thy commandment is exceeding broad.

renewed that life, there is no fear of its falling from our recollection. Experience teaches, and teaches effectually. How blessed a thing it is to have the precepts written on the heart with the golden pea of experience, and graven on the memory with the divine stylus of grace. Forgetfulness is a great evil in holy things; we see here the man of God fighting against it, and feeling sure of victory because he knew the life giving energy of the word in his own soul. That which quickens the heart is sure to quicken the memory. It seems singular that he should ascribe quickening to the precepts, and yet it lies in them and in all the words of the Lord alike. It is to be noted that when the Lord raised the dead he addressed to them the word of command. He said, "Lazarus, come forth," or "Maid, arise." We need not fear to address gospel precepts to dead sinners, since by them the Spirit gives them life. Remark that the Psalmist does not say that the precepts quickened him, but that the Lord quickened him by their means: thus he traces the life from tile channel to the source, and places the glory where it is due. Yet at the same time he prized the instruments of the blessing, and resolved never to forget them. He had already remembered them when he likened himself to a bottle in the smoke, and now he feels that whether in the smoke or in the fire the memory of the Lord's precepts shall never depart from him.

Verse 94. I am thine, save me. A comprehensive prayer with a prevailing argument. Consecration is a good plea for preservation. If we are conscious that we are the Lord's we may be confident that he will save us. We are the Lord's by creation, election, redemption, surrender, and acceptance; and hence our firm hope and assured belief that he will save us. A man will surely save his own child: Lord, save me. The need of salvation is better seen by the Lord's people than by any others, and hence their prayer—"save me"; they know that only God can save them, and hence they cry to him alone; and they know that no merit can be found in themselves, and hence they urge a reason fetched from the grace of God,—"I am thine." "For I have sought thy precepts." Thus had he proved that he was the Lord's.

Verse 95. The wicked have waited for me to destroy me: but I will consider thy testimonies. They were like wild beasts crouching by the way, or highway men waylaying a defenseless traveler; but the Psalmist went on his way without considering them, for he was considering something better, namely, the witness or testimony which God has borne to the sons of men. He did not allow the malice of the wicked to take him off from his holy study of the divine word. He was so calm that he could "consider"; so holy that he loved to consider the Lord's "testimonies"; so victorious over all their plots that he did not allow them to drive him from his pious contemplations. If the enemy cannot cause us to withdraw our thoughts from holy study, or our feet from holy walking, or our hearts from holy aspirations, lie has met with poor success in his assaults. The wicked are the natural enemies of holy men and holy thoughts; if they could, they would not only damage us but destroy us, and if they cannot do this today they will wait for further opportunities, ever hoping that their evil designs may be compassed. They have waited hitherto in vain, and they will have to wait much longer yet; for if we are so unmoved that we do not even give them a thought their hope of destroying us must be a very poor one.

Verse 96. I have seen an end of all perfection. He had seen its limit, for it went but a little way; he had seen its evaporation under the trials of life, its detection under the searching glance of truth, its exposure by the confession of the penitent. There is no perfection beneath the moon. Perfect men, in the absolute sense of the word, live only in a perfect world. Some men see no end to their own perfection, but this is because they are perfectly blind. The experienced believer has seen an end of all perfection in himself, in his brethren, in the best man's best works. It

JOHN CALVIN

from the Divine Law in such desperate circumstances, was as life to him.

93. I will never forget thy statutes. This verse contains a thanksgiving. As the law of the Lord had preserved him, he engages that he will never forget it. Yet he, at the same time, admonishes himself and others how necessary it is to cherish in the heart the remembrance of the Divine Law; for though we have found from experience its life-giving power, yet we easily allow it to pass from our memories, and on this account God afterwards justly punishes us, by leaving us for a long time to languish in our sadness.

94. I am thine, save me. In the first place, he takes encouragement to pray from the consideration, that he is one of God's own stamp and coinage, as we speak. In the second place, he proves that he is God's from the fact of his keeping his commandments. This ought not, however, to be understood as if he boasted of any merit which he possessed; as, in dealing with men, it is customary to adduce something meritorious which we have done as an argument for obtaining what we desire:—I have always loved and esteemed you, I have always studied to promote your honor and advantage; my service has always been ready at your command. But David rather brings forward the unmerited grace of God, and that alone; for no man, by any efforts of his own, acquires the high honor of being under the protection of God—an honor which proceeds solely from his free adoption. The blessing which God had conferred upon him is therefore here adduced as an argument why he should not forsake the work which he had commenced. When he affirms, that he was earnestly intent upon the Divine commandments, that also depended upon the Divine calling; for he did not begin to apply his mind to God's commandments before he was called and received into his household. As he desires, in this verse, that the Lord would save him, so, in the next verse, he expresses the need he had of being saved, saying, that the wicked sought for him to destroy him; by which he, at the same time, declares the constancy of his godliness, inasmuch as he then set his mind upon the law of God—a point worthy of special notice. Those who, at other times, would the forward and willing to follow God, know not to what side to turn themselves when they are assailed by the wicked, and, in that case, are very prone to follow unhallowed counsel. It is therefore a great virtue to do God the honor of resting contented with his promises alone, when the wicked conspire for our destruction, and when, to all human appearance, our life is in jeopardy. To consider God's testimonies is, in this place, equivalent to applying our minds to the word of God, which sustains us against all assaults, effectually allays all fears, and restrains us from following any perverse counsels.

96. In all perfection, I have seen the end. The prophet again, using other words, commends the same truth which he had taught in the first verse of this part—that the word of God is not subject to change, because it is elevated far above the perishable elements of this world. He here asserts, that there is nothing under heaven so perfect and stable, or so complete, in all respects, as not to have an end; and that the Divine word

MATTHEW HENRY

does not say, Thou art mine (as Dr. Manton observes), though that follows of course, because that were a higher challenge; but, I am thine, expressing himself in a more humble and dutiful way of resignation; nor does he say, I am thus, but, I am thine, not pleading his own good property or qualification, but God's propriety in him: "I am thine, not my own, not the world's."

2. He proves his claim: "I have sought thy precepts; I have carefully enquired concerning my duty and diligently endeavored to do it." This will be the best evidence that we belong to God; all that are his, though they have not found perfection, are seeking it.

3. He improves his claim: "I am thine; save me; save me from sin, save me from ruin." Those that have in sincerity given up themselves to God to be his may be sure that he will protect them and preserve them to his heavenly kingdom, Mal. iii. 18.

95

Here,

1. David complains of the malice of his enemies: The wicked (and none but such would be enemies to so good a man) have waited for me to destroy me. They were very cruel, and aimed at no less than his destruction; they were very crafty, and sought all opportunities to do him a mischief; and they were confident (they expected, so some read it), that they should destroy him; they thought themselves sure of their prey.

2. He comforts himself in the word of God as his protection: "While they are contriving my destruction, I consider thy testimonies, which secure to me my salvation." God's testimonies are then likely to be our support, when we consider them, and dwell in our thoughts upon them.

96

Here we have David's testimony from his own experience,

1. Of the vanity of the world and its insufficiency to make us happy: I have seen an end of all perfection. Poor perfection which one sees an end of! Yet such are all those things in this world which pass for perfections. David, in his time, had seen Goliath, the strongest, overcome, Asahel, the swiftest, overtaken, Ahithophel, the wisest, befooled, Absalom, the fairest, deformed; and, in short, he had seen an end of perfection, of all perfection. He saw it by faith; he saw it by observation.

2. Of the fullness of the word of God, and its sufficiency for our satisfaction: But thy commandment is broad, exceedingly broad. The word of God reaches to all cases, to all times. The divine law lays a restraint upon the whole man, is designed to sanctify us wholly. The divine promise (for that also is commanded) extends itself to all our burdens, wants, and grievances, and has that in it which will make a portion and happiness for us when we have seen an end of all perfection.

Psalm 119

Mem

97-100
97 O how love I thy law! it is my meditation all the day.
98 Thou through thy commandments hast made me wiser than mine enemies: for they are ever with me.
99 I have more understanding than all my teachers: for thy testimonies are my meditation.
100 I understand more than the ancients, because I keep thy precepts.

would be well if some who profess to be perfect could even see the beginning of perfection, for we fear they cannot have begun aright, or they would not talk so exceeding proudly.

Verse 97. O how love I thy law! It is a note of exclamation. He loves so much that he must express his love, and in making the attempt he perceives that it is inexpressible—and therefore cries, "O how I love!" We not only reverence but love the law, we obey it out of love, and even when it chides us for disobedience we love it none the less. The law is God's law, and therefore it is our love. We love it for its holiness, and pine to be holy; we love it for its wisdom, and study to be wise; we love it for its perfection, and long to be perfect. Those who know the power of the gospel perceive an infinite loveliness in the law as they see it fulfilled and embodied in Christ Jesus.

Verse 98. Thou through thy commandments hast made me wiser than mine enemies. The commands were his book, but God was his teacher. The letter can make us knowing, but only the divine Spirit can make us wise. Wisdom is knowledge put to practical use. Wisdom comes to us through obedience: "If any man will do his will he shall know of the doctrine." We learn not only from promise, and doctrine, and sacred history, but also from precept and command; in fact, from the commandments we gather the most practical wisdom and that which enables us best to cope with our adversaries. A holy life is the highest wisdom and the surest defense.

Verse 99. I have more understanding than all my teachers. That which the Lord had taught him had been useful in the camp, and now he finds it equally valuable in the schools. Our teachers are not always to be trusted; in fact, we may not follow any of them implicitly, for God holds us to account for our personal judgments. It behooves us then to follow closely the chart of the Word of God, that we may be able to save the vessel when even the pilot errs. If our teachers should be in all things sound and safe, they will be right glad for us to excel them, and they will ever be ready to own that the teaching of the Lord is better than any teaching which they can give us. Disciples of Christ who sit at his feet are often better skilled in divine things than doctors of divinity.

Verse 100. I understand more than the ancients, because I keep thy precepts. The men of old age, and the men of old time, were outdone by the holier and more youthful learner. He had been taught to observe in heart and life the precepts of the Lord, and this was more than the most venerable sinner had ever learned, more than the philosopher of antiquity had so much as aspired to know. He had the word with him, and so outstripped his foes; lie meditated on it, and so outran his friends; he practiced it, and so outshone his elders. The instruction derived from Holy Scripture is useful in many directions, superior from many points of view, unrivalled everywhere and in every way. As our soul may make her boast in the Lord, so may we boast in his word. "There is none like it: give it me," said David as to Goliath's sword, and we may say the same as to the word of the Lord. If men prize antiquity they have it here. The ancients are had in high repute, but what did they all know compared with that which we perceive in the divine precepts? "The old is better" says one: but the oldest of all is the best of all, and what is that but the word of the Ancient of days

Verse 101. I have refrained my feet from every evil way, that I might keep thy word. There is no treasuring up the holy word unless there is a casting out of all unholiness: if we keep the good word we must let go the evil. David had zealously watched his steps and put a check upon his conduct,—he had refrained his feet. No one evil way could entice him, for he knew that if he went astray but in one road he had practically left the way of righteousness, therefore he avoided every false way. The bypaths were smooth and flowery, but he knew right well that they were alone possesses such amplitude as to surpass all bounds and limits.

Psalm 119:97-104

97. O how have I loved thy law! Not contented with a simple affirmation, the prophet exclaims, by way of interrogation, that he was inflamed with incredible love to the law of God; and, in proof of this, he adds, that he was continually engaged in meditating upon it. If any person boasts that he loves the Divine Law, and yet neglects the study of it, and applies his mind to other things, he betrays the grossest hypocrisy; for the love of the law, and especially such an ardent love of it as the prophet here expresses, always produces continual meditation upon it. And, assuredly, unless God's law inflame and ravish our hearts with the love of it, many allurements will quickly steal upon us, and lead us away to vanity. The prophet, then, here commends such a love of the law, as, possessing all our senses, effectually excludes all the deceits and corruption's to which we are otherwise too much inclined.
98. Thou hast made me wiser than my adversaries. He here declares, that he was more learned than his adversaries, his instructors, and the aged, because he was a scholar of God's law. It is in a different sense that he describes himself as endued with understanding above his adversaries, from that in which he describes himself as wiser than his teachers. He surpassed his enemies, because their cunning and artifices availed them nothing when they employed these to the utmost to effect his destruction. The malice of the wicked is always goading them to do mischief; and as they are often artful and deceitful, we are afraid lest our simplicity should be imposed upon by their deceits, unless we use the same crafts and underhand dealings which they practice. Accordingly, the prophet glories, that he found in God's law enough to enable him to escape all their snares.
101. I have restrained my feet from every evil path He intimates that he proclaimed war against every vice, that he might wholly devote himself to the service of God. From this we learn the profitable lesson, that in order to our keeping God's Law, we must, from the commencement, beware lest our feet should step aside into crooked by-paths; for with a nature so corrupted as ours is, amidst so many allurements, and with minds so fickle, we are in the greatest danger of being led astray; yea, it is a rare miracle if any man hold on in his life in a right course, without turning aside in one direction or another. The faithful, therefore, have need to exercise the greatest circumspection, in order to keep their feet from going astray.
In the next verse, David commends his own constancy in observing the Law. He declares that ever since he had learned from God the right manner of living, he had pursued the right course. As the way is so slippery, and our feet so feeble, and our whole disposition so prone to go astray after innumerable errors, no small exertions are requisite on our part, in order to avoid declining from God's judgments. But we must attend to the manner of teaching to which the Psalmist refers; for

13. MEM.

97
Here is,
1. David's inexpressible love to the word of God: O how love I thy law! He protests his affection to the word of God with a holy vehemency; he found that love to it in his heart which, considering the corruption of his nature and the temptations of the world, he could not but wonder at, and at that grace which had wrought it in him.
2. An unexceptionable evidence of this. What we love we love to think of; by this it appeared that David loved the word of God that it was his meditation. He not only read the book of the law, but digested what he read in his thoughts.

98-100
We have here an account of David's learning, not that of the Egyptians, but of the Israelites indeed.
I. The good method by which he got it. In his youth he minded business in the country as a shepherd; from his youth he minded business in the court and camp. Which way then could he get any great stock of learning? He tells us here how he came by it; he had it from God as the author: Thou hast made me wise. All true wisdom is from God. He had it by the word of God as the means, by his commandments and his testimonies. These are able to make us wise to salvation and to furnish the man of God for every good work.
1. These David took for his constant companions: "They are ever with me, ever in my mind, ever in my eye." A good man, wherever he goes, carries his Bible along with him, if not in his hands, yet in his head and in his heart.
2. These he took for the delightful subject of his thoughts; they were his meditation, not only as matters of speculation for his entertainment, as scholars meditate on their notions, but as matters of concern, for his right management, as men of business think of their business, that they may do it in the best manner.
3. These he took for the commanding rules of all his actions: I keep thy precepts, that is, I make conscience of doing my duty in every thing. The best way to improve in knowledge is to abide and abound in all the instances of serious godliness.
II. The great eminency he attained to in it. By studying and practicing God's commandments, and making them his rule, he learnt to behave himself wisely in all his ways, 1 Sam. xviii. 14. 2. He outwitted his enemies; God, by these means, made him wiser to baffle and defeat their designs against him than they were to lay them.

101
Here is,
1. David's care to avoid the ways of sin: "I have refrained my feet from the evil ways they were ready

Psalm 119

101-104
101 I have refrained my feet from every evil way, that I might keep thy word.
102 I have not departed from thy judgments: for thou hast taught me.
103 How sweet are thy words unto my taste! yea, sweeter than honey to my mouth!
104 Through thy precepts I get understanding: therefore I hate every false way.

evil, and so he turned his feet away, and held on along the strait and thorny pathway which leads to God. It is a pleasure to look back upon self conquests,—"I have refrained," and a greater delight still to know that we did this out of no mere desire to stand well with our fellows, but with the one motive of keeping the law of the Lord. Sin avoided that obedience may be perfected is the essence of this verse; or it may be that the Psalmist would teach us that there is no real reverence for the book where there is not carefulness to avoid every transgression of its precepts. How can we keep God's word if we do not keep our own works from becoming vile?

Verse 102. I have not departed from thy judgments: for thou hast taught me. They are well taught whom God teaches. What we learn from the Lord we never forget. God's instruction has a practical effect—we follow his way when he teaches us; and it has an abiding effect,—we do not depart from holiness. Read this verse in connection with the preceding and you get the believer's "I have," and his "I have not": he is good both positively and negatively. What he did, namely, "refrained his feet," preserved him from doing that which otherwise he might have done, namely, "departed from thy judgments." He who is careful not to go an inch aside will not leave the road. He who never touches the intoxicating cup will never be drunk. He who never utters an idle word will never be profane. If we begin to depart a little we can never tell where we shall end. The Lord brings us to persevere in holiness by abstinence from the beginning of sin; but whatever be the method he is the worker of our perseverance, and to him be all the glory.

Verse 103. How sweet are thy words into my taste. He had not only heard the words of God, but fed upon them: they affected his palate as well as his ear. God's words are many and varied, and the whole of them make up what we call "the word": David loved them each one, individually, arid the whole of them as a whole; he tasted an indescribable sweetness in them. He expresses the fact of their sweetness, but as he cannot express the degree of their sweetness he cries, "How sweet!" Being God's words they were divinely sweet to God's servant; he who put the sweetness into them had prepared the taste of his servant to discern and enjoy it. David makes no distinction between promises and precepts, doctrines and threatenings; they are all included in God's words, and all are precious in his esteem. Oh for a deep love to all that the Lord has revealed, whatever form it may take. Yea, sweeter than honey to my mouth. When he did not only eat but also speak the word, by instructing others, he felt an increased delight in it. The sweetest of all temporal things fall short of the infinite deliciousness of the eternal word. Honey itself is outstripped of the Lord Widen the Psalmist fed on it he in sweetness by the word found it sweet; but when he bore witness of it it became sweeter still. How wise it will be on our part to keep the word on our palate by meditation and on our tongue by confession. It must be sweet to our taste when we think of it, or it will not be Sweet to our mouth when we talk of it.

Verse 104. Through thy precepts I get understanding. God's direction is our instruction. Obedience to the divine will begets wisdom of mind and action. As God's way is always best, those who follow it are sure to be justified by the result. If the Lawgiver were foolish his law would be the same, and obedience to such a law would involve us in a thousand mistakes; but as the reverse is the case, we may count ourselves happy to have such a wise, prudent, and beneficial law to be the rule of our lives. We are wise if we obey and we grow wise by obeying!

Verse 105. Thy word is a lamp unto my feet. We are walkers through the city of this world, and we are often called to go out into its darkness; let us never venture there without the light giving word, lest we slip with our feet. Each man should use the word of God personally, practically, and though all, without exception, to whom God's word is preached, are taught, yet scarce one in ten so much as tastes it; yea, scarce one in a hundred profits to the extent of being enabled, thereby, to proceed in a right course to the end. A peculiar manner of teaching is, therefore, here pointed out—that which consists in God's drawing his chosen people to himself. I have been brought, as if the Psalmist had said, into the way of salvation, and preserved in it by the secret influence of the Holy Spirit.

103. O how sweet have been thy words to my palate! He again repeats what he had previously stated in different words, that he was so powerfully attracted by the sweetness of the Divine Law, as to have no desire after any other delight. It is possible that a man may be affected with reverence towards the Law of God; but no one will cheerfully follow it, save he who has tasted this sweetness. God requires from us no slavish service: he will have us to come to him cheerfully, and this is the very reason why the prophet commends the sweetness of God's word so often in this psalm.

104. By thy statutes I have acquired understanding. The prophet seems here to invert the order he has just now laid down. He observed that he had kept his feet from going astray, that he might observe God's Law, and now he institutes a contrary order, beginning with the observance of the Law; for he declares that he had been taught by the word of God before he amended his faults.

Yet these two things are not inconsistent,—that the faithful should withdraw themselves from their wanderings, in order to frame their life according to the rule of God's word, and that when they are already advanced a considerable way in a holy life, the fear of God being then more vigorous in them, they should regard all vices with more intense hatred. The beginning of a good life, unquestionably, is when a man endeavors to purge himself from vices; and the more a man has made progress in a good life, he will burn with a, proportionate zeal in his detestation of vices and in shunning them. Moreover, we are taught by the words of the prophet, that the reason why men are so involved in falsehoods, and entangled in perverse errors, is, because they have not learned wisdom from the word of God. As the whole world are given to folly, those who wander astray plead in excuse, that it is difficult for them to guard against the allurements of vice. But the remedy will be near at hand, if we follow the counsel of the prophet; that is to say, if, instead of leaning on our own wisdom, we seek understanding from the word of God, in which he not only shows what is right. but also fortifies our minds, and puts us on our guard against all the deceits of Satan, and all the impostures of the world. Would to God that, at the present day, this were thoroughly impressed on the minds of all who boast themselves of being Christians; for then they would not be continually driven about, as the greater part of them are, with such inconstancy, according to the conflicting impulses of prevailing opinions. As Satan is so sedulously exerting himself to spread abroad the mists of error, let us apply ourselves with the greater earnestness to the acquisition of this wisdom.

to step aside into. I checked myself and drew back as soon as I was aware that I was entering into temptation." Though it was a broad way, a green way, a pleasant way, and a way that many walked in, yet, being a sinful way, it was an evil way, and he refrained his feet from it, foreseeing the end of that way.

2. His care to be found in the way of duty; That I might keep thy word, and never transgress it.

102

Here is,

1. David's constancy in his religion. He had not departed from God's judgments; he had not chosen any other rule than the word of God, nor had he willfully deviated from that rule. A constant adherence to the ways of God in trying times will be a good evidence of our integrity.

2. The cause of his constancy: "For thou hast taught me; that is, they were divine instructions that I learned; I was satisfied that the doctrine was of God, and therefore I stuck to it." Or rather, "It was divine grace in my heart that enabled me to receive those instructions."

103-104

Here is,

1. The wonderful pleasure and delight which David took in the word of God; it was sweet to his taste, sweeter than honey. There is such a thing as a spiritual taste, an inward savor and relish of divine things.

2. The unspeakable profit and advantage he gained by the word of God.

(1.) It helped him to a good head: "Through thy precepts I get understanding to discern between truth and falsehood, good and evil, so as not to mistake either in the conduct of my own life or in advising others."

(2.) It helped him to a good heart: "Therefore, because I have got understanding of the truth, I hate every false way, and am steadfastly resolved not to turn aside into it." Observe here,

[1.] The way of sin is a false way; it deceives, and will ruin, all that walk in it; it is the wrong way, and yet it seems to a man right, Prov. xiv. 12.

[2.] It is the character of every good man that he hates the way of sin, and hates it because it is a false way; he not only refrains his feet from it (v. 101), but he hates it, has an antipathy to it and a dread of it.

[3.] Those who hate sin as sin will hate all sin, hate every false way, because every false way leads to destruction. And,

[4.] The more understanding we get by the word of God the more rooted will our hatred of sin be (for to depart from evil, that is understanding, Job xxviii. 28), and the more ready we are in the scriptures the better furnished we are with answers to temptation.

Psalm 119

Nun

105-108

105 Thy word is a lamp unto my feet, and a light unto my path.

106 I have sworn, and I will perform it, that I will keep thy righteous judgments.

107 I am afflicted very much: quicken me, O LORD, according unto thy word.

108 Accept, I beseech thee, the freewill offerings of my mouth, O LORD, and teach me thy judgments.

habitually, that he may see his way and see what lies in it. When darkness settles down upon all around me, the word of the Lord, like a flaming torch, reveals my way. Having no fixed lamps in eastern towns, in old time each passenger carried a lantern with him that he might not fall into the open sewer, or stumble over the heaps of ordure which defiled the road. This is a true picture of our path through this dark world: we should not know the way, or how to walk in it, if Scripture, like a blazing flambeau, did not reveal it. One of the most practical benefits of Holy Writ is guidance in the acts of daily life: it is not sent to astound us with its brilliance, but to guide us by its instruction. It is true the head needs illumination, but even more the feet need direction, else head and feet may both fall into a ditch. Happy is the man who personally appropriates God's word, and practically uses it as his comfort and counselor,—a lamp to his own feet.

Verse 106. I have sworn, and I will perform it, that I will keep thy righteous judgments. Under the influence of the clear light of knowledge he had firmly made up his mind, and solemnly declared his resolve in the sight of God. Perhaps mistrusting his own fickle mind, he had pledged himself in sacred form to abide faithful to the determinations and decisions of his God. Whatever path might open before him, he was sworn to follow that only upon which the lamp of the word was shining. The Scriptures are God's judgments, or verdicts, upon great moral questions; these are all righteous, and hence righteous men should be resolved to keep them at all hazards, since it must always be right to do right.

Verse 107. I am afflicted very much. According to the last verse he had been sworn in as a soldier of the Lord, and in this next verse he is called to suffer hardness in that capacity. Our service of the Lord does not screen us from trial, but rather secures it for us. The Psalmist was a consecrated man, and yet a chastened man; nor were his chastisements light; for it seemed as if the more he was obedient the more he was afflicted. He evidently felt the rod to be cutting deep, and this he pleads before the Lord. He speaks not by way of murmuring, but by way of pleading; from the very much affliction he argues for very much quickening.

Verse 108. Accept, I beseech thee, the freewill offerings of my mouth, O Lord. The living praise the living God, and therefore the quickened one presents his sacrifice. He offers prayer, praise, confession, and testimony—these, presented with his voice in the presence of an audience, were the tribute of his mouth unto Jehovah. He trembles lest these should be so ill uttered as to displease the Lord, and therefore he implores acceptance. He pleads that the homage of his mouth was cheerfully and spontaneously rendered; all his utterances were freewill offerings. There can be no value in extorted confessions: God's revenues are not derived from forced taxation, but from freewill donation. There can be no acceptance where there is no willingness; there is no work of free grace where there is no fruit of free will. Acceptance is a favor to be sought from the Lord with all earnestness, for without it our offerings are worse than useless. What a wonder of grace that the Lord will accept anything of such unworthy ones as we are!

And teach me thy judgments. When we render unto the Lord our best, we become all the more concerned to do better. If, indeed, the Lord shall accept us, we then desire to be further instructed, that we may be still more acceptable, After quickening we need teaching: life without light, or zeal without knowledge, would be but half a blessing. These repeated cries for teaching show the humility of the man of God, and also discover to us our own need of similar instruction. Our judgment needs educating till it knows, agrees with, and acts upon, the judgments of the Lord.

JOHN CALVIN

Psalm 119:105-112

105. Thy word is a lamp to my feet. In this verse the Psalmist testifies that the Divine Law was his schoolmaster and guide in leading a holy life. He thus, by his own example, prescribes the same rule to us all; and it is highly necessary to observe this rule; for while each of us follows what seems good in his own estimation, we become entangled in inextricable and frightful mazes. The more distinctly to understand his intention, it is to be noted, that the word of God is set in opposition to all human counsels. What the world judges right is often crooked and perverse in the judgment of God, who approves of no other manner of living, than that which is framed according to the rule of his law. It is also to be observed, that David could not have been guided by God's word, unless he had first renounced the wisdom of the flesh, for it is only when we are brought to do this, that we begin to be of a teachable disposition.

106. I have sworn, and will perform. Here the Psalmist speaks of his own constancy. He had declared a little before, that during the whole course of his life, he had not declined from God's law, and now he speaks of the purpose of his mind. By the word swear, he intimates that he had solemnly pledged himself to God not to alter his determination. The true manner of keeping God's law is to receive and embrace what he commands heartily, and, at the same time, uniformly, that our ardor may not forthwith abate, as is often the case.

107. I am greatly afflicted, O Jehovah! This verse teaches, that God did not cherish the fathers under the law in his bosom so delicately as not to exercise them with grievous temptations; for the Psalmist declares that he was not afflicted lightly, or in an ordinary degree, but above measure. His prayer to be quickened implies that he was at the point of death. He, however, at the same time, shows, that though he was besieged by death, he yet fainted not, because he leaned upon God—a point worthy of special notice; for though, at the beginning, we may call upon God with much alacrity, yet when the trial increases in severity, our hearts quail, and, in the extremity of fear, our confidence is extinguished. Yet the prophet implores God for grace, not in order to his life being preserved in safety, but in order to his recovering the life he had lost, which indicates both the low condition to which he was reduced, and his continued confidence in God. We must also observe attentively the last part of the clause, according to thy word We will pray coldly, or rather we will not pray at all, if God's promise does not inspire us with courage in our sorrow and distress. In short, as we have said elsewhere, it is indispensably necessary that we should have this key at hand, in order to our having free access to the throne of grace.

108. O Jehovah! I beseech thee, let the free-will-offerings of my mouth. The prophet affirms that nothing was more precious to him than to understand the doctrine of the law. Lord, as if he had said, do thou, according to thy good pleasure, accept the sacrifices which I offer thee; and as my chief desire is, to be instructed aright in thy law, grant that I may be a partaker of this blessing, which I am so anxious to

MATTHEW HENRY

14. NUN.

105
Observe here,

1. The nature of the word of God, and the great intention of giving it to the world; it is a lamp and a light. It discovers to us, concerning God and ourselves, that which otherwise we could not have known; it shows us what is amiss, and will be dangerous; it directs us in our work and way, and a dark place indeed the world would be without it.

2. The use we should make of it. It must be not only a light to our eyes, to gratify them, and fill our heads with speculations, but a light to our feet and to our path, to direct us in the right ordering of our conversation, both in the choice of our way in general and in the particular steps we take in that way, that we may not take a false way nor a false step in the right way.

106
Here is,

1. The notion David had of religion; it is keeping God's righteous judgments. God's commands are his judgments, the dictates of infinite wisdom. They are righteous judgments, consonant to the eternal rules of equity, and it is our duty to keep them carefully.

2. The obligation he here laid upon himself to be religious, binding himself, by his own promise, to that which he was already bound to by the divine precept, and all little enough. "I have sworn (I have lifted up my head to the Lord, and I cannot go back) and therefore must go forward: I will perform it."

107
Here is,

1. The representation David makes of the sorrowful condition he was in: I am afflicted very much, afflicted in spirit; he seems to mean that especially. He labored under many discouragements; without were fightings, within were fears. This is often the lot of the best saints; therefore think it not strange if sometimes it be ours.

2. The recourse he has to God in this condition; he prays for his grace: "Quicken me, O Lord! make me lively, make me cheerful; quicken me by afflictions to greater diligence in my work. Quicken me, that is, deliver me out of my afflictions, which will be as life from the dead." He pleads the promise of God, guides his desires by it, and grounds his hopes upon it: Quicken me according to thy word. David resolved to perform his promises to God (v. 106) and therefore could, with humble boldness, beg of God to make good his word to him.

108
Two things we are here taught to pray for, in reference to our religious performances:

1. Acceptance of them. This we must aim at in all we do in religion, that, whether present or absent, we

Psalm 119

109-112

109 My soul is continually in my hand: yet do I not forget thy law.
110 The wicked have laid a snare for me: yet I erred not from thy precepts.
111 Thy testimonies have I taken as an heritage for ever: for they are the rejoicing of my heart.
112 I have inclined mine heart to perform thy statutes alway, even unto the end.

Those judgments are not always so clear as to be seen at once; we need to be taught in them till we admire their wisdom and adore their goodness as soon as ever we perceive them.

Verse 109. My soul is continually in my hand. He lived in the midst of danger. He had to be always fighting for existence—hiding in caves, or contending in battles. This is a very uncomfortable and trying state of affairs, and men are apt to think any expedient justifiable by which they can end such a condition: but David did not turn aside to find safety in am, for he says, Yet do I not forget thy law. They say that all things are fair in love and war; but the holy man thought not so: while he carried his life in his hand, he also carried the law in his heart. No danger of body should make us endanger our souls by forgetting that which is right. Trouble makes many a man forget his duty, and it would have had the same effect upon the Psalmist if he had not obtained quickening (Ps 119:107) and teaching (Ps 119:108). In his memory of the Lord's law lay his safety; he was certain not to be forgotten of God, for God was not forgotten of him. It is a special proof of grace when nothing can drive truth out of our thoughts, or holiness out of our lives. If we remember the law even when death stares us in the face, we may be well assured that the Lord is remembering us.

Verse 110. The wicked have laid a snare for me. Spiritual life is the scene of constant danger: the believer lives with his life in his hand, and meanwhile all seem plotting to take it from him, by cunning if they cannot by violence. We shall not find it an easy thing to live the life of the faithful. Wicked spirits and wicked men will leave no stone unturned for our destruction. If all other devices fail, and even hidden pits do not succeed, the wicked still persevere in their treacherous endeavors, and, becoming craftier still, they set snares for the victim of their hate. The smaller species of game are usually taken by this method, by gin, or trap, or net, or noose. Wicked men are quite indifferent as to the manner in which they can destroy the good man—they think no more of him than if he were a rabbit or a rat: cunning and treachery are always the allies of malice, and everything like a generous or chivalrous feeling is unknown among the graceless, who treat the godly as if they were vermin to be exterminated. When a man knows that he is thus assailed, he is too apt to become timorous, and rush upon some hasty device for deliverance, not without sin in the endeavor; but David calmly kept his way, and was able to write,

Verse 111. Thy testimonies have I taken as an heritage for ever. He chose them as his lot, his portion, his estate; and what is more, he laid hold upon them and made them so,—taking them into possession and enjoyment. David's choice is our choice. If we might have our desire, we would desire to keep the commands of God perfectly. To know the doctrine, to enjoy the promise, to practice the command,—be this a kingdom large enough for me. Here we have an inheritance which cannot fade and cannot be alienated; it is for ever, and ours for ever, if we have so taken it. Sometimes, like Israel at the first coming into Canaan, we have to take our heritage by hard fighting, and, if so, it is worthy of all our labor and suffering; but always it has to be taken by a decided choice of the heart and grip of the will. What God gives we must take.

Verse 112. I have inclined mine heart to perform thy statutes alway, even unto the end. He was not half inclined to virtue, but heartily inclined to it. His whole heart was bent on practical, persevering godliness. He was resolved to keep the statutes of the Lord with all his heart, throughout all his time, without erring or ending. He made it his end to keep the law unto the end, and that without end. He had by prayer, and meditation, and resolution made his whole being lean towards God's commands; or as we should say in other words—the grace of God had inclined him to incline his heart in a sanctified direction.

obtain. We should mark all the places in which the knowledge of divine truth is preferred to all the other benefits bestowed upon mankind; and doubtless, since it contains in it the pledge of everlasting salvation, there is good reason why it should be esteemed as an inestimable treasure. Yet the prophet begins at a point remote from this, praying that God would vouchsafe to approve of and accept his services.

109. My soul is continually in my hand. He declares, that no calamities, afflictions, or dangers, which he had experienced: had withdrawn him from the service of God, and the observance of his law. To bear his soul in his hand, is equivalent to his being in danger of his life, so that the soul was, as it were abandoned to the wind. Thus Job, (Job 13:14,) when he pines in his miseries: and is looking for death every moment, and dreading it, complains that his soul was in his hand; as if he had said, It is plucked from its own dwelling-place: and is under the dominion of death.

110. The wicked have laid a snare for me The meaning of this verse is similar to that of the preceding. The prophet shows more definitely in what respect he carried his life in his hand; namely, because, being hemmed in on all sides by the snares of the wicked, he saw scarcely any hope of life. We have previously observed how difficult it is to avoid wandering from the ways of the Lord, when our enemies, by their subtle arts, endeavor to effect our destruction.

111. I have thy testimonies as an inheritance for ever. He again confirms the sentiment, which cannot be too often repeated, That the law of God was more precious to him than all the pleasures, riches, and possessions, of the world. The prophet, to stir us up by his own example, asserts, that he took such pleasure in God's, testimonies as to esteem nothing more precious. It is love only which leads us to set a value on any object; and, therefore, it is requisite, in order to our observing the Divine law with the reverence due to it, that we begin with this delight in it.

112. I have inclined my heart to perform thy statutes. In this verse he describes the right observance of the law, which consists in our cheerfully and heartily preparing ourselves for doing what the law commands. Slavish and constrained obedience differs little from rebellion. The prophet, therefore, in order briefly to define what it is to serve God, asserts, that he applied not only his hands, eyes, or feet, to the keeping of the law, but that he began with the affection of the heart. Instead of the verb incline, the verb extend might with propriety be employed; but I am inclined to rest in the more generally received interpretation, which is, that he devoted himself with sincere affection of heart to the observance of the law. This inclination of the heart is opposed to the wandering lusts which rise up against God, and drag us any where rather than incline us to a virtuous life. The prophet does not here boast of what he had done by his own strength, for he now repeats the very same word which he had employed before, when he said, Incline my heart to these testimonies. If that prayer was not feigned, he doubtless acknowledged by it that it was the peculiar work of the Holy Spirit to incline and frame our hearts to God.

may be accepted of the Lord. What David here earnestly prays for the acceptance of are the free-will-offerings, not of his purse, but of his mouth, his prayers and praises.

2. Assistance in them: Teach me thy judgments. We cannot offer any thing to God which we have reason to think he will accept of, but what he is pleased to instruct us in the doing of; and we must be as earnest for the grace of God in us as for the favor of God towards us.

109-110

Here is,

1. David in danger of losing his life. There is but a step between him and death, for the wicked have laid a snare for him; Saul did so many a time, because he hated him for his piety. Wherever he was he found some design or other laid against him to take away his life, for it was that they aimed at. What they could not effect by open force they hoped to compass by treachery, which made him say, My soul is continually in my hand.

2. David in no danger of losing his religion, notwithstanding this, thus in jeopardy every hour and yet constant to God and his duty. None of these things move him.

111-112

The psalmist here in a most affectionate manner, like an Israelite indeed, resolves to stick to the word of God and to live and die by it.

I. He resolves to portion himself in it, and there to seek his happiness, nay, there to enjoy it; "Thy testimonies (the truths, the promises, of thy word) have I taken as a heritage for ever, for they are the rejoicing of my heart." The present delight he took in them was an evidence that the good things contained in them were in his account the best things, and the treasure which he set his heart upon.

1. He expected an eternal happiness in God's testimonies. The covenant God had made with him was an everlasting covenant, and therefore he took it as a heritage for ever.

2. He enjoyed a present satisfaction in them: They are the rejoicing of my heart, because they will be my heritage for ever. It requires the heart of a good man to see his portion in the promise of God and not in the possessions of this world.

II. He resolves to govern himself by it and thence to take his measures: I have inclined my heart to do thy statutes. We must look for comfort only in the way of duty, and that duty must be done with full consent and complacency, and with constancy and perseverance. He would perform God's statutes always, in all instances, in the duty of every day, in a constant course of holy walking, and this to the end, without weariness. This is following the Lord fully.

Psalm 119

Samekh

113-116
113 I hate vain thoughts: but thy law do I love.
114 Thou art my hiding place and my shield: I hope in thy word.
115 Depart from me, ye evildoers: for I will keep the commandments of my God.
116 Uphold me according unto thy word, that I may live: and let me not be ashamed of my hope.

Verse 113. I hate vain thoughts: but thy law do I love. In this paragraph the Psalmist deals with thoughts and things and persons which are the opposite of God's holy thoughts and ways. He is evidently in great fear of the powers of darkness, and of their allies, and his whole soul is stirred up to stand against them with a determined opposition. Just as he began the octave, Ps 119:97, with "O how I love thy law," so here he begins with a declaration of hatred against that which breaks the law. The opposite of the fixed and infallible law of God is the wavering, changing opinion of men: David had an utter contempt and abhorrence for this; all his reverence and regard went to the sure word of testimony. In proportion to his love to the law was his hate of man's inventions. The thoughts of men are vanity; but the thoughts of God are verity.
Verse 114. Thou art my hiding place and my shield. To his God he ran for shelter from vain thoughts; there he hid himself away from their tormenting intrusions, and in solemn silence of the soul he found God to be his hiding place. When called into the world, if he could not be alone with God as his hiding place, he could have the Lord with him as his shield, and by this means he could ward off the attacks of wicked suggestions. This is an experimental verse, and it testifies to that which the writer knew of his own personal knowledge: he could not fight with his own thoughts, or escape from them, till he flew to his God, and then he found deliverance. Observe that he does not speak of God's word as being his double defense, but he ascribes that to God himself. When we are beset by very spiritual assaults, such as those which arise out of vain thoughts, we shall do well to fly distinctly to the person of our Lord, and to cast ourselves upon his real presence. Happy is he who can truly say to the triune God, "Thou art my hiding place." He has beheld God under that glorious covenant aspect which ensures to the beholder the surest consolation. I hope in thy word. And well he might, since he had tried and proved it: he looked for protection from all danger, and preservation from all temptation to him who had hitherto been the tower of his defense on former occasions.
Verse 115. Depart from me, ye evil doers. Those who make a conscience of their thoughts are not likely to tolerate evil company. If we fly to God from vain thoughts, much more shall we avoid vain men. Kings are all too apt to be surrounded by a class of men who flatter them, and at the same time take liberty to break the laws of God: David purged his palace of such parasites; he would not harbor them beneath his roof. No doubt they would have brought upon him an ill name, for their doings would have been imputed to him, since the acts of courtiers are generally set down as acts of the court itself; therefore the king sent them packing bag and baggage, saying,—"Depart from me." Herein he anticipated the sentence of the last great day, when the Son of David shall say, "Depart from me, ye workers of iniquity." We cannot thus send all malefactors out of our houses, but it will often become a duty to do so where there is right and reason for it. A house is all the better for being rid of liars, pilferers, lewd talkers, and slanderers. We are bound at all hazards to keep ourselves clear of such companions as come to us by our own choice if we have any reason to believe that their character is vicious.
Verse 116. Uphold me according unto thy word, that I may have. It was so necessary that the Lord should hold up his servant, that he could not even live without it. Our soul would die if the Lord did not continually sustain it, and every grace which makes spiritual life to be truly life would decay if he withdrew his upholding hand. It is a sweet comfort that this great necessity of upholding is provided for in the word, and we have not to ask for it as for an uncovenanted mercy, but simply to plead for the fulfillment of a promise, saying, "Uphold me according to thy word." He who has given us eternal life hath in that gift secured to us all that is

JOHN CALVIN

Psalm 119:113-120

113. I have hated crooked thoughts. As the branches of a tree shoot out transversely, entangled and intertwined, so the thoughts of the human mind are, in like manner, confusedly mingled together, turning and twisting about in all directions. The crooked inventions of the human heart are set in opposition to the law of God, which alone is right.
114. Thou art my hiding place and my shield. The meaning is, that the prophet, persuaded that the only way in which he could be safe, was by lying hid under the wings of God, confided in his promises, and, therefore, feared nothing. And, assuredly, the faithful should hold it as a settled principle, that amidst the many dangers to which they are exposed, the preservation of their life is entirely owing to the protection of God; in order that they may be excited to flee to him, and leaning upon his word, may confidently wait for the deliverance which he has promised. This confidence, That God is our refuge and our shield, is, no doubt, derived from the word; but we must remember that there is here a mutual relation—that, when we have learned from the word of God that we have in him a safe hiding-place, this truth is to be cherished and confirmed in our hearts, under a consciousness of our absolute need of the divine protection. Besides, although his power ought abundantly to suffice in inspiring us with the hope of salvation, yet we should always set the word before us, that our faith may not fail when his aid is slow in coming.
115. Depart from me, ye wicked! If godliness does not increase in us in proportion to the sense and experience we have of God's grace, we betray base ingratitude. This, then, is a true and useful doctrine; but the prophet meant to convey a different sentiment in this place. As he saw how great a hindrance the ungodly are to us, he banishes them to a distance from him; or rather, he testifies that he will beware of entangling himself in their society.
116. Sustain me by thy word, and I shall live. We are said to fall from God's word when we fall from the faith of it; and in like manner, so long as we repose upon the truth and certainty of it, he is our sustainer. But, as the prophet well knew that there is not strength in man adequate to this, he asks from God ability to persevere as the singular gift of the Holy Spirit. It follows, then, that true stability is to be found no where else but in the word of God; and that no man can steadfastly lean upon it but he who is strengthened by the power of the Holy Spirit. We must therefore always beseech God, who alone is the author and finisher of faith, to maintain in us this grace.
In the next verse, the prophet means to say, that whenever God withdrew his word, it would be all over with his safety; but that, if he were established by the Divine power, there was nothing of which he would have reason to be afraid. The Psalmist adds, that he will continue to persevere in this meditation during the whole of his life.
118. Thou hast trodden under foot all those who wander from thy statutes. By treading under foot he means, that God overthrows all the despisers of his law, and casts them down

MATTHEW HENRY

15. SAMECH.

113
Here we have,
1. David's dread of the risings of sin, and the first beginnings of it: I hate vain thoughts. He does not mean that he hated them in others, for there he could not discern them, but he hated them in his own heart. Every good man makes conscience of his thoughts, for they are words to God.
2. David's delight in the rule of duty: But thy law do I love, which forbids those vain thoughts, and threatens them. The more we love the law of God the more we shall get the mastery of our vain thoughts, the more hateful they will be to us, as being contrary to the whole law, and the more watchful we shall be against them, lest they draw us from that which we love.

114
Here is,
1. God's care of David to protect and defend him, which he comforted himself with when his enemies were very malicious against him: Thou art my hiding-place and my shield. David, when Saul pursued him, often betook himself to close places for shelter; in war he guarded himself with his shield. Now God was both these to him, a hiding-place to preserve him from danger and a shield to preserve him in danger, his life from death and his soul from sin.
2. David's confidence in God. He is safe, and therefore he is easy, under the divine protection: "I hope in thy word, which has acquainted me with thee and assured me of thy kindness to me." Those who depend on God's promise shall have the benefit of his power and be taken under his special protection.

115
Here is,
1. David's firm and fixed resolution to live a holy life: I will keep the commandments of my God. Bravely resolved! like a saint, like a soldier; for true courage consists in a steady resolution against all sin and for all duty. Those that would keep God's commandments must be often renewing their resolutions to do so.
2. His farewell to bad company, pursuant to this resolution: Depart from me, you evil-doers. Though David, as a good magistrate, was a terror to evil-doers, yet there were many such, even about court, intruding near his person; these he here abdicates, and resolves to have no conversation with them.

116-117
Here,
1. David prays for sustaining grace; for this grace sufficient he besought the Lord twice: Uphold me; and again, Hold thou me up. He sees himself not only unable to go on in his duty by any strength of his own, but in danger of falling into sin unless he was

Psalm 119

117-120

117 Hold thou me up, and I shall be safe: and I will have respect unto thy statutes continually.
118 Thou hast trodden down all them that err from thy statutes: for their deceit is falsehood.
119 Thou puttest away all the wicked of the earth like dross: therefore I love thy testimonies.
120 My flesh trembleth for fear of thee; and I am afraid of thy judgments.

essential thereto, and as gracious upholding is one of the necessary things we may be sure that we shall have it.
Verse 117. Hold thou me up: as a nurse holds up a little child. "And I shall be safe," and not else; for unless thou hold me up I shall be falling about like an infant that is weak upon its knees. We are saved by past grace, but we are not safe unless we receive present grace. The Psalmist had vowed to keep the Lord's commands, but here he pleads with the Lord to keep him: a very sensible course of procedure. Our version roads the word "uphold," and then "hold up;" and truly we need this blessing in every shape in which it can come, for in all manner of ways our adversaries seek to cast us down. To be safe is a happy condition; there is only one door to it, and that is to be held up by God himself; thank God, that door is open to the least among us.
And I will have respect unto thy statutes continually. In obedience is safety; in being held up is obedience. No man will outwardly keep the Lord's statutes for long together unless he has an inward respect for them, and this will never be unless the hand of the Lord perpetually upholds the heart in holy love.
Verse 118. Thou hast trodden down all them that err from thy statutes. There is no holding up for them; they are thrown down and then trodden down, for they choose to go down into the wandering ways of sin. Sooner or later God will set his foot on those who turn their foot from his commands: it has always been so, and it always will be so to the end. If the salt has lost its savor, what is it fit for but to be trodden under foot? God puts away the wicked like dross, which is only fit to be cast out as road metal to be trodden down.
Verse 119. Thou puttest away all the wicked of the earth like dross. He does not trifle with them, or handle them with kid gloves. No, he judges them to be the scum of the earth, and he treats them accordingly by putting them away. He puts them away from his church, away from their honors, away from the earth, and at last away from himself. "Depart," saith he, "ye cursed." If even a good man feels forced to put away the evil doers from him, much more must the thrice holy God put away the wicked. They looked like precious metal, they were intimately mixed up with it, they were laid up in the same heap; but the Lord is a refiner, and every day He removes some of the wicked from among his people, either by making a shameful discovery of their hypocrisy or by consuming them from off the earth. They are put away as dross, never to be recalled. As the metal is the better for losing its alloy, so is the church the better for having the wicked removed. These wicked ones are "of the earth,"—"the wicked of the earth," and they have no right to be with those who are not of the world; the Lord perceives them to be out of place and injurious, and therefore he puts them away, all of them, leaving none of them to deteriorate his church. The process will one day be perfect; no dross will be spared, no gold will be left impure. Where shall we be when that great work is finished.
Verse 120. My flesh trembleth for fear of thee. Such was his awe in the presence of the Judge of all the earth, whose judgment he had just now been considering, that he did exceedingly fear and quake. Even the grosser part of his being,—his flesh, felt a solemn dread at the thought of offending one so good and great, who would so effectually sever the wicked from among the just. Alas, poor flesh, this is the highest thing to which thou canst attain!
And I am afraid of thy judgments. God's words of judgment are solemn, and his deeds of judgment are terrible; they may well make us afraid. At the thought of the Judge of all,—his piercing eye, his books of record, his day of assize, and the operations of his justice,—we may well cry for cleansed thoughts, and hearts, and ways, lest his judgments should light on us.

from that loftiness which they assume to themselves. The phrase is directed against the foolish, or rather frantic, confidence with which the wicked are inflated, when they recklessly deride the judgments of God; and, what is more, scruple not to magnify themselves against him, as if they were not subject to his power. The last clause is to be particularly noticed: for their deceit is falsehood. By these words the prophet teaches, that the wicked gain nothing by their wiles, but that they are rather entangled in them, or at length discover that they were mere sleight of hand.
119. Thou hast made all the wicked of the earth to cease as dross. The meaning of this verse is similar to that of the preceding. By the similitude employed, there is described a sudden and an unexpected change, when their imaginative glory and happiness become dissipated in smoke. It is to be observed, that the vengeance of God against the wicked is not all at once manifested, so that they completely perish, or are exterminated from the earth; but as God, in rooting them out one after another, shows himself to be the judge of the world, and that he is purging the earth of them, it is not wonderful to find the prophet speaking of their destruction in this manner; for the Hebrew verbs often denote a continued act. As God, then, executes his judgments by little and little, and often suspends punishment until he see that the wicked abuse his long-suffering; it becomes us, on our part, to continue patiently waiting until, as a heathen writer observes, he compensate the delay of the punishment, by its severity when inflicted. Those who are not induced to commit themselves to the protection of God, whenever, by lifting up his hand, he shows that the world is governed by his power, must certainly be very perverse; but when, of his own good pleasure, he offers himself to us by his word, those who do not make haste to embrace so great a boon are stupid indeed. On the other hand, when he connives for a long time at the wickedness of men, devout affection, which should ravish us with the love of God's word, languishes.
120. My flesh hath trembled for fear of thee. At first sight the prophet seems to contradict himself. He had just now said, that, by God's severity, he was gently drawn to love his testimonies; now he declares, that he was seized with terror. But although these two effects differ widely from each other, yet, if we consider by what kind of discipline God forms us to reverence his law, we will perceive that they entirely harmonize. We require to be subdued by fear that we may desire and seek after the favor of God. Since fear, then, is the beginning of love, the prophet testifies, that he was awakened by a heart-felt fear of God to look well to himself. Nor is the mortification of the flesh so easy a matter, as that every one should consent to enter upon it, without the constraint of violent means; and, therefore, it is not wonderful if God struck his servant with terror, that, in this way, he might bend his mind to a holy fear of him. It is an evidence of no common wisdom to tremble before God when he executes his judgments, of which the majority of mankind take no notice. We are then taught by these words of the prophet, that we ought to consider attentively the judgments of God, that they

prevented by divine grace; and therefore he is thus earnest for that grace to uphold him in his integrity (Ps. xli. 12), to keep him from falling and to keep him from tiring, that he might neither turn aside to evil-doing nor be weary of well-doing.
2. He pleads earnestly for this grace.
(1.) He pleads the promise of God, his dependence upon the promise, and his expectation from it: "Uphold me, according to thy word, which word I hope in; and, if it be not performed, I shall be made ashamed of my hope, and be called a fool for my credulity."
(2.) He pleads the great need he had of God's grace and the great advantage it would be of to him: Uphold me, that I may live, intimating that he could not live without the grace of God; he should fall into sin, into death, into hell, if God did not hold him up.

118-120
Here is,
I. God's judgment on wicked people, on those that wander from his statutes, that take their measures from other rules and will not have God to reign over them. All departure from God's statutes is certainly an error, and will prove a fatal one.
1. He treads them all down. He brings them to ruin, to utter ruin, to shameful ruin; he makes them his footstool. Though they are ever so high, he can bring them low (Amos ii. 9); he has done it many a time, and he will do it, for he resists the proud and will triumph over those that oppose his kingdom.
2. He puts them all away like dross. Wicked people are as dross, which, though it be mingled with the good metal in the ore, and seems to be of the same substance with it, must be separated from it.
II. The reasons of these judgments. God casts them off because they err from his statutes and because their deceit is falsehood and because they go about to deceive others with their hypocritical pretences of good and their crafty projects of mischief.
III. The improvement David made of these judgments. He took notice of them and received instruction from them. The ruin of the wicked helped to increase,
1. His love to the word of God. "I see what comes of sin; therefore I love thy testimonies, which warn me to take heed of those dangerous courses and keep me from the paths of the destroyer." We see the word of Go fulfilled in his judgments on sin and sinners, and therefore we should love it.
2. His fear of the wrath of God: My flesh trembles for fear of thee. Instead of insulting over those who fell under God's displeasure, he humbled himself.
(1.) To reverence his terrible majesty, and to stand in awe of him.
(2.) To fear lest we offend him and become obnoxious to his wrath. Good men have need to be restrained from sin by the terrors of the Lord, especially when judgment begins at the house of God and hypocrites are discovered and put away as dross.

Psalm 119

Ayin

121-124

121 I have done judgment and justice: leave me not to mine oppressors.
122 Be surety for thy servant for good: let not the proud oppress me.
123 Mine eyes fail for thy salvation, and for the word of thy righteousness.
124 Deal with thy servant according unto thy mercy, and teach me thy statutes.

Verse 121. I have done judgment and justice. This was a great thing for an Eastern ruler to say at any time, for these despots mostly cared more far gain than justice. Some of them altogether neglected their duty, and would not even do judgment at all, preferring their pleasures to their duties; and many more of them sold their judgments to the highest bidders by taking bribes, or regarding the persons of men. Some rulers gave neither judgment nor justice, others gave judgment without justice, but David gave judgment and justice, and saw that his sentences were carried out. He could claim before the Lord that he had dealt out even handed justice, and was doing so still.

Verse 122. Be surety for thy servant for good. Answer for me. Do not leave thy poor servant to die by the hand of his enemy and thine. Take up my interests and weave them with thine own, and stand for me. As my Master, undertake thy servants' cause, and represent me before the faces of haughty men till they see what an august ally I have in the Lord my God. Let not the proud oppress me. Thine interposition will answer the purpose of my rescue: when the proud see that thou art my advocate they will hide their heads. We should have been crushed beneath our proud adversary the devil if our Lord Jesus had not stood between us and the accuser, and become a surety for us. It is by his suretyship that we escape like a bird from the snare of the fowler. What a blessing to be able to leave our matters in our Surety's hands, knowing that all will be well, since he has an answer for every accuser, a rebuke for every reviler.

Verse 123. Mine eyes fail for thy salvation. He wept, waited, and watched for God's saving hand, and these exercises tried the eyes of his faith till they were almost ready to give out. He looked to God alone, he looked eagerly, he looked long, he looked till his eyes ached. The mercy is, that if our eyes fail, God does not fail, nor do his eyes fail. Eyes are tender things, and so are our faith, hope and expectancy: the Lord will not try them above what they are able to bear. "And for the word of thy righteousness:" a word that would silence the unrighteous words of his oppressors. His eyes as well as his ears waited for the Lord's word: he looked to see the divine word come forth as a fiat for his deliverance. He was "waiting for the verdict"—the verdict of righteousness itself. How happy are we if we have righteousness on our side; for then that which is the sinners' terror is our hope, that which the proud dread is our expectation and desire. David left his reputation entirely in the Lord's hand, and was eager to be cleared by the word of the Judge rather than by any defense of his own. He knew that he had done right, and, therefore, instead of avoiding the supreme court, he begged for the sentence which he knew would work out his deliverance. He even watched with eager eyes for the judgment and the deliverance, the word of righteousness from God which meant salvation to himself.

Verse 124. Deal with thy servant according unto thy mercy. Here he recollects himself: although before men he was so clear that he could challenge the word of righteousness, yet before the Lord, as his servant, he felt that he must appeal to mercy. We feel safest here. Our heart has more rest in the cry, "God be merciful to me," than in appealing to justice. It is well to be able to say, "I have done judgment and justice," and then to add in all lowliness, yet "deal with thy servant according unto thy mercy." The title of servant covers a plea; a master should clear the character of his servant if he be falsely accused, and rescue him from those who would oppress him; and, moreover, the master should show mercy to a servant? even if he deal severely with a stranger. The Lord condescendingly deals, or has communications with his servants, not spurning them, but communing with them; and this he does in a tender and merciful way, for in any other form of dealing we should be crushed into the dust.

may not only gently instruct us, but that they may also strike us with such terror as will lead us to true repentance.

Psalm 119:121-128

121. I have done judgment and righteousness. The Prophet implores the help of God against the wicked who troubled him, and he does so in such a manner as at the same time to testify that the harassing treatment he received from them was on his part altogether undeserved. If we would have God to come down to succor us, it becomes us to see to it that we meet him with the testimony of a good conscience. As He everywhere promises his aid to the afflicted who are unrighteously oppressed, it is no superfluous protestation which the Prophet makes, that he had not provoked his enemies, but had restrained himself from all injury and wrong-doing, and had not even attempted to requite evil for evil. In asserting that he had at all times done judgment, he means that whatever rite wicked practiced, he steadfastly persevered in following after integrity, and never turned aside from what was just and right in any of his public or private transactions.
122. Become surety for thy servant for good. God is said metaphorically to become surety for us, just as if, on finding us indebted in a large sum of money, he discharged us of the obligation, by paying down the money to our creditor. The prayer is to this effect, That God would not suffer the wicked to exercise, their cruelty against us at their pleasure, but that he would interpose as a defender to save us. By these words the Prophet intimates, that he was in extreme danger, and that he had nothing else left him in which to hope but the help of God.
123. My eyes have failed for thy salvation. He testifies that he had been afflicted with severe troubles, and that not for a short time only, but for a period so protracted as might have exhausted his patience and occasioned despondency. But so far was this from being the effect they produced, that he declares that in all these long and wearisome conflicts his heart had never sunk into despair.
124. Deal with thy servant according to thy goodness. The two clauses of this verse must be read correctly; for he does not first separately desire God to deal well with him, and next desire him to be his master and teacher. He rather beseeches him in the exercise of that goodness and mercy, which he is wont to display towards all his people, to instruct him in his law. The object of the Prophet's request then is, that God would teach him in his statutes. But he begins with the divine mercy, employing it as an argument to prevail with God to grant him what he desires. This prayer then must be resolved thus: Lord, deal gently with me, and manifest thy goodness towards me by instructing me in thy commandments. Our whole happiness undoubtedly consists in our having that true wisdom which is to be derived from the word of God; and our only hope of obtaining this wisdom lies in God's being pleased to display his mercy and goodness towards us. The Prophet, therefore, magnifies the greatness and excellence of the benefit of being instructed in the divine law, when he requests that it may be bestowed upon him as a free gift.

16. AIN.

121-122
David here appeals to God,
1. As his witness that he had not done wrong; he could truly say, "I have done judgment and justice, that is, I have made conscience of rendering to all their due, and have not by force or fraud hindered any of their right." Take him as a king, he executed judgment and justice to all his people, 2 Sam. viii. 15. Take him in a private capacity, he could appeal to Saul himself that there was no evil or transgression in his hand, 1 Sam. xxiv. 11. Note, Honesty is the best policy and will be our rejoicing in the day of evil.
2. As his Judge, that he might not be wronged. Having done justice for others that were oppressed, he begs that God would do him justice and avenge him of his adversaries: "Be surety for thy servant, for good; undertake for me against those that would run me down and ruin me." He is sensible that he cannot make his part good himself, and therefore begs that God would appear for him. Christ is our surety with God; and, if he be so, Providence shall be our surety against all the world.

123
David, being oppressed, is here waiting and wishing for the salvation of the Lord, which would make him easy.
1. He cannot but think that it comes slowly: My eyes fail for thy salvation. His eyes were towards it and had been long so. He looked for help from heaven but it did not come so soon as he expected, so that his eyes began to fail, and he was sometimes ready to despair.
2. Yet he cannot hope that it comes surely; for he expects the word of God's righteousness, and no other salvation than what is secured by that word, which cannot fall to the ground because it is a word of righteousness.

124-125
Here is David's petition for divine instruction: "Teach me thy statutes; give me to know all my duty; when I am in doubt, and know not for certain what is my duty, direct me, and make it plain to me; now that I am afflicted, oppressed, and my eyes are ready to fail for thy salvation, let me know what my duty is in this condition." In difficult times we should desire more to be told what we must do than what we may expect.

126
Here is,
1. A complaint of the daring impiety of the wicked. David, having in himself a holy indignation at it, humbly represents it to God: "Lord, there are those that have made void thy law, have set thee and thy government at defiance, and have done what in them lay to cancel and vacate the obligation of thy

Psalm 119

125-128
125 I am thy servant; give me understanding, that I may know thy testimonies.
126 It is time for thee, LORD, to work: for they have made void thy law.
127 Therefore I love thy commandments above gold; yea, above fine gold.
128 Therefore I esteem all thy precepts concerning all things to be right; and I hate every false way.

Verse 125. I am thy servant. This is the third time he has repeated this title in this one section: he is evidently fond of the name, and conceives it to be very effective plea. We who rejoice that we are sons of God are by no the less delighted to be his servants. Did not the firstborn Son assume the servant's form and fulfill the servant's labor to the full? What high, honor can the younger brethren desire than to be made like the Heir of things.

Give me understanding, that I may know thy testimonies. In the verse he sought teaching; but here he goes much further, and craves understanding. Usually, if the instructor supplies the teaching, the finds the understanding; but in our case we are far more dependent, must beg for understanding as well as teaching: this the ordinary cannot give, and we are thrice happy that our Divine Tutor can furnish us with it. We are to confess ourselves fools, and then our Lord will make us wise, as well as give us knowledge. The best understanding is that which enables us to render perfect obedience and to exhibit intelligent faith, and it is this which David desires,—"understanding, that I may know thy testimonies." Some would rather not know these things; they prefer to be at ease in the dark rather than possess the light which leads to repentance and diligence.

Verse 126. It is time for thee, Lord, to work: For they have made void thy law. David was a servant, and therefore it was always his time to work: but being oppressed by a sight of man's ungodly behavior, he feels that his Master's hand is wanted, and therefore he appeals to him to work against the working of evil. Men make void the law of God by denying it to be his law, by promulgating commands and doctrines in opposition to it, by setting up tradition in its place, or by utterly disregarding and scorning the authority of the lawgiver. Then sin becomes fashionable, and a holy walk is regarded as a contemptible puritanism; vice is styled pleasure.

Verse 127. Therefore I love thy commandments above gold; yea, above fine gold. As it was God's time to work so it was David's time to love. So far from being swayed by the example of evil men, so as to join them in slighting the Scriptures, he was the rather led into a more vehement love of them. As he saw the commandments slighted by the ungodly, his heart was in sympathy with God, and he felt a burning affection for his holy precepts. It is the mark of a true believer that he does not depend upon others for his religion, but drinks water out of his own well, which springs up even when the cisterns of earth are all dried. Our holy poet amid a general depreciation of the law felt his own esteem of it rising so high that gold and silver sank in comparison. Wealth brings with it so many conveniences that men naturally esteem it, and gold as the symbol of it is much set by; and yet, in the judgment of the wise, God's laws are more enriching, and bring with them more comfort than all the choicest treasures. The Psalmist could not boast that he always kept the commands; but he could declare that he loved them; he was perfect in heart, and would fain have been perfect in life. He judged God's holy commands to be better than the best earthly thing, yea, better than the best sort of the best earthly thing; and this esteem was confirmed and forced into expression by those very oppositions of the world which drive hypocrites to forsake the Lord and his ways.

Verse 128. Therefore I esteem all thy precepts concerning all things to be right. Because the ungodly found fault with the precepts of God, therefore David was all the more sure of their being right. The censure of the wicked is a certificate of merit; that which they sanction we may justly suspect, but that which they abominate we may ardently, admire. The good man's delight in God's law is unreserved, he believes in all God's precepts concerning all things.

Verse 129. Thy commands are wonderful. Full of wonderful revelations, commands and promises. Wonderful in their nature, as being free from all

JOHN CALVIN

125. I am thy servant, give me understanding. Here the prayer of the preceding verse is repeated. The repetition shows how ardently he wished the blessing prayed for, and how earnest and importunate he was in pleading with God for it. By the words he expresses still more plainly in what way it is that God teaches his own people—that he does so by illuminating with sound knowledge their understandings, which otherwise would be blind. It would profit us little to have the divine law sounding in our ears, or to have it exhibited in writing before our eyes, and to have it expounded by the voice of man, did not God correct our slowness of apprehension, and render us docile by the secret influence of his Spirit. We are not to suppose that David advances any meritorious claims before God when he boasts of being his servant.
126. It is time for thee, O Jehovah! to be doing. It being the object of the Prophet to imprecate upon the impious and wicked the vengeance which they have deserved, he says, that the fit time for executing it had now arrived, inasmuch as they had carried to a great extent their wanton forwardness against God. The general verb doing is more emphatic than if one more specific had been used. The language is as if he had said, that God would seem to delay too long, if he did not now execute the office of a judge. It is the peculiar work of God to restrain the wicked, and even to punish them severely when he finds that their repentance is utterly hopeless.
127. And therefore I have loved thy statutes above gold. This verse, I have no doubt, is connected with the preceding. I understand the Psalmist as intimating, that the reason why he esteemed God's law as more valuable than gold and precious stones, was because he had fixed in his mind a thorough persuasion of the truth, that although God may connive for a time at wickedness, the making havoc of all uprightness and equity will not always remain unpunished. Yea, the more he saw the wicked outrageously breaking forth into wickedness, the more was he incited by a holy indignation burning in his heart, to love the law.
This is a passage deserving of special attention, for the baneful influence of evil example is well known, every man thinking that he may lawfully do whatever is commonly practiced around him. Whence it comes to pass, that evil company carries us away like a tempest. The more diligently then ought we to meditate on this doctrine, That when the wicked claim to themselves an unbridled liberty, it behoves us to contemplate with the eyes of faith the judgments of God, in order to our being thereby quickened to the observance of the divine law.
128. Therefore I have esteemed all thy commandments to be altogether right. The extreme impiety of our age especially demands of all the faithful that they should exercise themselves in this holy zeal. Profane men strive to outdo one another in scornfully aspersing the doctrine of salvation, and endeavor to bring God's sacred Word into contempt by their derisive jeers. Others pour forth their blasphemies without intermission. We cannot, therefore, avoid being chargeable with the crime of treacherous indifference, if our hearts are not warmed with zeal, and unless we burn with a holy jealousy. The Prophet not merely says, that he approved of

MATTHEW HENRY

commands." Those that sin through infirmity transgress the law, but presumptuous sinners do in effect make void the law, saying, Who is the Lord? What is the Almighty, that we should fear him? It is possible a godly man may sin against the commandment, but a wicked man would sin away the commandment, would repeal God's laws and enact his own lusts. This is the sinfulness of sin and the malignity of the carnal mind.
2. A desire that God would appear, for the vindication of his own honor: "It is time for thee, Lord, to work, to do something for the effectual confutation of atheists and infidels, and the silencing of those that set their mouth against the heavens." God's time to work is when vice has become most daring and the measure of iniquity is full. Now will I arise, saith the Lord. Some read it, and the original will bear it, It is time to work for thee, O Lord! it is time for every one in his place to appear on the Lord's side—against the threatening growth of profaneness and immorality. We must do what we can for the support of the sinking interests of religion, and, after all, we must beg of God to take the work into his own hands.

127-128
David here, as often in this psalm, professes the great love he had to the word and law of God; and, to evidence the sincerity of it, observe,
1. The degree of his love. He loved his Bible better than he loved his money—above gold, yea, above fine gold. Gold, fine gold, is what most men set their hearts upon; nothing charms them and dazzles their eyes so much as gold does. It is fine gold, a fine thing in their eyes; they will venture their souls, their God, their all, to get and keep it. But David saw that the word of God answers all purposes better than money does, for it enriches the soul towards God; and therefore he loved it better than gold, for it had done that for him which gold could not do, and would stand him in stead when the wealth of the world would fail him.
2. The ground of his love. He loved all God's commandments because he esteemed them to be right, all reasonable and just, and suited to the end for which they were made. They are all as they should be, and no fault can be found with them; and we must love them because they bear God's image and are the revelations of his will. If we thus consent to the law that it is good, we shall delight in it after the inner man.
3. The fruit and evidence of this love: He hated every false way. The way of sin being directly contrary to God's precepts, which are right, is a false way, and therefore those that have a love and esteem for God's law hate it and will not be reconciled to it.

Psalm 119

Pe

129-132

129 Thy testimonies are wonderful: therefore doth my soul keep them.
130 The entrance of thy words giveth light; it giveth understanding unto the simple.
131 I opened my mouth, and panted: for I longed for thy commandments.
132 Look thou upon me, and be merciful unto me, as thou usest to do unto those that love thy name.

error, and bearing within themselves overwhelming self evidence of their truth; wonderful in their effects as instructing, elevating, strengthening, and comforting the soul. Jesus the eternal Word is called Wonderful, and all the uttered words of God are wonderful in their degree. Those who know them best wonder at them most. It is wonderful that God should have borne testimony at all to sinful men, and more wonderful still that his testimony should be of such a character, so clear, so full, so gracious, so mighty. Therefore doth my soul keep them. Their wonderful character so impressed itself upon his mind that he kept them in his memory: their wonderful excellence so charmed his heart that he kept them in his life. Some men wonder at the words of God, and use them for their speculation; but David was always practical, and the more he wondered the more he obeyed. Note that his religion was soul work; not with head and hand alone did he keep the testimonies; but his soul, his truest and most real self, held fast to them.

Verse 130. The entrance of thy words giveth light. No sooner do they gain admission into the soul than they enlighten it: what light may be expected from their prolonged indwelling! Their very entrance floods the mind with instruction for they are so full, so clear; but, on the other hand, there must be such an "entrance," or there will be no illumination. The mere hearing of the word with the external car is of small value by itself, but when the words of God enter into the chambers of the heart then light is scattered on all sides. The word finds no entrance into some minds because they are blocked up with self conceit, or prejudice, or indifference; but where due attention is given, divine illumination must surely follow upon a knowledge of the mind of God. Oh, that thy words, like the beams of the sun, may enter through the window of my understanding, and dispel the darkness of my mind!

Verse 131. I opened my mouth, and panted. So animated was his desire that he looked into the animal world to find a picture of it. He was filled with an intense longing, and was not ashamed to describe it by a most expressive, natural, and yet singular symbol. Like a stag that has been hunted in the chase, and is hard pressed, and therefore pants for breath, so did the Psalmist pant for the entrance of God's word into his soul. Nothing else could content him. All that the world could yield him left him still panting with open mouth. For I longed for thy commandments. Longed to know them, longed to obey them, longed to be conformed to their spirit, longed to teach them to others. He was a servant of God, and his industrious mind longed to receive orders; he was a learner in the school of grace, and his eager spirit longed to be taught of the Lord.

Verse 132. Look thou upon me. A godly man cannot long be without prayer. During the previous verses he had been expressing his love to God's word, but here he is upon his knees again. This prayer is specially short, but exceedingly sententious, "Look thou upon me." While he stood with open mouth panting for the commandments, he besought the Lord to look upon him, and let his condition and his unexpressed longings plead for him. He desires to be known of God, and daily observed by him. He wishes also to be favored with the divine smile which is included in the word—"look." If a look from us to God has saving efficacy in it, what may we not expect from a look from God to us. And be merciful unto me. Christ's look at Peter was a look of mercy, and all the looks of the heavenly Father are of the same kind. If he looked in stern justice his eyes would not endure us, but looking in mercy he spares and blesses us. If God looks and sees us panting, he will not fail to be merciful to us.

Verse 133. Order my steps in thy word. This is one of the Lord's customary mercies to his chosen,—"He keepeth the feet of his saints." By his grace he enables us to put our feet step by step in the very place which his word ordains. This prayer seeks a very choice favor, namely,

God's law wholly and without exception, but he adds, that he hated every way of lying, or every false way.

Psalm 119:129-136

129. Thy testimonies are marvelous. I have given this translation to avoid an ambiguous form of expression. The Prophet does not simply mean, that the doctrine of the law is wonderful, but that it contains high and hidden mysteries. Accordingly he declares, that the sublime and admirable wisdom which he found comprehended in the divine law led him to regard it with reverence. This is to be carefully marked, for the law of God is proudly despised by the great majority of mankind, when they do not duly taste its doctrine, nor acknowledge that God speaks from his throne in heaven, that, the pride of the flesh being abased, he may raise us upward by the apprehension of faith.
130. The entrance of thy word is light. The amount is, that the light of the truth revealed in God's word, is so distinct that the very first sight of it illuminates the mind. It is as if the Prophet had—"Not only do those who have attained an accurate acquaintance with the whole law, and who have made the study of it the business of their lives, discern there a clear light, but also those who have studied it even very imperfectly, and who have only, so to speak, entered the porch." Now we must reason from the less to the greater. If novices begin to be enlightened at their first entrance, what will be the case when a man is admitted to a full and perfect knowledge?
131. I opened my mouth and panted. By these words the Psalmist would have us to understand that he was inflamed with such love to and longing for the divine law, that lie was unceasingly sighing after it. In comparing himself to such as are hungry, or to such as burn with parching thirst, he has used a very appropriate metaphor. As such persons indicate the vehemence of their desire by opening the mouth, and by distressful panting, as if they would suck up the whole air, even so the Prophet affirms that he himself was oppressed with continual uneasiness. The opening of the mouth, then, and the drawing of breath, are. set in opposition to a cold assent to the word of God. Here the Holy Spirit teaches with what earnestness of soul the knowledge of divine truth is to be sought.
132. Look upon me, and be merciful to me. In this verse he beseeches God to have a regard to him: as he is accustomed always to look to those who are his people. He next adds the purpose for which he desires that God would look upon him, namely, that he may be relieved from his miseries. This, then, is the prayer of an afflicted man, who, when apparently destitute of all help, and unable to come to any other conclusion than that he is neglected and forsaken of God, yet reflects with himself, that, for God to forsake him, was foreign to his nature and to his usual manner of procedure. It is as if he had said—Although I can perceive no token of thy favor, yea, although my condition is so wretched and desperate, that, judging according to sense and reason, I deem that thou hast turned the back: upon me; yet, as from the beginning of the

17. PE.

129
See here how David was affected towards the word of God.
1. He admired it, as most excellent in itself: Thy testimonies are wonderful. The word of God gives us admirable discoveries of God, and Christ, and another world; admirable proofs of divine love and grace. The majesty of the style, the purity of the matter, the harmony of the parts, are all wonderful. Its effects upon the consciences of men, both for conviction and comfort, are wonderful; and it is a sign that we are not acquainted with God's testimonies, or do not understand them, if we do not admire them.
2. He adhered to it as of constant use to him: "Therefore doth my soul keep them, as a treasure of inestimable value, which I cannot be without." We do not keep them to any purpose unless our souls keep them.

130
Here is,
1. The great use for which the word of God was intended, to give light, that is, to give understanding, to give us to understand that which will be of use to us in our travels through this world; and it is the outward and ordinary means by which the Spirit of God enlightens the understanding of all that are sanctified. God's testimonies are not only wonderful for the greatness of them, but useful, as a light in a dark place.
2. Its efficacy for this purpose. It admirably answers the end; for even the entrance of God's word gives light. If we begin at the beginning, and take it before us, we shall find that the very first verses of the Bible give us surprising and yet satisfying discoveries of the origin of the universe, about which, without that, the world is utterly in the dark.

131
Here is,
1. The desire David had towards the word of God: I longed for thy commandments. When he was under a forced absence from God's ordinances he longed to be restored to them again.
2. The degree of that desire appearing in the expressions of it: I opened my mouth and panted, as one overcome with heat, or almost stifled, pants for a mouthful of fresh air. Thus strong, thus earnest, should our desires be towards God and the remembrance of his name, Ps. xlii. 1, 2. Luke xii. 50.

132
Here is,
1. David's request for God's favor to himself: "Look graciously upon me; let me have thy smiles, and the light of thy countenance. Take cognizance of me and my affairs, and be merciful to me; let me taste the

Psalm 119

133-136
133 Order my steps in thy word: and let not any iniquity have dominion over me.
134 Deliver me from the oppression of man: so will I keep thy precepts.
135 Make thy face to shine upon thy servant; and teach me thy statutes.
136 Rivers of waters run down mine eyes, because they keep not thy law.

that every distinct act, every step, might be arranged and governed by the will of God. This does not stop short of perfect holiness, neither will the believer's desires be satisfied with anything beneath that blessed consummation. And let not any iniquity have dominion over me. This is the negative side of the blessing. We ask to do all that is right, and to fall under the power of nothing that is wrong. God is our sovereign, and we would have every thought in subjection to his sway. Believers have no choice, darling sins to which they would be willing to bow. They pant for perfect liberty from the power of evil, and being conscious that they cannot obtain it of themselves, they cry unto God for it.
Verse 134. Deliver me from the oppression of man. David had tasted all the bitterness of this great evil. It had made him an exile from his country, and banished him from the sanctuary of the Lord: therefore he pleads to be saved from it. It is said that oppression makes a wise man mad, and no doubt it has made many a righteous man sinful. Oppression is in itself wicked, and it drives men to wickedness. We little know how much of our virtue is due to our liberty; if we had been in bonds under haughty tyrants we might have yielded to them, and instead of being confessors we might now have been apostates. He who taught us to pray, "Lead us not into temptation," will sanction this prayer, which is of much the same tenor, since to be oppressed is to be tempted. So will I keep thy statutes. When the stress of oppression was taken off he would go his own way, and that way would be the way of the Lord. Although we ought not to yield to the threatenings of men, yet many do so; the wife is sometimes compelled by the oppression of her husband to act against her conscience: children and servants, and even whole nations have been brought into the same difficulty. Their sins will be largely laid at the oppressor's door, and it usually pleases God ere long to overthrow these powers and dominions which compel men to do evil. The worst of it is that some persons, when the pressure is taken off from them, follow after unrighteousness of their own accord. These give evidence of being sinners in grain. As for the righteous, it happens to them as it did to the apostles of old, "Being let go, they went to their own company." When saints are freed from the tyrant they joyfully pay homage to their king.
Verse 135. Make thy face to shine upon thy servant. Oppressors frown, but do thou smile. They darken my life, but do thou shine upon me, and all will be bright. The Psalmist again declares that he is God's servant, and he seeks for no favor from others, but only from his own Lord and Master. And teach me thy statutes. This is the favor which he considers to be the shining of the face of God upon him. If the Lord will be exceeding gracious, and make him his favorite, he will ask no higher blessing than still to be taught the royal statutes. See how he craves after holiness; this is the choicest of all gems in his esteem. As we say among men that a good education is a great fortune, so to be taught of the Lord is a gift of special grace. The most favored believer needs teaching; even when he walks in the light of God's countenance he has still to be taught the divine statutes or he will transgress.
Verse 136. Rivers of waters run down mine eyes, because they keep not thy law. He wept in sympathy with God to see the holy law despised and broken. He wept in pity for men who were thus drawing down upon themselves the fiery wrath of God. His grief was such that he could scarcely give it vent; his tears were not mere drops of sorrow, but torrents of woe. In this he became like the Lord Jesus, who beheld the city, and wept over it; and like unto Jehovah himself, who hath no pleasure in the death of him that dieth, but that be turn unto him and live. The experience of this verse indicates a great advance upon anything we have had before: the psalm and the Psalmist are both growing. That man is a ripe believer who sorrows because of the sins of others. In Ps

world to the present day, thou hast testified, by numberless proofs, that thou art merciful to thy servants, I beseech time that, acting according to this rule, thou wouldst now exercise the like loving-kindness towards me.
133. Direct my steps according to thy word. By these words he shows, as he has often done before in other places, that the only rule of living well is for men to regulate themselves wholly by the law of God. We have already repeatedly seen in this Psalm, that so long as men allow themselves to wander after their own inventions, God rejects whatever they do, however laborious the efforts they may put forth. But as the Prophet declares that men's lives are then only framed aright when they yield themselves wholly to the obeying of God, so, on the other hand, he confesses that to do this is not within their own will or power.
134. Deliver me from the oppression of men. When recounting what had befallen himself, the Prophet shows, by his own example, that all the godly are exposed to rapine and oppression, and that, like sheep in the mouths of wolves, they will be inevitably destroyed unless God defend them. As very few are governed by the Spirit of God, it is no wonder if all love of equity is banished from the world, and if all men are found everywhere rushing into all kinds of wickedness, some impelled by cruelty, and others devoted to fraud and deceit.
135. Make thy face to shine upon thy servant. There is here the repetition of a prayer which we have several times met with before in this Psalm. The Prophet intimates, that he regarded nothing as of more importance than rightly to understand the divine law. When he beseeches God to make his face to shine upon his servant, he, in the first place, seeks to win the fatherly favor of God—for nothing is to be hoped for from Him unless we have an interest in his favor—but he at the same time, shows the greatness of the blessing. There is no testimony of the love of God, as if he had said, which I am more desirous to obtain than to be enabled to make progress in his law. Whence we gather that he preferred divine truth to all the possessions of the world. Would to God that this affection were vigorous in our hearts!
136. Rivers of waters run from my eyes. Here David affirms that he was inflamed with no ordinary zeal for the glory of God, inasmuch as he dissolved wholly into tears on account of the contempt put upon the divine law. He speaks hyperbolically; but still he truly and plainly expresses the disposition of mind with which he was endued; and it corresponds with what he says in altogether place, "The zeal of thine house hath eaten me up." (Psalm 69:9.) Wherever the Spirit of God reigns, he excites this ardent zeal, which burns the hearts of the godly when they see the commandment of the Most High God accounted as a thing of nought. It is not enough that each of us endeavor to please God; we must also desire that his law may be held in estimation by all men. In this way holy Lot, as the Apostle Peter testifies, vexed his soul when he beheld Sodom a sink of all kinds of wickedness. (2 Peter 2:8.) If, in former times, the ungodliness of the world extorted from the children of God such bitter grief, so great is the corruption into which we at this day are fallen, that those

sweetness of thy mercy and receive the gifts of thy mercy."
2. His acknowledgment of his favor to all his people: As thou usest to do unto those that love thy name. This is either a plea for mercy, or a description of the favor and mercy he desired—"that which thou usest to bestow on those that love thy name, which thou bearest to thy chosen," Ps. cvi. 4, 5.

133
Here David prays for two great spiritual blessings, and is, in this verse, as earnest for the good work of God in him as, in the verse before, for the good-will of God towards him. He prays,
1. For direction in the paths of duty: "Order my steps in thy word; having led me into the right way, let every step I take in that way be under the guidance of thy grace." We ought to walk by rule.
2. For deliverance from the power of sin: "Let no iniquity have dominion over me, so as to gain my consent to it, and that I should be led captive by it." The dominion of sin is to be dreaded and deprecated by every one of us.

134
Here David prays that he might live a quiet and peaceable life, and might not be harassed and discomposed by those that studied to be vexatious: "Deliver me from the oppression of man—man, whom God can control, and whose power is limited. Let them know themselves to be but men (Ps. ix. 20), and let me be delivered out of the hands of my enemies, that I may serve God without fear; so will I keep thy precepts."

135
David here, as often as elsewhere, writes himself God's servant, a title he gloried in, though he was a king. He is very ambitious of his Master's favor, accounting that his happiness and chief good.

136
Here we have David in sorrow.
1. It is a great sorrow, to such a degree that he weeps rivers of tears. Commonly, where there is a gracious heart, there is a weeping eye, in conformity to Christ, who was a man of sorrows and acquainted with grief. David had prayed for comfort in God's favor (v. 135), now he pleads that he was qualified for that comfort, and those that do so shall be comforted, Isa. lxi. 3.
2. It is godly sorrow. He wept not for his troubles, though they were many, but for the dishonor done to God: Because they keep not thy law, either because my eyes keep not thy law, so some (the eye is the inlet and outlet of a great deal of sin, and therefore it ought to be a weeping eye), or, rather, they, that is, those about me, v. 139. Note, The sins of sinners are the sorrows of saints. We must mourn for that which we cannot mend.

Psalm 119

Tsadhe

137-140

137 Righteous art thou, O LORD, and upright are thy judgments.

138 Thy testimonies that thou hast commanded are righteous and very faithful.

139 My zeal hath consumed me, because mine enemies have forgotten thy words.

140 Thy word is very pure: therefore thy servant loveth it.

119:120 his flesh trembled at the presence of God, and here it seems to melt and flow away in floods of tears. None are so affected by heavenly things as those who are much in the study of the word, and are thereby taught the truth and essence of things. Carnal men are afraid of brute force, and weep over losses and crosses; but spiritual men feel a holy fear of the Lord himself, and most of all lament when they see dishonor cast upon his holy name.

Verse 137. Righteous art thou, O LORD. The Psalmist has not often used the name of Jehovah in this vast composition. The whole psalm shows him to have been a deeply religious man, thoroughly familiar with the things of God; and such persons never use the holy name of God carelessly, nor do they even use it at all frequently in comparison with the thoughtless and the ungodly. Familiarity begets reverence in this case. Here he uses the sacred name in worship. He praises God by ascribing to him perfect righteousness. God is always right, and he is always actively light, that is, righteous. This quality is bound up in our very idea of God. We cannot imagine an unrighteous God.

Verse 138. Thy testimonies that thou hast commanded are righteous and very faithful. All that which God hath testified in his word is right and truthful. It is righteous, and may be relied upon for the present; it is faithful, and may be trusted in for the future. About every portion of the inspired testimonies there is a divine authority, they are issued and published by God's command, and they bear the impress of the royal style which carries omnipotence about it. Not only the precepts but the promises also are commanded of the Lord, and so are all the teachings of Scripture. It is not left to our choice whether we will accept them or no; they are issued by royal command, and are not to be questioned. Their characteristic is that they are like the Lord who has proclaimed them, they are the essence of justice and the soul of truth. God's word is righteous and cannot be impeached; it is faithful and cannot be questioned it is true from the beginning, and it will be true unto the end. Dwell upon that "sweet word"—"very faithful." What a mercy that we have a God to deal with who is scrupulously faithful, true to all the items and details of his promises, punctual to time, steadfast during all time. Well may we risk all upon a word which is" ever faithful, ever sure."

Verse 139. In the last two verses David spoke concerning his God and his law; here he speaks of himself, and says, My zeal hath consumed me, because mine enemies have forgotten thy words: this was no doubt occasioned by his having so clear a sense of the admirable character of God's word. His zeal was like a fire burning within his soul. The sight of man's forgetfulness of God acted as a fierce blast to excite the fire to a more vehement flame, and it blazed until it was ready to consume him. David could not bear that men should forget God's words. He was ready to forget himself, aye, to, consume himself, because these men forgot God. The ungodly were David s enemies: his enemies, because they hated him for his godliness; his enemies, because he abhorred them for their ungodliness. These men had gone so far in iniquity that they not only violated and neglected the commands of God, but they appeared actually to have forgotten them. This put David into a great heat; he burned with indignation. How dare they trample on sacred things! How could they utterly ignore the commands of God himself! He was astonished, and filled with holy anger.

Verse 140. Thy word is very pure. It is truth distilled, holiness in its quintessence. In the word of God there is no admixture of error or sin. It is pure in its sense, pure in its language, pure in its spirit, pure in its influence, and all this to the very highest degree—"very pure." "Therefore thy servant loveth it," which is a proof that he himself was pure in heart, for only those who are pure love God's word because of its purity. His heart was knit to the word because of its glorious holiness

JOHN CALVIN

who can look upon the present state of things unconcerned and without tears, are thrice, yea four times, insensible.

Psalm 119:137-144

137. O Jehovah! thou art righteous. All men indeed grant that God is righteous; but the Prophet has expressed more than the common sort of men, yea than the whole world, perceive in reference to this subject; for in designating God righteous, he means, that as soon as we depart from Him, we will not find a particle of righteousness anywhere else. When he adds that the evidence and testimony of this righteousness are to be seen in the law, he teaches us that God is robbed of his praise, if we do not subscribe to all his commandments. To the same purpose is the following verse, which declares that God has taught in his law full and perfect righteousness and truth.
139. My zeal hath consumed me. The Psalmist speaks of his persecutors, by whom it is certain he had been subjected to much trouble. But although they were virulent and cruel towards him, he avows that it was not so much his own private wrongs which offended him as the violation of God's law; yea rather, that he was so consumed with grief on that account as not to be affected at all with his own individual troubles. This is an example from which much profit may be derived. We are too tender and delicate in bearing wrongs; and hence it is that if we are but touched with a finger, we are instantly inflamed with anger, whilst at the same time we are but coldly affected at the most grievous offenses committed against God. But if we are animated with the zeal that inspired the Prophet it will carry us away to another kind of sorrow, which will take entire possession of our souls.
140. Thy word is exceedingly refined. In this verse he intimates that the cause of his zeal was the love which he bore to heavenly doctrine. For to be displeased with or severely to condemn the contempt of divine truth, unless we are bound to it by the cords of love, is pure hypocrisy. And he affirms that his love to God's word was not a rash, or a blind and inconsiderate affection, but that he loved it, because like gold or silver which has been refined, it was pure and free from all dregs and dross.
141. I am, insignificant and despised. The meaning is, that although he was tried with poverty and many other calamities, he steadily persevered in the exercise of true godliness, and in the observance of the law. On that account, as he states, he was despised by wicked men. Every man gives praise to God just in proportion as he is gorged with his benefits; and very few will be found applying their minds to the service of God, unless they have all their wishes gratified. Hence it comes to pass that hypocrites, as long as they are pampered to the full, accumulate riches and increase in power, are very lavish in praising God. But let them be treated in some degree roughly, and immediately the blessed name of God is heard of no more. Since then men are ordinarily mercenary in serving God, let us learn from the Prophet's example that true godliness is disinterested, so that when under its influence we cease not to praise God, although he may afflict us with adversity and make

MATTHEW HENRY

18. TZADDI.

137-138
Here is,
1. The righteousness of God, the infinite rectitude and perfection of his nature. As he is what he is, so he is what he should be, and in every thing acts as becomes him; there is nothing wanting, nothing amiss, in God; his will is the eternal rule of equity, and he is righteous, for he does all according to it.
2. The righteousness of his government. He rules the world by his providence, according to the principles of justice, and never did, nor ever can do, any wrong to any of his creatures: Upright are thy judgments, the promises and threatenings and the executions of both. Every word of God is pure, and he will be true to it; he perfectly knows the merits of every cause and will judge accordingly.
3. The righteousness of his commands, which he has given to be the rule of our obedience: "Thy testimonies that thou hast commanded, which are backed with thy sovereign authority, and to which thou dost require our obedience, are exceedingly righteous and faithful, righteousness and faithfulness itself."

139
Here is,
1. The great contempt which wicked men put upon religion: My enemies have forgotten thy words. They have often heard them, but so little did they heed them that they soon forgot them, they willingly forgot them, not only through carelessness let them slip out of their minds, but contrived how to cast them behind their backs.
2. The great concern which godly men show for religion. David reckoned those his enemies who forgot the words of God because they were enemies to religion, which he had entered into a league with, offensive and defensive. And therefore his zeal even consumed him, when he observed their impieties.

140
Here is,
1. David's great affection for the word of God: Thy servant loves it. Every good man, being a servant of God, loves the word of God, because it lets him know his Master's will and directs him in his Master's work.
2. The ground and reason of that affection; he saw it to be very pure, and therefore he loved it. Our love to the word of God is then an evidence of our love to God when we love it for the sake of its purity, because it bears the image of God's holiness and is designed to make us partakers of his holiness.

141
Here is,
1. David pious and yet poor. He was a man after God's own heart, one whom the King of kings did delight to honor, and yet small and despised in his

Psalm 119

141-144
141 I am small and despised: yet do not I forget thy precepts.
142 Thy righteousness is an everlasting righteousness, and thy law is the truth.
143 Trouble and anguish have taken hold on me: yet thy commandments are my delights.
144 The righteousness of thy testimonies is everlasting: give me understanding, and I shall live.

and truth. He admired it, delighted in it, sought to practice it, and longed to come under its purifying power.
Verse 141. I am small and despised: yet do I not forget thy precepts. That fault of forgetfulness which he condemned in others (Ps 119:139) could not be charged upon himself. His enemies made no account of him, regarded him as a man without power or ability, and therefore looked down upon him. He appears to accept the situation and humbly take the lowest room, but he carries God's word with him. How many a man has been driven to do some ill action in order to reply to the contempt of his enemies: to make himself conspicuous he has either spoken or acted in a manner which he could not justify. The beauty of the Psalmist's piety was that it was calm and well balanced, and as he was not carried away by flattery, so was he not overcome by shame. If small, he the more jealously attended to the smaller duties; and if despised, he was the more in earnest to keep the despised commandments of God.
Verse 142. Thy righteousness is an everlasting righteousness. Having in a previous verse ascribed righteousness to God, he now goes on to declare that that righteousness is unchanging and endures from age to age. This is the joy and glory of the saints, that what God is he always will be, and his mode of procedure towards the sons of men is immutable: having kept his promise, and dealt out justice among his people, he will do so world without end. Both the righteousnesses and the unrighteousnesses of men come to an end, but the righteousness of God is without end. And thy law is the truth. As God is love, so his law is the truth, the very essence of truth, truth applied to ethics, truth in action, truth upon the judgment seat. We hear great disputes about, "What is truth?" The holy Scriptures are the only answer to that question. Note, that they are not only true, but the truth itself. We may not say of them that they contain the truth, but that they are the truth: "thy law is the truth." There is nothing false about the law or preceptory part of Scripture. Those who are obedient thereto shall find that they are walking in a way consistent with fact, while those who act contrary thereto are walking in a vain show.
Verse 143. Trouble and anguish have taken hold on me. This affliction may have arisen from his circumstances, or from the cruelty of his enemies, or from his own internal conflicts, but certain it is that he was the subject of much distress, a distress which apprehended him, and carried him away a captive to its power. His griefs, like fierce dogs, had taken hold upon him; he felt their teeth. He had double trouble: trouble without and anguish within, as the apostle Paul put it, "without were rightings and within were fears."
Verse 144. The righteousness of thy testimonies is everlasting. First he had said that God's testimonies were righteous, then that they were everlasting, and now that their righteousness is everlasting. Thus he gives us a larger and more detailed account of the word of God the longer he is engaged in writing upon it. The more we say in praise of holy writ, the more we may say and the more we can say. God's testimonies to man cannot be assailed, they are righteous from beginning to end; and though ungodly men have opposed the divine justice, especially in the plan of salvation, they have always failed to establish any charge against the Most High. Long as the earth shall stand, long as there shall be a single intelligent creature in the universe, it will be confessed that God's plans of mercy are in all respects marvelous proofs of his love of justice: even that he may be gracious Jehovah will not be unjust.

us despised in the eyes of the world. These upbraiding words of Christ in John 6:26, ought, no doubt, to be carefully attended to, "Ye seek me, not because ye saw the miracles, but because ye did eat of the loaves, and were filled." (John 6:26) The persons then who serve God ingenuously and sincerely, are such as continue steadfast. in his fear, although their condition in this world may be mean and despised; in short, they are such as seek not their reward on earth, but through heat and cold, poverty and danger, slanders and mockeries, persevere with unwearied steps in the course of their warfare.

142. Thy righteousness is an everlasting righteousness. Here the law of God is honored by the additional encomium, that it is everlasting righteousness and truth; as if it had been said, that all other rules of life, with whatever attractions they may appear to be recommended, are but a shadow, which quickly vanishes away. The Psalmist, no doubt, indirectly contrasts the doctrine of the law with all the human precepts which were ever delivered, that he may bring all the faithful in subjection to it, since it is the school of perfect wisdom. There may be more of plausibility in the refined and subtle disquisition's of men; but there is in them nothing firm or solid at bottom, as there is in God's law. This firmness of the divine law he proves in the following verse from one instance—the continual comfort he found in it when grievously harassed with temptations. And the true test of the profit we have reaped from it is, when we oppose to all the distresses of whatever kind which may straiten us, the consolation derived from the word of God, that thereby all sadness may be effaced from our minds.

144. The righteousness of thy testimonies endureth forever. The Psalmist repeats what lie had already before stated, that there is a great dissimilarity between the righteousness of God's testimonies and man's inventions; the splendor of the last quickly vanishing away, whereas the other continues steadfast for ever. He repeats this twice; for although the world is forced to attribute the praise of righteousness to the law of God, yet the majority of mankind are carried away after their own speculations, so that there is nothing more difficult than to hold us fast in our obedience to God. David's drift is to show that everlasting righteousness is not comprehended elsewhere than in God's law, and that it is in vain to seek for it anywhere else; and there is accordingly here laid down a clearer definition of righteousness, which is, that righteousness consists in our keeping ourselves within the bounds of the law. As to the last clause of the verse, Give me understanding and I shall live, I read it in connection with the preceding clause; for although David desires to have his mind enlightened by God, yet he does not conceive of any other way by which he was to obtain an enlightened understanding than by his profiting aright in the study of the law. Farther, he here teaches, that men cannot, properly speaking, be said to live when they are destitute of the light of heavenly wisdom; and as the end for which men are created is not that, like swine or asses, they may stuff their bellies, but that they may exercise themselves in the knowledge and service of God, when they turn away from such employment, their life is worse than a thousand deaths.

own account and in the account of many others. God has chosen the foolish things of the world, and it has been the common lot of his people to be a despised people.

2. David poor and yet pious, small and despised for his strict and serious godliness, yet his conscience can witness for him that he did not forget God's precepts. He would not throw off his religion, though it exposed him to contempt, for he knew that was designed to try his constancy.

142

Observe,

1. That God's word is righteousness, and it is an everlasting righteousness. It is the rule of God's judgment, and it is consonant to his counsels from eternity and will direct his sentence for eternity. The word of God will judge us, it will judge us in righteousness, and by it our everlasting state will be determined.

2. That God's word is a law, and that law is truth. See the double obligation we are under to be governed by the word of God. We are reasonable creatures, and as such we must be ruled by truth, acknowledging the force and power of it. If the principles be true, the practices must be agreeable to them, else we do not act rationally. We are creatures, and therefore subjects, and must be ruled by our Creator; and whatever he commands we are bound to obey as a law.

143

These two verses are almost a repetition of the two foregoing verses, but with improvement.

1. David again professes his constant adherence to God and his duty, notwithstanding the many difficulties and discouragements he met with. He had said (v. 141), I am small and despised, and yet adhere to my duty. Here he finds himself not only mean, but miserable, as far as this world could make him so: Trouble and anguish have taken hold on me—trouble without, anguish within; they surprised him, they seized him, they held him. All this trouble and anguish did not put his mouth out of taste for the comforts of the word of God.

2. He again acknowledges the everlasting righteousness of God's word as before (v. 142): The righteousness of thy testimonies is everlasting and cannot be altered; and, when it is admitted in its power into a soul, it is there an abiding principle, a well of living water, John iv. 14.

(1.) His prayer for grace: Give me understanding. Those that know much of the word of God should still covet to know more; for there is more to be known.

(2.) His hope of glory: "Give me this renewed understanding, and then I shall live, shall live for ever, shall be eternally happy, and shall be comforted, for the present, in the prospect of it." This is life eternal, to know God, John xvii. 3.

Psalm 119

Qoph

145-148

145 I cried with my whole heart; hear me, O LORD: I will keep thy statutes.
146 I cried unto thee; save me, and I shall keep thy testimonies.
147 I prevented the dawning of the morning, and cried: I hoped in thy word.
148 Mine eyes prevent the night watches, that I might meditate in thy word.

Verse 145. I cried with my whole heart. His prayer was a sincere, plaintive, painful, natural utterance, as of a creature in pain. We cannot tell whether at all times he used his voice when he thus cried; but we are informed of something which is of much greater consequence, he cried with his heart. Heart cries are the essence of prayer. He mentions the unity of his heart in this holy engagement. His whole soul pleaded with God, his entire affections, his united desires all went out towards the living God. It is well when a man can say as much as this of his prayers: it is to be feared that many never cried to God with their whole heart in all their lives. There may be no beauty of elocution about such prayers, no length of expression, no depth of doctrine, nor accuracy of diction; but if the whole heart be in them they will find their way to the heart of God.

Verse 146. I cried unto thee. Again he mentions that his prayer was unto God alone. The sentence imports that he prayed vehemently, and very often; and that it had become one of the greatest facts of his life that he cried unto God. "Save me." This was his prayer; very short, but very full. He needed saving, none but the Lord could save him, to him he cried, "Save me" from the dangers which surround me, from the enemies that pursue me, from the temptations which beset me, from the sins which accuse me. He did not multiply words, and men never do so when they are in downright earnest. He did not multiply objects, and men seldom do so when they are intent upon the one thing needful: "save me" was his one and only prayer.

And I shall keep thy testimonies. This was his great object in desiring salvation, that he might be able to continue in a blameless life of obedience to God, that he might be able to believe the witness of God, and also to become himself a witness for God. It is a great thing when men seek salvation for so high an end. He did not ask to be delivered that he might sin with impunity; his cry was to be delivered from sin itself. He had vowed to keep the statutes or laws, here he resolves to keep the testimonies or doctrines, and so to be sound of head as well as clean of hand. Salvation brings all these good things in its train. David had no idea of a salvation which would allow him to live in sin, or abide in error: he knew right well that there is no saving a man while he abides in disobedience and ignorance.

Verse 147. I prevented the dawning of the morning, and cried. He was up before the sun, and began his pleadings before the dew began to leave the grass. Whatever is worth doing is worth doing speedily. This is the third time that he mentions that he cried. He cried, and cried, and cried again. His supplications had become so frequent, fervent, and intense, that he might hardly be said to be doing anything else from morning to night but crying unto his God. So strong was his desire after salvation that he could not rest in his bed; so eagerly did he seek it that at the first possible moment he was on his knees.

Verse 148. Mine eyes prevent the night watches. Or rather, the watches. Before the watchman cried the hour, he was crying to God. He did not need to be informed as to how the hours were flying, for every hour his heart was flying towards heaven. He began the day with prayer, and he continued in prayer through the watches of the day, and the watches of the night. The soldiers changed guard, but David did not change his holy occupation. Specially, however, at night did he keep his eyes open, and drive away sleep, that he might maintain communion with his God. He worshipped on from watch to watch as travelers journey from stage to stage. That I might meditate in thy word. This had become meat and drink to him. Meditation was the food of his hope, and the solace of his sorrow: the one theme upon which his thoughts ran was that blessed "word" which he continually mentions, and in which his heart rejoices. He preferred study to slumber; and he learned to forego his necessary sleep for much more necessary devotion. It is instructive to find

JOHN CALVIN

Psalm 119:145-152

145 I have cried with my whole heart. This verse may be so read and connected as that in the end of it the Psalmist may show what he desired in crying; and thus the meaning would be, that as he was inflamed with an intense desire to keep the law, he continually made supplication to God on that subject. But the subsequent verse compels us to take a different view, for the same thing is, no doubt, there again repeated. The Prophet then requests that God would hear him; and in token of his gratitude he promises to keep God's commandments. He simply uses the indefinite term cry; and thus he does not express what the prayers were which he offered up to God, but only shows, that while the children of this world are distracted by a multiplicity of objects, he directed all the affections of his heart exclusively to God, because he depended solely on him. As the world is compelled to acknowledge that God is the author of all good things, many formal prayers proceed from that principle. It was the consideration of this which led David to affirm that he prayed with his whole heart. When he shall have obtained his requests, he proposes to himself the glory of God as his end, resolving to devote himself with so much the more ardent affection to the work of serving him. Although God declares that he is served aright by the sacrifice of praise, yet David, to distinguish himself from hypocrites who profane the name of God by their cold and feigned praises, with good reason declares that he will give thanks by his life and works.

In the following verse he makes no new statement; but he speaks more expressly. In the first place, he says that he cried to God; and next he adds, that he commended his welfare to Him by prayer; thereby intimating that whether he was in safety, or whether imminent danger threatened him with death, he uniformly reposed upon God, being fully persuaded that the only way in which he could continue safe was by having him for the guardian and protector of his welfare.

147. I have prevented the twilight. David expresses the most eager haste when he says, that he prevented the dawn of the morning by his prayers. The verb cry always conveys the idea of earnestness; referring, as it does, not so much to the loudness of the voice as to the vehemency and ardor of the mind. In mentioning his haste, his object is the better to set forth his perseverance; for he tells us, that although he betook himself to prayer with such promptitude, yet he did not immediately become weary of that exercise, like the unbelieving, who, if God does not suddenly grant them their requests, murmur and complain against him. Thus, in conjoining patience of hope with earnestness of desire, he shows what is the true manner of praying; even as Paul, in Philippians 4:6, when he exhorts us to "let our requests be made known unto God with thanksgiving," (Philippians 4:6) admonishes us, while engaged in the exercise of prayer, to bridle our turbulent affections, because one of the ends of prayer is to nourish our hope. Nor is the mention made of the word in the close of the verse superfluous; for it is only by having the Word of God continually before our eyes, that we can bridle the wanton impetuosity of our corrupt nature.

MATTHEW HENRY

19. KOPH.

145-146
Here we have,

I. David's good prayers, by which he sought to God for mercy; these he mentions here, not as boasting of them, or trusting to any merit in them, but reflecting upon them with comfort, that he had taken the appointed way to comfort. Observe here,

1. That he was inward with God in prayer; he prayed with his heart, and prayer is acceptable no further than the heart goes along with it. Lip-labor, if that be all, is lost labor.

2. He was importunate with God in prayer; he cried, as one in earnest, with fervor of affection and a holy vehemence and vigor of desire.

3. That he directed his prayer to God: I cried unto thee. Whither should the child go but to his father when any thing ails him?

4. That the great thing he prayed for was salvation: Save me.

5. That he was earnest for an answer; and not only looked up in his prayers, but looked up after them, to see what became of them (Ps. v. 3): "Lord, hear me, and let me know that thou hearest me."

II. David's good purposes, by which he bound himself to duty when he was in the pursuit of mercy. "I will keep thy statutes; I am resolved that by thy grace I will;" for, if we turn away our ear from hearing the law, we cannot expect an answer of peace to our prayers, Prov. xxviii. 9.

147-148
David goes on here to relate how he had abounded in the duty of prayer, much to his comfort and advantage: he cried unto God, that is, offered up to him his pious and devout affections with all seriousness. Observe,

I. The handmaids of his devotion. The two great exercises that attended his prayers, and were helpful to them, were,

1. Hope in God's word, which encouraged him to continue instant in prayer, though the answer did not come immediately: "I cried, and hoped that at last I should speed, because the vision is for an appointed time, and at the end it will speak and not lie. I hoped in thy word, which I knew would not fail me."

2. Meditation in God's word. Reading the word will not serve, but we must meditate in it.

II. The hours of his devotion. He anticipated the dawning of the morning, nay, and the night-watches. See here,

1. That David was an early riser, which perhaps contributed to his eminency. He was none of those that say, Yet a little sleep.

2. That he began the day with God. The first thing he did in the morning, before he admitted any business, was to pray, when his mind was most fresh and in the best frame. If our first thoughts in the morning be of

Psalm 119

149-152

149 Hear my voice according unto thy loving kindness: O LORD, quicken me according to thy judgment.
150 They draw nigh that follow after mischief: they are far from thy law.
151 Thou art near, O LORD; and all thy commandments are truth.
152 Concerning thy testimonies, I have known of old that thou hast founded them for ever.

meditation so constantly connected with fervent prayer: it is the fuel which sustains the flame. How rare an article is it in these days.

Verse 149. Hear my voice according unto thy lovingkindness. Men find it very helpful to use their voices in prayer; it is difficult long to maintain the intensity of devotion unless we hear ourselves speak; hence David at length broke through his silence, arose from his quiet meditations, and began crying with voice as well as heart unto the Lord his God. Note, that he does not plead his own descryings, nor for a moment appeal for payment of a debt on account of merit; he takes the free-grace way, and puts it, "according unto thy lovingkindness." When God hears player according to his lovingkindness he overlooks all the imperfections of the prayer, he forgets the sinfulness of the offerer, and in pitying love he grants the desire though the suppliant be unworthy. It is according to God's lovingkindness to answer speedily, to answer frequently, to answer abundantly, yea, exceeding abundantly above all that we ask or even think. Lovingkindness is one of the sweetest words in our language. Kindness has much in it that is most precious, but loving kindness is doubly dear; it is the cream of kindness.

Verse 150. They draw nigh that follow after mischief. He could hear their footfalls close behind him. They are not following him for his benefit, but for his hurt, and therefore the sound of their approach is to be dreaded. They are not prosecuting a good object, but persecuting a good man. As if they had not enough mischief in their own hearts, they are hunting after more. He sees them going a steeple chase over hedge and ditch in order to bring mischief to himself, and he points them out to God, and entreats the Lord to fix his eyes upon them, and deal with them to their confusion. They were already upon him, and he was almost in their grip, and therefore he cries the more earnestly. They are far from thy law. A mischievous life cannot be an obedient one. Before these men could become persecutors of David they were obliged to get away from the restraints of God's law. They could not hate a saint and yet love the law. Those who keep God's law neither do harm to themselves nor to others. Sin is the greatest mischief in the world. David mentions this to the Lord in prayer, feeling some kind of comfort in the fact that those who hated him hated God also, and found it needful to get away from God before they could be free to act their cruel part towards himself. When we know that our enemies are God's enemies, and ours because they are his, we may well take comfort to ourselves.

Verse 151. Thou art near, O Lord. Near as the enemy might be, God was nearer: this is one of the choicest comforts of the persecuted child of God. The Lord is near to hear our cries, and to speedily afford us succor. He is near to chase away our enemies, and to give us rest and peace. And all thy commandments are truth. God neither commands a lie, nor lies in his commands. Virtue is truth in action, and this is what God commands. Sin is falsehood in action, and this is what God forbids. If all God's commands are truth, then the true man will be glad to keep near to them, and therein he will find the true God near him. This sentence will be the persecuted man's protection from tile false hearts that seek to do him mischief: God is near and God is true, therefore his people are safe. If at any time we fall into danger through keeping the commands of God we need not suppose that we have acted unwisely: we may, on the contrary, be quite sure that we are in the right way; for God's precepts are right and true. It is for this very reason that wicked men assail us: they hate the truth, and therefore hate those who do the truth. Their opposition may be our consolation; while God's presence upon our side is our glory and delight.

Verse 152. Concerning thy testimonies, I have known of old that thou hast founded them for ever. David found of old that God had founded them of old, and that they Would stand firm throughout all ages. It is a

JOHN CALVIN

148. My eyes have prevented the night watchers. The Psalmist here intimates, that he was more sedulously intent on meditating upon the law of God than watchmen of the night were to keep watch.
149. Hear my voice, O Jehovah! according to thy mercy. In the first place he declares, that the goodness of God was the only ground of his hope of being heard by him. Whatever blessings the saints may plead for in prayer, their opening argument must be the free and unmerited grace of God. Nor is the term judgments in the second clause to be taken in a different sense. As God has revealed his goodness in his word, his word is the source from which we must derive our assurance of his goodness. The Prophet, then, sensible that he had need of the divine mercy, betook himself directly to the word, in which God, sweetly alluring men to himself, promises that his grace will be ready and open for all. That each, therefore, may be confidently persuaded that God will be merciful to him in particular, let him learn from the example of the Prophet to entreat God to show himself such as he has promised to be.
150. The pursuers of malice have drawn near. David says, that those who are vehemently bent on malice are pursuing him close behind, and that they rush upon him with such violence in order to do him mischief, as plainly to indicate that they are far off from God's law, since they east far from them all regard to uprightness and equity. It was a most wretched condition for him to be in, to behold his enemies, who had shaken off all fear of God and reverence for his law, ready with uplifted hand to smite him to death, had not God been near to defend him, as he adds in the subsequent verse.
151. Thou, O Jehovah! art near. He encourages himself from the consolatory consideration, that God, when he sees his own people sore pressed, comes forward. seasonably to afford them succor; even as Paul on this subject says, "Be not over-careful, the Lord is at hand, let your moderation be known to all men " (Philippians 4:5).

The concluding sentence of the verse is to this effect, That God never forsakes nor disappoints his people in their necessity, because he is true to his promises; and in them he assures us, that the welfare of his people will always be the object of his care. That therefore we may be fully persuaded that the hand of God is always ready to repulse the assaults of our enemies, let us retain a settled belief of the truth, that he does not in vain promise in his word to be the guardian of our welfare.
152. I have known from thy testimonies from the beginning. The Prophet not only knew the everlasting steadfastness which characterizes the testimonies of God; but that he had also derived this knowledge from the testimonies themselves. He therefore says, that he had learned from God's testimonies, or had been taught by them, that they are established for ever. This indeed is the chief point of faith, That the word of God is not only distinguished for fidelity and steadfastness for a time, but that it continues unchangeable for ever.

MATTHEW HENRY

God they will help to keep us in his fear all the day long.

149
Here,
1. David applies to God for grace and comfort with much solemnity. He begs of God to hear his voice: "Lord, I have something to say to thee; shall I obtain a gracious audience?" Well, what has he to say? What is his petition and what is his request? It is not long, but it has much in a little: "Lord, quicken me; stir me up to that which is good, and make me vigorous, and lively, and cheerful in it. Let habits of grace be drawn out into act."
2. He encourages himself to hope that he shall obtain his request; for he depends,
(1.) Upon God's lovingkindness: "He is good, therefore he will be good to me, who hope in his mercy. His lovingkindness manifested to me will help to quicken me, and put life into me."
(2.) Upon God's judgment, that is, his wisdom ("He knows what I need, and what is good for me, and therefore will quicken me"), or his promise, the word which he has spoken, mercy secured by the new covenant: Quicken me according to the tenor of that covenant.

150-151
Here is,
I. The apprehension David was in of danger from his enemies.
1. They were very malicious, and industrious in prosecuting their malicious designs: They follow after mischief, any mischief they could do to David or his friends; they would let slip no opportunity nor let fall any pursuit that might be to his hurt.
2. They were very impious, and had no fear of God before their eyes: They are far from thy law, setting themselves as far as they can out of the reach of its convictions and commands.
II. The assurance David had of protection with God: "They draw nigh to destroy me, but thou art near, O Lord! to save me, not only mightier than they and therefore able to help me against them, but nearer than they and therefore ready to help."

152
This confirms what he had said in the close of the foregoing verses, All thy commandments are truth; he means the covenant, the word which God has commanded to a thousand generations. This is firm, as true as truth itself. For,
1. God has founded it so; he has framed it for a perpetuity. Such is the constitution of it, and so well ordered is it in all things, that it cannot but be sure.
2. David had found it so, both by a work of God's grace upon his heart and by the works of his providence on his behalf.

Psalm 119

Resh

153-156

153 Consider mine affliction, and deliver me: for I do not forget thy law.
154 Plead my cause, and deliver me: quicken me according to thy word.
155 Salvation is far from the wicked: for they seek not thy statutes.
156 Great are thy tender mercies, O LORD: quicken me according to thy judgments.

very blessed thing to be so early taught of God that we know substantial doctrines even from our youth. Those who think that David was a young man when he wrote this psalm will find it rather difficult to reconcile this verse with the theory; it is much more probable that he was now grown grey, and was looking back upon what he had known long before. He knew at the very first that the doctrines of God's word were settled before the world began, that they had never altered, and never could by any possibility be altered.

Verse 153. Consider mine affliction, and deliver me. The writer has a good case, though it be a grievous one, and he is ready, yea anxious, to submit it to the divine arbitration. His matters are right, and he is ready to lay them before the supreme court. His manner is that of one who feels safe at the throne. Yet there is no impatience: he does not ask for hasty action, but for consideration. In effect he cries—"Look into my grief, and see whether I do not need to be delivered. From my sorrowful condition judge as to the proper method and time for my rescue." The Psalmist desires two things, and these two things blended: first, a full consideration of his sorrow; secondly, deliverance; and, then, that this deliverance should come with a consideration of his affliction. It should be the desire of every gracious man who is in adversity that the Lord should look upon his need, and relieve it in such a way as shall be most for the divine glory, and for his own benefit.

Verse 154. Plead my cause, and deliver me. In the last verse he had prayed, "Deliver me," and here he specifies one method in which that deliverance might be vouchsafed, namely, by the advocacy of his cause. In providence the Lord has many ways of clearing the slandered of the accusations brought against them. He can make it manifest to all that they have been belied, and in this way he can practically plead their cause. He can, moreover, raise up friends for the godly who will leave no stone unturned till their characters are cleared; or he can smite their enemies with such fearfulness of heart that they will be forced to confess their falsehood, and thus the righteous will be delivered without tile striking of a blow. Alexander reads it, "Strive my strife, and redeem me"—that is, stand in my stead, bear my burden, fight my fight, pay my price, and bring me out to liberty. When we feel ourselves dumb before the foe, here is a prayer made to our hand. What a comfort that if we sin we have an advocate, and if we do not sin the same pleader is engaged on our side.

Verse 155. Salvation is far from the wicked. By their perseverance in evil they have almost put themselves out of the pale of hope. They talk about being saved, but they cannot have known anything of it or they would not remain wicked. Every step they have taken in the path of evil has removed them further from the kingdom of grace: they go from one degree of hardness to another till their hearts become as stone. When they fall into trouble it will be irremediable. Yet they talk big, as if they either needed no salvation or could save themselves whenever their fancy turned that way.

Verse 156. This verse is exceedingly like verse one hundred and forty nine, and yet it is no vain repetition. There is such a difference in the main idea that the one verse stands out distinct from the other. In the first case he mentions his prayer, but leaves the method of its accomplishment with the wisdom or judgment of God; while here he pleads no prayer of his own, but simply the mercies of the Lord, and begs to be quickened by judgments rather than to be left to spiritual lethargy. We may take it for granted that an inspired author is never so short of thought as to be obliged to repeat himself: where we think we have the same idea in this psalm we are misled by our neglect of careful study. Each verse is a distinct pearl. Each blade of grass in this field has its own drop of heavenly dew.

JOHN CALVIN

Psalm 119:153-160

153. Behold my affliction and rescue me. The Psalmist teaches by his own example that those who are devoted to the service and fear of God, must not be discouraged though they are not rewarded for it in this world. Their condition upon earth is one of warfare, and therefore they should not be dismayed by diversity, but rather rest satisfied with the consolatory consideration, that the gate of prayer is open to them. Yet the Prophet does not boast of his, endeavors to keep the law, as if he would have God to pay him wages for his service, but only to show that he was one of God's servants, just as he has spoken of his hope that he was so in other places.
154. Debate thy cause, and redeem me. In this verse David specifics the kind of his affliction, which was the wrongful and harassing treatment which he met with at the hands of evil and unprincipled men.
155. Safety is far from the wicked. Fully persuaded that the world is governed by the secret providence of God, who is a just judge, the Prophet draws from that source the doctrine, That the wicked are far removed from safety, and safety from them. Hence proceeds the confidence of prayer; for as God is turned away from the despisers of his word, so he is ready to succor his servants. It is to be noticed, that when the Prophet saw that his enemies were elated by their prosperity, he on the contrary lifted up his heart by faith that thus he might come to the settled persuasion that all their delights were cursed and tended to destruction. Whenever then the wicked prosper in the world according to their wishes, so that being pampered to the full they exult in their own fatness, let us learn, in order to defend ourselves, to lay hold upon this buckler which the Holy Spirit is holding out to us, namely, that they shall at length miserably perish, because they seek not the commandments of God. From this we draw a contrary doctrine, That although genuine believers, whilst they walk sincerely in the fear of God may be as sheep appointed to the slaughter, yet their salvation, which is under the special care and protection of God's secret providence, is just at hand. In this sense the Prophet adds in the following verse,
156. O Jehovah,! thy tender mercies are many; as if he had said that no offenders are safe but those who betake themselves to the divine mercy. Farther, to encourage himself to approach God with the greater confidence, he not only says that God is merciful, but he mightily magnifies and extols his compassion's. From this we gather that he was so contented with them, as not to seek any aid from his own merits.
157. My persecutors and oppressors are many. The Psalmist here as in other places testifies, that although lie had been provoked by many injuries, yet he had not departed from the right way; which was an evidence of great and singular constancy. It is an easy matter to act well when we are among the good; but if wicked men afflict us, if one man openly assault us by force, if another rob us of our property, if a third circumvent us by wiles, and a fourth attack us by calumnies, it is difficult for us to persevere in our integrity, and we rather begin to howl among the wolves. Besides, the license which is

MATTHEW HENRY

20. RESH.

153-154
Here, I. David prays for succor in distress. Is any afflicted? let him pray; let him pray as David does here.
1. He has an eye to God's pity, and prays, "Consider my affliction; take it into thy thoughts, and all the circumstances of it, and sit not by as one unconcerned." God is never unmindful of his people's afflictions, but he will have us to put him in remembrance (Isa. xliii. 26), to spread our case before him, and then leave it to his compassionate consideration to do in it as in his wisdom he shall think fit, in his own time and way.
2. He has an eye to God's power and prays, Deliver me; and again, "Deliver me; consider my troubles and bring me out of them." God has promised deliverance (Ps. 1.15) and we may pray for it, with submission to his will and with regard to his glory, that we may serve him the better.
3. He has an eye to God's righteousness, and prays, "Plead my cause; be thou my patron and advocate, and take me for thy client." David had a just cause, but his adversaries were many and mighty, and he was in danger of being run down by them; he therefore begs of God to clear his integrity and silence their false accusations.
II. He pleads his dependence upon the word of God and his obedient regard to its directions: Quicken and deliver me according to thy word of promise, for I do not forget thy precepts.

155
Here is,
1. The description of wicked men. They do not only do God's statutes, but they do not so much as seek them; they do not acquaint themselves with them, nor so much as desire to know their duty, nor in the least endeavor to do it. Those are wicked indeed who do not think the law of God worth enquiring after, but are altogether regardless of it, being resolved to live at large and to walk in the way of their heart.
2. Their doom: Salvation is far from them. They cannot upon any good grounds promise themselves temporal deliverance. Let not that man think that he shall receive any thing of the Lord.

156
Here,
1. David admires God's grace: Great are thy tender mercies, O Lord! The goodness of God's nature, as it is his glory, so it is the joy of all the saints. His mercies are tender, for he is full of compassion; they are many, they are great, a fountain that can never be exhausted.
2. He begs for God's grace, reviving quickening grace, according to his judgments, that is, according to the tenor of the new covenant.

Psalm 119

157-160
157 Many are my persecutors and mine enemies; yet do I not decline from thy testimonies.
158 I beheld the transgressors, and was grieved; because they kept not thy word.
159 Consider how I love thy precepts: quicken me, O LORD, according to thy loving kindness.
160 Thy word is true from the beginning: and every one of thy righteous judgments endureth for ever.

Verse 157. Many are my persecutors and mine enemies. Those who actually assail me, or who secretly abhor me, are many. He sets this over against the many tender mercies of God. It seems a strange thing that a truly godly man, as David was, should have many enemies; but it is inevitable. The disciple cannot be loved where his Master is hated. The seed of the serpent must oppose the seed of the woman: it is their nature. Yet do I not decline from thy testimonies. He did not deviate from the truth of God, but proceeded in the straight way, however many adversaries might endeavor to block up his path. Some men have been led astray by one enemy, but here is a saint who held on his way in the teeth of many persecutors. There is enough in the testimonies of God to recompense us for pushing forward against all the hosts that may combine against us. So long as they cannot drive or draw us into a spiritual decline our foes have done us no great harm, and they have accomplished nothing by their malice. If we do not decline they are defeated. If they cannot make us sin they have missed their mark. Faithfulness to the truth is victory over our enemies.
Verse 158. I beheld the transgressors. I saw the traitors; I understood their character, their object, their way, and their end. I could not help seeing them, for they pushed themselves into my way. As I was obliged to see them I fixed my eyes on them, to learn what I could from them. And was grieved. I was sorry to see such sinners. I was sick of them, disgusted with them, I could not endure them. I found no pleasure in them, they were a sad sight to me, however fine their clothing or witty their chattering. Even when they were most mirthful a sight of them made my heart heavy; I could not tolerate either them or their doings. Because they kept not thy word. My grief was occasioned more by their sin against God than by their enmity against myself. I could bear their evil treatment of my words, but not their neglect of thy word. Thy word is so precious to me that those who will not keep it move me to indignation; I cannot keep the company of those who keep not God's word. That they should have no love for me is a trifle; but to despise the teaching of the Lord is abominable.
Verse 159. Consider, or see, how I love thy precepts. A second time he asks for consideration. As he said before, "Consider mine affliction," so now he says, "Consider mine affection." He loved the precepts of God—loved them unspeakably loved them so as to be grieved with those who did not love them. This is a sure test: many there are who have a warm side towards the promises, but as for the precepts, they cannot endure them. The Psalmist so loved everything that was good and excellent that he loved all God had commanded. The precepts are all of them wise and holy, therefore the man of God loved them extremely, loved to know them, to think of them, to reclaim them, and principally to practice them. He asked the Lord to remember and consider this, not upon the ground of merit, but that it should serve as an answer to the slanderous accusations which at this lime were the great, sting of his sorrow.
Verse 160. The sweet singer finishes up this section in the same way as the last by dwelling upon the sureness of the truth of God. It will be well for the reader to note the likeness between Ps 119:144, 152, and the present one. Thy word is true. Whatever the transgressors may say, God is true, and his word is true. The ungodly are false, but God's word is true. They charge us with being false, but our solace is that God's true word will clear us. From the beginning. God's word has been true from the first moment in which it was spoken, true throughout the whole of history, true to us from the instant in which we believed it, and true to us before we were true to it. Some read it, "Thy word is true from the head;" true as a whole, true from top to bottom. Experience had taught David this lesson, and experience is teaching us the same. The Scriptures are as true in Genesis as in Revelation, and the five books of: Moses are as inspired as the four Gospels.

allowed them of doing what they please without the fear of being punished, is a powerful engine for shaking our faith, because, when God thus winks at the wicked, he seems to abandon us for a prey. The Prophet therefore, by God's testimonies, means not only the rule of holy and righteous living, but also the promises. Lord, as if he had said, I have not turned away from the path of integrity, although the conduct of the wicked has presented me with a temptation to do so; nor have I shaken off nay confidence in thy grace, but have waited patiently for thy succor. Both these are necessary.

158. I saw the perfidious and child them. In this verse the Psalmist proceeds yet farther, declaring that he was inflamed with a holy zeal when he saw the law of God despised by the wicked. In short, we are admonished by the example of the Prophet, that we ought to feel such displeasure at the contempt of God's word as that our heart grows hot even to chiding. In the first place, then, let grief affect us inwardly; and next, whenever opportunity shall present itself, let; us strenuously endeavor to repress the forwardness and pride of the wicked, and let us not hesitate to do so from the fear of provoking their resentment against us.

159. Behold, O Jehovah how I have loved thy commandments. When the saints speak of their own piety before God they are not chargeable with obtruding their own merits as the ground of their confidence; but they regard this as, a settled principle, that God, who distinguishes his servants from the profane and wicked, will be merciful to them because they seek him with their whole heart. Besides, an unfeigned love of God's law is an undoubted evidence of adoption, since this love is the work of the Holy Spirit. The Prophet, therefore, although he arrogates nothing to himself, very properly adduces his own piety for the purpose, of encouraging himself to entertain the more assured hope of obtaining his request, through the grace of God which he had experienced.

160. The beginning of thy word is truth. The design of the Prophet it is not difficult to perceive; but the words admit of being understood in two ways. This sentence contains the profitable doctrine, that if we are finished with eyes of understanding, we will no sooner cast our eyes upon heavenly doctrine than the truth of it will meet our view. Others, however, give a different explanation, and perhaps with no less propriety, eliciting this sense, That the word of God has been from the beginning certain and infallible truth, and will continue so even to the end. These two clauses hang very well together—that God has been true to his word from the beginning, and that he will continue to be so everlastingly and immutably. The interpretation which refers the word judgment to the works of God and not to his doctrine, I would not altogether condemn, yet it is not in harmony with the context. Let us then retain this sense, That from the time when God began to speak he has always been faithful to his promises, and has never disappointed the hope of his people; and that the course of this faithfulness has been so uniform, that from the beginning even to the end his word is true and faithful.

157

Here is,

1. David surrounded with difficulties and dangers: Many are my persecutors and my enemies. When Saul the king was his persecutor and enemy no marvel that many more were so: multitudes will follow the pernicious ways of abused authority. David, being a public person, had many enemies, but withal he had many friends, who loved him and wished him well; let him set the one over-against the other. In this David was a type both of Christ and his church. The enemies, the persecutors, of both, are many, very many.

2. David established in the way of his duty, notwithstanding: "Yet do I not decline from thy testimonies, as knowing that while I adhere to them God is for me; and then no matter who is against me." A man who is steady in the way of his duty, though he may have many enemies, needs fear none.

158

Here is,

1. David's sorrow for the wickedness of the wicked. He beheld the transgressors, those whose sins were open before all men, and it grieved him to see them dishonor God, serve Satan, debauch the world, and ruin their own souls.

2. The reason of that sorrow. He was grieved, not because they were vexatious to him, but because they were provoking to God: They kept not thy word. Those that hate sin truly hate it as sin, as a transgression of the law of God and a violation of his word.

159

Here is,

1. David's appeal to God concerning his love to his precepts: "Lord, thou knowest all things, thou knowest that I love them; consider it then, and deal with me as thou usest to deal with those that love thy word, which thou hast magnified above all thy name."

2. His petition thereupon: "Quicken me, to do my duty with vigor; revive me, keep me alive, not according to any merit of mine, though I love thy word, but according to thy lovingkindness."

160

David here comforts himself with the faithfulness of God's word, for the encouragement of himself and others to rely upon it.

1. It has always been found faithful hitherto, and never failed any that ventured upon it; It is true from the beginning. Ever since God began to reveal himself to the children of men all he said was true and to be trusted.

2. It will be found faithful to the end, because righteous: "Every one of thy judgments remains for ever unalterable and of perpetual obligation, adjusting men's everlasting doom."

Psalm 119

Sin and Shin

161-164

161 Princes have persecuted me without a cause: but my heart standeth in awe of thy word.
162 I rejoice at thy word, as one that findeth great spoil.
163 I hate and abhor lying: but thy law do I love.
164 Seven times a day do I praise thee because of thy righteous judgments.

Verse 161. Princes have persecuted me without a cause. Such persons ought to have known better; they should have had sympathy with one of their own rank. A man expects a fair trial at the hand of his peers: it is ignoble to be prejudiced. Moreover, if honor be banished from all other breasts it should remain in the bosom of kings, and honor forbids the persecution of the innocent. Princes are appointed to protect the innocent and avenge the oppressed, and it is a shame when they themselves become the assailants of the righteous. It was a sad case when the man of God found himself attacked by the judges of the earth, for eminent position added weight and venom to their enmity. It was well that the sufferer could truthfully assert that this persecution was without cause.

Verse 162. I rejoice at thy word, as one that findeth great spoil. His awe did not prevent his joy; his fear of God was not of the kind which perfect love casts out, but of the sort which it nourishes. He trembled at the word of the Lord, and yet rejoiced at it. He compares his joy to that of one who has been long in battle, and has at last won the victory and is dividing the spoil. This usually falls to the lot of princes, and though David was not one with them in their persecutions, yet he had his victories, and his spoil was equal to their greatest gains. The profits made in searching the Scriptures were greater than the trophies of war. We too have to fight for divine truth; every doctrine costs us a battle, but when we gain a full understanding of it by personal struggles it becomes doubly precious to us. In these days godly men have a full share of battling for the word of God; may we have for our spoil a firmer hold upon the priceless word. Perhaps, however, the Psalmist may have rejoiced as one who comes upon hidden treasure for which lie had not fought, in which case we find the analogy in the man of God who, while reading the Bible, makes grand and blessed discoveries of the grace of God laid up for him,—discoveries which surprise him, for he looked not to find such a prize. Whether we come by the truth as finders or as warriors fighting for it, the heavenly treasure should be equally dear to us. With what quiet joy does the ploughman steal home with his golden find! How victors shout as they share the plunder! How glad should that man be who has discovered his portion in the promises of holy writ, and is able to enjoy it for himself, knowing by the witness of the Holy Spirit that it is all his own.

Verse 163. I hate and abhor lying. A double expression for an inexpressible loathing. Falsehood in doctrine, in life, or in speech, falsehood in any form or shape, had become utterly detestable to the Psalmist. This was a remarkable state for an Oriental, for generally lying is the delight of Easterns, and the only wrong they see in it is a want of skill in its exercise so that the liar is found out. David himself had made much progress when he had come to this. He does not, however, alone refer to falsehood in conversation; he evidently intends perversity in faith and teaching. He set down all opposition to the God of truth as lying, and then he turned his whole soul against it in the most intense form of indignation. Godly men should detest false doctrine even as they abhor a lie. But thy law do I love, because it is all truth. His love was as ardent as his hate. True men love truth, and hate lying. It is well for us to know which way our hates and loves run, and we may do essential service to others by declaring what are their objects. Both love and hate are contagious, and when they are sanctified the wider their influence the better.

Verse 164. Seven times a day do I praise thee because of thy righteous judgments. He labored perfectly to praise his perfect God, and therefore fulfilled the perfect number of songs. Seven may also intend frequency. Frequently he lifted up his heart in thanksgiving to God for his divine teachings in the word, and for his divine actions m providence. With his

JOHN CALVIN

Psalm 119:161-168

161. Princes have persecuted me without a cause. Here the Psalmist, informs us that sore and grievous as his temptation had been, he was restrained by the fear of God from desiring to attempt anything unworthy of the character of a godly man. We are prone to fall into despair when princes who are armed with power to overwhelm us are hostile to and molest us. The evil is also aggravated from the consideration that it is the very persons who ought to be as bucklers to defend us, who employ their strength in hurting us. Yea, when the afflicted are stricken by those in high places, they in a manner think that the hand of God is against them. There was also this peculiarity in the case of the Prophet, that he had to encounter the grandees of the chosen people—men whom God had placed in such honorable stations, to the end they might be the pillars of the Church.

162. I have rejoiced at thy word as one who hath found great spoil. No gain, it is well known, brings greater joy than that which conquerors acquire from the spoil of their enemies; for to the gain there is added the glory of triumph; and when profit comes on a sudden, the delight experienced is from that circumstance the greater. This is the reason why David compares the knowledge he had obtained of heavenly doctrine with spoils rather than with other riches; for by these words he intimates that his greatest joy was derived from the word of God, to which no gain however desirable could at all approach. From this was learn that he was contented with the word of God as a thing in which was all his delight, and in which he found solid felicity; which could not be, but, in the way of his first withdrawing his heart from all depraved desires. Nor is it wonderful to find David placing the whole sum of a happy life in the word of God, in which he well knew the treasure of eternal life to be included and offered to him by means of free adoption.

163. I have hated and abhorred deceit. In this verse he declares that he was cleansed from corrupt affections that he might bestow upon the law of God such honor and estimation as it deserved.

164. Seven times a day have I praised thee. By the adverb seven times, the Prophet means that he was continually or very often engaged in celebrating the praises of God; just as it is said in Proverbs 24:16, "A just man falleth seven times," when he often falls into divers temptations. This diligence in praising God shows that David not only spoke reverently and honorably of the divine law, but that he accounted it an inestimable boon conferred upon the human race. It was not simply admiration which constrained him to this commendation, but a principle of gratitude; for he saw that nothing more excellent could be bestowed upon men than their being renewed to a blessed and an endless life by the incorruptible seed of heavenly truth. Yet scarcely one in a hundred of those to whom God offers this treasure puts himself to the trouble of giving God thanks for it even in an ordinary manner. On the contrary, there reigns such vile ingratitude everywhere in the world, that some scornfully

MATTHEW HENRY

21. SCHIN.

161

David here lets us know,

1. How he was discouraged in his duty by the fear of man: Princes persecuted him. They looked upon him as a traitor and an enemy to the government, and under that notion sought his life, and bade him go serve other gods, 1 Sam. xxvi. 19.

2. How he was kept to his duty, notwithstanding, by the fear of God: "They would make me stand in awe of them and their word, and do as they bid me; but my heart stands in awe of thy word, and I am resolved to please God, and keep in with him, whoever is displeased and falls out with me."

162

Here is,

1. The pleasure David took in the word of God. He rejoiced at it, rejoiced that God had made such a discovery of his mind, that Israel was blessed with that light when other nations sat in darkness, that he was himself let into the understanding of it and had had experience of the power of it.

2. The degree of that pleasure—as one that finds great spoil. This supposes a victory over the enemy. It is through much opposition that a soul comes to this, to rejoice in God's word.

163

Love and hatred are the leading affections of the soul; if those be fixed aright, the rest move accordingly. Here we have them fixed aright in David.

1. He had a rooted antipathy to sin; he could not endure to think of it: I hate and abhor lying, which may be taken for all sin, inasmuch as by it we deal treacherously and perfidiously with God and put a cheat upon ourselves.

2. He had a rooted affection to the word of God: Thy law do I love. And therefore he abhorred lying, for lying is contrary to the whole law of God; and the reason why he loved the law of God was because of the truth of it.

164

David, in this psalm, is full of complaints, yet those did neither jostle out his praises nor put him out of tune for them; whatever condition a child of God is in he does not want matter for praise and therefore should not want a heart. See here,

1. How often David praised God—Seven times a day, that is, very frequently, not only every day, but often every day.

2. What he praised God for—because of thy righteous judgments. We must praise God for his precepts, which are all just and good, for his promises and threatenings and the performance of both in his providence.

Psalm 119

165-168

165 Great peace have they which love thy law: and nothing shall offend them.
166 LORD, I have hoped for thy salvation, and done thy commandments.
167 My soul hath kept thy testimonies; and I love them exceedingly.
168 I have kept thy precepts and thy testimonies: for all my ways are before thee.

voice he extolled the righteousness of the Judge of all the earth. As often as ever he thought of God's ways a song leaped to his lips. At the sight of the oppressive princes, and at the hearing of the abounding falsehood around him, he felt all the more bound to adore and magnify God, who in all things is truth and righteousness. When others rob us of our praise it should be a caution to us not to fall into the same conduct towards our God, who is so much more worthy of honor. If we praise God when we are persecuted our music will be all the sweeter to him because of our constancy in suffering. If we keep clear of all lying, our song will be the more acceptable because it comes out of pure lips. If we never flatter men we shall be the better condition for honoring the Lord. Do we praise God seven times a day? Do we praise him once in seven days?

Verse 165. Great peace have they which love thy law. What a charming verse is this! It dwells not with those who perfectly keep the law, for where should such men be found? but with those who love it, whose hearts and hands are made to square with its precepts and demands. These men are ever striving, with all their hearts, to walk in obedience to the law, and though they are often persecuted they have peace, yea, great peace; for they have learned the secret of the reconciling blood, they have felt the power of the comforting Spirit, and they stand before the Father as men accepted. The Lord has given them to feel his peace, which passed all understanding.

Verse 166. Lord, I have hoped for thy salvation, and done thy commandments. Here we have salvation by grace, and the fruits thereof. All David's hope was fixed upon God, he looked to him alone for salvation; and then he endeavored most earnestly to fulfill the commands of his law. Those who place least reliance upon good works are very frequently those who have tile most of them; that same divine teaching which delivers us from confidence in our own doings leads us to abound in every good work to the glory of God. In times of trouble there are two things to be done, the first is to hope in God, and the second is to do that which is right. The first without the second would be mere presumption: the second without the first mere formalism. It is well if in looking back we can claim to have acted in the way which is commanded of the Lord. If we have acted rightly towards God we are sure that lie will act kindly with us.

Verse 167. My soul hath kept thy testimonies. My outward life has kept thy precepts, and my inward life—my soul, has kept thy testimonies. God has borne testimony to many sacred truths, and these we hold fast as for life itself. The gracious man stores up the truth of God within his heart as a treasure exceedingly dear and precious—he keeps it. His secret soul, his inmost self, becomes the guardian of these divine teachings which are his sole authority in soul matters. And I love them exceedingly. This was why he kept them, and having kept them this was the result of the keeping. He did not merely store up revealed truth by way of duty, but because of a deep, unutterable affection for it. He felt that he could sooner die than give up any part of the revelation of God. The more we store our minds with heavenly truth, the more deeply shall we be in love with it: the more we see the exceeding riches of the Bible the more will our love exceed measure, and exceed expression.

Verse 168. I have kept thy precepts and thy testimonies. Both the practical and the doctrinal parts of God's word he had stored up, and preserved, and followed. It is a blessed thing to see the two forms of the divine word, equally known, equally valued, equally confessed: there should be no picking and choosing as to the mind of God. We know those who endeavor to be careful as to the precepts, but who seem to think that the doctrines of the gospel are mere matters of opinion, which they may shape for themselves. This is not a perfect condition of things.

JOHN CALVIN

reject divine truth, and others despise or slight it, while others rail and gnash their teeth against it if they find anything in it which does not please them.

165. Great peace have they who love thy law. If we take the word peace for a prosperous or happy condition of life—a sense in which the Hebrews often employ it—the word rendered stumbling-block, to correspond with it, will be used for adversity; as if it had been said, that those who love God's law shall continually prosper and retain their position, although the whole world should fall into ruins. But a different interpretation will be equally appropriate, namely, that they have great peace, because, being persuaded that both their persons and their life are acceptable to God, they calmly repose themselves on a good conscience. This tranquil state of conscience, this serenity of mind, is justly reckoned the chief point of a happy life, that is to say it is so, when it proceeds from God's being reconciled to us, and from his fatherly favor shining in our hearts. The Prophet justly teaches that we attain this peace from the love of the law; for whoever would make it to depend upon anything else, will be from time to time trembling at every little blast. If this sense is adopted, the word stumbling-block, in the second clause, will signify all the troubles and disquietudes of mind with which all who lean not upon God's word are miserably distressed and tormented, and with which they are driven about either by their own depraved passions, or by the caprice of other men. But in whatever way understand these two words, peace and stumbling-block, the design of the Prophet will remain the same, which is to show, that those who are not devoted to God are miserable; for although they may applaud themselves for a time, yet they will meet with many stumbling-blocks to drive them suddenly out of their course.

166. O Jehovah! I have waited for thy salvation. It is not without cause that the Prophet often repeats this sentence, which is in all men's mouths, there being nothing easier than to ascribe to God the praise and office of saving, while yet there is hardly to be met with in the world a single example of steadfast hope, when men come to wrestle with temptations for any length of time.

168. I have kept thy commandments and thy testimonies. What the Psalmist had expressed more strongly, he now repeats more simply, adding there to reason. He abbreviates the statement as made in the preceding verse only by here omitting the word soul, which he there uses, whilst to commandments he joins testimonies, in order the more distinctly to show that he does not speak exclusively of the rule of an upright and holy life, but also comprehends the whole covenant of salvation. And, assuredly, the doctrine of the law could not be so sweet and attractive from its commanding what is right, did it not at the same time exhibit the free favor of God. The reason which the Prophet assigns for his keeping God's commandments and testimonies—for all my ways are before thee—is to this effect, That the truth, which he well knew, that nothing is hidden from God, served as a bridle to keep him devoted to the cultivation of godliness.

MATTHEW HENRY

165

Here is an account of the happiness of good men, who are governed by a principle of love to the word of God, who make it their rule and are ruled by it.

1. They are easy, and have a holy serenity; none enjoy themselves more than they do: Great peace have those that love thy law, abundant satisfaction in doing their duty and pleasure in reflecting upon it.

2. They are safe, and have a holy security: Nothing shall offend them; nothing shall be a scandal, snare, or stumbling-block, to them, to entangle them either in guilt or grief.

166

Here is the whole duty of man; for we are taught,

1. To keep our eye upon God's favor as our end: "Lord, I have hoped for thy salvation, not only temporal but eternal salvation. I have hoped for that as my happiness and laid up my treasure in it; I have hoped for it as thine, as a happiness of thy preparing, thy promising, and which consists in being with thee. Hope of this has raised me above the world, and borne me up under all my burdens in it."

2. To keep our eye upon God's word as our rule: I have done thy commandments, that is, I have made conscience of conforming myself to thy will in every thing. Observe here how God has joined these two together, and let no man put them asunder. We cannot, upon good grounds, hope for God's salvation, unless we set ourselves to do his commandments, Rev. xxii. 14.

167-168

David's conscience here witnesses for him,

I. That his practices were good.

1. He loved God's testimonies, he loved them exceedingly. Our love to the word of God must be a superlative love (we must love it better than the wealth and pleasure of this world), and it must be a victorious love, such as will subdue and mortify our lusts and extirpate carnal affections.

2. He kept them, his soul kept them. Bodily exercise profits little in religion; we must make heart-work of it or we make nothing of it. The soul must be sanctified and renewed, and delivered into the mould of the word; the soul must be employed in glorifying God, for he will be worshipped in the spirit. We must keep both the precepts and the testimonies.

II. That he was governed herein by a good principle: "Therefore I have kept thy precepts, because by faith I have seen thy eye always upon me; all my ways are before thee; thou knowest every step I take and strictly observest all I say and do. Thou dost see and accept all that I say and do well; thou dost see and art displeased with all I say and do amiss." Note, The consideration of this, that God's eye is upon us at all times, should make us very careful in every thing to keep his commandments, Gen. xvii. 1.

Psalm 119

Taw

169-172

169 Let my cry come near before thee, O LORD: give me understanding according to thy word.
170 Let my supplication come before thee: deliver me according to thy word.
171 My lips shall utter praise, when thou hast taught me thy statutes.
172 My tongue shall speak of thy word: for all thy commandments are righteousness.

We have known others again who are very rigid as to the doctrines, and painfully lax with reference to the precepts. This also is far from right. When the two are "kept" with equal earnestness then have we the perfect man. For all my ways are before thee. Probably he means to say that this was the motive of his endeavoring to be right both in head and heart, because he knew that God saw him, and under the sense of the divine presence he was afraid to err.

Verse 169. Let my cry come near before thee, O LORD. He is tremblingly afraid lest he should not be heard. He is conscious that his prayer is nothing better than the cry of a poor child, or the groan of a wounded beast. He dreads lest it should be shut out from the ear of the Most High, but he very boldly prays that it may come before God, that it may be in his sight, under his notice, and looked upon with his acceptance; yea, he goes further, and entreats, "Let my cry come near before thee, O Lord." He wants the Lord's attention to his prayer to be very close and considerate. He uses a figure of speech and personifies his prayer. We may picture his prayer as Esther, venturing into the royal presence, entreating an audience, and begging to find favor in the sight of the blessed and only Potentate. It is a very sweet thing to a suppliant when he knows of a surety that his prayer has obtained audience, when it has trodden the sea of glass before the throne, and has come even to the footstool of the glorious seat around which heaven and earth adore. It is to Jehovah that this prayer is expressed with trembling earnestness—our translators, filled with holy reverence, translate the word, "O LORD." We crave audience of none else, for we have confidence in none beside.

Verse 170. Let my supplication come before thee. It is the same entreaty with a slight change of words. He humbly calls his cry a supplication, a sort of beggar's petition; and again he asks for audience and for answer. There might be hindrances in the way to an audience, and he begs for their removal—let it come. Other believers are heard—let my prayer come before thee. Deliver me according to thy word. Rid me of mine adversaries, clear me of my slanderers, preserve me from my tempters, and bring me up out of all my afflictions, even as thy word has led me to expect thou wilt do. It is for this that he seeks understanding. His enemies would succeed through his folly, if they succeeded at all; but if he exercised a sound discretion they would be baffled, and he would escape from them. The Lord in answer to prayer frequently delivers his children by making them wise as serpents as well as harmless as doves.

Verse 171. My lips shall utter praise, when thou hast taught we thy statutes. He will not always be pleading for himself, he will rise above all selfishness, and render thanks for the benefit received. He promises to praise God when he has obtained practical instruction in the life of godliness: this is something to praise for, no blessing is more precious. The best possible praise is that which proceeds from men who honor God, not only with their lips, but in their lives. We learn the music of heaven in the school of holy living. He whose life honors the Lord is sure to be a man of praise. David would not only be grateful in silence, but he would express that gratitude in appropriate terms: his lips would utter what his life had practiced. Eminent disciples are wont to speak well of the master who instructed them, and this holy man, when taught the statutes of the Lord, promises to give all the glory to him to whom it is due.

Verse 172. My tongue shall speak of thy word. When he had done singing he began preaching. God's tender mercies are such that they may be either said or sung. When the tongue speaks of God's word it has a most fruitful subject; such speaking will be as a tree of life, whose leaves shall be for the healing of the people. Men will gather together to listen to such talk, and they will treasure it up in their hearts. The worst of us is that for the most part we are full of our own words, and speak but little of God's word. Oh, that we could come to the same resolve as this godly man, and say henceforth, "My tongue

JOHN CALVIN

Psalm 119:169-174

169. Let my cry come near into thy presence. The Psalmist repeats that his chief desire, and what he, most of all pressed after, regarding everything else as of secondary importance, was to make progress in the study of the divine law. By the word cry he denotes earnestness. I am anxious, as if he had said, above all things, and am chiefly inflamed with this desire, (even as it is just and reasonable,) that the light of understanding by which we excel the lower animals, and approach very near to God, may be preferred by me to all earthly advantages.
170. Let my prayer come into thy presence. After having made supplication that the gift of right understanding might be imparted to him, the Psalmist now implores God for deliverance, by which he acknowledges that lie was continually involved in multiplied dangers from which he found it impossible to escape, unless God stretched forth his hand from heaven to his aid. We know, indeed, that whenever any distress was pressing hard behind him, he called upon God for succor; but as he does not here specify any particular distress, I have no doubt that, in commending his life in general terms to the protection of God, he thought again and again how he was shut up on every side by innumerable deaths, from which lie could not escape if God did not prove his continual deliverer. But this is an inestimable comfort to us, that God assures us that in all dangers he will be ready and prepared to help us.
171. My lips shall speak praise. David now shows in another way than in the preceding verse, how high a privilege lie accounted it to be admitted by God among the number of His disciples, and to profit aright in His school, by declaring that, if so privileged, he will hasten forward to render thanks to him with fluent tongue.
172. My tongue shall speak of thy word. Here the Psalmist says, that when he shall have profited in God's law he will also employ himself in teaching it to others. This order is undoubtedly to be observed, That divine truth take root in our hearts before we engage in the work of teaching it to others. Yet every man, according to the measure of his faith, ought to communicate to his brethren what he has received, that the doctrine, whose use and fruit God would have to be displayed for the common edification of the Church, may not be buried.
173. Let thy hand be to succor me. As he had devoted himself to the doctrine of the law, David requests that the hand of God may be stretched forth for his aid. Farther, by these words he declares, that those who yield themselves to God to be governed by His word have continually need of His help. The more sincerely any individual studies to be a good man, so much the more numerous are the ways in which Satan troubles him, and so much the more are the enemies multiplied who molest him on all sides. But when God sees those who once embraced the truth of his word remaining steadfast in their resolution, he is so much the more inclined to aid them. By the word choose in the second clause, the Psalmist has expressed that nothing had hindered him from devoting himself to the

MATTHEW HENRY

22. TAU.

169-170
Here we have,
I. A general petition for audience repeated: Let my cry come near before thee; and again, Let my supplication come before thee. He calls his prayer his cry, which denotes the fervency and vehemence of it, and his supplication, which denotes the humility of it. We must come to God as beggars come to our doors for an alms. He is concerned that his prayer might come before God, might come near before him, that is, that he might have grace and strength by faith and fervency to lift up his prayers, that no guilt might interpose to shut out his prayers and to separate between him and God, and that God would graciously receive his prayers and take notice of them. His prayer that his supplication might come before God implied a deep sense of his unworthiness, and a holy fear that his prayer should come short or miscarry, as not fit to come before God; nor would any of our prayers have had access to God if Jesus Christ had not approached to him as an advocate for us.
II. Two particular requests, which he is thus earnest to present:
1. That God, by his grace, would give him wisdom to conduct himself well under his troubles: Give me understanding; he means that wisdom of the prudent which is to understand his way; "Give me to know thee and myself, and my duty to thee."
2. That God, by his providence, would rescue him out of his troubles: Deliver me, that is, with the temptation make a way to escape, 1 Cor. x. 13.
III. The same general plea to enforce these requests—according to thy word. This directs and limits his desires: "Lord, give me such an understanding as thou hast promised and such a deliverance as thou hast promised; I ask for no other."

171
Here is,
1. A great favor which David expects from God, that he will teach him his statutes. This he had often prayed for in this psalm, and urged his petition for it with various arguments; and now that he is drawing towards the close of the psalm he speaks of it as taken for granted.
2. The grateful sense he promises to have of that favor: My lips shall utter praise when thou hast taught me. Then he shall have cause to praise God. Those that are taught of God have a great deal of reason to be thankful, for this is the foundation of all these spiritual blessings, which are the best blessings, and the earnest of eternal blessings.

172
Observe here,
1. The good knowledge David had of the word of God; he knew it so well that he was ready to own, with the

Psalm 119

173-176

173 Let thine hand help me; for I have chosen thy precepts.
174 I have longed for thy salvation, O LORD; and thy law is my delight.
175 Let my soul live, and it shall praise thee; and let thy judgments help me.
176 I have gone astray like a lost sheep; seek thy servant; for I do not forget thy commandments.

shall speak of thy word." Then should we break through our sinful silence; we should no more be cowardly and half hearted, but should be true witnesses for Jesus. It is not only of God's works that we are to speak, but of his word. We may extol its truth, its wisdom, its preciousness, its grace, its power; and then we may tell of all it has revealed, all it has promised, all it has commanded, all it has effected. The subject gives us plenty of sea room; we may speak on for ever: the tale is for ever telling, yet untold.

Verse 173. Let thine hand help me. Give me practical succor. Do not entrust me to my friends or thy friends, but put thine own hand to the work. Thy hand has both skill and power, readiness and force: display all these qualities on my behalf. I am willing to do the utmost that I am able to do; but what I need is thine help, and this is so urgently required that if I have it not I shall sink. Do not refuse thy succor. Great as thy hand is, let it light on me, even me. The prayer reminds me of Peter walking on the sea and beginning to sink; he, too, cried, "Lord, help me," and the hand of his Master was stretched out for his rescue. For I have chosen, thy precepts.

Verse 174. I have lounged for thy salvation, O LORD. He speaks like old Jacob on his deathbed; indeed, all saints, both in prayer and in death, appear as one, in word, and deed, and mind. He knew God's salvation, and yet he longed for it; that is to say, he had experienced a share of it, and he was therefore led to expect something yet higher and more complete. There is a salvation yet to come, when we shall be clean delivered from the body of this death, set free from all the turmoil and trouble of this mortal life, raised above the temptations and assaults of Satan, and brought near unto our God, to be like him and with him for ever and ever. I have longed for thy salvation, O Jehovah; and thy law is my delight. The first clause tells us what the saint longs for, and this informs us what is his present satisfaction. God's law, contained in the ten commandments, gives joy to believers. God's law, that is, the entire Bible, is a well spring of consolation and enjoyment to all who receive it. Though we have not yet reached the fullness of our salvation, yet we find in God's word so much concerning a present salvation that we are even now delighted.

Verse 175. Let my soul live. Fill it full of life, preserve it from wandering into the ways of death, give it to enjoy the indwelling of the Holy Ghost, let it live to the fullness of life, to the utmost possibilities of its new created being. And it shall praise thee. It shall praise thee for life, for new life, for eternal life, for thou art the Lord and Giver of life. The more it shall live, the more it shall praise, and when it shall live in perfection it shall praise thee in perfection. Spiritual life is prayer and praise. And let thy judgments help me. While I read the record of what thou hast done, in terror or in love, let me be quickened and developed. While I see thy hand actually at work upon me, and upon others, chastening sin, and smiling upon righteousness, let me be helped both to live aright and to praise thee. Let all thy deeds in providence instruct me, and help me to overcome sin and to practice holiness.

Verse 176. This is the finale, the conclusion of the whole matter: I have gone astray like a lost sheep—often, willfully, wantonly, and even hopelessly, but for thine interposing grace. In times gone by, before I was afflicted, and before thou hadst fully taught me thy statutes, I went astray. "I went astray" from the practical precepts, from the instructive doctrines, and from the heavenly experiences which thou hadst set before me. I lost my road, and I lost myself. Even now I am apt to wander, and, in fact, have roamed already; therefore, Lord, restore me. Seek thy servant. He was not like a dog, that somehow or other can find its way back; but he was like a lost sheep, which goes further and further away from home; yet still he was a sheep, and the Lord's sheep, his property, and precious in his sight, and therefore he hoped to be sought in order to be restored.

law of God. No man will apply this mind to the love of the law without a great struggle, since the thoughts of every man are drawn away to a variety of objects, by the depraved affections of the flesh. This choosing then spoken of shows that it is not through ignorance or an inconsiderate zeal that the children of God desire above all things heavenly doctrine; but as they partake of the flexibility of mind common to men, and feel the various impulses of the flesh, they purposely subdue their minds to the obedience of God.

174. I have longed for thy salvation, O Jehovah! Although all men desire to be in happy circumstances, and no man avowedly repudiates God's favor; yet so confused and uncertain are the ideas which they entertain of that in which a life of happiness or propriety consists, that very few are to be found directing their aspirations to God. Some are carried away by their own ambition, some are wholly possessed with avarice, and others burn with lust, all imagining, that the farther they recede from God, everything will prosper so much the better with them. In short, in proportion as each man is desirous to be safe, in the same proportion does he provoke the anger of God, by seeking the means of his safety in all directions.

175. Let my soul live and let it praise thee. As the verbs are in the future tense, shall live, shall praise, this sentence may be expounded thus: Lord, when thou shalt have bestowed life upon me, I will endeavor, by celebrating thy praises, to show that I am not ungrateful. If this sense is approved, the sentence will be a kind of rejoicing, in which the Prophet, depending upon the divine promises, confidently proclaims, that his life will continue in safety.

176. I have wandered like a lost sheep. He is not to be understood as here confessing his sins,—an opinion erroneously held by many,—as if he had been drawn into the trails of Satan; for this is inconsistent with the second clause, in which he denies that he had forgotten God's law. The two clauses of this verse ought to be connected together by although, or notwithstanding, as if the Prophet had said, Although I have wandered about like a lost sheep, yet I have not forgotten the law of God. His meaning, I conceive, is, that he wandered, because, being chased by the force and violence of his enemies, he transported himself from place to place in great fear, in quest of retreats in which he might hide himself. This similitude would therefore very properly apply to him, because, although driven away and hunted after by his persecutors, he yet never turned aside from the law of God. Moreover, as the wolves pursued him everywhere, he prays God to bring him back and give him a place of safety and tranquility, that he may at length cease from any longer wandering hither and thither, and being as a vagabond. He had a very good ground for believing that he would be heard in the fact, that although provoked by manifold wrongs he yet never swerved from the fear of God—a statement which, however, ought to be referred rather to the general course of his life than to particular acts. Although when he fell into adultery he continued for a time in a state of insensibility, yet it cannot be denied that in his adversities he was restrained by a holy patience, so as to persevere in following after righteousness.

utmost satisfaction, that all God's commandments are not only righteous, but righteousness itself, the rule and standard of righteousness.

2. The good use he resolved to make of that knowledge: My tongue shall speak of thy word, not only utter praise for it to the glory of God, but discourse of it for the instruction and edification of others, as that which he himself was full of and as that which he desired others also might be filled with.

173-174

Here,

1. David prays that divine grace would work for him: Let thy hand help me. He finds his own hands are not sufficient for him, nor can any creature lend him a helping hand to any purpose; therefore he looks up to God in hopes that the hand that had made him would help him.

2. He pleads what divine grace had already wrought in him as a pledge of further mercy, being a qualification for it. Three things he pleads:

(1.) That he had made religion his serious and deliberate choice.

(2.) That his heart was upon heaven: I have longed for thy salvation.

(3.) That he took pleasure in doing his duty: "Thy law is my delight. Not only I delight in it, but it is my delight, the greatest delight I have in this world."

175

David's heart is still upon praising God; and therefore,

1. He prays that God would give him time to praise him: "Let my soul live, and it shall praise thee, that is, let my life be prolonged, that I may live to thy glory." The reason why a good man desires to live is that he may praise God in the land of the living, and do something to his honor.

2. He prays that God would give him strength to praise him: "Let thy judgments help me; let all ordinances and all providences" (both are God's judgments) "further me in glorifying God; let them be the matter of my praise and let them help to fit me for that work."

176

Here is,

1. A penitent confession: I have gone astray, or wander up and down, like a lost sheep.

2. A believing petition: Seek thy servant, as the good shepherd seeks a wandering sheep to bring it back again, Ezek. xxxiv. 12.

3. An obedient plea: "Though I have gone astray, yet I have not wickedly departed, I do not forget thy commandments." Thus he concludes the psalm with a penitent sense of his own sin and believing dependence on God's grace. With these a devout Christian will conclude his duties, will conclude his life; he will live and die repenting and praying.

Psalm 120

Title
A Song of degrees.

1 In my distress I cried unto the LORD, and he heard me.
2 Deliver my soul, O LORD, from lying lips, and from a deceitful tongue.
3 What shall be given unto thee? or what shall be done unto thee, thou false tongue?
4 Sharp arrows of the mighty, with coals of juniper.
5 Woe is me, that I sojourn in Mesech, that I dwell in the tents of Kedar!
6 My soul hath long dwelt with him that hateth peace.
7 I am for peace: but when I speak, they are for war.

Psalm 120

Suddenly we have left the continent of the vast Hundred and Nineteenth Psalm for the islands and islets of the Songs of Degrees. It may be well to engage in protracted devotion upon a special occasion, but this must cast no slur upon the sacred brevities which sanctify the godly life day by day. He who inspired the longest psalm was equally the author of the short compositions which follow it.
TITLE. A SONG OF DEGREES. We have already devoted a sufficient space to the consideration of this title in its application to this psalm and the fourteen compositions which succeed it. These appear to us to be Pilgrim Psalms, but we are not sure that they were always sung in company; for many of them are in the first person singular. No doubt there were solitary pilgrims as well as troops who went to the house of God in company, and for these lonely ones hymns were prepared.
SUBJECT. A certain author supposes that this hymn was sung by an Israelite upon leaving his house to go up to Jerusalem. He thinks that the good man had suffered from the slander of his neighbors, and was glad to get away from their gossip, and spend his time in the happier engagements of the holy feasts. It may be so, but we hope that pious people were not so foolish as to sing about their bad neighbors when they were leaving them, for a few days. If they wished to leave their houses in safety, and to come home to kind surroundings, it would have been the height of folly to provoke those whom they were leaving behind by singing aloud a psalm of complaint against them. We do not know why this ode is placed first among the Psalms of Degrees, and we had rather hazard no conjecture of our own. We prefer the old summary of the translators—"David prayeth against Doeg"—to any far fetched supposition: and if this be the scope of the psalm, we see at once why it suggested itself to David at the station where the ark abode, and from which he had come to remove it. He came to fetch away the ark, and at the place where he found it he thought of Doeg, and poured out his complaint concerning him. The author had been grievously calumniated, and had been tortured into bitterness by the false charges of his persecutors, and here is his appeal to the great Arbiter of right and wrong before whose judgment seal no man shall suffer from slanderous tongues.

EXPOSITION
Verse 1. In my distress. Slander occasions distress of the most grievous kind.
Verse 2. Deliver my soul, O Lord, from lying lips. It will need divine power to save a man from these deadly instruments. Lips are soft: but when they are lying lips they suck away the life of character and are as murderous as razors.
Verse 3. What shall be given unto thee? It is the worst of offences—this detraction, calumny, and slander. Judgment sharp and crushing would be measured out to it if men were visited for their transgressions.
Verse 4. Sharp arrows of the mighty. Swift, sure, and sharp shall be the judgment. Their words were as arrows, and so shall their punishment be.
Verse 5. Woe is me, that sojourn in Mesech, that I dwell in the tents of Kedar! Gracious men are vexed with the conversation of the wicked.
Verse 6. My soul hath long dwelt with him that hateth peace. Long, long enough, too long had he been an exile among such barbarians. A peace maker is a blessing, but a peace hater is a curse.
Verse 7. I am for peace. Properly, "I am peace"; desirous of peace, peaceful, forbearing,—in fact, peace itself. But when I speak, they are for war. David and David's Lord endured the same trial.

JOHN CALVIN

Psalm 120

1-4
1. I cried to Jehovah in my distress. The name of the author of the Psalm is not expressed, but the style of it throughout presents David to our view. Although, therefore, I cannot positively affirm, yet I am rather inclined to think that it was composed by him. Nor will it be improper, in my judgment, to explain it as if his name had been mentioned in the inscription. This, then, being granted, I would observe that although David, when in this verse he affirms that the Lord had heard him, gives thanks to him, yet his chief purpose was to set forth, in the form of complaint, how wickedly and cruelly Saul's flatterers employed all their ingenuity and power to accomplish his destruction.
2. O Jehovah! deliver my soul from the lip of falsehood. David now points out the kind of his affliction, declaring that he was loaded with false accusations. In charging his enemies with lying and falsehood, he asserts his own innocence of the crimes which they slanderously imputed to him. His complaint therefore amounts to this, that as he was conscious of having committed no fault, he was assaulted by the wicked contrary to all law, human and divine.
3. What shall the tongue of deceit give thee? The Prophet aggravates the malice of his enemies by asserting that they were so wickedly inclined as to be driven to evil speaking when they saw no prospect of deriving any advantage from such a course of conduct. He however seems to express more than this,—he seems farther to intimate, that after they have poured forth all the venom of their calumnies, their attempts will nevertheless be vain and ineffectual.
4. The arrows of a strong man sharpened, with coals of juniper. Here the Psalmist amplifies in another way the malice of such as distress the simple and innocent by their calumnies, affirming that they throw out their injurious reports just like a man who should draw an arrow, and with it pierce through the body of his neighbor; and that their calumnies were like coals of juniper, which penetrate more effectually, and burn more intensely the substances with which they come in contact than any other kind of coals.

5-7
5. Alas for me! that I have been a sojourner in Mesech. David complains that he was doomed to linger for a long time among a perverse people; his condition resembling that of some wretched individual who is compelled to live till he grows old in sorrowful exile.
6. My soul hath long dwelt with him who hateth peace. The Psalmist now shows, without figure, and, so to speak, points with the finger to those whom he had before indirectly marked out by the terms Mesech and Kedar, namely, the perfidious Israelites, who had degenerated from the holy fathers, and who rather wore the mask of Israelites than were the true seed of Israel. Let us, however, remember, that if God does not immediately stretch forth his hand in our behalf, it is our duty to bear the wearisomeness occasioned by delay.

MATTHEW HENRY

Psalm 120

1-4 Confession and complaints.
Here is,
I. Deliverance from a false tongue obtained by prayer. David records his own experience of this.

1. He was brought into distress, into great distress, by lying lips and a deceitful tongue. There were those that sought his ruin, and had almost effected it, by lying.
(1.) By telling lies to him. They flattered him with professions and protestations of friendships, and promises of kindness and service to him, that they might the more securely and without suspicion carry on their designs against him, and might have an opportunity, by betraying his counsels, to do him a mischief.
(2.) By telling lies of him. They forged false accusations against him and laid to his charge things that he knew not.

2. In this distress he had recourse to God by faithful and fervent prayer: I cried unto the Lord. Having no fence against false tongues, he appealed to him who has all men's hearts in his hand, who has power over the consciences of bad men, and can, when he pleases, bridle their tongues.

3. He obtained a gracious answer to this prayer. God heard him; so that his enemies, though they carried their designs very far, were baffled at last, and could not prevail to do him the mischief they intended.
II. The doom of a false tongue foretold by faith, v. 3, 4. As God will preserve his people from this mischievous generation, so he will reckon with their enemies, Ps. xii. 3, 7.

5-7 Mournful complaints.
The psalmist here complains of the bad neighborhood into which he was driven; and some apply the two foregoing verses to this: "What shall the deceitful tongue give, what shall it do to those that lie open to it? What shall a man get by living among such malicious deceitful men? Nothing but sharp arrows and coals of juniper," all the mischiefs of a false and spiteful tongue.
1. He was forced to live at a distance from the ordinances of God.
2. He was forced to live among wicked people, who were, upon many accounts, troublesome to him. He dwell in the tents of Kedar, where the shepherds were probably in an ill name for being litigious, like the herdsmen of Abraham and Lot. See here,
(1.) The character of a very good man in David, who could truly say, though he was a man of war, I am for peace.
(2.) The character of the worst of bad men in David's enemies. Such were Christ's enemies. If we meet with such enemies, we must not think it strange. Be not overcome of evil, try to overcome evil with good.

Psalm 121

Title
A Song of degrees.

1 I will lift up mine eyes unto the hills, from whence cometh my help.
2 My help cometh from the LORD, which made heaven and earth.
3 He will not suffer thy foot to be moved: he that keepeth thee will not slumber.
4 Behold, he that keepeth Israel shall neither slumber nor sleep.
5 The LORD is thy keeper: the LORD is thy shade upon thy right hand.
6 The sun shall not smite thee by day, nor the moon by night.
7 The LORD shall preserve thee from all evil: he shall preserve thy soul.
8 The LORD shall preserve thy going out and thy coming in from this time forth, and even for evermore.

Psalm 121

TITLE, ETC. This bears no other title than "A Song of degrees". It is several steps in advance of its predecessor, for it tells of the peace of God's house, and the guardian care of the Lord, while Psalm 120 bemoans the departure of peace from the good man's abode, and his exposure to the venomous assaults of slanderous tongues. In the first instance his eyes looked around with anguish, but here they look up with hope. From the constant recurrence of the word keep, we are led to name this song "a Psalm to the keeper of Israel". Were it not placed among the Pilgrim Psalms we should regard it as a martial hymn, fitted for the evensong of one who slept upon the tented field. It is a soldier's song as well as a traveler's hymn. There is an ascent in the psalm itself which rises to the greatest elevation of restful confidence.

EXPOSITION
Verse 1. I will lift up mine eyes unto the hills, from whence cometh my help. It is wise to look to the strong for strength. Dwellers in valleys are subject to many disorders for which there is no cure but a sojourn in the uplands, and it is well when they shake off their lethargy and resolve upon a climb. Down below they are the prey of marauders, and to escape from them the surest method is to fly to the strongholds upon the mountains.
Verse 2. My help cometh from the LORD, which made heaven and earth. What we need is help,—help powerful, efficient, constant: we need a very present help in trouble. What a mercy that we have it in our God.
Verse 3. He will not suffer thy foot to be moved. Though the paths of life are dangerous and difficult, yet we shall stand fast, for Jehovah will not permit our feet to slide; and if he will not suffer it we shall not suffer it.
Verse 4. Behold, he that keepeth Israel shall neither slumber nor sleep. The consoling truth must be repeated: it is too rich to be dismissed in a single line. It were well if we always imitated the sweet singer, and would dwell a little upon a choice doctrine, sucking the honey from it.
Verse 5. The Lord is thy keeper. Here the preserving One, who had been spoken of by pronouns in the two previous verses, is distinctly named—Jehovah is thy keeper. What a mint of meaning lies here: the sentence is a mass of bullion, and when coined and stamped with the king's name it will bear all our expenses between our birthplace on earth and our rest in heaven.
Verse 6. The sun shall not smite thee by day, nor the moon by night. None but the Lord could shelter us from these tremendous forces. These two great lights rule the day and the night, and under the lordship of both we shall labor or rest in equal safety.
Verse 7. The Lord shall preserve thee from all evil, or keep thee from all evil. It is a great pity that our admirable translation did not keep to the word keep all through the psalm, for all along it is one. God not only keeps his own in all evil times but from all evil influences and operations, yea, from evils themselves. This is a far reaching word of covering: it includes everything and excludes nothing.
Verse 8. The Lord shall preserve thy going out and thy coming in from this time forth, and even for evermore. When we go out in the morning to labor, and come home at eventide to rest, Jehovah shall keep us. When we go out in youth to begin life, and come in at the end to die, we shall experience the same keeping. Our exits and our entrances are under one protection. Three times have we the phrase, "Jehovah shall keep", as if the sacred Trinity thus sealed the word to make it sure: ought not all our fears to be slain by such a threefold flight of arrows? What anxiety can survive this triple promise? This keeping is eternal; continuing from this time forth, even for evermore.

JOHN CALVIN

Psalm 121

1-2

l. I will lift up my eyes to the mountains. The inspired writer, whoever he was, seems, in the opening of the Psalm, to speak in the person of an unbelieving man. As God prevents his believing people with his blessings, and meets them of his own accord, so they, on their part, immediately cast their eyes directly upon him.

These two verses ought to be read connectedly, bringing out this sense: When I shall have lifted up my eyes to the mountains, then I will at length experience that I have fallen into a rash and unprofitable mistake, until I direct them to God alone, and keep them fixed upon him. It is at the same time to be observed, that God in this place is not in vain honored with the title of Creator of heaven and earth; it being intended hereby tacitly to rebuke the ingratitude of men, when they cannot rest contented with his power.

3-5

3. He will not suffer thy foot to stumble. Here the Prophet, in order to recall the faithful to the right path, and to defeat the influence of all the allurements which are wont to distract their minds, affirms that whatever advantages worldly men are accustomed to desire or hope for from the world, true believers will find abundantly and at hand in God alone.

4. Behold! he who keepeth Israel will not slumber nor sleep. To recall each individual to the consideration of the common covenant, he represents the Divine providence as extending to the whole body of the Church.

6-8

6. The sun shall not smite thee by day. By these forms of expression the Psalmist magnifies the advantages which result to us from our having God present with us; and, by the figure synecdoche, under one particular, he declares in general that the faithful shall be safe from all adversities, defended as they are by Divine power. The language is metaphorical, the cold of night and the heat of day denoting all kind of inconveniences. The sense then is, that although God's people may be subject in common with others to the miseries of human life, yet his shadow is always at their side to shield them from thereby receiving any harm.

8. Jehovah will keep thy going out and thy coming in. The sense is, Whatever thou shalt undertake or engage in during thy life shall come to a happy and successful termination. God no doubt directs by his Holy Spirit the, deliberations of his servants; but it appears to me, that this passage is rather to be referred to prosperous issues. If, however, any one would give it a more extended meaning I have no objection. It is enough for me to embrace that sense which is indisputably certain and solid, That God will be the continual guide of his people, so that stretching out his hand to them he will conduct them according to their hearts' desire from the beginning even to the end.

MATTHEW HENRY

Psalm 121

1-8 Confidence in God.

This psalm teaches us,

I. To stay ourselves upon God as a God of power and a God all-sufficient for us. David did so and found the benefit of it.

1. We must not rely upon creatures, upon men and means, instruments and second causes, nor make flesh our arm.

2. We must see all our help laid up in God, in his power and goodness, his providence and grace; and from him we must expect it to come.

3. We must fetch in help from God, by faith in his promises, and a due regard to all his institutions: "I will lift up my eyes to the hills" (probably he meant the hills on which the temple was built, Mount Moriah, and the holy hill of Zion, where the ark of the covenant, the oracle, and the altars were); "I will have an eye to the special presence of God in his church, and with his people (his presence by promise) and not only to his common presence."

II. To comfort ourselves in God when our difficulties and dangers are greatest.

1. God himself has undertaken to be our protector: The Lord is thy keeper, v. 5.

2. The same that is the protector of the church in general is engaged for the preservation of every particular believer, the same wisdom, the same power, the same promises. He that keepeth Israel (v. 4) is thy keeper, v. 5.

3. He is a wakeful watchful keeper: "He that keepeth Israel, that keepeth thee, O Israelite! shall neither slumber nor sleep; he never did, nor ever will, for he is never weary; he not only does not sleep, but he does not so much as slumber; he has not the least inclination to sleep."

4. He not only protects those whom he is the keeper of, but he refreshes them: He is their shade.

5. He is always near to his people for their protection and refreshment.

6. He is not only at their right hand, but he will also keep the feet of his saints.

7. He will protect them from all the malignant influences of the heavenly bodies (v. 6): The sun shall not smite thee with his heat by day nor the moon with her cold and moisture by night.

8. His protection will make them safe in every respect: "The Lord shall preserve thee from all evil, the evil of sin and the evil of trouble. "

9. It is the spiritual life, especially, that God will take under his protection.

10. He will keep us in all our ways: "He shall preserve thy going out and thy coming in. Thou shalt be under his protection in all thy journeys and voyages, outward-bound or homeward-bound, as he kept Israel in the wilderness, in their removes and rests. He will keep thee in life and death. God will protect his church and his saints always.

Psalm 122

Title
A Song of degrees of David.

1-4
1 I was glad when they said unto me, Let us go into the house of the LORD.
2 Our feet shall stand within thy gates, O Jerusalem.
3 Jerusalem is builded as a city that is compact together:
4 Whither the tribes go up, the tribes of the LORD, unto the testimony of Israel, to give thanks unto the name of the LORD.

Psalm 122

TITLE AND SUBJECT. This brief but spirited Psalm is entitled "A Song of Degrees of David", and thus we are informed as go its author, and the occasion for which it was designed: David wrote it for the people to sing at the time of their goings up to the holy feasts at Jerusalem. It comes third in the series, and appears to be suitable to be sung when the people had entered the gates, and their feet stood within the city. It was most natural that they should sing of Jerusalem itself, and invoke peace and prosperity upon the Holy City, for it was the center of their worship, and the place where the Lord revealed himself above the mercy seat. Possibly the city was not all built in David's day, but he wrote under the spirit of prophecy, and spoke of it as it would be in the age of Solomon; a poet has license to speak of things, not only as they are, but as they will be when they come to their perfection. Jerusalem, or the Habitation of Peace, is used as the key word of this Psalm, wherein we have in the original many happy allusions to the salem, or peace, which they implored upon Jerusalem. When they stood within the triple walls, all things around the pilgrims helped to explain the words which they sang within her ramparts of strength. One voice led the Psalm with its personal "I," but ten thousand brethren and companions united with the first musician and swelled the chorus of the strain.

EXPOSITION
Verse 1. I was glad when they said unto me, Let us go into the house of the LORD. Good children are pleased to go home, and glad to hear their brothers and sisters call them thither. David's heart was in the worship of God, and he was delighted when he found others inviting him to go where his desires had already gone: it helps the ardor of the most ardent to hear others inviting them to a holy duty. The word was not "go," but "let us go"; hence the ear of the Psalmist found a double joy in it. He was glad for the sake of others: glad that they wished to go themselves, glad that they had the courage and liberality to invite others. He knew that it would do them good; nothing better can happen to men and their friends than to love the place where God's honor dwelleth. What a glorious day shall that be when many people shall go and say, "Come ye, and let us go up to the mountain of the Lord, to the house of the God of Jacob, and he will teach us of his ways, and we will walk in his paths."
Verse 2. Our feet shall stand within thy gates, O Jerusalem; or, better, "our feet are standing." The words imply present and joyous standing within the walls of the city of peace; or perhaps the pilgrims felt so sure of getting there that they antedated the joy, and spoke as if they were already there, though they were as yet only on the road. If we are within the church we may well triumph in the fact. While our feet are standing in Jerusalem our lips may well be singing. Outside the gates all is danger, and one day all will be destruction; but within the gates all is safely, seclusion, serenity, salvation, and glory. The gates are opened that we may pass in, and they are only shut that our enemies may not follow us. The Lord loveth the gates of Zion, and so do we when we are enclosed within them. What a choice favor, to be a citizen of the New Jerusalem!
Verse 3. Jerusalem is builded as a city that is compact together. David saw in vision the city built; no more a waste, or a mere collection of tents, or a city upon paper, commenced but not completed. God's mercy to the Israelitish nation allowed of peace and plenty, sufficient for the uprise and perfecting of its capital: that City flourished in happy times, even as the church is only built up when all the people of God are prospering. Thanks be to God, Jerusalem is builded: the Lord by his glorious appearing has built up Zion. Furthermore, it is not erected as a set of booths, or a conglomeration of hovels, but as a city, substantial, architectural, designed, arranged, and defended. The church is a permanent and important

JOHN CALVIN

Psalm 122

In this Psalm David congratulates himself and the whole Church upon the fact, that a seat had at length been appointed for the ark of the covenant, and that God had chosen a place where his name should be continually called upon. Afterwards, to incite and encourage the faithful to engage in the worship of the sanctuary, he briefly declares, that the prosperous condition of the people depended upon God's having chosen the seat of royalty to be at Jerusalem, from whence it was his purpose to defend, maintain, and assist his people.

1-3
1. I was glad when they said to me. God had often told Moses, that his Sanctuary would one day have a certain and fixed place of abode; yet from the time of Moses, for the space of more than a thousand years, the Ark of the Covenant had been carried about from place to place, as if it had been in a state of pilgrimage. At length it was revealed to David, that mount Zion was the spot where God would have his ark to be settled, and his temple built. Now, as David himself received this revelation with exceeding great joy, so he affirms that he was glad to find the whole people with one consent agreeing thereto.
2. Our feet shall be standing within thy gates, O Jerusalem! David rehearses the language in which all the godly in common expressed themselves—that they should at length stand with sure footing in Jerusalem, because it was the will of God there to establish his Sanctuary, which hitherto had often changed its lodgings, and had been carried from place to place. By such a pilgrimage state of the ark, God reminded the people that he had not without cause spoken by Moses what I have a little ago adverted to. Thus, whenever the ark of the covenant was conveyed from one place to another, God thereby stirred up the hearts of his servants to desire and pray that a certain settled place might be appointed to it.
3. Jerusalem is built as a city. Here David begins to celebrate the praises of Jerusalem; and he does this with the design of encouraging the people to persevere with uniform steadfastness in their obedience. It was of great importance for the minds of the godly, instead of being drawn hither and thither, to be kept constantly fixed on that city, which was the bond of a holy unity. When the people came to be divided into two bodies, that was the commencement of melancholy devastation. It is not surprising, then, to find David commending with such earnestness the place which God had chosen, knowing, as he did, that the prosperity of the Church depended upon the children of Abraham worshipping God there in purity, according to the appointed observances of the law; and next, upon their acknowledging the royal seat which the same God had erected there by his own authority, and had taken under his own protection When it is said that Jerusalem is built as a city, it is not to be understood as referring only to the walls, or towers, or ditches of that city, but chiefly to the good order and holy polity by which it was

MATTHEW HENRY

Psalm 122

1-5 The pleasures of public worship.
Here we have,
I. The pleasure which David and other pious Israelites took in approaching to and attending upon God in public ordinances, v. 1, 2.

1. The invitation to them was very welcome. David was himself glad, and would have every Israelite to say that he was glad, when he was called upon to go up to the house of the Lord. Note,
(1.) It is the will of God that we should worship him in concert, that many should join together to wait upon him in public ordinances. We ought to worship God in our own houses, but that is not enough; we must go into the house of the Lord, to pay our homage to him there, and not forsake the assembling of ourselves together.
(2.) We should not only agree with one another, but excite and stir up one another, to go to worship God in public. Let us go; not, "Do you go and pray for us, and we will stay at home;" but, We will go also, Zech. viii. 21. Not, "Do you go before, and we will follow at our leisure;" or, "We will go first, and you shall come after us;" but, "Let us go together, for the honor of God and for our mutual edification and encouragement."

2. The prospect of them was very pleasing. They speak it with a holy triumph (v. 2): Our feet shall stand within thy gates, O Jerusalem! Those that came out of the country, when they found the journey tedious, comforted themselves with this, that they should be in Jerusalem shortly, and that would make amends for all the fatigues of their journey. We shall stand there as servants; it is desirable to have a place in Jerusalem, though it be among those that stand by (Zech. iii. 7), though it be the door keeper's place, Ps. lxxxiv. 10. We have now got a resting-place for the ark, and where it is there will we be.
II. The praises of Jerusalem, as Ps. xlviii. 12.

1. It is the beautiful city, not only for situation, but for building. It is built into a city, the houses not scattered, but contiguous, and the streets fair and spacious. It is built uniform, compact together, the houses strengthening and supporting one another. Though the city was divided into the higher and lower town, yet the Jebusites being driven out, and it being entirely in the possession of God's people, it is said to be compact together. It was a type of the gospel-church, which is compact together in holy love and Christian communion, so that it is all as one city.

2. It is the holy city, v. 4. It is the place where all Israel meet one another: Thither the tribes go up, from all parts of the country, as one man, under the character of the tribes of the Lord, in obedience to his command. It is the place appointed for their general rendezvous; and they come together to receive instruction from God.

3. It is the royal city (v. 5): There are set thrones of judgment. Therefore the people had reason to be in

Psalm 122

5-9
5 For there are set thrones of judgment, the thrones of the house of David.
6 Pray for the peace of Jerusalem: they shall prosper that love thee.
7 Peace be within thy walls, and prosperity within thy palaces.
8 For my brethren and companions' sakes, I will now say, Peace be within thee.
9 Because of the house of the LORD our God I will seek thy good.

institution, founded on a rock, builded with art, and arranged with wisdom. The city of God had this peculiarity about it, that it was not a long, straggling street, or a city of magnificent distances (as some mere skeleton places have been styled), but the allotted space was filled, the buildings were a solid block, a massive unity: this struck the dwellers in villages, and conveyed to them the idea of close neighborhood, sure standing, and strong defense.

Verse 4. Whither the tribes go up, the tribes of the LORD. When there is unity within there will be gatherings from without: the tribes go up to a compact center. Note that Israel was one people, but yet it was in a sense divided by the mere surface distinction of tribes; and this may be a lesson to us that all Christendom is essentially one, though from various causes we are divided into tribes. Let us as much as possible sink the tribal individuality in the national unity, so that the church may be many waves, but one sea; many branches, but one tree; many members, but one body.

Verse 5. For there are set thrones of judgment. If discontented with the petty judgments of their village lords, the people could bring their hard matters to the royal seat, and the beloved King would be sure to decide aright; for the judgment thrones were The thrones of the house of David. We who come to the church and its public worship are charmed to come to the throne of God, and to the throne of the reigning Savior.

Verse 6. Pray for the peace of Jerusalem. Peace was her name, pray that her condition may verify her title. Abode of Peace, peace be to thee. Here was a most sufficient reason for rejoicing at the thought of going up to the house of the Lord, since that sacred shrine stood in the center of an area of peace: well might Israel pray that such peace should be continued. In a church peace is to be desired, expected, promoted, and enjoyed. If we may not say "Peace at any price," yet we may certainly cry "Peace at the highest price."

Verse 7. Peace be within thy walls. See how the poet personifies the church, and speaks to it: his heart is with Zion, and therefore his conversation runs in that direction. A second time is the sweet favor of peace earnestly sought after: "There is none like it, give it me." Walls were needed to keep out the foe, but it was asked of the Lord that those walls might prove sufficient for her security. May the munitions of rock so securely defend the city of God that no intruder may ever enter within her enclosure.

Verse 8. For my brethren and companions' sakes, I will now say, Peace be within thee. It is to the advantage of all Israel that there should be peace in Jerusalem. It is for the good of every Christian, yea, of every man, that there should be peace and prosperity in the church. Here our humanity and our common philanthropy assist our religious prayer. By a flourishing church our children, our neighbors, our fellow countrymen are likely to be blest. Moreover, we cannot but pray for a cause with which our dearest relatives and choicest friends are associated: if they labor for it, we must and will pray for it.

Verse 9. Because of the house of the LORD our God I will seek thy good. He prays for Jerusalem because of Zion. How the church salts and savors all around it. The presence of Jehovah, our God, endears to us every place wherein he reveals his glory. Well may we seek her good within whose walls there dwells God who alone is good. We are to live for God's cause, and to be ready to die for it. First we love it (Ps 122:6) and then we labor for it, as in this passage: we see its good, and then seek its good. If we can do nothing else we can intercede for it. Our covenant relation to Jehovah as our God binds us to pray for his people,—they are "the house of the Lord our God." If we honor our God we desire the prosperity of the church.

distinguished, although I allow that there is some allusion to its ancient state.

4-5

4. Thither the tribes ascended. David here invests Jerusalem with two titles of honor, calling it the sacred and regularly appointed place for calling upon the name of God; and next, the royal sea, to which the whole people were to have recourse for obtaining justice. All our salvation depends upon these two points; first, that Christ has been given to us to be our priest; and, secondly, that he has been established king to govern us. This God showed to his ancient people under figures. The sanctuary erected on mount Zion was intended to keep their faith fixed upon the spiritual priesthood of Christ; and in like manner, by the kingdom of David, there was presented to their view an image of the kingdom of Christ. The Psalmist, therefore, says in the first place, that the tribes or families of God shall come to Jerusalem; and then he immediately adds, that there the seat of judgment is erected, on which he and his posterity will sit.

5. For there were set thrones for judgment. He means, that the throne of the kingdom was fixed or established at Jerusalem, or that there it had its permanent seat. Among that people some order of judgments had always existed. these, however, had formerly been in an unsettled state, and frequently changed, but God at length ordained, in the person of David, a new government which should flow in a continual course; for it was his will that the children of David should succeed their father in this royal dignity from age to age until the coming of Christ.

6-9

6. Pray ye for the peace of Jerusalem. David now exhorts all the devout worshippers of God to make supplication for the prosperity of the holy city. The more effectually to stir them up to such exercise, he promises that, in this way the divine blessing will descend upon them. The reason why he was so deeply concerned about the prosperity of Jerusalem was, as we have formerly stated—and he again repeats the same thing at the end of the Psalm—because the welfare of the whole Church was inseparably connected with that kingdom and priesthood.

7. Peace be within thy bulwarks, etc. The two clauses express the same sentiment, and, therefore, the meaning of the first is gathered from the second. The term peace signifies nothing else than prosperity. The amount is, that David prays for the prosperity of the Church through its whole extent.

8. For the sake of my brethren and neighbors. If then the salvation of our brethren is regarded by us as an object of importance, if religion is with us a matter of heart-work, we ought, at the same time, as much as in us lies, to take an interest in the prosperity of the Church.

9. Because of the house of Jehovah our God, etc. In this verse he adds a second reason why he cared for the Church—that he did so, because the worship of God so far from remaining entire would go to ruin unless Jerusalem continued standing.

love with Jerusalem, because justice was administered there by a man after God's own heart. The civil interests of the people were as well secured as their ecclesiastical concerns; and very happy they were in their courts of judicature, which were erected in Jerusalem, as with us in Westminster Hall. Observe, What a goodly sight it was to see the testimony of Israel and the thrones of judgment such near neighbors, and they are good neighbors, which may greatly befriend one another. Let the testimony of Israel direct the thrones of judgment, and the thrones of judgment protect the testimony of Israel.

6-9 Prayer for the Church.

Here,

I. David calls upon others to wish well to Jerusalem, v. 6, 7. Pray for the peace of Jerusalem, for the welfare of it, for all good to it, particularly for the uniting of the inhabitants among themselves and their preservation from the incursions of enemies. This we may truly desire, that in the peace thereof we may have peace; and this we must earnestly pray for, for it is the gift of God, and for it he will be enquired of. Those that can do nothing else for the peace of Jerusalem can pray for it, which is something more than showing their good-will; it is the appointed way of fetching in mercy. The peace and welfare of the gospel church, particularly in our land, is to be earnestly desired and prayed for by every one of us. Now,

1. We are here encouraged in our prayers for Jerusalem's peace: Those shall prosper that love thee. We must pray for Jerusalem, not out of custom, nor for fashion's sake, but out of a principle of love to God's government of man and man's worship of God.

2. We are here directed in our prayers for it and words are put into our mouths (v. 7): Peace be within thy walls. He teaches us to pray for all the inhabitants in general, and for the princes and rulers especially.

II. He resolves that whatever others do he will approve himself a faithful friend to Jerusalem,

1. In his prayers: "I will now say, now I see the tribes so cheerfully resorting hither to the testimony of Israel, and the matter settled, that Jerusalem must be the place where God will record his name, now I will say, Peace be within thee."

2. In his endeavors, with which he will second his prayers: "I will, to the utmost of my power, seek thy good." Whatever lies within the sphere of our activity to do for the public good we must do it, else we are not sincere in praying for it. Now it might be said, No thanks to David to be so solicitous for the welfare of Jerusalem; it was his own city, and the interests of his family were lodged in it. This is true; yet he professes that this was not the reason why he was in such care for the welfare of Jerusalem, but it proceeded from the warm regard he had for the communion of saints, and for the ordinances of God: He had set his affections to the house of his God (1 Chron. xxix. 3).

Psalm 123

Title
A Song of degrees.

1 Unto thee lift I up mine eyes, O thou that dwellest in the heavens.
2 Behold, as the eyes of servants look unto the hand of their masters, and as the eyes of a maiden unto the hand of her mistress; so our eyes wait upon the LORD our God, until that he have mercy upon us.
3 Have mercy upon us, O LORD, have mercy upon us: for we are exceedingly filled with contempt.
4 Our soul is exceedingly filled with the scorning of those that are at ease, and with the contempt of the proud.

Psalm 123

TITLE. A Song of degrees. We are climbing. The first step (Ps. 120) saw us lamenting our troublesome surroundings, and the next saw us lifting or eyes to the hills and resting in assured security; from this we rose to delight in the house of the Lord; but here we look to the Lord himself, and this is the highest ascent of all by many degrees. The eyes are now looking above the hills, and above Jehovah's footstool on earth, to his throne in the heavens. Let us know it as "the Psalm of the eyes". Old authors call it Oculus "Sperans", or the eye of hope. It is a short Psalm, written with singular art, containing one thought, and expressing if in a most engaging manner. Doubtless it would be a favorite song among the people of God. It has been conjectured that this brief song, or rather sigh, may have first been heard in the days of Nehemiah, or under the persecutions of Antiochus. It may be so, but there is no evidence of it; it seems to us quite as probable that afflicted ones in all periods after David's time found this psalm ready to their hand If it appears to describe days remote from David, it is all the more evident that the Psalmist was also a prophet, and sang what he saw in vision.

EXPOSITION
Verse 1. Unto thee lift I up mine eyes. It is good to have some one to look up to. The Psalmist looked so high that he could look no higher. Not to the hills, but to the God of the hills he looked. He believed in a personal God, and knew nothing of that modern pantheism which is nothing more than atheism wearing a fig leaf. The uplifted eyes naturally and instinctively represent the state of heart which fixes desire, hope, confidence, and expectation upon the Lord. God is everywhere, and yet it is most natural to think of him as being above us, in that glory land which lies beyond the skies.
Verse 2. Behold—for it is worthy of regard among men, and O that the Majesty of heaven would also note it, and speedily send the mercy which our waiting spirits seek. See, O Lord, how we look to thee, and in thy mercy look on us. This Behold has, however, a call to us to observe and consider. Whenever saints of God have waited upon the Lord their example has been worthy of earnest consideration. Sanctification is a miracle of grace; therefore let us behold it.
Verse 3. Have mercy upon us, O Lord, have mercy upon us. He hangs upon the word "mercy," and embodies it in a vehement prayer: the very word seems to hold him, and he harps upon it. It is well for us to pray about everything, and turn everything into prayer; and especially when we are reminded of a great necessity we should catch at it as a keynote, and pitch our tune to it. The reduplication of the prayer before us is meant to express the eagerness of the Psalmist's spirit and his urgent need: what he needed speedily he begs for importunately. Note that he has left the first person singular for the plural. All the saints need mercy; they all seek it; they shall all have it.
Verse 4. Our soul is exceedingly filled with the scorning of those that are at ease. Knowing no troubles of their own, the easy ones grow cruel and deride the people of the Lord. Having the godly already in secret contempt, they show it by openly scorning them. Note those who do this: they are not the poor, the humble, the troubled, but those who have a merry life of it, and are self content. They are in easy circumstances; they are easy in heart through a deadened conscience, and so they easily come to mock at holiness; they are easy from needing nothing, and from having no severe toil exacted from them; they are easy as to any anxiety to improve, for their conceit of themselves is boundless.

JOHN CALVIN

Psalm 123

In this Psalm, the faithful oppressed with the cruel tyranny of their enemies, beseech God to deliver them, there being no other source of hope left for them except in his protection.

1-4

1. I lift my eyes to thee, who dwellest in the heavens. It is uncertain at what time, or even by what Prophet, this Psalm was composed. I do not think it probable that David was its author; because, when he bewails the persecutions which he suffered in the time of Saul, it is usual with him to interpose some particular references to himself. My opinion, then, rather is, that this form of prayer was composed for all the godly by some Prophet, either when the Jews were captives in Babylon, or when Antiochus Epiphanes exercised towards them the most relentless cruelty. Be this as it may, the Holy Spirit, by whose inspiration the Prophet delivered it to the people, calls upon us to have recourse to God, when—ever wicked men unrighteously and proudly persecute, not one or two of the faithful only, but the whole body of the Church.

2. Behold as the eyes of servants look to the hand of their masters. This similitude is very suitable to the present case. It implies that without the protection of God true believers have no comfort, are completely disarmed and exposed to all manner of wrongs, have neither strength nor courage to resist; in short, that their safety depends entirely upon aid derived from another. We know how shamefully servants were treated in ancient times, and what reproaches might be cast upon them, whilst yet they durst not move a finger to repel the outrage. Being therefore deprived of all means of defending themselves, the only thing which remained for them to do was, what is here stated, to crave the protection of their masters.

3. Have mercy upon us, O Jehovah! etc. The Psalmist prosecutes and confirms the preceding doctrine. He had said that the godly, finding themselves utterly broken in spirit and cast down, intently directed their eyes to the hand of God: now he adds that they are filled with reproach. From this we learn that the wicked not only assaulted them by such ways of violence as suggested themselves to their minds, but that by their mockery they as it were trampled under foot the children of God. The repetition of the prayer, Have mercy upon us, which is a sign of vehement and ardent desire, indicates that they were reduced to the last degree of misery. When insult is added to wrongs, there is nothing which inflicts a deeper wound upon well constituted minds. The Prophet therefore complains chiefly of that, as if it were the consummation of all calamities. He says that rich and proud men treated the Church with insolent triumph; for it commonly happens that those who are elevated hi the world, look down with contempt upon the people of God. The luster of their honor and power dazzles their eyes, so that they make no account of God's spiritual kingdom. This passage teaches us, that it is no new thing for the Church to be held in contempt by the children of this world who abound in riches.

MATTHEW HENRY

Psalm 123

1-4 Grateful acknowledgments.
We have here,

I. The solemn profession which God's people make of faith and hope in God, v. 1, 2. Observe,

1. The title here given to God: O thou that dwellest in the heavens. Our Lord Jesus has taught us, in prayer, to have an eye to God as our Father in heaven; not that he is confined there, but there especially he manifests his glory, as the King in his court. Heaven is a place of prospect and a place of power; he that dwells there beholds thence all the calamities of his people and thence can send to save them.

2. The regard here had to God. The psalmist himself lifted up his eyes to him. The eyes of a good man are ever towards the Lord, Ps. xxv. 15. In every prayer we lift up our soul, the eye of our soul, to God, especially in trouble, which was the case here. The eyes of the people waited on the Lord, v. 2. We find mercy coming towards a people when the eyes of man, as of all the tribes of Israel, are towards the Lord, Zech. ix. 1.

II. The humble address which God's people present to him in their calamitous condition (v. 3, 4), wherein,

1. They sue for mercy, not prescribing to God what he shall do for them, nor pleading any merit of their own why he should do it for them, but, Have mercy upon us, O Lord! have mercy upon us. We find little mercy with men; their tender mercies are cruel; there are cruel mockings. But this is our comfort, that with the Lord there is mercy and we need desire no more to relieve us, and make us easy, than the mercy of God. Whatever the troubles of the church are, God's mercy is a sovereign remedy.

2. They set forth their grievances: We are exceedingly filled with contempt. Reproach is the wound, the burden, they complain of. Observe,

(1.) Who were reproached: "We, who have our eyes up to thee." Those who are owned of God are often despised and trampled on by the world. Some translate the words which we render, those that are at ease, and the proud, so as to signify the persons that are scorned and contemned. "Our soul is troubled to see how those that are at peace, and the excellent ones, are scorned and despised." The saints are a peaceable people and yet are abused (Ps. xxxv. 20), the excellent ones of the earth and yet undervalued, Lam. iv. 1, 2.

(2.) Who did reproach them. Taking the words as we read them, they were the epicures who lived at ease, carnal sensual people, Job xii. 5. The scoffers are such as walk after their own lusts and serve their own bellies, and the proud such as set God himself at defiance and had a high opinion of themselves; they trampled on God's people, thinking they magnified themselves by vilifying them.

Psalm 124

Title
A Song of degrees of David.

1 If it had not been the LORD who was on our side, now may Israel say;
2 If it had not been the LORD who was on our side, when men rose up against us:
3 Then they had swallowed us up quick, when their wrath was kindled against us:
4 Then the waters had overwhelmed us, the stream had gone over our soul:
5 Then the proud waters had gone over our soul.
6 Blessed be the LORD, who hath not given us as a prey to their teeth.
7 Our soul is escaped as a bird out of the snare of the fowlers: the snare is broken, and we are escaped.
8 Our help is in the name of the LORD, who made heaven and earth.

Psalm 124

TITLE. A Song of degrees of David. Of course the superfine critics have pounced upon this title as inaccurate, but we are at liberty to believe as much or as little of their assertions as we may please. They declare that there are certain ornaments of language in this little ode which were unknown in the Davidic period. It may be so; but in their superlative wisdom they have ventured upon so many other questionable statements that we are not bound to receive this dictum. Assuredly the manner of the song is very like to David's, and we are unable to see why he should be excluded from the authorship. Whether it be his composition or no, it breathes the same spirit as that which animates the unchallenged songs of the royal composer.
DIVISION. This short Psalm contains an acknowledgement of favor received by way of special deliverance (1-5), then a grateful act of worship in blessing Jehovah (6, 7), and, lastly, a declaration of confidence in the Lord for all future time of trial. May our experience lead us to the same conclusion as the saints of David's time. From all confidence in man may we be rescued by a holy reliance upon our God.

EXPOSITION
Verse 1. If it had not been the Lord who was on our side, now may Israel say. The glorious Lord became our ally; he took our part, and entered into treaty with us.
Verse 2. If it had not been the Lord who was on our side, when men rose up against us. When all men combined, and the whole race of men seemed set upon stamping out the house of Israel, what must have happened if the covenant Lord had not interposed? When they stirred themselves, and combined to make an assault upon our quietude and safety, what should we have done in their rising if the Lord had not also risen?
Verse 3. Then they had swallowed us up quick, when their wrath was kindled against us. They were eager for our destruction and would have swallowed us up alive and whole in a single instant.
Verse 4. Then the waters had overwhelmed us. Rising irresistibly, like the Nile, the flood of opposition would soon have rolled over our heads. Across the mighty waste of waters we should have cast an anxious eye, but looked in vain for escape. The motto of a royal house is, "Tossed about but not submerged": we should have needed an epitaph rather than an epigram, for we should have been driven by the torrent and sunken, never to rise again.
Verse 5. Then the proud waters had gone over our soul. The figure represents the waves as proud, and so they seem to be when they overleap the bulwarks of a frail bark, and threaten every moment to sink her. In all the persecutions of the church a cruel contempt has largely mingled with the oppression, and this is overpowering to the soul.
Verse 6. Blessed be the Lord, who hath not given us as a prey to their teeth. Leaving the metaphor of a boiling flood, he compares the adversaries of Israel to wild beasts who desired to make the godly their prey. Their teeth are prepared to tear, and they regard the godly as their victims. The Lord is heartily praised for not permitting his servants to be devoured when they were between the jaws of the raging ones.
Verse 7. Our soul is escaped as a bird out of the snare of the fowlers. Our soul is like a bird for many reasons; but in this case the point of likeness is weakness, folly, and the ease with which it is enticed into the snare.
Verse 8. Our help, our hope for the future, our ground of confidence in all trials present and to come is in the name of the Lord. Jehovah's revealed character is our foundation of confidence, his person is our sure fountain of strength. Who made heaven and earth. Our Creator is our preserver.

JOHN CALVIN

Psalm 124

1-5
1. But for Jehovah, who was on our side. Most probably David here sets forth a known history, and exhorts the faithful to reflect upon the divine succor which they had already actually experienced.
2. But for Jehovah who was on our side. It is not without cause that he twice repeats the same sentence. So long as we are in danger our fear is immoderate; but no sooner are we delivered than we lessen the greatness of our calamity, and Satan, deceiving us by this artifice, leads us to obscure the grace of God.
4. The waters had then overwhelmed us. He embellishes by an elegant metaphor the preceding sentiment, comparing the dreadful impetuosity of the enemies of the Jews to an inundation, which swallows up whatever it meets with in its overflowing course. And he continues to preserve the character of a man affrighted. He names the waters, next the torrent, thirdly, the proud or impetuous waters. He says, over us, and over our soul, as if, by presenting the thing to the eye, he intended to strike terror into the people.

6-8
6. Blessed be Jehovah! The Psalmist now exhorts the godly to a grateful acknowledgment of the divine goodness, and as it were puts words into their mouth. Here also he shows by another similitude, that it would have been all over with them had not God succored them; affirming that they were delivered not otherwise than if some one had plucked the prey from the teeth of a wild and cruel beast. Of the same import is the third similitude, That they were on all sides entrapped and entangled in the snares of their enemies, even as little birds caught in the net lie stretched under the hand of the fowler; and that when they were delivered, it was just as if one should set at liberty birds which had been taken. The amount is, that the people of God, feeble, without counsel, and destitute of aid, had not only to deal with blood-thirsty and furious beasts, but were also ensnared by bird-nets and stratagems, so that being greatly inferior to their enemies as well in policy as in open force, they were besieged by many deaths. From this it may be easily gathered that they were miraculously preserved.
8. Our help is in the name of Jehovah. David here extends to the state of the Church in all ages that which the faithful had already experienced. As I interpret the verse, he not only gives thanks to God for one benefit, but affirms that the Church cannot continue safe except in so far as she is protected by the hand of God. His object is to animate the children of God with the assured hope, that their life is in perfect safety under the divine guardianship. The contrast between the help of God, and other resources in which the world vainly confides, as we have seen in Psalm 20:7, "Some trust in chariots, and some in horses, but we will remember the name of the Lord our God," is to be noticed, that the faithful may betake themselves exclusively to his succor, and depending upon it, may fearlessly despise whatever Satan and the world may plot against them.

MATTHEW HENRY

Psalm 124

1-5 The security of God's people.
The people of God, being here called upon to praise God for their deliverance, are to take notice,
I. Of the malice of men, by which they were reduced to the very brink of ruin. Let Israel say that there was but a step between them and death: the more desperate the disease appears to have been the more does the skill of the Physician appear in the cure. Observe,
1. Whence the threatening danger came: Men rose up against us, creatures of our own kind, and yet bent upon our ruin. Homo homini lupus—Man is a wolf to man. But what was the matter with these men? Why their wrath was kindled against us (v. 3); something or other they were angry at, and then no less would serve than the destruction of those they had conceived a displeasure against. Wrath is cruel and anger is outrageous. Their wrath was kindled as fire ready to consume us. They were proud; and the wicked in his pride doth persecute the poor. They were daring in their attempt; they rose up against us, rose in rebellion, with a resolution to swallow us up alive.
2. How far it went, and how fatal it would have been if it had gone a little further: "We should have been devoured as a lamb by a lion, not only slain, but swallowed up, so that there would have been no relics of us remaining, swallowed up with so much haste, ere we were aware, that we should have gone down alive to the pit. We should have been deluged as the low grounds by a land-flood or the sands by a high spring-tide."
II. Of the goodness of God, by which they were rescued from the very brink of ruin: "The Lord was on our side; and, if he had not been so, we should have been undone."

6-8 The security of God's people.
Here the psalmist further magnifies the great deliverance God had lately wrought for them.
I. That their hearts might be the more enlarged in thankfulness to him (v. 6): Blessed be the Lord. God is the author of all our deliverances, and therefore he must have the glory of them. We were delivered,
1. Like a lamb out of the very jaws of a beast of prey.
2. Like a bird, a little bird (the word signifies a sparrow), out of the snare of the fowler.
II. That their hearts, and the hearts of others, might be the more encouraged to trust in God in the like dangers (v. 8): Our help is in the name of the Lord. It is a comfort to all that lay the interests of God's Israel near their hearts that Israel's God is the same that made the world, and therefore will have a church in the world, and can secure that church in times of the greatest danger and distress. In him therefore let the church's friends put their confidence, and they shall not be put to confusion.

Psalm 125

Title
A Song of degrees.

1 They that trust in the LORD shall be as mount Zion, which cannot be removed, but abideth for ever.
2 As the mountains are round about Jerusalem, so the LORD is round about his people from henceforth even for ever.
3 For the rod of the wicked shall not rest upon the lot of the righteous; lest the righteous put forth their hands unto iniquity.
4 Do good, O LORD, unto those that be good, and to them that are upright in their hearts.
5 As for such as turn aside unto their crooked ways, the LORD shall lead them forth with the workers of iniquity: but peace shall be upon Israel.

Psalm 125

TITLE. A Song of Degrees. Another step is taken in the ascent, another station in the pilgrimage is reached: certainly a rise in the sense is here perceptible, since full assurance concerning years to come is a higher form of faith than the ascription of farther escapes to the Lord. Faith has praised Jehovah for past deliverances, and t, ere she rises to a confident jury in the present and future safety of believers. She asserts that they shall forever secure who trust themselves with the Lord. We can imagine the pilgrims chanting this song when perambulating the city walls.

We do not assert that David wrote this Psalm, but we have as much ground for doing so as others have for declaring that it was written after the captivity. It would seem provable that all the Pilgrim Psalms were composed, or, at least, compiled by the same writer, and as some of them are certainly by David, there is too conclusive reason for taking away the rest from him.

DIVISION. First we have a song of holy confidence (Ps 125:1-2); then a promise, Ps 125:3; followed by a prayer, Ps 125:4; and a note of warning.

EXPOSITION

Verse 1. They that trust in the LORD shall be as mount Zion. The emphasis lies upon the object of their trust, namely, Jehovah the Lord. What a privilege to be allowed to repose in God. How condescending is Jehovah to become the confidence of his people! To trust elsewhere is vanity; and the more implicit such misplaced trust becomes the more bitter will be the ensuing disappointment; but to trust in the living God is sanctified common sense which needs no excuse, its result shall be its best vindication.

Verse 2. As the mountains are round about Jerusalem, so the LORD is round about his people from henceforth even for ever. The hill of Zion is the type of the believer's constancy, and the surrounding mountains are made emblems of the all surrounding presence of the Lord. The mountains around the holy city, though they do not make a circular wall, are, nevertheless, set like sentinels to guard her gates. God doth not enclose his people within ramparts and bulwarks, making their city to be a prison; but yet he so orders the arrangements of his providence that his saints are as safe as if they dwelt behind the strongest fortifications. What a double security the two verses set before us!

Verse 3. For the rod of the wicked shall not rest upon the lot of the righteous. The people of God are not to expect immunity from trial because the Lord surrounds them, for they may feel the power and persecution of the ungodly. Isaac, even in Abraham's family, was mocked by Ishmael. Assyria laid its scepter even upon Zion itself. The graceless often bear rule and wield the rod.

Verse 4. Do good, O LORD, unto those that be good, and to them that are upright in their hearts. Men to be good at all must be good at heart. Those who trust in the Lord are good; for faith is the root of righteousness, and the evidence of uprightness. Faith in God is a good and upright thing, and its influence makes the rest of the man good and upright.

Verse 5. As for such as turn aside unto their crooked ways, the LORD shall lead them forth with the workers of iniquity. Two kinds of men are always to be found, the upright and the men of crooked ways. Alas, there are some who pass from one class to another, not by a happy conversion, turning from the twisting lanes of deceit into the highway of truth, but by an unhappy declension leaving the main road of honesty and holiness for the bypaths of wickedness.

JOHN CALVIN

Psalm 125

As the faithful being mingled in this world with the ungodly seem to be exposed to all the ills of life in the same manner as other people, the Prophet, comparing them to Jerusalem, shows that they are defended by an invincible bulwark. And if God at any time suffer them to be plagued by the malice of the wicked, he exhorts them to be of good hope. He however at the same time distinguishes between true and false Israelites, that hypocrites may not apply to themselves what is here said concerning the safety of the righteous.

1-2
1. They who confide in Jehovah are as mount Zion. The present Psalm differs from the preceding in this—that while in the other it was said that the Church had been preserved by the power of God, without any human means, the Holy Spirit, in the one before us, teaches that in the time to come she shall always continue in perfect safety, because she is defended by the invincible power of God. When the Church is emblematically described by the situation of the city of Jerusalem, the design of the Prophet is to encourage each of the faithful to believe, that the safety promised in common to all the chosen people belongs to him. But in exhibiting to the eyes a visible image of the Church, he accommodates himself to the rudeness of those who, detained by the dullness of the flesh, still continue settled down in the earth.

3-5
3. For the scepter of the wicked shall not rest upon the lot of the just. This is, as it were, a correction of the preceding sentence. The Psalmist had said that the hand of God was extended on all sides to defend his Church. But as we are disposed to draw the divine promises to our own advantage, in the way of interpreting them as securing our exemption from all trouble, we are here warned that the guardianship of God does not secure us from being sometimes exercised with the cross and afflictions, and that therefore the faithful ought not to promise themselves a delicate and easy life in this world, it being enough for them not to be abandoned of God when they stand in need of his help.
4. Do good, O Jehovah to the good. The Prophet has already promised to all the faithful the seasonable help of God; but still he has recourse to prayer, and that not without cause; for although faith may sustain us, yet, as our carnal sense and reason are wavering, we ought to mingle prayers for our confirmation.
5. But those who turn aside into their crooked paths, etc. The meaning is, that God does not always connive at the wickedness of those who, while boasting of a hollow and counterfeit profession, wander hither and thither according to their own lust, or even corrupt the simple, and draw them into the same excess of sinning with themselves. I have no doubt that the Psalmist here speaks of hypocrites, who are so hardened by temporary impunity, as to claim to. themselves a place among the holiest of men.

MATTHEW HENRY

Psalm 125

1-3 The security of God's people.
Here are three very precious promises made to the people of God, which, though they are designed to secure the welfare of the church in general, may be applied by particular believers to themselves, as other promises of this nature may. Here is,
I. The character of God's people, to whom these promises belong. Many call themselves God's people who have no part nor lot in this matter. But those shall have the benefit of them and may take the comfort of them who are righteous (v. 3), righteous before God, righteous to God, and righteous to all men, for his sake justified and sanctified.
II. The promises themselves.
1. That their hearts shall be established by faith: those minds shall be truly stayed that are stayed on God: They shall be as Mount Zion. The church in general is called Mount Zion (Heb. xii. 22), and it shall in this respect be like Mount Zion, it shall be built upon a rock, and its interests shall be so well secured that the gates of hell shall not prevail against it.
2. That, committing themselves to God, they shall be safe, under his protection, from all the insults of their enemies, as Jerusalem had a natural fastness and fortification in the mountains that were round about it, v. 2. Those mountains not only sheltered it from winds and tempests, and broke the force of them, but made it also very difficult of access for an enemy; such a defense is God's providence to his people.
3. That their troubles shall last no longer than their strength will serve to bear them up under them, v. 3.
(1.) It is supposed that the rod of the wicked may come, may fall, upon the lot of the righteous. The rod of their power may oppress them; the rod of their anger may vex and torment them.
(2.) It is promised that, though it may come upon their lot, it shall not rest there; it shall not continue so long as the enemies design, and as the people of God fear.
(3.) It is considered as a reason of this promise that if the trouble should continue over-long the righteous themselves would be in temptation to put forth their hands to iniquity, to join with wicked people in their wicked practices, to say as they say and do as they do.

4-5 The security of God's people.
Here is,
1. The prayer the psalmist puts up for the happiness of those that are sincere and constant (v. 4): Do good, O Lord! unto those that are good. This teaches us to pray for all good people, to make supplication for all saints; and we may pray in faith for them, being assured that those who do well shall certainly be well dealt with.
2. The prospect he has of the ruin of hypocrites and deserters; he does not pray for it, but he predicts it.

Psalm 126

Title
A Song of degrees.

1 When the LORD turned again the captivity of Zion, we were like them that dream.
2 Then was our mouth filled with laughter, and our tongue with singing: then said they among the heathen, The LORD hath done great things for them.
3 The LORD hath done great things for us; whereof we are glad.
4 Turn again our captivity, O LORD, as the streams in the south.
5 They that sow in tears shall reap in joy.
6 He that goeth forth and weepeth, bearing precious seed, shall doubtless come again with rejoicing, bringing his sheaves with him.

Psalm 126

TITLE. A Song of Degrees. This is the seventh Step, and we may therefore expect to meet with some special perfection of joy in it; nor shall we look in vain. We see here not only that Zion abides, but that her joy returns after sorrow. Abiding is not enough, fruitfulness is added. The pilgrims went from blessing to blessing in their psalmody as they proceeded on their holy way. Happy people to whom ever ascent was a song, every halt a hymn. Here the trustor becomes a sower: faith works by love, obtains a present bliss, and secures a harvest of delight.
There is nothing in this psalm by which we can decide its date, further than this,—that it is a song after a great deliverance from oppression. "Turning captivity" by no means requires an actual removal into banishment to fill out the idea; rescue from any dire affliction or crushing tyranny would be fitly described as "captivity turned." Indeed, the passage is not applicable to captives in Babylon, for it is Zion itself which is in captivity and not a part of her citizens: the holy city was in sorrow and distress; though it could not be removed, the prosperity could be diminished. Some dark cloud lowered over the beloved capital, and its citizens prayed "Turn again our captivity. O Lord."
This psalm is in its right place and most fittingly follows its predecessor, for as in Ps 125:1-5, we read that the rod of the wicked shall not rest upon the lot of the righteous, we here see it removed from them to their great joy. The word "turn" would seem to be the keynote of the song: it is a Psalm of conversion—conversion from captivity; and it may well be used to set forth the rapture of a pardoned soul when the anger of the Lord is turned away from it. We will call it, "Leading captivity captive."
DIVISIONS. The Psalm divides itself into a narrative (Ps 126:1-2), a song (Ps 126:3), a prayer (Ps 126:4), and a promise (Ps 126:5-6).

EXPOSITION
Verse 1. When the Lord turned again the captivity of Zion, we were like them that dream. Being in trouble, the gracious pilgrims remember for their comfort times of national woe which were succeeded by remarkable deliverances. Then sorrow was gone like a dream.
Verse 2. Then was our mouth filled with laughter, and our tongue with singing. So full were they of joy that they could not contain themselves. They must express their joy and yet they could not find expression for it.
Verse 3. The LORD hath done great things for us; whereof we are glad. They did not deny the statement which reflected so much glory upon Jehovah: with exultation they admitted and repeated the statement of Jehovah's notable dealings with them.
Verse 4. Turn again our captivity, O LORD. Remembering the former joy of a past rescue they cry to Jehovah for a repetition of it. When we pray for the turning of our captivity, it is wise to recall former instances thereof: nothing strengthens faith more effectually than the memory of a previous experience.
Verse 5. They that sow in tears shall reap in joy. Hence, present distress must not be viewed as if it would last for ever; it is not the end, by any means, but only a means to the end. Sorrow is our sowing, rejoicing shall be our reaping.
Verse 6. He. The general assurance is applied to each one in particular. That which is spoken in the previous verse in the plural—"they", is here repeated in the singular—"he." Yes, good husbandman, doubtless you will gather sheaves from your sowing. Because the Lord has written doubtless, take heed that you do not doubt.

Psalm 126

1-3

1. When Jehovah brought back the captivity of Zion, etc. I have no doubt that the Psalm was composed upon the return of the Jewish people from the Babylonish captivity. Now, whoever was the author of it, whether one of the Levites or one of the Prophets, he affirms that the manner of their deliverance was too wonderful to be attributed to fortune, in order to lead the faithful to the conclusion that the prophecy of Jeremiah, which had assigned seventy years as the term of the captivity, was truly fulfilled. (Jeremiah 25:12, and Jeremiah 29:10.)

2. Now shall our mouth be filled with laughter. The Prophet would have the people so to rejoice on account of their return, as not to bury in forgetfulness the grace of God. He therefore describes no ordinary rejoicing, but such as so fills their minds as to constrain them to break forth into extravagance of gesture and of voice. At the same time he intimates that there was good ground for this joy, in which it became the children of God to indulge, on account of their return to their own land. As there was at that period nothing more wretched than for them to live in captivity, in which they were in a manner dispossessed of the inheritance God had promised them; so there was nothing which ought to have been more desirable to them than to be restored. Their restoration to their own country having been therefore a proof of their renewed adoption by God, it is not surprising to find the Prophet asserting that their mouth was filled with laughter, and their tongue with exultation. With a similar joy does it become us at the present day to exult when God gathers together his Church and it is an undoubted evidence that we are steel-hearted, if her miserable dispersion does not produce in our minds grief and lamentation.

4-6

4. O Jehovah! bring back our captivity. The second part of the Psalm contains a prayer that God would gather together the residue of the captives. The Holy Spirit endited this form of prayer for the Jews who were already come home to their own country, that they might not forget their poor brethren who were still in exile. All the Jews, no doubt, had a door opened to them to come out of the land of their captivity, but the number of those who partook of this benefit was small.

5. They who sow in tears shall reap in joy. This sentence, in my opinion, ought not less to be extended to the future than understood of the past. The carrying away of the Jews into Babylon was to them as a seed-time; God having, by the prophecy of Jeremiah, encouraged them to hope for the harvest. Still, it was not without very great heaviness and anguish of heart that they were dragged into such long continued captivity. It was, as if in the time of dearth the poor husbandman were compelled to abridge himself of his ordinary food in order to provide for the coming year; and although this is a hard and distressing case, he is yet moved to sow from the hope of the harvest.

Psalm 126

1-3 The deliverance from captivity.
Here is,

1. The deliverance God has wrought for them: He turned again the captivity of Zion. It is possible that Zion may be in captivity for the punishment of her degeneracy, but her captivity shall be turned again when the end is answered and the work designed by it is effected. Cyrus, for reasons of state, proclaimed liberty to God's captives, and yet it was the Lord's doing, according to his word many years before.
2. The pleasing surprise that this was to them. They were amazed at it.
3. The notice which their neighbors took of it: They said among the heathen, Jehovah, the God of Israel, has done great things for that people, such as our gods cannot do for us.
4. The acknowledgments which they themselves made of it, v. 3.

4-6 Hope for the sorrowful.
We have here,

1. A prayer for the perfecting of their deliverance (v. 4): "Turn again our captivity. Let those that have returned to their own land be eased of the burdens which they are yet groaning under. Let those that remain in Babylon have their hearts stirred up, as ours were, to take the benefit of the liberty granted."
2. A promise for their encouragement to wait for it, assuring them that, though they had now a sorrowful time, yet it would end well.

(1.) Suffering saints have a season of tears. They are in tears often; they share in the calamities of human life, and commonly have a greater share in them than others. But they sow in tears; they do the duty of an afflicted state and so answer the intentions of the providences they are under. Weeping must not hinder sowing; when we suffer ill we must be doing well. Thus does a good man sow in tears.

(2.) They shall have a harvest of joy. The troubles of the saints will not last always, but, when they have done their work, shall have a happy period. The captives in Babylon were long sowing in tears, but at length they were brought forth with joy, and then they reaped the benefit of their patient suffering, and brought their sheaves with them to their own land, in their experiences of the goodness of God to them. Job, and Joseph, and David, and many others, had harvests of joy after a sorrowful seedness. Those that sow in the tears of godly sorrow shall reap in the joy of a sealed pardon and a settled peace. Those that sow to the spirit, in this vale of tears, shall of the spirit reap life everlasting, and that will be a joyful harvest indeed. Blessed are those that mourn, for they shall be for ever comforted.

Psalm 127

Title
A Song of degrees for Solomon.

1 Except the LORD build the house, they labor in vain that build it: except the LORD keep the city, the watchman waketh but in vain.
2 It is vain for you to rise up early, to sit up late, to eat the bread of sorrows: for so he giveth his beloved sleep.
3 Lo, children are an heritage of the LORD: and the fruit of the womb is his reward.
4 As arrows are in the hand of a mighty man; so are children of the youth.
5 Happy is the man that hath his quiver full of them: they shall not be ashamed, but they shall speak with the enemies in the gate.

Psalm 127

TITLE. A Song of Degrees for Solomon. It was meet that the builder of the holy house should be remembered by the pilgrims to its sacred shrine. The title probably indicates that David wrote it for his wise son, in whom he so greatly rejoiced, and whose name Jedidiah, or "beloved of the Lord", is introduced into the second verse. The spirit of his name, "Solomon, or peaceable", breathes through the whole of this most charming song. If Solomon himself was the author, it comes fitly from him who reared the house of the Lord. Observe how in each of these songs the heart is fixed upon Jehovah only. Read the first verses of these Psalms, from Psalm 120 to the present song, and they run thus: "I cried unto the Lord", "I will lift up mine eyes to the hills", "Let us go unto the house of the Lord." "Unto thee will I lift up mine eyes", "If it had not been the Lord", "They that trust in the Lord." "When the Lord turned again the captivity." The Lord and the Lord alone is thus lauded at each step of these songs of the ascents. O for a life whose every halting place shall suggest a new song unto the Lord!
SUBJECT. God's blessing on his people as their one great necessity and privilege is here spoken of. We are here taught that builders of houses and cities, systems and fortunes, empires and churches all labor in vain without the Lord; but under the divine favor they enjoy perfect rest. Sons, who are in the Hebrew called "builders", are set forth as building up families under the same divine blessing, to the great honor and happiness of their parents. It is THE BUILDER'S PSALM. "Every house is builded by some man, but he that built all things is God", and unto God be praise.

EXPOSITION
Verse 1. Except the LORD build the house, they labor in vain that build it. The word vain is the keynote here, and we hear it ring out clearly three times. Men desiring to build know that they must labor, and accordingly they put forth all their skill and strength; but let them remember that if Jehovah is not with them their designs will prove failures.
Verse 2. It is vain for you to rise up early, to sit up late, to eat the bread of sorrows. Because the Lord is mainly to be rested in, all carking care is mere vanity and vexation of spirit. We are bound to be diligent, for this the Lord blesses; we ought not to be anxious, for that dishonors the Lord, and can never secure his favor.
Verse 3. Lo, children are an heritage of the LORD. This points to another mode of building up a house, namely, by leaving descendants to keep our name and family alive upon the earth. Without this what is a man's purpose in accumulating wealth!
Verse 4. As arrows are in the hand of a mighty man; so are children of the youth. Children born to men in their early days, by God's blessing become the comfort of their riper years. A man of war is glad of weapons which may fly where he cannot: good sons are their father's arrows speeding to hit the mark which their sires aim at. What wonders a good man can accomplish if he has affectionate children to second his desires, and lend themselves to his designs!
Verse 5. Happy is the man that hath his quiver full of them. Those who have no children bewail the fact; those who have few children see them soon gone, and the house is silent, and their life has lost a charm; those who have many gracious children are upon the whole the happiest. Of course a large number of children means a large number of trials; but when these are met by faith in the Lord it also means a mass of love, and a multitude of joys.

JOHN CALVIN

Psalm 127

This Psalm shows that the order of society, both political and domestic, is maintained solely by the blessing of God, and not by the policy, diligence, or wisdom of men; and that the procreating of children is his peculiar gift.

1-2
1. Except Jehovah build the house. There is no reason why the Jews should deny that this Psalm was composed by Solomon. In affirming that God governs the world and the life of man, he does so for two reasons: First, whatever prosperous event may fall out to men, their ingratitude is instantly manifested by their ascribing it wholly to themselves; and thus God is defrauded of the honor which is his due. Solomon, to correct such a perverse error, declares, that nothing happens prosperously to us except in so far as God blesses our proceedings. Secondly, his purpose was to beat down the foolish presumption of men, who, setting God aside, are not afraid to undertake to do anything, whatever it may be, in exclusive reliance upon their own wisdom and strength.
2. It is vain for you in hastening to rise early. Solomon now expresses more plainly that men in vain wear themselves out with toiling, and waste themselves by fasting to acquire riches, since these also are a benefit bestowed only by God. The more effectually to move them, he addresses himself to every man in particular. It is, says he, in vain for you He particularizes two means which are thought to contribute in an eminent degree to the amassing of riches. It is not surprising to find those growing rich in a short time who spare no exertion, but consume night and day in plying their occupations, and allow themselves only scanty fare from the product of their labor.

3-5
3. Lo! children are the heritage of Jehovah. Solomon here adduces one instance in which, in a particular manner, he would have us to recognize the truth which he has hitherto asserted generally—that the life of men is governed by God. Nothing seems more natural than for men to be produced of men. The majority of mankind dream, that after God had once ordained this at the beginning, children were thenceforth begotten solely by a secret instinct of nature, God ceasing to interfere in the matter; and even those who are endued with some sense of piety, although they may not deny that He is the Father and Creator of the human race, yet do not acknowledge that his providential care descends to this particular case, but rather think that men are created by a certain universal motion.
5. They shall not be ashamed when they speak with their enemies in the gate. Here Solomon describes such children as, distinguished by uprightness and integrity, have no hesitation in rendering an account of their life, that they may shut the mouths of the malevolent and of calumniators. He teaches us that the children which we ought to wish for, are not such as may violently oppress the wretched and suffering, but such as will practice uprightness, and be willing to live in obedience to the laws.

MATTHEW HENRY

Psalm 127

1-4 Dependence on providence; God the giver of prosperity.
We are here taught to have a continual regard to the divine Providence in all the concerns of this life. Solomon was cried up for a wise man, and would be apt to lean to his own understanding and forecast, and therefore his father teaches him to look higher, and to take God along with him in his undertakings. He was to be a man of business, and therefore David instructed him how to manage his business under the direction of his religion. Parents, in teaching their children, should suit their exhortations to their condition and occasions. We must have an eye to God,
I. In all the affairs and business of the family, even of the royal family, for kings' houses are no longer safe than while God protects them. We must depend upon God's blessing and not our own contrivance,
1. For the raising of a family: Except the Lord build the house, by his providence and blessing, those labor in vain, though ever so ingenious, that build it. We may understand it of the material house: except the Lord bless the building it is to no purpose for men to build.
2. For the securing of a family or a city (for this is what the psalmist particularly mentions): if the guards of the city cannot secure it without God, much less can the good man of the house save his house from being broken up.
3. For the enriching of a family; this is a work of time and thought, but cannot be effected without the favor of Providence any more than that which is the product of one happy turn: "It is vain for you to rise up early and sit up late, and so to deny yourselves your bodily refreshments, in the eager pursuit of the wealth of the world."
II. In the increase of the family. He shows,
1. That children are God's gift, v. 3. If children are withheld it is God that withholds them (Gen. xxx. 2); if they are given, it is God that gives them (Gen. xxxiii. 5); and they are to us what he makes them, comforts or crosses.
2. That they are a good gift, and a great support and defense to a family: As arrows are in the hand of a mighty man, who knows how to use them for his own safety and advantage, so are children of the youth, that is, children born to their parents when they are young, which are the strongest and most healthful children, and are grown up to serve them by the time they need their service; or, rather, children who are themselves young; they are instruments of much good to their parents and families, which may fortify themselves with them against their enemies. The family that has a large stock of children is like a quiver full of arrows, of different sizes we may suppose, but all of use one time or other; children of different capacities and inclinations may be several ways serviceable to the family.

Psalm 128

Title
A Song of degrees.

1 Blessed is every one that feareth the LORD; that walketh in his ways.
2 For thou shalt eat the labor of thine hands: happy shalt thou be, and it shall be well with thee.
3 Thy wife shall be as a fruitful vine by the sides of thine house: thy children like olive plants round about thy table.
4 Behold, that thus shall the man be blessed that feareth the LORD.
5 The LORD shall bless thee out of Zion: and thou shalt see the good of Jerusalem all the days of thy life.
6 Yea, thou shalt see thy children's children, and peace upon Israel.

Psalm 128

TITLE. A Song of Degrees. There is an evident ascent from the last Psalm: that did but hint at the way in which a house may be built up, but this draws a picture of that house built, and adorned with domestic bliss through the Lord's own benediction. There is clearly an advance in age, for here we go beyond children to children's children; and also a progress in happiness, for children which in the last Psalm were arrows are here Olive plants, and instead of speaking "with the enemies in the gate" we done with "peace upon Israel." Thus we rise step by step, and sing as we ascend.
SUBJECT. It is a family hymn, a song for a marriage, or a birth, or for any day in which a happy household has met to praise the Lord. Like all the songs of degrees, it has an eye to Zion and Jerusalem, which are both expressly mentioned, and it closes like Psalms 125, 130, and 131, with an allusion to Israel. It is a short Psalm, but exceedingly full and suggestive. Its poetry is of the highest order. Perhaps in no country can it be better understood than in our own, for we above all nations delight to sing of "Home, sweet home."

EXPOSITION
Verse 1. Blessed is every one that feareth the Lord. The last Psalm ended with a blessing,—for the word there translated "happy" is the same as that which is here rendered "blessed": thus the two songs are joined by a catch word. There is also in them a close community of subject. The fear of God is the corner stone of all blessedness. We must reverence the ever blessed God before we can be blessed ourselves.
Verse 2. For thou shalt eat the labor of thine hands. The general doctrine in Ps 128:1 here receives a personal application: note the change to the second person: "thou shalt eat", etc. This is the portion of God's saints,—to work, and to find a reward in so doing. God is the God of laborers.
Verse 3. Thy wife. To reach the full of earthly felicity a man must not be alone. A helpmeet was needed in Paradise, and assuredly she is not less necessary out of it. He that findeth a wife findeth a good thing. It is not every man that feareth the Lord who has a wife; but if he has, she shall share in his blessedness and increase it.
Verse 4. To the Lord alone we must look for it. The possession of riches will not ensure it; the choice of a healthy and beautiful bride will not ensure it; the birth of numerous comely children will not ensure it: there must be the blessing of God, the influence of piety, the result of holy living.
Verse 5. The Loud shall bless thee out of Zion. A spiritual blessing shall be received by the gracious man, and this shall crown all his temporal mercies. He is one among the many who make up God's inheritance; his tent is part and parcel of the encampment around the tabernacle; and therefore, when the benediction is pronounced at the center it shall radiate to him in his place.
Verse 6. Yea, thou shalt see thy children's children. This is a great pleasure. Men live their young lives over again in their grandchildren. And peace upon Israel. With this sweet word Psalm 126 was closed. It is a favorite formula. Let God's own heritage be at peace, and we are all glad of it. We count it our own prosperity for the chosen of the Lord to find rest and quiet. Jacob was sorely tossed about; his life knew little of peace; but yet the Lord delivered him out of all his tribulations, and brought him to a place of rest in Goshen for a while, and afterwards to sleep with his fathers in the cave of Machpelah. His glorious Seed was grievously afflicted and at last crucified; but he has risen to eternal peace, and in his peace we dwell.

JOHN CALVIN

Psalm 128

1-3

1. Blessed is the man who feareth Jehovah. In the preceding Psalm it was stated that prosperity in all human affairs, and in the whole course of our life, is to be hoped for exclusively from the grace of God; and now the Prophet admonishes us that those who desire to be partakers of the blessing of God must with sincerity of heart devote themselves wholly to him; for he will never disappoint those who serve him. The first verse contains a summary of the subject-matter of the Psalm; the remaining portion being added only by way of exposition. The maxim "that those are blessed who fear God, especially in the present life," is so much with variance with the common opinion of men, that very few will give it their assent.

2. For when thou shalt eat the labor of thy hands thou shalt be blessed. Here the Prophet, confirming the doctrine stated in the first verse, teaches us that we ought to form a different estimate of what happiness consists hi from that formed by the world, which makes a happy life to consist in ease, honors, and great wealth. He recalls God's servants to the practice of moderation, which almost all men refuse to exercise.

3. Thy wife shall be as a fruitful vine on the sides of thy house. Here again it is promised, as in the preceding Psalm, that God will make those who honor him fruitful in a numerous offspring. The majority of mankind indeed desire to have issue, and this desire may be said to be implanted in them by nature; but many, when they have obtained children, soon become cloyed therewith.

4-6

4. Lo! surely, thus blessed shall be the man who feareth Jehovah. The preceding doctrine, that even in the outward condition of God's servants while in this transitory state there is afforded such evidence of the divine favor and goodness as demonstrates that we do not lose our labor in serving him, is here confirmed by the Prophet.

5. Jehovah shall bless thee from Zion. Although the gifts of God often present themselves before our eyes, yet through the obscurity which false imaginations throw around them our perception of them is dim and imperfect. Hence this repetition of the sentiment, That whenever true believers meet with any prosperous events in the course of their life, it is the effect of the divine blessing, is not to be deemed superfluous. The persons described are said to be blessed from Zion, to lead them to call to remembrance the covenant into which God had entered with them, for he had graciously promised to be favorable to the observers of his law; and these principles of godliness they had imbibed from their infancy. The Prophet, therefore, declares that it is no novel doctrine or something before unheard of which he adduces, the law having long ago taught them that it is made manifest even by the temporary benefits conferred on those who serve God, that the pains taken in serving him are not thrown away; and he affirms that of this they shall actually have the experience.

MATTHEW HENRY

Psalm 128

1-6 Blessedness of the godly.

It is here shown that godliness has the promise of the life that now is and of that which is to come.

I. It is here again and again laid down as an undoubted truth that those who are truly holy are truly happy. Those whose blessed state we are here assured of are such as fear the Lord and walk in his ways, such as have a deep reverence of God upon their spirits and evidence it by a regular and constant conformity to his will. Such are blessed (v. 1), and shall be blessed, v. 4. God blesses them, and his pronouncing them blessed makes them so. They are blessed now, they shall be blessed still, and for ever. This blessedness, arising from this blessing, is here secured,

1. To all the saints universally: Blessed is everyone that fears the Lord, whoever he be; in every nation he that fears God.

2. To such a saint in particular: Thus shall the man be blessed, not only the nation, the church in its public capacity, but the particular person in his private interests.

3. We are encouraged to apply it to ourselves (v. 2): "Happy shalt thou be; thou mayest take the comfort of the promise, and expect the benefit of it. "

II. Particular promises are here made to godly people, which they may depend upon, as far as is for God's glory and their good; and that is enough.

1. That, by the blessing of God, they shall get an honest livelihood and live comfortably upon it.

2. That they shall have abundance of comfort in their family-relations. As a wife and children are very much a man's care, so, if by the grace of God they are such as they should be, they are very much a man's delight, as much as any creature-comfort.

(1.) The wife shall be as a vine by the sides of the house.

(2.) The children shall be as olive plants, likely in time to be olive-trees, and, though wild by nature, yet grafted into the good olive, and partaking of its root and fatness, Rom. xi. 17.

3. That they shall have those things which God has promised and which they pray for: The Lord shall bless thee out of Zion, where the ark of the covenant was, and where the pious Israelites attended with their devotions.

4. That they shall live long, to enjoy the comforts of the rising generations: "Thou shalt see thy children's children, as Joseph, Gen. 1.23. Thy family shall be built up and continued, and thou shalt have the pleasure of seeing it."

5. That they shall see the welfare of God's church, and the land of their nativity, which every man who fears God is no less concerned for than for the prosperity of his own family. A good man can have little comfort in seeing his children's children, unless withal he see peace upon Israel.

Psalm 129

Title
A Song of degrees.

1 Many a time have they afflicted me from my youth, may Israel now say:
2 Many a time have they afflicted me from my youth: yet they have not prevailed against me.
3 The plowers plowed upon my back: they made long their furrows.
4 The LORD is righteous: he hath cut asunder the cords of the wicked.
5 Let them all be confounded and turned back that hate Zion.
6 Let them be as the grass upon the housetops, which withereth afore it groweth up:
7 Wherewith the mower filleth not his hand; nor he that bindeth sheaves his bosom.
8 Neither do they which go by say, The blessing of the LORD be upon you: we bless you in the name of the LORD.

Psalm 129

TITLE. A Song of Degrees. I fail to see how this is a step beyond the previous Psalm; and yet it is clearly the song of an older and more tried individual, who looks back upon a life of affliction in which he suffered all along, even from his youth. Inasmuch as patience is a higher, or at least more difficult, grace than domestic love, the ascent or progress may perhaps be seen in that direction. Probably if we knew more of the stations on the road to the Temple we should see a reason for the order of these Psalms; but as that information cannot be obtained, we must take the songs as we find them, and remember that, as we do not now go on pilgrimages to Zion, it is our curiosity and not oar necessity which is a loser by our not knowing the cause of the arrangement of the songs in this Pilgrim Psalter.
AUTHOR, ETC. It does not seem to us at all needful to ascribe this Psalm to a period subsequent to the captivity...indeed, it is more suitable to a time when as yet the enemy bad not so far prevailed as to have carried the people indo a distant land. It is a mingled hymn of sorrow and of strong resolve. Though sorely smitten, the afflicted one is heart whole, and scorns to yield in the least degree to the enemy. The poet sings the trials of Israel, Ps 129:1-3; the interposition of the Lord, Ps 129:4; and the unblessed condition of Israel's foes, Ps 129:5-8. It is a rustic song, full of allusions to husbandry. It reminds us of the books of Ruth and Amos.

EXPOSITION
Verse 1. Many a time have they afflicted me from my youth, may Israel now say. In her present hour of trial she may remember her former afflictions and speak of them for her comfort, drawing from them the assurance that he who has been with her for so long will not desert her in the end.
Verse 2. Many a time have they afflicted, me from my youth. Israel repeats her statement of her repeated afflictions. The fact was uppermost in her thoughts, and she could not help soliloquizing upon it again and again. These repetitions are after the manner of poetry: thus she makes a sonnet out of her sorrows, music out of her miseries.
Verse 3. The plowers plowed up on my back. The scourgers tore the flesh as ploughmen furrow a field. The people were maltreated like a criminal given over to the lictors with their cruel whips; the back of the nation was scored and furrowed by oppression. It is a grand piece of imagery condensed into few words.
Verse 4. The LORD is righteous. Whatever men may be, Jehovah remains just, and will therefore keep covenant with his people and deal out justice to their oppressors. Here is the hinge of the condition: this makes the turning point of Israel's distress.
Verse 5. Let them all be confounded and turned back that hate Zion. It is but justice that those who hate, harass, and hurt the good should be brought to naught.
Verse 6. Let them be as the grass upon the housetops, which withereth afore it groweth up. Grass on the housetop is soon up and soon down. Such is and such ought to be the lot of the enemies of God's people. Transient is their prosperity; speedy is their destruction.
Verse 7. Wherewith the mower filleth not his hand; nor he that bindeth sheaves his bosom. Easterners carry their corn in their bosoms, but in this case there was nothing to bear home. Thus do the wicked come to nothing.
Verse 8. Neither do they which go by say, The blessing of the LORD be upon you: we bless you in the name of the LORD. In harvest times men bless each other in the name of the Lord; but there is nothing in the course and conduct of the ungodly man to suggest the giving or receiving of a benediction.

JOHN CALVIN

Psalm 129

1-4
1. They have often afflicted me from my youth. This Psalm was probably composed at a time when the Church of God, reduced to a state of extreme distress, or dismayed by some great danger, or oppressed with tyranny, was on the verge of total destruction. It is as if the Prophet; had said, When God's faithful ones are with difficulty drawing their breath under the burden of temptations, it is a seasonable time for them to reflect on the manner in which he has exercised his people from the beginning, and from age to age. As soon as God has given loose reins to our enemies to do as they please we are distressed with sorrow, and our thoughts are wholly engrossed with the evils which presently harass us. Hence proceeds despair; for we do not remember that the patience of the fathers was subjected to the like trial, and that nothing happens to us which they did not experience.
3. The ploughers have ploughed upon my back. Here the Prophet, by an apparent similitude, embellishes his preceding statement respecting the grievous afflictions of the Church. He compares the people of God to a field through which a plough is drawn. He says that the furrows were made long, so that no corner was exempted from being cut up by the ploughshare. These words vividly express the fact—that the cross has always been planted on the back of the Church, to make long and wide furrows.

5-8
5. All who hate Zion shall be confounded, and tutored backward. Whether we take this as a prayer or a promise, the Prophet has a respect to the time to come. Since all the verbs are in the future tense, it is certainly a very appropriate interpretation to understand him as deriving from times past instruction as to what is to be hoped for in future. In whichever way we understand the passage, he declares that the faithful have no reason to be discouraged when they behold their enemies raised on high. The grass which grows upon the house-tops is not, on account of its higher situation, more valuable than the blade of corn which in the low ground is trampled under foot.
7. With which the mower hath not filled his hand. We have here an additional confirmation of the truth, that although the wicked mount high or elevate themselves, and form an extravagant opinion of their own importance, yet they continue mere grass, not bringing forth any good fruit, nor reaching a state of ripeness, but swelling only with fresh appearance.

To make this obvious, the Psalmist sets them in opposition to fruit-bearing herbs, which in valleys and low grounds produce fruit for men. In fine, he affirms that they deserve to be hated or despised of all, whereas commonly every one in passing by the corn fields blesses them and prays for the harvest? Farther, he has borrowed this illustration of his doctrine from the affairs of ordinary life, we are taught that whenever there is a hopeful prospect of a good harvest, we ought to beseech God, whose peculiar province it is to impart fertility to the earth, that he would give full effect to his blessing.

MATTHEW HENRY

Psalm 129

1-4 Domestic happiness.
The church of God, in its several ages, is here spoken of, or, rather, here speaks, as one single person, now old and gray-headed, but calling to remembrance the former days, and reflecting upon the times of old. And, upon the review, it is found,
1. That the church has been often greatly distressed by its enemies on earth: Israel may now say, "I am the people that has been oppressed more than any people, that has been as a speckled bird, pecked at by all the birds round about," Jer. xii. 9. The gospel-church, ever since it had a being, has been at times afflicted; and it bore this yoke most of all in its youth, witness the ten persecutions which the primitive church groaned under. The ploughers ploughed upon my back, v. 3. We read (Ps. cxxv. 3) of the rod of the wicked upon the lot of the righteous, where we rather expected the plough, to mark it out for themselves; here we read of the plough of the wicked upon the back of the righteous, where we rather expected to find the rod.
2. That the church has been always graciously delivered by her friend in heaven. The enemies' projects have been defeated. They have afflicted the church, in hopes to ruin it, but they have not gained their point.

5-8 God's regard for His Church.
The psalmist, having triumphed in the defeat of the many designs that had been laid as deep as hell to ruin the church, here concludes his psalm as Deborah did her song, So let all thy enemies perish, O Lord! Judg. v. 31.
I. There are many that hate Zion, that hate Zion's God, his worship, and his worshippers, that have an antipathy to religion and religious people, that seek the ruin of both, and do what they can that God may not have a church in the world.
II. We ought to pray that all their attempts against the church may be frustrated, that in them they may be confounded.
III. No wise man will pray God to bless the mowers or reapers, v. 8. Observe,
1. It has been an ancient and laudable custom not only to salute and wish a good day to strangers and travelers, but particularly to pray for the prosperity of harvest-laborers.
2. Religious expressions, being sacred things, must never be made use of in light and ludicrous actions.
3. It is a dangerous thing to let the church's enemies have our good wishes in their designs against the church. If we wish them God speed, we are partakers of their evil deeds, 2 John 11. When it is said, None will bless them, and show them respect, more is implied, namely, that all wise and good people will cry out shame on them, and beg God to defeat them.

Psalm 130

Title
A Song of degrees.

1 Out of the depths have I cried unto thee, O LORD.
2 Lord, hear my voice: let thine ears be attentive to the voice of my supplications.
3 If thou, LORD, shouldest mark iniquities, O Lord, who shall stand?
4 But there is forgiveness with thee, that thou mayest be feared.
5 I wait for the LORD, my soul doth wait, and in his word do I hope.
6 My soul waiteth for the Lord more than they that watch for the morning: I say, more than they that watch for the morning.
7 Let Israel hope in the LORD: for with the LORD there is mercy, and with him is plenteous redemption.
8 And he shall redeem Israel from all his iniquities.

Psalm 130

TITLE. A Song of Degrees. It would be hard to see any upward step from the preceding to the present Psalm, and therefore it is possible that the steps or ascents are in the song itself: certainly it does rise rapidly out of the depths of anguish to the heights of assurance. It follows well upon 129: when we have overcome the trials which arise from man we are the better prepared to meet those sharper sorrows which arise out of our matters towards God. He who has borne the scourges of the wicked is trained in all patience to wait the dealings of the Holy Lord. We name this the DE PROFUNDIS PSALM: "Out of the depths" is the leading word of it: out of those depths we cry, wait, watch, and hope. In this Psalm we hear of the pearl of redemption, Ps 130:7-8: perhaps the sweet singer would never have found that precious thing had he not been cast into the depths. "Pearls lie deep."
DIVISION. The first two verses (Ps 130:1-2) reveal an intense desire; and the next two are a humble confession of repentance and faith, Ps 130:3-4. In Ps 130:5-6 waiting watchfulness is declared and resolved upon; and in Ps 130:7-8 joyful expectation, both for himself and all Israel, finds expression.

EXPOSITION
Verse 1. Out of the depths have I cried unto thee, O LORD. This is the Psalmist's statement and plea: he had never ceased to pray even when brought into the lowest state. The depths usually silence all they engulf, but they could not close the mouth of this servant of the Lord. Deep places beget deep devotion. Depths of earnestness are stirred by depths of tribulation. Diamonds sparkle most amid the darkness. Prayer de profundis gives to God gloria in excelsis.
Verse 2. Lord, hear my voice. It is all we ask; but nothing less will content us. If the Lord will but hear us we will leave it to his superior wisdom to decide whether he will answer us or no.
Verse 3. If thou, LORD, shouldest mark iniquities, O Lord, who shall stand. If JAH, the all seeing, should in strict justice call every man to account for every want of conformity to righteousness, where would any one of us be?
Verse 4. But there is forgiveness with thee. Free, full, sovereign pardon is in the hand of the great King: it is his prerogative to forgive, and he delights to exercise it. Because his nature is mercy, and because he has provided a sacrifice for sin, therefore forgiveness is with him for all that come to him confessing their sins.
Verse 5. I wait for the LORD, my soul doth wait. Expecting him to come to me in love, I quietly wait for his appearing; I wait upon him in service, and for him in faith. For God I wait and for him only: if he will manifest himself I shall have nothing more to wait for.
Verse 6. My soul waiteth for the Lord more than they that watch for the morning. Men who guard a city, and women who wait by the sick, long for daylight. David, however, waited more than these, waited longer, waited more longingly, waited more expectantly.
Verse 7. Let Israel hope in the LORD. Or, "Hope thou, Israel, in Jehovah." Jehovah is Israel's God; therefore, let Israel hope in him. What one Israelite does he wishes all Israel to do.
Verse 8. And he shall redeem Israel from all his iniquities. Our iniquities are our worst dangers: if saved from these, we are saved altogether; but there is no salvation from them except by redemption. What a blessing is promised here: the Lord shall certainly redeem his believing people from all their sins. Well may the redemption be plenteous since it concerns all Israel and all iniquities!

JOHN CALVIN

Psalm 130

1-4
1. Out of the deep places have I cried to thee, O Jehovah! It is to be noticed that the Prophet speaks of himself as sending forth his voice, as it were from out of a deep gulf, feeling himself overwhelmed with calamities. As the miseries to which there is no prospect of a termination commonly bring despair in their train, nothing is more difficult than for persons, when involved in grievous and deep sorrow, to stir up their minds to the exercise of prayer. And it is wonderful, considering that whilst we enjoy peace and prosperity we are cold in prayer, (because then our hearts are in a state of infatuated security,) how in adversities, which ought to quicken us, we are still more stupefied. But the Prophet derives confidence in coming to the time one of grace from the very troubles, cares, dangers and sorrow into which he was plunged.
3. If thou, O God! shoudst mark iniquities. Here the Prophet acknowledges that although grievously afflicted he had justly deserved such punishment, as had been inflicted upon him. As by his own example he gives a rule which the whole Church ought to observe, let no man presume to intrude himself into the presence of God, but in the way of humbly deprecating his wrath.
4. But with thee there is forgiveness. This verse leads us farther. Though all men confess with the mouth that there is no human being in the world whom God may not justly adjudge to everlasting death, should it so please him, yet how few are persuaded of the truth which the Prophet now adds, that the grace of which they stand in need shall not be denied them?

5-6
5. I have waited for Jehovah. After having testified in general that God is ready to show mercy to poor sinners who betake themselves to him, the Psalmist concludes that he is thereby encouraged to entertain good hope. From this we also gather that even in the inward feelings of his heart he had maintained quietness and patience before God.
6. My soul hath waited for the Lord before the watchers of the morning. In this verse he expresses both the ardor and the perseverance of his desire. In saying that he anticipated the watchmen, he shows by this similitude with what diligence and alacrity he breathed after God.

7-8
7. But let Israel hope in Jehovah. After having spoken of himself, and exhibited in his own person an example for all to follow, he now applies the doctrine to the whole body of the Church. It is to be noticed that the foundation upon which he would have the hope of all the godly to rest is the mercy of God, the source from which redemption springs.
8. And he shall redeem Israel from all his iniquities. Here the Psalmist applies more closely to the Church what he has said in the preceding verse. He concludes that it is not to be doubted that God will prove himself the deliverer of the people whom he has chosen.

MATTHEW HENRY

Psalm 130

1-4 God's regard for His Church.
In these verses we are taught,
I. Whatever condition we are in, though ever so deplorable, to continue calling upon God, v. 1. The best men may sometimes be in the depths, in great trouble and affliction, and utterly at a loss what to do, in the depths of distress and almost in the depths of despair, the spirit low and dark, sinking and drooping, cast down and disquieted.
II. While we continue calling upon God to assure ourselves of an answer of peace from him; for this is that which David in faith prays for (v. 2): Lord, hear my voice, my complaint and prayer, and let thy ears be attentive to the voice both of my afflictions and of my supplications.
III. We are taught to humble ourselves before the justice of God as guilty in his sight, and unable to answer him for one of a thousand of our offences (v. 3): If thou, Lord, shouldst mark iniquities, O Lord! who shall stand? His calling God Lord twice, in so few words, Jah and Adonai, is very emphatic, and intimates a very awful sense of God's glorious majesty and a dread of his wrath.
IV. We are taught to cast ourselves upon the pardoning mercy of God, and to comfort ourselves with that when we see ourselves obnoxious to his justice, v. 4. Here is,
1. God's grace discovered, and pleaded with him, by a penitent sinner: But there is forgiveness with thee. It is our unspeakable comfort, in all our approaches to God, that there is forgiveness with him, for that is what we need.
2. Our duty designed in that discovery, and inferred from it.

5-8 Encouragement to trust in and depend upon God. Here,
I. The psalmist engages himself to trust in God and to wait for him, v. 5, 6. Observe,
1. His dependence upon God, expressed in a climax, it being a song of degrees, or ascents.
2. The ground of that dependence: In his word do I hope.
3. The degree of that dependence: "more than those that watch for the morning, who are well-assured that the morning will come; and so am I that God will return in mercy to me."
II. He encourages all the people of God in like manner to depend upon him and trust in him. Let all that devote themselves to God cheerfully stay themselves upon him (v. 7, 8), for two reasons:
1. Because the light of nature discovers to us that there is mercy with him.
2. Because the light of the gospel discovers to us that there is redemption with him, contrived by him, and to be wrought out in the fullness of time; it was in the beginning hidden in God.

Psalm 131

Title
A Song of degrees of David.

1 Lord, my heart is not haughty, nor mine eyes lofty: neither do I exercise myself in great matters, or in things too high for me.
2 Surely I have behaved and quieted myself, as a child that is weaned of his mother: my soul is even as a weaned child.
3 Let Israel hope in the LORD from henceforth and for ever.

Psalm 131

TITLE. A Song of Degrees of David. It is both by David and of David: he is the author and the subject of it, and many incidents of his life may be employed to illustrate it. Comparing all the Psalms to gems, we should liken this to a pearl: how beautifully it will adorn the neck of patience. It is one of the shortest Psalms to read, but one of the longest to learn. It speaks of a young child, but it contains the experience of a man in Christ. Lowliness and humility are here seen in connection with a sanctified heart, a will subdued to the mind of God, and a hope looking to the Lord alone happy is the man who can without falsehood use these words as his own; for he wears about him the likeness of his Lord, who said, "I am meek and lowly in heart." The Psalm is in advance of all the Songs of Degrees which have preceded it; for loveliness is one of the highest attainments in the divine life. There are also steps in this Song of Degrees: it is a short ladder, if we count the words; but yet it rises to a great height, reaching from deep humility to fixed confidence. Le Blanc thinks that this is a song of the Israelites who returned from Babylon with, humble hearts, weaned from their idols. At any rate, after any spiritual captivity let it be the expression of our hearts.

EXPOSITION
Verse 1. LORD, my heart is not haughty. The Psalm deals with the Lord, and is a solitary colloquy with him, not a discourse before men. We have a sufficient audience when we speak with the Lord, and we may say to him many things which were not proper for the ears of men. The holy man makes his appeal to Jehovah, who alone knows the heart: a man should be slow to do this upon any matter, for the Lord is not to be trifled with; and when anyone ventures on such an appeal he should be sure of his case. He begins with his heart, for that is the center of our nature, and if pride be there it defiles everything; just as mire in the spring causes mud in all the streams.
Neither do I exercise myself in great matters. As a private man he did not usurp the power of the king or devise plots against him: he minded his own business, and left others to mind theirs. As a thoughtful man he did not pry into things unrevealed; he was not speculative, self conceited or opinionated. As a secular person he did not thrust himself into the priesthood as Saul had done before him, and as Uzziah did after him. It is well so to exercise ourselves unto godliness that we know our true sphere, and diligently keep to it. Many through wishing to be great have failed to be good: they were not content to adorn the lowly stations which the Lord appointed them, and so they have rushed at grandeur and power, and found destruction where they looked for honor.
Verse 3. Let Israel hope in the LORD from henceforth and for ever. See how lovingly a man who is weaned from self thinks of others! David thinks of his people, and loses himself in his care for Israel. How he prizes the grace of hope! He has given up the things which are seen, and therefore he values the treasures which are not seen except by the eyes of hope. There is room for the largest hope when self is gone, ground for eternal hope when transient things no longer hold the mastery of our spirits. This verse is the lesson of experience: a man of God who had been taught to renounce the world and live upon the Lord alone, here exhorts all his friends and companions to do the same. He found it a blessed thing to live by hope, and therefore he would have all his kinsmen do the same. Let all the nation hope, let all their hope be in Jehovah, let them at once begin hoping "from henceforth", and let them continue hoping "for ever." Weaning takes the child out of a temporary condition into a state in which he will continue for the rest of his life: to rise above the world is to enter upon a heavenly existence which can never end.

Psalm 131

David, having it as his object in this Psalm to encourage the people to fight strenuously under his banner, and to exhort and excite the godly to acknowledge him as entitled to their obedience, declares that he had always submitted himself to the guidance of God, and had done nothing without his call and commission.

1. O Jehovah! My heart has not been elated. David had been made head over God's people, and in order to prove that he was their lawful prince, entitled to the allegiance of the faithful, he is desirous to show that he had not been influenced, in anything which he had attempted, by ambition or pride, but had submitted himself with a quiet and humble spirit to the divine disposal. In this he teaches us a very useful lesson, and one by which we should be ruled in life—to be contented with the lot which God has marked out for us, to consider what he calls us to, and not to aim at fashioning our own lot √ to be moderate in our desires, to avoid entering upon rash undertakings, and to confine ourselves cheerfully within our own sphere, instead of attempting great things. He denies that his heart had been lifted up, for this is the true cause of all unwarranted rashness and presumption in conduct.

2-3
2. If I have not set, etc. He here employs a figure which appropriately explains what he meant, and likens himself to a weaned child; by which is intended, that he dismissed all the anxieties which disquiet the man of ambition, and was willing to be satisfied with small things. This assertion, which some might be inclined to disbelieve, he makes with an oath, expressed in that particular form of which I have elsewhere taken notice, in which the imprecation is not directly brought forward, but left to be understood, to teach us caution in the use of God's name.
As to the words, to set his soul like a child, is as if he had said, that he would frame it into such a likeness. The quiet of soul he alludes to is opposed to those tumultuous desires by which many cause disquietude to themselves, and are the means of throwing the world into agitation. The figure of childhood is elsewhere used in another sense, to convey reprehension. (Isaiah 28:9.) "Whom shall I teach knowledge? them that are weaned from the milk? and drawn from the breasts?" where the Prophet censures the people for their slowness of apprehension, and being as incapable of profiting by instruction as infants. In the passage now before us, what is recommended is that simplicity of which Christ spake,
"Unless ye become like this little child, ye shall in no wise enter into the kingdom of God." (Matthew 18:3) The vain desires with which men are carried away, originate in their seeking to be wise and careful above what is necessary. David adds accordingly, my soul over me is quieted, not as expressing the language of self-confidence, but speaking as if his soul lay sweetly and peacefully on his bosom, undisturbed by inordinate desires.

Psalm 131

1-3 Humble Confidence.
Here are two things which will be comforts to us:
I. Consciousness of our integrity. This was David's rejoicing, that his heart could witness for him that he had walked humbly with his God, notwithstanding the censures he was under and the temptations he was in.

1. He aimed not at a high condition, nor was he desirous of making a figure in the world, but, if God had so ordered, could have been well content to spend all his days, as he did in the beginning of them, in the sheep-folds. His own brother, in a passion, charged him with pride (1 Sam. xvii. 28), but the charge was groundless and unjust. God, who searches the heart, knew,
(1.) That he had no conceited opinion of himself, or his own merits: Lord, my heart is not haughty. Humble saints cannot think so well of themselves as others think of them, are not in love with their own shadow, nor do they magnify their own attainments or achievements. The love of God reigning in the heart will subdue all inordinate self-love.
(2.) That he had neither a scornful nor an aspiring look: "My eyes are not lofty, either to look with envy upon those that are above me or to look with disdain upon those that are below me." Where there is a proud heart there is commonly a proud look (Prov. vi. 17), but the humble publican will not so much as lift up his eyes.
(3.) That he did not employ himself in things above his station, in things too great or too high for him. He did not employ himself in studies too high; he made God's word his meditation, and did not amuse himself with matters of nice speculation or doubtful disputation, or covet to be wise above what is written. To know God and our duty is learning sufficiently high for us.

2. He was well reconciled to every condition that God placed him in (v. 2): I have behaved and quieted myself as a child that is weaned of his mother. As he had not proudly aimed at the kingdom, so, since God had appointed him to it, he had not behaved insolently towards any, nor been restless in his attempts to get the crown before the time set.
II. Confidence in God; and this David recommends to all Israel of God, no doubt from his own experience of the benefit of it (v. 3): Let Israel hope in the Lord, and let them continue to do so henceforth and for ever. Though David could himself wait patiently and quietly for the crown designed him, yet perhaps Israel, the people whose darling he was, would be ready to attempt something in favor of him before the time; and therefore endeavors to quiet them too, and bids them hope in the Lord that they should see a happy change of the face of affairs in due time. Thus it is good to hope and quietly to wait for the salvation of the Lord.

Psalm 132

Title
A Song of degrees.

1-6
1 Lord, remember David, and all his afflictions:
2 How he sware unto the LORD, and vowed unto the mighty God of Jacob;
3 Surely I will not come into the tabernacle of my house, nor go up into my bed;
4 I will not give sleep to mine eyes, or slumber to mine eyelids,
5 Until I find out a place for the LORD, an habitation for the mighty God of Jacob.
6 Lo, we heard of it at Ephratah: we found it in the fields of the wood.

Psalm 132

TITLE. A Song of Degrees. A joyful song indeed: let all pilgrims to the New Jerusalem sing it often. The degrees or ascents are very visible; the theme ascends step by step from, "afflictions" to a "crown", from "remember David", to, "I will make the horn of David to bud." The latter half is like the over arching sky bending above "the fields of the wood" which are found in the resolves and prayers of the former portion.
DIVISION. Our translators have rightly divided this Psalm. It contains a statement of David's anxious care to build a house for the Lord (Ps 132:1-7); a prayer at the removal of the Ark (Ps 132:8-10); and a pleading of the divine covenant and its promises (Ps 132:11-18).

EXPOSITION
Verse 1. LORD, remember David, and all his afflictions. With David the covenant was made, and therefore his name is pleaded on behalf of his descendants, and the people who would be blessed by his dynasty.
Verse 2. How he sware unto the Lord, and vowed unto the mighty God of Jacob. Moved by intense devotion, David expressed his resolve in the form of a solemn vow, which was sealed with an oath.
Verse 3. Surely I will not come into the tabernacle of my house, nor go up into my bed. David meant well, but he spake more than he could carry out. His language was hyperbolical, and the Lord knew what he meant: zeal does not always measure its terms, for it is not thoughtful of the criticisms of men, but is carried away with love to the Lord, who reads the hearts of his people.
Verse 4. I will not give sleep to mine eyes, or slumber to wine eyelids. He could not enjoy sleep till he had done his best to provide a place for the ark. It is a strong expression, and it is not to be coolly discussed by us. Remember that the man was all on fire, and he was writing poetry also, and therefore his language is not that which we should employ in cold blood.
Verse 5. Until I find out a place for the Lord, an habitation for the mighty God of Jacob. He resolved to find a place where Jehovah would allow his worship to be celebrated, a house where God would fix the symbol of his presence, and commune with his people. At that time, in all David's land, there was no proper place for that ark whereon the Lord had placed the mercy seat, where prayer could be offered, and where the manifested glory shone forth. All things had fallen into decay, and the outward forms of public worship were too much disregarded; hence the King resolves to be first and foremost in establishing a better order of things. Yet one cannot help remembering that the holy resolve of David gave to a place and a house much more importance than the Lord himself ever attached to such matters.
Verse 6. Meanwhile, where was the habitation of God among men? He was wont to shine forth from between the cherubim, but where was the ark? It was like a hidden thing, a stranger in its own land. Lo, we heard of it at Ephratah. Rumors came that it was somewhere in the land of Ephraim, in a temporary lodging; rather an object of dread than of delight. Is it not wonderful that so renowned a symbol of the presence of the Lord should be lingering in neglect—a neglect so great that it was remarkable that we should have heard of its whereabouts at all? When a man begins to think upon God and his service it is comforting that the gospel is heard of.
Verse 7. We will go into his tabernacles. Having found the place where he dwells we will hasten thereto. He has many dwellings in one in the various courts of his house, and each of these shall receive the reverence due: in each the priest shall offer for us the appointed service; and our hearts shall go where our bodies may not enter. David is not alone, he is represented as having sought for the ark with others, for so the word "we" implies; and now they are glad to attend him in his pilgrimage to the chosen shrine,

Psalm 132

1-5

1. O Jehovah! remember David. The name of David is prominently mentioned, because it was to him that the continuance of the kingdom and Temple was promised, and though dead, this could not affect the truthfulness of God's word. The Church could very properly pray in the manner which is here done, that God would perform what he had promised to his servant David, not as a private individual, but in favor of all his people.

2. Who sware to Jehovah. One affliction of David is particularly mentioned, That he was filled with perplexity on account of the situation of the Ark. Moses had commanded the people ages before to worship God in the place which he had chosen. (Deuteronomy 12:5.) David knew that the full time had now arrived when the particular place should be made apparent, and yet was in some hesitation—a state of things which was necessarily attended with much anxiety, especially to one who was so ardently attached to the worship of God, and so vehemently desirous to have the fixed presence of God with the nation, for its defense and government.

6-9

6. Lo! we heard of it at Ephratha. This verse is obscure, and we need not wonder at the difficulty which interpreters have felt in ascertaining its meaning. The simple way to understand the word Ephratha is to apply it to David personally, and not so much to the place of that name, the declaration of the Psalmist being to this effect √ that now when God had chosen a king from Ephratha, the place would necessarily at the same time be marked out for the Ark of the Covenant. It is said, have heard, for the fixing of the place of the Sanctuary depended upon the will of God; nor until this was declared could men determine it according to their own fancy. The fact that now upon David's mounting the throne this illustrious oracle concerning the permanent settlement of the Temple was to take effect, afforded good ground of thanksgiving. We have proof here that the people of God did not deposit the Ark at random in any place, but had express directions from God himself as to the place where he would be worshipped √ all proper worship proceeding from faith, while faith cometh by hearing. (Romans 10:17.) Mount Zion had no peculiar excellencies almost to recommend it; but having once heard that it was the object of God's choice, they show that they consider it wrong to call the matter in question.

7. We will go into his habitations. Here he dictates to all the Lord's people a common form of mutual exhortation to the duty of going up to the place which had been pointed out by the Angel. The clearer the intimation God may have given of his will, the more alacrity should we show in obeying it. Accordingly, the Psalmist intimates that now when the people had ascertained beyond all doubt the place of God's choice, they should admit of no procrastination, and show all the more alacrity as God was calling them more closely, and

Psalm 132

1-10 Solomon's prayer for divine favor.

In these verses we have Solomon's address to God for his favor to him and to his government, and his acceptance of his building a house to God's name. Observe,

I. What he pleads, two things:

1. That what he had done was in pursuance of the pious vow which his father David had made to build a house for God. Solomon was a wise man, yet pleads not any merit of his own: "I am not worthy, for whom thou shouldst do this; but, Lord, remember David, with whom thou madest the covenant."

2. That it was in pursuance of the expectations of the people of Israel, v. 6, 7.

(1.) They were inquisitive after the ark; for they lamented its obscurity, 1 Sam. vii. 2. They heard of it at Ephratah (that is, at Shiloh, in the tribe of Ephraim); there they were told it had been, but it was gone.

(2.) They were resolved to attend it: "Let us but have a convenient place, and we will go into his tabernacle, to pay our homage there; we will worship at his footstool as subjects and suppliants, which we neglected to do, for want of such a place, in the days of Saul," 1 Chron. xiii. 3.

II. What he prays for, v. 8-10.

1. That God would vouchsafe, not only to take possession of, but to take up his residence in, this temple which he had built: Arise, O Lord! into thy rest, and let this be it, thou, even the ark of thy strength, the pledge of thy presence, thy mighty presence.

2. That God would give grace to the ministers of the sanctuary to do their duty: Let thy priests be clothed with righteousness; let them appear righteous both in their administrations and in their conversations, and let both be according to the rule.

3. That the people of God might have the comfort of the due administration of holy ordinances among them: Let thy saints shout for joy. They did so when the ark was brought into the city of David (2 Sam. vi. 15); they will do so when the priests are clothed with righteousness.

4. That Solomon's own prayer, upon occasion of the dedicating of the temple, might be accepted of God: "Turn not away the face of thy anointed, that is, deny me not the things I have asked of thee, send me not away ashamed."

11-18 God's choice of Zion; God's promises to Zion.

These are precious promises, confirmed by an oath, that the heirs of them might have strong consolation, Heb. vi. 17, 18. Here is,

I. The choice God made of David's house and Zion hill. Both were of divine appointment.

1. God chose David's family for the royal family and confirmed his choice by an oath, v. 11, 12. David, being a type of Christ, was made king with an oath: The Lord hath sworn and will not repent, will not turn

Psalm 132

7-12

7 We will go into his tabernacles: we will worship at his footstool.
8 Arise, O LORD, into thy rest; thou, and the ark of thy strength.
9 Let thy priests be clothed with righteousness; and let thy saints shout for joy.

10 For thy servant David's sake turn not away the face of thine anointed.
11 The LORD hath sworn in truth unto David; he will not turn from it; Of the fruit of thy body will I set upon thy throne.
12 If thy children will keep my covenant and my testimony that I shall teach them, their children shall also sit upon thy throne for evermore.

saying, "We found it, we will go." Because these are the Lord's courts we will resort to them. We will worship at his footstool. The best ordered earthly house can be no more than the footstool of so great a King. His ark can only reveal the glories of his feet, according to his promise that he will make the place of his feet glorious: yet thither will we hasten with joy, in glad companionship, and there will we adorn him. Where Jehovah is, there shall he be worshipped. It is well not only to go to the Lord's house, but to worship there: we do but profane his tabernacles if we enter them for any other purpose. Before leaving this verse let us note the ascent of this Psalm of degrees—"We heard...we found...we will go...we will worship."

Verse 11. Here we come to a grand covenant pleading of the kind which is always prevalent with the Lord. The LORD hath sworn in truth unto, David. We cannot urge anything with God which is equal to his own word and oath. Jehovah swears that our faith may have strong confidence in it: he cannot forswear himself. He swears in truth, for he means every word that he utters; men may be perjured, but none will be so profane as to imagine this of the God of truth. By Nathan this covenant of Jehovah was conveyed to David, and there was no delusion in it. He will not turn from it. Jehovah is not a changeable being. He never turns from his purpose, much less from his promise solemnly ratified by oath.

Verse 12. If thy children will keep my covenant and my testimony that I shall teach them. There is a condition to the covenant so far as it concerned kings of David's line before the coming of the true Seed; but he has fulfilled that condition, and made the covenant indefeasible henceforth and for ever as to himself and the spiritual seed in him. Considered as it related to temporal things it was no small blessing for David's dynasty to be secured the throne upon good behavior.

Verse 13. For the LORD hath chosen Zion. It was no more than any other Canaanite town till God chose it, David captured it, Solomon built it, and the Lord dwelt in it. So was the church a mere Jebusite stronghold till grace chose it, conquered it, rebuilt it, and dwelt in it. Jehovah has chosen his people, and hence they are his people. He has chosen the church, and hence it is what it is. Thus in the covenant David and Zion, Christ and his people, go together. David is for Zion, and Zion for David: the interests of Christ and his people are mutual. He hath desired it for his habitation. David's question is answered. The Lord has spoken: the site of the temple is fixed: the place of the divine manifestation is determined. Indwelling follows upon election, and arises out of it: Zion is chosen, chosen for a habitation of God.

Verse 14. This is my rest for ever. Oh, glorious words! It is God himself who here speaks. Think of rest for God! A Sabbath for the Eternal and a place of abiding for the Infinite. He calls Zion my rest. Here his love remains and displays itself with delight. "He shall rest in his love." And this forever. He will not seek another place of repose, nor grow weary of his saints. In Christ the heart of Deity is filled with content, and for his sake he is satisfied with his people, and will be so world without end. These august words declare a distinctive choice—this and no other; a certain choice—this which is well known to me; a present choice—this which is here at this moment. God has made his election of old, he has not changed it, and he never will repent of it: his church was his rest and is his rest still. As he will not turn from his oath, so he will never turn from his choice. Oh, that we may enter into his rest, may be part and parcel of his church, and yield by our loving faith a delight to the mind of him who taketh pleasure in them that fear him, in them that hope in his mercy.

Verse 15. I will abundantly bless her provision. It must be so. How can we be without a blessing when the Lord is among us? We live upon his word, we are clothed by his charity, we are armed by his power: all sorts of provision are in him, and how can they be otherwise than blessed? The provision is to be abundantly blessed; then it will be abundant and blessed.

with a more privileged familiarity, to himself, now that he had selected a certain place of rest amongst them.

8. Arise, O Jehovah? Such language as this, inviting the great God who fills heaven and earth to come into a new place of residence, might seem strange and harsh, but the external symbols of religion which God had appointed are spoken of in these exalted terms to put honor upon them, and the better to ensure to them the regard of God's people. Should God institute no medium of intercourse, and call us to a direct communication with heaven, the great distance at which we stand from him would strike us with dismay, and paralyze invocation. Although, therefore, he does not thereby change place himself, he is felt by us to draw sensibly nearer. It was thus that he descended amongst his ancient people by the Ark of the Covenant, which he designed to be a visible emblem of his power and grace being present amongst them. Accordingly, the second clause of the verse is of an exegetical character, informing the Church that God was to be understood as having come in the sense of making a conspicuous display of his power in connection with the Ark. Hence it is called the Ark of his strength, not a mere dead idle shadow to look upon, but what certainly declared God's nearness to his Church. By the rest spoken of we are to understand Mount Zion, because, as we shall see afterwards, God was ever afterwards to be worshiped only in that place.

9. Let thy priests, etc. He now prays in general for the prosperity of the Church, as what stood intimately connected with the previous statement, the promotion of our best interests being the great end for which God dwells amongst us.

10-12

10. For thy servant David's sake, etc. We may infer with certainty from Solomon's prayer, that they are a request that God would show favor to the king. The same expression is employed by Bathsheba in the request which she made to her son Solomon, "Turn not away thy face," meaning that he would not cast her out of his sight. (1 Kings 2:20.) It is an expression tantamount to shewing displeasure; and we might say a word or two in reference to it because the other idea of referring the words to our Redeemer is plausible, and might mislead persons of little discernment. Nothing more, then, is here asked than that God would not despise and reject the prayers which David had preferred in the name of all the people. The favor is asked for David's sake, only because God had made a covenant with him.

11. Jehovah sware unto David. Here he brings out the idea still more clearly, that the only thing he had respect to in David was the free promise which God had made to him. He takes notice of the fact, as confirmatory to his faith, that God had ratified the promise by oath.

12. If thy sons keep my covenant. We must remember that the covenant was perfectly gratuitous, so far as related to God's promise of sending a Savior and Redeemer, because this stood connected with the original adoption of those to whom the promise was made, which was itself free. Indeed the treachery and rebellion of the nation did not prevent God

from it. Did David swear to the Lord (v. 2) that he would find him a house? The Lord swore to David that he would build him a house; for God will be behind with none of his people in affections or assurances. The promise made to David refers,

(1.) To a long succession of kings that should descend from his loins: Of the fruit of thy body will I set upon thy throne, which was fulfilled in Solomon; David himself lived to see it with great satisfaction, 1 Kings i. 48.

(2.) To an everlasting successor, a king that should descend from his loins of the increase of whose government and peace there shall be no end. St. Peter applies this to Christ, nay, he tells us that David himself so understood it. Acts ii. 30, He knew that God had sworn with an oath to him that of the fruit of his loins, according to the flesh, he would raise up Christ to sit on his throne; and in the fullness of time he did so, and gave him the throne of his father David, Luke i. 32.

2. God chose Zion hill for the holy hill, and confirmed his choice by the delight he took in it, v. 13, 14. He chose the Mount Zion which he loved (Ps. lxxviii. 68); he chose it for the habitation of his ark, and said of it, This is my rest for ever, and not merely my residence for a time, as Shiloh was. Zion was the city of David; he chose it for the royal city because God chose it for the holy city. God said, Here will I dwell, and therefore David said, Here will I dwell, for here he adhered to his principle, It is good for me to be near to God. Zion must be here looked upon as a type of the gospel-church, which is called Mount Zion (Heb. xii. 22), and in it what is here said of Zion has its full accomplishment. Zion was long since ploughed as a field, but the church of Christ is the house of the living God (1 Tim. iii. 15), and it is his rest for ever, and shall be blessed with his presence always, even to the end of the world. The delight God takes in his church, and the continuance of his presence with his church, are the comfort and joy of all its members.

II. The choice blessings God has in store for David's house and Zion hill. Whom God chooses he will bless.

1. God, having chosen Zion hill, promises to bless that,

(1.) With the blessings of the life that now is; for godliness has the promise of them, v. 15. The earth shall yield her increase; where religion is set up there shall be provision, and in blessing God will bless it (Ps. lixivia. 6); he will surely and abundantly bless it. And a little provision, with an abundant blessing upon it, will be more serviceable, as well as more comfortable, than a great deal without that blessing. God's people have a special blessing upon common enjoyments, and that blessing puts a peculiar sweetness into them. Nay, the promise goes further: I will satisfy her poor with bread. Zion has her own poor to keep; and it is promised that God will take care even of them.

Psalm 132

13-18
13 For the LORD hath chosen Zion; he hath desired it for his habitation.
14 This is my rest for ever: here will I dwell; for I have desired it.
15 I will abundantly bless her provision: I will satisfy her poor with bread.
16 I will also clothe her priests with salvation: and her saints shall shout aloud for joy.
17 There will I make the horn of David to bud: I have ordained a lamp for mine anointed.
18 His enemies will I clothe with shame: but upon himself shall his crown flourish.

Daily provision, royal pie vision, satisfying provision, overflowingly joyful provision the church shall receive; and the divine benediction shall cause us to receive it with faith, to feed upon it by experience, to grow upon it by sanctification, to be strengthened by it to labor, cheered by it to patience, and built up by it to perfection.
Verse 16. More is promised than was prayed for. See how the ninth verse asks for the priests to be clad in righteousness, and the answer is, I will also clothe her priests with salvation. God is wont to do exceeding abundantly, above all that we ask or even think. Righteousness is but one feature of blessing, salvation is the whole of it. What cloth of gold is this! What more than regal array! Garments of salvation! we know who has woven them, who has dyed them, and who has given them to his people. These are the best robes for priests and preachers, for princes and people; there is none like them; give them me. Not every priest shall be thus clothed, but only her priests, those who truly belong to Zion by faith which is in Christ Jesus who hath made them priests unto God.
Verse 17. There will I make the horn of David to bud. In Zion David's dynasty shall develop power and glory. In our notes from other authors we have included a description of the growth of the horns of stags, which is the natural fact from which we conceive the expression in the text to be borrowed. As the stag is made noble and strong by the development of his horns, so the house of David shall advance from strength to strength. This was to be by the work of the Lord—"there will I make", and therefore it would be sure and solid growth. When God makes us to bud none can cause us to fade. When David's descendants left the Lord and the worship of his house, they declined in all respects, for it was only through the Lord, and in connection will his worship that their horn would bud. I have ordained a lamp for mine anointed. David's name was to be illustrious, and brilliant as a lamp; it was to continue shining like a lamp in the sanctuary; it was thus to be a comfort to the people, and an enlightenment to the nations. God would not suffer the light of David to go out by the extinction of his race: his holy ordinances had decreed that the house of his servant should remain in the midst of Israel. What a lamp is our Lord Jesus! A light to lighten the Gentiles, and the glory of his people Israel. As the anointed—the true Christ, he shall be the light of heaven itself. Oh for grace to receive our illumination and our consolation from Jesus Christ alone.
Verse 18. His enemies will I clothe with shame. They shall be utterly defeated, they shall loathe their evil design, they shall be despised for having hated the Ever Blessed One. Their shame they will be unable to hide, it shall cover them: God will array them in it for ever, and it shall be their convict dress to all eternity. But upon himself shall his crown flourish. Green shall be his laurels of victory. He shall win and wear the crown of honor, and his inherited diadem shall increase in splendor. Is it not so to this hour with Jesus? His kingdom cannot fail, his imperial glories cannot fade. It is himself that we delight to honor; it is to himself that the honor comes, and upon himself that it flourishes. If others snatch at his crown their traitorous aims are defeated; but he in his own person reigns with ever growing splendor.
"Crown him, crown him,
Crowns become the victor's brow."

JOHN CALVIN

from sending forth his Son, and this was a public proof that he was not influenced by the consideration of their good conduct. Hence Paul says, (Romans 3:3,) "What if some did not believe is therefore the truth of God of none effect?" intimating that God had not withdrawn his favor from the Jews, having chosen them freely of his grace. We know, too, that notwithstanding their efforts, as if it had been of set purpose, to destroy the promises, God met their malicious opposition with displays of his marvelous love, made his truth and faithfulness to emerge in a most triumphant manner, and showed that he stood firm to his own purpose, independently of any merit of theirs.

13-16

13. Seeing that Jehovah has chosen Zion. By coupling the kingdom with the priesthood and sanctuary service, he declares it still more emphatically to have been of divine and not human appointment.

14. This is my rest for ever. The same truth is here put into the mouth of God, to give it additional weight; and it is declared not to have been in vain that the Temple had been erected, since God would show effectually and by practical testimonies the delight which he had in the worship of his own appointment. God's resting, or talking up his habitation, are expressions which denote his being present with men in the manifestation of his power.

15. Blessing I will bless, etc. God's dwelling in the midst of the people was what constituted the great source of their blessedness; and now some of the proofs are mentioned which he would give of his fatherly regard, such as preparing and administering their ordinary food, relieving their wants, clothing their priests with salvation, and filling all his people with joy and gladness. This it was necessary should be added, for unless we have ocular demonstration of the divine goodness, we are not spiritual enough to rise upwards to the apprehension of it. We have a twofold demonstration of it in the matter of our daily food; first in the earth's being enriched so as to furnish us with corn, and wine, and oil; and again in the earth's produce being multiplied, through a secret power, so as to provide us with sufficient nourishment.

17-18

17. There will I make, etc. He reverts to the state of the kingdom, which God had promised to take under his care and protection. It is necessary that we should attend to the peculiar force of the words employed √ I will make the horn of David to bud. Now there can be no doubt as to the meaning of the term horn, which in Hebrew is very commonly used to signify force or power; but we are to mark that by the horn budding there is an allusion to the humble original of the kingdom, and the singular restorations which it underwent.

18. His enemies will I clothe with shame. The priests were said above "to be clothed with righteousness and salvation," now the enemies of David are represented as "clothed with shame." It is not enough that all go well within. God must keep us from the various harms and evils which come upon us from without.

MATTHEW HENRY

[1.] By his providence they shall be kept from wanting; they shall have provision enough. If there be scarcity, the poor are the first that feel it, so that it is a sure sign of plenty if they have sufficient. Zion's poor shall not want, for God has obliged all the sons of Zion to be charitable to the poor, according to their ability, and the church must take care that they be not neglected, Acts vi. 1.

[2.] By his grace they shall be kept from complaining; though they have but dry bread, yet they shall be satisfied. Zion's poor have, of all others, reason to be content with a little of this world, because they have better things prepared for them. And this may be understood spiritually of the provision that is made for the soul in the word and ordinances; God will abundantly bless that for the nourishment of the new man, and satisfy the poor in spirit with the bread of life. What God sanctifies to us we shall and may be satisfied with.

(2.) With the blessings of the life that is to come, things pertaining to godliness (v. 16), which is an answer to the prayer, v. 9.

[1.] It was desired that the priests might be clothed with righteousness; it is here promised that God will clothe them with salvation.

[2.] It was desired that the saints might shout for joy; it is promised that they shall shout aloud for joy. God gives more than we ask, and when he gives salvation he will give an abundant joy.

2. God, having chosen David's family, here promises to bless that also with suitable blessings.

(1.) Growing power: There, in Zion, will I make the horn of David to bud, v. 17. The royal dignity shall increase more and more, and constant additions he made to the luster of it. Christ is the horn of salvation (denoting a powerful salvation) which God has raised up in the house of his servant David.

(2.) Lasting honor: I have ordained a lamp for my anointed. Thou wilt light my candle, Ps. xviii. 28. That lamp is likely to burn brightly which God ordains. A lamp is a successor, for, when a lamp is almost out, another may be lighted by it; it is a succession, for by this means David shall not want a man to stand before God. Christ is the lamp and the light of the world.

(3.) Complete victory: "His enemies, who have formed designs against him, will I clothe with shame, when they shall see their designs baffled." Let the enemies of all good governors expect to be clothed with shame, and especially the enemies of the Lord Jesus and his government.

(4.) Universal prosperity: Upon himself shall his crown flourish, that is, his government shall be more and more his honor. This was to have its full accomplishment in Jesus Christ, whose crown of honor and power shall never fade, nor the flowers of it wither. The crowns of earthly princes endure not to all generations (Prov. xxvii. 24), but Christ's crown shall endure to all eternity and the crowns reserved for his faithful subjects are such as fade not away.

Psalm 133

Title
A Song of degrees of David.

1 Behold, how good and how pleasant it is for brethren to dwell together in unity!
2 It is like the precious ointment upon the head, that ran down upon the beard, even Aaron's beard: that went down to the skirts of his garments;
3 As the dew of Hermon, and as the dew that descended upon the mountains of Zion: for there the LORD commanded the blessing, even life for evermore.

Psalm 133

TITLE. A Song of Degrees of David. We see no reason for depriving David of the authorship of this sparkling sonnet. He knew by experience the bitterness occasioned by divisions in families, and was well prepared to celebrate in choicest Psalmody the blessing of unity for which he sighed. Among the "songs of degrees", this hymn has certainly attained unto a good degree, and even in common literature it is frequently quoted for its perfume and dew. In this Psalm there is no wry word, all is "sweetness and light",—a notable ascent from Psalm 110 with which the Pilgrims set out. That is full of war and lamentation, but this sings of peace and pleasantness. The visitors to Zion were about to return, and this may have been their hymn of joy because they had seen such union among the tribes who had gathered at the common altar. The previous Psalm, which sings o f the covenant, had also reveal ed the center of Israel's unity in the Lord's anointed and the promises made to him. No wonder that brethren dwell in unity when God dwells among them, and finds his rest in them. Our translators have given to this Psalm an admirable explanatory heading, "The benefit of the communion of saints." These good men often hit off the meaning of a passage in a few words.

EXPOSITION
Verse 1. Behold. It is a wonder seldom seen, therefore behold it! It may be seen, for it is the characteristic of real saints,—therefore fail not to inspect it! It is well worthy of admiration; pause and gaze upon it! It will charm you into imitation, therefore note it well! God looks on with approval, therefore consider it with attention. How good and holy pleasant it is for brethren to dwell together in unity! No one can tell the exceeding excellence of such a condition; and so the Psalmist uses the word "how" twice;—Behold how good! and how pleasant! He does not attempt to measure either the good or the pleasure, but invites us to behold for ourselves. The combination of the two adjectives "good" and "pleasant", is more remarkable than the conjunction of two stars of the first magnitude: for a thing to be "good" is good, but for it also to be pleasant is better. All men love pleasant things, and yet it frequently happens that the pleasure is evil; but here the condition is as good as it is pleasant, as pleasant as it is good, for the same "how" is set before each qualifying word.
Verse 2. It is like the precious ointment upon the head. In order that we may the better behold brotherly unity David gives us a resemblance, so that as in a glass we may perceive its blessedness. It has a sweet perfume about it, comparable to that precious ointment with which the first High Priest was anointed at his ordination. It is a holy thing, and so again is like the oil of consecration which was to be used only in the Lord's service.
Verse 3. As the dew of Hermon, and as the dew that descended upon the mountains of Zion. From the loftier mountains the moisture appears to be wafted to the lesser hills: the dews of Hermon fall on Zion. The Alpine Lebanon ministers to the minor elevation of the city of David; and so does brotherly love descend from the higher to the lower, refreshing and enlivening in its course. Holy concord is as dew, mysteriously blessed, full of life and growth for all plants of grace. It brings with it so much benediction that it is as no common dew, but As that of Hermon which is specially copious, and far reaching. The proper rendering is, "As the dew of Hermon that descended upon the mountains of Zion", and this tallies with the figure which has been already used; and sets forth by a second simile the sweet descending diffusiveness of brotherly unity.

JOHN CALVIN

Psalm 133

A Psalm of thanksgiving for that holy concord which prevailed in the nation, and which the Lord's people are earnestly exhorted to maintain.

1-3

1. Behold how good, etc. I have no doubt that David in this Psalm renders thanks to God for the peace and harmony which had succeeded a long and melancholy state of confusion and division in the kingdom, and that he would exhort all individually to study the maintenance of peace. This is the subject enlarged upon, at least so far as the shortness of the Psalm admits of it. There was ample ground to praise the goodness of God in the highest terms, for uniting in one a people which had been so deplorably divided. When he first came to the kingdom the larger part of the nation considered him in the light of an enemy to the public good, and were alienated from him. Indeed so mortal was the feud which existed, that nothing else than the destruction of the party in opposition seemed to hold out the prospect of peace. The hand of God was wonderfully seen, and most unexpectedly, in the concord which ensued among them, when these who had been inflamed with the most violent antipathy cordially coalesced. This peculiarity in the circumstances which called forth the Psalm has been unfortunately by interpreters, who have considered that David merely passes a general commendation upon brotherly union, without any such particular reference. The exclamation with which the Psalm opens, Behold! is particularly expressive, not only as setting the state of things visibly before our eyes, but suggesting a tacit contrast between the delightfulness of peace and those civil commotions which had well√nigh rent the kingdom asunder. He sets forth the goodness of God in exalted terms, the Jews having by long experience of intestine feuds, which had gone far to ruin the nation, learned the inestimable value of union.

3. Like the precious ointment upon the head. We have here clear proof that David holds all true union among brethren to take its rise from God, and to have this for its legitimate object, that all may be brought to worship God in purity, and call upon iris name with one consent. Would the similitude have been borrowed from holy ointment if it had not been to denote, that religion must always hold the first place? Any concord, it is thus insinuated, which may prevail amongst men, is insipid, if not pervaded by a sweet savor of God's worship. We maintain, therefore, that men are to be united amongst themselves in mutual affection, with this as the great end., that they may be placed together under the government of God. If there be any who disagree with these terms, we would do well rather to oppose them strenuously, than purchase peace at the expense of God's honor. We must hold, that when mention is made of the Priest, it is to intimate, that concord takes its rise in the true and pure worship of God, while by the beard and skirts of the garments, we are led to understand that the peace which springs from Christ as the head, is diffused through the whole length and breadth of the Church.

MATTHEW HENRY

Psalm 133

1-3 Brotherly love.

Here see,

I. What it is that is commended—brethren's dwelling together in unity, not only not quarrelling, and devouring one another, but delighting in each other with mutual endearments, and promoting each other's welfare with mutual services.

II. How commendable it is: Behold, how good and how pleasant it is! It is good in itself, agreeable to the will of God, the conformity of earth to heaven. It is good for us, for our honor and comfort. It is pleasant and pleasing to God and all good men; it brings constant delight to those who do thus live in unity. Behold, how good! We cannot conceive or express the goodness and pleasantness of it.

III. How the pleasantness of it is illustrated.

1. It is fragrant as the holy anointing oil, which was strongly perfumed, and diffused its odors, to the great delight of all the bystanders, when it was poured upon the head of Aaron, or his successor the high priest, so plentifully that it ran down the face, even to the collar or binding of the garment, v. 2.

(1.) This ointment was holy. So must our brotherly love be, with a pure heart, devoted to God. We must love those that are begotten for his sake that begat, 1 John v. 1.

(2.) This ointment was a composition made up by a divine dispensatory; God appointed the ingredients and the quantities. Thus believers are taught of God to love one another; it is a grace of his working in us.

(3.) It was very precious, and the like to it was not to be made for any common use. Thus holy love is, in the sight of God, of great price; and that is precious indeed which is so in God's sight.

(4.) It was grateful both to Aaron himself and to all about him. So is holy love; it is like ointment and perfume which rejoice the heart. Christ's love to mankind was part of that oil of gladness with which he was anointed above his fellows.

(5.) Aaron and his sons were not admitted to minister unto the Lord till they were anointed with this ointment, nor are our services acceptable to God without this holy love; if we have it not we are nothing, 1 Cor. xiii. 1, 2.

2. It is fructifying. It is profitable as well as pleasing; it is as the dew; it brings abundance of blessings along with it, as numerous as the drops of dew.

IV. The proof of the excellency of brotherly love. Loving people are blessed people. For,

1. They are blessed of God, and therefore blessed indeed: There, where brethren dwell together in unity, the Lord commands the blessing, a complicated blessing, including all blessings.

2. They are everlastingly blessed. The blessing which God commands on those that dwell in love is life for evermore; that is the blessing of blessings.

Psalm 134

Title
A Song of degrees.

1 Behold, bless ye the LORD, all ye servants of the LORD, which by night stand in the house of the LORD.
2 Lift up your hands in the sanctuary, and bless the LORD.
3 The LORD that made heaven and earth bless thee out of Zion.

Psalm 134

TITLE. A Song of Degrees. We have now reached the last of the Gradual Psalms. The Pilgrims are going home, and are singing the last song in their psalter. They leave early in the morning, before the day has fully commenced, for the journey is long for many of them. While yet the night lingers they are on the move. As soon as they are outside the gates they see the guards upon the temple wall, and the lamps shining from the windows of the chambers which surround the sanctuary; therefore, moved by the sight, they chant a farewell to the perpetual attendants upon the holy shrine. Their parting exhortation arouses the priests to pronounce upon them a blessing out of the holy place: this benediction is contained in the third verse. The priests as good as say, "You have desired us to bless the Lord, and now we pray the Lord to bless you."
The Psalm teaches us to pray for those who are continually ministering before the Lord, and it invites all ministers to pronounce benedictions upon their loving and prayerful people.

EXPOSITION
Verse 1. Behold. By this call the pilgrims bespeak the attention of the night watch. They shout to them—Behold! The retiring pilgrims stir up the holy brotherhood of those who are appointed to keep the watch of the house of the Lord. Let them look around them upon the holy place, and everywhere "behold" reasons for sacred praise. Let them look above them at night and magnify him that made heaven and earth, and lighted the one with stars and the other with his love. Let them see to it that their hallelujahs never come to an end. Their departing brethren arouse them with the shrill cry of "Behold!" Behold!—see, take care, be on the watch, diligently mind your work, and incessantly adore and bless Jehovah's name.
Verse 2. Lift up your hands in the sanctuary. In the holy place they must be busy, full of strength, wide awake, energetic, and moved with holy ardor. Hands, heart, and every other part of their manhood must be upraised, elevated, and consecrated to the adoring service of the Lord. As the angels praise God day without night, so must the angels of the churches be instant in season and out of season. And bless the LORD. This is their main business. They are to bless men by their teaching, but they must yet more bless Jehovah with their worship. Too often men look at public worship only from the side of its usefulness to the people; but the other matter is of even higher importance: we must see to it that the Lord God is adored, extolled, and had in reverence. For a second time the word "bless" is used, and applied to Jehovah. Bless the Lord, O my soul, and let every other soul bless him. There will be no drowsiness about even midnight devotion if the heart is set upon blessing God in Christ Jesus, which is the gospel translation of God in the sanctuary.
Verse 3. This last verse is the answer from the temple to the pilgrims preparing to depart as the day breaks. It is the ancient blessing of the high priest condensed, and poured forth upon each individual pilgrim. The LORD that made heaven and earth bless thee out of Zion. Ye are scattering and going to your homes one by one; may the benediction come upon you one by one. You have been up to Jehovah's city and temple at his bidding; return each one with such a benediction as only he can give—divine, infinite, effectual, eternal. You are not going away from Jehovah's works or glories, for he made the heaven above you and the earth on which you dwell. He is your Creator, and he can bless you with untold mercies; he can create joy and peace in your hearts, and make for you a new heaven and a new earth.

JOHN CALVIN

Psalm 134

An exhortation to praise God, addressed to the people of God generally, but more particularly to the Priests and Levites.

1-3

1. Behold! bless ye Jehovah. The Psalm begins with the demonstrative adverb Behold! setting the matter of their duty before their eyes, for they were to be stimulated to devotion by looking constantly to the Temple. We are to notice the Psalmist's design in urging the duty of praise so earnestly upon them. Many of the Levites, through the tendency which there is in all men to abuse ceremonies, considered that nothing more was necessary than standing idly in the Temple, and thus overlooked the principal part of their duty. The Psalmist would show that merely to keep nightly watch over the Temple, kindle the lamps, and superintend the sacrifices, was of no importance, unless they served God spiritually, and referred all outward ceremonies to that which must be considered the main sacrifice √ the celebration of God's praises.

You may think it a very laborious service, as if he had said, to stand at watch in the Temple, while others sleep in their own houses; but the worship which God requires is something more excellent than this, and demands of you to sing his praises before all the people. In the second verse he reminds them in addition, of the form observed in calling upon the name of the Lord. For why do men lift their hands when they pray? Is it not that their hearts may be raised at the same time to God? It is thus that the Psalmist takes occasion to reprehend their carelessness in either standing idle in the Temple, or trifling and indulging in vain conversation, and thus failing to worship God in a proper manner.

3. Jehovah bless thee out of Zion! We have conclusive proof in my opinion from this verse that the Psalm is to be considered as referring to the priests and Levites only, for to them it properly belonged under the law to bless the people. (Numbers 6:23.) The Psalmist had first told them to bless God; now he tells them to bless the people in his name. Not that God meant by any such injunction that the people might themselves indulge in a life of carnal security. What God intended was, that the priests should lead the way in divine service, and the people take example by what was done in the temple, and practice it individually in their private houses. The duty of blessing the people was enjoined upon the priests, as representing Christ's person. Since many, however, are apt, when they hear God spoken of as Creator, to conceive of him as standing at a distance from them, and doubt their access to him, the Psalmist also mentions a symbol of God's nearness to his people √ and this that they might be encouraged to approach him with the freedom and unrestrained confidence of persons who are invited to come to the bosom of a Father. By looking to the heavens, then, they were to discover the power of God √ by looking to Zion, his dwelling√place, they were to recognize his fatherly love.

MATTHEW HENRY

Psalm 134

1-3 A call to bless God.

This psalm instructs us concerning a two-fold blessing:

I. Our blessing God, that is, speaking well of him, which here we are taught to do, v. 1, 2.

1. It is a call to the Levites to do it. They were the servants of the Lord by office, appointed to minister in holy things; they attended the sanctuary, and kept the charge of the house of the Lord, Num. iii. 6, &c. Some of them did by night stand in the house of the Lord, to guard the holy things of the temple, that they might not be profaned, and the rich things of the temple, that they might not be plundered. While the ark was in curtains there was the more need of guards upon it. They attended likewise to see that neither the fire on the altar nor the lamps in the candlestick went out. Probably it was usual for some devout and pious Israelites to sit up with them; we read of one that departed not from the temple night or day, Luke ii. 37. Now these are here called upon to bless the Lord. Thus they must keep themselves awake by keeping themselves employed. Thus they must redeem time for holy exercises.

2. It is a call to us to do it, who, as Christians, are made priests to our God, and Levites, Isa. lxvi. 21. We are the servants of the Lord; we have a place and a name in his house, in his sanctuary; we stand before him to minister to him. Even by night we are under his eye and have access to him. Let us therefore bless the Lord, and again bless him; think and speak of his glory and goodness. Let us lift up our hands in prayer, in praise, in vows; let us do our work with diligence and cheerfulness, and an elevation of mind. This exhortation is ushered in with Behold! a note commanding attention. Look about you, Sirs, when you are in God's presence, and conduct yourselves accordingly.

II. God's blessing us, and that is doing well for us, which we are here taught to desire, v. 3. Whether it is the watchmen's blessing their captain, or the Levites' blessing the high priest, or whoever was their chief (as many take it, because it is in the singular number, The Lord bless thee), or whether the blessing is pronounced by one upon many ("The Lord bless thee, each of you in particular, thee and thee; you that are blessing God, the Lord bless you"), is not material. We may learn,

1. That we need desire no more to make us happy than to be blessed of the Lord, for those whom he blesses are blessed indeed.

2. That blessings out of Zion, spiritual blessings, the blessings of the covenant, and of communion with God, are the best blessings.

3. It is a great encouragement to us, when we come to God for a blessing, that it is he who made heaven and earth, and therefore has all the blessings of both at his disposal, the upper and nether springs.

Psalm 135

1-7

1 Praise ye the LORD. Praise ye the name of the Lord; praise him, O ye servants of the LORD.

2 Ye that stand in the house of the LORD, in the courts of the house of our God.

3 Praise the LORD; for the LORD is good: sing praises unto his name; for it is pleasant.

4 For the LORD hath chosen Jacob unto himself, and Israel for his peculiar treasure.

5 For I know that the LORD is great, and that our Lord is above all gods.

6 Whatsoever the LORD pleased, that did he in heaven, and in earth, in the seas, and all deep places.

7 He causeth the vapors to ascend from the ends of the earth; he maketh lightnings for the rain; he bringeth the wind out of his treasuries.

Psalm 135

GENERAL REMARKS. This Psalm has no title. It is mainly made up of selections from other Scriptures. It has been called a mosaic, and compared to a tessellated pavement. At the outset, its first two verses (Ps 135:1-2) are taken from Ps 134:1-3; while the latter part of Ps 135:2 and the commencement of Ps 135:3 put us in mind of Ps 116:19; and Ps 135:4 suggests De 7:6. Does not Ps 135:5 remind us of Ps 95:3? As for Ps 135:7, it is almost identical with Jer 10:13, which may have been taken from it. The passage contained in Ps 135:13 is to be found in Ex 3:15, and Ps 135:14 in De 32:36. The closing verses, Ps 135:8-12, are in Psalms 136. From Ps 135:15 to the end the strain is a repetition of Ps 115:1-18 This process of tracing the expressions to other sources might be pushed further without straining the quotations; the whole Psalm is a compound of many choice extracts, and yet it has all the continuity and freshness of an original poem. The Holy Spirit occasionally repeats himself; not because he has any lack of thoughts or words, but because it is expedient for us that we hear the same things in the same form. Yet, when our great Teacher uses repetition, it is usually with instructive variations, which deserve our careful attention.

DIVISION. The first fourteen verses contain an exhortation to praise Jehovah for his goodness (Ps 135:3), for his electing love (Ps 135:4), his greatness (Ps 135:5-7) his judgments (Ps 135:8-12), his unchanging character (Ps 135:13), and his love towards his people. This is followed by a denunciation of idols (Ps 135:15-18), and a further exhortation to bless the name of the Lord. It is a song full of life, vigor, variety, and devotion.

EXPOSITION

Verse 1. Praise ye the LORD, or, Hallelujah. Let those who are themselves full of holy praise labor to excite the like spirit in others. It is not enough for us to praise God ourselves, we are quite unequal to such a work; let us call in all our friends and neighbors, and if they have been slack in such service, let us stir them up to it with loving exhortations.

Verse 2. Ye that stand in the house of the Lord, in the courts of the house of our God. You are highly favored; you are the domestics of the palace, nearest to the Father of the heavenly family, privileged to find your home in his house; therefore you must, beyond all others, abound in thanksgiving.

Verse 3. Praise the LORD. Do it again; continue to do it; do it better and more heartily; do it in growing numbers; do it at once. There are good reasons for praising the Lord, and among the first is this—for the LORD is good. He is so good that there is none good in the same sense or degree. He is so good that all good is found in him, flows from him, and is rewarded by him.

Verse 4. For the LORD hath chosen Jacob unto himself. Jehovah hath chosen Jacob. Should not the sons of Jacob praise him who has so singularly favored them. Election is one of the most forcible arguments for adoring love. Chosen! chosen unto himself!—who can be grateful enough for being concerned in this privilege. "Jacob have I loved", said Jehovah, and he gave no reason for his love except that he chose to love.

Verse 5. For I know that the LORD is great, and that our Lord is above all gods. The greatness of God is as much a reason for adoration as his goodness, when we are once reconciled to him. God is great positively great comparatively, and great superlatively—"above all gods." Of this the Psalmist had an assured personal persuasion. He says positively, "I know." It is knowledge worth possessing. He knew by observation, inspiration, and realization; he was no agnostic, he was certain and clear upon the matter.

Verse 6. Whatsoever the LORD pleased, that did he in heaven, and in earth, in the seas, and all deep places. His will is carried out throughout all space. The king's warrant runs in every portion of the universe. The heathen divided the great domain; but Jupiter does not rule in heaven, nor Neptune

JOHN CALVIN

Psalm 135

1-4

1. Praise ye the name of Jehovah. Though this Psalm begins almost in the same manner with the preceding, the Psalmist would not appear to be addressing the Levites exclusively, but the people generally, since the reasons given for praising God are equally applicable to all God's children. No mention is made of night watching, or of their standing constantly in the Temple. But indeed, as it was the special duty of the priests to take the lead in this devotional exercise, to give out, if we might use such an expression, and sing the praises of God before the people, there is no reason why we should not suppose that they are primarily addressed, and stirred up to their duty. We need only to examine the words more closely in order to be convinced that the people are included as next in order to the priests. For the Psalmist addresses the servants of God who stand in the temple, then those who are in the courts, whereas no notice was taken of the courts in the former Psalm. Mention seems to be made of courts in the plural number, because the priests had their court; and then there was another common to all the people, for by the law spoken of, (Leviticus 16:17,) they were prohibited from entering the sanctuary. To prevent any feeling of disgust which might arise from the very frequent repetition of this exhortation to the praises of God, it is only necessary to remember, as was already observed, that there is no sacrifice in which he takes greater delight than the expression of our gratitude. Thus, (Psalm 50:14,) "Sacrifice unto the Lord thanksgiving, and pay your vows to the Most High;" and, (Psalm 116:12, 13,) "What shall I render unto the Lord for all his benefits? I will take the cup of salvation, and call upon the name of the Lord."

5-7

5. For I know that Jehovah is great. We have here a general description of the power of God, to show the Israelites that the God they worshipped was the same who made the world, and rules over all according to his will, neither is there any other besides him. He would not exclude others when he speaks of having known himself the greatness of God, but is rather to be considered as taking occasion from his own experience to stir up men generally to attend to this subject, and awake to the recognition of what lies abundantly open to observation. The immensity of God is what none can comprehend; still his glory, so far as was seen fit, has been sufficiently manifested to leave all the world without excuse for ignorance.

6. Whatsoever doth please him, etc. This is that immeasurable greatness of the divine being, of which he had just spoken. He not only founded heaven and earth at first, but governs all things according to his power. To own that God made the world, but maintain that he sits idle in heaven, and takes no concern in the management of it, is to cast an impious aspersion upon his power; and yet the idea, absurd as it is, obtains wide currency amongst men. They would not say, perhaps, in so many words, that they believed that God slept

MATTHEW HENRY

Psalm 135

1-4 Majesty and goodness of God.
Here is,
1. The duty we are called to—to praise the Lord, to praise his name; praise him, and again praise him. We must not only thank him for what he has done for us, but praise him for what he is in himself and has done for others; take all occasions to speak well of God and to give his truths and ways a good word.
2. The persons that are called upon to do this—the servants of the Lord, the priests and Levites that stand in his house, and all the devout and pious Israelites that stand in the courts of his house to worship there, v. 2. Those that have most reason to praise God who are admitted to the privileges of his house, and those see most reason who there behold his beauty and taste his bounty; from them it is expected, for to that end they enjoy their places. Who should praise him if they do not?
3. The reasons why we should praise God.
(1.) Because he whom we are to praise is good.
(2.) Because the work is its own wages: Sing praises to his name, for it is pleasant.
(3.) Because of the peculiar privileges of God's people (v. 4): The Lord hath chosen Jacob to himself, and therefore Jacob is bound to praise him; for therefore God chose a people to himself that they might be unto him for a name and a praise (Jer. xiii. 11).

5-14 Majesty and goodness of God.
The psalmist had suggested to us the goodness of God, as the proper matter of our cheerful praises; here he suggests to us the greatness of God as the proper matter of our awful praises; and on this he is most copious, because this we are less forward to consider.
I. He asserts the doctrine of God's greatness (v. 5): The Lord is great, great indeed, who knows no limits of time or place. He asserts it with assurance, "I know that he is so; know it not only by observation of the proofs of it, but by belief of the revelation of it. I know it; I am sure of it; I know it by my own experience of the divine greatness working on my soul."
II. He proves him to be a great God by the greatness of his power, v. 6.
1. He has an absolute power, and may do what he will: Whatsoever the Lord pleased, that did he, and none could control him, or say unto him, What doest thou? He does what he pleases, because he pleases, and gives not an account of any of his matters.
2. He has an almighty power and can do what he will; if he will work, none shall hinder.
3. This absolute almighty power is of universal extent; he does what he will in heaven, in earth, in the seas, and in all the deep places that are in the bottom of the sea or the bowels of the earth. The gods of the heathen can do nothing; but our God can do any thing and does do every thing.

Psalm 135

8-14
8 Who smote the firstborn of Egypt, both of man and beast.
9 Who sent tokens and wonders into the midst of thee, O Egypt, upon Pharaoh, and upon all his servants.
10 Who smote great nations, and slew mighty kings;
11 Sihon king of the Amorites, and Og king of Bashan, and all the kingdoms of Canaan:
12 And gave their land for an heritage, an heritage unto Israel his people.
13 Thy name, O LORD, endureth for ever; and thy memorial, O LORD, throughout all generations.
14 For the LORD will judge his people, and he will repent himself concerning his servants.

on the sea, nor Pluto in the lower regions; Jehovah rules over all. His decree is not defeated, his purpose is not frustrated: in no one point is his good pleasure set aside. The word "whatsoever" is of the widest range and includes all things, and the four words of place which are mentioned comprehend all space; therefore the declaration of the text knows neither limit nor exception.

Verse 7. He causeth the vapors to ascend from the ends of the earth. Here we are taught the power of God in creation. The process of evaporation is passed by unnoticed by the many, because they see it going on all around them; the usual ceases to be wonderful to the thoughtless, but it remains a marvel to the instructed. When we consider upon what an immense scale evaporation is continually going on, and how needful it is for the existence of all life, we may well admire the wisdom and the power which are displayed therein.

Verse 8. Who smote the firstborn of Egypt, both of man and beast. Herein the Lord is to be praised; for this deadly smiting was an act of justice against Egypt, and of love to Israel.

Verse 9. Who sent tokens and wonders into the midst of thee, O Egypt, upon Pharaoh, and upon all his servants. The Lord is still seen by the Psalmist as sending judgments upon rebellious men; he keeps before us the personal action of God, "who sent tokens", etc. The more distinctly God is seen the better. Even in plagues he is to be seen, as truly as in mercies.

Verse 10. Who smote great nations, and slew mighty kings. The nations of Canaan joined in the desperate resistance offered by their monarchs, and so they were smitten; while their kings, the ringleaders of the fight, were slain.

Verse 11. Sihon king of the Amorites, and Og king of Bashan. These two kings were the first to oppose, and they were amongst the most notable of the adversaries: their being smitten is therefore a special object of song for loyal Israelites. The enmity of these two kings was wanton and unprovoked, and hence their overthrow was the more welcome to Israel.

Verse 12. And gave their land for an heritage, an heritage unto Israel his people. Jehovah is Lord Paramount, and permits men to hold their lands upon lease, terminable at his pleasure. The nations of Canaan had become loathsome with abominable vices, and they were condemned by the great Judge of all the earth to be cut off from the face of the country which they defiled.

Verse 13. Thy name, O LORD, endureth for ever. God's name is eternal, and will never be changed. His character is immutable; his fame and honor also shall remain to all eternity. There shall always be life in the name of Jesus, and sweetness and consolation. Those upon whom the Lord's name is named in verity and truth shall be preserved by it, and kept from all evil, world without end.

Verse 14. For the LORD will judge his people. He will exercise personal discipline over them, and not leave it to their foes to maltreat them at pleasure. When the correction is ended he will arise and avenge them of their oppressors, who for a while were used by him as his rod. He may seem to forget his people, but it is not so; he will undertake their cause and deliver them. The judges of Israel were also her deliverers, and such is the Lord of hosts: in this sense—as ruling, preserving, and delivering his chosen—Jehovah will judge his people.

Verse 15. The idols of the heathen are silver and gold, the work of men's hands. Their essential material is dead metal, their attributes are but the qualities of senseless substances, and what of form and fashion they exhibit they derive from the skill and labor of those who worship them. It is the height of insanity to worship metallic manufactures. Though silver and gold are useful to us when we rightly employ them, there is nothing about them which can entitle them to reverence and worship. If we did not know the sorrowful fact to be indisputable, it would seem to be impossible that in heaven, but in imagining, as they do, that he resigns the reins to chance or fortune, they leave him the mere shadow of a power, such as is not manifested in effects; whereas Scripture teaches us that it is a real practical power, by which he governs the whole world as he does according to his will.

7. Causing the clouds to ascend. The Psalmist touches upon one or two particulars, in illustration of the point that nothing takes place of itself, but by the hand and counsel of God. Our understandings cannot comprehend a thousandth part of God's works, and it is only a few examples which he brings forward to be considered in proof of the doctrine of a divine providence which he had just announced. He speaks of the clouds ascending from the ends of the earth; for the vapors which rise out of the earth form clouds, when they accumulate more densely together. Now who would think that the vapors which we see ascending upwards would shortly darken the sky, and impend above our heads? It strikingly proves the power of God, that these thin vapors, which steam up from the ground:, should form a body over-spreading the whole atmosphere.

8-12

8. He smote the first-born of Egypt. He now reverts to those more special benefits, by which God had laid his Church and chosen people under obligation to his service. As it was the Lord's believing people only whom he addressed, the chief point singled out as the subject of praise is God's having adopted them, small as they were in numbers, from the mass of the human family. Again, there was the fact of his having set himself in opposition, for their sakes, to great kingdoms and mighty nations.

10. He smote great nations. He comes now to speak of the end for which God delivered them from their bondage. He did not lead his people out of Egypt, and then leave them to wander as they might, but brought them forth that he might settle them in the promised inheritance. This the Psalmist mentions as another signal proof of the favor of God, and his unwearied kindness to them; for having once taken the children of Abraham by the hand, he led them on, in the continued exercise of his power, till he put them in possession of the promised land.

13-14

13. O Jehovah! thy name is for ever. There are many reasons why the name of God ought always to be kept up in the world, but here the Psalmist speaks more especially of that everlasting praise which is due to him for preserving his Church and people, the cause being immediately added—that God will judge his people The whole world is a theater for the display of the divine goodness, wisdom, justice, and power, but the Church is the orchestra, as it were—the most conspicuous part of it; and the nearer the approaches are that God makes to us the more intimate and condescending the communication of his benefits, the more attentively are we called to consider them. The term judging in the Hebrew expresses whatever belongs to just and legitimate government,

III. He gives instances of his great power,

1. In the kingdom of nature, v. 7. All the powers of nature prove the greatness of the God of nature, from whom they are derived and on whom they depend. The chain of natural causes was not only framed by him at first, but is still preserved by him.

(1.) It is by his power that exhalations are drawn up from the terraqueous globe. The heat of the sun raises them, but it has that power from God, and therefore it is given as an instance of the glory of God that nothing is hidden from the heat of the sun, Ps. xix. 6.

(2.) It is he who, out of those vapors so raised, forms the rain, so that the earth is no loser by the vapors it sends up, for they are returned with advantage in fruitful showers.

(3.) Out of the same vapors (such is his wonderful power) he makes lightnings or the rain; by them he opens the bottles of heaven, and shakes the clouds, that they may water the earth.

(4.) The same exhalations, to serve another purpose, are converted into winds.

2. In the kingdoms of men; and here he mentions the great things God had formerly done for his people Israel, which were proofs of God's greatness as well as of his goodness, and confirmations of the truth of the scriptures of the Old Testament, which began to be written by Moses, the person employed in working those miracles. Observe God's sovereign dominion and irresistible power,

(1.) In bringing Israel out of Egypt, humbling Pharaoh by many plagues, and so forcing him to let them go.

(2.) In destroying the kingdoms of Canaan before them, v. 10. Those that were in possession of the land designed for Israel had all possible advantages for keeping possession. The people were numerous, and warlike, and confederate against Israel. They were great nations. Yet, if a great nation has a meek and mean-spirited prince, it lies exposed; but these great nations had mighty kings, and yet they were all smitten and slain—Sihon and Og, and all the kingdoms of Canaan, v. 10, 11. No power of hell or earth can prevent the accomplishment of the promise of God when the time, the set time, for it has come.

(3.) In settling them in the land of promise. He that gives kingdoms to whomsoever he pleases gave Canaan to be a heritage to Israel his people. It came to them by inheritance, for their ancestors had the promise of it, though not the possession; and it descended as an inheritance to their seed. This was done long before, yet God is now praised for it; and with good reason, for the children were now enjoying the benefit of it.

IV. He triumphs in the perpetuity of God's glory and grace.

1. Of his glory (v. 13): Thy name, O God! endures for ever. God's manifestations of himself to his people have everlasting fruits and consequences. What God doeth it shall be for ever, Eccl. iii. 14. His name

Psalm 135

15-21
15 The idols of the heathen are silver and gold, the work of men's hands.
16 They have mouths, but they speak not; eyes have they, but they see not;
17 They have ears, but they hear not; neither is there any breath in their mouths.
18 They that make them are like unto them: so is every one that trusteth in them.
19 Bless the LORD, O house of Israel: bless the sLORD, O house of Aaron:
20 Bless the LORD, O house of Levi: ye that fear the LORD, bless the LORD.
21 Blessed be the LORD out of Zion, which dwelleth at Jerusalem. Praise ye the LORD.

intelligent beings could bow down before substances which they must themselves refine from the ore, and fashion into form. One would think it less absurd to worship one's own hands than to adore that which those hands have made.

Verse 16. They have mouths. For their makers fashioned them like themselves. An opening is made where the mouth should be, and yet it is no mouth, for they eat not, they speak not. They cannot communicate with their worshippers; they are dumb as death. If they cannot even speak, they are not even so worthy of worship as our children at school. Jehovah speaks, and it is done: but these images utter never a word. Surely, if they could speak, they would rebuke their votaries. Is not their silence a still more powerful rebuke? When our philosophical teachers deny that God has made any verbal revelation of himself they also confess that their god is dumb. Eyes have they, but they see not.

Verse 17. They have ears, and very large ones, too, if we remember certain of the Hindu idols. But they hear not. Useless are their ears; in fact, they are mere counterfeits and deceits. Ears which men make are always deaf: the secret of hearing is wrapped up with the mystery of life, and both are in the unsearchable mind of the Lord. It seems that these heathen gods are dumb, and blind, and deaf—a pretty bundle of infirmities to be found in a deity! Neither is there any breath in their mouths; they are dead, no sign of life is perceptible; and breathing, which is of the essence of animal life, they never knew.

Verse 18. They that make them are like unto them. they are as blockish, as senseless, as stupid as the gods they have made, and, like them they are the objects of divine abhorrence, and shall be broken in pieces in due time. So is every one that trusteth in them. The idol worshippers are as bad as the idol makers; for if there were none to worship, there would be no market for the degrading manufacture. Idolaters, are spiritually dead, they are the mere images of men, their best being is gone, they are not what they seem.

Verse 19. Bless the LORD, O house of Israel. All of you, in all your tribes, praise the one Jehovah. Each tribe, from Reuben to Benjamin, has its own special cause for blessing the Lord, and the nation as a whole has substantial reasons for pouring out benedictions upon his name. Those whom God has named "the house of Israel", a family of prevailing princes, ought to show their loyalty by thankfully bowing before their sovereign Lord. Bless the LORD, O house of Aaron. These were elected to high office and permitted to draw very near to the divine presence; therefore they beyond all others were bound to bless the Lord.

Verse 20. Bless the LORD, O house of Levi. These helped the priests in other things, let them aid them in this also. The house of Israel comprehends all the chosen seed; then we come down to the smaller but more central ring of the house of Aaron, and now we widen out to the whole tribe of Levi. Let reverence and adoration spread from man to man until the whole lump of humanity shall be leavened. The house of Levi had choice reasons for blessing God: read the Levite story and see. Remember that the whole of the Levites were set apart for holy service, and supported by the tribes allotted to them; therefore they were in honor bound above all others to worship Jehovah with cheerfulness.

the future tense denoting continued action apparently, as it often does, so that what the Psalmist says is tantamount to this—that God would always watch over and preserve his people, and that being thus under God's guardian care, they would be placed in safety. Or we may suppose that the Psalmist employs the future tense to teach us that, under affliction, we must have a sustained hope, not giving way to despondency, though God may seem to have overlooked and deserted us, since whatever temporary delays there may be of his help, he will appear as our judge and defender at the proper season, and when he sees that we have been sufficiently humbled. This may recommend itself the more to be the true meaning, because the Psalmist seems to allude to the expression of Moses, (Deuteronomy 32:36,) whose very words indeed, he quotes. As some alleviation under the divine chastisements which the people would suffer, Moses foretold that God would come forth as their judge, to help and deliver them when in extremity. And this the writer of the present Psalm, whoever he may have been, makes use of with a general application to the Church, declaring that God would never allow it to be altogether destroyed, since upon the event of its destruction he would cease to be a King. To propose changing the tense of the verb into the past, and understand it of God having shown himself to be the judge of his people against the Egyptians, puts a feeble sense upon the passage, and one which does not suit with the context, either of this Psalm or of the address of Moses.

15-21

15. The images of the nations, etc. In upbraiding the stupidity of the heathen, who thought that they could not have God near them in any other way than by resorting to idol worship, he reminds the Israelites of the signal mercy which they had enjoyed, and would have them abide the more deliberately by the simplicity and purity of God's worship, and avoid profane superstitions. He declares, that idolaters only draw down heavier judgments upon themselves, the more zealous they are in the service of their idols. And there is no doubt, that, in denouncing the awful judgments which must fall upon the worshippers of false gods, it is his object to deter such as had been brought up under the word of God from following their example. In Psalm 115 the exhortation given is to trust or hope in the Lord; here, to bless him. The Levites are mentioned in addition to the house of Aaron, there being two orders of priesthood. Every thing else in the two Psalms is the same, except that, in the last verse: the Psalmist here joins himself, along with the rest of the Lord's people, in blessing God. He says, out of Zion, for when God promised to hear their prayers from that place, he thereby gave good ground why they should praise him from it. The reason is stated, that he dwelt in Jerusalem; which is not to be understood in the low and gross sense that he was confined to any such narrow residence; but in the sense, that he was there as to the visible manifestation of his favor, experience showing, that while his majesty is such as to fill heaven and earth, his power and. grace were vouchsafed in a particular manner to his own people.

endures for ever in the constant and everlasting praises of his people; his memorial endures, has endured hitherto, and shall still endure throughout all generations of the church. This seems to refer to Exod. iii. 15, where, when God had called himself the God of Abraham, Isaac, and Jacob.

2. Of his grace. He will be kind to his people. He will plead their cause against others that contend with them. He will judge his people, that is, he will judge for them, and will not suffer them to be run down.

15-21 An invitation to praise.

The design of these verses is,

I. To arm the people of God against idolatry and all false worship, by showing what sort of gods they were that the heathen worshipped, as we had it before, Ps. cxv. 4, &c.

1. They were gods of their own making; being so, they could have no power but what their makers gave them, and then what power could their makers receive from them? The images were the work of men's hands, and the deities that were supposed to inform them were as much the creatures of men's fancy and imagination.

2. They had the shape of animals, but could not perform the least act, no, not of the animal life.

3. Their worshippers were therefore as stupid and senseless as they were, both those that made them to be worshipped and those that trusted in them when they were made, v. 18.

II. To stir up the people of God to true devotion in the worship of the true God, v. 19-21. The more deplorable the condition of the Gentile nations that worship idols is the more are we bound to thank God that we know better. Therefore,

1. Let us set ourselves about the acts of devotion, and employ ourselves in them: Bless the Lord, and again and again, bless the Lord. In the parallel place (Ps. cxv. 9-11), by way of inference from the impotency of idols, the duty thus pressed upon us is to trust in the Lord; here to bless him; by putting our trust in God we give glory to him, and those that depend upon God shall not want matter of thanksgiving to him. All persons that knew God are here called to praise him—the house of Israel (the nation in general), the house of Aaron and the house of Levi (the Lord's ministers that attended in his sanctuary), and all others that feared the Lord, though they were not of the house of Israel.

2. Let God have the glory of all: Blessed be the Lord. The tribute of praise arises out of Zion. All God's works do praise him, but his saints bless him; and they need not go far to pay their tribute, for he dwells in Jerusalem, in his church, which they are members of, so that he is always nigh unto them to receive their homage. The condescensions of his grace, in dwelling with men upon the earth, call for our grateful and thankful returns, and our repeated Hallelujahs.

Psalm 136

1-8

1 O give thanks unto the LORD; for he is good: for his mercy endureth for ever.
2 O give thanks unto the God of gods: for his mercy endureth for ever.
3 O give thanks to the Lord of lords: for his mercy endureth for ever.
4 To him who alone doeth great wonders: for his mercy endureth for ever.
5 To him that by wisdom made the heavens: for his mercy endureth for ever.
6 To him that stretched out the earth above the waters: for his mercy endureth for ever.
7 To him that made great lights: for his mercy endureth for ever:
8 The sun to rule by day: for his mercy endureth for ever:

Psalm 136

We know not by whom this Psalm was written, but we do know that it was sung in Solomon's temple (2Ch 7:3,6), and by the armies of Jehoshaphat when they sang themselves into victory in the wilderness of Tekoa. From the striking form of it we should infer that it was a popular hymn among the Lord's ancient people. Most hymns with a solid, simple chorus become favorites with congregations, and this is sure to have been one of the best beloved. It contains nothing but praise. It is tuned to rapture, and can only be fully enjoyed by a devoutly grateful heart.

It commences with a threefold praise to the Triune Lord (Ps 136:1-3), then it gives us six notes of praise to the Creator (Ps 136:4-9), six more upon deliverance from Egypt (Ps 134:10-15), and seven upon the journey through the wilderness and the entrance into Canaan. Then we have two happy verses of personal gratitude for present mercy (Ps 134:23-24), one (Ps 134:25) to tell of the Lord's universal providence, and a closing verse to excite to never ending praise.

EXPOSITION

Verse 1. O give thanks unto the LORD. The exhortation is intensely earnest: the Psalmist pleads with the Lord's people with an "O", three times repeated. Thanks are the least that we can offer, and these we ought freely to give. The inspired writer calls us to praise Jehovah for all his goodness to us, and all the greatness of his power in blessing his chosen. We thank our parents, let us praise our heavenly Father; we are grateful to our benefactors, let us give thanks unto the Giver of all good.

Verse 2. O give thanks unto the God of gods. If there be powers in heaven or on earth worthy of the name of gods he is the God of them; from him their dominion comes, their authority is derived from him, and their very existence is dependent upon his will.

Verse 3. O give thanks to the Lord of lords. There are lords many, but Jehovah is the Lord of them. All lordship is vested in the Eternal. He makes and administers law, he rules and governs mind and matter, he possesses in himself all sovereignty and power.

Verse 4. To him who alone doeth great wonders. Jehovah is the great Thaumaturge, the unrivalled Wonder worker. None can be likened unto him, he is alone in wonderland, the Creator and Worker of true marvels, compared with which all other remarkable things are as child's play. His works are all great in wonder even when they are not great in size; in fact, in the minute objects of the microscope we behold as great wonders as even the telescope can reveal.

Verse 5. To him that by wisdom made the heavens. His goodness appears in creating the upper regions. He set his wisdom to the task of fashioning a firmament, or an atmosphere suitable for a world upon which mortal men should dwell. What a mass of wisdom lies hidden in this one creating act!

Verse 6. To him that stretched out the earth above the waters. Lifting it up from the mingled mass, the dank morass, the bottomless bog, of mixed land and sea; and so fitting it to be the abode of man. Who but the Lord could have wrought this marvel? Few even think of the divine wisdom and power which performed all this of old; yet, if a continent can be proved to have risen or fallen an inch within historic memory, the fact is recorded in the "transactions" of learned societies, and discussed at every gathering of philosophers. For his mercy endureth for ever, as is seen in the original upheaval and perpetual upstanding of the habitable land, so that no deluge drowns the race.

Verse 7. To him that made great lights. This also is a creating miracle worthy of our loudest thanks. What could men have done without light? Though they had the heavens above them, and dry land to move upon, yet what could they see, and where could they go without light? Thanks be to the Lord, who has not consigned us to darkness.

JOHN CALVIN

Psalm 136

The Psalmist reminds the Lord's people, that unless they were assiduous in his praises, they were chargeable with defrauding him of what was justly due to him for his benefits. And, in mentioning each benefit, he takes particular notice of the mercy of God, to teach us how necessary it is to the proper celebration of his praises that we own everything which we receive from him to be bestowed gratuitously.

1-9

1. For his mercy, etc. The insertion of this clause again and again in so many short and abrupt sentences, may seem a vain repetition, but verses repeated by way of chorus are both allowed and admired in profane poets, and why should we object to the reiteration in this instance, for which the best reasons can be shown. Men may not deny the divine goodness to be the source and Fountain of all their blessings, but the graciousness of his bounty is far from being fully and sincerely recognized, though the greatest stress is laid upon it in Scripture. Paul in speaking of it, (Romans 3:23,) calls it emphatically by the general term of the glory of God, intimating, that while God should be praised for all his works, it is his mercy principally that we should glorify. It is evident from what we read in sacred history, that it was customary for the Levites. according to the regulation laid down by David for conducting the praises of God, to sing by response, "for his mercy endureth for ever." The practice was followed by Solomon in the dedication of the Temple, (2 Chronicles 7:3, 6,) and by Jehoshaphat in that solemn triumphal song mentioned in 2 Chronicles 20:21, of the same book. [Before proceeding to recite God's works, the Psalmist declares his supreme Deity, and dominion, not that such comparative language implies that there is anything approaching.] Deity besides him, but there is a disposition in men, whenever they see any part of his glory displayed, to conceive of a God separate from him, thus impiously dividing the Godhead into parts, and even proceeding so far as to frame gods of wood and stone. There is a depraved tendency in all to take delight in a multiplicity of gods.

4. Who alone hath done great wonders. Under this term he comprehends all God's works from the least to the greatest, that he may awaken our admiration of them, for notwithstanding the signal marks of inconceivably great wisdom and divine power of God which are inscribed upon them we are apt through thoughtlessness to undervalue them. He declares that whatever is worthy of admiration is exclusively made and done by God, to teach us that we cannot transfer the smallest portion of the praise due to him without awful sacrilege, there being no vestige of divinity in the whole range of heaven and earth with which it is lawful to compare or equal him. He then proceeds to praise the wisdom of God, as particularly displayed in the skill with which the heavens are framed, giving evidence in a surprising degree of the fine discrimination with which they are adorned. Next he comes to speak of the earth, that he may

MATTHEW HENRY

Psalm 136

1-9 Exhortations to thanksgiving.

The duty we are here again and again called to is to give thanks, to offer the sacrifice of praise continually, not the fruits of our ground or cattle, but the fruit of our lips, giving thanks to his name, Heb. xiii. 15. We are never so earnestly called upon to pray and repent as to give thanks; for it is the will of God that we should abound most in the most pleasant exercises of religion, in that which is the work of heaven. Now here observe,

1. Whom we must give thanks to—to him that we receive all good from, to the Lord, Jehovah, Israel's God (v. 1), the God of gods, the God whom angels adore, from whom magistrates derive their power, and by whom all pretended deities are and shall be conquered (v. 2), to the Lord of lords, the Sovereign of all sovereigns, the stay and supporter of all supports; v. 3. In all our adorations we must have an eye to God's excellency as transcendent, and to his power and dominion as incontestably and uncontrollably supreme.

2. What we must give thanks for, not as the Pharisee that made all his thanksgivings terminate in his own praise (God, I thank thee, that I am so and so), but directing them all to God's glory.

(1.) We must give thanks to God for his goodness and mercy (v. 1): Give thanks to the Lord, not only because he does good, but because he is good (all the streams must be traced up to the fountain), not only because he is merciful to us, but because his mercy endures for ever, and will be drawn out to those that shall come after us. We must give thanks to God, not only for that mercy which is now handed out to us here on earth, but for that which shall endure for ever in the glories and joys of heaven.

(2.) We must give God thanks for the instances of his power and wisdom. In general (v. 4), he along does great wonders. The contrivance is wonderful, the design being laid by infinite wisdom; the performance is wonderful, being put in execution by infinite power. He alone does marvelous things; none besides can do such things, and he does them without the assistance or advice of any other. More particularly,

[1.] He made the heavens, and stretched them out, and in them we not only see his wisdom and power, but we taste his mercy in their benign influences; as long as the heavens endure the mercy of God endures in them, v. 5.

[2.] He raised the earth out of the waters when he caused the dry land to appear, that it might be fit to be a habitation for man, and therein also his mercy to man still endures (v. 6); for the earth hath he given to the children of men, and all its products.

[3.] Having made both heaven and earth, he settled a correspondence between them, notwithstanding their distance, by making the sun, moon, and stars, which he placed in the firmament of heaven, to shed

Psalm 136

9-17
9 The moon and stars to rule by night: for his mercy endureth for ever.
10 To him that smote Egypt in their firstborn: for his mercy endureth for ever:
11 And brought out Israel from among them: for his mercy endureth for ever:
12 With a strong hand, and with a stretched out arm: for his mercy endureth for ever.
13 To him which divided the Red sea into parts: for his mercy endureth for ever:
14 And made Israel to pass through the midst of it: for his mercy endureth for ever:
15 But overthrew Pharaoh and his host in the Red sea: for his mercy endureth for ever.
16 To him which led his people through the wilderness: for his mercy endureth for ever.
17 To him which smote great kings: for his mercy endureth for ever:

Verse 8. The sun to rule by day. We cannot be too specific in our praises; after mentioning great lights, we may sing of each of them, and yet not outwear our theme. The influences of the sun are too many for us to enumerate them all, but untold benefits come to all orders of beings by its light, warmth, and other operations. Whenever we sit in the sunshine, our gratitude should be kindled.

Verse 9. The moon and stars to rule by night. No hour is left without rule. Blessed be God, he leaves us never to the doom of anarchy. The rule is one of light and benediction. The moon with her charming changes, and the stars in their fixed spheres gladden the night. When the season would be dark and dreary because of the absence of the sun, forth come the many minor comforters. The sun is enough alone; but when he is gone a numerous band cannot suffice to give more than a humble imitation of his radiance.

Verse 10. We have heard of the glory of the world's creation, we are now to praise the Lord for the creation of his favored nation by their Exodus from Egypt. Because the monarch of Egypt stood in the way of the Lord's gracious purposes it became needful for the Lord to deal with him in justice; but the great design was mercy to Israel, and through Israel mercy to succeeding ages, and to all the world.

Verse 11. And brought out Israel from among them. Scattered as the tribes were up and down the country, and apparently held in a grasp which would never be relaxed, the Lord wrought their deliverance, and severed them from their idolatrous task masters.

Verse 12. With a strong hand, and with a stretched out arm. Not only the matter but the manner of the Lord's mighty acts should be the cause of our praise. We ought to bless the Lord for adverbs as well as adjectives. In the Exodus the great power and glory of Jehovah were seen. He dashed in pieces the enemy with his right hand. He led forth his people in no mean or clandestine manner.

Verse 13. To him which divided the Red sea into parts. He made a road across the sea bottom, causing the divided waters to stand like walls on either side. Men deny miracles; but, granted that there is a God, they become easy of belief. Since it requires me to be an atheist that I may logically reject miracles, I prefer the far smaller difficulty of believing in the infinite power of God.

Verse 14. And made Israel to pass through the midst of it. HE gave the people courage to follow the predestined track through the yawning abyss, which might well have terrified a veteran host. It needed no little generalship to conduct so vast and motley a company along a way so novel and apparently so dangerous. He made them to pass, by the untrodden road; he led them down into the deep and up again on the further shore in perfect order, keeping their enemies back by the thick darkness of the cloudy pillar. Herein is the glory of God set forth, as all his people see it in their own deliverance from sin.

Verse 15. But overthrew Pharaoh and his host in the Red sea. Here comes the thunder clap. Though we hear them sounding peal upon peal, yet the judgments of the Lord were only loud mouthed mercies speaking confusion to the foe, that the chosen might tremble before him no longer.

Verse 16. To him which led his people through the wilderness. He led them into it, and therefore he was pledged to lead them through it. They were "his people", and yet they must go into the wilderness, and the wilderness must remain as barren as ever it was; but in the end they must come out of it into the promised land. God's dealings are mysterious, but they must be right, simply because they are his. The people knew nothing of the way, but they were led; they were a vast host, yet they were all led; there were neither roads nor tracks, but being led by unerring wisdom they never lost their way.

Verse 17. To him which smote great kings. Within sight of their inheritance Israel had to face powerful enemies. Kings judged to be great because of the lead us to form a proper estimate of this great and memorable work of God, stretching forth as it does a bare and dry superficies above the waters. As these elements are of a spherical form, the waters, if not kept within their limits, would naturally cover the earth, were it not that God has seen fit to secure a place of habitation for the human family. This philosophers themselves are forced to admit as one of their principles and maxims. The earth's expanded surface, and the vacant space uncovered with water, has been justly considered therefore one of the great wonders of God. And it is ascribed to his mercy, because his only reason for displacing the waters from their proper seat was that regard which he had in his infinite goodness for the interests of man.

7. Who made the great lights, etc.—Moses calls the sun and moon the two great lights, and there is little doubt that the Psalmist here borrows the same phraseology. What is immediately added about the stars, is, as it were, accessory to the others. It is true, that the other planets are larger than the moon, but it is stated as second in order on account of its visible effects. The Holy Spirit had no intention to teach astronomy; and, in proposing instruction meant to be common to the simplest and most uneducated persons, he made use by Moses and the other Prophets of popular language, that none might shelter himself under the pretext of obscurity, as we will see men sometimes very readily pretended an incapacity to understand, when anything deep or recondite is submitted to their notice. Accordingly, as Saturn though bigger than the moon is not so to the eye owing to his greater distance, the Holy Spirit would rather speak childishly than unintelligibly to the humble and unlearned. The same remark may be made upon what the Psalmist adds regarding God's having assigned the sun and moon their respective parts, making the one to rule the day, and the other to rule the night, by which we are not to understand that they exercise any government, but that the administrative power of God is very manifest in this distribution. The sun in illuminating the earth through the day, and the, moon and stars by night, may be said to yield a reverential homage to God.

10-16

10. Who smote the Egyptians in, their first-born. We notice that the Egyptians are well said to have been smitten in their first-born, because they continued in their outrageous obstinacy under the other plagues, though occasionally terrified by them, but were broken and subdued by this last plague, and submitted. As it was not intended to recount all the wonders successively done in Egypt, the whole is summed up in one word when it is said, that he led his people forth from the midst of it with a mighty and a stretched out arm. For pressed down as they were on every side, it was only by a wonderful display of divine power that they could effect an escape. The figure of an outstretched arm is appropriate, for we stretch out the arm when any great effort is required; so that this implies that God put forth an extraordinary and not a common or slight display of his power in redeeming his people.

13. Who divided the Red Sea. Moses plainly and explicitly asserts that the heaps of waters stood up on both sides, from

their light and influences upon this earth, v. 7-9. These are called the great lights because they appear so to us, for otherwise astronomers could tell us that the moon is less than many of the stars, but, being nearer to the earth, it seems much greater. They are said to rule, not only because they govern the seasons of the year, but because they are useful to the world, and benefactors are the best rulers, Luke xxii. 25. But the empire is divided, one rules by day, the other by night (at least, the stars), and yet all are subject to God's direction and disposal. Those rulers, therefore, which the Gentiles idolized, are the world's servants and God's subjects. Sun, stand thou still, and thou moon.

10-22 Divine mercy celebrated.

The great things God did for Israel, when he first formed them into a people, and set up his kingdom among them, are here mentioned, as often elsewhere in the psalms, as instances both of the power of God and of the particular kindness he had for Israel. See Ps. cxxxv. 8, &c.

1. He brought them out of Egypt, v. 10-12. That was a mercy which endured long to them, and our redemption by Christ, which was typified by that, does indeed endure for ever, for it is an eternal redemption. Of all the plagues of Egypt, none is mentioned but the death of the first-born, because that was the conquering plague; by that God, who in all the plagues distinguished the Israelites from the Egyptians, brought them at last from among them, not by a wile, but with a strong hand and an arm stretched out to reach far and do great things. These miracles of mercy, as they proved Moses's commission to give law to Israel, so they laid Israel under lasting obligations to obey that law, Exod. xx. 2.

2. He forced them a way through the Red Sea, which obstructed them at their first setting out. By the power he has to control the common course of nature he divided the sea into two parts, between which he opened a path, and made Israel to pass between the parts, now that they were to enter into covenant with him; see Jer. xxxiv. 18. He not only divided the sea, but gave his people courage to go through it when it was divided, which was an instance of God's power over men's hearts, as the former of his power over the waters. And, to make it a miracle of justice as well as mercy, the same Red Sea that was a lane to the Israelites was a grave to their pursuers. There he shook off Pharaoh and his host.

3. He conducted them through a vast howling wilderness (v. 16); there he led them and fed them. Their camp was victualled and fortified by a constant series of miracles for forty years; though they loitered and wandered there, they were not lost. And in this the mercy of God, and the constancy of that mercy, were the more observable because they often provoked him in the wilderness and grieved him in the desert.

Psalm 136

18-26

18 And slew famous kings: for his mercy endureth for ever:
19 Sihon king of the Amorites: for his mercy endureth for ever:
20 And Og the king of Bashan: for his mercy endureth for ever:
21 And gave their land for an heritage: for his mercy endureth for ever:
22 Even an heritage unto Israel his servant: for his mercy endureth for ever.
23 Who remembered us in our low estate: for his mercy endureth for ever:
24 And hath redeemed us from our enemies: for his mercy endureth for ever.
25 Who giveth food to all flesh: for his mercy endureth for ever.
26 O give thanks unto the God of heaven: for his mercy endureth for ever.

armies at their back blocked up their road. This difficulty soon disappeared, for the Lord smote their adversaries, and a single stroke sufficed for their destruction.

Verse 18. And slew famous kings. What good was their fame to them? As they opposed God they became infamous rather than famous. Their deaths made the Lord's fame to increase among the nations while their fame ended in disgraceful defeat. For his mercy endureth for ever. Israelitish patriots felt that they, could never have too much of this music; God had protected their nation, and they chanted his praises with unwearied iteration.

Verse 19. Sihon king of the Amorites. Let the name be mentioned that the mercy may be the better remembered. Sihon smote Moab, but he could not smite Israel, for the Lord smote him. He was valiant and powerful, so as to be both great and famous; but as he willfully refused to give a peaceful passage to the Israelites, and fought against them in malice, there was no choice for it but to let him run into that destruction which he courted.

Verse 20. And Og the king of Bashan. He was of the race of the giants, but he was routed like a pygmy when he entered the lists with Israel's God. The Lord's people were called upon to fight against him, but it was God who won the victory. The fastnesses of Bashan were no defense against Jehovah.

Verse 21. And gave their land for an heritage. As Lord of the whole earth he transferred his estate from one tenant to another. The land did not become the property of the Israelites by their own sword and bow, but by a grant from the throne.

Verse 22. Even an heritage unto Israel his servant. Repetitions are effective in poetry, and the more so if there be some little variation in them, bringing out into fuller light some point which else had not been noticed. The lands of the heathen kings were given to "Israel", the name by which the chosen seed is here mentioned for the third time in the Psalm, with the addition of the words, "his servant."

Verse 23. Who remembered us in our low estate. Personal mercies awake the sweetest song—"he remembered us." Our prayer is, "Lord, remember me", and this is our encouragement—he has remembered us. For the Lord even to think of us is a wealth of mercy.

Verse 24. And hath redeemed us from our enemies. Israel's enemies brought the people low; but the Lord intervened, and turned the tables by a great redemption. The expression implies that they had become like slaves, and were not set free without price and power; for they needed to be "redeemed."

Verse 25. Who giveth food to all flesh. Common providence, which cares for all living things, deserves our most devout thanks. If we think of heavenly food, by which all saints are supplied, our praises rise to a still greater height; but meanwhile the universal goodness of God in feeding all his creatures is as worthy of praise as his special favors to the elect nation.

Verse 26. O give thanks unto the God of heaven. The title is full of honor. The Lord is God in the highest realms, and among celestial beings. His throne is set in glory, above all, out of reach of foes, in the place of universal oversight. He who feeds ravens and sparrows is yet the glorious God of the highest realms.

which we infer that the space between was one and undivided. But as the people passed through in troops, and not one by one, the pathway being so broad as to admit of their passing freely men and women, with their families and cattle, the Psalmist very properly mentions divisions, with a reference to the people who passed through, this circumstance not a little enhancing the mercy of God, that they saw large depths or channels dried up, so that they had no difficulty in advancing in troops abreast. Another circumstance which confirmed or enhanced the mercy shown, was, that Pharaoh was shortly afterwards drowned; for the very different issue proved that it could not be owing to any hidden cause of a merely natural kind, that some should have perished, while others passed over with entire safety. The distinction made afforded a conspicuous display of God's mercy in saving his people. Much is included in the single expression that God was the leader of his people through the wilderness. It was only by a succession of miracles of various kinds that they could have been preserved for forty years in a parched wilderness. So that we are to comprehend, under what is here stated, the various proofs of divine goodness and power which are mentioned by Moses as having been vouchsafed, in feeding his people with bread from heaven—in making water to flow from the rock—in protecting them under the cloud from the heat of the sun—giving them a sign of his presence in the pillar of fire—preserving their raiment entire—shielding them and their little ones in their exile wanderings.

17-26

23. Who remembered us in our humiliation. The six verses taken from the previous Psalm I pass over without observation; and I shall only touch very briefly upon the others, which do not need lengthened consideration. We may just observe that the Psalmist represents every age as affording' displays of the same goodness as had been shown to their fathers, since God had never failed to help his people by a continued succession of deliverances. It was a more notable proof of his mercy to interpose for the nation at a time when it was nearly overwhelmed by calamities, than to preserve it in its entire state and under a more even course of affairs, there being something in the emergency to awaken attention and arrest the view. Besides, in all the deliverances which God grants his people, there is an accompanying remission of their sins. In the close he speaks of the paternal providence of God as extending not only to all mankind, but to every living creature, suggesting that we have no reason to feel surprise at his sustaining the character of a kind and provident father to his own people, when he condescends to care for the cattle, and the asses of the field, and the crow, and the sparrow. Men are much better than brute beasts, and there is a great difference between some men and others, though not in merit, yet as regards the privilege of the divine adoption, and the Psalmist is to be considered as reasoning from the less to the greater, and enhancing the superior mercy which God shows to his own children.

4. He destroyed kings before them, to make room for them (v. 17, 18), not deposed and banished them, but smote and slew them, in which appeared his wrath against them, but his mercy, his never-failing mercy, to Israel. And that which magnified it was that they were great kings and famous kings, yet God subdued them as easily as if they had been the least, and weakest, and meanest, of the children of men. They were wicked kings, and then their grandeur and luster would not secure them from the justice of God. It is good to enter into the detail of God's favors and not to view them in the gross, and in each instance to observe, and own, that God's mercy endureth for ever.

5. He put them in possession of a good land, v. 21, 22. He whose the earth is, and the fullness thereof, the world and those that dwell therein, took land from one people and gave it to another, as pleased him. The iniquity of the Amorites was now full, and therefore it was taken from them. Israel was his servant. As he said to the Egyptians, Let my people go, so to the Canaanites, Let my people in, that they may serve me. In this God's mercy to them endureth for ever, because it was a figure of the heavenly Canaan, the mercy of our Lord Jesus Christ unto eternal life.

23-26 Divine mercy celebrated.

God's everlasting mercy is here celebrated,

1. In the redemption of his church, v. 23, 24. In the many redemptions wrought for the Jewish church out of the hands of their oppressors, but especially in the great redemption of the universal church, of which these were types, we have a great deal of reason to say, "He remembered us, the children of men, in our low estate, in our lost estate, for his mercy endureth for ever; he sent his Son to redeem us from sin, and death, and hell, and all our spiritual enemies, for his mercy endureth for ever; he was sent to redeem us, and not the angels that sinned, for his mercy endureth for ever."

2. In the provision he makes for all the creatures (v. 25): He gives food to all flesh. It is an instance of the mercy of God's providence that wherever he has given life he gives food agreeable and sufficient; and he is a good housekeeper that provides for so large a family.

3. In all his glories, and all his gifts (v. 26): Give thanks to the God of heaven. This denotes him to be a glorious God, and the glory of his mercy is to be taken notice of in our praises. The riches of his glory are displayed in the vessels of his mercy, Rom. ix. 23. It also denotes him to be the great benefactor, for every good and perfect gift is from above, from the Father of lights, the God of heaven; and we should trace every stream to the fountain. This and that particular mercy may perhaps endure but a while, but the mercy that is in God endures for ever; it is an inexhaustible fountain.

Psalm 137

1-4
1 By the rivers of Babylon, there we sat down, yea, we wept, when we remembered Zion.
2 We hanged our harps upon the willows in the midst thereof.
3 For there they that carried us away captive required of us a song; and they that wasted us required of us mirth, saying, Sing us one of the songs of Zion.
4 How shall we sing the LORD's song in a strange land?

Psalm 137

This plaintive ode is one of the most charming compositions in the whole Book of Psalms for its poetic power. If it were not inspired it would nevertheless occupy a high place in poesy, especially the former portion of it, which is tender and patriotic to the highest degree. In the later verses (Ps 137:7-9), we have utterances of burning indignation against the chief adversaries of Israel,—an indignation as righteous as it was fervent. Let those find fault with it who have never seen their temple burned, their city ruined, their wives ravished, and after children slain; they might not, perhaps, be quite so velvet mouthed if they had suffered after this fashion. It is one thing to talk of the bitter feeling which moved captive Israelites in Babylon, and quite another thing to be captives ourselves under a savage and remorseless power, which knew not how to show mercy, but delighted in barbarities to the defenseless. The song is such as might fitly be sung in the Jews' wailing place. It is a fruit of the Captivity in Babylon, and often has it furnished expression for sorrows which else had been unutterable. It is an opalesque Psalm within whose mild radiance there glows afire which strikes the beholder with wonder.

EXPOSITION

Verse 1. By the rivers of Babylon, there we sat down. Water courses were abundant in Babylon, wherein were not only natural streams but artificial canals: it was place of broad rivers and streams. Glad to be away from the noisy streets, the captives sought the river side, where the flow of the waters seemed to be in sympathy with their tears. It was some slight comfort to be out of the crowd, and to have a little breathing room, and therefore they sat down, as if to rest a while and solace themselves in their sorrow. In little groups they sat down and made common lamentation, mingling their memories and their tears. The rivers were well enough, but, alas, they were the rivers of Babylon, and the ground whereon the sons of Israel sat was foreign soil, and therefore they wept.

Verse 2. We hanged our harps upon the willows in the midst thereof. The drooping branches appeared to weep as we did, and so we gave to them our instruments of music; the willows could as well make melody as we, for we had no mind for minstrelsy. In the midst of the willows, or in the midst of the rivers, or in the midst of Babylon, it matters little which, they hung their harps aloft—those harps which once in Zion's halls the soul of music shed. Better to hang them up than to dash them down: better to hang them on willows than profane them to the service of idols. Sad indeed is the child of sorrow when he grows weary of his harp, from which in better days he had been able to draw sweet solaces. Music hath charms to give unquiet spirits rest; but when the heart is sorely sad it only mocks the grief which flies to it. Men put away their instruments of mirth when a heavy cloud darkens their souls.

Verse 3. For there they that carried us away captive required of us a song. It was ill to be a singer at all when it was demanded that this talent should go into bondage to an oppressor's will. Better be dumb than be forced to please an enemy with forced song. What cruelty to make a people sigh, and then require them to sing! Shall men be carried away from home and all that is dear to them, and yet chant merrily for the pleasure of their unfeeling captors? This is studied torture: the iron enters into the soul. It is indeed "woe to the conquered" when they are forced to sing to increase the triumph of their conquerors.

Verses 3-4. St. John Chrysostom observes the improvement such tribulation effected in the Jews, who previously derided, nay, even put to death, some of the prophets; but now that they were captives in a foreign land, they would not attempt to expose their sacred hymns to the ridicule of the Gentiles.

JOHN CALVIN

Psalm 137

At the Babylonish captivity the established order of God's worship was overthrown, and the Psalmist complains, in the name of the Church at large, of the taunts which the enemy east upon the name of God, addressing at the same time a word of comfort to his people under their captivity, to cheer them with the hope of deliverance.

1-4
1. By the rivers of Babylon there we sat down. It is a great mistake to suppose that it is David who here prophetically apprises the people of God of the captivity which should come upon them. The Prophets in speaking of future events employ very different language. What is brought under notice is the event as now historically come, and matter of experience.

We shall briefly explain the scope of the Psalmist. There was danger that the Jews when cast off in such a melancholy manner should lose hold altogether of their faith and of their religion. Considering how ready we are, when mixed up with the wicked and ungodly, to fall into superstition or evil practices, it was to be feared that they might wax profane amongst the population of Babylon. The people of the Lord might be thrown into despondency, besides, by their captivity, the cruel bondage they were subjected to, and the other indignities which they had to endure. The writer of this Psalm, whose name is unknown, drew up a form of lamentation, that by giving expression to their sufferings in sighs and prayers, they might keep alive the hope of that deliverance which they despaired of. Another end he has in view, is to warn them against, the decline of godliness in an irreligious land, and against; defilement with the contaminations of the heathen. Accordingly he denounces merited judgment upon the children of Edom, and declares that Babylon, whose prosperity, short-lived as it was destined to be in itself, eclipsed at that time the rest of the world, was an object of pity, and near to destruction. The length of time during which the captivity lasted, may of itself convince us how useful and even necessary it must have been to support the fainting minds of God's people. They must have been ready to acquiesce in the corrupt practices of the heathen, unless endued with surprising mental fortitude through a period of seventy years.
2. We hanged our harps upon the willows. He deplores the suspension of the songs of praise, which God had enjoined in his Temple. The Levites were set over the department of singing, and led the way among the people in this devotional exercise. When willows are mentioned, this denotes the pleasantness of the banks, which were planted with willows for coolness. But the Psalmist says that these shades, however delightful, could not dispel a grief which was too deeply seated to admit of common consolations or refreshment.
3. Then they that carried us away captive, etc. We may be certain that the Israelites were treated with cruel severity under this barbarous tyranny to which they were subjected. And the worst affliction of all was, that their conquerors reproachfully insulted them, and even mocked them, their

MATTHEW HENRY

Psalm 137

1-6 The sorrows of captivity.
We have here the daughter of Zion covered with a cloud, and dwelling with the daughter of Babylon; the people of God in tears, but sowing in tears. Observe,
I. The mournful posture they were in as to their affairs and as to their spirits.
1. They were posted by the rivers of Babylon, in a strange land, a great way from their own country, whence they were brought as prisoners of war.
2. There they sat down to indulge their grief by poring on their miseries. Jeremiah had taught them under this yoke to sit alone, and keep silence, and put their mouths in the dust, Lam. iii. 28, 29. "We sat down, as those that expected to stay, and were content, since it was the will of God that it must be so."
3. Thoughts of Zion drew tears from their eyes; and it was not a sudden passion of weeping, such as we are sometimes put into by a trouble that surprises us, but they were deliberate tears (we sat down and wept), tears with consideration—we wept when we remembered Zion, the holy hill on which the temple was built. Their affection to God's house swallowed up their concern for their own houses.
II. The abuses which their enemies put upon them when they were in this melancholy condition, v. 3. They had carried them away captive from their own land and then wasted them in the land of their captivity, took what little they had from them. But this was not enough; to complete their woes they insulted over them: They required of us mirth and a song. Now,
1. This was very barbarous and inhuman; even an enemy, in misery, is to be pitied and not trampled upon. It argues a base and sordid spirit to upbraid those that are in distress either with their former joys or with their present griefs, or to challenge those to be merry who, we know, are out of tune for it. This is adding affliction to the afflicted.
2. It was very profane and impious. No songs would serve them but the songs of Zion, with which God had been honored; so that in this demand they reflected upon God himself as Belshazzar, when he drank wine in temple-bowls. Their enemies mocked at their Sabbaths, Lam. i. 7.
III. The patience wherewith they bore these abuses, v. 4. They had laid by their harps, and would not resume them, no, not to ingratiate themselves with those at whose mercy they lay; they would not answer those fools according to their folly.
IV. The constant affection they retained for Jerusalem, the city of their solemnities, even now that they were in Babylon. Though their enemies banter them for talking so much of Jerusalem, and even doting upon it, their love to it is not in the least abated; it is what they may be jeered for, but will never be jeered out of, v. 5, 6. Observe,
1. How these pious captives stood affected to Jerusalem.

Psalm 137

5-9
5 If I forget thee, O Jerusalem, let my right hand forget her cunning.
6 If I do not remember thee, let my tongue cleave to the roof of my mouth; if I prefer not Jerusalem above my chief joy.
7 Remember, O LORD, the children of Edom in the day of Jerusalem; who said, Rase it, rase it, even to the foundation thereof.
8 O daughter of Babylon, who art to be destroyed; happy shall he be, that rewardeth thee as thou hast served us.
9 Happy shall he be, that taketh and dasheth thy little ones against the stones.

Verse 4. How shall we sing the LORD's song in a strange land How shall they sing at all? sing in a strange land? sing Jehovah's song among the uncircumcised? No, that must not be; it shall not be. With one voice they refuse, but the refusal is humbly worded by being put in the form of a question. If the men of Babylon were wicked enough to suggest the defiling of holy things for the gratification of curiosity, or for the creation of amusement, the men of Zion had not so hardened their hearts as to be willing to please them at such a fearful cost. There are many things which the ungodly could do, and think nothing of the doing thereof, which gracious men cannot venture upon. The question "How can I?" or "How shall we?" comes of a tender conscience and denotes an inability to sin which is greatly to be cultivated.
Verse 5. If I forget thee, O Jerusalem, let my right hand forget her cunning. To sing Zion's songs for the pleasure of Zion's foes, would be to forget the Holy City Each Jew declares for himself that he will not do this; for the pronoun alters from "we" to "I." Individually the captives pledge themselves to fidelity to Jerusalem, and each one asserts that he had sooner forget the art which drew music from his harp strings than use it for Babel's delectation.
Verse 6. If I do not remember thee, let my tongue cleave to the roof of my mouth. Thus the singers imprecate eternal silence upon their mouths if they forget Jerusalem to gratify Babylon. The players on instruments and the sweet songsters are of one mind: the enemies of the Lord will get no mirthful tune or song from them.
Verse 7. Remember, O LORD, the children of Edom in the day of Jerusalem. The case is left in Jehovah's hands. He is a God of recompenses, and will deal out justice with impartiality. The Edomites ought to have been friendly with the Israelites, from kinship; but there was a deep hatred and cruel spite displayed by them.
Verse 8. O daughter of Babylon, who art to be destroyed. Or the destroyer: let us accept the word either way, or both ways: the destroyer would be destroyed, and the Psalmist in vision saw her as already destroyed. It is usual to speak of a city as a virgin daughter. Babylon was in her prime and beauty, but she was already doomed for her crimes.
Verse 9. Happy shall he be, that taketh and dasheth thy little ones against the stones. Fierce was the heart of the Jew who had seen his beloved city the scene of such terrific butchery. His heart pronounced like sentence upon Babylon. She should be scourged with her own whip of wire. The desire for righteous retribution is rather the spirit of the law than of the gospel; and yet in moments of righteous wrath the old fire will burn; and while justice survives in the human breast it will not lack for fuel among the various tyrannies which still survive. We shall be wise to view this passage as a prophecy. History informs us that it was literally fulfilled: the Babylonian people in their terror agreed to destroy their own offspring, and men thought themselves happy when they had put their own wives and children to the sword. Horrible as was the whole transaction, it is a thing to be glad of if we take a broad view of the world's welfare; for Babylon, the gigantic robber, had for many a year slaughtered nations without mercy, and her fall was the rising of many people to a freer and safer state. The murder of innocent infants can never be sufficiently deplored, but it was an incident of ancient warfare which the Babylonians had not omitted in their massacres, and, therefore, they were not spared it themselves. The revenges of providence may be slow, but they are ever sure.

design being less to wound the hearts of these miserable exiles, than to cast blasphemies upon their God. The Babylonians had no desire to hear their sacred songs, and very likely would not have suffered them to engage in the public praises of God, but they speak ironically, and insinuate it as a reproach upon the Levites that they should be silent, when it was their custom formerly to sing sacred songs. Is your God dead, as if they had said, to whom your praises were formerly addressed?

4. How shall we sing, etc. The Psalmist puts a lofty and magnanimous answer into the mouth of the Lord's people to their insolent reproach, which is this, that they abstained from their songs, as from their legal sacrifices, because the land where they now were was polluted. The Chaldeans thought the Jews were bound down permanently to this place of their exile; the Psalmist, when he calls it a foreign land, suggests that it was but the place of their temporary stay. But the main idea is, that Chaldea was not worthy of the honor of having God's praises sung in it.

5-9

5. If I shall forget thee, O Jerusalem! This confirms what was said in the former verse, and leaves us in no difficulty to understand what the Psalmist meant by it. For here God's people declare, and with the solemnity of an oath, that the remembrance of the holy city would be ever engraven upon their hearts, and never, under any circumstances, effaced. Having spoken of song, and of the instruments of music, the Psalmist's appeal is made in terms which correspond—that his hand would forager its cunning, and his tongue cleave to his palate, or the roof of his mouth. The meaning is, that the Lord's people, while they mourn under personal trials, should be still more deeply affected by public calamities which befall the Church, it being reasonable that the zeal of God's house should have the highest place in our hearts, and rise above all mere private considerations.

7. Remember, O Jehovah! the children of Edom. Vengeance was to be executed upon the other neighboring nations which had conspired to destroy Jerusalem, so that they are all doubtless included here under the children of Edom, who are specified, a part, for the whole, either because they showed more hatred and cruelty than the rest, or that theirs were not so easily borne, considering that they were brethren, and of one blood, being the posterity of Esau, and that the Israelites had, by God's commandment, spared the Edomites, when they devoted all beside them to destruction. (Deuteronomy 2:4.) It was, therefore, the height of cruelty in them to invite the Babylonians to destroy their own brethren, or fan the flames of their hostility.

8. O daughter of Babylon laid waste! The Psalmist discerns the coming judgment of God, though not yet apparent, by the eye of faith, as the Apostle well calls faith "the beholding of things not seen." (Hebrews 11:1.) Incredible as it might appear that any calamity should overtake so mighty an empire as Babylon then was, he sees in the glass of the Word its destruction and overthrow.

(1.) Their heads were full of it. It was always in their minds; they remembered it; they did not forget it, though they had been long absent from it.

(2.) Their hearts were full of it. They preferred it above their chief joy, and therefore they remembered it and could not forget it.

2. How steadfastly they resolved to keep up this affection, which they express by a solemn imprecation of mischief to themselves if they should let it fall: "Let me be for ever disabled either to sing or play on the harp if I so far forget the religion of my country as to make use of my songs and harps for the pleasing of Babylon's sons or the praising of Babylon's gods. Let my right hand forget her art."

7-9 The sorrows of captivity.

The pious Jews in Babylon, having afflicted themselves with the thoughts of the ruins of Jerusalem, here please themselves with the prospect of the ruin of her impenitent implacable enemies; but this not from a spirit of revenge, but from a holy zeal for the glory of God and the honor of his kingdom.

I. The Edomites will certainly be reckoned with, and all others that were accessories to the destruction of Jerusalem, that were aiding and abetting, that helped forward the affliction (Zech. i. 15) and triumphed in it, that said, in the day of Jerusalem, the day of her judgment, "Raise it, raze it to the foundations; down with it, down with it; do not leave one stone upon another."

II. Babylon is the principal, and it will come to her turn too to drink of the cup of tremblings, the very dregs of it (v. 8, 9): O daughter of Babylon! proud and secure as thou art, we know well, by the scriptures of truth, thou art to be destroyed, or (as Dr. Hammond reads it) who art the destroyer. The destroyers shall be destroyed, Rev. xiii. 10. The destruction of Babylon being foreseen as a sure destruction (thou art to be destroyed), it is spoken of,

1. As a just destruction. She shall be paid in her own coin: "Thou shalt be served as thou hast served us, as barbarously used by the destroyers as we have been by thee."

2. As an utter destruction. The very little ones of Babylon, when it is taken by storm, and all in it are put to the sword, shall be dashed to pieces by the enraged and merciless conqueror.

3. As a destruction which should reflect honor upon the instruments of it. Happy shall those be that do it; for they are fulfilling God's counsels; and therefore he calls Cyrus, who did it, his servant, his shepherd, his anointed (Isa. xliv. 28; xlv. 1). They are making way for the enlargement of God's Israel, and happy are those who are in any way serviceable to that. The fall of the New-Testament Babylon will be the triumph of all the saints, Rev. xix. 1.

Psalm 138

Title
A Psalm of David.

1 I will praise thee with my whole heart: before the gods will I sing praise unto thee.
2 I will worship toward thy holy temple, and praise thy name for thy loving kindness and for thy truth: for thou hast magnified thy word above all thy name.
3 In the day when I cried thou answeredst me, and strengthenedst me with strength in my soul.
4 All the kings of the earth shall praise thee, O LORD, when they hear the words of thy mouth.
5 Yea, they shall sing in the ways of the LORD: for great is the glory of the LORD.
6 Though the LORD be high, yet hath he respect unto the lowly: but the proud he knoweth afar off.
7 Though I walk in the midst of trouble, thou wilt revive me: thou shalt stretch forth thine hand against the wrath of mine enemies, and thy right hand shall save me.
8 The LORD will perfect that which concerneth me: thy mercy, O LORD, endureth for ever: forsake not the works of thine own hands.

Psalm 138

TITLE. A Psalm of David. This Psalm is wisely placed. Whoever edited and arranged these sacred poems, he had an eye to apposition and contrast; for if in Ps 137:1-9 we see the need of silence before revilers, here we see the excellence of a brave confession. There is a time to be silent, lest we cast pearls before swine; and there is a time to speak openly, lest we be found guilty of cowardly not confessing. The Psalm is evidently of a Davidic character, exhibiting all the fidelity, courage, and decision of that King of Israel and Prince of Psalmists. Of course the critics have tried to rend the authorship from David on account of the mention of the temple, though it so happens that in one of the Psalms which is allowed to be David's the same word occurs. Many modern critics are to the word of God what blowflies are to the food of men: they cannot do any good, and unless relentlessly driven away they do great harm.

DIVISION. In full confidence David is prepared to own his God before the gods of the heathen, or before angels or rulers (Ps 138:1-3); he declares that he will instruct and convert kings and nations, till on very highway men shall sing the praises of the Lord (Ps 138:4-5). Having thus spoken, he utters his personal confidence in Jehovah, who will help his lowly servant, and preserve him from all the malice of wrathful foes.

EXPOSITION

Verse 1. I will praise thee with my whole heart. His mind is so taken up with God that he does not mention his name.

Verse 2. I will worship toward thy holy temple, or the place of God's dwelling, where the ark abode. He would worship God in God's own way.

Verse 3. In the day when I cried thou answerest me. No proof is so convincing as that of experience. No man doubts the power of prayer after he has received an answer of peace to his supplication. It is the distinguishing mark of the true and living God that he hears the pleadings of his people, and answers them; the gods hear not and answer not, but Jehovah's memorial is—"the God that heareth prayer."

Verse 4. All the kings of the earth shall praise thee, O Lord, when they hear the words of thy mouth. Kings have usually small care to hear the word of the Lord; but King David feels assured that if they do hear it they will feel its power. A little piety goes a long way in courts.

Verse 5. Yea, they shall sing in the ways of the LORD. Here is a double wonder—kings in God's ways, and kings singing there.

Verse 6. Though the Lord be high. In greatness, dignity, and power, Jehovah is higher than the highest. His nature is high above the comprehension of his creatures, and his glory even exceeds the loftiest soarings of imagination.

Verse 7. Though I walk in the midst of trouble, thou wilt revive me. If I am walking there now, or shall be doing so in years to come, I have no cause for fear; for God is with me, and will give me new life. When we are somewhat in trouble it is bad enough, but it is worse to penetrate into the center of that dark continent and traverse its midst: yet in such a case the believer makes progress, for he walks; he keeps to a quiet pace, for he does no more than walk; and he is not without the best of company, for his God is near to pour fresh life into him.

Verse 8. The Lord will perfect that which concerneth me. All my interests are safe in Jehovah's hands. God is concerned in all that concerns his servants. He will see to it that none of their precious things shall fail of completion; their life, their strength, their hopes, their graces, their pilgrimage, shall each and all be perfected. Jehovah himself will see to this and therefore it is most sure.

JOHN CALVIN

Psalm 138

1-5
1. I will praise thee with my whole heart. As David had been honored to receive distinguishing marks of the divine favor, he declares his resolution to show more than ordinary gratitude. This is exercise which degenerates and is degraded in the case of hypocrites to a mere sound of empty words, but he states that he would return thanks to God not with the lips only, but with sincerity of heart, for by the whole heart is meant a heart which is sincere and not double.
2. I will worship towards the temple of thy holiness. He intimates that he would show more than private gratitude, and, in order to set an example before others, come in compliance with the precept of the law into the sanctuary. He worshipped God spiritually, and yet would lift his eyes to those outward symbols which were the means then appointed for drawing the minds of God's people upwards. He singles out the divine mercy and truth as the subject of his praise.
3. In the day when I cried to thee, etc. Frequently God prevents our prayers, and surprises us, as it were, sleeping: but commonly he stirs us up to prayer by the influence of his Spirit, and this to illustrate his goodness the more by our finding that he crowns our prayers with success.
4. Let all kings of the earth praise thee. Here he declares that the goodness he had experienced would be extensively known, and the report of it spread over all the world. In saying that even kings had heard the words of God's mouth, he does not mean to aver that they had been taught in the true religion so as to be prepared for becoming members of the Church, but only that it would be well known everywhere that the reason of his having been preserved in such a wonderful manner was God's having anointed him king by his commandment.

6-8
6. Because Jehovah the exalted, etc. In this verse he passes commendation upon God's general government of the world. The thing of all others most necessary to be known is, that he is not indifferent to our safety; for though in words we are all ready to grant this, our disbelief of it is shown by the feat we betray upon the slightest appearance of danger, and we would not give way to such alarm if we had a solid persuasion of our being under his fatherly protection.
7. Should I walk in the midst of trouble, etc. On the slightest approach of danger we are immoderately afraid, as if our emergencies precluded the hope of Divine deliverance. This is faith's true office, to see life in the midst of death, and to trust the mercy of God.
8. Jehovah will recompense upon me, etc. Having once been delivered by an act of Divine mercy, David concludes that what had been done would be perfected, as God's nature is unchangeable, and he cannot divest himself of that goodness which belongs to him.

MATTHEW HENRY

Psalm 138

1-5 Grateful praise.
I. How he would praise God, compare Ps. cxi. 1.
1. He will praise him with sincerity and zeal—"With my heart, with my whole heart, with that which is within me and with all that is within me, with uprightness of intention and fervency of affection, inward impressions agreeing with outward expressions."
2. With freedom and boldness: Before the gods will I sing praise unto thee.
3. In the way that God had appointed: I will worship towards thy holy temple. The priests alone went into the temple; the people, at the nearest, did but worship towards it, and that they might do at a distance. Christ is our temple, and towards him we must look with an eye of faith, as Mediator between us and God, in all our praises of him.
II. What he would praise God for.
1. For the fountain of his comforts—for thy lovingkindness and for thy truth.
2. For the streams flowing from that fountain, in which he himself had tasted that the Lord is gracious, v. 3.
III. What influence he hoped that his praising God would have upon others, v. 4, 5. Now,
1. This may have reference to the kings that were neighbors to David, as Hiram and others. "They shall all praise thee."
2. It may look further, to the calling of the Gentiles and the discipling of all nations by the gospel of Christ, of whom it is said that all kings shall fall down before him, Ps. lxxii. 11.

6-8 God's care of His people.
David here comforts himself with three things:
I. The favor God bears to his humble people (v. 6): Though the Lord be high, and neither needs any of his creatures nor can be benefited by them, yet has he respect unto the lowly.
II. The care God takes of his afflicted oppressed people, v. 7. David, though a great and good man, expects to walk in the midst of trouble, but encourages himself with hope,
1. That God would comfort him: "When my spirit is ready to sink and fail, thou shalt revive me, and make me easy and cheerful under my troubles."
2. That he would protect him, and plead his cause.
III. The assurance we have that whatever good work God has begun in and for his people he will perform it (v. 8): The Lord will perfect that which concerns me,
1. That which is most needful for me.
2. That which we are most concerned about. Every good man is most concerned about his duty to God and his happiness in God. Our hopes that we shall persevere must be founded, not upon our own strength, for that will fail us, but upon the mercy of God, for that will not fail.

Psalm 139

Title
To the chief Musician. A Psalm of David.

1-8
1 O lord, thou hast searched me, and known me.
2 Thou knowest my downsitting and mine uprising, thou understandest my thought afar off.
3 Thou compassest my path and my lying down, and art acquainted with all my ways.
4 For there is not a word in my tongue, but, lo, O LORD, thou knowest it altogether.
5 Thou hast beset me behind and before, and laid thine hand upon me.
6 Such knowledge is too wonderful for me; it is high, I cannot attain unto it.
7 Whither shall I go from thy spirit? or whither shall I flee from thy presence?
8 If I ascend up into heaven, thou art there: if I make my bed in hell, behold, thou art there.

Psalm 139

One of the most notable of the sacred hymns. It sings the omniscience and omnipresence of God, inferring from these the overthrow of the powers of wickedness, since he who sees and hears the abominable deeds and words of the rebellious will surely deal with them according to his justice. The brightness of this Psalm is like unto a sapphire stone, or Ezekiel's "terrible crystal"; it flames out with such flashes of light as to turn night into day. Like a Pharos, this holy song casts a clear light even to the uttermost parts of the sea, and warns its against that practical atheism which ignores the presence of God, and so makes shipwreck of the soul.
TITLE. To the Chief Musician. The fast time this title occurred was in Ps 109:1-31. This sacred song is worthy of the most excellent of the singers, and is fitly dedicated to the leader of the Temple Psalmody, that he might set it to music, and see that it was devoutly sung in the solemn worship of the Most High. A Psalm of David. It bears the image and superscription of King David, and could have come from no other mint than that of the son of Jesse. Of course the critics take this composition away from David, on account of certain Aramaic expressions in it. We believe that upon the principles of criticism now in vogue it would be extremely easy to prove that Milton did not write Paradise Lost. We have yet to learn that David could not have used expressions belonging to "the language of the patriarchal ancestral house." Who knows how much of the antique speech may have been purposely retained among those nobler minds who rejoiced in remembering the descent of their race? Knowing to what wild inferences the critics have run in other matters, we have lost nearly all faith in them, and prefer to believe David to be the author of this Psalm, from internal evidences of style and matter, rather than to accept the determination of men whose modes of judgment are manifestly unreliable.

EXPOSITION
Verse 1. O LORD, thou hast searched me, and known me. He invokes in adoration Jehovah the all knowing God, and he proceeds to adore him by proclaiming one of his peculiar attributes. The divine knowledge is extremely thorough and searching; it is as if he had searched us, as officers search a man for contraband goods.
Verse 2. Thou knowest my downsitting and mine uprising. Me thou knowest, and all that comes of me. I am observed when I quietly sit down, and marked when I resolutely rise up. My most common and casual acts, my most needful and necessary movements, are noted by time, and thou knowest the inward thoughts which regulate them.
Verse 3. Thou compassest my path and my lying down. My path and my pallet, my running and my resting, are alike within the circle of thine observation.
Verse 4. For there is not a word in my tongue, but lo, O LORD, thou knowest it altogether. The unformed word, which lies within the tongue like a seed in the soil, is certainly and completely known to the Great Searcher of hearts.
Verse 5. Thou hast beset me behind and before. As though we were caught in an ambush, or besieged by an army which has wholly beleaguered the city walls, we are surrounded by the Lord. God has set us where we be, and beset us wherever we be. Behind us there is God recording our sins, or in grace blotting out the remembrance of them; and before us there is God foreknowing all our deeds, and providing for all our wants.
Verse 6. Such knowledge is too wonderful for me. I cannot grasp it. I can hardly endure to think of it. The theme overwhelms me. I am amazed and astounded at it. Such knowledge not only surpasses my comprehension, but even my imagination.
Verse 7. Here omnipresence is the theme,—a truth to which omniscience naturally leads up. Whither shall I go from thy spirit? Not that the Psalmist

JOHN CALVIN

Psalm 139

1-6
1. O Jehovah! thou hast searched me. David declares, in the outset of this Psalm, that he does not come before God with any idea of its being possible to succeed by dissimulation, as hypocrites will take advantage of secret refuges to prosecute sinful indulgences, but that he voluntarily lays bare his innermost heart for inspection, as one convinced of the impossibility of deceiving God. It is thine, he says, O God! to discover every secret thought, nor is there anything which can escape thy notice, He then insists upon particulars, to show that his whole life was known to God, who watched him in all his motions—when he slept, when he arose, or when he walked abroad.
4. For there is not a word, etc. The words admit a double meaning. Accordingly some understand them to imply that God knows what, we are about to say before the words are formed on our tongue; others, that though we speak not a word, and try by silence to conceal our secret intentions, we cannot elude his notice. Either rendering amounts to the same thing, and it is of no consequence which we adopt. The idea meant to be conveyed is, that while the tongue is the index of thought to man. being the great medium of communication, God, who knows the heart, is independent of words. And use is made of the demonstrative particle lo! to indicate emphatically that the innermost recesses of our spirit stand present to his view.
5. One who finds the way blocked up turns back; but David found himself hedged in behind as well as before. God by his hand, laid as it were upon men, holds them strictly under his inspection, so that they cannot move a hair's breadth without his knowledge.
6. Thy knowledge is wonderful above me. David exclaims against the folly of measuring God's knowledge by our own, when it rises prodigiously above us. Many when they hear God spoken of conceive of him as like unto themselves, and such presumption is most condemnable.

7-12
7. Whither shall I go from thy Spirit? I consider that David prosecutes the same idea of its being impossible that men by any subterfuge should elude the eye of God. By the Spirit of God we are not here, as in several other parts of Scripture, to conceive of his power merely, but his understanding and knowledge. In man the spirit is the seat of intelligence, and so it is here in reference to God, as is plain from the second part of the sentence, where by the face of God is meant his knowledge or inspection. David means in short that he could not change from one place to another without God seeing him, and following him with his eyes as he moved.
11. If I shall say, etc. David represents himself as a man using every possible method to make his escape from a situation of embarrassment. So having acknowledged that it was vain to dream of flight, he bethinks himself of another remedy, and says, If no speed of mine can bear me out of the range of

MATTHEW HENRY

Psalm 139

1-6 The omniscience of God.
David here lays down this great doctrine, That the God with whom we have to do has a perfect knowledge of us, and that all the motions and actions both of our inward and of our outward man are naked and open before him.
I. He lays down this doctrine in the way of an address to God; he says it to him, acknowledging it to him, and giving him the glory of it. Divine truths look fully as well when they are prayed over as when they are preached over, and much better than when they are disputed over. When we speak of God to him himself we shall find ourselves concerned to speak with the utmost degree both of sincerity and reverence, which will be likely to make the impressions the deeper.
II. He lays it down in a way of application to himself, not, "Thou hast known all," but, "Thou hast known me; that is it which I am most concerned to believe and which it will be most profitable for me to consider."
III. He descends to particulars: "Thou knowest me wherever I am and whatever I am doing, me and all that belongs to me."
1. "Thou knowest me and all my motions, my down-sitting to rest, my up-rising to work, with what temper of mind I compose myself when I sit down and stir up myself when I rise up, what my soul reposes itself in as its stay and support, what it aims at and reaches towards as its felicity and end."
2. "Thou knowest all my imaginations. Nothing is more close and quick than thought; it is always unknown to others; it is often unobserved by ourselves, and yet thou understandest my thought afar off. "
3. "Thou knowest me and all my designs and undertakings; thou compassest every particular path; thou siftest (or winnowest) my path" (so some), "so as thoroughly to distinguish between the good and evil of what I do," as by sifting we separate between the corn and the chaff.
4. "Thou knowest me in all my retirements; thou knowest my lying down; when I am withdrawn from all company, and am reflecting upon what has passed all day and composing myself to rest, thou knowest what I have in my heart and with what thought I go to bed."
5. "Thou knowest me, and all I say (v. 4): There is not a word in my tongue, not a vain word, nor a good word, but thou knowest it altogether, knowest what it meant, from what thought it came, and with what design it was uttered. There is not a word at my tongue's end, ready to be spoken, yet checked and kept in, but thou knowest it."
6. "Thou knowest me in every part of me.
IV. He speaks of it with admiration (v. 6): It is too wonderful for me; it is high. "Thou hast such a knowledge of me as I have not of myself, nor can have. I cannot take notice of all my own thoughts, nor

Psalm 139

9-16

9 If I take the wings of the morning, and dwell in the uttermost parts of the sea;
10 Even there shall thy hand lead me, and thy right hand shall hold me.
11 If I say, Surely the darkness shall cover me; even the night shall be light about me.
12 Yea, the darkness hideth not from thee; but the night shineth as the day: the darkness and the light are both alike to thee.
13 For thou hast possessed my reins: thou hast covered me in my mother's womb.
14 I will praise thee; for I am fearfully and wonderfully made: marvelous are thy works; and that my soul knoweth right well.
15 My substance was not hid from thee, when I was made in secret, and curiously wrought in the lowest parts of the earth.
16 Thine eyes did see my substance, yet being unperfect; and in thy book all my members were written, which in continuance were fashioned, when as yet there was none of them.

wished to go from God, or to avoid the power of the divine life; but he asks this question to set forth the fact that no one can escape from the all pervading being and observation of the Great Invisible Spirit.

Verse 8. If I ascend up into heaven, thou art there. Filling the loftiest region with his yet loftier presence, Jehovah is in the heavenly place, at home, upon his throne. The ascent, if it were possible, would be unavailing for purposes of escape.

Verse 9. If I take the wings of the morning, and dwell in the uttermost parts of the sea. If I could fly with all swiftness, and find a habitation where the mariner has not yet ploughed the deep, yet I could not reach the boundaries of the divine presence.

Verse 10. Even there shall thy hand lead me. We could only fly from God by his own power. The Lord would be leading, covering, preserving, sustaining us even when we were fugitives from him.

Verse 11. If I say, Surely the darkness shall cover me. Dense darkness may oppress me, but it cannot shut me out from thee, or thee from me. Thou seest as well without the light as with it, since thou art not dependent upon light which is thine own creature, for the full exercise of thy perceptions.

Verse 12. Yea, of a surety, beyond all denial. The darkness hideth not from thee; it veils nothing, it is not the medium of concealment in any degree what ever. It hides from men, but not from God. But the night shineth as the day: it is but another form of day: it shines, revealing all; it "shineth as the day,"—quite as clearly and distinctly manifesting all that is done.

Verse 13. For thou hast possessed my reins. Thou art the owner of my inmost parts and passions: not the indweller and observer only, but the acknowledged lord and possessor of my most secret self. The word "reins" signifies the kidneys, which by the Hebrews were supposed to be the seat of the desires and longings; but perhaps it indicates here the most hidden and vital portion of the man.

Verse 14. I will praise thee: a good resolve, and one which he was even now carrying out. Those who are praising God are the very men who will praise him. Those who wish to praise have subjects for adoration ready to hand.

Verse 15. My substance was not hid from thee. The substantial part of my being was before thine all seeing eye; the bones which make my frame were put together by thine hand. The essential materials of my being before they were arranged were all within the range of thine eye.

Verse 16. Thine eyes did see my substance, yet being unperfect. While as yet the vessel was upon the wheel the Potter saw it all. The Lord knows not only our shape, but our substance: this is substantial knowledge indeed. The Lord's observation of us is intent and intentional.

Verse 17. How precious also are thy thoughts unto me, O God! He is not alarmed at the fact that God knows all about him; on the contrary, he is comforted, and even feels himself to be enriched, as with a casket of precious jewels. That God should think upon him is the believer's treasure and pleasure.

Verse 18. If I should count them, they are more in number than the sand. This figure shows the thoughts of God to be altogether innumerable; for nothing can surpass in number the grains of sand which belt the main ocean and all the minor seas. The task of counting God's thoughts of love would be a never ending one. If we should attempt the reckoning we must necessarily fail, for the infinite falls not within the line of our feeble intellect. Even could we count the sands on the seashore, we should not then be able to number God's thoughts, for they are "more in number than the sand." This is not the hyperbole of poetry, but the solid fact of inspired statement: God thinks upon us infinitely: there is a limit to the act of creation, but not to the might of divine love.

Verse 19. Surely thou wilt slay the wicked, O God. There can be no doubt upon that head, for thou hast seen all their transgressions, which indeed have been done in thy presence; and thou hast long enough endured their

God's vision, yet, on the supposition of light being removed, the darkness might cover me, that I might have a short breath of respite. But this also he declares to be hopeless, as God sees equally well in the deepest darkness as at noon-day.

13-16

13. For thou hast possessed my reins. Apparently he prosecutes the same subject, though he carries it out somewhat farther, declaring that we need not be surprised at God's knowledge of the most secret thoughts of men, since he formed their hearts.

15. My strength was not hid from thee. That nothing is hid from God David now begins to prove from the way in which man is at first formed, and points out God's superiority to other artificers in this, that while they must have their work set before their eyes before they can form it, he fashioned us in our mother's womb. He next likens the womb of the mother to the lowest caverns or recesses of the earth. Should an artisan intend commencing a work in some dark cave where there was no light to assist him, how would he set his hand to it. In what way would he proceed? And what kind of workmanship would it prove? But God makes the most perfect work of all in the dark, for he fashions man in mother's womb.

16. Thine eyes beheld my shapelessness, etc. The embryo, when first conceived in the womb, has no form; and David speaks of God's having known him when he was yet a shapeless mass. The argument is from the greater to the less. If he was known to God before he had grown to certain definite shape, much less could he now elude his observation.

17-18

17. How precious also are thy thoughts unto me. The Psalmist is asserting the distinction between the righteous and the wicked. The context requires that he should still be considered as speaking of the matchless excellence of divine providence. He therefore repeats—and not without reason—what he had said before; for we apparently neglect or underestimate the singular proofs of the deep wisdom of God, exhibited in man's creation, and the whole superintendence and government of his life.

19-24

19. If thou shalt slay, etc. The sentiment seems to me that David would apply himself to the consideration of the divine judgments, and advance in godliness and in the fear of his name, so often as vengeance was taken upon the ungodly. There can be no question that God designs to make an example of them, that his elect ones may be taught by their punishment to withdraw themselves from their society. David was of himself well disposed to the fear and worship of God, and yet he needed a certain check, like other saints, as Isaiah says, (Isaiah 26:9,) "when God has sent abroad his judgments, the inhabitants of the earth shall learn righteousness," that is, to remain in the fear of the Lord. At the same time, I have no doubt that the Psalmist presents himself before God as witness of his integrity; as if he had said, that he came freely and

make such a judgment of myself as thou makest of me."

7-16 The omniscience of God.

It is of great use to us to know the certainty of the things wherein we have been instructed, that we may not only believe them, but be able to tell why we believe them, and to give a reason of the hope that is in us. David is sure that God perfectly knows him and all his ways,

I. Because he is always under his eye. David here acknowledges this also with application and sees himself thus open before God.

1. No flight can remove us out of God's presence: "Whither shall I go from thy Spirit, from thy presence, that is, from thy spiritual presence, from thyself, who art a Spirit?"

2. No veil can hide us from God's eye, no, not that of the thickest darkness, v. 11, 12. "If I say, Yet the darkness shall cover me, when nothing else will, alas! I find myself deceived; the curtains of the evening will stand me in no more stead than the wings of the morning; even the night shall be light about me. That which often favors the escape of a pursued criminal, and the retreat of a beaten army, will do me no kindness in fleeing from them."

II. Because he is the work of his hands. He that framed the engine knows all the motions of it. God made us, and therefore no doubt he knows us; he saw us when we were in the forming, and can we be hidden from him now that we are formed? This argument he insists upon (v. 13-16). Concerning the formation of man, of each of us,

1. The glory of it is here given to God, entirely to him; for it is he that has made us and not we ourselves. "I will praise thee, the author of my being; my parents were only the instruments of it." It was done,

(1.) Under the divine inspection.

(2.) By the divine operation. As the eye of God saw us then, so his hand wrought us; we were his work.

(3.) According to the divine model: In thy book all my members were written. Eternal wisdom formed the plan, and by that almighty power raised the noble structure.

2. Glorious things are here said concerning it. The generation of man is to be considered with the same pious veneration as his creation at first. Consider it,

(1.) As a great marvel, a great miracle we might call it, but that it is done in the ordinary course of nature.

(2.) As a great mystery, a mystery of nature: My soul knows right well that it is marvelous, but how to describe it for any one else I know not.

(3.) As a great mercy, that all our members in continuance were fashioned, according as they were written in the book of God's wise counsel, when as yet there was none of them; or, as some read it, and none of them was left out.

Psalm 139

17-24

17 How precious also are thy thoughts unto me, O God! how great is the sum of them!
18 If I should count them, they are more in number than the sand: when I awake, I am still with thee.
19 Surely thou wilt slay the wicked, O God: depart from me therefore, ye bloody men.
20 For they speak against thee wickedly, and thine enemies take thy name in vain.
21 Do not I hate them, O LORD, that hate thee? and am not I grieved with those that rise up against thee?
22 I hate them with perfect hatred: I count them mine enemies.
23 Search me, O God, and know my heart: try me, and know my thoughts:
24 And see if there be any wicked way in me, and lead me in the way everlasting.

provocations, which have been so openly manifest before thee. Crimes committed before the face of the Judge are not likely to go unpunished.

Verse 20. For they speak against thee wickedly. Why should I bear their company when their talk sickens me? They vent their treasons and blasphemies as often as they please, doing so without the slightest excuse or provocation; let them therefore be gone, where they may find a more congenial associate than I can be.

Verse 21. Do not I hate them, O LORD, that hate thee? He was a good hater, for he hated only those who hated good. Of this hatred he is not ashamed, but he sets it forth as a virtue to which he would have the Lord bear testimony. To love all men with benevolence is our duty; but to love any wicked man with complacency would be a crime.

Verse 22. I hate them with perfect hatred. He does not leave it a matter of question. He does not occupy a neutral position. His hatred to bad, vicious, blasphemous men is intense, complete, energetic. He is as whole hearted in his hate of wickedness as in his love of goodness.

I count them mine enemies. He makes a personal matter of it. They may have done him no ill, but if they are doing despite to God, to his laws, and to the great principles of truth and righteousness, David proclaims war against them. Wickedness passes men into favor with unrighteous spirits; but it excludes them from the communion of the just.

Verse 23. Search me, O God, and know my heart. David is no accomplice with traitors. He has disowned them in set form, and now he appeals to God that he does not harbor a trace of fellowship with them. He will have God himself search him, and search him thoroughly, till every point of his being is known, and read, and understood; for he is sure that even by such an investigation there will be found in him no complicity with wicked men. He challenges the fullest investigation, the innermost search: he had need be a true man who can put himself deliberately into such a crucible. Yet we may each one desire such searching; for it would be a terrible calamity to us for sin to remain in our hearts unknown and undiscovered. Try me, and know my thoughts. Exercise any and every test upon me. By fire and by water let me be examined. Read not alone the desires of my heart, but the fugitive thoughts of my head. Know with all penetrating knowledge all that is or has been in the chambers of my mind. What a mercy that there is one being who can know us to perfection!

Verse 24. And see if there be any wicked way in me. See whether there be in my heart, or in my life, any evil habit unknown to myself. If there be such an evil way, take me from it, take it from me. No matter how dear the wrong may have become, nor how deeply prejudiced I may have been in its favor, be pleased to deliver me therefrom altogether, effectually, and at once, that I may tolerate nothing which is contrary to thy mind. As I hate the wicked in their way, so would I hate every wicked way in myself. And lead me in the way everlasting. If thou hast introduced me already to the good old way, be pleased to keep me in it, and conduct me further and further along it. It is a way which thou hast set up of old, it is based upon everlasting principles, and it is the way in which immortal spirits will gladly run for ever and ever. There will be no end to it world without end. It lasts for ever, and they who are in it last for ever.

ingenuously to God's bar, as not being one of the wicked despisers of his name, nor having any connection with them.
20. Who have spoken of thee wickedly. He intimates the extent to which the wicked proceed when God spares them, and forbears to visit them with vengeance. They not merely conclude that they may perpetrate any crime with impunity, but openly blaspheme their Judge. He takes notice of their speaking wickedly, in the sense of their taking no pains to disguise their sin under plausible pretences, as persons who have some shame remaining will exercise a certain restraint upon their language, but they make no secret of the contempt they entertain for God.
21. Shall I not hold in hatred those that hate thee? He proceeds to mention how greatly he had profited by the meditation upon God into which he had been led, for, as the effect, of his having realized his presence before God's bar, and reflected upon the impossibility of escaping the eye of him who searches all deep places, he now lays down his resolution to lead a holy and pious life. In declaring his hatred of those who despised God, he virtually asserts thereby his own integrity, not as being free from all sin, but as being devoted to godliness, so that he detested in his heart everything which was contrary to it.
22. I hate them with perfect hatred. Literally it is, I hate them with perfection of hatred. He repeats the same truth as formerly, that such was his esteem for God's glory that he would have nothing' in common with those who despised him. He means in general that he gave no countenance to the works of darkness, for whoever connives at sin and encourages it through silence, wickedly betrays God's cause, who has committed the vindication of righteousness into our hands. David's example should teach us to rise with a lofty and bold spirit above all regard to the enmity of the wicked, when the question concerns the honor of God, and rather to renounce all earthly friendships than falsely pander with flattery to the favor of those who do everything to draw down upon themselves the divine displeasure. We have the more need to attend to this, because the keen sense we have of what concerns our private interest, honor, and convenience, makes us never hesitate to engage in contest when any one injures ourselves, while we are abundantly timid and cowardly in defending the glory of God.
23. Search me, O God! He insists upon this as being the only cause why he opposed the despisers of God, that he himself was a genuine worshipper of God, and desired others to possess the same character. It indicates no common confidence that he should submit, himself so boldly to the judgment of God. But being fully conscious of sincerity in his religion, it was not without due consideration that he placed himself so confidently before God's bar; neither must we think that he claims to be free from all sin, for he groaned under the felt burden of his transgressions. The saints in all that they say of their integrity still depend only upon free grace.
24. And lead me, etc. God will watch over his servant to whom he had already shown kindness to the end, and not forsake him in the midst of his days.

17-24 The omniscience of God.
Here the psalmist makes application of the doctrine of God's omniscience, divers ways.
I. He acknowledges, with wonder and thankfulness, the care God had taken of him all his days, v. 17, 18. God, who knew him, thought of him, and his thoughts towards him were thoughts of love, thoughts of good, and not of evil, Jer. xxix. 11. God's omniscience, which might justly have watched over us to do us hurt, has been employed for us, and has watched over us to do us good, Jer. xxxi. 28. God's counsels concerning us and our welfare have been,
II. He concludes from this doctrine that ruin will certainly be the end of sinners. God knows all the wickedness of the wicked, and therefore he will reckon for it: "Surely thou wilt slay the wicked, O God! for all their wickedness is open before thee, however it may be artfully disguised and colored over, to hide it from the eye of the world. However thou suffer them to prosper for a while, surely thou wilt slay them at last." Now observe,
1. The reason why God will punish them, because they daringly affront him and set him at defiance (v. 20): They speak against thee wickedly; they set their mouth against the heavens (Ps. lxxiii. 9), and shall be called to account for the hard speeches they have spoken against him, Jude 15.
2. The use David makes of this prospect which he has of the ruin of the wicked.
(1.) He defies them: "Depart from me, you bloody men; you shall not debauch me, for I will not admit your friendship nor have fellowship with you; and you cannot destroy me, for, being under God's protection, he shall force you to depart from me."
(2.) He detests them (v. 21, 22): "Lord, thou knowest the heart, and canst witness for me; do not I hate those that hate thee, and for that reason, because they hate thee? I hate them because I love thee, and hate to see such affronts and indignities put upon thy blessed name. Am not I grieved with those that rise up against thee, grieved to see their rebellion and to foresee their ruin, which it will certainly end in?"
III. He appeals to God concerning his sincerity, v. 23, 24.
1. He desires that as far as he was in the wrong God would discover it to him. Those that are upright can take comfort in God's omniscience as a witness of their uprightness, and can with a humble confidence beg of him to search and try them, to discover them to themselves and to discover them to others. He that means honestly could wish he had a window in his breast that any man may look into his heart.
2. He desires that, as far as he was in the right, he might be forwarded in it, which he that knows the heart knows how to do effectually: Lead me in the way everlasting.

Psalm 140

Title
To the chief Musician. A Psalm of David.

1-6
1 Deliver me, O LORD, from the evil man: preserve me from the violent man;
2 Which imagine mischiefs in their heart; continually are they gathered together for war.
3 They have sharpened their tongues like a serpent; adders' poison is under their lips. Selah.
4 Keep me, O LORD, from the hands of the wicked; preserve me from the violent man; who have purposed to overthrow my goings.
5 The proud have hid a snare for me, and cords; they have spread a net by the wayside; they have set gins for me. Selah.
6 I said unto the LORD, Thou art my God: hear the voice of my supplications, O LORD.

Psalm 140

This Psalm is in its proper place, and so fitly follows 139 that you might almost read right on, and make no break between the two. Serious injury would follow to the whole Book of Psalms if the order should be interfered with as certain wiseacres propose. It is The Cry Of A Hunted Soul the supplication of a believer incessantly persecuted and beset by cunning enemies, who hungered for his destruction. David was hunted like a partridge upon the mountains, and seldom obtained a moment's rest. This is his pathetic appeal to Jehovah for protection, an appeal which gradually intensifies into a denunciation of his bitter foes. With this sacrifice of prayer he offers the salt of faith; for in a very marked and emphatic manner he expresses his personal confidence in the Lord as the Protector of the oppressed, and as his own God and Defender. Few short Psalms are so rich in the jewelery of precious faith.
TO THE CHIEF MUSICIAN. The writer wished this experimental hymn to be under the care of the chief master of song, that it might neither be left unsung, nor chanted in a slovenly manner. Such trials and such rescues deserved to be had in remembrance, and to be set up among the choicest memorials of the Lord's goodness. We, too, have our songs which are of no ordinary kind, and these must be sung with our best powers of heart and tongue. We will offer them to the Lord by no other hand than that of "the Chief Musician."
A PSALM OF DAVID. The life of David wherein he comes in contact with Saul and Doeg is the best explanation of this Psalm; and surely there can be no reasonable doubt that David wrote it, and wrote it in the time of his exile and peril. The tremendous outburst at the end has in it the warmth which was so natural to David, who was never lukewarm in anything; yet it is to be noticed that concerning his enemies he was often hot in language through indignation, and yet he was cool in action, for he was not revengeful. His was no petty malice, but a righteous anger: he foresaw, foretold, and even desired the just vengeance of God upon the proud and wicked, and yet he would not avail himself of opportunities to revenge himself upon those who had done him wrong. It may be that his appeals to the great King cooled his anger, and enabled him to leave his wrongs unredressed by any personal act of violence. "Vengeance is mine; I will repay, saith the Lord"; and David when most wounded by undeserved persecution and wicked falsehood was glad to leave his matters at the foot of the throne, where they would be safe with the King of kings.

EXPOSITION
Verse 1. Deliver me, O LORD, from the evil man. It reads like a clause of the Lord's prayer, "Deliver us from evil." David does not so much plead against an individual as against the species represented by him, namely, the being whose best description is—"the evil man."
Verse 2. Which imagine mischiefs in their heart. They cannot be happy unless they are plotting and planning, conspiring and contriving. They seem to have but one heart, for they are completely agreed in their malice; and with all their heart and soul they pursue their victim. One piece of mischief is not enough for them; they work in the plural, and prepare many arrows for their bow.
Verse 3. They have sharpened their tongues like a serpent. The rapid motion of a viper's tongue gives you the idea of its sharpening it; even thus do the malicious move their tongues at such a rate that one might suppose them to be in the very act of wearing them to a point, or rubbing them to a keen edge.
Verse 4. Keep me, O LORD, from the hands of the wicked. To fall into their hands would be a calamity indeed. David in his most pitiable plight chose to fall into the hand of a chastising God rather than to be left in the power of men.

JOHN CALVIN

Psalm 140

1-5
To the chief Musician, etc. I cannot bring myself to restrict this Psalm to Doeg, as the great body of interpreters do, for the context will clearly show that it speaks of Saul, and of the counselors who ceased not to inflame the king—himself sufficiently incensed against the life of one who was a saint of God. Being as he was a figure of Christ, we need not wonder that the agents of the devil directed so much of their rage against him.
2. Who imagine mischief's in their heart. Here he charges them with inward malignity of heart. And it is plain that the reference is not to one man merely, for he passes to the plural number (in a manner sufficiently common,) reverting from the head to all his associates and copartners in guilt. Indeed what was formerly said in the singular number may be taken indefinitely, as grammarians say. In general he repeats that the hostility to which he was subjected arose from no cause of his. From this we learn that the more wickedly our enemies assail us, and the more of treachery and clandestine acts they manifest, the nearer is the promised aid of the Holy Spirit, who himself dictated this form of prayer by the mouth of David.
4. Keep me, O Jehovah! To complaints and accusations he now again adds prayer, from which it appears more clearly, as I observed already, that it is God whom he seeks to be his avenger. It is the same sentiment repeated, with one or two words changed; for he had said deliver me, now he says keep me, and for the wicked man he substitutes the hand of the wicked. He had spoken of their conceiving mischief, now of their plotting how they might ruin a poor unsuspecting individual. What he had said of their fraud and deceit he repeats in figurative language, which does not want emphasis. He speaks of nets spread out on every side to circumvent him, unless God interposed for his help.

6-10
6. I said to Jehovah. In these words he shows that his prayers were not merely those of the lips, as hypocrites will make loud appeals to God for mere appearance sake, but that he prayed with earnestness, and from a hidden principle of faith. Till we have a persuasion of being saved through the grace of God there can be no sincere prayer. We have here an excellent illustration of the nature of faith, in the Psalmist's turning himself away from man's view, that he may address God apart, hypocrisy being excluded in this internal exercise of the heart. This is true prayer—not the mere idle lifting up of the voice, but the presentation of our petitions from an inward principle of faith.
8. Grant not, O Jehovah! the desires of the wicked. We might render the words, Establish not, though the meaning would be the same—that God would restrain the desires of the wicked, and frustrate all their aims and attempts. We see from this that it is in his power, whenever he sees proper, to frustrate the unprincipled designs of men, and their wicked expectations, and to dash their schemes. When, therefore, it

MATTHEW HENRY

Psalm 140

1-7 Complaints and petitions.
In this, as in other things, David was a type of Christ, that he suffered before he reigned, was humbled before he was exalted, and that as there were many who loved and valued him, and sought to do him honor, so there were many who hated and envied him, and sought to do him mischief, as appears by these verses, where,
I. He gives a character of his enemies, and paints them out in their own colors, as dangerous men, whom he had reason to be afraid of, but wicked men, whom he had no reason to think the righteous God would countenance. There was one that seems to have been the ring-leader of them, whom he calls the evil man and the man of violence (v. 1, 4), probably he means Saul. The Chaldee paraphrased (v. 9) names both Doeg and Ahithophel; but between them there was a great distance of time. Violent men are evil men. But there were many besides this one who were confederate against David, who are here represented as the genuine offspring and seed of the serpent. For,
1. They are very subtle, crafty to do mischief; they have imagined it (v. 2), have laid the scheme with all the art and cunning imaginable. They have purposed and plotted to overthrow the goings of a good man (v. 4), to draw him into sin and trouble, to ruin him by blasting his reputation, crushing his interest, and taking away his life. For this purpose they have, like mighty hunters, hidden a snare, and spread a net, and set gins (v. 5), that their designs against him, being kept undiscovered, might be the more likely to take effect, and he might fall into their hands ere he was aware.
2. They are very spiteful, as full of malice as Satan himself: They have sharpened their tongues like a serpent, that infuses his venom with his tongue; and there is so much malignity in all they say that one would think there was nothing under their lips but adders' poison, v. 3.
3. They are confederate; they are many of them; but they are all gathered together against me for war, v. 2.
4. They are proud (v. 5), conceited of themselves and confident of their success; and herein also they resemble Satan, whose reigning ruining sin was pride.
II. He prays to God to keep him from them and from being swallowed up by them: "Lord, deliver me, preserve me, keep me (v. 1, 4); let them not prevail to take away my life, my reputation, my interest, my comfort, and to prevent my coming to the throne. Keep me from doing as they do, or as they would have me do, or as they promise themselves I shall do."
III. He triumphs in God, and thereby, in effect, he triumphs over his persecutors, v. 6, 7. When his

Psalm 140

7-13

7 O GOD the Lord, the strength of my salvation, thou hast covered my head in the day of battle.
8 Grant not, O LORD, the desires of the wicked: further not his wicked device; lest they exalt themselves. Selah.

9 As for the head of those that compass me about, let the mischief of their own lips cover them.
10 Let burning coals fall upon them: let them be cast into the fire; into deep pits, that they rise not up again.
11 Let not an evil speaker be established in the earth: evil shall hunt the violent man to overthrow him.
12 I know that the LORD will maintain the cause of the afflicted, and the right of the poor.
13 Surely the righteous shall give thanks unto thy name: the upright shall dwell in thy presence.

Verse 5. The proud have hid a snare for me. Proud as they are, they stoop to this mean action: they use a snare, and they hide it away, that their victim may be taken like a poor hare who is killed without warning—killed in its usual run, by a snare which it could not see.
Verse 6. I said unto the LORD, Thou art my God. Here was David's stay and hope. He was assured that Jehovah was his God, he expressed that assurance, and he expressed it before Jehovah himself.
Verse 7. O God the Lord, the strength of my salvation, thou hast covered my head in the day of battle. When he looked back upon past dangers and deliverances, the good man felt that he should have perished had not the Lord held a shield over his head.
Verse 8. Grant not, O LORD, the desires of the wicked. Even they are dependent upon thee they can do no more than thou dost permit. Thou dost restrain them; not a dog of them can move his tongue without thy leave and license.
Verse 9. As for the head of those that compass me about, let the mischief of their own lips cover them. To the Lord who had covered his head amid the din of arms the Psalmist appeals against his foes, that their heads may be covered in quite another sense—covered with the reward of their own malice.
Verse 10. Let burning coals fall upon them. Then will they know that the scattering of the firebrands is not the sport they thought it to be. When hailstones and coals of fire descend upon them, how will they escape? Even the skies above the wicked are able to deal out vengeance upon them.
Verse 11. Let not an evil speaker be established in the earth. For that would be an established plague, a perpetual curse. Men of false and cruel tongues are of most use when they go to fatten the soil in which they rot as carcases: while they are alive they are the terror of the good, and the torment of the poor. God will not allow the specious orators of falsehood to retain the power they temporarily obtain by their deceitful speaking.
Verse 12. I know that the Lord will maintain the cause of the afflicted, and, the right of the poor. All through the Psalm the writer is bravely confident, and speaks of things about which he had no doubt: in fact, no Psalm can be more grandly positive than this protest against slander. The slandered saint knew Jehovah's care for the afflicted, for lie had received actual proofs of it himself. "I will maintain it" is the motto of the great Defender of the rights of the needy. What confidence this should create within the bosoms of the persecuted and poverty stricken! The prosperous and wealthy can maintain their own cause, but those who are otherwise shall find that God helps those who cannot help themselves. Many talk as if the poor had no rights worth noticing, but they will sooner or later find out their mistake when the Judge of all the earth begins to plead with them.
Verse 13. Surely the righteous shall give thanks unto thy name. The former Psalm had its "surely", but this is a more pleasing one. As surely as God will slay the wicked he will save the oppressed, and fill their hearts and mouths with praises. Whoever else may be silent, the righteous will give thanks; and whatever they may suffer, the matter will end ill their living through the trial, and magnifying the Lord for his delivering grace. On earth ere long, and in heaven for ever, the pure in heart shall sing unto the Lord. How loud and sweet will be the songs of the redeemed in the millennial age, when the meek shall inherit the earth, and delight themselves in the abundance of peace!

is found impracticable to bring our enemies to a right state of mind, we are to pray that the devices which they have imagined may be immediately overthrown and thwarted.
9. David prays they may be sunk into deep pits, whence they may never rise. God sometimes heals those whom he has smitten with great severity; David cuts off the reprobate from the hope of pardon, as knowing them to be beyond recovery. Had they been disposable to repentance, he would have been inclinable on his part to mercy.

11-13
11. The man of tongue, etc. Whether his enemies wrought by treachery, or by open violence, he looks forward to God as his deliverer. The figure drawn from hunting is expressive. The hunter, by spreading his toils on all sides, leaves no way of escape for the wild beast; and the ungodly cannot by any subterfuge elude the divine judgments. Mischief hunts them into banishment's, for the more they look for impunity and escape, they only precipitate themselves more certainly upon destruction.
12. I have known; that God, etc. There can be no question that David here seals or corroborates his prayer by turning his thoughts and discourse to the providential judgments of God, for, as I have already said, doubtful prayer is no prayer at all. He declares it to be a thing known and ascertained that God cannot but deliver the afflicted. As he may connive for a time, however, and suffer good and upright persons to be grievously tried, David suggests as consideration which may meet this temptation, that God does so advisedly, that he may relieve those who are in affliction, and recover those who are oppressed. He accordingly says in express words that he will be the judge of the poor and the afflicted. In this way does he encourage both others and himself under continued troubles, till the time proper for deliverance arrive, intimating that though he might be universally considered an object of pity in being exposed to the fury of the wicked, and in not being immediately delivered by the hand of God, he would not give way to despair, but remember that it was the very part of God to undertake the cause of the poor.

He infers (Psalm 140:13) that the righteous would give thanks to God, and be safe under his help. Though the godly may be silenced for a time, and through the force of trouble may not raise the praises of God, David expresses his conviction that what was taken away would be speedily restored, and they would celebrate the loving kindness of the Lord with joy and alacrity. As this is not easily believed in circumstances of trial, the already referred to is inserted. We must endeavor, though with a struggle, to rise to a confident persuasion, that however low they may be brought, the Lord's people will be restored to prosperity, and will soon sing his praises. The second clause of the verse gives the reason of their thanksgivings. He speaks of this as being the ground of the praises of the righteous, that they experience God's care of them, and concern for their salvation. For to dwell before God's face is to be cherished and sustained by his fatherly regards.

enemies sharpened their tongues against him, did he sharpen his against them? No; adders' poison was under their lips, but grace was poured into his lips, witness what he here said unto the Lord, for to him he looked, to him he directed himself, when he saw himself in so much danger, through the malice of his enemies: and it is well for us that we have a God to go to. He comforted himself,
1. In his interest in God.
2. In his access to God.

8-13 Shame and confusion of persecutors.
Here is the believing foresight David had,
I. Of the shame and confusion of persecutors.
1. Their disappointment. This he prays for (v. 8), that their lusts might not be gratified, their lust of ambition, envy, and revenge: "Grant not, O Lord! the desires of the wicked, but frustrate them; let them not see the ruin of my interest, which they so earnestly wish to see; but hear the voice of my supplications."
2. Their destruction. This he prays for (as we read it); but some choose to read it rather as a prophecy, and the original will bear it. If we take it as a prayer, that proceeds from a spirit of prophecy, which comes all to one. He foretells the ruin,
(1.) Of his own enemies: "As for those that compass me about, and seek my ruin," "The mischief of their own lips shall cover their heads (v. 9); the evil they have wished to me shall come upon themselves, their curses shall be blown back into their own faces, and the very designs which they have laid against me shall turn to their own ruin," Ps. vii. 15, 16.
(2.) Of all others that are like them, v. 11. Evil speakers must expect to be shaken, for they shall never be established in the earth. What is got by fraud and falsehood, by calumny and unjust accusation, will not prosper, will not last. Wealth gotten by vanity will be diminished.
II. Here is his foresight of the deliverance and comfort of the persecuted, v. 12, 13.
1. God will do those justice, in delivering them, who, being wronged, commit themselves to him: "I know that the Lord will maintain the just and injured cause of his afflicted people, and will not suffer might always to prevail against right, though it be but the right of the poor, who have but little that they can pretend a right to."
2. They will do him justice (if I may so speak), in ascribing the glory of their deliverance to him: "Surely the righteous shall give thanks unto thy name when they find their cause pleaded with jealousy and prosecuted with effect." The closing words, The upright shall dwell in thy presence, denote both God's favor to them and their duty to God: "They shall attend upon thee as servants that keep in the presence of their masters, both to do them honor and to receive their commands." This is true thanksgiving, even thanks living; and this use we should make of all our deliverance, we should serve God the more closely and cheerfully.

Psalm 141

Title
A Psalm of David

1-5
1 Lord, I cry unto thee: make haste unto me; give ear unto my voice, when I cry unto thee.
2 Let my prayer be set forth before thee as incense; and the lifting up of my hands as the evening sacrifice.
3 Set a watch, O LORD, before my mouth; keep the door of my lips.
4 Incline not my heart to any evil thing, to practice wicked works with men that work iniquity: and let me not eat of their dainties.
5 Let the righteous smite me; it shall be a kindness: and let him reprove me; it shall be an excellent oil, which shall not break my head: for yet my prayer also shall be in their calamities.

Psalm 141

TITLE. A Psalm, Of David. Yes, David under suspicion, half afraid to speak lest he should speak unadvisedly while trying to clear himself; David slandered and beset by enemies; David censured even by saints, and taking it kindly; David deploring the condition of the godly party of whom he was the acknowledged heard: David waiting upon God with confident expectation. The Psalm is one of a group of four, and it bears a striking likeness to the other three. Its meaning lies so deep as to be in places exceedingly obscure, yet even upon its surface it has dust of gold. In its commencement the psalm is lighted up with the evening glow as the incense rises to heaven; then comes a night of language whose meaning we cannot see; and this gives place to morning light in which our eyes are unto the Lord.
DIVISION. The Psalmist cries for acceptance in prayer (Ps 141:1-2); Then he begs to be kept as to his speech, preserved in heart and deed, and delivered from every sort of fellowship with the ungodly. He prefers to be rebuked by the gracious rather than to be flattered by the wicked, and consoles himself with the confident assurance that be will one day be understood by the godly party, and made to be a comfort to them (Ps 141:3-6). In the last verses the slandered saint represents the condition of the persecuted church, looks away to God and pleads for rescue from his cruel enemies, and for the punishment of his oppressors.

EXPOSITION
Verse 1. Lord, I cry unto thee. This is my last resort: prayer never fails me. My prayer is painful and feeble, and worthy only to be called a cry; but it is a cry unto Jehovah, and this ennobles it. I have cried unto thee, I still cry to thee, and I always mean to cry to thee. To whom else could I go? What else can I do? Others trust to themselves, but I cry unto thee. The weapon of all prayer is one which the believer may always carry with him, and use in every time of need.
Verse 2. Let my prayer be set forth before thee as incense. As incense is carefully prepared, kindled with holy fire, and devoutly presented unto God, so let my prayer be. We are not to look upon prayer as easy work requiring no thought. It needs to be "set forth"; what is more, it must be set forth "before the Lord," by a sense of his presence and a holy reverence for his name: neither may we regard all supplication as certain of divine acceptance, it needs to be set forth before the Lord "as incense," concerning the offering of which there were rules to be observed, otherwise it would be rejected of God.
Verse 3. Set a watch, O LORD, before my mouth. That mouth had been used in prayer, it would be a pity it should ever be defiled with untruth, or pride, or wrath; yet so it will become unless carefully watched, for these intruders are ever lurking about the door. David feels that with all his own watchfulness he may be surprised into sin, and so he begs the Lord himself to keep him. When Jehovah sets the watch the city is well guarded: when the Lord becomes the guard of our mouth the whole man is well garrisoned.
Verse 4. To practice wicked works with men that work iniquity. The way the heart inclines the life soon tends: evil things desired bring forth wicked things practiced. Unless the fountain of life is kept pure the streams of life will soon be polluted. Alas, there is great power in company: even good men are apt to be swayed by association; hence the fear that we may practice wicked works when we are with wicked workers. We must endeavor not to be with them lest we sin with them. It is bad when the heart goes the wrong way alone, worse when the life runs in the evil road alone; but it is apt to increase unto a high degree of ungodliness when the backslider runs the downward path with a whole horde of sinners around him. Our practice will be our perdition if it be evil: it is an aggravation of sin rather than an excuse

Psalm 141

Whatever may have been the immediate cause pressing David to pray in the manner he does in this Psalm, it is plain that his desire is through divine grace to check and bridle his spirit, under injuries of a causeless and unprovoked description, so as not to break out into retaliation and revenge, and return evil for evil. Having attained to the exercise of forbearance, he seeks that God would judge between him and his enemies.

1-4

1. O Jehovah! I have cried unto thee. From such a manner of praying, it is evident that David was laboring under no small trial, as he repeats his requests, and insists upon receiving help. Without venturing to say anything definite upon the point, we would not disapprove of the conjecture that this Psalm was written by David with reference to the persecutions he suffered from Saul. He teaches us by his example to make application immediately to God, and not be tempted, as wicked men are, to renounce prayer, and rely on other resources. He says that he cried to God, not to heaven or earth, to men or to fortune, and other vain objects, which are made mention of, in the first place at least, in such cases by the ungodly. If they do address themselves to God, it is with murmurs and complaints, howling rather than praying.

In the second verse the allusion is evidently to the legal ceremonies. At that time the prayers of God's people were according to his own appointment sanctified through the offering up of incense and sacrifices, and David depended upon this promise.

The lifting up of the hands, evidently means prayer. And we can easily suppose that David here as elsewhere repeats the same thing twice.

3. Set a watch, O Jehovah! upon my mouth. As David was liable to be hurt at the unbridled and unprincipled rage of his enemies, so as to be tempted to act in a manner that might not be justifiable, he prays for divine direction, and not that he might be kept back from manual violence merely, but that his tongue might be restrained from venting reproach, or words of complaint. Even persons of the most self-possessed temper, if unwarrantably injured, will some—times proceed to make retaliation, through their resenting the unbecoming conduct of their enemies. David prays accordingly that his tongue might be restrained by the Lord from uttering any word which was out of joint.

Next he seeks that his heart be kept back from every mischievous device that might issue in revenge. The words added—that I may not eat of their delicacies, are to be understood figuratively, as a petition that he might not be tempted by the prosperity which they enjoyed in sin to imitate their conduct.

5-7

5. Let the righteous smite me, etc. While Satan tempts the wicked by his allurements, they, at the same time, deceive one

Psalm 141

1-4 Fervent supplications.

Mercy to accept what we do well, and grace to keep us from doing ill, are the two things which we are here taught by David's example to pray to God for.

I. David loved prayer, and he begs of God that his prayers might be heard and answered, v. 1, 2. David cried unto God. His crying denotes fervency in prayer; he prayed as one in earnest. His crying to God denotes faith and fixedness in prayer. And what did he desire as the success of his prayer?

1. That God would take cognizance of it: "Give ear to my voice; let me have a gracious audience." Those that cry in prayer may hope to be heard in prayer, not for their loudness, but their liveliness.

2. That he would visit him upon it: Make haste unto me. Those that know how to value God's gracious presence will be importunate for it and humbly impatient of delays. He that believes does not make haste, but he that prays may be earnest with God to make haste.

3. That he would be well pleased with him in it, well pleased with his praying and the lifting up of his hands in prayer, which denotes both the elevation and enlargement of his desire and the out-goings of his hope and expectation, the lifting up of the hand signifying the lifting up of the heart, and being used instead of lifting up the sacrifices which were heaved and waved before the Lord. Prayer is a spiritual sacrifice; it is the offering up of the soul, and its best affections, to God.

II. David was in fear of sin, and he begs of God that he might be kept from sin, knowing that his prayers would not be accepted unless he took care to watch against sin. We must be as earnest for God's grace in us as for his favor towards us.

1. He prays that he might not be surprised into any sinful words (v. 3): "Set a watch, O Lord! before my mouth, and, nature having made my lips to be a door to my words, let grace keep that door, that no word may be suffered to go out which may in any way tend to the dishonor of God or the hurt of others." Nehemiah prayed to the Lord when he set a watch, and so must we, for without him the watchman waketh but in vain.

2. That he might not be inclined to any sinful practices (v. 4): "Incline not my heart to any evil thing; whatever inclination there is in me to sin, let it be not only restrained, but mortified, by divine grace." We have need to pray that we may neither be drawn in by any allurement nor driven on by any provocation to do any sinful thing.

3. That he might not be ensnared by any sinful pleasures: "Let me not eat of their dainties. Let me not join with them in their feasts and sports, lest thereby I be inveigled into their sins." Better is a dinner of herbs, out of the way of temptation, than a stalled ox in it.

Psalm 141

6-10

6 When their judges are overthrown in stony places, they shall hear my words; for they are sweet.

7 Our bones are scattered at the grave's mouth, as when one cutteth and cleaveth wood upon the earth.

8 But mine eyes are unto thee, O GOD the Lord: in thee is my trust; leave not my soul destitute.

9 Keep me from the snares which they have laid for me, and the gins of the workers of iniquity.

10 Let the wicked fall into their own nets, whilst that I withal escape.

for it to say that it is our custom and our habit. It is God's practice to punish all who make a practice of iniquity.

Verse 5. Let the righteous smite me; it shall be a kindness. He prefers the bitters of gracious company to the dainties of the ungodly. He would rather be smitten by the righteous than feasted by the wicked. He gives a permit to faithful admonition, he even invites it—"let the righteous smite me." When the ungodly smile upon us their flattery is cruel; when the righteous smite us their faithfulness is kind.

Verse 6. This is a verse of which the meaning seems far to seek. Does it refer to the righteous among the Israelites? We think so. David surely means that when their leaders fell never to rise again, they would then turn to him and take delight in listening to his voice. When their judges are overthrown in stony places, they shall hear my words; for they are sweet. And so they did: the death of Saul made all the best of the nation look to the son of Jesse as the Lord's anointed; his words became sweet to them.

Verse 7. David's case seemed hopeless: the cause of God in Israel was as a dead thing, even as a skeleton broken, and rotten, and shoveled out of the grave, to return as dust to its dust. Our bones are scattered at the grave's mouth. There seemed to be no life, no cohesion, no form, order, or headship among the godly party in Israel: Saul had demolished it, and scattered all its parts, so that it did not exist as an organized whole. David himself was like one of these dried bones, and the rest of the godly were in much the same condition. There seemed to be no vitality or union among the holy seed; but their cause lay at death's door.

Verse 8. But mine eyes are unto thee, O GOD the Lord. He looked upward and kept his eyes fixed there. He regarded duty more than circumstances; he considered the promise rather than the external providence; and he expected from God rather than from men. He did not shut his eyes in indifference or despair, neither did he turn them to the creature in vain confidence, but he gave his eyes to his God, and saw nothing to fear. Jehovah his Lord is also his hope.

Verse 9. Keep me from, the snares which they have laid for me. He had before asked, in Ps 141:3, that the door of his mouth might be kept; but his prayer now grows into "Keep me." He seems more in trouble about covert temptation than concerning open attacks. Brave men do not dread battle, but they hate secret plots. We cannot endure to be entrapped like unsuspecting animals; therefore we cry to the God of wisdom for protection. And the gins of the workers of iniquity. These evil workers sought to catch David in his speech or acts. This was in itself a piece of in equity, and so of a piece with the rest of their conduct. They were bad themselves, and they wished either to make him like themselves, or to cause him to seem so. If they could not catch the good man in one way, they would try another; snares and gins should be multiplied, for anyhow they were determined to work his ruin. Nobody could preserve David but the Omniscient and Omnipotent One: he also will preserve us.

Verse 10. Let the wicked fall into their own nets, whilst that I withal escape. It may not be a Christian prayer, but it is a very just one, and it takes a great deal of grace to refrain from crying Amen to it; in fact, grace does not work towards making us wish otherwise concerning the enemies of holy men. Do we not all wish the innocent to be delivered, and the guilty to reap the result of their own malice? Of course we do, if we are just men. There can be no wrong in desiring that to happen in our own case which we wish for all good men. Yet is there a more excellent way.

JOHN CALVIN

another by flattery, which leads David to declare, that he would much rather be awakened to his duty by the severe rod of reproof, than be seduced through pleasing falsehoods. Among those who hold religion in contempt no reproof is administered to one who has contracted any sin, and, therefore, if we have any concern for our spiritual safety we will connect ourselves with good men, who restore such as have fallen by upright admonition, and bring back those who have erred to the right way. It is not agreeable to corrupt nature to be reproved when we sin, but, David had brought himself to that degree of docility and self-denial which led him to consider no reproof distasteful which he knew to proceed from the spirit of kindness.

6. Their judges have been thrown down upon stony places. It appears to me that the sense of David would be made very plain by reading, When their judges have been cast down from the rock, or upon stony places, they shall hear my words. David, on perceiving the rage which the common people expressed towards him, as carried away through the influence of error and misrepresentation, lays the blame upon their leaders. When their power should be taken away, he is confident that the simple, who had been misled, would be brought to a right mind.

Casting from the rocks, or upon stony places, is a metaphorical expression in reference to the high and dignified position in which they were placed.

7. As one who breaketh, etc. Here David complains that his enemies were not satisfied with inflicting upon him one death—death of a common description—but must first mangle him, and those associated with him, and then cast them into the grave.

8-10

8. Because to thee, O Jehovah! etc. If we reflect upon what was comprehended under the previous figure of their bones being broken, his praying in such circumstances is just as if the torn fragments of a mangled corpse should cry unto God. This may give us some idea of the courage of David, who could continue to direct his eyes to God even under such overwhelming difficulties; this being the very part faith ought to discharge, in making us collected and composed when our senses would otherwise be confounded. Great a miracle as it would have been for God to have preserved them in life, when their bones were scattered abroad, it was a double miracle to support their minds in the firm persuasion of their not perishing.

9. Keep me, etc. He owns himself to be shut up in the snares of his enemies, unless set free by a higher hand. In praying to God under the straits to which he was reduced, he proves what a high estimate he formed of what his mercy could effect, as elsewhere he says, that the issues from death belong to him. (Psalm 68:20.) God often delays interposing, that the deliverance may be the more signal; and afterwards he makes the devices of the wicked to recoil upon their own heads.

What follows admits of two meanings. Many read, I shall always pass. But we may suppose the order of the words changed and read, until I pass. He prays that his enemies should be held in the snare till he is safe.

MATTHEW HENRY

5-10 Reproofs of the righteous; complaints and petitions.

Here,

I. David desires to be told of his faults. His enemies reproached him with that which was false, which he could not but complain of; yet, at the same time, he desired his friends would reprove him for that which was really amiss in him, particularly if there was any thing that gave the least color to those reproaches (v. 5): let the righteous smite me; it shall be a kindness.

1. We must desire to be reproved for whatever is amiss in us, or is done amiss by us: "Lord, put it into the heart of the righteous to smite me and reprove me. If my own heart does not smite me, as it ought, let my friend do it; let me never fall under that dreadful judgment of being let alone in sin."

2. We must account it a piece of friendship. We must not only bear it patiently, but take it as a kindness; for reproofs of instruction are the way of life (Prov. vi. 23), are means of good to us, to bring us to repentance for the sins we have committed, and to prevent relapses into sin.

II. David hopes his persecutors will, some time or other, bear to be told of their faults, as he was willing to be told of his (v. 6): "When their judges" (Saul and his officers who judged and condemned David, and would themselves be sole judges) "are overthrown in stony places, among the rocks in the wilderness, then they shall hear my words, for they are sweet."

III. David complains of the great extremity to which he and his friends were reduced (v. 7): Our bones are scattered at the grave's mouth, out of which they are thrown up, so long have we been dead.

IV. David casts himself upon God, and depends upon him for deliverance: "But my eyes are unto thee (v. 8); for, when the case is ever so deplorable, thou canst redress all the grievances. From thee I expect relief, bad as things are, and in thee is my trust." Those that have their eye towards God may have their hopes in him.

V. He prays that God would succor and relieve him as his necessity required.

1. That he would comfort him: "Leave not my soul desolate and destitute; still let me see where my help is."

2. That he would prevent the designs of his enemies against him (v. 9): "Keep me from being taken in the snare they have laid for me; give me to discover it and to evade it." Be the gin placed with ever so much subtlety, God can and will secure his people from being taken in it.

3. That God would, in justice, turn the designs of his enemies upon themselves, and, in mercy, deliver him from being ruined by them (v. 10): let the wicked fall into their own net, the net which, intentionally, they procured for me, but which, meritoriously, they prepared for themselves.

Psalm 142

Title
Maschil of David. A Prayer when he was in the cave.

1 I cried unto the LORD with my voice; with my voice unto the LORD did I make my supplication.
2 I poured out my complaint before him; I shewed before him my trouble.
3 When my spirit was overwhelmed within me, then thou knewest my path. In the way wherein I walked have they privily laid a snare for me.
4 I looked on my right hand, and beheld, but there was no man that would know me: refuge failed me; no man cared for my soul.
5 I cried unto thee, O LORD: I said, Thou art my refuge and my portion in the land of the living.
6 Attend unto my cry; for I am brought very low: deliver me from my persecutors; for they are stronger than I.
7 Bring my soul out of prison, that I may praise thy name: the righteous shall compass me about; for thou shalt deal bountifully with me.

Psalm 142

TITLE. Maschil of David. This Maschil is written for our instruction. It teaches us principally by example how to order our prayer in times of distress. Such instruction is among the most needful, practical, and effectual parts of our spiritual education. He who has learned how to pray has been taught the most useful of the arts and sciences. The disciples said unto the Son of David, "Lord, teach, us to pray"; and here David gives us a valuable lesson by recording his own experience as to supplication from beneath a cloud.

A Prayer when he was in the cave. He was in one of his many lurking places, either Engedi, Adullam, or some other lone cavern wherein he could conceal himself from Saul and his blood hounds. Caves make good closets for prayer; their gloom and solitude are helpful to the exercise of devotion. Had David prayed as much in his palace as he did in his cave, he might never have fallen into the act which brought such misery upon his later days. SUBJECT. There can be little doubt that this song dates from the days when Saul was sorely persecuting David, and David himself was in soul trouble, probably produced by that weakness of faith which led him to associate with heathen princes. His fortunes were evidently at their lowest, and, what was worse, his repute had fearfully fallen; yet he displayed a true faith in God, to whom he made known his pressing sorrows. The gloom of the cave is over the psalm, and yet as if standing at the mouth of it the prophet poet sees a bright light a little beyond.

EXPOSITION

Verse 1. I cried unto the LORD with my voice. It was a cry of such anguish that he remembers it long after, and makes a record of it. In the loneliness of the cave he could use his voice as much as he pleased; and therefore he made its gloomy vaults echo with his appeals to heaven.

Verse 2. I poured out my complaint before him. His inward meditation filled his soul: the bitter water rose up to the brim; what was to be done?

Verse 3. When my spirit was overwhelmed within me, then thou knewest my path. The bravest spirit is sometimes sorely put to it. A heavy fog settles down upon the mind, and the man seems drowned and smothered in it; covered with a cloud, crushed with a load, confused with difficulties, conquered by impossibilities.

Verse 4. I looked on my right hand, and beheld, but there was no man that would know me. He did not miss a friend for want of looking for him, nor for want of looking in a likely place.

Verse 5. I cried unto thee, O Lord. As man would not regard him, David was driven to Jehovah, his God. Was not this a gain made out of a loss? Wealth gained by a failure? Anything which leads us to cry unto God is a blessing to us.

Verse 6. Attend unto my cry. Men of God look upon prayer as a reality, and they are not content without having an audience with God; moreover, they have such confidence in the Lord's condescending grace, that they hope he will even attend to that poor broken prayer which can only be described as a cry.

Verse 7. Bring my soul out of prison, that I may praise thy name. That God may be glorified is another notable plea for a suppliant. Escaped prisoners are sure to speak well of those who give them liberty; Soul emancipation is the noblest form of liberation, and calls for the loudest praise: he who is delivered from the dungeons of despair is sure to magnify the name of the Lord. We are in such a prison that only God himself can bring us out of it, and when he does so he will put a new song into our mouths.

JOHN CALVIN

Psalm 142

1-4
1. I cried to Jehovah, etc. It showed singular presence of mind in David that he was not paralyzed with fear, or that he did not in a paroxysm of fury take vengeance upon his enemy, as he easily might have done; and that he was not actuated by despair to take away his life, but composedly addressed himself to the exercise of prayer.

He tells us still more clearly in the next verse that he disburdened his ears unto God. To pour out one's thoughts and tell over his afflictions implies the reverse of those perplexing anxieties which men brood over inwardly to their own distress, and by which they torture themselves, and are chafed by their afflictions rather than led to God; or it implies the reverse of those frantic exclamations to which others give utterance who find no comfort in the superintending providence and care of God.

3. When, my spirit, etc. Though he owns here that he felt anxiety, yet he confirms what he had said as to the constancy of his faith. The figure which he uses of his spirit being perplexed, aptly represents the state of the mind in alternating between various resolutions when there was no apparent escape from danger, and increasing its distress by resorting to all kinds of devices.

4. On looking to the right hand, etc. He shows that there was good cause for the dreadful sufferings he experienced, since no human aid or comfort was to be expected, and destruction seemed inevitable.

When he speaks of having looked and yet not perceived a friend amongst men, he does not mean that he had turned his thoughts to earthly helps in forgetfulness of God, but that he had made such inquiry as was warrantable after one on the earth who might assist him. Had any person of the kind presented himself, he would no doubt have recognized him as an instrument in the hand of God's mercy, but it was God's purpose that he should be abandoned of all assistance from man, and that his deliverance from destruction should thus appear more extraordinary. In the expression, none seeking after my soul, the verb to seek after is used in a good sense, for being solicitous about any man's welfare or safety.

5-7
5. I cried unto thee, O Jehovah! With a view to hasten God's interposition, David complains of the low estate he was reduced to, and of his extremity; the term cry denoting vehemence.

He speaks of deliverance as being plainly needed, since he was now held a prisoner. By prison some suppose he alludes to the cave where he was lodged, but this is too restricted a meaning.

The sense which I have adopted is the simplest: That the mercy vouchsafed would be shown conspicuously to all as in a theater, proving a signal example to the righteous for establishment of their faith. The verb in the Hebrew, is of a more general signification than to repay, and means to confer a benefit, as I have shown elsewhere.

MATTHEW HENRY

Psalm 142

1-3 David's complaints.
In these verses observe,

I. How David complained to God, v. 1, 2. When the danger was over he was not ashamed to own (as great spirits sometimes are) the fright he had been in and the application he had made to God. Let no men of the first rank think it any diminution or disparagement to them, when they are in affliction, to cry to God, and to cry like children to their parents when any thing frightens them. David poured out his complaint, which denotes a free and full complaint; he was copious and particular in it. Two things David laid open to God, in this complaint:

1. His distress. He exhibited a remonstrance or memorial of his case: I showed before him my trouble, and all the circumstances of it.

2. His desire. When he made his complaint he made his supplication (v. 1), not claiming relief as a debt, but humbly begging it as a favor. Complainants must be suppliants, for God will be sought unto.

II. What he complained of: "In the way wherein I walked, suspecting no danger, have they privily laid a snare for me, to entrap me." Saul gave Michal his daughter to David on purpose that she might be a snare to him, 1 Sam. xviii. 21. This he complains of to God, that every thing was done with a design against him. If he had gone out of his way, and met with snares, he might have thanked himself; but when he met with them in the way of his duty he might with humble boldness tell God of them.

III. What comforted him in the midst of these complaints (v. 3): "When my spirit was overwhelmed within me, and ready to sink under the burden of grief and fear, when I was quite at a loss and ready to despair, then thou knewest my path, that is, then it was a pleasure to me to think that thou knewest it."

4-7 Complaints and petitions.
The psalmist here tells us, for our instruction,

1. How he was disowned and deserted by his friends, v. 4

2. How he then found satisfaction in God, v. 5.

3. How, in this satisfaction, he addressed himself to God (v. 5, 6): "Lord, give a gracious ear to my cry, the cry of my affliction, the cry of my supplication, for I am brought very low, and, if thou help me not, I shall be quite sunk. Lord, deliver me from my persecutors, either tie their hands or turn their hearts, break their power or blast their projects, restrain them or rescue me, for they are stronger than I, and it will be thy honor to take part with the weakest. Deliver me from them, or I shall be ruined by them, for I am not yet myself a match for them. Lord, bring my soul out of prison, not only bring me safe out of this cave, but bring me out of all my perplexities."

Psalm 143

Title
A Psalm of David.

1-6
1 Hear my prayer, O LORD, give ear to my supplications: in thy faithfulness answer me, and in thy righteousness.
2 And enter not into judgment with thy servant: for in thy sight shall no man living be justified.
3 For the enemy hath persecuted my soul; he hath smitten my life down to the ground; he hath made me to dwell in darkness, as those that have been long dead.
4 Therefore is my spirit overwhelmed within me; my heart within me is desolate.
5 I remember the days of old; I meditate on all thy works; I muse on the work of thy hands.
6 I stretch forth my hands unto thee: my soul thirsteth after thee, as a thirsty land. Selah.

Psalm 143

TITLE. A Psalm of David. It is so much like other Davidic psalms that we accept the title without a moment's hesitation. David's history illustrates it, and his spirit breathes in it. Why it has been set down as one of the seven Penitential Psalms we can hardly tell; for it is rather a vindication of his own integrity, and an indignant prayer against his slanderers, than a confession of fault. It is true the second verse proves that he never dreamed of justifying himself before the Lord; but even in it there is scarcely the brokenness of penitence. It seems to us rather martial than penitential, rather a supplication for deliverance from trouble than a weeping acknowledgment of transgression. We suppose that seven penitentials were needed by ecclesiastical rabbis, and therefore this was impressed into the service. In truth, it is a mingled strain, a box of ointment composed of divers ingredients, sweet and bitter, pungent and precious. It is the outcry of an overwhelmed spirit, unable to abide in the highest state of spiritual prayer, again and again descending to bewail its deep temporal distress; yet evermore struggling to rise to the best things. The singer moans at intervals; the petitioner for mercy cannot withhold his cries for vindication. His hands are outstretched to heaven, but at his girdle hangs a sharp sword, which rattles in its scabbard as he closes his psalm.
DIVISION. This psalm is divided by the Selah. We prefer to follow the natural cleavage, and therefore have made no other dissection of it. May the Holy Spirit lead us into its inner meaning.

EXPOSITION
Verse 1. Hear my prayer, O Lord, give ear to my supplications. In the preceding psalm he began by declaring that he had cried unto the Lord; here he begs to be favorably regarded by Jehovah the living God, whose memorial is that he heareth prayer. He knew that Jehovah did hear prayer, and therefore he entreated him to hear his supplication, however feeble and broken it might be. In two forms he implores the one blessing of gracious audience:—"hear" and "give ear." Gracious men are so eager to be heard in prayer that they double their entreaties for that boon.
Verse 2. And enter not into judgment with thy servant. He had entreated for audience at the mercy seat, but he has no wish to appear before the judgment seat. Though clear before men, he could not claim innocence before God.
Verse 3. For the enemy hath persecuted my soul. He has followed me up with malicious perseverance, and has worried me as often as I have been within his reach. The attack was upon the soul or life of the Psalmist: our adversaries mean us the worst possible evil, their attacks are no child's play, they hunt for the precious life.
Verse 4. Therefore is my spirit overwhelmed within me; my heart within me is desolate. David was no stoic: he felt his banishment, and smarted under the cruel assaults which were made upon his character. He felt perplexed and overturned, lonely and afflicted.
Verse 5. I remember the days of old. When we see nothing new which can cheer us, let us think upon old things. We once had merry days, days of deliverance, and joy and thanksgiving; why not again? Jehovah rescued his people in the ages which lie back, centuries ago; wily should he not do the like again? We ourselves have a rich past to look back upon; we have sunny memories, sacred memories, satisfactory memories, and these are as flowers for the bees of faith to visit, from whence they may make honey for present use.
Verse 6. I stretch forth my hands unto thee. He was eager for his God. His thoughts of God kindled in him burning desires, and these led to energetic expressions of his inward longings. As a prisoner whose feet are bound extends his hands in supplication when there is hope of liberty, so does

JOHN CALVIN

Psalm 143

1-3

1. Hear my prayer, O Jehovah! It is evident that the oppression of his enemies must have been extreme, when David laments his case in such earnest and pathetic terms. The introductory words show that the grief he felt was great. His reason for speaking of the justice and faithfulness of God in connection we have shown elsewhere. Under the term justice, or righteousness, we are not to suppose that he speaks of merit, or hire, as some ignorantly imagine, but of that goodness of God which leads him to defend his people.
2. And enter not into judgment, etc. When overtaken by adversity, we are ever to conclude that it is a rod of correction sent by God to stir us up to pray. Although he is far from taking pleasure in our trials, it is certain that our sins are the cause of his dealing towards us with this severity.
3. For the enemy hath persecuted my soul. Having acknowledged that he only suffered the just punishment of his sins, David comes now to speak of his enemies; for to have begun by speaking of them would have been a preposterous order. Their cruelty was shown in their not resting satisfied but with the destruction of one who was a saint of God; he declares that he must even now perish unless God should help him speedily.

4-7

4. And my spirit, etc. Hitherto he has spoken of the troubles that were without, now he acknowledges the feebleness of his spirits, from which it is evident that his strength, vas not like that of the rock, imperturbable or without feeling, but that, while overwhelmed with grief as to the feeling of the flesh, he owed his support entirely to faith and the grace of the Spirit. We are taught by his example not to give up in despair, however much we may be weakened by afflictions, as God will enable us to surmount them, if we only rise to him with our hearts amidst all our anxieties.

In the next verse David mentions that he had diligently sought means whereby to mitigate his grief. It is not to be wondered at, that many who spontaneously give themselves up to inaction, should sink under their trials, not using means to invigorate themselves by calling to remembrance the grace of God.
6. I have stretched forth my hands to thee. Here appears the good effect of meditation, that it stirred David up to pray; for if we reflect seriously upon the acting's of God towards his people, and towards ourselves in our own experience, this will necessarily lead out our minds to seek after him, under the alluring influence of his goodness.

8-12

8. Cause me to hear thy loving-kindness. In this verse he again prays that God would show him his favor visibly and effectually. The expression cause me to hear, may seem not very proper, as the goodness of God is rather felt than heard; but as the mere perception of God's benefits, without a

MATTHEW HENRY

Psalm 143

1-6 Complaints and petitions.
Here,
I. David humbly begs to be heard (v. 1), not as if he questioned it, but he earnestly desired it, and was in care about it, for, having desired it, and was in care about it, for having directed his prayer, he looked up to see how it sped, Hab. ii. 1. He is a suppliant to his God, and he begs that his requests may be granted: Hear my prayer; give ear to my supplications.
II. He humbly begs not to be proceeded against in strict justice, v. 2. He seems here, if not to correct, yet to explain, his plea (v. 1), Deliver me in thy righteousness; "I mean," says he, "the righteous promises of the gospel, not the righteous threatenings of the law; if I be answered according to the righteousness of this broken covenant of innocency, I am quite undone;" and therefore,
1. His petition is, "Enter not into judgment with thy servant; do not deal with me in strict justice, as I deserve to be dealt with."
2. His plea is, "In thy sight shall no man living be justified upon those terms, for no man can plead innocency nor any righteousness of his own, either that he has not sinned or that he does not deserve to die for his sins; nor that he has any satisfaction of his own to offer."
III. He complains of the prevalency of his enemies against him (v. 3): "Saul, that great enemy, has persecuted my soul, sought my life, with a restless malice, and has carried the persecution so far that he has already smitten it down to the ground. "
IV. He bemoans the oppression of his mind, occasioned by his outward troubles (v. 4): Therefore is my spirit overpowered and overwhelmed within me, and I am almost plunged in despair; when without are fightings within are fears, and those fears greater tyrants and oppressors than Saul himself and not so easily out-run.
V. He applies himself to the use of proper means for the relief of his troubled spirit. He had no force to muster up against the oppression of the enemy, but, if he can keep possession of nothing else, he will do what he can to keep possession of his own soul and to preserve his inward peace. In order to this,
1. He looks back, and remembers the days of old (v. 5), God's former appearances for his afflicted people and for him in particular.
2. He looks round, and takes notice of the works of God in the visible creation, and the providential government of the world: I meditate on all thy works. Many see them, but do not see the footsteps of God's wisdom, power, and goodness in them, and do not receive the benefit they might by them because they do not meditate upon them.
3. He looks up with earnest desires towards God and his favor (v. 6): "I stretch forth my hands unto thee, as one begging an alms, and big with expectation to

Psalm 143

7-12

7 Hear me speedily, O LORD: my spirit faileth: hide not thy face from me, lest I be like unto them that go down into the pit.
8 Cause me to hear thy loving kindness in the morning; for in thee do I trust: cause me to know the way wherein I should walk; for I lift up my soul unto thee.
9 Deliver me, O LORD, from mine enemies: I flee unto thee to hide me.
10 Teach me to do thy will; for thou art my God: thy spirit is good; lead me into the land of uprightness.
11 Quicken me, O LORD, for thy name's sake: for thy righteousness' sake bring my soul out of trouble.
12 And of thy mercy cut off mine enemies, and destroy all them that afflict my soul: for I am thy servant.

David. My soul thirsteth after thee, as a thirsty land. As the soil cracks, and yawns, and thus opens its mouth in dumb pleadings, so did the Psalmist's soul break with longings. No heavenly shower had refreshed him from the sanctuary: banished from the means of grace, his soul felt parched and dry, and he cried out, "My soul to thee"; nothing would content him but the presence of his God.

Verse 7. Hear me speedily, O LORD: my spirit faileth. If long delayed, the deliverance would come too late. The afflicted suppliant faints, and is ready to die. His life is ebbing out; each moment is of importance; it will soon be all over with him. No argument for speed can be more powerful than this.

Verse 8. Cause me to hear thy loving kindness in the morning; for in thee do I trust. Lord, my sorrow makes me deaf,—cause me to hear: there is but one voice that can cheer me—cause me to hear thy lovingkindness; that music I would fain enjoy at once—cause me to hear it in the morning, at the first dawning hour. A sense of divine love is to the soul both dawn and dew; the end of the night of weeping, the beginning of the morning of joy. Only God can take away from our weary ears the din of our care, and charm them with the sweet notes of his love. Our plea with the Lord is our faith: if we are relying upon him, he cannot disappoint us: "in thee do I trust" is a sound and solid argument with God. He who made the ear will cause us to hear: he who is love itself will have the kindness to bring his lovingkindness before our minds. Cause me to know the way wherein I should walk; for I lift up my soul unto thee. The Great First Cause must cause us to hear and to know. Spiritual senses are dependent upon God, and heavenly knowledge comes from him alone.

Verse 9. Deliver me, O LORD, from mine enemies. Many foes beset us, we cannot overcome them, we cannot even escape from them; but Jehovah can and will rescue us if we pray to him. The weapon of all prayer will stand us in better stead than sword and shield. I flee unto thee to hide me. This was a good result from his persecutions. That which makes us flee to our God may be an ill wind, but it blows us good. There is no cowardice in such flight, but much holy courage. God can hide us out of reach of harm, and even out of sight Of it. He is our hiding place; Jesus has made himself the refuge of his people: the sooner, and the more entirely we flee to him the better for us. Beneath the crimson canopy of our Lord's atonement believers are completely hidden; let us abide there and be at rest. In the seventh verse our poet cried, "Hide not thy face", and here he prays, "Hide me." Note also how often he uses the words "unto thee"; he is after his God; lie must travel in that direction by some means, even though he may seem to be beating a retreat; his whole being longs to be near the Lord. Is it possible that such thirsting for God will be left unsupplied? Never, while the Lord is love.

Verse 12. And of thy mercy cut off mine enemies, and destroy all them that afflict my soul. He believes that it will be so, and thus prophesies the event; for the words may be read as a declaration, and it is better so to understand them. We could not pray just so with our Christian light; but under Old Testament arrangements the spirit of it was congruous to the law. It is a petition which justice sanctions, but the spirit of love is not at home in presenting it. We, as Christians, turn the petition to spiritual use only. Yet David was of so generous a mind, and dealt so tenderly with Saul, that he could hardly have meant all that his words are made in our version to say. For I am lay servant; and therefore I hope that my Master will protect me in his service, and grant me victory while I fight his battles. It is a warrior's prayer, and smells of the dust and smoke of battle. It was heard, and therefore it was not asking amiss. Still there is a more excellent way.

believing apprehension and improvement of them, would do us little good, David very properly begins with hearing. We see how wicked men riot in the abundance of them, while yet they have no sense of the Lord's goodness, through want of attention to the word, and a believing apprehension of God as a father.

9. Deliver me, O Jehovah! from my enemies. This prayer is to the same effect, his enemies being so earnestly bent upon his destruction as to leave no way out for him.

10. Teach me that I may do thy will. He now rises to something higher, praying not merely for deliverance from outward troubles, but for the guidance of God's Spirit, that he might be kept in the path of rectitude. This is a request which should never be forgotten when temptations assail us with great severity, as it is peculiarly difficult to submit to God without resorting to unwarrantable methods of relief. As anxiety, fear, disease, languor, or pain, often tempt persons to particular steps, David's example should bad us to pray for divine restraint, and that we may not be hurried, through impulses of feeling, into unjustifiable courses.

11. For thy name's sake, O Jehovah! etc. By this expression he makes it still more clear that it was entirely of God's free mercy that he looked for deliverance; for, had he brought forward anything of his own, the cause would not have been in God, and only in God. He is said to help us for his own name's sake, when, although he discovers nothing in us to conciliate his favor, he is induced to interpose of his mere goodness. To the same effect is the term righteousness; for God, as I have said elsewhere, has made the deliverance of his people a means of illustrating his righteousness. He at the same time repeats what he had said as to the extraordinary extent of his afflictions: in seeking to be quickened or made alive, he declares himself to be exanimated, and that he must remain under the power of death, if the God who has the issues of life did not recover him by a species of resurrection.

12. And in thy mercy, etc. In this verse he repeats for the fifth or sixth time that he looked for life only of God's free mercy. Whatever severity may appear on the part of God when he destroys the wicked, David affirms that the vengeance taken upon them would be a proof of fatherly mercy to him. Indeed these two things often meet together—the severity and the goodness of God; for in stretching out his hand to deliver his own people, he directs the thunder of his indignation against their enemies. In short, he comes forth armed for the deliverance of his people. In calling himself, The servant of God, he by no means boasts of his services, but rather commends the grace of God, to whom he owed this privilege. This is not an honor to be got by our own struggles or exertions—to be reckoned among God's servants; it depends upon his free choice, by which he condescends before we are born to take us into the number and rank of his followers, as David elsewhere declares still more explicitly—"I am thy servant, truly I am thy servant, and the son of thine handmaid." (Psalm 116:16.) This is equivalent to making himself God's client, and committing his life to his protection.

receive something great, standing ready to lay hold on it and bid it welcome. My soul thirsteth after thee; it is to thee (so the word is), entire for thee, intent on thee."

7-12 Prayers for divine grace.
David here tells us what he said when he stretched forth his hands unto God; he begins not only as one in earnest, but as one in haste: "Hear me speedily, and defer no longer, for my spirit faileth. I am just ready to faint; reach the cordial—quickly, quickly, or I am gone." Three things David here prays for:

I. The manifestations of God's favor towards him, that God would be well pleased with him and let him know that he was so; this he prefers before any good, Ps. iv. 6.

1. He dreads God's frowns: "Lord, hide not thy face from me; Lord, be not angry with me, do not turn from me, as we do from one we are displeased with."

2. He entreats God's favor (v. 8): Cause me to hear thy lovingkindness in the morning. He cannot but think that God has a kindness for him, that he has some kind things to say to him, some good words and comfortable words; but the present hurry of his affairs, and tumult of his spirits, drowned those pleasing whispers; and therefore he begs, "Lord, do not only speak kindly to me, but cause me to hear it, to hear joy and gladness," Ps. li. 8.

II. The operations of God's grace in him. Those he is as earnest for as for the tokens of God's favor to him, and so should we be. He prays,

1. That he might be enlightened with the knowledge of God's will; and this is the first work of the Spirit, in order to his other works, for God deals with men as men, as reasonable creatures.

2. He prays that he might be enlivened to do his will (v. 11): "Quicken me, O Lord!—quicken my devotions, that they may be lively; quicken me to my duty, and quicken me in it; and this for thy name's sake." The best saints often find themselves dull, and dead, and slow, and therefore pray to God to quicken them.

III. The appearance of God's providence for him, 1. That God would, in his own way and time, give him rest from his troubles (v. 9): "Deliver me, O Lord! from my enemies, that they may not have their will against me; for I flee unto thee to hide me; I trust to thee to defend me in my trouble, and therefore to rescue me out of it." Preservations are pledges of salvation, and those shall find God their hiding-place who by faith make him such. He explains himself (v. 11): "For thy righteousness-sake, bring my soul out of trouble, for thy promise-sake, nay, for thy mercy-sake do not only deliver me from my outward trouble, but from the trouble of my soul, the trouble that threatens to overwhelm my spirit. Whatever trouble I am in, Lord, let not my heart be troubled."

Psalm 144

Title
A Psalm of David.

1-7
1 Blessed be the LORD my strength which teacheth my hands to war, and my fingers to fight:
2 My goodness, and my fortress; my high tower, and my deliverer; my shield, and he in whom I trust; who subdueth my people under me.
3 LORD, what is man, that thou takest knowledge of him! or the son of man, that thou makest account of him!
4 Man is like to vanity: his days are as a shadow that passeth away.
5 Bow thy heavens, O LORD, and come down: touch the mountains, and they shall smoke.
6 Cast forth lightning, and scatter them: shoot out thine arrows, and destroy them.
7 Send thine hand from above; rid me, and deliver me out of great waters, from the hand of strange children;

Psalm 144

Albeit that this Psalm is in some measure very similar to Ps 18:1-50, yet it is a new song, and in its latter portion it is strikingly so. Let the reader accept it as a new psalm, and not as a mere variation of an old one, or as two compositions roughly joined together. It is true that it would be a complete composition if the passage from Ps 144:12-15 were dropped; but there are other parts, of David's poems which might be equally self contained if certain verses were omitted; and the same might be said of many uninspired sonnets. It does not, therefore, follow that the latter part was added by another hand, nor even that the latter part was a fragment by the same author, appended to the first song merely with the view of preserving it. It seems to us to be highly probable that the Psalmist, remembering that he had trodden some of the same ground before, felt his mind moved to fresh thought, and that the Holy Spirit used this mood for his own high purposes. Assuredly the addendum is worthy of the greatest Hebrew poet, and it is so admirable in language, and so full of beautiful imagery, that persons of taste who were by no means overloaded with reverence have quoted it times without number, thus confessing its singular poetical excellence. To us the whole psalm appears to be perfect as it stands, and to exhibit such unity throughout that it would be a literary Vandalism, as well as a spiritual crime, to rend away one part from the other.
TITLE. Its title is "Of David", and its language is of David, if ever language can belong to any man. As surely as we could say of any poem, this is of Tennyson, or of Longfellow, we may say, This is of David. Nothing but the disease which closes the eye to manifest fact and opens it to fancy, could have led learned critics to ascribe this song to anybody but David. Alexander well says, "The Davidic origin of this psalm is as marked as that of any in the Psalter."
It is to God the devout warrior sings when he extols him as his strength and stay (Ps 144:1-2). Man he holds in small account, and wonders at the Lord's regard for him (Ps 144:3-4); but he turns in his hour of conflict to the Lord, who is declared to be "a man of war", whose triumphant interposition he implores (Ps 144:5-8). He again extols and entreats in Ps 144:9-11 and then closes with a delightful picture of the Lord's work for his chosen people, who are congratulated upon having such a God to be their God.

EXPOSITION
Verse 1. Blessed be the LORD my strength. He cannot delay the utterance of his gratitude, he bursts at once into a loud note of praise. His best word is given to his best friend—"Blessed be Jehovah." When the heart is in a right state it must praise God, it cannot be restrained; its utterances leap forth as waters forcing their way from a living spring.
Verse 2. Now our royal poet multiplies metaphors to extol his God. My goodness, and my fortress. The word for goodness signifies mercy. Whoever we may be, and wherever we may be, we need mercy such as can only be found in the infinite God.
Verse 3. LORD, what is man, that thou takest knowledge of him? What a contrast between Jehovah and man! The Psalmist turns from the glorious all sufficiency of God to the insignificance and nothingness of man.
Verse 4. Man is like to vanity. Adam is like to Abel. He is like that which is nothing at all. He is actually vain, and he resembles that unsubstantial empty thing which is nothing but a blown up nothing,—a puff, a bubble. Yet he is not vanity, but only like it. He is not so substantial as that unreal thing; he is only the likeness of it. Lord, what is a man? It is wonderful that God should think of such a pretentious insignificance.
Verse 5. Bow thy heavens, O LORD, and come down. The heavens are the Lord's own, and he who exalted them can bow them. His servant is

Psalm 144

1-4

1. Blessed be Jehovah, my strength. It is very evident that David, since he celebrates the favor of God in such high terms, had not only obtained the kingdom, but gained signal victories. When he calls God his strength, he acknowledges that any courage he had was given him from above, not only because he had been made from a country shepherd a mighty warrior, but because the constancy and perseverance he had shown was signally a gift from God.

2. My goodness, etc. Having experienced God's kindness in so many ways, he calls him "his goodness," meaning that whatever good he possessed flowed from him. The accumulation of terms, one upon another, which follows, may appear unnecessary, yet it tends greatly to strengthen faith. We know how unstable men's minds are, and especially how soon faith wavers, when they are assailed by some trial of more than usual severity.

3. O Jehovah! what is man, etc. He amplifies the goodness shown by God by instituting a comparison. Having declared how singularly he had been dealt with, he turns his eyes inward, and asks, "Who am I, that God should show me such condescension? "He speaks of man in general; only the circumstance is noticeable that he commends the mercy of God, by considering his lowly and abject condition. In other places he mentions grounds of humiliation of a more personal or private nature,—here he confines himself to what has reference to our common nature; and though even in discussing the nature of man there are other reasons he might have specified why he is unworthy of the regard and love of God, he briefly adverts to his being like the smoke, and as a shadow. We are left to infer that the riches of the divine goodness are extended to objects altogether unworthy in themselves.

5-8

5. O Jehovah! bow thy heavens. After extolling, as was due, the great goodness of God, he requests him to furnish such help for the preservation of the kingdom as was necessary in the present exigency. He employs almost the same phraseology in the eighteenth Psalm, but it is in praising God for help already extended, and to signify that he had been preserved from above in a wonderful and unusual manner.

7. Send thy hand, etc. In one word we are now made to see what was meant by the figures formerly used—that in the absence of all earthly help, God would put forth his hand from above, the greatness of the exigency making extraordinary help necessary. Accordingly he compares his enemies to great and deep waters. He calls them strangers, not in respect of generic origin, but character and disposition.

9-11

9. O God! I will sing a new song to thee. He again sets himself, with self-possession, to the exercise of praising God, not doubting but he would continue those mercies which he

Psalm 144

1-8 Grateful acknowledgments of divine goodness; prayer for success against enemies.

Here,

I. David acknowledges his dependence upon God and his obligations to him, v. 1, 2. A prayer for further mercy is fitly begun with a thanksgiving for former mercy; and when we are waiting upon God to bless us we should stir up ourselves to bless him. He gives to God the glory of two things:

1. What he was to him: Blessed be the Lord my rock (v. 1), my goodness, my fortress, v. 2. He has in the covenant engaged himself to be so, and encouraged us, accordingly, to depend upon him; all the saints, who by faith have made him theirs, have found him not only to answer but to out do their expectations.

2. What he had done for him. He was bred a shepherd, and seems not to have been designed by his parents, or himself for any thing more.

II. He admires God's condescension to man and to himself in particular (v. 3, 4): "Lord, what is man, what a poor little thing is he, that thou takest knowledge of him, that thou makest account of him, that he falls so much under thy cognizance and care, and that thou hast such a tender regard to any of that mean and worthless race as thou hast had to me!" Considering the many disgraces which the human nature lies under, we have reason to admire the honors God has put upon mankind in general (the saints especially, some in a particular manner, as David) and upon the Messiah (to whom those words are applied, Heb. ii. 6), who was highly exalted because he humbled himself to be found in fashion as a man, and has authority to execute judgment because he is the Son of man. A question to this purport David asked (Ps. viii. 4), and he illustrated the wonder by the consideration of the great dignity God has placed man in (Ps. viii. 5), Thou hast crowned him with glory and honor. Here he illustrates it by the consideration of the meanness and mortality of man, notwithstanding the dignity put upon him (v. 4): Man is like to vanity; so frail is he, so weak, so helpless, compassed about with so many infirmities, and his continuance here so very short and uncertain, that he is as like as may be to vanity itself.

III. He begs of God to strengthen him and give him success against the enemies that invaded him, v. 5-8. He does not specify who they were that he was in fear of, but says, Scatter them, destroy them. God knew whom he meant, though he did not name them. But afterwards he describes them (v. 7, 8).

1. David prays that God would appear, that he would do something extraordinary, for the conviction of those who preferred their dunghill-deities before the God of Israel (v. 5): "Bow thy heavens, O Lord! and make it evident that they are indeed thine, and that thou art the Lord of them, Isa. lxvi. 1. Let thy providence threaten my enemies."

Psalm 144

8-15

8 Whose mouth speaketh vanity, and their right hand is a right hand of falsehood.
9 I will sing a new song unto thee, O God: upon a psaltery and an instrument of ten strings will I sing praises unto thee.
10 It is he that giveth salvation unto kings: who delivereth David his servant from the hurtful sword.
11 Rid me, and deliver me from the hand of strange children, whose mouth speaketh vanity, and their right hand is a right hand of falsehood:
12 That our sons may be as plants grown up in their youth; that our daughters may be as corner stones, polished after the similitude of a palace:
13 That our garners may be full, affording all manner of store: that our sheep may bring forth thousands and ten thousands in our streets:
14 That our oxen may be strong to labor; that there be no breaking in, nor going out; that there be no complaining in our streets.
15 Happy is that people, that is in such a case: yea, happy is that people, whose God is the LORD.

struggling against bitter foes, and he finds no help in men, therefore he entreats Jehovah to come down to his rescue.

It is, indeed, a coming down for Jehovah to interfere in the conflicts of his

Verse 6. Cast forth lightning, and scatter them. The Eternal can hurl his lightnings wheresoever he pleases, and effect his purpose instantaneously.

Verse 7. Send thine hand from above. Let thy long and strong arm be stretched out till thine hand seizes my foes, and delivers me from them. Rid me, and deliver me out of great waters. Make a Moses of me,—one drawn out of the waters. My foes pour in upon me like torrents, they threaten to overwhelm me; save me from their force and fury; take them from me, and me from them.

Verse 8. Whose mouth speaketh vanity. No wonder that men who are vanity speak vanity. "When he speaketh a lie, he speaketh of his own." They cannot be depended upon, let them promise as fairly as they may: their solemn declarations are light as the foam of the sea, in no wise to be depended upon. Good men desire to be rid of such characters: of all men deceivers and liars are among the most disgusting to true hearts.

Verse 9. I will sing a new song unto thee, O God. Weary of the false, I will adore the true. Fired with fresh enthusiasm, my gratitude shall make a new channel for itself. I will sing as others have done; but it shall be a new song, such as no others have sung. That song shall be all and altogether for my God: I will extol none but the Lord, from whom my deliverance has come.

Verse 10. It is he that giveth salvation unto kings. Those whom the Lord sets up he will keep up. Kings, from their conspicuous position, are exposed to special danger, and when their lives and their thrones are preserved to them they should give the Lord the glory of it.

Verse 11. Because of what the Lord had done, David returns to his pleading. He begs deliverance from him who is ever delivering him. Rid me, and deliver me from the hand of strange children. This is in measure the refrain of the song, and the burden of the prayer. He desired to be delivered from his open and foreign adversaries, who had broken compacts, and treated treaties as vain things.

Verse 12. God's blessing works wonders for a people. That our sons may be as plants grown up in their youth. Our sons are of first importance to the state, since men take a leading part in its affairs; and that the young men are the older men will be. He desires that they may be like strong, well rooted, young trees, which promise great things.

Verse 13. That our garners may be full, affording all manner of store. A household must exercise thrift and forethought: it must have its granary as well as its nursery. Husbands should husband their resources; and should not only furnish their tables but fill their garners. Where there are happy households, there must needs be plentiful provision for them, for famine brings misery even where love abounds.

Verse 14. That our oxen may be strong to labor; so that the ploughing and cartage of the farm may be duly performed, and the husbandman's work may be accomplished without unduly taxing the cattle, or working them cruelly. That there be no breaking in, nor going out; no irruption of marauders, and no forced emigration; no burglaries and no evictions.

Verse 15. Happy is that people that is in such a case. Such things are not to be overlooked. Temporal blessings are not trifles, for the miss of them would be a dire calamity. It is a great happiness to belong to a people so highly favored. Yea, happy is that people, whose God is the LORD. This comes in as an explanation of their prosperity. Under the Old Testament Israel had present earthly rewards for obedience.

had once bestowed. The chief thing to be noticed is the subject of his songs, that God, who is the preserver of kings, had kept—and even rescued from the sword—David, whom he had made and anointed king by his authoritative decree.
10. By the hurtful sword, are doubtless meant all the dangers he had passed through for a series of years, which were such that he might be truly said to have come to the throne by deaths oft, and to have been settled upon the throne in the midst of them.

12-15
12. Because our sons, etc. These three concluding verses some consider as being a wish or a prayer. Others think that David congratulates himself, and all the people, that through the divine blessing every species of mercy was showered down prosperously upon them. I have no doubt that David commemorates, by way of thanksgiving, the liberality which God had shown to his people. But it consists very well with this, to suppose that he prays at the same time for the continuance or preservation of those divine benefits which must well-nigh be cut off altogether by wicked men and domestic foes, unless God should interpose, in the troubles and confusions which prevailed.
13. Our recesses full, etc. The meaning in short is, that there prevailed amongst the people such plenty, not only of wheat, but all kinds of produce, that every corner was filled to sufficiency with every variety.
14. Our oxen, etc. Notice that God's fatherly care of his people is celebrated on the account that he condescends to attend to every the smallest matter which concerns their advantage. As in the verse before he had ascribed the fruitfulness of the herds and flocks to God's goodness, so now the fattening of their oxen, to show that there is nothing relating to us here which he overlooks. As it would signify little to have abundance of everything unless we could enjoy it, he takes notice of it as another part of the Lord's kindness that the people were peaceable and quiet. 15. Happy the people, etc. He thus concludes that the divine favor had been sufficiently shown and manifested to his people. Should any object that it breathed altogether a gross and worldly spirit to estimate man's happiness by benefits of a transitory description, I would say in reply that we must read the two things in connection, that those are happy who recognize the favor of God in the abundance they enjoy, and have such a sense of it from these transitory blessings as leads them through a persuasion of his fatherly love to aspire after the true inheritance. There is no impropriety in calling those happy whom God blesses in this world, provided they do not show themselves blinded in the improvement and use which they make of their mercies, or foolishly and supinely overlook the author of them. The kind providence of God in not suffering us to want any of the means of life is surely a striking illustration of his wonderful love. What more desirable than to be the objects of God's care, especially if we have sufficient understanding to conclude from the liberality with which he supports us he is our Father?

2. That he would appear against his enemies, that he would fight from heaven against them, as sometimes he had done, by lightnings, which are his arrows (his fiery darts, against which the hardest steel is no armor of proof, so penetrating is the force of lightning), that he himself would shoot these arrows, who, we are sure, never misses his mark, but hits where he aims.
3. That he would appear for him, v. 7. He begs for their destruction, in order to his own deliverance and the repose of his people: "Send thy hand, thy power, from above, for that way we look for help; rid me and deliver me out of these great waters that are ready to overflow me." God's time to help his people is when they are sinking and all other helps fail.

9-15 Thanksgiving and petitions; national happiness desired.
The method is the same in this latter part of the psalm as in the former; David first gives glory to God and then begs mercy from him.
I. He praises God for the experiences he had had of his goodness to him and the encouragements he had to expect further mercy from him, v. 9, 10. In the midst of his complaints concerning the power and treachery of his enemies, here is a holy exultation in his God: I will sing a new song to thee, O God! a song of praise for new mercies, for those compassions that are new every morning.
II. He prays for the continuance of God's favor.

1. That he might be delivered from the public enemies, v. 11. Here he repeats his prayer and plea, v. 7, 8. His persecutors were still of the same character, false and perfidious, and who would certainly over-reach an honest man and be too hard for him: "Therefore, Lord, do thou deliver me from them, for they are a strange sort of people."

2. That he might see the public peace and prosperity: "Lord, let us have victory, that we may have quietness, which we shall never have while our enemies have it in their power to do us mischief." David, as a king, here expresses the earnest desire he had of the welfare of his people, wherein he was a type of Christ, who provides effectually for the good of his chosen. We have here,
(1.) The particular instances of that public prosperity which David desired for his people. A hopeful progeny (v. 12): "That our sons and our daughters may be in all respects such as we could wish." He means not those only of his own family, but those of his subjects, that are the seed of the next generation.
(2.) His reflection upon this description of the prosperity of the nation, which he so much desired (v. 15): Happy are the people that are in such a case (but it is seldom so, and never long so), yea, happy are the people whose God is the Lord.

Psalm 145

Title
David's Psalm of praise.

1-7
1 I will extol thee, my God, O king; and I will bless thy name for ever and ever.
2 Every day will I bless thee; and I will praise thy name for ever and ever.
3 Great is the LORD, and greatly to be praised; and his greatness is unsearchable.
4 One generation shall praise thy works to another, and shall declare thy mighty acts.
5 I will speak of the glorious honor of thy majesty, and of thy wondrous works.
6 And men shall speak of the might of thy terrible acts: and I will declare thy greatness.
7 They shall abundantly utter the memory of thy great goodness, and shall sing of thy righteousness.

Psalm 145

This is one of the alphabetical psalms, composed with much art, and, doubtless, so arranged that the memory might be aided. The Holy Spirit condescends to use even the more artificial methods of the poet, to secure attention, and impress the heart.
TITLE. David's Psalm Of Praise. It is David's, David's very own, David's favorite. It is David's Praise just as another (Ps 86:1-17) is David's Prayer. It is altogether praise, and praise pitched in a high key. David had blessed God many a time in other psalms, but this he regarded as his peculiar, his crown jewel of praise. Certainly David's praise is the best of praise, for it is that of a man of experience, of sincerity, of calm deliberation, and of intense warmth of the heart. It is not for any one of us to render David's praise, for David only could do that, but we may take David's psalm as a model, and aim at making our own personal adoration as much, like it as possible: we shall be long before we equal our model. Let each Christian reader present his own praise unto the Lord, and call it by his own name. What a wealth of varied praise will thus be presented through Christ Jesus!
DIVISION. The psalm does not fall into any marked divisions, but is one and indivisible. Our other translators have mapped out this song with considerable discernment. It is or a perfect arrangement, but it will suit our convenience in exposition. David praiseth God for his fame or glory (Ps 145:1-7), for his goodness (Ps 145:8-10), for his kingdom (Ps 145:11-13), for his providence (Ps 145:14-16), for his saving mercy (Ps 145:17-21).

EXPOSITION
Verse 1. I will extol thee, my God, O king. David as God's king adores God as his king. It is well when the Lord's royalty arouses our loyalty, and our spirit is moved to magnify his majesty. The Psalmist has extolled his Lord many a time before, he is doing so still, and he will do so in the future: praise is for all tenses.
Verse 2. Every day will I bless thee. Whatever the character of the day, or of my circumstances and conditions during that day, I will continue to glorify God. Were we well to consider the matter we should see abundant cause in each day for rendering special blessing unto the Lord.
Verse 3. Great is the LORD, and greatly to be praised. Worship should be somewhat like its object—great praise for a great God. There is no part of Jehovah's greatness which is not worthy of great praise. In some beings greatness is but vastness of evil: in him it is magnificence of goodness.
Verse 4. One generation shall praise thy works to another. There shall be a tradition of praise: melt shall hand on the service, they shall make it a point to instruct their descendants in this hallowed exercise. We look back upon the experience of our fathers, and sing of it; even thus shall our sons learn praise from the Lord's works among ourselves.
Verse 5. I will speak of the glorious honor of thy majesty. 'Tis fit that a king should speak of the majesty of the King of kings. David cannot give over the worship of God into the hands of others, even though all generations should undertake to perpetuate it: he must have his own individual share in it, and so he saith, "I will speak."
Verse 6. And men shall speak of the might of thy terrible acts. If unobservant of other matters these acts of judgment shall seize their attention and impress their minds so that they must talk about them. Did not men in our Savior's day speak of the falling tower of Siloam and the slaughtered Galileans? Are there not rumors of wars, when there are not even whispers of other things? Horrible news is sure to spread: under mercies men may be dumb, but concerning miseries they raise a great outcry. The force of dread is a power which loosens the tongue of the multitude: they are sure to talk of that which makes the ear to tingle and the hair to stand upright. While they are thus occupied with "fearsome facts",

JOHN CALVIN

Psalm 145

1-6

1. I will extol thee, my God and my king. David does not so much tell what he would do himself, as stir up and urge all others to this religious service of offering to God the praises due to his name. The design with which he declares God to be beneficent to the children of men is, to induce them to cultivate a pious gratitude, he insists upon the necessity of persevering in the exercise; for since God is constant in extending mercies, it would be highly improper in us to faint in his praises. As he thus gives his people new ground for praising him, so he stimulates them to gratitude, and to exercise it throughout the whole course of their life. In using the term daily, he denotes perseverance in the exercise. Afterwards he adds, that should he live through a succession of ages he would never cease to act in this manner. The repetitions used tend very considerably to give emphasis to his language. As it is probable that the Psalm was written at a time when the kingdom of David was in a flourishing condition, the circumstances deserves notice, that in calling God his king he gives both himself and other earthly princes their proper place, and does not allow any earthly distinctions to interfere with the glory due to God.

This is made still more manifest in the verse which follows, where, in speaking of the greatness of God as unmeasurable, he intimates that we only praise God aright when we are filled and overwhelmed with an ecstatic admiration of the immensity of his power. This admiration will form the fountain from which our just praises of him will proceed, according the measure of our capacity.

4. Generation to generation, etc. Here he insists upon the general truth, that all men were made and are preserved in life for this end, that they may devote themselves to the praise of God. And there is an implied contrast between the eternal name of God, and that immortality of renown which great men seem to acquire by their exploits.

7-13

7. They shall speak forth, etc. To celebrate the memory of the Lord's goodness, is the same with recalling to memory what we have personally experienced of his goodness. We cannot deny God's claim to praise in all his excellencies, but we are most sensibly affected by such proofs of his fatherly mercy as we have ourselves experienced. David makes use, therefore, of this alluring consideration to induce us the more readily and cheerfully to engage in the praises of God, or rather, (according to the figurative word already used,) to burst forth in celebration of them.

8. Jehovah is gracious, etc. He opens up the goodness of which he spoke by using several expressions, as that God is inclined to mercy, and that he helps us willingly, as one sympathizing with our miseries. It is to be noticed that David has borrowed the terms which he here applies to God from that celebrated passage in Exodus 34:6; and as the inspired writers drew their doctrine from the fountain of the law, we need not wonder

MATTHEW HENRY

Psalm 145

1-8 Grateful acknowledgments.

The entitling of this David's psalm of praise may intimate not only that he was the penman of it, but that he took a particular pleasure in it and sung it often; it was his companion wherever he went. In this former part of the psalm God's glorious attributes are praised, as, in the latter part of the psalm, his kingdom and the administration of it. Observe,

I. Who shall be employed in giving glory to God.

1. Whatever others do, the psalmist will himself be much in praising God. To this good work he here excites himself, engages himself, and has his heart much enlarged in it. What he does, that he will do, having more and more satisfaction in it. It was his duty; it was his delight. Observe,

(1.) How he expresses the work itself: "I will extol thee, and bless thy name (v. 1); I will speak well of thee, as thou hast made thyself known, and will therein express my own high thoughts of thee and endeavor to raise the like in others." When we speak honorably of God, this is graciously interpreted and accepted as an extolling of him. Again (v. 2): I will bless thee, I will praise thy name; the repetition intimates the fervency of his affection to this work, the fixedness of his purpose to abound in it, and the frequency of his performances therein. Again (v. 5): I will speak of thy honor, and (v. 6) I will declare thy greatness. He would give glory to God, not only in his solemn devotions, but in his common conversation.

(2.) How he expresses his resolution to persevere in it. He will be constant to this work: Every day will I bless thee.

2. He doubts not but others also would be forward to this work.

(1.) "They shall concur in it now; they shall join with me in it: When I declare thy greatness men shall speak of it (v. 6); they shall abundantly utter it" (v. 7), or pour it out (as the word is); they shall praise God with a gracious fluency, better than the most curious oratory. David's zeal would provoke many, and it has done so.

(2.) "They shall keep it up when I am gone, in an uninterrupted succession (v. 4): One generation shall praise thy works to another."

II. What we must give to God the glory of.

1. Of his greatness and his great works. We must declare, Great is the Lord, his presence infinite, his power irresistible, his brightness insupportable, his majesty awful, his dominion boundless, and his sovereignty incontestable; and therefore there is no dispute, but great is the Lord, and, if great, then greatly to be praised, with all that is within us, to the utmost of our power, and with all the circumstances of solemnity imaginable.

(1.) His majesty is glorious in the upper world, above the heavens, where he has set his glory; and when we are declaring his greatness we must not fail to

Psalm 145

8-14

8 The LORD is gracious, and full of compassion; slow to anger, and of great mercy.

9 The LORD is good to all: and his tender mercies are over all his works.

10 All thy works shall praise thee, O LORD; and thy saints shall bless thee.

11 They shall speak of the glory of thy kingdom, and talk of thy power;

12 To make known to the sons of men his mighty acts, and the glorious majesty of his kingdom.

13 Thy kingdom is an everlasting kingdom, and thy dominion endureth throughout all generations.

14 The LORD upholdeth all that fall, and raiseth up all those that be bowed down.

such as the drowning of a world, the destruction of the cities of the plain, the plagues of Egypt, the destruction at the Red Sea, and so forth, David would look at these affairs in another light, and sing another tune.

Verse 7. They shall abundantly utter the memory of thy great goodness. They shall pour forth grateful memories even as springs gush with water, plenteously, spontaneously, constantly, joyously. The Lord's redeemed people having been filled with his great goodness, shall retain the happy recollection of it, and shall be moved often and often to utter those recollections.

Verse 8. The Lord is gracious. Was it not in some such terms that the Lord revealed himself to Moses? Is not this Jehovah's glory? To all living men his aspect: he is gracious, or full of goodness and generosity. He treats creatures with kindness, his subjects with consideration, and his saints favor. His words and ways, his promises and his gifts, his plans and his poses all manifest his grace, or free favor. There is nothing suspicious, diced, morose, tyrannical, or unapproachable in Jehovah,—he is condescending and kind.

Verse 9. The LORD is good to all. No one, not even his fiercest enemy, can this; for the falsehood would be too barefaced, since the very existence lips which slander him is a proof that it is slander. He allows his live, he even supplies them with food, and smooths their way with many forts; for them the sun shines as brightly as if they were saints, and the rain waters their fields as plentifully as if they were perfect men.

Verse 10. All thy works shall praise thee, O LORD. There is a something about every creature which redounds to the honor of God. The skill, kindness, and power manifested in the formation of each living thing is in itself to the praise of God, and when observed by an intelligent mind the Lord is honored thereby. Some works praise him by their being, and others by their well being; some by their mere existence, and others by their hearty volition.

Verse 11. They shall speak of the glory of thy kingdom. Excellent themes for saintly minds. Those who bless God from their hearts rejoice to see him enthroned, glorified, and magnified in power. No subject is more profitable for humility, obedience, hope, and joy than that of the reigning power of the Lord our God. His works praise him, but they cannot crown him: this remains for holy hands and hearts. It is their high pleasure to tell of the glory of his kingdom in its justice, kindness, eternity, and so forth.

Verse 12. To make known to the sons of men his mighty acts. These glorious deeds ought to be known to all mankind; but yet few reckon such knowledge to be an essential part of education. As the State cannot teach these holy histories the people of God must take care to do it themselves. The work must be done for every age, for men have short memories in reference to their God, and the doings of his power.

Verse 13. Thy kingdom is an everlasting kingdom. His meditation has brought him near to God, and God near to him: he speaks to him in adoration, changing the pronoun from "his" to "thy." He sees the great King, and prostrates himself before him. It is well when our devotion opens the gate of heaven, and enters within the portal, to speak with God face to face, as a man speaketh with his friend. The point upon which the Psalmist's mind rests is the eternity of the divine throne,—"thy reign is a reign of all eternities." The Lord's kingdom is without beginning, without break, without bound, and without end.

Verse 14. The Lead upholdeth all that fall. Read this verse in connection with the preceding, and admire the unexpected contrast: he who reigns in glorious majesty, yet condescends to lift up and hold up those who are apt to fall. The form of the verb shows that he is always doing this; he is Jehovah upholding. His choice of the fallen, and the falling, as the subjects of his gracious help is specially to be noted.

that they set a high value upon the vision which is there recorded, and in which as clear and satisfactory a description of the nature of God is given us as can anywhere be found. David, therefore, in giving us a brief statement of what it was most important we should know in reference to God, makes use of the same terms employed there. Indeed no small part of the grace of God is to be seen in his alluring us to himself by such attractive titles.

9. Jehovah is good to all, etc. The truth here stated is of wider application than the former, for the declaration of David is to the effect, that not only does God, with fatherly indulgence and clemency, forgive sin, but is good to all without discrimination, as he makes his sun to rise upon the good and upon the wicked. (Matthew 5:45.) Forgiveness of sin is a treasure from which the wicked are excluded, but their sin and depravity does not prevent God from showering down his goodness upon them, which they appropriate without being at all sensible of it.

10. All thy works, etc. Though many would suppress God's praises, observing a wicked silence regarding them, David declares that they shine forth everywhere, appear of themselves, and are sounded, as it were, by the very dumb creatures. He then assigns the special work of declaring them to believers, who have eyes to perceive God's works, and know that they cannot be employed better than in celebrating his mercies.

14-16

14. Jehovah upholding all the falling. He gives instances of the goodness and mercy of God, such as make it evident that God reigns only for the promotion of the general welfare of mankind. By the falling, and those who are bowed down, he means figuratively those who are overwhelmed by adversity, and would sink at once, were not God to extend his hand for their support. God, in short, has respect to the troubles of men, and helps such as are in distress, so that all ought not only to look upon his divine government with reverence, but willingly and cordially submit themselves to it. Another lesson taught us is, that none will be disappointed who seeks comfort from God in his affliction.

15. The eyes of all hope in thee. David adduces an additional proof of God's goodness, in giving food to all living creatures, and thus showing himself in the character of the father of a family.

16. Thou openest thine hand, etc. The figure is a beautiful one. Most men pass over without observation the singular goodness of God apparent in this admirable ordering of things in nature, and David therefore represents him as stretching out his hand to distribute to the animals their food. We sinfully confine our attention to the earth which yields us our food, or to natural causes. To correct this error David describes God as opening his hands to put the food into our mouths.

17-21

17. Jehovah is righteous in all his ways. He does not now speak of God's goodness merely in providing all his creatures with

speak of the glorious honor of his majesty, the splendor of the glory of his majesty (v. 5), how brightly he shines in the upper world, so as to dazzle the eyes of the angels themselves, and oblige them to cover their faces, as unable to bear the luster of it.

(2.) His works are wondrous in this lower world. The preservation, maintenance, and government of all the creatures, proclaim the Creator very great. When therefore we declare his greatness we must observe the unquestionable proofs of it, and must declare his mighty acts (v. 4), speak of his wondrous works (v. 5), the might of his terrible acts, v. 6.

2. Of his goodness; this is his glory, Exod. xxxiii. 19. It is what he glories in (Exod. xxxiv. 6, 7), and it is what we must give him the glory of: They shall abundantly utter the memory of thy great goodness, v. 7. God's goodness is great goodness, the treasures of it can never be exhausted, nay, they can never be lessened, for he ever will be as rich in mercy as he ever was.

(1.) There is a fountain of goodness in God's nature (v. 8): The Lord is gracious to those that serve him; he is full of compassion to those that need him, slow to anger to those that have offended him, and of great mercy to all that seek him and sue to him. He is ready to give, and ready to forgive, more ready than we are to ask, than we are to repent.

(2.) There are streams of goodness in all the dispensations of his providence, v. 9. As he is good, so he does good; he is good to all, to all his creatures, from the highest angel to the meanest worm, to all but devils and damned sinners, that have shut themselves out from his goodness.

10-21 Grateful acknowledgments.

The greatness and goodness of him who is optimus et maximus—the best and greatest of beings, were celebrated in the former part of the psalm; here, in these verses, we are taught to give him the glory of his kingdom, in the administration of which his greatness and goodness shine so clearly, so very brightly. Observe, as before,

I. From whom the tribute of praise is expected (v. 10): All God's works shall praise him. They all minister to us matter for praise, and so praise him according to their capacity; even those that refuse to give him honor he will get himself honor upon.

II. For what this praise is to be given: They shall speak of thy kingdom. The kingdom of God among men is a thing to be often thought of and often spoken of. As, before, he had magnified God's greatness and goodness in general, so here he magnifies them with application to his kingdom. Consider then,

1. The greatness of his kingdom. It is great indeed, for all the kings and kingdoms of the earth are under his control. To show the greatness of God's kingdom, he observes,

(1.) The pomp of it. Would we by faith look within the veil, we should see, and, believing, we should speak

Psalm 145

15-21

15 The eyes of all wait upon thee; and thou givest them their meat in due season.
16 Thou openest thine hand, and satisfiest the desire of every living thing.
17 The LORD is righteous in all his ways, and holy in all his works.
18 The LORD is nigh unto all them that call upon him, to all that call upon him in truth.
19 He will fulfill the desire of them that fear him: he also will hear their cry, and will save them.
20 The LORD preserveth all them that love him: but all the wicked will he destroy.
21 My mouth shall speak the praise of the LORD: and let all flesh bless his holy name for ever and ever.

Verse 15. The eyes of all wait upon thee. They have learned to look to thee: it has become their nature to turn to thee for all they want. As children look to a father for all they need, so do the creatures look to God, the all sufficient Provider. It were well if all men had the eye of faith, and if all waited therewith upon the Lord. And thou givest them their meat in due season. They wait, and God gives.

Verse 16. Thou openest thine hand, and satisfiest the desire of every living thing. You alone provide, O Jehovah! Thou doest it liberally, with open hand; thou doest it easily, as if it were only to open thine hand; thou doest this at once as promptly as if all supplies were ready to hand. Living things have needs, and these create desires; the living God has suitable supplies at hand, and these he gives till inward satisfaction is produced, and the creature sighs no longer.

Verse 17. The LORD is righteous in all his ways, and holy in all his works. His ways and works are both worthy to be praised. Jehovah cannot be unjust or impure. Let his doings be what they may, they are in every case righteous and holy. This is the confession of the godly who follow his ways, and of the gracious who study his works. Whatever God is or does must be right. In the salvation of his people he is as righteous and holy as in any other of his ways and works: he has not manifested mercy at the expense of justice, but the rather he has magnified his righteousness by the death of his Son.

Verse 19. He will fulfill the desire of them that fear him: that is, those who reverence his name and his law. Inasmuch as they have respect unto his will, he will have respect unto their will. They shall have their way for they have his way in their hearts. A holy heart only desires what a holy God can give, and so its desire is filled full out of the fullness of the Lord. He also will hear their cry, and will save them. Divinely practical shall his nearness be, for he will work their deliverance. He will listen to their piteous cry, and then will send salvation from every ill. This he will do himself personally; he will not trust them to angels or saints.

Verse 21. My mouth shall speak the praise of the LORD. Whatever others may do, I will not be silent in the praise of the Lord: whatever others may speak upon, my topic is fixed once for all: I will speak the praise of Jehovah. I am doing it, and I will do it as long as I breathe. And let all flesh bless his holy name for ever and ever. Praise is no monopoly for one, even though he be a David; others are debtors, let them also be songsters. All men of every race, condition, or generation should unite to glorify God. No man need think that he will be rejected when he comes with his personal note of praise; all are permitted, invited, and exhorted to magnify the Lord. Specially should his holiness be adored: this is the crown, and in a certain sense the sum, of all his attributes. Only holy hearts will praise the holy name, or character of the Lord; oh, that all flesh were sanctified, then would the sanctity of God be the delight of all. Once let the song begin and there will be no end to it. It shall go on for ever and a clay, as the old folks used to say. If there were two forevers, or twenty forevers, they ought all to be spent in the praises of the ever living, ever blessing, ever blessed JEHOVAH. Blessed be the Lord for ever for having revealed to us his name, and blessed be that name as he has revealed it; yea, blessed be he above all that we can know, or think, or say. Our hearts revel in the delight of praising him. Our mouth, our mind, our lip, our life shall be our Lord's throughout this mortal existence, and when time shall be no more.

their daily food, but comprehends other parts of his providence, as in correcting men for their sins, restraining the wicked, trying the patience of his people under the cross, and governing the world by judgments which are often inscrutable to us. The ground upon which praise is here ascribed to God may seem a common one, being in every one's mouth; but in nothing is wisdom shown more than in holding fast the truth, that God is just in all his ways, so as to retain in our hearts an unabated sense of it amidst all troubles and confusions. Though all acknowledge God to be just, most men are no sooner overtaken by affliction than they quarrel with his severity: unless their wishes are immediately complied with, they are impatient, and nothing is more common than to hear his justice impeached. As it is everywhere abused by the wicked imputations men cast upon it, here it is very properly vindicated from such ungrateful treatment, and asserted to be constant and unfailing, however loudly the word may disparage it. It is expressly added, in all his ways and works, for we fail to give God due honor unless we recognize a consistent tenor of righteousness in the whole progress of his operation. Nothing is more difficult in the time of trouble, when God has apparently forsaken us, or afflicts us without cause, than to restrain our corrupt feelings from breaking out against his judgments.

18. Jehovah is near to all that call upon him. This truth is principally applicable to believers, whom God in the way of singular privilege invites to draw near him, promising that he will be favorable to their prayers. Faith, there is no doubt, lies idle and even dead without prayer, in which the spirit of adoption shows and exercises itself, and by which we evidence that all his promises are considered by us as stable and sure. The inestimable grace of God, in short, towards believers, appears in this, that he exhibits himself to them as a Father.

20. Jehovah preserves, etc. He insists upon the same truth,—that God is near to his people to help them in the time of need; this being a sure proof of his presence, that by his mercy they come safe and unhurt out of every danger which befalls them. It is worthy of our notice, that, instead of fear, he now speaks of love; for, in distinguishing believers by this title, that they love God, he intimates it to be the root of true godliness, that they submit themselves to him voluntarily, which again is the effect of faith. Till God draw us by the attractions of his grace, this placid submission will never follow. The love spoken of by David, however, is perhaps more extensive, as God's people not only attach themselves to him in the way of obedience to his authority aspire with their whole soul after this happiness. Still there can be no doubt, that the reference is to it here as the chief part of holiness and righteousness, as was said by Moses, "And now, O Israel, what does the Lord thy God require of thee," etc. (Deuteronomy 10:12.) This effect of godliness in securing our safety under the divine guardianship, David exemplifies by an opposition clause, declaring, that all the wicked shall, in the just judgment of God, miserably perish. That he might close as he had begun, he again affirms, that he will publish the praises of God, and urges all to the same duty by his example.

of the glory of his kingdom (v. 11), the glorious majesty of it (v. 12), for he has prepared his throne in the heavens, and it is high and lifted up, and surrounded with an innumerable company of angels.

(2.) The power of it: When they speak of the glory of God's kingdom they must talk of his power, the extent of it, the efficacy of it—his power, by which he can do any thing and does every thing he pleases (v. 11); and, as a proof of it, let them make known his mighty acts (v. 12), that the sons of men may be invited to yield themselves his willing subjects and so put themselves under the protection of such a mighty potentate.

(3.) The perpetuity of it, v. 13. The thrones of earthly princes totter, and the flowers of their crowns wither, monarchies come to an end; but, Lord, thy kingdom is an everlasting kingdom. God will govern the world to the end of time, when the Mediator, who is now entrusted with the administration of his kingdom, shall deliver it up to God, even the Father, that he may be all in all to eternity. His dominion endures throughout all generations, for he himself is eternal, and his counsels are unchangeable and uniform; and Satan, who has set up a kingdom in opposition to him, is conquered and in a chain.

2. The goodness of his kingdom. His royal style and title are, The Lord God, gracious and merciful; and his government answers to his title. The goodness of God appears in what he does,

(1.) For all the creatures in general (v. 15, 16): He provides food for all flesh, and therein appears his everlasting mercy, Ps. cxxxvi. 25. All the creatures live upon God, and, as they had their being from him at first, so from him they have all the supports of their being and on him they depend for the continuance of it.

(2.) For the children of men in particular, whom he governs as reasonable creatures. He does none of them any wrong, for (v. 17) the Lord is righteous in all his ways, and not unrighteous in any of them; he is holy, and acts like himself, with a perfect rectitude in all his works. He does all of them good, his own people in a special manner.

First, He supports those that are sinking, and it is his honor to help the weak, v. 14.

Secondly, He is very ready to hear and answer the prayers of his people, v. 18, 19.

Thirdly, He takes those under his special protection who have a confidence and complacency in him (v. 20).

Lastly, The psalmist concludes, with a resolution to give glory to God himself (v. 21): My mouth shall speak the praise of the Lord. When we have said what we can, in praising God, still there is more to be said, and therefore we must not only begin our thanksgivings with this purpose, as he did (v. 1), but conclude them with it, as he does here, because we shall presently have occasion to begin again.

Psalm 146

1-5

1 Praise ye the LORD.
Praise the LORD, O my soul.
2 While I live will I
praise the LORD: I will sing
praises unto my God while I
have any being.
3 Put not your trust in
princes, nor in the son of
man, in whom there is no
help.
4 His breath goeth forth,
he returneth to his earth; in
that very day his thoughts
perish.
5 Happy is he that hath
the God of Jacob for his
help, whose hope is in the
LORD his God:

Psalm 146

DIVISION. We are now among the Hallelujahs. The rest of our journey lies through the Delectable Mountains. All is praise to the close of the book. The key is high pitched: the music is upon the high sounding cymbals. O for a heart full of joyful gratitude, that we may run, and leap, and glorify God, even as these Psalms do.

Alexander thinks that this song may be regarded as composed of two equal parts; in the first we see the happiness of those who trust in God, and not in man (Ps 146:1-5), while the second gives the reason drawn from the Divine perfections (Ps 146:5-10). This might suffice for our purpose; but as there is really no break at all, we will keep it entire. It is "one pearl", a sacred censer of holy incense, pouring forth one sweet perfume.

EXPOSITION

Verse 1. Praise ye the LORD, or, Hallelujah. It is saddening to remember how this majestic word has been trailed in the mire of late. Its irreverent use is an aggravated instance of taking the name of Jehovah our God in vain. Let us hope that it has been done in ignorance by the ruder sort; but great responsibility lies with leaders who countenance and even copy this blasphemy. With holy awe let us pronounce the word HALLELUJAH, and by it summon ourselves and all others to adore the God of the whole earth. Men need to be called to praise; it is important that they should praise; and there are many reasons why they should do it at once. Let all who hear the word Hallelujah unite immediately in holy praise.

Verse 2. While I live will I praise the LORD. I shall not live here for ever. This mortal life will find a finis in death; but while it lasts I will laud the Lord my God. I cannot tell how long or short my life may be; but every hour of it shall be given to the praises of my God. While I live I'll love; and while I breathe I'll bless. It is but for a while, and I will not while that time away in idleness, but consecrate it to that same service which shall occupy eternity. As our life is the gift of God's mercy, it should be used for his glory. I will sing praises unto my God while I have any being. When I am no longer in being on earth, I hope to have a higher being in heaven, and there I will not only praise, but sing praises. Here I have to sigh and praise, but there I shall only sing and praise.

Verse 3. Put not your trust in princes. If David be the author this warning comes from a prince. In any case it comes from the Spirit of the living God. Men are always far too apt to depend upon the great ones of earth, and forget the Great One above; and this habit is the fruitful source of disappointment. Princes are only men, and men with greater needs than others; why, then, should we look to them for aid? They are in greater danger, are burdened with greater cares, and are more likely to be misled than other men; therefore, it is folly to select them for our confidence. Probably no order of men have been so false to their promises and treaties as men of royal blood. So live as to deserve their trust, but do not burden them with your trust.

Verse 4. His breath goeth forth, he returneth to his earth. His breath goes from his body, and his body goes to the grave. His spirit goes one way, and his body another. High as he stood, the want of a little air brings him down to the ground, and lays him under it. Man who comes from the earth returns to the earth: it is the mother and sister of his body, and he must needs lie among Ins kindred as soon as the spirit which was his life has made its exit. There is a spirit in man, and when that goes the man goes. The spirit returns to God who gave it, and the flesh to the dust out of which it was fashioned. This is a poor creature to trust in: a dying creature, a corrupting creature. Those hopes will surely fall to the ground which are built upon men who so soon lie under ground. In that very day his thoughts perish. Whatever he may have proposed to do, the proposal ends in smoke. He

JOHN CALVIN

Psalm 146

After stirring up himself, and others by his example, to praise God, David animadverts upon the diseased disposition, almost universally prevalent, to deceive ourselves by expectations entertained from various quarters. He, at the same time, points out the remedy—that our whole hope should be centered in God. To persuade us to resort to him more readily, he touches shortly upon some proofs of his power and mercy.

1-5

1. Praise Jehovah. The five last Psalms close with the same word with which they begin. But having in general called upon all to praise God, he addresses himself, or, which is the same thing, his soul, only that under the name of soul he addresses his inward self more emphatically. We may infer from this, that the influence which moved him was not volatile and superficial, (as many will blame themselves with remissness on this point, and then immediately lapse into it again,) but a staid and constant affection, followed up by activity, and proved by its effects not to be feigned. As David felt, that good endeavors are frustrated or hindered through the craft of Satan, he thinks it proper to apply a stimulus for exciting his own zeal, in the first place, before professing to be a leader or teacher to others. Although his heart was truly and seriously in the work, he would not rest in this, until he had acquired still greater ardor. And if it was necessary for David to stir himself up to the praises of God, how powerful a stimulant must we require for a more difficult matter when we aim at the divine life with self-denial. As to the religious exercise here mentioned, let us feel that we will never be sufficiently active in it, unless we strenuously exact it from ourselves. As God supports and maintains his people in the world with this view, that they may employ their whole life in praising him, David very properly declares, that he will do this to the end of his course.

3. Trust not in princes. This admonition is appropriately inserted, for one means by which men blind themselves is that of involving their minds through a number of inventions, and being thus prevented from engaging in the praises of God. That God may have the whole praise due to him, David exposes and overthrows those false stays on which we would otherwise be too much disposed to trust. His meaning is, that we should withdraw ourselves from man in general, but he names princes, from whom more is to be feared than common men.

5. Blessed is he, etc. As it would not have been enough to reprove the sin, he submits the remedy upon which the proper correction of it depends; and this is, that the hopes of men are only stable and well-founded when they rest entirely upon God. For even the wicked sometimes come the length of acknowledging the folly of trust in man. Accordingly they are often angry with themselves for being so inconsiderate as to expect deliverance from men; but by neglecting the remedy, they are not extricated from their error. The Psalmist

MATTHEW HENRY

Psalm 146

1-4 The divine bounty.

David is supposed to have penned this psalm; and he was himself a prince, a mighty prince; as such, it might be thought,

1. That he should be exempted from the service of praising God, that it was enough for him to see that his priests and people did it, but that he needed not to do it himself in his own person. Michal thought it a disparagement to him to dance before the ark; but he was so far from being of this mind that he would himself be first and foremost in the work, v. 1, 2. He considered his dignity as so far from excusing him from it that it rather obliged him to lead in it, and he thought it so far from lessening him that it really magnified him; therefore he stirred up himself to it and to make a business of it: Praise the Lord, O my soul! and he resolved to abide by it: "I will praise him with my heart, I will sing praises to him with my mouth. Herein I will have an eye to him as the Lord, infinitely blessed and glorious in himself, and as my God, in covenant with me."

2. It might be thought that he himself, having been so great a blessing to his country, should be adored, according to the usage of the heathen nations, who deified their heroes, that they should all come and trust in his shadow and make him their stay and strong-hold. "No," says David, "Put not your trust in princes (v. 3), not in me, not in any other; do not repose your confidence in them; do not raise your expectations from them. Be not too sure of their sincerity; some have thought they knew better how to reign by knowing how to dissemble. Be not too sure of their constancy and fidelity; it is possible they may both change their minds and break their words."

5-10 Encouragement to trust in God.

The psalmist, having cautioned us not to trust in princes (because, if we do, we shall be miserably disappointed), here encourages us to put our confidence in God, because, if we do so, we shall be happily secured: Happy is he that has the God of Jacob for his help, that has an interest in his attributes and promises, and has them engaged for him, and whose hope is in the Lord his God.

I. Let us take a view of the character here given of those whom God will uphold. Those shall have God for their help,

1. Who take him for their God, and serve and worship him accordingly.

2. Who have their hope in him, and live a life of dependence upon him, who have good thoughts of him, and encourage themselves in him, when all other supports fail.

II. Let us take a view of the great encouragements here given us to hope in the Lord our God.

1. He is the Maker of the world, and therefore has all power in himself, and the command of the powers of

Psalm 146

6-10

6 Which made heaven, and earth, the sea, and all that therein is: which keepeth truth for ever:
7 Which executeth judgment for the oppressed: which giveth food to the hungry. The LORD looseth the prisoners:
8 The LORD openeth the eyes of the blind: the LORD raiseth them that are bowed down: the LORD loveth the righteous:
9 The LORD preserveth the strangers; he relieveth the fatherless and widow: but the way of the wicked he turneth upside down.
10 The LORD shall reign for ever, even thy God, O Zion, unto all generations. Praise ye the LORD.

cannot think, and what he had thought of cannot effect itself, and therefore it dies.

Verse 5. Happy is he that hath the God of Jacob for his help. Heaped up is his happiness. He has happiness indeed: the true and the real delight is with him. The God of Jacob is the God of the covenant, the God of wrestling prayer, the God of the tried believer; he is the only living and true God. The God of Jacob is Jehovah, who appeared unto Moses, and led the tribes of Jacob out of Egypt, and through the wilderness. Those are happy who trust him, for they shall never be ashamed or confounded. The Lord never dies, neither do his thoughts perish: his purpose of mercy, like himself, endures throughout all generations. Hallelujah!

Verse 6. Which made heaven, and earth, the sea, and all that therein is. Wisely may we trust our Creator: justly may we expect to be happy in so doing. He who made heaven can make a heaven for us, and make us fit for heaven. He who made the earth can preserve us while we are on earth, and help us to make good use of it while we sojourn upon it. He who made the sea and all its mysteries can steer us across the pathless deeps of a troubled life, and make it a way for his redeemed to pass over. This God who still makes the world by keeping it in existence is assuredly able to keep us to his eternal kingdom and glory.

Verse 7. Which executeth judgment for the oppressed. He is a swift and impartial administrator of justice. Our King surpasses all earthly princes because he pays no deference to rank or wealth, and is never the respecter of persons. He is the friend of the down trodden, the avenger of the persecuted, the champion of the helpless. Safely may we trust our cause with such a Judge if it be a just one: happy are we to be under such a Ruler.

Verse 8. The LORD openeth the eyes of the blind. Jesus did this very frequently, and hereby proved himself to be Jehovah. He who made the eye can open it, and when he does so it is to his glory. How often is the mental eye closed in moral night! And who can remove this dreary effect of the fall but the Almighty God This miracle of grace he has performed in myriads of cases, and it is in each case a theme for loftiest praise. The Lord raiseth them that are bowed down. This also Jesus did literally, thus doing the work peculiar to God. Jehovah consoles the bereaved, cheers the defeated, solaces the despondent, comforts the despairing. Let those who are bowed to the ground appeal to him, and he will speedily upraise them.

Verse 9. The Lord preserveth the strangers. Many monarchs hunted aliens down, or transported them from place to place, or left them as outlaws unworthy of the rights of man; but Jehovah made special laws for their shelter within his domain.

Verse 10. The LORD shall reign for ever. Jehovah is King, and his kingdom can never come to an end. Neither does he die, nor abdicate, nor lose his crown by force. Glory be to his name, his throne is never in jeopardy. As the Lord ever liveth, so he ever reigneth. Even thy God, O Zion, unto all generations. Zion's God, the God of his worshipping people, is he who in every age shall reign. There will always be a Zion; Zion will always have Jehovah for her King; for her he will always prove himself to be reigning in great power. What should we do in the presence of so great a King, but enter into his courts with praise, and pay to him our joyful homage? Praise ye the LORD. Again they said Hallelujah. Again the sweet perfume arose from the golden vials full of sweet odors. Are we not prepared for an outburst of holy song? Do not we also say—Hallelujah? Here endeth this happy Psalm. Here endeth not the praise of the Lord, which shall ascend for ever and ever. Amen.

JOHN CALVIN

having condemned the infatuation, which we have seen to be natural to us all, wisely subjoins that they are blessed who trust in God. Jeremiah observes the same order. (Jeremiah 17:5, 7.)
"Cursed is he that trusteth in man, and maketh flesh his arm," etc., and then—"Blessed is the man whose hope the Lord is."

6-10
6. Who made heaven, etc. By all these epithets he confirms the truth previously stated. For though at first sight it may seem inappropriate to speak of the Creation, the power of God bears most pertinently upon his helping us whenever danger is near. We know how easily Satan tempts to distrust, and we are thrown into a state of trembling agitation by the slightest causes. Now, if we reflect that God is the Maker of heaven and earth, we will reasonably give him the honor of having the government of the world which he created in his hands and power. There is in this first ascription, then, a commendation of his power, which should swallow up all our fears. As it is not enough that God is merely able to help us, but as a promise is farther necessary, to the effect that he is willing and shall do it, David next declares that he is faithful and true, that, on discovering his willingness, no room may be left for hesitation.
7. Rendering right, etc. He instances other kinds both of the power and goodness of God, which are just so many reasons why we should hope in him. All of them bear upon the point, that the help of God will be ready and forthcoming to those who are in the lowest circumstances, that accordingly our miseries will be no barrier in the way of his helping us; nay, that such is his nature, that he is disposed to assist all in proportion to their necessity.
9. Jehovah guarding, etc. By strangers, orphans, and widows, the Psalmist means all those in general who are destitute of the help of man. While all show favor to those who are known to them and near to them, we know that strangers are, for the most part, exposed to injurious treatment. We find comparatively few who come forward to protect and redress widows and orphans; it seems lost labor, where there is no likelihood of compensation. Under these cases the Psalmist shows that whatever the grievance may be under which we suffer, the reason can only be with ourselves if God, who so kindly invites all who are in distress to come to him, does not stretch forth his arm for our help.
10. Jehovah shall reign, etc. He directs his discourse to the Church, that he may more effectually persuade all God's people of their really finding him to be such as he had just described. When he says that God is king for ever, we are to remember at the same time the purpose for which he reigns—taking our definition of it from the preceding ascription's. It follows that, whether living or dying, we shall be safe under the keeping of a king who reigns expressly for our salvation. Had he said no more than that Jehovah reigned for ever, we would have been ready to object the distance between us and his inconceivable greatness. He states, therefore, in express terms, his being bound by sacred covenant to his chosen people.

MATTHEW HENRY

all the creatures, which, being derived from him, depend upon him (v. 6): He made heaven and earth, the sea, and all that in them is, and therefore his arm is not shortened, that it cannot save.
2. He is a God of inviolable fidelity. We may venture to take God's word, for he keepeth truth for ever, and therefore no word of his shall fall to the ground; it is true from the beginning, and therefore true to the end.
3. He is the patron of injured innocency: He pleads the cause of the oppressed, and (as we read it) he executes judgment for them. He often does it in his providence, giving redress to those that suffer wrong and clearing up their integrity.
4. He is a bountiful benefactor to the necessitous: He gives food to the hungry; so God does in an ordinary way for the answering of the cravings of nature; so he has done sometimes in an extraordinary way, as when ravens fed Elijah.
5. He is the author of liberty to those that were bound: The Lord looseth the prisoners. He brought Israel out of the house of bondage in Egypt and afterwards in Babylon.
6. He gives sight to those that have been long deprived of it; The Lord can open the eyes of the blind, and has often given to his afflicted people to see that comfort which before they were not aware of; witness Gen. xxi. 19, and the prophet's servant, 2 Kings vi. 17. But this has special reference to Christ, (John ix. 32).
7. He sets that straight which was crooked, and makes those easy that were pained and ready to sink: He raises those that are bowed down, by comforting and supporting them under their burdens, and, in due time, removing their burdens.
8. He has a constant kindness for all good people: The Lord loveth the righteous, and they may with the more confidence depend upon his power when they are sure of his good-will.
9. He has a tender concern for those that stand in special need of his care: The Lord preserves the strangers. It ought not to pass without remark that the name of Jehovah is repeated here five times in five lines, to intimate that it is an almighty power that is engaged and exerted for the relief of the oppressed.
10. He will appear for the destruction of all those that oppose his kingdom and oppress the faithful subjects of it: The way of the wicked he turns upside down, and therefore let us hope in him, and not be afraid of the fury of the oppressor, as though he were ready to destroy.
11. His kingdom shall continue through all the revolutions of time, to the utmost ages of eternity, v. 10. Let this encourage us to trust in God at all times that the Lord shall reign for ever, in spite of all the malignity of the powers of darkness, even thy God, O Zion! unto all generations.

Psalm 147

1-7
1 Praise ye the LORD: for it is good to sing praises unto our God; for it is pleasant; and praise is comely.
2 The LORD doth build up Jerusalem: he gathereth together the outcasts of Israel.
3 He healeth the broken in heart, and bindeth up their wounds.
4 He telleth the number of the stars; he calleth them all by their names.
5 Great is our Lord, and of great power: his understanding is infinite.
6 The LORD lifteth up the meek: he casteth the wicked down to the ground.
7 Sing unto the LORD with thanksgiving; sing praise upon the harp unto our God:

Psalm 147

SUBJECT. This is a specially remarkable song. In it the greatness and the condescending goodness of the Lord are celebrated The God of Israel is set forth in his peculiarity of glory as caring for the sorrowing, the insignificant, and forgotten. The poet finds a singular joy in extolling one who is so singularly gracious. It is a Psalm of the city and of the field, of the first and the second creations, of the common wealth and of the church. It is good and pleasant throughout.

DIVISION. The, song appears to divide itself into three portions. From Ps 147:1-6, Jehovah is extolled for building up Zion, and blessing his mourners; from Ps 147:7-11, the like praise is given because of his provision for the lowly, and his pleasure in them; and then, from Ps 147:12-20, he is magnified for his work on behalf of his people, and the power of his word in nature and in grace. Let it be studied with joyful gratitude.

EXPOSITION

Verse 1. Praise ye the Lord, or Hallelujah: The flow of the broad river of the Book of Psalms ends in a cataract of praise. The present Psalm begins and ends with Hallelujah. Jehovah and happy praise should ever be associated in the mind of a believer.

Verse 2. The Lord doth build up Jerusalem. God appears both ill the material and spiritual world as a Builder and Maker, and therein he is to be praised. His grace, wisdom, and power are all seen in the formation and establishment of the chosen seat of his worship; once a city with material walls, but now a church composed of spiritual stones.

Verse 3. He healeth the broken in heart, and bindeth up their wounds. This the Holy Spirit mentions as a part of the glory of God, and a reason for our declaring his praise: the Lord is not only a Builder, but a Healer; he restores broken hearts as well as broken walls.

Verse 4. He telleth the number of the stars. None but he can count the mighty host, but as he made them and sustains them he can number them. To Jehovah stars are as mere coins, which the merchant tells as he puts them into his bag. He calleth them all by their names. He has an intimate acquaintance with each separate orb, so as to know its name or character.

Verse 5. Great is our Lord. Our Lord and King is great—magnanimous, infinite, inconceivably glorious. None can describe his majesty, or reckon up the number of his excellencies. And of great power. Doing as he wills, and willing to do mighty deeds. His acts reveal something of his might, but the mass of his power is hidden, for all things are possible with God, even the things impossible with men.

Verse 6. The LORD lifteth up the meek: he casteth the wicked down to the ground. He reverses the evil order of things. The meek are down, and he lifts them up; the wicked are exalted, anti he hurls them down to the dust. The Lord loves those who are reverent to himself, humble in their own eyes, and gentle to their fellow men: these he lifts up to hope, to peace, to power, to eternal honor. When God lifts a man, it is a lift indeed. Proud men are in their own esteem, high enough already; only those who are low will care to be lifted up, and only such will Jehovah upraise.

Verse 7. In this paragraph the contrast announced in the former section is enlarged upon from another point of view, namely, as it is seen in nature and in providence. Sing unto the LORD with, thanksgiving; or rather, "respond to Jehovah." He speaks to us in his works, let us answer him with our thanks. All that he does is gracious, every movement of Iris hand is goodness; therefore let our hearts reply with gratitude, and our lips with song. Our lives should be responses to divine love. Jehovah is ever engaged in giving, let us respond with thanksgiving. Sing praise upon the harp unto our God. Blend music with song. Under a dispensation of ritual the use of music was most commendable, and suitable in the great

JOHN CALVIN

Psalm 147

1-6

Praise ye God, etc. Though the benefits he speaks of are such as God extends to all men indiscriminately, it is plain that he addresses more especially God's people, who alone behold his works in an enlightened manner, whereas stupidity and blindness of mind deprive others of their understanding. Nor is his subject confined to the common benefits of God, but the main thing which he celebrates is his mercy, as shown to his chosen people. That the Church may address itself to the praises of God with more alacrity, he states that this kind of exercise is good, delightful, and pleasant, by which he indirectly censures a sin which is all but universal of becoming wearied at the very mention of God, and counting it our highest pleasure to forget both God and ourselves, that we may give way to unrestrained indulgence.

2. Jehovah building up, etc. He begins with the special mercy of God towards his Church and people, in choosing to adopt one nation out of all others, and selecting a fixed place where his name might be called upon. When he is here called the builder of Jerusalem, the allusion is not so much to the outward form and structure, as to the spiritual worship of God. It is a common figure in treating of the Church to speak of it as a building or temple. The meaning is, that the Church was not of human erection, but formed by the supernatural power of God; for it was from no dignity of the place itself that Jerusalem became the only habitation of God in our world, nor did it come to this honor by counsel, industry, effort or power of man, but because God was pleased to consecrate it to himself.

In the following verse he insists upon the same truth, the figure suggesting that though the Church labor under, and be oppressed by many diseases, God will speedily and easily recover it from all its wounds.

4. Numbering the multitude, etc. As the gathering together of the people of whom the Psalmist spoke might appear to be an impossibility, there seems some ground for the opinion of those who think that he confirms it in this verse. The connection they give to the Psalmist's words is this—that as it is at least not more difficult to gather men together who are outcast and scattered, than to number the stars, there was no reason why the wandering exile Israelites should despair of their return, provided they should resort with one consent to God as their only head.

6. Raising up, etc. The ascription of this to God fitly tends to confirm our hope under affliction, and prevent our souls from fainting under the cross. From this we may infer that although our fathers who lived under the Law were more gently dealt with, they knew something at least of that warfare with which God daily exercises us, in order to make us seek our true rest elsewhere than in this world.

7-11

7. Sing to Jehovah in thanksgiving. Again he exhorts to sing the praises of God, intimating at the same time that abundant

MATTHEW HENRY

Psalm 147

1-11 A call to praise God; reasons for praise.
Here,

I. The duty of praise is recommended to us. It is not without reason that we are thus called to it again and again: Praise you the Lord (v. 1), and again (v. 7), Sing unto the Lord with thanksgiving, sing praise upon the harp to our God (let all our praises be directed to him and center in him), for it is good to do so; it is our duty, and therefore good in itself; it is our interest, and therefore good for us. It is acceptable to our Creator and it answers the end of our creation. The law for it is holy, just, and good; the practice of it will turn to a good account. It is good, for

1. It is pleasant. Holy joy or delight are required as the principle of it, and that is pleasant to us as men; giving glory to God is the design and business of it, and that is pleasant to us as saints that are devoted to his honor. Praising God is work that is its own wages; it is heaven upon earth; it is what we should be in as in our element.

2. It is comely; it is that which becomes us as reasonable creatures, much more as people in covenant with God. In giving honor to God we really do ourselves a great deal of honor.

II. God is recommended to us as the proper object of our most exalted and enlarged praises, upon several accounts.

1. The care he takes of his chosen people, v. 2. Is Jerusalem to be raised out of small beginnings? Is it to be recovered out of its ruins? In both cases, The Lord builds up Jerusalem. The gospel-church, the Jerusalem that is from above, is of this building. He framed the model of it in his own counsels; he founded it by the preaching of his gospel; he adds to it daily such as shall be saved, and so increases it.

2. The comforts he has laid up for true penitents, v. 3. They are broken in heart, and wounded, humbled, and troubled, for sin, inwardly pained at the remembrance of it, as a man is that is sorely wounded. Their very hearts are not only pricked, but rent, under the sense of the dishonor they have done to God and the injury they have done to themselves by sin.

3. The sovereign dominion he has over the lights of heaven, v. 4, 5. The stars are innumerable, many of them being scarcely discernible with the naked eye, and yet he counts them, and knows the exact number of them, for they are all the work of his hands and the instruments of his providence.

4. The pleasure he takes in humbling the proud and exalting those of low degree (v. 6): The Lord lifts up the meek, who abase themselves before him, and whom men trample on; but the wicked, who conduct themselves insolently towards God and scornfully towards all mankind, who lift up themselves in pride and folly, he casteth down to the ground, sometimes by very humbling providences in this world, at

Psalm 147

8-14

8 Who covereth the heaven with clouds, who prepareth rain for the earth, who maketh grass to grow upon the mountains.
9 He giveth to the beast his food, and to the young ravens which cry.
10 He delighteth not in the strength of the horse: he taketh not pleasure in the legs of a man.
11 The LORD taketh pleasure in them that fear him, in those that hope in his mercy.
12 Praise the LORD, O Jerusalem; praise thy God, O Zion.
13 For he hath strengthened the bars of thy gates; he hath blessed thy children within thee.
14 He maketh peace in thy borders, and filleth thee with the finest of the wheat.

congregation: those of us who judge it to be less desirable for public worship, under a spiritual economy, because it has led to so many abuses, nevertheless rejoice in it in our privacy, and are by no means insensible to its charms. It seems profanation that choice minstrelsy should so often be devoted to unworthy themes: the sweetest harmonies should be consecrated to the honor of the Lord.

Verse 8. Who covereth the heaven with clouds. He works in all things, above as well as below. Clouds are not caused by accident, but produced by God himself, and made to assume degrees of density by which the blue firmament is hidden. A sky scape might seem to be a mere fortuitous concourse of vapors, but it is not so: the Great Artist's hand thus covers the canvas of the heavens.

Verse 9. He giveth to the beast his food. By causing the grass to grow on the hills the Lord feeds the cattle. God careth for the brute creation. Men tread grass under foot as though it were nothing, but God causeth it to grow: too often men treat their cattle with cruelty, but the Lord himself feedeth them. The great God is too good, and, indeed, too great to overlook things that are despised. Say not, "Doth God care for oxen?" Indeed he does, and he permits himself to be here described as giving them their food as husbandmen are wont to do.

Verse 10. He delighteth not in the strength of the horse. Not to great and strong animals doth the Creator in any measure direct his special thought; but in lesser living things he has equal pleasure. If man could act the Creator's part, he would take peculiar delight in producing noble quadrupeds like horses, whose strength and speed would reflect honor upon their maker; but Jehovah has no such feeling; lie cares as much for helpless birds in the nest as for the war horse in the pride of its power. He taketh not pleasure in the legs of a man. These are the athlete's glory, but God hath no pleasure in them.

Verse 11. The LORD taketh pleasure in them that fear him in those that hope in his mercy. While the bodily powers give no content to God, spiritual qualities are his delight. He cares most for those emotions which center in himself: the fear which he approves is fear of him, and the hope which he accepts is hope in his mercy. It is a striking thought that God should not only be at peace with some kinds of men, but even find a solace and a joy in their company. Oh! the matchless condescension of the Lord, that his greatness should take pleasure in the insignificant creatures of his hand.

Verse 12. Praise the Lord, O Jerusalem; praise thy God, O Zion. How the poet insists upon praise: he cries praise, praise, as if it were the most important of all duties. A peculiar people should render peculiar praise. The city of peace should be the city of praise; and the temple of the covenant God should resound with his glories. If nowhere else, yet certainly in Zion there should be joyful adoration of Zion's God.

Verse 13. For he hath strengthened the bars of thy gates. Her fortifications were finished, even to the fastenings of the gates, and God had made all sound and strong, even to her bolts and bars: thus her security against invading foes was guaranteed. This is no small mercy. Oh, that our churches were thus preserved from all false doctrine and unholy living! This must be the Lord's doing; and where he has wrought it his name is greatly to be praised.

Verse 14. He maketh peace in thy borders. Even to the boundaries quiet extends; no enemies are wrangling with the borderers. If there is peace there, we may be sure that peace is everywhere. "When a man's ways please the Lord he maketh even his enemies to be at peace with him." Peace is from the God of peace. Considering the differing constitutions, conditions, tastes, and opinions of men, it is a work of God when in large churches unbroken peace is found year after year; and it is an equal wonder if worldlings, instead of persecuting the godly, treat them with marked respect.

matter was not wanting, since new proofs still meet our eyes of his power, goodness, and wisdom. First he tells us that he covers the heavens with clouds, and this change would awaken our attention, were we not chargeable with so much thoughtlessness. Various as are the marvels to be seen in the heavens above us, were the same serenity always to continue, we would not have so wonderful a display of his power as when he suddenly veils them with clouds, withdrawing the light of the sun, and setting a new face as it were upon the world.
9. Who gives to the cattle their food. By giving an instance he explains more clearly what he had said, of God's providing food for every living creature. When he speaks of the cattle and the ravens being fed, and not of men, this is to give more emphasis to his argument. We know that it was for man's sake the world was made at all, and endued with fertility and plenty; and in proportion as we are nearer in the scale of existence to God, he shows us the more of his goodness. But if he condescends to notice the brute creation, it is plain that to us he will be a nurse and a father.
10. Not in the strength of the horse, etc. After the Psalmist has shown that there is proof of the divine goodness in every part of the world, he takes particular notice that men have no strength but what is given them from above, and this he adds with the express purpose of checking the pride by which almost all men are inflamed, and which leads them to trust in their own strength. The meaning of the passage is, that let man come in the preparation of his own strength, and with all the assistance's that seem to him most prevalent, this will only issue in smoke and vanity; nay, that in arrogating the very least to himself, this will only be a hindrance in the way of the mercy of God, by which alone we stand. The strength of the horse is mentioned by synecdoche to denote any kind of protection.

12-14
12. Celebrate Jehovah, O Jerusalem! Having spoken in general of the mercies of God, he again addresses his discourse to the Lord's people, who alone, as we have remarked already, can appreciate them, calling upon them to recognize with thanksgiving the blessings which others riot upon without acknowledgment. Under the name of Jerusalem, he comprises the whole Church, for in that place the faithful then held their religious assemblies, and flowed together as it were to the standard of the Lord. Although he will take occasion afterwards again to speak of the government of the world at large, he here commemorates the goodness of God as manifested to his own people, in protecting his own Church, bountifully cherishing it, enriching it abundantly with all blessings, and preserving it in peace and safety from all harm.

15-20
15. While he sends forth, etc. He again touches upon some instances of the operation of God, everywhere to be seen in the system of nature. And as the changes which take place in the air, and upon the earth, and which should be considered evidences of his power, may perhaps be regarded by the world as the effect of chance, the Psalmist, before proceeding to speak

furthest in the day when their faces shall be filled with everlasting shame. God proves himself to be God by looking on the proud and abasing them, Job xl. 12.
5. The provision he makes for the inferior creatures. Though he is so great as to command the stars, he is so good as not to forget even the fowls, v. 8, 9.
6. The complacency he takes in his people, v. 10, 11. In times when great things are doing, and there are great expectations of the success of them, it concerns us to know (since the issue proceeds from the Lord) whom, and what, God will delight to honor and crown with victory. It is not the strength of armies, but the strength of grace, that God is pleased to own.

12-20 Jerusalem and Zion called to praise to God; God's favor to Israel.
Jerusalem, and Zion, the holy city, the holy hill, are here called upon to praise God, v. 12. For where should praise be offered up to God but where his altar is? Where may we expect that glory should be given to him but in the beauty of holiness? Let the inhabitants of Jerusalem praise the Lord in their own houses; let the priests and Levites, who attend in Zion, the city of their solemnities, in a special manner praise the Lord. They have more cause to do it than others, and they lie under greater obligations to do it than others; for it is their business, it is their profession. "Praise thy God, O Zion! he is thine, and therefore thou art bound to praise him; his being thine includes all happiness, so that thou canst never want matter for praise." Jerusalem and Zion must praise God,
I. For the prosperity and flourishing state of their civil interests, v. 13, 14.
1. For their common safety. They had gates, and kept their gates barred in times of danger; but that would not have been an effectual security to them if God had not strengthened the bars of their gates and fortified their fortifications. The most probable means we can devise for our own preservation will not answer the end, unless God give his blessing with them; we must therefore in the careful and diligent use of those means, depend upon him for that blessing, and attribute the undisturbed repose of our land more to the wall of fire than to the wall of water round about us, Zech. ii. 5.
2. For the increase of their people. This strengthens the bars of the gates as much as any thing: He hath blessed thy children within thee, with that first and great blessing, Be fruitful, and multiply, and replenish the land. It is a comfort to parents to see their children blessed of the Lord (Isa. lxi. 9), and a comfort to the generation that is going off to see the rising generation numerous and hopeful, for which blessing God must be blessed.
3. For the public tranquility, that they were delivered from the terrors and desolations of war: He makes peace in thy borders, by putting an end to the wars that were, and preventing the wars that were threatened and feared. He makes peace within thy

Psalm 147

15-20

15 He sendeth forth his commandment upon earth: his word runneth very swiftly.
16 He giveth snow like wool: he scattereth the hoarfrost like ashes.
17 He casteth forth his ice like morsels: who can stand before his cold?
18 He sendeth out his word, and melteth them: he causeth his wind to blow, and the waters flow.
19 He sheweth his word unto Jacob, his statutes and his judgments unto Israel.
20 He hath not dealt so with any nation: and as for his judgments, they have not known them. Praise ye the LORD.

Verse 15. He sendeth forth his commandment upon earth. His messages fly throughout his dominions: upon earth his warrants are executed as well as in heaven. From his church his word goes forth; from Zion he missions the nations with the word of life. His word runneth very swiftly: his purposes of love are speedily accomplished. Oriental monarchs labored hard to establish rapid postal communication; the desire, will, and command of the Lord flash in an instant from pole to pole, yea, from heaven to earth.

Verse 16. Here follow instances of the power of God upon the elements. He giveth snow like wool. As a gift he scatters the snow, which falls in flakes like fleecy wool. Snow falls softly, covers universally, and clothes warmly, even as wool covers the sheep. The most evident resemblance lies in the whiteness of the two substances; but many other likenesses are to be seen by the observant eye. It is wise to see God in winter and in distress as well as in summer and prosperity. He who one day feeds us with the finest of the wheat, at another time robes us in snow: he is the same God in each case, and each form of his operation bestows a gift on men.

Verse 17. He casteth forth his ice like morsels. Such are the crumbs of hail which he casts forth, or the crusts of ice which he creates upon the waters. These morsels are his ice, and he casts them abroad. The two expressions indicate a very real presence of God in the phenomena of nature. Who can stand before his cold? None can resist the utmost rigors of cold any more than they can bear the vehemence of heat. God's withdrawals of light are a darkness that may be felt, and his withdrawals of heat are a cold which is absolutely omnipotent.

Verse 18. He sendeth out his word, and melteth them. When the frost is sharpest, and the ice is hardest, the Lord intervenes; and though he doth no more than send his word, yet the rocks of ice are dissolved at once, and the huge bergs begin to float into the southern seas. The phenomena of winter are not so abundant in Palestine as with us, yet they are witnessed sufficiently to cause the devout to bless God for the return of spring.

Verse 19. He sheweth his word unto Jacob, his statutes and his judgments unto Israel. He who is the Creator is also the Revealer. We are to praise the Lord above all things for his manifesting himself to us as he does not unto the world. Whatever part of his mind he discloses to us, whether it be a word of instruction, a statute of direction, or a judgment of government, we are bound to bless the Lord for it. He who causes summer to come in the place of winter has also removed the coldness and death from our hearts by the power of his word, and this is abundant cause for singing unto his name. As Jacob's seed of old were made to know the Lord, even so are we ill these latter days; wherefore, let his name be magnified among us. By that knowledge Jacob is ennobled into Israel, and therefore let him who is made a prevailing prince in prayer be also a chief musician in praise.

Verse 20. He hath not dealt so with any nation. Israel had clear and exclusive knowledge of God, while others were left in ignorance. Election is the loudest call for grateful adoration. And as for his judgments, they have not known them; or, and judgments they had not known them, as if not knowing the laws of God, they might be looked upon as having no laws at all worth mentioning. The nations were covered with darkness, and only Israel sat in the light. This was sovereign grace in its fullest noontide of power. Praise ye the Lord. When we have mentioned electing, distinguishing love, our praise can rise no higher, and therefore we close with one more hallelujah.

JOHN CALVIN

of the snow, hoar frost, and ice, expressly declares, that earth is governed by his power and control. The sending forth of his word is nothing else than the secret influence by which he regulates and governs all things, for without his orders and appointment no movement could take place among the elements, nor could they be borne, now one way and now another, upon their own spontaneous impulse without his foregoing secret decree. He says, that his word runneth quickly, because, when once God has intimated his will, all things concur to carry it into effect. If we do not hold fast by this principle, however acutely we may investigate second causes, all our perspicacity will come to nothing. It is thus that Aristotle, for example, has shown such ingenuity upon the subject of meteors, that he discusses their natural causes most exactly, while he omits the main point of all, upon which the merest child, at least having any religion, has the superiority over him. He must have little discernment who, in the sudden snows and hoar-frosts, does not perceive how quickly the word of God runs. If, then, we would avoid a senseless natural philosophy, we must always start with this principle, that everything in nature depends upon the will of God, and that the whole course of nature is only the prompt carrying into effect of his orders.

19. He announces his words to Jacob, etc. Here it is another word that is spoken of than what was formerly mentioned; for God speaks in a different way to the insensate works of his hands, which he silently subordinates to his will by secret laws impressed upon them, than he does to men who are endued with understanding, for these he teaches with articulate language, that they may obey him intelligently and with consent. Although the blessings formerly mentioned are not to be depreciated, they fall far short of this, that he has condescended to be the teacher of his chosen people, by communicating to them that religious doctrine which is a treasure of everlasting salvation. How little would it avail the Church that it were filled with the perishing enjoyments of time, and protected from hostile violence, did not its hope extend beyond this world. This, accordingly, is the grand proof of his love, that he has set before us in his word the light of eternal life. On this account it is appropriately mentioned here as the crowning part of true solid happiness. And let us learn from this, that we should embrace God's doctrine with affection, for we can conceive of nothing more delightful than that God should undertake our salvation, and give testimony of this by stretching out his hand to bring us to himself. For this is the design with which the doctrine has been given to us, that amidst the thick darkness of this world, and the devious errors into which Satan misleads the children of men, the great Father of us all may by it cast a foregoing light upon our path before gathering us to the inheritance of heaven. We are to notice, that the part which was sustained by Moses and the Prophets according to divine appointment is here ascribed to God himself, for we only put due honor upon the doctrine of religion, and estimate it at its proper worth when we rise to the consideration of God, who, in using the instrumentality of men, still claims to be considered our chief and only teacher.

MATTHEW HENRY

borders, that is, in all parts of the country, by composing differences among neighbors, that there may be no intestine broils and animosities, and upon thy borders, that they may not be attacked by invasions from abroad. If there be trouble any where, it is in the borders, the marches of a country; the frontier-towns lie most exposed, so that, if there be peace in the borders, there is a universal peace, a mercy we can never be sufficiently thankful for.

4. For great plenty, the common effect of peace: He filleth thee with the finest of the wheat—wheat, the most valuable grain, the fat, the finest of that, and a fullness thereof. What would they more? Canaan abounded with the best wheat (Deut. xxxii. 14) and exported it to the countries abroad, as appears, Ezek. xxvii. 17. The land of Israel was not enriched with precious stones nor spices, but with the finest of the wheat, with bread, which strengthens man's heart. This made it the glory of all lands, and for this God was praised in Zion.

II. For the wonderful instances of his power in the weather, particularly the winter-weather. He that protects Zion and Jerusalem is that God of power from whom all the powers of nature are derived and on whom they depend, and who produces all the changes of the seasons, which, if they were not common, would astonish us.

1. In general, whatever alterations there are in this lower world (and it is that world that is subject to continual changes) they are produced by the will, and power, and providence of God (v. 15): He sendeth forth his commandment upon earth, as one that has an incontestable authority to give orders.

2. In particular, frosts and thaws are both of them wonderful changes, and in both we must acknowledge the word of his power.

III. For his distinguishing favor to Israel, in giving them his word and ordinances, a much more valuable blessing than their peace and plenty (v. 14), as much as the soul is more excellent than the body. Jacob and Israel had God's statutes among them. They were under his peculiar government; the municipal laws of their nation were of his framing, and their constitution was a theocracy. They had the benefit of divine revelation; the great things of God's law were written to them. They had a priesthood of divine institution for all things pertaining to God, and prophets for all extraordinary occasions. Now this was,

1. A preventing mercy. They did not find out God's statutes and judgments of themselves, but God showed his word unto Jacob, and by that word he made known to them his statutes and judgments.

2. A distinguishing mercy, and upon that account the more obliging: "He hath not dealt so with every nation, not with any nation; and, as for his judgments, they have not known them, nor are likely to know them till the Messiah shall come and take down the partition-wall between Jew and Gentile, that the gospel may be preached to every creature."

Psalm 148

1-7
1 Praise ye the LORD. Praise ye the LORD from the heavens: praise him in the heights.
2 Praise ye him, all his angels: praise ye him, all his hosts.
3 Praise ye him, sun and moon: praise him, all ye stars of light.
4 Praise him, ye heavens of heavens, and ye waters that be above the heavens.
5 Let them praise the name of the LORD: for he commanded, and they were created.
6 He hath also stablished them for ever and ever: he hath made a decree which shall not pass.
7 Praise the LORD from the earth, ye dragons, and all deeps:

Psalm 148

The song is one and indivisible. It seems almost impossible to expound it in detail, for a living poem is not to be dissected verse by verse. It is a song of nature and of grace. As a flash of lightning flames through space, and enwraps both heaven and earth in one vestment of glory, so doth the adoration of the Lord in this Psalm light up all the universe, and cause it to glow with a radiance of praise. The song begins in the heavens, sweeps downward to dragons and all deeps, and then ascends again, till the people near unto Jehovah take up the strain. For its exposition the chief requisite is a heart on fire with reverent love to the Lord over all, who is to be blessed for ever.

EXPOSITION

Verse 1. Praise ye the LORD. Whoever ye may be that hear this word, ye are invited, entreated, commanded, to magnify Jehovah. Assuredly he has made you, and, if for nothing else, ye are bound, upon the ground of creatureship, to adore your Maker.

Verse 2. Praise ye him, all his angels. Living intelligences, perfect in character and in bliss, lift up your loudest music to your Lord, each one, of you. Not one bright spirit is exempted from this consecrated service. However many ye be, O angels, ye are all his angels, and therefore ye are bound, all of you, to render service to your Lord.

Verse 3. Praise ye him, sun and moon: praise him, all ye stars of light. The Psalmist enters into detail as to the heavenly hosts. As all, so each, must praise the God of each and all. The sun and moon, as joint rulers of day and night, are paired in praise: the one is the complement of the other, and so they are closely associated in the summons to worship.

Verse 4. Praise him, ye heavens of heavens. By these are meant those regions which are heavens to those who dwell in our heavens; or those most heavenly of abodes where the most choice of spirits dwell. As the highest of the highest, so the best of the best are to praise the Lord.

Verse 5. Let them praise the name of the LORD; for he commanded, and they were created. Here is good argument: The Maker should have honor from his works, they should tell forth his praise: and thus they should praise his name—by which his character is intended.

Verse 6. He hath also stablished them for ever and ever. The continued existence of celestial beings is due to the supporting might of Jehovah, and to that alone. They do not fail because the Lord does not fail them. Without his will these things cannot alter; he has impressed upon them laws which only he himself can change. Eternally his ordinances are binding upon them. Therefore ought the Lord to be praised because he is Preserver as well as Creator, Ruler as well as Maker.

Verse 7. Praise the LORD from the earth. The song descends to our abode, and so comes nearer home to us. We who are "bodies terrestrial", are to pour out our portion of praise from the golden globe of this favored planet. Jehovah is to be praised not only in the earth but from the earth, as if the adoration ran over from this planet into the general accumulation of worship. In Ps 148:1 the song was "from the heavens"; here it is "from the earth": songs coming down from heaven are to blend with those going up from earth. The "earth" here meant is our entire globe of land and water: it is to be made vocal everywhere with praise.

Verse 8. Fire and hail. Lightning and hailstones go together. In the plagues of Egypt they cooperated in making Jehovah known in all the terrors of his power. Fire and ice morsels are a contrast in nature, but they are combined in magnifying the Lord. Snow and vapors. Offsprings of cold, or creations of heat, be ye equally consecrated to his praise. Congealed or expanded vapors, falling flakes or rising clouds, should, rising or falling, still reveal the praises of the Lord. Stormy winds fulfilling his word. Though rushing with

JOHN CALVIN

Psalm 148

1-6

1. Praise Jehovah from the heavens. He seems here to include the stars as well as the angels, and, therefore, heaven itself, the air, and all that is gendered in it; for afterwards a division is made when he first calls upon angels, then upon the stars, and the waters of the firmament. With regard to the angels, created as they were for this very end—that they might be instant in this religious service, we need not wonder that they should be placed first in order when the praises of God are spoken of. Accordingly, in that remarkable vision which Isaiah describes, (Isaiah 6:3,) the cherubim cry out—"Holy, holy, holy, Lord God of Hosts." And in several other places of Scripture the angels are represented as praising God by such ascriptions.

3. Praise him, ye sun and moon. This passage gives no countenance to the dream of Plato, that the stars excel in sense and intelligence. Nor does the Psalmist give them the same place as he had just assigned to angels, but merely intimates that the glory of God is everywhere to be seen, as if they sang his praises with an audible voice. And here he tacitly reproves the ingratitude of man; for all would hear this symphony, were they at all attent upon considering the works of God. For doth not the sun by his light, and heat, and other marvelous effects, praise his Maker? The stars when they run their course, and at once adorn the heavens and give light to the earth, do they not sound the praises of God?

5. Let them praise the name, etc. As he speaks of things wanting intelligence, he passes to the third person, from which we infer that his reason for having spoken in the second person hitherto, was to make a deeper impression upon men. And he asks no other praise than that which may teach us that the stars did not make themselves, nor the rains spring from chance; for notwithstanding the signal proofs we constantly have before our eyes of the divine power, we with shameful carelessness overlook the great author. He says emphatically—for He Himself created, intimating that the world is not eternal, as wicked men conjecture, nor made by a concourse of atoms, but that this fair order of things which we see, suddenly sprang forth upon the commandment of God.

7-10

7. Praise Jehovah, etc. He now comes to the lower parts of the world; although deviating at the same time from the exact order, he mixes up such things as are produced in the air—lightning's, snow, ice, and storms. These should rather have been placed among the former class, but he has respect to the common apprehension of men. The scope of the whole is, that wherever we turn our eyes we meet with evidences of the power of God.

The passage contains instruction of various kinds, as, for example, that when dearth impends, however parched the earth may be by long continued heat, God can promptly send rain which will remove the drought at his pleasure. If

MATTHEW HENRY

Psalm 148

1-6 An invitation to praise.

We, in this dark and depressed world, know but little of the world of light and exaltation, and, conversing within narrow confines, can scarcely admit any tolerable conceptions of the vast regions above. But this we know,

I. That there is above us a world of blessed angels by whom God is praised, an innumerable company of them. Thousand thousands minister unto him, and ten thousand times ten thousand stand before him; and it is his glory that he has such attendants, but much more his glory that he neither needs them, nor is, nor can be, any way benefited by them. To that bright and happy world the psalmist has an eye here, v. 1, 2.

In general, to the heavens, to the heights. The heavens are the heights, and therefore we must lift up our souls above the world unto God in the heavens, and on things above we must set our affections.

In particular, he had an eye to God's angels, to his hosts, and calls upon them to praise God. That God's angels are his hosts is plain enough; as soon as they were made they were enlisted, armed, and disciplined; he employs them in fighting his battles, and they keep ranks, and know their place, and observe the word of command as his hosts.

II. That there is above us not only an assembly of blessed spirits, but a system of vast bodies too, and those bright ones, in which God is praised, that is, which may give us occasion (as far as we know any thing of them) to give to God the glory not only of their being, but of their beneficence to mankind. Observe,

1. What these creatures are that thus show us the way in praising God, and, whenever we look up and consider the heavens, furnish us with matter for his praises. There are the sun, moon, and stars, which continually, either day or night, present themselves to our view, as looking-glasses, in which we may see a faint shadow (for so I must call it, not a resemblance) of the glory of him that is the Father of lights, v. 3. The greater lights, the sun and moon, are not too great, too bright, to praise him; and the praises of the less lights, the stars, shall not be slighted.

2. Upon what account we are to give God the glory of them: Let them praise the name of the Lord, that is, let us praise the name of the Lord for them, and observe what constant and fresh matter for praise may be fetched from them.

(1.) Because he made them, gave them their powers and assigned them their places: He commanded them (great as they are) out of nothing, and they were created at a word's speaking. God created, and therefore may command; for he commanded, and so created; his authority must always be acknowledged and acquiesced in, because he once spoke with such authority.

Psalm 148

8-14

8 Fire, and hail; snow, and vapors; stormy wind fulfilling his word:
9 Mountains, and all hills; fruitful trees, and all cedars:
10 Beasts, and all cattle; creeping things, and flying fowl:
11 Kings of the earth, and all people; princes, and all judges of the earth:
12 Both young men, and maidens; old men, and children:
13 Let them praise the name of the LORD: for his name alone is excellent; his glory is above the earth and heaven.
14 He also exalteth the horn of his people, the praise of all his saints; even of the children of Israel, a people near unto him. Praise ye the LORD.

incalculable fury, the storm wind is still under law, and moves in order due, to carry out the designs of God. It is a grand orchestra which contains such wind instruments as these! He is a great leader who can keep all these musicians in concert, and direct both time and tune.

Verse 9. Mountains, and all hills. Towering steeps and swelling knolls alike declare their Creator. "All hills" are to be consecrated; we have no longer Ebal and Gerizim, the hill of the curse and the hill of the blessing, but all our Ebals are turned to Gerizims. Tabor and Hermon, Lebanon and Carmel, rejoice in the name of the Lord. The greater and the lesser mounts are one in their adoration.

Verse 10. Beasts, and all cattle. Animals fierce or tame; wild beasts and domestic cattle; let all these show forth the praises of Jehovah. Those are worse than beasts who do not praise our God. More than brutish are those who are willfully dumb concerning their Maker.

Verse 11. Kings of the earth, and all people: princes, and all judges of the earth. Now the poet has reached our own race, and very justly he would have rulers and subjects, chieftains and magistrates, unite in worshipping the sovereign Lord of all. Monarchs must not disdain to sing, nor must their people refrain from uniting with them. Those who lead in battle and those who decide in courts must neither of them allow their vocations to keep them from reverently adoring the Chief and Judge of all.

Verse 12. Both young men, and maidens; old men, and children. Both sexes and all ages are summoned to the blessed service of song. Those who usually make merry together are to be devoutly joyful together: those who make up the ends of families, that is to say, the elders and the juveniles, should make the Lord their one and only end. Old men should by their experience teach children to praise; and children by their cheerfulness should excite old men to song.

Verse 13. Let them praise the name of the LORD. All that is contained in the name or character of Jehovah is worthy of praise, and all the objects of his creating care will be too few to set it forth in its completeness. For his name alone is excellent. It alone dseserves to be exalted in praise, for alone it is exalted in worth. There is none like unto the Lord, none that for a moment can be compared unto him. His unique name should have a monopoly of praise. His glory is above the earth and heaven: it is therefore alone because it surpasses all others. His royal splendor exceeds all that earth and heaven can express.

Verse 14. He also exalteth the horn of his people. He hath made them strong, famous, and victorious. His goodness to all his creatures does not prevent his having a special favor to his chosen nation: he is good to all, but he is God to his people. He lifts up the down trodden, but he in a peculiar manner lifts up his people. When they are brought low he raises up a horn for them by sending them a deliverer; when they are in conflict he gives them courage and strength, so that they lift up their horn amid the fray; and when all is peaceful around them, he fills their horn with plenty, and they lift it up with delight. The praise of all his saints. He is their glory: to him they render praise; and he by his mercy to them evermore gives them further reasons for praise, and higher motives for adoration. He lifts up their horn, and they lift up his praise. He exalts them, and they exalt him. The Holy One is praised by holy ones. He is their God, and they are his saints; he makes them blessed, and they bless him in return. All nations are bidden in Ps 148:11 to praise the Lord; but here the call is specially addressed to his elect people, who know him beyond all others.

from incessant rains, on the other hand, the seed rot in the ground, or the crops do not come to maturity, we should pray for fair weather.

11-14

11. Kings of the earth, etc. He now turns his address to men, with a respect to whom it was that he called for a declaration of God's praises from creatures, both above and from beneath. As kings and princes are blinded by the dazzling influence of their station, so as to think the world was made for them, and to despise God in the pride of their hearts, he particularly calls them to this duty; and, by mentioning them first, he reproves their ingratitude in withholding their tribute of praise when they are under greater obligations than others. As all men originally stand upon a level as to condition, the higher persons have risen, and the nearer they have been brought to God, the more sacredly are they bound to proclaim his goodness. The more intolerable is the wickedness of kings and princes who claim exemption from the common rule, when they ought rather to inculcate it upon others and lead the way. He could have addressed his exhortation at once summarily to all men, as indeed he mentions peoples in general terms; but by thrice specifying princes he suggests that they are slow to discharge the duty, and need to be urged do it. Then follows a division according to age and sex, to show that all without exception are created for this end, and should unitedly devote their energies to it. As to old men, the more God has lengthened out their lives the more should they be exercised in singing his praises; but he joins young men with them, for though they have less experience from continued habit, it will be inexcusable if they do not acknowledge the great mercy of God in the vigor of their lives. In speaking of girls or virgins he conveys the truth that even the young women who are not so liberally educated as the male sex, being considered as born for domestic offices, will omit their duty if they do not join with the rest of the Church in praising God. It follows that all from the least to the greatest are bound by this common rule.

14. And hath exalted the horn, etc. The perfections of God are to be seen more conspicuously in the Church than in the constitution of the world at large, the Psalmist has added this sentence, as to the Church being protected by the divine hand, and armed with a power against all enemies which secures its safety in every danger. By the horn, as is well known, is meant strength or dignity. Accordingly the Psalmist means that God's blessing is apparent in his Church and among his chosen people, inasmuch as it only flourishes and is powerful through his strength. There is a tacit comparison implied between the Church of God and other hostile powers, for it needs divine guardianship as being exposed on all sides to attack. Hence the Psalmist infers that praise is to all the merciful ones of God, for they have ground given them in the singular goodness of his condescension both for self-congratulation and praise. In calling the children of Israel a people near unto God, he reminds them of the gracious covenant which God made with Abraham.

(2.) Because he still upholds and preserves them in their beings and posts, their powers and motions (v. 6): He hath established them for ever and ever, that is, to the end of time, a short ever, but it is their ever; they shall last as long as there is occasion for them. He hath made a decree, the law of creation, which shall not pass.

7-14 An invitation to praise.

Considering that this earth, and the atmosphere that surrounds it, are the very sediment of the universe, it concerns us to enquire after those considerations that may be of use to reconcile us to our place in it; and I know none more likely than this (next to the visit which the Son of God once made to it), that even in this world, dark and as bad as it is, God is praised: Praise you the Lord from the earth, v. 7. As the rays of the sun, which are darted directly from heaven, reflect back (though more weakly) from the earth, so should the praises of God, with which this cold and infected world should be warmed and perfumed.

I. Even those creatures that are not dignified with the powers of reason are summoned into this concert, because God may be glorified in them, v. 7-10. Let the dragons or whales, that sport themselves in the mighty waters (Ps. civ. 26), dance before the Lord, to his glory. Take a view of the surface of the earth (v. 9), and there are presented to our view the exalted grounds, mountains and all hills, from the barren tops of some of which, and the fruitful tops of others, we may fetch matter for praise. Pass we next to the animal kingdom, and there we find God glorified, even by the beasts that run wild, and all cattle that are tame and in the service of man, v. 10. Nay, even the creeping things have not sunk so low, nor do the flying fowl soar so high, as not to be called upon to praise the Lord.

II. Much more those creatures that are dignified with the powers of reason ought to employ them in praising God: Kings of the earth and all people, v. 11, 12. God is to be glorified in and for these, as in and for the inferior creatures, for their hearts are in the hand of the Lord and he makes what use he pleases of them.

III. Most of all his own people, who are dignified with peculiar privileges, must in a peculiar manner give glory to him, v. 14. Observe,

1. The dignity God has put upon his people, even the children of Israel, typical of the honor reserved for all true believers, who are God's spiritual Israel. He exalts their horn, their brightness, their plenty, their power.

2. The duty God expects from them in consideration of this. Let those whom God honors honor him: Praise you the Lord. Let him be the praise of all his saints, the object of their praise; for he is a praise to them. He is thy praise, and he is thy God, Deut. x. 21. Some by the horn of his people understand David, as a type of Christ, for it is through him that they are a people near to God.

Psalm 149

1-4
1 Praise ye the LORD. Sing unto the LORD a new song, and his praise in the congregation of saints.
2 Let Israel rejoice in him that made him: let the children of Zion be joyful in their King.
3 Let them praise his name in the dance: let them sing praises unto him with the timbrel and harp.
4 For the LORD taketh pleasure in his people: he will beautify the meek with salvation.

Psalm 149

We are almost at the last Psalm, and still among the Hallelujahs. This is "a new song", evidently intended for the new creation, and the men who are of new heart. It is such a song as may be sung at the coming of the Lord, when the new dispensation shall bring overthrow to the wicked and honor to all the saints. The tone is exceedingly jubilant and exultant. All through one hears the beat of the feet of dancing maidens, keeping time to the timbrel and harp.

EXPOSITION
Verse 1. Praise ye the LORD. Specially you, ye chosen people, whom he has made to be his saints. You have praised him aforetime, praise him yet again; yea, for ever praise him. With renewed zeal and fresh delight lift up your song unto Jehovah. Sing unto the LORD a new song. Sing, for it is the fittest method for expressing reverent praise. Sing a hymn newly composed, for you have now a new knowledge of God. He is ever new in his manifestations; his mercies are new every morning; his deliverances are new in every night of sorrow; let your gratitude and thanksgivings be new also. It is well to repeat the old; it is more useful to invent the new. Novelty goes well with heartiness. Our singing should be "unto the Lord"; the songs we sing should be of him and to him, "for of him, and to him, and through him are all things." Among our novelties there should be new songs: alas! men are fonder of making new complaints than new Psalms.
Verse 2. Let Israel rejoice in him that made him. Here is that new creation which calls for the new song. It was Jehovah who made Israel to be Israel, and the tribes to become a great nation: therefore let the Founder of the nation be had in perpetual honor. Joy and rejoicing are evidently to be the special characteristics of the new song. The religion of the dead in sin is more apt to chant dirges than to sing hallelujahs; but when we are made new in the spirit of our minds we joy and rejoice in him that made us. Our joy is in our God and King: we choose no lower delight.
Verse 3. Let them praise his name in the dance: let them sing praises unto him with the timbrel and harp. Thus let them repeat the triumph of the Red Sea, which was ever the typical glory of Israel. Miriam led the daughters of Israel in the dance when the Lord had triumphed gloriously; was it not most fit that she should? The sacred dance of devout joy is no example, nor even excuse, for frivolous dances, much less for lewd ones. Who could help dancing when Egypt was vanquished, and the tribes were free? Every mode of expressing delight was bound to be employed on so memorable an occasion. Dancing, singing, and playing on instruments were all called into requisition, and most fitly so. There are unusual seasons which call for unusual expressions of joy. When the Lord saves a soul its holy joy overflows, and it cannot find channels enough for its exceeding gratitude: if the man does not leap, or play, or sing, at any rate he praises God, and wishes for a thousand tongues with which to magnify his Savior. Who would wish it to be otherwise? Young converts are not to be restrained in their joy. Let them sing and dance while they can. How can they mourn now that their Bridegroom is with them? Let us give the utmost liberty to joy. Let us never attempt its suppression, but issue in the terms of this verse a double license for exultation. If any ought to be glad it is the children of Zion; rejoicing is more fit for Israel than for any other people: it is their own folly and fault that they are not oftener brimming with joy in God.
Verse 4. For the LORD taketh pleasure in his people; and therefore they should take pleasure in him. If our joy be pleasing to him let us make it full. What condescension is this on Jehovah's part, to notice, to love, and to delight in his chosen! Surely there is nothing in our persons, or our actions, which could cause pleasure to the Ever blessed One, were it not that he condescends to men of low estate. The thought of the Lord's taking

JOHN CALVIN

Psalm 149

If we may be allowed to compare this Psalm with the former ones, and the next, which is the last, the only difference is, that while the author of the Psalm, whoever he was, has hitherto spoken of God's special care and protection of his Church in connection with the common providential government of the world, here he speaks of his benefits to the Church exclusively. In the next Psalm mention is only made of the power of God in general.

1-4

1. Sing to Jehovah a new song. This exordium proves that the exhortation now given is addressed only to God's people; for the singular goodness which is particularly extended to them affords more ample matter of praise. The Psalmist had good reason therefore for animating the godly to look forward for the full accomplishment of the mercy of God, that they might be persuaded of divine protection until such time as the Messiah should arise who would gather all Israel. He calls this a new song, as we have noticed elsewhere, to distinguish it from those with which the saints commonly and daily praised God, for praise is their continued exercise. It follows that he speaks of some rare and unusual benefit, demanding signal and particular thanksgiving.

2. Let Israel rejoice in his Maker. He insists upon the same point, that the Lord's people should rest firmly persuaded that their family had not been chosen out in vain from the rest of the world, but that God would be mindful of his covenant, and not allow the mercies which he had extended to them to fail or become extinct. Although they had been temporarily deprived of the inheritance of the land of Canaan, which was the pledge of their adoption, the Psalmist calls God their Maker, and king of the sons of Zion, to remind them that when adopted to a pre-eminency above other nations, this was a species of new creation. So in Psalm 45:6, the Israelites are called "the work of God's hands," not merely because they were like other men created by him, but because he had formed them anew, and distinguished them with a new honor, that, of being separated front the whole human race.

4. For God hath taken pleasure in his people. The Psalmist accordingly mitigates the sadness of present evils by administering seasonable consolation, that God's people, when oppressed by troubles, might look forward with hope to the glorious deliverance which was yet unseen. The sum of the passage is—that God, who had fixed his love upon his chosen people, could not possibly abandon them to such miseries as they now suffered under.

5-9

5. They shall rejoice. In making mention here of joy, jubilee, and the high praises of God, he shows still more clearly from the effects which it would produce, that he does not speak of a common benefit of God; for had not the deliverance of the people been of a remarkable kind, there would have been no occasion for such joy, and even triumph. And by these

MATTHEW HENRY

Psalm 149

1-5 Saints admonished to praise God.

We have here,

I. The calls given to God's Israel to praise. All his works were, in the foregoing psalm, excited to praise him; but here his saints in a particular manner are required to bless him. Observe then,

1. Who are called upon to praise God. Israel in general, the body of the church (v. 2), the children of Zion particularly, the inhabitants of that holy hill.

2. What must be the principle of this praise, and that is holy joy in God: Let Israel rejoice, and the children of Zion be joyful, and the saints be joyful in glory.

3. What must be the expressions of this praise. We must by all proper ways show forth the praises of God: Sing to the Lord. We must entertain ourselves, and proclaim his name, by singing praises to him (v. 3), singing aloud (v. 5), for we should sing psalms with all our heart.

4. What opportunities must be taken for praising God, none must be let slip, but particularly,

(1.) We must praise God in public, in the solemn assembly (v. 1), in the congregation of saints. The more the better; it is the more like heaven.

(2.) We must praise him in private. Let the saints be so transported with their joy in God as to sing aloud upon their beds, when they awake in the night, full of the praises of God, as David, Ps. cxix. 62.

II. The cause given to God's Israel for praise.

1. God's doings for them.

They have reason to rejoice in God, to devote themselves to his honour and employ themselves in his service; for it is he that made them. He gave us our being as men, and we have reason to praise him for that, for it is a noble and excellent being. He gave Israel their being as a people, as a church, made them what they were, so very different from other nations. Let that people therefore praise him, for he formed them for himself, on purpose that they might show forth his praise, Isa. xliii. 21. Let Israel rejoice in his Makers (so it is in the original); for God said, Let us make man; and in this, some think, is the mystery of the Trinity.

2. God's dominion over them.

This follows upon the former: if he made them, he is their King; he that gave being no doubt may give law; and this ought to be the matter of our joy and praise that we are under the conduct and protection of such a wise and powerful King.

3. God's delight in them.

He is a king that rules by love, and therefore to be praised; for the Lord takes pleasure in his people, in their services, in their prosperity, in communion with them, and in the communications of his favour to them.

6-9 Israel admonished to praise God.

The Israel of God are here represented triumphing over their enemies, which is both the matter of their

Psalm 149

5-9
5 Let the saints be joyful in glory: let them sing aloud upon their beds.
6 Let the high praises of God be in their mouth, and a two-edged sword in their hand;
7 To execute vengeance upon the heathen, and punishments upon the people;
8 To bind their kings with chains, and their nobles with fetters of iron;
9 To execute upon them the judgment written: this honor have all his saints. Praise ye the LORD.

pleasure in us is a mine of joy never to be exhausted. He will beautify the meek with salvation. They are humble, and feel their need of salvation; he is gracious, and bestows it upon them.

Verse 5. Let the saints be joyful in glory. God has honored them, and put a rare glory upon them; therefore let them exult therein. Shall those to whom God is their glory be cast down and troubled? Nay, let their joy proclaim their honorable estate. Let them sing aloud upon their beds. Their exultation should express itself in shouts and songs, for it is not a feeling of which they have any need to be ashamed. That which is so fully justified by fact, may well be loudly proclaimed.

Verse 6. Let the high praises of God be in their mouth, and a two edged sword in their hand. It seems they are not always on their beds, but are ready for deeds of prowess. When called to fight, the meek are very hard to overcome; they are just as steady in conflict as they are steadfast in patience. Besides, their way of fighting is of an extraordinary sort, for they sing to God but keep their swords in their hands. They can do both things at once: if they do not wield the trowel and the sword, at least they sing and strike. In this Israel was not an example, but a type: we will not copy the chosen people in making literal war, but we will fulfill the emblem by carrying on spiritual war.

Verse 7. To execute vengeance upon the heathen, and punishments upon the people. This was once literally the duty of Israel: when they came into Canaan they fulfilled the righteous sentence of the Lord upon guilty nations. At this hour, under the gentler dispensation of grace, we wrestle not with flesh and blood; yet is our warfare none the less stern, and our victory none the less sure. All evil shall eventually be overthrown: the Lord shall display his justice against evildoers, and in that warfare his servants shall play their parts. The saints shall judge the world. Both the conflict and the victory at the end of it shall cause glory to God, and honor to his holy ones.

Verse 8. To bind their kings with chains, and their nobles with fetters of iron. Thus are the greatest enemies of Jehovah and his people reduced to shame, rendered helpless, and themselves punished. This was Israel's boast in actual fact, it is ours spiritually. The chief powers of evil shall be restrained and ultimately destroyed. Those who made captives of the godly shall themselves be made captive. The powers of evil cannot bind our King, but by his power their king shall be bound with a great chain, and shut up in the bottomless pit, that he may at length be trodden under the feet of saints.

Verse 9. To execute upon them the judgment written. Israel as a nation had this to do, and did it, and then they rejoiced in the God who gave success to their arms. We praise our God after another fashion; we are not executioners of justice, but heralds of mercy. It would be a sad thing for any one to misuse this text: lest any warlike believer should be led to do so, we would remind him that the execution must not go beyond the sentence and warrant; and we have received no warrant of execution against our fellow men. Christians have no commission of vengeance; it is theirs to execute the command of mercy, and that alone. This honor have all his saints. All the godly shared in the triumphs of the Lord when he smote Israel's foes. We have like honor, but it is shown in victories of another sort. All the holy ones are sent upon errands by their holy Lord. The Lord honors all his chosen here, and he will glorify them all hereafter: this rule is without exception.

expressions he intimates that the people would not be brought back from exile to be immediately dispersed again, but to flourish in the enjoyment of every species of blessing. He on this account makes mention of couches, teaching them to expect daily rest under the divine protection. He declares that they would be furnished with arms and power, not only to ward off enemies, but to put them to flight on every side, so as to reduce to subjection kings and nations which formerly ruled over them. By swords of a double-mouth, or two-edged, are meant such as cut on both sides, for at that time swords had but one edge.

7. To execute vengeance, etc. Both during their exile and after their return from it, this might seem to be altogether incredible. Nor did it take place before the advent of Christ; for though the Machabaei and their posterity reduced the neighboring nations to subjection, this was but a faint prelude and earnest to direct the thoughts of the Lord's people to what was approaching. But as Haggai prophesied that the glory of the second Temple would be greater than of the first, so here there is promised a more prosperous state than had ever existed. (Haggai 2:9.) Reduced as the Jews were in numbers, and low as was the state of things among them, the Psalmist announces to all nations which opposed and troubled them, that they would have the ascendancy. As they dwelt at Jerusalem only by sufferance, they were called to exercise faith in a promise which might appear visionary, and to raise their thoughts to the infinite power of God, which triumphs over all worldly obstacles. The vengeance spoken of is such as the Israelites would take, not under the influence of private resentment, but by commandment of God; and this we mention that none may infer that they are allowed to take vengeance for personal injuries.

The next verse, where mention is made of kings and nobles, is an amplification; for had he only spoken of peoples and nations, this might have been restricted to the common people and men of low condition. Here is something much greater—that kings and others of noble rank would be dragged to punishment in chains. But it is to be remembered that but a small part of this splendid prospect was realized until Christ appeared; for any small increase of prosperity which the people enjoyed was not worthy of any consideration, except in so far as by this help God sustained the drooping spirits of the people up to Christ's advent. Here the prediction of Jacob is to be noticed—"the scepter shall not depart from Judah, until Shiloh come." (Genesis 49:10) As the Psalmist treats here of the perfection of the prosperity of the people, it follows that he refers to the Messiah, that their expectation and desire of him might never cease either in their prosperity or adversity.

9. To perform the judgment, etc. He qualifies what he had said in the previous verses, in which he might have appeared to arm the Lord's people for deeds of warlike cruelty. Although God's people, therefore, have nothing of the strength of the giant, and will not move a finger without divine permission, and have a calm spirit, the Psalmist declares, that they have an honorable and splendid issue out of all their troubles.

praise (let them give to God the glory of those triumphs) and the recompence of their praise; those that are truly thankful to God for their tranquility shall be blessed with victory. Now this may be applied,

1. To the many victories which God blessed his people Israel with over the nations of Canaan and other nations that were devoted to destruction.

These began in Moses and Joshua, who, when they taught Israel the high praises of the Lord, did withal put a two-edged sword in their hand; David did so too, for, as he was the sweet singer of Israel, so he was the captain of their hosts, and taught the children of Judah the use of the bow (2 Sam. i. 18), taught their hands to war, as God had taught his. Thus he and they went on victoriously, fighting the Lord's battles, and avenging Israel's quarrels on those that had oppressed them; then they executed vengeance upon the heathen (the Philistines, Moabites, Ammonites, and others, 2 Sam. viii. 1, &c.) and punishments upon the people, for all the wrong they had done to God's people, v. 7. Their kings and nobles were taken prisoners (v. 8) and on some of them the judgment written was executed, as by Joshua on the kings of Canaan, by Gideon on the princes of Midian, by Samuel on Agag. The honor of this redounded to all the Israel of God; and to him who put it upon them they return it entirely in their hallelujahs. Jehoshaphat's army had at the same time the high praises of God in their mouth and a two-edged sword in their hand, for they went forth to war singing the praises of God, and then their sword did execution, 2 Chron. xx. 23. The kings of the earth that shall be employed in the destruction of the New-Testament Babylon will but execute the judgment written, Rev. xvii. 16, 17. But, since now no such special commissions can be produced, this will by no means justify the violence either of subjects against their princes or of princes against their subjects, or both against their neighbors, under pretence of religion; for Christ never intended that his gospel should be propagated by fire and sword or his righteousness wrought by the wrath of man. When the high praises of God are in our mouth with them we should have an olive-branch of peace in our hands.

2. To Christ's victories by the power of his gospel and grace over spiritual enemies. The word of God is the two-edged sword (Heb. iv. 12), the sword of the Spirit (Eph. vi. 17), Now,

(1.) With this two-edged sword the first preachers obtained a glorious victory over the powers of darkness.

(2.) With this two-edged sword believers fight against their own corruptions.

(3.) The complete accomplishment of this will be in the judgment of the great day, when the Lord shall come with ten thousands of his saints, to execute judgment upon all, Jude 14, 15.

KING JAMES VERSION

Psalm 150

1 Praise ye the LORD. Praise God in his sanctuary: praise him in the firmament of his power.
2 Praise him for his mighty acts: praise him according to his excellent greatness.
3 Praise him with the sound of the trumpet: praise him with the psaltery and harp.
4 Praise him with the timbrel and dance: praise him with stringed instruments and organs.
5 Praise him upon the loud cymbals: praise him upon the high sounding cymbals.
6 Let every thing that hath breath praise the LORD. Praise ye the LORD.

CHARLES H. SPURGEON

Psalm 150

We have now reached the last summit of the mountain chain of Psalms. It rises high into the clear azure, and its brow is bathed in the sunlight of the eternal world of worship, it is a rapture. The poet prophet is full of inspiration and enthusiasm. He slays not to argue, to teach, to explain; but cries with burning words, "Praise him, Praise him, Praise ye the LORD."

EXPOSITION

Verse 1. Praise ye the LORD. Hallelujah! The exhortation is to all things in earth or in heaven. Should they not all declare the glory of him for whose glory they are, and were created? Jehovah, the one God, should be the one object of adoration. To give the least particle of his honor to another is shameful treason; to refuse to render it to him is heartless robbery. Praise God in his sanctuary. Praise El, or the strong one, in his holy place. See how power is mentioned with holiness in this change of names. Praise begins at home.

Verse 2. Praise him for his mighty acts. Here is a reason for praise. In these deeds of power we see himself. These doings of his omnipotence are always on behalf of truth and righteousness. His works of creation, providence, and redemption, all call for praise; they are his acts, and his acts of might, therefore let him be praised for them. Praise him according to his excellent greatness. His being is unlimited, and his praise should correspond therewith. He possesses a multitude or a plenitude of greatness, and therefore he should be greatly praised.

Verse 3. Praise him with the sound of the trumpet. With the loudest, clearest note call the people together. Make all men to know that we are not ashamed to worship. Summon them with unmistakable sound to bow before their God. The sound of trumpet is associated with the grandest and most solemn events, such as the giving of the law, the proclamation of jubilee, the coronation of Jewish kings, and the raging of war. It is to be thought of in reference to the coming of our Lord in his second advent and the raising of the dead. If we cannot give voice to this martial instrument, at least let our praise be as decided and bold as if we could give a blast upon the horn. Let us never sound a trumpet before us to our own honor, but reserve all our trumpeting for God's glory.

Verse 4. Praise him with the timbrel and dance. Associated with the deliverance at the Red Sea, this form of worship set forth the most jubilant and exultant of worship. The hands and the feet were both employed, and the entire body moved in sympathy with the members. Are there not periods of life when we feel so glad that we would fain dance for joy? Let not such exhilaration be spent upon common themes, but let the name of God stir us to ecstasy.

Verse 5. Praise high upon the loud cymbals: praise him upon the high sounding cymbals. Let the clash of the loudest music be the Lord's: let the joyful clang of the loftiest notes be all for him. Praise has beaten the timbrel, swept the harp, and sounded the trumpet, and now for a last effort, awakening the most heavy of slumberers, and startling the most indifferent of onlookers, she dashes together the disks of brass, and with sounds both loud and high proclaims the glories of the Lord.

Verse 6. Let everything that hath breath praise the Lord. "Let all breath praise him": that is to say, all living beings. He gave them breath, let them breathe his praise. His name is in the Hebrew composed rather of breathings than of letters, to show that all breath comes from him: therefore let it be used for him. Join all ye living things in the eternal song. Be ye least or greatest, withhold not your praises.

JOHN CALVIN

JOHN CALVIN

Psalm 150

The argument of this Psalm is the same with that of the former.

1-6

1. Praise God in his sanctuary. This psalm in general commends the spiritual worship of God, which consists in sacrifices of praise. By the sanctuary there is little doubt that heaven is here meant, as is often the case elsewhere.

That the majesty of God may be duly reverenced, the Psalmist represents him as presiding on his throne in the heavens; and he enlarges upon the same truth in the second verse, celebrating his power and his greatness, which he had brought under our notice in the heavens, which are a mirror in which they may be seen. If we would have our minds kindled, then, to engage in this religious service, let us meditate upon his power and greatness, which will speedily dispel all such insensibility. Though our minds can never take in this immensity, the mere taste of it will deeply affect us. And God will not reject such praises as we offer according to our capacity.

3. Praise him with sound of trumpet. The children of God cannot apply themselves too diligently to the praises of God. Nor was it without reason that God under the law enjoined this multiplicity of songs, that he might lead men away from those vain and corrupt pleasures to which they are excessively addicted, to a holy and profitable joy. Our corrupt nature indulges in extraordinary liberties, many devising methods of gratification which are preposterous, while their highest satisfaction lies in suppressing all thoughts of God. This perverse disposition could only be corrected in the way of God's retaining a weak and ignorant people under many restraints, and constant exercises. The Psalmist, therefore, in exhorting believers to pour forth all their joy in the praises of God, enumerates, one upon another, all the musical instruments which were then in use, and reminds them that they ought all to be consecrated to the worship of God.

6. Whatever breathes, etc. The words may be extended to every kind of living creatures, as we have seen in the preceding psalms that the declaration of God's praises is assigned even to things wanting intelligence. But as men exclusively are often meant under the name of "flesh," so we may very well suppose that the words have reference here to men, who, although they have vital breath in common with the brute creation, obtain by way of distinction the name of breathing, as of living creatures. I am led to think this for the following reason: As yet the Psalmist has addressed himself in his exhortations to the people who were conversant with the ceremonies under the law, now he turns to men in general, tacitly intimating that a time was coming when the same songs, which were then only heard in Judea, would resound in every quarter of the globe. And in this prediction we have been joined in the same symphony with the Jews, that we may worship God with constant sacrifices of praise, until being gathered into the kingdom of heaven, we sing with elect angels an eternal hallelujah.

MATTHEW HENRY

Psalm 150

1-6 An invitation to praise God; all creatures called to praise God.

Observe here,

I. Whence this tribute of praise arises, and out of what part of his dominion it especially issues. It comes,

1. From his sanctuary; praise him there. Let his priests, let his people, that attend there, attend him with their praises. Where should he be praised, but there where he does, in a special manner, both manifest his glory and communicate his grace?

2. From the firmament of his power. Praise him because of his power and glory which appear in the firmament, its vastness, its brightness, and its splendid furniture; and because of the powerful influences it has upon this earth.

II. Upon what account this tribute of praise is due, upon many accounts, particularly,

1. The works of his power (v. 2): Praise him for his mighty acts; for his mightinesses (so the word is), for all the instances of his might, the power of his providence, the power of his grace, what he has done in the creation, government, and redemption of the world, for the children of men in general, for his own church and children in particular.

2. The glory and majesty of his being: Praise him according to his excellent greatness, according to the multitude of his magnificence (so Dr. Hammond reads it); not that our praises can bear any proportion to God's greatness, for it is infinite, but, since he is greater than we can express or conceive, we must raise our conceptions and expressions to the highest degree we can attain to.

III. In what manner this tribute must be paid, with all the kinds of musical instruments that were then used in the temple-service, v. 3-5. It is well that we are not concerned to enquire what sort of instruments these were; it is enough that they were well known then.

IV. Who must pay this tribute (v. 6): Let every thing that has breath praise the Lord. He began with a call to those that had a place in his sanctuary and were employed in the temple-service; but he concludes with a call to all the children of men, in prospect of the time when the Gentiles should be taken into the church, and in every place, as acceptably as at Jerusalem, this incense should be offered, Mal. i. 11. What have we our breath, our spirit, for, but to spend it in praising God; and how can we spend it better? Prayers are called our breathings, Lam. iii. 56. Let every one that breathes towards God in prayer, finding the benefit of that, breathe forth his praises too. Having breath, let the praises of God perfume our breath. Since therefore we must shortly breathe our last, while we have breath let us praise the Lord, and then we shall breathe our last with comfort, and, when death runs us out of breath, we shall remove to a better state to breathe God's praises in a freer better air.